The Broadview Introduction

to Philosophy

VOLUME I | KNOWLEDGE AND REALITY

The Broadview Introduction to

PHILOSOPHY

VOLUME I | KNOWLEDGE AND REALITY

edited by **ANDREW BAILEY**

broadview press

BROADVIEW PRESS – www.broadviewpress.com
Peterborough, Ontario, Canada

Founded in 1985, Broadview Press remains a wholly independent publishing house. Broadview's focus is on academic publishing; our titles are accessible to university and college students as well as scholars and general readers. With over 600 titles in print, Broadview has become a leading international publisher in the humanities, with world-wide distribution. Broadview is committed to environmentally responsible publishing and fair business practices.

Library and Archives Canada Cataloguing in Publication

Title: The Broadview introduction to philosophy / edited by Andrew Bailey.
Other titles: Introduction to philosophy
Names: Bailey, Andrew, 1969– editor.
Description: Includes bibliographical references. | Contents: Volume I: Knowledge and reality.
Identifiers: Canadiana 20190105038 | ISBN 9781554814015 (v. 1 ; softcover)
Subjects: LCSH: Philosophy—Introductions.
Classification: LCC BD21 .B76 2019 | DDC 100—dc23

Broadview Press handles its own distribution in North America:
PO Box 1243, Peterborough, Ontario K9J 7H5, Canada
555 Riverwalk Parkway, Tonawanda, NY 14150, USA
Tel: (705) 743-8990; Fax: (705) 743-8353
email: customerservice@broadviewpress.com

Distribution is handled by Eurospan Group in the UK, Europe, Central Asia, Middle East, Africa, India, Southeast Asia, Central America, South America, and the Caribbean. Distribution is handled by Footprint Books in Australia and New Zealand.

Canada

Broadview Press acknowledges the financial support of the Government of Canada for our publishing activities.

Book design by Michel Vrana
Cover image: borojoint, istockphoto.com

PRINTED IN CANADA

CONTRIBUTING EDITORS AND WRITERS

Editor
Andrew Bailey

Editorial Coordinator
Stephen Latta

Assistant Editor
Tara Bodie

Copyeditor
Robert M. Martin

Proofreaders
Stacey Aspinall
Joe Davies
Michel Pharand
Paige Pinto
Michael Roberts
Helena Snopek

Production Editors
Tara Lowes
Tara Trueman

Permissions Coordinator
Merilee Atos

Contributing Writers
Andrew Bailey
Laura Buzzard
Leslie Dema
Stephen Latta
Melissa MacAulay
Robert M. Martin
Andrew Reszitnyk
Nora Ruddock

CONTENTS

PART III: METAPHYSICS

ACKNOWLEDGMENTS

A number of academics provided valuable comments and input that helped to shape this book, including (but not limited to):

Ardis Anderson, University of Lethbridge
Shannon Dea, University of Waterloo
William J. Devlin, Bridgewater State University
Leigh Duffy, Buffalo State College
Mark Ereshefsky, University of Calgary
Erin Frykholm, University of Kansas
Hans V. Hansen, University of Windsor
W. Jim Jordan, University of Waterloo
Karl Laderoute, University of Lethbridge
Christinia Landry, Wilfrid Laurier University
Alison K. McConwell, University of Calgary
Joshua Mugg, Park University
Csaba Nyiri, Lourdes University
Brian Orend, University of Waterloo
Tina Strasbourg, Grande Prairie Regional College
Brynn Welch, University of Alabama at Birmingham
Byron Williston, Wilfrid Laurier University

This book is a successor to *First Philosophy: Fundamental Problems and Readings in Philosophy* (2nd ed.; Broadview Press, 2011). Thanks to Alan Belk, Lance Hickey, Peter Loptson, and Mark Migotti for pointing out errors and omissions in the first edition of that book. The editor would warmly welcome further corrections or suggestions for improvement.

Andrew Bailey
Department of Philosophy
The University of Guelph
abailey@uoguelph.ca

HOW TO USE THIS BOOK

This book is an introduction to philosophy. It is intended to be a reasonably representative—though very far from exhaustive—sampling of important philosophical questions, major philosophers and their most important works, periods of philosophical history, and styles of philosophical thought.* More than half of the included readings, however, were published since 1950, and another important aim of the book is to provide some background for *current* philosophical debates, to give the interested reader a springboard for the plunge into the exciting world of contemporary philosophy (debates about the nature of consciousness, say, or quantum theories of free will, or feminist ethics, or the status of scientific knowledge, or welfarist vs. libertarian accounts of social justice, or ...).

The aim of this book is to introduce philosophy through philosophy itself: it is not a book *about* philosophy but a book *of* philosophy, in which more than sixty great philosophers speak for themselves. Each of the readings is prefaced by a set of notes, but these notes are not intended to explain or summarize the reading. Instead, the goal of the notes is to provide *background information* helpful for understanding the reading—to remove as many of the unnecessary barriers to comprehension as possible, and to encourage a deeper and more sophisticated encounter with great works of philosophy. The notes to selections, therefore, do not stand alone and *certainly* are not a substitute for the reading itself: they are meant to be consulted in combination with the reading.

Readers can of course take or leave these notes as they choose, and read them (or not) in any order. One good way of proceeding, however, would be the following. First, read the selection (so that nothing said in the notes inadvertently taints your first impression of the piece). Then, go back and read some of the notes—the biographical sketch, information on the author's philo-

sophical project, structural and background information—and with these things in mind read the selection again. Spend some time *thinking* about the reading: ask yourself if you really feel you have a good grasp of what the author is trying to say, and then—no less importantly—ask yourself whether the author gives good reasons to believe that what is said is *true*. (The general Introduction tries to give some helpful suggestions for this process of critical reflection.) After this, it should be worthwhile going back to the notes, checking your impressions against any 'common misconceptions,' and then running through at least some of the suggestions for critical reflection. Finally, you might want to go on and read more material by the philosopher in question, or examine what other philosophers have said about those ideas: the suggestions for further reading, available at the companion website, will point you in the right direction.

The philosophical selections are also quite heavily annotated throughout by the editors, again in an effort to get merely contingent difficulties for comprehension out of the way and allow the reader to devote all her or his effort to understanding the philosophy itself. Many of the original texts also include their own notes, all of which have been presented here as endnotes following the reading, so as to keep those notes separate from the editors' annotations. The original endnotes are marked with numbers, while the added annotations are marked with symbols (*, †, ‡, etc.) and placed at the bottom of each page.

A word of explanation about the 'Suggestions for Critical Reflection' section: although the notes to the readings contain no philosophical critique of the selection, the questions in this section are largely intended to help the reader generate his or her own critique. As such, they are supposed to be thought-provoking, rather than straightforwardly easy to answer. They try to sug-

---

* There are two major exceptions to this. First, this book focuses exclusively on 'Western' philosophy—that is, roughly, on the philosophical traditions of Europe and of the descendants of European settlers in North America and Australasia. In particular, it does not attempt to encompass the rich philosophical heritage of Asia or Africa. Second, this collection under-represents an important strain of twentieth-century philosophy, 'Continental' philosophy, which includes thinkers such as Husserl, Heidegger, Sartre, Foucault, Derrida, and Habermas, and is characterized by such movements as existentialism, hermeneutics, structuralism, and deconstructionism.

gest fruitful avenues for critical thought (though they do not cover every possible angle of questioning, or even all the important ones), and only very rarely is there some particular 'right answer' to the question. Thus, these questions should not be considered a kind of 'self-test' to see if you understand the material: even people with a very good grasp of the material will typically be puzzled by the questions—because they are *supposed* to be puzzling questions.

The readings and their accompanying notes are designed to be 'modular'; that is, in general, one reading can be understood without the benefit of having read any of the other selections. This means that the selections can be read in any order. The current arrangement of the readings groups them by topic, and then orders them so that they follow a reasonably natural progression through a particular philosophical problem. However, quite different courses of study could be plotted through this book, emphasizing, say, philosophers grouped by nationality, by historical period, by philosophical approach, and so on. Furthermore, often readings from one section can quite naturally be brought into another (e.g., Descartes' *Meditations* into the Philosophy of Mind section).

The readings in this anthology are, so far as is practicable, 'complete': that is, they are entire articles, chapters, or sections of books. The editors feel it is important for students to be able to see an argument in the context in which it was originally presented; also, the fact that the readings are not edited to include only what is relevant to one particular philosophical concern means that they can be used in a variety of different ways following a variety of different lines of thought across the ages. Some instructors will wish to assign for their students shorter excerpts of some of these readings, rather than having them read all of the work included: the fact that complete, or almost complete, works of philosophy are included in this anthology gives instructors the freedom to select the excerpts that best fit their pedagogical aims.

The notes to the readings in this anthology are almost entirely a work of synthesis, and many books and articles were consulted in their preparation; it is impossible—without adding an immense apparatus of notes and references—to acknowledge them in detail. This is, I believe, appropriate for a textbook, but it is not intended to model good referencing practices for student essays. All the material and annotations accompanying the readings was written by the editors, and none of it (unless otherwise noted) was copied from other sources. Typically, the notes for each reading amalgamate information from up to a dozen or so sources; in a few instances, especially for biographical information on still-living philosophers, the notes rely heavily on a smaller number of sources (and I tried to indicate this in the text when it occurred).

INTRODUCTION

What Is Philosophy?

Philosophy, at least according to the origin of the word in classical Greek, is the "love of wisdom"—philosophers are lovers of wisdom. The first philosophers of the Western tradition lived on the shores of the Mediterranean in the sixth century BCE (that is, more than 2,500 years ago);* thinkers such as Thales, Xenophanes, Pythagoras, Heraclitus, and Protagoras tried systematically to answer questions about the ultimate nature of the universe, the standards of knowledge, the objectivity of moral claims, and the existence and nature of God. Questions like these are still at the core of the discipline today.

So what is philosophy? It can be characterized either as a particular sort of *method*, or in terms of its *subject matter*, or as a kind of intellectual *attitude*.

PHILOSOPHY AS A METHOD

One view is that philosophers study the same things—the same world—as, for example, scientists do, but that they do so in a different, and complementary, way. In particular, it is often claimed that while scientists draw conclusions from empirical *observations* of the world, philosophers use *rational arguments* to justify claims about the world. For instance, both scientists and philosophers are involved in contemporary studies of the human mind. Neuroscientists and psychologists are busily mapping out correlations between brain states and mental states—finding which parts of the visual cortex play a role in dreaming, for example—and building computer models of intelligent information processing (such as software for self-driving vehicles). Philosophers are also involved in cognitive science, trying to discover just what would *count* as discovering that dreaming is really nothing more than certain electro-chemical events in the brain, or would count as building a computer which feels pain or genuinely has beliefs. These second kinds of questions are crucial to the whole project of cognitive science, but they are not empirical, scientific questions: there simply is no fact about the brain that a scientist could observe to answer them. And so these questions—which are part of cognitive science—are dealt with by philosophers.

Here are two more examples. Economists study the distribution of wealth in society, and develop theories about how wealth and other goods can come to be distributed one way rather than another (e.g., concentrated in a small proportion of the population, as in Brazil, or spread more evenly across society, as in Sweden). However, questions about which kind of distribution is more *just*, which kind of society is best to live in, are not answered within economic theory—these are philosophical questions. Medical professionals are concerned with facts about sickness and death, and often have to

---

* In the East, Lao-Tzu, the founder of Taoism, probably lived at about the same time in China. Buddha and Confucius were born a few decades later. In India, an oral literature called the Veda had been asking philosophical questions since at least 1500 BCE.

make decisions about the severity of an illness or weigh the risk of death from a certain procedure. Philosophers also examine the phenomenon of death, but ask different questions: for example, they ask whether people can survive their own deaths (i.e., if there is a soul), whether death is really a harm for the person who dies, under what conditions—if any—we should assist people in committing suicide, and so on.

One reason why philosophers deal differently with phenomena than scientists do is that philosophers are using different techniques of investigation. The core of the philosophical method is the application of *rational thought* to problems. There are (arguably) two main aspects to this: the use of conceptual or linguistic *analysis* to clarify ideas and questions, and the use of formal or informal *logic* to argue for certain answers to those questions.

For example, questions about the morality of abortion often pivot on the following question: is a fetus a *person* or not? A person is, roughly, someone who has a similar moral status to a normal adult human being. Being a person is not simply *the same thing* as being a member of the human species, however, since it is at least possible that some human beings are not persons (brain-dead individuals in permanent comas, for example?) and some persons might not be human beings (intelligent life from other planets, or gorillas, perhaps?). If it turns out that a fetus *is* a person, abortion will be morally problematic— it may even be a kind of murder. On the other hand, if a fetus is no more a person than, say, one of my kidneys, abortion may be as morally permissible as a transplant. So *is* a fetus a person? How would one even go about discovering the answer to this question? Philosophers proceed by using *conceptual analysis*. What we need to find out, first of all, is what makes something a person—what the essential difference is between persons and non-persons—and then we can apply this general account to human fetuses to see if they satisfy the definition. Put another way, we need to discover precisely what the word "person" means.

Since different conceptual analyses will provide importantly different answers to questions about the morality of abortion, we need to *justify* our definition: we need to give reasons to believe that one particular analysis of personhood is correct. This is where logic comes in: logic is the study of arguments, and its techniques are designed to distinguish between good arguments—by which we should be persuaded—and bad arguments, which we should not find persuasive. (The next main section of this introduction will tell you a little more about logic.)

PHILOSOPHY AS A SUBJECT MATTER

Another way of understanding philosophy is to say that philosophers study a special set of issues, and that it is this subject matter which defines the subject. Philosophical questions fit three major characteristics:

1. They are of deep and lasting interest to human beings;
2. They have answers, but the answers have not yet been settled on;
3. The answers cannot be decided by science, faith, or common sense.

Philosophers try to give the best possible answers to such questions. That is, they seek the one answer which is more justified than any other possible answer. There are lots of questions which count as philosophical, according to these criteria. All can be classified as versions of one of three basic philosophical questions.

The first foundational philosophical question is *What exists?* For example: Does God exist? Are quarks really real, or are they just fictional postulates of a particular scientific theory? Are numbers real? Do persons exist, and what is the difference between a person and her physical body, or between a person and a 'mere animal'? The various questions of existence are studied by the branch of philosophy called Metaphysics, and by its various sub-fields such as Philosophy of Mind and the study of Personal Identity.

The second fundamental philosophical question is *What do we know?* For example, can we be sure that a scientific theory is actually true, or is it merely the currently dominant simplification of reality? The world appears to us to be full of colors and smells, but can we ever find out whether it really is colored or smelly (i.e., even if no one is perceiving it)? Everyone believes that 5+6=11, but what makes us so sure of this—could we be wrong, and if not, why not? The branch of philosophy which deals with these kinds of questions is called Epistemology. Philosophy of Science examines the special claims to knowledge made by the natural sciences, and Logic is the study of the nature of rational justification.

The third major philosophical question is *What should we do?* If I make a million dollars selling widgets or playing basketball, is it okay for me to keep all of that money and do what I want with it, or do I have some kind of moral obligation to give a portion of my income to the less well off? If I could get out of trouble by telling a lie, and no one else will really be harmed by my lie, is it alright to do so? Is Mozart's *Requiem* more or less artistically valuable than The Beatles' *Sgt. Pepper's Lonely Hearts Club Band*? Questions like these are addressed by Value Theory, which includes such philosophical areas as Ethics, Aesthetics, Political Philosophy, and Philosophy of Law.

PHILOSOPHY AS AN ATTITUDE

A third view is that philosophy is a state of being—a kind of intellectual independence. Philosophy is a reflective activity, an attitude of critical and systematic thoughtfulness. To be philosophical is to continue to question the assumptions behind every claim until we come to our most basic beliefs about reality, and then to critically examine those beliefs. For example, most of us assume that criminals are responsible for their actions, and that this is at least partly why we punish them. But *are* they responsible for what they do? We know that social pressures are very powerful in affecting our behavior. Is it unfair to make individuals entirely responsible for society's effects on them when those effects are negative? How much of our personal identity is bound up with the kind of community we belong to, and how far are we free to choose our own personalities and values? Furthermore, it is common to believe that the brain is the physical cause of all our behavior, that the brain is an entirely physical organ, and that all physical objects are subject to deterministic causal laws. If all of this is right, then presumably all human behavior is just the result of complex causal laws affecting our brain and body, and we could no more choose our actions than a falling rock could choose to take a different route down the mountainside. If this is true, then can we even make sense of the notion of moral responsibility? If it is not true, then where does free will come from and how (if at all) does it allow us to escape the laws of physics? Here, a questioning attitude towards our assumptions about criminals has shown that we might not have

properly considered the bases of our assumptions. This ultimately leads us to fundamental questions about the place of human beings in the world.

Here are three quotations from famous philosophers which give the flavor of this view of philosophy as a critical attitude:

Socrates, one of the earliest Western philosophers, who lived in Greece around 400 BCE, is said to have declared that it "is the greatest good for a man, to talk every day about virtue and the other things you hear me converse about when I examine both myself and others, and that the unexamined life is not worth living for a man."[*]

Immanuel Kant—the most important thinker of the late eighteenth century—called this philosophical state of being "Enlightenment."

> Enlightenment is the emergence of man from the immaturity for which he is himself responsible. Immaturity is the inability to use one's understanding without the guidance of another. Man is responsible for his own immaturity, when it is caused, by lack not of understanding, but of the resolution and the courage to use it without the guidance of another. *Sapere aude*! Have the courage to use your own reason! is the slogan of Enlightenment.[†]

Finally, in the twentieth century, Bertrand Russell wrote the following assessment of the value of philosophy:

> Philosophy is to be studied, not for the sake of any definite answers to its questions, since no definite answers can, as a rule, be known to be true, but rather for the sake of the questions themselves; because these questions enlarge our conception of what is possible, enrich our intellectual imagination and diminish the dogmatic assurance which closes the mind against speculation; but above all because, through the greatness of the universe which philosophy contemplates, the mind also is rendered great, and becomes capable of that union with the universe which constitutes its highest good.[‡]

---

[*]   Plato, *Apology* 38a, in *The Apology and Related Dialogues*, ed. Andrew Bailey, trans. Cathal Woods and Ryan Pack (Broadview, 2016), 75–76.

[†]   Immanuel Kant, "An Answer to the Question: What Is Enlightenment?" in *Practical Philosophy*, ed. Mary J. Gregor (Cambridge University Press, 1996), 17.

[‡]   Bertrand Russell, *The Problems of Philosophy* (Oxford University Press, 1912), 93–94.

SUGGESTIONS FOR CRITICAL REFLECTION

1. Here are some more examples of phenomena which are studied by both scientists and philosophers: color, sense perception, medical practices like abortion and euthanasia, human languages, mathematics, quantum mechanics, the evolution of species, democracy, taxation. What contribution (if any) might philosophers make to the study of these topics?

2. How well does *mathematics* fit into the division between science and philosophy described above? How does *religion* fit into this classification?

3. Here are a few simple candidate definitions of "person": a person is anything which is capable of making rational decisions; a person is any creature who can feel pain; a person is any creature with a soul; a person is any creature which has the appropriate place in a human community. Which of these, if any, do you think are plausible? What are the consequences of these definitions for moral issues like abortion or vegetarianism? Try to come up with a more sophisticated conceptual analysis of personhood.

4. Do you think criminals are responsible for their actions?

5. Should society support philosophy, and to what degree (e.g., should tax dollars be spent paying philosophers to teach at public universities? Why (not)?)?

A Brief Introduction to Arguments

EVALUATING ARGUMENTS

The main tool of philosophy is the *argument*. An argument is any sequence of statements intended to establish—or at least to make plausible—some particular claim. For example, if I say that Vancouver is a better place to live in than Toronto because it has a beautiful setting between the mountains and the ocean, is more relaxed, and has a lower cost of living, then I am making an argument. The claim which is being defended is called the *conclusion*, and the statements which together are supposed to show that the conclusion is (likely to be) true are called the *premises*. Often arguments will be strung together in a sequence, with the conclusions of earlier arguments featuring as premises of the later ones. For example, I might go on to argue that since Vancouver is a better place to live in than Toronto, and since one's living conditions are a big part of what determines one's happiness, then the people who live in Vancouver must, in general, be happier than those living in Toronto. Usually, a work of philosophy is primarily made up of chains of argumentation: good philosophy consists of good arguments; bad philosophy contains bad arguments.

What makes the difference between a good and a bad argument? It's important to notice, first of all, that the difference is *not* that good arguments have true conclusions and bad arguments have false ones. A perfectly good argument might, unluckily, happen to have a conclusion that is false. For example, you might argue that you know this rope will bear my weight because you know that the rope's rating is greater than my weight, you know that the rope's manufacturer is a reliable one, you have a good understanding of the safety standards which are imposed on rope makers and vendors, and you have carefully inspected this rope for flaws. Nevertheless, it still might be the case that this rope is the one in 50 million which has a hidden defect causing it to snap. If so, that makes me unlucky, but it doesn't suddenly make your argument a bad one—we were still being quite reasonable when we trusted the rope. On the other hand, it is very easy to give appallingly bad arguments for true conclusions: Every sentence beginning with the letter "c" is true; "Chickens lay eggs" begins with the letter "c"; therefore, chickens lay eggs.

But there is a deeper reason why the evaluation of arguments doesn't begin by assessing the truth of the conclusion. The whole point of making arguments is to establish *whether or not* some particular claim is true or false. An argument works by starting from some claims which, ideally, everyone is willing to accept as true—the premises—and then showing that something interesting—something *new*—follows from them: i.e., an argument tells you that *if* you believe these premises, *then* you should also believe this conclusion. In general, it would be unfair, therefore, to simply reject the conclusion and suppose that the argument must be a bad one—in fact, it would often be intellectually dishonest. If the argument *were* a good one, then it would show you that you might be *wrong* in supposing its conclusion to be false; and to refuse to accept this is not to respond to the argument but simply to ignore it.*

It follows that there are exactly two reasonable ways to criticize an argument. The first is to question the truth of the *premises*. The second is to question the claim that if the premises are true then the conclusion is true as well—that is, one can critique the *strength* of the argument. Querying the truth of the premises (i.e., asking whether it's really true that Vancouver is cheaper than Toronto) is fairly straightforward. The thing to bear in mind is that you will usually be working backwards down a chain of argumentation: that is, each premise of a philosopher's main argument will often be supported by sub-arguments, and the controversial premises in these sub-arguments might be defended by further arguments, and so on. Normally it is not enough to merely demand to know whether some particular premise is true: one must look for *why* the arguer thinks it is true, and then engage with *that* argument.

Understanding and critiquing the strength of an argument (either your own or someone else's) is somewhat more complex. In fact, this is the main subject of most books and courses in introductory logic. When dealing with the strength of an argument, it is usual to divide arguments into two classes: *deductive* arguments and *inductive* arguments. Good deductive arguments are the strongest possible kind of argument: if their premises are true, then their conclusion *must necessarily* be true. For example, if all bandicoots are rat-like marsupials, and if Billy is a bandicoot, then it cannot possibly be false that Billy is a rat-like marsupial. On the other hand, good inductive arguments establish that, if the premises are true, then the conclusion is *highly likely* (but not absolutely certain) to be true as well. For example, I may notice that the first bandicoot I see is rat-like, and the second one is, and the third, and so on; eventually, I might reasonably conclude that all bandicoots are rat-like. This is a good argument for a probable conclusion, but nevertheless the conclusion can never be shown to be *necessarily* true. Perhaps a non-rat-like bandicoot once existed before I was born, or perhaps there is one living now in an obscure corner of New Guinea, or perhaps no bandicoot

so far has ever been non-rat-like but at some point, in the future, a bandicoot will be born that in no way resembles a rat, and so on.

DEDUCTIVE ARGUMENTS AND VALIDITY

The strength of deductive arguments is an on/off affair, rather than a matter of degree. Either these arguments are such that if the premises are true then the conclusion necessarily must be, or they are not. Strong deductive arguments are called *valid*; otherwise, they are called *invalid*. The main thing to notice about validity is that its definition is an *if ... then ...* statement: *if* the premises *were* true, then the conclusion *would* be. For example, an argument can be valid even if its premises and its conclusion are not true: all that matters is that if the premises *had* been true, the conclusion necessarily would have been as well. This is an example of a valid argument:

1. Either bees are rodents or they are birds.
2. Bees are not birds.
3. Therefore bees are rodents.

If the first premise were true, then (since the second premise is already true) the conclusion would *have* to be true—that's what makes this argument valid. This example makes it clear that validity, though a highly desirable property in an argument, is not enough all by itself to make a good argument: good deductive arguments are both valid *and* have true premises. When arguments are good in this way they are called *sound*: sound arguments have the attractive feature that they necessarily have true conclusions. To show that an argument is unsound, it is enough to show that it is either invalid or has a false premise.

It bears emphasizing that even arguments which have true premises and a true conclusion can be unsound. For example:

1. Only US citizens can become the President of America.

---

* Of course, occasionally, you might legitimately know for sure that the conclusion is false, and then you could safely ignore arguments which try to show it is true: for example, after the rope breaks, I could dismiss your argument that it is safe (again, though, this would not show that your argument was bad, just that I need not be persuaded that the conclusion is true). However, this will not do for philosophical arguments: all interesting philosophy deals with issues where, though we may have firm opinions, we cannot just insist that we know all the answers and can therefore afford to ignore relevant arguments.

2. George W. Bush is a US citizen.
3. Therefore, George W. Bush was elected President of America.

This argument is not valid, and therefore it should not convince anyone who does not already believe the conclusion to start believing it. It is not valid because the conclusion could have been false even though the premises were true: Bush could have lost to Gore in 2000, for example. The question to ask, in thinking about the validity of arguments, is this: Is there a coherent possible world, which I can even *imagine*, in which the premises are true and the conclusion false? If there is, then the argument is invalid.

When assessing the deductive arguments that you encounter in philosophical work, it is often useful to try to lay out, as clearly as possible, their *structure*. A standard and fairly simple way to do this is simply to pull out the logical connecting phrases and to replace, with letters, the sentences they connect. Five of the most common and important 'logical operators' are *and*, *or*, *it is not the case that*, *if ... then ...*, and *if and only if....* For example, consider the following argument: "If God is perfectly powerful (omnipotent) and perfectly good, then no evil would exist. But evil does exist. Therefore, God cannot be both omnipotent and perfectly good; so either God is not all-powerful or he is not perfectly good." The structure of this argument could be laid bare as follows:

1. If (O and G) then not-E.
2. E.
3. Therefore, not-(O and G).
4. Therefore, either not-O or not-G.

Revealing the structure in this way can make it easier to see whether or not the argument is valid. And in this case, it is valid. In fact, no matter what O, G, and E stand for—no matter how we fill in the blanks—*any* argument of this form must be valid. You could try it yourself—invent random sentences to fill in for O, G, and E, and no matter how hard you try, you will never produce an argument with all true premises and a false conclusion.* What this shows is that validity is often a property of the *form* or structure

of an argument. (This is why deductive logic is known as "formal logic." It is not formal in the sense that it is stiff and ceremonious, but because it has to do with argument forms.)

Using this kind of shorthand, therefore, it is possible to describe certain general argument forms which are *invariably* valid and which—since they are often used in philosophical writing—it can be handy to look out for. For example, a very common and valuable form of argument looks like this: if P then Q; P; therefore Q. This form is often called *modus ponens*. Another—which appears in the previous argument about God and evil—is *modus tollens*: if P then Q; not-Q; therefore not-P. A *disjunctive syllogism* works as follows: either P or Q; not-P; therefore Q. A *hypothetical syllogism* has the structure: if P then Q; if Q then R; therefore if P then R. Finally, a slightly more complicated but still common argument structure is sometimes called a *constructive dilemma*: either P or Q; if P then R; if Q then R; therefore R.

INDUCTIVE ARGUMENTS AND INDUCTIVE STRENGTH

I noted above that the validity of deductive arguments is a yes/no affair—that a deductive argument is either extremely strong or it is hopelessly weak. This is not true for inductive arguments. The strength of an inductive argument—the amount of support the premises give to the conclusion—is a matter of degree, and there is no clear dividing line between the 'strong' inductive arguments and the 'weak' ones. Nevertheless, some inductive arguments are obviously much stronger than others, and it is useful to think a little bit about what factors make a difference.

There are lots of different types and structures of inductive arguments; here I will briefly describe four which are fairly representative and commonly encountered in philosophy. The first is *inductive generalization*. This type of argument is the prototypical inductive argument—indeed, it is often what people mean when they use the term "induction"—and it has the following form:

1. *x* per cent of observed Fs are G.
2. Therefore *x* per cent of all Fs are G.

---

* Since the argument about God and evil is valid, then we are left with only two possibilities. Either all its premises are true, and then it is sound and its conclusion must inescapably be true. Or one of its premises is false, in which case the conclusion might be false (though we would still not have shown that it is false). The only way to effectively critique this argument, therefore, is to argue against one of the claims 1 and 2.

That is, inductive generalizations work by inferring a claim about an entire *population* of objects from data about a *sample* of those objects. For example:

(a) Every swan I have ever seen is white, so all swans (in the past and future, and on every part of the planet) are white.
(b) Every swan I have ever seen is white, so probably all the swans around here are white.
(c) 800 of the 1,000 rocks we have taken from the Moon contain silicon, so probably around 80% of the Moon's surface contains silicon.
(d) We have tested two very pure samples of copper in the lab and found that each sample has a boiling point of 2,567°C; we conclude that 2,567°C is the boiling point for copper.
(e) Every intricate system I have seen created (such as houses and watches) has been the product of intelligent design, so therefore all intricate systems (including, for example, frogs and volcanoes) must be the product of intelligent design.

The two main considerations when assessing the strength of inductive generalizations are the following. First, ask how *representative* is the sample? How likely is it that whatever is true of the sample will also be true of the population as a whole? For instance, although the sample size in argument (c) is much larger than that in argument (d), it is much more likely to be biased: we know that pure copper is very uniform, so a small sample will do; but the surface of the Moon might well be highly variable, and so data about the areas around moon landings may not be representative of the surface as a whole. Second, it is important to gauge how cautious and *accurate* the conclusion is, given the data—how far beyond the evidence does it go? The conclusion to argument (a) is a much more radical inference from the data than that in argument (b); consequently, though less exciting, the conclusion of argument (b) is much better supported by the premise.

A second type of inductive argument is an *argument from analogy*. It most commonly has the following form:

1. Object (or objects) *A* and object (or objects) *B* are alike in having features F, G, H, ...
2. *B* has feature X.
3. Therefore *A* has feature X as well.

These examples illustrate arguments from analogy:

(a) Human brains and dolphin brains are large, compared to body size. Humans are capable of planning for the future. So, dolphins must also be capable of planning for the future.
(b) Humans and dolphins are both mammals and often grow to more than five feet long. Humans are capable of planning for the future. So, dolphins must also be capable of planning for the future.
(c) Eagles and robins are alike in having wings, feathers, claws, and beaks. Eagles kill and eat sheep. Therefore, robins kill and eat sheep.
(d) Anselm's ontological argument has the same argumentative form as Gaunilo's "Lost Island" argument. But Gaunilo's argument is a patently bad argument. So there must be something wrong with the ontological argument.
(e) An eye and a watch are both complex systems in which all of the parts are inter-dependent and where any small misadjustment could lead to a complete failure of the whole. A watch is the product of intelligent design. Therefore, the eye must also be the product of intelligent design (i.e., God exists).

The strength of an argument from analogy depends mostly on two things: first, the degree of *positive relevance* that the noted similarities (F, G, H ...) have to the target property X; and second, the absence of *relevant dissimilarities*—properties which *A* has but *B* does not, which make it *less* likely that *A* is X. For example, the similarity (brain size) between humans and dolphins cited in argument (a) is much more relevant to the target property (planning) than are the similarities cited in argument (b). This, of course, makes (a) a much stronger argument than (b). The primary problem with argument (c), on the other hand, is that we know that robins are much smaller and weaker than eagles and this dissimilarity makes it far less likely that they kill sheep.

A third form of inductive argument is often called *inference to the best explanation* or sometimes *abduction*. This kind of argument works in the following way. Suppose we have a certain quantity of data to explain (such as the behavior of light in various media, or facts about the complexity of biological organisms, or a set of ethical claims). Suppose also that we have a number of theories which account for this data in different ways (e.g., the theory that light is a particle, or the theory that light is a wave, or the theory that it is somehow both). One way of arguing for the truth of one of these theories, over the others, is to show that one theory provides a much *better explanation* of the data than the others. What counts as making a theory a better explanation can be a bit tricky, but some basic criteria would be:

1. The theory predicts all the data we know to be true.
2. The theory explains all this data in the most economical and theoretically satisfying way (scientists and mathematicians often call this the most *beautiful* theory).
3. The theory predicts some *new* phenomena which turn out to exist and which would be a big surprise if one of the competing theories were true. (For example, one of the clinchers for Einstein's theory of relativity was the observation that starlight is bent by the sun's gravity. This would have been a big surprise under the older Newtonian theory, but was predicted by Einstein's theory.)

Here are some examples of inferences to the best explanation:

(a) When I inter-breed my pea plants, I observe certain patterns in the properties of the plants produced (e.g., in the proportion of tall plants, or of plants which produce wrinkled peas). If the properties of pea plants were generated randomly, these patterns would be highly surprising. However, if plants pass on packets of information (genes) to their offspring, the patterns I have observed would be neatly explained. Therefore, genes exist.

(b) The biological world is a highly complex and inter-dependent system. It is highly unlikely that such a system would have come about (and would continue to hang together) from the purely random motions of particles. It would be much less surprising if it were the result of conscious design from a super-intelligent creator. Therefore, the biological world was deliberately created (and therefore, God exists).

(c) The biological world is a highly complex and inter-dependent system. It is highly unlikely that such a system would have come about (and would continue to hang together) from the purely random motions of particles. It would be much less surprising if it were the result of an evolutionary process of natural selection which mechanically preserves order and eliminates randomness, and which (if it existed) would produce a world much like the one we see around us. Therefore, the theory of evolution is true.

The final type of inductive argument that I want to mention here is usually called *reductio ad absurdum*, which means "reduction to absurdity." It is always a negative argument, and has this structure:

1. Suppose (for the sake of argument) that position *p* were true.
2. If *p* were true then something else, *q*, would also have to be true.
3. However *q* is absurd—it can't possibly be true.
4. Therefore *p* can't be true either.

In fact, this argument style can be either inductive or deductive, depending on how rigorous premises 2 and 3 are. If *p* logically implies *q*, and if *q* is a logical contradiction, then it is deductively certain that *p* can't be true (at least, assuming the classical laws of logic). On the other hand, if *q* is merely absurd but not literally *impossible*, then the argument is inductive: it makes it highly likely that *p* is false, but does not prove it beyond all doubt.

Here are a few examples of *reductio* arguments:

(a) Suppose that gun control were a good idea. That would mean it's a good idea for the government to gather information on anything we own which, in the wrong hands, could be a lethal weapon, such as kitchen knives and baseball bats. But that would be ridiculous. This shows gun control cannot be a good idea.

(b) If you think that fetuses have a right to life because they have hearts and fingers and toes, then you must believe that anything with a heart, fingers, and toes has a right to life. But that would be absurd. Therefore, a claim like this about fetuses cannot be a good argument against abortion.

(c) Suppose, for the sake of argument, that this is not the best possible world. But that would mean God had either deliberately chosen to create a sub-standard world or had failed to notice that this was not the best of all possible worlds, and either of these options is absurd. Therefore, it must be true that this is the best of all possible worlds.

(d) "The anti-vitalist says that there is no such thing as vital spirit. But this claim is self-refuting. The speaker can be taken seriously only if his claim cannot. For if the claim is true, then the speaker does not have vital spirit and must be dead. But if he is dead, then his statement is a meaningless string of noises, devoid of reason and truth."*

The critical questions to ask about *reductio* arguments are simply: *Does* the supposedly absurd consequence follow from the position being attacked? and Is it *really* absurd?

A FEW COMMON FALLACIES

Just as it can be useful to look for common patterns of reasoning in philosophical writing, it can also be helpful to be on guard for a few recurring fallacies—and, equally importantly, to take care not to commit them in your own philosophical writing. Here are four common ones:

Begging the question does not mean, as the media would have us believe, stimulating one to ask a further question; instead, it means to assume as true (as one of your premises) the very same thing which you are supposedly attempting to prove. This fallacy is sometimes called *circular reasoning* or even (the old Latin name) *petitio principii*. To argue, for example, that God exists because (a) the Bible says that God exists, (b) God wrote the Bible, and (c) God would not lie, is to commit a blatant case of begging the question. In this case, of course, one would have no reason to accept the premises as true unless one *already* believed the conclusion. Usually, however, arguments that beg the question are a little more disguised. For example, "Adultery is immoral, since sexual relations outside marriage violate ethical principles," or "Terrorism is bad, because it encourages further acts of terrorism," are both instances of circular reasoning.

Arguing *ad hominem* means attacking or rejecting a position not because the arguments for it are poor, but because the person presenting those arguments is unattractive in some way: i.e., an attack is directed at the person (which is what *ad hominem* means) rather than at their argument. The following are implicit *ad hominem* arguments: "You say churches have too much influence on society? Well, Hitler and Stalin would agree with you!" and "We shouldn't trust the claim, by philosophers such as Anselm, Aquinas, and Leibniz, that God exists, since they were all Christian philosophers and so of course they were biased." Such attacks are fallacious because they have nothing at all to do with how reasonable a claim is: even if the claim is false, *ad hominem* attacks do nothing to show this.

Straw person arguments are particularly devious, and this fallacy can be hard to spot (or to avoid committing) unless great care is taken. The *straw person* fallacy consists in misrepresenting someone else's position so that it can be more easily criticized. It is like attacking a dummy stuffed with straw instead of a real opponent. For example, it's not uncommon to see attacks on "pro-choice" activists for thinking that abortion is a good thing. However, whatever the merits of either position, this objection is clearly unfair—no serious abortion advocates think it is a positively *good thing* to have an abortion; at most they claim that (at least in some circumstances) it is a lesser evil than the alternative. Here's an even more familiar example, containing two straw persons, one after the other: "We should clean out the closets. They're getting a bit messy." "Why, we just went through those closets last year. Do we have to clean them out every day?" "I never said anything about cleaning them out every day. You just want to keep all your junk forever, which is simply ridiculous."

Arguments from ignorance, finally, are based on the assumption that lack of evidence *for* something is evidence that it is false, or that lack of evidence *against* something is evidence for its truth. Generally, neither of these assumptions is reliable. For example, even if we could find no good proof to show that God exists, this would not, all by itself, suffice to show that God does *not* exist: it would still be possible, for example, that God exists but transcends our limited human reason. Consider the following 'argument' by Senator Joseph McCarthy, about some poor official in the State Department: "I do not have much information on this except the general statement of the agency that there is nothing in the files to disprove his Communist connections."†

---

* This example is from Paul Churchland's "Eliminative Materialism and the Propositional Attitudes," *Journal of Philosophy* 78 (1981). (Note, however, that it is not Churchland's argument.)

† McCarthy on the Senate floor, quoted by Richard H. Rovere in *Senator Joe McCarthy* (University of California Press, 1996), 132.

SUGGESTIONS FOR CRITICAL REFLECTION

1. Suppose some deductive argument has a premise which is necessarily false. Is it a valid argument?
2. Suppose some deductive argument has a conclusion which is necessarily true. Is it a valid argument? From this information alone, can you tell whether it is sound?
3. Is the following argument form valid: if P then Q; Q; therefore P? How about: if P then Q; not-P; so not-Q?
4. No inductive argument is strong enough to *prove* that its conclusion is true: the best it can do is to show that the conclusion is highly probable. Does this make inductive arguments bad or less useful? Why don't we restrict ourselves to using only deductive arguments?
5. Formal logic provides mechanical and reliable methods for assessing the validity of deductive arguments. Do you think there might be some similar system for evaluating the strength of inductive arguments?
6. I have listed four important fallacies; can you identify any other common patterns of poor reasoning?

Introductory Tips on Reading and Writing Philosophy

READING PHILOSOPHY

As you will soon find out, if you haven't already, it is not easy to read philosophy. It can be exhilarating, stimulating, life-changing, or even annoying, but it isn't easy. There are no real shortcuts for engaging with philosophy (though the notes accompanying the readings in this book are intended to remove a few of the more unnecessary barriers); however, there are two things to remember which will help you get the most out of reading philosophy—*read it several times*, and *read it actively*.

Philosophical writing is not like a novel, a historical narrative, or even a textbook: it is typically dense, compressed, and written to contribute to an on-going debate with which you may not yet be fully familiar. This means, no matter how smart you are, it is highly unlikely that you will get an adequate understanding of any halfway interesting piece of philosophy the first time through, and it may even take two or three more readings before it really becomes clear. Furthermore, even after that point, repeated readings of good philosophy will usually reveal new and interesting nuances to the writer's position, and occasionally you will notice some small point that seems to open a mental door and show you what the author is trying to say in a whole new way. As they say, if a piece of philosophy isn't worth reading at least twice, it isn't worth reading once. Every selection in this book, I guarantee, is well worth reading once.

As you go through a piece of philosophy, it is very important to engage with it: instead of just letting the words wash over you, you should make a positive effort, first, to

understand, and then, to critically assess the ideas you encounter. On your first read-through it is a good idea to try to formulate a high-level understanding of what the philosopher is attempting: What are the main claims? What is the overall structure of the arguments behind them? At this stage, it can be useful to pay explicit attention to section headings and introductory paragraphs.

Ideally during a second reading, you should try to reconstruct the author's arguments and sub-arguments in more detail. To help yourself understand them, consider jotting down their outlines on a sheet of paper. At this point, it can be extremely fruitful to pay attention to special definitions or distinctions used by the author in the arguments. It is also helpful to consider the historical context in which the philosopher wrote, and to look for connections to ideas found in other philosophical works.

Finally, on third and subsequent readings, it is valuable to expressly look for *objections* to the writer's argument (Are the premises true? Is the argument strong?), *unclarities* in position statements, or *assumptions* they depend upon, but do not argue for. I make these suggestions partly because the process of critical assessment is helpful in coming to understand a philosopher's work; but more importantly for the reason that—perhaps contrary to popular opinion—philosophers are typically playing for very high stakes. When philosophers write about whether God exists, whether science is a rational enterprise, or whether unfettered capitalism creates a just society, they are seriously interested in discovering the *answers* to these questions. The arguments they make, if they are good enough, will be strong reasons to believe one thing rather than another. If you are reading philosophy properly, you must sincerely join the debate and be honestly prepared to be persuaded—but it is also important not to let yourself be persuaded too easily.

WRITING PHILOSOPHY

Writing philosophy consists, in roughly equal measures, of *thinking* about philosophy and then of trying to express your ideas *clearly and precisely*. This makes it somewhat unlike other writing: the point of writing philosophy is not, alas, to entertain, nor to explain some chunk of knowledge, nor to trick or cajole the reader into accepting a certain thesis. The point of philosophical writing is, really, to *do* philosophy. This means that, since philosophy is based on arguments, most philosophical essays will have the underlying structure of an argument. They will seek to defend some particular philosophical claim by developing one or more good arguments for that claim.*

There is no particular template to follow for philosophical writing (there are lots of different kinds of good philosophical writing—lots of different ways of arguing well), but here are seven suggestions you might find useful:

1. Take your time. Spend time thinking, and then leave yourself enough time to get the writing right.

2. After you've thought for a while, begin by making an outline of the points you want to make (rather than immediately launching into prose). Then write several drafts, preferably allowing some cooling-off time between drafts so you can come back refreshed and with a more objective eye. Be prepared for the fact that writing a second draft doesn't mean merely tinkering with what you've already got, but starting at the beginning and writing it again.

3. Strive to be clear. Avoid unnecessary jargon, and use plain, simple words whenever possible; concrete examples can be extremely useful in explaining what you mean. It's also worth remembering that the clarity of a piece of writing has a lot to do with

its structure. Ideally, the argumentative structure of your essay should be obvious to the reader, and it is a good idea to use your introduction to give the reader a 'road map' of the argument to follow.

4. Aim for precision. Make sure the *thesis* of your essay is spelled out in sufficient detail that the reader is left in no doubt about what you are arguing for (and therefore what the implications will be, if your arguments are strong ones). Also, take care to define important terms so the reader knows exactly what you mean by them. Terms should normally be defined under any of the following three conditions: (a) the word is a technical term whose meaning a layperson probably won't know (e.g., "intrinsic value"); (b) it is an ordinary word whose meaning is not sufficiently clear or precise for philosophical purposes (e.g., "abortion"); or (c) it is an ordinary word that you are going to use to mean something other than what it normally means (e.g., "person").

5. Focus. Everything you write should directly contribute to establishing your thesis. Anything which is unnecessary for your arguments should be eliminated. Make every word count. Also, don't be over-ambitious; properly done, philosophy moves at a fairly slow pace—it is unlikely that anyone could show adequately that, for example, there is no such thing as matter in three pages or less.

6. Argue as well and as carefully as you can. Defend your position using reason and not rhetoric; critically assess the strength of your arguments, and consider the plausibility of your premises. It's important to consider alternatives to your own position and possible counter-arguments; don't be afraid to raise and attempt to reply to objections to your position. (If you make a serious objection, one which you cannot answer, perhaps you should change your position.)

7. When you think you are finished, read the essay out loud and/or give it to someone else to read—at a minimum, this is a good way of checking for ease of reading, and it may reveal problems with your essay or argument that hadn't previously occurred to you.

---

* The conclusion of a philosophical essay, however, need not always be something like: "God exists," or "Physical objects are not colored." It could just as legitimately be something like: "Philosopher A's third argument is flawed," or "When the arguments of philosopher A and those of philosopher B are compared, B wins," or "No one has yet given a good argument to show either P or not-P," or even "Philosopher A's argument is not, as is widely thought, X, but instead it is Y." Though these kinds of claims are, perhaps, less immediately exciting than the first two examples, they are still philosophical claims, they still need to be argued for, and they can be extremely important in an overall debate about, say, the existence of God.

Does God Exist?

The philosophy of religion is the sub-field of philosophy concerned with the rational evaluation of the truth of religious claims; in particular, the philosophy of religion deals most centrally with claims about the existence, nature, and activities of God. For example, one might ask, is it coherent to say that God is absolutely all-powerful?* Can God be *both* all-knowing and unchanging?† If God is all-knowing—and so knows everything that I am going to do—then in what sense can human beings really be said to have free will? Does God exist eternally, or instead is God somehow 'outside' of time altogether? Does God listen to and answer prayers? Does God ever cause miracles to occur? Does God punish sinners, and if so then what counts as sin and how does the deity punish it? How can a deity consign souls to eternal damnation and yet still be considered benevolent? Could God command us to torture little children for fun, and if he did so would this be a moral duty? If God is inexpressibly mysterious, as some religious creeds assert, then how does one know what one believes in if one believes in God? And so on.

The religious proposition singled out for philosophical evaluation in this chapter is something like the following:

---

* Consider, for instance, this old quandary: can God make a stone so heavy that even God cannot lift it? Whichever way this question is answered, it seems that there must be at least one thing which God cannot do.

† After all, as the world changes over time, so must the facts which God knows to be true at that time. What God knew to be true ten seconds ago will differ from what he knows to be true now, which will be different again from what will be true in ten seconds, and so on. So (it appears) God's beliefs must be constantly changing if they are to remain true, so God cannot be eternally unchanging.

that there exists one, and exactly one, deity who is eternal, immaterial, all-powerful, all-knowing, and perfectly morally good, and who created the universe and all its inhabitants. The first seven readings in this chapter introduce (and evaluate) the three main arguments in favor of the existence of such an entity and the most important argument against its existence.

One of the earliest philosophical arguments for the existence of God comes from Saint Anselm in the eleventh century and is called the *ontological argument*. The ontological argument tries to show that God *necessarily* exists since God's existence is logically entailed by the concept of God. This argument, a version of which also appears in Descartes's *Meditations* in the Epistemology chapter of this volume, is criticized in the Anselm reading by a monk called Gaunilo, and also in the selections in this chapter from Aquinas and Hume.

The second main type of argument for the existence of God is what is called the *cosmological argument*. Arguments of this type start from observations about the world (the 'cosmos'), such as that every event has a cause, or that all natural things depend for their existence on something else, and infer from this that there must be some entity—a creator and a sustainer—which necessarily exists and upon which everything else depends for its existence. Aquinas presents three cosmological arguments, the first three of his 'Five Ways.'

Finally, the third main variety of argument for the existence of God is the so-called *teleological argument*, often known as the *argument from design*. These arguments begin from the premise that the natural world shows signs of intelligent design or purpose (the Greek for purpose is *telos*) and from this draw the conclusion that the universe must have had an intelligent designer—God. The fifth of Aquinas's arguments for God is a member of this species, Paley defends it strongly, and the argument from design is also presented, but then roundly criticized, by Hume.

Perhaps the most important argument *against* the existence of God is known as the *problem of evil*. This argument essentially claims that the existence of evil is incompatible with the existence of a powerful and benevolent God; since evil clearly does exist, God cannot. The problem of evil is addressed briefly by Aquinas, but turned into a serious difficulty for the existence of God

by Hume in Parts X and XI of his *Dialogues Concerning Natural Religion*. Leibniz provides a classic defense of theism against the problem of evil (a 'theodicy'), but a modern philosopher, J.L. Mackie, argues that the problem of evil is logically unbeatable. Marilyn McCord Adams provides a nuanced account from a Christian point of view of what she calls "the deepest of religious problems."

The final three readings in this chapter, Blaise Pascal's "The Wager," William Clifford's "The Ethics of Belief," and William James's "The Will to Believe," ask what we should do if it turns out that there *is* no rational reason to believe in God. Pascal argues that, even though as finite beings we cannot comprehend God or be sure of his existence, a rational person should nevertheless believe in God. In contrast, Clifford makes a passionate case that "it is wrong always, everywhere, and for anyone, to believe anything upon insufficient evidence," while in response James argues that, even if we can have no good intellectual reasons for faith, we nevertheless have the right to choose to believe in God for emotional or "passional" reasons instead.

If you want to explore this area of philosophy in more depth, there are many books available which discuss the philosophy of religion. Some of the more philosophically informed ones are: Brian Davies, *An Introduction to the Philosophy of Religion* (Oxford University Press, 2004); Anthony Flew, *God, Freedom and Immortality* (Prometheus Books, 1984); John Hick, *Arguments for the Existence of God* (Macmillan, 1970); John Hick, *Philosophy of Religion* (Prentice-Hall, 1990); Anthony Kenny, *The God of the Philosophers* (Oxford University Press, 1987); Alvin Plantinga, *God and Other Minds* (Cornell University Press, 1990); William Rowe, *Philosophy of Religion* (Wadsworth, 2006); Bertrand Russell, *Why I Am Not a Christian* (Simon and Schuster, 1957); Richard Swinburne, *The Existence of God* (Oxford University Press, 1979); Charles Taliaferro, *Contemporary Philosophy of Religion: An Introduction* (Blackwell, 1998); and Keith Yandell, *Philosophy of Religion: A Contemporary Introduction* (Routledge, 2016). Two useful reference texts are *A Companion to Philosophy of Religion*, edited by Philip Quinn and Charles Taliaferro (Blackwell, 2010), and William Wainwright, ed., *The Oxford Handbook of Philosophy of Religion* (Oxford University Press, 2007).

ST. ANSELM OF CANTERBURY

Proslogion

Who Was St. Anselm of Canterbury?

Anselm was born in 1033 to a noble family in Aosta, Italy, but after his mother's death (when he was 23) he repudiated his inherited wealth and the political career for which his father had prepared him and took up the life of a wandering scholar. In 1060 he became a monk at the Benedictine abbey of Bec in Normandy, rose rapidly through various positions of authority, and was elected Abbot in 1078. He was highly successful as Abbot, attracting monks from all over Europe and confirming Bec in its position as one of the main centers of learning of the time; during this time he became internationally known as a leading intellectual and established himself as a spiritual counselor to kings from Ireland to Jerusalem. In 1093, much against his will, he succeeded his old teacher Lanfranc as Archbishop of Canterbury, the head of the church in England. His tenure as Archbishop was stormy in the extreme: the king of England at the time, William Rufus, "seems to have combined the virtues of an American gangster with those of a South American dictator,"[*] and was determined to make the wealthy and powerful church subservient to royal authority. Anselm, by contrast, considered himself effectively co-ruler of England on the Pope's behalf, and he resisted William's encroachments fiercely and bravely. Anselm was exiled from England twice (for a total of more than five years), but eventually reached a compromise with William's brother and successor, Henry I, after the Pope threatened the king's excommunication.[†] He died in Canterbury in 1109, at the age of 76.

Anselm is often considered the most impressive philosopher and theologian of the early Middle Ages (i.e., between about 500 and 1100 CE). His major philosophical works are *Monologion* (which means "soliloquy"), *Proslogion* (Latin for "allocution," a formal speech or address), and a series of dialogues: *On the Grammarian*, *On Truth*, and *On Free Will*. His most important theological writing is *Cur Deus Homo*, or "Why God Became Man." In his final, unfinished work he tried to unravel the mystery of how a soul could come into existence. When he was told that he was soon to die, he is supposed to have replied, characteristically, "If it is His will I shall gladly obey, but if He should prefer me to stay with you just long enough to solve the question of the origin of the soul which I have been turning over in my mind, I would gratefully accept the chance, for I doubt whether anybody else will solve it when I am gone."

What Was Anselm's Overall Philosophical Project?

The original title of Anselm's *Proslogion* was *Faith Seeking Understanding*, and this encapsulates Anselm's consuming theological interest: he wanted to apply the tools of reason in order to better understand some (though not all) of what he already believed on the basis of faith. In fact, Anselm is often credited with being the first major thinker in the medieval Christian tradition to place great importance on the rational justification of theology, not (according to Anselm) because faith by itself is inadequate, but because rational proofs can improve our grasp of the nature of God. Anselm thought of the search for religious truth as not so much accumulating facts

---

[*]   Max Charlesworth, from his introduction to *St. Anselm's Proslogion* (Clarendon Press, 1965), 17.

[†]   To excommunicate someone is to ban them from membership in the church and so, in the Catholic tradition, to exclude them from all the sacraments, such as attending mass and receiving absolution for sins. Since it was believed that this would prevent those excommunicated from entering heaven, it was considered an extremely serious punishment.

about God but as coming to a better personal *acquaintance* with God, as one might come to know more about a friend over time. Since we clearly cannot sit down with God over a cup of coffee and chat, this process of finding out more about God depends to a large degree on careful, rational thought about God's nature.

Anselm is best remembered for originating one of the most stimulating and controversial of the arguments for the existence of God, the so-called Ontological Argument. ("Ontological" means "concerning what exists"; in this context, the idea is that we can come to know about God's 'pure' existence, without any sensory contact with God or his effects.) The Ontological Argument, if it works, not only proves as a matter of logic that God exists but also proves that God has a certain nature—that he is wise, good, infinite, powerful, and so on. The selection from Anselm given here is his presentation of this argument from the *Proslogion*, then a critique of the argument from Gaunilo, a monk from the Abbey of Marmoutier near Tours, and finally Anselm's response to that criticism. (Although Anselm's response to Gaunilo can be challenging reading, coming to grips with his compressed arguments is exhilarating, and important for better understanding his argument in the *Proslogion*.)

What Is the Structure of This Reading?

After a preface, in which he explains how the idea for the Ontological Argument came to him, Anselm lays out the Ontological Argument in Chapters 2 and 3 of the *Proslogion*. His argument has three parts:

(a) That something-than-which-nothing-greater-can-be-thought must really exist (Chapter 2).
(b) That furthermore it must necessarily exist: that is, it exists in such a way that it cannot be conceived by the human mind as not existing (first part of Chapter 3).
(c) That the entity described in (a) and (b) must be God (second part of Chapter 3).

In Chapter 4 Anselm responds to a possible objection to part (b) of the argument. In Chapter 5 he briefly draws some conclusions about the nature of God.

In the next section Gaunilo of Marmoutiers responds "on behalf of the Fool." Gaunilo's most important objections are:

(a) That God cannot be meaningfully thought about by human beings (Paragraph 4). Anselm responds to this in parts of Replies 1, 2, 8, and 9.
(b) That even if we could think about God, thinking about things doesn't show all by itself that they exist (Paragraphs 2 and 5). Anselm deals with this in Replies 1, 2, and 6.
(c) That if the Ontological Argument establishes the existence of God, it ought also to establish the existence of the "Lost Island," which is absurd (Paragraph 6). Anselm's response—which, rightly or wrongly, doesn't take the objection very seriously—is at the start of Reply 3.
(d) That that-than-which-a-greater-cannot-be-thought can be thought not to exist (Paragraph 7). Anselm answers in Replies 1, 3, and 9.

Some Useful Background Information

1. The Ontological Argument is an "*a priori*" argument: it purports to prove the existence of God on the basis of reason alone, independently of sensory experience and empirical science. Anselm wants to show that the *idea* of God (all by itself) proves that God must exist.

2. Anselm makes use of various distinctions that it is useful to be aware of. The first is between two kinds of existence: existence in the mind (in Latin, "in intellectu") and existence in actual reality ("in re"). Something can exist in the mind but not in reality: for example, I can imagine a gold dinosaur and this dinosaur exists only *in intellectu* but not *in re*. Or something can exist in reality but not in anyone's mind: for example, a particular rock no one has ever seen, on the dark side of the Moon. Or something can exist in *both* the mind and reality: the Eiffel Tower, for instance, is both *in re* and *in intellectu* since it is both in Paris and in our thoughts. Finally, some unreal thing no one has ever thought of would be neither *in re* nor *in intellectu*.

3. Then there is a distinction between two ways of thinking about an idea: this is the difference between merely thinking the words that express an idea and actually thinking about the thing itself. As Anselm puts it, "in one sense a thing is thought when the word signifying it is thought; in another sense when the very object which the thing is is understood." For example, the Fool might think to himself, "God does not exist," but if he does not really know what God is, then for him only "the sound of the letters or syllables" exists *in intellectu* and not actually God himself. This is sometimes explained in terms of the meaning of words or ideas: some of the ideas you think about really are meaningful to you (such as "Paris"), but some only *seem* meaningful when all you are really doing is silently mouthing the words (such as, perhaps, "crapulous"). Notice that, on this way of talking, ideas can be meaningful for us even if we do not know *everything* about their objects. For example, I don't need to have ever visited Paris to think meaningfully about that city; similarly, Anselm held that we can think about God even though God might be unimaginably greater than any picture we can form in our mind.

4. Finally, a third distinction is raised by Gaunilo and discussed by Anselm in his reply. This is the technical distinction between *thinking* (in Latin, "cogitare") and *understanding* ("intelligere"). For Anselm and Gaunilo, to think or conceive is to entertain possibilities—it's to consider things that may not actually be true and treat them (perhaps only temporarily) as if they were. For example, although I know I currently exist I could perhaps conceive of myself as not existing; although it may turn out to be false that extraterrestrials will visit the Earth within fifty years, I can certainly think that they will. By contrast, "understanding" is what philosophers today would call a 'success term': by definition, you cannot *understand* something to be true (or real) if it is in fact false (or unreal). Thus, according to Gaunilo, we could, strictly speaking, only understand the phrase "God exists" if in fact God does exist.

One important question we can now ask is the following: can we think meaningfully about things that are *not* possible? For example, can we think about square circles or married bachelors?

According to Anselm, the answer to this question is no: we can, as it were, think the *words* "square circle," but we can't really think about the things themselves. What this means, significantly, is that for Anselm anything we can properly think about must really be possible.

Some Common Misconceptions

1. Anselm is not just claiming that we can prove something exists by simply *thinking* of it existing: he realizes that not every concept which includes the idea of existence is actually exemplified. For example, we can invent a concept of an existing unicorn—a *glunicorn*, defined as a unicorn that exists. But still there is no such thing. He thinks that the concept of God (that is, that-than-which-a-greater-cannot-be-thought) is a *uniquely special* concept in this respect; God, according to Anselm, has a unique kind of reality.

2. The unwary sometimes suppose that Anselm argues in the following way: God exists in our minds (*in intellectu*); our minds exist in the world (*in re*); therefore God must also exist in the world. This, however, is not his argument. (If it were, it would merely establish that the *concept* of God exists, while Anselm wants to show that God *himself* exists. Furthermore, when Anselm says things exist *in intellectu* it's not at all clear that he literally wants to say they are *located inside our heads*; the Eiffel Tower which is the object of our thoughts is the very same one as that which is located in Paris.)

3. Anselm (perhaps contrary to what Aquinas says about him in the next reading) does not think that the existence of God is simply self-evident: that is, he doesn't think either (a) that we all already know that God exists, or (b) that merely to say "God does not exist" is to say something obviously self-contradictory (like saying "triangles have four sides"). What he does think is that *after* hearing his argument, it becomes obvious that God must exist. Similarly, he does not claim that everyone already has the concept of God (e.g., that we are born with the knowledge of God); his claim is rather that everyone can grasp that concept if it is explained to them.

How Important and Influential Is This Passage?

Rejected as mere verbal trickery by many subsequent philosophers (including St. Thomas Aquinas, in the next selection; the influential nineteenth-century philosopher Arthur Schopenhauer called it a "charming joke"), the Ontological Argument was nevertheless popular throughout the Middle Ages, was revived by René Descartes and Gottfried Leibniz in the seventeenth and eighteenth centuries, was influentially used by G.W.F. Hegel in the nineteenth century, and is still attractive to some philosophers today. Many more contemporary philosophers think it fallacious, but it has proved frustratingly difficult to uncontroversially pin down precisely what is wrong with this 'many-faced' argument. Early in the twentieth century developments in the logic of predicates (predicates are 'describing phrases' like "... is green" or "... is taller than ...") bolstered Immanuel Kant's objection that "existence is not a predicate" (see question 5 at the end of the reading). However, more recent developments in the logic of possibility and necessity (called modal logic) have apparently given the argument a new lease on life.

Proslogion

PREFACE AND CHAPTERS 2–5*

Preface

After I had published, at the pressing entreaties of several of my brethren, a certain short tract[†] as an example of meditation on the meaning of faith from the point of view of one seeking, through silent reasoning within himself, things he knows not—reflecting that this was made up of a connected chain of many arguments, I began to wonder if perhaps it might be possible to find one single argument that for its proof required no other save itself, and that by itself would suffice to prove that God really exists, that He is the supreme good needing no other and is He whom all things have need of for their being and well-being, and also to prove whatever we believe about the Divine Being. But as often and as diligently as I turned my thoughts to this, sometimes it seemed to me that I had almost reached what I was seeking, sometimes it eluded my acutest thinking completely, so that finally, in desperation, I was about to give up what I was looking for as something impossible to find. However, when I had decided to put aside this idea altogether, lest by uselessly occupying my mind it might prevent other ideas with which I could make some progress, then, in spite of my unwillingness and my resistance to it, it began to force itself upon me more and more pressingly. So it was that one day when I was quite worn out with resisting its importunacy, there came to me, in the very conflict of my thoughts, what I had despaired of finding, so that I eagerly grasped the notion which in my distraction I had been rejecting.

Judging, then, that what had given me such joy to discover would afford pleasure, if it were written down, to anyone who might read it, I have written the following short tract dealing with this question as well as several others, from the point of view of one trying to raise his mind to contemplate God and seeking to understand what he believes. In my opinion, neither this tract nor the other I mentioned before deserves to be called a book or to carry its author's name, and yet I did not think they should be sent forth without some title (by which, so to speak, they might invite those

---

* The *Proslogion* was written between 1077 and 1078. Gaunilo's reply was written shortly after it appeared, and Anselm's response quickly after that. The translation reprinted here, of all three works, is by M.J. Charlesworth and appears in *Anselm of Canterbury: The Major Works*, ed. Brian Davies and G.R. Evans (Oxford World's Classics, 1998).

† The *Monologion*, probably written one year before the *Proslogion*.

into whose hands they should come, to read them); so I have given to each its title, the first being called *An Example of Meditation on the Meaning of Faith*, and the sequel *Faith in Quest of Understanding*.

However, as both of them, under these titles, had already been copied out by several readers, a number of people (above all the reverend Archbishop of Lyons, Hugh, apostolic delegate to Gaul, who commanded me by his apostolic authority) have urged me to put my name to them. For the sake of greater convenience I have named the first book *Monologion*, that is, a soliloquy; and the other *Proslogion*, that is, an allocution.

...

Chapter 2. *That God truly exists*

Well then, Lord, You who give understanding to faith, grant me that I may understand, as much as You see fit, that You exist as we believe You to exist, and that You are what we believe You to be. Now we believe that You are something than which nothing greater can be thought. Or can it be that a thing of such a nature does not exist, since 'the Fool has said in his heart, there is no God'?* But surely, when this same Fool hears what I am speaking about, namely, 'something-than-which-nothing-greater-can-be-thought,' he understands what he hears, and what he understands is in his mind, even if he does not understand that it actually exists. For it is one thing for an object to exist in the mind, and another thing to understand that an object actually exists. Thus, when a painter plans beforehand what he is going to execute, he has [the picture] in his mind, but he does not yet think that it actually exists because he has not yet executed it. However, when he has actually painted it, then he both has it in his mind and understands that it exists because he has now made it. Even the Fool, then, is forced to agree that something-than-which-nothing-greater-can-be-thought exists in the mind, since he understands this when he hears it, and whatever is understood is in the mind. And surely that-than-which-a-greater-cannot-be-thought cannot exist in the mind alone. For if it exists solely in the mind, it can be thought to exist in reality also, which is greater. If then that-than-which-a-greater-cannot-be-thought exists in the mind alone, this same that-than-which-a-greater-*cannot*-be-thought is that-than-which-a-greater-*can*-be-thought. But this is obviously impossible. Therefore there is absolutely no doubt that something-than-which-a-greater-cannot-be-thought exists both in the mind and in reality.

Chapter 3. *That God cannot be thought not to exist*

And certainly this being so truly exists that it cannot be even thought not to exist. For something can be thought to exist that cannot be thought not to exist, and this is greater than that which can be thought not to exist. Hence, if that-than-which-a-greater-cannot-be-thought can be thought not to exist, then that-than-which-a-greater-cannot-be-thought is not the same as that-than-which-a-greater-cannot-be-thought, which is absurd. Something-than-which-a-greater-cannot-be-thought exists so truly then, that it cannot be even thought not to exist.

And You, Lord our God, are this being. You exist so truly, Lord my God, that You cannot even be thought not to exist. And this is as it should be, for if some intelligence could think of something better than You, the creature would be above its Creator and would judge its Creator—and that is completely absurd. In fact, everything else there is, except You alone, can be thought of as not existing. You alone, then, of all things most truly exist and therefore of all things possess existence to the highest degree; for anything else does not exist as truly, and so possesses existence to a lesser degree. Why then did 'the Fool say in his heart, there is no God' when it is so evident to any rational mind that You of all things exist to the highest degree? Why indeed, unless because he was stupid and a fool?

Chapter 4. *How 'the Fool said in his heart' what cannot be thought*

How indeed has he 'said in his heart' what he could not think; or how could he not think what he 'said in

---

* This quotation is from the first line of Psalms 13 and 52 in the Vulgate version of the Bible, 14 and 53 in the King James version. Later citations in this reading also refer to the Vulgate.

his heart,' since to 'say in one's heart' and to 'think' are the same? But if he really (indeed, since he really) both thought because he 'said in his heart' and did not 'say in his heart' because he could not think, there is not only one sense in which something is 'said in one's heart' or thought. For in one sense a thing is thought when the word signifying it is thought; in another sense when the very object which the thing is is understood. In the first sense, then, God can be thought not to exist, but not at all in the second sense. No one, indeed, understanding what God is can think that God does not exist, even though he may say these words in his heart either without any [objective] signification or with some peculiar signification. For God is that-than-which-nothing-greater-can-be-thought. Whoever really understands this understands clearly that this same being so exists that not even in thought can it not exist. Thus whoever understands that God exists in such a way cannot think of Him as not existing.

I give thanks, good Lord, I give thanks to You, since what I believed before through Your free gift I now so understand through Your illumination, that if I did not want to *believe* that You existed, I should nevertheless be unable not to *understand* it.

Chapter 5. That God is whatever it is better to be than not to be and that, existing through Himself alone, He makes all other beings from nothing

What then are You, Lord God, You than whom nothing greater can be thought? But what are You save that supreme being, existing through Yourself alone, who made everything else from nothing? For whatever is not this is less than that which can be thought of; but this cannot be thought about You. What goodness, then, could be wanting to the supreme good, through which every good exists? Thus You are just, truthful, happy, and whatever it is better to be than not to be—for it is better to be just rather than unjust, and happy rather than unhappy.

Pro Insipiente

("ON BEHALF OF THE FOOL"),

BY GAUNILO OF MARMOUTIERS

Paragraph 1

To one doubting whether there is, or denying that there is, something of such a nature than which nothing greater can be thought, it is said here [in the *Proslogion*] that its existence is proved, first because the very one who denies or doubts it already has it in his mind, since when he hears it spoken of he understands what is said; and further, because what he understands is necessarily such that it exists not only in the mind but also in reality. And this is proved by the fact that it is greater to exist both in the mind and in reality than in the mind alone. For if this same being exists in the mind alone, anything that existed also in reality would be greater than this being, and thus that which is greater than everything would be less than some thing and would not be greater than everything, which is obviously contradictory. Therefore, it is necessarily the case that that which is greater than everything, being already proved to exist in the mind, should exist not only in the mind but also in reality, since otherwise it would not be greater than everything.

Paragraph 2

But he [the Fool] can perhaps reply that this thing is said already to exist in the mind only in the sense that I understand what is said. For could I not say that all kinds of unreal things, not existing in themselves in any way at all, are equally in the mind since if anyone speaks about them I understand whatever he says? Unless perhaps it is manifest that this being is such that it can be entertained in the mind in a different way from unreal or doubtfully real things, so that I am not said to think of or have in thought what is heard, but to understand and have it in mind, in that I cannot really think of this being in any other way save by understanding it, that is to say, by grasping by certain knowledge that the thing itself actually exists. But if this is the case, first, there will be no difference between having an object in mind (taken as preceding in time), and understanding that the object actually exists (taken as following in time), as in the case of the picture which exists first in the mind of the painter and then in the completed work. And thus it would be scarcely conceivable that, when this object had been spoken of and heard, it could not be thought not to exist in the same way in which God can [be thought] not to exist. For if He cannot, why put forward this whole argument against anyone denying or doubting that there is something of this kind? Finally, that it is such a thing that, as soon as it is thought of, it cannot but be certainly perceived by the mind as indubitably existing, must be proved to me by some indisputable argument and not by that proposed, namely, that it must already be in my mind when I understand what I hear. For this is in my view like [arguing that] any things doubtfully real or even unreal are capable of existing if these things are mentioned by someone whose spoken words I might understand, and, even more, that [they exist] if, though deceived about them as often happens, I should believe them [to exist]—which argument I still do not believe!

Paragraph 3

Hence, the example of the painter having the picture he is about to make already in his mind cannot support this argument. For this picture, before it is actually made, is contained in the very art of the painter and such a thing in the art of any artist is nothing but a certain part of his very understanding, since as St. Augustine says,* 'when the artisan is about actually to make a box he has it beforehand in his art. The box which is actually made is not a living thing, but the box which is in his art is a living thing since the soul of the artist, in which these things exist before their actual realization, is a living thing.' Now how are these things living in the living soul of the artist unless they are identical with the knowledge or understanding of the soul itself? But, apart from those things which are

known to belong to the very nature of the mind itself, in the case of any truth perceived by the mind by being either heard or understood, then it cannot be doubted that this truth is one thing and that the understanding which grasps it is another. Therefore even if it were true that there was something than which nothing greater could be thought, this thing, heard and understood, would not, however, be the same as the not-yet-made picture is in the mind of the painter.

Paragraph 4

To this we may add something that has already been mentioned, namely, that upon hearing it spoken of I can so little think of or entertain in my mind this being (that which is greater than all those others that are able to be thought of, and which it is said can be none other than God Himself) in terms of an object known to me either by species or genus, as I can think of God Himself, whom indeed for this very reason I can even think does not exist. For neither do I know the reality itself, nor can I form an idea from some other things like it since, as you say yourself, it is such that nothing could be like it. For if I heard something said about a man who was completely unknown to me so that I did not even know whether he existed, I could nevertheless think about him in his very reality as a man by means of that specific or generic notion by which I know what a man is or men are. However, it could happen that, because of a falsehood on the part of the speaker, the man I thought of did not actually exist, although I thought of him nevertheless as a truly existing object—not this particular man but any man in general. It is not, then, in the way that I have this unreal thing in thought or in mind that I can have that object in my mind when I hear 'God' or 'something greater than everything' spoken of. For while I was able to think of the former in terms of a truly existing thing which was known to me, I know nothing at all of the latter save for the verbal formula, and on the basis of this alone one can scarcely or never think of any truth. For when one thinks in this way, one thinks not so much of the word itself, which is indeed a real thing (that is to say, the sound of the letters or syllables), as of the meaning

---

*   St. Augustine of Hippo, a north-African bishop who lived from 354 until 430, was the most important early Christian theologian and Anselm's major intellectual influence. This quote is from his *Treatises on the Gospel of John*.

of the word which is heard. However, it [that which is greater than everything] is not thought of in the way of one who knows what is meant by that expression—thought of, that is, in terms of the thing [signified] or as true in thought alone. It is rather in the way of one who does not really know this object but thinks of it in terms of an affection of his mind produced by hearing the spoken words, and who tries to imagine what the words he has heard might mean. However, it would be astonishing if he could ever [attain to] the truth of the thing. Therefore, when I hear and understand someone saying that there is something greater than everything that can be thought of, it is agreed that it is in this latter sense that it is in my mind and not in any other sense. So much for the claim that that supreme nature exists already in my mind.

Paragraph 5

That, however, [this nature] necessarily exists in reality is demonstrated to me from the fact that, unless it existed, whatever exists in reality would be greater than it and consequently it would not be that which is greater than everything that undoubtedly had already been proved to exist in the mind. To this I reply as follows: if something that cannot even be thought in the true and real sense must be said to exist in the mind, then I do not deny that this also exists in my mind in the same way. But since from this one cannot in any way conclude that it exists also in reality, I certainly do not yet concede that it actually exists, until this is proved to me by an indubitable argument. For he who claims that it actually exists because otherwise it would not be that which is greater than everything does not consider carefully enough whom he is addressing. For I certainly do not yet admit this greater [than everything] to be any truly existing thing; indeed I doubt or even deny it. And I do not concede that it exists in a different way from that—if one ought to speak of 'existence' here—when the mind tries to imagine a completely unknown thing on the basis of the spoken words alone. How then can it be proved to me on that basis that that which is greater than everything truly exists in reality (because it is evident that it is greater

than all others) if I keep on denying and also doubting that this is evident and do not admit that this greater [than everything] is either in my mind or thought, not even in the sense in which many doubtfully real and unreal things are? It must first of all be proved to me then that this same greater than everything truly exists in reality somewhere, and then only will the fact that it is greater than everything make it clear that it also subsists in itself.

Paragraph 6

For example: they say that there is in the ocean somewhere an island which, because of the difficulty (or rather the impossibility) of finding that which does not exist, some have called the 'Lost Island.' And the story goes that it is blessed with all manner of priceless riches and delights in abundance, much more even than the Happy Isles,* and, having no owner or inhabitant, it is superior everywhere in abundance of riches to all those other lands that men inhabit. Now, if anyone [were to] tell me that it is like this, I shall easily understand what is said, since nothing is difficult about it. But if he should then go on to say, as though it were a logical consequence of this: You cannot any more doubt that this island that is more excellent than all other lands truly exists somewhere in reality than you can doubt that it is in your mind; and since it is more excellent to exist not only in the mind alone but also in reality, therefore it must needs be that it exists. For if it did not exist, any other land existing in reality would be more excellent than it, and so this island, already conceived by you to be more excellent than others, will not be more excellent. If, I say, someone wishes thus to persuade me that this island really exists beyond all doubt, I should either think that he was joking, or I should find it hard to decide which of us I ought to judge the bigger fool—I, if I agreed with him, or he, if he thought that he had proved the existence of this island with any certainty, unless he had first convinced me that its very excellence exists in my mind precisely as a thing existing truly and indubitably and not just as something unreal or doubtfully real.

---

* The mythical land—often located where the sun sets in the West—where people in classical times believed the souls of heroes lived in bliss.

Paragraph 7

Thus first of all might the Fool reply to objections. And if then someone should assert that this greater [than everything] is such that it cannot be thought not to exist (again without any other proof than that otherwise it would not be greater than everything), then he could make this same reply and say: When have I said that there truly existed some being that is 'greater than everything,' such that from this it could be proved to me that this same being really existed to such a degree that it could not be thought not to exist? That is why it must first be conclusively proved by argument that there is some higher nature, namely that which is greater and better than all the things that are, so that from this we can also infer everything else which necessarily cannot be wanting to what is greater and better than everything. When, however, it is said that this supreme being cannot be *thought* not to exist, it would perhaps be better to say that it cannot be *understood* not to exist nor even to be able not to exist. For, strictly speaking, unreal things cannot be *understood*, though certainly they can be *thought* of in the same way as the Fool *thought* that God does not exist. I know with complete certainty that I exist, but I also know at the same time nevertheless that I can not-exist. And I *understand* without any doubt that that which exists to the highest degree, namely God, both exists and cannot not exist. I do not know, however, whether I can *think* of myself as not existing while I know with absolute certainty that I do exist; but if I can, why cannot [I do the same] with regard to anything else I know with the same certainty? If however I cannot, this will not be the distinguishing characteristic of God [namely, to be such that He cannot be thought not to exist].

Paragraph 8

The other parts of this tract* are argued so truly, so brilliantly and so splendidly, and are also of so much worth and instinct with so fragrant a perfume of devout and holy feeling, that in no way should they be rejected because of those things at the beginning (rightly intuited, but less surely argued out). Rather the latter should be demonstrated more firmly and so everything received with very great respect and praise.

Anselm's Reply to Gaunilo

Since it is not the Fool, against whom I spoke in my tract, who takes me up, but one who, though speaking on the Fool's behalf, is an orthodox Christian and no fool, it will suffice if I reply to the Christian.

Reply 1

You say then—you, whoever you are, who claim that the Fool can say these things—that the being than-which-a-greater-cannot-be-thought is not in the mind except as what cannot be thought of, in the true sense, at all. And [you claim], moreover, that what I say does not follow, namely, that 'that-than-which-a-greater-cannot-be-thought' exists in reality from the fact that it exists in the mind, any more than that the Lost Island most certainly exists from the fact that, when it is described in words, he who hears it described has no doubt that it exists in his mind. I reply as follows: If 'that-than-which-a-greater-cannot-be-thought' is neither understood nor thought of, and is neither in the mind nor in thought, then it is evident that *either* God is not that-than-which-a-greater-cannot-be-thought *or* is not understood nor thought of, and is not in the mind nor in thought. Now my strongest argument that this is false is to appeal to your faith and to your conscience. Therefore 'that-than-which-a-greater-cannot-be-thought' is truly understood and thought and is in the mind and in thought. For this reason, [the arguments] by which you attempt to prove the contrary are either not true, or what you believe follows from them does not in fact follow.

Moreover, you maintain that, from the fact that that-than-which-a-greater-cannot-be-thought is understood, it does not follow that it is in the mind, nor that,

---

* *The Proslogion* has 26 chapters, of which only chapters two to five—those containing the ontological argument about which Gaunilo has complaints—are reprinted here.

if it is in the mind, it therefore exists in reality. I insist, however, that simply if it can be thought it is necessary that it exists. For 'that-than-which-a-greater-cannot-be-thought' cannot be thought save as being without a beginning. But whatever can be thought as existing and does not actually exist can be thought as having a beginning of its existence. Consequently, 'that-than-which-a-greater-cannot-be-thought' cannot be thought as existing and yet not actually exist. If, therefore, it can be thought as existing, it exists of necessity.

Further: even if it can be thought of, then certainly it necessarily exists. For no one who denies or doubts that there is something-than-which-a-greater-cannot-be-thought, denies or doubts that, if this being were to exist, it would not be capable of not-existing either actually or in the mind—otherwise it would not be that-than-which-a-greater-cannot-be-thought. But, whatever can be thought as existing and does not actually exist, could, if it were to exist, possibly not exist either actually or in the mind. For this reason, if it can merely be thought, 'that-than-which-a-greater-cannot-be-thought' cannot not exist. However, let us suppose that it does not exist even though it can be thought. Now, whatever can be thought and does not actually exist would not be, if it should exist, 'that-than-which-a-greater-cannot-be-thought.' If, therefore, it were 'that-than-which-a-greater-cannot-be-thought' it would not be that-than-which-a-greater-cannot-be-thought, which is completely absurd. It is, then, false that something-than-which-a-greater-cannot-be-thought does not exist if it can merely be thought; and it is all the more false if it can be understood and be in the mind.

I will go further: It cannot be doubted that whatever does not exist in any one place or at any one time, even though it does exist in some place or at some time, can however be thought to exist at no place and at no time, just as it does not exist in some place or at some time. For what did not exist yesterday and today exists can thus, as it is understood not to have existed yesterday, be supposed not to exist at any time. And that which does not exist here in this place, and does exist elsewhere can, in the same way as it does not exist here, be thought not to exist anywhere. Similarly with a thing some of whose particular parts do not exist in the place and at the time its other parts exist—all of its parts, and therefore the whole thing itself, can be

thought to exist at no time and in no place. For even if it be said that time always exists and that the world is everywhere, the former does not, however, always exist as a whole, nor is the other as a whole everywhere; and as certain particular parts of time do not exist when other parts do exist, therefore they can be even thought not to exist at any time. Again, as certain particular parts of the world do not exist in the same place where other parts do exist, they can thus be supposed not to exist anywhere. Moreover, what is made up of parts can be broken up in thought and can possibly not exist. Thus it is that whatever does not exist as a whole at a certain place and time can be thought not to exist, even if it does actually exist. But 'that-than-which-a-greater-cannot-be-thought' cannot be thought not to exist if it does actually exist, otherwise, if it exists it is not that-than-which-a-greater-cannot-be-thought, which is absurd. In no way, then, does this being not exist as a whole in any particular place or at any particular time; but it exists as a whole at every time and in every place.

Do you not consider then that that about which we understand these things can to some extent be thought or understood, or can exist in thought or in the mind? For if it cannot, we could not understand these things about it. And if you say that, because it is not completely understood, it cannot be understood at all and cannot be in the mind, then you must say [equally] that one who cannot see the purest light of the sun directly does not see daylight, which is the same thing as the light of the sun. Surely then 'that-than-which-a-greater-cannot-be-thought' is understood and is in the mind to the extent that we understand these things about it.

Reply 2

I said, then, in the argument that you criticize, that when the Fool hears 'that-than-which-a-greater-cannot-be-thought' spoken of he understands what he hears. Obviously if it is spoken of in a known language and he does not understand it, then either he has no intelligence at all, or a completely obtuse one.

Next I said that, if it is understood it is in the mind; or does what has been proved to exist necessarily in actual reality not exist in any mind? But you will say that, even if it is in the mind, yet it does not follow that it is understood. Observe then that, from the fact that it is understood, it does follow that it is in the mind. For, just as what is thought is thought by means of a thought, and what is thought by a thought is thus, as thought, *in* thought, so also, what is understood is understood by the mind, and what is understood by the mind is thus, as understood, *in* the mind. What could be more obvious than this?

I said further that if a thing exists even in the mind alone, it can be thought to exist also in reality, which is greater. If, then, it (namely, 'that-than-which-a-greater-cannot-be-thought') exists in the mind alone, it is something than which a greater *can* be thought. What, I ask you, could be more logical? For if it exists even in the mind alone, cannot it be thought to exist also in reality? And if it can [be so thought], is it not the case that he who thinks this thinks of something greater than it, if it exists in the mind alone? What, then, could follow more logically than that, if 'that-than-which-a-greater-cannot-be-thought' exists in the mind alone, it is the same as that-than-which-a-greater-*can*-be-thought? But surely 'that-than-which-a-greater-*can*-be-thought' is not for any mind [the same as] 'that-than-which-a-greater-*cannot*-be-thought.' Does it not follow, then, that 'that-than-which-a-greater-*cannot*-be-thought,' if it exists in anyone's mind, does not exist in the mind alone? For if it exists in the mind alone, it is that-than-which-a-greater-*can*-be-thought, which is absurd.

Reply 3

You claim, however, that this is as though someone asserted that it cannot be doubted that a certain island in the ocean (which is more fertile than all other lands and which, because of the difficulty or even the impossibility of discovering what does not exist, is called the 'Lost Island') truly exists in reality since anyone easily understands it when it is described in words. Now, I truly promise that if anyone should discover for me something existing either in reality or in the mind alone—except 'that-than-which-a-greater-cannot-be-thought'—to which the logic of my argument would apply, then I shall find that Lost Island and give it,

never more to be lost, to that person. It has already been clearly seen, however, that 'that-than-which-a-greater-cannot-be-thought' cannot be thought not to exist, because it exists as a matter of such certain truth. Otherwise it would not exist at all. In short, if anyone says that he thinks that this being does not exist, I reply that, when he thinks of this, either he thinks of something than which a greater cannot be thought, or he does not think of it. If he does not think of it, then he does not think that what he does not think of does not exist. If, however, he does think of it, then indeed he thinks of something which cannot be even thought not to exist. For if it could be thought not to exist, it could be thought to have a beginning and an end—but this cannot be. Thus, he who thinks of it thinks of something that cannot be thought not to exist; indeed, he who thinks of this does not think of it as not existing, otherwise he would think what cannot be thought. Therefore 'that-than-which-a-greater-cannot-be-thought' cannot be thought not to exist.

Reply 4

You say, moreover, that when it is said that this supreme reality cannot be *thought* not to exist, it would perhaps be better to say that it cannot be *understood* not to exist or even to be able not to exist. However, it must rather be said that it cannot be *thought*. For if I had said that the thing in question could not be *understood* not to exist, perhaps you yourself (who claim that we cannot understand—if this word is to be taken strictly—things that are unreal) would object that nothing that exists can be understood not to exist. For it is false [to say that] what exists does not exist, so that it is not the distinguishing characteristic of God not to be able to be understood not to exist. But, if any of those things which exist with absolute certainty can be understood not to exist, in the same way other things that certainly exist can be understood not to exist. But, if the matter is carefully considered, this objection cannot be made apropos* [the term] 'thought.' For even if none of those things that exist can be *understood* not to exist, all however can be *thought* as not existing, save that which exists to a supreme degree. For in fact all

---

*   With respect to, concerning.

those things (and they alone) that have a beginning or end or are made up of parts and, as I have already said, all those things that do not exist as a whole in a particular place or at a particular time can be thought as not existing. Only that being in which there is neither beginning nor end nor conjunction of parts, and that thought does not discern save as a whole in every place and at every time, cannot be thought as not existing.

Know then that you can think of yourself as not existing while yet you are absolutely sure that you exist. I am astonished that you have said that you do not know this. For we think of many things that we know to exist, as not existing; and [we think of] many things that we know not to exist, as existing—not judging that it is really as we think but imagining it to be so. We *can*, in fact, think of something as not existing while knowing that it does exist, since we can [think of] the one and know the other at the same time. And we *cannot* think of something as not existing if yet we know that it does exist, since we cannot think of it as existing and not existing at the same time. He, therefore, who distinguishes these two senses of this assertion will understand that [in one sense] nothing can be thought as not existing while yet it is known to exist, and that [in another sense] whatever exists, save that-than-which-a-greater-cannot-be-thought, can be thought of as not existing even when we know that it does exist. Thus it is that, on the one hand, it is the distinguishing characteristic of God that He cannot be thought of as not existing, and that, on the other hand, many things, the while they do exist, cannot be thought of as not existing. In what sense, however, one can say that God can be thought of as not existing I think I have adequately explained in my tract.

Reply 5

As for the other objections you make against me on behalf of the Fool, it is quite easy to meet them, even for one weak in the head, and so I considered it a waste of time to show this. But since I hear that they appear to certain readers to have some force against me, I will deal briefly with them.

First, you often reiterate that I say that that which is greater than everything exists in the mind, and that if it is in the mind, it exists also in reality, for otherwise that which is greater than everything would not be that which is greater than everything. However,

nowhere in all that I have said will you find such an argument. For 'that which is greater than everything' and 'that-than-which-a-greater-cannot-be-thought' are not equivalent for the purpose of proving the real existence of the thing spoken of. Thus, if anyone should say that 'that-than-which-a-greater-cannot-be-thought' is not something that actually exists, or that it can possibly not exist, or even can be thought of as not existing, he can easily be refuted. For what does not exist can possibly not exist, and what can not exist can be thought of as not existing. However, whatever can be thought of as not existing, if it actually exists, is not that-than-which-a-greater-cannot-be-thought. But if it does not exist, indeed even if it should exist, it would not be that-than-which-a-greater-cannot-be-thought. But it cannot be asserted that 'that-than-which-a-greater-cannot-be-thought' is not, if it exists, that-than-which-a-greater-cannot-be-thought, or that, if it should exist, it would not be that-than-which-a-greater-cannot-be-thought. It is evident, then, that it neither does not exist nor can not exist or be thought of as not existing. For if it does exist in another way it is not what it is said to be, and if it should exist [in another way] it would not be [what it was said to be].

However it seems that it is not as easy to prove this in respect of what is said to be greater than everything. For it is not as evident that that which can be thought of as not existing is not that which is greater than everything, as that it is not that-than-which-a-greater-cannot-be-thought. And, in the same way, neither is it indubitable that, if there is something which is 'greater than everything,' it is identical with 'that-than-which-a-greater-cannot-be-thought'; nor, if there were [such a being], that no other like it might exist—as this is certain in respect of what is said to be 'that-than-which-a-greater-cannot-be-thought.' For what if someone should say that something that is greater than everything actually exists, and yet that this same being can be thought of as not existing, and that something greater than it can be thought, even if this does not exist? In this case can it be inferred as evidently that [this being] is therefore not that which is greater than everything, as it would quite evidently be said in the other case that it is therefore not that-than-which-a-greater-cannot-be-thought? The former [inference] needs, in fact, a premiss in addition to this which is said to be 'greater than everything'; but the latter needs nothing save this utterance itself, namely, 'that-than-which-a-greater-cannot-be-thought.' Therefore, if what 'that-than-which-a-greater-cannot-be-thought' of itself proves concerning itself cannot be proved in the same way in respect of what is said to be 'greater than everything,' you criticize me unjustly for having said what I did not say, since it differs so much from what I did say.

If, however, it can [be proved] by means of another argument, you should not have criticized me for having asserted what can be proved. Whether it can [be proved], however, is easily appreciated by one who understands that it can [in respect of] 'that-than-which-a-greater-cannot-be-thought.' For one cannot in any way understand 'that-than-which-a-greater-cannot-be-thought' without [understanding that it is] that which alone is greater than everything. As, therefore, 'that-than-which-a-greater-cannot-be-thought' is understood and is in the mind, and is consequently judged to exist in true reality, so also that which is greater than everything is said to be understood and to exist in the mind, and so is necessarily inferred to exist in reality itself. You see, then, how right you were to compare me with that stupid person who wished to maintain that the Lost Island existed from the sole fact that being described it was understood.

Reply 6

You object, moreover, that any unreal or doubtfully real things at all can equally be understood and exist in the mind in the same way as the being I was speaking of. I am astonished that you urge this [objection] against me, for I was concerned to prove something which was in doubt, and for me it was sufficient that I should first show that it was understood and existed in the mind *in some way or other*, leaving it to be determined subsequently whether it was in the mind alone as unreal things are, or in reality also as true things are. For, if unreal or doubtfully real things are understood and exist in the mind in the sense that, when they are spoken of, he who hears them understands what the speaker means, nothing prevents what I have spoken of being understood and existing in the mind. But how are these [assertions] consistent, that is, when you assert that if someone speaks of unreal things you would understand whatever he says, and that, in the case of a thing which is not entertained

in thought in the same way as even unreal things are, you do not say that you think of it or have it in thought upon hearing it spoken of, but rather that you understand it and have it in mind since, precisely, you cannot think of it save by understanding it, that is, knowing certainly that the thing exists in reality itself? How, I say, are both [assertions] consistent, namely that unreal things are understood, and that 'to understand' means knowing with certainty that something actually exists? You should have seen that nothing [of this applies] to me. But if unreal things are, in a sense, understood (this definition applying not to every kind of understanding but to a certain kind) then I ought not to be criticized for having said that 'that-than-which-a-greater-cannot-be-thought' is understood and is in the mind, even before it was certain that it existed in reality itself.

Reply 7

Next, you say that it can hardly be believed that when this [that-than-which-a-greater-cannot-be-thought] has been spoken of and heard, it cannot be thought not to exist, as even it can be thought that God does not exist. Now those who have attained even a little expertise in disputation and argument could reply to that on my behalf. For is it reasonable that someone should therefore deny what he understands because it is said to be [the same as] that which he denies since he does not understand it? Or if that is denied [to exist] which is understood only to some extent and is the same as what is not understood at all, is not what is in doubt more easily proved from the fact that it is in some mind than from the fact that it is in no mind at all? For this reason it cannot be believed that anyone should deny 'that-than-which-a-greater-cannot-be-thought' (which, being heard, he understands to some extent), on the ground that he denies God whose meaning he does not think of in any way at all. On the other hand, if it is denied on the ground that it is not understood completely, even so is not that which is understood in some way easier to prove than that which is not understood in any way? It was therefore not wholly without reason that, to prove against the Fool that God exists, I proposed 'that-than-which-a-greater-cannot-be-thought,' since he would understand this in some way, [whereas] he would understand the former [God] in no way at all.

Reply 8

In fact, your painstaking argument that 'that-than-which-a-greater-cannot-be-thought' is not like the not-yet-realized painting in the mind of the painter is beside the point. For I did not propose [the example] of the foreknown picture because I wanted to assert that what was at issue was in the same case, but rather that so I could show that something not understood as existing exists in the mind.

Again, you say that upon hearing of 'that-than-which-a-greater-cannot-be-thought' you cannot think of it as a real object known either generically or specifically or have it in your mind, on the grounds that you neither know the thing itself nor can you form an idea of it from other things similar to it. But obviously this is not so. For since everything that is less good is similar in so far as it is good to that which is more good, it is evident to every rational mind that, mounting from the less good to the more good we can from those things than which something greater can be thought conjecture a great deal about that-than-which-a-greater-cannot-be-thought. Who, for example, cannot think of this (even if he does not believe that what he thinks of actually exists) namely, that if something that has a beginning and end is good, that which, although it has had a beginning, does not, however, have an end, is much better? And just as this latter is better than the former, so also that which has neither beginning nor end is better again than this, even if it passes always from the past through the present to the future. Again, whether something of this kind actually exists or not, that which does not lack anything at all, nor is forced to change or move, is very much better still. Cannot this be thought? Or can we think of something greater than this? Or is not this precisely to form an idea of that-than-which-a-greater-cannot-be-thought from those things than which a greater can be thought? There is, then, a way by which one can form an idea of 'that-than-which-a-greater-cannot-be-thought.' In this way, therefore, the Fool who does not accept the sacred authority [of Revelation] can easily be refuted if he denies that he can form an idea from other things of 'that-than-which-a-greater-cannot-be-thought.'

But if any orthodox Christian should deny this let him remember that "the invisible things of God from the creation of the world are clearly seen through the things that have been made, even his eternal power and Godhead."*

Reply 9

But even if it were true that [the object] that-than-which-a-greater-cannot-be-thought cannot be thought of nor understood, it would not, however, be false that [the formula] 'that-than-which-a-greater-cannot-be-thought' could be thought of and understood. For just as nothing prevents one from saying 'ineffable'† although one cannot specify what is said to be ineffable; and just as one can think of the inconceivable—although one cannot think of what 'inconceivable' applies to—so also, when 'that-than-which-a-greater-cannot-be-thought' is spoken of, there is no doubt at all that what is heard can be thought of and understood even if the thing itself cannot be thought of and understood. For if someone is so witless as to say that there is not something than-which-a-greater-cannot-be-thought, yet he will not be so shameless as to say that he is not able to understand and think of what he was speaking about. Or if such a one is to be found, not only should his assertion be condemned, but he himself condemned. Whoever, then, denies that there is something than-which-a-greater-cannot-be-thought, at any rate understands and thinks of the denial he makes, and this denial cannot be understood and thought about apart from its elements. Now, one element [of the denial] is 'that-than-which-a-greater-cannot-be-thought.' Whoever, therefore, denies this understands and thinks of 'that-than-which-a-greater-cannot-be-thought.' It is evident, moreover, that in the same way one can think of and understand that which cannot not exist. And one who thinks of this thinks of something greater than one who thinks of what can not exist. When, therefore, one thinks of that-than-which-a-greater-cannot-be-thought, if one thinks of what can not exist, one does not think of that-than-which-a-greater-cannot-be-thought. Now the same thing cannot at the same time be thought of and not thought of. For this reason he

---

* A biblical quote, from St. Paul's Epistle to the Romans (1:20).

† "Ineffable" means unutterable or indescribable—incapable of being expressed.

who thinks of that-than-which-a-greater-cannot-be-thought does not think of something that can not exist but something that cannot not exist. Therefore what he thinks of exists necessarily, since whatever can not exist is not what he thinks of.

Reply 10

I think now that I have shown that I have proved in the above tract, not by a weak argumentation but by a sufficiently necessary one, that something-than-which-a-greater-cannot-be-thought exists in reality itself, and that this proof has not been weakened by the force of any objection. For the import of this proof is in itself of such force that what is spoken of is proved (as a necessary consequence of the fact that it is understood or thought of) both to exist in actual reality and to be itself whatever must be believed about the Divine Being. For we believe of the Divine Being whatever it can, absolutely speaking, be thought better to be than not to be. For example, it is better to be eternal than not eternal, good than not good, indeed goodness itself than not goodness-itself. However, nothing of this kind cannot but be that-than-which-a-greater-cannot-be-thought. It is, then, necessary that 'that-than-which-a-greater-cannot-be-thought' should be whatever must be believed about the Divine Nature.

I thank you for your kindness both in criticizing and praising my tract. For since you praised so fulsomely those parts that appeared to you to be worthy of acceptance, it is quite clear that you have criticized those parts that seemed to you to be weak, not from any malice but from good will. ∎

Suggestions for Critical Reflection

1. If Anselm's argument is sound, what if anything does it tell us about God (in addition to the fact that he exists)?

2. The concepts 'bachelor' or 'unicorn' do not entail that such things exist. Why does Anselm think that the concept 'God' is importantly different? Is he right? What about the concept of 'an integer between 10 and 12': do you think this concept might commit us to the existence of the number 11? Does this show that not all existence claims are empirical?

3. What do you think about Anselm's distinction between two kinds of existence (*in re* and *in intellectu*)? Do you agree that being thought about is a kind of existence?

4. Does Gaunilo's example of the "Lost Island" show that Anselm has made a mistake? If so, does it show *what* mistake (or mistakes) has been made?

5. The famous eighteenth-century German philosopher Immanuel Kant argued that the flaw in the Ontological Argument is that it mistakenly treats existence as a property. When we say that leopards are spotted we are ascribing a property (being covered in spots) to leopards; however, Kant would argue, when we say that leopards exist, we are not pointing to all the leopards and saying that they have the property of existence. (If it were a property, then it would make sense to say that some leopards have it, and some don't. But which leopards don't?) Instead, we are saying something not about actual leopards but about the concept 'leopard': we are saying that something in the actual world fits that concept. If we say that Boy Scouts are honest, we might go on to talk about some Boy Scout who is *perfectly* honest—who possesses the property of honesty to perfection. However, if we say that Boy Scouts exist, it is incoherent to try to point to the perfectly existing Boy Scout. Existence, therefore, is not a property, and so (according to Kant's argument) we have no reason to believe that a being which possesses all the properties of the most perfect thing—i.e., which is that-than-which-a-greater-cannot-be-thought—must exist. What do you think of this objection to the Ontological Argument? Is it decisive?

6. Suppose we agree with Anselm (against Kant) that existence *is* a perfection. Does this mean that an actual serial killer is more perfect than a merely fictional one?

7. Another objection to the Ontological Argument is the following: we may (as human beings) be able to *think* of an absolutely perfect being, but (contrary

to Anselm's assumption) it does not follow from this that an absolutely perfect being is actually *possible*. That is, although we are unable to see what is logically impossible in the idea of a perfect being, it might nevertheless still *be* logically impossible; and since we can't rule this out, we can't show *a priori* that God exists. What do you think of this objection? If it works, what implications does it have for our knowledge of possibility?

8. Finally, a third possible objection to Anselm's Ontological Argument: Even if Anselm succeeds in showing that the being-than-which-nothing-greater-can-be-thought must be *thought of* as existing, it still doesn't follow that it actually *does* exist. To conceive of something as being a certain way, the argument goes, does not mean that it actually *is* that way, or even that one must *believe* that it is that way: for example, one can conceive of the sky as being bright green, even though it isn't. So, for God, we can and perhaps must conceive of God as existing, but it doesn't follow that God does exist (or even that we must believe that God exists). What do you think of this objection? How do you think Anselm might respond to it?

ST. THOMAS AQUINAS

The Existence of God

(FROM *SUMMA THEOLOGIAE*)

Who Was St. Thomas Aquinas?

Saint Thomas was born in 1225 in Roccasecca in southern Italy, the son of the count of Aquino. At the age of five he was sent to be educated at the great Benedictine abbey of Monte Casino, and at 14 he went to university in Naples. His father expected him to join the respectable and wealthy Benedictine order of monks. However, when he was 19 Aquinas instead joined the recently formed Dominican order of celibate, mendicant (begging) friars. These monks had adopted a life of complete poverty and traveled Europe studying and teaching the gospel. Thomas's father was outraged, and—according to legend—he locked Aquinas in the family castle for a year and offered him bribes, including a beautiful prostitute, to join the Benedictines instead. Aquinas is said to have grabbed a burning brand from the fire and chased away the prostitute; his family eventually allowed him to leave and travel to Paris. He went on to study Greek and Islamic philosophy, natural science, and theology in Paris and Cologne under Albertus Magnus ("Albert the Great"), a Dominican who was famed for his vast learning. His colleagues in Cologne nicknamed Aquinas "the dumb ox" because of his reserved personality and large size; Albertus is said to have responded that Thomas's bellowing would be heard throughout the world. In 1256 Aquinas was made a regent master (professor) at the University of Paris. He taught in Paris and Naples until, on December 6, 1273, he had a deeply religious experience after which he stopped writing. "All that I have written seems to me like straw compared to what has now been revealed to me," he said. He died four months later.

Aquinas became known to later ages as the Angelic Doctor, and was canonized in 1323. In fact, starting shortly after his death, miraculous powers (such as healing the blind) were attributed to Aquinas's corpse, and the Cistercian monks who possessed the body became concerned that members of the Dominican order would steal their treasure: as a safeguard, they "exhumed the corpse of Brother Thomas from its resting place, cut off the head and placed it in a hiding place in a corner of the chapel," so that even if the body were stolen they would still have the skull. His sister was given one of his hands.

Aquinas wrote voluminously—over eight million words of closely reasoned prose, especially amazing considering he was not yet 50 when he died. He is said to have committed the entire Bible to memory, and was able to dictate to six or seven secretaries at one time. (His own handwriting was so unintelligible it has been dubbed the *litera inintelligibilis*.) His two major works, both written in Latin, are *Summa contra Gentiles* and *Summa Theologiae*. The first (written between 1259 and 1264) defends Christianity against a large number of objections, without assuming in advance that Christianity is true—it was reputedly written as a handbook for missionaries seeking to convert Muslims and others to Catholicism. The second (written between 1265 and 1273) attempts to summarize Catholic doctrine in such a way that it is consistent with rational philosophy and the natural science of the day.

What Was Aquinas's Overall Philosophical Project?

Aquinas was the most important European philosopher of the Middle Ages. His great achievement was that he brought together Christian theology with the insights of classical Greek philosophy—especially the work of Aristotle—and created a formidably systematic and powerful body of thought. Much of this system, as part of the medieval tradition called "scholasticism," became the standard intellectual world view for Christian Europe for hundreds of years: it formed the basis of European science and philosophy until the intellectual Renaissance of the sixteenth century, and still underpins much Catholic theology.* In 1879 Pope Leo XIII recognized the philosophical system of Aquinas as the official doctrine of the Catholic Church.

The writings of the classical philosophers like Plato and Aristotle were lost to Western Europe for centuries after the fall of the Roman empire, but they were preserved by Jewish, Byzantine, and Islamic scholars on the Eastern and Southern shores of the Mediterranean. Starting in the sixth century CE these writings, translated into Latin, trickled back into non-Arabic Europe and by the thirteenth century, when Aquinas was writing, most of the texts of Plato and Aristotle were again available to Western thinkers. In particular, in the second half of the twelfth century, Aristotle's writings on physics and metaphysics came to light, triggering a deep intellectual conflict in Western Europe. Christian theology is ultimately based on *faith* or scriptural revelation, while the conclusions of Plato and Aristotle are supported by *reason*. When theology and philosophy disagree—and in particular, when philosophers provide us with a rationally compelling argument against a theological claim—which are we to believe? Many conservative Christian theologians at the time viewed classical philosophy as a pagan threat to Christian dogma, but Aquinas was deeply impressed by the work of Aristotle—he considered him the greatest of all philosophers, often referring to him in his writings as simply "The Philosopher"—and set out to reconcile Aristotle's writings with Catholic doctrine. He did this, it is important to note, not because he wanted to remove any threat to Christianity from pagan science, but because he thought that much of what Aristotle had to say was *demonstrably true*.

Aquinas's reconciliation project had two prongs. First, he tried to show whenever possible that Aristotelian thought did not conflict with Christianity but actually supported it: thus faith could be conjoined with reason—religion could be combined with science—by showing how the human powers of reason allowed us to *better understand* the revealed truths of Catholicism.

Second, Aquinas argued that when Aristotle's conclusions did conflict with revealed truth, his arguments were not rationally compelling—but that neither were there any rationally compelling arguments on the other side. For example, Aristotle argued that the universe is eternal and uncreated; Christianity holds that the universe was created a finite amount of time ago by God. Aquinas tried to show that *neither* position is provable. In situations like this, Aquinas argued, we discover that reason falls short and some truths can only be known on the basis of faith.

Together, these two kinds of argument were intended to show that there is no conflict between reason and faith and in fact, rational argument, properly carried out, can only strengthen faith, either by further supporting points of doctrine and making them comprehensible to the rational mind, or by revealing the limits of reason. Importantly, this only works when we reason rigorously and *well*. The foolish, according to Aquinas, might be led into error by arguments which are only apparently persuasive, and one important solution to this problem is not to suppress reason but to *encourage* trained, critical, rational reflection on such arguments. (Of course, this solution, Aquinas realized, was not appropriate for the poor and uneducated; the peasants should instead be urged to rely upon their faith.)

Aquinas distinguished sharply between philosophy and theology. He held that theology begins from faith in God and interprets all things as creatures of God, while philosophy moves in the other direction: it starts with the concrete objects of sense perception—such as animals, rocks, and trees—and reasons towards more general conceptions, eventually making its way to God. In our selection from *Summa Theologiae* Aquinas is doing philosophy, and so all five of the proofs for the existence of God given in the Third Article are based upon Aristotelian science—that is, each proof starts from what intellectuals in the thirteenth century thought was a properly rational understanding of ordinary objects, and shows that this scientific understanding leads us to God. Properly understood, according to Aristotle, the natural phenomena appealed to in all of the "five ways" can only be ultimately explained—even *within* a completed science—by bringing in God.

---

* Although Aquinas's work is usually considered the keystone of scholasticism, he didn't create the tradition single-handedly. Other prominent scholastics—who did not all agree with Aquinas—were Peter Abelard (France, 1079–1142), John Duns Scotus (Scotland, c. 1266–1308), William of Occam (England, c. 1285–1349), and Jean Buridan (France, c. 1295–1358).

What Is the Structure of This Reading?

This reading is a good example of the medieval 'scholastic' method of doing philosophy. Aquinas begins by dividing up his subject matter—which is the knowledge of God—into a sequence of more precise questions. Question 2 of Part I of the *Summa Theologiae* is about God's essence, and in particular about whether God exists. He breaks down this question into three parts, and in each part—called an 'Article'—Aquinas lays out his view, and then answers a series of objections. The First Article considers whether God's existence is *self-evident*: that is, whether it is simply obvious to everyone who considers the matter that God must exist. Aquinas claims that it is not self-evident (except to the learned), and so some kind of argument will be needed to convince the unbeliever. In this section Aquinas argues against the Ontological Argument for the existence of God (see the previous section on Anselm's *Proslogion*). The Second Article discusses whether God's existence can be rationally demonstrated at all, or whether it is something that must be merely accepted on faith: Aquinas argues that God's existence can be proven. Finally, the Third Article lays out this proof; in fact, Aquinas thinks there are no fewer than *five* good arguments for the existence of God (his famous "five ways").

Some Useful Background Information

1. All five of Aquinas's arguments for the existence of God have the same basic form. They all move from some familiar empirical fact about the world to the conclusion that there must be some 'transcendent cause' upon which these facts depend. A 'transcendent cause' is a cause which transcends—lies beyond—the natural world; that is, it is a cause which is not itself *part* of the ever-changing physical universe but which *explains* the existence and nature of that universe.

2. In his first argument for the existence of God Aquinas uses the word "motion" in a somewhat technical sense. Aquinas is not just talking about a change of position but about *all* change in the physical world: the motion of the tides, the growth of a plant, the erosion of a mountain range, or someone baking a cake. Furthermore, in Aristotelian science, all motion or change is a transformation from a state of 'potentiality' to a state of 'actuality.' For example, imagine a row of dominoes standing next to each other. Each domino is *actually* standing up, but it is *potentially* falling down. When one domino is knocked down, it bumps into the next domino in the series and converts that potentiality into actuality—it makes the domino fall down. For Aristotle and Aquinas *all* change is this kind of movement, from being only potentially X into being actually X.

3. One important thing to notice about the domino example is that a domino cannot be toppled by something only *potentially* falling down—the domino next to it must be *actually* falling to have any effect. In other words, mere potentiality cannot make anything happen at all—or, to put it yet another way, a domino cannot knock *itself* over. This last claim is crucial for Aquinas's argument in the First Way to work.

4. The Aristotelian notion of an 'efficient cause' plays a key role in Aquinas's Second Way. The 'efficient cause' of something, according to Aristotle, is simply the agent (the object or substance) which brings it about: for example, the 'efficient cause' of tides is the moon's gravity. It's worth noticing that, sometimes, the continuing presence of an effect requires the continuation of the cause. If the moon's gravity went away, ocean tides would also subside; if the force causing the moon to orbit the Earth disappeared, according to Aristotelian science, the moon would stop moving.* Thus, if God is ultimately the 'efficient cause' of, say, the movements of the tides, God must still be presently acting as that cause.

5. When Aquinas talks about 'merely possible' being in the Third Way he again does not use this phrase in quite the modern sense. For modern philosophers, something is 'merely possible' if it might not have existed—for example, the book you are holding has 'merely possible' (or contingent) being,

---

* Notice that this is importantly different from modern science. Today, we know that motions like planetary orbits, once started, simply continue forever unless some force stops them—this is Newton's first law of motion.

in this modern sense, because under other circumstances it might never have been written at all. By contrast, many modern philosophers would agree that mathematical objects, like the number two, have necessary existence—there are no possible circumstances in which the number two could fail to exist. But this is not quite what Aquinas means by 'possible' and 'necessary': for him, something has 'merely possible' being if it is *generated* and *corruptible*. Something is generated if there was a time at which it didn't exist—a time at which it came into being. Something is corruptible if there will be a time at which it ceases to exist. Since things can't come into existence for no reason at all (according to Aquinas), all non-necessary beings must have been generated by *something else*. For example, this book was generated by me, I was generated by my parents, and so on.

6. Aquinas also distinguishes between two different sorts of necessary (i.e., eternal) being. Some entities have necessary being but were nevertheless created by something else (God). For example, suppose that angels are non-corruptible, eternal beings; nevertheless, they have this nature only because God has created them in that way, so their necessary being is derivative of the necessary being of God. God himself, by contrast, is eternal and uncreated—the necessity of his being is, so to speak, built-in, rather than derived from some other source; God is necessarily necessary.

7. In the Fifth Way, the empirical fact from which Aquinas begins is this: different kinds of things, like water and air and plants, co-operate with each other in such a way that a stable order of nature is produced and maintained. They seem to act 'for the sake of a goal,' which is to say, for a particular *purpose*. For example, heat causes water to evaporate; this water then condenses as clouds and falls as rain; as it falls it nourishes plants and animals, and finally runs back into lakes and oceans where it once again evaporates; and so on. This co-operative cycle is stable and self-perpetuating, but the entities that make it up—the water, plants, and so on—do not *intend* for this to happen: they just, as a matter of fact, act in a way that preserves the system.

Some Common Misconceptions

1. Aquinas does not say that *everything* must have a cause, or that all creation involves a change in the creator. If he did say that, he would have to admit that God must himself have a cause, or that God must himself be moved. When Aquinas asserts that God is the 'first' element of a series, he means that God is importantly different than the other members of that series: God is not a changeable thing, for example, but is instead an Unmoved Mover who brings into existence even the phenomenon of change itself.

2. Although Aquinas thinks that the world in fact began a finite amount of time ago, he does not argue that the notion of an infinite time is rationally incoherent: "By faith alone do we hold, and by no demonstration can it be proved, that the world did not always exist," he says in *Summa Theologiae* (Part I, Question 46, Article 2). But this is not inconsistent with Aquinas's attempt to rationally demonstrate that there must have been a first cause. He thinks he can prove that the world must have been created by God—i.e., that God is the ultimate or underlying cause of the world—but, he argues in a treatise called *On the Eternity of the World*, no one can demonstrate that God's on-going creation of the world might not be spread over an infinitely long period of time. (Analogously, we might loosely say that the curvature of space causes gravitational effects and the curvature of space could conceivably continue forever.) Aquinas, that is, thought of God not just as a temporally first cause of the universe, back at the beginning of time like a supernatural Big Bang, but as the most fundamental cause of everything that happens in the natural world throughout time.

3. When Aquinas says that God is a necessary being, he means (roughly) that God's existence does not depend on the existence of anything else. He does not mean that God's existence is what modern philosophers would call "logically necessary." If God were logically necessary, then it would be impossible for God not to exist—it would be self-contradictory to assert that God does not exist, like saying that some bachelors are married. Aquinas does not think that it is self-contradictory to say that God does not exist, just that it is demonstrably false.

4. Aquinas was well aware that his Five Ways, even if they are sound, only prove the *existence* of God and, by themselves, fail to establish important positive conclusions about the nature of God (e.g., his moral goodness). In the section of the *Summa Theologiae* which comes after our selection, he goes on to give arguments about God's nature. Furthermore, Aquinas was aware he had not yet proved that there can be only one God, and he goes on to try to show—on the basis of philosophical arguments—that any entity whose necessary being is essential rather than derived must be simple, perfect, infinite, immutable, eternal, and one—i.e., if there is a God at all, there can be only one God (*Summa Theologiae* Part I, Questions 3 to 11).

5. Although Aquinas appeals to empirical facts as the premises of his arguments for God, he does not think his *conclusion* that God exists is a merely empirical hypothesis. For example, he does not think any amount of future scientific research could ever cast doubt on his arguments. Contrast that with, for example, the claim that electrons are the unseen cause of the pictures that appear on our television sets. It might be that future scientific advances could call into question our present sub-atomic theory, and so cast doubt on the existence of electrons: maybe all the phenomena we explain by talking about electrons can be better explained by talking about some other kind of invisible particle, or about some other category of thing altogether. By contrast, according to Aquinas, our proofs of the existence of God do not depend on the truth of some particular scientific theory; they follow from the mere existence of change, causation, and contingent beings, *however* these things are ultimately explained by science.

How Important and Influential Is This Passage?

Aquinas thought that, although the existence of God is not self-evident, reason is capable of proving to the careful thinker that God exists. The "five ways" he lists in this passage include versions of many of the most important arguments for God's existence, and—as a convenient, short, and very capable outline of the main arguments—this section from Aquinas's *Summa Theologiae* has been at the center of debate about the existence of God for hundreds of years.

Summa Theologiae*

PART I, QUESTION 2: DOES GOD EXIST?

Article 1: Is the Existence of God Self-Evident?

THOMAS'S ANSWER

A proposition can be self-evident in two different ways. In one way, a proposition is self-evident in itself but not to us; in another way, a proposition is self-evident in itself and also to us. A proposition of either sort is self-evident if the meaning of the predicate term is included in the meaning of the subject term. For example, "a human being is an animal" is self-evident, because the meaning of "animal" [the predicate] is included in the meaning of "human being" [the subject], because being an animal is a part of what it means to be human. Now, if the meaning of the subject and predicate is known to everyone, then the proposition will be self-evident to everyone, as is the case in the first principles of demonstration, the terms

---

* This part of the *Summa Theologiae* was written around 1265. The translation used here, by Steven Baldner, is taken from *Thomas Aquinas: Basic Philosophical Writings* (Broadview Press, 2018). This translation rearranges and abridges the original texts for the sake of clarity and understanding.

of which are basic, common, and known to everyone. These are terms like "being" and "non-being," "whole" and "part," and so forth. On the other hand, if the terms of a self-evident proposition are not known to everyone, the proposition will still be self-evident in itself, but it will not be self-evident to those who do not know the meanings of the terms. It can thus happen, as Boethius says, that "some terms and propositions are self-evident only to those with specialized knowledge."* For example, the proposition, "incorporeal beings do not exist in any place," is self-evident only to those with specialized knowledge.

Accordingly, I say that the proposition, "God exists," is self-evident in itself, because the predicate is identical with the subject, for God is his own being, as will be shown later. However, because we do not know what God is, the proposition "God exists" is not self-evident to us and must be demonstrated to us by means of things that are better known to us, although they are of a lesser nature than God. That is, we must demonstrate the existence of God through the effects that God causes.

OBJECTION 1

A truth is self-evident if the knowledge of that truth is naturally in us, as is the case with first principles. John of Damascus, in the beginning of his book, says that "the knowledge of the existence of God is naturally implanted in everyone."† Therefore, the existence of God is self-evident.

REPLY TO OBJECTION 1

It is true that a general and confused knowledge of God is naturally implanted in everyone. This can be seen in our desire for ultimate happiness, for God is our ultimate happiness, and the fact that we have a natural desire for happiness indicates that we have some natural knowledge of what we desire. Such a natural desire for happiness, however, does not give us any clear knowledge that God exists. If I know, for example, that some person is approaching, that knowledge does not tell me that it is Peter who is approaching, even if in fact it is Peter. Similarly, everyone desires the ultimate human good, but some people think that this good is riches, others think that it is pleasure, and others have other wrong ideas.

OBJECTION 2

A proposition is called self-evident if it is known to be true as soon as the meaning of its terms are known. Aristotle says that the first principles of demonstrations are known to be true in this way.‡ If, for example, you know what a "whole" is and what a "part" is, you immediately know that "any whole is greater than one of its parts." Likewise, if you understand the meaning of the word "God," you immediately know that God exists. The word "God" means "that than which nothing greater can be thought." It is, however, greater to exist both in reality and in the mind than to exist in the mind alone. Hence, when you understand the word "God" and have this meaning in your mind, you immediately know that God also exists in reality. Therefore, the existence of God is self-evident.

REPLY TO OBJECTION 2

It is quite possible that someone who hears the word "God" will not understand it to mean "that than which a greater cannot be thought," because some people think that God is something physical. Still, even if someone should understand the meaning of "God" as "that than which a greater cannot be thought," it does not follow that he or she would understand this to mean that God would exist in reality as something outside of the mind. The real existence of God cannot be shown unless it is granted that "that than which a greater cannot be thought" exists in some way, but this is precisely what atheists deny.

---

* An aristocratic Christian Roman from the early sixth century, Boethius translated Aristotle's logical writings and wrote several theological treatises. See *How Substances Are Good in Virtue of Their Existence without Being Substantial Goods* (*De hebdomadibus*), Rule 1.

† John of Damascus was an eighth-century monk in Jerusalem. This quote is taken from *An Exposition of the Orthodox Faith* (*De fide orthodoxa*), Bk. 1, Chs. 1 and 3.

‡ Aristotle, *Posterior Analytics* 1.3, 72b18–22.

OBJECTION 3

The existence of truth is self-evident, because anyone who attempts to deny the existence of truth must affirm the existence of truth in the process; for if truth did not exist, it would be true that truth did not exist. If anything is true, it is necessary that truth exists. God, however, is Truth Itself, as is written in John 16:6, "I am the way, the truth, and the life." Therefore, the existence of God is self-evident.

REPLY TO OBJECTION 3

The existence of truth in some general sense is self-evident, but the existence of the First Truth [i.e., God] is not self-evident to us.

Article 2: Is It Possible to Prove the Existence of God?

THOMAS'S ANSWER

There are two kinds of proof. One kind of proof is an argument from cause to effect, and this is a proof from what is absolutely prior to what is posterior. The other kind of proof is an argument from effect to cause, and this is an argument from what is prior in our knowledge [to what is posterior in our knowledge]. When an effect is better known to us than its cause, our knowledge proceeds from the effect to the cause of that effect. From any given effect a proof can be given of its proper cause, provided that the effect is better known to us. Since the effect always depends on its cause, for any given effect there must be a pre-existent cause. Hence, the existence of God, which is not self-evident to us, can be proven through the effects that are known to us.

OBJECTION 1

The existence of God is an article of faith. Whatever belongs to the faith cannot be proven, because proofs or demonstrations produce *knowledge*, but faith is about "the things that cannot be known."* Therefore, the existence of God cannot be proven.

REPLY TO OBJECTION 1

The existence of God and other truths of this sort that can be known by natural reason, truths about which Paul was speaking in Romans 1:20,† are not articles of faith; rather, they are *preambles* to the articles of faith. This is an indication that faith presupposes natural knowledge, just as grace‡ presupposes nature, and as whatever is brought to perfection presupposes a prior state of imperfection. Furthermore, there is no reason why a truth that can be proven and known could be taken on faith by someone who does not grasp the proof.

OBJECTION 2

In order to give a proof, the nature of the thing to be proven must be known. It is not possible, however, for us to know what God is, for we can only understand what God is not, according to John of Damascus.§

REPLY TO OBJECTION 2

When a proof is given from effect to cause, it is necessary to understand about the cause only that it is the cause of the given effect, because the proper definition of the cause cannot be given. This is especially so in the case of God. Whenever we prove the existence of something, we can only know what the name of the cause means; we cannot know the real nature of the

---

* Hebrews 11:1.

† "The invisible things of God can be known through those things that have been made by God." This verse from St. Paul was generally taken by medieval theologians to indicate that we can know God's existence philosophically from a consideration of the world God has made. St. Paul was a Jewish Roman citizen who lived in Jerusalem in the first century CE and who became an important missionary and the most significant founder of the church after his conversion to Christianity on the road to Damascus. He is often considered to be something like the second founder of Christianity.

‡ Grace is the unmerited favor or protection of God.

§ John of Damascus, *An Exposition of the Orthodox Faith* (*De fide orthodoxa*), Bk. 1, Ch. 4.

cause. This is so because the nature of something cannot be discovered until after its existence is known. The names of God are given to God from the effects that he causes, as will be discussed later.

OBJECTION 3

The only way to prove the existence of God is through the effects caused by God. The effects, however, are not proportionate to the cause, because he is infinite and the effects are finite. There can be no proportion between the infinite and the finite. Since a cause cannot be proven through an effect that is not proportionate to it, it seems that it is not possible to prove the existence of God.

REPLY TO OBJECTION 3

From effects that are not proportionate to their cause it is not possible to have a perfect knowledge of the cause, but nevertheless from any effect known to us it is possible to demonstrate the existence of the cause, as I have said. Hence, from the effects caused by God it is possible to demonstrate that God exists, although we are not able to attain a perfect knowledge of God's essence through such effects.

Article 3: Does God Exist?

THOMAS'S ANSWER

The existence of God can be proven in five ways.

The first and most manifest way is through motion. It is a fact and obvious to our senses that some things are moved in this world. Whatever is moved is moved by something else. This is so because nothing is moved unless it is first in a potential state toward the goal to which it is moved. The cause of motion, on the other hand, is in an actual state. For example, fire, which is actually hot, makes wood, which is potentially hot, to be actually so. In this way the fire moves and changes the wood. It is not possible that the same thing can be simultaneously in an actual and in a potential state in exactly the same way. What is actually hot cannot at the same time be potentially hot but is, rather, potentially cold. It is, therefore, impossible that something be simultaneously, in exactly the same respect, both the mover and the thing moved. In other words, it is impossible that

anything can move itself. Therefore, whatever is moved must be moved by something other than itself.

Furthermore, it is not possible to suppose an infinite number of movers, for if there is no first mover, then there are no other movers, either. The other, secondary movers are only movers because they are moved by the primary mover. For example, the stick [secondary mover] is moved by the hand [primary mover]. It is, therefore, necessary to come to some primary mover, which is moved by no other mover, and this everyone understands to be God.

The second way is taken from what it means to be an efficient cause. We find in the things of our experience that there is an order among efficient causes, which means that it is never possible for anything to be the efficient cause of itself. If something were the efficient cause of itself, it would have to be prior to itself, which is impossible.

Furthermore, it is not possible that there be an infinite number of efficient causes. This is so because in all series of coordinated efficient causes, the first is the cause of the intermediate cause, and the intermediate cause is the cause of the last cause. It does not matter how many intermediate causes there are; if the cause is removed, the effect is removed. Therefore, if there is no first efficient cause, neither will there be any intermediate efficient cause or a last efficient cause. Clearly, however, there *are* efficient causes. It is necessary, therefore, to recognize some first efficient cause, which everyone calls God.

The third way is taken from a consideration of what is possible and what is necessary. It goes like this. We find some things that are possible to be or not to be, because some things are generated and destroyed, and such things have the possibility either to be or not to be. It is impossible, however, that anything of this nature can exist forever, because whatever can possibly not exist at some time will not exist. If, therefore, all things could possibly not exist, at some time or other, nothing would exist. This is clearly not the case, for it would mean that now nothing would exist, since something can only come to exist from what already does exist. If there were nothing in existence, it would have been impossible for anything to begin to exist, and thus there would be nothing existing now, which is clearly false. It cannot, therefore, be the case that all beings are merely possible beings; it must be the case that some are necessarily existing. Whatever is necessarily existing either has the cause of its necessity from something else or not.

Again, it is not possible to have an infinite number of causes of necessity, just as we saw above that it is not possible to have an infinite number of efficient causes. It is, therefore, necessary to recognize the existence of something that exists necessarily through itself and does not have the cause of its necessity from outside of itself. This being is the cause of necessity in other things, and everyone calls this God.

The fourth way is taken from the grades of being in things. We find that some things have more goodness, more truth, more nobility, and so forth, than other things. We say "more" or "less" about different things because we recognize a "most." For example, things are more or less hot, because we recognize a maximum in heat.* Similarly, there is something that is the maximum in truth, goodness, and nobility, and consequently, the maximum in being, as Aristotle said.† Whatever is the maximum in its category is the cause of all the other things in the category. Fire, for example, is the hottest of things and is the cause of heat in all other cases, as Aristotle said in the same place. There is, therefore, something that is the cause of being and goodness in all things, and this we call God.

The fifth way is taken from the order of things. We see that some things that lack knowledge, such as natural bodies, operate for the sake of a goal. This is apparent from the fact that they always or for the most part operate in the same way, and in this way achieve what is best. It is clear that they achieve their goal, not by chance, but by intention. Those things that lack knowledge do not tend toward a goal unless they are so directed by intelligence, as the arrow is directed to the target by the archer. There is, therefore, some intelligent being, by whom all natural things are ordered to a goal, and this we call God.

OBJECTION 1

If one of two contrary things is infinite, the other contrary‡ cannot possibly exist. God, by his very name, is understood to be an infinitely good being. If, therefore, God does exist, no evil could possibly exist. Evil, however, does exist in the world. Therefore, God does not exist.

REPLY TO OBJECTION 1

As Augustine says, "Since God is supremely good, he would not permit anything of evil to exist in his works, unless he were so omnipotent and good that he would bring good even out of evil."§ It is characteristic of the infinite goodness of God that he allows evils to exist and that he brings good out of them.

OBJECTION 2

We must not suppose more causes than we need in order to explain effects. It seems, however, that everything that happens in the world can be explained by causes other than God, if we suppose that God does not exist. Natural things can be explained entirely by causes in nature, and artificial things can be explained by human reason and will. There is no need, therefore, to suppose that God exists.

REPLY TO OBJECTION 2

Since nature operates for determinate goals by the direction of a superior cause, it is necessary to recognize that even those things that occur by nature are caused by God as the first cause. Furthermore, as has been shown, it is necessary to find a cause beyond human reason and will, because these things are changeable and can fail. It is necessary that all moveable and possibly failing beings be caused by something that is absolutely immobile and necessary in itself, as has been shown. ■

---

* For Thomas, the maximum in heat would be the element of fire, understood to be something like one of our chemical elements. Any fire he experienced would have been a lesser version of that elemental fire.

† Aristotle, *Metaphysics* 2.1, 993b22–30.

‡ Contraries are properties which cannot both apply to a thing at the same time, though they can both fail to apply, e.g., being red all over and green all over, or being ugly and beautiful, or being wise and stupid.

§ St. Augustine of Hippo, a north-African bishop who lived from 354 until 430, was the most important early Christian theologian and philosopher. This quote is from his *Enchiridion on Faith, Hope, and Charity*, Ch. 3, 11.

Suggestions for Critical Reflection

1. Do any of Aquinas's five arguments actually prove that God exists? If none of them work, does this show that God does *not* exist?

2. Do Aquinas's five arguments establish the existence of a *personal* God—of a God who resembles the Christian conception of him? Does Aquinas show that there can be only *one* God, or are his arguments compatible with the existence of numerous gods?

3. Aquinas claims that there cannot be an infinite hierarchy of causes. Is he right about this? Do you think he gives compelling arguments for his claim? We are quite familiar with infinite sequences, such as the succession of integers (... -3, -2, -1, 0, 1, 2, 3 ...). Should Aquinas be worried about such infinite series? Why or why not?

4. Aquinas asserts that if everything were merely possible (and not necessary), then there would have to be some time in the past at which nothing at all existed. Does this follow? What might Aquinas have had in mind when he made this move?

5. For Aquinas, could anything have *both* possible and necessary being? Does this fit with your intuitions about possibility and necessity? What, if anything, is the connection between something being eternal and it having necessary being—for example, in your view, could something necessarily exist, but only for a finite amount of time, or could something that might not have existed at all be eternal?

6. Aquinas asserts that we must have an idea of *the best*, before we can judge anything to be *better than* something else. Do you agree with this claim? Support your answer with examples.

7. To what extent do you think that Aquinas's arguments depend on specifically Aristotelian science? How much does the fact that Aristotelian science has now been discredited in favor of post-Newtonian science cast doubt on his arguments?

DAVID HUME

FROM *Dialogues Concerning Natural Religion*

Who Was David Hume?

David Hume has been called the most important philosopher ever to have written in English. He was born to a strict Calvinist family in Edinburgh, Scotland's capital, in 1711, and spent his youth there and in Ninewells, his family's small land-holding near the border with England. Little is known of Hume's early childhood. His father, Joseph, died when he was two, and he was educated by his mother Katherine, who never re-married. He was a precociously intelligent and well-read child,* and by the age of 16 he had begun composing his first philosophical master-work, *A Treatise of Human Nature*, on which he was to work, more or less continuously, for the next ten years.

Hume spent the years between 1723 and 1726 (i.e., between the ages of 12 and 15) studying a wide range of subjects at the University of Edinburgh but, like many students of that era, did not take a degree. His father and grandfather had both been lawyers, and his family expected him also to go into law, but, Hume later wrote, he found the law "nauseous" and discovered in himself "an unsurmountable aversion to every thing but the pursuits of philosophy and general learning."†

Hume continued to read and write and, as a result of his feverish intellectual activity—motivated by his belief that he had made a major philosophical discovery— he suffered a nervous breakdown in 1734. He was forced to put philosophy aside for several months, during which he attempted life as a businessman at Bristol, in the employ of a Portsmouth merchant, but found that it didn't suit him; then he left Britain for France. There, in the following three years, living frugally in the countryside in Anjou (and using up all his savings), he completed most of his book.

Hume's *A Treatise of Human Nature* was published anonymously when he was 27. Hume later wrote, it "fell dead-born from the press, without reaching such distinction as even to excite a murmur among the zealots." Hume's career as an intellectual and man of letters seemed to have ended before it had begun, and Hume blamed not the substance of his work but its style. "I was carry'd away by the Heat of Youth & Invention to publish too precipitately. So vast an Undertaking, plan'd before I was one and twenty, & compos'd before twenty-five, must necessarily be very defective. I have repented my Haste a hundred, & a hundred times." Hume returned to Scotland to live with his mother, and began to re-cast the material of the *Treatise* into two new books, which have become philosophical classics in their own right: *An Enquiry Concerning Human Understanding* (1748) and *An Enquiry Concerning the Principles of Morals* (1751). However, both these books—though more successful than the *Treatise*—were slow to become influential during Hume's own lifetime.

Needing money, Hume got his first real job at the age of 34 and spent a well-paid year as tutor to a mad nobleman (the Marquess of Annandale). In 1746 Hume accepted a position as secretary to General St. Clair's military expedition to Canada (which never reached Canada and ended, oddly enough, with a brief attack on the French coast), and for two years after that was part of a secret diplomatic and military embassy by St. Clair to the courts of Vienna and Turin. During this period Hume was twice refused academic appointments at Scottish universities—first Edinburgh, then Glasgow—because of his reputation as a religious skeptic. Shortly afterwards, between 1755 and 1757, unsuccessful attempts were made in Edinburgh to have Hume excommunicated from the Church of Scotland.

---

* As his mother put it, in her Scottish dialect: "Our Davie's a fine good-natured crater [creature], but uncommon wake-minded [uncommonly weak-minded]."

† David Hume, "The Life of David Hume, Esq. Written by Himself," reprinted in *The Cambridge Companion to Hume*, ed. David Fate Norton (Cambridge University Press, 1993), 351, 352, 356.

In 1752 Hume was offered the Keepership of the Advocates' Library at Edinburgh and there, poorly paid but surrounded by books, he wrote the colossal six-volume *History of England*, which (though unpopular at first) eventually became his first major literary success. At this time he also published a controversial *Natural History of Religion*.

In 1763 Hume was made secretary of the English embassy at Paris, where he found himself very much in fashion and seems to have enjoyed the experience. There he fell in love with, but failed to win the hand of, the Comtesse de Boufflers, the mistress of a prominent French nobleman. (It was suggested this might have been partly because at the time, when Hume was in his fifties, he had come to resemble "a fat well-fed Bernardine monk."*) In 1767, back in Scotland and now a fairly wealthy man, Hume was appointed an Under-Secretary of State, a senior position in the British civil service.

By the time Hume died in 1776, of cancer of the bowel, he had become respected as one of Europe's leading men of letters and a principal architect of the Enlightenment. His death gave him the reputation of something of a secular saint, as he faced his incurable condition with cheerfulness and resignation and refused to abandon his religious skepticism. In a short autobiography, written just before he died, Hume described his own character:

> I was ... a man of mild dispositions, of command of temper, of an open, social, and cheerful humour, capable of attachment, but little susceptible of enmity, and of great moderation in all my passions. Even my love of literary fame, my ruling passion, never soured my temper, notwithstanding my frequent disappointments. My company was not unacceptable to the young and careless,† as well as to the studious and literary; and as I took a particular pleasure in the company of modest women, I had no reason to be displeased with the reception I met from them.... I cannot say there is no vanity in making this funeral oration of myself, but I hope it is not a misplaced one; and this is a matter of fact which is easily cleared and ascertained.

What Was Hume's Overall Philosophical Project?

Hume can be called the first 'post-skeptical' modern philosopher. He was wholly convinced (by, among others, the writings of his predecessors Descartes, Locke, and Berkeley) that no knowledge that goes beyond the mere data of our own minds has anything like secure and reliable foundations: that is, he believed, we have no certain knowledge of the inner workings of the physical world and its laws, or of God, or of absolute moral 'truth,' or even of our own 'real selves.' All we have secure knowledge of is our own mental states and their relations: our sensory impressions, our ideas, our emotions, and so on.

Despite all this, Hume's philosophical project was a positive one: he wanted to develop a new, constructive science of human nature that would provide a defensible foundation for all the sciences, including ethics, physics and politics. Where Hume's predecessors tried in vain to argue against philosophical skepticism, Hume assumed that a certain kind of skepticism was actually true and tried to go beyond it, to say something positive about how we are to get on with our lives (including our lives as scientists and philosophers).

Much of Hume's philosophical writing, therefore, begins by showing the unstoppable power of skepticism in some domain—such as skepticism about causation or objective ethical truths—and then goes on to show how we can still talk sensibly about causation or ethics after all. The selection from *An Enquiry Concerning Human Understanding* which appears later in this volume follows this pattern. The structure of Hume's *Dialogues*, however, is more complex. Exactly what Hume's own religious views were remains a matter of some controversy, but a strong case can be made that Hume felt substantial conclusions about the existence and nature of God cannot be founded in experience and therefore cannot be made sense of at all. Hume may, in other words, have been unremittingly skeptical about religion.

One of the central aspects of both Hume's skeptical and constructive philosophy is his strictly empirical methodology—a development of what was called in Hume's day 'the experimental method.' His science of human nature is based firmly on the experimental meth-

---

*   A quotation attributed to Diderot, who was, nevertheless, a friend of Hume's.
†   Without cares (carefree).

ods of the natural sciences, which emphasize the data of experience and observation, sometimes combined with mathematical or logical reasoning. Any other method of investigation—such as an appeal to 'innate intuition,' for example—is illegitimate. As Hume put it,

> If we take in our hand any volume; of divinity or school metaphysics, for instance; let us ask, Does it contain any abstract reasoning concerning quantity or number? No. Does it contain any experimental reasoning concerning matter of fact and existence? No. Commit it then to the flames: for it can contain nothing but sophistry and illusion.*

This assumption that all human knowledge is either a "matter of fact" or a matter of "relations of ideas"—the product of experience or of reason—is often known as 'Hume's Fork.' You can find more about this in the Hume reading from the Philosophy of Science chapter of this volume.

This general philosophical attitude is also applied to religion. Hume's two main writings on religion are the *Dialogues Concerning Natural Religion* (which was published only after Hume's death, due to its controversial religious skepticism) and *The Natural History of Religion*. The former examines the rational basis for belief in God; the latter is a historical study of religion's origins in human nature and society: that is, Hume studies both the *reasons* for religious belief, and the *causes* of religious belief. In the *Dialogues*, written in the 1750s, Hume raises powerful doubts about whether we could ever have good reasons for believing in God—all religion, if Hume is right, may be no more than "mere superstition." Why then is religious belief so common? In *The Natural History of Religion*, published in 1757, Hume argues that the causes of religious belief are independent of rationality and are instead based on human fear of the unpredictable and uncontrollable influences in our lives—such as the forces of nature—which we try to propitiate through worship. Furthermore, Hume suggests, religious belief is more harmful than it is beneficial. Even apart from the suffering and strife which they have historically caused, religions invent spurious sins (like suicide) which Hume argued are not really harmful, and create "frivolous merits" not grounded in any genuine good (such as attending certain ceremonies and abstaining from particular foods).

In his *Enquiry Concerning the Principles of Morals* Hume develops a secular alternative to religiously-based morality; the theory of moral life he develops there is based entirely upon an analysis of human nature and human needs and is completely independent of religion. (Hume is often thought of as the original founder of the moral doctrine called "utilitarianism.")

What Is the Structure of This Reading?

There are three speakers in this dialogue: Cleanthes, who advocates the argument from design; Demea, who defends both mysticism and, occasionally, a kind of cosmological argument; and Philo, who plays the role of a skeptical critic of both of the others. The dialogue contains 12 sections: the second, third, fifth, ninth and part of the tenth are included here. In Parts II, III, and V Hume's characters discuss the argument from design; in Part IX they debate the cosmological argument; and in Part X Hume uses the character of Philo to raise the problem of evil. Here is how these selections fit into the flow of the whole work:

[PART I. Introductory discussion of the relationship between religion and philosophy.]

PART II. Demea and Philo claim that the nature of God is inaccessible, since it goes beyond human experience. Cleanthes presents the argument from design (to show that experience can give results about God), but Philo objects to the argument as being weak, even for an empirical argument. Cleanthes defends the analogy between a house and the universe and Philo re-presents the design argument for Demea's benefit, but then presents several objections to it.

PART III. Cleanthes defends the argument against Philo's objections, and Demea responds.

[PART IV. The three discuss the question of whether the nature of God's mind is at all similar to ours (e.g., in containing a set of ideas), and thus whether we can intelligibly speak of God as a designer. Philo suggests that to say the universe is created by a mind like ours invites us to ask what caused the ordered ideas that make up that mind (ideas don't just appear and fall into a certain pattern all by themselves, any more than matter does), and then we have an infinite regress. Cleanthes responds to this argument, and Philo replies.]

---

*   David Hume, *An Enquiry Concerning Human Understanding*, ed. Lorne Falkenstein (Broadview Press, 2011), 202.

PART V. Philo goes on to reconsider the principle "like effects prove like causes," and to suggest what consequences this would have for our idea of God as a cause "proportioned to the effect."

[PART VI. Philo next suggests that reasoning very like the argument from design will show that God is not the cause of the universe, but its mind or soul, and the material universe is God's body—his point is that, if this conclusion is unacceptable, something must be wrong with the arguments for both conclusions. Cleanthes responds, arguing (in part) that the universe cannot have been infinite and so cannot be God, and Philo in turn argues for its infinity.]

[PART VII. Philo next objects that reasoning very like the argument from design will show that a more plausible cause for the universe is not a human-like designer, but the kind of "generation or vegetation" which we observe giving rise to plants and animals. We have no good evidence, he argues, to think that reason—thought—is the only creative power in the universe.]

[PART VIII. Here Philo hypothesizes that more or less random motions of matter, over an endless duration of time, would eventually produce a complex world just like ours, and once formed this world would persist for some time. Cleanthes objects that this is implausible. Philo agrees, but asserts that it is no more implausible than any other hypothesis and so "a total suspension of judgment is here our only reasonable resource."]

PART IX. Faced with the failure of the argument from design ("the argument *a posteriori*"), Demea urges a return to cosmological and ontological arguments (which he calls "the argument *a priori*"). His argument is rejected by Cleanthes.

PART X. The speakers discuss the problem of evil. Why would a good and powerful God allow pain, hardship, and misery to exist in the world? And does not the existence of evil in the world cast doubt upon our inference from the apparent design of the world to a benevolent designer?

[PART XI. The three continue the discussion of the problem of evil. They examine four sources of evil, but it is suggested that at best they may establish the compatibility of evil with God and that they block any inference from a world containing evil to an infinitely good God. On the contrary, Philo suggests, the existence of evil means that we should infer an amoral origin of the universe.]

[PART XII. After Demea's departure Philo completely reverses himself and admits that the argument from design does indeed show the existence of God; he claims, however, that it nevertheless tells us little about God's nature or about how human beings should behave.]

Some Useful Background Information

1. Probably, none of the three speakers in the dialogue fully and uniquely represents Hume's own views. Philo certainly comes closest to Hume's own position, but all three of the characters have philosophically important points to make. At the end of the *Dialogues* Hume offers no decisive verdict, but instead leaves his readers to grapple with the questions he raises. Furthermore, Hume's writing is often ironic, or intended to protect himself from charges of atheism: for example, claims by the various speakers that God's nature and existence is obvious to any rational thinker should be taken with a pinch of salt.

   It's important for the modern reader to understand that Hume had good reason to fear becoming known as an atheist. As recently as 1619 atheists were executed in Europe by having their tongues pulled out and then being burnt to death, and even in the eighteenth century there were stiff legal penalties in Britain for impiety: for example, in 1763, 70-year-old Peter Annet was sentenced to a year of hard labor for questioning the accounts of miracles in the Old Testament. At a minimum, a reputation for atheism could easily lead to social and professional isolation and, despite his caution, Hume himself felt some of these sorts of effects (such as twice being denied university posts).

2. In his *Dialogues* Hume is operating with certain distinctions that it is useful to be aware of. *Natural religion* (or natural theology) is religious belief that can be proven on the basis of public evidence, available to believer and unbeliever alike (such as facts about causation, or the concept of God). This is contrasted with *revealed religion* (or revelation), which is based on privileged information given only to believers (such as scripture).

   Theism is the belief in a unique, all-powerful God who created the universe, and who remains active—sustaining the universe, answering prayers, granting revelations, and so on. Typically, evidence for the existence of God the creator is thought to be part of natural religion, while claims about the continuing activity of God (often called God's "immanence" or "providence") are more often based on revelation. *Deism* is a philosophical view that accepts rational arguments for the existence of God—accepts natural theology—but is skeptical of revelation and so denies the Christian (or Judaic or Islamic) revelation of an immanent God.

Deism was a fairly influential view during Hume's lifetime. It held that God was the first cause of the universe and its laws, but subsequently did not intervene, leaving the universe to operate by itself, and leaving humans without divine contact. Hume always vigorously denied that he himself was a deist. In fact, his arguments in the *Dialogues* are much more focused on deism than on theism, since what he is attacking is natural religion. Elsewhere in his writings, however, Hume levels a brief but seminal criticism at revealed religion, and especially at the idea that miracles can be evidence of the existence and nature of God (Section X of *An Enquiry Concerning Human Understanding*). Many modern commentators (but by no means all of them) believe that Hume was in fact some kind of 'attenuated deist': that is, he may have thought that rational argument—and especially the argument from design—did make it at least somewhat likely that God exists, but it can tell us little about God's nature.

Anthropomorphism, by contrast, is a view which not only says that we can understand God but that we can appropriately describe God in language that draws its meaning from human activities and qualities, using such adjectives as "beautiful," "merciful," "fatherly," or "wise." ("Anthropomorphism" is from Greek words meaning "having the shape of a man.") This is a view Hume portrays Demea and Philo as rejecting.

3. Within natural religion, Hume (like other eighteenth-century thinkers) distinguishes between two types of argument, which he calls "the argument *a priori*" and "the argument *a posteriori*." The argument *a priori*, for Hume, is usually the cosmological argument for a First Cause. The argument *a posteriori* is the argument from design. See the introduction to this chapter on philosophy of religion for a little more information on these types of argument.

A Common Misconception

The *Dialogues* are deliberately written to be somewhat "literary" and philosophically ambiguous. Thus, for example, though many of the arguments he raises for and against are clear and compelling, it is not a clearcut matter whether Hume himself would totally reject the argument from design, or tentatively endorse it, or whether he thinks the problem of evil conclusively eliminates the possibility of a morally benevolent Deity. It is left up to readers to make these kinds of final judgments, on the basis of the arguments they encounter in reading the *Dialogues*.

How Important and Influential Is This Passage?

In one of his last letters, Hume wrote of the *Dialogues*: "Some of my Friends flatter me, that it is the best thing I ever wrote."[*] After his death the skeptical ideas developed by Hume were gradually transmitted to the main flow of European culture (via thinkers such as Immanuel Kant, Baron d'Holbach, and the poet Percy Shelley), and by the nineteenth century Hume and others were considered to have so thoroughly overthrown the rational basis for belief in God that important religious philosophers such as Friedrich Schleiermacher (1768–1834) and Søren Kierkegaard (1813–55) began to try to place religion less on a foundation of evidence and argument than on subjective experience and faith. Hume's own writings on religion, however, were neglected by philosophers and theologians until the 1930s (when interest in Hume was stimulated by changes in philosophical fashion, and especially the rise of a kind of radical empiricism called "logical positivism"). Since the 1960s the *Dialogues* have been widely considered the most formidable attack on the rationality of belief in God ever mounted by a philosopher.

---

[*] David Hume, letter of 8th June 1776, in *The Letters of David Hume*, ed. J.Y.T. Greig (Clarendon Press, 1935).

FROM *Dialogues Concerning Natural Religion**

Part II

I must own,[†] Cleanthes, said Demea, that nothing can more surprise me, than the light in which you have all along put this argument. By the whole tenor of your discourse, one would imagine that you were maintaining the being of a God, against the cavils[‡] of atheists and infidels; and were necessitated to become a champion for that fundamental principle of all religion. But this, I hope, is not by any means a question among us. No man, no man at least of common sense, I am persuaded, ever entertained a serious doubt with regard to a truth so certain and self-evident. The question is not concerning the being, but the nature of God. This, I affirm, from the infirmities of human understanding, to be altogether incomprehensible and unknown to us. The essence of that supreme mind, his attributes, the manner of his existence, the very nature of his duration; these, and every particular which regards so divine a Being, are mysterious to men. Finite, weak, and blind creatures, we ought to humble ourselves in his august presence; and, conscious of our frailties, adore in silence his infinite perfections, which eye hath not seen, ear hath not heard, neither hath it entered into the heart of man to conceive.[§] They are covered in a deep cloud from human curiosity. It is profaneness to attempt penetrating through these sacred obscurities. And, next to the impiety of denying his existence, is the temerity[¶] of prying into his nature and essence, decrees and attributes.

But lest you should think that my piety has here got the better of my philosophy, I shall support my opinion, if it needs any support, by a very great authority. I might cite all the divines,[**] almost, from the foundation of Christianity, who have ever treated of this or any other theological subject: But I shall confine myself, at present, to one equally celebrated for piety and philosophy. It is Father Malebranche,[††] who, I remember, thus expresses himself. "One ought not so much," says he, "to call God a spirit, in order to express positively what he is, as in order to signify that he is not matter. He is a Being infinitely perfect: of this we cannot doubt. But in the same manner as we ought not to imagine, even supposing him corporeal, that he is clothed with a human body, as the Anthropomorphites[‡‡] asserted, under colour that that figure was the most perfect of any; so, neither ought we to imagine that the spirit of God has human ideas, or bears any resemblance to our spirit, under colour that we know nothing more perfect than a human mind. We ought rather to believe, that as he comprehends[§§] the perfections of matter without being material ... he comprehends also the perfections of created spirits without being spirit, in the manner we conceive spirit: That his true name is, He that is; or, in other words, Being without restriction, All Being, the Being infinite and universal."

After so great an authority, Demea, replied Philo, as that which you have produced, and a thousand more which you might produce, it would appear ridiculous in me to add my sentiment, or express my approbation[¶¶] of your doctrine. But surely, where reasonable men treat these subjects, the question can never be concerning

---

* Hume's *Dialogues* were first published in 1779, three years after Hume's death. This is a reprint of that edition, with some modernized spelling and capitalization.
† I must admit.
‡ Petty or unnecessary objections.
§ This is paraphrased from the Bible: 1 Corinthians 2:9.
¶ Audacity or impudence, rashness.
** Priests or theologians.
†† Malebranche (1638–1715) was an important French philosopher and follower of Descartes; his main work was *On the Search for the Truth* (1675), and it is from this that Philo is quoting.
‡‡ See the background information, above.
§§ Includes.
¶¶ Approval.

the being, but only the nature, of the Deity. The former truth, as you well observe, is unquestionable and self-evident. Nothing exists without a cause; and the original cause of this universe (whatever it be) we call God; and piously ascribe to him every species of perfection. Whoever scruples* this fundamental truth, deserves every punishment which can be inflicted among philosophers, to wit,† the greatest ridicule, contempt, and disapprobation. But as all perfection is entirely relative, we ought never to imagine that we comprehend the attributes of this divine Being, or to suppose that his perfections have any analogy or likeness to the perfections of a human creature. Wisdom, thought, design, knowledge; these we justly ascribe to him; because these words are honourable among men, and we have no other language or other conceptions by which we can express our adoration of him. But let us beware, lest we think that our ideas anywise correspond to his perfections, or that his attributes have any resemblance to these qualities among men. He is infinitely superior to our limited view and comprehension; and is more the object of worship in the temple, than of disputation in the schools.

In reality, Cleanthes, continued he, there is no need of having recourse to that affected scepticism so displeasing to you, in order to come at this determination. Our ideas reach no further than our experience. We have no experience of divine attributes and operations. I need not conclude my syllogism. You can draw the inference yourself. And it is a pleasure to me (and I hope to you too) that just reasoning and sound piety here concur in the same conclusion, and both of them establish the adorably mysterious and incomprehensible nature of the supreme Being.

Not to lose any time in circumlocutions,‡ said Cleanthes, addressing himself to Demea, much less in replying to the pious declamations of Philo; I shall briefly explain how I conceive this matter. Look round the world: contemplate the whole and every part of it: you will find it to be nothing but one great machine, subdivided into an infinite number of lesser machines, which again admit of subdivisions to a degree beyond what human senses and faculties can trace and explain. All these various machines, and even their most minute parts, are adjusted to each other with an accuracy which ravishes into admiration all men who have ever contemplated them. The curious adapting of means to ends, throughout all nature, resembles exactly, though it much exceeds, the productions of human contrivance; of human designs, thought, wisdom, and intelligence. Since, therefore, the effects resemble each other, we are led to infer, by all the rules of analogy, that the causes also resemble; and that the Author of nature is somewhat similar to the mind of man, though possessed of much larger faculties, proportioned to the grandeur of the work which he has executed. By this argument *a posteriori*, and by this argument alone, do we prove at once the existence of a Deity, and his similarity to human mind and intelligence.

I shall be so free, Cleanthes, said Demea, as to tell you, that from the beginning, I could not approve of your conclusion concerning the similarity of the Deity to men; still less can I approve of the mediums by which you endeavour to establish it. What! No demonstration of the being of God! No abstract arguments! No proofs *a priori*! Are these, which have hitherto been so much insisted on by philosophers, all fallacy, all sophism?§ Can we reach no further in this subject than experience and probability? I will not say that this is betraying the cause of a Deity: But surely, by this affected candour, you give advantages to atheists, which they never could obtain by the mere dint of argument and reasoning.

What I chiefly scruple in this subject,¶ said Philo, is not so much that all religious arguments are by Cleanthes reduced to experience, as that they appear not to be even the most certain and irrefragable** of that inferior kind. That a stone will fall, that fire will burn, that the earth has solidity, we have observed a thousand and a thousand times; and when any new instance of this nature is presented, we draw without hesitation the accustomed inference. The exact

---

* To scruple is to feel doubt or hesitation.
† "To wit" is a phrase meaning "that is to say."
‡ Unnecessarily wordy or roundabout language.
§ A sophism is a clever but misleading argument.
¶ Scruple in this subject: feel doubt about this subject.
** Unanswerable, undeniable.

similarity of the cases gives us a perfect assurance of a similar event; and a stronger evidence is never desired nor sought after. But wherever you depart, in the least, from the similarity of the cases, you diminish proportionably the evidence; and may at last bring it to a very weak analogy, which is confessedly liable to error and uncertainty. After having experienced the circulation of the blood in human creatures, we make no doubt that it takes place in Titius and Mævius:* but from its circulation in frogs and fishes, it is only a presumption, though a strong one, from analogy, that it takes place in men and other animals. The analogical reasoning is much weaker, when we infer the circulation of the sap in vegetables from our experience that the blood circulates in animals; and those, who hastily followed that imperfect analogy, are found, by more accurate experiments, to have been mistaken.

If we see a house, Cleanthes, we conclude, with the greatest certainty, that it had an architect or builder; because this is precisely that species of effect which we have experienced to proceed from that species of cause. But surely you will not affirm, that the universe bears such a resemblance to a house, that we can with the same certainty infer a similar cause, or that the analogy is here entire and perfect. The dissimilitude is so striking, that the utmost you can here pretend to is a guess, a conjecture, a presumption concerning a similar cause; and how that pretension will be received in the world, I leave you to consider.

It would surely be very ill received, replied Cleanthes; and I should be deservedly blamed and detested, did I allow, that the proofs of a Deity amounted to no more than a guess or conjecture. But is the whole adjustment of means to ends in a house and in the universe so slight a resemblance? The economy of final causes?† The order, proportion, and arrangement of every part? Steps of a stair are plainly

contrived, that human legs may use them in mounting; and this inference is certain and infallible. Human legs are also contrived for walking and mounting; and this inference, I allow, is not altogether so certain, because of the dissimilarity which you remark; but does it, therefore, deserve the name only of presumption or conjecture?

Good God! cried Demea, interrupting him, where are we? Zealous defenders of religion allow, that the proofs of a Deity fall short of perfect evidence! And you, Philo, on whose assistance I depended in proving the adorable‡ mysteriousness of the divine nature, do you assent to all these extravagant§ opinions of Cleanthes? For what other name can I give them? or, why spare my censure, when such principles are advanced, supported by such an authority, before so young a man as Pamphilus?¶

You seem not to apprehend, replied Philo, that I argue with Cleanthes in his own way; and, by showing him the dangerous consequences of his tenets,** hope at last to reduce him to our opinion. But what sticks most with you, I observe, is the representation which Cleanthes has made of the argument a posteriori; and finding that that argument is likely to escape your hold and vanish into air, you think it so disguised, that you can scarcely believe it to be set in its true light. Now, however much I may dissent, in other respects, from the dangerous principles of Cleanthes, I must allow that he has fairly represented that argument; and I shall endeavour so to state the matter to you, that you will entertain no further scruples with regard to it.

Were a man to abstract from every thing which he knows or has seen, he would be altogether incapable, merely from his own ideas, to determine what kind of scene the universe must be, or to give the preference to one state or situation of things above another. For as nothing which he clearly conceives could be esteemed

---

* That is, randomly chosen, generic human beings: John or Jane Doe.

† Hume uses the word "economy" in its now somewhat archaic sense to mean an orderly arrangement or system (of any type, not necessarily a financial system or necessarily one characterized by frugality). "Final causes" are one of the four types of causation (material, formal, efficient, final) identified by Aristotle: final causes are, roughly, the reasons for things, the purposes that explain them. For example, the structure of a can opener can be explained in terms of its purpose: it has a sharp pointy bit, for instance, because it is supposed to bite into the metal top of a can.

‡ In this context, 'adorable' doesn't mean cute. It means, worthy of adoration, that is, of worshipful veneration.

§ Excessive, unreasonable.

¶ The character who is supposed to be listening to this dialogue and later writing it down.

** Opinions or doctrines.

impossible or implying a contradiction, every chimera* of his fancy would be upon an equal footing; nor could he assign any just reason why he adheres to one idea or system, and rejects the others which are equally possible.

Again; after he opens his eyes, and contemplates the world as it really is, it would be impossible for him at first to assign the cause of any one event, much less of the whole of things, or of the universe. He might set his fancy a rambling; and she might bring him in an infinite variety of reports and representations. These would all be possible; but being all equally possible, he would never of himself give a satisfactory account for his preferring one of them to the rest. Experience alone can point out to him the true cause of any phenomenon.

Now, according to this method of reasoning, Demea, it follows, (and is, indeed, tacitly allowed by Cleanthes himself,) that order, arrangement, or the adjustment of final causes, is not of itself any proof of design; but only so far as it has been experienced to proceed from that principle. For aught† we can know *a priori*, matter may contain the source or spring of order originally within itself, as well as mind does; and there is no more difficulty in conceiving, that the several elements, from an internal unknown cause, may fall into the most exquisite arrangement, than to conceive that their ideas, in the great universal mind, from a like internal unknown cause, fall into that arrangement. The equal possibility of both these suppositions is allowed. But, by experience, we find (according to Cleanthes) that there is a difference between them. Throw several pieces of steel together, without shape or form; they will never arrange themselves so as to compose a watch: stone, and mortar, and wood, without an architect, never erect a house. But the ideas in a human mind, we see, by an unknown, inexplicable economy, arrange themselves so as to form the plan of a watch or house. Experience, therefore, proves, that there is an original principle of order in mind, not in matter. From similar effects we infer similar causes. The adjustment of means to ends is alike in the universe, as in a machine of human contrivance. The causes, therefore, must be resembling.

I was from the beginning scandalized, I must own, with this resemblance, which is asserted, between the Deity and human creatures; and must conceive it to imply such a degradation of the supreme Being as no sound theist could endure. With your assistance, therefore, Demea, I shall endeavour to defend what you justly call the adorable mysteriousness of the divine Nature, and shall refute this reasoning of Cleanthes, provided he allows that I have made a fair representation of it.

When Cleanthes had assented, Philo, after a short pause, proceeded in the following manner.

That all inferences, Cleanthes, concerning fact, are founded on experience; and that all experimental reasonings are founded on the supposition that similar causes prove similar effects, and similar effects similar causes; I shall not at present much dispute with you. But observe, I entreat you, with what extreme caution all just reasoners proceed in the transferring of experiments to similar cases. Unless the cases be exactly similar, they repose no perfect confidence in applying their past observation to any particular phenomenon. Every alteration of circumstances occasions a doubt concerning the event; and it requires new experiments to prove certainly, that the new circumstances are of no moment or importance. A change in bulk, situation, arrangement, age, disposition of the air, or surrounding bodies; any of these particulars may be attended with the most unexpected consequences: and unless the objects be quite familiar to us, it is the highest temerity to expect with assurance, after any of these changes, an event similar to that which before fell under our observation. The slow and deliberate steps of philosophers here, if any where, are distinguished from the precipitate march of the vulgar,‡ who, hurried on by the smallest similitude, are incapable of all discernment or consideration.

But can you think, Cleanthes, that your usual phlegm§ and philosophy have been preserved in so wide a step as you have taken, when you compared to the universe houses, ships, furniture, machines, and, from their similarity in some circumstances, inferred

---

* A chimera is a mythological beast; that is, an imaginary thing.
† For all, for anything.
‡ The common people (from the Latin for "the common people," *vulgus*).
§ Calmness or coolness.

a similarity in their causes? Thought, design, intelligence, such as we discover in men and other animals, is no more than one of the springs and principles of the universe, as well as heat or cold, attraction or repulsion, and a hundred others, which fall under daily observation. It is an active cause, by which some particular parts of nature, we find, produce alterations on other parts. But can a conclusion, with any propriety,* be transferred from parts to the whole? Does not the great disproportion bar all comparison and inference? From observing the growth of a hair, can we learn any thing concerning the generation of a man? Would the manner of a leaf's blowing, even though perfectly known, afford us any instruction concerning the vegetation of a tree?

But, allowing that we were to take the operations of one part of nature upon another, for the foundation of our judgement concerning the origin of the whole (which never can be admitted); yet why select so minute, so weak, so bounded a principle, as the reason and design of animals is found to be upon this planet? What peculiar privilege has this little agitation of the brain which we call thought, that we must thus make it the model of the whole universe? Our partiality† in our own favour does indeed present it on all occasions; but sound philosophy ought carefully to guard against so natural an illusion.

So far from admitting, continued Philo, that the operations of a part can afford us any just conclusion concerning the origin of the whole, I will not allow any one part to form a rule for another part, if the latter be very remote from the former. Is there any reasonable ground to conclude, that the inhabitants of other planets possess thought, intelligence, reason, or any thing similar to these faculties in men? When nature has so extremely diversified her manner of operation in this small globe, can we imagine that she incessantly copies herself throughout so immense a universe? And if thought, as we may well suppose, be confined merely to this narrow corner, and has even there so limited a sphere of action, with what propriety can we assign it

for the original cause of all things? The narrow views of a peasant, who makes his domestic economy the rule for the government of kingdoms, is in comparison a pardonable sophism.

But were we ever so much assured, that a thought and reason, resembling the human, were to be found throughout the whole universe, and were its activity elsewhere vastly greater and more commanding than it appears in this globe; yet I cannot see, why the operations of a world constituted, arranged, adjusted, can with any propriety be extended to a world which is in its embryo state, and is advancing towards that constitution and arrangement. By observation, we know somewhat of the economy, action, and nourishment of a finished animal; but we must transfer with great caution that observation to the growth of a foetus in the womb, and still more to the formation of an animalcule‡ in the loins of its male parent. Nature, we find, even from our limited experience, possesses an infinite number of springs§ and principles, which incessantly discover¶ themselves on every change of her position and situation. And what new and unknown principles would actuate her in so new and unknown a situation as that of the formation of a universe, we cannot, without the utmost temerity, pretend to determine.

A very small part of this great system, during a very short time, is very imperfectly discovered to us; and do we thence pronounce decisively concerning the origin of the whole?

Admirable conclusion! Stone, wood, brick, iron, brass, have not, at this time, in this minute globe of earth, an order or arrangement without human art and contrivance; therefore the universe could not originally attain its order and arrangement, without something similar to human art. But is a part of nature a rule for another part very wide of the former? Is it a rule for the whole? Is a very small part a rule for the universe? Is nature in one situation, a certain rule for nature in another situation vastly different from the former?

---

* Appropriateness; fittingness.

† Bias.

‡ A sperm cell. It was thought at the time that these were tiny animals.

§ Origins.

¶ Reveal, disclose, exhibit.

And can you blame me, Cleanthes, if I here imitate the prudent reserve of Simonides, who, according to the noted story,[*] being asked by Hiero, What God was? desired a day to think of it, and then two days more; and after that manner continually prolonged the term, without ever bringing in his definition or description? Could you even blame me, if I had answered at first, that I did not know, and was sensible[†] that this subject lay vastly beyond the reach of my faculties? You might cry out sceptic and railler,[‡] as much as you pleased: but having found, in so many other subjects much more familiar, the imperfections and even contradictions of human reason, I never should expect any success from its feeble conjectures, in a subject so sublime, and so remote from the sphere of our observation. When two species of objects have always been observed to be conjoined together, I can infer, by custom, the existence of one wherever I see the existence of the other; and this I call an argument from experience. But how this argument can have place, where the objects, as in the present case, are single, individual, without parallel, or specific resemblance, may be difficult to explain. And will any man tell me with a serious countenance, that an orderly universe must arise from some thought and art like the human, because we have experience of it? To ascertain this reasoning, it were requisite that we had experience of the origin of worlds; and it is not sufficient, surely, that we have seen ships and cities arise from human art and contrivance....

Philo was proceeding in this vehement manner, somewhat between jest and earnest, as it appeared to me, when he observed some signs of impatience in Cleanthes, and then immediately stopped short. What I had to suggest, said Cleanthes, is only that you would not abuse terms, or make use of popular expressions to subvert philosophical reasonings. You know, that the vulgar often distinguish reason from experience, even where the question relates only to

matter of fact and existence; though it is found, where that reason is properly analysed, that it is nothing but a species of experience. To prove by experience the origin of the universe from mind, is not more contrary to common speech, than to prove the motion of the earth from the same principle. And a caviller[§] might raise all the same objections to the Copernican system,[¶] which you have urged against my reasonings. Have you other earths, might he say, which you have seen to move? Have....

Yes! cried Philo, interrupting him, we have other earths. Is not the moon another earth, which we see to turn round its centre? Is not Venus another earth, where we observe the same phenomenon? Are not the revolutions of the sun also a confirmation, from analogy, of the same theory? All the planets, are they not earths, which revolve about the sun? Are not the satellites moons, which move round Jupiter and Saturn, and along with these primary planets round the sun? These analogies and resemblances, with others which I have not mentioned, are the sole proofs of the Copernican system; and to you it belongs to consider, whether you have any analogies of the same kind to support your theory.

In reality, Cleanthes, continued he, the modern system of astronomy is now so much received by all inquirers, and has become so essential a part even of our earliest education, that we are not commonly very scrupulous in examining the reasons upon which it is founded. It is now become a matter of mere curiosity to study the first writers on that subject, who had the full force of prejudice to encounter, and were obliged to turn their arguments on every side in order to render them popular and convincing. But if we peruse Galileo's famous Dialogues concerning the system of the world,[**] we shall find, that that great genius, one of the sublimest that ever existed, first bent all his endeavours to prove, that there was no foundation for

---

[*]   Cicero, *De Natura Deorum* ("On the Nature of the Gods").

[†]   Aware or conscious.

[‡]   A "railler" is one who rails: complains vehemently or bitterly.

[§]   One who cavils, i.e., finds fault or makes petty criticisms.

[¶]   The model of the solar system introduced by Polish astronomer Nicolaus Copernicus (1473–1543) in which the planets move in circular orbits around the sun (rather than orbiting the Earth, as in the older theory).

[**]   *Dialogue Concerning the Two Chief World Systems* (1632).

the distinction commonly made between elementary and celestial substances.* The schools,† proceeding from the illusions of sense, had carried this distinction very far; and had established the latter substances to be ingenerable,‡ incorruptible, unalterable, impassable;§ and had assigned all the opposite qualities to the former. But Galileo, beginning with the moon, proved its similarity in every particular to the earth; its convex figure, its natural darkness when not illuminated, its density, its distinction into solid and liquid, the variations of its phases, the mutual illuminations of the earth and moon, their mutual eclipses, the inequalities of the lunar surface, &c. After many instances of this kind, with regard to all the planets, men plainly saw that these bodies became proper objects of experience; and that the similarity of their nature enabled us to extend the same arguments and phenomena from one to the other.

In this cautious proceeding of the astronomers, you may read your own condemnation, Cleanthes; or rather may see, that the subject in which you are engaged exceeds all human reason and inquiry. Can you pretend to show any such similarity between the fabric of a house, and the generation of a universe? Have you ever seen nature in any such situation as resembles the first arrangement of the elements? Have worlds ever been formed under your eye; and have you had leisure to observe the whole progress of the phenomenon, from the first appearance of order to its final consummation? If you have, then cite your experience, and deliver your theory.

Part III

How the most absurd argument, replied Cleanthes, in the hands of a man of ingenuity and invention, may acquire an air of probability! Are you not aware, Philo, that it became necessary for Copernicus and his first disciples to prove the similarity of the terrestrial and celestial matter; because several philosophers, blinded by old systems, and supported by some sensible¶ appearances, had denied this similarity? But that it is by no means necessary, that theists should prove the similarity of the works of nature to those of art; because this similarity is self-evident and undeniable? The same matter, a like form; what more is requisite to show an analogy between their causes, and to ascertain the origin of all things from a divine purpose and intention? Your objections, I must freely tell you, are no better than the abstruse** cavils of those philosophers who denied motion;†† and ought to be refuted in the same manner, by illustrations, examples, and instances, rather than by serious argument and philosophy.

Suppose, therefore, that an articulate voice were heard in the clouds, much louder and more melodious than any which human art could ever reach: Suppose, that this voice were extended in the same instant over all nations, and spoke to each nation in its own language and dialect: suppose, that the words delivered not only contain a just sense and meaning, but convey some instruction altogether worthy of a benevolent Being, superior to mankind: Could you possibly hesitate a moment concerning the cause of this voice? And must you not instantly ascribe it to some design or purpose? Yet I cannot see but all the same objections (if they merit that appellation‡‡) which lie against the system of theism, may also be produced against this inference.

Might you not say, that all conclusions concerning fact were founded on experience: that when we hear an articulate voice in the dark, and thence infer a man,

---

* Between the material of which earthly things are made and the stuff of which the "celestial bodies" (stars and planets) are made.
† The medieval philosophical system called "scholasticism"; see the notes to the Aquinas reading in this chapter for more information.
‡ Not capable of being produced.
§ Not capable of being affected.
¶ Perceptual; appearances that can be sensed or experienced.
** Difficult to understand, obscure.
†† For example, the Greek philosopher Zeno of Elea (born in about 490 BCE), the originator of the so-called Zeno's paradoxes about motion.
‡‡ Name.

it is only the resemblance of the effects which leads us to conclude that there is a like resemblance in the cause: but that this extraordinary voice, by its loudness, extent, and flexibility to all languages, bears so little analogy to any human voice, that we have no reason to suppose any analogy in their causes: and consequently, that a rational, wise, coherent speech proceeded, you know not whence, from some accidental whistling of the winds, not from any divine reason or intelligence? You see clearly your own objections in these cavils, and I hope too you see clearly, that they cannot possibly have more force in the one case than in the other.

But to bring the case still nearer the present one of the universe, I shall make two suppositions, which imply not any absurdity or impossibility. Suppose that there is a natural, universal, invariable language, common to every individual of human race; and that books are natural productions, which perpetuate themselves in the same manner with animals and vegetables, by descent and propagation.* Several expressions of our passions contain a universal language: all brute animals have a natural speech, which, however limited, is very intelligible to their own species. And as there are infinitely fewer parts and less contrivance in the finest composition of eloquence, than in the coarsest organised body, the propagation of an *Iliad* or *Æneid*† is an easier supposition than that of any plant or animal.

Suppose, therefore, that you enter into your library, thus peopled by natural volumes, containing the most refined reason and most exquisite beauty; could you possibly open one of them, and doubt, that its original cause bore the strongest analogy to mind and intelligence? When it reasons and discourses; when it expostulates, argues, and enforces its views and topics; when it applies sometimes to the pure intellect, sometimes to the affections; when it collects, disposes, and adorns every consideration suited to the subject; could you persist in asserting, that all this, at the bottom, had really no meaning; and that the first

formation of this volume in the loins of its original parent proceeded not from thought and design? Your obstinacy, I know, reaches not that degree of firmness: even your sceptical play and wantonness‡ would be abashed at so glaring an absurdity.

But if there be any difference, Philo, between this supposed case and the real one of the universe, it is all to the advantage of the latter. The anatomy of an animal affords many stronger instances of design than the perusal of Livy or Tacitus;§ and any objection which you start in the former case, by carrying me back to so unusual and extraordinary a scene as the first formation of worlds, the same objection has place on the supposition of our vegetating library. Choose, then, your party, Philo, without ambiguity or evasion; assert either that a rational volume is no proof of a rational cause, or admit of a similar cause to all the works of nature.

Let me here observe too, continued Cleanthes, that this religious argument, instead of being weakened by that scepticism so much affected by you, rather acquires force from it, and becomes more firm and undisputed. To exclude all argument or reasoning of every kind, is either affectation or madness. The declared profession of every reasonable sceptic is only to reject abstruse, remote, and refined arguments; to adhere to common sense and the plain instincts of nature; and to assent, wherever any reasons strike him with so full a force that he cannot, without the greatest violence, prevent it. Now the arguments for natural religion are plainly of this kind; and nothing but the most perverse, obstinate metaphysics can reject them. Consider, anatomise the eye; survey its structure and contrivance;¶ and tell me, from your own feeling, if the idea of a contriver does not immediately flow in upon you with a force like that of sensation. The most obvious conclusion, surely, is in favour of design; and it requires time, reflection, and study, to summon up those frivolous, though abstruse objections, which

---

* By (biological) reproduction.
† Two well-known works of classical literature, the former written by Homer and the latter by Virgil.
‡ Recklessness.
§ Two Roman historians. Livy (59 BCE–17 CE) wrote a 142-volume history of Rome (of which only 35 volumes survive) from its foundation to his own time, while Tacitus (55–120 CE) wrote about the period of Roman history from 14 to 96 CE.
¶ Design.

can support infidelity.* Who can behold the male and female of each species, the correspondence of their parts and instincts, their passions, and whole course of life before and after generation, but must be sensible, that the propagation of the species is intended by nature? Millions and millions of such instances present themselves through every part of the universe; and no language can convey a more intelligible irresistible meaning, than the curious adjustment of final causes. To what degree, therefore, of blind dogmatism must one have attained, to reject such natural and such convincing arguments?

Some beauties in writing we may meet with, which seem contrary to rules, and which gain the affections, and animate the imagination, in opposition to all the precepts of criticism, and to the authority of the established masters of art. And if the argument for theism be, as you pretend, contradictory to the principles of logic; its universal, its irresistible influence proves clearly, that there may be arguments of a like irregular nature. Whatever cavils may be urged, an orderly world, as well as a coherent, articulate speech, will still be received as an incontestable proof of design and intention.

It sometimes happens, I own, that the religious arguments have not their due influence on an ignorant savage and barbarian; not because they are obscure and difficult, but because he never asks himself any question with regard to them. Whence arises the curious structure of an animal? From the copulation of its parents. And these whence? From their parents? A few removes set the objects at such a distance, that to him they are lost in darkness and confusion; nor is he actuated by any curiosity to trace them further. But this is neither dogmatism nor scepticism, but stupidity: a state of mind very different from your sifting, inquisitive disposition, my ingenious friend. You can trace causes from effects: you can compare the most distant and remote objects: and your greatest errors proceed not from barrenness of thought and invention, but from too luxuriant a fertility, which suppresses your natural good sense, by a profusion of unnecessary scruples and objections.

Here I could observe, Hermippus,† that Philo was a little embarrassed and confounded: But while he hesitated in delivering an answer, luckily for him, Demea broke in upon the discourse, and saved his countenance.

Your instance, Cleanthes, said he, drawn from books and language, being familiar, has, I confess, so much more force on that account: but is there not some danger too in this very circumstance; and may it not render us presumptuous, by making us imagine we comprehend the Deity, and have some adequate idea of his nature and attributes? When I read a volume, I enter into the mind and intention of the author: I become him, in a manner, for the instant; and have an immediate feeling and conception of those ideas which revolved in his imagination while employed in that composition. But so near an approach we never surely can make to the Deity. His ways are not our ways. His attributes are perfect, but incomprehensible. And this volume of nature contains a great and inexplicable riddle, more than any intelligible discourse or reasoning.

The ancient Platonists,‡ you know, were the most religious and devout of all the pagan philosophers; yet many of them, particularly Plotinus,§ expressly declare, that intellect or understanding is not to be ascribed to the Deity; and that our most perfect worship of him consists, not in acts of veneration, reverence, gratitude, or love; but in a certain mysterious self-annihilation, or total extinction of all our faculties. These ideas are, perhaps, too far stretched; but still it must be acknowledged, that, by representing the Deity as so intelligible and comprehensible, and so similar to a human mind, we are guilty of the grossest and most narrow partiality, and make ourselves the model of the whole universe.

All the sentiments of the human mind, gratitude, resentment, love, friendship, approbation, blame, pity, emulation, envy, have a plain reference to the state and

---

* Lack of (religious) faith.
† The character to whom Pamphilus, the narrator, is supposed to be sending his written record of the dialogue.
‡ Followers of the philosophy of Plato.
§ An Egyptian philosopher, founder of a movement today called Neoplatonism, who lived from 205 to 270 CE. His main work is called *The Enneads*.

situation of man, and are calculated for preserving the existence and promoting the activity of such a being in such circumstances. It seems, therefore, unreasonable to transfer such sentiments to a supreme existence, or to suppose him actuated by them; and the phenomena besides of the universe will not support us in such a theory. All our ideas, derived from the senses, are confessedly false and illusive; and cannot therefore be supposed to have place in a supreme intelligence: and as the ideas of internal sentiment, added to those of the external senses, compose the whole furniture of human understanding, we may conclude, that none of the materials of thought are in any respect similar in the human and in the divine intelligence. Now, as to the manner of thinking; how can we make any comparison between them, or suppose them any wise resembling? Our thought is fluctuating, uncertain, fleeting, successive, and compounded; and were we to remove these circumstances, we absolutely annihilate its essence, and it would in such a case be an abuse of terms to apply to it the name of thought or reason. At least if it appear more pious and respectful (as it really is) still to retain these terms, when we mention the supreme Being, we ought to acknowledge, that their meaning, in that case, is totally incomprehensible; and that the infirmities of our nature do not permit us to reach any ideas which in the least correspond to the ineffable sublimity of the Divine attributes.

...

Part V

But to show you still more inconveniences, continued Philo, in your anthropomorphism, please to take a new survey of your principles. Like effects prove like causes. This is the experimental argument; and this, you say too, is the sole theological argument. Now, it is certain, that the liker* the effects are which are seen, and the liker the causes which are inferred, the stronger is the argument. Every departure on either side diminishes the probability, and renders the experiment less conclusive. You cannot doubt of the principle; neither ought you to reject its consequences.

All the new discoveries in astronomy, which prove the immense grandeur and magnificence of the works of nature, are so many additional arguments for a Deity, according to the true system of theism; but, according to your hypothesis of experimental theism, they become so many objections, by removing the effect still further from all resemblance to the effects of human art and contrivance....

The discoveries by microscopes, as they open a new universe in miniature, are still objections, according to you, arguments, according to me. The further we push our researches of this kind, we are still led to infer the universal cause of all to be vastly different from mankind, or from any object of human experience and observation.

And what say you to the discoveries in anatomy, chemistry, botany? ... These surely are no objections, replied Cleanthes; they only discover new instances of art and contrivance. It is still the image of mind reflected on us from innumerable objects. Add, a mind *like the human*, said Philo. I know of no other, replied Cleanthes. And the liker the better, insisted Philo. To be sure, said Cleanthes.

Now, Cleanthes, said Philo, with an air of alacrity and triumph, mark the consequences. *First*, by this method of reasoning, you renounce all claim to infinity in any of the attributes of the Deity. For, as the cause ought only to be proportioned to the effect, and the effect, so far as it falls under our cognisance, is not infinite; what pretensions have we, upon your suppositions, to ascribe that attribute to the divine Being? You will still insist, that, by removing him so much from all similarity to human creatures, we give in to the most arbitrary hypothesis, and at the same time weaken all proofs of his existence.

Secondly, you have no reason, on your theory, for ascribing perfection to the Deity, even in his finite capacity, or for supposing him free from every error, mistake, or incoherence, in his undertakings. There are many inexplicable difficulties in the works of nature, which, if we allow a perfect Author to be proved *a priori*, are easily solved, and become only seeming difficulties, from the narrow capacity of man, who cannot trace infinite relations. But according to your method of reasoning, these difficulties become all real; and perhaps will be insisted on, as new instances of likeness to human art and contrivance. At least, you must

---

*   The more similar.

acknowledge, that it is impossible for us to tell, from our limited views, whether this system contains any great faults, or deserves any considerable praise, if compared to other possible, and even real systems. Could a peasant, if the *Æneid** were read to him, pronounce that poem to be absolutely faultless, or even assign to it its proper rank among the productions of human wit, he, who had never seen any other production?

But were this world ever so perfect a production, it must still remain uncertain, whether all the excellences of the work can justly be ascribed to the workman. If we survey a ship, what an exalted idea must we form of the ingenuity of the carpenter who framed so complicated, useful, and beautiful a machine? And what surprise must we feel, when we find him a stupid mechanic, who imitated others, and copied an art, which, through a long succession of ages, after multiplied trials, mistakes, corrections, deliberations, and controversies, had been gradually improving? Many worlds might have been botched and bungled, throughout an eternity, ere this system was struck out; much labour lost, many fruitless trials made; and a slow, but continued improvement carried on during infinite ages in the art of world-making. In such subjects, who can determine, where the truth; nay, who can conjecture where the probability, lies; amidst a great number of hypotheses which may be proposed, and a still greater which may be imagined?

And what shadow of an argument, continued Philo, can you produce, from your hypothesis, to prove the unity of the Deity? A great number of men join in building a house or ship, in rearing a city, in framing a commonwealth; why may not several deities combine in contriving and framing a world? This is only so much greater similarity to human affairs. By sharing the work among several, we may so much further limit the attributes of each, and get rid of that extensive power and knowledge, which must be supposed in one deity, and which, according to you, can only serve to weaken the proof of his existence. And if such foolish, such vicious creatures as man, can yet often unite in framing and executing one plan, how much more those deities or dæmons,† whom we may suppose several degrees more perfect?

To multiply causes without necessity, is indeed contrary to true philosophy: but this principle applies not to the present case. Were one deity antecedently proved by your theory, who were possessed of every attribute requisite to the production of the universe; it would be needless, I own (though not absurd) to suppose any other deity existent. But while it is still a question, whether all these attributes are united in one subject, or dispersed among several independent beings, by what phenomena in nature can we pretend to decide the controversy? Where we see a body raised in a scale, we are sure that there is in the opposite scale, however concealed from sight, some counterpoising weight equal to it; but it is still allowed to doubt, whether that weight be an aggregate of several distinct bodies, or one uniform united mass. And if the weight requisite very much exceeds any thing which we have ever seen conjoined in any single body, the former supposition becomes still more probable and natural. An intelligent being of such vast power and capacity as is necessary to produce the universe, or, to speak in the language of ancient philosophy, so prodigious an animal exceeds all analogy, and even comprehension.

But farther, Cleanthes: men are mortal, and renew their species by generation; and this is common to all living creatures. The two great sexes of male and female, says Milton,‡ animate the world. Why must this circumstance, so universal, so essential, be excluded from those numerous and limited deities? Behold, then, the theogony§ of ancient times brought back upon us.

And why not become a perfect anthropomorphite? Why not assert the deity or deities to be corporeal, and to have eyes, a nose, mouth, ears, &c.? Epicurus¶ maintained, that no man had ever seen reason but in a human figure; therefore the gods must have a human

---

* An epic poem written in Latin by Virgil (70–19 BCE), describing the wanderings of the hero Aeneas for the seven years between his escape of the destruction of Troy and his settling in Italy.
† In the Ancient Greek religion these were demigods, half-way between the human and the gods.
‡ English poet John Milton (1608–74), best known for his epic poem *Paradise Lost*.
§ An account of the genealogy of the gods: the theory of their family tree, so to speak.
¶ A Greek philosopher (341–270 BCE) best known for defending an atomistic view of the world that sees it as built up entirely from an infinite number of tiny indestructible particles.

figure. And this argument, which is deservedly so much ridiculed by Cicero, becomes, according to you, solid and philosophical.

In a word, Cleanthes, a man who follows your hypothesis is able perhaps to assert, or conjecture, that the universe, sometime, arose from something like design: but beyond that position he cannot ascertain one single circumstance; and is left afterwards to fix every point of his theology by the utmost license of fancy and hypothesis. This world, for aught he knows, is very faulty and imperfect, compared to a superior standard; and was only the first rude essay* of some infant deity, who afterwards abandoned it, ashamed of his lame performance: it is the work only of some dependent, inferior deity; and is the object of derision to his superiors: it is the production of old age and dotage in some superannuated deity; and ever since his death, has run on at adventures,† from the first impulse and active force which it received from him.... You justly give signs of horror, Demea, at these strange suppositions; but these, and a thousand more of the same kind, are Cleanthes's suppositions, not mine. From the moment the attributes of the Deity are supposed finite, all these have place. And I cannot, for my part, think that so wild and unsettled a system of theology is, in any respect, preferable to none at all.

These suppositions I absolutely disown, cried Cleanthes: they strike me, however, with no horror, especially when proposed in that rambling way in which they drop from you. On the contrary, they give me pleasure, when I see, that, by the utmost indulgence of your imagination, you never get rid of the hypothesis of design in the universe, but are obliged at every turn to have recourse to it. To this concession I adhere steadily; and this I regard as a sufficient foundation for religion.

...

Part IX

But if so many difficulties attend the argument *a posteriori*, said Demea, had we not better adhere to that simple and sublime argument *a priori*, which, by offering to us infallible demonstration, cuts off at once all doubt and difficulty? By this argument, too, we may prove the infinity of the divine attributes, which, I am afraid, can never be ascertained with certainty from any other topic. For how can an effect, which either is finite, or, for aught we know, may be so; how can such an effect, I say, prove an infinite cause? The unity too of the divine nature, it is very difficult, if not absolutely impossible, to deduce merely from contemplating the works of nature; nor will the uniformity alone of the plan, even were it allowed, give us any assurance of that attribute. Whereas the argument *a priori*....

You seem to reason, Demea, interposed Cleanthes, as if those advantages and conveniences in the abstract argument were full proofs of its solidity. But it is first proper, in my opinion, to determine what argument of this nature you choose to insist on; and we shall afterwards, from itself, better than from its useful consequences, endeavour to determine what value we ought to put upon it.

The argument, replied Demea, which I would insist on, is the common one.‡ Whatever exists must have a cause or reason of its existence; it being absolutely impossible for any thing to produce itself, or be the cause of its own existence. In mounting up, therefore, from effects to causes, we must either go on in tracing an infinite succession, without any ultimate cause at all; or must at last have recourse to some ultimate cause, that is *necessarily* existent: now, that the first supposition is absurd, may be thus proved. In the infinite chain or succession of causes and effects, each single effect is determined to exist by the power and efficacy of that cause which immediately preceded; but the whole eternal chain or succession, taken together, is not determined or caused by any thing; and yet it is evident that it requires a cause or reason, as much as any particular object which begins to exist in time. The question is still reasonable, why this particular succession of causes existed from eternity, and not any other succession, or no succession at all. If there be no necessarily existent being, any supposition which

---

* "Rude essay" means a rough attempt or primitive effort.
† At random; recklessly, without due consideration or thought.
‡ Hume takes this argument primarily from Samuel Clarke's *A Discourse Concerning the Being and Attributes of God* (1705), which was very influential in its time.

can be formed is equally possible; nor is there any more absurdity in nothing's having existed from eternity, than there is in that succession of causes which constitutes the universe. What was it, then, which determined something to exist rather than nothing, and bestowed being on a particular possibility, exclusive of the rest? *External* causes, there are supposed to be none. *Chance* is a word without a meaning. Was it *nothing*? But that can never produce any thing. We must, therefore, have recourse to a necessarily existent Being, who carries the *reason* of his existence in himself, and who cannot be supposed not to exist, without an express contradiction. There is, consequently, such a Being; that is, there is a Deity.

I shall not leave it to Philo, said Cleanthes, though I know that the starting* objections is his chief delight, to point out the weakness of this metaphysical reasoning. It seems to me so obviously ill-grounded, and at the same time of so little consequence to the cause of true piety and religion, that I shall myself venture to show the fallacy of it.

I shall begin with observing, that there is an evident absurdity in pretending to demonstrate a matter of fact, or to prove it by any arguments *a priori*. Nothing is demonstrable, unless the contrary implies a contradiction. Nothing, that is distinctly conceivable, implies a contradiction. Whatever we conceive as existent, we can also conceive as non-existent. There is no being, therefore, whose non-existence implies a contradiction. Consequently there is no being, whose existence is demonstrable. I propose this argument as entirely decisive, and am willing to rest the whole controversy upon it.

It is pretended that the Deity is a necessarily existent Being; and this necessity of his existence is attempted to be explained by asserting, that if we knew his whole essence or nature, we should perceive it to be as impossible for him not to exist, as for twice two not to be four. But it is evident that this can never happen, while our faculties remain the same as at present. It will still be possible for us, at any time, to conceive the non-existence of what we formerly conceived to exist; nor can the mind ever lie under a necessity of supposing any object to remain always in being; in the same manner as we lie under a necessity of always conceiving twice two to be four. The words, therefore, *necessary existence*, have no meaning; or, which is the same thing, none that is consistent.

But further, why may not the material universe be the necessarily existent Being, according to this pretended explication of necessity? We dare not affirm that we know all the qualities of matter; and for aught we can determine, it may contain some qualities, which, were they known, would make its non-existence appear as great a contradiction as that twice two is five. I find only one argument employed to prove, that the material world is not the necessarily existent Being: and this argument is derived from the contingency both of the matter and the form of the world. "Any particle of matter," it is said, "may be *conceived* to be annihilated; and any form may be *conceived* to be altered. Such an annihilation or alteration, therefore, is not impossible."† But it seems a great partiality‡ not to perceive, that the same argument extends equally to the Deity, so far as we have any conception of him; and that the mind can at least imagine him to be non-existent, or his attributes to be altered. It must be some unknown, inconceivable qualities, which can make his non-existence appear impossible, or his attributes unalterable: and no reason can be assigned, why these qualities may not belong to matter. As they are altogether unknown and inconceivable, they can never be proved incompatible with it.

Add to this, that in tracing an eternal succession of objects, it seems absurd to inquire for a general cause or first Author. How can any thing, that exists from eternity, have a cause, since that relation implies *a priority* in time, and a beginning of existence?

In such a chain, too, or succession of objects, each part is caused by that which preceded it, and causes that which succeeds it. Where then is the difficulty? But the whole, you say, wants§ a cause. I answer, that the uniting of these parts into a whole, like the uniting of several distinct countries into one kingdom, or

---

* A hunting metaphor: to start game (such as birds) is to startle them out of their hiding place.
† This paraphrases an argument found in Clarke.
‡ Unfair bias.
§ Lacks.

several distinct members into one body, is performed merely by an arbitrary act of the mind, and has no influence on the nature of things. Did I show you the particular causes of each individual in a collection of twenty particles of matter, I should think it very unreasonable, should you afterwards ask me, what was the cause of the whole twenty. This is sufficiently explained in explaining the cause of the parts.

Though the reasonings which you have urged, Cleanthes, may well excuse me, said Philo, from starting any further difficulties, yet I cannot forbear insisting still upon another topic. It is observed by arithmeticians, that the products of 9* compose always either 9, or some lesser product of 9, if you add together all the characters of which any of the former products is composed. Thus, of 18, 27, 36, which are products of 9, you make 9 by adding 1 to 8, 2 to 7, 3 to 6. Thus, 369 is a product also of 9; and if you add 3, 6, and 9, you make 18, a lesser product of 9. To a superficial observer, so wonderful a regularity may be admired as the effect either of chance or design: but a skilful algebraist immediately concludes it to be the work of necessity, and demonstrates, that it must for ever result from the nature of these numbers. Is it not probable, I ask, that the whole economy of the universe is conducted by a like necessity, though no human algebra can furnish a key which solves the difficulty? And instead of admiring the order of natural beings, may it not happen, that, could we penetrate into the intimate nature of bodies, we should clearly see why it was absolutely impossible they could ever admit of any other disposition? So dangerous is it to introduce this idea of necessity into the present question! And so naturally does it afford an inference directly opposite to the religious hypothesis!

But dropping all these abstractions, continued Philo, and confining ourselves to more familiar topics, I shall venture to add an observation, that the argument *a priori* has seldom been found very convincing, except to people of a metaphysical head, who have accustomed themselves to abstract reasoning, and who, finding from mathematics, that the understanding frequently leads to truth through obscurity, and, contrary to first appearances, have transferred the same habit of thinking to subjects where it ought not to have place. Other people, even of good sense and the best inclined to religion, feel always some deficiency in such arguments, though they are not perhaps able to explain distinctly where it lies; a certain proof that men ever did, and ever will derive their religion from other sources than from this species of reasoning.

Part X

It is my opinion, I own, replied Demea, that each man feels, in a manner, the truth of religion within his own breast, and, from a consciousness of his imbecility and misery, rather than from any reasoning, is led to seek protection from that Being, on whom he and all nature is dependent. So anxious or so tedious are even the best scenes of life, that futurity† is still the object of all our hopes and fears. We incessantly look forward, and endeavour, by prayers, adoration, and sacrifice, to appease those unknown powers, whom we find, by experience, so able to afflict and oppress us. Wretched creatures that we are! What resource for us amidst the innumerable ills of life, did not religion suggest some methods of atonement, and appease those terrors with which we are incessantly agitated and tormented?

I am indeed persuaded, said Philo, that the best, and indeed the only method of bringing every one to a due sense of religion, is by just representations of the misery and wickedness of men. And for that purpose a talent of eloquence and strong imagery is more requisite than that of reasoning and argument. For is it necessary to prove what every one feels within himself? It is only necessary to make us feel it, if possible, more intimately and sensibly.

The people, indeed, replied Demea, are sufficiently convinced of this great and melancholy truth. The miseries of life; the unhappiness of man; the general corruptions of our nature; the unsatisfactory enjoyment of pleasures, riches, honours; these phrases have become almost proverbial in all languages. And who can doubt of what all men declare from their own immediate feeling and experience?

...

---

*   Numbers generated by multiplying 9 together with some other number: e.g., 9×1 = 9, 9×2 = 18, etc.
†   Existence after death.

And can any man hope by a simple denial (for the subject scarcely admits of reasoning), to bear down the united testimony of mankind, founded on sense and consciousness?

And why should man, added he, pretend to an exemption from the lot of all other animals? The whole earth, believe me, Philo, is cursed and polluted. A perpetual war is kindled amongst all living creatures. Necessity, hunger, want, stimulate the strong and courageous: fear, anxiety, terror, agitate the weak and infirm. The first entrance into life gives anguish to the new-born infant and to its wretched parent: weakness, impotence, distress, attend each stage of that life: and it is at last finished in agony and horror.

Observe too, says Philo, the curious artifices of nature, in order to embitter the life of every living being. The stronger prey upon the weaker, and keep them in perpetual terror and anxiety. The weaker too, in their turn, often prey upon the stronger, and vex and molest them without relaxation. Consider that innumerable race of insects, which either are bred on the body of each animal, or, flying about, infix their stings in him. These insects have others still less than themselves, which torment them. And thus on each hand, before and behind, above and below, every animal is surrounded with enemies, which incessantly seek his misery and destruction.

Man alone, said Demea, seems to be, in part, an exception to this rule. For by combination in society, he can easily master lions, tigers, and bears, whose greater strength and agility naturally enable them to prey upon him.

On the contrary, it is here chiefly, cried Philo, that the uniform and equal maxims of nature are most apparent. Man, it is true, can, by combination, surmount all his real enemies, and become master of the whole animal creation: but does he not immediately raise up to himself imaginary enemies, the dæmons of his fancy, who haunt him with superstitious terrors, and blast every enjoyment of life? His pleasure, as he imagines, becomes, in their eyes, a crime: his food and repose give them umbrage and offence: his very sleep and dreams furnish new materials to anxious fear: and

even death, his refuge from every other ill, presents only the dread of endless and innumerable woes. Nor does the wolf molest more the timid flock, than superstition does the anxious breast of wretched mortals.

Besides, consider, Demea: This very society, by which we surmount those wild beasts, our natural enemies; what new enemies does it not raise to us? What woe and misery does it not occasion? Man is the greatest enemy of man. Oppression, injustice, contempt, contumely,* violence, sedition, war, calumny,† treachery, fraud; by these they mutually torment each other; and they would soon dissolve that society which they had formed, were it not for the dread of still greater ills, which must attend their separation.

But though these external insults, said Demea, from animals, from men, from all the elements, which assault us, form a frightful catalogue of woes, they are nothing in comparison of those which arise within ourselves, from the distempered condition of our mind and body. How many lie under the lingering torment of diseases?...

The disorders of the mind, continued Demea, though more secret, are not perhaps less dismal and vexatious. Remorse, shame, anguish, rage, disappointment, anxiety, fear, dejection, despair; who has ever passed through life without cruel inroads from these tormentors? How many have scarcely ever felt any better sensations? Labour and poverty, so abhorred by every one, are the certain lot of the far greater number; and those few privileged persons, who enjoy ease and opulence, never reach contentment or true felicity. All the goods of life united would not make a very happy man; but all the ills united would make a wretch indeed; and any one of them almost (and who can be free from every one?) nay often the absence of one good (and who can possess all?) is sufficient to render life ineligible.‡

...

And is it possible, Cleanthes, said Philo, that after all these reflections, and infinitely more, which might be suggested, you can still persevere in your anthropomorphism, and assert the moral attributes of the Deity, his justice, benevolence, mercy, and rectitude,

---

* Disgrace or insult.
† Slander.
‡ Unworthy of being chosen, undesirable.

to be of the same nature with these virtues in human creatures? His power we allow is infinite: whatever he wills is executed: but neither man nor any other animal is happy: therefore he does not will their happiness. His wisdom is infinite: He is never mistaken in choosing the means to any end: but the course of nature tends not to human or animal felicity:* therefore it is not established for that purpose. Through the whole compass of human knowledge, there are no inferences more certain and infallible than these. In what respect, then, do his benevolence and mercy resemble the benevolence and mercy of men?

Epicurus's old questions are yet unanswered. Is he willing to prevent evil, but not able? Then is he impotent. Is he able, but not willing? Then is he malevolent. Is he both able and willing? Whence then is evil? … ∎

Suggestions for Critical Reflection

1. Do you think that Hume was an atheist, or a skeptic about God? What's the difference?

2. How close is the analogy between a machine and the universe? How about between an animal or plant and the universe? Do differences or similarities between the two things compared—e.g., between machines and the world—suggest important differences or similarities between their (alleged) designers?

3. "Experience, therefore, proves, that there is an original principle of order in mind, not in matter." Why does Philo say this? How important is it to the argument he is recreating?

4. Do you agree with Hume that "like effects prove like causes" (i.e., that similar effects demonstrate similar causes)?

5. Cleanthes says that "[t]he anatomy of an animal affords many stronger instances of design than the perusal of Livy or Tacitus," by which he means that an animal shows more evidence of being created by an intelligent thing than a book does. Why does Cleanthes say this? How plausible do you find this claim?

6. Does the existence of order in nature *need* to be explained (or, for example, might it just be the result of random chance)? If it does require an explanation, can it only be explained by an appeal to an intelligent Designer? If we explain the order of nature by postulating a Designer, must we then go on to explain the Designer (and then explain the explanation of that Designer, and so on)?

7. Do you think that the existence of suffering makes it impossible to believe in an omnipotent and benevolent God? Do you think that the existence of suffering makes it impossible to infer the existence of an omnipotent and benevolent God from the evidence of design that we observe in the world? Are these two different questions?

8. What do you think of Hume's claim (in Part IX) that: "Whatever we conceive as existent, we can also conceive as non-existent"? If correct, how would this principle affect *a priori* attempts to prove the existence of God?

---

*   Happiness.

WILLIAM PALEY

FROM *Natural Theology*

Who Was William Paley?

William Paley (1743–1805) was an Anglican priest and theologian. He was born in Peterborough, the child of an earnest, intelligent mother and a father who became headmaster of Giggleswick School, Yorkshire, where Paley was educated until going up to Christ's College, Cambridge. Paley's first two years at Cambridge were spent "happily, but unprofitably," as he wrote in his memoirs, in company with friends "where we were not immoral, but idle and rather expensive." He enjoyed, then as throughout his life, angling, visiting the theater, and attending trials at the Old Bailey, the central criminal court of England and Wales. At the start of his third year at university, however, he was scolded by one of his friends for wasting his intellectual talents, and this seems to have changed Paley's relatively idle ways. Two years later he graduated from Christ's College as Senior Wrangler, the title given annually to the top mathematics undergraduate at Cambridge University. (This is considered a major intellectual achievement—arguably, between the mid-eighteenth and the early twentieth century, the most prestigious academic prize in the British Empire.)

After three years as a schoolmaster's assistant and then a Latin tutor, Paley returned to Cambridge to become a fellow of Christ's College, where he taught moral philosophy and religion for the following ten years, earning a reputation as one of the University's most popular lecturers.

In 1767 Paley was ordained a priest and became an Anglican clergyman. In 1776 he married Jane Hewitt, the daughter of a local spirit merchant, with whom he went on to have eight children, and took up his first parish in what is now Cumbria, in the northwest of England. Although Paley was unambitious and indifferent to promotion within the church,[*] he had the respect of several influential clerical friends who moved him around different parishes until eventually he become Archdeacon of Carlisle (1782) and then Subdean of Lincoln (1795). In the same year, 1795, Paley was offered a doctorate of divinity from Cambridge and was also granted one of the most well-paid church positions in England, the rectory of Bishopwearmouth.

Paley was a popular, humorous, and easy-going man—which no doubt, in addition to his prodigious intellect, contributed to his somewhat charmed clerical career—but he was also a sincere and conscientious vicar. He was in favor (within limits) of toleration and free intellectual inquiry within the church, publicly and vehemently campaigned against the slave trade,[†] and took seriously his pastoral duties—such as visiting the sick, helping feed the poor, writing inspiring sermons, acting as a magistrate, and establishing Sunday Schools—and wrote instructional pamphlets for his curates to guide and encourage them in those activities as well. He does not seem to have been particularly concerned for his own reputation, and some contemporaries found him lacking in the dignity appropriate to a man of his position: "The familiarity of his manners, his almost perpetual jests, his approximations to coarseness of language, weakened the splendour of his literary reputation."[‡]

Paley's reputation today is not as an original thinker but as a defender of orthodox Anglican views, boiled down to plain language and laid out as arguments that are intended to be rationally compelling. *The Principles*

---

[*] Paley was contemptuous of patronage (the practice of seeking favors and jobs from wealthy or politically powerful benefactors), coining the term "rooting" for "that baseness and servility which like swine rooting in a dunghill will perform the basest acts for a rich patron, to gain his protection and good benefice." See the entry on Paley by James E. Crimmins in the *Oxford Dictionary of National Biography* (2004).

[†] He publicly supported the American colonies against the British Crown during the American Revolutionary War (1775–83), believing that an American victory would lead to the end of slavery.

[‡] Henry Digby Best, *Literary and Personal Memorials* (1829), 182, cited in James Crimmins's entry on Paley in the *Oxford Dictionary of National Biography* (2004).

of Moral and Political Philosophy is one of the best state-ments of eighteenth-century (theologically-based) util-itarianism: an ethical view based on the principle that morally appropriate behavior will not harm others but instead will increase their happiness. This book was one of the most influential philosophical texts of its time, even being cited in debates in British Parliament and in US Congress. It was a set textbook at Cambridge until the early twentieth century—it was required reading for Charles Darwin as a student, for instance—and during his lifetime made Paley quite a lot of money.

Natural Theology, the book from which this reading is excerpted, was written at the end of Paley's life, and in-tended to be a preface or foundation to the rest of Paley's writings. In it he argues that the general happiness or well-being that can be observed in the physical, natural, and social order of things is evidence for God's creation of the universe. This idea was far from original to Paley—you can see in the previous reading that it had already been raised and extensively objected to by David Hume, for example—but Paley's use of analogies, and espe-cially the analogy between the world and a clockwork watch (though this also is not original to Paley*) made this an especially influential and well-received presen-tation of the argument. Paley's writings were much more influential than Hume's until the 1840s; *Natural Theology* was another Paley best-seller, and Darwin also read this book as an undergraduate and reported in his memoirs that he was charmed and initially persuaded by it.

Paley suffered for several years from an intestinal com-plaint which he nicknamed 'the scorpion' and, like Hume (see the introduction to the previous reading), he was ad-mired by those who knew him for his fortitude in dealing with this illness while he was completing *Natural Theology*. He died in 1805 and is buried in Carlisle Cathedral.

What Is the Structure of This Reading?

Paley argues that, even if we knew nothing at all about watches, just encountering a watch would immediately show to us that it had been created by an intelligent de-signer (Chapter I). If we were to discover a special watch that was able to somehow produce copies of itself, this would not make us less likely to think that the watch had

a designer but in fact we would naturally assume that the original watch—from which all the rest were produced as copies—had an even more intelligent designer (Chap-ter II). The natural world—and in Paley's specific exam-ple, the eye—is in many respects very similar to a com-plex mechanism, such as a watch or a telescope. Since these complex mechanisms are the product of intelligent design, this suggests that the natural world must be, too (Chapter III); and this conclusion follows even if some of the processes and structures we observe in nature ap-parently fall short of perfection, or it is unclear to us what their purposes are (Chapter V).

Some Useful Background Information

1. The Argument from Design, in Paley's version, has the form of an Argument from Analogy (see A Brief Introduction to Arguments in the introductory material to this book). This is a fairly common argu-ment structure that exhibits the following pattern:
    i.   Some thing A is similar to some other thing B, in several key ways that we already know about.
    ii. We know thing A has some additional fea-ture X that is of interest to us.
    iii. Therefore thing B very likely has feature X as well (since A and B are so similar in other ways).

    Assessing the strength of arguments from analogy is a complex matter, but generally the more known similarities there are between A and B, the more fundamental those similarities are, and the more relevant they are to whether something is X or not, the stronger the argument is.
2. The Argument from Design is also often known as the Teleological Argument, from the idea that the universe has a *telos*, ancient Greek for a goal or a purpose.

Some Common Misconceptions

1. Paley begins by asking the reader to imagine finding a watch lying on the ground in a remote

---

*   In fact, this analogy, used as evidence of divine creation, goes back at least to writings in the 1680s.

natural setting—a heath, or moorland—and wondering how it came to be there. The question Paley is asking is not why the watch is lying on the ground there, but how the watch came to exist in the first place. The point of specifying that the watch is discovered in a natural setting is to leave open the (*prima facie*) possibility that the watch might have grown there, or always been there, or been formed by some sort of process of erosion, or in some other way come into existence without having been constructed by some intelligent watch designer. Of course, Paley immediately then suggests that we should be incredulous at any other suggestion than that a sentient watchmaker had created the watch (and it had somehow then found its way onto the heath).

FROM *Natural Theology**

Chapter I: State of the Argument

In crossing a heath, suppose I pitched my foot against a *stone*, and were asked how the stone came to be there, I might possibly answer, that, for anything I knew to the contrary, it had lain there forever: nor would it perhaps be very easy to show the absurdity of this answer. But suppose I had found a *watch* upon the ground, and it should be inquired how the watch happened to be in that place, I should hardly think of the answer which I had before given, that, for anything I knew, the watch might have always been there. Yet why should not this answer serve for the watch as well as for the stone? Why is it not as admissible in the second case, as in the first? For this reason, and for no other, viz.† that, when we come to inspect the watch, we perceive (what we could not discover in the stone) that its several parts are framed and put together for a purpose, *e.g.* that they are so formed and adjusted as to produce motion, and that motion so regulated as to point out the hour of the day; that, if the several parts had been differently shaped from what they are, of a different size from what they are, or placed after any other manner, or in any other order, than that in which they are placed, either no motion at all would have been carried on in the machine, or none which would have answered the use that is now served by it. To reckon up a few of the plainest of these parts, and of their offices, all tending to one result:—We see a cylindrical box containing a coiled elastic spring, which, by its endeavour to relax itself, turns round the box. We next observe a flexible chain (artificially wrought for the sake of flexure) communicating the action of the spring from the box to the fusee.‡ We then find a series of wheels, the teeth of which, catch in, and apply to, each other, conducting the motion from the fusee to the balance, and from the balance to the pointer; and at the same time, by the size and shape of those wheels, so regulating that motion, as to terminate in causing an index,§ by an equable and measured progression, to pass over a given space in a given time. We take notice that the wheels are made of brass, in order to keep them from rust; the springs of steel, no other metal being so elastic; that over the face of the watch there is placed glass, a material employed in no other part of the work, but, in the room of which, if there had been any other than a transparent substance, the hour could not be seen without opening the case. This mechanism being observed (it requires indeed an examination of the instrument, and perhaps some previous knowledge of the subject, to perceive and understand it; but being once, as we have said, observed and understood),

---

* From *Natural Theology: or, Evidences of the Existence and Attributes of the Deity, Collected from the Appearances of Nature* (Philadelphia, 1802), 1–17, 42–43.

† "Viz.": that is.

‡ A fusee is a cone-shaped pulley with a chain wound around it in a spiral (used so that as the mainspring unwinds it exerts a constant force).

§ In this context, the index is the hand of the watch (in general, something that indicates a value or quantity).

the inference, we think, is inevitable; that the watch must have had a maker; that there must have existed, at some time and at some place or other, an artificer or artificers, who formed it for the purpose which we find it actually to answer; who comprehended its construction,* and designed its use.

I. Nor would it, I apprehend, weaken the conclusion, that we had never seen a watch made; that we had never known an artist capable of making one; that we were altogether incapable of executing such a piece of workmanship ourselves, or of understanding in what manner it was performed; all this being no more than what is true of some exquisite remains of ancient art, of some lost arts, and to the generality of mankind, of the more curious productions of modern manufacture. Does one man in a million know how oval frames are turned?† Ignorance of this kind exalts our opinion of the unseen and unknown artist's skill, if he be unseen and unknown, but raises no doubt in our minds of the existence and agency of such an artist, at some former time, and in some place or other. Nor can I perceive that it varies at all the inference, whether the question arise concerning a human agent, or concerning an agent of a different species, or an agent possessing, in some respects, a different nature.

II. Neither, secondly, would it invalidate our conclusion, that the watch sometimes went wrong, or that it seldom went exactly right. The purpose of the machinery, the design, and the designer, might be evident, and in the case supposed would be evident, in whatever way we accounted for the irregularity of the movement, or whether we could account for it or not. It is not necessary that a machine be perfect, in order to shew with what design it was made: still less necessary, where the only question is, whether it were made with any design at all.

III. Nor, thirdly, would it bring any uncertainty into the argument, if there were a few parts of the watch, concerning which we could not discover, or had not yet discovered, in what manner they conduced to the general effect;‡ or even some parts, concerning which we could not ascertain, whether they conduced to that effect in any manner whatever. For, as to the first branch of the case; if, by the loss, or disorder, or decay of the parts in question, the movement of the watch were found in fact to be stopped, or disturbed, or retarded, no doubt would remain in our minds as to the utility or intention of these parts, although we should be unable to investigate the manner§ according to which, or the connexion by which, the ultimate effect depended upon their action or assistance: and the more complex is the machine, the more likely is this obscurity to arise. Then, as to the second thing supposed, namely, that there were parts which might be spared, without prejudice to the movement of the watch, and that we had proved this by experiment— these superfluous parts, even if we were completely assured that they were such, would not vacate the reasoning¶ which we had instituted concerning other parts. The indication of contrivance** remained, with respect to them, nearly as it was before.

IV. Nor, fourthly, would any man in his sense think the existence of the watch, with its various machinery, accounted for, by being told that it was one out of possible combinations of material forms; that whatever he had found in the place where he found the watch, must have contained some internal configuration or other; and that this configuration might be the structure now exhibited, viz. of the works of a watch, as well as†† a different structure.

V. Nor, fifthly, would it yield his inquiry more satisfaction to be answered, that there existed in things a principle of order, which had disposed the parts of the watch into their present form and situation. He never knew a watch made by the principle of order; nor can he even form to himself an idea of what is meant by a principle of order, distinct from the intelligence of the watchmaker....

---

* "Comprehended its construction": designed it, worked out how to make it.
† Shaped into a rounded form using a cutting tool.
‡ "Conduced to the general effect": contributed to the overall function of the watch.
§ "Although we should be unable to investigate the manner": even if we couldn't work out how.
¶ "Would not vacate the reasoning": would not make the argument unsound.
** Evidence of design.
†† Just as probably as.

Chapter II: State of the Argument Continued

Suppose, in the next place, that the person, who found the watch, should after some time, discover, that, in addition to all the properties which he had hitherto observed in it, it possessed the unexpected property of producing, in the course of its movement, another watch like itself; (the thing is conceivable;) that it contained within it a mechanism, a system of parts, a mould for instance, or a complex adjustment of lathes, files, and other tools, evidently and separately calculated for this purpose; let us inquire, what effect ought such a discovery to have upon his former conclusion?

I. The first effect would be to increase his admiration of the contrivance, and his conviction of the consummate skill of the contriver. Whether he regarded the object of the contrivance, the distinct apparatus, the intricate, yet in many parts intelligible, mechanism by which it was carried on, he would perceive, in this new observation, nothing but an additional reason for doing what he had already done; for referring the construction of the watch to design, and to supreme art.* If that construction *without* this property, or, which is the same thing, before this property had been noticed, proved intention and art to have been employed about it; still more strong would the proof appear, when he came to the knowledge of this farther property, the crown and perfection of all the rest.

II. He would reflect, that though the watch before him were, *in some sense*, the maker of the watch which was fabricated in the course of its movements, yet it was in a very different sense from that in which a carpenter, for instance, is the maker of a chair; the author of its contrivance, the cause of the relation of its parts to their use. With respect to these, the first watch was no cause at all to the second: in no such sense as this was it the author of the constitution and order, either of the parts which the new watch contained, or of the parts by the aid and instrumentality of which it was produced.... Therefore,

III. Though it be now no longer probable, that the individual watch which our observer had found was made immediately by the hand of an artificer, yet doth not this alteration in any-wise affect the inference, that an artificer had been originally employed and concerned in the production. The argument from design remains as it was. Marks of design and contrivance are no more accounted for now than they were before. In the same thing, we may ask for the cause of different properties. We may ask for the cause of the colour of a body, of its hardness, of its heat; and these causes may be all different. We are now asking for the cause of that subserviency to an use, that relation to an end,† which we have remarked in the watch before us. No answer is given to the question by telling us that a preceding watch produced it. There cannot be design without a designer; contrivance without a contriver; order without choice; arrangement, without anything capable of arranging; subserviency and relation to a purpose, without that which could intend a purpose; means suitable to an end, and executing their office in accomplishing that end, without the end ever having been contemplated, or the means accommodated to it. Arrangement, disposition of parts, subserviency of means to an end, relation of instruments to a use, imply the presence of intelligence and mind. No one, therefore, can rationally believe, that the insensible, inanimate‡ watch, from which the watch before us issued, was the proper cause of the mechanism we so much admire in it; could be truly said to have constructed the instrument, disposed its parts, assigned their office, determined their order, action, and mutual dependency, combined their several motions into one result, and that also a result connected with the utilities of other beings.§ All these properties, therefore are as much unaccounted for as they were before.

IV. Nor is anything gained by running the difficulty farther back, *i.e.* by supposing the watch before us to have been produced from another watch, that from a former, and so on indefinitely. Our going back ever so far brings us no nearer to the least degree

---

* Skill or craft of the highest order.

† "That subserviency to an use, that relation to an end": the property of the watch as being something that was designed to serve the function ('end') of telling the time.

‡ Not capable of thought or deliberate action.

§ "The utilities of other beings": the needs of other entities, i.e., of human beings to tell what time it is.

of satisfaction upon the subject. Contrivance is still unaccounted for. We still want a contriver. A designing mind is neither supplied by this supposition, nor dispensed with. If the difficulty were diminished the further we went back, by going back indefinitely we might exhaust it. And this is the only case to which this sort of reasoning applies. Where there is a tendency, or, as we increase the number of terms, a continual approach towards a limit, *there*, by supposing the number of terms to be what is called infinite, we may conceive the limit to be attained: but where there is no such tendency, or approach, nothing is effected by lengthening the series. There is no difference, as to the point in question, (whatever there may be as to many points) between one series and another; between a series which is finite, and a series which is infinite.... The machine, which we are inspecting, demonstrates, by its construction, contrivance and design. Contrivance must have had a contriver; design, a designer; whether the machine immediately proceeded from another machine, or not. That circumstance alters not the case. That other machine may, in like manner, have proceeded from a former machine: nor does that alter the case: contrivance must have had a contriver. That former one from one preceding it: no alteration still: a contriver is still necessary. No tendency is perceived, no approach towards a diminution of this necessity. It is the same with any and every succession of these machines; a succession of ten, of a hundred, of a thousand; with one series as with another; a series which is finite, as with a series which is infinite. In whatever other respects they may differ, in this they do not. In all, equally, contrivance and design are unaccounted for.

The question is not simply, How came the first watch into existence? which question, it may be pretended, is done away by supposing the series of watches thus produced from one another to have been infinite, and consequently to have had no such *first*, for which it was necessary to provide a cause. This, perhaps, would have been nearly the state of the question, if nothing had been before us but an unorganized, unmechanised substance, without mark or indication of contrivance. It might be difficult to shew that such substance could not have existed from eternity, either in succession (if it were possible, which I think it is not, for unorganized bodies to spring from one another), or by individual perpetuity.* But that is not the question now. To suppose it to be so, is to suppose that it made no difference whether we had found a watch or a stone. As it is, the metaphysics of that question have no place; for, in the watch which we are examining, are seen contrivance, design; an end, a purpose; means for the end, adaptation to the purpose. And the question, which irresistibly presses upon our thoughts, is, whence this contrivance and design? The thing required is the intending mind, the adapting hand, the intelligence by which that hand was directed. This question, this demand, is not shaken off, by increasing a number or succession of substances, destitute of these properties;† nor the more, by increasing that number to infinity....

V. ...The conclusion which the *first* examination of the watch, of its works, construction, and movement, suggested, was, that it must have had, for the cause and author of that construction, an artificer, who understood its mechanism, and designed its use. This conclusion is invincible. A *second* examination presents us with a new discovery. The watch is found, in the course of its movement, to produce another watch, similar to itself: and not only so, but we perceive in it a system or organization, separately calculated for that purpose. What effect would this discovery have or ought it to have, upon our former inference? What, as hath already been said, but to increase, beyond measure, our admiration of the skill which had been employed in the formation of such a machine? Or shall it, instead of this, all at once turn us round to an opposite conclusion, viz. that no art or skill whatever has been concerned in the business, although all other evidences of art and skill remain as they were, and this last and supreme piece of art be now added to the rest? Can this be maintained without absurdity? Yet this is atheism.

Chapter III: Application of the Argument

This is atheism: for every indication of contrivance, every manifestation of design, which existed in the

---

* By one thing to exist for eternity.
† Lacking the properties of being designed, for a particular purpose, by a designer.

watch, exists in the works of nature; with the differ-ence, on the side of nature, of being greater and more, and that in a degree which exceeds all computation. I mean that the contrivances of nature surpass the contrivances of art, in the complexity, subtlety, and curiosity of the mechanism; and still more, if possible, do they go beyond them in number and variety: yet, in a multitude of cases, are not less evidently accommo-dated to their end, or suited to their office, than are the most perfect productions of human ingenuity.

I know no better method of introducing so large a subject, than that of comparing a single thing with a single thing; an eye, for example, with a telescope. As far as the examination of the instrument goes, there is precisely the same proof that the eye was made for vision, as there is that the telescope was made for assisting it. They are made upon the same principles; both being adjusted to the laws by which the trans-mission and refraction of rays of light are regulated. I speak not of the origin of the laws themselves; but, such laws being fixed, the construction, in both cases, is adapted to them. For instance; these laws require, in order to produce the same effect, that the rays of light, in passing from water into the eye, should be refracted by a more convex surface, than when it passes out of air into the eye. Accordingly we find, that the eye of a fish, in that part of it called the crys-talline lens, is much rounder than the eye of terrestrial animals. What plainer manifestation of design can there be than this difference? What could a mathe-matical instrument-maker have done more, to shew his knowledge of his principle, his application of that knowledge, his suiting of his means to his end; I will not say to display the compass* or excellence of his skill and art, for in these all comparison is indecorous, but to testify counsel, choice, consideration, purpose?

To some it may appear a difference sufficient to destroy all similitude between the eye and the telescope, that the one is a perceiving organ, the other an unperceiving instrument. The fact is, that they are both instruments. And, as to the mechanism, at least as to mechanism being employed, and even as to the kind of it, this circumstance varies not the analogy at all. For, observe, what the constitution of the eye is. It is necessary, in order to produce distinct vision, that an image or picture of the object be formed at the bottom of the eye.† Whence this necessity arises, or how the picture is connected with the sensation, or contributes to it, it may be difficult, nay we will con-fess, if you please, impossible for us to search out. But the present question is not concerned in the inquiry. It may be true, that, in this, and in other instances, we trace mechanical contrivance a certain way; and that then we come to something which is not mechan-ical, or which is inscrutable. But this affects not the certainty of our investigation, as far as we have gone. The difference between an animal and an automatic statue,‡ consists in this,—that, in the animal, we trace the mechanism to a certain point, and then we are stopped; either the mechanism becoming too subtile§ for our discernment, or something else beside the known laws of mechanism taking place; whereas, in the automaton,¶ for the comparatively few motions of which it is capable, we trace the mechanism through-out. But, up to the limit, the reasoning is as clear and certain in the one case as in the other. In the example before us, it is a matter of certainty, because it is a matter which experience and observation demonstrate, that the formation of an image at the bottom of the eye is necessary to perfect vision. The image itself can be shewn.** Whatever affects the distinctness of the image, affects the distinctness of the vision. The formation then of such an image being necessary (no matter how), to the sense of sight, and to the exercise of that sense, the apparatus by which it is formed is constructed and put together, not only with infinitely

---

*   Extent, range.
†   "At the bottom of the eye": i.e., on the retina (at the back of the eye).
‡   A statue with a hidden mechanism inside, making it move.
§   Subtle; in this context, hard to see or understand.
¶   Automatic statue.
** For example, French philosopher and scientist René Descartes recommended placing the eye from a fresh corpse in a hole in the wall of a dark box and scraping away the back of the eye until one could see the inverted image cast upon the retina (in *Optics*, published in 1637).

more art, but upon the self-same principles of art, as in the telescope or the camera obscura.* The perception arising from the image may be laid out of the question: for the production of the image, these are instruments of the same kind. The end is the same; the means are the same. The purpose in both is alike. The lenses of the telescope, and the humours of the eye† bear a complete resemblance to one another, in their figure, their position, and in their power over the rays of light, viz. in bringing each pencil‡ to a point at the right distance from the lens; namely, in the eye, at the exact place where the membrane is spread to receive it. How is it possible, under circumstances of such close affinity, and under the operation of equal evidence, to exclude contrivance from the one, yet to acknowledge the proof of contrivance having been employed, as the plainest and clearest of all propositions, in the other?

The resemblance between the two cases is still more accurate, and obtains in more points than we have yet represented, or than we are, on the first view of the subject, aware of. In dioptric telescopes§ there is an imperfection of this nature. Pencils of light, in passing through glass lenses, are separated into different colours, thereby tingeing the object, especially the edges of it, as if it were viewed through a prism. To correct this inconvenience had been long a desideratum¶ in the art. At last it came into the mind of a sagacious optician, to inquire how this matter was managed in the eye; in which there was exactly the same difficulty to contend with as in the telescope. His observation taught him, that, in the eye, the evil was cured by combining together lenses composed of different substances, i.e. of substances which possessed different refracting powers. Our artist borrowed from thence his hint; and produced a correction of the defect by imitating, in glasses made from different materials, the effects of the different humours through which the rays of light pass before they reach the bottom of the eye. Could this be in the eye without purpose, which suggested to the optician the only effectual means of attaining that purpose?** ...

Chapter V: Application of the Argument Continued

Every observation which was made in our first chapter, concerning the watch, may be repeated with strict propriety†† concerning the eye; concerning animals; concerning plants; concerning, indeed, all the organized parts of the works of nature. As,

I. When we are inquiring simply after the *existence* of an intelligent Creator, imperfection, inaccuracy, liability to disorder, occasional irregularities, may subsist, in a considerable degree, without inducing any doubt into the question: just as a watch may frequently go wrong, seldom perhaps exactly right, may be faulty in some parts, defective in some, without the smallest ground of suspicion from thence arising that it was not a watch; not made; or not made for the purpose ascribed to it. When faults are pointed out, and when a question is started‡‡ concerning the skill of the artist, or the dexterity with which the work is executed, then indeed, in order to defend these qualities from accusation, we must be able, either to expose some intractableness and imperfection in the materials, or point out some invincible difficulty in the execution, into which imperfection and difficulty, the matter of complaint may be resolved; or if we cannot do this, we must adduce such specimens of consummate art and contrivance, proceeding from the same hand, as

---

* A camera obscura is a dark chamber in which an image of the external scene is projected through a pinhole in one wall and appears as a reversed and inverted image on a surface opposite to the opening. This optical phenomenon has been known for thousands of years, and was in common use in the seventeenth and eighteenth centuries as an aid to drawing.

† The fluids inside the eyeball.

‡ Ray of light.

§ Telescopes that create their image using a convex lens.

¶ Something desired.

** That is, could something in the eye that was random and not part of a design have been the only effective solution to the optician's technical difficulty? (This is a rhetorical question, to which Paley thinks the obvious answer is 'no.')

†† "With strict propriety": very properly.

‡‡ "A question is started": someone raises the question.

may convince the inquirer of the existence, in the case before him, of impediments like those which we have mentioned, although, what from the nature of the case is very likely to happen, they be unknown and unperceived by him. This we must do in order to vindicate the artist's skill, or, at least, the perfection of it; as we must also judge of his intention, and of the provision employed in fulfilling that intention, not from an instance in which they fail, but from the great plurality of instances in which they succeed. But, after all, these are different questions from the question of the artist's existence; or, which is the same, whether the thing before us be a work of art* or not: and the question ought always to be kept separate in the mind. So likewise it is in the works of nature. Irregularities and imperfections are of little or no weight in the consideration, when that consideration relates simply to the existence of a Creator. When the argument respects his attributes, they are of weight; but are then to be taken in conjunction (the attention is not to rest upon them, but they are to be taken in conjunction) with the unexceptionable evidences† which we possess, of skill, power, and benevolence, displayed in other instances; which evidences may, in strength, number, and variety be such, and may so overpower apparent blemishes, as to induce us, upon the most reasonable ground, to believe, that these last ought to be referred to some cause, though we be ignorant of it, other than defect of knowledge or of benevolence‡ in the author.... ∎

Suggestions for Critical Reflection

1. Although Paley's key argument is typically described as resting on an analogy between a clockwork watch and the universe, this reading begins with a *disanalogy* between a watch and a stone. What is going on here? How exactly does Paley's larger argument work? It would be a good idea to lay it out according to the Argument from Analogy pattern described above. What precisely is Paley trying to persuade us to believe?

2. Paley distinguishes between arguments for the existence of a creator, and arguments concerning the nature of that creator. Why does he make this distinction? Are both arguments equally persuasive?

3. David Hume, in the previous reading, makes several criticisms of the argument from design. How effective are these criticisms against Paley's version of the argument?

---

* In this context, a work of art is something created through skilled craftwork.
† Undeniable examples.
‡ "Referred to some cause ... other than defect of knowledge or of benevolence": assumed to be caused by something different from any failing in the creator.

GOTTFRIED LEIBNIZ

Theodicy

Who Was Gottfried Leibniz?

Gottfried Wilhelm Leibniz was born in 1646 in Leipzig (a major city in Saxony, the east-central region of what is now Germany). His father Friedrich, a professor of moral philosophy at the University of Leipzig, died when he was six, but the young Gottfried had already been infected with a love of learning. He taught himself Latin at the age of seven or eight, and he read widely in his late father's large library. He went to the University of Leipzig at the age of 14, and then at 20 moved on to the University of Altdorf near Nuremberg, graduating with degrees in law and philosophy. However, he had no intention of pursuing an academic career, and after turning down a position as professor of law at the University of Altdorf, he got employment with the Elector of Mainz* in 1667 as part of a project to recodify and systematize the laws of Germany.

In 1672 Leibniz was sent to Paris, the leader of a devious political embassy trying to persuade the French king Louis XIV to invade Egypt and expel the Turks (and thus weaken the French economy and turn their attention away from Germany). Leibniz never got to present this idea to the French court, but he spent four years in Paris—at that time the intellectual capital of Europe—where he studied mathematics and philosophy and had his first significant encounter with the "mechanical philosophy" of Galileo, Bacon, Descartes, Gassendi, Hobbes, and others (see the Descartes reading in the Epistemology chapter of this volume for more details). Intoxicated with the philosophical excitement of the time, Leibniz plunged into the new philosophy and began the development of his own philosophical and scientific system. His early work was relatively amateurish, and he was very disappointed to be refused a research position with the Paris Academy of Sciences. However, it

was during this period that Leibniz independently, but more or less simultaneously with Isaac Newton, invented the differential calculus (the mathematics of the variation of a function with respect to changes in independent variables, a tool crucial to the development of the new Newtonian science because it allowed the formal representation of rates of change). He was later to feud bitterly and publicly with Newton over who was the first to invent it.

Leibniz returned to Germany in 1676 and became Court Councilor and Librarian to the Duke of Brunswick in Hanover, where he lived until his death in 1714. During this period he took on a wide variety of jobs—including geologist, mining engineer (unsuccessfully supervising the draining of the silver mines in the Harz mountains), diplomat, linguist, and historian—but all the while continued with his philosophical work in a series of letters, essays, and two books. He never married (though at age 50 he made a marriage proposal that he quickly thought better of). He spent months at a time without leaving his study, eating at irregular hours, falling asleep over a book at one or two in the morning and waking at seven or eight to continue his reading. He was quick to anger and resented criticism, but he was also swift to regain his good humor. In his old age he was, unfortunately, a figure of ridicule at the Court of Hanover, an irascible old fossil in a huge black wig, wearing old-fashioned, overly ornate clothes (he was also, ironically, disliked by the townspeople because it was rumored he was an atheist). When he died only one mourner attended his funeral, even though by then he was widely recognized in Europe as an important scholar and original thinker.

Leibniz was a man who sought synthesis and reconciliation between opposing points of view wherever possible. He believed, as he put it in the last year of his life, that "the majority of the philosophical sects are right in

---

* The political leader and archbishop of the region of Mainz, in Germany. Some German rulers were called "Electors," as they had the right to elect their overall ruler, the Holy Roman Emperor.

the greater part of what they affirm, but not so much in what they deny."* Perhaps because his childhood years were a time of great unrest in Europe—the aftermath of the Thirty Years' War between the Holy Roman Empire, France, Sweden, and Spain (1618–48)—Leibniz was, throughout his life, interested in political and religious reconciliation; for example, he had an ambitious scheme to reunite the Catholic and Protestant churches in Germany. Part of his plan to promote peace was a project to develop an ideal, universal language, which would promote communication and understanding between divided peoples. In his physics and philosophy he generally aimed to bring together the old Aristotelian-Scholastic tradition, which he learned as a student, with the new mechanical philosophy he encountered in France.

What Was Leibniz's Overall Philosophical Project?

Leibniz the philosopher was, first and foremost, a metaphysician. Metaphysics, in this sense, can be thought of as the study of 'ultimate reality'—that is, of the essential nature of the fundamental substances that make up the world (such as, perhaps, matter and spirit). Leibniz placed a particular weight on this understanding of substance as "the key to philosophy": he believed that his own theory of substance was "so rich, that there follow from it most of the most important truths about God, the soul, and the nature of body, which are generally either unknown or unproved."†

A good way to begin to understand his account of substance is to think about the following disagreement, which Leibniz had with the influential French philosopher René Descartes, who lived in the generation just prior to Leibniz. Descartes held that matter was a substance, but he thought of it as a *single*, continuous, extended lump of stuff. For Descartes, the whole material universe is fundamentally one single thing, spread out across all of space. In other words, there is only one material substance. On the other hand, Descartes believed that there are many mental substances (though they all

belong to the same *category* of substance, i.e., they are all minds): God is one (infinite, uncreated, etc.) mental substance, and each finite human mind is another. My mind is a different individual substance from your mind, for example, but according to Descartes our bodies are both part of the same substance.

It is Descartes's view of material substance with which Leibniz disagreed. He firmly rejected the notion that a single substance can 'include' a large number of separable bits, and insisted that reality must consist of a large number of discrete individual things rather than of a continuous expanse of 'stuff.' As it is sometimes put, for Leibniz "substantiality requires individuality"—i.e., substances are indivisible, complete beings that have a special kind of 'substantial unity.' The whole of material reality simply could not be a single substance, according to Leibniz, because it blatantly fails to have the right kind of unity. For example, a pile of stones or flock of sheep is not a substance since its unity (as a single heap or flock) is only *accidental*; on the other hand, a human being is a substance, according to Leibniz, because that unity is not accidental but is, so to speak, built in to one's personhood: it is what he called a unity *per se*, a unity "in itself."

The importance of all this for Leibniz's philosophical system is that he took very seriously the idea that reality is fundamentally made up of a collection of indivisible substances—which Leibniz calls "substantial forms"— each of which possesses substantial unity and so is complete in itself. At least by the time of his later philosophy, Leibniz held that all of reality is made up of a large collection of immaterial substances (roughly, minds or souls) which he called *monads*: the material world is an "appearance" that somehow "results" from the activities of purely immaterial minds. Furthermore, since these monads are complete in themselves, their "substantial form" encompasses their whole nature—their parts and structure, their causal powers and activities, their whole life-cycle of changing states are all derived from their substantial forms. Hence, to fully know the form of a human soul, for example, would be to know everything about its nature, according to Leibniz: one would be able

---

*   Gottfried Leibniz, letter to Nicolas Remond of 10th January 1714, in *Die philosophischen Schriften von Gottfried Wilhelm Leibniz*, Vol. III, ed. C.I. Gerhardt (1875), 60.

†   Gottfried Leibniz, *Reflections on the Advancement of True Metaphysics and Particularly on the Nature of Substance Explained by Force* (1694), section 4.

to predict and understand each and every activity of that soul, throughout its entire history.

Another consequence of Leibniz's metaphysics is that it presents *physics* in an important new light. Leibniz was writing during the heyday of the "new" or "mechanical" philosophy—typified by Descartes's philosophy and Newton's physics—which sought to explain all the phenomena of the material world, not in terms of mysterious forces or essences, but solely in terms of the complex collisions between bits of matter. Leibniz was part of this "new philosophy" movement—he agreed, in general terms, with the view that physics should be thought of as the study of matter in motion. Where he disagreed with many of his contemporaries, however, was over the concept of *physical force*—over the mechanism by which motion is transferred from one body to another (or conserved in a single moving body, like a planet). This was a matter of great interest and controversy in the seventeenth century, and was a far from trivial question. If a car rear-ends another vehicle waiting in neutral at a stop light, for example, it will cause the front car to roll forward. What philosophers of Leibniz's time were puzzled by was just exactly *what* is this invisible power which is transmitted from the first car to the second, and furthermore what keeps the second car moving when it is no longer being pushed by the first? In short, the movement of three-dimensional bodies through space was thought to be well understood, but what makes the bodies move in the first place was much more mysterious.

A natural response to this problem, at the time, was to turn to God as an explanation of this mystery. One such theory was called "occasionalism," and its most famous supporter was a French philosopher called Nicolas Malebranche (1638–1715). According to occasionalism, God is the true cause of all physical motion: God watches over the world and, when one body is hit by another moving body, this is the occasion for God to step in and cause the first body to move; similarly, God is constantly acting to keep moving bodies (like the Moon) in motion—without his intervention they would immediately halt. Leibniz, however, held that this role was beneath the dignity of God. It is far more worthy of God to have produced entities capable of initiating their own movements. And Leibniz's metaphysical framework allowed him, he thought, to explain how God has done this: reality consists in substantial forms, and these forms are active in their very nature—their movement is, once again, 'built in' to the individuals in the world at the moment of their creation, so God does not have to intervene 'from the outside' to bring about natural phenomena.

Interestingly, on this view, the fundamental individuals in the world (monads) do not really *interact* with each other; rather, they each independently run through the sequence of activities 'pre-programmed' by their forms, and God has designed the world—by creating the substantial forms in a certain way—so that all these activities mesh together. Leibniz called this "the system of pre-established harmony." For example, if I see a cat in the room, this perception is *not* caused in me by the cat, according to Leibniz, but arises in me "spontaneously from [my] own nature"; meanwhile, however, God has so arranged things so that what I see corresponds to reality—that is, there really is a cat in the room.

What Is the Structure of This Reading?

This reading is broken down into eight different "objections": each objection is an argument against the traditional conception of God (that God is an infinitely good, wise, and powerful being) premised either on the presence of evil in the world or on Leibniz's own theory that this is the greatest of all possible worlds. The first objection is in the form of the traditional "problem of evil," but then there follow arguments to show that God is unjust in punishing sin, or culpable for the existence of sin, or insufficiently caring for his creation, or unfree to choose what kind of world he will create. Leibniz responds to each of these objections, trying to show that his philosophical system can answer all of them: in other words, he tries to defend the *possibility* of a God that is omniscient, omnipotent, and perfectly benevolent.

Some Useful Background Information

1. The title of Leibniz's book, *Theodicy*, is a word meaning "the vindication of God's power and goodness despite the existence of evil." That is, a theodicy is an attempt to respond to the problem of evil.
2. This reading is structured as a set of syllogisms, plus Leibniz's responses to them. A syllogism is an argument, and usually one of a particular form: it consists of two premises and a conclusion. Many

of the arguments considered by Leibniz are a type of "categorical syllogism" and have the following form:

All *M* is *P*.
All *S* is *M*.
Therefore all *S* is *P*.

In arguments of this form, the first line is called the "major premise" (since it includes *P*, the predicate of the conclusion, which is known as the "major term") and the second line is the "minor premise" (since it includes *S*, the subject of the conclusion, which is known as the "minor term"). "Prosyllogisms" are syllogisms that have as their conclusion one of the premises of another syllogism—that is, they are what would often be called today "sub-arguments."

3. According to Leibniz there are "two great principles" on which "our reasonings are founded." They are the "principle of contradiction" and the "principle of sufficient reason." It is the principle of contradiction "in virtue of which we judge as false anything that involves contradiction, and as true whatever is opposed or contradictory to what is false" (*Monadology*, section 31). For example, suppose that, if some claim *P* were true, then it would follow logically that some other claim (*Q*) would have to be both true and false. To say that *Q* is both true and false is to express a contradiction: "*Q* and not-*Q*." Since (arguably) no proposition can be both true and false at the same time (i.e., no contradictions are true), this shows as a matter of logic that *P* could not possibly be true, and hence (according to Leibniz) *P* must be false or, to put the same thing another way, not-*P* must be true.

The principle of sufficient reason says "no fact could ever be true or existent ... unless there were a sufficient reason why it was thus and not otherwise," as Leibniz puts it in the *Monadology*. In the case of necessary truths, they must be true because of the principle of contradiction—because their opposites must be false. In the case of contingent truths, their "sufficient reason," according to Leibniz, is "the principle of the best": that is, God could only have created the best possible world, and that is why the world is the way it is.

4. Although Leibniz probably did not invent the notion of a "possible world" (the concept can also be found in the work of his contemporary, Nicolas Malebranche, as early as 1674), he is generally thought of as the main developer of this way of talking prior to the twentieth century. The language of possible worlds is fairly straightforward, but has proved to be a powerful tool for thinking clearly and precisely about possibility, contingency, and necessity. In this way of talking, a "world" is a complete state of affairs: it is not just, say, a planet, but an entire universe, extended throughout space and time. A world is "possible" if it is logically consistent: that is, if it does not involve a contradiction. One way to think of this is to say that a possible world is a way the actual universe *might have been*. For example, the cover of this book might have been plaid, or the Vietnam War might never have taken place, or cats might have turned out to be robotic spies from outer space, or the laws of physics might have been different; and so there are possible worlds in which all these things are the case. (The actual world, of course, is also a possible world, since it too is a way the actual world could have been!) On the other hand, there are some differences from the actual world that are *not* possible (i.e., which appear in no possible universe). For example, two plus two must always equal four, oculists must (by definition) always be eye doctors, and the sky could never be red all over and blue all over at the same time. According to Leibniz, God necessarily and eternally has in his mind the ideas of each of these infinitely many possible worlds, and he has chosen just one of them—the best one—to make actual through an act of creation.

5. When Leibniz says that the actual world is the best of all possible worlds, he means this in both of two different ways. First, he means that it is "metaphysically" the best possible world: God has designed it in such a way that the maximum amount of variety and richness in the natural world is produced using the simplest and most efficient possible set of natural laws. Second, he means that it is "morally" the best possible world: it has been designed with the happiness of human beings as its primary aim.

Some Common Misconceptions

1. In Voltaire's novel *Candide* (1759), Leibniz is lampooned, in the person of the character Dr. Pangloss, for his thesis that this is the best of all possible worlds: Voltaire makes it seem that Leibniz's optimism is a foolish and wickedly complacent response to the evils of our world. However, Leibniz does not deny the existence of evil: he is perfectly aware that sometimes 'bad things happen to good people.' Nor does Leibniz claim that the existence of evil is necessary: he thinks that God could have made a world that did not contain evil, or could have chosen not to create any world at all. What Leibniz does think is that God *could not have made any world which is better than this one*: that is, any possible world that contains less evil than the actual world is, nevertheless, for some reason, a less good world than the actual one. Thus, precisely the amount of evil which does exist—no more and no less—is necessary for this world to be the best of all possible worlds.

2. Leibniz does not think it is incumbent upon him to prove that this actually is the best of all possible worlds. In order to counter the problem of evil, Leibniz merely has to show that the existence of evil is *consistent* with the existence of a benevolent, all-powerful God—that is, he just has to show that this *might* be the best of all possible worlds even though it contains evil. (Nevertheless, "in order to make the matter clearer," Leibniz does his best to show that "this universe must be in reality better than every other possible universe.")

3. Leibniz does not think that whatever is true is true by absolute necessity. Although this is the best of all possible worlds and the only one which God, given his nature, could have made actual, there is nevertheless a huge number of non-actual but possible worlds, that God in some sense could have created but did not.

How Important and Influential Is This Passage?

This particular passage is not an especially influential and important piece of philosophy, nor is Leibniz's *Theodicy* today thought to be a central part of his writings (although it was the only philosophical book he published during his lifetime). On the other hand, Leibniz's idea that this is the best of all possible worlds—his defense of which is summarized in this selection, but which is spelled out in more detail in several places in his writings—is perhaps one of the most notorious ideas in all of philosophy. The idea of possible worlds, which Leibniz developed as part of his theodicy, has also been of great influence on twentieth-century philosophy, as a useful tool for thinking about possibility and necessity. (For example, when philosophers today want to say that something is necessarily true they will often assert that it is "true at all possible worlds.")

Theodicy

ABRIDGEMENT OF THE ARGUMENT
REDUCED TO SYLLOGISTIC FORM[*]

Some intelligent persons have desired that this supplement be made, and I have the more readily yielded to their wishes as in this way I have an opportunity again to remove certain difficulties and to make some observations which were not sufficiently emphasized in the work itself.

Objection I

i.   Whoever does not choose the best is lacking in power, or in knowledge, or in goodness.
ii. God did not choose the best in creating this world.
iii. Therefore, God has been lacking in power, or in knowledge, or in goodness.

Answer

I deny the minor, that is, the second premise of this syllogism; and our opponent proves it by this:[†]

Prosyllogism

i.   Whoever makes things in which there is evil, which could have been made without any evil, or the making of which could have been omitted, does not choose the best.
ii. God has made a world in which there is evil, a world, I say, which could have been made without any evil, or the making of which could have been omitted altogether.
iii. Therefore, God has not chosen the best.

Answer

I grant the minor [premise] of this prosyllogism; for it must be confessed that there is evil in this world which God has made, and that it was possible to make a world without evil, or even not to create a world at all, for its creation has depended on the free will of God; but I deny the major, that is, the first of the two premises of the prosyllogism, and I might content myself with simply demanding its proof; but in order to make the matter clearer, I have wished to justify this denial by showing that the best plan is not always that which seeks to avoid evil, since it may happen that *the evil is accompanied by a greater good*. For example, a general of an army will prefer a great victory with a slight wound to a condition without wound and without victory. We have proved this more fully in the large work by making it clear, by instances taken from mathematics and elsewhere, that an imperfection in the part may be required for a greater perfection in the whole. In this I have followed the opinion of St. Augustine,[‡] who has said a hundred times, that God has permitted evil in order to bring about good, that is, a greater good; and that of Thomas Aquinas (in libr. II. *sent. dist.* 32, qu. I, art. 1),[§] that the permitting of

---

[*]   The *Theodicy* was first published in 1710. This translation from the original French was made by George M. Duncan and comes from *The Philosophical Works of Leibnitz*, published in 1890 by Tuttle, Morehouse & Taylor. Numbering of the premises of the various syllogisms has been added.

[†]   "Our opponent proves it by this": our opponent tries to justify this premise with the following argument.

[‡]   Augustine, a north-African bishop who lived in the early fifth century, was a highly important early Christian theologian and philosopher. Some of his influential writings on the problem of evil appear in his book *Enchiridion* (which means "handbook"); his other important works include *City of God* and the autobiographical *Confessions*.

[§]   Leibniz is here referring to St. Thomas Aquinas's commentary on a work called the *Sentences* by Peter Lombard (specifically, to the first article of the first question of Part 32 of Book II of the commentary). Lombard was bishop of Paris between 1150 and 1152, and his *Sentences* became a standard textbook for thirteenth-century students of theology.

evil tends to the good of the universe. I have shown that the ancients called Adam's fall* *felix culpa*, a happy sin, because it had been retrieved with immense advantage by the incarnation of the Son of God, who has given to the universe something nobler than anything that ever would have been among creatures except for it. For the sake of a clearer understanding, I have added, following many good authors, that it was in accordance with order and the general good that God allowed to certain creatures the opportunity of exercising their liberty, even when he foresaw that they would turn to evil, but which he could so well rectify; because it was not fitting that, in order to hinder sin, God should always act in an extraordinary manner. To overthrow this objection, therefore, it is sufficient to show that a world with evil might be better than a world without evil; but I have gone even farther, in the work, and have even proved that this universe must be in reality better than every other possible universe.

Objection II

i.   If there is more evil than good in intelligent creatures, then there is more evil than good in the whole work of God.
ii. Now, there is more evil than good in intelligent creatures.
iii. Therefore, there is more evil than good in the whole work of God.

Answer

I deny the major and the minor of this conditional syllogism. As to the major, I do not admit it at all, because this pretended deduction from a part to the whole, from intelligent creatures to all creatures, supposes tacitly and without proof that creatures destitute of reason cannot enter into comparison nor into account with those which possess it. But why may it not be that the surplus of good in the non-intelligent creatures which fill the world, compensates for, and even incomparably surpasses, the surplus of evil in the rational creatures? It is true that the value of the latter is greater; but, in compensation, the others are beyond comparison the more numerous, and it may be that the proportion of number and quantity surpasses that of value and of quality.

As to the minor, that is no more to be admitted; that is, it is not at all to be admitted that there is more evil than good in the intelligent creatures. There is no need even of granting that there is more evil than good in the human race, because it is possible, and in fact very probable, that the glory and the perfection of the blessed are incomparably greater than the misery and the imperfection of the damned, and that here the excellence of the total good in the smaller number exceeds the total evil in the greater number. The blessed approach the Divinity, by means of a Divine Mediator, as near as may suit these creatures,† and make such progress in good as is impossible for the damned to make in evil, approach as nearly as they may to the nature of demons. God is infinite, and the devil is limited; the good may and does go to infinity, while evil has its bounds. It is therefore possible, and is credible, that in the comparison of the blessed and the damned, the contrary of that which I have said might happen in the comparison of intelligent and non-intelligent creatures, takes place; namely, it is possible that in the comparison of the happy and the unhappy, the proportion of degree exceeds that of number, and that in the comparison of intelligent and non-intelligent creatures, the proportion of number is greater than that of value. I have the right to suppose that a thing is possible so long as its impossibility is not proved; and indeed that which I have here advanced is more than a supposition.

But in the second place, if I should admit that there is more evil than good in the human race, I have still good grounds for not admitting that there is more evil than good in all intelligent creatures. For there is an inconceivable number of genii,‡ and perhaps of other rational creatures. And an opponent could not

---

*   According to the Old Testament Book of Genesis, the expulsion of Adam and Eve from the Garden of Eden for disobedience to God, and the consequent lapse of the human race into the human condition of suffering and "original sin."

†   Good and religious people, with the assistance of divine entities like the Virgin Mary, can become as much like God (in goodness) as is possible for mere created beings.

‡   Supernatural spirits, such as the various types of angels.

prove that in all the City of God, composed as well of genii as of rational animals without number and of an infinity of kinds, evil exceeds good. And although in order to answer an objection, there is no need of proving that a thing is, when its mere possibility suffices; yet, in this work, I have not omitted to show that it is a consequence of the supreme perfection of the Sovereign of the universe, that the kingdom of God is the most perfect of all possible states or governments, and that consequently the little evil there is, is required for the consummation of the immense good which is found there.

Objection III

i. If it is always impossible not to sin, it is always unjust to punish.
ii. Now, it is always impossible not to sin; or, in other words, every sin is necessary.
iii. Therefore, it is always unjust to punish.
The minor of this is proved thus:

First Prosyllogism

i. All that is predetermined* is necessary.
ii. Every event is predetermined.
iii. Therefore, every event (and consequently sin also) is necessary.
Again this second minor is proved thus:

Second Prosyllogism

i. That which is future, that which is foreseen, that which is involved in the causes, is predetermined.
ii. Every event is such.
iii. Therefore, every event is predetermined.

Answer

I admit in a certain sense the conclusion of the second prosyllogism, which is the minor of the first; but I shall deny the major of the first prosyllogism, namely, that every thing predetermined is necessary; understanding by the necessity of sinning, for example, or by the impossibility of not sinning, or of not performing any action, the necessity with which we are here concerned, that is, that which is essential and absolute, and which destroys the morality of an action and the justice of punishments. For if anyone understood another necessity or impossibility, namely, a necessity which should be only moral, or which was only hypothetical (as will be explained shortly); it is clear that I should deny the major of the objection itself. I might content myself with this answer and demand the proof of the proposition denied; but I have again desired to explain my procedure in this work, in order to better elucidate the matter and to throw more light on the whole subject, by explaining the necessity which ought to be rejected and the determination which must take place. That *necessity* which is contrary to morality and which ought to be rejected, and which would render punishment unjust, is an insurmountable necessity which would make all opposition useless, even if we should wish with all our heart to avoid the necessary action, and should make all possible efforts to that end. Now, it is manifest that this is not applicable to voluntary actions, because we would not perform them if we did not choose to. Also their prevision† and predetermination are not absolute, but presuppose the will: if it is certain that we shall perform them, it is not less certain that we shall choose to perform them. These voluntary actions and their consequences will not take place no matter what we do or whether we wish them or not; but, *through* that which we shall do and through that which we shall wish to do, which leads to them. And this is involved in prevision and in predetermination, and even constitutes their ground. And the necessity of such an event is called conditional or hypothetical, or the necessity of consequence, because it supposes the will, and the other *requisites*; whereas the necessity which destroys morality and renders punishment unjust and reward useless, exists in things which will be whatever we may do or whatever we may wish to do, and, in a word, is in that which is essential; and this is what is called an absolute necessity. Thus it is to no purpose, as regards what is absolutely necessary, to make prohibitions or commands, to propose penalties

---

* Predetermined means "fixed in advance."
† Being seen (by God) before they happened.

or prizes, to praise or to blame; it will be none the less. On the other hand, in voluntary actions and in that which depends upon them, precepts* armed with power to punish and to recompense are very often of use and are included in the order of causes which make an action exist. And it is for this reason that not only cares and labours but also prayers are useful; God having had these prayers in view before he regulated things and having had that consideration for them which was proper. This is why the precept which says *ora et labora* (pray and work), holds altogether good; and not only those who (under the vain pretext of the necessity of events) pretend that the care which business demands may be neglected, but also those who reason against prayer, fall into what the ancients even then called the *lazy sophism*.† Thus the predetermination of events by causes is just what contributes to morality instead of destroying it, and causes incline the will, without compelling it. This is why the *determination* in question is not a necessitation—it is certain (to him who knows all) that the effect will follow this inclination; but this effect does not follow by a necessary consequence, that is, one the contrary of which implies contradiction. It is also by an internal inclination such as this that the will is determined, without there being any necessity. Suppose that one has the greatest passion in the world (a great thirst, for example), you will admit to me that the soul can find some reason for resisting it, if it were only that of showing its power. Thus, although one may never be in a perfect indifference of equilibrium and there may be always a preponderance of inclination for the side taken, it, nevertheless, never renders the resolution taken absolutely necessary.

Objection IV

i. Whoever can prevent the sin of another and does not do so but rather contributes to it although he is well informed of it, is accessory to it.

ii. God can prevent the sin of intelligent creatures; but he does not do so, and rather contributes to it by his concurrence‡ and by the opportunities which he brings about, although he has a perfect knowledge of it.

iii. Hence, etc.

Answer

I deny the major of this syllogism. For it is possible that one could prevent sin, but ought not, because he could not do it without himself committing a sin, or (when God is in question) without performing an unreasonable action. Examples have been given and the application to God himself has been made. It is possible also that we contribute to evil and that sometimes we even open the road to it, in doing things which we are obliged to do; and, when we do our duty or (in speaking of God) when, after thorough consideration, we do that which reason demands, we are not responsible for the results, even when we foresee them. We do not desire these evils; but we are willing to permit them for the sake of a greater good which we cannot reasonably help preferring to other considerations. And this is a *consequent* will, which results from *antecedent* wills by which we will the good. I know that some persons, in speaking of the antecedent and consequent will of God, have understood by the *antecedent* that which wills that all men should be saved; and by the *consequent*, that which wills, in consequence of persistent sin, that some should be damned. But these are merely illustrations of a more general idea, and it may be said for the same reason that God, by his antecedent will, wills that men should not sin; and by his consequent or final and decreeing will (that which is always followed by its effect), he wills to permit them to sin, this permission being the result of superior reasons. And we have the right to say in general that the antecedent will of God tends to the production of good and the prevention of evil, each taken in itself and as if alone (*particulariter*

---

* Laws or principles.

† The 'lazy sophism' was an argument for fatalism, proposed by the Stoic philosopher Chrysippus (280–208 BCE) and strongly criticized by the Roman poet and philosopher Cicero (106–43 BCE). It runs roughly as follows: Whatever will be, will be; Therefore nothing you can do will change things; Therefore any action to try to influence events is pointless—you might just as well do nothing.

‡ God's maintaining things in existence by a kind of continuous divine act of will.

et secundum quid, Thom. I, qu. 19, art. 6),* according to the measure of the degree of each good and of each evil; but that the divine consequent or final or total will tends toward the production of as many goods as may be put together, the combination of which becomes in this way determined, and includes also the permission of some evils and the exclusion of some goods, as the best possible plan for the universe demands. Arminius,† in his *Anti-perkinsus*, has very well explained that the will of God may be called consequent, not only in relation to the action of the creature considered beforehand in the divine under-standing, but also in relation to other anterior‡ divine acts of will. But this consideration of the passage cited from Thomas Aquinas, and that from Scotus (I. dist. 46, qu. XI),§ is enough to show that they make this distinction as I have done here. Nevertheless, if anyone objects to this use of terms let him substitute *deliberating* will, in place of antecedent, and final or decreeing will, in place of consequent. For I do not wish to dispute over words.

Objection V

i. Whoever produces all that is real in a thing, is its cause.
ii. God produces all that is real in sin.
iii. Hence, God is the cause of sin.

Answer

I might content myself with denying the major or the minor, since the term *real* admits of interpretations which would render these propositions false. But in order to explain more clearly, I will make a distinc-tion. *Real* signifies either that which is positive only, or, it includes also privative¶ beings: in the first case, I deny the major and admit the minor; in the second case, I do the contrary. I might have limited myself to this, but I have chosen to proceed still farther and give the reason for this distinction. I have been very glad therefore to draw attention to the fact that every reality purely positive or absolute is a perfection; and that imperfection comes from limitation, that is, from the privative: for to limit is to refuse progress, or the greatest possible progress. Now God is the cause of all perfections and consequently of all realities considered as purely positive. But limitations or privations result from the original imperfection of creatures, which limits their receptivity. And it is with them as with a loaded vessel, which the river causes to move more or less slowly according to the weight which it carries: thus its speed depends upon the river, but the retarda-tion which limits this speed comes from the load. Thus in the *Theodicy*, we have shown how the creature, in causing sin, is a defective cause;** how errors and evil inclinations are born of privation; and how privation is accidentally efficient;†† and I have justified the opinion of St. Augustine (lib. I. *ad Simpl.* qu. 2)‡‡ who explains,

---

* This is a reference to Part I, Question 19, Article 6 of St. Thomas Aquinas's *Summa Theologiae*.

† Jacob Arminius (1560–1609) was a Protestant Dutch theologian who rejected the doctrine of predestination—i.e., he denied that God has already decided who will be damned and who will be saved, even before they are born.

‡ Earlier.

§ The Scottish philosopher and theologian John Duns (c. 1266–1308), who is usually referred to as Duns Scotus ("Duns the Scot"). The reference is to section 46 of the first part of Scotus's commentary on the *Sentences* by Peter Lombard.

¶ A privation is an absence, or lack, or some quality or attribute. In medieval terminology, "privation" was the name of the state in which matter was supposed to exist before the process of generation begins, which gives it some form or other—i.e., before the "stuff" of matter became stars, or rocks, or trees, or anything at all.

** Caused by some defect or limitation, rather than by some "positive" quality of the creature.

†† Privation, or limitation, doesn't necessarily cause anything at all—it does not have an essential power to have effects (be 'efficient'). Instead, privation can 'accidentally' have certain effects due to the surrounding circumstances. (By analogy, a hole in the ground doesn't normally, by its nature, suck surrounding objects into it; but in certain circum-stances—e.g., when combined with somebody who isn't looking where they're going—the hole can be a partial cause of an object falling into it.)

‡‡ A reference to question 2 of Book I of Augustine's work *To Simplicianus, On Seven Different Questions*, written in about 395 CE.

for example, how God makes the soul obdurate,* not by giving it something evil, but because the effect of his good impression is limited by the soul's resistance and by the circumstances which contribute to this resistance, so that he does not give it all the good which would overcome its evil. *Nec (inquit) ab illo erogatur aliquid quo homo fit deterior, sed tantum quo fit melior non erogatur.*† But if God had wished to do more, he would have had to make either other natures for creatures or other miracles to change their natures, things which the best plan could not admit. It is as if the current of the river must be more rapid than its fall admitted or that the boats should be loaded more lightly, if it were necessary to make them move more quickly. And the original limitation or imperfection of creatures requires that even the best plan of the universe could not receive more good, and could not be exempt from certain evils, which, however, are to result in a greater good. There are certain disorders in the parts which marvellously enhance the beauty of the whole; just as certain dissonances, when properly used, render harmony more beautiful. But this depends on what has already been said in answer to the first objection.

Objection VI

i. Whoever punishes those who have done as well as it was in their power to do, is unjust.
ii. God does so.
iii. Hence, etc.

Answer

I deny the minor of this argument. And I believe that God always gives sufficient aid and grace to those who have a good will, that is, to those who do not reject this grace by new sin. Thus I do not admit the damnation of infants who have died without baptism or outside of the church; nor the damnation of adults who have acted according to the light which God has given them. And I believe that *if any one has followed the light which has been given him*, he will undoubtedly receive greater light when he has need of it, as the late

M. Hulseman, a profound and celebrated theologian at Leipzig, has somewhere remarked; and if such a man has failed to receive it during his lifetime he will at least receive it when at the point of death.

Objection VII

i. Whoever gives only to some, and not to all, the means which produces in them effectively a good will and salutary final faith, has not sufficient goodness.
ii. God does this.
iii. Hence, etc.

Answer

I deny the major of this. It is true that God could overcome the greatest resistance of the human heart; and does it, too, sometimes, either by internal grace, or by external circumstances which have a great effect on souls; but he does not always do this. Whence comes this distinction? it may be asked, and why does his goodness seem limited? It is because, as I have already said in answering the first objection, it would not have been in order always to act in an extraordinary manner, and to reverse the connection of things. The reasons of this connection, by means of which one is placed in more favourable circumstances than another, are hidden in the depths of the wisdom of God: they depend upon the universal harmony. The best plan of the universe, which God could not fail to choose, made it so. We judge from the event itself; since God has made it, it was not possible to do better. Far from being true that this conduct is contrary to goodness, it is supreme goodness which led him to it. This objection with its solution might have been drawn from what was said in regard to the first objection; but it seemed useful to touch upon it separately.

Objection VIII

i. Whoever cannot fail to choose the best, is not free.

---

* Stubbornly wicked.
† "Nor (he says) is man provided by him [God] with anything by which he becomes worse, but it is only that there is not furnished that by which he becomes better."

ii. God cannot fail to choose the best.
iii. Hence, God is not free.

Answer

I deny the major of this argument; it is rather true liberty, and the most perfect, to be able to use one's free will for the best, and to always exercise this power, without ever being turned aside either by external force or by internal passions, the first of which causes slavery of the body, the second, slavery of the soul. There is nothing less servile, and nothing more in accordance with the highest degree of freedom, than to be always led toward the good, and always by one's own inclination, without any constraint and without any displeasure. And to object therefore that God had need of external things, is only a sophism.* He created them freely; but having proposed to himself an end, which is to exercise his goodness, wisdom has determined him to choose the means best fitted to attain this end. To call this a need, is to take that term in an unusual sense which frees it from all imperfection, just as when we speak of the wrath of God.

Seneca† has somewhere said that God commanded but once but that he obeys always, because he obeys laws which he willed to prescribe to himself: *semel jussit, semper paret*.‡ But he might better have said that God always commands and that he is always obeyed; for in willing, he always follows the inclination of his own nature, and all other things always follow his will. And as this will is always the same, it cannot be said that he obeys only that will which he formerly had. Nevertheless, although his will is always infallible and always tends toward the best, the evil, or the lesser good, which he rejects, does not cease to be possible in itself; otherwise the necessity of the good would be geometrical§ (so to speak), or metaphysical, and altogether absolute; the contingency of things would be destroyed, and there would be no choice. But this sort of necessity, which does not destroy the possibility of the contrary, has this name only by analogy; it becomes effective, not by the pure essence of things, but by that which is outside of them, above them, namely, by the will of God. This necessity is called moral, because, to the sage, *necessity* and *what ought to be* are equivalent things; and when it always has its effect, as it really has in the perfect sage, that is, in God, it may be said that it is a happy necessity. The nearer creatures approach to it, the nearer they approach to perfect happiness. Also this kind of necessity is not that which we try to avoid and which destroys morality, rewards and praise. For that which it brings, does not happen whatever we may do or will, but because we will it so. And a will to which it is natural to choose well, merits praise so much the more; also it carries its reward with it, which is sovereign happiness. And as this constitution of the divine nature gives entire satisfaction to him who possesses it, it is also the best and the most desirable for the creatures who are all dependent on God. If the will of God did not have for a rule the principle of the best, it would either tend toward evil, which would be the worst; or it would be in some way indifferent to good and to evil, and would be guided by chance: but a will which would allow itself always to act by chance, would not be worth more for the government of the universe than the fortuitous concourse¶ of atoms, without there being any divinity therein. And even if God should abandon himself to chance only in some cases and in a certain way (as he would do, if he did not always work entirely for the best and if he were capable of preferring a lesser work to a greater, that is, an evil to a good, since that which prevents a greater good is an evil), he would be imperfect, as well as the object of his choice; he would not merit entire confidence; he would act without reason in such a case, and the government of the universe would be like certain games, equally divided between reason and chance. All this proves that this objection which is made against the choice of the best, perverts the notions of the free and of the necessary, and represents to us the best even as evil: which is either malicious or ridiculous. ■

---

* An argument which seems valid on the surface but which actually isn't.
† A Roman playwright, philosopher, and statesman, who lived from about 5 BCE to 65 CE. He was widely known for his ethical writings, and his death by suicide was taken as a model of Stoic virtuous action.
‡ "He commanded once, but obeys always."
§ Mathematical.
¶ "Fortuitous concourse" means "coming and moving together by chance."

Suggestions for Critical Reflection

1. Leibniz asserts "the best plan is not always that which seeks to avoid evil." This may be true for human beings, such as military leaders who need to risk casualties in order to win battles, but how plausible a claim is it for an omnipotent deity—for a being whose actions are not constrained by the behavior of opponents or competitors, or even by the laws of physics?

2. Where do you think human free will enters into Leibniz's picture? Is it compatible with, or even entailed by, this being the best of all possible worlds? Why do you think that Leibniz says it would be "unfitting" for God to interfere with human freedom in order to hinder sin?

3. Where does *God's* freedom fit into a theory like Leibniz's? If God could only have created the best possible world (i.e., this world), then in what sense can we say that God is free? What do you think of Leibniz's response to this problem?

4. What do you think of Leibniz's claim that "every reality purely positive or absolute is a perfection; and that imperfection comes from limitation, that is, from the privative"? Do you agree that all evil consists in the *absence* of something that could have made things better, rather than the presence of something that is positively bad?

5. It sometimes appears that Leibniz argues in the following way: this must be the best of all possible worlds because a perfect God made it, and therefore it is possible that a perfect God exists. Do you think Leibniz does make this argument, and if so, does this strike you as a good argument? If it's a bad argument, how serious a problem is this for Leibniz's theodicy?

6. Do you think that there is a "universal harmony," and if so, does it make sense of all the evil in the world? Does it make sense of it by showing that the evil is necessary for some "higher purpose," or alternatively by showing that it is not *really* evil in the first place?

J.L. MACKIE

Evil and Omnipotence

Who Was J.L. Mackie?

John Leslie Mackie was born in Sydney, Australia, in 1917 and educated at the University of Sydney and Oriel College, Oxford. After serving in the Australian army during the Second World War, he taught at the University of Sydney from 1946 to 1954 and then at Otago University in Dunedin, New Zealand. In 1963 he moved permanently to England, and from 1967 until his death in 1981 he was a Fellow of University College, Oxford. He wrote six books and many philosophical papers, mostly on topics in metaphysics, ethics, the history of philosophy, and the philosophy of religion.

Mackie is probably best known for his 'error theory' of moral values. This holds that:

1. There are no objective moral values.
2. All ordinary moral judgments include a claim to objectivity, and so,   "
3. All ordinary moral judgments are false.

Mackie therefore argued that morality is not discovered but is *created* by human beings. We should scrap traditional moral theory, he said, and, instead of treating moral theory as descriptive of moral facts, we should understand morality as a device for encouraging empathy with the points of view of others.

Mackie's work, like most Australian analytical philosophy of this century, is notable for its dislike of obfuscation and obscurantism, and for its careful attempts at clarity and precision. "Evil and Omnipotence" is well known as probably the best short modern defense of an argument called "the problem of evil."

What Is the Structure of This Reading?

Mackie begins by introducing an argument against the existence of God (or, at least, of God as traditionally conceived) called "the problem of evil." He lays out its logical form (as a paradox), and tries to make clear its theological importance. He briefly discusses a kind of response to this paradox, which he does think is adequate, but claims that such a response would be unacceptable to those who believe in God. Believers must thus attempt to give other solutions to the paradox, but Mackie argues that all of these attempts fail (and, he suggests, typically only seem as plausible as they do because of their vagueness and lack of clarity).

First, there are "half-hearted" responses which, Mackie says, really fail to address the problem. Then there are four more serious responses: (1) good cannot exist without evil; (2) evil is necessary as a means to good; (3) the universe is better with some evil in it; (4) evil is due to human free will. (These responses fall naturally into two groups: 1 and 2, and 3 and 4.) Mackie argues carefully that all four of these responses to the problem of evil are fallacious.

In the course of his attack on the free-will response to the problem of evil, Mackie develops a further argument which he calls "the Paradox of Omnipotence." He argues that this paradox shows it is *logically impossible* that any (temporal) being could exist which had absolutely unlimited power.

The upshot of all this, Mackie concludes, is that God (as he is described by, say, Christianity) cannot possibly exist.

Some Useful Background Information

When Mackie talks about "evil" in this article, he follows normal philosophical usage in this context. In everyday language the word "evil" tends to suggest an especially wicked kind of moral badness; however, "the problem of evil," though it certainly includes extreme ethical badness, is much broader in its scope than that. It's important to realize that, according to the argument from evil, any kind of 'sub-optimality' can be a problem for the existence of God. Therefore examples of 'evil' range along the spectrum from such mild harms as a nasty pimple, a job that does not give 100 per cent satisfaction, or a mountain that would be just a little more beautiful if it were a slightly different shape, right up to major earthquakes, epidemics, and oil spills in the Alaskan wilderness. Moral 'evils' can be as minor as breaking a trivial promise or making a slightly cutting remark, or as serious as rape, torture, and genocide.

A Common Misconception

Mackie is not arguing (directly) that God does not exist: he is arguing that nothing like the *theistic conception* of God can exist. That is, although some sort of God—perhaps an extremely powerful but somehow limited being, like, say, the classical Greek god Zeus—can escape the problem of evil, the sort of God envisaged by the main monotheistic religions such as Christianity, Judaism, and Islam cannot possibly be real. For many if not most of the people who believe in God, this is not a trivial conclusion: if it is a sound argument, the problem of evil shows that God, if he exists at all, must be either limited in his power, or limited in his knowledge, or not entirely morally good.

Evil and Omnipotence*

The traditional arguments for the existence of God have been fairly thoroughly criticised by philosophers. But the theologian can, if he wishes, accept this criticism. He can admit that no rational proof of God's existence is possible. And he can still retain all that is essential to his position, by holding that God's existence is known in some other, non-rational way. I think, however, that a more telling criticism can be made by way of the traditional problem of evil. Here it can be shown, not that religious beliefs lack rational support, but that they are positively irrational, that the several parts of the essential theological doctrine are inconsistent with one another, so that the theologian can maintain his position as a whole only by a much more extreme rejection of reason than in the former case. He must now be prepared to believe, not merely what cannot be proved, but what can be *disproved* from other beliefs that he also holds.

The problem of evil, in the sense in which I shall be using the phrase, is a problem only for someone who believes that there is a God who is both omnipotent† and wholly good. And it is a logical problem, the problem of clarifying and reconciling a number of beliefs: it is not a scientific problem that might be solved by further observations, or a practical problem that might be solved by a decision or an action. These points are obvious; I mention them only because they are sometimes ignored by theologians, who sometimes parry a statement of the problem with such remarks as "Well, can you solve the problem yourself?" or "This is a mystery which may be revealed to us later," or "Evil is something to be faced and overcome, not to be merely discussed."

In its simplest form the problem is this: God is omnipotent; God is wholly good; and yet evil exists. There seems to be some contradiction between these three propositions, so that if any two of them were true the third would be false. But at the same time all three are essential parts of most theological positions: the theologian, it seems, at once *must* adhere and *cannot consistently* adhere to all three. (The problem does not arise only for theists,‡ but I shall discuss it in the form in which it presents itself for ordinary theism.)

---

* This article was originally published in 1955 in the journal *Mind* (64, 254 [April 1955]: 200–12).

† "Omnipotent" means all-powerful; able to do anything at all. (Or at least anything that is not logically incoherent: God could make pigs fly, but even God, perhaps, could not make a male vixen or create a leaf that is—at the same time—both entirely green and not entirely green. This issue is discussed later in the article.)

‡ For those who believe in one, powerful, benevolent God who created and watches over the universe.

However, the contradiction does not arise immediately; to show it we need some additional premises, or perhaps some quasi-logical rules connecting the terms 'good,' 'evil,' and 'omnipotent.' These additional principles are that good is opposed to evil, in such a way that a good thing always eliminates evil as far as it can, and that there are no limits to what an omnipotent thing can do. From these it follows that a good omnipotent thing eliminates evil completely, and then the propositions that a good omnipotent thing exists, and that evil exists, are incompatible.

A. Adequate Solutions

Now once the problem is fully stated it is clear that it can be solved, in the sense that the problem will not arise if one gives up at least one of the propositions that constitute it. If you are prepared to say that God is not wholly good, or not quite omnipotent, or that evil does not exist, or that good is not opposed to the kind of evil that exists, or that there are limits to what an omnipotent thing can do, then the problem of evil will not arise for you.

There are, then, quite a number of adequate solutions of the problem of evil, and some of these have been adopted, or almost adopted, by various thinkers. For example, a few have been prepared to deny God's omnipotence, and rather more have been prepared to keep the term 'omnipotence' but severely to restrict its meaning, recording quite a number of things that an omnipotent being cannot do. Some have said that evil is an illusion, perhaps because they held that the whole world of temporal, changing things is an illusion, and that what we call evil belongs only to this world, or perhaps because they held that although temporal things are much as we see them, those that we call evil are not really evil. Some have said that what we call evil is merely the privation of good,* that evil in

a positive sense, evil that would really be opposed to good, does not exist. Many have agreed with Pope[†] that disorder is harmony not understood, and that partial evil is universal good. Whether any of these views is true is, of course, another question. But each of them gives an adequate solution of the problem of evil in the sense that if you accept it this problem does not arise for you, though you may, of course, have *other* problems to face.

But often enough these adequate solutions are only *almost* adopted. The thinkers who restrict God's power, but keep the term 'omnipotence,' may reasonably be suspected of thinking, in other contexts, that his power is really unlimited. Those who say that evil is an illusion may also be thinking, inconsistently, that this illusion is itself an evil. Those who say that "evil" is merely privation of good may also be thinking, inconsistently, that privation of good is an evil. (The fallacy here is akin to some forms of the "naturalistic fallacy" in ethics,[‡] where some think, for example, that "good" is just what contributes to evolutionary progress, and that evolutionary progress is itself good.) If Pope meant what he said in the first line of his couplet, that "disorder" is only harmony not understood, the "partial evil" of the second line must, for consistency, mean "that which, taken in isolation, falsely appears to be evil," but it would more naturally mean "that which, in isolation, really is evil." The second line, in fact, hesitates between two views, that "partial evil" isn't really evil, since only the universal quality is real, and that "partial evil" is really an evil, but only a little one.

In addition, therefore, to adequate solutions, we must recognise unsatisfactory inconsistent solutions, in which there is only a half-hearted or temporary rejection of one of the propositions which together constitute the problem. In these, one of the constituent propositions is explicitly rejected, but it is covertly re-asserted or assumed elsewhere in the system.

---

* The privation of good: the absence of good (some sort of regrettable lack or absence in the world).

† Alexander Pope (1688–1744), an English writer best known for his mock-epic poems such as *The Rape of the Lock*. This quotation comes from his *Essay on Man, Epistle I*: "All nature is but art, unknown to thee; All chance, direction, which thou canst not see; All discord, harmony, not understood; All partial evil, universal good: And, spite of pride, in erring reason's spite, One truth is clear, Whatever is, is right."

‡ This is the alleged fallacy of identifying an ethical concept with a "natural" (i.e., non-moral) notion, such as analyzing moral goodness as evolutionary fitness or the sensation of pleasure.

B. Fallacious Solutions

Besides these half-hearted solutions, which explicitly reject but implicitly assert one of the constituent propositions, there are definitely fallacious solutions which explicitly maintain all the constituent propositions, but implicitly reject at least one of them in the course of the argument that explains away the problem of evil.

There are, in fact, many so-called solutions which purport to remove the contradiction without abandoning any of its constituent propositions. These must be fallacious, as we can see from the very statement of the problem, but it is not so easy to see in each case precisely where the fallacy lies. I suggest that in all cases the fallacy has the general form suggested above: in order to solve the problem one (or perhaps more) of its constituent propositions is given up, but in such a way that it appears to have been retained, and can therefore be asserted without qualification in other contexts. Sometimes there is a further complication: the supposed solution moves to and fro between, say, two of the constituent propositions, at one point asserting the first of these but covertly abandoning the second, at another point asserting the second but covertly abandoning the first. These fallacious solutions often turn upon some equivocation with the words 'good' and 'evil,' or upon some vagueness about the way in which good and evil are opposed to one another, or about how much is meant by 'omnipotence.' I propose to examine some of these so-called solutions, and to exhibit their fallacies in detail. Incidentally, I shall also be considering whether an adequate solution could be reached by a minor modification of one or more of the constituent propositions, which would, however, still satisfy all the essential requirements of ordinary theism.

1. "GOOD CANNOT EXIST WITHOUT EVIL" OR "EVIL IS NECESSARY AS A COUNTERPART TO GOOD."

It is sometimes suggested that evil is necessary as a counterpart to good, that if there were no evil there could be no good either, and that this solves the problem of evil. It is true that it points to an answer to the question "Why should there be evil?" But it does so only by qualifying some of the propositions that constitute the problem.

First, it sets a limit to what God can do, saying that God cannot create good without simultaneously creating evil, and this means either that God is not omnipotent or that there are some limits to what an omnipotent thing can do. It may be replied that these limits are always presupposed, that omnipotence has never meant the power to do what is logically impossible, and on the present view the existence of good without evil would be a logical impossibility. This interpretation of omnipotence may, indeed, be accepted as a modification of our original account which does not reject anything that is essential to theism, and I shall in general assume it in the subsequent discussion. It is, perhaps, the most common theistic view, but I think that some theists at least have maintained that God can do what is logically impossible. Many theists, at any rate, have held that logic itself is created or laid down by God, that logic is the way in which God arbitrarily chooses to think. (This is, of course, parallel to the ethical view that morally right actions are those which God arbitrarily chooses to command, and the two views encounter similar difficulties.*) And *this* account of logic is clearly inconsistent with the view that God is bound by logical necessities—unless it is possible for an omnipotent being to bind himself, an issue which we shall consider later, when we come to the Paradox of Omnipotence. This solution of the problem of evil cannot, therefore, be consistently adopted along with the view that logic is itself created by God.

But, secondly, this solution denies that evil is opposed to good in our original sense. If good and evil are counterparts, a good thing will not "eliminate evil as far as it can." Indeed, this view suggests that good and evil are not strictly qualities of things at all. Perhaps the suggestion is that good and evil are related in much the same way as great and small. Certainly, when the term 'great' is used relatively as a condensation of 'greater than so-and-so', and 'small' is used correspondingly, greatness and smallness are

[handwritten note: Wouldn't this make evil "good" for allowing good to exist?]

---

* This ethical view is often called Divine Command Theory, and the usual label for its main problem is "the Euthyphro Dilemma" (from a dialogue by Plato in which the problem is first raised).

counterparts and cannot exist without each other. But in this sense greatness is not a quality, not an intrinsic feature of anything; and it would be absurd to think of a movement in favour of greatness and against smallness in this sense. Such a movement would be self-defeating, since relative greatness can be promoted only by a simultaneous promotion of relative smallness. I feel sure that no theists would be content to regard God's goodness as analogous to this—as if what he supports were not the *good* but the *better*, and as if he had the paradoxical aim that all things should be better than other things.

This point is obscured by the fact that 'great' and 'small' seem to have an absolute as well as a relative sense. I cannot discuss here whether there is absolute magnitude or not, but if there is, there could be an absolute sense for 'great,' it could mean of at least a certain size, and it would make sense to speak of all things getting bigger, of a universe that was expanding all over, and therefore it would make sense to speak of promoting greatness. But in *this* sense great and small are not logically necessary counterparts: either quality could exist without the other. There would be no logical impossibility in everything's being small or in everything's being great.

Neither in the absolute nor in the relative sense, then, of 'great' and 'small' do these terms provide an analogy of the sort that would be needed to support this solution of the problem of evil. In neither case are greatness and smallness both necessary counterparts and mutually opposed forces or possible objects for support and attack.

It may be replied that good and evil are necessary counterparts in the same way as any quality and its logical opposite: redness can occur, it is suggested, only if non-redness also occurs. But unless evil is merely the privation of good, they are not logical opposites, and some further argument would be needed to show that they are counterparts in the same way as genuine logical opposites. Let us assume that this could be given. There is still doubt of the correctness of the metaphysical principle that a quality must have a real opposite: I suggest that it is not really impossible that everything should be, say, red, that the truth is merely that if everything were red we should not notice redness,

and so we should have no word 'red'; we observe and give names to qualities only if they have real opposites. If so, the principle that a term must have an opposite would belong only to our language or to our thought, and would not be an ontological principle,* and, correspondingly, the rule that good cannot exist without evil would not state a logical necessity of a sort that God would just have to put up with. God might have made everything good, though we should not have noticed it if he had.

But, finally, even if we concede that this is an ontological principle, it will provide a solution for the problem of evil only if one is prepared to say, "Evil exists, but only just enough evil to serve as the counterpart of good." I doubt whether any theist will accept this. After all, the *ontological* requirement that non-redness should occur would be satisfied even if all the universe, except for a minute speck, were red, and, if there were a corresponding requirement for evil as a counterpart to good, a minute dose of evil would presumably do. But theists are not usually willing to say, in all contexts, that all the evil that occurs is a minute and necessary dose.

2. "EVIL IS NECESSARY AS A MEANS TO GOOD."

It is sometimes suggested that evil is necessary for good not as a counterpart but as a means. In its simple form this has little plausibility as a solution of the problem of evil, since it obviously implies a severe restriction of God's power. It would be a causal law that you cannot have a certain end without a certain means, so that if God has to introduce evil as a means to good, he must be subject to at least some causal laws. This certainly conflicts with what a theist normally means by omnipotence. This view of God as limited by causal laws also conflicts with the view that causal laws are themselves made by God, which is more widely held than the corresponding view about the laws of logic. This conflict would, indeed; be resolved if it were possible for an omnipotent being to bind himself, and this possibility has still to be considered. Unless a favourable answer can be given to this question, the suggestion that evil is necessary as a means to good solves the problem of

---

* That is, not a principle constraining what exists.

evil only by denying one of its constituent propositions, either that God is omnipotent or that 'omnipotent' means what it says.

3. "THE UNIVERSE IS BETTER WITH SOME EVIL IN IT THAN IT COULD BE IF THERE WERE NO EVIL."

Much more important is a solution which at first seems to be a mere variant of the previous one, that evil may contribute to the goodness of a whole in which it is found, so that the universe as a whole is better as it is, with some evil in it, than it would be if there were no evil. This solution may be developed in either of two ways. It may be supported by an aesthetic analogy, by the fact that contrasts heighten beauty, that in a musical work, for example, there may occur discords which somehow add to the beauty of the work as a whole. Alternatively, it may be worked out in connexion with the notion of progress, that the best possible organisation of the universe will not be static, but progressive, that the gradual overcoming of evil by good is really a finer thing than would be the eternal unchallenged supremacy of good.

In either case, this solution usually starts from the assumption that the evil whose existence gives rise to the problem of evil is primarily what is called physical evil, that is to say, pain. In Hume's rather half-hearted presentation of the problem of evil, the evils that he stresses are pain and disease, and those who reply to him argue that the existence of pain and disease makes possible the existence of sympathy, benevolence, heroism, and the gradually successful struggle of doctors and reformers to overcome these evils. In fact, theists often seize the opportunity to accuse those who stress the problem of evil of taking a low, materialistic view of good and evil, equating these with pleasure and pain, and of ignoring the more spiritual goods which can arise in the struggle against evils.

But let us see exactly what is being done here. Let us call pain and misery 'first order evil' or 'evil (1).' What contrasts with this, namely, pleasure and happiness, will be called 'first order good' or 'good (1).' Distinct from this is 'second order good' or 'good (2)' which somehow emerges in a complex situation in which evil (1) is a necessary component—logically, not merely causally, necessary. (Exactly *how* it emerges does not matter: in the crudest version of this solution good (2) is simply the heightening of happiness by the contrast with misery, in other versions it includes sympathy with suffering, heroism in facing danger, and the gradual decrease of first order evil and increase of first order good.) It is also being assumed that second order good is more important than first order good or evil, in particular that it more than outweighs the first order evil it involves.

Now this is a particularly subtle attempt to solve the problem of evil. It defends God's goodness and omnipotence on the ground that (on a sufficiently long view) this is the best of all logically possible worlds, because it includes the important second order goods, and yet it admits that real evils, namely first order evils, exist. But does it still hold that good and evil are opposed? Not, clearly, in the sense that we set out originally: good does not tend to eliminate evil in general. Instead, we have a modified, a more complex pattern. First order good (e.g., happiness) *contrasts with* first order evil (e.g., misery): these two are opposed in a fairly mechanical way; some second order goods (e.g., benevolence) try to maximise first order good and minimise first order evil; but God's goodness is not this, it is rather the will to maximise *second* order good. We might, therefore, call God's goodness an example of a third order goodness, or good (3). While this account is different from our original one, it might well be held to be an improvement on it, to give a more accurate description of the way in which good is opposed to evil, and to be consistent with the essential theist position.

There might, however, be several objections to this solution. First, some might argue that such qualities as benevolence—and *a fortiori*[*] the third order goodness which promotes benevolence—have a merely derivative value, that they are not higher sorts of good, but merely means to good (1), that is, to happiness, so that it would be absurd for God to keep misery in existence in order to make possible the virtues of benevolence, heroism, etc. The theist who adopts the present solution must, of course, deny this, but he can do so with some plausibility, so I should not press this objection.

---

[*] All the more, for an even stronger reason.

Secondly, it follows from this solution that God is not in our sense benevolent or sympathetic: he is not concerned to minimise evil (1), but only to promote good (2); and this might be a disturbing conclusion for some theists.

But, thirdly, the fatal objection is this. Our analysis shows clearly the possibility of the existence of a *second* order evil, an evil (2) contrasting with good (2) as evil (1) contrasts with good (1). This would include malevolence, cruelty, callousness, cowardice, and states in which good (1) is decreasing and evil (1) increasing. And just as good (2) is held to be the important kind of good, the kind that God is concerned to promote, so evil (2) will, by analogy, be the important kind of evil, the kind which God, if he were wholly good and omnipotent, would eliminate. And yet evil (2) plainly exists, and indeed most theists (in other contexts) stress its existence more than that of evil (1). We should, therefore, state the problem of evil in terms of second order evil, and against this form of the problem the present solution is useless.

An attempt might be made to use this solution again, at a higher level, to explain the occurrence of evil (2): indeed the next main solution that we shall examine does just this, with the help of some new notions. Without any fresh notions, such a solution would have little plausibility: for example, we could hardly say that the really important good was a good (3), such as the increase of benevolence in proportion to cruelty, which logically required for its occurrence the occurrence of some second order evil. But even if evil (2) could be explained in this way, it is fairly clear that there would be third order evils contrasting with this third order good: and we should be well on the way to an infinite regress, where the solution of a problem of evil, stated in terms of evil (n), indicated the existence of an evil (n + 1), and a further problem to be solved.

4. "EVIL IS DUE TO HUMAN FREEWILL."

Perhaps the most important proposed solution of the problem of evil is that evil is not to be ascribed to God at all, but to the independent actions of human beings, supposed to have been endowed by God with freedom of the will. This solution may be combined with the preceding one: first order evil (e.g., pain) may be justified as a logically necessary component in second order good (e.g., sympathy) while second order evil (e.g., cruelty) is not *justified*, but is so ascribed to human beings that God cannot be held responsible for it. This combination evades my third criticism of the preceding solution.

The freewill solution also involves the preceding solution at a higher level. To explain why a wholly good God gave men freewill although it would lead to some important evils, it must be argued that it is better on the whole that men should act freely, and sometimes err, than that they should be innocent automata,* acting rightly in a wholly determined way. Freedom, that is to say, is now treated as a third order good, and as being more valuable than second order goods (such as sympathy and heroism) would be if they were deterministically produced, and it is being assumed that second order evils, such as cruelty, are logically necessary accompaniments of freedom, just as pain is a logically necessary pre-condition of sympathy.

I think that this solution is unsatisfactory primarily because of the incoherence of the notion of freedom of the will: but I cannot discuss this topic adequately here, although some of my criticisms will touch upon it.

First I should query the assumption that second order evils are logically necessary accompaniments of freedom. I should ask this: if God has made men such that in their free choices they sometimes prefer what is good and sometimes what is evil, why could he not have made men such that they always freely choose the good? If there is no logical impossibility in a man's freely choosing the good on one, or on several, occasions, there cannot be a logical impossibility in his freely choosing the good on every occasion. God was not, then, faced with a choice between making innocent automata and making beings who, in acting freely, would sometimes go wrong: there was open to him the obviously better possibility of making beings who would act freely but always go right. Clearly, his failure to avail himself of this possibility is inconsistent with his being both omnipotent and wholly good.

If it is replied that this objection is absurd, that the making of some wrong choices is logically necessary

---

* Robots.

for freedom, it would seem that 'freedom' must here mean complete randomness or indeterminacy, including randomness with regard to the alternatives good and evil, in other words that men's choices and consequent actions can be "free" only if they are not determined by their characters. Only on this assumption can God escape the responsibility for men's actions; for if he made them as they are, but did not determine their wrong choices, this can only be because the wrong choices are not determined by men as they are. But then if freedom is randomness, how can it be a characteristic of *will*? And, still more, how can it be the most important good? What value or merit would there be in free choices if these were random actions which were not determined by the nature of the agent?

I conclude that to make this solution plausible two different senses of 'freedom' must be confused, one sense which will justify the view that freedom is a third order good, more valuable than other goods would be without it, and another sense, sheer randomness, to prevent us from ascribing to God a decision to make men such that they sometimes go wrong when he might have made them such that they would always freely go right.

This criticism is sufficient to dispose of this solution. But besides this there is a fundamental difficulty in the notion of an omnipotent God creating men with free will, for if men's wills are really free this must mean that even God cannot control them, that is, that God is no longer omnipotent. It may be objected that God's gift of freedom to men does not mean that he cannot control their wills, but that he always *refrains* from controlling their wills. But why, we may ask, should God refrain from controlling evil wills? Why should he not leave men free to will rightly, but intervene when he sees them beginning to will wrongly? If God could do this, but does not, and if he is wholly good, the only explanation could be that even a wrong free act of will is not really evil, that its freedom is a value which outweighs its wrongness, so that there would be a loss of value if God took away the wrongness and the freedom together. But this is utterly opposed to what theists say about sin in other contexts. The present solution of the problem of evil, then, can be maintained only in the form that God has made men so free that he *cannot* control their wills.

This leads us to what I call the Paradox of Omnipotence: can an omnipotent being make things

which he cannot subsequently control? Or, what is practically equivalent to this, can an omnipotent being make rules which then bind himself? (These are practically equivalent because any such rules could be regarded as setting certain things beyond his control, and *vice versa*.) The second of these formulations is relevant to the suggestions that we have already met, that an omnipotent God creates the rules of logic or causal laws, and is then bound by them.

It is clear that this is a paradox: the questions cannot be answered satisfactorily either in the affirmative or in the negative. If we answer "Yes," it follows that if God actually makes things which he cannot control, or makes rules which bind himself, he is not omnipotent once he has made them: there are *then* things which he cannot do. But if we answer "No," we are immediately asserting that there are things which he cannot do, that is to say that he is already not omnipotent.

It cannot be replied that the question which sets this paradox is not a proper question. It would make perfectly good sense to say that a human mechanic has made a machine which he cannot control: if there is any difficulty about the question it lies in the notion of omnipotence itself.

This, incidentally, shows that although we have approached this paradox from the free will theory, it is equally a problem for a theological determinist. No one thinks that machines have free will, yet they may well be beyond the control of their makers. The determinist might reply that anyone who makes anything determines its ways of acting, and so determines its subsequent behaviour: even the human mechanic does this by his *choice* of materials and structure for his machine, though he does not know all about either of these: the mechanic thus determines, though he may not foresee, his machine's actions. And since God is omniscient, and since his creation of things is total, he both determines and foresees the ways in which his creatures will act. We may grant this, but it is beside the point. The question is not whether God *originally* determined the future actions of his creatures, but whether he can *subsequently* control their actions, or whether he was able in his original creation to put things beyond his subsequent control. Even on determinist principles the answers "Yes" and "No" are equally irreconcilable with God's omnipotence.

Before suggesting a solution of this paradox, I would point out that there is a parallel Paradox of

Sovereignty. Can a legal sovereign* make a law restricting its own future legislative power? For example, could the British parliament make a law forbidding any future parliament to socialise banking, and also forbidding the future repeal of this law itself? Or could the British parliament, which was legally sovereign in Australia in, say, 1899, pass a valid law, or series of laws, which made it no longer sovereign in 1933? Again, neither the affirmative nor the negative answer is really satisfactory. If we were to answer "Yes," we should be admitting the validity of a law which, if it were actually made, would mean that parliament was, no longer sovereign. If we were to answer "No," we should be admitting that there is a law, not logically absurd, which parliament cannot validly make, that is, that parliament is not now a legal sovereign. This paradox can be solved in the following way. We should distinguish between first order laws, that is laws governing the actions of individuals and bodies other than the legislature, and second order laws, that is laws about laws, laws governing the actions of the legislature itself. Correspondingly, we should distinguish two orders of sovereignty, first order sovereignty (sovereignty (1)) which is unlimited authority to make first order laws, and second order sovereignty (sovereignty (2)) which is unlimited authority to make second order laws. If we say that parliament is sovereign we might mean that any parliament at any time has sovereignty (1), or we might mean that parliament has both sovereignty (1) and sovereignty (2) at present, but we cannot without contradiction mean both that the present parliament has sovereignty (2) and that every parliament at every time has sovereignty (1), for if the present parliament has sovereignty (2) it may use it to take away the sovereignty (1) of later parliaments. What the paradox shows is that we cannot ascribe to any continuing institution legal sovereignty in an inclusive sense.

The analogy between omnipotence and sovereignty shows that the paradox of omnipotence can be solved in a similar way. We must distinguish between first order omnipotence (omnipotence (1)), that is

unlimited power to act, and second order omnipotence (omnipotence (2)), that is unlimited power to determine what powers to act things shall have. Then we could consistently say that God all the time has omnipotence (1), but if so no beings at any time have powers to act independently of God. Or we could say that God at one time had omnipotence (2), and used it to assign independent powers to act to certain things, so that God thereafter did not have omnipotence (1). But what the paradox shows is that we cannot consistently ascribe to any continuing being omnipotence in an inclusive sense.

An alternative solution of this paradox would be simply to deny that God is a continuing being, that any times can be assigned to his actions at all. But on this assumption (which also has difficulties of its own) no meaning can be given to the assertion that God made men with wills so free that he could not control them. The paradox of omnipotence can be avoided by putting God outside time, but the freewill solution of the problem of evil cannot be saved in this way, and equally it remains impossible to hold that an omnipotent God *binds himself* by causal or logical laws.

Conclusion

Of the proposed solutions of the problem of evil which we have examined, none has stood up to criticism. There may be other solutions which require examination, but this study strongly suggests that there is no valid solution of the problem which does not modify at least one of the constituent propositions in a way which would seriously affect the essential core of the theistic position.

Quite apart from the problem of evil, the paradox of omnipotence has shown that God's omnipotence must in any case be restricted in one way or another, that unqualified omnipotence cannot be ascribed to any being that continues through time. And if God and his actions are not in time, can omnipotence, or power of any sort, be meaningfully ascribed to him? ■

---

* A sovereign in Mackie's sense is a person or group with unlimited authority over others.

Suggestions for Critical Reflection

1. Why do responses like "Evil is something to be faced and overcome, not to be merely discussed" or "God works in mysterious ways, but I have faith" fail to deal rationally with the problem of evil (if they do)?

2. What do you think goodness is? Do you think evil is merely the absence of goodness (or *vice versa*), or can something be neither good nor evil (nor both)?

3. Is the universe better with some evil in it than it would be without any? (For example, do you think a life of successful struggle against adversity is more valuable than one of uninterrupted pleasure? If so, why?) What do you make of Mackie's arguments against this claim?

4. Could *all* evil be due to human free will? If even some of it is, should God have given us free will (if he did)? Is it coherent to think that God could have made us so that we have free will but nevertheless always choose some particular option (the best one) on every occasion?

5. Do you agree that the notion of omnipotence must have *some* limits? For example, could God have made the number four smaller than the number three, or created things that are neither rocks nor non-rocks, or made violent murder a moral duty? If even an "omnipotent" deity must be restricted in these ways, how serious a problem is this for the traditional picture of God? How much does Mackie's "paradox of omnipotence" add to these worries?

MARILYN MCCORD ADAMS

Horrendous Evils and the Goodness of God

Who Was Marilyn McCord Adams?

Marilyn McCord Adams (1943–2017) was an American academic who worked in the philosophy of religion, medieval philosophy, and Christian theology. She received a PhD in philosophy from Cornell University and a Doctor of Divinity degree from the University of Oxford, where she was the first woman to serve as the Regius Professor of Divinity. Beyond her academic work, Adams was heavily involved in Christian practice, serving as a priest of the Episcopal Church and advocating for the inclusion of homosexual and other LGBT people within the church. From 1966 to her death from cancer in 2017, Adams was married to Robert Merrihew Adams, also an accomplished philosopher of religion.

What Is the Structure of This Reading?

In most formulations, the problem of evil is presented as a general objection applicable to most monotheistic* belief systems: a God that is all-knowing, all-powerful, and benevolent would not create (or permit) evil. Rather than respond on behalf of all monotheistic religions, Adams deliberately narrows the focus of this paper to address whether Christianity in particular is compatible with evil.

Adams argues that the problem of evil takes two distinct forms. The first is the question of whether the existence of God is compatible with evil in a logical sense. This is the formulation of the problem that is most often addressed in modern academic philosophy. Some, such as J.L. Mackie, argue that the existence of evil disproves God, while Alvin Plantinga and others hold that evils are compatible with God and may be a necessary part of a greater good.

Separate from but related to this is a more personal formulation of the problem of evil, which is Adams's focus in this paper. Here, the issue is not whether the good outweighs evil in the world on the whole, but whether the good balances with (or "defeats") horrendous evil within the context of an individual life. For a person who has experienced horrendous evil—and Adams offers a number of upsetting examples—does the notion that evil is outweighed by other goods offer any consolation?

According to Adams, this second, personal formulation of the problem cannot be adequately addressed through general observations about the balance of good or the requirements and limitations of an all-powerful, all-knowing creator. Rather, in order for Christianity to offer an adequate response, Adams believes that one must draw on other aspects of the Christian belief system. More specifically, horrendous evils may be overcome or "engulfed" by *transcendent* goods, involving "beatific,† face-to-face intimacy with God," which exceed other non-transcendent experiences. She offers several examples of such goods, and proposes that they may not only engulf or balance with horrendous evils, but also defeat those evils and establish the overall goodness of the sufferer's life.

Some Useful Background Information

Adams makes several references to the views of Ivan Karamazov, a fictional character in *The Brothers Karamazov*, written by Russian novelist Fyodor Dostoevsky. Ivan, the most rational and skeptical of three brothers, conveys a variation of the problem of evil. The following passage depicts part of a conversation between Ivan and his religiously inclined younger brother Alyosha. Note the use of first-person pronouns—Ivan isn't making a general argument about God's existence; rather, he frames the issue in terms of his own capacity to accept the existence of God in a world with undeniable evil:

---

*   A monotheistic belief system is one that posits the existence of a single god.
†   Blissfully happy.

"I want to forgive. I want to embrace. I don't want more suffering. And if the sufferings of children go to swell the sum of sufferings which was necessary to pay for truth, then I protest that the truth is not worth such a price. I don't want the mother to embrace the oppressor who threw her son to the dogs! She dare not forgive him! Let her forgive him for herself, if she will, let her forgive the torturer for the immeasurable suffering of her mother's heart. But the sufferings of her tortured child she has no right to forgive; she dare not forgive the torturer, even if the child were to forgive him! And if that is so, if they dare not forgive, what becomes of harmony? Is there in the whole world a being who would have the right to forgive and could forgive? I don't want harmony. From love for humanity I don't want it. I would rather be left with the unavenged suffering. I would rather remain with my unavenged suffering and unsatisfied indignation, even if I were wrong. Besides, too high a price is asked for harmony; it's beyond our means to pay so much to enter on it. And so I hasten to give back my entrance ticket, and if I am an honest man I am bound to give it back as soon as possible. And that I am doing. It's not God that I don't accept, Alyosha, only I most respectfully return Him the ticket."

"That's rebellion," murmured Alyosha, looking down.

"Rebellion? I am sorry you call it that," said Ivan earnestly. "One can hardly live in rebellion, and I want to live. Tell me yourself, I challenge you—answer. Imagine that you are creating a fabric of human destiny with the object of making men happy in the end, giving them peace and rest at last, but that it was essential and inevitable to torture to death only one tiny creature—that baby beating its breast with its fist, for instance—and to found that edifice on its unavenged tears, would you consent to be the architect on those conditions? Tell me, and tell the truth."

*"No, I wouldn't consent," said Alyosha softly.**

Horrendous Evils and the Goodness of God[†]

I: Introduction

Over the past thirty years, analytic philosophers of religion have defined 'the problem of evil' in terms of the *prima facie*[‡] difficulty in consistently maintaining

    (1) God exists, and is omnipotent, omniscient,[§] and perfectly good

and

    (2) Evil exists.

In a crisp and classic article 'Evil and Omnipotence',[1] J.L. Mackie emphasized that the problem is not that (1) and (2) are logically inconsistent by themselves, but that they together with quasi-logical rules formulating attribute-analyses—such as

    (P1) A perfectly good being would always eliminate evil so far as it could,

and

    (P2) There are *no limits* to what an omnipotent being can do,

* Fyodor Dostoyevsky, *The Brothers Karamazov* (1880), trans. Constance Garnett (The Lowell Press, 1912), lightly modernized for this volume.

† From Marilyn McCord Adams and Stewart Sutherland, "Horrendous Evils and the Goodness of God," *Proceedings of the Aristotelian Society*, Supplementary Volumes 63 (1989): 297–310.

‡ Latin for "first impression." Adams uses the term several times in this article, primarily in reference to "prima facie reasons"—that is, to reasons or conclusions that we can hold as true unless there is evidence to the contrary.

§ To be omnipotent is to be all-powerful, and to be omniscient is to be all-knowing.

—constitute an inconsistent premiss-set. He added, of course, that the inconsistency might be removed by substituting alternative and perhaps more subtle analyses, but cautioned that such replacements of (P1) and (P2) would save 'ordinary theism' from his charge of positive irrationality, only if true to its 'essential requirements'.[2]

In an earlier paper 'Problems of Evil: More Advice to Christian Philosophers',[3] I underscored Mackie's point and took it a step further. In debates about whether the argument from evil can establish the irrationality of religious belief, care must be taken, both by the atheologians* who deploy it and the believers who defend against it, to insure that the operative attribute-analyses accurately reflect that religion's understanding of Divine power and goodness. It does the atheologian no good to argue for the falsity of Christianity on the ground that the existence of an omnipotent, omniscient, pleasure-maximizer is incompossible† with a world such as ours, because Christians never believed God was a pleasure-maximizer anyway. But equally, the truth of Christianity would be inadequately defended by the observation that an omnipotent, omniscient egoist could have created a world with suffering creatures, because Christians insist that God loves other (created) persons than Himself. The extension of 'evil' in (2) is likewise important. Since Mackie and his successors are out to show that 'the several parts of the *essential* theological doctrine are inconsistent with *each other*',[4] they can accomplish their aim only if they circumscribe the extension of 'evil'‡ as their religious opponents do. By the same token, it is not enough for Christian philosophers to explain how the power, knowledge, and goodness of God could coexist with some evils or other; a full account must exhibit the compossibility§ of Divine perfection with evils in the amounts and of the kinds found in the actual world (and evaluated as such by Christian standards).

The moral of my earlier story might be summarized thus: where the internal coherence of a system of religious beliefs is at stake, successful arguments for its inconsistency must draw on premises (explicitly or implicitly) internal to that system or obviously acceptable to its adherents; likewise for successful rebuttals or explanations of consistency. The thrust of my argument is to push both sides of the debate towards more detailed attention to and subtle understanding of the religious system in question.

As a Christian philosopher, I want to focus in this paper on the problem for the truth of Christianity raised by what I shall call 'horrendous' evils. Although our world is riddled with them, the Biblical record punctuated by them, and one of them—viz., the passion of Christ, according to Christian belief, the judicial murder of God by the people of God—is memorialized by the Church on its most solemn holiday (Good Friday) and in its central sacrament (the Eucharist), the problem of horrendous evils is largely skirted by standard treatments for the good reason that they are intractable by them. After showing why, I will draw on other Christian materials to sketch ways of meeting this, the deepest of religious problems.

II: Defining the Category

For present purposes, I define 'horrendous evils' as 'evils the participation in (the doing or suffering of) which gives one reason *prima facie* to doubt whether one's life could (given their inclusion in it) be a great good to one on the whole'. Such reasonable doubt arises because it is so difficult humanly to conceive how such evils could be overcome. Borrowing [Roderick] Chisholm's contrast between *balancing off* (which occurs when the opposing values of *mutually exclusive* parts¶ of a whole partially or totally cancel each other out) and *defeat* (which cannot occur by the mere addition to the whole of a new part of opposing value, but involves some 'organic unity' among the values of parts and wholes, as when the positive aesthetic value of a whole painting defeats the ugliness of a small colour patch),[5] horrendous evils seem *prima*

---

* An atheologian is someone who is opposed to a theologian; a theorist of atheism.
† In this context, "incompossible" can be read as "incompatible."
‡ Circumscribe the extension of 'evil': define which things count as evil.
§ Ability or possibility of coexistence.
¶ Mutually exclusive parts are such that it's not possible for them to exist together.

facie, not only to balance off but to engulf the positive value of a participant's life. Nevertheless, that very horrendous proportion, by which they threaten to rob a person's life of positive meaning, cries out not only to be engulfed, but to be made meaningful through positive and decisive defeat.

I understand this criterion to be objective, but relative to individuals. The example of habitual complainers, who know how to make the worst of a good situation, shows individuals not to be incorrigible experts on what ills would defeat the positive value of their lives. Nevertheless, nature and experience endow people with different strengths; one bears easily what crushes another. And a major consideration in determining whether an individual's life is/has been a great good to him/her on the whole, is invariably and appropriately how it has seemed to him/her.[6]

I offer the following list of paradigmatic* horrors: the rape of a woman and axing off of her arms, psychophysical torture whose ultimate goal is the disintegration of personality, betrayal of one's deepest loyalties, cannibalizing one's own offspring, child abuse of the sort described by Ivan Karamazov,[†] child pornography, parental incest, slow death by starvation, participation in the Nazi death camps, the explosion of nuclear bombs over populated areas, having to choose which of one's children shall live and which be executed by terrorists, being the accidental and/or unwitting agent of the disfigurement or death of those one loves best. I regard these as *paradigmatic* because I believe most people would find in the doing or suffering of them *prima facie* reason to doubt the positive meaning of their lives. Christian belief counts the crucifixion of Christ another. On the one hand, death by crucifixion seemed to defeat Jesus' Messianic vocation; for according to Jewish law, death by hanging from a tree made its victim ritually accursed, definitively excluded from the compass of God's people, *a fortiori*[‡] disqualified from being the Messiah. On the other hand, it represented the defeat of its perpetrators' leadership vocations, as those who were to prepare the people of God

for the Messiah's coming, kill and ritually accurse the true Messiah, according to later theological understanding, God Himself.

III: *The Impotence of Standard Solutions*

For better or worse, the by-now-standard strategies for 'solving' the problem of evil are powerless in the face of horrendous evils.

3.1: SEEKING THE REASON WHY

In his model article 'Hume on Evil',[7] [Nelson] Pike takes up Mackie's challenge, arguing that (P1) fails to reflect ordinary moral intuitions (more to the point, I would add, Christian beliefs), and traces the abiding sense of trouble to the hunch that an omnipotent, omniscient being could have no reason compatible with perfect goodness for permitting (bringing about) evils, because all legitimate excuses arise from ignorance or weakness. Solutions to the problem of evil have thus been sought in the form of counter-examples to this latter claim, i.e., logically possible reasons why that would excuse even an omnipotent, omniscient God! The putative logically possible reasons offered have tended to be *generic* and *global*: generic insofar as some *general* reason is sought to cover all sorts of evils; global insofar as they seize upon some feature of the world as a whole. For example, philosophers have alleged that the desire to make a world with one of the following properties—'the best of all possible worlds',[8] 'a world a more perfect than which is impossible', 'a world exhibiting a perfect balance of retributive justice',[9] 'a world with as favourable a balance of (created) moral good over moral evil as God can weakly actualize'[10]—would constitute a reason compatible with perfect goodness for God's creating a world with evils in the amounts and of the kinds found in the actual world. Moreover, such general reasons are presented as so powerful as to do away with any need to catalogue types of evils one by one, and

---

* A paradigmatic example is one that is clear and unambiguous, and which may serve as a model to determine what other cases count as examples of the concept at issue.

† A character in Fyodor Dostoevsky's *The Brothers Karamazov*. See the introduction to this reading.

‡ Latin for "from the stronger." An *a fortiori* inference is one that draws a weaker conclusion on the basis of a stronger conclusion that has already been reached.

examine God's reason for permitting each in particular. [Alvin] Plantinga explicitly hopes that the problem of horrendous evils can thus be solved without being squarely confronted.[11]

3.2: THE INSUFFICIENCY OF GLOBAL DEFEAT

A pair of distinctions is in order here: (i) between two dimensions of Divine goodness in relation to creation—viz., 'producer of global goods' and 'goodness to' or 'love of individual created persons'; and (ii) between the overbalance/defeat of evil by good on the global scale, and the overbalance/defeat of evil by good within the context of an individual person's life.[12] Correspondingly, we may separate two problems of evil parallel to the two sorts of goodness mentioned in (i).

In effect, generic and global approaches are directed to the first problem: they defend Divine goodness along the first (global) dimension by suggesting logically possible strategies for the global defeat of evils. But establishing God's excellence as a producer of global goods does not automatically solve the second problem, especially in a world containing horrendous evils. For God cannot be said to be good or loving to any created persons the positive meaning of whose lives He allows to be engulfed in and/or defeated by evils—that is, individuals within whose lives horrendous evils remain undefeated. Yet, the only way unsupplemented global and generic approaches could have to explain the latter, would be by applying their general reasons-why to particular cases of horrendous suffering.

Unfortunately, such an exercise fails to give satisfaction. Suppose for the sake of argument that horrendous evil could be included in maximally perfect world orders; its being partially constitutive of such an order would assign it that generic and global positive meaning. But would knowledge of such a fact, defeat for a mother the *prima facie* reason provided by her cannibalism of her own infant, to wish that she had never been born? Again, the aim of perfect retributive balance confers meaning on evils imposed. But would

knowledge that the torturer was being tortured give the victim who broke down and turned traitor under pressure, any more reason to think his/her life worthwhile? Would it not merely multiply reasons for the torturer to doubt that his/her life could turn out to be a good to him/her on the whole? Could the truck-driver who accidentally runs over his beloved child find consolation in the idea that this middle-known[13] but unintended side-effect was part of the price God accepted for a world with the best balance of moral good over moral evil He could get?

Not only does the application to horrors of such generic and global reasons for Divine permission of evils fail to solve the second problem of evil; it makes it worse by adding *generic prima facie* reasons to doubt whether human life would be a great good to individual human beings in possible worlds where such Divine motives were operative. For, taken in isolation and made to bear the weight of the whole explanation, such reasons-why draw a picture of Divine indifference or even hostility to the human plight. Would the fact that God permitted horrors because they were constitutive means to His end of global perfection, or that He tolerated them because He could obtain that global end anyway, make the participant's life more tolerable, more worth living for him/her? Given radical human vulnerability to horrendous evils, the ease with which humans participate in them, whether as victim or perpetrator, would not the thought that God visits horrors on anyone who caused them, simply because s/he deserves it, provide one more reason to expect human life to be a nightmare?

Those willing to split the two problems of evil apart might adopt a divide-and-conquer strategy, by simply denying Divine goodness along the second dimension. For example, many Christians do not believe that God will insure an overwhelmingly good life to each and every person He creates. Some say the decisive defeat of evil with good is promised only within the lives of the obedient, who enter by the narrow gate.* Some speculate that the elect† may be few. Many recognize that the sufferings of this present life are as nothing compared to the hell of eternal torment,

---

* The reference is to Matthew 7:13: "Enter through the narrow gate. For wide is the gate and broad is the road that leads to destruction, and many enter through it" (New International Version).

† Here, "the elect" means, roughly, "those who are chosen by God."

designed to defeat goodness with horrors within the lives of the damned.

Such a road can be consistently travelled only at the heavy toll of admitting that human life in worlds such as ours is a bad bet. Imagine (adapting Rawls' device*) persons in a pre-original position, considering possible worlds containing managers of differing power, wisdom, and character, and subjects of varying fates. The question they are to answer about each world is whether they would willingly enter it as a human being, from behind a veil of ignorance as to which position they would occupy. Reason would, I submit, dictate a negative verdict for worlds whose omniscient and omnipotent manager permits pre-mortem horrors that remain undefeated within the context of the human participant's life; *a fortiori*, for worlds in which some or most humans suffer eternal torment.

3.3: INACCESSIBLE REASONS

So far, I have argued that generic and global solutions are at best incomplete: however well their account of Divine motivating reasons deals with the first problem of evil, the attempt to extend it to the second fails by making it worse. This verdict might seem *prima facie* tolerable to standard generic and global approaches and indicative of only a minor modification in their strategy: let the above-mentioned generic and global reasons cover Divine permission of non-horrendous evils, and find other *reasons* compatible with perfect goodness *why* even an omnipotent, omniscient God would permit horrors.

In my judgment, such an approach is hopeless. As Plantinga[14] points out, where horrendous evils are concerned, not only do we not know God's *actual* reason for permitting them; we cannot even *conceive* of any plausible candidate sort of reason consistent with worthwhile lives for human participants in them.

IV: The How of God's Victory

Up to now, my discussion has given the reader cause to wonder whose side I am on anyway? For I have insisted, with rebels like Ivan Karamazov and John Stuart Mill,[†] on spot-lighting the problem horrendous evils pose. Yet, I have signalled my preference for a vision of Christianity that insists on both dimensions of Divine goodness, and maintains not only (a) that God will be good enough to created persons to make human life a good bet, but also (b) that each created person will have a life that is a great good to him/her on the whole. My critique of standard approaches to the problem of evil thus seems to reinforce atheologian Mackie's verdict of 'positive irrationality' for such a religious position.

4.1: WHYS VERSUS HOWS

The inaccessibility of reasons-why seems especially decisive. For surely an all-wise and all-powerful God, who loved each created person enough (a) to defeat any experienced horrors within the context of the participant's life, and (b) to give each created person a life that is a great good to him/her on the whole, would not permit such persons to suffer horrors for no reason.[15] Does not our inability even to conceive of plausible candidate reasons suffice to make belief in such a God positively irrational in a world containing horrors? In my judgment, it does not.

To be sure, motivating reasons come in several varieties relative to our conceptual grasp: There are (i) reasons of the sort we can readily understand when we are informed of them (e.g., the mother who permits her child to undergo painful heart surgery because it is the only humanly possible way to save its life). Moreover, there are (ii) reasons we would be cognitively, emotionally, and spiritually equipped to grasp if only we had a larger memory or wider attention span (analogy: I may be able to memorize small town street plans; memorizing the road networks of the entire country

---

* In *A Theory of Justice* (1971), philosopher John Rawls posited a thought experiment in which people in an "original position" determine the rules of society after placing themselves behind a "veil of ignorance" in which they are unaware of their own life circumstances, including ethnicity, gender, social status, and conception of what is good.

† John Stuart Mill (1806–73) was an English philosopher known especially for his defenses of liberty, utilitarian moral reasoning, and women's rights. See his *Three Essays on Religion*.

is a task requiring more of the same, in the way that proving Gödel's theorem* is not). Some generic and global approaches insinuate that Divine permission of evils has motivating reasons of this sort. Finally, (iii) there are reasons that we are cognitively, emotionally, and/or spiritually too immature to fathom (the way a two-year old child is incapable of understanding its mother's reasons for permitting the surgery). I agree with Plantinga that our ignorance of Divine reasons for permitting horrendous evils is not of types (i) or (ii), but of type (iii).

Nevertheless, if there are varieties of ignorance, there are also varieties of reassurance. The two-year old heart patient is convinced of its mother's love, not by her cognitively inaccessible reasons, but by her intimate care and presence through its painful experience. The story of Job suggests something similar is true with human participation in horrendous suffering: God does not give Job His reasons-why, and implies that Job isn't smart enough to grasp them; rather Job is lectured on the extent of Divine power, and sees God's goodness face to face! Likewise, I suggest, to exhibit the logical compossibility of both dimensions of Divine goodness with horrendous suffering, it is not necessary to find logically possible reasons *why* God might permit them. It is enough to show *how* God can be good enough to created persons despite their participation in horrors— by defeating them within the context of the individual's life and by giving that individual a life that is a great good to him/her on the whole.

4.2: WHAT SORT OF VALUABLES?

In my opinion, the reasonableness of Christianity can be maintained in the face of horrendous evils only by drawing on resources of religious value theory. For one way for God to be *good to* created persons is by relating them appropriately to relevant and great goods. But philosophical and religious theories differ importantly on what valuables they admit into their ontology.† Some maintain that 'what you see is what you get', but nevertheless admit a wide range of valuables, from sensory pleasures, the beauty of nature and cultural artifacts, the joys of creativity, to loving personal intimacy. Others posit a transcendent good (e.g., the Form of the Good in Platonism, or God, the Supremely Valuable Object, in Christianity). In the spirit of Ivan Karamazov, I am convinced that the depth of horrific evil cannot be accurately estimated without recognizing it to be incommensurate‡ with any package of merely non-transcendent goods and so unable to be balanced off, much less defeated thereby.

Where the *internal* coherence of Christianity is the issue, however, it is fair to appeal to its own store of valuables. From a Christian point of view, God is a being a greater than which cannot be conceived, a good incommensurate with both created goods and temporal evils. Likewise, the good of beatific, face-to-face intimacy with God is simply incommensurate with any merely non-transcendent goods or ills a person might experience. Thus, the good of beatific face-to-face intimacy with God would *engulf* (in a sense analogous to Chisholmian balancing off) even the horrendous evils humans experience in this present life here below, and overcome any *prima facie* reasons the individual had to doubt whether his/her life would or could be worth living.

4.3: PERSONAL MEANING, HORRORS DEFEATED

Engulfing personal horrors within the context of the participant's life would vouchsafe to that individual a life that was a great good to him/her on the whole. I am still inclined to think it would guarantee that immeasurable Divine goodness to any person thus benefited. But there is good theological reason for Christians to believe that God would go further, beyond engulfment to defeat. For it is the nature of persons to look for meaning, both in their lives and in the world. Divine respect for and commitment to created personhood would drive God to make all those sufferings which threaten to destroy the positive meaning of a person's life meaningful through positive defeat.

---

* Gödel's theorem: one of three theorems in formal logic established by Kurt Gödel by 1931, the most famous of which asserts that no formal axiomatic system is capable of proving all truths about the arithmetic of the natural numbers.

† In this context, an ontology is an account of what things exist.

‡ Having no shared standard of measurement, not comparable with.

How could God do it? So far as I can see, only by integrating participation in horrendous evils into a person's relationship with God. Possible dimensions of integration are charted by Christian soteriology.* I pause here to sketch three.[16] (i) First, because God in Christ participated in horrendous evil through His passion and death, human experience of horrors can be a means of *identifying* with Christ, either through *sympathetic* identification (in which each person suffers his/her own pains, but their similarity enables each to know what it is like for the other) or through *mystical* identification (in which the created person is supposed literally to experience a share of Christ's pain[17]). (ii) Julian of Norwich's[†] description of heavenly welcome suggests the possible defeat of horrendous evil through Divine gratitude. According to Julian, before the elect have a chance to thank God for all He has done for them, God will say, 'Thank you for all your suffering, the suffering of your youth'. She says that the creature's experience of Divine gratitude will bring such full and unending joy as could not be merited by the whole sea of human pain and suffering throughout the ages.[18] (iii) A third idea identifies temporal suffering itself with a vision into the inner life of God, and can be developed several ways. Perhaps, contrary to medieval theology, God is not impassible,[‡] but rather has matched capacities for joy and for suffering. Perhaps, as the Heidelberg catechism[§] suggests, God responds to human sin and the sufferings of Christ with an agony beyond human conception.[19] Alternatively, the inner life of God may be, strictly speaking and in and of itself, beyond both joy and sorrow. But, just as (according to Rudolf Otto[¶]) humans experience Divine presence now as *tremendum* (with deep dread and anxiety), now as *fascinans* (with ineffable attraction), so perhaps our deepest suffering as much as our highest joys may themselves be direct visions into the inner life of God, imperfect but somehow less obscure in proportion to their intensity. And if a face-to-face vision of God is a good for humans incommensurate with any non-transcendent goods

or ills, so any vision of God (including horrendous suffering) would have a good aspect insofar as it is a vision of God (even if it has an evil aspect insofar as it is horrendous suffering). For the most part, horrors are not recognized as experiences of God (any more than the city slicker recognizes his visual image of a brown patch as a vision of Beulah the cow in the distance). But, Christian mysticism might claim, at least from the post-mortem perspective of the beatific vision, such sufferings will be seen for what they were, and retrospectively no one will wish away any intimate encounters with God from his/her life-history of this world. The created person's experience of the beatific vision together with his/her knowledge that intimate Divine presence stretched back over his/her pre-mortem life and reached down into the depths of his/her worst suffering, would provide retrospective comfort independent of comprehension of the reasons-why akin to the two-year-old's assurance of its mother's love. Taking this third approach, Christians would not need to commit themselves about what in any event we do not know: viz., whether we will (like the two-year-old) ever grow up enough to understand the reasons why God permits our participation in horrendous evils. For by contrast with the best of earthly mothers, such Divine intimacy is an incommensurate good and would cancel out for the creature any need to know why.

V: Conclusion

The worst evils demand to be defeated by the best goods. Horrendous evils can be overcome only by the goodness of God. Relative to human nature, participation in horrendous evils and loving intimacy with God are alike disproportionate: for the former threatens to engulf the good in an individual human life with evil, while the latter guarantees the reverse engulfment of evil by good. Relative to one another, there is also disproportion, because the good that God *is*, and intimate relationship with Him, is incommensurate

---

* Soteriology is the study of salvation.
† Julian of Norwich (c. 1342–c. 1416) was a Christian mystic and holy woman; she is the author of *Revelations of Divine Love*, in which she recounts personal visions of God.
‡ Impassibility is the theological doctrine that God does not experience pain or pleasure from the actions of any other being.
§ *The Heidelberg Catechism* (1563) is a statement of Christian doctrine recognized by many Protestant denominations.
¶ Rudolf Otto (1869–1937) was a prominent German Lutheran theologian.

with created goods and evils alike. Because intimacy with God so outscales relations (good or bad) with any creatures, integration into the human person's relationship with God confers significant meaning and positive value even on horrendous suffering. This result coheres with basic Christian intuition: that the powers of darkness are stronger than humans, but they are no match for God!

Standard generic and global solutions have for the most part tried to operate within the territory common to believer and unbeliever, within the confines of religion-neutral value theory. Many discussions reflect the hope that substitute attribute-analyses, candidate reasons-why and/or defeaters could issue out of values shared by believers and unbelievers alike. And some virtually make this a requirement on an adequate solution. Mackie knew better how to distinguish the many charges that may be levelled against religion. Just as philosophers may or may not find the existence of God plausible, so they may be variously attracted or repelled by Christian values of grace and redemptive sacrifice. But agreement on truth-value is not necessary to consensus on internal consistency. My contention has been that it is not only legitimate, but, given horrendous evils, necessary for Christians to dip into their richer store of valuables to exhibit the consistency of (1) and (2).[20] I would go one step further: assuming the pragmatic and/or moral (I would prefer to say, broadly speaking, religious) importance of believing that (one's own) human life is worth living, the ability of Christianity to exhibit how this could be so despite human vulnerability to horrendous evil, constitutes a pragmatic/moral/religious consideration in its favour, relative to value schemes that do not.

To me, the most troublesome weakness in what I have said, lies in the area of conceptual underdevelopment. The contention that God suffered in Christ or that one person can experience another's pain require detailed analysis and articulation in metaphysics and philosophy of mind. I have shouldered some of this burden elsewhere,[21] but its full discharge is well beyond the scope of this paper.[22] ∎

Suggestions for Critical Reflection

1. In this paper, Adams addresses a personal form of the problem of evil rather than the global/generic question of whether evil is compatible with goodness. Indeed, she claims that it would be "hopeless" to seek out reasons as to why God would permit horrendous evils. Does this mean that horrendous evil is logically incompatible with an all-powerful, all-knowing, benevolent God, and if so does that mean that the "global" formulation of the problem remains unanswered? Can the personal form of the problem of evil be separated from the global question?

2. Adams focuses on evils suffered by the individual, arguing that such sufferings may be outweighed in a Christian's life by his or her relationship with God. In a companion piece originally published alongside this paper, Stewart Sutherland points out that we may also have difficulty justifying evils in the lives of other people, as when we observe or hear of terrible harms to innocents. This is the kind of evil that most bothers Ivan Karamazov when he reflects on the horrors faced by the mother of a tortured child. Does Adams's argument hold equally with regard to horrendous evils affecting other people? That is, in the context of one's own life, can the goodness one receives through a relationship with God outweigh the horrendous evils that affect not only oneself but also other people? Or would this be a selfish form of reasoning?

3. What exactly do you think Adams means by the "positive meaning" of a life? Is this notion clear?

4. Does Adams's argument—or a variation of it—hold equally for all Christians, or does it only apply to some denominations? Does it hold equally for other monotheistic religions? Which particular beliefs would have to be shared by other religions in order for Adams's arguments to apply?

5. Adams defines horrendous evils as those which give one "reason *prima facie* to doubt whether one's life could ... be a great good to one on the whole." She offers a Christian response to those evils: "the powers of darkness are stronger than humans, but they are no match for God!" Where

does this leave the non-Christian? Is it possible to adequately respond to an evil that causes one to doubt the goodness of one's life without appealing to God or other supernatural entities?

Notes

1   J.L. Mackie, 'Evil and Omnipotence', *Mind*, 1955; reprinted in Nelson Pike, *God and Evil*, Prentice-Hall Inc., Englewood Cliffs, N.J., 1964, pp. 46–60.

2   Mackie, *op. cit.*, p. 47.

3   Marilyn McCord Adams, 'Problems of Evil: More Advice to Christian Philosophers', *Faith and Philosophy*, April 1988, pp. 121–43.

4   Mackie, *op. cit.*, pp. 46–47.

5   Roderick Chisholm, 'The Defeat of Good and Evil' (unpublished version).

6   Cf. Malcolm's astonishment at Wittgenstein's dying exclamation that he had had a wonderful life, *Ludwig Wittgenstein: A Memoir*, Oxford University Press, London, 1962, p. 100.

7   'Hume on Evil', *Philosophical Review* LXXII (1963), pp. 180–97; reprinted in *God and Evil*, p. 88.

8   Following Leibniz, Pike draws on this feature as part of what I have called his 'Epistemic Defense' ('Problems of Evil: More Advice to Christian Philosophers', pp. 124–25).

9   Augustine, *On Free Choice of Will* III. 93–102, implies that there is a maximum value for created worlds, and a plurality of worlds that meets it. All of these contain rational free creatures; evils are foreseen but unintended side-effects of their creation. No matter what they choose, however, God can order their choices into a maximally perfect universe by establishing an order of retributive justice.

10 Plantinga takes this line in numerous discussions, in the course of answering Mackie's objection to the Free Will Defence, that God should have made sinless free creatures. Plantinga insists that, given incompatibilist freedom in creatures, God cannot strongly actualize any world He wants. It is logically possible that a world with evils in the amounts and of the kinds found in this world is the best that He could do, Plantinga argues, given His aim of getting some moral goodness in the world.

11 Alvin Plantinga, 'Self-Profile', in *Alvin Plantinga*, edited by James E. Tomberlin and Peter van Inwagen, D. Reidel Publishing Company (Dordrecht, Boston, Lancaster, 1985), p. 38.

12 I owe the second of these distinctions to a remark by Keith DeRose in our Fall 1987 seminar on the problem of evil at UCLA.

13 Middle knowledge, or knowledge of what is 'in between' the actual and the possible, is the sort of knowledge of what a free creature *would do* in every situation in which that creature could possibly find himself: Following Luis de Molina and Francisco Suarez, Alvin Plantinga ascribes such knowledge to God, prior in the order of explanation to God's decision about which free creatures to actualize (in *The Nature of Necessity*, Oxford University Press, 1974, chapter IX, pp. 164–93). Robert Merrihew Adams challenges this idea in his article 'Middle Knowledge and the Problem of Evil', *American Philosophical Quarterly* 14 (1977); reprinted in *The Virtue of Faith*, Oxford University Press, 1987, pp. 77–93.

14 Alvin Plantinga, 'Self-Profile', *Alvin Plantinga*, pp. 34–35.

15 This point was made by William Fitzpatrick in our Fall 1987 seminar on the problem of evil at UCLA.

16 In my paper 'Redemptive Suffering: A Christian Solution to the Problem of Evil', *Rationality, Religious Belief, and Moral Commitment: New Essays in Philosophy of Religion*, ed. by Robert Audi and William J. Wainwright, Cornell University Press, 1986, pp. 248–67, I sketch how horrendous suffering can be meaningful by being made a vehicle of divine redemption for victim, perpetrator, and onlooker, and thus an occasion of the victim's collaboration with God. In 'Separation and Reversal in Luke-Acts', forthcoming in *Philosophy and the Christian Faith*, ed. by Thomas Morris, Notre Dame University Press, Notre Dame, Indiana, 1988, I attempt to chart the redemptive plotline there, whereby horrendous sufferings are made meaningful by being woven into the redemptive plot. My considered opinion is that such collaboration would be too strenuous for the human condition were it not to be supplemented by a more explicit and beatific divine intimacy.

17 For example, Julian of Norwich tells us that she prayed for and received the latter (*Revelations of Divine Love*, chapter 17). Mother Theresa of Calcutta seems to construe Matthew 25:31–46 to mean that the poorest and the least *are* Christ, and that their sufferings *are* Christ's (Malcolm Muggeridge, *Something Beautiful for God*, Harper & Row, Publishers, New York 1960, pp. 72–75).

18 *Revelations of Divine Love*, chapter 14. I am grateful to Houston Smit for recognizing this scenario of Julian's as a case of Chisholmian defeat.

19 Cf. Plantinga, 'Self-Profile', *Alvin Plantinga*, p. 36.

20 I develop this point at some length in 'Problems of Evil: More Advice to Christian Philosophers', pp. 127–35.

21 For example in 'The Metaphysics of the Incarnation in Some Fourteenth Century Franciscans', *Essays Honoring Allan B. Wolter*, edited by William A. Frank and Girard J. Etzkorn, The Franciscan Institute, St. Bonaventure, N.Y. 1985, pp. 21–57.

22 In the development of these ideas, I am indebted to the members of our Fall 1987 seminar on the problem of evil at UCLA—especially to Robert Merrihew Adams (its co-leader) and to Keith De Rose, William Fitzpatrick, and Houston Smit. I am also grateful to the Very Reverend Jon Hart Olson for many conversations in mystical theology.

BLAISE PASCAL

The Wager, FROM *Pensées*

Who Was Blaise Pascal?

Blaise Pascal (1623–62) was a French scientific prodigy, one of the most important mathematicians of the seventeenth century, and a Catholic theologian. He was born in France's Auvergne region and his mother died when he was three. The family moved to Paris in 1631, where Pascal and his siblings were educated entirely by his father Étienne (who never remarried). Pascal was a brilliant child, especially interested in mathematics, and even before he was sixteen was developing new proofs and corresponding with some of the leading mathematicians of his day—some of whom, such as René Descartes, initially refused to believe they were reading the work of a child.

When Pascal was 16 the French government, enmeshed in the very expensive Thirty Years' War, defaulted on the government's bonds where the Pascals' money was invested, and the family was suddenly plunged from living in relative comfort to hard times. To make matters worse, Pascal's father soon had to flee Paris, leaving his children behind, because of his (understandable) opposition to the government's fiscal policies. For several months Blaise and his two sisters were in the care of a neighbor, Madame Sainctot, a society beauty who ran one of the most glamorous 'salons'—regular intellectual gatherings/parties—in Paris.

Pascal's father was eventually able to find an appointment as the king's tax collector for the city of Rouen, and began to rebuild the family's financial fortunes. But Rouen's tax records were in complete disarray because of recent failed popular uprisings, and the job of rebuilding those records was a tedious and grinding one. In order to help his father with the endless calculations required, the 18-year-old Pascal built the first of a series of mechanical calculators, capable of addition and subtraction, which he developed and refined over the following decade. There was a prior abortive attempt by Wilhelm Schickard in Germany in the 1620s to build a mechanical calculator, but Pascal's machine was probably the first properly functional calculator ever built; it would be another 200 years before the study of mechanical calculation took a further jump forward, including the work of Charles Babbage and his difference engine, and eventually became modern computer engineering.

In mathematics, Pascal's role in the development of probability theory was his most influential contribution. Originally applied to gambling—as we see in this selection—his ideas, partly developed in correspondence with the French lawyer and mathematician Pierre de Fermat, have strongly influenced the development of modern economics, actuarial science, and social science, and were an important basis for Leibniz's formulation of the calculus.

In addition to his achievements in mathematics, Pascal did important work in the experimental sciences, especially on the properties of fluids and air pressure, and he created influential experiments which sought to demonstrate the then-controversial existence of a vacuum.

In 1654, when he was 31, Pascal—already dabbling with religion after the illness and death of his father and the departure of his younger sister, Jacqueline, to a convent—had an intense night-time religious vision that changed his life. He followed his sister in converting to a theological movement within Catholicism that emphasized original sin and human depravity, and hence the necessity of divine grace for salvation, as well as the doctrine of predestination, which holds that the fate of individual human souls has already been decided by God.[*] It was at this time that Pascal began his reli-

---

[*] This movement was known by its detractors as Jansenism, after the Dutch theologian Cornelius Jansen (1585–1638). It was suppressed by the French monarch, King Louis XIV, and by the mainstream of the Catholic church, including Pope Alexander VII and the Jesuits.

gious writings, though he also continued his mathematical work.* During this period he was also increasingly plagued by painful poor health—based on an autopsy performed after his death, it's clear he had a brain lesion, but it is speculated that he may also have had both tuberculosis and stomach cancer—and he lived frugally and abstained from sensual pleasures. What he published in this period—including the *Lettres provinciales* (The Provincial Letters, 1656–57)—established Pascal's reputation as one of the greatest writers of French prose.

What Is the Structure of This Reading?

Pensées ('Thoughts') is a collection of fragments of writing that Pascal had been preparing to put together as a major defense of Christianity. He died, aged 39, before the book, his life's work, could be completed. Over the centuries since his death several editors and translators have published different arrangements of the material, but the proper order of the fragments is disputed.

The fragment reprinted here is the most well-known section of the *Pensées*, and is part of a series of thoughts where Pascal argues that we do not require certainty in order to believe in religion—and that such a certainty is unavailable because of our limited and finite understanding. It is rational to believe in God even though we cannot be certain of God's existence and nature, Pascal argues, because this is a question on which we are forced to make a choice (with major consequences for how we should live), and since we must choose an option, the rational choice is to believe in God and the Christian religion.

Some Useful Background Information

1. Although Pascal became a fervent defender of Catholicism, and was an internationally known scientist and mathematician with many aristocratic friends, he was not really a member of the establishment and many of his ideas were radical and unsettling at the time. After his conversion to a brand of Catholicism rather like his sister's

'Jansenism,' Pascal became embroiled in a public and legal battle with the powerful Jesuit order. His *Provincial Letters* contained scathing—and humorous—criticisms of Jesuit casuistry and had to be published anonymously, or Pascal was in real danger of prosecution.

2. Pascal's Wager is often described as an example of what has come to be called decision theory, which is the branch of probability theory that examines how to make decisions in situations of uncertainty. The two key concepts of decision theory are *preferences* and *prospects*: how much do you want different outcomes to occur, and how likely are those outcomes? At its simplest, combining weightings for preferences with judgments of prospects will produce an *expected value* for each possible option, and then the rational agent will choose the option with the highest expected value.

Suppose that you are considering playing a betting game where you toss a fair coin twice and if heads comes up both times you win $8, but on any other result you must pay $2. We can represent the values of the different outcomes in a table:

Option	You win	You lose
1. You bet	$8	-$2
2. You don't bet	$0	$0

Consider option 1. The probability of getting two heads is 1/4. The probability of *not* getting two heads is therefore 3/4. The expected value of choice one, betting, is therefore ($8 x 1/4) + (-$2 x 3/4) = $2 + -$1.50 = $0.50.

If you choose option 2 and don't place a bet, then you are guaranteed to neither gain nor lose money, and so your expected value is $0. The expected value of option 1 thus exceeds the expected value of option 2, so—in this simple version of decision theory—you should take the bet.

---

* Pascal also found time to inaugurate what is probably the first bus line in history, when his plan for a many-seated carriage to move passengers around Paris was implemented.

The Wager, FROM *Pensées**

§233

...We know that there is an infinite, and are ignorant of its nature. As we know it to be false that numbers are finite, it is therefore true that there is an infinity in number. But we do not know what it is. It is false that it is even, it is false that it is odd; for the addition of a unit can make no change in its nature. Yet it is a number, and every number is odd or even (this is certainly true of every finite number). So we may well know that there is a God without knowing what He is. Is there not one substantial truth, seeing there are so many things which are not the truth itself?

We know then the existence and nature of the finite, because we also are finite and have extension.† We know the existence of the infinite, and are ignorant of its nature, because it has extension like us, but not limits like us. But we know neither the existence nor the nature of God, because He has neither extension nor limits.

But by faith we know His existence; in glory‡ we shall know His nature. Now, I have already shown that we may well know the existence of a thing, without knowing its nature.

Let us now speak according to natural lights.§

If there is a God, He is infinitely incomprehensible, since, having neither parts nor limits, He has no affinity to us.¶ We are then incapable of knowing either what He is or if He is. This being so, who will dare to undertake the decision of the question? Not we, who have no affinity to Him.

Who then will blame Christians for not being able to give a reason for their belief, since they profess a religion for which they cannot give a reason? They declare, in expounding it to the world, that it is a foolishness, *stultitiam*;** and then you complain that they do not prove it! If they proved it, they would not keep their word; it is in lacking proofs, that they are not lacking in sense.†† "Yes, but although this excuses those who offer it as such,‡‡ and takes away from them the blame of putting it forward without reason, it does not excuse those who receive it." Let us then examine this point, and say, "God is, or He is not." But to which side shall we incline? Reason can decide nothing here. There is an infinite chaos which separated us. A game is being played at the extremity of this infinite distance where heads§§ or tails will turn up. What will you wager? According to reason, you can do neither the one thing nor the other; according to reason, you can defend neither of the propositions.

Do not then reprove for error those who have made a choice; for you know nothing about it. "No, but I blame them for having made, not this choice, but a choice; for again both he who chooses heads and he who chooses tails are equally at fault, they are both in the wrong. The true course is not to wager at all."

Yes; but you must wager. It is not optional. You are embarked. Which will you choose then? Let us see. Since you must choose, let us see which interests you least. You have two things to lose, the true and the good; and two things to stake, your reason and your will, your knowledge and your happiness; and your

---

* From *Pensées*, trans. W.F. Trotter (E.P. Dutton & Co., 1958).

† "We also are finite and have extension": we are limited beings with spatial boundaries.

‡ In heaven, after death.

§ "According to natural lights": in accord with the power of reasoning we all have by virtue of being human.

¶ No similarity or commonality with us.

** This is a reference to the Bible, 1 Corinthians 1:18: "For the message of the cross is foolishness to those who are perishing, but to us who are being saved it is the power of God." *Stultitiam* is Latin for being a fool.

†† "It is in lacking proofs, that they are not lacking in sense": it is by being without proof that they show that they are not without sense.

‡‡ Propose it without giving a reason.

§§ The word Pascal uses for heads is *croix*, which subtly relates the gambler's choice to the Christian message of the cross referenced just above.

nature has two things to shun, error and misery. Your reason is no more shocked in choosing one rather than the other, since you must of necessity choose. This is one point settled. But your happiness? Let us weigh the gain and the loss in wagering that God is. Let us estimate these two chances. If you gain, you gain all; if you lose, you lose nothing. Wager, then, without hesitation that He is.—"That is very fine. Yes, I must wager; but I may perhaps wager too much."—Let us see. Since there is an equal risk of gain and of loss, if you had only to gain two lives, instead of one,* you might still wager. But if there were three lives to gain, you would have to play (since you are under the necessity of playing), and you would be imprudent, when you are forced to play, not to chance your life† to gain three at a game where there is an equal risk of loss and gain. But there is an eternity of life and happiness. And this being so, if there were an infinity of chances, of which one only would be for you,‡ you would still be right in wagering one to win two, and you would act stupidly, being obliged to play, by refusing to stake one life against three at a game in which out of an infinity of chances there is one for you, if there were an infinity of an infinitely happy life to gain. But there is here an infinity of an infinitely happy life to gain, a chance of gain against a finite number of chances of loss, and what you stake is finite. It is all divided;§ wherever the infinite is and there is not an infinity of chances of loss against that of gain, there is no time to hesitate, you must give all. And thus, when one is forced to play, he must renounce reason to preserve his life, rather than risk it for infinite gain, as likely to happen as the loss of nothingness.¶

For it is no use to say it is uncertain if we will gain, and it is certain that we risk, and that the infinite distance between the *certainty* of what is staked and the *uncertainty* of what will be gained, equals the finite good which is certainly staked against the uncertain infinite. It is not so, as every player stakes a certainty to gain an uncertainty, and yet he stakes a finite certainty to gain a finite uncertainty, without transgressing against reason. There is not an infinite distance between the certainty staked and the uncertainty of the gain; that is untrue. In truth, there is an infinity between the certainty of gain and the certainty of loss. But the uncertainty of the gain is proportioned to the certainty of the stake according to the proportion of the chances of gain and loss. Hence it comes that, if there are as many risks on one side as on the other, the course is to play even;** and then the certainty of the stake is equal to the uncertainty of the gain, so far is it from fact that there is an infinite distance between them. And so our proposition is of infinite force, when there is the finite to stake in a game where there are equal risks of gain and of loss, and the infinite to gain. This is demonstrable; and if men are capable of any truths, this is one.

"I confess it, I admit it. But, still, is there no means of seeing the faces of the cards?"—Yes, Scripture and the rest, etc. "Yes, but I have my hands tied and my mouth closed; I am forced to wager, and am not free. I am not released, and am so made that I cannot believe.†† What, then, would you have me do?"

True. But at least learn your inability to believe, since reason brings you to this, and yet you cannot believe.‡‡ Endeavour then to convince yourself, not by increase of proofs of God, but by the abatement

---

* "To gain two lives, instead of one": to stand to win two lives instead of one.
† To bet your life.
‡ "If there were an infinity of chances, of which one only would be for you": even if there were an infinite number of outcomes where you lose and only one where you win.
§ It is already mathematically determined.
¶ "Infinite gain, as likely to happen as the loss of nothingness": an infinite gain which is just as likely to happen as a loss which (by comparison) amounts to nothing.
** "The course is to play even": the odds are even.
†† "I am not released, and am so made that I cannot believe": I am not free to choose (what I believe) and I am built in such a way that I cannot believe in God.
‡‡ "But at least learn your inability to believe, since reason brings you to this, and yet you cannot believe": but at least realize that if you can't believe it is not because reason prevents you, since it doesn't (but because your emotions or prejudices do).

of your passions. You would like to attain faith, and do not know the way; you would like to cure yourself of unbelief, and ask the remedy for it. Learn of those who have been bound like you, and who now stake all their possessions.* These are people who know the way which you would follow, and who are cured of an ill of which you would be cured. Follow the way by which they began; by acting as if they believed, taking the holy water, having masses said, etc. Even this will naturally make you believe, and deaden your acuteness.†—"But this is what I am afraid of."—And why? What have you to lose?

But to show you that this leads you there, it is this which will lessen the passions, which are your stumbling-blocks.

The end of this discourse.—Now, what harm will befall you in taking this side? You will be faithful, honest, humble, grateful, generous, a sincere friend, truthful. Certainly you will not have those poisonous pleasures, glory and luxury; but will you not have others? I will tell you that you will thereby gain in this life, and that, at each step you take on this road, you will see so great certainty of gain, so much nothingness in what you risk, that you will at last recognise that you have wagered for something certain and infinite, for which you have given nothing.

"Ah! This discourse transports me, charms me," etc.

If this discourse pleases you and seems impressive, know that it is made by a man who has knelt, both before and after it, in prayer to that Being, infinite and without parts,‡ before whom he lays all he has, for you also to lay before Him all you have for your own good and for His glory, that so strength may be given to lowliness.

...

§277

The heart has its reasons, which reason does not know. We feel it in a thousand things. I say that the heart naturally loves the Universal Being, and also itself naturally, according as it gives itself to them; and it hardens itself against one or the other at its will. You have rejected the one, and kept the other. Is it by reason that you love yourself? ∎

Suggestions for Critical Reflection

1. "[Y]ou must wager. It is not optional." Why do you think Pascal insists on this? Is he right?

2. "And so our proposition is of infinite force, when there is the finite to stake in a game where there are equal risks of gain and of loss, and the infinite to gain. This is demonstrable; and if men are capable of any truths, this is one." This is arguably the heart of Pascal's Wager: what exactly is he saying here? How persuasive is it?

3. Some may object that, while it is all very well to say that we should choose to believe in God, beliefs are not the sort of thing we can simply choose to have or not have. This kind of objection has been made to Pascal's Wager many times. How adequately do you think he deals with the problem? Imagine that somebody offered you $100 if you would sincerely believe that all the dogs and cats on earth were controlled by aliens on the planet Zarkon. Could you sincerely believe it? Suppose we can bring ourselves to believe in something, by a process other than reasoning (i.e., by a process other than relying on evidence or argument): how authentic would such a belief be?

4. Pascal was a scientist and a mathematician, and one of the key figures in the development of the scientific method; in science, reason is supreme in the pursuit of truth and the emotions or presumptions have no role. Yet in the *Pensées* he argues (using

---

* "Stake all their possessions": wager all they have.

† Pascal uses the word *abêtira*, which implies becoming more like an unthinking, instinctive animal than a human being, who is separated from the beasts by possessing the (in this case unhelpful) capacity to reason.

‡ Indivisible.

reason) that reason has no role in the apprehension of religious truth. This can seem to have an air of paradox. Is it in fact paradoxical? What do you think is going on here?

5. Although Pascal's Wager can seem fairly straightforward as an argument, there is disagreement among commentators as to what it is actually supposed to show. Is it intended to establish that *the only rational option* is to bet that God exists (to choose to be religious)? Or is it really meant to show that logical reasoning *cannot support either* faith or a lack of faith and that therefore, since there is no good reason to choose one over the other, we need some other principle to allow us to decide (since we have no choice except to decide)? Think carefully about the difference between these two interpretations. Which do you think is the right one? Irrespective of what Pascal actually intended, which do you think is the more plausible argument?

6. Suppose Pascal persuades us that we should choose to be religious. Which religion should you choose, and how would you make this decision?

7. What are the limits of reason?

WILLIAM K. CLIFFORD

The Ethics of Belief

Who Was William Clifford?

William Kingdon Clifford (1845–79) was an English mathematician and philosopher. Professor of mathematics at Trinity College, Cambridge, and then at University College London, he is credited with formalizing the field of geometric algebra (a system of transformations for geometric objects) and was also the first to suggest that gravitation might be an expression of spatial geometry— preceding Einstein by more than a quarter of a century. As a philosopher his commitment to clarity of thought, and his sense that it was a public duty to combat error and obscurantism, led him to clash with certain aspects of religious feeling. Darwin's ground-shaking work on evolution was still fresh and newly shocking in the 1870s, and was widely perceived to be inconsistent with Christian theology; Clifford was thus writing in an era in which the modern science seemed to be at odds with religion, and he was perceived to be a notorious and outspoken opponent of spirituality. Clifford was indeed an enemy of dogmatic religion, and he also held ethical and metaphysical views that might be seen to be in tension with some religious views, and (as the essay reprinted here demonstrates) fiercely attacked the role of 'blind faith' in belief.*

In both ethics and metaphysics, Clifford—in the spirit of Darwin—was a sort of naturalist and evolutionist. He defended the view that every elementary piece of matter has a mental aspect—indeed, is essentially "mind-stuff" as he put it—and that these atoms of proto-mentality combine together to make glimmerings of sentience in simpler organisms and, eventually, human consciousness. In this way, minds can be seen as the natural result of increasing complexity in the organization of an underlying (quasi-mental) substance rather than something radically new in nature. Ethically, Clifford postulated the existence of a "tribal self" that developed over historical time, as societies changed and the moral law developed, and is expressed in each individual as a conscience that prescribes behaviors that contribute to the good of the whole 'tribe'. One of his philosophical concerns was to fight against the distortion of this moral voice by the improper demands of dogmatic and priest-ridden religion, which he saw as putting the claims of a particular sect above those of society in general. In his 1877 essay "The Ethics of Religion," Clifford proclaimed that "if men were no better than their religions, the world would be a hell, indeed."

Clifford was born in Exeter and educated at Kings College London and Cambridge. In his mid-twenties he took part in an expedition to Italy to observe a solar eclipse, where he survived a shipwreck on the coast of Sicily. In 1875 he married Lucy Lane, who would become a prominent novelist and journalist. He suffered a breakdown, possibly brought on by overwork, in 1876; eventually recovering, he was able to resume his work, but his health remained poor and he died in 1879 of tuberculosis, at the age of only 33.

By all accounts, Clifford was a somewhat eccentric but brilliant person. He was a highly original thinker, with views that were often contentious or ahead of their time, but he was a very popular teacher, a well-respected scholar, and a sociable person who enjoyed parties and (like his counterpart Charles Dodgson, a.k.a. Lewis Carroll) wrote and published fairy stories for children. The contemporary philosopher Edward Clodd wrote in his book *Memories* (1916) that at Clifford's gatherings "you were sure to meet some one worth the knowing. There was no smart set to fill their empty time and waste yours

---

*   At the time Clifford was a student and then a Fellow there, all Cambridge students had to sign the Thirty-nine Articles of Protestant Faith each year affirming their allegiance to the Church of England. Clifford signed in 1863 and 1864, fretted over it but eventually signed in 1865, and then refused to sign in 1866. This should have required his expulsion from the university, but for reasons that are unclear this did not happen and he was elected to a Fellowship at Trinity College in 1868.

in inane gossip; no prigs to irritate you with their affectation; and no pedants to bore you with their academic vagueness, but just a company of sane and healthy men and women, gentle and simple, who wanted to meet one another and have a full, free talk."

What Is the Structure of This Reading?

In Part I, Clifford argues for his famous conclusion that "it is wrong always, everywhere, and for anyone, to believe anything upon insufficient evidence." In the second part he argues that this stance—a philosophical position which has come to be called 'evidentialism'—does not lead to radical skepticism or to moral anarchy. Clifford goes on to make a fairly lengthy examination, not included in this reading, of "under what circumstances it is lawful to believe on the testimony of others." (This discussion deals with cases discussed by William James in the next reading of this book: the conflicting testimony of religious prophets such as Mohammed and Buddha, as well as the examples of a chemist and an Arctic explorer. Clifford argues that the testimony of an individual has weight only insofar as "there are reasonable grounds for supposing that he knew the truth of what he was saying"—and Clifford argues that supernatural or universal claims can never be justified in this way.) In the final section of the essay, Clifford discusses "when and why we may believe that which goes beyond our own experience, or even beyond the experience of mankind."

A Common Misconception

Clifford's conclusion that it is always wrong to believe anything without sufficient evidence applies not only to cases where the available evidence underdetermines a particular conclusion, but also requires us as individuals to *seek out* the evidence on an issue before we reach a conclusion. We should not allow ourselves to believe something based on inadequate evidence, and the evidence we have might be inadequate either because it is a difficult question that is hard to answer conclusively, or because we have been lazy or biased in uncovering and assessing the evidence that does exist.

The Ethics of Belief *

I. The Duty of Inquiry

A shipowner was about to send to sea an emigrant-ship.† He knew that she was old, and not overwell built at the first; that she had seen many seas and climes, and often had needed repairs. Doubts had been suggested to him that possibly she was not seaworthy. These doubts preyed upon his mind, and made him unhappy; he thought that perhaps he ought to have her thoroughly overhauled and refitted, even though this should put him to great expense. Before the ship sailed, however, he succeeded in overcoming these melancholy reflections. He said to himself that she had gone safely through so many voyages and weathered so many storms that it was idle to suppose she would not come safely home from this trip also. He would put his trust in Providence, which could hardly fail to protect all these unhappy families that were leaving their fatherland to seek for better times elsewhere. He would dismiss from his mind all ungenerous suspicions about the honesty of builders and contractors. In such ways he acquired a sincere and comfortable conviction that his vessel was thoroughly safe and seaworthy; he watched her departure with a light heart, and benevolent wishes

---

* This essay was published in *Contemporary Review* 29 (1877), 289–309, and reprinted in Clifford's *Lectures and Essays* (1879).

† That is, a sailing ship carrying emigrants to start new lives in another country; a common example at the time Clifford was writing would be emigrants from Europe, particularly Germany or Ireland, to the United States.

for the success of the exiles in their strange new home that was to be; and he got his insurance-money when she went down in mid-ocean and told no tales.

What shall we say of him? Surely this, that he was verily guilty of the death of those men. It is admitted that he did sincerely believe in the soundness of his ship; but the sincerity of his conviction can in no wise help him, because *he had no right to believe on such evidence as was before him.* He had acquired his belief not by honestly earning it in patient investigation, but by stifling his doubts. And although in the end he may have felt so sure about it that he could not think otherwise, yet inasmuch as he had knowingly and willingly worked himself into that frame of mind, he must be held responsible for it.

Let us alter the case a little, and suppose that the ship was not unsound after all; that she made her voyage safely, and many others after it. Will that diminish the guilt of her owner? Not one jot. When an action is once done, it is right or wrong for ever; no accidental failure of its good or evil fruits* can possibly alter that. The man would not have been innocent, he would only have been not found out. The question of right or wrong has to do with the origin of his belief, not the matter of it; not what it was, but how he got it; not whether it turned out to be true or false, but whether he had a right to believe on such evidence as was before him.

There was once an island in which some of the inhabitants professed a religion teaching neither the doctrine of original sin nor that of eternal punishment. A suspicion got abroad that the professors of this religion† had made use of unfair means to get their doctrines taught to children. They were accused of wresting the laws of their country in such a way as to remove children from the care of their natural and legal guardians; and even of stealing them away and keeping them concealed from their friends and relations. A certain number of men formed themselves into a society for the purpose of agitating the public about this matter. They published grave accusations against individual citizens of the highest position and character, and did all in their power to injure these citizens in their exercise of their professions. So great was the noise they made,

that a Commission was appointed to investigate the facts; but after the Commission had carefully inquired into all the evidence that could be got, it appeared that the accused were innocent. Not only had they been accused on insufficient evidence, but the evidence of their innocence was such as the agitators might easily have obtained, if they had attempted a fair inquiry. After these disclosures the inhabitants of that country looked upon the members of the agitating society, not only as persons whose judgment was to be distrusted, but also as no longer to be counted honourable men. For although they had sincerely and conscientiously believed in the charges they had made, *yet they had no right to believe on such evidence as was before them.* Their sincere convictions, instead of being honestly earned by patient inquiring, were stolen by listening to the voice of prejudice and passion.

Let us vary this case also, and suppose, other things remaining as before, that a still more accurate investigation proved the accused to have been really guilty. Would this make any difference in the guilt of the accusers? Clearly not; the question is not whether their belief was true or false, but whether they entertained it on wrong grounds. They would no doubt say, "Now you see that we were right after all; next time perhaps you will believe us." And they might be believed, but they would not thereby become honourable men. They would not be innocent, they would only be not found out. Every one of them, if he chose to examine himself *in foro conscientiae,*‡ would know that he had acquired and nourished a belief, when he had no right to believe on such evidence as was before him; and therein he would know that he had done a wrong thing....

In the two supposed cases which have been considered, it has been judged wrong to believe on insufficient evidence, or to nourish belief by suppressing doubts and avoiding investigation. The reason of this judgment is not far to seek: it is that in both these cases the belief held by one man was of great importance to other men. But forasmuch as no belief held by one man, however seemingly trivial the belief, and however obscure the believer, is ever actually insignificant or without its effect on the fate of mankind,

---

* "Its good or evil fruits": the good or bad things that happen because of it.
† People who profess—affirm their allegiance to—the religion.
‡ *In foro conscientiae* is Latin for "before the tribunal of one's personal conscience."

we have no choice but to extend our judgment to all cases of belief whatever. Belief, that sacred faculty which prompts the decisions of our will, and knits into harmonious working all the compacted energies of our being, is ours not for ourselves but for humanity. It is rightly used on truths which have been established by long experience and waiting toil, and which have stood in the fierce light of free and fearless questioning. Then it helps to bind men together, and to strengthen and direct their common action. It is desecrated when given to unproved and unquestioned statements, for the solace and private pleasure of the believer; to add a tinsel splendour* to the plain straight road of our life and display a bright mirage beyond it; or even to drown the common sorrows of our kind by a self-deception which allows them not only to cast down, but also to degrade us. Whoso would deserve well of his fellows in this matter will guard the purity of his beliefs with a very fanaticism of jealous care, lest at any time it should rest on an unworthy object, and catch a stain which can never be wiped away.

It is not only the leader of men, statesmen, philosopher, or poet, that owes this bounden duty to mankind. Every rustic who delivers in the village alehouse his slow, infrequent sentences, may help to kill or keep alive the fatal superstitions which clog his race. Every hard-worked wife of an artisan may transmit to her children beliefs which shall knit society together, or rend it in pieces. No simplicity of mind, no obscurity of station, can escape the universal duty of questioning all that we believe.

It is true that this duty is a hard one, and the doubt which comes out of it is often a very bitter thing. It leaves us bare and powerless where we thought that we were safe and strong. To know all about anything is to know how to deal with it under all circumstances. We feel much happier and more secure when we think we know precisely what to do, no matter what happens, than when we have lost our way and do not know where to turn. And if we have supposed ourselves to know all about anything, and to be capable of doing what is fit in regard to it, we naturally do not like to find that we are really ignorant and powerless, that we

have to begin again at the beginning, and try to learn what the thing is and how it is to be dealt with—if indeed anything can be learnt about it. It is the sense of power attached to a sense of knowledge that makes men desirous of believing, and afraid of doubting.

This sense of power is the highest and best of pleasures when the belief on which it is founded is a true belief, and has been fairly earned by investigation. For then we may justly feel that it is common property, and holds good for others as well as for ourselves. Then we may be glad, not that *I* have learned secrets by which I am safer and stronger, but that *we men* have got mastery over more of the world; and we shall be strong, not for ourselves but in the name of Man and his strength. But if the belief has been accepted on insufficient evidence, the pleasure is a stolen one. Not only does it deceive ourselves by giving us a sense of power which we do not really possess, but it is sinful, because it is stolen in defiance of our duty to mankind. That duty is to guard ourselves from such beliefs as from pestilence,† which may shortly master our own body and then spread to the rest of the town. What would be thought of one who, for the sake of a sweet fruit, should deliberately run the risk of bringing a plague upon his family and his neighbours?

And, as in other such cases, it is not the risk only which has to be considered; for a bad action is always bad at the time when it is done, no matter what happens afterwards. Every time we let ourselves believe for unworthy reasons, we weaken our powers of self-control, of doubting, of judicially and fairly weighing evidence. We all suffer severely enough from the maintenance and support of false beliefs and the fatally wrong actions which they lead to, and the evil born when one such belief is entertained is great and wide. But a greater and wider evil arises when the credulous‡ character is maintained and supported, when a habit of believing for unworthy reasons is fostered and made permanent. If I steal money from any person, there may be no harm done from the mere transfer of possession; he may not feel the loss, or it may prevent him from using the money badly. But I cannot help doing this great wrong towards Man, that I make myself

---

* A superficial or misleading appearance of value.
† Infectious disease.
‡ Too ready to believe things on inadequate evidence; gullible.

dishonest. What hurts society is not that it should lose its property, but that it should become a den of thieves, for then it must cease to be society. This is why we ought not to do evil, that good may come; for at any rate this great evil has come, that we have done evil and are made wicked thereby. In like manner, if I let myself believe anything on insufficient evidence, there may be no great harm done by the mere belief; it may be true after all, or I may never have occasion to exhibit it in outward acts. But I cannot help doing this great wrong towards Man, that I make myself credulous. The danger to society is not merely that it should believe wrong things, though that is great enough; but that it should become credulous, and lose the habit of testing things and inquiring into them; for then it must sink back into savagery.

The harm which is done by credulity in a man is not confined to the fostering of a credulous character in others, and consequent support of false beliefs. Habitual want of care about what I believe leads to habitual want of care in others about the truth of what is told to me. Men speak the truth to one another when each reveres the truth in his own mind and in the other's mind; but how shall my friend revere the truth in my mind when I myself am careless about it, when I believe things because I want to believe them, and because they are comforting and pleasant? Will he not learn to cry, "Peace," to me, when there is no peace?* By such a course I shall surround myself with a thick atmosphere of falsehood and fraud, and in that I must live. It may matter little to me, in my cloud-castle of sweet illusions and darling lies; but it matters much to Man that I have made my neighbours ready to deceive. The credulous man is father to the liar and the cheat; he lives in the bosom of this his family, and it is no marvel if he should become even as they are. So closely are our duties knit together, that whoso shall keep the whole law, and yet offend in one point, he is guilty of all.

To sum up: it is wrong always, everywhere, and for anyone, to believe anything upon insufficient evidence.

If a man, holding a belief which he was taught in childhood or persuaded of afterwards, keeps down and pushes away any doubts which arise about it in his mind, purposely avoids the reading of books and the company of men that call into question or discuss it, and regards as impious those questions which cannot easily be asked without disturbing it—the life of that man is one long sin against mankind....

Inquiry into the evidence of a doctrine is not to be made once for all, and then taken as finally settled. It is never lawful to stifle a doubt; for either it can be honestly answered by means of the inquiry already made, or else it proves that the inquiry was not complete.

"But," says one, "I am a busy man; I have no time for the long course of study which would be necessary to make me in any degree a competent judge of certain questions, or even able to understand the nature of the arguments."

Then he should have no time to believe.

II. The Weight of Authority

Are we then to become universal sceptics, doubting everything, afraid always to put one foot before the other until we have personally tested the firmness of the road? Are we to deprive ourselves of the help and guidance of that vast body of knowledge which is daily growing upon the world, because neither we nor any other one person can possibly test a hundredth part of it by immediate experiment or observation, and because it would not be completely proved if we did? Shall we steal and tell lies because we have had no personal experience wide enough to justify the belief that it is wrong to do so?

There is no practical danger that such consequences will ever follow from scrupulous care and self-control in the matter of belief. Those men who have most nearly done their duty in this respect have found that certain great principles, and these most fitted for the guidance of life, have stood out more and more clearly in proportion to the care and honesty with which they were tested, and have acquired in this way a practical certainty. The beliefs about right and wrong which guide our actions in dealing with men in society, and the beliefs about physical nature which guide our actions in dealing with animate and

---

* An allusion to the Bible, Jeremiah 6:14 and 8:11: "They have healed the wound of my people lightly, saying, 'Peace, peace,' when there is no peace."

inanimate bodies, these never suffer from investigation; they can take care of themselves, without being propped up by "acts of faith," the clamour of paid advocates, or the suppression of contrary evidence. Moreover there are many cases in which it is our duty to act upon probabilities, although the evidence is not such as to justify present belief; because it is precisely by such action, and by observation of its fruits, that evidence is got which may justify future belief. So that we have no reason to fear lest a habit of conscientious inquiry should paralyze the actions of our daily life....

What shall we say of that authority, more venerable and august than any individual witness, the time-honoured tradition of the human race? An atmosphere of beliefs and conceptions has been formed by the labours and struggles of our forefathers, which enables us to breathe amid the various and complex circumstances of our life. It is around and about us and within us; we cannot think except in the forms and processes of thought which it supplies. Is it possible to doubt and to test it? and if possible, is it right?

We shall find reason to answer that it is not only possible and right, but our bounden duty; that the main purpose of the tradition itself is to supply us with the means of asking questions, of testing and inquiring into things; that if we misuse it, and take it as a collection of cut-and-dried statements to be accepted without further inquiry, we are not only injuring ourselves here, but, by refusing to do our part towards the building up of the fabric which shall be inherited by our children, we are tending to cut off ourselves and our race from the human line....

In regard, then, to the sacred tradition of humanity, we learn that it consists, not in propositions or statements which are to be accepted and believed on the authority of the tradition, but in questions rightly asked, in conceptions which enable us to ask further questions, and in methods of answering questions. The value of all these things depends on their being tested day by day. The very sacredness of the precious deposit imposes upon us the duty and the responsibility of testing it, of purifying and enlarging it to the utmost of our power. He who makes use of its results to stifle his own doubts, or to hamper the inquiry of others, is guilty of a sacrilege which centuries shall never be able to blot out. When the labours and questionings of honest and brave men shall have built up the fabric of known truth to a glory which we in this generation can neither hope for nor imagine, in that pure and holy temple he shall have no part nor lot, but his name and his works shall be cast out into the darkness of oblivion for ever.

III. *The Limits of Inference*

The question, in what cases we may believe that which goes beyond our experience, is a very large and delicate one, extending to the whole range of scientific method, and requiring a considerable increase in the application of it before it can be answered with anything approaching to completeness. But one rule, lying on the threshold of the subject, of extreme simplicity and vast practical importance, may here be touched upon and shortly laid down.

A little reflection will show us that every belief, even the simplest and most fundamental, goes beyond experience when regarded as a guide to our actions. A burnt child dreads the fire, because it believes that the fire will burn it to-day just as it did yesterday; but this belief goes beyond experience, and assumes that the unknown fire of to-day is like the known fire of yesterday. Even the belief that the child was burnt yesterday goes beyond *present* experience, which contains only the memory of a burning, and not the burning itself; it assumes, therefore, that this memory is trustworthy, although we know that a memory may often be mistaken. But if it is to be used as a guide to action, as a hint of what the future is to be, it must assume something about that future, namely, that it will be consistent with the supposition that the burning really took place yesterday; which is going beyond experience. Even the fundamental "I am," which cannot be doubted,* is no guide to action until it takes to itself "I shall be," which goes beyond experience. The question is not, therefore, "May we believe what goes beyond experience?" for this is involved in the very nature of belief; but "How far and in what manner may we add to our experience in forming our beliefs?"

And an answer, of utter simplicity and universality, is suggested by the example we have taken: a burnt

---

* See Descartes's *Meditations* elsewhere in this book.

child dreads the fire. We may go beyond experience by assuming that what we do not know is like what we do know; or, in other words, we may add to our experience on the assumption of a uniformity in nature. What this uniformity precisely is, how we grow in the knowledge of it from generation to generation, these are questions which for the present we lay aside, being content to examine two instances which may serve to make plainer the nature of the rule.

From certain observations made with the spectroscope, we infer the existence of hydrogen in the sun. By looking into the spectroscope when the sun is shining on its slit, we see certain definite bright lines: and experiments made upon bodies on the earth have taught us that when these bright lines are seen hydrogen is the source of them. We assume, then, that the unknown bright lines in the sun are like the known bright lines of the laboratory, and that hydrogen in the sun behaves as hydrogen under similar circumstances would behave on the earth.

But are we not trusting our spectroscope too much? Surely, having found it to be trustworthy for terrestrial substances, where its statements can be verified by man, we are justified in accepting its testimony in other like cases; but not when it gives us information about things in the sun, where its testimony cannot be directly verified by man?

Certainly, we want to know a little more before this inference can be justified; and fortunately we do know this. The spectroscope testifies to exactly the same thing in the two cases; namely, that light-vibrations of a certain rate are being sent through it. Its construction is such that if it were wrong about this in one case, it would be wrong in the other. When we come to look into the matter, we find that we have really assumed the matter of the sun to be like the matter of the earth, made up of a certain number of distinct substances; and that each of these, when very hot, has a distinct rate of vibration, by which it may be recognized and singled out from the rest. But this is the kind of assumption which we are justified in using when we add to our experience. It is an assumption of uniformity in nature, and can only be checked by comparison with many similar assumptions which we have to make in other such cases.

But is this a true belief, of the existence of hydrogen in the sun? Can it help in the right guidance of human action?

Certainly not, if it is accepted on unworthy grounds, and without some understanding of the process by which it is got at. But when this process is taken in as the ground of the belief, it becomes a very serious and practical matter. For if there is no hydrogen in the sun, the spectroscope—that is to say, the measurement of rates of vibration—must be an uncertain guide in recognizing different substances; and consequently it ought not to be used in chemical analysis—in assaying, for example—to the great saving of time, trouble, and money. Whereas the acceptance of the spectroscopic method as trustworthy has enriched us not only with new metals, which is a great thing, but with new processes of investigation, which is vastly greater.

For another example, let us consider the way in which we infer the truth of an historical event—say the siege of Syracuse in the Peloponnesian war.* Our experience is that manuscripts exist which are said to be and which call themselves manuscripts of the history of Thucydides;† that in other manuscripts, stated to be by later historians, he is described as living during the time of the war; and that books, supposed to date from the revival of learning, tell us how these manuscripts had been preserved and were then acquired. We find also that men do not, as a rule, forge books and histories without a special motive; we assume that in this respect men in the past were like men in the present; and we observe that in this case no special motive was present. That is, we add to our experience on the assumption of a uniformity in the characters of men. Because our knowledge of this uniformity is far less complete and exact than our knowledge of that which obtains in physics, inferences of the historical kind are more precarious and less exact than inferences in many other sciences.

---

* The final phase of the Peloponnesian War (431–404 BCE) began when Athens launched a failed raid against Syracuse, eventually leading to surrender to Sparta.

† Thucydides (c. 460–c. 400 BCE) was an Athenian general and chronicler of the war, from whom most of the surviving contemporary accounts have come.

But if there is any special reason to suspect the character of the persons who wrote or transmitted certain books, the case becomes altered. If a group of documents give internal evidence that they were produced among people who forged books in the names of others, and who, in describing events, suppressed those things which did not suit them, while they amplified such as did suit them; who not only committed these crimes, but gloried in them as proofs of humility and zeal; then we must say that upon such documents no true historical inference can be founded, but only unsatisfactory conjecture.

We may, then, add to our experience on the assumption of a uniformity in nature; we may fill in our picture of what is and has been, as experience gives it us, in such a way as to make the whole consistent with this uniformity. And practically demonstrative inference—that which gives us a right to believe in the result of it—is a clear showing that in no other way than by the truth of this result can the uniformity of nature be saved.

No evidence, therefore, can justify us in believing the truth of a statement which is contrary to, or outside of, the uniformity of nature. If our experience is such that it cannot be filled up consistently with uniformity, all we have a right to conclude is that there is something wrong somewhere; but the possibility of inference is taken away; we must rest in our experience, and not go beyond it at all. If an event really happened which was not a part of the uniformity of nature, it would have two properties: no evidence could give the right to believe it to any except those whose actual experience it was; and no inference worthy of belief could be founded upon it at all.

Are we then bound to believe that nature is absolutely and universally uniform? Certainly not; we have no right to believe anything of this kind. The rule only tells us that in forming beliefs which go beyond our experience, we may make the assumption that nature is practically uniform so far as we are concerned. Within the range of human action and verification, we may form, by help of this assumption, actual beliefs; beyond it, only those hypotheses which serve for the more accurate asking of questions.

To sum up:—

We may believe what goes beyond our experience, only when it is inferred from that experience by the assumption that what we do not know is like what we know.

We may believe the statement of another person, when there is reasonable ground for supposing that he knows the matter of which he speaks, and that he is speaking the truth so far as he knows it.

It is wrong in all cases to believe on insufficient evidence; and where it is presumption* to doubt and to investigate, there it is worse than presumption to believe. ■

Suggestions for Critical Reflection

1. "But forasmuch as no belief held by one man, however seemingly trivial the belief, and however obscure the believer, is ever actually insignificant or without its effect on the fate of mankind, we have no choice but to extend our judgment to all cases of belief whatever." How plausible is this claim of Clifford's? If it is not plausible, or if things are more complicated than Clifford allows here, what effect does this have on his overall argument and its conclusion?

2. Clifford argues that our duty to believe only on the basis of sufficient evidence is a duty not only to ourselves but to our community and, indeed, to all of humanity. Why do you think he argues for this stronger conclusion? Would it have been sufficient, or even possible, for him to have argued for a weaker one?

3. "[A] bad action is always bad at the time when it is done, no matter what happens afterwards." Is it? Why is this important to Clifford's argument do you think? If you have studied some ethical theory you

---

*   Arrogance, overstepping the bounds of what is appropriate.

might want to consider what sort of general value theory Clifford is committed to: is he a consequentialist, a deontologist, a virtue theorist, or something else? (For instance, one view might be that he is a consequentialist but restricts his concern to a particular *sort* of consequence.)

4. Clifford raises a high bar for belief. In section II of this essay, he addresses the question of whether this bar is impractically high and argues that it is not. Is he right?

5. "There are many cases in which it is our duty to act upon probabilities, although the evidence is not such as to justify present belief." When Clifford says this, is he being consistent with the rest of his position? What significance do you think this addition has to his view?

6. In part III of his essay, Clifford appeals to "a uniformity in nature" as part of his justification for our believing things that go beyond our own experience. How well justified is this assumption itself? If it is not well justified, how much of a problem is this for Clifford? If you have read the David Hume reading on induction in the Philosophy of Science section of this book you might consider his critique of this assumption.

7. Clifford's position in this essay is typically contrasted with William James's response in "The Will to Believe" (see the next reading). Once you have read James's essay, you should carefully consider what exactly these two thinkers disagree about (and whether there are, perhaps surprising, things about which they agree; e.g., the pragmatic nature of belief?), and make your own assessment of which position is the more plausible.

WILLIAM JAMES

The Will to Believe

Who Was William James?

William James was a popular essayist, one of the philosophical originators of pragmatism (often considered the first uniquely American philosophy), and one of the founders of academic psychology in America. He was born in 1842 in a New York hotel room. His family lived on a substantial inheritance from William's paternal grandfather (after whom he was named), and his father spent his time in the independent study of theology. Shortly after the birth of William's brother Henry—who was to become a famous novelist, author of *The Portrait of a Lady* and *The Bostonians*—the family moved to Europe, living in London, Paris, and Windsor. There, while William was still a young boy, his father had a violent nervous breakdown and found solace in religious mysticism and the "theosophy" of Emanuel Swedenborg.* The family sailed back to New York in 1847, only to return to Europe seven years later in search of a good education for the children: William was educated at a multilingual boarding school near Geneva, the Collège Impérial at Boulogne, and finally the University of Geneva.

As a young man, James was interested in science and painting. Back in Newport, Rhode Island, he embarked on a career as a painter, but quickly switched to the study of chemistry at Harvard in 1861. By then James had already begun his life-long habit of ingesting various, often hallucinogenic, chemicals (such as chloral hydrate, amyl nitrate, or mescaline) out of a scientific interest to see what effect they might have on him. After helping to care for his younger brother Wilky, badly wounded during the Civil War (during and after which the James family made attempts to help the black slaves of the South), James entered Harvard Medical School

in 1864. He took part in a scientific expedition to Brazil the following year, but was badly seasick on the trip out and suffered temporary blindness from catching a mild form of smallpox in Rio de Janeiro (he suffered from intermittent trouble with his eyes for the rest of his life). Though he decided at that point that he was "cut out for a speculative rather than an active life," he stayed with the expedition as it sailed up the Amazon. Back in Massachusetts, he continued to suffer from ill health and depression, and contemplated suicide.

He spent the period between 1867 and 1868 studying experimental psychology in Germany, and returned to Harvard to take and pass his examination for an M.D. but then sank into black depression, including bouts of insomnia and nervousness. He resolved never to marry for fear of passing mental illness onto his children. One of the causes of his depression in these years was his inability either to convince himself that modern science had not proved that free will was an illusion, or to resign himself to living in a deterministic, mechanical universe. Famously, in 1870, he apparently decided to shake off this particular worry and simply decided to believe in free will *despite* all the evidence against it: he wrote in his diary, "my first act of free will shall be to believe in free will."† Nevertheless, in 1872 James had a "crisis" which probably resembled that which had changed his father's life 28 years earlier: "Suddenly there fell upon me without any warning, just as if it came out of the darkness, a horrible fear of my own existence.... I became a mass of quivering fear. After this the universe was changed for me altogether...."‡

Probably a psychological lifeline for James at this point was the offer in 1873 to teach comparative anatomy and physiology at Harvard (though he hesitated over

---

* Swedenborg (1688–1772) was a Swedish scientist and mystic, an important influence on the artist William Blake and poet W.B. Yeats, as well as on the James family.
† William James, "Diary" for April 30th, 1870, in *The Letters of William James*, ed. Henry James, Jr. (Atlantic Monthly Press, 1920), Volume I, 147–48.
‡ William James, *The Varieties of Religious Experience* (1902), Lectures VI and VII. In William James, *The Essential Writings*, ed. Bruce Wilshire (State University of New York Press, 1984), 232.

accepting it, and delayed taking up the appointment for a year due to ill health). By 1877 James was a permanent professor of physiology at Harvard, though he lectured less on physiology than on the relatively new subject of psychology under the auspices of the philosophy department. In 1878 he married Alice Gibbens; "I have found in marriage a calm and repose I never knew before." His first son, Harry, was born the following year.

In 1889 he became the first Alford Professor of Psychology at Harvard University, and the next year he finally completed his first major work, *The Principles of Psychology* (he had signed the book contract in 1878). This book, a modern-day classic, met with instant acclaim. In 1897 he published *The Will to Believe, and Other Essays in Popular Psychology* and the next year, *Human Immortality: Two Supposed Objections to the Doctrine*, then, in 1899, one of his most popular books during his own lifetime, *Talks to Teachers on Psychology, and to Students on Some of Life's Ideals*. The 1902 publication of *The Varieties of Religious Experience* met with international praise and sales that substantially boosted James's income.

Throughout his life James's work was dogged by persistent health problems and nervous exhaustion, and in 1903 he tried to resign from Harvard but was persuaded to stay with a reduced teaching load. In 1906 James took a temporary appointment at Stanford University in California, but it was cut short by the great San Francisco earthquake of that year (which James witnessed, and apparently found quite exhilarating). In 1907 he finally retired from Harvard and published *Pragmatism: A New Name for Some Old Ways of Thinking*; this is arguably the most famous single work of American philosophy. That book was followed by *A Pluralistic Universe*, *The Meaning of Truth*, and the posthumous *Some Problems in Philosophy*, all of which try to develop and defend James's overall philosophical framework. James died of a chronic heart condition at his farmhouse in New Hampshire in 1910.

What Was James's Overall Philosophical Project?

James's philosophical work, including "The Will to Believe" and his other essays on religious belief, is rooted in a general metaphysical framework that James came

to call "radical empiricism." Radical empiricism has three central elements, each of which has far-reaching philosophical implications.

First, there is James's emphasis on careful attention to what is "directly experienced." He thought philosophers and psychologists had generally failed to look carefully enough at what is actually delivered in experience, and to counteract this he defended what is called "the introspective method" in psychology—essentially, learning to pay close attention to the contents of one's own thought. James argued, as early as *The Principles of Psychology*, that philosophers have tended to read too much into what we experience: for example, he argued (like David Hume) that there is no soul or ego or spiritual medium of thought to be seen if we actually look inside ourselves for such a thing. On the other hand, according to James, philosophers (such as Hume) have failed to notice that there is *more* to our experience than is traditionally assumed. We do not simply undergo discrete, repeatable lumps of experience, but experience a continuous stream of thought which includes transitions and relations between the more stable 'substantive' ideas; thus "we ought to say a feeling of *and*, a feeling of *if*, a feeling of *but*, and a feeling of *by*, quite as readily as we say a feeling of *blue* or a feeling of *cold*."*

Second, James rejected the traditional duality of mind and matter. Instead he postulated "a world of pure experience." Ultimately, according to James, the universe is made up not of some kind of 'stuff' but of a huge set of 'pure experiences.' Some of these experiences make up our streams of individual consciousness and, of those, some are taken by us (on the basis of their relations with other experiences) to be 'mental' and some 'physical.'

Third, James felt that he was able, on the basis of this picture of the nature of the universe, to solve the vexing problem of the *meaning of thought* (which philosophers today call "the problem of intentionality"). The problem is this: what is it about your thoughts, your sensations, or your words that makes them *about* some particular object in the external world? What is it, for example, about the word or the thought "cow" that connects it to a certain species of large, smelly mammal? According to James, the answer is relatively simple: your sensation of the cow just is the cow. The succession of pure experiences that makes up the cow, and the sequence of pure experiences that is your stream

---

* William James, *The Principles of Psychology* (1890) (Harvard University Press, 1981), 238.

of consciousness (which is *you*) simply intersect, just as two lines can cross at a point; at that intersection is an experience that is simultaneously both thought and object of thought, mental and non-mental, you and the cow.

Our *idea* of a cow, then, is certainly *about* cows, but that 'aboutness' can now be understood in terms of the prospects for future intersections between, if you like, cow sequences and our personal autobiography. Roughly, for James, the meaning of an idea—including religious and moral ideas like *God* and *free will*—is its "cash-value" in terms of future experience. Importantly, this includes not only predictions about sensations that we might expect lie in store for us, but also the effects such an idea will have on our future behavior; how it will change *us*, and thus affect our future experience. This is the core doctrine of what James called "Pragmatism." "To attain perfect clearness in our thoughts of an object, then, we need only consider what conceivable effects of a practical kind the object may involve—what sensations we are to expect from it, and what reactions we must prepare."*

Finally, once we know how ideas get their meaning, we can ask what it is for an idea to be *true*. For James, the answer is its "workability." Given his radical empiricism and his pragmatism, truth can't possibly consist, for James, in a kind of correspondence or matching between an idea and some sort of external reality—James has rejected that whole way of talking. For an idea to be called 'true' is not for it to have some special property or value at the moment it occurs but instead it is for it to have particularly *beneficial* effects on our future conduct and our future experiences. An idea might turn out to be true because it is especially valuable for predicting scientific events (such as eclipses, for example), or its truth might lie in the way it is spiritually ennobling to all those who believe in it.

This, then, is a sketch of James's final world-view. This over-arching philosophical structure did not come to James all at once; it was shaped and reshaped, piece by piece, over his lifetime. Its motivation, one of James's key intellectual driving forces, was the tension that he felt between science and religion: between the cold but intelligent detachment and determinism of his 'scientific conscience,' and his attachment to the ideals of free will, morality, and an interested God. "The Will to Believe" was

one of James's earlier—and, at the time and ever since, highly popular—attempts to resolve this contradiction.

What Is the Structure of This Reading?

"The Will to Believe," James announces at the outset, is to be "an essay in justification of faith." He starts out by making three distinctions between types of "options" (living or dead, forced or avoidable, momentous or trivial) and suggests that his essay is to be about options that are living, forced, and momentous—what James calls "genuine options."

James begins his discussion of this kind of option—in the second section of the paper—by immediately considering the objection that it is in some way "preposterous" to say that we could or should simply *choose* what to believe. He responds that not only can we and do we believe things on the basis of "our non-intellectual nature," but furthermore that we must and should do so— that willingness to believe is (morally and intellectually) "lawful." He tries to tie this view to the rejection of what he calls "absolutism" in science and the endorsement of "empiricism," and to the quest to "believe truth" rather than merely "avoid error."

In Section VIII James begins to present his actual arguments for the claim that "there are some options between opinions in which [our passional nature] must be regarded both as an inevitable and as a lawful determinant of our choice." He does so partly by arguing that this must be true for what he earlier called *genuine* options, and he gives as examples moral questions, issues to do with personal relationships, and—at greater length—religious faith. One of his central claims in this section is that "a rule of thinking which would absolutely prevent me from acknowledging certain kinds of truth if those truths were really there, would be an irrational rule."

Some Background Information

1. James refers to a number of people in his essay that may no longer be familiar to modern audiences. Here is a run-down of the names James drops, in the order of their appearance:

---

* William James, *Pragmatism* (Harvard University Press, 1975), 29.

- Leslie Stephen (1832–1904): a British writer, editor, and biographer best known as the editor of the *Dictionary of National Biography* and as novelist Virginia Woolf's father.
- Fridtjof Nansen (1861–1930): a Norwegian explorer, zoologist, and politician who led an Arctic expedition from 1893 to 1896.
- Blaise Pascal (1623–62): a French mathematician, physicist and philosopher. James is referring to the book *Pensées*, published (posthumously) in 1670.
- Arthur Hugh Clough (1819–61): a British poet. The quote is from a poem sometimes known as "Steadfast."
- Thomas Henry Huxley (1825–95): a British biologist and writer, known for championing Darwin's theory of evolution. The quotation is from "The Influence upon Morality of a Decline in Religious Belief" (1878, published as part of a symposium to which Clifford also contributed).
- William Kingdon Clifford (1845–79): a British mathematician, philosopher, and well-known agnostic who died an early death from tuberculosis. James quotes extensively from his "The Ethics of Belief," published in *Contemporary Review* 29 (1877).
- Arthur James Balfour (1848–1930): a philosopher who went on to be British prime minister from 1902 to 1905 and then foreign secretary (1916–19). James is thinking of Balfour's essay "Authority and Reason," published in 1895.
- John Henry Newman (1801–91): an English theologian who converted to Roman Catholicism in 1845 and became a cardinal in 1879.
- Johann Zöllner (1834–82): a German astrophysicist who researched psychic phenomena and defended the existence of a "fourth dimension."
- Charles Howard Hinton (1853–1907): an English mathematician who also, independently, postulated a "fourth dimension."
- Thomas Reid (1710–96): a Scottish philosopher and opponent of the 'skepticism' of David Hume.
- Herbert Spencer (1820–1903): an English philosopher who tried to apply the scientific theory of evolution to philosophy and ethics. He coined the phrase "the survival of the fittest."
- August Wiesmann (1834–1914): a German biologist and one of the founders of modern genetics, who defended the view that hereditary characteristics are transmitted by a germinal plasm (and so ruled out the transmission of acquired characteristics).
- Charles Secrétan (1815–95): A (rather obscure) late nineteenth-century Swiss philosopher.

2. James's position in "The Will to Believe" is often thought to be a good example of the philosophical position called fideism. This is the thesis that religious belief is based on faith and not on either evidence or reasoning. In other words, the fundamental claims of religion cannot be established by either science or reason but nevertheless (perhaps because we should not place reason ahead of God) they should be believed to be true. Fideism comes in various flavors. Perhaps the mildest is the view, held by St. Augustine and Pascal, that faith must come before reason: that is, only faith can persuade us that religious doctrines are true, but once we believe, we can use our intellect to come to better understand them and to see *why* they are true and rational. The most extreme version is typified in the writings of the nineteenth-century Danish philosopher Søren Kierkegaard. Kierkegaard went so far as to say that some central tenets of Christianity—e.g., that God became incarnate in the person of Jesus Christ—are actually self-contradictory, and thus irrational, so belief in them requires a "leap into faith" which cannot in any way be justified.

Some Common Misconceptions

1. James is not anti-science: he does not want to eliminate the scientific attitude in favor of a religious one, but to show that science leaves open the possibility of religious faith and that it can do so without merely ignoring religion or granting it a special sphere insulated from normal rational inquiry.
2. James does not argue that we *must* be religious but only that, even though we are reasonable and scientifically educated people, we still *can* be religious. Religious belief is, for James, a personal choice.

The Will to Believe*

In the recently published *Life* by Leslie Stephen of his brother, Fitz-James, there is an account of a school to which the latter went when he was a boy. The teacher, a certain Mr. Guest, used to converse with his pupils in this wise: "Gurney, what is the difference between justification and sanctification?—Stephen, prove the omnipotence of God!" etc. In the midst of our Harvard freethinking and indifference we are prone to imagine that here at your good old orthodox College conversation continues to be somewhat upon this order; and to show you that we at Harvard have not lost all interest in these vital subjects, I have brought with me to-night something like a sermon on justification by faith to read to you,—I mean an essay in justification *of* faith, a defence of our right to adopt a believing attitude in religious matters, in spite of the fact that our merely logical intellect may not have been coerced. "The Will to Believe," accordingly, is the title of my paper.

I have long defended to my own students the lawfulness of voluntarily adopted faith; but as soon as they have got well imbued with the logical spirit, they have as a rule refused to admit my contention to be lawful philosophically, even though in point of fact they were personally all the time chock-full of some faith or other themselves. I am all the while, however, so profoundly convinced that my own position is correct, that your invitation has seemed to me a good occasion to make my statements more clear. Perhaps your minds will be more open than those with which I have hitherto had to deal. I will be as little technical as I can, though I must begin by setting up some technical distinctions that will help us in the end.

I.

Let us give the name of *hypothesis* to anything that may be proposed to our belief; and just as the electricians speak of live and dead wires, let us speak of any hypothesis as either *live* or *dead*. A live hypothesis is one which appeals as a real possibility to him to whom it is proposed. If I ask you to believe in the Mahdi,[†] the notion makes no electric connection with your nature,—it refuses to scintillate with any credibility at all. As an hypothesis it is completely dead. To an Arab, however (even if he be not one of the Mahdi's followers), the hypothesis is among the mind's possibilities: it is alive. This shows that deadness and liveness in an hypothesis are not intrinsic properties, but relations to the individual thinker. They are measured by his willingness to act. The maximum of liveness in an hypothesis, means willingness to act irrevocably. Practically, that means belief; but there is some believing tendency wherever there is willingness to act at all.

Next, let us call the decision between two hypotheses an *option*. Options may be of several kinds. They may be—1, *living* or *dead*; 2, *forced* or *avoidable*; 3, *momentous* or *trivial*; and for our purposes we may call an option a *genuine* option when it is of the forced, living, and momentous kind.

1. A living option is one in which both hypotheses are live ones. If I say to you: "Be a theosophist[‡] or be a Mohammedan,"[§] it is probably a dead option, because for you neither hypothesis is likely to be alive. But if I say: "Be an agnostic or be a Christian," it is otherwise: trained as you are, each

---

* This essay was an address to the Philosophical Clubs of Yale and Brown Universities, and was first published in the *New World* in June 1896. This reprint is based on the text in *The Will to Believe, and Other Essays in Popular Philosophy* (Longmans, Green & Co., 1897).

† In Islam, a messianic leader who, it is believed, will appear shortly before the end of the world to establish a reign of righteousness.

‡ A member of a religious sect, the Theosophical Society, founded in New York in 1875, which incorporates aspects of Buddhism and Brahmanism.

§ A Muslim.

hypothesis makes some appeal, however small, to your belief.

2. Next, if I say to you: "Choose between going out with your umbrella or without it," I do not offer you a genuine option, for it is not forced. You can easily avoid it by not going out at all. Similarly, if I say, "Either love me or hate me," "Either call my theory true or call it false," your option is avoidable. You may remain indifferent to me, neither loving nor hating, and you may decline to offer any judgment as to my theory. But if I say, "Either accept this truth or go without it," I put on you a forced option, for there is no standing place outside of the alternative. Every dilemma based on a complete logical disjunction, with no possibility of not choosing, is an option of this forced kind.

3. Finally, if I were Dr. Nansen and proposed to you to join my North Pole expedition, your option would be momentous; for this would probably be your only similar opportunity, and your choice now would either exclude you from the North Pole sort of immortality altogether or put at least the chance of it into your hands. He who refuses to embrace a unique opportunity loses the prize as surely as if he tried and failed. *Per contra*,[*] the option is trivial when the opportunity is not unique, when the stake is insignificant, or when the decision is reversible if it later prove unwise. Such trivial options abound in the scientific life. A chemist finds an hypothesis live enough to spend a year in its verification: he believes in it to that extent. But if his experiments prove inconclusive either way, he is quit for his loss of time,[†] no vital harm being done.

It will facilitate our discussion if we keep all these distinctions well in mind.

II.

The next matter to consider is the actual psychology of human opinion. When we look at certain facts, it seems as if our passional and volitional nature lay at the root of all our convictions. When we look at others, it seems as if they could do nothing when the intellect had once said its say. Let us take the latter facts up first.

Does it not seem preposterous on the very face of it to talk of our opinions being modifiable at will? Can our will either help or hinder our intellect in its perceptions of truth? Can we, by just willing it, believe that Abraham Lincoln's existence is a myth, and that the portraits of him in *McClure's Magazine*[‡] are all of some one else? Can we, by any effort of our will, or by any strength of wish that it were true, believe ourselves well and about when we are roaring with rheumatism in bed, or feel certain that the sum of the two one-dollar bills in our pocket must be a hundred dollars? We can say any of these things, but we are absolutely impotent to believe them; and of just such things is the whole fabric of the truths that we do believe in made up,—matters of fact, immediate or remote, as Hume said,[§] and relations between ideas, which are either there or not there for us if we see them so, and which if not there cannot be put there by any action of our own.

In Pascal's *Thoughts* there is a celebrated passage known in literature as Pascal's wager.[¶] In it he tries to force us into Christianity by reasoning as if our concern with truth resembled our concern with the stakes in a game of chance. Translated freely his words are these: You must either believe or not believe that God is—which will you do? Your human reason cannot say. A game is going on between you and the nature of things which at the day of judgment will bring out either heads or tails. Weigh what your gains and your losses would be if you should stake all you have on heads, or God's existence: if you win in such case, you gain eternal beatitude;[**] if you lose, you lose nothing

---

[*]   "On the other hand."
[†]   That is, free to stop with no penalty except for the loss of his time.
[‡]   An influential American muckraking periodical, founded in 1893.
[§]   See the Hume selections in this chapter and in the section on the Philosophy of Science.
[¶]   See the Pascal selection in this chapter.
[**] Blessedness or happiness.

at all. If there were an infinity of chances, and only one for God in this wager, still you ought to stake your all on God; for though you surely risk a finite loss by this procedure, any finite loss is reasonable, even a certain one is reasonable, if there is but the possibility of infinite gain. Go, then, and take holy water, and have masses said; belief will come and stupefy your scruples,—*Cela vous fera croire et vous abêtira.** Why should you not? At bottom, what have you to lose?

You probably feel that when religious faith expresses itself thus, in the language of the gaming table, it is put to its last trumps.† Surely Pascal's own personal belief in masses and holy water had far other springs; and this celebrated page of his is but an argument for others, a last desperate snatch at a weapon against the hardness of the unbelieving heart. We feel that a faith in masses and holy water adopted wilfully after such a mechanical calculation—would lack the inner soul of faith's reality; and if we were ourselves in the place of the Deity, we should probably take particular pleasure in cutting off believers of this pattern from their infinite reward. It is evident that unless there be some pre-existing tendency to believe in masses and holy water, the option offered to the will by Pascal is not a living option. Certainly no Turk ever took to masses and holy water on its account; and even to us Protestants these means of salvation seem such foregone impossibilities that Pascal's logic, invoked for them specifically, leaves us unmoved. As well might the Mahdi write to us, saying, "I am the Expected One whom God has created in his effulgence.‡ You shall be infinitely happy if you confess me; otherwise you shall be cut off from the light of the sun. Weigh, then, your infinite gain if I am genuine against your finite sacrifice if I am not!" His logic would be that of Pascal; but he would vainly use it on us, for the hypothesis he offers us is dead. No tendency to act on it exists in us to any degree.

The talk of believing by our volition seems, then, from one point of view, simply silly. From another point of view it is worse than silly, it is vile. When one turns to the magnificent edifice of the physical sciences, and sees how it was reared; what thousands of disinterested moral lives of men lie buried in its mere foundations; what patience and postponement, what choking down of preference, what submission to the icy laws of outer fact are wrought into its very stones and mortar; how absolutely impersonal it stands in its vast augustness,—then how besotted and contemptible seems every little sentimentalist who comes blowing his voluntary smoke-wreaths, and pretending to decide things from out of his private dream! Can we wonder if those bred in the rugged and manly school of science should feel like spewing such subjectivism out of their mouths? The whole system of loyalties which grow up in the schools of science go dead against its toleration; so that it is only natural that those who have caught the scientific fever should pass over to the opposite extreme, and write sometimes as if the incorruptibly truthful intellect ought positively to prefer bitterness and unacceptableness to the heart in its cup.

It fortifies my soul to know
That, though I perish, Truth is so—

sings Clough, while Huxley exclaims: "My only consolation lies in the reflection that, however bad our posterity may become, so far as they hold by the plain rule of not pretending to believe what they have no reason to believe, because it may be to their advantage so to pretend [the word 'pretend' is surely here redundant], they will not have reached the lowest depth of immorality." And that delicious *enfant terrible*§ Clifford writes: "Belief is desecrated when given to unproved and unquestioned statements for the solace and private pleasure of the believer…. Whoso would deserve well of his fellows in this matter will guard the purity of his belief with a very fanaticism of jealous care, lest at any time it should rest on an unworthy object, and catch a stain which can never be wiped away…. If [a] belief has been accepted on insufficient evidence [even though the belief be true, as Clifford on the same page explains] the pleasure is a stolen

---

* "That will make you believe and will stupefy you."
† Near to death, in desperate straits.
‡ Radiance.
§ 'Bad boy'—a person whose behavior or ideas shock or embarrass those with more conventional attitudes.

one.... It is sinful because it is stolen in defiance of our duty to mankind. That duty is to guard ourselves from such beliefs as from a pestilence which may shortly master our own body and then spread to the rest of the town.... It is wrong always, everywhere, and for every one, to believe anything upon insufficient evidence."

III.

All this strikes one as healthy, even when expressed, as by Clifford, with somewhat too much of robustious pathos in the voice. Free-will and simple wishing do seem, in the matter of our credences,* to be only fifth wheels to the coach. Yet if any one should thereupon assume that intellectual insight is what remains after wish and will and sentimental preference have taken wing, or that pure reason is what then settles our opinions, he would fly quite as directly in the teeth of the facts.

It is only our already dead hypotheses that our willing nature is unable to bring to life again. But what has made them dead for us is for the most part a previous action of our willing nature of an antagonistic kind. When I say 'willing nature,' I do not mean only such deliberate volitions as may have set up habits of belief that we cannot now escape from,—I mean all such factors of belief as fear and hope, prejudice and passion, imitation and partisanship, the circumpressure of our caste and set. As a matter of fact we find ourselves believing, we hardly know how or why. Mr. Balfour gives the name of 'authority' to all those influences, born of the intellectual climate, that make hypotheses possible or impossible for us, alive or dead. Here in this room, we all of us believe in molecules and the conservation of energy, in democracy and necessary progress, in Protestant Christianity and the duty of fighting for 'the doctrine of the immortal Monroe,'† all for no reasons worthy of the name. We see into these matters with no more inner clearness, and probably with much less, than any disbeliever in them might possess. His unconventionality would probably have some grounds to show for its conclusions; but for us, not insight, but the *prestige* of the opinions, is what makes the spark shoot from them and light up our sleeping magazines‡ of faith. Our reason is quite satisfied, in nine hundred and ninety-nine cases out of every thousand of us, if it can find a few arguments that will do to recite in case our credulity is criticized by someone else. Our faith is faith in someone else's faith, and in the greatest matters this is most the case. Our belief in truth itself, for instance, that there is a truth, and that our minds and it are made for each other,—what is it but a passionate affirmation of desire, in which our social system backs us up? We want to have a truth; we want to believe that our experiments and studies and discussions must put us in a continually better and better position towards it; and on this line we agree to fight out our thinking lives. But if a pyrrhonistic sceptic§ asks us *how we know* all this, can our logic find a reply? No! certainly it cannot. It is just one volition against another,—we willing to go in for life upon a trust or assumption which he, for his part, does not care to make.[1]

As a rule we disbelieve all facts and theories for which we have no use. Clifford's cosmic emotions find no use for Christian feelings. Huxley belabors the bishops because there is no use for sacerdotalism¶ in his scheme of life. Newman, on the contrary, goes over to Romanism,** and finds all sorts of reasons good for staying there, because a priestly system is for him an organic need and delight. Why do so few 'scientists' even look at the evidence for telepathy, so called? Because they think, as a leading biologist, now dead, once said to me, that even if such a thing were true, scientists ought to band together to keep it suppressed and concealed. It would undo the uniformity of Nature and all sorts of other things without which scientists cannot carry on their pursuits. But if this

---

* Beliefs.
† This is the "Monroe Doctrine," set out by American president James Monroe in 1823, which states that the US would regard attempts by European powers to establish new colonies or otherwise interfere in the Americas as acts of aggression.
‡ A storehouse of explosive ammunition.
§ A radical skeptic, one who is determined to withhold assent from almost all beliefs.
¶ The institution of the priesthood.
** Roman Catholicism.

very man had been shown something which as a scientist he might *do* with telepathy, he might not only have examined the evidence, but even have found it good enough. This very law which the logicians would impose upon us—if I may give the name of logicians to those who would rule out our willing nature here—is based on nothing but their own natural wish to exclude all elements for which they, in their professional quality of logicians, can find no use.

Evidently, then, our non-intellectual nature does influence our convictions. There are passional tendencies and volitions which run before and others which come after belief, and it is only the latter that are too late for the fair; and they are not too late when the previous passional work has been already in their own direction. Pascal's argument, instead of being powerless, then seems a regular clincher, and is the last stroke needed to make our faith in masses and holy water complete. The state of things is evidently far from simple; and pure insight and logic, whatever they might do ideally, are not the only things that really do produce our creeds.

IV.

Our next duty, having recognized this mixed-up state of affairs, is to ask whether it be simply reprehensible and pathological, or whether, on the contrary, we must treat it as a normal element in making up our minds. The thesis I defend is, briefly stated, this: *Our passional nature not only lawfully may, but must, decide an option between propositions, whenever it is a genuine option that cannot by its nature be decided on intellectual grounds; for to say, under such circumstances, "Do not decide, but leave the question open," is itself a passional decision,—just like deciding yes or no,—and is attended with the same risk of losing the truth.* The thesis thus abstractly expressed will, I trust, soon become quite clear. But I must first indulge in a bit more of preliminary work.

V.

It will be observed that for the purposes of this discussion we are on 'dogmatic' ground,—ground, I mean, which leaves systematic philosophical scepticism altogether out of account. The postulate that there is truth, and that it is the destiny of our minds to attain it, we are deliberately resolving to make, though the sceptic will not make it. We part company with him, therefore, absolutely, at this point. But the faith that truth exists, and that our minds can find it, may be held in two ways. We may talk of the *empiricist* way and of the *absolutist* way of believing in truth. The absolutists in this matter say that we not only can attain to knowing truth, but we can *know* when we have attained to knowing it; while the empiricists think that although we may attain it, we cannot infallibly know when. To *know* is one thing, and to know for certain *that* we know is another. One may hold to the first being possible without the second; hence the empiricists and the absolutists, although neither of them is a sceptic in the usual philosophic sense of the term, show very different degrees of dogmatism in their lives.

If we look at the history of opinions, we see that the empiricist tendency has largely prevailed in science, while in philosophy the absolutist tendency has had everything its own way. The characteristic sort of happiness, indeed, which philosophies yield has mainly consisted in the conviction felt by each successive school or system that by it bottom-certitude had been attained. "Other philosophies are collections of opinions, mostly false; *my* philosophy gives standing-ground forever,"—who does not recognize in this the key-note of every system worthy of the name? A system, to be a system at all, must come as a *closed* system, reversible in this or that detail, perchance, but in its essential features never!

Scholastic orthodoxy,* to which one must always go when one wishes to find perfectly clear statement, has beautifully elaborated this absolutist conviction in a doctrine which it calls that of 'objective evidence.' If, for example, I am unable to doubt that I now exist before you, that two is less than three, or that if all

---

* The dominant philosophy of the Middle Ages, combining remnants of ancient Greek philosophy (especially Aristotle) with Christian theology.

men are mortal then I am mortal too, it is because these things illumine my intellect irresistibly. The final ground of this objective evidence possessed by certain propositions is the *adæquatio intellectus nostri cum rê.** The certitude it brings involves an *apititudinem ad extorquendum certum assensum*† on the part of the truth envisaged, and on the side of the subject a *quietem in cognitione,*‡ when once the object is mentally received, that leaves no possibility of doubt behind; and in the whole transaction nothing operates but the *entitas ipsa*§ of the object and the *entitas ipsa* of the mind. We slouchy modern thinkers dislike to talk in Latin,—indeed, we dislike to talk in set terms at all; but at bottom our own state of mind is very much like this whenever we uncritically abandon ourselves: You believe in objective evidence, and I do. Of some things we feel that we are certain: we know, and we know that we do know. There is something that gives a click inside of us, a bell that strikes twelve, when the hands of our mental clock have swept the dial and meet over the meridian hour.¶ The greatest empiricists among us are only empiricists on reflection: when left to their instincts, they dogmatize like infallible popes. When the Cliffords tell us how sinful it is to be Christians on such 'insufficient evidence,' insufficiency is really the last thing they have in mind. For them the evidence is absolutely sufficient, only it makes the other way. They believe so completely in an anti-Christian order of the universe that there is no living option: Christianity is a dead hypothesis from the start.

VI.

But now, since we are all such absolutists by instinct, what in our quality of students of philosophy ought we to do about the fact? Shall we espouse and endorse it? Or shall we treat it as a weakness of our nature from which we must free ourselves, if we can?

I sincerely believe that the latter course is the only one we can follow as reflective men. Objective evidence and certitude are doubtless very fine ideals to play with, but where on this moonlit and dream-visited planet are they found? I am, therefore, myself a complete empiricist so far as my theory of human knowledge goes. I live, to be sure, by the practical faith that we must go on experiencing and thinking over our experience, for only thus can our opinions grow more true; but to hold any one of them—I absolutely do not care which—as if it never could be reinterpretable or corrigible,** I believe to be a tremendously mistaken attitude, and I think that the whole history of philosophy will bear me out. There is but one indefectibly certain truth, and that is the truth that pyrrhonistic scepticism itself leaves standing,—the truth that the present phenomenon of consciousness exists. That, however, is the bare starting-point of knowledge, the mere admission of a stuff to be philosophized about. The various philosophies are but so many attempts at expressing what this stuff really is. And if we repair to our libraries what disagreement do we discover! Where is a certainly true answer found? Apart from abstract propositions of comparison (such as two and two are the same as four), propositions which tell us nothing by themselves about concrete reality, we find no proposition ever regarded by any one as evidently certain that has not either been called a falsehood, or at least had its truth sincerely questioned by some one else. The transcending of the axioms of geometry, not in play but in earnest, by certain of our contemporaries (as Zöllner and Charles H. Hinton), and the rejection of the whole Aristotelian logic by the Hegelians, are striking instances in point.

No concrete test of what is really true has ever been agreed upon. Some make the criterion external to the moment of perception, putting it either in revelation, the *consensus gentium,*†† the instincts of the heart, or the systematized experience of the race. Others make the perceptive moment its own test,—Descartes, for instance, with his clear and distinct ideas guaranteed by the veracity of God; Reid with his 'common-sense';

---

*   "Perfect correspondence of our understanding with the thing."
†   "The aptitude to force a certain agreement."
‡   "Repose in knowledge," i.e., passive acceptance of knowledge.
§   "Being itself," real being.
¶   Noon; i.e., the hour when the sun is at its meridian, its highest point in the sky.
**   Correctable.
††   "Public consensus."

and Kant with his forms of synthetic judgment *a priori*.* The inconceivability of the opposite; the capacity to be verified by sense; the possession of complete organic unity or self-relation, realized when a thing is its own other,—are standards which, in turn, have been used. The much lauded objective evidence is never triumphantly there; it is a mere aspiration or *Grenzbegriff*,† marking the infinitely remote ideal of our thinking life. To claim that certain truths now possess it, is simply to say that when you think them true and they *are* true, then their evidence is objective, otherwise it is not. But practically one's conviction that the evidence one goes by is of the real objective brand, is only one more subjective opinion added to the lot. For what a contradictory array of opinions have objective evidence and absolute certitude been claimed! The world is rational through and through,—its existence is an ultimate brute fact; there is a personal God,—a personal God is inconceivable; there is an extra-mental physical world immediately known,—the mind can only know its own ideas; a moral imperative exists,—obligation is only the resultant of desires; a permanent spiritual principle is in every one,—there are only shifting states of mind; there is an endless chain of causes,—there is an absolute first cause; an eternal necessity,—a freedom; a purpose,—no purpose; a primal One,—a primal Many; a universal continuity,—an essential discontinuity in things; an infinity,—no infinity. There is this,—there is that; there is indeed nothing which some one has not thought absolutely true, while his neighbor deemed it absolutely false; and not an absolutist among them seems ever to have considered that the trouble may all the time be essential, and that the intellect, even with truth directly in its grasp, may have no infallible signal for knowing whether it be truth or no. When, indeed, one remembers that the most striking practical application to life of the doctrine of objective certitude has been the conscientious labors of the Holy Office of the Inquisition,‡

one feels less tempted than ever to lend the doctrine a respectful ear.

But please observe, now, that when as empiricists we give up the doctrine of objective certitude, we do not thereby give up the quest or hope of truth itself. We still pin our faith on its existence, and still believe that we gain an ever better position towards it by systematically continuing to roll up experiences and think. Our great difference from the scholastic lies in the way we face. The strength of his system lies in the principles, the origin, the *terminus a quo*§ of his thought; for us the strength is in the outcome, the upshot, the *terminus ad quem*.¶ Not where it comes from but what it leads to is to decide. It matters not to an empiricist from what quarter an hypothesis may come to him: he may have acquired it by fair means or by foul; passion may have whispered or accident suggested it; but if the total drift of thinking continues to confirm it, that is what he means by its being true.

VII.

One more point, small but important, and our preliminaries are done. There are two ways of looking at our duty in the matter of opinion,—ways entirely different, and yet ways about whose difference the theory of knowledge seems hitherto to have shown very little concern. *We must know the truth*; and *we must avoid error*,—these are our first and great commandments as would-be knowers; but they are not two ways of stating an identical commandment, they are two separable laws. Although it may indeed happen that when we believe the truth *A*, we escape as an incidental consequence from believing the falsehood *B*, it hardly ever happens that by merely disbelieving *B* we necessarily believe *A*. We may in escaping *B* fall into believing other falsehoods, *C* or *D*, just as bad as *B*; or we may escape *B* by not believing anything at all, not even *A*.

Believe truth! Shun error—these, we see, are two materially different laws; and by choosing between

---

* See the readings in Epistemology from Descartes and Kant elsewhere in this volume.

† From Kant's *Critique of Pure Reason*, this literally means a concept at the edge or limit of our understanding; it is often translated "limiting concept."

‡ A tribunal formerly held in the Roman Catholic Church and directed at the forceful suppression of heresy; its best known variant is the notorious Spanish Inquisition of the late fifteenth century.

§ "The point from which it comes."

¶ "The point to which it goes."

them we may end by coloring differently our whole intellectual life. We may regard the chase for truth as paramount, and the avoidance of error as secondary; or we may, on the other hand, treat the avoidance of error as more imperative, and let truth take its chance. Clifford, in the instructive passage which I have quoted, exhorts us to the latter course. Believe nothing, he tells us, keep your mind in suspense forever, rather than by closing it on insufficient evidence incur the awful risk of believing lies. You, on the other hand, may think that the risk of being in error is a very small matter when compared with the blessings of real knowledge, and be ready to be duped many times in your investigation rather than postpone indefinitely the chance of guessing true. I myself find it impossible to go with Clifford. We must remember that these feelings of our duty about either truth or error are in any case only expressions of our passional life. Biologically considered, our minds are as ready to grind out falsehood as veracity, and he who says, "Better go without belief forever than believe a lie!" merely shows his own preponderant private horror of becoming a dupe. He may be critical of many of his desires and fears, but this fear he slavishly obeys. He cannot imagine any one questioning its binding force. For my own part, I have also a horror of being duped; but I can believe that worse things than being duped may happen to a man in this world: so Clifford's exhortation has to my ears a thoroughly fantastic* sound. It is like a general informing his soldiers that it is better to keep out of battle forever than to risk a single wound. Not so are victories either over enemies or over nature gained. Our errors are surely not such awfully solemn things. In a world where we are so certain to incur them in spite of all our caution, a certain lightness of heart seems healthier than this excessive nervousness on their behalf. At any rate, it seems the fittest thing for the empiricist philosopher.

VIII.

And now, after all this introduction, let us go straight at our question. I have said, and now repeat it, that not only as a matter of fact do we find our passional nature influencing us in our opinions, but that there are some options between opinions in which this influence must be regarded both as an inevitable and as a lawful determinant of our choice.

I fear here that some of you my hearers will begin to scent danger, and lend an inhospitable ear. Two first steps of passion you have indeed had to admit as necessary,—we must think so as to avoid dupery, and we must think so as to gain truth; but the surest path to those ideal consummations, you will probably consider, is from now onwards to take no further passional step.

Well, of course, I agree as far as the facts will allow. Wherever the option between losing truth and gaining it is not momentous, we can throw the chance of *gaining truth* away, and at any rate save ourselves from any chance of *believing falsehood*, by not making up our minds at all till objective evidence has come. In scientific questions, this is almost always the case; and even in human affairs in general, the need of acting is seldom so urgent that a false belief to act on is better than no belief at all. Law courts, indeed, have to decide on the best evidence attainable for the moment, because a judge's duty is to make law as well as to ascertain it, and (as a learned judge once said to me) few cases are worth spending much time over: the great thing is to have them decided on *any* acceptable principle, and got out of the way. But in our dealings with objective nature we obviously are recorders, not makers, of the truth; and decisions for the mere sake of deciding promptly and getting on to the next business would be wholly out of place. Throughout the breadth of physical nature facts are what they are quite independently of us, and seldom is there any such hurry about them that the risks of being duped by believing a premature theory need be faced. The questions here are always trivial options, the hypotheses are hardly living (at any rate not living for us spectators), the choice between believing truth or falsehood is seldom forced. The attitude of sceptical balance is therefore the absolutely wise one if we would escape mistakes. What difference, indeed, does it make to most of us whether we have or have not a theory of the Röntgen rays,† whether we believe or not in mind-stuff, or have a conviction about the causality of conscious states? It

---

* Outrageous, unreal—the result of a fantasy.
† Named for Wilhelm Röntgen, the German physicist who discovered them, these are today called X-rays.

makes no difference. Such options are not forced on us. On every account it is better not to make them, but still keep weighing reasons *pro et contra*[*] with an indifferent hand.

I speak, of course, here of the purely judging mind. For purposes of discovery such indifference is to be less highly recommended, and science would be far less advanced than she is if the passionate desires of individuals to get their own faiths confirmed had been kept out of the game. See for example the sagacity which Spencer and Weismann now display. On the other hand, if you want an absolute duffer in an investigation, you must, after all, take the man who has no interest whatever in its results: he is the warranted incapable, the positive fool. The most useful investigator, because the most sensitive observer, is always he whose eager interest in one side of the question is balanced by an equally keen nervousness lest he become deceived.[2] Science has organized this nervousness into a regular *technique*, her so-called method of verification; and she has fallen so deeply in love with the method that one may even say she has ceased to care for truth by itself at all. It is only truth as technically verified that interests her. The truth of truths might come in merely affirmative form, and she would decline to touch it. Such truth as that, she might repeat with Clifford, would be stolen in defiance of her duty to mankind. Human passions, however, are stronger than technical rules. "Le coeur a ses raisons," as Pascal says, "que la raison ne connaît pas;"[†] and however indifferent to all but the bare rules of the game the umpire, the abstract intellect, may be, the concrete players who furnish him the materials to judge of are usually, each one of them, in love with some pet 'live hypothesis' of his own. Let us agree, however, that wherever there is no forced option, the dispassionately judicial intellect with no pet hypothesis, saving us, as it does, from dupery at any rate, ought to be our ideal.

The question next arises: Are there not somewhere forced options in our speculative questions, and can

we (as men who may be interested at least as much in positively gaining truth as in merely escaping dupery) always wait with impunity till the coercive evidence shall have arrived? It seems *a priori* improbable that the truth should be so nicely adjusted to our needs and powers as that. In the great boarding-house of nature, the cakes and the butter and the syrup seldom come out so even and leave the plates so clean. Indeed, we should view them with scientific suspicion if they did.

IX.

Moral questions immediately present themselves as questions whose solution cannot wait for sensible proof. A moral question is a question not of what sensibly exists, but of what is good, or would be good if it did exist. Science can tell us what exists; but to compare the *worths*, both of what exists and of what does not exist, we must consult not science, but what Pascal calls our heart. Science herself consults her heart when she lays it down that the infinite ascertainment of fact and correction of false belief are the supreme goods for man. Challenge the statement, and science can only repeat it oracularly,[‡] or else prove it by showing that such ascertainment and correction bring man all sorts of other goods which man's heart in turn declares. The question of having moral beliefs at all or not having them is decided by our will. Are our moral preferences true or false, or are they only odd biological phenomena, making things good or bad for *us*, but in themselves indifferent? How can your pure intellect decide? If your heart does not *want* a world of moral reality, your head will assuredly never make you believe in one. Mephistophelian[§] scepticism, indeed, will satisfy the head's play-instincts much better than any rigorous idealism can. Some men (even at the student age) are so naturally cool-hearted that the moralistic hypothesis never has for them any pungent life, and in their supercilious presence the hot young moralist always feels strangely ill at ease. The appearance of knowingness is on their side, of *naïveté*, and

---

[*] "For and against."
[†] "The heart has its reasons which reason knows nothing of."
[‡] In the manner of an oracle: solemnly and enigmatically, but without giving reasons.
[§] Mephistopheles is the devil to whom, according to a sixteenth-century German legend, Faust sold his soul: something is "Mephistophelian," therefore, if it is fiendish and tricky.

gullibility on his. Yet, in the inarticulate heart of him, he clings to it that he is not a dupe, and that there is a realm in which (as Emerson says) all their wit and intellectual superiority is no better than the cunning of a fox.* Moral scepticism can no more be refuted or proved by logic than intellectual scepticism can. When we stick to it that there *is* truth (be it of either kind), we do so with our whole nature, and resolve to stand or fall by the results. The sceptic with his whole nature adopts the doubting attitude; but which of us is the wiser, Omniscience only knows.

Turn now from these wide questions of good to a certain class of questions of fact, questions concerning personal relations, states of mind between one man and another. *Do you like me or not?*—for example. Whether you do or not depends, in countless instances, on whether I meet you half-way, am willing to assume that you must like me, and show you trust and expectation. The previous faith on my part in your liking's existence is in such cases what makes your liking come. But if I stand aloof, and refuse to budge an inch until I have objective evidence, until you shall have done something apt, as the absolutists say, *ad extorquendum assensum meum,*† ten to one your liking never comes. How many women's hearts are vanquished by the mere sanguine insistence of some man that they *must* love him! he will not consent to the hypothesis that they cannot. The desire for a certain kind of truth here brings about that special truth's existence; and so it is in innumerable cases of other sorts. Who gains promotions, boons, appointments, but the man in whose life they are seen to play the part of live hypotheses, who discounts them, sacrifices other things for their sake before they have come, and takes risks for them in advance? His faith acts on the powers above him as a claim, and creates its own verification.

A social organism of any sort whatever, large or small, is what it is because each member proceeds to his own duty with a trust that the other members will simultaneously do theirs. Wherever a desired result is achieved by the co-operation of many independent persons, its existence as a fact is a pure consequence of the precursive‡ faith in one another of those immediately concerned. A government, an army, a commercial system, a ship, a college, an athletic team, all exist on this condition, without which not only is nothing achieved, but nothing is even attempted. A whole train of passengers (individually brave enough) will be looted by a few highwaymen, simply because the latter can count on one another, while each passenger fears that if he makes a movement of resistance, he will be shot before any one else backs him up. If we believed that the whole car-full would rise at once with us, we should each severally rise, and train-robbing would never even be attempted. There are, then, cases where a fact cannot come at all unless a preliminary faith exists in its coming. *And where faith in a fact can help create the fact,* that would be an insane logic which should say that faith running ahead of scientific evidence is the 'lowest kind of immorality' into which a thinking being can fall. Yet such is the logic by which our scientific absolutists pretend to regulate our lives!

X.

In truths dependent on our personal action, then, faith based on desire is certainly a lawful and possibly an indispensable thing.

But now, it will be said, these are all childish human cases, and have nothing to do with great cosmical matters, like the question of religious faith. Let us then pass on to that. Religions differ so much in their accidents§ that in discussing the religious question we must make it very generic and broad. What then do we now mean by the religious hypothesis? Science says things are; morality says some things are better than other things; and religion says essentially two things.

First, she says that the best things are the more eternal things, the overlapping things, the things in the universe that throw the last stone, so to speak, and say the final word. "Perfection is eternal,"—this phrase of Charles Secrétan seems a good way of putting this first affirmation of religion, an affirmation

---

* A reference to the poet Ralph Waldo Emerson's essay "The Sovereignty of Ethics" (1884).
† "To force my unqualified assent."
‡ Preceding.
§ Non-essential properties or attributes.

which obviously cannot yet be verified scientifically at all.

The second affirmation of religion is that we are better off even now if we believe her first affirmation to be true.

Now, let us consider what the logical elements of this situation are *in case the religious hypothesis in both its branches be really true.* (Of course, we must admit that possibility at the outset. If we are to discuss the question at all, it must involve a living option. If for any of you religion be a hypothesis that cannot, by any living possibility be true, then you need go no farther. I speak to the 'saving remnant' alone.) So proceeding, we see, first, that religion offers itself as a *momentous* option. We are supposed to gain, even now, by our belief, and to lose by our non-belief, a certain vital good. Secondly, religion is a *forced* option, so far as that good goes. We cannot escape the issue by remaining sceptical and waiting for more light, because, although we do avoid error in that way *if religion be untrue*, we lose the good, *if it be true*, just as certainly as if we positively chose to disbelieve. It is as if a man should hesitate indefinitely to ask a certain woman to marry him because he was not perfectly sure that she would prove an angel after he brought her home. Would he not cut himself off from that particular angel-possibility as decisively as if he went and married some one else? Scepticism, then, is not avoidance of option; it is option of a certain particular kind of risk. *Better risk loss of truth than chance of error,*—that is your faith-vetoer's exact position. He is actively playing his stake as much as the believer is; he is backing the field against the religious hypothesis, just as the believer is backing the religious hypothesis against the field. To preach scepticism to us as a duty until 'sufficient evidence' for religion be found, is tantamount therefore to telling us, when in presence of the religious hypothesis, that to yield to our fear of its being error is wiser and better than to yield to our hope that it may be true. It is not intellect against all passions, then; it is only intellect with one passion laying down its law. And by what, forsooth, is the supreme wisdom of this passion warranted? Dupery for dupery, what proof is there that dupery through hope is so much worse than dupery through fear? I, for one, can see no proof; and I simply refuse obedience to the scientist's command to imitate his kind of option, in a case where my own stake is important

enough to give me the right to choose my own form of risk. If religion be true and the evidence for it be still insufficient, I do not wish, by putting your extinguisher upon my nature (which feels to me as if it had after all some business in this matter), to forfeit my sole chance in life of getting upon the winning side,— that chance depending, of course, on my willingness to run the risk of acting as if my passional need of taking the world religiously might be prophetic and right.

All this is on the supposition that it really may be prophetic and right, and that, even to us who are discussing the matter, religion is a live hypothesis which may be true. Now, to most of us religion comes in a still further way that makes a veto on our active faith even more illogical. The more perfect and more eternal aspect of the universe is represented in our religions as having personal form. The universe is no longer a mere *It* to us, but a *Thou*, if we are religious; and any relation that may be possible from person to person might be possible here. For instance, although in one sense we are passive portions of the universe, in another we show a curious autonomy, as if we were small active centres on our own account. We feel, too, as if the appeal of religion to us were made to our own active good-will, as if evidence might be forever withheld from us unless we met the hypothesis half-way. To take a trivial illustration: just as a man who in a company of gentlemen made no advances, asked a warrant for every concession, and believed no one's word without proof, would cut himself off by such churlishness from all the social rewards that a more trusting spirit would earn—so here, one who should shut himself up in snarling logicality and try to make the gods extort his recognition willy-nilly, or not get it at all, might cut himself off forever from his only opportunity of making the gods' acquaintance. This feeling, forced on us we know not whence, that by obstinately believing that there are gods (although not to do so would be so easy both for our logic and our life) we are doing the universe the deepest service we can, seems part of the living essence of the religious hypothesis. If the hypothesis *were* true in all its parts, including this one, then pure intellectualism, with its veto on our making willing advances, would be an absurdity; and some participation of our sympathetic nature would be logically required. I, therefore, for one, cannot see my way to accepting the agnostic rules for truth-seeking, or wilfully agree to keep my willing nature out of the game. I cannot do so for this plain reason, that *a rule of thinking which would absolutely prevent me from acknowledging certain kinds of truth if those kinds of truth were really there, would be an irrational rule.* That for me is the long and short of the formal logic of the situation, no matter what the kinds of truth might materially be.

I confess I do not see how this logic can be escaped. But sad experience makes me fear that some of you may still shrink from radically saying with me, *in abstracto,** that we have the right to believe at our own risk any hypothesis that is live enough to tempt our will. I suspect, however, that if this is so, it is because you have got away from the abstract logical point of view altogether, and are thinking (perhaps without realizing it) of some particular religious hypothesis which for you is dead. The freedom to 'believe what we will' you apply to the case of some patent superstition; and the faith you think of is the faith defined by the schoolboy when he said, "Faith is when you believe something that you know ain't true." I can only repeat that this is misapprehension. *In concreto,*† the freedom to believe can only cover living options which the intellect of the individual cannot by itself resolve; and living options never seem absurdities to him who has them to consider. When I look at the religious question as it really puts itself to concrete men, and when I think of all the possibilities which both practically and theoretically it involves, then this command that we shall put a stopper on our heart, instincts, and courage, and *wait*— acting of course meanwhile more or less as if religion were *not* true[3]—till doomsday, or till such time as our intellect and senses working together may have raked in evidence enough,—this command, I say, seems to me the queerest idol ever manufactured in the philosophic cave. Were we scholastic absolutists, there might be more excuse. If we had an infallible intellect with its objective certitudes, we might feel ourselves disloyal to such a perfect organ of knowledge in not trusting to it exclusively, in not waiting for its releasing word. But if we are empiricists, if we believe that no bell in us tolls to let us know for certain when truth

is in our grasp, then it seems a piece of idle fantasticality to preach so solemnly our duty of waiting for the bell. Indeed we *may* wait if we will,—I hope you do not think that I am denying that,—but if we do so, we do so at our peril as much as if we believed. In either case we *act*, taking our life in our hands. No one of us ought to issue vetoes to the other, nor should we bandy words of abuse. We ought, on the contrary, delicately and profoundly to respect one another's mental freedom: then only shall we bring about the intellectual republic; then only shall we have that spirit of inner tolerance without which all our outer tolerance is soulless, and which is empiricism's glory; then only shall we live and let live, in speculative as well as in practical things.

I began by a reference to Fitz-James Stephen; let me end by a quotation from him. "What do you think of yourself? What do you think of the world? ... These are questions with which all must deal as it seems good to them. They are riddles of the Sphinx,‡ and in some way or other we must deal with them.... In all important transactions of life we have to take a leap in the dark.... If we decide to leave the riddles unanswered, that is a choice; if we waver in our answer, that, too, is a choice: but whatever choice we make, we make it at our peril. If a man chooses to turn his back altogether on God and the future, no one can prevent him; no one can show beyond reasonable doubt that he is mistaken. If a man thinks otherwise and acts as he thinks, I do not see that any one can prove that he is mistaken. Each must act as he thinks best; and if he is wrong, so much the worse for him. We stand on a mountain pass in the midst of whirling snow and blinding mist, through which we get glimpses now and then of paths which may be deceptive. If we stand still we shall be frozen to death. If we take the wrong road we shall be dashed to pieces. We do not certainly know whether there is any right one. What must we do? 'Be strong and of a good courage.' Act for the best, hope for the best, and take what comes.... If death ends all, we cannot meet death better."[4] ■

---

* "In the abstract."

† "In concrete (or actual) cases."

‡ In Greek legend, the Sphinx devoured all who could not solve its riddle. (Oedipus succeeded.)

Suggestions for Critical Reflection

1. The American judge Oliver Wendell Holmes, a close friend, once complained that James was inclined "to turn down the lights so as to give miracle a chance," shielding religious issues from the bright light of truth and careful, scientific inquiry. Do you agree with this criticism? How do you think James responded?

2. Do you think James's position in this essay is best understood as saying religious belief is in fact rational, or that religious belief is not rational but nevertheless 'lawful'?

3. James sometimes seems to talk as if we could and should believe things on the basis of our *will*, our decision to do so, and sometimes as if it's a matter of having some beliefs based on *emotion* ("our passional nature") rather than intellect. Do you think there's a conflict between these two ways of talking? If so, which do you think James really meant?

4. James takes W.K. Clifford's essay "The Ethics of Belief"—which is the reading before this one—as a foil to his own position in "The Will to Believe." If you have read Clifford's piece, how do you think his arguments stand up to James's criticisms? Clifford begins his essay with the story of a ship owner who suppresses his own doubts about the seaworthiness of his vessel and, "putting his trust in Providence," allows the ship to sail, carrying its load of immigrants to their death at sea. James never mentions this example—what do you think he would say about it?

5. Some critics of "The Will to Believe" have complained that James seems to be imagining only cases where we have no evidence at all, either for or against a particular possibility, and simply ignoring the much more common case where we are in possession of some evidence and have to weigh the balance of probabilities. Do you agree that James does this, and if so, is it a mistake on his part?

6. Another common criticism of this essay is that the religious belief James defends is highly attenuated: no more than the belief that "perfection is eternal." Do you share this reaction? Is this all that James is defending, in the end? In what way, if so, is this a "momentous" choice?

7. If you have read the Mackie selection "Evil and Omnipotence" you might want to ask yourself how James could respond to Mackie's claim that belief in a Christian/Islamic/Judaic (etc.) God is internally inconsistent and hence that no reasonable person should hold such a belief. Can James and Mackie *both* be right? If not, which of them is (if either)?

8. In *The Varieties of Religious Experience*, James defines 'truth' basically as what's good for you. He argues that religious belief is good for you. It follows that religious belief is true. Is this consistent with the main point in this essay? Is this basically different from Pascal's main point?

Notes

1 Compare the admirable page 310 in S.H. Hodgson's *Time and Space*, London, 1865.

2 Compare Wilfrid Ward's Essay, "The Wish to Believe," in his *Witnesses to the Unseen*, Macmillan & Co., 1893.

3 Since belief is measured by action, he who forbids us to believe religion to be true, necessarily also forbids us to act as we should if we did believe it to be true. The whole defence of religious faith hinges upon action. If the action required or inspired by the religious hypothesis is in no way different from that dictated by the naturalistic hypothesis, then religious faith is a pure superfluity, better pruned away, and controversy about its legitimacy is a piece of idle trifling, unworthy of serious minds. I myself believe, of course, that the religious hypothesis gives to the world an expression which specifically determines our reactions, and makes them in a large part unlike what they might be on a purely naturalistic scheme of belief.

4 *Liberty, Equality, Fraternity*, p. 353, 2nd edition. London, 1874.

Epistemology

IS THE EXTERNAL WORLD THE WAY IT APPEARS TO BE?

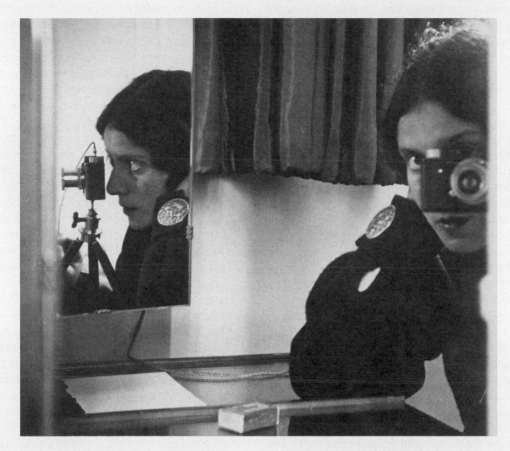

'Epistemology' is the theory of knowledge (the word comes from the Greek *epistēmē*, meaning knowledge). Epistemology can be thought of as arranged around three fundamental questions:

i) *What is knowledge?* For example, what is the difference between believing something that happens to be true and actually *knowing* it to be true? How much justification or proof do we need (if any) before we can be said to know something? Or does knowledge have more to do with, say, the *reliability* of our beliefs than our arguments for them? What is the difference between the

conclusions of good science and those of, for example, astrology? Or between astrology and religion?

ii) *What can we know?* What are the scope and limits of our knowledge? Can we ever really *know* about the real, underlying nature of the universe? Can we aspire to religious knowledge (e.g., of the true nature of God), or to ethical knowledge (as opposed to mere ethical belief or opinion), or to reliable knowledge of the historical past or the future? Can I ever know what you are thinking, or even *that* you are thinking? Do I even really know what *I* am thinking: e.g., might I have beliefs and desires that I am unaware of, perhaps because they are repressed or simply non-conscious?

iii) *How do we know that we know?* That is, how can we *justify* our claims to know things? What counts as 'enough' justification for a belief? Where does our knowledge—if we have any at all—come from in the first place? Do we acquire knowledge only through sense-experience, or can we also come to know important things through the power of our own naked reason? Do we have some beliefs which are especially 'basic'— which can be so reliably known that they can form a foundation for all our other beliefs? Or, by contrast, do all our pieces of knowledge fit together like the answers in a giant crossword puzzle, with each belief potentially up for grabs if the rest of the puzzle changes?

The epistemological question that is the focus of this chapter is sometimes called 'the problem of the external world.' In its starkest form, it is simply this: are *any* of our beliefs about the world outside our own heads justified? Can we be sure that any of them at all are *true*? For example, I currently believe that there is a laptop computer in front of me, and a soft-drink can on the table to my left, and a window to my right out of which I can see trees and grass and other houses. Furthermore, I not only believe that these objects exist but I also believe that they have a certain nature: that the pop can is colored red; that the trees outside are further away from me in space than the window I am looking through; that the houses are three-dimensional objects with solid walls, and that they continue to exist even when I close my eyes or turn away; that my computer will continue to behave in a (relatively!) predictable way in accordance with the laws of physics and of computing. But are any of these beliefs of mine justified: do any of them cross the threshold into being *knowledge*, as opposed to mere conjecture? And if some of them are known and not others, *which* are the ones I really know? Which are the beliefs to which a rational person should be committed, and which are the ones a rational person should jettison?

It may seem that these kinds of questions should be fairly straightforward to answer. *Of course* I know that my soda can exists and is really red; it should be pretty easy just to think for a while and give my compelling reasons for having this belief—the reasons which make this belief much more likely to be true than, say, the belief that the can is a figment of my imagination, or is really colorless. However, it turns out, the problem of the external world is a very challenging problem indeed, and

one which has been an important philosophical issue since at least the seventeenth century.

The first five readings in this chapter explore different aspects of the problem of the external world. First, we might ask, does the external world exist *at all*—is there any such thing as a world outside my own head, or might reality be just a dream or some sort of illusion? Plato uses the analogy of a cave to illustrate the view that the world we perceive is merely a superficial shadow cast by a quite different reality, which can only be known through the intellect and not the senses. In the modern era, Descartes seminally raises the question of whether the world we experience could be radically different from the way we perceive it to be and then tries to satisfactorily answer this conundrum. However, in 'solving' this problem, Descartes comes to the conclusion that only some of the things we commonsensically believe about the real nature of the external world are true or justifiable. The Locke reading can be thought of as extending this insight and making it more precise through his discussion of the distinction between 'primary qualities' (which resemble our ideas of them) and 'secondary qualities' (which do not). Locke also raises a somewhat different question: what can we know about the sort of 'stuff' that the external world is made of—if it is 'matter,' then what can we say about the kind of *substance* which is matter?

Kant, faced with what by this time seemed the intractable problem of proving that mind-independent material objects exist and resemble our ideas of them, attempted to make a radical break with the philosophical assumptions which he thought had generated the puzzle in the first place. Instead of assuming that our mental representations of the world are passive pictures of reality (which, like a portrait, could either be a good likeness or misleadingly inaccurate), he argued that our minds actually *interact* with data from the external world to *create* 'empirical reality.' For example, he claims, we cannot be mistaken in believing that external objects are three-dimensional, persist through time, and interact causally with each other, since all these features of reality are essential features of empirical experience: it is impossible, according to Kant, that anyone could have an experience that was not arranged in this way.

G.E. Moore represents one twentieth-century approach to the problem of the external world. He defends a 'common sense' approach to the problem of the external world, and with great care tries to show that there are many perfectly good proofs available to show that things exist external to our minds: for example, one can solve the problem of the external world by showing that at least two hands exist, and you can do this, Moore thinks, by simply waving your hands in front of your face.

The final four readings in this section introduce some key epistemological innovations of the twentieth century. Gettier's article "Is Justified True Belief Knowledge?" presents a deep problem for the basic philosophical intuition—which in some form goes all the way back to Plato—that any belief that is both true and properly justified counts as an instance of knowledge. Meanwhile, Lorraine Code challenges another generally historically-unquestioned assumption: that the ideal knower should be as objective as possible, such that any item of knowledge should be equally justifiable no matter what standpoint one occupies. Instead, Code argues, knowers are *situated*, and what they (can) know reflects their particular perspectives (as, for example, a woman rather than a man). Jennifer Saul explores the consequences of implicit bias, and argues compellingly that it gives rise to something similar to—and more pressingly serious than—philosophical skepticism. And Lee Hester and Jim Cheney provide an introduction to Indigenous (Native American, First Nations, Métis, or Inuit) ways of knowing and contrast them strikingly with Western forms of epistemology.

There are several good introductory epistemology textbooks currently available if you want more background information. For example: Robert Audi, *Epistemology* (Routledge, 2010); Jonathan Dancy, *Introduction to Contemporary Epistemology* (Blackwell, 1991); Richard Feldman, *Epistemology* (Prentice Hall, 2002); Alvin Goldman and Matthew McGrath, *Epistemology: A Contemporary Introduction* (Oxford University Press, 2014); Keith Lehrer, *Theory of Knowledge* (Westview, 2000); Robert M. Martin, *Epistemology: A Beginner's Guide* (OneWorld, 2014); Adam Morton, *A Guide through the Theory of Knowledge* (Blackwell, 2008); Jennifer Nagel, *Knowledge: A Very Short Introduction* (Oxford University Press, 2014); Pollock and Cruz, *Contemporary Theories of Knowledge* (Rowman & Littlefield, 1999); Matthias Steup, *An Introduction to Contemporary Epistemology* (Prentice Hall, 1996); Steup and Sosa, eds., *Contemporary Debates in Epistemology* (Blackwell, 2013); and Michael Williams, *Problems of Knowledge* (Oxford University Press, 2001). There are also several useful reference works on epistemology: Dancy, Sosa, and Steup, eds., *A Companion to Epistemology* (Blackwell, 2010); Paul K. Moser, *The Oxford Handbook of Epistemology* (Oxford University Press, 2005); Greco and Sosa, eds., *The Blackwell Guide to Epistemology* (Blackwell, 1999); and Bernecker and Pritchard, eds., *The Routledge Companion to Epistemology* (Routledge, 2011).

PLATO

The Allegory of the Cave

Who Was Plato?

The historical details of Plato's life are shrouded in uncertainty. He is traditionally thought to have been born in about 427 BCE and to have died in 347 BCE. His family, who lived in the Greek city-state of Athens, was aristocratic and wealthy. Legend has it that Plato's father, Ariston, was descended from Codrus, the last king of Athens, and his mother, Perictione, was related to the great Solon, who wrote the first Athenian constitution. While Plato was still a boy, his father died and his mother married Pyrilampes, a friend of the revered Athenian statesman Pericles who in the 450s had transformed Athens into one of the greatest cities in the Greek world.

As a young man, Plato probably fought in the Athenian army against Sparta during the Peloponnesian war (431–404 BCE)—which Athens lost—and he may have served again when Athens was involved in the Corinthian war (395–386 BCE).

Given his family connections, Plato looked set for a prominent role in Athenian political life, and, as it happened, when he was about 23, a political revolution occurred in Athens which could have catapulted Plato into public affairs. The coup swept the previous democratic rulers—who had just lost the war against Sparta—out of power and into exile, and replaced them with the so-called Thirty Tyrants, several of whom were Plato's friends and relatives. Plato, an idealistic young man, expected this would usher in a new era of justice and good government, but he was soon disillusioned when the new regime was even more violent and corrupt than the old. He withdrew from public life in disgust. The rule of the Thirty lasted only about 90 days before the exiled democrats were restored to power, and Plato—impressed by their relative lenience towards the coup leaders—apparently thought again about entering politics. But then, in 399 BCE, the city rulers arrested Plato's old friend and mentor, Socrates, and accused him of the trumped-up charge of impiety towards the city's gods and of corrupting the youth of Athens. Socrates was convicted by a jury of the townspeople, and—since he declared that he would rather die than give up philosophy, even though he was given a chance to escape—he was executed by being forced to drink poison.

> The result was that I, who had at first been full of eagerness for public affairs, when I considered all this and saw how things were shifting about every which way, at last became dizzy. I didn't cease to consider ways of improving this particular situation, however, and, indeed, of reforming the whole constitution. But as far as action was concerned, I kept waiting for favorable moments and finally saw clearly that the constitutions of all actual cities are bad and that their laws are almost beyond redemption without extraordinary resources and luck as well. Hence I was compelled to say in praise of the true philosophy that it enables us to discern what is just for a city or an individual in every case and that the human race will have no respite from evils until those who are really and truly philosophers acquire political power or until, through some divine dispensation, those who rule and have political authority in cities become real philosophers.*

After the death of Socrates, it appears that Plato, along with some other philosophical followers of Socrates, fled Athens and went to the city of Megara in east-

---

* This is a quotation from the so-called *Seventh Letter*, supposed to have been written by Plato when he was 70 years old. It is not certain that Plato actually wrote this document, but if it was not his, it was probably written by one of his disciples shortly after his death. See Plato, *Seventh Letter*, translated by C.D.C. Reeve in his "Introduction" to Plato's *Republic*, trans. G.M.A. Grube, revised by C.D.C. Reeve (Hackett, 1992), ix–x. The later fragmentary quote is from the translation of the *Seventh Letter* by Glen R. Morrow, in *Plato: Complete Works*, ed. John M. Cooper and D.S. Hutchinson (Hackett, 1997), 1648.

central Greece to stay with the philosopher Eucleides (a follower of the great Greek philosopher Parmenides of Elea). He may also have visited Egypt, though his travels at this time are shrouded in myth. It appears that Plato started doing philosophy in earnest at about this time, and his earliest writings date from this point. Almost all of Plato's writings are in the form of dialogues between two or more characters and, in most of them, the character leading the discussion is Socrates. Since Plato never wrote himself into any of his dialogues, it is usually—though not uncontroversially—assumed that the views expressed by the character of Socrates more or less correspond with those that Plato is trying to put forward in his dialogues.

Later, when Plato was about 40, he made another trip away from Athens, visiting Italy to talk with the Pythagorean philosophers. Plato was deeply impressed by Pythagorean philosophy—especially their emphasis on mathematics—but he was horrified by the luxury and sensuality of life in Italy, "with men gorging themselves twice a day and never sleeping alone at night."

After Italy, Plato visited Syracuse on the island of Sicily where, during a long stay, he became close friends with Dion, the brother-in-law of the ruling tyrant Dionysius I.* Dion became Plato's pupil, and (according to legend) came to prefer the philosophical life of moral goodness to the pleasure, luxury, and power of his surroundings. Exactly what happened next is historically unclear, but there is some reason to believe Plato was captured by a displeased Dionysius, sold into slavery, and subsequently rescued from the slave market when his freedom was purchased by an unidentified benevolent stranger.

On Plato's return to Athens, he bought land in a precinct named for an Athenian hero called Academus, and there, in about 385, he founded the first European university (or at least, the first of which there is any real historical knowledge). Because of its location, this school was called the Academy, and it was to remain in existence for over 900 years, until 529 CE. For most of the rest of his life, Plato stayed at the Academy, directing its studies, and he probably wrote the *Republic* there (in about 380 BCE). Very quickly, the school became a vital center for research in all kinds of subjects, both theoretical and practical. It was probably one of the first cradles for the subjects of metaphysics, epistemology, psychology, ethics, politics, aesthetics, and mathematical science, and members were invited, by various Greek city-states, to help draft new political constitutions.

In 368 Dionysius I of Sicily died and Dion persuaded his successor, Dionysius II, to send for Plato to advise him on how the state should be run. Plato, by now about 60, agreed with some misgivings, possibly hoping to make the younger Dionysius an example of a philosopher-king and to put the doctrines of the *Republic* into practice. However, the experiment was a disastrous failure. Dionysius II—though he gave himself airs as a philosopher—had no inclination to learn philosophy and mathematics in order to become a better ruler. Within four months Dion was banished, and Plato returned to Greece shortly afterwards. However, four years later Dionysius II convinced Plato to return, pressuring him with testimonials from eminent philosophers describing Dionysius's love for philosophy, and bribing him by offering to reinstate Dion at Syracuse within a year. Once again, the king proved false: he not only kept Dion in exile but confiscated and sold his lands and property. Plato was imprisoned on Sicily for nearly two years until, in 360, he finally escaped and returned to Athens for good. He died 13 years later, at the ripe old age of 80.†

What Was Plato's Overall Philosophical Project?

Plato is probably the single person with the best claim to being the inventor of western philosophy. His thought encompassed nearly all the areas central to philosophy today—metaphysics, epistemology, ethics, political theory, aesthetics, and the philosophy of science and mathematics—and, for the first time in European history, dealt with them in a unified way.‡ Plato thought of

---

* Indeed, Plato later wrote a poem about Dion and spoke of being driven out of his mind with love for him.

† Dion, meanwhile, attempted to recover his position at Syracuse by force—an endeavor Plato, wisely, refused to support—and was later assassinated by Callippus, a supposed friend and fellow member of the Academy.

‡ In fact the mathematician and philosopher Alfred North Whitehead (1861–1947) famously was moved to say that "The safest general characterization of the European philosophical tradition is that it consists of a series of footnotes

philosophy as a special discipline with its own intellectual method, and he was convinced it had foundational importance in human life. Only philosophy, Plato thought, could provide genuine understanding, since only philosophy scrutinized the assumptions that other disciplines left unquestioned. Furthermore, according to Plato, philosophy reveals a realm of comprehensive and unitary hidden truths—indeed, a whole level of reality that the senses cannot detect—which goes far beyond everyday common sense and which, when properly understood, has the power to revolutionize the way we live our lives and organize our societies. Philosophy, and only philosophy, holds the key to genuine human happiness and well-being.

This realm of objects which Plato claimed to have discovered is generally known as that of the Platonic Forms. The Forms—according to Plato—are changeless, eternal objects, which lie outside of both the physical world and the minds of individuals, and which can only be encountered through pure thought rather than through sensation. One of Plato's favorite examples of a Form is the mathematical property of Equality. In a dialogue called the *Phaedo* he argues that Equality itself cannot be identical with two equal sticks, or with any other group of physical objects of equal length, since we could always be mistaken about whether any two observed objects are really equal with one another, but we could not possibly be mistaken about Equality itself and somehow take *it* to be unequal. When two sticks are equal in length, therefore, they "participate in" Equality—it is their relation to Equality which makes them equal rather than unequal—but Equality itself is an abstract object which exists over and above all the instances of equal things. The form of Equality is what one succeeds in understanding when one has a proper conception of what Equality really is in itself: real knowledge, therefore, comes not from observation but from acquaintance with the Forms. Other central examples of Platonic Forms are Sameness, Number, Motion, Beauty, Justice, Piety, and (the most important Form of all) Goodness.

What Is the Structure of This Reading?

The *Republic* is written in the form of a dramatic dialogue. The narrator, Socrates, speaking directly to the reader, is describing a recent philosophical conversation he had with various other characters. In this excerpt the person he is speaking to is Glaucon (who was actually one of Plato's brothers). In this selection, Socrates—who, in this case, is usually thought to be expressing the views of Plato himself—describes the relation of the ordinary world of perceivable, concrete objects to the realm of the Forms, using the allegory of a cave. Ordinary people, lacking the benefit of a philosophical education, are like prisoners trapped underground in a cave since birth and forced to look only at shadows cast on the wall in front of them by puppets behind their backs, dancing in front of a fire. With the proper philosophical encouragement, they can—if they have the courage to do so—break their bonds and turn around to see that what they believed was reality was really only an illusory puppet show. The philosophers among them can even leave the cave to encounter the true reality—of which even the puppets are only copies—illuminated by the light of the sun which, for Plato, represents the form of the Good. The perceptible world is thus merely an imperfect image of—and sustained by—the quasi-divine, eternal realm of the unchanging and unobservable Forms.

Some Useful Background Information

1. Implicit in the story Socrates tells is a hierarchy of things, each of which corresponds to something in his analogy. From 'worst' to 'best' these are: the shadows of artificial objects (cast by the fire), the artificial objects themselves, the fire, the shadows or reflections of natural objects (cast by the sun), natural objects, and the sun. The corresponding levels in the analogy are (roughly): perceptions or images, material objects, light,* mathematical objects, abstract ideas or forms, and the form of the Good.

---

to Plato." Alfred North Whitehead, *Process and Reality*, corrected edition, ed. D.R. Griffin and D.W. Sherburne (Free Press, 1978), 39.

* So notice that, a bit confusingly, the fire in the cave is an allegory for the sun in real life, while the sun in Socrates's story is an allegory for the Good.

How Important and Influential Is This Passage?

Plato's vivid cave allegory has been influencing Western thought and culture for two thousand years. Sometimes emphasis is placed on its epistemological importance and Plato's theory of Forms as being the fundamental reality. Other readers are most struck by its political resonance, as a plea for the importance of education and philosophical clear-sightedness in our leaders, or as an account of what it means to be really free. In contemporary culture it is frequently referenced either explicitly or implicitly, in movies such as *The Matrix*, *Dark City*, *The Truman Show* and *City of Ember*, and books like Ray Bradbury's *Fahrenheit 451* and Emma Donoghue's *Room*.

"The Allegory of the Cave"*

FROM REPUBLIC, BOOK VII (514A–517C)

And now, I said, let me show in a figure† how far our nature is enlightened or unenlightened:—Behold! human beings living in a underground den, which has a mouth open towards the light and reaching all along the den; here they have been from their childhood, and have their legs and necks chained so that they cannot move, and can only see before them, being prevented by the chains from turning round their heads. Above and behind them a fire is blazing at a distance, and between the fire and the prisoners there is a raised way; and you will see, if you look, a low wall built along the way, like the screen which marionette players have in front of them, over which they show the puppets.

I see.

And do you see, I said, men passing along the wall carrying all sorts of vessels, and statues and figures of animals made of wood and stone and various materials, which appear over the wall? Some of them are talking, others silent.

You have shown me a strange image, and they are strange prisoners.

Like ourselves, I replied; and they see only their own shadows, or the shadows of one another, which the fire throws on the opposite wall of the cave?

True, he said; how could they see anything but the shadows if they were never allowed to move their heads?

And of the objects which are being carried in like manner they would only see the shadows?

Yes, he said.

And if they were able to converse with one another, would they not suppose that they were naming what was actually before them?

Very true.

And suppose further that the prison had an echo which came from the other side, would they not be sure to fancy when one of the passers-by spoke that the voice which they heard came from the passing shadow?

No question, he replied.

To them, I said, the truth would be literally nothing but the shadows of the images.

That is certain.

And now look again, and see what will naturally follow if the prisoners are released and disabused of their error. At first, when any of them is liberated and compelled suddenly to stand up and turn his neck round and walk and look towards the light, he will suffer sharp pains; the glare will distress him, and he will be unable to see the realities of which in his former state he had seen the shadows; and then conceive some one saying to him, that what he saw before was an illusion, but that now, when he is approaching nearer to being and his eye is turned towards more real existence, he has a clearer vision,—what will be his

---

* This translation of the beginning of Book VII of Plato's *Republic* (380 BCE) is by Benjamin Jowett (1888).

† An imaginary form.

reply? And you may further imagine that his instructor is pointing to the objects as they pass and requiring him to name them,—will he not be perplexed? Will he not fancy that the shadows which he formerly saw are truer than the objects which are now shown to him?

Far truer.

And if he is compelled to look straight at the light, will he not have a pain in his eyes which will make him turn away to take refuge in the objects of vision which he can see, and which he will conceive to be in reality clearer than the things which are now being shown to him?

True, he said.

And suppose once more, that he is reluctantly dragged up a steep and rugged ascent, and held fast until he is forced into the presence of the sun himself, is he not likely to be pained and irritated? When he approaches the light his eyes will be dazzled, and he will not be able to see anything at all of what are now called realities.

Not all in a moment, he said.

He will require to grow accustomed to the sight of the upper world. And first he will see the shadows best, next the reflections of men and other objects in the water, and then the objects themselves; then he will gaze upon the light of the moon and the stars and the spangled heaven; and he will see the sky and the stars by night better than the sun or the light of the sun by day?

Certainly.

Last of all he will be able to see the sun, and not mere reflections of him* in the water, but he will see him in his own proper place, and not in another; and he will contemplate him as he is.

Certainly.

He will then proceed to argue that this is he who gives the season and the years, and is the guardian of all that is in the visible world, and in a certain way the cause of all things which he and his fellows have been accustomed to behold?

Clearly, he said, he would first see the sun and then reason about him.

And when he remembered his old habitation, and the wisdom of the den and his fellow-prisoners, do you not suppose that he would felicitate† himself on the change, and pity them?

Certainly, he would.

And if they were in the habit of conferring honours among themselves on those who were quickest to observe the passing shadows and to remark which of them went before, and which followed after, and which were together; and who were therefore best able to draw conclusions as to the future, do you think that he would care for such honours and glories, or envy the possessors of them? Would he not say with Homer, "Better to be the poor servant of a poor master,"‡ and to endure anything, rather than think as they do and live after their manner?

Yes, he said, I think that he would rather suffer anything than entertain these false notions and live in this miserable manner.

Imagine once more, I said, such an one coming suddenly out of the sun to be replaced in his old situation; would he not be certain to have his eyes full of darkness?

To be sure, he said.

And if there were a contest, and he had to compete in measuring the shadows with the prisoners who had never moved out of the den, while his sight was still weak, and before his eyes had become steady (and the time which would be needed to acquire this new habit of sight might be very considerable), would he not be ridiculous? Men would say of him that up he went and down he came without his eyes; and that it was better not even to think of ascending; and if any one tried to loose another and lead him up to the light, let them only catch the offender, and they would put him to death.

---

* Jowett translates Socrates as calling the sun "him," indicating that for Plato the sun represents the form of the Good.

† Congratulate.

‡ Socrates is paraphrasing an exclamation by Achilles's ghost to Odysseus in Homer's epic poem the *Odyssey* (c. 725 BCE): "By god, I'd rather slave on earth for another man—Some dirt-poor tenant farmer who scrapes to keep alive—Than rule down here over all the breathless dead" (trans. Robert Fagles).

No question, he said.

This entire allegory, I said, you may now append, dear Glaucon, to the previous argument;* the prison-house is the world of sight, the light of the fire is the sun, and you will not misapprehend me if you interpret the journey upwards to be the ascent of the soul into the intellectual world according to my poor belief, which, at your desire, I have expressed—whether rightly or wrongly God knows. But, whether true or false, my opinion is that in the world of knowledge the idea of good appears last of all, and is seen only with an effort; and, when seen, is also inferred to be the universal author of all things beautiful and right, parent of light and of the lord of light in this visible world, and the immediate source of reason and truth in the intellectual; and that this is the power upon which he who would act rationally either in public or private life must have his eye fixed. ■

Suggestions for Critical Reflection

1. What do you think Socrates has in mind when he talks about certain special people breaking the chains that hold them in the cave and ascending to the light of the sun? What is this an allegory for? How can we achieve this—what sort of process would this be?

2. Given what Socrates says here, what do you think is his view of the knowledge we gain from our senses? Given what Socrates says here, what do you think is his view of material objects—the things that we perceive with our senses?

3. Why do you think Socrates emphasizes how difficult it is to break out of the cave, and how hard it is to get used to the new understanding of reality that this reveals?

---

*   These previous arguments are known as the analogy of the sun (*Republic* 508b–509c) and the analogy of the divided line (509d–511e).

RENÉ DESCARTES

Meditations on First Philosophy

Who Was René Descartes?

René Descartes was born in 1596 in a small town nestled below the vineyards of the Loire in western France; at that time the town was called La Haye, but it was later renamed Descartes in his honor. His early life was probably unhappy: he suffered from ill health, his mother had died a year after he was born, and he didn't get on well with his father. (When René sent his father a copy of his first published book, his father's only reported reaction was that he was displeased to have a son "idiotic enough to have himself bound in vellum."*) At the age of about 10 he went to the newly founded college of La Flèche to be educated by the Jesuits. Descartes later called this college "one of the best schools in Europe," and it was there that he learned the medieval 'scholastic' science and philosophy that he was later decisively to reject. Descartes took a law degree at the University of Poitiers and studied mathematics and mechanics; then, at 21, joined first the Dutch army of Prince Maurice of Nassau and then the forces of Maximilian of Bavaria. As a soldier he saw little action, traveling around Europe supported by his family's wealth. During this period, he had resolved "to seek no knowledge other than that which could be found either in myself or in the great book of the world," developing an intense interest in mathematics, which stayed with him for the rest of his life. In fact, Descartes was one of the most important figures in the development of algebra, which is the branch of mathematics that allows abstract relations to be described without using specific numbers, and which is therefore capable of unifying arithmetic and geometry:†

I came to see that the exclusive concern of mathematics is with questions of order or method, and that it is irrelevant whether the measure in question involves numbers, shapes, stars, sounds, or any other object whatsoever. This made me realize that there must be a general science which explains all the points that can be raised concerning order and measure irrespective of subject matter. (From *Rules for the Direction of our Native Intelligence* [1628])

This insight led Descartes directly to one of the most significant intellectual innovations of the modern age: the conception of science as the exploration of abstract mathematical descriptions of the world.

It was also during this time—in 1619—that Descartes had the experience said to have inspired him to take up the life of a philosopher, and which, perhaps, eventually resulted in the form of the *Meditations*. Stranded by bad weather near Ulm on the river Danube, Descartes spent the day in a *poêle* (a stoveheated room‡) engaged in intense philosophical speculations. That night he had three vivid dreams which he later described as giving him his mission in life. In the first dream Descartes felt himself attacked by phantoms and then a great wind; he was then greeted by a friend who gave him a message about a gift. On awaking after this first dream, Descartes felt a sharp pain which made him fear that the dream was the work of some deceitful evil demon. Descartes eventually fell back asleep and immediately had the second dream: a loud thunderclap, which woke him in terror believing that the room was filled with fiery sparks. The third and last dream was a pleasant one, in which he found an encyclopedia on a table next to a poetry anthol-

---

* Vellum is the parchment made from animal skin that was used to make books.

† He invented the method still used to quantify locations on a graph: Cartesian coordinates (that adjective is derived from the Latin version of his name, 'Cartesius').

‡ Sometimes Descartes's words are taken in what might be their literal meaning, that he spent time in a stove. But although there is other evidence of his eccentricity, this seems an uncharitable translation.

ogy, open to a poem which begins with the line "Which road in life shall I follow?" A man then appeared and said "*Est et non*"—"it is and is not." While still asleep, Descartes apparently began to speculate about the meaning of his dreams, and decided, among other things, that the gift of which his friend spoke in the first dream was the gift of solitude, the dictionary represented systematic knowledge, and "*Est et non*" spoke of the distinction between truth and falsity as revealed by the correct scientific method. Descartes concluded that he had a divine mission to found a new philosophical system to underpin all human knowledge.

In 1628, at the age of 32, Descartes settled in Holland (at the time the most intellectually vibrant nation in Europe), where he lived for most of his remaining life. It was only then that he began sustained work in metaphysics and mathematical physics. His family was wealthy enough that Descartes, who cultivated very modest tastes, was free of the necessity to earn a living and could devote his time to scientific experimentation and writing. By 1633 he had prepared a book on cosmology and physics, called *Le Monde* (The World), in which he accepted Galileo's revolutionary claim that the Earth orbits the sun (rather than the other way around), but when he heard that Galileo had been condemned by the Inquisition of the Catholic Church, Descartes withdrew the work from publication.* In 1637 he published (in French) a sample of his scientific work, *Optics, Meteorology, and Geometry*, together with an introduction called *Discourse on the Method of Rightly Conducting One's Reason and Reaching the Truth in the Sciences*. Criticisms of this methodology led Descartes to compose his philosophical masterpiece, *Meditations on First Philosophy*, first published in Latin in 1641. (A French translation, prepared under Descartes's supervision and incorporating his changes, was published in 1647.) In 1644 he published a summary of his scientific and philosophical views, the *Principles of Philosophy*, which he hoped would become a standard university textbook, replacing the medieval texts used at the time. His last work, published in 1649, was *The Passions of the Soul*,

which attempted to extend his scientific methodology to ethics and psychology.

Descartes never married, but in 1635 he had a daughter, Francine, with a serving woman called Hélène Jans. He made arrangements for the care and education of the girl, but she died of scarlet fever at the age of five, a devastating shock for Descartes.

In 1649 Descartes accepted an invitation to visit Stockholm and give philosophical instruction to Queen Kristina of Sweden. He was required to give tutorials at the royal palace at five o'clock in the morning; ever since he was a sickly schoolboy he had habitually stayed in bed until 11 am, and it is said that the strain of this sudden break in his habits caused him to catch pneumonia; he died in February 1650. His dying words are said to have been, "*mon âme; il faut partir*"—my soul, it's time to part. His body was returned to France but, apparently, his head was secretly kept in Sweden; in the 1820s a skull bearing the faded inscription "René Descartes" was discovered in Stockholm and is now on display in the Museum of Natural History in Paris.

What Was Descartes's Overall Philosophical Project?

Descartes lived at a time when the accumulated beliefs of centuries—assumptions based on religious doctrine, straightforward observation, and common sense—were being gradually but remorselessly stripped away by exciting new discoveries. (The most striking example of this was the evidence mounting against the centuries-old belief that an unmoving Earth is the center of the universe, orbited by the moon, sun, stars, and all the other planets.) In this intellectual climate, Descartes became obsessed by the thought that no lasting scientific progress was possible without a systematic method for sifting through our preconceived assumptions and distinguishing between those that are reliable and those that are false. Descartes's central intellectual goal was to develop just such a reliable scientific method, and then to construct a coherent and unified theory of the world

---

* Descartes was very aware of the threat from Catholic authorities' opposition to his ideas, and afraid of it. After his death, all his works were placed on the Index of Prohibited Works by the Church, with the note that they would remain there "until corrected." (The Church announced in 1966 that the prohibition of items on this list was no longer to be considered law, but the Index was still retained as a moral guide.)

and of humankind's place within it. This theory, he hoped, would replace scholasticism, the deeply flawed medieval system of thought based on the science of Aristotle and Christian theology.

A key feature of Descartes's system is that all knowledge should be based on utterly reliable foundations, discovered through the systematic rejection of any assumptions that can possibly be called into doubt. Then, as in mathematics, complex conclusions could be reliably derived from these foundations by chains of valid reasoning—of simple and certain inferences. The human faculty of *reason* was therefore of the greatest importance. Furthermore, Descartes urged that scientific knowledge of the external world should be rooted, not in the deceptive and variable testimony of the senses, but in the concepts of pure mathematics. That is, Cartesian science tries to reduce all physics to "what the geometers call *quantity*, and take as the object of their demonstrations, i.e., that to which every kind of division shape and motion is applicable" (*Principles of Philosophy*, 1644). (There is, however, for Descartes, a place for empirical investigation in science—not as a tool for producing general understanding, but rather to determine the real external existences of particular things.)

These ideas (though they have never been uncritically and uniformly accepted) have come to permeate the modern conception of science, including Descartes's influential metaphor of a unified "tree of knowledge," with metaphysics as the roots, physics as the trunk, and the special sciences (like biology, anthropology, or ethics) as the branches. His most important and lasting influence on scientific thought is his idea that the physical world is a unified whole, governed by very basic universal mathematical and physical laws, and that finding these is the most basic job of science. One much less familiar, and less lasting, aspect of Descartes's method for the production of knowledge is the central role played by God in his system. For Descartes, all human knowledge of the world around us essentially relies upon our prior knowledge that a non-deceiving God exists. Science, properly understood, not only does not conflict with religion but actually *depends* on religion, he believed.

Finally, one of the best-known results of Descartes's metaphysical reflections is "Cartesian dualism." This doctrine states that mind and body are two completely different substances—that the mind is a nonphysical self in which all the operations of thought take place, and which can be wholly separated from the body after death. Like much of Descartes's work, this theory came to have the status of a more or less standard view for some 300 years after his death, but at the time it was a radical philosophical innovation, breaking with the traditional Aristotelian conception of mental activity as a kind of *attribute* of the physical body (rather than as something entirely separable from the body).

What Is the Structure of This Reading?

The *Meditations* is not intended to be merely an exposition of philosophical arguments and conclusions, but is supposed to be an exercise in philosophical reflection for the reader—as Bernard Williams has put it, "the 'I' that appears throughout them from the first sentence on does not specifically represent [Descartes]: it represents anyone who will step into the position it marks, the position of the thinker who is prepared to reconsider and recast his or her beliefs, as Descartes supposed we might, from the ground up."* Descartes aims to convince us of the truth of his conclusions by making us conduct the arguments ourselves. (It is interesting to note that the structure of the *Meditations* was modeled on the "spiritual exercises" that students at Jesuit schools, such as the one Descartes attended, were required to undertake in order to learn to move away from the world of the senses and to focus on God.)

In the First Meditation the thinker applies a series of progressively more radical doubts to his or her preconceived opinions, which leaves her unsure whether she knows anything at all. But then in the Second Meditation the thinker finds a secure foundational belief in her indubitable awareness of her own existence. The rest of this meditation is a reflection on the thinker's own nature as a "thinking thing." In the Third Meditation the thinker realizes that final certainty can only be achieved through the existence of a non-deceiving God, and argues from the idea of God found in her own mind to the conclusion that God must really exist and be the cause of this idea (this is sometimes nicknamed the "Trademark Argument," from the notion that our possession of the

---

* This appears in his introductory essay to the Cambridge University Press edition of the *Meditations* (1996).

idea of God is God's "trademark" on his creation). The Fourth Meditation urges that the way to avoid error in our judgments is to restrict our beliefs to things of which we are clearly and distinctly certain. The Fifth Meditation introduces Cartesian science by discussing the mathematical nature of our knowledge of matter, and also includes a second proof for God's existence which resembles the eleventh-century "ontological argument" of St. Anselm. Finally, in the Sixth Meditation, the thinker re-establishes our knowledge of the real existence of the external world, argues that mind and body are two distinct substances, and reflects on how mind and body are related.

Some Useful Background Information

1. Descartes makes frequent use of the terms "substance," "essence," and "accident." A substance is, roughly, a bearer of attributes, i.e., a thing that has properties, what the properties are properties *of*. The essence of a substance is its fundamental intrinsic nature, a property without which that thing, of that sort, could not exist. Descartes held that for every substance there is exactly one property which is its essence. A substance's "accidents"* are all the rest of its properties, the ones which are not part of its essence.

    Take, for example, a red ball: its redness, the spherical shape, the rubbery feel, and so on, are all properties—accidents—of the ball, and the ball's substance is the "stuff" that underlies and possesses these properties. According to Descartes, the fundamental nature of this stuff— its essence—is that it is extended in three dimensions, that it fills space.

    For Descartes and his contemporaries there is also another important aspect to the idea of substance. Unlike an instance of a property, which cannot exist all by itself (there can't be an occurrence of redness without there being something which is red—some bit of substance which is the bearer of that property), substances are not dependent for their existence on something else. In

fact, for Descartes, this is actually the *definition* of a substance: "By 'substance' we can understand nothing other than a thing which exists in such a way as to depend on no other things for its existence" (*Principles of Philosophy*). So, for instance, a tree is not really a substance, since trees do depend for their existence on other things (such as soil, light, past trees, and so on). On the other hand, according to Descartes, matter itself—all matter, taken as a whole—is a substance. Matter cannot be destroyed or created (except by God), it can only change its local form, gradually moving from the form of a tree to the form of a rotting tree trunk to the form of soil, for example.

2. Descartes relies quite heavily in the *Meditations* on a three-fold contrast between intellect (or understanding), the will, and sensation and imagination. He explains this distinction in some detail in the Sixth Meditation, but the basic distinction is as follows: Sensation and imagination involve the presentation of ideas, especially mental images. The word 'Imagination' here has a more particular sense than the current one, which includes any sort of speculation or invention; Descartes's notion is an earlier one, involving the having of mental images—pictures in the mind's eye, so to speak. The understanding is our intellectual apprehension of ideas, the faculty by which the mind considers the contents of thoughts (indeed, without understanding, mere sensations have no content at all). The will is our ability to either assent or dissent to these ideas—it is our faculty of judgment. An act of will (assent) is necessary for there to be a belief at all, according to Descartes—a mere idea by itself can be neither accurate nor erroneous.

    Two key details are worth bearing in mind for a fuller appreciation of Descartes's arguments in the *Meditations*. First, although the understanding/ imagination distinction would have been quite familiar at the time, Descartes departs from the intellectual tradition of Aristotle in holding that sensation and imagination, though they certainly intimately involve the body, are modes of the mind. (Aristotle and his followers held that only

---

* Strictly speaking, Descartes thought of accidents as being 'modes' of the one essential property of the substance (rather than being really separate properties): shape, for example, is a mode of being extended in space.

the intellect is properly mental.) Furthermore, Descartes emphasized that our sensations, by themselves, tell us nothing about the world—only our understanding generates judgments. This is arguably the central point of the famous wax example, in the Second Meditation.

Second, Descartes believed that the understanding is a passive, rather than an active, mental faculty: it takes in the deliveries of sensation, for example, and produces thoughts almost automatically, according to the way in which God has created us. By contrast, the will (also given to us by God) is an active mental faculty. We cannot choose how the world appears to us, but we can choose whether or not to certify those judgments as accurate. In this way, for Descartes, error is almost a moral failing—a failure of the will. Our mistakes are not God's fault, but our own.

3. A related phrase frequently used by Descartes in the *Meditations* is the "natural light." Descartes has in mind here what in earlier writings he calls "the light of reason"—the pure inner light of the intellect, a faculty given to us by God, which allows us to see the truth of the world much more clearly than we can with the confused and fluctuating testimony of the senses.

4. Descartes, following the scholastic jargon of the time, calls the representational content of an idea its "objective reality" (he uses this term in his attempted proof of the existence of God in the Third Meditation). Confusingly, for something to have merely objective reality in this sense is for it to belong to the mental world of ideas, and not to the mind-independent external world at all.

For example, if I imagine Santa Claus as being fat and jolly, then Descartes would say that fatness is "objectively" present in my idea—an idea of fatness forms part of my idea of Santa Claus. By contrast, the baby beluga at the Chicago aquarium is fat, but its fatness is not merely the *idea* of fatness but an actual property of the beluga. In general, for any idea *I* that represents a thing *X* which has the property of being F, F-ness will be present formally in *X* but objectively in *I*.

What Descartes and his contemporaries call "formal reality," then, is just the reality something has simply by virtue of existing. Since ideas exist (they are modes of a thinking substance), they have both formal reality—the idea itself—and objective reality—the content of the idea.

5. Although Descartes's talk of a non-physical "soul" was in accord with contemporary Christian theology, his reasons for holding that the mind is immortal and non-material (given largely in the Second and Sixth Meditations) were not primarily religious ones. Descartes does not think of the soul as being especially "spiritual" or as being identical with our "better nature," for example. For Descartes the word "soul" simply means the same as the word "mind," and encompasses the whole range of conscious mental activity, including the sensations of sight, touch, sound, taste, and smell; emotions (such as joy or jealousy); and cognitive activities like believing, planning, desiring, or doubting. For Descartes the mind, or soul, is also to be distinguished from the brain: our brains, since they are extended material things, are part of our body and not our mind.

6. Descartes's metaphysics was a radical departure from the then-prevailing Aristotelian view of nature. In very brief summary, Aristotelians saw natural bodies as being composed of both form and matter. Matter cannot exist without form, and a thing's form determines its nature: that is, a thing's form makes it what it is—a horse, a tree, a cloud—by determining its characteristic development and behavior. There are four basic substances—earth, air, fire, and water—and four basic qualities—hot, cold, wet, and dry. Most natural bodies are made up of mixtures of elements, and they belong to different kinds (such as species, or types of minerals) defined by their forms. In this way, Aristotelian science made no distinction between biological processes, such as growth or nutrition, and other natural phenomena such as burning or gravity: they are all the playing out of essential forms, principles of growth and change, that are 'built in' to the entities involved. For the Aristotelian, then, scientific explanation will be a matter of identifying the multifarious forms—the essential natures—of all the different items in the natural world. Furthermore, the objects that we encounter in nature really have the properties they appear to have to our senses—color, texture, taste, odor, and so on—and what it is for us to perceive the world is a transfer of these qualities from

external objects to our sense organs (where they are received in our sensory soul as a "form without matter"). One final important aspect of Aristotelian science: the changing, natural realm in which we live is located at the center of the universe (due to the tendency of earth and water, because of their natures, to seek the center and thus collect there), but there is a radical discontinuity between this world and the heavenly spheres—literally, crystalline spheres in which the moon, sun, planets and stars were thought to be embedded—which are unchanging, and not even made of the familiar four elements but of a completely different fifth element (called quintessence).

One of the interpretive tasks in reading the *Meditations* (which Descartes secretly thought of as being designed to present his new and, for his audience highly counter-intuitive, physics) is to discover the differences between the Aristotelian tradition and Descartes's own account. Some of the Cartesian departures to look for are: that different natural kinds differ only in the sizes, shapes, and motions of the particles that make them up; that matter does not contain within it its own principle of motion and change but is 'passive' and subject to external forces; that the qualities we encounter in sense experience do not resemble the causes of those experiences; and that the whole material world, including the heliocentric solar system, is governed by the same small set of laws of motion.

Some Common Misconceptions

1. The *Meditations* describe a process, in which the thinker moves from pre-reflective starting points towards a clearer understanding of knowledge. As a consequence, not everything that Descartes writes—especially in the earlier meditations—is something that he, or the thinker, will agree with by the time they have completed the process. (For example, he begins by saying that "[u]p to this point, what I have accepted as very true I have

derived either from the senses or through the senses," which is a principle he later rejects.)

2. Descartes is not a skeptic. Although he is famous for the skeptical arguments put forward in the First Meditation, he uses these only in order to go beyond them.* It is a bit misleading, however, to think of Descartes as setting out in the *Meditations* to defeat skepticism: his main interest is probably not in proving the skeptic wrong, but in discovering the first principles upon which a proper science can be built. He uses skepticism, surprisingly, in order to create knowledge—to show that a properly constituted science would have nothing to fear from even the most radical doubts of the skeptic. Thus, for example, Descartes does not at any point argue that we should actually believe that the external world does not exist—instead, he suspends his belief in external objects until he has a chance to properly build a foundation for this belief (and by the end of the *Meditations* he is quite certain that the external world exists).

3. The "method of doubt" which Descartes uses in the *Meditations* is not an everyday method—it is not supposed to be an appropriate technique for making day-to-day decisions, or even for doing science or mathematics. Most of the time it would be hugely impractical for us to call into question everything that we might possibly doubt, to question all our presuppositions, before we make a judgment. Instead the method of the *Meditations* is supposed to be a once-in-a-lifetime exercise, by which we discover and justify the basic "first principles" that we rely on in everyday knowledge. In short, we always have to rely on certain assumptions when we make decisions or do science, and this is unavoidable but dangerous; the exercise of the *Meditations* can ensure that the assumptions we rely upon are absolutely secure.

4. Although "I think therefore I am" (or "I am, I exist") is the first step in Descartes's reconstruction of human knowledge in the *Meditations*, it is nevertheless not the first piece of *knowledge* that he recognizes—it does not arise out of a

---

* In one of his letters, Descartes noted that, when ancient medical authorities such as Galen or Hippocrates wrote about the causes of disease, no one accused them of telling people how to get sick; in the same way, Descartes complained, "I put forward these reasons for doubting not to convince people of them but, on the contrary, in order to refute them."

complete knowledge vacuum. Before the thinker can come to know that "I think therefore I am" is true, Descartes elsewhere admits that she must know, for example, what is meant by thinking, and that doubting is a kind of thought, and that in order to think one must first exist. Therefore, it is best to think of "I think therefore I am," not as the first item of knowledge, but as the first *non-trivial* piece of secure knowledge about the world that a thinker can have. It's a piece of information not just about concepts or logic but actually about the world—but, according to Descartes, it's information we can only get if we *already* (somehow) possess a certain set of concepts.

5. It is sometimes supposed that Descartes thought that all knowledge could be mathematically deduced from the foundational beliefs that remain after he has applied his method of doubt. But this is not quite right. He thought that the proper *concepts and terms*, which science must use to describe the world, were purely mathematical and were deducible through pure rational reflection. But he also recognized that only through empirical investigation can we discover which scientific descriptions, expressed in the proper mathematical terms, are actually *true* of the world. For example, reason tells us (according to Descartes—and this was a radically new idea at the time) that matter can be defined simply in terms of extension in three dimensions, and that the laws which guide the movements of particles can be understood mathematically. However, only experience can tell us how the bits of matter in, for example, the human body are actually arranged.

6. Descartes does not conclude that error is impossible, even for those who adopt the proper intellectual methods of science. He argues only that *radical and systematic* error is impossible for the conscientious thinker. For example, even after completing Descartes's course of meditations we might still occasionally be tricked by perceptual illusions, or think we are awake when in fact we are dreaming; what Descartes thinks he has blocked, however, is the possibility that such errors show that our entire picture of reality might be wrong.

7. Descartes's project is to show how, by setting our knowledge of the world on firm foundations, we can overcome any skeptical doubts and have confidence in the conception of reality that results. It is less widely appreciated, however, that the common-sense picture of the world, as it is apparently revealed to our senses, with which Descartes begins is very different from the worldview with which we are left at the end of the *Meditations*. Descartes does not merely rescue common sense from skepticism; instead, he replaces a naïve view of the world with a more modern, scientific one.

8. Descartes is sometimes portrayed as making the following (bad) argument to establish that mind is distinct from body: I can doubt that my body exists; I cannot doubt that my mind exists; there is therefore at least one property that my mind has which my body lacks (i.e., being doubtable); and therefore mind and body are not identical. Descartes does seem to make an argument which resembles this (in the Second Meditation), but he later denied that this is really what he meant, and he formulates much stronger—though perhaps still flawed—arguments for dualism in the Sixth Meditation.

How Important and Influential Is This Text?

Descartes is one of the most widely studied Western philosophers, and his *Meditations on First Philosophy* is his philosophical masterpiece and most important work. John Cottingham, an expert on Descartes, has written of the *Meditations* that

> The radical critique of preconceived opinions or prejudices which begins that work seems to symbolize the very essence of philosophical inquiry. And the task of finding secure foundations for human knowledge, a reliable basis for science and ethics, encapsulates, for many, what makes philosophy worth doing.*

---

* This appears in his Introduction to the *Cambridge Companion to Descartes* (1992).

"I think therefore I am" ("*cogito ergo sum*" in Latin) is the most famous dictum in the history of philosophy. Note that this is not what it is often popularly taken to be: praise of the intellectual life as the real source of human identity. It's rather Descartes's foundational claim beginning his reconstruction of indubitable truth. These exact words, by the way, never appear in the *Meditations*—they are found in other writings by Descartes, including *Discourse on the Method* and the *Principles of Philosophy*; the *Meditations*, however, contains Descartes's most complete account of how this principle, today simply often called "the Cogito," is established.

The importance of Descartes's work to the history of thought is profound. He is commonly considered the first great philosopher of the modern era, since his work was central in sweeping away medieval scholasticism based on Aristotelian science and Christian theology and replacing it with the methods and questions that have dominated philosophy ever since.* This change from scholastic to modern modes of thought was also crucial to the phenomenal growth of natural science and mathematics beginning in the seventeenth century. In recent years, however, it has been fashionable to blame Descartes for what have been seen as philosophical dead ends, and many of the assumptions which he built into philosophy have been questioned (this is one of the reasons why the philosophy of the second half of the twentieth century and beyond has been so exciting).

Meditations on First Philosophy

IN WHICH THE EXISTENCE OF GOD AND THE DIFFERENCE BETWEEN THE HUMAN SOUL AND BODY ARE DEMONSTRATED[†]

Synopsis of the Six Following Meditations

In the First Meditation I set down the reasons which enable us to place everything in doubt, especially material things, at least as long as we do not have foundations for the sciences different from those we have had up to now. Although at first glance the usefulness of such a widespread doubt is not apparent, it is, in fact, very great, because it frees us from all prejudices, sets down the easiest route by which we can detach our minds from our senses, and finally makes it impossible for us to doubt anymore those things which we later discover to be true.

In the Second Meditation, the mind, using its own unique freedom, assumes that all those things about whose existence it can entertain the least doubt do not exist, and recognizes that during this time it is impossible that it itself does not exist. And that is also extremely useful, because in this way the mind can easily differentiate between those things pertaining to it,

---

* Alan Gewirth went so far as to write, in 1970, "the history of twentieth-century philosophy ... consists in a series of reactions to Descartes's metaphysics. Examples of these reactions are Ryle's castigations of the Cartesian mind-body dualism, Sartre's and Hare's attacks on Cartesian intellectualism and intuitionism, Chomsky's support of Cartesian innatism, and the opposed views taken on Cartesian doubt by Russell and Husserl on the one hand and by Moore, Dewey, Austin, and the later Wittgenstein on the other" ("The Cartesian Circle Reconsidered," *The Journal of Philosophy* 67: 668–85).

† Translated by Ian Johnston, Vancouver Island University, 2012. Translator's Note: This translation is based upon the first Latin edition of Descartes's *Meditations* (1641). I have incorporated most of the relatively few corrections made to that text in the second Latin edition (1642), none of which is particularly important. I have also inserted a number of additions made to the Latin text in the first French edition (1647), which was supervised by Descartes, who approved of the result. These additions from the French edition are inserted here only where they help to clarify the meaning of the original Latin (for example, by clarifying Descartes's Latin pronouns). Other changes in the French text I have ignored. Words in square brackets are insertions and additions from the first French edition.

that is, to its intellectual nature, and those pertaining to the body. However, since at this point some people may perhaps expect an argument [proving] the immortality of the soul, I think I should warn them that I have tried to avoid writing anything which I could not accurately demonstrate and that, therefore, I was unable to follow any sequence of reasoning other than the one used by geometers. That means I start by setting down everything on which the proposition we are looking into depends, before I reach any conclusions about it. Now, the first and most important prerequisite for understanding the immortality of the soul is to form a conception of the soul that is as clear as possible, one entirely distinct from every conception [we have] of the body. And that I have done in this section. After that, it is essential also for us to know that all those things we understand clearly and distinctly are true in a way which matches precisely how we think of them. This I was unable to prove before the Fourth Meditation. We also need to have a distinct conception of corporeal* nature. I deal with that point partly in this Second Meditation and partly in the Fifth and Sixth Meditations, as well. And from these we necessarily infer that all those things we conceive clearly and distinctly as different substances, in the same way we think of the mind and the body, are, in fact, truly different substances, distinct from one another, a conclusion I have drawn in the Sixth Meditation. This conclusion is also confirmed in the same meditation from the fact that we cannot think of the body as anything other than something divisible, and, by contrast, [cannot think of] the mind as anything other than something indivisible. For we cannot conceive of half a mind, in the same way we can with a body, no matter how small. Hence, we realize that their natures are not only different but even, in some respects, opposites. However, I have not pursued the matter any further in this treatise for two reasons: (1) because these points are enough to show that the annihilation of the mind does not follow from the corruption of the body, so we mortals thus ought to entertain hopes of another life;

and (2) because the premises on the basis of which we can infer the immortality of the mind depend upon an explanation of all the principles of physics. For (2), first of all, we would have to know that all substances without exception—or those things which, in order to exist, must be created by God—are by their very nature incorruptible and can never cease to exist, unless God, by denying them his concurrence,† reduces them to nothing, and then, second, we would have to understand that a body, considered generally, is a substance and thus it, too, never dies. But the human body, to the extent that it differs from other bodies, consists merely of a certain arrangement of parts, with other similar accidental‡ properties; whereas, the human mind is not made up of any accidental properties; in this way, but is a pure substance. For even if all the accidental properties of the mind were changed—if, for example, it were to think of different things or have different desires and perceptions, and so on—that would not mean it had turned into a different mind. But the human body becomes something different from the mere fact that the shape of some of its parts has changed. From this it follows that the [human] body does, in fact, perish very easily, but that the mind, thanks to its nature, is immortal.

In the Third Meditation I have set out what seems to me a sufficiently detailed account of my main argument to demonstrate the existence of God. However, in order to lead the minds of the readers as far as possible from the senses, in this section I was unwilling to use any comparisons drawn from corporeal things, and thus many obscurities may still remain. But these, I hope, have later been entirely removed in the replies [I have made] to the objections.§ For instance, among all the others, there is the issue of how the idea of a supremely perfect being, which is present within us, could have so much objective reality that it is impossible for it not to originate from a supremely perfect cause. This is illustrated [in the replies] by the comparison with a wholly perfect machine, the idea of which exists in the mind of some craftsman. For just as the

---

* Bodily, physical.

† The continuous divine action which many Christians think necessary to maintain things in existence.

‡ See the section in the Introduction, "Some Useful Background Information," for an explanation of "accidental" here, and for a number of other confusing or obscure terms that Descartes uses at various points in *Meditations*.

§ Descartes refers to the set of objections and replies he published at the end of *Meditations*, not reprinted here.

objective ingenuity of this idea must have some cause, that is, the technical skill of this craftsman or of someone else from whom he got the idea, so the idea of God, which is in us, cannot have any cause other than God Himself.

In the Fourth Meditation, I establish that all the things which we perceive clearly and distinctly are true, and at the same time I explain what constitutes the nature of falsity; these are things that we have to know both to confirm what has gone before and to understand what still remains. (However, in the meantime I must observe that in this part I do not deal in any way with sin, that is, with errors committed in pursuit of good and evil, but only with those which are relevant to judgments of what is true and false. Nor do I consider matters relevant to our faith or to the conduct of our lives, but merely those speculative truths we can know only with the assistance of our natural light.)

In the Fifth Meditation, I offer a general explanation of corporeal* nature and, in addition, also demonstrate the existence of God in a new argument, in which, however, several difficulties may, once again, arise. These I have resolved later in my replies to the objections. And finally, I point out in what sense it is true that the certainty of geometrical demonstrations depends upon a knowledge of God.

Finally, in the Sixth Meditation, I differentiate between the understanding and the imagination and describe the principles of this distinction. I establish that the mind is truly distinct from the body, and I point out how, in spite of that, it is so closely joined to the body that they form, as it were, a single thing. I review all the errors which customarily arise through the senses and explain the ways in which such errors can be avoided. And then finally, I set down all the reasons which enable us to infer the existence of material things. I believe these are useful not because they demonstrate the truth of what they prove—for example, that there truly is a world, that human beings have bodies, and things like that, which no one of sound mind ever seriously doubted—but rather because, when we examine these reasons, we see that they are neither as firm or as evident as those by which we arrive at a knowledge of our own minds and of God,

so that the latter are the most certain and most evident of all things which can be known by the human intellect. The proof of this one point was the goal I set out to attain in these *Meditations*. For that reason I am not reviewing here, as they arise [in this treatise], various [other] questions I have dealt with elsewhere.

First Meditation: Concerning Those Things Which Can Be Called into Doubt

It is now several years since I noticed how from the time of my early youth I had accepted many false claims as true, how everything I had later constructed on top of those [falsehoods] was doubtful, and thus how at some point in my life I needed to tear everything down completely and begin again from the most basic foundations, if I wished to establish something firm and lasting in the sciences. But this seemed an immense undertaking, and I kept waiting until I would be old enough and sufficiently mature to know that no later period of my life would come [in which I was] better equipped to undertake this disciplined enquiry. This reason made me delay for so long that I would now be at fault if, by [further] deliberation, I used up the time which still remains to carry out that project. And so today, when I have conveniently rid my mind of all worries and have managed to find myself secure leisure in solitary withdrawal, I will at last find the time for an earnest and unfettered general demolition of my [former] opinions.

Now, for this task it will not be necessary to show that every opinion I hold is false, something which I might well be incapable of ever carrying out. But reason now convinces me that I should withhold my assent from opinions which are not entirely certain and indubitable, no less than from those which are plainly false; so if I uncover any reason for doubt in each of them, that will be enough to reject them all. For that I will not need to run through them separately, a task that would take forever, because once the foundations are destroyed, whatever is built above them will collapse on its own. Thus, I shall at once assault the very principles upon which all my earlier beliefs rested.

Up to this point, what I have accepted as true I have derived either from the senses or through the

---

* Physical (i.e., not mental).

senses. However, sometimes I have discovered that these are mistaken, and it is prudent never to place one's entire trust in things which have deceived us even once.

However, although from time to time the senses deceive us about minuscule things or those further away, it could well be that there are still many other matters about which we cannot entertain the slightest doubt, even though we derive [our knowledge] of them from sense experience—for example, the fact that I am now here, seated by the fire, wearing a winter robe, holding this paper in my hands, and so on. And, in fact, how could I deny that these very hands and this whole body are mine, unless perhaps I were to compare myself with certain insane people whose brains are so troubled by the stubborn vapours of black bile* that they constantly claim that they are kings, when, in fact, they are very poor, or that they are dressed in purple, when they are nude, or that they have earthenware heads, or are complete pumpkins, or made of glass? But these people are mad, and I myself would appear no less demented if I took something from them and applied it to myself as an example.

A brilliant piece of reasoning! But nevertheless I am a person who sleeps at night and experiences in my dreams all the things these [mad] people do when wide awake, sometimes even less probable ones. How often have I had an experience like this: while sleeping at night, I am convinced that I am here, dressed in a robe and seated by the fire, when, in fact, I am lying between the covers with my clothes off! At the moment, my eyes are certainly wide open and I am looking at this piece of paper, this head which I am moving is not asleep, and I am aware of this hand as I move it consciously and purposefully. None of what happens while I am asleep is so distinct. Yes, of course—but nevertheless I recall other times when I have been deceived by similar thoughts in my sleep. As I reflect on this matter carefully, it becomes completely clear to me that there are no certain indicators which ever enable us to differentiate between being awake and being asleep, and this is astounding; in my confusion I am almost convinced that I may be sleeping.

So then, let us suppose that I am asleep and that these particular details—that my eyes are open, that I am moving my head, that I am stretching out my hand—are not true, and that perhaps I do not even have hands like these or a whole body like this. We must, of course, still concede that the things we see while asleep are like painted images, which could only have been made as representations of real things. And so these general things—these eyes, this head, this hand, and this entire body—at least are not imaginary things but really do exist. For even when painters themselves take great care to form sirens and satyrs with the most unusual shapes, they cannot, in fact, give them natures which are entirely new. Instead, they simply mix up the limbs of various animals or, if they happen to come up with something so new that nothing at all like it has been seen before and thus [what they have made] is completely fictitious and false, nonetheless, at least the colours which make up the picture certainly have to be real. For similar reasons, although these general things—eyes, head, hand, and so on—could also be imaginary, still we are at least forced to concede the reality of certain even simpler and more universal objects, out of which, just as with real colours, all those images of things that are in our thoughts, whether true or false, are formed.

Corporeal nature appears, in general, to belong to this class [of things], as well as its extension,† the shape of extended things, their quantity or their size and number, the place where they exist, the time which measures how long they last, and things like that.

Thus, from these facts perhaps we are not reaching an erroneous conclusion [by claiming] that physics, astronomy, medicine, and all the other disciplines which rely upon a consideration of composite objects are indeed doubtful, but that arithmetic, geometry, and the other [sciences] like them, which deal with only the simplest and most general matters and have little concern whether or not they exist in the nature of things, contain something certain and indubitable. For whether I am awake or asleep, two and three always add up to five, a square does not have more than four sides, and it does not seem possible to suspect that such manifest truths could be false.

---

* One of the four basic bodily fluids then thought to be associated with disease when in imbalance.

† Something's extension is its spatial magnitude—the volume of space it occupies.

Nevertheless, a certain opinion has for a long time been fixed in my mind—that there is an all-powerful God who created me and [made me] just as I am. But how do I know He has not arranged things so that there is no earth at all, no sky, no extended thing, no shape, no magnitude, no place, and yet seen to it that all these things appear to me to exist just as they do now? Besides, given that I sometimes judge that other people make mistakes with the things about which they believe they have the most perfect knowledge, might I not in the same way be wrong every time I add two and three together, or count the sides of a square, or do something simpler, if that can be imagined? Perhaps God is unwilling to deceive me in this way, for He is said to be supremely good. But if it is contrary to the goodness of God to have created me in such a way that I am always deceived, it would also seem foreign to His goodness to allow me to be occasionally deceived. The latter claim, however, is not one that I can make.

Perhaps there may really be some people who prefer to deny [the existence of] such a powerful God, rather than to believe that all other things are uncertain. But let us not seek to refute these people, and [let us concede] that everything [I have said] here about God is a fiction. No matter how they assume I reached where I am now, whether by fate, or chance, or a continuous series of events, or in some other way, given that being deceived and making mistakes would seem to be something of an imperfection, the less power they attribute to the author of my being, the greater the probability that I will be so imperfect that I will always be deceived. I really do not have a reply to these arguments. Instead, I am finally compelled to admit that there is nothing in the beliefs which I formerly held to be true about which one cannot raise doubts. And this is not a reckless or frivolous opinion, but the product of strong and well-considered reasoning. And therefore, if I desire to discover something certain, in future I should also withhold my assent from those former opinions of mine, no less than [I do] from opinions which are obviously false.

But it is not sufficient to have called attention to this point. I must [also] be careful to remember it. For these habitual opinions constantly recur, and I have made use of them for so long and they are so familiar that they have, as it were, acquired the right to seize hold of my belief and subjugate it, even against my wishes, and I will never give up the habit of deferring to and relying on them, as long as I continue to assume that they are what they truly are: opinions which are to some extent doubtful, as I have already pointed out, but still very probable, so that it is much more reasonable to believe them than to deny them. For that reason, I will not go wrong, in my view, if I deliberately turn my inclination into its complete opposite and deceive myself, [by assuming] for a certain period that these earlier opinions are entirely false and imaginary, until I have, as it were, finally brought the weight of both my [old and my new] prejudices into an equal balance, so that corrupting habits will no longer twist my judgment away from the correct perception of things. For I know that doing this will not, for the time being, lead to danger or error and that it is impossible for me to indulge in excessive distrust, since I am not concerned with actions at this point, but only with knowledge.

Therefore, I will assume that it is not God, who is supremely good and the fountain of truth, but some malicious demon, at once omnipotent and supremely cunning, who has been using all the energy he possesses to deceive me. I will suppose that sky, air, earth, colours, shapes, sounds, and all other external things are nothing but the illusions of my dreams, set by this spirit as traps for my credulity. I will think of myself as if I had no hands, no eyes, no flesh, no blood, nor any senses, and yet as if I still falsely believed I had all these things. I shall continue to concentrate resolutely on this meditation, and if, in doing so, I am, in fact, unable to learn anything true, I will at least do what is in my power and with a resolute mind take care not to agree to what is false or to enable the deceiver to impose anything on me, no matter how powerful and cunning [he may be]. But this task is onerous, and laziness brings me back to my customary way of life. I am like a prisoner who in his sleep may happen to enjoy an imaginary liberty and who, when he later begins to suspect that he is asleep, fears to wake up and willingly cooperates with the pleasing illusions [in order to prolong them]. In this way, I unconsciously slip back into my old opinions and am afraid to wake up, in case from now on I would have to spend the period of challenging wakefulness that follows this peaceful relaxation not in the light, but in the inextricable darkness of the difficulties I have just raised.

Second Meditation: Concerning the Nature of the Human Mind and the Fact That It Is Easier to Know Than the Body

Yesterday's meditation threw me into so many doubts that I can no longer forget them or even see how they might be resolved. Just as if I had suddenly fallen into a deep eddying current, I am hurled into such confusion that I am unable to set my feet on the bottom or swim to the surface. However, I will struggle along and try once again [to follow] the same path I started on yesterday—that is, I will reject everything which admits of the slightest doubt, just as if I had discovered it was completely false, and I will proceed further in this way, until I find something certain, or at least, if I do nothing else, until I know for certain that there is nothing certain. In order to shift the entire earth from its location, Archimedes asked for nothing but a fixed and immovable point.* So I, too, ought to hope for great things if I can discover something, no matter how small, which is certain and immovable.

Therefore, I assume that everything I see is false. I believe that none of those things my lying memory represents has ever existed, that I have no senses at all, and that body, shape, extension, motion, and location are chimeras.† What, then, will be true? Perhaps this one thing: there is nothing certain.

But how do I know that there exists nothing other than the items I just listed, about which one could not entertain the slightest momentary doubt? Is there not some God, by whatever name I call him, who places these very thoughts inside me? But why would I think this, since I myself could perhaps have produced them? So am I then not at least something? But I have already denied that I have senses and a body. Still, I am puzzled, for what follows from this? Am I so bound up with my body and my senses that I cannot exist without them? But I have convinced myself that there is nothing at all in the universe—no sky, no earth, no minds, no bodies. So then, is it the case that I, too, do not exist? No, not at all: if I persuaded myself of

something, then I certainly existed. But there is some kind of deceiver, supremely powerful and supremely cunning, who is constantly and intentionally deceiving me. But then, if he is deceiving me, there again is no doubt that I exist—for that very reason. Let him trick me as much as he can, he will never succeed in making me nothing, as long as I am aware that I am something. And so, after thinking all these things through in great detail, I must finally settle on this proposition: the statement *I am, I exist* is necessarily true every time I say it or conceive of it in my mind.

But I do yet understand enough about what this *I* is, which now necessarily exists. Thus, I must be careful I do not perhaps unconsciously substitute something else in place of this *I* and in that way make a mistake even here, in the conception which I assert is the most certain and most evident of all. For that reason, I will now reconsider what I once believed myself to be, before I fell into this [present] way of thinking. Then I will remove from that whatever could, in the slightest way, be weakened by the reasoning I have [just] brought to bear, so that, in doing this, by the end I will be left only with what is absolutely certain and immovable.

What then did I believe I was before? Naturally, I thought I was a human being. But what is a human being? Shall I say a *rational animal*? No. For then I would have to ask what an *animal* is and what *rational* means, and thus from a single question I would fall into several greater difficulties. And at the moment I do not have so much leisure time that I wish to squander it with subtleties of this sort. Instead I would prefer here to attend to what used to come into my mind quite naturally and spontaneously in earlier days every time I thought about what I was. The first thought, of course, was that I had a face, hands, arms, and this entire mechanism of limbs, the kind one sees on a corpse, and this I designated by the name *body*. Then it occurred to me that I ate and drank, walked, felt, and thought. These actions I assigned to the *soul*. But I did not reflect on what this *soul* might be, or else I imagined it as some

---

*   Archimedes was an ancient Greek scientist. He also asked for a long-enough lever.

†   In Greek mythology, a female fire-breathing monster with a lion's head, a goat's body, and a serpent's tail; more generally, an absurd or horrible idea or wild fancy.

kind of attenuated substance, like wind, or fire, or aether,* spread all through my denser parts. However, I had no doubts at all about my body—I thought I had a clear knowledge of its nature. Perhaps if I had attempted to describe it using the mental conception I used to hold, I would have explained it as follows: By a *body* I understand everything that is appropriately bound together in a certain form and confined to a place; it fills a certain space in such a way as to exclude from that space every other body; it can be perceived by touch, sight, hearing, taste, or smell, and can also be moved in various ways, not, indeed, by itself, but by something else which makes contact with it. For I judged that possessing the power of self-movement, like the ability to perceive things or to think, did not pertain at all to the nature of body. Quite the opposite in fact, so that when I found out that faculties rather similar to these were present in certain bodies, I was astonished.

But what [am I] now, when I assume that there is some extremely powerful and, if I may be permitted to speak like this, malevolent and deceiving being who is deliberately using all his power to trick me? Can I affirm that I possess even the least of all those things which I have just described as pertaining to the nature of body? I direct my attention [to this], think [about it], and turn [the question] over in my mind. Nothing comes to me. It is tedious and useless to go over the same things once again. What, then, of those things I used to attribute to the soul, like eating, drinking, or walking? But given that now I do not possess a body, these are nothing but imaginary figments. What about sense perception? This, too, surely does not occur without the body. And in sleep I have apparently sensed many objects which I later noticed I had not [truly] perceived. What about thinking? Here I discover something: thinking does exist. This is the only thing which cannot be detached from me. *I am, I exist*—that is certain. But for how long? Surely for as long as I am thinking. For it could perhaps be the case that, if I were to abandon thinking altogether, then in that moment I would completely cease to be. At this point I am not agreeing to anything except what is necessarily true. Therefore, strictly speaking, I am

merely a thinking thing, that is, a mind or spirit, or understanding, or reason—words whose significance I did not realize before. However, I am something real, and I truly exist. But what kind of thing? As I have said, a thing that thinks.

And what else besides? I will let my imagination roam. I am not that interconnection of limbs we call a human body. Nor am I even some attenuated air which filters through those limbs—wind, or fire, or vapour, or breath, or anything I picture to myself. For I have assumed those things were nothing. Let this assumption hold. Nonetheless, I am still something. Perhaps it could be the case that these very things which I assume are nothing, because they are unknown to me, are truly no different from that *I* which I do recognize. I am not sure, and I will not dispute this point right now. I can render judgment only on those things which are known to me: I know that I exist. I am asking what this *I* is—the thing I know. It is very certain that knowledge of this *I*, precisely defined like this, does not depend on things whose existence I as yet know nothing about and therefore on any of those things I conjure up in my imagination. And this phrase *conjure up* warns me of my mistake, for I would truly be conjuring something up if I imagined myself to be something, since imagining is nothing other than contemplating the form or the image of a physical thing. But now I know for certain that I exist and, at the same time, that it is possible for all those images and, in general, whatever relates to the nature of body to be nothing but dreams [or chimeras]. Having noticed this, it seems no less foolish for me to say "I will let my imagination work, so that I may recognize more clearly what I am" than if I were to state, "Now I am indeed awake, and I see some truth, but because I do yet not see it with sufficient clarity, I will quite deliberately go to sleep, so that in my dreams I will get a truer and more distinct picture of it." Therefore, I realize that none of those things which I can understand with the aid of my imagination is pertinent to this idea I possess about myself and that I must be extremely careful to summon my mind back from such things, so that it may perceive its own nature with the utmost clarity, on its own.

---

* Aether is the fifth element of medieval alchemy, and the idea has its origins in the classical Greek notion of the pure atmosphere beyond the sky in which the gods were thought to live, and which they breathed, analogous to (but different from) the air of the terrestrial atmosphere.

But what then am I? A thinking thing. What is this? It is surely something that doubts, understands, affirms, denies, is willing, is unwilling, and also imagines and perceives.

This is certainly not an insubstantial list, if all [these] things belong to me. But why should they not? Surely I am the same I who now doubts almost everything, yet understands some things, who affirms that this one thing is true, denies all the rest, desires to know more, does not wish to be deceived, imagines many things, even against its will, and also notices many things which seem to come from the senses? Even if I am always asleep and even if the one who created me is also doing all he can to deceive me, what is there among all these things which is not just as true as the fact that I exist? Is there something there that I could say is separate from me? For it is so evident that I am the one who doubts, understands, and wills, that I cannot think of anything which might explain the matter more clearly. But obviously it is the same I that imagines, for although it may well be the case, as I have earlier assumed, that nothing I directly imagine is true, nevertheless, the power of imagining really exists and forms part of my thinking. Finally, it is the same I that feels, or notices corporeal things, apparently through the senses: for example, I now see light, hear noise, and feel heat. But these are false, for I am asleep. Still, I certainly seem to see, hear, and grow warm—and this cannot be false. Strictly speaking, this is what in me is called sense perception and, taken in this precise meaning, it is nothing other than thinking.

From these thoughts, I begin to understand somewhat better what I am. However, it still appears that I cannot prevent myself from thinking that corporeal things, whose images are formed by thought and which the senses themselves investigate, are much more distinctly known than that obscure part of me, the *I*, which is not something I can imagine, even though it is really strange that I have a clearer sense of those things whose existence I know is doubtful, unknown, and alien to me than I do of something which is true and known, in a word, of my own self. But I realize what the trouble is. My mind loves to wander and is not yet allowing itself to be confined within the limits of the truth. All right, then, let us at this point for once give it completely free rein, so that a little later on, when the time comes to pull back, it will consent to be controlled more easily.

Let us consider those things we commonly believe we understand most distinctly of all, that is, the bodies we touch and see—not, indeed, bodies in general, for those general perceptions tend to be somewhat more confusing, but rather one body in particular. For example, let us take this [piece of] beeswax. It was collected from the hive very recently and has not yet lost all the sweetness of its honey. It [still] retains some of the scent of the flowers from which it was gathered. Its colour, shape, and size are evident. It is hard, cold, and easy to handle. If you strike it with your finger, it will give off a sound. In short, everything we require to be able to recognize a body as distinctly as possible appears to be present. But watch. While I am speaking, I bring the wax over to the fire. What is left of its taste is removed, its smell disappears, its colour changes, its shape is destroyed, its size increases, it turns to liquid, and it gets hot. I can hardly touch it. And now, if you strike it, it emits no sound. After [these changes], is what remains the same wax? We must concede that it is. No one denies this; no one thinks otherwise. What then was in [this piece of wax] that I understood so distinctly? Certainly nothing I apprehended with my senses, since all [those things] associated with taste, odour, vision, touch, and sound have now changed. [But] the wax remains.

Perhaps what I now think is as follows: the wax itself was not really that sweetness of honey, that fragrance of flowers, that white colour, or that shape and sound, but a body which a little earlier was perceptible to me in those forms, but which is now [perceptible] in different ones. But what exactly is it that I am imagining in this way? Let us consider that point and, by removing those things which do not belong to the wax, see what is left over. It is clear that nothing [remains], other than something extended, flexible, and changeable. But what, in fact, do *flexible* and *changeable* mean? Do these words mean that I imagine that this wax can change from a round shape to a square one or from [something square] to something triangular? No, that is not it at all. For I understand that the wax has the capacity for innumerable changes of this kind, and yet I am not able to run through these innumerable changes by using my imagination. Therefore, this conception [I have of the wax] is not produced by the faculty of imagination. What about extension? Is not the extension of the wax also unknown? For it becomes greater when the wax melts, greater [still] when it boils, and once again [even] greater, if the heat is increased. And I would not be judging correctly what wax is if I did not believe that it could also be extended in various other ways, more than I could ever grasp in my imagination. Therefore, I am forced to admit that my imagination has no idea at all what this wax is and that I perceive it only with my mind. I am talking about this [piece of] wax in particular, for the point is even clearer about wax in general. But what is this wax which can be perceived only by the mind? It must be the same as the wax I see, touch, and imagine—in short, the same wax I thought it was from the beginning. But we should note that the perception of it is not a matter of sight, or touch, or imagination, and never was, even though that seemed to be the case earlier, but simply of mental inspection, which could be either imperfect and confused as it was before, or clear and distinct as it is now, depending on the lesser or greater degree of attention I bring to bear on those things out of which the wax is composed.

However, now I am amazed at how my mind is [weak and] prone to error. For although I am considering these things silently within myself, without speaking aloud, I still get stuck on the words themselves and am almost deceived by the very nature of the way we speak. For if the wax is there [in front of us], we say that we see the wax itself, not that we judge it to be there from the colour or shape. From that I could immediately conclude that I recognized the wax thanks to the vision in my eyes, and not simply by mental inspection. But by analogy, suppose I happen to glance out of the window at people crossing the street; in normal speech I also say I see the people themselves, just as I do with the wax. But what am I really seeing other than hats and coats, which could be concealing automatons* underneath? However, I judge that they are people. And thus what I thought I was seeing with my eyes I understand only with my faculty of judgment, which is in my mind.

But someone who wishes [to elevate] his knowledge above the common level should be ashamed to have based his doubts in the forms of speech which ordinary people use, and so we should move on to consider next whether my perception of what wax is was more perfect and more evident when I first perceived it and believed I knew it by my external senses, or at least by my so-called *common sense*,† in other words, by the power of imagination, or whether it is more perfect now, after I have investigated more carefully both what wax is and how it can be known. To entertain doubts about this matter would certainly be silly. For in my first perception of the wax what was distinct? What did I notice there that any animal might not be capable of capturing? But when I distinguish the wax from its external forms and look at it as something naked, as if I had stripped off its clothing, even though there could still be some error in my judgment, it is certain that I could not perceive it in this way without a human mind.

But what am I to say about this mind itself, in other words, about myself? For up to this point I am not admitting there is anything in me except mind. What, I say, is the *I* that seems to perceive this wax so distinctly? Do I not know myself not only much more truly and certainly, but also much more distinctly and clearly than I know the wax? For if I judge that the wax exists from the fact that I see it, then from the very fact that I see the wax it certainly follows much more clearly that I myself also exist. For it could be that what I see is not really wax. It could be the case that I do not have eyes at all with which to see anything. But when I see or think I see (at the moment I am not differentiating between these two), it is completely impossible that I, the one doing the thinking, am not something. For similar reasons, if I judge that the wax exists from the fact that I am touching it, the same conclusion follows once again, namely, that I exist. The result is clearly the same if [my judgment rests] on the fact that I imagine the wax or on any other reason at all. But these observations I have made about the wax can be applied to all other things located outside of me. Furthermore, if my perception of the wax seemed more distinct after it was drawn to my attention, not merely by sight or touch, but by several [other] causes, I must concede that I now

---

* Mechanical person-imitations; robots.

† This is the supposed mental faculty which unites the data from the five external senses—sight, smell, sound, touch, and taste—into a single sensory experience. The notion goes back to Aristotle, and is different from what we call "common sense" today.

understand myself much more distinctly, since all of those same reasons capable of assisting my perception either of the wax or of any other body whatsoever are even better proofs of the nature of my mind! However, over and above this, there are so many other things in the mind itself which can provide a more distinct conception of its [nature] that it hardly seems worthwhile to review those features of corporeal things which might contribute to it.

And behold—I have all on my own finally returned to the place where I wanted to be. For since I am now aware that bodies themselves are not properly perceived by the senses or by the faculty of imagination, but only by the intellect, and are not perceived because they are touched or seen, but only because they are understood, I realize this obvious point: there is nothing I can perceive more easily or more clearly than my own mind. But because it is impossible to rid oneself so quickly of an opinion one has long been accustomed to hold, I would like to pause here, in order to impress this new knowledge more deeply on my memory with a prolonged meditation.

Third Meditation: Concerning God and the Fact That He Exists

Now I will close my eyes, stop up my ears, and withdraw all my senses. I will even blot out from my thinking all images of corporeal things, or else, since this is hardly possible, I will dismiss them as empty and false images of nothing at all, and by talking only to myself and looking more deeply within, I will attempt, little by little, to acquire a greater knowledge of and more familiarity with myself. I am a thinking thing—in other words, something that doubts, affirms, denies, knows a few things, is ignorant of many things, wills, refuses, and also imagines and feels. For, as I have pointed out earlier, although those things which I sense or imagine outside of myself are perhaps nothing, nevertheless, I am certain that the thought processes I call sense experience and imagination, given that they are only certain modes of thinking, do exist within me.

In these few words, I have reviewed everything I truly know, or at least [everything] that, up to this point, I was aware I knew. Now I will look around more diligently, in case there are perhaps other things in me that I have not yet considered. I am certain that I am a thinking thing. But if that is the case, do I not

then also know what is required for me to be certain about something? There is, to be sure, nothing in this first knowledge other than a certain clear and distinct perception of what I am affirming, and obviously this would not be enough for me to be certain about the truth of the matter, if it could ever happen that something I perceived just as clearly and distinctly was false. And now it seems to me that now I can propose the following general rule: all those things I perceive very clearly and very distinctly are true.

However, before now I have accepted as totally certain and evident many things that I have later discovered to be doubtful. What, then, were these things? [They were], of course, the earth, the sky, the stars, and all the other things I used to grasp with my senses. But what did I clearly perceive in them? Obviously I was observing in my mind ideas or thoughts of such things. And even now I do not deny that those ideas exist within me. However, there was something else which I held to be true and which, because I was in the habit of believing it, I also thought I perceived clearly, although I really was not perceiving it at all, namely, that certain things existed outside of me from which those ideas proceeded and which were like them in every way. And here was where I went wrong, or, if anyway I was judging truthfully, that certainly was not the result of the strength of my perception.

What [then was] true? When I was thinking about something very simple and easy in arithmetic or geometry—for example, that two and three added together make five, and things of that sort—was I not recognizing these with sufficient clarity at least to affirm that they were true? Later on, to be sure, I did judge that such things could be doubted, but the only reason I did so was that it crossed my mind that some God could perhaps have placed within me a certain kind of nature, so that I deceived myself even about those things which appeared most obvious. And every time this preconceived opinion about the supreme power of God occurs to me, I cannot but confess that if He wished, it would be easy for Him to see to it that I go astray, even in those matters which I think I see as clearly as possible with my mind's eye. But whenever I turn my attention to those very things which I think I perceive with great clarity, I am so completely persuaded by them, that I spontaneously burst out with the following words: Let whoever can deceive me, do so; he will still never succeed in making me nothing, not while I think I am something, or in making it true someday that I never existed, since it is true that I exist now, or perhaps even in making two and three, when added together, more or less than five, or anything like that, in which I clearly recognize a manifest contradiction. And since I have no reason to think that some God exists who is a deceiver and since, up to this point, I do not know enough to state whether there is a God at all, it is clear that the reason for any doubt which rests on this supposition alone is very tenuous and, if I may say so, metaphysical. However, to remove even that doubt, as soon as the occasion presents itself, I ought to examine whether God exists and, if He does, whether He can be a deceiver. For as long as this point remains obscure, it seems to me that I can never be completely certain about anything else.

But now an orderly arrangement would seem to require that I first divide all of my thoughts into certain kinds and look into which of these [kinds], strictly speaking, contain truth or error. Some of my thoughts are, so to speak, images of things, and for these alone the name *idea* is appropriate, for example, when I think of a man, or a chimera, or the sky, or an angel, or God. But other thoughts, in addition to these, possess certain other forms. For example, when I will, when I fear, when I affirm, and when I deny, I always apprehend something as the object of my thinking, but in my thought I also grasp something more than the representation of that thing. In this [group of thoughts], some are called volitions* or feelings, and others judgments.

Now, where ideas are concerned, if I consider these only in and of themselves, not considering whether they refer to anything else, they cannot, strictly speaking, be false. For whether I imagine a goat or a chimera, it is no less true that I imagine one than it is that I imagine the other. And we also need have no fear of error in willing or in feeling, for although I can desire something evil or even things which have never existed, that still does not make the fact that I desire them untrue. And thus, all that remains are judgments, in which I must take care not

to be deceived. But the most important and most frequent error I can discover in judgments consists of the fact that I judge the ideas within me are similar to or conform to certain things located outside myself. For obviously, if I considered ideas themselves only as certain modes of my thinking, without considering their reference to anything else, they would hardly furnish me any material for making a mistake.

Of these ideas, some, it seems to me, are innate,† others come from outside, and still others I have myself made up. For the fact that I understand what a thing is, what truth is, and what thinking is I seem to possess from no source other than my own nature. But if I now hear a noise, see the sun, or feel heat, I have up to now judged that [these sensations] come from certain things placed outside of me. And, finally, sirens, hippogriffs,‡ and such like are things I myself dream up. But perhaps I could also believe that all [these ideas] come from outside, or else are all innate, or else are all made up, for I have not yet clearly perceived their true origin.

However, the most important point I have to explore here concerns those ideas which I think of as being derived from objects existing outside me: What reason leads me to suppose that these ideas are similar to those objects? It certainly seems that I am taught to think this way by nature. Furthermore, I know by experience that these [ideas] do not depend on my will and therefore not on me myself, for they often present themselves to me even against my will. For example, whether I will it or not, I now feel heat, and thus I believe that the feeling or the idea of heat reaches me from some object apart from me, that is, from [the heat] of the fire I am sitting beside. And nothing is more obvious than my judgment that this object is sending its own likeness into me rather than something else.

I will now see whether these reasons are sufficiently strong. When I say here that I have been taught to think this way by nature, I understand only that I have been carried by a certain spontaneous impulse to believe it, not that some natural light has revealed its truth to me. There is an important difference between

---

* Acts of decision-making.
† Inborn—an idea that is already inside me.
‡ In Greek mythology, sirens are half woman, half bird; hippogriffs are combinations of horse and griffin (which is part eagle, part lion).

these two things. For whatever natural light reveals to me—for example, that from the fact that I am doubting it follows that I exist, and things like that—cannot admit of any possible doubt, because there cannot be another faculty [in me] as trustworthy as natural light, one which could teach me that the ideas [derived from natural light] are not true. But where natural impulses are concerned, in the past, when there was an issue of choosing the good thing to do, I often judged that such impulses were pushing me in the direction of something worse, and I do not see why I should place more trust in them in any other matters.

Moreover, although those ideas do not depend on my will, it is not therefore the case that they must come from objects located outside of me. For just as those impulses I have been talking about above are within me and yet seem to be different from my will, so perhaps there is also some other faculty in me, one I do not yet understand sufficiently, which produces those ideas, in the same way they have always appeared to be formed in me up to now while I sleep, without the help of any external objects [which they represent].

Finally, even if these ideas did come from things different from me, it does not therefore follow that they have to be like those things. Quite the contrary, for in numerous cases I seem to have often observed a great difference [between the object and the idea]. So, for example, I find in my mind two different ideas of the sun. One, which is apparently derived from the senses and should certainly be included among what I consider ideas coming from outside, makes the sun appear very small to me. However, the other, which is derived from astronomical reasoning, that is, elicited by certain notions innate in me or else produced by me in some other manner, makes the sun appear many times larger than the earth. Clearly, these two [ideas] cannot both resemble the sun which exists outside of me, and reason convinces [me] that the one which seems to have emanated most immediately from the sun itself is the least like it.

All these points offer me sufficient proof that previously, when I believed that certain things existed apart from me that conveyed ideas or images of themselves, whether by my organs of sense or by some other means, my judgment was not based on anything certain but only on some blind impulse.

However, it crosses my mind that there is still another way of exploring whether certain things of which I have ideas within me exist outside of me. To the extent that those ideas are [considered] merely certain ways of thinking, of course, I do not recognize any inequality among them, and they all appear to proceed from me in the same way. But to the extent that one idea represents one thing, while another idea represents something else, it is clear that they are very different from each other. For undoubtedly those that represent substances to me and contain in themselves more objective reality, so to speak, are something more than those that simply represent modes or accidents.* And, once again, that idea thanks to which I am aware of a supreme God—eternal, infinite, omniscient, omnipotent,† the Creator of all things that exist outside of Him—certainly has more objective reality in it than those ideas through which finite substances are represented.

Now, it is surely evident by natural light that there must be at least as much [reality] in the efficient and total cause as there is in the effect of this cause. For from where, I would like to know, can the effect receive its reality if not from its cause? And how can the cause provide this reality to the effect, unless the cause also possesses it? But from this it follows that something cannot be made from nothing and also that what is more perfect, that is, contains more reality in itself, cannot be produced from what is less perfect. This is obviously true not only of those effects whose reality is [what the philosophers call] actual or formal, but also of those ideas in which we consider only [what they call] objective reality. For example, some stone which has not previously existed cannot now begin to exist, unless it is produced by something which has in it, either formally or eminently, everything that goes into the stone,‡ and heat cannot be brought into an object which was not warm previously, except by

---

* See the Introduction for background information on "substance," "accident," "objective reality," and "formal reality."
† To be omniscient is to be all-knowing; to be omnipotent is to be infinitely powerful.
‡ That is, it has either the same properties as the stone (e.g., a certain hardness) or possesses even more perfect or pronounced versions of those properties (e.g., perfect hardness). An effect is "eminently" in a cause when the cause is more perfect than the effect.

something which is of an order at least as perfect as heat, and so on with all the other examples. But beyond this, even the idea of heat or of the stone cannot exist within me, unless it is placed in me by some cause containing at least as much reality as I understand to be in the heat or in the stone. For although that cause does not transfer anything of its own reality, either actual or formal, into my idea, one should not therefore assume that [this cause] must be less real. Instead, [we should consider] that the nature of the idea itself is such that it requires from itself no formal reality other than what it derives from my own thinking, of which it is a mode [that is, a way or style of thinking]. But for the idea to possess this objective reality rather than another, it must surely obtain it from some cause in which there is at least as much formal reality as the objective reality contained in the idea itself. For if we assume that something can be discovered in the idea which was not present in its cause, then it must have obtained this from nothing. But no matter how imperfect the mode of being may be by which a thing is objectively present in the understanding through its idea, that mode is certainly not nothing, and therefore [this idea] cannot come from nothing.

And although the reality which I am considering in my ideas is only objective, I must not imagine that it is unnecessary for the same reality to exist formally in the causes of those ideas, that it is sufficient if [the reality] in them is objective as well. For just as that mode of existing objectively belongs to ideas by their very nature, so the mode of existing formally belongs to the causes of [these] ideas, at least to the first and most important causes, by their nature. And although it may well be possible for one idea to be born from another, still this regress cannot continue on *ad infinitum*,* for we must finally come to some first [idea], whose cause is, as it were, the archetype [or original idea], which formally contains the entire reality that exists only objectively in the idea. And thus natural light makes it clear to me that ideas exist within me as certain images that can, in fact, easily fall short of the perfection of the things from which they were derived but that cannot contain anything greater or more perfect than those things do.

And the more time and care I take examining these things, the more clearly and distinctly I recognize their truth. But what am I finally to conclude from them? It is clear that if the objective reality of any of my ideas is so great that I am certain that the same reality is not in me either formally or eminently and that therefore I myself cannot be the cause of that idea, it necessarily follows that I am not alone in the world but that some other thing also exists which is the cause of that idea. But if I do not find any such idea within me, then I will obviously have no argument that confirms for me the existence of anything beyond myself. For I have been searching very diligently and have not been able to find any other argument up to now.

But of these ideas of mine, apart from the one which reveals my own self to me, about which there can be no difficulty, there is another [that represents] God [to me], and there are others which represent corporeal and inanimate things, as well as others representing angels, animals, and finally other men who resemble me.

As far as concerns those ideas which display other human beings or animals or angels, I understand readily enough that I could have put these together from ideas I have of myself, of corporeal things, and of God, even though there might be no people apart from me or animals or angels in the world.

Where the ideas of corporeal things are concerned, I see nothing in them so great that it seems as if it could not have originated within me. For if I inspect these ideas thoroughly and examine them individually in the same way I did yesterday with the idea of the wax, I notice that there are only a very few things I perceive in them clearly and distinctly—for example, magnitude or extension in length, breadth, and depth; shape, which emerges from the limits of that extension; position, which different forms derive from their relation to each other; and motion or a change of location. To these one can add substance, duration, and number. However, with the other things, like light, colours, sounds, odours, tastes, heat, cold, and other tactile qualities, my thoughts of them involve so much confusion and obscurity, that I still do not know whether they are true or false—in other words, whether the ideas I have of these [qualities] are ideas of things or of non-things. For although I observed a little earlier that falsehood (or, strictly speaking, formal falsehood) could occur only in judgments, nonetheless

---

* Forever (to infinity).

there is, in fact, a certain other material falsehood in ideas, when they represent a non-thing as if it were a thing. Thus, for example, ideas which I have of heat and cold are so unclear and indistinct that I am not able to learn from them whether cold is merely a lack of heat, or heat a lack of cold, or whether both of these are real qualities, or whether neither [of them is]. And because there can be no ideas which are not, as it were, ideas of things, if it is indeed true that cold is nothing other than a lack of heat, the idea which represents cold to me as if it were something positive and real will not improperly be called false, and that will also hold for all other ideas [like this].

To such ideas I obviously do not have to assign any author other than myself, for, if they are, in fact, false, that is, if they represent things which do not exist, my natural light informs me that they proceed from nothing—in other words, that they are in me only because there is something lacking in my nature, which is not wholly perfect. If, on the other hand, they are true, given that the reality they present to me is so slight that I cannot distinguish the object from something which does not exist, then I do not see why I could not have come up with them myself.

As for those details which are clear and distinct in my ideas of corporeal things, some of them, it seems to me, I surely could have borrowed from the idea of myself, namely, substance, duration, number, and other things like that. I conceive of myself as a thinking and non-extended thing, but of the stone as an extended thing which does not think; so there is a great difference between the two; but nevertheless, I think of both as *substance*, something equipped to exist on its own. In the same way, when I perceive that I now exist and also remember that I have existed for some time earlier and when I have various thoughts whose number I recognize, I acquire ideas of *duration* and *number*, which I can then transfer to any other things I choose. As for all the other qualities from which I put together my ideas of corporeal things, that is, extension, shape, location, and motion, they are, it is true, not formally contained in me, since I am nothing other than a thinking thing, but because they are merely certain modes of a substance and I, too, am a substance, it seems that they could be contained in me eminently.

And so the only thing remaining is the idea of God. I must consider whether there is anything in this idea for which I myself could not have been the origin. By the name *God* I understand a certain infinite, [eternal, immutable,] independent, supremely intelligent, and supremely powerful substance by which I myself was created, along with everything else that exists (if, [in fact], anything else does exist). All of these [properties] are clearly [so great] that the more diligently I focus on them, the less it seems that I could have brought them into being by myself alone. And thus, from what I have said earlier, I logically have to conclude that God necessarily exists.

For although the idea of a substance is, indeed, in me—because I am a substance—that still does not mean [that I possess] the idea of an infinite substance, since I am finite, unless it originates in some other substance which is truly infinite.

And I should not think that my perception of the infinite comes, not from a true idea, but merely from a negation of the finite, in [the same] way I perceive rest and darkness by a negation of motion and light. For, on the contrary, I understand clearly that there is more reality in an infinite substance than in a finite one and that therefore my perception of the infinite is somehow in me before my perception of the finite—in other words, my perception of God comes before my perception of myself. For how would I know that I am doubting or desiring, or, in other words, that something is lacking in me and that I am not entirely perfect, unless some idea of a perfect being was in me and I recognized my defects by a comparison?

And one cannot claim that this idea of God might well be materially false and thus could have come from nothing, the way I observed a little earlier with the ideas of heat and cold and things like that. Quite the reverse: for [this idea] is extremely clear and distinct and contains more objective reality than any other, and thus no idea will be found which is more inherently true and in which there is less suspicion of falsehood. This idea, I say, of a supremely perfect and infinite being is utterly true, for although it may well be possible to imagine that such a being does not exist, it is still impossible to imagine that the idea of Him does not reveal anything real to me, in the way I talked above about the idea of cold. This idea of a perfect Being is also entirely clear and distinct, for whatever I see clearly and distinctly which is real and true and which introduces some perfection is totally contained within [this idea]. The fact that I cannot comprehend the infinite or that there are innumerable other things in God that I do not understand or even perhaps have any way of contacting in my thoughts—all this is irrelevant. For something finite, like myself, cannot comprehend the nature of the infinite, and it is sufficient that I understand this very point and judge that all things which I perceive clearly and which I know convey some perfection, as well as innumerable others perhaps which I know nothing about, are in God, either formally or eminently, so that the idea I have of Him is the truest, clearest, and most distinct of all the ideas within me.

But perhaps I am something more than I myself understand, and all those perfections which I attribute to God are potentially in me somehow, even though they are not yet evident and are not manifesting themselves in action. For I already know by experience that my knowledge is gradually increasing, and I do not see anything which could prevent it from increasing more and more to infinity. Nor do I even know of any reasons why, with my knowledge augmented in this way, I could not, with its help, acquire all the other perfections of God or, finally, why, if the power [to acquire] those perfections is already in me, it would not be sufficient to produce the idea of those perfections.

And yet none of these things is possible. For, in the first place, although it is true that my knowledge is gradually increasing and that there are potentially many things within me which have not yet been realized, still none of these is relevant to the idea of God, in which, of course, nothing at all exists potentially. For the very fact that my knowledge is increasing little by little is the most certain argument for its imperfection. Beyond that, even if my knowledge is always growing more and more, nonetheless, that does not convince me that it will ever be truly infinite, since it can never reach a stage where it is not capable of increasing any further. But I judge that God is actually infinite, so that nothing can possibly be added to His perfection. And lastly, I perceive that the objective existence of an idea cannot be produced from a being that is merely potential, which, strictly speaking, is nothing, but only from something which actually or formally exists.

Obviously everything in all these thoughts is evident to the natural light in anyone who reflects carefully [on the matter]. But when I pay less attention and when images of sensible* things obscure the vision in my mind, I do not so readily remember why the idea of a being more perfect than myself must necessarily proceed from some entity that is truly more perfect than me. Therefore, I would like to enquire further whether I, who possess this idea [of God], could exist if such a being did not exist.

If that were the case, then from whom would I derive my existence? Clearly from myself or from my parents or from some other source less perfect than God. For we cannot think of or imagine anything more perfect than God or even anything equally perfect.

However, if I originated from myself, then I would not doubt or hope, and I would lack nothing at all, for I would have given myself all the perfections of which I have any idea within me, and thus I myself would be God. I must not assume that those things which I lack might be more difficult to acquire than those now within me. On the contrary, it clearly would have been much more difficult for me—that is, a thinking thing or substance—to emerge from nothing than to acquire a knowledge of the many things about which I am ignorant, for knowing such things is merely an accident of that thinking substance. And surely if I had obtained from myself that greater perfection [of being the author of my own existence], then I could hardly have denied myself the perfections which are easier to acquire, or, indeed, any of those I perceive contained in the idea of God, since, it seems to me, none of them is more difficult to produce. But if there were some perfections more difficult to acquire, they would certainly appear more difficult to me, too, if, indeed, everything else I possessed was derived from myself, because from them I would learn by experience that my power was limited.

And I will not escape the force of these arguments by assuming that I might perhaps have always been the way I am now, as if it followed from that assumption that I would not have to seek out any author for my own existence. For since the entire period of my life can be divided into innumerable parts each one of which is in no way dependent on the others, therefore, just because I existed a little while ago, it does not follow

---

* I.e., things that can be perceived with the physical senses.

that I must exist now, unless at this very moment some cause is, at it were, creating me once again—in other words, preserving me. For it is clear to anyone who directs attention to the nature of time that, in order for the existence of anything at all to be preserved in each particular moment it lasts, that thing surely needs the same force and action which would be necessary to create it anew if it did not yet exist. Thus, one of the things natural light reveals is that preservation and creation are different only in the ways we think of them.

Consequently, I now ought to ask myself whether I have any power which enables me to bring it about that I, who am now existing, will also exist a little later on, for since I am nothing other than a thinking thing—or at least since my precise concern at the moment is only with that part of me which is a thinking thing—if such a power is in me, I would undoubtedly be conscious of it. But I experience nothing [of that sort], and from this fact alone I recognize with the utmost clarity that I depend upon some being different from myself.

But perhaps that being is not God, and I have been produced by my parents or by some other causes less perfect than God. But [that is impossible]. As I have already said before, it is clear that there must be at least as much [reality] in the cause as in the effect and that thus, since I am a thinking thing and have a certain idea of God within me, I must concede that whatever I finally designate as my own cause is also a thinking substance containing the idea of all the perfections I attribute to God. It is possible once again to ask whether that cause originates from itself or from something else. If it comes from itself, then, given what I have said, it is obvious that the cause itself is God. For clearly, if it derives its power of existing from itself, it also undoubtedly has the power of actually possessing all the perfections whose idea it contains within itself, that is, all those that I think of as existing in God. But if it is produced from some other cause, then I ask once again in the same way whether this cause comes from itself or from some other cause, until I finally reach a final cause, which will be God.

For it is clear enough that this questioning cannot produce an infinite regress, particularly because the issue I am dealing with here is a matter not only of the cause which once produced me but also—and most importantly—of the cause which preserves me at the present time.

And I cannot assume that perhaps a number of partial causes came together to produce me and that from one of them I received the idea of one of the perfections I attribute to God and from another the idea of another perfection, so that all those perfections are indeed found somewhere in the universe, but they are not all joined together in a single being who is God. Quite the contrary, [for] the unity and simplicity—or the inseparability of all those things present in God—is one of the principal perfections which I recognize in Him. And surely the idea of this unity of all His perfections could not have been placed in me by any cause from which I did not acquire ideas of the other perfections as well, for no single cause could have made it possible for me to understand that those perfections were joined together and inseparable, unless at the same time it enabled me to recognize what those perfections were.

And finally, concerning my parents, even if everything I have ever believed about them is true, it is perfectly clear that they are not the ones who preserve me and that, to the extent that I am a thinking thing, there is no way they could have even made me. Instead they merely produced certain arrangements in the material substance which, as I have judged the matter, contains me—that is, contains my mind, for that is all I assume I am at the moment. And thus the fact that my parents contributed to my existence provides no problem for my argument. Given all this, however, from the mere fact that I exist and that I have the idea of a supremely perfect being, or God, I must conclude that I have provided an extremely clear proof that God does, indeed, exist.

All that is left now is to examine how I have received that idea from God. For I have not derived it from the senses, and it has never come to me unexpectedly, as habitually occurs with the ideas of things I perceive with the senses, when those ideas of external substances impinge, or seem to impinge, on my sense organs. Nor is it something I just made up, for I am completely unable to remove anything from it or add anything to it. Thus, all that remains is that the idea is innate in me, just as the idea of myself is also innate in me.

And obviously it is not strange that God, when He created me, placed that idea within me, so that it would be, as it were, the mark of the master craftsman impressed in his own work—not that it is at all necessary for this mark to be different from the work itself. But the fact that God created me makes it highly believable that He made me in some way in His image and likeness, and that I perceive this likeness, which contains the idea of God, by the same faculty with which I perceive myself. In other words, when I turn my mind's eye onto myself, I not only understand that I am an incomplete thing, dependent on something else, and one that aspires [constantly] to greater and better things without limit, but at the same time I also realize that the one I depend on contains within Himself all those greater things [to which I aspire], not merely indefinitely and potentially, but actually and infinitely, and thus that He is God. The entire force of my argument rests on the fact that I recognize I could not possibly exist with the sort of nature I possess, namely, having the idea of God within me, unless God truly existed as well—that God, I say, whose idea is in me—the Being having all those perfections which I do not grasp but which I am somehow capable of touching in my thoughts, and who is entirely free of any defect. These reasons are enough to show that He cannot be a deceiver, for natural light clearly demonstrates that every fraud and deception depends upon some defect.

But before I examine this matter more carefully and at the same time look into other truths I could derive from it, I wish to pause here for a while to contemplate God himself, to ponder His attributes, and to consider, admire, and adore the beauty of His immense light, to the extent that the eyes of my darkened intellect can bear it. For just as we believe through faith that the supreme happiness of our life hereafter consists only in this contemplation of the Divine Majesty, so we know from experience that the same [contemplation] now, though far less perfect, is the greatest joy we are capable of in this life.

Fourth Meditation: Concerning Truth and Falsity

In these last few days, I have grown accustomed to detaching my mind from my senses, and I have clearly noticed that, in fact, I perceive very little with any certainty about corporeal things and that I know a great deal more about the human mind and even more about God. As a result, I now have no difficulty directing my thoughts away from things I [perceive with the senses or] imagine, and onto those purely intellectual matters divorced from all material substance. And clearly the idea I have of the human mind, to the extent that it is a thinking thing that has no extension in length, breadth, and depth and possesses nothing else which the body has, is much more distinct than my idea of any corporeal substance. Now, when I direct my attention to the fact that I have doubts, in other words, that [I am] something incomplete and dependent, the really clear and distinct idea of an independent and complete being, that is, of God, presents itself to me. From this one fact—that there is an idea like this in me—or else because of the fact that I, who possess this idea, exist, I draw the clear conclusion that God also exists and that my entire existence depends on Him every single moment [of my life]. Thus, I believe that the human intellect can know nothing with greater clarity and greater certainty. And now it seems to me I see a way by which I can go from this contemplation of the true God, in whom all the treasures of science and wisdom are hidden, to an understanding of everything else.

First of all, I recognize that it is impossible that God would ever deceive me, for one discovers some sort of imperfection in everything false or deceptive. And although it may appear that the ability to deceive is evidence of a certain cleverness or power, the wish to deceive undoubtedly demonstrates either malice or mental weakness, and is therefore not found in God.

Then, I know from experience that there is in me a certain faculty of judgment, which I certainly received from God, like all the other things within me. Since He is unwilling to deceive me, He obviously did not give me the kind of faculty that could ever lead me into error, if I used it correctly.

There would remain no doubt about this, if it did not seem to lead to the conclusion that I could never make mistakes. For if whatever is within me I have from God and if He did not give me any power to commit errors, it would appear that I could never make a mistake. Now, it is true that as long as I am thinking only about God and directing myself totally to Him, I detect no reason for errors or falsity. But after a while, when I turn back to myself, I know by experience that I am still subject to innumerable errors. When I seek out their cause, I notice that I can picture not only a certain real and positive [idea] of God, or of a supremely perfect being, but also, so to speak, a certain negative idea of nothingness, or of something removed as far as possible from every perfection, and [I recognize] that I am, as it were, something intermediate between God and nothingness—that is, that

I am situated between a supreme being and non-being in such a way that, insofar as I was created by a supreme being, there is, in fact, nothing in me which would deceive me or lead me into error, but insofar as I also participate, to a certain extent, in nothingness or non-being—in other words, given that I myself am not a supreme being—I lack a great many things. Therefore, it is not strange that I am deceived. From this I understand that error, to the extent that it is error, is not something real which depends on God, but is merely a defect. Thus, for me to fall into error, it is not necessary that I have been given a specific power to do this by God. Instead, I happen to make mistakes because the power I have of judging what is true [and what is false], which I do have from God, is not infinite within me.

However, this is not yet entirely satisfactory, for error is not pure negation, but rather the privation or lack of a certain knowledge that somehow ought to be within me. But to anyone who thinks about the nature of God, it does not seem possible that He would place within me any power that is not a perfect example of its kind or that lacks some perfection it ought to have. For [if it is true] that the greater the skill of the craftsman, the more perfect the works he produces, what could the supreme maker of all things create which was not perfect in all its parts? And there is no doubt that God could have created me in such a way that I was never deceived, and, similarly, there is no doubt that He always wills what is best. So then, is it better for me to make mistakes or not to make them?

As I weigh these matters more attentively, it occurs to me, first, that I should not find it strange if I do not understand the reasons for some of the things God does; thus I should not entertain doubts about His existence just because I happen to learn from experience about certain other things and do not grasp why or how He has created them. For given the fact that I already know my nature is extremely infirm and limited and that, by contrast, the nature of God is immense, incomprehensible, and infinite,

I understand sufficiently well that He is capable of innumerable things about whose causes I am ignorant. For that reason alone, I believe that the entire class of causes we are in the habit of searching out as *final causes** is completely useless in matters of physics, for I do not think I am capable of investigating the final purposes of God without appearing foolhardy.

It also occurs to me that, whenever we look into whether the works of God are perfect, we should not examine one particular creature by itself, but rather the universal totality of things. For something which may well justly appear, by itself, very imperfect, is utterly perfect [if we think of it] as part of the [entire] universe. And although, given my wish to doubt everything, I have up to now recognized nothing as certain, other than the existence of myself and God, nonetheless, since I have observed the immense power of God, I cannot deny that He may have created many other things or at least is capable of creating them and therefore that I may occupy a place in a universe of things.

After that, by examining myself more closely and looking into the nature of my errors (the only things testifying to some imperfection in me), I observe that they proceed from two causes working together simultaneously, namely, from the faculty of knowing, which I possess, and from the faculty of choosing, or from my freedom to choose—in other words from both the intellect and the will together. For through my intellect alone I [do not affirm or deny anything, but] simply grasp the ideas of things about which I can make a judgment, and, if I consider my intellect in precisely this way, I find nothing there which is, strictly speaking, an error. For although countless things may well exist of which I have no idea at all within me, I still should not assert that I am deprived of them, in the proper sense of that word, [as if that knowledge were something my understanding was entitled to thanks to its nature]. I can only make the negative claim that I do not have them, for obviously I can produce no reason which enables me to prove that God ought to have

---

* The final cause of something is (roughly) the purpose or reason for that thing's existence: e.g., the final cause of a statue might be an original idea or artistic goal in the sculptor's head which prompted her to make that particular statue. This terminology goes back to Aristotle, and involves a contrast between final causes and three other sorts of cause— material causes (the marble out of which the statue is hewn), formal causes (the shape—the form—of the statue), and efficient causes (the sculptor's craft in making the statue).

given me a greater power of understanding than He has provided. And although I know that a craftsman is an expert, still I do not assume that he must therefore place in each of his works all the perfections he is capable of placing in some. Moreover, I certainly cannot complain that I have received from God a will or a freedom to choose that is insufficiently ample and perfect. For I clearly know from experience that my will is not circumscribed by any limits. And what seems to me particularly worthy of notice is the fact that, apart from my will, there is nothing in me so perfect or so great that I do not recognize that it could be still more perfect or even greater. For, to consider an example: if I think about the power of understanding, I see at once that in me it is very small and extremely limited. At the same time, I form an idea of another understanding which is much greater, even totally great and infinite, and from the mere fact that I can form this idea, I see that it pertains to the nature of God. By the same reasoning, if I examine my faculty of memory or of imagination or any other faculty, I find none at all which I do not recognize as tenuous and confined in me and immense in God. It is only my will or my freedom to choose which I experience as so great in me that I do not apprehend the idea of anything greater. Thus, through my will, more than through anything else, I understand that I bear a certain image of and resemblance to God. For although the will is incomparably greater in God than in myself—because the knowledge and power linked to it make it much stronger and more efficacious and because, with respect to its object, His will extends to more things—nonetheless, if I think of the will formally and precisely in and of itself, His does not appear greater than mine. For the power of will consists only in the ability to do or not to do [something] (that is, to affirm or to deny, to follow or to avoid)—or rather in this one thing alone, that whether we affirm or deny, follow or avoid [something] which our understanding has set before us, we act in such a way that we do not feel that any external force is determining what we do. For to be free, I do not have to be inclined in two [different] directions. On the contrary, the more I am inclined to one—whether that is because I understand that the principle of the true and the good are manifestly in it or because that is the way God has arranged the inner core of my thinking—the more freely I choose it. Clearly divine grace and natural knowledge never

diminish liberty, but rather increase and strengthen it. However, the indifference I experience when there is no reason urging me to one side more than to the other is the lowest degree of liberty. It does not demonstrate any perfection in [the will], but rather a defect in my understanding or else a certain negation. For if I always clearly perceived what is true and good, I would never need to deliberate about what I ought to be judging or choosing, and thus, although I would be entirely free, I could never be indifferent.

For these reasons, however, I perceive that the power of willing, which I have from God, considered in itself, is not the source of my errors. For it is extremely ample and perfect. And the source is not my power of understanding. For when I understand something, I undoubtedly do so correctly, since my [power of] understanding comes from God, and thus it is impossible for it to deceive me. So from where do my errors arise? Surely from the single fact that my will ranges more widely than my intellect, and I do not keep it within the same limits but extend it even to those things which I do not understand. Since the will does not discriminate among these things, it easily turns away from the true and the good, and, in this way, I make mistakes and transgress.

For example, in the past few days, when I was examining whether anything in the world existed and I observed that, from the very fact that I was exploring this [question], it clearly followed that I existed, I was not able [to prevent myself] from judging that what I understood so clearly was true, not because I was forced to that conclusion by any external force, but because a great light in my understanding was followed by a great inclination in my will, and thus the less I was indifferent to the issue, the more spontaneous and free was my belief. For example: now I know that I exist, to the extent I am a thinking thing; but I am in doubt about whether this thinking nature within me (rather, which I myself *am*) is of that corporeal nature also revealed to me. I assume that up to this point no reason has offered itself to my understanding which might convince me that I am, or am not, of corporeal nature. From this single fact it is clear that I am indifferent as to which of the two I should affirm or deny, or whether I should even make any judgment in the matter.

Furthermore, this indifference extends not merely to those things about which the understanding knows nothing at all, but also, in general, to everything which it does not recognize with sufficient clarity at the time when the will is deliberating about them. For, however probable the conjectures [may be] which draw me in one direction, the mere knowledge that they are only conjectures and not certain and indubitable reasons is enough to urge me to assent to the opposite view. In the past few days I have learned this well enough by experience, once I assumed that all those things I had previously accepted as absolutely true were utterly false, because of the single fact that I discovered they could in some way be doubted.

But when I do not perceive that something is true with sufficient clarity and distinctness, if, in fact, I abstain from rendering judgment, I am obviously acting correctly and am not deceived. But if at that time I affirm or deny, [then] I am not using my freedom to choose properly. If I make up my mind [and affirm] something false, then, of course I will be deceived. On the other hand, if I embrace the alternative, then I may, indeed, hit upon the truth by chance, but that would not free me from blame, since natural light makes it clear that a perception of the understanding must always precede a determination of the will. And it is in this incorrect use of the freedom of the will that one finds the privation which constitutes the nature of error. Privation, I say, inheres in this act of the will, to the extent that it proceeds from me, but not in the faculty I have received from God, nor even in the act, insofar as it depends upon Him.

For I have no cause to complain at all about the fact that God has not given me a greater power of understanding or a more powerful natural light than He has, because it is in the nature of a finite intellect not to understand many things and it is in the nature of a created intellect to be finite. Instead, I should thank Him, who has never owed me anything, for His generosity, rather than thinking that He has deprived me of something He did not provide or else has taken it away.

And I also have no reason to complain on the ground that He gave me a will more extensive than my understanding. For since the will consists of only a single thing and is, so to speak, indivisible, it does not seem that its nature is such that anything could be removed [without destroying it]. And, of course, the more extensive my will, the more I ought to show gratitude to the one who gave it to me.

And finally I also ought not to complain because God concurs with me in bringing out those acts of will or those judgments in which I am deceived. For those actions are true and good in every way, to the extent that they depend on God, and in a certain way there is more perfection in me because I am capable of eliciting these actions than if I were not. But privation, in which one finds the only formal reason for falsity and failure, has no need of God's concurrence, because it is not a thing, and if one links it to Him as its cause, one should not call it privation but merely negation. For obviously it is not an imperfection in God that He has given me freedom to assent or not to assent to certain things, when He has not placed a clear and distinct perception of them in my understanding. However, it is undoubtedly an imperfection in me that I do not use that liberty well and that I bring my judgment to bear on things which I do not properly understand. Nonetheless, I see that God could easily have created me so that I never made mistakes, even though I remained free and had a limited understanding. For example, He could have placed in my intellect a clear and distinct perception of everything about which I would ever deliberate, or He could have impressed on my memory that I should never make judgments about things which I did not understand clearly and distinctly, and done that so firmly that it would be impossible for me ever to forget. And I readily understand that, if God had made me that way, insofar as I have an idea of this totality, I would have been more perfect than I am now. But I cannot therefore deny that there may somehow be more perfection in this whole universe of things because some of its parts are not immune to errors and others are—more perfection than if all things were entirely alike. And I have no right to complain just because the part God wanted me to play in the universe is not the most important and most perfect of all.

Besides, even if I am unable to avoid errors in the first way [mentioned above], which depends upon a clear perception of all those things about which I need to deliberate, I can still use that other [method], which requires me only to remember to abstain from rendering judgment every time the truth of something is not evident. For although experience teaches me that I have a weakness which renders me incapable of keeping [my mind] always focused on one and the same thought, I can still see to it that by attentive and frequently repeated meditation I remember that fact every time the occasion demands. In this way I will acquire the habit of not making mistakes.

Since the greatest and preeminent perfection of human beings consists in this ability to avoid mistakes, I think that with the discovery in today's meditation of the cause of error and falsity I have gained a considerable gift. Clearly the source of mistakes can be nothing other than what I have identified. For as long as I keep my will restrained when I deliver judgments, so that it extends itself only to those things which reveal themselves clearly and distinctly to my understanding, I will surely be incapable of making mistakes, because every clear and distinct perception is undoubtedly something [real]. Therefore, it cannot exist from nothing but necessarily has God as its author—God, I say, that supremely perfect being, who would contradict His nature if He were deceitful. And thus, [such a perception] is unquestionably true. I have learned today not only what I must avoid in order to ensure that I am never deceived, but also at the same time what I must do in order to reach the truth. For I will assuredly reach that if I only pay sufficient attention to all the things I understand perfectly and distinguish these from all the other things which I apprehend confusedly and obscurely. In future, I will pay careful attention to this matter.

Fifth Meditation: Concerning the Essence of Material Things, and, Once Again, Concerning the Fact That God Exists

Many other [issues] concerning the attributes of God are still left for me to examine, [as well as] many things about myself, that is, about the nature of my mind. However, I will perhaps return to those at another time. Now (after I have taken note of what I must avoid and what I must do to arrive at the truth) nothing seems to be more pressing than for me to attempt to emerge from the doubts into which I have fallen in the last few days and to see whether I can know anything certain about material things.

But before I look into whether any such substances exist outside of me, I ought to consider the ideas of them, insofar as they are in my thinking, and see which of them are distinct and which confused.

For example, I distinctly imagine quantity (which philosophers commonly refer to as 'continuous' quantity)—that is, the length, breadth and depth of the quantity, or rather, of the object being quantified. Further, I enumerate the various parts of the object, and assign to those parts all sorts of sizes, shapes, locations, and local movements, and to those movements all sorts of durations.

And in this way I not only clearly observe and acquire knowledge of those things when I examine them in general, but later, by devoting my attention to them, I also perceive innumerable particular details about their shapes, number, motion, and so on, whose truth is so evident and so well suited to my nature, that when I discover them for the first time, it seems that I am remembering what I used to know, rather than learning anything new, or else noticing for the first time things which were truly within me earlier, although I had not previously directed my mental gaze on them.

I believe that the most important issue for me to consider here is that I find within me countless ideas of certain things which, even if they perhaps do not exist outside of me at all, still cannot be called nothing. Although in a certain sense I can think of them whenever I wish, still I do not create them. They have their own true and immutable natures. For example, when I imagine a triangle whose particular shape perhaps does not exist and has never existed outside my thinking, it nevertheless has, in fact, a certain determinate nature or essence or form which is immutable and eternal, which I did not produce, and which does not depend upon my mind; this is clearly shown in the fact that I can demonstrate the various properties of that triangle, namely, that the sum of its three angles is equal to two right angles, that the triangle's longest side has its endpoints on the lines made by the triangle's largest angle, and so on. These properties I now recognize clearly whether I wish to or not, although earlier, when I imagined the triangle [for the first time], I was not thinking of them at all and therefore did not invent them.

In this case it is irrelevant if I tell [myself] that perhaps this idea of a triangle came to me from external things through my sense organs, on the ground that I have certainly now and then seen objects possessing a triangular shape. For I am able to think up countless other shapes about which there can be no suspicion that they ever flowed into me through my senses, and yet [I can] demonstrate various properties about them, no less than I can about the triangle. All these properties are *something* and not pure nothingness, since I conceive of them clearly and distinctly, and, as I have shown above, thus they must be true. Besides, even if I had not proved this, the nature of my mind is certainly such that I cannot refuse to assent to them, at least for as long as I am perceiving them clearly. And I remember that, even in those earlier days, when I was attracted as strongly as possible to objects of sense experience, I always maintained that the most certain things of all were those kinds of truth which I recognized clearly as shapes, numbers, or other things pertinent to arithmetic or geometry or to pure and abstract mathematics generally.

But if it follows from the mere fact that I can draw the idea of some object from my thinking that all things which I perceive clearly and distinctly as pertaining to that object really do belong to it, can I not also derive from this an argument which proves that God exists? For clearly I find the idea of Him, that is, of a supremely perfect being, within me just as much as I do the idea of some shape or number. I know that [actual and] eternal existence belongs to His nature just as clearly and distinctly as [I know] that what I prove about some shape or number also belongs to the nature of that shape or number. And therefore, even if all the things I have meditated on in the preceding days were not true, for me the existence of God ought to have at least the same degree of certainty as [I have recognized] up to this point in the truths of mathematics.

At first glance, however, this argument does not look entirely logical but [appears to] contain some sort of sophistry.* For, since in all other matters I have been accustomed to distinguish existence from essence, I can easily persuade myself that [existence] can also be separated from the essence of God and thus that I [can] think of God as not actually existing. However, when I think about this more carefully, it becomes clear that one cannot separate existence from the essence of God, any more than one can separate the fact that the sum of the three angles in a triangle is equal to two right angles from the essence of a triangle, or separate the idea of a valley from the idea of a mountain. Thus, it is no less contradictory to think of a God (that is, of a supremely perfect being) who lacks existence (that is, who lacks a certain perfection) than it is to think of a mountain without a valley.†

Nonetheless, although I cannot conceive of God other than as something with existence, any more than I can of a mountain without a valley, the truth is that just because I think of a mountain with a valley, it does not therefore follow that there is any mountain in the world. In the same way, just because I think of God as having existence, it does not seem to follow that God therefore exists. For my thinking imposes no necessity on things, and in the same way as I can imagine a horse with wings, even though no horse has wings, so I could perhaps attribute existence to God, even though no God exists.

But this [objection] conceals a fallacy. For from the fact that I cannot think of a mountain without a valley, it does not follow that a mountain and valley exist anywhere, but merely that the mountain and valley, whether they exist or not, cannot be separated from each other. However, from the fact that I cannot think of God without existence, it does follow that existence is inseparable from God, and thus that He truly does exist. Not that my thought brings this about or imposes any necessity on anything, but rather, by contrast, because the necessity of the thing itself, that is, of the existence of God, determines that I must think this way. For I am not free to think of God without existence (that is, of a supremely perfect being lacking a supreme perfection) in the same way that I am free to imagine a horse with wings or without them.

Suppose somebody objects: Agreed that once one has assumed that God has every perfection it is in fact necessary to admit that He exists (because existence is part of perfection), but it is not necessary to make that assumption, just as it is unnecessary to assume that all quadrilaterals [can] be inscribed in a circle. For if one assumed that, one would have to conclude that any rhombus could be inscribed in a circle—but

---

* That is, clever-sounding but deceptive reasoning.
† That is, an upslope without a downslope.

this is clearly false.* But this objection is invalid. For although it may not be necessary for me ever to entertain any thought of God, nevertheless, whenever I do happen to think of a first and supreme being, and, as it were, to derive an idea of Him from the storehouse of my mind, I have to attribute to Him all perfections, even though I do not enumerate them all at that time or attend to each one of them individually. And this necessity is obviously sufficient to make me conclude correctly, once I have recognized that existence is a perfection, that a first and supreme being exists. In the same way, it is not necessary that I ever imagine any triangle, but every time I wish to consider a rectilinear† figure with only three angles, I have to attribute to it those [properties] from which I correctly infer that its three angles are no greater than two right angles, although at that time I may not notice this. But when I think about which figures [are capable of being] inscribed in a circle, it is not at all necessary that I believe every quadrilateral is included in their number. On the contrary, I cannot even imagine anything like that, as long as I do not wish to admit anything unless I understand it clearly and distinctly. Thus, there is a great difference between false assumptions of this kind and the true ideas which are innate in me, of which the first and most important is the idea of God. For, in fact, I understand in many ways that this [idea] is not something made up which depends upon my thought but [is] the image of a true and immutable nature: first, because I cannot think of any other thing whose essence includes existence, other than God alone; second, because I am unable to conceive of two or more Gods of this sort, and because, given that I have already assumed that one God exists, I see clearly that it is necessary that He has previously existed from [all] eternity and will continue [to exist] for all eternity; and finally because I perceive many other things in God, none of which I can remove or change.

But, in fact, no matter what reasoning I finally use by way of proof, I always come back to the point that the only things I find entirely persuasive are those I perceive clearly and distinctly. Among the things I

perceive in this way, some are obvious to everyone, while others reveal themselves only to those who look into them more closely and investigate more diligently, but nevertheless once the latter have been discovered, they are considered no less certain than the former. For example, even though the fact that the hypotenuse of a right triangle is opposite the largest angle of the triangle is more apparent than the fact that the square of the hypotenuse is equal to the sum of the squares of the other two sides, nonetheless, after we have initially recognized the second fact, we are no less certain of its truth [than we are of the other]. But where God is concerned, if I were not overwhelmed with prejudices, and if images of perceptible things were not laying siege to my thinking on all sides, there is certainly nothing I would recognize sooner or more easily than Him. For what is more inherently evident than that there is a supreme being; in other words, that God exists, for existence [necessarily and eternally] belongs to His essence alone?

And although it required careful reflection on my part to perceive this [truth], nonetheless I am now not only as sure about it as I am about all the other things which seem [to me] most certain, but also, I see that the certainty of everything else is so dependent on this very truth that without it nothing could ever be perfectly known.

For although my nature is such that, as long as I perceive something really clearly and distinctly, I am unable to deny that it is true, nevertheless, because I am also by nature incapable of always fixing my mental gaze on the same thing in order to perceive it clearly, [and because] my memory may often return to a judgment I have previously made at a time when I am not paying full attention to the reasons why I made such a judgment, other arguments can present themselves which, if I knew nothing about God, might easily drive me to abandon that opinion. Thus, I would never have any true and certain knowledge, but merely vague and changeable opinions. For example, when I consider the nature of a triangle, it is, in fact, very evident to me (given that I am well versed in the

---

* Quadrilaterals are four-sided figures. A figure can be inscribed in a circle when a circle can be drawn that passes through each corner. Rhombuses are figures with four sides of equal length. Squares (a type of rhombus) can be inscribed in a circle, but rhombuses not containing four right angles cannot.
† Formed by straight lines.

principles of geometry) that its three angles are equal to two right angles, and, as long as I focus on the proof of this fact, it is impossible for me not to believe that it is true. But as soon as I turn my mental gaze away from that, although I still remember I perceived it very clearly, it could still easily happen that I doubt whether it is true, if, in fact, I had no knowledge of God. For I can convince myself that nature created me in such a way that I am sometimes deceived by those things I think I perceive as clearly as possible, especially when I remember that I have often considered many things true and certain that I later judged to be false, once other reasons had persuaded me.

However, after I perceived that God exists, because at the same time I also realized that all other things depend on Him and that He is not a deceiver, I therefore concluded that everything I perceive clearly and distinctly is necessarily true. Thus, even if I am not fully attending to the reasons why I have judged that something is true, if I only remember that I have perceived it clearly and distinctly, no opposing argument can present itself that would force me to have doubts. Instead, I possess true and certain knowledge about it—and not just about that, but about all other matters which I remember having demonstrated at any time, for example, [about the truths] of geometry and the like. For what argument could I now bring against them? What about the fact that I am created in such a manner that I often make mistakes? But now I know that I cannot be deceived about those things which I understand clearly. What about the fact that I used to consider many other things true and certain which I later discovered to be false? But I was not perceiving any of these [things] clearly and distinctly, and, in my ignorance of this rule [for confirming] the truth, I happened to believe them for other reasons which I later discovered to be less firm. What then will I say? Perhaps I am dreaming (an objection I recently made to myself), or else everything I am now thinking is no more true than what happens when I am asleep? But even this does not change anything: for surely even though I am asleep, if what is in my intellect is clear, then it is absolutely true.

In this way I fully recognize that all certainty and truth in science depend only on a knowledge of the true God, so much so that, before I knew Him,

I could have no perfect knowledge of anything else. But now I am able to understand innumerable things completely and clearly, about both God Himself and other intellectual matters, as well as about all those things in corporeal nature that are objects of study in pure mathematics.

Sixth Meditation: Concerning the Existence of Material Things and the Real Distinction between Mind and Body

It remains for me to examine whether material things exist. At the moment, I do, in fact, know that they *could* exist, at least insofar as they are objects of pure mathematics, since I perceive them clearly and distinctly. For there is no doubt that God is capable of producing everything which I am capable of perceiving in this way, and I have never judged that there is anything He cannot create, except in those cases where there might be a contradiction in my clear perception of it. Moreover, from my faculty of imagination, which I have learned by experience I use when I turn my attention to material substances, it seems to follow that they exist. For when I consider carefully what the imagination is, it seems nothing other than a certain application of my cognitive faculty to an object which is immediately present to it and which therefore exists.

In order to clarify this matter fully, I will first examine the difference between imagination and pure understanding. For example, when I imagine a triangle, not only do I understand that it is a shape composed of three lines, but at the same time I also see those three lines as if they were, so to speak, present to my mind's eye. This is what I call imagining. However, if I wish to think about a chiliagon, even though I understand that it is a figure consisting of one thousand sides just as well as I understand that a triangle is a figure consisting of three sides, I do not imagine those thousand sides in the same way, nor do I see [them], as it were, in front of me. And although, thanks to my habit of always imagining something whenever I think of a corporeal substance, it may happen that [in thinking of a chiliagon] I create for myself a confused picture of some shape, nevertheless, it is obviously not a chiliagon, because it is no different from the shape I would also picture to myself if I were thinking of a myriagon* or of any other figure with many sides. And that shape is no help at all in recognizing those properties which distinguish the chiliagon from other polygons. However, if it is a question of a pentagon, I can certainly understand its shape just as [well as] I can the shape of a chiliagon, without the assistance of my imagination. But, of course, I can also imagine the pentagon by applying my mind's eye to its five sides and to the area they contain. From this I clearly recognize that, in order to imagine things, I need a certain special mental effort that I do not use to understand them, and this new mental effort reveals clearly the difference between imagination and pure understanding.

Furthermore, I notice that this power of imagining, which exists within me, insofar as it differs from the power of understanding, is not a necessary part of my own essence, that is, of my mind. For even if I did not have it, I would still undoubtedly remain the same person I am now. From this it would seem to follow that my imagination depends upon something different from [my mind]. I understand the following easily enough: If a certain body—my body—exists, and my mind is connected to it in such a way that whenever my mind so wishes it can direct itself (so to speak) to examine that body, then thanks to this particular body it would be possible for me to imagine corporeal things. Thus, the only difference between imagination and pure understanding would be this: the mind, while it is understanding, in some way turns its attention to itself and considers one of the ideas present in itself, but when it is imagining, it turns its attention to the body and sees something in it which conforms to an idea which it has either conceived by itself or perceived with the senses. I readily understand, as I have said, that the imagination *could* be formed in this way, if the body exists, and because I can think of no other equally convenient way of explaining it, I infer from this that the body probably exists—but only probably—and although I am looking into everything carefully, I still do not yet see how from this distinct idea of corporeal nature which I find in my imagination I can derive any argument which necessarily concludes that anything corporeal exists.

However, I am in the habit of imagining many things apart from the corporeal nature which is the object of study in pure mathematics, such as colours, sounds, smells, pain, and things like that, although not so distinctly. And since I perceive these better with my senses, through which, with the help of my memory, they appear to have reached my imagination, then in order to deal with them in a more appropriate manner, I ought to consider the senses at the same time as well and see whether those things which I perceive by this method of thinking, which I call sensation, will enable me to establish some credible argument to prove the existence of corporeal things.

First of all, I will review in my mind the things that I previously believed to be true, because I perceived them with my senses, along with the reasons for those beliefs. Then I will also assess the reasons why I later called them into doubt. And finally I will consider what I ought to believe about them now.

To begin with, then, I sensed that I had a head, hands, feet, and other limbs making up that body which I looked on as if it were a part of me or perhaps even my totality. I sensed that this body moved around among many other bodies which could affect it in different ways, either agreeably or disagreeably. I judged which ones were agreeable by a certain feeling of pleasure and which ones were disagreeable by a feeling of pain. Apart from pain and pleasure, I also felt inside me sensations of hunger, thirst, and other appetites of this kind, as well as certain physical inclinations towards joy, sadness, anger, and other similar emotions. And outside myself, besides the extension, shapes, and motions of bodies, I also had sensations in them of hardness, heat, and other tactile qualities and, in addition, of light, colours, smells, tastes, and sounds. From the variety of these, I distinguished sky, land, sea, and other bodies, one after another. And because of the ideas of all those qualities which presented themselves to my thinking, although I kept sensing these as merely my own personal and immediate ideas, I reasonably believed that I was perceiving certain objects entirely different from my thinking, that is, bodies from which these ideas proceeded. For experience taught me that these ideas reached me without my consent, so that I was unable to sense any object, even if I wanted to, unless it was present to my organs of sense, and I was unable not to sense it when

---

* A myriagon is a 10,000-sided polygon.

it was present. And since the ideas I perceived with my senses were much more vivid, lively, and sharp, and even, in their own way, more distinct than any of those which I myself intentionally and deliberately shaped by meditation or which I noticed impressed on my memory, it did not seem possible that they could have proceeded from myself. Thus, the only conclusion left was that they had come from some other things. Because I had no conception of these objects other than what I derived from those ideas themselves, the only thought my mind could entertain was that [the objects] were similar to [the ideas they produced]. And since I also remembered that earlier I had used my senses rather than my reason and realized that the ideas which I myself formed were not as vivid, lively, and sharp as those which I perceived with my senses and that most of the former were composed of parts of the latter, I easily convinced myself that I had nothing at all in my intellect which I had not previously had in my senses. I also maintained, not without reason, that this body, which, by some special right, I called my own, belonged to me more than any other object, for I could never separate myself from it, as I could from other [bodies], I felt every appetite and emotion in it and because of it, and finally, I noticed pain and the titillation of pleasure in its parts, but not in any objects placed outside it. But why a certain strange sadness of spirit follows a sensation of pain and a certain joy follows from a sensation of [pleasurable] titillation, or why some sort of twitching in the stomach, which I call hunger, is urging me to eat food, while the dryness of my throat [is urging me] to drink, and so on—for that I had no logical explanation, other than that these were things I had learned from nature. For there is clearly no relationship (at least, none I can understand) between that twitching [in the stomach] and the desire to consume food, or between the sensation of something causing pain and the awareness of sorrow arising from that feeling. But it seemed to me that all the other judgments I made about objects of sense experience I had learned from nature. For I had convinced myself that that was how things happened, before I thought about any arguments which might prove it.

However, many later experiences have gradually weakened the entire faith I used to have in the senses. For, now and then, towers which seemed round from a distance appeared square from near at hand, immense statues standing on the tower summits did not seem large when I viewed them from the ground, and in countless other cases like these I discovered that my judgments were deceived in matters dealing with external senses. And not just with external [senses], but also with internal ones as well. For what could be more internal than pain? And yet I heard that people whose legs or arms had been cut off sometimes still seemed to feel pain in the part of their body which they lacked. Thus, even though I were to feel pain in one of my limbs, I did not think I could be completely certain that it was the limb which caused my pain. To these reasons for doubting sense experience, I recently added two extremely general ones. First, there was nothing I ever thought I was sensing while awake that I could not also think I was sensing now and then while asleep, and since I do not believe that those things I appear to sense in my sleep come to me from objects placed outside me, I did not see why I should give more credit to those I appear to sense when I am awake. Second, because I was still ignorant—or at least was assuming I was ignorant—of the author of my being, there seemed to be nothing to prevent nature from constituting me in such a way that I would make mistakes, even in those matters which seemed to me most true. As for the reasons which had previously convinced me of the truth of what I apprehended with my senses, I had no difficulty refuting them. For since nature seemed to push me to accept many things which my reason opposed, I believed I should not place much trust in those things nature taught. And although perceptions of the senses did not depend upon my will, I did not believe that was reason enough for me to conclude that they must come from things different from myself, because there could well be some other faculty in me, even one I did not yet know, which produced them.

But now that I am starting to gain a better understanding of myself and of the author of my being, I do not, in fact, believe that I should rashly accept all those things I appear to possess from my senses, but, at the same time, [I do not think] I should call everything into doubt.

First, since I know that all those things I understand clearly and distinctly could have been created by God in a way that matches my conception of them, the fact that I can clearly and distinctly understand one thing, distinguishing it from something else, is sufficient to convince me that the two of them are different, because they can be separated from each other, at least by God. The power by which this [separation] takes place is irrelevant to my judgment that they are distinct. And therefore, given the mere fact that I know I exist and that, at the moment, I look upon my nature or essence as absolutely nothing other than that I am a thinking thing, I reasonably conclude that my essence consists of this single fact: I am a thinking thing. And although I may well possess (or rather, as I will state later, although I certainly do possess) a body which is very closely joined to me, nonetheless, because, on the one hand, I have a clear and distinct idea of myself, insofar as I am merely a thinking thing, without extension, and, on the other hand, [I have] a distinct idea of body, insofar as it is merely an extended thing which does not think, it is certain that my mind is completely distinct from my body and can exist without it.

Moreover, I discover in myself faculties for certain special forms of thinking, namely, the faculties of imagining and feeling. I can conceive of myself clearly and distinctly as a complete being without these, but I cannot do the reverse and think of these faculties without me, that is, without an intelligent substance to which they belong. For the formal conception of them includes some act of intellection by which I perceive that they are different from me, just as [shapes, movement, and the other] modes [or accidents of bodies are different] from the object [to which they belong]. I also recognize certain other faculties [in me], like changing position, assuming various postures, and so on, which certainly cannot be conceived, any more than those previously mentioned, apart from some substance to which they belong, and therefore they, too, cannot exist without it. However, it is evident that these [faculties], if indeed they [truly] exist, must belong to some corporeal or extended substance, and not to any intelligent substance, since the clear and distinct conception of them obviously contains some [form of] extension, but no intellectual activity whatsoever. Now, it is, in fact, true that I do have a certain passive faculty of perception, that is, of receiving and recognizing ideas of sensible things. But I would be unable to use this power unless some active

faculty existed, as well, either in me or in some other substance capable of producing or forming these ideas. But this [active faculty] clearly cannot exist within me, because it presupposes no intellectual activity at all, and because, without my cooperation and often even against my will, it produces those ideas. Therefore I am left to conclude that it exists in some substance different from me that must contain, either formally or eminently, all the reality objectively present in the ideas produced by that faculty (as I have just observed above).* This substance is either a body, that is, something with a corporeal nature which obviously contains formally everything objectively present in the ideas, or it must be God, or some other creature nobler than the body, one that contains [those same things] eminently. But since God is not a deceiver, it is very evident that He does not transmit these ideas to me from Himself directly or even through the intervention of some other creature in which their objective reality is contained, not formally but only eminently. For since he has given me no faculty whatsoever for recognizing such a source, but by contrast, has endowed me with a powerful tendency to believe that these ideas are sent out from corporeal things, I do not see how it would be possible not to think of Him as a deceiver, if these [ideas] were sent from any source other than corporeal things. And therefore corporeal things exist. However, perhaps they do not all exist precisely in the ways I grasp them with my senses, since what I comprehend with my senses is very obscure and confused in many things. But at least [I should accept as true] all those things in them which I understand clearly and distinctly, that is, generally speaking, everything which is included as an object in pure mathematics.

But regarding other material things which are either merely particular, for example that the sun is of such and such a magnitude and shape, and so on, or less clearly understood, for example light, sound, pain, and things like that, although these may be extremely doubtful and uncertain, nonetheless, because of the very fact that God is not a deceiver and thus it is impossible for there to be any falsity in my opinions which I cannot correct with another faculty God has given me, I have the sure hope that I can reach the

---

* For more on the distinction between formal and objective presence, see the "Some Useful Background Information" section of the introduction to this reading.

truth even in these matters. And clearly there is no doubt that all those things I learn from nature contain some truth. For by the term *nature*, generally speaking, I understand nothing other than either God himself or the coordinated structure of created things established by God, and by the term *my nature*, in particular, nothing other than the combination of all those things I have been endowed with by God.

However, there is nothing that nature teaches me more emphatically than the fact that I have a body, which does badly when I feel pain, which needs food or drink when I suffer from hunger or thirst, and so on. And therefore I should not doubt that there is some truth in this.

For through these feelings of pain, hunger, thirst, and so on, nature teaches me that I am not only present in my body in the same way a sailor is present onboard a ship, but also that I am bound up very closely and, so to speak, mixed in with it, so that my body and I form a certain unity. For if that were not the case, then when my body was injured, I, who am merely a thinking thing, would not feel any pain because of it; instead, I would perceive the wound purely with my intellect, just as a sailor notices with his eyes if something is broken on his ship. And when my body needed food or drink, I would understand that clearly and not have confused feelings of hunger and thirst. For those sensations of thirst, hunger, pain, and so on are really nothing other than certain confused ways of thinking, which arise from the union and, as it were, the mixture of the mind with the body.

Moreover, nature also teaches me that various other bodies exist around my own and that I should pursue some of these and stay away from others. And certainly from the fact that I sense a wide diversity of colours, sounds, odours, tastes, heat, hardness, and similar things, I reasonably conclude that in the bodies from which these different sense perceptions come there are certain variations which correspond to these perceptions, even if they are perhaps not like them. And given the fact that I find some of these sense perceptions pleasant and others unpleasant, it is entirely certain that my body, or rather my totality, since I am composed of body and mind, can be affected by various agreeable and disagreeable bodies surrounding it.

However, many other things which I seemed to have learned from nature I have not really received from her, but rather from a certain habit I have of accepting careless judgments [about things]. And thus it could easily be the case that these judgments are false—for example, [the opinion I have] that all space in which nothing at all happens to stimulate my senses is a vacuum, that in a warm substance there is something completely similar to the idea of heat which is in me, that in a white or green [substance] there is the same whiteness or greenness which I sense, that in [something] bitter or sweet there is the same taste as I sense, and so on, that stars and towers and anything else some distance away have bodies with the same size and shape as the ones they present to my senses, and things of that sort. But in order to ensure that what I perceive in this matter is sufficiently distinct, I should define more accurately what it is precisely that I mean when I say I have learned something from nature. For here I am taking the word *nature* in a more restricted sense than *the combination of all those things which have been bestowed on me by God*. For this combination contains many things which pertain only to the mind, such as the fact that I perceive that what has been done cannot be undone, and all the other things I grasp by my natural light [without the help of the body]. Such things are not under discussion here. This combination also refers to many things which concern only the body, like its tendency to move downward, and so on, which I am also not dealing with [here]. Instead, I am considering only those things which God has given me as a combination of mind and body. And so nature, in this sense, certainly teaches me to avoid those things which bring a sensation of pain and to pursue those which [bring] a sensation of pleasure, and such like, but, beyond that, it is not clear that with those sense perceptions nature teaches us that we can conclude anything about things placed outside of us without a previous examination by the understanding, because to know the truth about them seems to belong only to the mind and not to that combination [of body and mind]. And so, although a star does not make an impression on my eyes any greater than the flame of a small candle, nonetheless, that fact does not incline me, in any real or positive way, to believe that the star is not larger [than the flame], but from the time of my youth I have made this judgment without any reason [to support it]. And although I feel heat when I come near the fire, and even pain if I get too close to it, that is really no reason to believe that there is something in the fire similar to that heat I feel, any more than there is something similar to the pain. The only thing [I can conclude] is that there is something in the fire, whatever it might be, which brings out in us those sensations of heat or pain. So, too, although in some space there is nothing which stimulates my senses, it does not therefore follow that the space contains no substances. But I see that in these and in a great many other matters, I have grown accustomed to undermine the order of nature, because, of course, these sense perceptions are, strictly speaking, given to me by nature merely to indicate to my mind which things are agreeable or disagreeable to that combination of which it is a part, and for that purpose they are sufficiently clear and distinct. But then I use them as if they were dependable rules for immediately recognizing the essence of bodies placed outside me. However, about such bodies they reveal nothing except what is confusing and obscure.

In an earlier section, I have already examined sufficiently why my judgments may happen to be defective, in spite of the goodness of God. However, a new difficulty crops up here concerning those very things which nature reveals to me as objects I should seek out or avoid, and also concerning the internal sensations, in which I appear to have discovered errors: for example, when someone, deceived by the pleasant taste of a certain food, eats a poison hidden within it [and thus makes a mistake]. Of course, in this situation, the person's nature urges him only to eat food which has a pleasant taste and not the poison, of which he has no knowledge at all. And from this, the only conclusion I can draw is that my nature does not know everything. There is nothing astonishing about that, because a human being is a finite substance and thus is capable of only limited perfection.

However, we are frequently wrong even in those things which nature urges [us to seek]. For example, sick people are eager for drink or food which will harm them soon afterwards. One could perhaps claim that such people make mistakes because their nature has been corrupted. But this does not remove the difficulty, for a sick person is no less a true creature of God than a healthy one, and thus it seems no less contradictory that God has given the person a nature which deceives him. And just as a clock made out of wheels and weights observes all the laws of nature with the same accuracy when it is badly made and does not indicate the hours correctly as it does when it completely satisfies the wishes of the person who made it, in the same way, if I look on the human body as some kind of machine composed of bones, nerves, muscles, veins, blood, and skin, as if no mind existed in it, the body would still have all the same motions it now has in those movements that are not under the control of the will and that, therefore, do not proceed from the mind [but merely from the disposition of its organs]. I can readily acknowledge, for example, that in the case of a body sick with dropsy,* it would be quite natural for it to suffer from a parched throat, which usually conveys a sensation of thirst to the mind, and for its nerves and other parts also to move in such a way that it takes a drink and thus aggravates the illness. And when nothing like this is harming the body, it is equally natural for it to be stimulated by a similar dryness in the throat and to take a drink to benefit itself. Now, when I consider the intended purpose of the clock, I could say that, since it does not indicate the time correctly, it is deviating from its own nature, and, in the same way, when I think of the machine of the human body as something formed for the motions which usually take place in it, I might believe that it, too, is deviating from its own nature, if its throat is dry when a drink does not benefit its own preservation. However, I am fully aware that this second meaning of the word *nature* is very different from the first. For it is merely a term that depends on my own thought, a designation with which I compare a sick person and a badly constructed clock with the idea of a healthy person and a properly constructed clock, and thus, the term is extrinsic to these objects. But by that [other use of the term *nature*] I understand something that is really found in things and that therefore contains a certain measure of the truth.

Now, when I consider a body suffering from dropsy, even though I say that its nature has been corrupted, because it has a dry throat and yet does not need to drink, clearly the word *nature* is merely an extraneous term. However, when I consider the composite, that is, the mind united with such a body, I am not dealing with what is simply a term but with a true error of nature, because this composite is thirsty when drinking

---

* An abnormal accumulation of watery fluid in the body (now called edema).

will do it harm. And thus I still have to enquire here why the goodness of God does not prevent its nature, taken in this sense, from being deceitful.

At this point, then, my initial observation is that there is a great difference between the mind and the body, given that the body is, by its very nature, always divisible, whereas the mind is completely indivisible. For, in fact, when I think of [my mind], that is, when I think of myself as purely a thinking thing, I cannot distinguish any parts within me. Instead, I understand that I am something completely individual and unified. And although my entire mind seems to be united with my entire body, nonetheless, I know that if a foot or arm or any other part of the body is sliced off, that loss will not take anything from my mind. And I cannot call the faculties of willing, feeling, understanding, and so on parts of the mind because it is the same single mind that wishes, feels, and understands. By contrast, I cannot think of any corporeal or extended substance that my thought is not capable of dividing easily into parts. From this very fact, I understand that the substance is divisible. (This point alone would be enough to teach me that the mind is completely different from the body, if I did not already know that well enough from other sources.)

Furthermore, I notice that the mind is not immediately affected by all parts of the body, but only by the brain, or perhaps even by just one small part of it, namely, the one in which our *common sense** is said to exist. Whenever this part is arranged in the same particular way, it delivers the same perception to the mind, even though the other parts of the body may be arranged quite differently at the time. This point has been demonstrated in countless experiments, which I need not review here.

In addition, I notice that the nature of my body is such that no part of it can be moved by any other part some distance away which cannot also be moved in the same manner by any other part lying between them, even though the more distant part does nothing. So, for example, in a rope ABCD [which is taut throughout], if I pull on part D at the end, then the movement of the first part, A, will be no different than it would

be if I pulled at one of the intermediate points, B or C, while the last part, D, remained motionless. And for a similar reason, when I feel pain in my foot, physics teaches me that this sensation occurs thanks to nerves spread throughout the foot. These nerves stretch from there to the brain, like cords, and when they are pulled in my foot, they also pull the inner parts of the brain, where they originate, and stimulate in them a certain motion which nature has established to influence the mind with a sense of pain apparently present in the foot. However, since these nerves have to pass through the shin, the thigh, the loins, the back, and the neck in order to reach the brain from the foot, it can happen that, even if that portion of the nerves which is in the foot is not affected, but only one of the intermediate portions, the motion created in the brain is exactly the same as the one created there by an injured foot. As a result, the mind will necessarily feel the identical pain. And we should assume that the same is true with any other sensation whatsoever.

Finally, I notice that, since each of those motions created in that part of the brain which immediately affects the mind introduces into it only one particular sensation, we can, given this fact, come up with no better explanation than that this sensation, out of all the ones which could be introduced, is the one which serves to protect human health as effectively and frequently as possible [when a person is completely healthy]. But experience testifies to the fact that all sensations nature has given us are like this, and thus we can discover nothing at all in them which does not bear witness to the power and benevolence of God. Thus, for example, when the nerves in the foot are moved violently and more than usual, their motion, passing through the spinal cord to the inner core of the brain, gives a signal there to the mind which makes it feel something—that is, it feels as if there is a pain in the foot. And that stimulates [the mind] to do everything it can to remove the cause of the pain as something injurious to the foot. Of course, God could have constituted the nature of human beings in such a way that this same motion in the brain communicated something else to the mind, for example, a sense of

---

* Descartes is probably thinking of the pineal gland here, a tiny structure located between the two hemispheres of the brain; this is because he believed it to be the only anatomical structure of the brain which existed as a single part, rather than one half of a pair.

its own movements, either in the brain, or in the foot, or in any of the places in between—in short, of anything you wish. But nothing else would have served so well for the preservation of the body. In the same way, when we need a drink, a certain dryness arises in the throat which moves its nerves and, with their assistance, the inner parts of the brain. And this motion incites in the mind a sensation of thirst, because in this whole situation nothing is more useful for us to know than that we need a drink to preserve our health. The same is true for the other sensations.

From this it is clearly evident that, notwithstanding the immense goodness of God, human nature, given that it is composed of mind and body, cannot be anything other than something that occasionally deceives us. For if some cause, not in the foot, but in some other part through which the nerves stretch between the foot and the brain, or even in the brain itself, stimulates exactly the same motion as that which is normally aroused when a foot is injured, then pain will be felt as if it were in the foot, and the sensation will naturally be deceiving. Since that same motion in the brain is never capable of transmitting to the mind anything other than the identical sensation and since [the sensation] is habitually aroused much more frequently from an injury in the foot than from anything else in another place, it is quite reasonable that it should always transmit to the mind a pain in the foot rather than a pain in any other part of the body. And if sometimes dryness in the throat does not arise, as it usually does, from the fact that a drink is necessary for the health of the body, but from some different cause, as occurs in a patient suffering from dropsy, it is much better that it should deceive us in a case like that than if it were, by contrast, always deceiving us when the body is quite healthy. The same holds true with the other sensations.

This reflection is the greatest help, for it enables me not only to detect all the errors to which my nature is prone, but also to correct or to avoid them easily. For since I know that, in matters concerning what is beneficial to the body, all my senses show [me] what is true much more frequently than they deceive me, and since I can almost always use several of them to examine the same matter and, in addition, [can use] my memory, which connects present events with earlier ones, as well as my understanding, which has now ascertained all the causes of my errors, I should no longer fear that those things which present themselves to me every day through my senses are false. And I ought to dismiss all those exaggerated doubts of the past few days as ridiculous, particularly that most important [doubt] about sleep, which I did not distinguish from being awake. For now I notice a significant distinction between the two of them, given that our memory never links our dreams to all the other actions of our lives, as it [usually] does with those things which take place when we are awake. For clearly, if someone suddenly appears to me when I am awake and then immediately afterwards disappears, as happens in my dreams, so that I have no idea where he came from or where he went, I would reasonably judge that I had seen some apparition or phantom created in my brain [similar to the ones created when I am asleep], rather than a real person. But when certain things occur and I notice distinctly the place from which they came, where they are, and when they appeared to me, and when I can link my perception of them to the rest of my life as a totality, without a break, then I am completely certain that this is taking place while I am awake and not in my sleep. And I should not have the slightest doubt about the truth of these perceptions if, after I have called upon all my senses, my memory, and my understanding to examine them, I find nothing in any of them which contradicts any of the others. For since God is not a deceiver, it must follow that in such cases I am not deceived. But because, in dealing with what we need to do, we cannot always take the time for such a scrupulous examination, we must concede that human life is often prone to error concerning particular things and that we need to acknowledge the frailty of our nature. ∎

Suggestions for Critical Reflection

1. Descartes, in the *Meditations*, has traditionally been seen as raising and then trying to deal with the problem of radical skepticism: that is, according to this interpretation, he raises the possibility that (almost) all our beliefs might be radically mistaken and then argues that this is, in fact, impossible. A more recent line of interpretation, though, sees Descartes not as attempting to answer the skeptic, but as trying to replace naïve empirical assumptions about science with a more modern, mathematical view—in particular, that Descartes is trying to show our most fundamental pieces of knowledge about mind, God, and the world come not from sensory experience, but directly from the intellect. Which interpretation do you think is more plausible? Could they both be right? If Descartes does want to refute skepticism, is he successful in doing so? If his goal is to overturn naïve scholastic empiricism, do you think he manages to do that?

2. Descartes's foundational claim is "I think therefore I am." How does Descartes justify this claim? Does he have, or need, an *argument* for it? Is an argument that justifies this claim even possible?

3. Descartes writes, in the Third Meditation, "[t]here cannot be another faculty [in me] as trustworthy as natural light, one which could teach me that the ideas [derived from natural light] are not true." What do you think he means by this? Is he right? How important to his arguments is it that he be right about this?

4. Eighteenth-century Scottish philosopher David Hume dryly said, of the *Meditations*, "To have recourse to the veracity of the supreme Being, in order to prove the veracity of our senses, is surely making a very unexpected circuit" (Section XII of *An Enquiry Concerning Human Understanding*, 1748). What do you think? Does Descartes establish the existence of God?

5. On Descartes's picture, do you think an atheist can have any knowledge? Why or why not?

6. It seems to be crucial to Descartes's arguments (especially those in the Fourth Meditation) that God is not responsible for our errors, that what we believe—and, indeed, whether we believe or simply suspend our belief—is something that is under our direct control: that we can freely will to believe or not. Does this seem plausible to you? (Could you really decide not to believe that, say, your body exists?) How might Descartes argue for this position? If it cannot be defended, how problematic would this be for the project of the *Meditations*?

7. A famous objection to Descartes's conclusions in the *Meditations* (raised for the first time by some of his contemporaries) is today known as the problem of the Cartesian Circle. Descartes says in the Third Meditation, "Whatever I perceive very clearly and distinctly is true." Call this the CDP (Clear and Distinct Perception) Principle. It is this principle that he thinks will allow him to reconstruct a body of reliable scientific knowledge on the foundations of the Cogito. However, he immediately admits, the CDP Principle will only work if we cannot ever make mistakes about what we clearly and distinctly perceive; to show this, Descartes tries to prove that God exists and has created human beings such that what we clearly and distinctly see to be evidently true really is true. But how does Descartes prove God exists? Apparently, by arguing that we have a clear and distinct idea of God, and so it must be true that God exists. That is, the objection runs, Descartes relies upon the CDP Principle to prove that the CDP Principle is reliable—and this argument just goes in a big circle and doesn't prove anything. What do you think of this objection?

8. "How do I know that I am not ten thinkers thinking in unison?" (Elizabeth Anscombe, "The First Person" [1975]). What, if anything, do you think Descartes has proved about the nature of the self?

9. How adequate are Descartes's arguments for mind-body dualism? If mind and body are two different substances, do you think this might cause other philosophical problems to arise? For example, how might mind and body interact if they are radically different and have no properties in common? How could we come to know things about other people's minds? How could we be sure whether animals have minds or not, and if they do what they might be like?

10. Descartes recognized no physical properties but size, shape, and motion. Where do you think Descartes would say colors, tastes, smells, and so on come from?

JOHN LOCKE

FROM *An Essay Concerning Human Understanding*

Who Was John Locke?

John Locke was born in the Somerset countryside, near the town of Bristol, in 1632. His parents were small landowners—minor gentry—who subjected the young Locke to a strict Protestant upbringing. Thanks to the influence of one of his father's friends, Locke was able to gain a place at Westminster School, at the time the best school in England, where he studied Greek, Latin, and Hebrew. He went on to Christ Church College, Oxford, and graduated with a BA in 1656. Shortly afterwards he was made a senior student of his college—a kind of teaching position—which he was to remain at until 1684, when the king of England, Charles II, personally (and illegally) demanded his expulsion.

During the 1650s and early 1660s Locke lectured on Greek and rhetoric at Oxford, but he was idle and unhappy and became increasingly bored by the traditional philosophy of his day. He developed an interest in medicine and physical science (in 1675 he tried and failed to gain the degree of Doctor of Medicine) and in 1665 left the confines of the academic world and began to make his way into the world of politics and science. In the winter of 1665–66 he was ambassador to the German state of Brandenburg, where his first-hand observation of religious toleration between Calvinists, Lutherans, Catholics, and Anabaptists made a big impression on him.

A chance encounter in 1666 was the decisive turning-point in Locke's life: he met a nobleman called Lord Ashley, then the Chancellor of the Exchequer, and soon went to live at Ashley's London house as his confidant and medical advisor. In 1668, Locke was responsible for a life-saving surgical operation on Ashley, implanting a small silver spigot to drain off fluid from a cyst on his liver; the lord never forgot his gratitude (and wore the small tap in his side for the rest of his life). Under Ashley's patronage, Locke had both the leisure to spend several years working on his *Essay Concerning Human Understanding* and a sequence of lucrative and interesting government positions, including one as part of a group drafting the constitution of the new colony of Carolina in the Americas.

Ashley's support was also essential in giving Locke—an introverted and hyper-sensitive soul who suffered for most of his life from bad asthma and general poor health—the confidence to do original philosophy. Locke never married, was a life-long celibate, shied away from drinking parties and a hectic social life, but enjoyed the attentions of lady admirers, and throughout his life he had many loyal friends and got on especially well with some of his friends' children.

Locke spent from 1675 until 1679 traveling in France (where he expected to die of tuberculosis, but survived—Locke spent a large portion of his life confidently expecting an early death), and when he returned to England it was to a very unsettled political situation. The heir to the British throne, Charles II's younger brother James, was a Catholic, and his succession was feared by many politicians, including Ashley—who was, by this time, the Earl of Shaftesbury—and his political party, the Whigs. Their greatest worry was that the return of a Catholic monarchy would mean the return of religious oppression to England, as was happening in parts of Europe. Charles, however, stood by his brother and in 1681 Shaftesbury was sent to prison in the Tower of London, charged with high treason. Shaftesbury was acquitted by a grand jury, but he fled to Holland and died a few months later (spending his last few hours, the story goes, discussing a draft of Locke's *Essay* with his friends). Locke, in danger as a known associate of Shaftesbury's, followed his example in 1683 and secretly moved to the Netherlands, where he had to spend a year underground evading arrest by the Dutch government's agents on King Charles's behalf. While in Holland he rewrote material for the *Essay*, molding it towards its final state, and published an abridgement of the book, which immediately attracted international attention, in a French scholarly periodical.

In 1689 the political tumult in England had subsided enough for Locke to return—James's brief reign (as James II) had been toppled by the Protestant William of Orange and his queen Mary—and he moved as a permanent house-guest to an estate called Oates about 25 miles from London. He returned to political life (though he refused re-appointment as ambassador to Branden-burg, on grounds of ill health), and played a significant role in loosening restrictions on publishers and authors.

It was in this year, when Locke was 57, that the re-sults of his 30 years of thinking and writing were sud-denly published in a flood. First, published anonymously, came the *Letter on Toleration*, then *Two Treatises on Government*. In the *Two Treatises*—which proved influ-ential in the liberal movements of the next century that culminated in the French and American revolutions—Locke argued that the authority of monarchs is limited by individuals' rights and the public good. Finally, *An Essay Concerning Human Understanding* was published under his own name, to almost instant acclaim; the pub-lication of this book catapulted Locke overnight to what we would now think of as international superstardom.

These three were his most important works, but Locke—by now one of the most famous men in En-gland—continued to write and publish until his death 15 years later. He wrote, for example, works on the prop-er control of the currency for the English government; *Some Thoughts Concerning Education* (which, appar-ently, was historically important in shaping the toilet-training practices of the English educated classes); a work on the proper care and cultivation of fruit trees; and a careful commentary on the *Epistles* of St. Paul. He died quietly, reading in his study, in October 1704.

What Was Locke's Overall Philosophical Project?

Locke is the leading proponent of a school of philosophy now often called "British empiricism." Some of the central platforms of this doctrine are as follows: First, human be-ings are born like a blank, white sheet of paper—a *tabula rasa*—without any innate knowledge but with certain nat-ural powers, and we use these powers to adapt ourselves to the social and physical environment into which we are born. Two especially important natural powers are the capacity for conscious sense experience and for feeling pleasure and pain, and it is from the interaction of these capacities with the environment that we acquire all of our ideas, knowledge, and habits of mind. All meaningful lan-guage must be connected to the ideas that we thus ac-quire, and the abuse of language to talk about things of which we have no idea is a serious source of intellectual errors—errors that can have harmful consequences for

social and moral life, as well as the growth of the sciences. British empiricism—whose other main exponents were Thomas Hobbes (1588–1679), George Berkeley (1685–1753), and David Hume (1711–76)—was generally opposed to re-ligious fervor and sectarian strife, and cautious about the human capacity for attaining absolute knowledge about things that go beyond immediate experience.

An Essay Concerning Human Understanding is Locke's attempt to present a systematic and detailed empiricist account of the human mind and human knowl-edge. It also includes an account of the nature of lan-guage, and touches on philosophical issues to do with logic, religion, metaphysics, and ethics. Locke was also consciously interested in defending a certain modern way of thinking against the habits of the past: instead of relatively uncritical and conservative acceptance of Greek and Roman history, literature and philosophy, and of Christian theology, Locke defended independent thought, secular values, and the power of modern ideas and social change to produce useful results.

Locke was optimistic about the power and accuracy of his own theory of human understanding—and thus about the powers of human beings to come to know the world—but he nevertheless thought it was a *limited* power. There are some things human beings just cannot ever come to know with certainty, Locke thought, and we should be humble in our attempts to describe reality. Thus, there are some domains in which, according to Locke, our human capacities are sufficient to produce certain knowledge: mathematics, morality, the existence of God, and the ex-istence of things in the world corresponding to our 'sim-ple ideas' (i.e., roughly, the things we perceive). However, there are other areas where the best we can do is to make skillful guesses: these more difficult questions have to do with the underlying nature and workings of nature—that is, with scientific theory—and with the details of religious doctrine. God has given us the capacity to effectively get by in the world by making these careful guesses, accord-ing to Locke, but he has not given us the capacity to ever know for sure whether our guesses are correct or not. (This is one reason why Locke believed we should be tol-erant of other people's religious beliefs.)

What Is the Structure of This Reading?

An Essay Concerning Human Understanding is divided into four books, each of which is further divided into chapters, which in turn are divided into sections. Book I is primarily an attack on the notion, which Locke found especially in Descartes, that human beings are born with certain "innate ideas"—concepts and knowledge which are not the product of experience but which are, perhaps, implanted in us by God. Book II develops Locke's alternative empiricist theory of ideas: here he describes the different sorts of ideas human beings have (such as our ideas of external objects, space, time, number, cause and effect, and so on), and tries to show how these ideas all derive ultimately from reflection on our own sense-experience. In Book III Locke describes the workings of language, and in particular defends the thesis that all meaningful language derives that meaning from its connections to our ideas. Finally, Book IV is where Locke considers the question of human knowledge and asks how much justification there is for our beliefs about God and nature, concluding that, although limited, the scope of our knowledge is more than enough for practical purposes.

The first two selections collected here come from Book II (and so are about ideas), and the third from Book IV (and so is about knowledge). The first selection asks how much our ideas resemble those things in the world that cause them and, among other things, describes and defends an important distinction between "primary" and "secondary" qualities. The second extract deals with the topic of "substance," the 'stuff' of the material world. The third approaches head-on the issue of the extent and limits of our knowledge of the external world.

Some Useful Background Information

1. Locke writes in a very straightforward and clear style—he deliberately set out to write informally, for a general educated readership—but his language is the English of the seventeenth century and some readers might find this difficult. Here is a short glossary of the words which might be either unfamiliar or used in an unfamiliar way. Other terms are defined in the footnotes of this reading.

    Apprehension: understanding, perception
    Bare/barely: mere/merely
    Denominate: apply a name to something
    Doth: does
    Figure: shape
    Hath: has

    Manna: the sweet dried juice of the Mediterranean ash tree and other plants, which can be used as a mild laxative (also, a substance miraculously supplied as food to the Israelites in the wilderness, according to the Bible)
    Peculiar: particular, specific
    Sensible/insensible: able to be sensed/invisible to the senses
    V.g.: for example
    Viz.: in other words, that is
    Without: outside (of us)

2. Locke's notion of an *idea* is central to his philosophy—which is even sometimes called "the way of ideas"—and he uses the word in his own special and carefully worked out way. For Locke, ideas are not activities of the mind but instead are the *contents* of the mind—they are the things we think about, the objects of our thought. (In fact, for Locke, thought consists entirely in the succession of ideas through consciousness.) Thus, for example, the things we believe, know, remember, or imagine are what Locke would call ideas.

    As the term suggests, Locke probably assumes ideas are mental entities—they are things that exist in our minds rather than in the external world. Certainly, there are no ideas floating around that are not part of someone's consciousness; every idea is necessarily the object of some act of thinking. Furthermore, ideas are the *only* things we directly think about—our thought and our mental experience, for Locke, is internally rather than externally directed: it is an experience of our ideas and the operations of our mind, not directly of the world. When Locke uses the word "perception," for example, he often means the mind's perception (awareness) of its own ideas, not, as we would usually mean, perception of objects outside our own minds.

    However, this is not to say that we don't think about or perceive the external world; Locke commonsensically thought that we saw trees, tasted apples, heard the speech of other human beings, and so on. But it does mean that all our thought and perception is mediated by ideas, which intervene between us and external reality. The ideas we have before our minds are the "immediate objects of perception," and the things those ideas represent are the "indirect objects of perception." Yet it is important to remember that, for Locke, ideas *do* naturally and evidently represent things beyond themselves (although not necessarily the whole, or even the most important aspects, of the nature of those things)—Locke does not believe for a moment that we are locked inside our own heads.

Locke distinguishes between lots of different types of ideas, but one especially important contrast is between simple and complex ideas. A simple idea is "nothing but one uniform appearance, or conception in the mind, and is not distinguishable into different ideas," whereas complex ideas are compounded out of more than one simple idea. For example, redness is a simple idea, while the idea of a London double-decker bus is a complex idea. For Locke, all simple ideas are acquired from experience, either through sense perception or through the perception of our own thoughts (often called "introspection"): we are not free to simply invent or ignore such ideas, as they are physically caused by the things they represent. However, we are free to construct complex ideas out of this raw material as we like, and we can do so in various ways: we can add simple ideas together into a single idea (e.g., the idea of a horse), or we can compare two ideas and perceive the relation that holds between them (e.g., the idea of being taller than), or we can generalize about simple ideas to form abstract ideas (e.g., the idea of time or infinity).

3. Locke held the modern (at the time) "corpuscular" theory of matter, which was developed by Pierre Gassendi (1592–1655) and Robert Boyle (1627–91) and which, though a "mechanical philosophy," contradicted some important elements of Descartes's physical theory. As a corpuscularian, Locke thought that the physical world was made up of tiny indestructible particles, invisible to the human eye, moving around in empty space, and having only the following properties: solidity, extension in three dimensions, shape (or "figure"), motion or rest, number, location ("situation"), volume ("bulk"), and texture. All the phenomena of the material world are built out of or caused by these particles and their properties and powers. Thus, collections of particles big enough to be visible have certain properties (which Locke called "qualities"), e.g., the shape and size of a gold nugget, its color, malleability, luster, chemical inertness, and so on. Our perception of the world—that is to say, our

experience of these qualities—is brought about by invisible streams of tiny particles emanating from the objects in our environment and striking our sense-receptors (our eyes, ears, skin, and so on). Locke and his contemporaries thought this stimulation of our senses causes complex reactions in our "animal spirits," and this is what gives rise to our ideas. Animal spirits were supposed to be a fine fluid (itself made up of tiny particles) flowing through our nervous system and carrying signals from one place to another and ultimately to our brain.

Some Common Misconceptions

1. In reading Locke, it is important not to confuse ideas with qualities. Ideas are mental entities; they constitute our *experience* of the world. Qualities are non-mental attributes of chunks of matter in the world; they are the things ideas are *about*. Thus, in Locke's view, our idea of color should not be confused with the property of color itself. The distinction between primary and secondary qualities, then, is mainly a distinction between types of physical property (though it does have implications for the taxonomy of our ideas).

2. The secondary qualities not only include colors, tastes, smells, sounds, and feels; they also include properties like solubility, brittleness, flammability, being nutritious, being a pain-killer, and so on.

3. It is sometimes thought Locke argued that secondary qualities do not really exist, and that color, smell, taste, and so on are only ideas in our mind. But this is not so. Locke does think that material objects in the world really have secondary qualities, but he argues that we have misunderstood the *nature* of these qualities in a particular way.

4. In thinking about the nature of the secondary qualities it is helpful to consider the nature of their connection with our ideas of them. In this context, two concepts are useful but are sometimes confused with each other. The first notion is that of *perceiver-relativity*: this is the idea that how something *seems* depends on who is perceiving it. To say that "beauty is in the eye of the beholder" is to make a claim about perceiver-relativity; more interestingly, being poisonous is an example of a perceiver-relative property, since substances that are poisonous to one

kind of perceiver might not be poisonous to others (e.g., chemicals called avermectins are lethal to many invertebrates but harmless to mammals). The second, different, notion is of *perceiver-dependence*: this is the idea that the very existence of something depends upon being perceived or thought about. An example of this would be a conscious visual image—there can be no such thing as a conscious image that is not in anybody's consciousness, and so mental images must be mind-dependent.

5. In the third selection below, when Locke is writing about substance, his main topic is the *idea* of substance, not substance itself. That is, he does not ask (directly) whether substance really exists; instead, his question is, do we have an idea of substance? And whatever his conclusions about the idea of substance, Locke denied being skeptical about the actual existence of substance.

How Important and Influential Is This Passage?

"The *Essay* has long been recognized as one of the great works of English literature of the seventeenth century, and one of the epoch-making works in the history of philosophy. It has been one of the most repeatedly re-printed, widely disseminated and read, and profoundly influential books of the past three centuries."* So writes Peter Nidditch, an expert on Locke's philosophy. Locke's *Essay* is often credited with being the most thorough and plausible formulation and defense of empiricism ever written, and it has exercised a huge influence on, especially, English-speaking philosophers right up until the present day (though with a period in the philosophical wilderness during the 1800s). In the eighteenth century Locke was widely considered as important for philosophy, and for what we would today call psychology, as Newton was for physics.

Although the distinction between primary and secondary qualities was certainly not invented by Locke, his account of it was very influential and was taken as the standard line in subsequent discussions of this important idea. Furthermore, the problem Locke raised about the coherence of our idea of material substance has been an important metaphysical problem since he formulated it, and was an important motivator for Berkeley's ideas.

FROM *An Essay Concerning Human Understanding*†

Book II, Chapter VIII: Some Further Considerations Concerning Our Simple Ideas

§1. Concerning the simple ideas of Sensation, it is to be considered, that whatsoever is so constituted in nature as to be able, by affecting our senses, to cause any perception in the mind, doth thereby produce in the understanding a simple idea, which, whatever be the external cause of it, when it comes to be taken notice of by our discerning faculty, it is by the mind looked on and considered there to be a real positive idea in the understanding, as much as any other whatsoever; though, perhaps, the cause of it be but a privation‡ of the subject.

§2. Thus the ideas of heat and cold, light and darkness, white and black, motion and rest, are equally clear and positive ideas in the mind, though, perhaps, some of the causes which produce them are barely

---

*   P.H. Nidditch, "Introduction" to *An Essay Concerning Human Understanding* (Oxford University Press, 1975), vii.

†   Locke's *An Essay Concerning Human Understanding* was first published in 1690. The excerpts given here are from the sixth edition of 1710, reprinted from Locke's 10-volume *Collected Works* (first published in 1714 and reprinted with corrections in 1823).

‡   A privation is a loss or absence of something.

privations in subjects, from whence our senses derive those ideas. These the understanding, in its view of them, considers all as distinct positive ideas, without taking notice of the causes that produce them; which is an inquiry not belonging to the idea, as it is in the understanding, but to the nature of the things existing without us. These are two very different things, and carefully to be distinguished; it being one thing to perceive and know the idea of white or black, and quite another to examine what kind of particles they must be, and how ranged in the superficies,* to make any object appear white or black.

§3. A painter or dyer, who never inquired into their causes, hath the ideas of white and black, and other colours, as clearly, perfectly, and distinctly in his understanding, and perhaps more distinctly, than the philosopher, who hath busied himself in considering their natures, and thinks he knows how far either of them is in its cause positive or privative; and the idea of black is no less positive in his mind than that of white, however the cause of that colour in the external object may be only a privation.

...

§7. To discover the nature of our ideas the better, and to discourse of them intelligibly, it will be convenient to distinguish them as they are ideas or perceptions in our minds; and as they are modifications of matter in the bodies that cause such perceptions in us: that so we may not think (as perhaps usually is done) that they are exactly the images and resemblances of something inherent in the subject; most of those of sensation being in the mind no more the likeness of something existing without us, than the names that stand for them are the likeness of our ideas, which yet upon hearing they are apt to excite in us.

§8. Whatsoever the mind perceives in itself, or is the immediate object of perception, thought, or understanding, that I call idea; and the power to produce any idea in our mind, I call quality of the subject wherein that power is. Thus a snow-ball having the power to produce in us the ideas of white, cold, and round, the powers to produce those ideas in us, as they are in the snow-ball, I call qualities; and as they are sensations or perceptions in our understandings, I call them ideas; which ideas, if I speak of sometimes as in

the things themselves, I would be understood to mean those qualities in the objects which produce them in us.

§9. Qualities thus considered in bodies are, first, such as are utterly inseparable from the body, in what state soever it be; such as in all the alterations and changes it suffers, all the force can be used upon it, it constantly keeps; and such as sense constantly finds in every particle of matter which has bulk enough to be perceived; and the mind finds inseparable from every particle of matter, though less than to make itself singly be perceived by our senses: v.g. take a grain of wheat, divide it into two parts; each part has still solidity, extension, figure, and mobility; divide it again, and it retains still the same qualities, and so divide it on, till the parts become insensible, they must retain still each of them all those qualities. For division (which is all that a mill, or pestle, or any other body, does upon another, in reducing it to insensible parts) can never take away either solidity, extension, figure, or mobility from any body, but only makes two or more distinct separate masses of matter, of that which was but one before; all which distinct masses, reckoned as so many distinct bodies, after division make a certain number. These I call original or primary qualities of body, which I think we may observe to produce simple ideas in us, viz. solidity, extension, figure, motion or rest, and number.

§10. Secondly, such qualities which in truth are nothing in the objects themselves, but powers to produce various sensations in us by their primary qualities, i.e., by the bulk, figure, texture, and motion of their insensible parts, as colours, sounds, tastes, &c. these I call secondary qualities. To these might be added a third sort, which are allowed to be barely powers; though they are as much real qualities in the subject as those which I, to comply with the common way of speaking, call qualities, but for distinction, secondary qualities. For the power in fire to produce a new colour, or consistency, in wax or clay, by its primary qualities, is as much a quality in fire, as the power it has to produce in me a new idea or sensation of warmth or burning, which I felt not before, by the same primary qualities, viz. the bulk, texture, and motion of its insensible parts.

---

* Outside surfaces.

§11. The next thing to be considered is, how bodies produce ideas in us; and that is manifestly by impulse,* the only way which we can conceive bodies to operate in.

§12. If then external objects be not united to our minds, when they produce ideas therein, and yet we perceive these original qualities in such of them as singly fall under our senses, it is evident that some motion must be thence continued by our nerves, or animal spirits, by some parts of our bodies, to the brains or the seat of sensation, there to produce in our minds the particular ideas we have of them. And since the extension, figure, number, and motion of bodies, of an observable bigness, may be perceived at a distance by the sight, it is evident some singly imperceptible bodies must come from them to the eyes, and thereby convey to the brain some motion, which produces these ideas which we have of them in us.

§13. After the same manner, that the ideas of these original qualities are produced in us, we may conceive that the ideas of secondary qualities are also produced, viz. by the operation of insensible particles on our senses. For it being manifest that there are bodies, and good store of bodies, each whereof are so small that we cannot, by any of our senses, discover either their bulk, figure, or motion, as is evident in the particles of the air and water, and others extremely smaller than those; perhaps as much smaller than the particles of air and water as the particles of air and water are smaller than peas or hail-stones: let us suppose at present, that the different motions and figures, bulk and number of such particles, affecting the several organs of our senses, produce in us those different sensations, which we have from the colours and smells of bodies; *v.g.* that a violet, by the impulse of such insensible particles of matter of peculiar figures and bulks, and in different degrees and modifications of their motions, causes the ideas of the blue colour and sweet scent of that flower to be produced in our minds, it being no more impossible to conceive that God should annex such ideas to such motions, with which they have no similitude, than that he should annex the idea of pain to the motion of a piece of steel dividing our flesh, with which that idea hath no resemblance.

§14. What I have said concerning colours and smells may be understood also of tastes and sounds, and other the like sensible qualities; which, whatever reality we by mistake attribute to them, are in truth nothing in the objects themselves, but powers to produce various sensations in us, and depend on those primary qualities, viz. bulk, figure, texture, and motion of parts as I have said.

§15. From whence I think it easy to draw this observation, that the ideas of primary qualities of bodies are resemblances of them, and their patterns do really exist in the bodies themselves, but the ideas produced in us by these secondary qualities have no resemblance of them at all. There is nothing like our ideas, existing in the bodies themselves. They are, in the bodies we denominate from them, only a power to produce those sensations in us; and what is sweet, blue, or warm in idea, is but the certain bulk, figure, and motion of the insensible parts, in the bodies themselves, which we call so.

§16. Flame is denominated hot and light; snow white and cold; and manna white and sweet, from the ideas they produce in us: which qualities are commonly thought to be the same in those bodies that those ideas are in us, the one the perfect resemblance of the other, as they are in a mirror; and it would by most men be judged very extravagant† if one should say otherwise. And yet he that will consider that the same fire, that at one distance produces in us the sensation of warmth, does at a nearer approach produce in us the far different sensation of pain, ought to bethink himself what reason he has to say, that his idea of warmth, which was produced in him by the fire, is actually in the fire; and his idea of pain, which the same fire produced in him the same way, is not in the fire. Why are whiteness and coldness in snow, and pain not, when it produces the one and the other idea in us, and can do neither but by the bulk, figure, number, and motion of its solid parts?

§17. The particular bulk, number, figure, and motion of the parts of fire, or snow, are really in them, whether any one's senses perceive them or no; and therefore they may be called real qualities, because they really exist in those bodies: but light, heat, whiteness,

---

* Causal impact.
† Odd or peculiar.

or coldness, are no more really in them than sickness or pain is in manna. Take away the sensation of them; let not the eyes see light or colours, nor the ears hear sounds; let the palate not taste, nor the nose smell; and all colours, tastes, odours, and sounds, as they are such particular ideas, vanish and cease, and are reduced to their causes, i.e., bulk, figure, and motion of parts.

§18. A piece of manna of a sensible bulk is able to produce in us the idea of a round or square figure, and, by being removed from one place to another, the idea of motion. This idea of motion represents it as it really is in manna moving: a circle or square are the same, whether in idea or existence, in the mind or in the manna; and this, both motion and figure, are really in the manna, whether we take notice of them or no: this every body is ready to agree to. Besides, manna, by the bulk, figure, texture, and motion of its parts, has a power to produce the sensations of sickness, and sometimes of acute pains or gripings* in us. That these ideas of sickness and pain are not in the manna, but effects of its operations on us, and are nowhere when we feel them not: this also every one readily agrees to. And yet men are hardly to be brought to think, that sweetness and whiteness are not really in manna; which are but the effects of the operations of manna, by the motion, size, and figure of its particles on the eyes and palate; as the pain and sickness caused by manna are confessedly nothing but the effects of its operations on the stomach and guts, by the size, motion, and figure of its insensible parts, (for by nothing else can a body operate, as has been proved); as if it could not operate on the eyes and palate, and thereby produce in the mind particular distinct ideas, which in itself it has not, as well as we allow it can operate on the guts and stomach, and thereby produce distinct ideas, which in itself it has not. These ideas being all effects of the operations of manna, on several parts of our bodies, by the size, figure, number, and motion of its parts; why those produced by the eyes and palate should rather be thought to be really in the manna than those produced by the stomach and guts; or why the pain and sickness, ideas that are the effect of manna, should be thought to be nowhere when they are not felt: and

yet the sweetness and whiteness, effects of the same manna on other parts of the body, by ways equally as unknown, should be thought to exist in the manna, when they are not seen or tasted, would need some reason to explain.

§19. Let us consider the red and white colours in porphyry:† hinder light from striking on it, and its colours vanish, it no longer produces any such ideas in us; upon the return of light it produces these appearances on us again. Can any one think any real alterations are made in the porphyry by the presence or absence of light; and that those ideas of whiteness and redness are really in porphyry in the light, when it is plain it has no colour in the dark? It has, indeed, such a configuration of particles, both night and day, as are apt, by the rays of light rebounding from some parts of that hard stone, to produce in us the idea of redness, and from others the idea of whiteness; but whiteness or redness are not in it at any time, but such a texture that hath the power to produce such a sensation in us.

§20. Pound an almond, and the clear white colour will be altered into a dirty one, and the sweet taste into an oily one. What real alteration can the beating of the pestle make in any body, but an alteration of the texture of it?

§21. Ideas being thus distinguished and understood, we may be able to give an account how the same water, at the same time, may produce the idea of cold by one hand and of heat by the other; whereas it is impossible that the same water, if those ideas were really in it, should at the same time be both hot and cold: for if we imagine warmth, as it is in our hands, to be nothing but a certain sort and degree of motion in the minute particles of our nerves or animal spirits, we may understand how it is possible that the same water may, at the same time, produce the sensations of heat in one hand, and cold in the other; which yet figure never does, that never producing the idea of a square by one hand, which has produced the idea of a globe by another. But if the sensation of heat and cold be nothing but the increase or diminution of the motion of the minute parts of our bodies, caused by the corpuscles‡ of any other body, it is easy to be understood,

---

*   Pains in the bowels.
†   A hard red rock filled with large red or white crystals.
‡   Small particles.

that if that motion be greater in one hand than in the other; if a body be applied to the two hands, which has in its minute particles a greater motion, than in those of one of the hands, and a less than in those of the other; it will increase the motion of the one hand and lessen it in the other, and so cause the different sensations of heat and cold that depend thereon.

§22. I have in what just goes before been engaged in physical inquiries a little further than perhaps I intended. But it being necessary to make the nature of sensation a little understood, and to make the difference between the qualities in bodies, and the ideas produced by them in the mind, to be distinctly conceived, without which it were impossible to discourse intelligibly of them, I hope I shall be pardoned this little excursion into natural philosophy, it being necessary in our present inquiry to distinguish the primary and real qualities of bodies, which are always in them (viz. solidity, extension, figure, number, and motion, or rest; and are sometimes perceived by us, viz. when the bodies they are in are big enough singly to be discerned), from those secondary and imputed qualities, which are but the powers of several combinations of those primary ones, when they operate, without being distinctly discerned; whereby we may also come to know what ideas are, and what are not, resemblances of something really existing in the bodies we denominate from them.

§23. The qualities, then, that are in bodies, rightly considered, are of three sorts. First, The bulk, figure, number, situation, and motion, or rest of their solid parts; those are in them, whether we perceive them or no; and when they are of that size that we can discover them, we have by these an idea of the thing, as it is in itself, as is plain in artificial things. These I call primary qualities.

Secondly, The power that is in any body, by reason of its insensible primary qualities, to operate after a peculiar manner on any of our senses, and thereby produce in us the different ideas of several colours, sounds, smells, tastes, &c. These are usually called sensible qualities.

Thirdly, The power that is in any body, by reason of the particular constitution of its primary qualities, to make such a change in the bulk, figure, texture, and motion of another body, as to make it operate on our senses, differently from what it did before. Thus the sun has a power to make wax white, and fire to make lead fluid. These are usually called powers.

The first of these, as has been said, I think may be properly called real, original, or primary qualities; because they are in the things themselves, whether they are perceived or no; and upon their different modifications it is that the secondary qualities depend.

The other two are only powers to act differently upon other things, which powers result from the different modifications of those primary qualities.

§24. But, though the two latter sorts of qualities are powers barely, and nothing but powers, relating to several other bodies, and resulting from the different modifications of the original qualities, yet they are generally otherwise thought of: for the second sort, viz. the powers to produce several ideas in us by our senses, are looked upon as real qualities in the things thus affecting us; but the third sort are called and esteemed barely powers, *v.g.* the idea of heat, or light, which we receive by our eyes or touch from the sun, are commonly thought real qualities, existing in the sun, and something more than mere powers in it. But when we consider the sun in reference to wax, which it melts or blanches, we look on the whiteness and softness produced in the wax, not as qualities in the sun, but effects produced by powers in it: whereas, if rightly considered, these qualities of light and warmth, which are perceptions in me when I am warmed or enlightened by the sun, are no otherwise in the sun, than the changes made in the wax, when it is blanched or melted, are in the sun. They are all of them equally powers in the sun, depending on its primary qualities; whereby it is able, in the one case, so to alter the bulk, figure, texture, or motion of some of the insensible parts of my eyes or hands, as thereby to produce in me the idea of light or heat; and in the other, it is able so to alter the bulk, figure, texture, or motion of the insensible parts of the wax, as to make them fit to produce in me the distinct ideas of white and fluid.

§25. The reason why the one are ordinarily taken for real qualities, and the other only for bare powers, seems to be, because the ideas we have of distinct colours, sounds, &c., containing nothing at all in them of bulk, figure, or motion, we are not apt to think them the effects of these primary qualities, which appear not, to our senses, to operate in their production, and with which they have not any apparent congruity or conceivable connection. Hence it is that we are so forward to imagine, that those ideas are the resemblances of something really existing in the objects themselves: since sensation discovers nothing of bulk, figure, or motion of parts in their production; nor can reason show how bodies, by their bulk, figure, and motion, should produce in the mind the ideas of blue or yellow, &c. But, in the other case, in the operations of bodies changing the qualities one of another, we plainly discover, that the quality produced hath commonly no resemblance with anything in the thing producing it; wherefore we look on it as a bare effect of power. For, through receiving the idea of heat or light from the sun, we are apt to think it is a perception and resemblance of such a quality in the sun; yet when we see wax, or a fair face, receive change of colour from the sun, we cannot imagine that to be the reception or resemblance of anything in the sun, because we find not those different colours in the sun itself. For our senses being able to observe a likeness or unlikeness of sensible qualities in two different external objects, we forwardly enough conclude the production of any sensible quality in any subject to be an effect of bare power, and not the communication of any quality, which was really in the efficient,* when we find no such sensible quality in the thing that produced it. But our senses not being able to discover any unlikeness between the idea produced in us, and the quality of the object producing it, we are apt to imagine, that our ideas are resemblances of something in the objects, and not the effects of certain powers placed in the modification of their primary qualities, with which primary qualities the ideas produced in us have no resemblance.

§26. To conclude, beside those before-mentioned primary qualities in bodies, viz. bulk, figure, extension, number, and motion of their solid parts; all the rest whereby we take notice of bodies, and distinguish them one from another, are nothing else but several powers in them, depending on those primary qualities; whereby they are fitted, either by immediately operating on our bodies to produce several different ideas in us; or else, by operating on other bodies, so to change their primary qualities, as to render them capable of producing ideas in us different from what before they did. The former of these, I think, may be called secondary qualities, immediately perceivable: the latter, secondary qualities, mediately perceivable.

Book II, Chapter XXIII: Of Our Complex Ideas of Substances [§§1–6]

§1. The mind being, as I have declared, furnished with a great number of the simple ideas, conveyed in by the senses, as they are found in exterior things, or by reflection on its own operations, takes notice also, that a certain number of these simple ideas go constantly together; which being presumed to belong to one thing, and words being suited to common apprehensions, and made use of for quick dispatch, are called, so united in one subject, by one name; which, by inadvertency, we are apt afterward to talk of and consider as one simple idea, which indeed is a complication of many ideas together; because, as I have said, not imagining how these simple ideas can subsist by themselves, we accustom ourselves to suppose some substratum wherein they do subsist, and from which they do result; which therefore we call substance.

§2. So that if any one will examine himself concerning his notion of pure substance in general, he will find he has no other idea of it at all, but only a supposition of he knows not what support of such qualities, which are capable of producing simple ideas in us; which qualities are commonly called accidents.† If any one should be asked, what is the subject wherein colour or weight inheres, he would have nothing to say, but the solid extended parts: and if he were demanded, what is it that solidity and extension adhere in, he would not be in a much better case than the Indian‡ before mentioned who, saying that the world was supported by a great elephant, was asked what the elephant rested on; to which his answer was a great tortoise. But being again pressed to know what gave support to the broad-backed tortoise, replied, something, he knew not what. And thus here, as in all other cases where we use words without having clear and distinct ideas, we talk like children; who, being questioned what such a thing is, which they know not, readily give this satisfactory answer, that it is something: which in truth signifies no more, when so used, either by children or men, but that they know not what; and that the thing they pretend to know,

---

* The cause.
† "Accidents" in philosophical usage means non-essential characteristics.
‡ A person from the subcontinent of India (rather than a native of North America).

and talk of, is what they have no distinct idea of at all, and so are perfectly ignorant of it, and in the dark. The idea then we have, to which we give the general name substance, being nothing but the supposed, but unknown support of those qualities we find existing, which we imagine cannot subsist, "*sine re substante*," without something to support them, we call that support *substantia*; which, according to the true import of the word, is, in plain English, standing under or upholding.

§3. An obscure and relative idea of substance in general being thus made, we come to have the ideas of particular sorts of substances, by collecting such combinations of simple ideas as are, by experience and observation of men's senses taken notice of to exist together, and are therefore supposed to flow from the particular internal constitution, or unknown essence of that substance. Thus we come to have the ideas of a man, horse, gold, water, &c. of which substances, whether any one has any other clear idea, farther than of certain simple ideas co-existent together, I appeal to every one's own experience. It is the ordinary qualities observable in iron, or a diamond, put together, that make the true complex idea of those substances, which a smith or a jeweller commonly knows better than a philosopher; who, whatever substantial forms he may talk of, has no other idea of those substances, than what is framed by a collection of those simple ideas which are to be found in them: only we must take notice, that our complex ideas of substances, besides all those simple ideas they are made up of, have always the confused idea of something to which they belong, and in which they subsist. And therefore when we speak of any sort of substance, we say it is a thing having such or such qualities; as body is a thing that is extended, figured, and capable of motion; spirit, a thing capable of thinking; and so hardness, friability,* and power to draw iron, we say, are qualities to be found in a loadstone.† These, and the like fashions of speaking, intimate, that the substance is supposed always something besides the extension, figure, solidity, motion, thinking, or other observable ideas, though we know not what it is.

§4. Hence, when we talk or think of any particular sort of corporeal substances, as horse, stone, &c., though the idea we have of either of them be but the complication or collection of those several simple ideas of sensible qualities, which we used to find united in the thing called horse or stone; yet, because we cannot conceive how they should subsist alone, nor one in another, we suppose them existing in and supported by some common subject; which support we denote by the name substance, though it be certain we have no clear or distinct idea of that thing we suppose a support.

§5. The same thing happens concerning the operations of the mind, viz. thinking, reasoning, fearing, &c., which we concluding not to subsist of themselves, nor apprehending how they can belong to body, or be produced by it, we are apt to think these the actions of some other substance, which we call spirit: whereby yet it is evident, that having no other idea or notion of matter, but something wherein those many sensible qualities which affect our senses do subsist; by supposing a substance wherein thinking, knowing, doubting, and a power of moving, &c. do subsist, we have as clear a notion of the substance of spirit, as we have of body; the one being supposed to be (without knowing what it is) the substratum to those simple ideas we have from without; and the other supposed (with a like ignorance of what it is) to be the substratum to those operations we experiment‡ in ourselves within. It is plain then, that the idea of corporeal substance in matter is as remote from our conceptions and apprehensions, as that of spiritual substance, or spirit: and therefore, from our not having any notion of the substance of spirit, we can no more conclude its non-existence, than we can for the same reason deny the existence of body; it being as rational to affirm there is no body, because we have no clear and distinct idea of the substance of matter, as to say there is no spirit, because we have no clear and distinct idea of the substance of a spirit.

§6. Whatever therefore be the secret, abstract nature of substance in general, all the ideas we have of particular distinct sorts of substances are nothing

---

* Brittleness, crumbliness.

† A piece of magnetite (iron oxide) that has magnetic properties.

‡ Here, "experiment" means "experience."

but several combinations of simple ideas co-existing in such, though unknown, cause of their union, as make the whole subsist of itself. It is by such combinations of simple ideas, and nothing else, that we represent particular sorts of substances to ourselves; such are the ideas we have of their several species in our minds; and such only do we, by their specific names, signify to others, *v.g.* man, horse, sun, water, iron: upon hearing which words, every one who understands the language, frames in his mind a combination of those several simple ideas, which he has usually observed, or fancied to exist together under that denomination; all which he supposes to rest in, and be as it were, adherent to that unknown common subject, which inheres not in anything else. Though, in the mean time it be manifest, and every one upon inquiry into his own thoughts will find, that he has no other idea of any substance, *v.g.* let it be gold, horse, iron, man, vitriol,* bread, but what he has barely of those sensible qualities, which he supposes to inhere, with a supposition of such a substratum, as gives, as it were, a support to those qualities or simple ideas, which he has observed to exist united together. Thus the idea of the sun, what is it but an aggregate of those several simple ideas, bright, hot, roundish, having a constant regular motion, at a certain distance from us, and perhaps some other? As he who thinks and discourses of the sun has been more or less accurate in observing those sensible qualities, ideas, or properties, which are in that thing which he calls the sun.

Book IV, Chapter XI: Of Our Knowledge of the Existence of Other Things

§1. The knowledge of our own being we have by intuition. The existence of a God, reason clearly makes known to us, as has been shown.[†]

The knowledge of the existence of any other thing we can have only by sensation: for there being no necessary connection of real existence with any idea a man hath in his memory, nor of any other existence but that of God, with the existence of any particular man; no particular man can know the existence of any other being, but only when, by actual operating upon him, it makes itself perceived by him. For, the having the idea of anything in our mind no more proves the existence of that thing, than the picture of a man evidences[‡] his being in the world, or the visions of a dream make thereby a true history.

§2. It is therefore the actual receiving of ideas from without, that gives us notice of the existence of other things, and makes us know that something doth exist at that time without us, which causes that idea in us, though perhaps we neither know nor consider how it does it: for it takes not from the certainty of our senses, and the ideas we receive by them, that we know not the manner wherein they are produced: *v.g.* whilst I write this, I have, by the paper affecting my eyes, that idea produced in my mind, which, whatever object causes, I call white; by which I know that that quality or accident (i.e., whose appearance before my eyes always causes that idea) doth really exist, and hath a being without me. And of this, the greatest assurance I can possibly have, and to which my faculties can attain, is the testimony of my eyes, which are the proper and sole judges of this thing, whose testimony I have reason to rely on as so certain, that I can no more doubt, whilst I write this, that I see white and black, and that something really exists, that causes that sensation in me, than that I write or move my hand; which is a certainty as great as human nature is capable of, concerning the existence of anything but a man's self alone, and of God.

§3. The notice we have by our senses of the existing of things without us, though it be not altogether so certain as our intuitive knowledge, or the deductions of our reason, employed about the clear abstract ideas of our own minds; yet it is an assurance that deserves the name of knowledge. If we persuade ourselves that our faculties act and inform us right, concerning the existence of those objects that affect them, it cannot pass for an ill-grounded confidence: for I think nobody can,

---

*   Sulfuric acid.

†   These two claims were argued for in his previous two chapters (IX and X). Intuition, for Locke, is roughly direct knowledge—something we can directly see to be true—and is to be contrasted with the indirect knowledge we get from sensation, memory, or reason.

‡   In this context, "evidences" can be read as "shows."

in earnest, be so sceptical as to be uncertain of the existence of those things which he sees and feels. At least, he that can doubt so far (whatever he may have with his own thoughts) will never have any controversy* with me; since he can never be sure I say anything contrary to his own opinion. As to myself, I think God has given me assurance enough of the existence of things without me; since by their different application I can produce in myself both pleasure and pain, which is one great concernment of my present state. This is certain, the confidence that our faculties do not herein deceive us, is the greatest assurance we are capable of concerning the existence of material beings. For we cannot act anything, but by our faculties; nor talk of knowledge itself, but by the helps of those faculties, which are fitted to apprehend even what knowledge is. But besides the assurance we have from our senses themselves, that they do not err in the information they give us, of the existence of things without us, when they are affected by them, we are further confirmed in this assurance by other concurrent reasons.

§4. First, it is plain those perceptions are produced in us by exterior causes affecting our senses; because those that want the organs of any sense never can have the ideas belonging to that sense produced in their minds. This is too evident to be doubted: and therefore we cannot but be assured that they come in by the organs of that sense, and no other way. The organs themselves, it is plain, do not produce them; for then the eyes of a man in the dark would produce colours, and his nose smell roses in the winter: but we see nobody gets the relish of a pine-apple till he goes to the Indies, where it is, and tastes it.

§5. Secondly, because sometimes I find that I cannot avoid the having those ideas produced in my mind. For though when my eyes are shut, or windows fast, I can at pleasure recall to my mind the ideas of light, or the sun, which former sensations had lodged in my memory; so I can at pleasure lay by that idea, and take into my view that of the smell of a rose, or taste of sugar. But, if I turn my eyes at noon towards the sun, I cannot avoid the ideas, which the light, or sun, then produces in me. So that there is a manifest difference between the ideas laid up in my memory (over which,

if they were there only, I should have constantly the same power to dispose of them, and lay them by at pleasure) and those which force themselves upon me, and I cannot avoid having. And therefore it must needs be some exterior cause, and the brisk acting of some objects without me, whose efficacy I cannot resist, that produces those ideas in my mind, whether I will or no. Besides, there is nobody who doth not perceive the difference in himself between contemplating the sun, as he hath the idea of it in his memory, and actually looking upon it; of which two his perception is so distinct, that few of his ideas are more distinguishable one from another. And therefore he hath certain knowledge, that they are not both memory, or the actions of his mind, and fancies only within him; but that actual seeing hath a cause without.

§6. Thirdly, add to this, that many of those ideas are produced in us with pain, which afterwards we remember without the least offence.† Thus, the pain of heat or cold, when the idea of it is revived in our minds, gives us no disturbance; which, when felt, was very troublesome, and is again, when actually repeated; which is occasioned by the disorder the external object causes in our bodies when applied to it. And we remember the pains of hunger, thirst, or the head-ache, without any pain at all; which would either never disturb us, or else constantly do it, as often as we thought of it, were there nothing more but ideas floating in our minds, and appearances entertaining our fancies, without the real existence of things affecting us from abroad. The same may be said of pleasure, accompanying several actual sensations: and though mathematical demonstration depends not upon sense, yet the examining them by diagrams gives great credit to the evidence of our sight, and seems to give it a certainty approaching to that of demonstration itself. For it would be very strange that a man should allow it for an undeniable truth, that two angles of a figure, which he measures by lines and angles of a diagram, should be bigger one than the other; and yet doubt of the existence of those lines and angles, which by looking on he makes use of to measure that by.

§7. Fourthly, our senses in many cases bear witness to the truth of each other's report, concerning the

---

* Disagreement, argument.
† Painful sensation.

existence of sensible things without us. He that sees a fire may, if he doubt whether it be anything more than a bare fancy, feel it too; and be convinced, by putting his hand in it: which certainly could never be put into such exquisite pain by a bare idea or phantom,* unless that the pain be a fancy too; which yet he cannot, when the burn is well, by raising the idea of it, bring upon himself again.

Thus I see, whilst I write this, I can change the appearance of the paper: and by designing the letters, tell beforehand what new idea it shall exhibit the very next moment, by barely drawing my pen over it: which will neither appear (let me fancy as much as I will) if my hands stand still; or though I move my pen, if my eyes be shut: nor, when those characters are once made on the paper, can I choose afterwards but see them as they are; that is, have the ideas of such letters as I have made. Whence it is manifest, that they are not barely the sport and play of my own imagination, when I find that the characters, that were made at the pleasure of my own thought, do not obey them; nor yet cease to be, whenever I shall fancy it; but continue to affect my senses constantly and regularly, according to the figures I made them. To which if we will add, that the sight of those shall, from another man, draw such sounds as I beforehand design they shall stand for; there will be little reason left to doubt that those words I write do really exist without me, when they cause a long series of regular sounds to affect my ears, which could not be the effect of my imagination, nor could my memory retain them in that order.

§8. But yet, if after all this any one will be so sceptical as to distrust his senses, and to affirm that all we see and hear, feel and taste, think and do, during our whole being, is but the series and deluding appearances of a long dream, whereof there is no reality; and therefore will question the existence of all things, or our knowledge of any thing; I must desire him to consider, that, if all be a dream, then he doth but dream that he makes the question; and so it is not much matter that a waking man should answer him. But yet, if he pleases, he may dream that I make him this answer, that the certainty of things existing *in rerum natura*,† when we have the testimony of our senses for it, is not only as great as our frame can attain to, but as our condition needs. For, our faculties being suited not to the full extent of being, nor to a perfect, clear, comprehensive knowledge of things free from all doubt and scruple; but to the preservation of us, in whom they are, and accommodated to the use of life; they serve to our purpose well enough, if they will but give us certain notice of those things which are convenient or inconvenient to us. For he that sees a candle burning, and hath experimented the force of its flame, by putting his finger in it, will little doubt that this is something existing without him, which does him harm, and puts him to great pain: which is assurance enough, when no man requires greater certainty to govern his actions by than what is as certain as his actions themselves. And if our dreamer pleases to try whether the glowing heat of a glass furnace be barely a wandering imagination in a drowsy man's fancy; by putting his hand into it he may perhaps be wakened into a certainty greater than he could wish, that it is something more than bare imagination. So that this evidence is as great as we can desire, being as certain to us as our pleasure or pain, i.e., happiness or misery; beyond which we have no concernment, either of knowing or being. Such an assurance of the existence of things without us is sufficient to direct us in the attaining the good, and avoiding the evil, which is caused by them; which is the important concernment we have of being made acquainted with them.

§9. In fine, then, when our senses do actually convey into our understandings any idea, we cannot but be satisfied that there doth something at that time really exist without us, which doth affect our senses, and by them give notice of itself to our apprehensive faculties, and actually produce that idea which we then perceive: and we cannot so far distrust their testimony, as to doubt that such collections of simple ideas as we have observed by our senses to be united together, do really exist together. But this knowledge extends as far as the present testimony of our senses, employed about particular objects that do then affect them, and no further. For if I saw such a collection of simple ideas, as is wont to be called man, existing together one minute since, and am now alone, I cannot be certain that the same

---

* "Phantom" here and "fancy" earlier both mean illusion, hallucination, imaginary object.

† "In the nature of things," or sometimes, more specifically "in physical reality."

man exists now, since there is no necessary connection of his existence a minute since with his existence now: by a thousand ways he may cease to be, since I had the testimony of my senses for his existence. And if I cannot be certain that the man I saw last to-day is now in being, I can less be certain that he is so who hath been longer removed from my senses, and I have not seen since yesterday, or since the last year: and much less can I be certain of the existence of men that I never saw. And, therefore, though it be highly probable that millions of men do now exist, yet, whilst I am alone writing this, I have not that certainty of it which we strictly call knowledge; though the great likelihood of it puts me past doubt, and it be reasonable for me to do several things upon the confidence that there are men (and men also of my acquaintance, with whom I have to do) now in the world: but this is but probability, not knowledge.

§10. Whereby yet we may observe how foolish and vain a thing it is for a man of a narrow knowledge, who having reason given him to judge of the different evidence and probability of things, and to be swayed accordingly,—how vain, I say, it is to expect demonstration and certainty in things not capable of it, and refuse assent to very rational propositions, and act contrary to very plain and clear truths, because they cannot be made out so evident, as to surmount every the least (I will not say reason but) pretence of doubting. He that, in the ordinary affairs of life would admit of* nothing but direct plain demonstration, would be sure of nothing in this world, but of perishing quickly. The wholesomeness of his meat or drink would not give him reason to venture on it: and I would fain† know, what it is he could do upon such grounds as are capable of no doubt, no objection.

§11. As when our senses are actually employed about any object, we do know that it does exist; so by our memory we may be assured, that heretofore things that affected our senses have existed. And thus we have knowledge of the past existence of several things whereof, our senses having informed us, our memories still retain the ideas; and of this we are past all doubt, so long as we remember well. But this knowledge also reaches no further than our senses have formerly assured us. Thus, seeing water at this instant, it is an unquestionable truth to me that water doth exist: and remembering that I saw it yesterday, it will also be always true, and as long as my memory retains it, always an undoubted proposition to me, that water did exist the 10th of July, 1688, as it will also be equally true that a certain number of very fine colours did exist, which at the same time I saw upon a bubble of that water: but, being now quite out of sight both of the water and bubbles too, it is no more certainly known to me that the water doth now exist, than that the bubbles or colours therein do so; it being no more necessary that water should exist to-day, because it existed yesterday, than that the colours or bubbles exist to-day, because they existed yesterday; though it be exceedingly much more probable, because water hath been observed to continue long in existence but bubbles and the colours on them, quickly cease to be.

§12. What ideas we have of spirits,‡ and how we come by them, I have already shown. But though we have those ideas in our minds, and know we have them there, the having the ideas of spirits does not make us know that any such things do exist without us, or that there are any finite spirits, or any other spiritual beings but the eternal God. We have ground from revelation, and several other reasons, to believe with assurance that there are such creatures: but our senses not being able to discover them, we want the means of knowing their particular existences. For we can no more know, that there are finite spirits really existing, by the idea we have of such beings in our minds, than by the ideas any one has of fairies, or centaurs, he can come to know that things answering those ideas do really exist.

And therefore concerning the existence of finite spirits, as well as several other things, we must content ourselves with the evidence of faith; but universal certain propositions concerning this matter are beyond our reach. For however true it may be, *v.g.* that all the intelligent spirits that God ever created do still exist; yet it can never make a part of our certain knowledge.

---

* "Admit of": accept.
† Gladly, happily.
‡ Spiritual beings such as angels.

These and the like propositions we may assent to as highly probable, but are not, I fear, in this state capable of knowing. We are not then to put others upon demonstrating, nor ourselves upon search of universal certainty, in all those matters, wherein we are not capable of any other knowledge, but what our senses give us in this or that particular.

§13. By which it appears that there are two sorts of propositions: 1. There is one sort of propositions concerning the existence of any thing answerable to such an idea: as having the idea of an elephant, phoenix,* motion, or an angel, in my mind, the first and natural inquiry is, Whether such a thing does anywhere exist? And this knowledge is only of particulars. No existence of anything without us, but only of God, can certainly be known farther than our senses inform us. 2. There is another sort of propositions, wherein is expressed the agreement or disagreement of our abstract ideas, and their dependence on one another. Such propositions may be universal and certain. So having the idea of God and myself, of fear and obedience, I cannot but be sure that God is to be feared and obeyed by me: and this proposition will be certain, concerning man in general, if I have made an abstract idea of such a species, whereof I am one particular. But yet this proposition, how certain soever, that men ought to fear and obey God proves not to me the existence of men in the world, but will be true of all such creatures, whenever they do exist: which certainty of such general propositions depends on the agreement or disagreement to be discovered in those abstract ideas.

§14. In the former case, our knowledge is the consequence of the existence of things producing ideas in our minds by our senses: in the latter, knowledge is the consequence of the ideas (be they what they will) that are in our minds, producing there general certain propositions. Many of these are called *aeternae veritates*,† and all of them indeed are so; not from being written all or any of them in the minds of all men; or that they were any of them propositions in any one's mind till he, having got the abstract ideas, joined or separated them by affirmation or negation. But wheresoever we can suppose such a creature as man is, endowed with such faculties, and thereby furnished with such ideas as we have, we must conclude, he must needs, when he applies his thoughts to the consideration of his ideas, know the truth of certain propositions that will arise from the agreement or disagreement which he will perceive in his own ideas. Such propositions are therefore called eternal truths, not because they are eternal propositions actually formed, and antecedent to the understanding, that at any time makes them; nor because they are imprinted on the mind from any patterns, that are anywhere out of the mind, and existed before: but because being once made about abstract ideas, so as to be true, they will, whenever they can be supposed to be made again at any time past or to come, by a mind having those ideas, always actually be true. For names being supposed to stand perpetually for the same ideas, and the same ideas having immutably the same habitudes‡ one to another; propositions concerning any abstract ideas that are once true, must needs be eternal verities. ■

---

* Mythological bird that dies in flame and is regenerated from its ashes.

† "Eternal verities"—things that are eternally true.

‡ Relations, connections.

Suggestions for Critical Reflection

1. It is relatively easy to see roughly how Locke's distinction between primary and secondary qualities is supposed to go, but harder to see what Locke's *argument* for this distinction is. Do you think Locke backs up his claims with arguments? If so, how strong do you think they are? In the end, how plausible is the primary/secondary quality distinction?

2. Similarly, while it is relatively easy to see roughly how Locke's distinction between primary and secondary qualities is supposed to go, it is harder to see *precisely* how the distinction works. For example, what might Locke mean by saying that our ideas of primary qualities resemble their causes while our ideas of secondary qualities do not? Does this really make any sense? If it doesn't, then what other criterion should we use to help us make the distinction?

3. There has recently been some controversy about Locke's position on substance. The traditional view is that Locke defended substance, but was wrong to do so since his own arguments had effectively shown that we could have no such idea. The notion of substance in question here is that of a "bare particular" or "substratum"—that which underlies properties, as opposed to any of the properties themselves. A more recent interpretation holds that Locke did indeed defend some notion of substance, but one which is more defensible. This is the idea of substance as the "real essence" of something: roughly, for Locke, something's real essence is supposed to be the (unknown) set of properties that forms the causal basis for the observable properties of that thing (just as the atomic structure of gold is responsible for its color, softness, shininess, and so on). Which of these

two conceptions of substance do you find the more plausible? (Can you see why philosophers have typically found the notion of a substratum difficult to make sense of?) Which of these notions of substance do you think fits better with what Locke actually says? Do you perhaps prefer a third interpretation?

4. What do you make of Locke's response to skepticism about the existence of the external world? Does it convince you? Do you find plausible the way Locke carefully divides up different types of knowledge about the external world and gives different answers for them?

5. What kind of entity might a Lockean idea be? What, if anything, is it made of? How determinate must it be? For example, if I clearly perceive the idea of a speckled hen, must we say that I perceive (have the idea of) a particular number of speckles, say 12,372? If not, does that mean the idea does not *have* a determinate number of speckles (even though it's a perfectly clear idea and not blurry at all)? What kind of object could *that* be? Some recent commentators, such as John Yolton, have tried to defend Locke from these kinds of puzzles by suggesting that Locke never meant ideas to be mental *things* at all: what, then, could they be instead?

6. How could an idea, in Locke's sense, really be *caused* by material objects in the external world? What could the last few steps of this causal chain be like?

7. If ideas are the objects of our thought—the things we "perceive" in thought—then what is it that does the perceiving, do you think? Can we distinguish it from the succession of ideas?

IMMANUEL KANT

FROM *Critique of Pure Reason*

Who Was Immanuel Kant?

Immanuel Kant—by common consent the most important philosopher of the past 300 years, and arguably the most important of the past 2,300—was born in 1724 on the coast of the Baltic Sea, in Königsberg, a regionally important harbor city in East Prussia.* Kant spent his whole life living in this town, and never ventured outside its region. His family were devout members of an evangelical Protestant sect (rather like the Quakers or early Methodists) called the Pietists, and Pietism's strong emphasis on moral responsibility, hard work, and personal faith over religious dogma had a deep effect on Kant's character. Kant's father was a craftsman (making harnesses and saddles for horses) and his family was fairly poor; Kant's mother, whom he loved deeply, died when he was 13.

Kant's life is notorious for its outward uneventfulness. He was educated at a strict Lutheran school in Königsberg, and after graduating from the University of Königsberg in 1746 (where he supported himself by some tutoring but also by his skill at billiards and card games) he served as a private tutor to various local families until he became a lecturer at the university in 1755. However, his position—that of *Privatdozent*—carried no salary, and Kant was expected to support himself by the income from his lecturing. Financial need caused Kant to lecture for 30 or more hours a week on a wide range of subjects (including mathematics, physics, geography, anthropology, ethics, and law). During this period Kant published several scientific works and his reputation as a scholar grew; he turned down opportunities for professorships in other towns (Erlangen and Jena), his heart being set on a professorship in Königsberg. Finally, at the age of 46, Kant became professor of logic and metaphysics at the University of Königsberg, a position he held until his retirement 26 years later in 1796. After a tragic period of senility, he died in 1804 and was buried with pomp and circumstance in the "professors' vault" in the Königsberg cathedral.†

Kant's days were structured by a rigorous and unvarying routine—indeed, it is often said that the housewives of Königsberg were able to set their clocks by the regularity of his afternoon walk. He never married (though twice he nearly did), had very few close friends, and lived by all accounts an austere and outwardly unemotional life. He was something of a hypochondriac, hated noise, and disliked all music except military marches. Nevertheless, anecdotes by those who knew him give the impression of a warm, impressive, rather noble human being, capable of great kindness and dignity and sparkling conversation. He did not shun society, and in fact his regular daily routine included an extended lunchtime gathering at which he and his guests—drawn from the cosmopolitan stratum of Königsberg society—would discuss politics, science, philosophy, and poetry.

Kant's philosophical life is often divided into three phases: his "pre-Critical" period, his "silent" period, and his "Critical" period. His pre-Critical period began in 1747 when he published his first work (*Thoughts on the True Estimation of Living Forces*) and ended in 1770 when he wrote his Inaugural Dissertation—*Concerning the Form and Principles of the Sensible and Intelligible World*—and became a professor. Between 1770 and 1780, Kant published almost nothing. In 1781, however, at the age of 57, Kant made his first major contribution to philosophy with his monumental *Critique of Pure Reason* (written, Kant said, over the course of a few months "as if in flight"). He spent the next 20 years in unrelenting intellectual labor, trying to develop and answer the new problems laid out in this masterwork. First, in order to clarify and simplify the system of the *Critique* for the

---

* Prussia is a historical region that included what is today northern Germany, Poland, and the western fringes of Russia.
† His corpse is no longer there: in 1950 his sarcophagus was broken open by unknown vandals and his remains stolen and never recovered.

educated public, Kant published the much shorter *Prolegomena to Any Future Metaphysics* in 1783. In 1785 came Kant's *Foundations of the Metaphysics of Morals*, and in 1788 he published what is now known as his "second Critique": the *Critique of Practical Reason*. His third and final Critique, the *Critique of Judgment*, was published in 1790—an amazing body of work produced in less than 10 years.

By the time he died, Kant had already become known as a great philosopher, with a permanent place in history. Over his grave was inscribed a quotation from the *Critique of Practical Reason*, which sums up the impulse for his philosophy: "Two things fill the mind with ever new and increasing admiration and reverence, the more often and more steadily one reflects on them: the starry heavens above me and the moral law within me."*

What Was Kant's Overall Philosophical Project?

Kant began his philosophical career as a follower of rationalism. Rationalism was an important seventeenth- and eighteenth-century intellectual movement begun by Descartes and developed by Leibniz and his follower Christian Wolff, which held that all knowledge was capable of being part of a single, complete "science": that is, all knowledge can be slotted into a total, unified system of *a priori*, and certainly true, claims capable of encompassing everything that exists in the world, whether we have experience of it or not. In other words, for the German rationalists of Kant's day, metaphysical philosophy—which then included theoretical science—was thought of as being very similar to pure mathematics. Rationalism was also, in Kantian terminology, "dogmatic" as opposed to "critical": that is, it sought to construct systems of knowledge without first attempting a careful examination of the scope and limits of possible knowledge. (This is why Kant's rationalist period is usually called his pre-Critical phase.)

In 1781, after 10 years of hard thought, Kant rejected this rationalistic view of philosophy: he came to the view that metaphysics, as traditionally understood, is so far from being a rational science that it is not even a body of

knowledge at all. Three major stimuli provoked Kant into being "awakened from his dogmatic slumber," as he put it. First, in about 1769, Kant came to the conclusion that he had discovered several "antinomies"—sets of two contradictory propositions *both* of which can apparently be *rationally proven* to be true of reality (if we assume that our intellectual concepts apply to reality at all) and yet which can't both be true. For example, Kant argued that rational arguments are available to prove both that reality is finite but also that it is infinite, and that it is composed of indivisible atoms yet also infinitely divisible. Since both halves of these two pairs can't possibly be true at the same time, Kant argued that this casts serious doubt on the power of pure reason to draw metaphysical conclusions.

Second, Kant was worried about the conflict between free will and natural causality (this is a theme that appears throughout Kant's Critical works). He was convinced that genuine morality must be based on *freely* choosing—or "willing"—to do what is right. To be worthy of moral praise, in Kant's view, one must choose to do *X* rather than *Y*, not because some law of nature causes you to do so, but because your rational self is convinced that it is the right thing to do.† Yet he also thought that the rational understanding of reality sought by the metaphysicians could only be founded on universally extending the laws we find in the scientific study of nature—and this includes universal causal determination, the principle that nothing (including choosing *X* over *Y*) happens without a cause. This, for Kant, produces an antinomy: some actions are free (i.e., *not* bound by the laws of nature) and yet everything that happens *is* determined by a law of nature.

Kant resolved this paradox by arguing that the scientific view of reality (including that pursued by the rationalists) must in principle be *incomplete*. Roughly, he held that although we can only rationally understand reality by thinking of it as causally deterministic and governed by scientific laws, our intellectual reason can never encompass *all* of reality. According to Kant, there must be a level of ultimate reality which is beyond the scope of pure reason, and which allows for the free activity of what Kant calls "practical reason" (which therefore holds open the possibility of genuine morality).

---

*   Immanuel Kant, *Critique of Practical Reason*, ed. Mary Gregor (Cambridge University Press, 1997), 133.

†   For more on Kant's ethical views, see his *Foundations of the Metaphysics of Morals*.

The third alarm bell to rouse Kant from his pre-Critical dogmatism was his reading of the Scottish philosopher David Hume. Hume was not a rationalist but instead represented the culmination of the other main seventeenth- and eighteenth-century stream of philosophical thought, usually called empiricism. Instead of thinking of knowledge as a unified, systematic, *a priori* whole, as the rationalists did, empiricists like Locke and Hume saw knowledge as being a piecemeal accumulation of claims derived primarily, not from pure logic, but from *sensation*—from our experience of the world. Science, for Hume, is thus not *a priori* but *a posteriori*: for example, we cannot just *deduce* from first principles that heavy objects tend to fall to the ground, as the rationalists supposed we could; we can only learn this by observing it to happen in our experience. The trouble was that Hume appeared to Kant (and to many others) to have shown that experience is simply *inadequate* for establishing the kind of metaphysical principles that philosophers have traditionally defended: no amount of sense-experience could ever either prove or disprove that God exists, that substance is imperishable, that we have an immortal soul, or even that there exist mind-independent "physical" objects which interact with each other according to causal laws of nature. Not just what we now think of as "philosophy" but theoretical science itself seemed to be called into question by Hume's "skeptical" philosophy. Since Kant was quite sure that mathematics and the natural sciences were genuine bodies of knowledge, he needed to show how such knowledge was possible despite Hume's skepticism: that is, as well as combating the excessive claims of rationalism, he needed to show how empiricism went wrong in the other direction.

Prior to Kant, seventeenth- and eighteenth-century philosophers divided knowledge into exactly two camps: "truths of reason" (or "relations of ideas") on the one hand, and "truths of fact" (or "matters of fact") on the other. Rationalism was characterized by the doctrine that all final, complete knowledge was a truth of reason: that is, it was made up entirely of claims that could be proven *a priori* as being necessarily true, as a matter of logic, since it would be self-contradictory for them to be false. Empiricists, on the other hand, believed that all genuinely *informative* claims were truths of fact: if we wanted to find out about the world itself, rather than merely the logical relations between our own concepts, we had to rely upon the (*a posteriori*) data of sensory experience.

Kant, however, reshaped this distinction in a new framework which, he argued, cast a vital new light upon the nature of metaphysics. Instead of merely drawing a distinction between truths of reason and truths of fact, Kant replaced this with *two* separate distinctions: that between "*a priori*" and "*a posteriori*" propositions, and that between "analytic" and "synthetic" judgments. On this more complex scheme, the rationalists' truths of reason turn out to be "analytic *a priori*" knowledge, while empirical truths of fact are "synthetic *a posteriori*" propositions. But, Kant pointed out, this leaves open the possibility that there is at least a *third* type of knowledge: *synthetic a priori* judgments. These are judgments which we know *a priori* and thus do not need to learn from experience, but which nevertheless go beyond merely "analytic" claims about the definitions of words and the logical relationships of our own concepts. Kant's central claim in the *Critique of Pure Reason* is that he is the first philosopher in history to understand that the traditional claims of metaphysics—questions about God, the soul, free will, the underlying nature of space, time and matter—consist entirely of synthetic *a priori* propositions. (He also argues that pure mathematics is synthetic *a priori* as well.)

Kant's question therefore becomes: *How* is synthetic *a priori* knowledge possible? After all, the source of this knowledge can be neither experience (since it is *a priori*) nor the logical relations of ideas (since it is synthetic), so where could this kind of knowledge possibly come from? Once we have discovered the conditions of synthetic *a priori* knowledge, we can ask what its limits are: in particular, we can ask whether the traditional claims of speculative metaphysics meet those conditions, and thus whether they can be known to be true.

In bald (and massively simplified) summary, Kant's answer to these questions in the *Critique of Pure Reason* is the following. Synthetic *a priori* knowledge is possible insofar as it is knowledge of the *conditions of our experience of the world* (or indeed, of any *possible* experience). For example, for Kant, our judgments about the fundamental nature of space and time are not claims about our experiences themselves, nor are they the results of logic: instead, the forms of space and time are the conditions under which anybody is capable of having experience *at all*—one *can* only undergo sensations (either perceived or imaginary) that are arranged in space, and spread out in time; anything else is just impossible. So we can know *a priori*, but not analytically, that space and time must have a certain nature, since they are the forms of (the very possibility of) our experience.

Kant, famously, described this insight as constituting a kind of "Copernican revolution" in philosophy: just as Copernicus set cosmology on a totally new path by suggesting (in 1543) that the Earth orbits the Sun and not the other way around, so Kant wanted to breathe new life into philosophy by suggesting that, rather than assuming that "all our knowledge must conform to objects," we might instead "suppose that objects must conform to our knowledge."* That is, rather than merely passively representing mind-independent objects in a "real" world, Kant held that the mind actively *constitutes* its objects—by *imposing* the categories of time, space, and causation onto our sensory experience, the subject actually *creates* the only kind of reality to which it has access. (This is why Kant's philosophy is often called "transcendental idealism." However, Kant is not a full-out idealist in the way that, say, Berkeley is. He does not claim that the *existence* of objects is mind-dependent—only God's mind is capable of this kind of creation, according to Kant. Instead, the *a priori properties* of objects are what we create, by the structures of our cognition.)

When we turn to speculative metaphysics, however, we try to go beyond experience and its conditions—we attempt to move beyond what Kant called the "phenomena" of experience, and to make judgments about the nature of a reality that lies behind our sensory experience, what Kant called the "noumenal" realm. And here pure reason reaches its limits. If we ask about the nature of "things in themselves," independently of our experience of them, or if we try to show whether a supra-sensible God really exists, then our faculty of reason is powerless to demonstrate that these synthetic *a priori* judgments are either true or false—these metaphysical questions are neither empirical, nor logical, nor about the basic categories of our experience, so there is simply no way to answer them. The questions are meaningful ones (human beings crave answers to them) but they are beyond the scope of our faculty of reason. In short, we can have knowledge only of things that can be objects of possible experience, and cannot know anything that transcends the phenomenal realm.

This result, according to Kant, finally lets philosophy cease its constant oscillation between dogmatism and skepticism. It sets out the area in which human cognition is capable of attaining lasting truth (theoretical science—the metaphysics of experience—and mathematics), and that in which reason leads to self-contradiction and illusion (speculative metaphysics). Importantly, for Kant, this Copernican revolution provides *morality* with all the metaphysical support it needs, by clearing an area for free will.

What Is the Structure of This Reading?

Kant begins by conceding to the empiricists that, as a matter of psychological fact, we acquire a lot of knowledge through our experience of the world. But, he claims, this does not by itself show that all our knowledge is really *empirical*, and in Section I he draws a distinction between "pure" and "empirical" knowledge in order to make this issue clearer. In the next section he lays out two criteria for distinguishing between pure and empirical knowledge and uses these criteria to argue that we do in fact have a quantity of important pure *a priori* knowledge. However, in Section III, Kant claims that a lot of what we think can be known *a priori* is actually mere fabrication: what is needed, therefore, is a way of accurately *telling the difference* between reliable and unreliable *a priori* judgments. The first step in doing this, according to Kant, is to draw a distinction between analytic and synthetic judgments. He proceeds to do this in Section IV. He then argues, in Section V, that all our interesting *a priori* knowledge—mathematics, the principles of natural science, metaphysics—is synthetic. The "general problem of pure reason," therefore (Section VI), is to develop an account of how synthetic *a priori* judgments are possible, which will in turn tell us when they are reliable and when they are not. According to Kant, we must replace dogmatic philosophy with *critical* and *transcendental* philosophy: i.e., we must undertake a critique of pure reason, as Kant explains in Section VII.

---

* Immanuel Kant, *Critique of Pure Reason*, ed. Norman Kemp Smith (Palgrave, 1929), 24–25.

Some Useful Background Information

1. A priori is Latin for "what is earlier" and a posteriori means "what comes after." These terms were used as early as the fourteenth century to mark a distinction (which dates back to Aristotle) between two different directions of reasoning: in this usage, now out of date, an a priori argument reasons from a ground to its consequence, while to argue a posteriori is to argue backwards from a consequence to its ground. For example, Descartes's "trademark" argument for the existence of God in the Third Meditation is a posteriori in this archaic sense since it starts from his idea of God and moves to the 'only' possible cause of that idea, which is God himself. By contrast, St. Anselm of Canterbury's ontological argument is a priori in the medieval sense since, while it also begins with the idea of God, it does not argue 'backwards' to the cause of the idea but 'forwards' to the idea's (alleged) logical consequence, which is the necessary existence of God.

   The *modern* usage of *a priori* and *a posteriori*, however, was formulated in the late seventeenth and eighteenth centuries, primarily by Leibniz and Kant, and has now wholly replaced the older meanings. The selection from Kant reprinted here includes the classic statement of the distinction (though the new usage first appeared much earlier—see, for example, section eight of Leibniz's *Discourse on Metaphysics*, published in 1686). One thing to notice is that the distinction is no longer one between two different directions of reasoning but instead distinguishes primarily between two different types of *knowledge*: the standard example of *a priori* knowledge is the truths of mathematics, and of *a posteriori* knowledge, the results of the natural sciences. This distinction between kinds of knowledge then motivates a similar distinction between two kinds of proposition, two kinds of concept, and two kinds of justification.

   Kant himself prefers to use the words "pure" and "empirical" for *a priori* and *a posteriori* knowledge themselves, and usually reserves the terms "*a priori*" and "*a posteriori*" to describe the sources of this knowledge—the way in which it is acquired.

2. At the end of the Introduction to the *Critique*, Kant says that there are "two stems of human knowledge": sensibility and understanding. This is an important assumption of Kant's, and is reflected throughout the reading given here (in, for example, Kant's distinction between intuitions and concepts). Furthermore, it structures the way in which Kant proceeds with his critique of pure reason after the introduction: he deals firstly with what he calls the Transcendental Aesthetic,* which has to do with the faculty of sensibility, and secondly with the Transcendental Analytic, which applies to the faculty of understanding. The faculty of sensibility, according to Kant, is our capacity to passively receive objects into our mental world; this is achieved primarily through sensation, but these sensations are possible only if the objects are intuited: that is, roughly, represented as concretely existing in space and time. The faculty of understanding, on the other hand, is our capacity to actively produce knowledge through the application of *concepts*. When concepts are compared with each other, we produce logical knowledge; when concepts (such as space, time, and causation) are combined with intuitions we get empirical knowledge. (However, when concepts that arise out of our knowledge of the empirical world are applied to a realm beyond experience we do not get *any* kind of knowledge, according to Kant: he calls these metaphysical concepts *ideas*, the three most important of which are God, freedom, and immortality.)

A Common Misconception

Some people, on reading Kant for the first time, are thrown off by the word "transcendental." For Kant, transcendental knowledge is knowledge about the necessary conditions for the possibility of experience (for example, "every event has a cause" is a transcendental claim, according to Kant). Thus, transcendental knowledge is *not*,

---

* When Kant uses the word "aesthetic"—as in "the transcendental aesthetic"—he means generally "having to do with sense-perception" rather than merely "beautiful."

as would be easy to assume, knowledge of *things which are transcendent* (i.e., of things which lie beyond the empirical world, such as God and other spirits). Therefore Kant's "transcendental philosophy" has nothing to do with, say, Transcendental Meditation.

How Important and Influential Is This Passage?

Within just a few years of the publication of the *Critique of Pure Reason*, Kant was recognized by many of his intellectual contemporaries as one of the great philosophers of all time. The first *Critique* is a candidate for being the single most important philosophical book ever written, and can be thought of as decisively changing the path of Western philosophy. In particular, it did away with the assumption that knowledge is a fixed and stable thing which can be more or less passively received into

the mind through either experience or reason, and replaced it with a picture that sees human beings as active *participants* in the construction of our representations of the world. That is, the mind is not a passive receptacle of data but is instead an active *filter* and *creator* of our reality. The implications of this view are still being explored by philosophers today.

The distinction between analytic and synthetic propositions which Kant formulates in the selection reprinted here, as well as being foundational to his new philosophical system, has also had a great impact on philosophy. From the end of the eighteenth century until the 1950s it was generally accepted as marking a fundamental and important difference between kinds of knowledge. Today, however, the distinction has been thrown into question by philosophers who doubt that we can really make good sense of one concept "containing" or being "synonymous" with another.

FROM *Critique of Pure Reason*

INTRODUCTION*

I. The Distinction between Pure and Empirical Knowledge

There can be no doubt that all our knowledge begins with experience. For how should our faculty† of knowledge be awakened into action did not objects affecting our senses partly of themselves produce representations, partly arouse the activity of our understanding to compare these representations, and, by combining or separating them, work up the raw material of the sensible impressions‡ into that knowledge of objects

which is entitled experience? In the order of time, therefore, we have no knowledge antecedent to experience, and with experience all our knowledge begins.

But though all our knowledge begins with experience, it does not follow that it all arises out of experience. For it may well be that even our empirical knowledge is made up of what we receive through impressions and of what our own faculty of knowledge (sensible impressions serving merely as the occasion) supplies from itself. If our faculty of knowledge makes any such addition, it may be that we are not in a position to distinguish it

---

* Kant's *Critique of Pure Reason*, as first published in German in 1781, is usually called the "A" edition. A significantly different second edition, the "B" edition, was published in 1787. The translation used here, of the Introduction to the "B" edition, was made in 1929 by Norman Kemp Smith (Copyright 2007, Palgrave Macmillan).

† A "faculty," in this sense, is an inherent mental power or capacity, such as the faculty of speech or the faculty of memory.

‡ A "sensible impression" is an effect produced on the mind which is received by the faculty of sensory perception. Sensible impressions are, roughly, the data we receive from the world (such as, perhaps, colors, sounds, pains, and so on) out of which our conscious perceptual experience (say the experience of being bitten by a squirrel) is constructed.

from the raw material, until with long practice of attention we have become skilled in separating it.

This, then, is a question which at least calls for closer examination, and does not allow of any off-hand answer:—whether there is any knowledge that is thus independent of experience and even of all impressions of the senses. Such knowledge is entitled *a priori*, and distinguished from the *empirical*, which has its sources *a posteriori*, that is, in experience.

The expression '*a priori*' does not, however, indicate with sufficient precision the full meaning of our question. For it has been customary to say, even of much knowledge that is derived from empirical sources, that we have it or are capable of having it *a priori*, meaning thereby that we do not derive it immediately from experience, but from a universal rule—a rule which is itself, however, borrowed by us from experience. Thus we would say of a man who undermined the foundations of his house, that he might have known *a priori* that it would fall, that is, that he need not have waited for the experience of its actual falling. But still he could not know this completely *a priori*. For he had first to learn through experience that bodies are heavy, and therefore fall when their supports are withdrawn.

In what follows, therefore, we shall understand by *a priori* knowledge, not knowledge independent of this or that experience, but knowledge absolutely independent of all experience. Opposed to it is empirical knowledge, which is knowledge possible only *a posteriori*, that is, through experience. *A priori* modes of knowledge are entitled pure when there is no admixture of anything empirical. Thus, for instance, the proposition, 'every alteration has its cause', while an *a priori* proposition, is not a pure proposition, because alteration is a concept which can be derived only from experience.

II. We Are in Possession of Certain Modes of A priori *Knowledge, and Even the Common Understanding Is Never without Them*

What we here require is a criterion by which to distinguish with certainty between pure and empirical knowledge. Experience teaches us that a thing is so and so, but not that it cannot be otherwise. First, then, if we have a proposition which in being thought is thought as *necessary*, it is an *a priori* judgment; and if, besides, it is not derived from any proposition except one which also has the validity of a necessary judgment, it is an absolutely *a priori* judgment. Secondly, experience never confers on its judgments true or strict but only assumed and comparative *universality*, through induction.* We can properly only say, therefore, that so far as we have hitherto observed, there is no exception to this or that rule. If, then, a judgment is thought with strict universality, that is, in such manner that no exception is allowed as possible, it is not derived from experience, but is valid absolutely *a priori*. Empirical universality is only an arbitrary extension of a validity holding in most cases to one which holds in all, for instance, in the proposition, 'all bodies are heavy'. When, on the other hand, strict universality is essential to a judgment, this indicates a special source of knowledge, namely, a faculty of *a priori* knowledge. Necessity and strict universality are thus sure criteria of *a priori* knowledge, and are inseparable from one another. But since in the employment of these criteria the contingency of judgments is sometimes more easily shown than their empirical limitation, or, as sometimes also happens, their unlimited universality can be more convincingly proved than their necessity, it is advisable to use the two criteria separately, each by itself being infallible.

Now it is easy to show that there actually are in human knowledge judgments which are necessary and in the strictest sense universal, and which are therefore pure *a priori* judgments. If an example from the sciences be desired, we have only to look to any of the propositions of mathematics; if we seek an example from the understanding in its quite ordinary employment, the proposition, 'every alteration must have a cause', will serve our purpose. In the latter case, indeed, the very concept of a cause so manifestly contains the concept of a necessity of connection with an effect and of the strict universality of the rule, that the concept would be altogether lost if we attempted to derive it, as

---

* Induction is the inference of a general law from particular instances. For example, if you see that one chickadee is chirpy, and you see that the next chickadee is chirpy, and so on, eventually you might conclude that all chickadees are chirpy. See the Philosophy of Science chapter of this volume for further discussion of induction.

Hume has done,* from a repeated association of that which happens with that which precedes, and from a custom of connecting representations, a custom originating in this repeated association, and constituting therefore a merely subjective necessity. Even without appealing to such examples, it is possible to show that pure *a priori* principles are indispensable for the possibility of experience, and so to prove their existence *a priori*. For whence could experience derive its certainty, if all the rules, according to which it proceeds, were always themselves empirical, and therefore contingent? Such rules could hardly be regarded as first principles. At present, however, we may be content to have established the fact that our faculty of knowledge does have a pure employment, and to have shown what are the criteria of such an employment.

Such *a priori* origin is manifest in certain concepts, no less than in judgments. If we remove from our empirical concept of a body, one by one, every feature in it which is [merely] empirical, the colour, the hardness or softness, the weight, even the impenetrability, there still remains the space which the body (now entirely vanished) occupied, and this cannot be removed. Again, if we remove from our empirical concept of any object, corporeal or incorporeal, all properties which experience has taught us, we yet cannot take away that property through which the object is thought as substance or as inhering in a substance (although this concept of substance is more determinate than that of an object in general). Owing, therefore, to the necessity with which this concept of substance forces itself upon us, we have no option save to admit that it has its seat in our faculty of *a priori* knowledge.

III. Philosophy Stands in Need of a Science Which Shall Determine the Possibility, the Principles, and the Extent of All A priori Knowledge

But what is still more extraordinary than all the preceding is this, that certain modes of knowledge leave the field of all possible experiences and have the appearance of extending the scope of our judgments beyond all limits of experience, and this by means of concepts to which no corresponding object can ever be given in experience.

It is precisely by means of the latter modes of knowledge, in a realm beyond the world of the senses, where experience can yield neither guidance nor correction, that our reason carries on those enquiries which owing to their importance we consider to be far more excellent, and in their purpose far more lofty, than all that the understanding can learn in the field of appearances. Indeed we prefer to run every risk of error rather than desist from such urgent enquiries, on the ground of their dubious character, or from disdain and indifference. These unavoidable problems set by pure reason itself are *God, freedom,* and *immortality*. The science which, with all its preparations, is in its final intention directed solely to their solution is metaphysics; and its procedure is at first dogmatic, that is, it confidently sets itself to this task without any previous examination of the capacity or incapacity of reason for so great an undertaking.

Now it does indeed seem natural that, as soon as we have left the ground of experience, we should, through careful enquiries, assure ourselves as to the foundations of any building that we propose to erect, not making use of any knowledge that we possess without first determining whence it has come, and not trusting to principles without knowing their origin. It is natural, that is to say, that the question should first be considered, how the understanding can arrive at all this knowledge *a priori*, and what extent, validity, and worth it may have. Nothing, indeed, could be more natural, if by the term 'natural' we signify what fittingly and reasonably ought to happen. But if we mean by 'natural' what ordinarily happens, then on the contrary nothing is more natural and more intelligible than the fact that this enquiry has been so long neglected. For one part of this knowledge, the mathematical, has long been of established reliability, and

---

* Kant is referring to Hume's *An Enquiry Concerning Human Understanding*, which was published in 1748 and translated into German by 1755. (Hume's earlier book, the *Treatise of Human Nature*, was not translated into German until 1791, and Kant probably had no first-hand acquaintance with most of it.) See the Hume reading in the Philosophy of Science chapter of this volume for more information on this philosopher and his views, and especially for some of his views on causation.

so gives rise to a favourable presumption as regards the other part,* which may yet be of quite different nature. Besides, once we are outside the circle of experience, we can be sure of not being *contradicted* by experience. The charm of extending our knowledge is so great that nothing short of encountering a direct contradiction can suffice to arrest us in our course; and this can be avoided, if we are careful in our fabrications—which none the less will still remain fabrications. Mathematics gives us a shining example of how far, independently of experience, we can progress in *a priori* knowledge. It does, indeed, occupy itself with objects and with knowledge solely in so far as they allow of being exhibited in intuition.† But this circumstance is easily overlooked, since the intuition, in being thought, can itself be given *a priori*, and is therefore hardly to be distinguished from a bare and pure concept. Misled by such a proof of the power of reason, the demand for the extension of knowledge recognises no limits. The light dove, cleaving the air in her free flight, and feeling its resistance, might imagine that its flight would be still easier in empty space. It was thus that Plato left the world of the senses, as setting too narrow limits to the understanding, and ventured out beyond it on the wings of the ideas, in the empty space of the pure understanding. He did not observe that with all his efforts he made no advance—meeting no resistance that might, as it were, serve as a support upon which he could take a stand, to which he could apply his powers, and so set his understanding in motion. It is, indeed, the common fate of human reason to complete its speculative structures as speedily as may be, and only afterwards to enquire whether the foundations are reliable. All sorts of excuses will then be appealed to, in order to reassure us of their solidity, or rather indeed to enable us to dispense altogether with so late and so dangerous an enquiry. But

what keeps us, during the actual building, free from all apprehension and suspicion, and flatters us with a seeming thoroughness, is this other circumstance, namely, that a great, perhaps the greatest, part of the business of our reason consists in analysis of the concepts which we already have of objects. This analysis supplies us with a considerable body of knowledge, which, while nothing but explanation or elucidation of what has already been thought in our concepts, though in a confused manner, is yet prized as being, at least as regards its form, new insight. But so far as the matter or content is concerned, there has been no extension of our previously possessed concepts, but only an analysis of them. Since this procedure yields real knowledge *a priori*, which progresses in an assured and useful fashion, reason is so far misled as surreptitiously to introduce, without itself being aware of so doing, assertions of an entirely different order, in which it attaches to given concepts others completely foreign to them, and moreover attaches them *a priori*. And yet it is not known how reason can be in position to do this. Such a question is never so much as thought of. I shall therefore at once proceed to deal with the difference between these two kinds of knowledge.

IV. The Distinction between Analytic and Synthetic Judgments

In all judgments in which the relation of a subject to the predicate‡ is thought (I take into consideration affirmative judgments only, the subsequent application to negative judgments being easily made), this relation is possible in two different ways. Either the predicate B belongs to the subject A, as something which is (covertly) contained in this concept A; or outside the concept A, although it does indeed stand in connection with it. In the one case I entitle the judgment

---

* Metaphysics.

† By "intuition" (*Anschauung*) Kant means the direct perception of an object. An intuition is a mental representation that is *particular* and *concrete*, rather like an image. The main contrast, for Kant, is with *concepts*, which he thinks of as abstract and general representations. For example, the concept of redness is an idea that can apply to many things at once (lots of different things can be red all at the same time); by contrast, an intuition of redness is a sensory impression of some particular instance of red—it is an apprehension of *this* redness.

‡ A predicate is a describing-phrase, and the subject of a sentence is the thing being described. An affirmative judgment says that some predicate is true of (or "satisfied by") a subject, while a negative judgment says that a subject does not satisfy that predicate. For example, "this nectarine is ripe" is an affirmative judgment (where the nectarine is the subject and '___ is ripe' is the predicate); "this nectarine is not juicy" is a negative judgment.

analytic, in the other synthetic. Analytic judgments (affirmative) are therefore those in which the connection of the predicate with the subject is thought through identity;* those in which this connection is thought without identity should be entitled synthetic. The former, as adding nothing through the predicate to the concept of the subject, but merely breaking it up into those constituent concepts that have all along been thought in it, although confusedly, can also be entitled explicative. The latter, on the other hand, add to the concept of the subject a predicate which has not been in any wise thought in it, and which no analysis could possibly extract from it; and they may therefore be entitled ampliative. If I say, for instance, 'All bodies are extended', this is an analytic judgment. For I do not require to go beyond the concept which I connect with 'body' in order to find extension as bound up with it. To meet with this predicate, I have merely to analyse the concept, that is, to become conscious to myself of the manifold† which I always think in that concept. The judgment is therefore analytic. But when I say, 'All bodies are heavy', the predicate is something quite different from anything that I think in the mere concept of body in general; and the addition of such a predicate therefore yields a synthetic judgment.

Judgments of experience, as such, are one and all synthetic. For it would be absurd to found an analytic judgment on experience. Since, in framing the judgment, I must not go outside my concept, there is no need to appeal to the testimony of experience in its support. That a body is extended is a proposition that holds *a priori* and is not empirical. For, before appealing to experience, I have already in the concept of body all the conditions required for my judgment. I have only to extract from it, in accordance with the principle of contradiction,‡ the required predicate, and in so doing

can at the same time become conscious of the necessity of the judgment—and that is what experience could never have taught me. On the other hand, though I do not include in the concept of a body in general the predicate 'weight', none the less this concept indicates an object of experience through one of its parts, and I can add to that part other parts of this same experience, as in this way belonging together with the concept. From the start I can apprehend the concept of body analytically through the characters of extension, impenetrability, figure, etc., all of which are thought in the concept. Now, however, looking back on the experience from which I have derived this concept of body, and finding weight to be invariably connected with the above characters, I attach it as a predicate to the concept; and in doing so I attach it synthetically, and am therefore extending my knowledge. The possibility of the synthesis of the predicate 'weight' with the concept of 'body' thus rests upon experience. While the one concept is not contained in the other, they yet belong to one another, though only contingently, as parts of a whole, namely, of an experience which is itself a synthetic combination of intuitions.

But in *a priori* synthetic judgments this help is entirely lacking. [I do not here have the advantage of looking around in the field of experience.] Upon what, then, am I to rely, when I seek to go beyond the concept A, and to know that another concept B is connected with it? Through what is the synthesis made possible? Let us take the proposition, 'Everything which happens has its cause'. In the concept of 'something which happens', I do indeed think an existence which is preceded by a time, etc., and from this concept analytic judgments may be obtained. But the concept of a 'cause' lies entirely outside the other concept, and signifies something different from 'that which happens', and is not therefore

---

* By "identity" here Kant means self-identity: for example, to say that rapper Eminem *is identical with* Slim Shady (or that Beyoncé is identical with Sasha Fierce, or even that Cicero is identical with Tully) is to say that they are not two different people but are one and the same person being named in different ways. Another example, more relevant to Kant's concerns in this passage, is that being a vixen *is identical with* being a female fox: these are just two different ways of describing one and the same property.

† "Manifold" = composed of many parts. For example, in the judgment that all uncles are male, the concept *uncle* has as one of its "parts" the concept *male*. So that is an analytic judgment.

‡ The principle of contradiction states that a proposition and its negation cannot both be true. For example it can't *both* be true that it is now Sunday *and* true that it is not now Sunday; if it is true that the spiny anteater lays eggs, then it is not true that it is false that the spiny anteater lays eggs. As Aristotle once pithily put it, "nothing can both be and not be at the same time in the same respect."

in any way contained in this latter representation. How come I then to predicate of that which happens something quite different, and to apprehend that the concept of cause, though not contained in it, yet belongs, and indeed necessarily belongs to it? What is here the unknown = X which gives support to the understanding when it believes that it can discover outside the concept A a predicate B foreign to this concept, which it yet at the same time considers to be connected with it? It cannot be experience, because the suggested principle has connected the second representation with the first, not only with greater universality, but also with the character of necessity, and therefore completely *a priori* and on the basis of mere concepts. Upon such synthetic, that is, ampliative principles, all our *a priori* speculative knowledge must ultimately rest; analytic judgments are very important, and indeed necessary, but only for obtaining that clearness in the concepts which is requisite for such a sure and wide synthesis as will lead to a genuinely new addition to all previous knowledge.

V. In All Theoretical Sciences of Reason Synthetic A priori Judgments Are Contained as Principles

1. *All mathematical judgments, without exception, are synthetic.* This fact, though incontestably certain and in its consequences very important, has hitherto escaped the notice of those who are engaged in the analysis of human reason, and is, indeed, directly opposed to all their conjectures. For as it was found that all mathematical inferences proceed in accordance with the principle of contradiction* (which the nature of all apodeictic† certainty requires), it was supposed that the fundamental propositions of the science can themselves be known to be true through that principle. This is an erroneous view. For though a synthetic proposition can indeed be discerned in accordance with the principle of contradiction, this can only be if another synthetic proposition is presupposed, and if it can then be apprehended as following from this other

proposition; it can never be so discerned in and by itself. First of all, it has to be noted that mathematical propositions, strictly so called, are always judgments *a priori*, not empirical; because they carry with them necessity, which cannot be derived from experience. If this be demurred to, I am willing to limit my statement to *pure* mathematics, the very concept of which implies that it does not contain empirical, but only pure *a priori* knowledge.

We might, indeed, at first suppose that the proposition 7 + 5 = 12 is a merely analytic proposition, and follows by the principle of contradiction from the concept of a sum of 7 and 5. But if we look more closely we find that the concept of the sum of 7 and 5 contains nothing save the union of the two numbers into one, and in this no thought is being taken as to what that single number may be which combines both. The concept of 12 is by no means already thought in merely thinking this union of 7 and 5; and I may analyse my concept of such a possible sum as long as I please, still I shall never find the 12 in it. We have to go outside these concepts, and call in the aid of the intuition which corresponds to one of them, our five fingers, for instance, or, as Segner does in his *Arithmetic*,‡ five points, adding to the concept of 7, unit by unit, the five given in intuition. For starting with the number 7, and for the concept of 5 calling in the aid of the fingers of my hand as intuition, I now add one by one to the number 7 the units which I previously took together to form the number 5, and with the aid of that figure [the hand] see the number 12 come into being. That 5 should be added to 7, I have indeed already thought in the concept of a sum = 7 + 5, but not that this sum is equivalent to the number 12. Arithmetical propositions are therefore always synthetic. This is still more evident if we take larger numbers. For it is then obvious that, however we might turn and twist our concepts, we could never, by the mere analysis of them, and without the aid of intuition, discover what [the number is that] is the sum.

Just as little is any fundamental proposition of pure geometry analytic. That the straight line between two

---

* By showing that they must be true, since if they were false this would lead to a contradiction.

† For Kant, an apodeictic proposition states what *must* be the case, i.e., what is necessary. (By contrast, in Kant's terminology, an "assertoric" proposition states what *is* the case—i.e., what is actual—and a "problematic" proposition asserts what *can* be the case, i.e., what is possible.)

‡ The book Kant refers to is Johann Segner's *Anfangsgründe der Arithmetik*, translated from the original Latin, the second edition of which was published in 1773.

points is the shortest, is a synthetic proposition. For my concept of *straight* contains nothing of quantity, but only of quality. The concept of the shortest is wholly an addition, and cannot be derived, through any process of analysis, from the concept of the straight line. Intuition, therefore, must here be called in; only by its aid is the synthesis possible. What here causes us commonly to believe that the predicate of such apodeictic judgments is already contained in our concept, and that the judgment is therefore analytic, is merely the ambiguous character of the terms used. We are required to join in thought a certain predicate to a given concept, and this necessity is inherent in the concepts themselves. But the question is not what we *ought* to join in thought to the given concept, but what we *actually* think in it, even if only obscurely; and it is then manifest that, while the predicate is indeed attached necessarily to the concept, it is so in virtue of an intuition which must be added to the concept, not as thought in the concept itself.

Some few fundamental propositions, presupposed by the geometrician, are, indeed, really analytic, and rest on the principle of contradiction. But, as identical propositions,* they serve only as links in the chain of method and not as principles; for instance, $a = a$; the whole is equal to itself; or $(a + b) > a$, that is, the whole is greater than its part. And even these propositions, though they are valid according to pure concepts, are only admitted in mathematics because they can be exhibited in intuition.

2. *Natural science (physics) contains* a priori *synthetic judgments as principles*. I need cite only two such judgments: that in all changes of the material world the quantity of matter remains unchanged; and that in all communication of motion, action and reaction must always be equal. Both propositions, it is evident, are not only necessary, and therefore in their origin *a priori*, but also synthetic. For in the concept of matter I do not think its permanence, but only its presence in the space which it occupies. I go outside and beyond the concept of matter, joining to it *a priori* in thought something which I have not thought *in* it. The proposition is not, therefore, analytic, but synthetic, and yet is thought *a priori*; and so likewise are the other propositions of the pure part of natural science.

3. *Metaphysics*, even if we look upon it as having hitherto failed in all its endeavours, is yet, owing to the nature of human reason, a quite indispensable science, and *ought to contain* a priori *synthetic knowledge*. For its business is not merely to analyse concepts which we make for ourselves *a priori* of things, and thereby to clarify them analytically, but to extend our *a priori* knowledge. And for this purpose we must employ principles which add to the given concept something that was not contained in it, and through *a priori* synthetic judgments venture out so far that experience is quite unable to follow us, as, for instance, in the proposition, that the world must have a first beginning, and such like. Thus metaphysics consists, at least *in intention*, entirely of *a priori* synthetic propositions.

VI. The General Problem of Pure Reason

Much is already gained if we can bring a number of investigations under the formula of a single problem. For we not only lighten our own task, by defining it accurately, but make it easier for others, who would test our results, to judge whether or not we have succeeded in what we set out to do. Now the proper problem of pure reason is contained in the question: How are *a priori* synthetic judgments possible?

That metaphysics has hitherto remained in so vacillating a state of uncertainty and contradiction, is entirely due to the fact that this problem, and perhaps even the distinction between analytic and synthetic judgments, has never previously been considered. Upon the solution of this problem, or upon a sufficient proof that the possibility which it desires to have explained does in fact not exist at all, depends the success or failure of metaphysics. Among philosophers, David Hume came nearest to envisaging this problem, but still was very far from conceiving it with sufficient definiteness and universality. He occupied himself exclusively with the synthetic proposition regarding the connection of an effect with its cause (*principium causalitatis*†), and he believed himself to have shown that such an *a priori* proposition is entirely impossible. If we accept his conclusions, then all that we call metaphysics is a mere delusion whereby we fancy

---

* As assertions of identities (or non-identities).
† "The principle of causality."

ourselves to have rational insight into what, in actual fact, is borrowed solely from experience, and under the influence of custom has taken the illusory semblance of necessity. If he had envisaged our problem in all its universality, he would never have been guilty of this statement, so destructive of all pure philosophy. For he would then have recognised that, according to his own argument, pure mathematics, as certainly containing *a priori* synthetic propositions, would also not be possible; and from such an assertion his good sense would have saved him.

In the solution of the above problem, we are at the same time deciding as to the possibility of the employment of pure reason in establishing and developing all those sciences which contain a theoretical *a priori* knowledge of objects, and have therefore to answer the questions:

How is pure mathematics possible?
How is pure science of nature possible?

Since these sciences actually exist, it is quite proper to ask *how* they are possible; for that they must be possible is proved by the fact that they exist.[1] But the poor progress which has hitherto been made in metaphysics, and the fact that no system yet propounded can, in view of the essential purpose of metaphysics, be said really to exist, leaves everyone sufficient ground for doubting as to its possibility.

Yet, in a certain sense, this *kind of knowledge* is to be looked upon as given; that is to say, metaphysics actually exists, if not as a science, yet still as natural disposition (*metaphysica naturalis**). For human reason, without being moved merely by the idle desire for extent and variety of knowledge, proceeds impetuously, driven on by an inward need, to questions such as cannot be answered by any empirical employment of reason, or by principles thence derived. Thus in all men, as soon as their reason has become ripe for speculation, there has always existed and will always continue to exist some kind of metaphysics. And so we have the question:

How is metaphysics, as natural disposition, possible?

That is, how from the nature of universal human reason do those questions arise which pure reason propounds to itself, and which it is impelled by its own need to answer as best it can?

But since all attempts which have hitherto been made to answer these natural questions—for instance, whether the world has a beginning or is from eternity—have always met with unavoidable contradictions, we cannot rest satisfied with the mere natural disposition to metaphysics, that is, with the pure faculty of reason itself, from which, indeed, some sort of metaphysics (be it what it may) always arises. It must be possible for reason to attain to certainty whether we know or do not know the objects of metaphysics, that is, to come to a decision either in regard to the objects of its enquiries or in regard to the capacity or incapacity of reason to pass any judgment upon them, so that we may either with confidence extend our pure reason or set to it sure and determinate limits. This last question, which arises out of the previous general problem, may, rightly stated, take the form:

How is metaphysics, as science, possible?

Thus the critique of reason, in the end, necessarily leads to scientific knowledge; while its dogmatic employment, on the other hand, lands us in dogmatic assertions to which other assertions, equally specious,† can always be opposed—that is, in *scepticism*.

This science cannot be of any very formidable prolixity,‡ since it has to deal not with the objects of reason, the variety of which is inexhaustible, but only with itself and the problems which arise entirely from within itself, and which are imposed upon it by its own nature, not by the nature of things which are distinct from it. When once reason has learnt completely to understand its own power in respect of objects which can be presented to it in experience, it should easily be able to determine, with completeness and certainty, the extent and the limits of its attempted employment beyond the bounds of all experience.

We may, then, and indeed we must, regard as abortive all attempts, hitherto made, to establish a metaphysic *dogmatically*. For the analytic part in any

---

* "Natural metaphysics."
† Superficially plausible, but actually false.
‡ Tedious length.

such attempted system, namely, the mere analysis of the concepts that inhere in our reason *a priori*, is by no means the aim of, but only a preparation for, metaphysics proper, that is, the extension of its *a priori* synthetic knowledge. For such a purpose, the analysis of concepts is useless, since it merely shows what is contained in these concepts, not how we arrive at them *a priori*. A solution of this latter problem is required, that we may be able to determine the valid employment of such concepts in regard to the objects of all knowledge in general. Nor is much self-denial needed to give up these claims, seeing that the undeniable, and in the dogmatic procedure of reason also unavoidable, contradictions of reason with itself have long since undermined the authority of every metaphysical system yet propounded. Greater firmness will be required if we are not to be deterred by inward difficulties and outward opposition from endeavouring, through application of a method entirely different from any hitherto employed, at last to bring to a prosperous and fruitful growth a science indispensable to human reason—a science whose every branch may be cut away but whose root cannot be destroyed.

VII. *The Idea and Division of a Special Science, under the Title "Critique of Pure Reason"*

In view of all these considerations, we arrive at the idea of a special science which can be entitled the Critique of Pure Reason. For reason is the faculty which supplies the principles of *a priori* knowledge. Pure reason is, therefore, that which contains the principles whereby we know anything absolutely *a priori*. An organon* of pure reason would be the sum-total of those principles according to which all modes of pure *a priori* knowledge can be acquired and actually brought into being. The exhaustive application of such an organon would give rise to a system of pure reason. But as this would be asking rather much, and as it is still doubtful whether, and in what cases, any extension of our knowledge be here possible, we can regard a science of the mere examination of pure reason, of its sources and

limits, as the *propaedeutic*† to the system of pure reason. As such, it should be called a critique, not a doctrine, of pure reason. Its utility, in speculation, ought properly to be only negative, not to extend, but only to clarify our reason, and keep it free from errors—which is already a very great gain. I entitle *transcendental* all knowledge which is occupied not so much with objects as with the mode of our knowledge of objects in so far as this mode of knowledge is to be possible *a priori*. A system of such concepts might be entitled transcendental philosophy. But that is still, at this stage, too large an undertaking. For since such a science must contain, with completeness, both kinds of *a priori* knowledge, the analytic no less than the synthetic, it is, so far as our present purpose is concerned, much too comprehensive. We have to carry the analysis so far only as is indispensably necessary in order to comprehend, in their whole extent, the principles of *a priori* synthesis, with which alone we are called upon to deal. It is upon this enquiry, which should be entitled not a doctrine, but only a transcendental critique, that we are now engaged. Its purpose is not to extend knowledge, but only to correct it, and to supply a touchstone of the value, or lack of value, of all *a priori* knowledge. Such a critique is therefore a preparation, so far as may be possible, for an organon; and should this turn out not to be possible, then at least for a canon,‡ according to which, in due course, the complete system of the philosophy of pure reason—be it in extension or merely in limitation of its knowledge—may be carried into execution, analytically as well as synthetically. That such a system is possible, and indeed that it may not be of such great extent as to cut us off from the hope of entirely completing it, may already be gathered from the fact that what here constitutes our subject-matter is not the nature of things, which is inexhaustible, but the understanding which passes judgment upon the nature of things; and this understanding, again, only in respect of its *a priori* knowledge. These *a priori* possessions of the understanding, since they have not to be sought for without, cannot remain hidden from us, and in all probability are sufficiently small in extent to

---

* An instrument of thought, especially a system of logic or a method for reasoning. (Aristotle's logical writings were historically grouped together as the *Organon*, and Francis Bacon's influential 1620 book on the scientific method was called the *Novum* [new] *Organon*.)

† Preliminary or introductory instruction (from the Greek, meaning "to teach beforehand").

‡ A general principle or criterion.

allow of our apprehending them in their completeness, of judging as to their value or lack of value, and so of rightly appraising them. Still less may the reader here expect a critique of books and systems of pure reason; we are concerned only with the critique of the faculty of pure reason itself. Only in so far as we build upon this foundation do we have a reliable touchstone for estimating the philosophical value of old and new works in this field. Otherwise the unqualified historian or critic is passing judgments upon the groundless assertions of others by means of his own, which are equally groundless.

Transcendental philosophy is only the idea of a science, for which the critique of pure reason has to lay down the complete architectonic* plan. That is to say, it has to guarantee, as following from principles, the completeness and certainty of the structure in all its parts. It is the system of all principles of pure reason. And if this critique is not itself to be entitled a transcendental philosophy, it is solely because, to be a complete system, it would also have to contain an exhaustive analysis of the whole of *a priori* human knowledge. Our critique must, indeed, supply a complete enumeration of all the fundamental concepts that go to constitute such pure knowledge. But it is not required to give an exhaustive analysis of these concepts, nor a complete review of those that can be derived from them. Such a demand would be unreasonable, partly because this analysis would not be appropriate to our main purpose, inasmuch as there is no such uncertainty in regard to analysis as we encounter in the case of synthesis, for the sake of which alone our whole critique is undertaken; and partly because it would be inconsistent with the unity of our plan to assume responsibility for the completeness of such an analysis and derivation, when in view of our purpose we can be excused from doing so. The analysis of these *a priori* concepts, which later we shall have to enumerate, and the derivation of other concepts from them, can easily, however, be made complete when once they have been established as exhausting the principles of synthesis, and if in this essential respect nothing be lacking in them.

The critique of pure reason therefore will contain all that is essential in transcendental philosophy. While it is the complete idea of transcendental philosophy, it is not equivalent to that latter science; for it carries the analysis only so far as is requisite for the complete examination of knowledge which is *a priori* and synthetic.

What has chiefly to be kept in view in the division of such a science, is that no concepts be allowed to enter which contain in themselves anything empirical, or, in other words, that it consist in knowledge wholly *a priori*. Accordingly, although the highest principles and fundamental concepts of morality are *a priori* knowledge, they have no place in transcendental philosophy, because, although they do not lay at the foundation of their precepts the concepts of pleasure and pain, of the desires and inclinations, etc., all of which are of empirical origin, yet in the construction of a system of pure morality these empirical concepts must necessarily be brought into the concept of duty, as representing either a hindrance, which we have to overcome, or an allurement, which must not be made into a motive. Transcendental philosophy is therefore a philosophy of pure and merely speculative reason. All that is practical, so far as it contains motives, relates to feelings, and these belong to the empirical sources of knowledge.

If we are to make a systematic division of the science which we are engaged in presenting, it must have first a *doctrine of the elements*,† and secondly, a *doctrine of the method of pure reason*. Each of these chief divisions will have its subdivisions, but the grounds of these we are not yet in a position to explain. By way of introduction or anticipation we need only say that there are two stems of human knowledge, namely, *sensibility*‡ and *understanding*, which perhaps spring from a common, but to us unknown, root. Through the former, objects are given to us; through the latter, they are thought. Now in so far as sensibility may be found to contain *a priori* representations constituting the condition under which objects are given to us, it will belong to transcendental philosophy. And since the conditions under which alone the objects of human knowledge are given must precede those under which they are thought, the transcendental doctrine of sensibility will constitute the first part of the science of the elements. ∎

---

* Having to do with the scientific systematization of knowledge.
† The "elements" are the constituents of cognition, which for Kant are intuitions and concepts.
‡ The power of sensation.

Suggestions for Critical Reflection

1. Kant's two distinctions—between *a priori* and *a posteriori* propositions, and between analytic and synthetic propositions—allow him to distinguish between *four* different types of knowledge. However, he only entertains the possibility of *three* of those classes of proposition: the analytic *a priori*, synthetic *a priori*, and synthetic *a posteriori*. What is it about the notion of *analytic a posteriori* knowledge which causes Kant to dismiss it as incoherent? Is Kant right about this?

2. There is another distinction between types of propositions which Kant was clearly aware of, and which is often listed along with the *a priori*/*a posteriori* and analytic/synthetic contrasts: this is the distinction between propositions which are *necessarily* true, and those which are only *contingently* true. (A proposition is necessarily true if it is true no matter what—if no change you could possibly make to the world would make it false. A proposition is contingent if it is possibly, but not necessarily, true.) How, if at all, might this necessary/contingent distinction complicate Kant's classification of knowledge? For example, could some synthetic *a posteriori* propositions be necessary and others be contingent?

3. How adequate is Kant's criterion for the distinction between analytic and synthetic propositions? If you try out this distinction on a number of examples, do you find you can easily tell which are analytic and which synthetic? (How about, for example, "nothing is red all over and green all over at the same time," "water is H_2O," "all tigers are mammals," "2 is less than 3," "contradictions are impossible," or "every event has a cause"?)

4. Kant argues that mathematical knowledge is synthetic rather than analytic. Do you think he is right, or do you think it is more plausible to say that mathematics deals entirely with the *analytic* relations between our mathematical *concepts*? If Kant is wrong about mathematics being synthetic, how much harm do you think this causes to his overall philosophical framework—for example, would he then be in danger of turning into just a German Hume?

5. Kant claims that some of the principles of natural science are synthetic *a priori*: that is, they are not learned from experience but are in some sense *prior* to experience. (As he hints at the beginning of the reading, Kant's view is that although all our knowledge *begins* with experience it does not all *arise* out of experience.) How plausible do you find this claim? How radical is it—what implications might it have for the way we think of the relationship between our minds and external reality?

6. Kant claims that the judgment that all events have causes is necessary and *a priori*. But quantum physics routinely deals with events that are claimed to be without determining cause. Kant also claims that the judgment that space is Euclidean is necessary and *a priori* (that is, that, for example, plane triangles in space must have interior angles adding up to two right angles). But Einstein's theory postulates that this is false, and that has been borne out by observation. Have these sciences shown that Kant was mistaken? What damage (if any) do these findings do to Kant's system?

7. Do you share Kant's skepticism about speculative metaphysics? If so, do you agree with his reasons for rejecting it? If not, where does Kant go wrong?

8. Are there really any such things as synthetic *a priori* propositions, or are all *a priori* propositions really analytic and all synthetic propositions really *a posteriori*?

Note

1 Many may still have doubts as regards pure natural science. We have only, however, to consider the various propositions that are to be found at the beginning of (empirical) physics, properly so called, those, for instance, relating to the permanence in the quantity of matter, to inertia, to the equality of action and reaction, etc., in order to be soon convinced that they constitute a *physica pura*, or *rationalis*, which well deserves, as an independent science, to be separately dealt with in its whole extent, be that narrow or wide.

G.E. MOORE

Proof of an External World

Who Was G.E. Moore?

George Edward Moore was a leading figure in the generation of philosophers—including Bertrand Russell and the young Ludwig Wittgenstein—which set British philosophy on a new path at the start of the twentieth century by founding the important stream of thought called "analytic philosophy" (which, in somewhat altered form, is still dominant today in the English-speaking philosophical world).

Born to middle-class, devoutly religious parents in a London suburb in 1873, Moore studied Greek and Latin (but, by his own admission, no science at all) at Dulwich College, and then went up to Trinity College, Cambridge, to study classics. Bertrand Russell, who was a student there at the same time, persuaded Moore to switch to the study of philosophy, and after his undergraduate education Moore won (on his second attempt) a six-year prize fellowship at Trinity. It paid £200 a year, plus board and lodging in college, from 1898 until 1904.

During these early years of his philosophical career Moore had two notable triumphs. First, he published papers (in particular "The Refutation of Idealism," in 1903) which, it turned out, signaled the death knell of the then-dominant form of philosophy in Britain—a philosophy called "absolute idealism" which, roughly, held that the universe is constituted, not of matter, but of the thought of an absolute spirit. Second, he wrote a book on ethics called *Principia Ethica* (also published in 1903) which influentially declared that all previous ethical theories were guilty of a major fallacy, the "naturalistic fallacy" of trying to define moral values in non-ethical terms. By contrast, Moore said, goodness is an intrinsic, unanalyzable quality known to us by intuition. This book, as well as having a major influence on professional philosophers, became the manifesto for a group of artists and writers known as the Bloomsbury Group, which included Virginia and Leonard Woolf, E.M. Forster, John Maynard Keynes, Lytton Strachey, and Clive Bell.

In his later work, Moore became known for his defense of common sense: he believed that whenever a philosophical doctrine contradicts common sense, it was more likely that the philosophical argument had gone awry than that common sense had done so. He disagreed with those philosophers (such as Russell and Wittgenstein) who held that our ordinary language concealed philosophical errors that needed to be eliminated in an artificial, perfect, logical language. Similarly, he did not think that our everyday beliefs were false and in need of replacement by more rigorous philosophical or scientific claims. What, then, is the role of philosophy according to Moore? It is to *analyze* our everyday beliefs and find out what, exactly, they are telling us. What, for example, Moore asks, do we really *mean* when we say, "I think that table over there exists outside of my mind"?

Moore left Cambridge in 1904, lived in Edinburgh and London for a while, but then returned to Cambridge as a university lecturer in 1911. He spent the rest of his life there, except for a lengthy visit to the United States shortly after his retirement in 1939. In 1916 he married one of his students (a "Miss D.M. Ely," who for some reason always called him either "Moore" or "Bill"), and had two sons, one of whom became a poet and the other a musician. Moore quickly became one of the most well-respected philosophers in Britain and, partly under his influence, Cambridge was the most important center for philosophy in the world during these years. Though he had a rather retiring personality, Moore's acute intelligence and his intense concern to lay out problems with total precision and thereby get matters exactly right seems to have exerted a powerful and uplifting influence on those around him. A British philosopher from the generation after Moore's, Gilbert Ryle, said of him:

> For some of us there still lives the Moore whose voice is never quite resuscitated by his printed words. This is the Moore whom we met at Cambridge and at the annual Joint Session of the Mind Association and the Aristotelian Society. Moore was a dynamo of courage. He gave us courage not by making concessions, but by making no concessions to our youth or to our shyness. He treated us

as corrigible and therefore as responsible thinkers. He would explode at our mistakes and muddles with just that genial ferocity with which he would explode at the mistakes and muddles of philosophical high-ups, and with just the genial ferocity with which he would explode at mistakes and muddles of his own. He would listen with minute attention to what we said, and then, without a trace of discourtesy or courtesy, treat our remarks simply on their merits, usually, of course, and justly inveighing against their inadequacy, irrelevance or confusedness, but sometimes, without a trace of politeness or patronage, crediting them with whatever positive utility he thought that they possessed. If, as sometimes happened, he found in someone's interposition the exposure of a confusion or a fallacy of his own, he would announce that this was so, confess to his own unbelievable muddle-headedness or slackness of reasoning, and then with full acknowledgment, adopt and work with the clarification.*

What Is the Structure of This Reading?

Moore begins by introducing the problem he will be discussing: the problem of the existence of the external world. He does not proceed immediately to try to answer it, however, but begins by trying to clarify exactly what the question is asking (and thus what would count as a correct answer). He starts with the phrase "things outside of us" and sets out to refine it into a more exact expression, ending up with "things which are to be met with in space." Then he tries to make clearer what precisely this means, contrasting it with "things which are presented in space" in order to do so: this involves showing, first, that some things presented in space are not to be met with in space, and second that some things to be met with in space are not presented in space. Moore now claims (though he admits he has not succeeded in making the notion *absolutely* clear) he has said enough to show that, if only he can prove there exist some things which are to be met with in space (such as tables, stars, and sheets of paper), it would trivially follow that "there are things to be met with in space" is true.

Moore now faces another problem: even if he can prove that there are things to be met with in space, why should we admit that these objects are *external to our minds*? That is, how can Moore prove that tables, even though they are importantly different from after-images, are not nevertheless another kind of mental object? Moore's reasoning needs to be followed carefully here, but his central idea is that statements about things external to our minds are logically independent of claims about experience. That is, for example, it being true that a sheet of paper exists does not logically entail the truth of the claim that someone is perceiving that paper, whereas to say that someone is seeing double at a particular time *commits* one to the claim that someone is having an experience of a double image at that time.

Moore points out that this means that "external to our minds" is not synonymous with "to be met with in space," but suggests that if something *is* to be met with in space then it must also be external to our minds. Moore is now at the point in his argument where, he says, if he can just show that two things are to be met with in space this will prove that some external things exist and so definitively answer his original question. *Can* he show that at least two things are to be met with in space? He can, he says, and demonstrates by proving that his two hands exist.

Philosophers, however, will wonder if it can really be so simple? *Did* Moore actually prove that his hands exist outside of his (and our) mind? Moore completes his paper by attempting to defend his argument against possible objections and showing that it satisfies the three "conditions necessary for a rigorous proof."

Some Common Misconceptions

Moore is sometimes caricatured as merely gesticulating with his hands in the air and claiming that he has proved the external world exists. Although there is *some* truth to this, you should be able to see that what Moore is doing is much more complicated and careful than mere hand-waving.

> "Moore," I said, "have you any apples in that basket?" "No," he replied and smiled seraphically as was his wont. I decided to try a different logical tack.

---

*   Gilbert Ryle, "G.E. Moore," in his *Collected Papers*, Vol. I (Hutchinson, 1971), 270–71.

"Moore," I said, "do you then have some apples in that basket?" "No," he said once again. Now I was in a logical cleft-stick, so to speak, and had but one way out. "Moore," I said, "do you then have apples in that basket?" "Yes," he replied, and from that day forth we remained the very best of friends.

This piece of comedy—written by Jonathan Miller for the 1960s show *Beyond the Fringe*—illustrates another common but over-hasty perception of Moore's philosophical method. This is the impression that Moore's work consisted in making, for their own sake, a sequence of trivial and unnecessary logical distinctions and clarifications which perhaps sound clever but which are irrelevant to the "big" concerns of philosophy. You should decide for yourself how fruitful Moore's method of analysis is, but it is certainly untrue that Moore was not at least sincerely *attempting* to deal with real, important philosophical questions by, for example, distinguishing carefully between the logic of the phrases "to be met with in space" and "presented in space."

*Proof of an External World**

In the Preface to the second edition of Kant's *Critique of Pure Reason* some words occur, which, in Professor Kemp Smith's translation, are rendered as follows:[†]

> It still remains a scandal to philosophy ... that the existence of things outside of us ... must be accepted merely on *faith*, and that, if anyone thinks good to doubt their existence, we are unable to counter his doubts by any satisfactory proof.[1]

It seems clear from these words that Kant thought it a matter of some importance to give a proof of "the existence of things outside of us" or perhaps rather (for it seems to me possible that the force of the German words is better rendered in this way) of "the existence of *the* things outside of us"; for had he not thought it important that a proof should be given, he would scarcely have called it a "scandal" that no proof had been given. And it seems clear also that he thought that the giving of such a proof was a task which fell properly within the province of philosophy; for, if it did not, the fact that no proof had been given could not possibly be a scandal to *philosophy*.

Now, even if Kant was mistaken in both of these two opinions there seems to me to be no doubt whatever that it is of some importance and also a matter which falls properly within the province of philosophy, to discuss the question what sort of proof, if any, can be given of "the existence of things outside of us." And to discuss this question was my object when I began to write the present lecture. But I may say at once that, as you will find, I have only, at most, succeeded in saying a very small part of what ought to be said about it.

The words "it ... remains a scandal to philosophy ... that we are unable ..." would, taken strictly, imply that, at the moment at which he wrote them, Kant himself was unable to produce a satisfactory proof of the point in question. But I think it is unquestionable that Kant himself did not think that he personally was at the time unable to produce such a proof. On the contrary, in the immediately preceding sentence, he has declared that he has, in the second edition of his *Critique*, to which he is now writing the Preface, given a "rigorous proof" of this very thing; and has added that he believes this proof of his to be "the only possible proof." It is true that in this preceding sentence he does not describe the proof which he has given as a proof of "the existence of things outside of us" or of "the existence of the things outside of us," but describes it instead as a proof of "the objective reality

*   This paper was first published in 1939 in the *Proceedings of the British Academy* (Volume 25, 273–300).
†   The introduction to the second (or "B") edition of the *Critique of Pure Reason* appears as a reading in this section. More information about Kant appears in the notes to that selection.

of outer intuition." But the context leaves no doubt that he is using these two phrases, "the objective reality of outer intuition" and "the existence of things (*or* "the things") outside of us," in such a way that whatever is a proof of the first is also necessarily a proof of the second. We must, therefore, suppose that when he speaks as if *we* are unable to give a satisfactory proof, he does not mean to say that he himself, as well as others, is *at the moment* unable; but rather that, until he discovered the proof which he has given, both he himself and every-body else *were* unable. Of course, if he is right in thinking that he has given a satisfactory proof, the state of things which he describes came to an end as soon as his proof was published. As soon as that happened, anyone who read it was able to give a satisfactory proof by simply repeating that which Kant had given, and the "scandal" to philosophy had been removed once for all.

If, therefore, it were certain that the proof of the point in question given by Kant in the second edition is a satisfactory proof, it would be certain that at least one satisfactory proof can be given; and all that would remain of the question which I said I proposed to discuss would be, firstly, the question as to what *sort* of a proof this of Kant's is, and secondly the question whether (contrary to Kant's own opinion) there may not perhaps be other proofs, of the same or of a different sort, which are also satisfactory. But I think it is by no means certain that Kant's proof is satisfactory. I think it is by no means certain that he did succeed in removing once for all the state of affairs which he considered to be a scandal to philosophy. And I think, therefore, that the question whether it is possible to give *any* satisfactory proof of the point in question still deserves discussion.

But what is the point in question? I think it must be owned that the expression "things outside of us" is rather an odd expression, and an expression the meaning of which is certainly not perfectly clear. It would have sounded less odd if, instead of "things outside of us" I had said "external things," and perhaps also the meaning of this expression would have seemed to be clearer; and I think we make the meaning of "external things" clearer still if we explain that this phrase has been regularly used by philosophers as short for

"things external to *our minds*." The fact is that there has been a long philosophical tradition, in accordance with which the three expressions "external things," "things external to *us*," and "things external to *our minds*" have been used as equivalent to one another, and have, each of them, been used as if they needed no explanation. The origin of this usage I do not know. It occurs already in Descartes; and since he uses the expressions as if they needed no explanation, they had presumably been used with the same meaning before. Of the three, it seems to me that the expression "external to *our minds*" is the clearest, since it at least makes clear that what is meant is not "external to *our bodies*"; whereas both the other expressions might be taken to mean this: and indeed there has been a good deal of confusion, even among philosophers, as to the relation of the two conceptions "external things" and "things external to *our bodies*." But even the expression "things external to our minds" seems to me to be far from perfectly clear; and if I am to make really clear what I mean by "proof of the existence of things outside of us," I cannot do it by merely saying that by "outside of us" I mean "external to our minds."

There is a passage (*Kritik der reinen Vernunft*, A373)* in which Kant himself says that the expression "outside of us" "carries with it an unavoidable ambiguity." He says that "sometimes it means something which exists *as a thing in itself* distinct from us, and sometimes something which merely belongs to external *appearance*"; he calls things which are "outside of us" in the first of these two senses "objects which might be called external in the transcendental sense," and things which are so in the second "*empirically external* objects"; and he says finally that, in order to remove all uncertainty as to the latter conception, he will distinguish empirically external objects from objects which might be called "external" in the transcendental sense, "by calling them outright things which are *to be met with in space*."

I think that this last phrase of Kant's, "things which are to be met with in space," does indicate fairly clearly what sort of things it is with regard to which I wish to inquire what sort of proof, if any, can be given that there are any things of that sort. My body, the bodies of other men, the bodies of animals, plants of

---

*   *Critique of Pure Reason*, first ("A") edition, p. 373 (of the original German).

all sorts, stones, mountains, the sun, the moon, stars, and planets, houses and other buildings, manufactured articles of all sorts—chairs, tables, pieces of paper, etc., are all of them "things which are to be met with in space." In short, all things of the sort that philosophers have been used to call "physical objects," "material things," or "bodies" obviously come under this head. But the phrase "things that are to be met with in space" can be naturally understood as applying also in cases where the names "physical object," "material thing," or "body" can hardly be applied. For instance, shadows are sometimes to be met with in space, although they could hardly be properly called "physical objects," "material things," or "bodies"; and although in one usage of the term "thing" it would not be proper to call a shadow a "thing," yet the phrase "things which are to be met with in space" can be naturally understood as synonymous with "whatever can be met with in space," and this is an expression which can quite properly be understood to include shadows. I wish the phrase "things which are to be met with in space" to be understood in this wide sense; so that if a proof can be found that there ever have been as many as two different shadows it will follow at once that there have been at least two "things which were to be met with in space," and this proof will be as good a proof of the point in question as would be a proof that there have been at least two "physical objects" of no matter what sort.

The phrase "things which are to be met with in space" can, therefore, be naturally understood as having a very wide meaning—a meaning even wider than that of "physical object" or "body," wide as is the meaning of these latter expressions. But wide as is its meaning, it is not, in one respect, so wide as that of another phrase which Kant uses as if it were equivalent to this one; and a comparison between the two will, I think, serve to make still clearer what sort of things it is with regard to which I wish to ask what proof, if any, can be given that there are such things.

The other phrase which Kant uses as if it were equivalent to "things which are to be met with in space" is used by him in the sentence immediately preceding that previously quoted in which he declares that the expression "things outside of us" "carries with it an unavoidable ambiguity" (A373). In this preceding sentence he says that an "empirical object" "is called *external*, if it is presented (*vorgestellt*) *in space*." He

treats, therefore, the phrase "presented in space" as if it were equivalent to "to be met with in space." But it is easy to find examples of "things," of which it can hardly be denied that they are "presented in space," but of which it could, quite naturally, be emphatically denied that they are "to be met with in space." Consider, for instance, the following description of one set of circumstances under which what some psychologists have called a "negative after-image" and others a "negative after-sensation" can be obtained. "If, after looking steadfastly at a white patch on a black ground, the eye be turned to a white ground, a grey patch is seen for some little time" (Foster's *Text-book of Physiology*, IV, iii, 3, p. 1266; quoted in Stout's *Manual of Psychology*, 3rd edition, p. 280). Upon reading these words recently, I took the trouble to cut out of a piece of white paper a four-pointed star, to place it on a black ground, to "look steadfastly" at it, and then to turn my eyes to a white sheet of paper: and I did find that I saw a grey patch for some little time—I not only saw a grey patch, but I saw it on the white ground, and also this grey patch was of roughly the same shape as the white four-pointed star at which I had "looked steadfastly" just before—it also was a four-pointed star. I repeated this simple experiment successfully several times. Now each of those grey four-pointed stars, one of which I saw in each experiment, was what is called an "after-image" or "after-sensation"; and can anybody deny that each of these after-images can be quite properly said to have been "presented in space"? I saw each of them on a real white background, and, if so, each of them was "presented" on a real white background. But though they were "presented in space" everybody, I think, would feel that it was gravely misleading to say that they were "to be met with in space." The white star at which I "looked steadfastly," the black ground on which I saw it, and the white ground on which I saw the after-images, were, of course, "to be met with in space": they were, in fact, "physical objects" or surfaces of physical objects. But one important difference between them, on the one hand, and the grey after-images, on the other, can be quite naturally expressed by saying that the latter were *not* "to be met with in space." And one reason why this is so is, I think, plain. To say that so and so was at a given time "to be met with in space" naturally suggests that there are conditions such that *any one* who fulfilled them might, conceivably, have "perceived" the "thing" in question—might have seen it, if it was a visible object, have felt it, if it was a tangible one, have heard it, if it was a sound, have smelt it, if it was a smell. When I say that the white four-pointed paper star, at which I looked steadfastly, was a "physical object" and was "to be met with in space," I am implying that *anyone*, who had been in the room at the time, and who had normal eyesight and a normal sense of touch, might have seen and felt it. But, in the case of those grey after-images which I saw, it is not conceivable that anyone besides myself should have seen any one of them. It is, of course, quite conceivable that other people, if they had been in the room with me at the time, and had carried out the same experiment which I carried out, would have seen grey after-images *very like* one of those which I saw: there is no absurdity in supposing even that they might have seen after-images *exactly* like one of those which I saw. But there is an absurdity in supposing that any one of the after-images which I saw could also have been seen by anyone else: in supposing that two different people can ever see the very same after-image. One reason, then, why we should say that none of those grey after-images which I saw was "to be met with in space," although each of them was certainly "presented in space" to me, is simply that none of them could conceivably have been seen by anyone else. It is natural so to understand the phrase "to be met with in space," that to say of anything which a man perceived that it was to be met with in space is to say that it might have been perceived by *others* as well as by the man in question.

Negative after-images of the kind described are, therefore, one example of "things" which, though they must be allowed to be "presented in space," are nevertheless *not* "to be met with in space," and are *not* "external to our minds" in the sense with which we shall be concerned. And two other important examples may be given.

The first is this. It is well known that people sometimes see things double, an occurrence which has also been described by psychologists by saying that they have a "double image," or two "images," of some object at which they are looking. In such cases it would certainly be quite natural to say that each of the two "images" is "presented in space": they are seen,

one in one place, and the other in another, in just the same sense in which each of those grey after-images which I saw was seen at a particular place on the white background at which I was looking. But it would be utterly unnatural to say that, when I have a double image, each of the two images is "to be met with in space." On the contrary it is quite certain that *both* of them are not "to be met with in space." If both were, it would follow that somebody else might see the *very same* two images which I see; and, though there is no absurdity in supposing that another person might see a pair of images exactly similar to a pair which I see, there is an absurdity in supposing that anyone else might see the *same identical pair*. In every case, then, in which anyone sees anything double, we have an example of at least one "thing" which, though "presented in space" is certainly not "to be met with in space."

And the second important example is this. Bodily pains can, in general, be quite properly said to be "presented in space." When I have a toothache, I feel it *in* a particular region of my jaw or *in* a particular tooth; when I make a cut on my finger smart by putting iodine on it, I feel the pain in a particular place in my finger; and a man whose leg has been amputated may feel a pain *in* a place where his foot might have been if he had not lost it. It is certainly perfectly natural to understand the phrase "presented in space" in such a way that if, in the sense illustrated, a pain is felt *in* a particular place, that pain is "presented in space." And yet of pains it would be quite unnatural to say that they are "to be met with in space," for the same reason as in the case of after-images or double images. It is quite conceivable that another person should feel a pain exactly like one which I feel, but there is an absurdity in supposing that he could feel *numerically the same** pain which I feel. And pains are in fact a typical example of the sort of "things" of which philosophers say that they are *not* "external" to our minds, but "within" them. Of any pain which I feel they would say that it is necessarily *not* external to my mind but *in* it.

And finally it is, I think, worth while to mention one other class of "things," which are certainly not "external" objects and certainly not "to be met with in space," in the sense with which I am concerned, but which yet some philosophers would be inclined to

---

* One and the same, self-identical with.

say are "presented in space," though they are not "presented in space" in quite the same sense in which pains, double images, and negative after-images of the sort I described are so. If you look at an electric light and then close your eyes, it sometimes happens that you see, for some little time, against the dark background which you usually see when your eyes are shut, a bright patch similar in shape to the light at which you have just been looking. Such a bright patch, if you see one, is another example of what some psychologists have called "after-images" and others "after-sensations"; but, unlike the negative after-images of which I spoke before, it is seen when your eyes are shut. Of such an after-image, seen with closed eyes, some philosophers might be inclined to say that this image too was "presented in space," although it is certainly not "to be met with in space." They would be inclined to say that it is "presented in space," because it certainly is presented as at some little distance from the person who is seeing it: and how can a thing be presented as at some little distance from me, without being "presented in space"? Yet there is an important difference between such after-images, seen with closed eyes, and after-images of the sort I previously described—a difference which might lead other philosophers to deny that these after-images, seen with closed eyes, are "presented in space" at all. It is a difference which can be expressed by saying that when your eyes are shut, you are not seeing any part of *physical* space at all—of the space which is referred to when we talk of "things which are to be met with in *space*." An after-image seen with closed eyes certainly is presented in *a* space, but it may be questioned whether it is proper to say that it is presented in *space*.

It is clear, then, I think, that by no means everything which can naturally be said to be "presented in space" can also be naturally said to be "a thing which is to be met with in space." Some of the "things," which are presented in space, are very emphatically *not* to be met with in space: or, to use another phrase, which may be used to convey the same notion, they are emphatically *not* "physical realities" at all. The conception "presented in space" is therefore, in one respect, much wider than the conception "to be met with in space": many "things" fall under the first conception which do not fall under the second—many after-images, one at least of the pair of "images" seen whenever anyone sees double, and most bodily pains, are "presented in space," though none of them are to be met with in space. From the

fact that a "thing" is presented in space, it by no means follows that it is to be met with in space. But just as the first conception is, in one respect, wider than the second, so, in another, the second is wider than the first. For there are many "things" to be met with in space, of which it is not true that they are presented in space. From the fact that a "thing" is to be met with in space, it by no means follows that it is presented in space. I have taken "to be met with in space" to imply, as I think it naturally may, that a "thing" *might be* perceived; but from the fact that a thing *might be* perceived, it does not follow that it is perceived; and if it is not actually perceived, then it will not be presented in space. It is characteristic of the sorts of "things," including shadows, which I have described as "to be met with in space," that there is no absurdity in supposing with regard to any one of them which is, at a given time, perceived, both (1) that it might have existed at that very time, without being perceived; (2) that it might have existed at another time, without being perceived at that other time; and (3) that during the whole period of its existence, it need not have been perceived at any time at all. There is, therefore, no absurdity in supposing that many things, which were at one time to be met with in space, never were "presented" at any time at all, and that many things which *are* to be met with in space now, are not now "presented" and also never were and never will be. To use a Kantian phrase, the conception of "things which are to be met with in space," embraces not only objects of actual experience, but also objects *of possible* experience; and from the fact that a thing is or was an object of *possible* experience, it by no means follows that it either was or is or will be "presented" at all.

I hope that what I have now said may have served to make clear enough what sorts of "things" I was originally referring to as "things outside us" or "things external to our minds." I said that I thought that Kant's phrase "things that are to be met with in space" indicated fairly clearly the sorts of "things" in question; and I have tried to make the range clearer still, by pointing out that this phrase only serves the purpose, if (*a*) you understand it in a sense, in which many "things," e.g., after-images, double images, bodily pains, which might be said to be "presented in space," are nevertheless *not* to be reckoned as "things that are to be met with in space," and (*b*) you realise clearly that there is no contradiction in supposing that there have been and are "to be met with in space" things which never have been, are not now, and never will be perceived, nor in supposing that among those of them which have at some time been perceived many existed at times at which they were not being perceived. I think it will now be clear to everyone that, since I do not reckon as "external things" after-images, double images, and bodily pains, I also should not reckon as "external things," any of the "images" which we often "see with the mind's eye" when we are awake, nor any of those which we see when we are asleep and dreaming; and also that I was so using the expression "external" that from the fact that a man was at a given time having a visual hallucination, it will follow that he was seeing at that time something which was *not* "external" to his mind, and from the fact that he was at a given time having an auditory hallucination, it will follow that he was at the time hearing a sound which was *not* "external" to his mind. But I certainly have not made my use of these phrases, "external to our minds" and "to be met with in space," so clear that in the case of every kind of "thing" which might be suggested, you would be able to tell at once whether I should or should not reckon it as "external to our minds" and "to be met with in space." For instance, I have said nothing which makes it quite clear whether a reflection which I see in a looking-glass is or is not to be regarded as "a thing that is to be met with in space" and "external to our minds," nor have I said anything which makes it quite clear whether the sky is or is not to be so regarded. In the case of the sky, everyone, I think, would feel that it was quite inappropriate to talk of it as "a thing that is to be met with in space"; and most people, I think, would feel a strong reluctance to affirm, without qualification, that reflections which people see in looking-glasses are "to be met with in space." And yet neither the sky nor reflections seen in mirrors are in the same position as bodily pains or after-images in the respect which I have emphasised as a reason for saying of these latter that they are *not* to be met with in space—namely that there is an absurdity in supposing that *the very same* pain which I feel could be felt by someone else or that *the very same* after-image which I see could be seen by someone else. In the case of reflections in mirrors we should quite naturally, in certain circumstances, use language which implies that another person may see the same reflection which we

see. We might quite naturally say to a friend: "Do you see that reddish reflection in the water there? I can't make out what it's a reflection of," just as we might say, pointing to a distant hill-side: "Do you see that white speck on the hill over there? I can't make out what it is." And in the case of the sky, it is quite obviously *not* absurd to say that other people see it as well as I.

It must, therefore, be admitted that I have not made my use of the phrase "things to be met with in space," nor therefore that of "external to our minds," which the former was used to explain, so clear that in the case of every kind of "thing" which may be mentioned, there will be no doubt whatever as to whether things of that kind are or are not "to be met with in space" or "external to our minds." But this lack of a clear-cut definition of the expression "things that are to be met with in space," does not, so far as I can see, matter for my present purpose. For my present purpose it is, I think, sufficient if I make clear, in the case of many kinds of things, that I am so using the phrase "things that are to be met with in space," that, in the case of each of these kinds, from the proposition that there are things of that kind it *follows* that there are things to be met with in space. And I have, in fact, given a list (though by no means an exhaustive one) of kinds of things which are related to my use of the expression "things that are to be met with in space" in this way. I mentioned among others the bodies of men and of animals, plants, stars, houses, chairs, and shadows; and I want now to emphasise that I am so using "things to be met with in space" that, in the case of each of these kinds of "things," from the proposition that there are "things" of that kind it *follows* that there are things to be met with in space: e.g., from the proposition that there are plants or that plants exist it *follows* that there are things to be met with in space, from the proposition that shadows exist, it *follows* that there are things to be met with in space, and so on, in the case of all the kinds of "things" which I mentioned in my first list. That this should be clear is sufficient for my purpose, because, if it is clear, then it will also be clear that, as I implied before, if you have proved that two plants exist, or that a plant and a dog exist, or that a dog and a shadow exist, etc., etc., you will *ipso facto** have proved that there are things to be met with in space: you will not require *also*

---

* (Latin): "by that very fact," "by the fact itself."

to give a separate proof that from the proposition that there are plants it *does* follow that there are things to be met with in space.

Now with regard to the expression "things that are to be met with in space" I think it will readily be believed that I may be using it in a sense such that no proof is required that from "plants exist" there follows "there are things to be met with in space"; but with regard to the phrase "things external to our minds" I think the case is different. People may be inclined to say: "I can see quite clearly that from the proposition 'At least two dogs exist at the present moment' there *follows* the proposition 'At least two things are to be met with in space at the present moment,' so that if you can prove that there are two dogs in existence at the present moment you will *ipso facto* have proved that two things at least are to be met with in space at the present moment. I can see that you do not also require a separate proof that from 'Two dogs exist' 'Two things are to be met with in space' *does* follow; it is quite obvious that there couldn't be a dog which wasn't to be met with in space. But it is not by any means so clear to me that if you can prove that there are two dogs or two shadows, you will *ipso facto* have proved that there are two things *external to our minds*. Isn't it possible that a dog, though it certainly must be 'to be met with in space,' might *not* be an external object—an object external to our minds? Isn't a separate proof required that anything that is to be met with in space must be external to our minds? Of course, if you are using 'external' as a mere synonym for 'to be met with in space,' no proof will be required that dogs are external objects: in that case, if you can prove that two dogs exist, you will *ipso facto* have proved that there are some external things. But I find it difficult to believe that you, or anybody else, do really use 'external' as a mere synonym for 'to be met with in space'; and if you don't, isn't some proof required that whatever is to be met with in space must be external to our minds?"

Now Kant, as we saw, asserts that the phrases "outside of us" or "external" are in fact used in two very different senses; and with regard to one of these two senses, that which he calls the "transcendental" sense, and which he tries to explain by saying that it is a sense in which "external" means "existing *as a thing in itself* distinct from us," it is notorious that he himself held that things which are to be met with in space are *not* "external" in that sense.* There is, therefore, according to him, *a* sense of "external," a sense in which the word has been commonly used by philosophers—such that, if "external" be used in that sense, then from the proposition "Two dogs exist" it will *not* follow that there are some external things. What this supposed sense is I do not think that Kant himself ever succeeded in explaining clearly; nor do I know of any reason for supposing that philosophers ever have used "external" in a sense, such that in *that* sense things that are to be met with in space are *not* external. But how about the other sense, in which, according to Kant, the word "external" has been commonly used—that which he calls "empirically external"? How is this conception related to the conception "to be met with in space"? It may be noticed that, in the passages which I quoted (A373), Kant himself does not tell us at all clearly what he takes to be the proper answer to this question. He only makes the rather odd statement that, in order to remove all uncertainty as to the conception "empirically external," he will distinguish objects to which it applies from those which might be called "external" in the transcendental sense, by "calling them outright things which are *to be met with in space*." These odd words certainly suggest, as one possible interpretation of them, that in Kant's opinion the conception "empirically external" is *identical* with the conception "to be met with in space"—that he does think that "external," when used in this second sense, is a mere synonym for "to be met with in space." But, if this is his meaning, I do find it very difficult to believe that he is right. Have philosophers, in fact, ever used "external" as a mere synonym for "to be met with in space"? Does he himself do so?

I do not think they have, nor that he does himself; and, in order to explain how they have used it, and how the two conceptions "external to our minds" and "to be met with in space" are related to one another, I

---

* Basically, this is because, for Kant, the things we "meet with in space" are always *appearances* of things, rather than "things in themselves" (the hidden nature behind those appearances). That is, we never meet with "things in themselves" in space, so if *those* things are what we mean by "the things external to us" then none of the things which we *do* meet with in space could be external. See the notes to the Kant selection in this section for more information.

think it is important expressly to call attention to a fact which hitherto I have only referred to incidentally: namely the fact that those who talk of certain things as "external to" our minds, do, in general, as we should naturally expect, talk of other "things," with which they wish to contrast the first, as "in" our minds. It has, of course, been often pointed out that when "in" is thus used, followed by "my mind," "your mind," "his mind," etc., "in" is being used metaphorically. And there are some metaphorical uses of "in," followed by such expressions, which occur in common speech, and which we all understand quite well. For instance, we all understand such expressions as "I had you in mind, when I made that arrangement" or "I had you in mind, when I said that there are some people who can't bear to touch a spider." In these cases "I was thinking of you" can be used to mean the same as "I had you in mind." But it is quite certain that this particular metaphorical use of "in" is not the one in which philosophers are using it when they contrast what is "in" my mind with what is "external" to it. On the contrary, in their use of "external," you will be external to my mind even at a moment when I have you in mind. If we want to discover what this peculiar metaphorical use of "*in* my mind" is, which is such that nothing, which is, in the sense we are now concerned with, "external" to my mind, can ever be "in" it, we need, I think, to consider instances of the sort of "things" which they would say are "in" my mind in this special sense. I have already mentioned three such instances, which are, I think, sufficient for my present purpose: any bodily pain which I feel, any after-image which I see with my eyes shut, and any image which I "see" when I am asleep and dreaming, are typical examples of the sort of "thing" of which philosophers have spoken as "*in* my mind." And there is no doubt, I think, that when they have spoken of such things as my body, a sheet of paper, a star—in short "physical objects" generally—as "external," they have meant to emphasize some important difference which they feel to exist between such things as these and such "things" as a pain, an after-image seen with closed eyes, and a dream-image. But *what* difference? What difference do they feel to exist between a bodily pain which I feel or an after-image which I see with closed eyes, on the one hand, and my body itself, on the other—what difference which leads them to say that whereas the bodily pain and the after-image are "in" my mind, my body itself is

not "in" my mind—not even when I am feeling it and seeing it or thinking of it? I have already said that one difference which there is between the two, is that my body is to be met with in space, whereas the bodily pain and the after-image are not. But I think it would be quite wrong to say that this is *the* difference which has led philosophers to speak of the two latter as "in" my mind, and of my body as *not* "in" my mind.

The question what the difference is which has led them to speak in this way, is not, I think, at all an easy question to answer; but I am going to try to give, in brief outline, what I *think* is a right answer.

It should, I think, be noted, first of all, that the use of the word "mind," which is being adopted when it is said that any bodily pains which I feel are "in my mind," is one which is not quite in accordance with any usage common in ordinary speech, although we are very familiar with it in philosophy. Nobody, I think, would say that bodily pains which I feel are "in my mind," unless he was also prepared to say that it is *with* my mind that I feel bodily pains; and to say this latter is, I think, not quite in accordance with common non-philosophic usage. It is natural enough to say that it is with my mind that I remember, and think, and imagine, and feel *mental* pains—e.g., disappointment, but not, I think, quite so natural to say that it is with my mind that I feel *bodily* pains, e.g., a severe headache; and perhaps even less natural to say that it is with my mind that I see and hear and smell and taste. There is, however, a well-established philosophical usage according to which seeing, hearing, smelling, tasting, and having a bodily pain are just as much *mental* occurrences or processes as are remembering, or thinking, or imagining. This usage was, I think, adopted by philosophers, because they saw a real resemblance between such statements as "I saw a cat," "I heard a clap of thunder," "I smelt a strong smell of onions," "My finger smarted horribly," on the one hand, and such statements as "I remembered having seen him," "I was thinking out a plan of action," "I pictured the scene to myself," "I felt bitterly disappointed," on the other—a resemblance which puts all these statements in one class together, as contrasted with other statements in which "I" or "my" is used, such as, e.g., "I was less than four feet high," "I was lying on my back," "My hair was very long." What is the resemblance in question? It is a resemblance which might be expressed by saying that all the first eight statements are the sort of statements which furnish data for psychology, while the three latter are not. It is also a resemblance which may be expressed, in a way now common among philosophers, by saying that in the case of all the first eight statements, if we make the statement more specific by adding a date, we get a statement such that, if it is true, then it *follows* that I was "having an experience" at the date in question, whereas this does not hold for the three last statements. For instance, if it is true that I saw a cat between 12 noon and 5 minutes past, today, it *follows* that I was "having some experience" between 12 noon and 5 minutes past, today; whereas from the proposition that I was less than four feet high in December 1877, it does not *follow* that I had any experiences in December 1877. But this philosophic use of "having an experience" is one which itself needs explanation, since it is not identical with any use of the expression that is established in common speech. An explanation, however, which is, I think, adequate for the purpose, can be given by saying that a philosopher, who was following this usage, would say that I was at a given time "having an experience" if and only if either (1) I was conscious at the time or (2) I was dreaming at the time or (3) something else was true of me at the time, which resembled what is true of me when I am conscious and when I am dreaming, in a certain very obvious respect in which what is true of me when I am dreaming resembles what is true of me when I am conscious, and in which what would be true of me, if at any time, for instance, I had a vision, would resemble both. This explanation is, of course, in some degree vague; but I think it is clear enough for our purpose. It amounts to saying that, in this philosophic usage of "having an experience," it would be said of me that I was, at a given time, having *no* experience, if I was at the time neither conscious nor dreaming nor having a vision nor *anything else of the sort*; and, of course, this is vague in so far as it has not been specified what else would be *of the sort*: this is left to be gathered from the instances given. But I think this is sufficient: often at night when I am asleep, I am neither conscious nor dreaming nor having a vision nor *anything else of the sort*—that is to say, I am having no experiences. If this explanation of this philosophic usage of "having an experience" is clear enough, then I think that what has been meant by saying that any pain which I feel or any after-image which I see with my eyes closed is "*in my*

mind," can be explained by saying that what is meant is neither more nor less than that there would be a contradiction in supposing *that very same pain* or *that very same after-image* to have existed at a time at which I was having no experience; or, in other words, that from the proposition, with regard to any time, that *that* pain or *that* after-image existed at that time, it *follows* that I was having some experience at the time in question. And if so, then we can say that the felt difference between bodily pains which I feel and after-images which I see, on the one hand, and my body on the other, which has led philosophers to say that any such pain or after-image is "*in my mind*," whereas my body *never* is but is always "outside of" or "external to" my mind, is just this, that whereas there is a contradiction in supposing a pain which I feel or an after-image which I see to exist at a time when I am having no experience, there is no contradiction in supposing my body to exist at a time when I am having no experience; and we can even say, I think, that just this and nothing more is what they have meant by these puzzling and misleading phrases "in my mind" and "external to my mind."

But now, if to say of anything, e.g., my body, that it is external to my mind, means merely that from a proposition to the effect that it existed at a specified time, there in no case follows the further proposition that I was having an experience at the time in question, then to say of anything that it is external to *our* minds, will mean similarly that from a proposition to the effect that it existed at a specified time, it in no case follows that any of us were having experiences at the time in question. And if by *our* minds be meant, as is, I think, usually meant, the minds of human beings living on the earth, then it will follow that any pains which animals may feel, any after-images they may see, any experiences they may have, though not external to *their* minds, yet are external to *ours*. And this at once makes plain how different is the conception "external to our minds" from the conception "to be met with in space"; for, of course, pains which animals feel or after-images which they see are no more to be met with in space than are pains which *we* feel or after-images which *we* see. From the proposition that there are external objects—objects that are not in any of *our* minds, it does *not* follow that there are things to be met with in space; and hence "external to our minds" is not a mere synonym for "to be met with in space": that is to say, "external to our minds" and "to be met with in space" are two different conceptions. And the true relation between these conceptions seems to me to be this. We have already seen that there are ever so many kinds of "things," such that, in the case of each of these kinds, from the proposition that there is at least one thing of that kind there *follows* the proposition that there is at least one thing to be met with in space: e.g., this follows from "There is at least one star," from "There is at least one human body," from "There is at least one shadow," etc. And I think we can say that of every kind of thing of which this is true, it is also true that from the proposition that there is at least one "thing" of that kind there *follows* the proposition that there is at least one thing external to our minds: e.g., from "There is at least one star" there follows not only "There is at least one thing to be met with in space" but also "There is at least one external thing," and similarly in all other cases. My reason for saying this is as follows. Consider any kind of thing, such that anything of that kind, if there is anything of it, must be "to be met with in space": e.g., consider the kind "soap-bubble." If I say of anything which I am perceiving, "That is a soap-bubble," I am, it seems to me, certainly implying that there would be no contradiction in asserting that it existed before I perceived it and that it will continue to exist, even if I cease to perceive it. This seems to me to be part of what is meant by saying that it is a real soap-bubble, as distinguished, for instance, from an hallucination of a soap-bubble. Of course, it by no means follows, that if it really is a soap-bubble, it did in fact exist before I perceived it or will continue to exist after I cease to perceive it: soap-bubbles are an example of a kind of "physical object" and "thing to be met with in space," in the case of which it is notorious that particular specimens of the kind often do exist only so long as they are perceived by a particular person. But a thing which I perceive would not be a soap-bubble unless its existence at any given time were logically *independent* of my perception of it at that time; unless that is to say, from the proposition, with regard to a particular time, that it existed at that time, it *never* follows that I perceived it at that time. But, if it is true that it would not be a soap-bubble, unless it *could* have existed at any given time without being perceived by me at that time, it is certainly also true that it would not be a soap-bubble, unless it *could* have existed at any given time, without its being true that I was having any experience

of any kind at the time in question: it would not be a soap-bubble, unless, whatever time you take, from the proposition that it existed at that time it does *not* follow that I was having any experience at that time. That is to say, from the proposition with regard to anything which I am perceiving that it is a soap-bubble, *follows* the proposition that it is external to *my* mind. But if, when I say that anything which I perceive is a soap-bubble, I am implying that it is external to *my* mind, I am, I think, certainly also implying that it is also external to all other minds: I am implying that it is not a thing of a sort such that things of that sort can only exist at a time when somebody is having an experience. I think, therefore, that from any proposition of the form "There's a soap-bubble!" there does really *follow* the proposition "There's an external object!" "There's an object external to all our minds!" And, if this is true of the kind "soap-bubble," it is certainly also true of any other kind (including the kind "unicorn") which is such that, if there are any things of that kind, it follows that there are *some* things to be met with in space.

I think, therefore, that in the case of all kinds of "things," which are such that if there is a pair of things, both of which are of one of these kinds, or a pair of things one of which is of one of them and one of them of another, then it will follow at once that there are some things to be met with in space, it is true also that if I can prove that there are a pair of things, one of which is of one of these kinds and another of another, or a pair both of which are of one of them, then I shall have proved *ipso facto* that there are at least two "things outside of us." That is to say, if I can prove that there exist now both a sheet of paper and a human hand, I shall have proved that there are now "things outside of us"; if I can prove that there exist now both a shoe and sock, I shall have proved that there are now "things outside of us," etc.; and similarly I shall have proved it, if I can prove that there exist now two sheets of paper, or two human hands, or two shoes, or two socks, etc. Obviously, then, there are thousands of different things such that, if, at any time, I can prove any one of them, I shall have proved the existence of things outside of us. Cannot I prove any of these things?

It seems to me that, so far from its being true, as Kant declares to be his opinion, that there is only one possible proof of the existence of things outside of us, namely the one which he has given, I can now give a large number of different proofs, each of which is a perfectly rigorous proof; and that at many other times I have been in a position to give many others. I can prove now, for instance, that two human hands exist. How? By holding up my two hands, and saying, as I make a certain gesture with the right hand, "Here is one hand," and adding, as I make a certain gesture with the left, "and here is another." And if, by doing this, I have proved *ipso facto* the existence of external things, you will all see that I can also do it now in numbers of other ways: there is no need to multiply examples.

But did I prove just now that two human hands were then in existence? I do want to insist that I did; that the proof which I gave was a perfectly rigorous one; and that it is perhaps impossible to give a better or more rigorous proof of anything whatever. Of course, it would not have been a proof unless three conditions were satisfied; namely (1) unless the premiss which I adduced as proof of the conclusion was different from the conclusion I adduced it to prove; (2) unless the premiss which I adduced was something which I *knew* to be the case, and not merely something which I believed but which was by no means certain, or something which, though in fact true, I did not know to be so; and (3) unless the conclusion did really follow from the premiss. But all these three conditions were in fact satisfied by my proof. (1) The premiss which I adduced in proof was quite certainly different from the conclusion, for the conclusion was merely "Two human hands exist at this moment"; but the premiss was something far more specific than this—something which I expressed by showing you my hands, making certain gestures, and saying the words "Here is one hand, and here is another." It is quite obvious that the two were different, because it is quite obvious that the conclusion might have been true, even if the premiss had been false. In asserting the premiss I was asserting much more than I was asserting in asserting the conclusion. (2) I certainly did at the moment *know* that which I expressed by the combination of certain gestures with saying the words "There is one hand and here is another." I *knew* that there was one hand in the place indicated by combining a certain gesture with my first utterance of "here" and that there was another in the different place indicated by combining a certain gesture with my second utterance of "here." How absurd it would be to suggest that I did not know it, but only believed it, and that perhaps it was not the case! You might as well suggest that I do not know that

I am now standing up and talking—that perhaps after all I'm not, and that it's not quite certain that I am! And finally (3) it is quite certain that the conclusion did follow from the premiss. This is as certain as it is that if there is one hand here and another here *now*, then it follows that there are two hands in existence *now*.

My proof, then, of the existence of things outside of us did satisfy three of the conditions necessary for a rigorous proof. Are there any other conditions necessary for a rigorous proof, such that perhaps it did not satisfy one of them? Perhaps there may be; I do not know; but I do want to emphasise that, so far as I can see, we all of us do constantly take proofs of this sort as absolutely conclusive proofs of certain conclusions—as finally settling certain questions, as to which we were previously in doubt. Suppose, for instance, it were a question whether there were as many as three misprints on a certain page in a certain book. A says there are, B is inclined to doubt it. How could A prove that he is right? Surely he *could* prove it by taking the book, turning to the page, and pointing to three separate places on it, saying "There's one misprint here, another here, and another here": surely that is a method by which it *might* be proved! Of course, A would not have proved, by doing this, that there were at least three misprints on the page in question, unless it was certain that there was a misprint in each of the places to which he pointed. But to say that he *might* prove it in this way, is to say that it *might* be certain that there was. And if such a thing as that could ever be certain, then assuredly it was certain just now that there was one hand in one of the two places I indicated and another in the other.

I did, then, just now, give a proof that there were *then* external objects; and obviously, if I did, I could *then* have given many other proofs of the same sort that there were external objects *then*, and could now give many proofs of the same sort that there are external objects *now*.

But, if what I am asked to do is to prove that external objects have existed in *the past*, then I can give many different proofs of this also, but proofs which are in important respects of a different *sort* from those just given. And I want to emphasise that, when Kant says it is a scandal not to be able to give a proof of the existence of external objects, a proof of their existence in the past would certainly *help* to remove the scandal of which he is speaking. He says that, if it occurs to anyone to question their existence, we ought to be able to confront him with a satisfactory proof. But by a person who questions their existence, he certainly means not merely a person who questions whether any exist at the moment of speaking, but a person who questions whether any have *ever* existed; and a proof that some have existed in the past would certainly therefore be relevant to *part* of what such a person is questioning. How then can I prove that there have been external objects in the past? Here is one proof. I can say: "I held up two hands above this desk not very long ago; therefore two hands existed not very long ago; therefore at least two external objects have existed at some time in the past, QED."* This is a perfectly good proof, provided I *know* what is asserted in the premiss. But I do know that I held up two hands above this desk not very long ago. As a matter of fact, in this case you all know it too. There's no doubt whatever that I did. Therefore I have given a perfectly conclusive proof that external objects have existed in the past; and you will all see at once that, if this is a conclusive proof, I could have given many others of the same sort, and could now give many others. But it is also quite obvious that this sort of proof differs in important respects from the sort of proof I gave just now that there were two hands existing *then*.

I have, then, given two conclusive proofs of the existence of external objects. The first was a proof that two human hands existed at the time when I gave the proof; the second was a proof that two human hands had existed at a time previous to that at which I gave the proof. These proofs were of a different sort in important respects. And I pointed out that I could have given, then, many other conclusive proofs of both sorts. It is also obvious that I could give many others of both sorts now. So that, if these are the sort of proof that is wanted, nothing is easier than to prove the existence of external objects.

But now I am perfectly well aware that, in spite of all that I have said, many philosophers will still feel that I have not given any satisfactory proof of the point in question. And I want briefly, in conclusion, to say something as to why this dissatisfaction with my proofs should be felt.

One reason why, is, I think, this. Some people understand "proof of an external world" as including a proof of things which I haven't attempted to prove and haven't proved. It is not quite easy to say *what* it is that they want proved—*what* it is that is such that unless they got a proof of it, they would not say that they had a proof of the existence of external things; but I can make an approach to explaining what they want by saying that if I had proved the propositions which I used as *premisses* in my two proofs, then they would perhaps admit that I had proved the existence of external things, but, in the absence of such a proof (which, of course, I have neither given nor attempted to give), they will say that I have not given what they mean by a proof of the existence of external things. In other words, they want a proof of what I assert *now* when I hold up my hands and say "Here's one hand and here's another"; and, in the other case, they want a proof of what I assert *now* when I say "I did hold up two hands above this desk just now." Of course, what they really want is not merely a proof of these two propositions, but something like a general statement as to how *any* propositions of this sort may be proved. This, of course, I haven't given; and I do not believe it can be given: if this is what is meant by proof of the existence of external things, I do not believe that any proof of the existence of external things is possible. Of course, in some cases what might be called a proof of propositions which seem like these can be got. If one of you suspected that one of my hands was artificial he might be said to get a proof of my proposition "Here's one hand, and here's another," by coming up and examining the suspected hand close up, perhaps touching and pressing it, and so establishing that it really was a human hand. But I do not believe that any proof is possible in nearly all cases. How am I to prove now that "Here's one hand, and here's another"? I do not believe I can do it. In order to do it, I should need to prove for one thing, as Descartes pointed out, that I am not now dreaming. But how can I prove that I am not? I have, no doubt, conclusive reasons for asserting that I am not now dreaming; I have conclusive evidence that I am awake: but that is a very different thing from being able to prove it. I could not tell you what all my evidence is; and I should require to do this at least, in order to give you a proof.

---

*   *Quod erat demonstrandum* (Latin): "which was to be demonstrated."

But another reason why some people would feel dissatisfied with my proofs is, I think, not merely that they want a proof of something which I haven't proved, but that they think that, if I cannot give such extra proofs, then the proofs that I have given are not conclusive proofs at all. And this, I think, is a definite mistake. They would say: "If you cannot prove your premiss that here is one hand and here is another, then you do not know it. But you yourself have admitted that, if you did not know it, then your proof was not conclusive. Therefore your proof was not, as you say it was, a conclusive proof." This view that, if I cannot prove such things as these, I do not know them, is, I think, the view that Kant was expressing in the sentence which I quoted at the beginning of this lecture, when he implies that so long as we have no proof of the existence of external things, their existence must be accepted merely on *faith*. He means to say, I think, that if I cannot prove that there is a hand here, I must accept it merely as a matter of faith—I cannot know it. Such a view, though it has been very common among philosophers, can, I think, be shown to be wrong—though shown only by the use of premisses which are not known to be true, unless we do know of the existence of external things. I can know things, which I cannot prove; and among things which I certainly did know, even if (as I think) I could not prove them, were the premisses of my two proofs. I should say, therefore, that those, if any, who are dissatisfied with these proofs merely on the ground that I did not know their premisses, have no good reason for their dissatisfaction. ■

Suggestions for Critical Reflection

1. Do you think Moore is attempting to refute philosophical skepticism in this paper, or do you think he might be trying to do something slightly different or more focused? Does his proof of the existence of the external world, if it works, show that skepticism must be false? Do you think Moore even takes the possibility of skepticism *seriously*? (And if not, should he?)

2. Do you think that Moore manages to prove that the things which are "to be met with in space" (such as shrubbery or furniture) *must* be "external to our minds"? And even if he does that, does he also show that trees and tables must be external to *any* mind at all (even God's)?

3. How, if at all, does Moore *justify* his claim that he knows his hands exist? Is this a good enough justification (at least, good enough for what Moore is trying to do)?

4. In a lecture at the University of Michigan, Moore pointed overhead, and claimed that the existence of that skylight was an example of a common-sense belief that was undeniably certain. At this claim, his audience stirred and murmured: they knew that the "skylight" in Hill Auditorium was a painted illusion. Is there a moral in this anecdote about Moore's methodology?

5. Moore's defense of his final proof that objects exist in the external world may depend upon making a distinction between proving something and proving *that one knows* that thing. Do you think this is a viable distinction? Put it this way: could someone know *p* without knowing that they know *p*?

Note

1 B xxxix, note: Kemp Smith, p. 34. The German words are "so bleibt es immer ein Skandal der Philosophie ..., das Dasein der Dinge ausser uns ..., bloss auf *Glauben* annehmen zu müssen, und wenn es jemand einfällt es zu bezweifeln, ihm keinen genugtuenden Beweis entgegenstellen zu können."

EDMUND L. GETTIER

Is Justified True Belief Knowledge?

Who Is Edmund Gettier?

Edmund Gettier's career has been one of the most unusual in contemporary academic philosophy. His first teaching job was at Wayne State University, in Detroit, Michigan. During the early sixties, the chair of his department suggested that, as tenure consideration approached, some publication might help. The result was "Is Justified True Belief Knowledge?" This article took up all of three pages of a 1963 issue of *Analysis*, but it's the best-known article ever published in epistemology. All Gettier did there was present two examples, but these two showed that the most basic assumption of epistemology since Plato was wrong. Eminent philosopher David Lewis cited Gettier and Gödel as perhaps the only thinkers ever who conclusively refuted a philosophical theory.*

Opinions differ on the extent of the remainder of Gettier's publication dossier. One of his friends thinks there's a second article in print; another believes there are two additional articles.† The Philosopher's Index lists only two others, both translations; the title listed for one of these, clearly translated into Hungarian and back, is "If Knowledge Is a Justified True Belief?"‡

But Gettier has not been relaxing since his career began in the late 1950s. His friends agree that, coupled with his "massive indifference to the usual trappings of an academic career," Gettier has shown an "abiding, deep commitment to philosophy."§ Colleagues and students have enjoyed decades of energetic, creative philosophical interchange. In 1967 Gettier moved to the University of Massachusetts, Amherst, where he is now Professor Emeritus.

What Was Gettier's Overall Philosophical Project?

Gettier attacks a widely-accepted analysis of the concept of *knowledge*. The analysis of knowledge Gettier attacks is the claim that the necessary and sufficient conditions for S (a subject) knowing that P (a proposition) are that (a) P is true; (b) S believes P; and (c) S has justification for this belief.

What Is the Structure of This Reading?

Gettier begins with two assumptions. The first is that one can have justification for believing something that's false.

A tiny bit of background in logic is necessary to understand the second. Logicians say that a statement P is *entailed* by another statement Q when it's logically impossible for P to be false given the truth of Q. So, for example, *The picnic is off* is entailed by *It's raining* and *If it's raining, the picnic is off*.

Gettier's second assumption is that whenever P is entailed by Q, and a person believes Q, and is justified in this belief, and deduces P from Q, and accepts P on this basis, then that person is justified in believing P. Suppose, for example, you believe, with good justification, that it's raining and if it's raining, the picnic is off. And so you deduce from this, and accordingly believe, that the picnic is off. According to Gettier's second assumption, you're justified in believing that the picnic is off.

The second assumption seems quite reasonable. After all, the fact that one's belief that Q is justified means that you'd count Q as likely to be true; and the fact that

---

*   *Philosophical Papers*, Vol. I (Oxford University Press, 1983), x.

†   The first opinion is from Robert C. Sleigh, Jr., "Knowing Edmund Gettier," *Philosophical Analysis: A Defense by Example*, ed. David F. Austin (Kluwer, 1987), xiv; the second is from Austin's Preface to that book, xii.

‡   *Magyar Filozofiai Szemle*, nos. 1–2 (1995), 231–33.

§   Sleigh, xiii.

Q entails P means that P is likely to be true also; so you'd also be justified in believing P.

Applying these reasonable assumptions to Smith's belief in each of Gettier's two examples, we'd conclude that Smith is justified in his belief in both cases. Since both beliefs are true, they should count as knowledge, under the traditional analysis of knowledge as justified true belief; but in neither case would we agree that Smith's true beliefs are knowledge.

There has been an enormous amount of discussion in print concerning what to do about Gettier's examples (and other similar sorts of examples, known as Gettier-type cases). Some philosophers have tried to propose a theory of justification that would better account for our judgments about the beliefs of Smith (and the believers in other Gettier-type cases). Others have argued that what's needed is that an additional condition (aside from justified true belief) be added for the correct analysis of knowledge.

Some Useful Background Information

1. In Gettier's time, but less frequently nowadays, philosophers believed their job (or one of them) was to provide analyses of concepts; an analysis, in this sense, provides the conditions for the concept's application, and it was generally thought that the ideal analysis of any concept would provide a list of *necessary* and *sufficient* application conditions.

   The *necessary conditions* for the application of a concept are those such that if something doesn't meet those conditions, the concept doesn't apply to it. Thus, for example, one of the necessary conditions for being someone's brother is being male. You can't be anyone's brother unless you're male. The sufficient conditions are those such that if something does meet these conditions, the concept does apply to it. Thus, being someone's male sibling is sufficient for the application of the concept *brother*. In this case, being someone's

male sibling is also necessary. So it's necessary and sufficient; and the successful analysis of the concept *brother* is given by providing this list of conditions which are each necessary and together sufficient: (a) male, (b) somebody's sibling.*

2. It's clear, and hardly needs argument, that believing P is necessary for knowing P. If you don't believe it, you wouldn't be said to know it. And the truth of P is another obvious necessary condition; your beliefs that are in fact false aren't knowledge, even though you think they are. The third necessary condition—that P be justified—needs a bit more explanation. This is added to distinguish between genuine knowledge and just a lucky guess. If S believes some true P merely because of a hunch, S's belief has no firm grounding, no justification, so it doesn't merit being called knowledge. When Fred wins the lottery, and says he knew he'd win, what he says is false. He may have been firmly convinced he'd win, but he had no justification for this, so he didn't know it. (Note that one may sometimes have justification for a false belief, when a large preponderance of evidence points toward it. But then it's not knowledge either.)

3. The places in Plato's writing Gettier mentions in a footnote, where Plato appears to suggest that knowledge is justified true belief, are these:

From Plato, *Theaetetus*†

SOCRATES: But, my friend, if true opinion and knowledge were the same thing in law courts, the best of judges could never have true opinion without knowledge; in fact, however, it appears that the two are different.

THEAETETUS: Oh yes, I remember now, Socrates, having heard someone make the distinction, but I had forgotten it. He said that knowledge was true opinion accompanied by reason, but that unreasoning true opinion was outside of the sphere of knowledge; and matters of which there is not a rational explanation are unknowable—yes, that is

---

* This is supposed to be a simple example of a conceptual analysis, but it's worth noticing that even in a case as elementary as this there are hidden complexities: What if the male-female gender binary is problematic? What does it mean to be a sibling—must this be a biological notion? Analysis is rarely as straightforward as it may initially seem.

† Both this and the following translation are from Benjamin Jowett.

what he called them—and those of which there is are knowable.

From Plato, *Meno*

SOCRATES: Well, and a person who had a right opinion as to which was the way, but had never been there and did not really know, might give right guidance, might he not?

MENO: Certainly.

SOCRATES: And so long, I presume, as he has right opinion about that which the other man really knows, he will be just as good a guide—if he thinks the truth instead of knowing it—as the man who has the knowledge.

MENO: Just as good.

SOCRATES: Hence true opinion is as good a guide to rightness of action as knowledge; and this is a point we omitted just now in our consideration of the nature of virtue, when we stated that knowledge is the only guide of right action; whereas we find there is also true opinion.

MENO: So it seems.

SOCRATES: Then right opinion is just as useful as knowledge.

MENO: With this difference, Socrates, that he who has knowledge will always hit on the right way, whereas he who has right opinion will sometimes do so, but sometimes not.

SOCRATES: How do you mean? Will not he who always has right opinion be always right, so long as he opines rightly?

MENO: It appears to me that he must; and therefore I wonder, Socrates, this being the case, that knowledge should ever be more prized than right opinion, and why they should be two distinct and separate things.

SOCRATES: Well, do you know why it is that you wonder, or shall I tell you?

MENO: Please tell me.

SOCRATES: It is because you have not observed with attention the images of Daedalus.* But perhaps there are none in your country.

MENO: What is the point of your remark?

SOCRATES: That if they are not fastened up they play truant and run away; but, if fastened, they stay where they are.

MENO: Well, what of that?

SOCRATES: To possess one of his works which is let loose does not count for much in value; it will not stay with you any more than a runaway slave: but when fastened up it is worth a great deal, for his productions are very fine things. And to what am I referring in all this? To true opinion. For these, so long as they stay with us, are a fine possession, and effect all that is good; but they do not care to stay for long, and run away out of the human soul, and thus are of no great value until one makes them fast with causal reasoning. And this process, friend Meno, is recollection,† as in our previous talk we have agreed. But when once they are fastened, in the first place they turn into knowledge, and in the second, are abiding. And this is why knowledge is more prized than right opinion: the one transcends the other by its trammels.

MENO: Upon my word, Socrates, it seems to be very much as you say.

---

* Socrates refers here to the legend that the first sculptor, Daedalus, put mechanisms inside his works that made them move.

† Socrates argues earlier in this dialogue that real knowledge comes from recollection of the general Forms of things encountered before birth.

Is Justified True Belief Knowledge?*

Various attempts have been made in recent years to state necessary and sufficient conditions for someone's knowing a given proposition. The attempts have often been such that they can be stated in a form similar to the following:[1]

(a) S knows that P   *IFF*[†]
   (i)   P is true,
   (ii)   S believes that P, and
   (iii)   S is justified in believing that P.

For example, Chisholm has held that the following gives the necessary and sufficient conditions for knowledge:[2]

(b) S knows that P   *IFF*
   (i)   S accepts P,
   (ii)   S has adequate evidence for P, and
   (iii)   P is true.

Ayer has stated the necessary and sufficient conditions for knowledge as follows:[3]

(c) S knows that P   *IFF*
   (i)   P is true,
   (ii)   S is sure that P is true, and
   (iii)   S has the right to be sure that P is true.

I shall argue that (a) is false in that the conditions stated therein do not constitute a *sufficient* condition for the truth of the proposition that S knows that P. The same argument will show that (b) and (c) fail if "has adequate evidence for" or "has the right to be sure that" is substituted for "is justified in believing that" throughout.

I shall begin by noting two points. First, in that sense of 'justified' in which S's being justified in believing P is a necessary condition of S's knowing that P, it is possible for a person to be justified in believing a proposition that is in fact false. Secondly, for any proposition P, if S is justified in believing P, and P entails Q, and S deduces Q from P and accepts Q as a result of this deduction, then S is justified in believing Q. Keeping these two points in mind, I shall now present two cases in which the conditions stated in (a) are true for some proposition, though it is at the same time false that the person in question knows that proposition.

Case I

Suppose that Smith and Jones have applied for a certain job. And suppose that Smith has strong evidence for the following conjunctive proposition:[‡]

(d) Jones is the man who will get the job, and Jones has ten coins in his pocket.

Smith's evidence for (d) might be that the president of the company assured him that Jones would in the end be selected, and that he, Smith, had counted the coins in Jones's pocket ten minutes ago. Proposition (d) entails:

(e) The man who will get the job has ten coins in his pocket.

Let us suppose that Smith sees the entailment from (d) to (e), and accepts (e) on the grounds of (d), for which he has strong evidence. In this case, Smith is clearly justified in believing that (e) is true.

But imagine, further, that unknown to Smith, he himself, not Jones, will get the job. And, also, unknown to Smith, he himself has ten coins in his pocket. Proposition (e) is then true, though proposition (d), from which Smith inferred (e), is false. In our example, then, all of the following are true: (*i*) (e) is true, (*ii*) Smith believes that (e) is true, and (*iii*) Smith is justified in believing that (e) is true. But it is equally

---

*   "Is Justified True Belief Knowledge?" *Analysis* 23 (June 1963): 121–23.
†   'IFF' is an abbreviation for 'If and only if.' 'X if and only if Y' means if X then Y, and if Y then X.
‡   A conjunctive proposition is a statement composed of two propositions connected by 'and.' "It's raining and it's Tuesday" is an example. A conjunctive proposition is true when both of its components are true; otherwise, it's false.

clear that Smith does not *know* that (e) is true; for (e) is true in virtue of the number of coins in Smith's pocket, while Smith does not know how many coins are in Smith's pocket, and bases his belief in (e) on a count of the coins in Jones's pocket, whom he falsely believes to be the man who will get the job.

Case II

Let us suppose that Smith has strong evidence for the following proposition:

(f)   Jones owns a Ford.

Smith's evidence might be that Jones has at all times in the past within Smith's memory owned a car, and always a Ford, and that Jones has just offered Smith a ride while driving a Ford. Let us imagine, now, that Smith has another friend, Brown, of whose whereabouts he is totally ignorant. Smith selects three place-names quite at random, and constructs the following three propositions:

(g)   Either Jones owns a Ford, or Brown is in Boston;

(h)   Either Jones owns a Ford, or Brown is in Barcelona;

(i)   Either Jones owns a Ford, or Brown is in Brest-Litovsk.

Each of these propositions is entailed by (f).* Imagine that Smith realizes the entailment of each of these propositions he has constructed by (f), and proceeds to accept (g), (h), and (i) on the basis of (f). Smith has correctly inferred (g), (h), and (i) from a proposition for which he has strong evidence. Smith is therefore completely justified in believing each of these three propositions. Smith, of course, has no idea where Brown is.

But imagine now that two further conditions hold. First, Jones does *not* own a Ford, but is at present driving a rented car. And secondly, by the sheerest coincidence, and entirely unknown to Smith, the place mentioned in proposition (h) happens really to be the place where Brown is. If these two conditions hold then Smith does *not* know that (h) is true, even though (*i*) (h) *is* true, (*ii*) Smith does believe that (h) is true, and (*iii*) Smith is justified in believing that (h) is true.

These two examples show that definition (a) does not state a *sufficient* condition for someone's knowing a given proposition. The same cases, with appropriate changes, will suffice to show that neither definition (b) nor definition (c) do so either. ■

Suggestions for Critical Reflection

1.   Sometimes you say, "I just know that …" when what you're saying is merely that you feel certain. But most philosophers would say that feeling certain that P is not a sufficient condition for knowing that P. Do you agree? Why or why not? Perhaps a more likely claim is that feeling certain that P is a necessary condition for knowing that P. Do you agree? Why or why not?

2.   One suggestion to deal with Gettier-type cases is to add an additional necessary condition to the traditional analysis: that S's belief not be the result of S's inference from a false belief. But consider this example: S believes that there are sheep in the field, and this is true; but what S in fact has seen is really a large furry dog. So S doesn't know there are sheep there. It's sometimes thought that there's no inference from a false belief in this case—why might this be, and do you agree? If so, why might this show the inadequacy of the current proposal?

3.   Another suggestion is that S's belief has to have been arrived at by a generally reliable method.

---

*   Note that a statement 'P' entails 'P or Q,' where 'Q' is any proposition at all. That's because a disjunctive proposition—one composed by connecting two component propositions with 'or'—is true when (at least) one of its components is true. So assuming that P is true, then it follows that P or anything-at-all must also be true.

But consider this example: S's watch has kept perfect time for years, so looking at her watch is a generally reliable way of finding out what time it is. Today, S looks at her watch at exactly 1 pm, and the watch shows 1:00. S believes correctly that it's 1 pm. But the watch stopped the previous night at 1 am. So S doesn't know that it's 1 pm. This is sometimes taken to show the inadequacy of this proposal—does it?

4. Here's a third troublesome Gettier-type case. S knows a barn when she sees one. But today, unbeknownst to her, she's traveling in an area where they're making a movie, and set designers have built a large number of barn-facades that look just like real barns from the road. By fortunate coincidence, S sees, however, what is the only real barn in the area, and believes (correctly) that there's a real barn there. Does S know that there's a (real) barn there? Is this true belief justified, given that S is an excellent barn-detector?

Notes

1   Plato seems to be considering some such definition at *Theaetetus* 201, and perhaps accepting one at *Meno* 98. [See "Some Useful Background Information" in the introduction to this reading.]

2   Roderick M. Chisholm, *Perceiving: A Philosophical Study* (Ithaca, NY: Cornell University Press, 1957), 16.

3   A.J. Ayer, *The Problem of Knowledge* (London: Macmillan, 1956), 34.

LORRAINE CODE

Is the Sex of the Knower Epistemologically Significant?

Who Is Lorraine Code?

Lorraine Code (1937–) is Distinguished Research Professor Emerita at York University, Toronto, Canada, and is a Fellow of the Royal Society of Canada. She received her undergraduate degree from Queen's University and her PhD from the University of Guelph, both in Ontario. The author or editor of 10 books and many papers, her main areas of interest are epistemology, ethics, feminist philosophy, gender studies, and the politics of knowledge. A key theme of her work over her distinguished career has been a multifaceted critique of the ways that apparently neutral knowledge claims are in fact political and ethical, and when unexamined often cause harm to people and the environment. For example, she has argued that traditional philosophical epistemology fails to acknowledge the role of social and political relations in the formation of knowledge, and because of this that it allows for and even encourages the exploitation of various groups of disempowered people, and of the natural world. Code was named the Distinguished Woman Philosopher for 2009 by the US Society for Women in Philosophy, and in 2016 she received the Ursula Franklin Award in Gender Studies.

How Important and Influential Is This Passage?

An idea which has moved from the fringes to the mainstream of philosophical ethics and social/political theory in the past few decades is *feminism*. The notion that women have, throughout history, been systematically subordinated and disparaged by male-dominated society—and that this immoral situation must be changed not only through the reform of social structures but also by adjustments to some of our most basic philosophical concepts and assumptions—was once controversial but is now widely accepted by the philosophical community. Thus, there is today a range of feminist projects to critique traditional ways of doing philosophy, and the present article illustrates one of these.

Feminist epistemology examines the assumptions which lie at the basis of traditional epistemology—such as that the ideal knower is perfectly rational and objective, or that the paradigm model for knowledge-acquisition is the scientific method—and subjects them to critical assessment from a feminist point of view. The central concept of feminist epistemology is that of a *situated knower*—and thus of situated knowledge: knowledge that reflects the particular perspectives of the subject—and a central feminist argument is that gender is a particularly important way of being situated. Code lays out these ideas in a clear and careful way.

Is the Sex of the Knower Epistemologically Significant?*

The Question

A question that focuses on the knower, as the title of this chapter does, claims that there are good reasons for asking who that knower is.[1] Uncontroversial as such a suggestion would be in ordinary conversations about knowledge, academic philosophers commonly treat 'the knower' as a featureless abstraction. Sometimes, indeed, she or he is merely a place holder in the proposition 'S knows that p'. Epistemological analyses of the proposition tend to focus on the 'knowing that', to determine conditions under which a knowledge claim can legitimately be made. Once discerned, it is believed, such conditions will hold across all possible utterances of the proposition. Indeed, throughout the history of modern philosophy the central 'problem of knowledge' has been to determine necessary and sufficient conditions for the possibility and justification of knowledge claims. Philosophers have sought ways of establishing a relation of correspondence between knowledge and 'reality' and/or ways of establishing the coherence of particular knowledge claims within systems of already-established truths. They have proposed methodologies for arriving at truth, and criteria for determining the validity of claims to the effect that 'S knows that p'. Such endeavors are guided by the putatively self-evident principle that truth once discerned, knowledge once established, claim their status as truth and knowledge by virtue of a grounding in or coherence within a permanent, objective, ahistorical, and circumstantially neutral framework or set of standards.

The question 'Who is S?' is regarded neither as legitimate nor as relevant in these endeavors. As inquirers into the nature and conditions of human knowledge, epistemologists commonly work from the assumption that they need concern themselves only with knowledge claims that meet certain standards of *purity*. Questions about the circumstances of knowledge acquisition serve merely to clutter and confuse the issue with contingencies and other impurities. The

question 'Who is S?' is undoubtedly such a question. If it matters who S is, then it must follow that something peculiar to S's character or nature could bear on the validity of the knowledge she or he claims: that S's *identity* might count among the conditions that make that knowledge claim possible. For many philosophers, such a suggestion would undermine the cherished assumption that knowledge can—and should—be evaluated on its own merits. More seriously still, a proposal that it matters who the knower is looks suspiciously like a move in the direction of epistemological relativism. For many philosophers, an endorsement of relativism signals the end of knowledge and of epistemology.

Broadly described, epistemological relativists hold that knowledge, truth, or even 'reality' can be understood only in relation to particular sets of cultural or social circumstances, to a theoretical framework, a specifiable range of perspectives, a conceptual scheme, or a form of life. Conditions of justification, criteria of truth and falsity, and standards of rationality are likewise relative: there is no universal, unchanging framework or scheme for rational adjudication among competing knowledge claims.

Critics of relativism often argue that relativism entails incommensurability: that a relativist cannot evaluate knowledge claims comparatively. This argument is based on the contention that epistemological relativism entails conceptual relativism: that it contextualizes language just as it contextualizes knowledge, so that there remains no 'common' or neutral linguistic framework for discussion, agreement, *or* disagreement. Other critics maintain that the very concept 'knowledge' is rendered meaningless by relativism: that the only honest—and logical—move a relativist can make is once and for all to declare her or his skepticism. Where there are no universal standards, the argument goes, there can be no knowledge worthy of the name. Opponents often contend that relativism is simply incoherent because of its inescapable self-referentiality.

---

* This is Chapter One of Lorraine Code's *What Can She Know? Feminist Theory and the Construction of Knowledge* (Cornell University Press, 1991), 1–26. Copyright © 1991 by Cornell University.

Relativism, they argue, is subject to the same constraints as every other claim to knowledge and truth. Any claim for the truth of relativism must itself be relative to the circumstances of the claimant; hence relativism itself has no claim to objective or universal truth. In short, relativism is often perceived as a denial of the very possibility of epistemology.[2]

Now posing the question 'Who is S?'—that is, 'Who is the knowing subject?'—does indeed count as a move in the direction of relativism, and my intention in posing it is to suggest that the answer has epistemological import. But I shall invoke certain caveats* to demonstrate that such a move is not the epistemological disaster that many theorists of knowledge believe it to be.

It is true that, on its starkest construal, relativism may threaten to slide into subjectivism, into a position for which knowledge claims are indistinguishable from expressions of personal opinion, taste, or bias. But relativism need not be construed so starkly, nor do its *limitations* warrant exclusive emphasis. There are advantages to endorsing a measure of epistemological relativism that make of it an enabling rather than a constraining position. By no means the least of these advantages is the fact that relativism is one of the more obvious means of avoiding reductive explanations, in terms of drastically simplified paradigms of knowledge, monolithic explanatory modes, or privileged, decontextualized positions. For a relativist, who contends that there can be many valid ways of knowing any phenomenon, there is the possibility of taking several constructions, many perspectives into account. Hence relativism keeps open a range of interpretive possibilities. At the same time, because of the epistemic choices it affirms, it creates stringent accountability requirements of which knowers have to be cognizant. Thus it introduces a moral-political component into the heart of epistemological enquiry.[3]

There probably is no absolute authority, no practice of all practices or scheme of all schemes. Yet it does not follow that conceptual schemes, practices, and paradigms are radically idiosyncratic or purely subjective. Schemes, practices, and paradigms evolve out of communal projects of inquiry. To sustain viability and authority, they must demonstrate their adequacy in enabling people to negotiate the everyday world and to cope with the decisions, problems, and puzzles they encounter daily. From the claim that no single scheme has absolute explanatory power, it does not follow that all schemes are equally valid. Knowledge is qualitatively variable: some knowledge is *better* than other knowledge. Relativists are in a good position to take such qualitative variations into account and to analyze their implications.

Even if these points are granted, though, it would be a mistake to believe that posing the 'Who is S?' question indicates that the circumstances of the knower are *all* that counts in knowledge evaluation. The point is, rather, that understanding the circumstances of the knower makes possible a more *discerning* evaluation. The claim that certain of those circumstances are epistemologically significant—the sex of the knower, in this instance—by no means implies that they are definitive, capable of bearing the entire burden of justification and evaluation. This point requires special emphasis. Claiming epistemological significance for the sex of the knower might seem tantamount to a dismissal, to a contention that S made such a claim only because of his or her sex. Dismissals of this sort, both of women's knowledge *and* of their claims to be knowers in any sense of the word, are only too common throughout the history of western thought. But claiming that the circumstances of the knower are not epistemologically definitive is quite different from claiming that they are of no epistemological consequence. The position I take in this book is that the sex of the knower is one of a cluster of *subjective* factors (i.e., factors that pertain to the circumstances of cognitive agents) constitutive of received conceptions of knowledge and of what it means to be a knower. I maintain that subjectivity and the specificities of cognitive agency can and must be accorded central epistemological significance, yet that so doing does not commit an inquirer to outright subjectivism. Specificities count, and they require a place in epistemological evaluation, but they cannot tell the whole story.

Knowers and the Known

The only thing that is clear about S from the standard proposition 'S knows that p' is that S is a (would-be)

---

*   A caveat is a warning or a reservation.

knower. Although the question 'Who is S?' rarely arises, certain assumptions about S as knower permeate epistemological inquiry. Of special importance for my argument is the assumption that knowers are self-sufficient and solitary individuals, at least in their knowledge-seeking activities. This belief derives from a long and venerable heritage, with its roots in Descartes's quest for a basis of perfect certainty on which to establish his knowledge. The central aim of Descartes's endeavors is captured in this claim: "I shall have the right to conceive high hopes if I am happy enough to discover one thing only which is certain and indubitable."[4] That "one thing," Descartes believed, would stand as the fixed, pivotal, Archimedean point* on which all the rest of his knowledge would turn. Because of its systematic relation to that point, his knowledge would be certain and indubitable.

Most significant for this discussion is Descartes's conviction that his quest will be conducted in a private, introspective examination of the contents of his own mind. It is true that, in the last section of the *Discourse on the Method*, Descartes acknowledges the benefit "others may receive from the communication of [his] reflection," and he states his belief that combining "the lives and labours of many"[5] is essential to progress in scientific knowledge. It is also true that this individualistically described act of knowing exercises the aspect of the soul that is common to and alike in all knowers: namely, the faculty of reason. Yet his claim that knowledge seeking is an introspective activity of an individual mind accords no relevance either to a knower's embodiment or to his (or her) intersubjective relations. For each knower, the Cartesian route to knowledge is through private, abstract thought, through the efforts of reason unaided either by the senses or by consultation with other knowers. It is this individualistic, self-reliant, private aspect of Descartes's philosophy that has been influential in shaping subsequent epistemological ideals.

Reason is conceived as autonomous in the Cartesian project in two ways, then. Not only is the quest for certain knowledge an independent one, undertaken separately by each rational being, but it is a journey of reason alone, unassisted by the senses. For Descartes believed that sensory experiences had the effect of distracting reason from its proper course.

The custom of formulating knowledge claims in the 'S knows that p' formula is not itself of Cartesian origin. The point of claiming Cartesian inspiration for an assumption implicit in the formulation is that the knower who is commonly presumed to be the subject of that proposition is modeled, in significant respects, on the Cartesian pure inquirer. For epistemological purposes, all knowers are believed to be alike with respect both to their cognitive capacities and to their methods of achieving knowledge. In the empiricist tradition this assumption is apparent in the belief that simple, basic observational data can provide the foundation of knowledge just because perception is invariant from observer to observer, in standard observation conditions. In fact, a common way of filling the places in the 'S knows that p' proposition is with substitutions such as "Peter knows that the door is open" or "John knows that the book is red." It does not matter who John or Peter is.

Such knowledge claims carry implicit beliefs not only about would-be knowers but also about the knowledge that is amenable to philosophical analysis. Although (Cartesian) rationalists and empiricists differ with respect to what kinds of claim count as foundational, they endorse similar assumptions about the relation of foundational claims to the rest of a body of knowledge. With 'S knows that p' propositions, the belief is that such propositions stand as paradigms for knowledge in general. Epistemologists assume that knowledge is analyzable into propositional 'simples' whose truth can be demonstrated by establishing relations of correspondence to reality, or coherence within a system of known truths. These relatively simple knowledge claims (i.e., John knows that the book is red) could indeed be made by most 'normal' people who know the language and are familiar with the objects named. Knowers would seem to be quite self-sufficient in acquiring such knowledge. Moreover, no

---

* Archimedes was an ancient Greek scientist. His famous claim is that if there were a solid point on which he could stand outside the earth, with a long enough lever, he could move the earth. An "Archimedean point" is now understood more broadly as a viewpoint from which one could see some subject of inquiry in its objective entirety. Descartes's reference to this is in the Second Meditation.

one would claim to know "a little" that the book is red or to be in the process of acquiring knowledge about the openness of the door. Nor would anyone be likely to maintain that S knows better than W does that the door is open or that the book is red. Granting such examples paradigmatic status creates the mistaken assumption that all knowledge worthy of the name will be like this.

In some recent epistemological discussion, emphasis has shifted away from simple perceptual claims toward processes of evaluating the 'warranted assertability' of more complex knowledge claims. In such contexts it does make sense to analyze the degree or extent of the knowledge claimed. Yet claims of the simple, perceptual sort are still most commonly cited as exemplary. They are assumed to have an all-or-nothing character; hence they seem not to admit of qualitative assessment. Granting them exemplary status implies that, for knowledge in general, it is appropriate to ask about neither the circumstances of the knowing process nor who the knower is. There would be no point to the suggestion that her or his identity might bear on the *quality* of the knowledge under discussion.

Proposing that the sex of the knower is significant casts doubt both on the autonomy of reason and on the (residual) exemplary status of simple observational knowledge claims. The suggestion that reason might function differently according to whose it is and in what circumstances its capacities are exercised implies that the manner of its functioning is dependent, in some way, on those circumstances, not independent from them. Simple perceptual examples are rendered contestable for their tendency to give a misleading impression of how knowledge is constructed and established and to suppress diversities in knowledge acquisition that derive from the varied circumstances—for example, the sex—of different knowers.

Just what am I asking, then, with this question about the epistemological *significance* of the sex of the knower? First, I do not expect that the question will elicit the answer that the sex of the knower is pertinent among conditions for the existence of knowledge, in the sense that taking it into account will make it possible to avoid skepticism. Again, it is unlikely that information about the sex of the knower could count among criteria of evidence or means of justifying knowledge claims. Nor is it prima facie obvious that

the sex of the knower will have a legitimate bearing on the qualitative judgments that could be made about certain claims to know. Comparative judgments of the following kind are not what I expect to elicit: that if the knower is female, her knowledge is likely to be better grounded; if the knower is male, his knowledge will likely be more coherent.

In proposing that the sex of the knower is epistemologically significant, I am claiming that the scope of epistemological inquiry has been too narrowly defined. My point is not to denigrate projects of establishing the best foundations possible or of developing workable criteria of coherence. I am proposing that even if it is not possible (or not *yet* possible) to establish an unassailable foundationalist or coherentist position, there are numerous questions to be asked about knowledge whose answers matter to people who are concerned to know well. Among them are questions that bear not just on criteria of evidence, justification, and warrantability, but on the 'nature' of cognitive agents: questions about their character; their material, historical, cultural circumstances; their interests in the inquiry at issue. These are questions about how credibility is established, about connections between knowledge and power, about the place of knowledge in ethical and aesthetic judgments, and about political agendas and the responsibilities of knowers. I am claiming that all of these questions are epistemologically significant.

The Sex of the Knower

What, then, of the sex of the knower? In the rest of this chapter ... I examine some attempts to give content to the claim that the sex of the knower *is* epistemologically significant.[6] Many of these endeavors have been less than satisfactory. Nonetheless, I argue that the claim itself is accurate.

Although it has rarely been spelled out prior to the development of feminist critiques, it has long been tacitly assumed that S is male. Nor could S be just any man, the apparently infinite substitutability of the 'S' term notwithstanding. The S who could count as a model, paradigmatic knower has most commonly—if always tacitly—been an adult (but not old), white, reasonably affluent (latterly middle-class) educated man of status, property, and publicly acceptable accomplishments. In theory of knowledge he has been allowed to stand for all men.[7] This assumption does not merely derive from habit or coincidence, but is a manifestation of engrained philosophical convictions. Not only has it been taken for granted that knowers properly so-called are male, but when male philosophers have paused to note this fact, as some indeed have done, they have argued that things are as they should be. Reason may be alike in all men, but it would be a mistake to believe that 'man', in this respect, 'embraces woman'. Women have been judged incapable, for many reasons, of achieving knowledge worthy of the name. It is no exaggeration to say that anyone who wanted to *count* as a knower has commonly had to be male.

In the *Politics*, Aristotle observes: "The freeman rules over the slave after another manner from that in which the male rules over the female, or the man over the child; although the parts of the soul are present in all of them, they are present in different degrees. For the slave has no deliberative faculty at all; the woman has, but it is without authority, and the child has, but it is immature."[8] Aristotle's assumption that a woman will naturally be ruled by a man connects directly with his contention that a woman's deliberative faculty is "without authority." Even if a woman could, in her sequestered, domestic position, acquire deliberative skills, she would remain reliant on her husband for her sources of knowledge and information. She must be ruled by a man because, in the social structure of the *polis*,* she enjoys neither the autonomy nor the freedom to put into visible practice the results of the deliberations she may engage in, in private. If she can claim no authority for her rational, deliberative endeavors, then her chances of gaining recognition as a knowledgeable citizen are seriously limited, whatever she may do.[9]

Aristotle is just one of a long line of western thinkers to declare the limitations of women's cognitive capacities.[10] Rousseau maintains that young men and women should be educated quite differently because of women's inferiority in reason and their propensity to be dragged down by their sensual natures. For Kierkegaard, women are merely aesthetic beings: men alone can attain the (higher) ethical and religious levels of existence. And for Nietzsche, the Apollonian (intellectual) domain is the male preserve, whereas women are Dionysian (sensuous) creatures. Nineteenth-century philosopher and linguist Wilhelm von Humboldt, who writes at length about women's knowledge, sums up the central features of this line of thought as follows: "A sense of truth exists in [women] quite literally as a sense: ... their nature also contains a lack or a failing of analytic capacity which draws a strict line of demarcation between ego and world; therefore, they will not come as close to the ultimate investigation of truth as man."[11] The implication is that women's knowledge, if ever the products of their projects deserve that label, is inherently and inevitably *subjective*—in the most idiosyncratic sense—by contrast with the best of men's knowledge.

Objectivity, quite precisely construed, is commonly regarded as a defining feature of knowledge per se.[12] So if women's knowledge is declared to be *naturally* subjective, then a clear answer emerges to my question. The answer is that if the would-be knower is female, then her sex is indeed epistemologically significant, for it disqualifies her as a knower in the fullest sense of that term. Such disqualifications will operate differently for women of different classes, races, ages, and allegiances, but in every circumstance they will operate asymmetrically for women and for men. Just what is to be made of these points—how their epistemological significance is to be construed—is the subject of this book.

The presuppositions I have just cited claim more than the rather simple fact that many kinds of knowledge and skill have, historically, been inaccessible to women on a purely practical level. It is true, historically speaking, that even women who were the racial and social 'equals' of standard male knowers were only rarely able to become learned. The thinkers I have cited (and others like them) claim to find a rationale for this state of affairs through appeals to dubious 'facts' about women's natural incapacity for rational thought. Yet deeper questions still need to be asked: Is there knowledge that is, quite simply, inaccessible to members of the female, or the male, sex? Are there kinds of knowledge that only men, or only women, can acquire? Is the sex of the knower crucially determining in this respect, across all other specificities? The answers to these questions should not address only the *practical*

---

* Ancient Greek city-state, e.g., Athens.

possibilities that have existed for members of either sex. Such practical possibilities are the constructs of complex social arrangements that are themselves constructed out of historically specific choices, and are, as such, open to challenge and change.

Knowledge, as it achieves credence and authoritative status at any point in the history of the male-dominated mainstream, is commonly held to be a product of the individual efforts of human knowers. References to Pythagoras's theorem, Copernicus's revolution, and Newtonian and Einsteinian physics signal an epistemic community's attribution of path-breaking contributions to certain of its individual members. The implication is that *that* person, single-handedly, has effected a leap of progress in a particular field of inquiry. In less publicly spectacular ways, other cognitive agents are represented as contributors to the growth and stability of public knowledge.

Now any contention that such contributions are the results of independent endeavor is highly contestable. As I argue elsewhere,[13] a complex of historical and other sociocultural factors produces the conditions that make 'individual' achievement possible, and 'individuals' themselves are socially constituted.[14] The claim that individual *men* are the creators of the authoritative (often Kuhn*-paradigm-establishing) landmarks of western intellectual life is particularly interesting for the fact that the contributions—both practical and substantive—of their lovers, wives, children, servants, neighbors, friends, and colleagues rarely figure in analyses of their work.[15]

The historical attribution of such achievements to specific cognitive agents does, nonetheless, accord a significance to individual efforts which raises questions pertinent to my project. It poses the problem, in another guise, of whether aspects of human specificity could, in fact, constitute conditions for the existence of knowledge or determine the kinds of knowledge that a knower can achieve. It would seem that such incidental physical attributes as height, weight, or hair color would not count among factors that would determine a person's capacities to know (though the arguments that

skin color *does* count are too familiar). It is not necessary to consider how much Archimedes weighed when he made his famous discovery,[†] nor is there any doubt that a thinner or a fatter person could have reached the same conclusion. But in cultures in which sex differences figure prominently in virtually every mode of human interaction,[16] being female or male is far more fundamental to the construction of subjectivity than are such attributes as size or hair color. So the question is whether femaleness or maleness are the kinds of subjective factor (i.e., factors about the circumstances of a knowing subject) that are constitutive of the form and content of knowledge. Attempts to answer this question are complicated by the fact that sex/gender does not function uniformly and universally, even in western societies. Its implications vary across class, race, age, ability, and numerous other interwoven specificities. A separated analysis of sex/gender, then, always risks abstraction and is limited in its scope by the abstracting process. Further, the question seems to imply that sex and gender are themselves constants, thus obscuring the processes of *their* sociocultural construction. Hence the formulation of adequately nuanced answers is problematic and necessarily partial.

Even if it should emerge that gender-related factors play a crucial role in the construction of knowledge, then, the inquiry into the epistemological significance of the sex of the knower would not be complete. The task would remain of considering whether a distinction between 'natural' and socialized capacity can retain any validity. The equally pressing question as to how the hitherto devalued products of *women's* cognitive projects can gain acknowledgment as 'knowledge' would need to be addressed so as to uproot entrenched prejudices about knowledge, epistemology, and women. 'The epistemological project' will look quite different once its tacit underpinnings are revealed.

Reclaiming 'the Feminine'

Whether this project could or should emerge in a *feminist epistemology* is quite another question.

---

*   Philosopher of science Thomas Kuhn, who is most associated with the notion that paradigms—roughly, sets of key experimental concepts and results—govern scientific research.

†   The principle, which Archimedes is said to have discovered in his bath, that the apparent loss of weight of a body when immersed in a liquid is equal to the weight of the liquid displaced.

Investigations that start from the conviction that the sex of the knower is epistemologically significant will surely question received conceptions of the nature of knowledge and challenge the hegemony* of mainstream epistemologies. Some feminist theorists have maintained that there are distinctively female—or feminine—ways of knowing: neglected ways, from which the label 'knowledge', traditionally, is withheld. Many claim that a recognition of these 'ways of knowing' should prompt the development of new, rival, or even separate epistemologies. Others have adopted Mary O'Brien's brilliant characterization of mainstream epistemology as "malestream,"[17] claiming that one of the principal manifestations of its hegemony is its suppression of female—or 'feminine'—knowledge. In this section I sketch some classic and more recent arguments in favor of feminine 'ways of knowing' and offer a preliminary analysis of their strengths and shortcomings.

Claims that there are specifically female or feminine ways of knowing often find support in the contention that women's significantly different experiences (different, that is, from men's experiences) lead them to know 'the world' differently (i.e., from the ways men do). A putatively different female consciousness, in turn, generates different theories of knowledge, politics, metaphysics, morality, and aesthetics. Features of women's experiences commonly cited are a concern with the concrete, everyday world; a connection with objects of experience rather than an objective distance from them; a marked affective† tone; a respect for the environment; and a readiness to listen perceptively and responsibly to a variety of 'voices' in the environment, both animate and inanimate, manifested in a tolerance of diversity.

Many of these features are continuous with the attributes with which the dominant discourse of affluent western societies characterizes a good mother. Indeed, one of the best-known advocates of a caring, maternal approach both to knowledge and to a morality based on that knowledge is Sara Ruddick, in her now-classic article "Maternal Thinking." Maternal thinking, Ruddick believes, grows out of the *practice* of caring for and establishing an intimate connection with another being—a growing child. That practice is marked by a "unity of reflection, judgment and emotion ... [which is] ... no more relative to its particular reality (the growing child) than the thinking that arises from scientific, religious, or other practice"[18] is relevant to scientific or religious matters alone. Just as scientific or religious thought can structure a knower's characteristic approach to experiences and knowledge in general, Ruddick believes that attitudes and skills developed in the attentive and painstaking practices of caring for infants and small children are generalizable across cognitive domains.

Ruddick's celebration of values traditionally associated with mothering and femininity is not the first such in the history of feminist thought. Among nineteenth-century American feminists, both Margaret Fuller and Matilda Gage praised women's intuition as a peculiarly insightful capacity. Fuller, for example, believed that women have an intuitive perception that enables them to "seize and delineate with unerring discrimination" the connections and links among the various life forms that surround them.[19] In this respect, she maintains, women are superior to men. And Gage believed that women have unique intellectual capacities, manifested especially in an intuitive faculty that does not "need a long process of ratiocination" for its operations.[20] Both Fuller and Gage, albeit in quite different contexts, advocate legitimizing this suppressed and undervalued faculty whose deliverances, they believe, are attuned to and hence better able to reveal the secrets of nature and (for Gage) of spirituality, than masculine ratiocinative practices.‡

This nineteenth-century belief in the powers of female intuition is echoed in the work of two of the best-known twentieth-century radical feminists, Shulamith Firestone and Mary Daly. For Firestone, there are two sharply contrasting modes or styles of response to experience: an "aesthetic response," which she links to femaleness and characterizes as "subjective, intuitive, introverted, wishful, dreamy or fantastic, concerned with the subconscious (the id), emotional,

---

* Domination, especially political or social domination.
† Showing moods, feelings, values.
‡ Practices having to do with reasoning.

even temperamental (hysterical)"; and a technological response, which she describes as masculine: "objective, logical, extroverted, realistic, concerned with the conscious mind (the ego), rational, mechanical, pragmatic and down-to-earth, stable."[21] Firestone's claim is not that the aesthetic (= the feminine) should dominate, but that there should be a fusion between the two modes. To overcome patriarchal domination, she believes, it is vital for the aesthetic principle to manifest itself in all cultural and cognitive activity and for technology to cease operating to exclude affectivity.

Daly's concern with spirituality and with the celebration of witchcraft places her closer to Gage than to Fuller. Daly invokes the metaphor of spinning to describe the creation of knowledge and to connect the process with women's traditional creative activities. She claims that "Gyn/Ecology Spins around, past, and through the established fields, opening the coffers/coffins in which 'knowledge' has been stored, re-stored, re-covered ... [where] its meaning will be hidden from the Grave Keepers of tradition." These "Grave Keepers" are the arbiters of knowledge in patriarchal culture: the men who determine the legitimacy of knowledge claims. In consequence of their forced adherence to masculine epistemic norms, Daly contends, "women are encouraged, that is, dis-couraged, to adapt to a maintenance level of cognition and behavior by all the myth-masters and enforcers." Gyn/Ecology is a process of breaking the "spell of patriarchal myth"—by which Daly means all 'received' knowledge in patriarchal cultures—"bounding into freedom"; weaving "the tapestries of [one's] own creation."[22] Once freed from patriarchal myth, women will acquire the knowledge they need to validate their pleasures and powers as marks of their own authority and to unmask patriarchy. Daly's is a vision of female empowerment.

Some theorists maintain that research into the lateralization of brain function reveals 'natural' female-male cognitive differences. The findings of this research are frequently interpreted to indicate that in men, "left-brain" functions predominate, whereas "right-brain" functioning is better developed in women. Evidence that women have better verbal skills and fine motor coordination, whereas men are more adept at spatial skills, mathematics, and abstract thinking, is cited as proof of the existence of female and male cognitive differences. Depending on the political orientation of the inquirer, such findings are read either as confirmations of male supremacy and female inferiority or as indications of a need to revalue 'the feminine'. Among the celebratory interpretations are Gina Covina's claim that women, whom she describes as more "rightbrained" than men, deal with experience "in a diffuse non-sequential way, assimilating many different phenomena simultaneously, finding connections between separate bits of information." By contrast, men, whom she labels "leftbrained," engage typically in thinking that is "focused narrowly enough to squeeze out human or emotional considerations ... [and to enable] ... men to kill (people, animals, plants, natural processes) with free consciousnesses."[23] For Covina, there are 'natural' female-male differences. They are marked not just descriptively but evaluatively.

If brain-lateralization studies, or theories like Daly's and Firestone's, can be read as demonstrations of women's and men's necessarily different cognitive capacities, then my title question requires an affirmative answer. But it is not clear that such conclusions follow unequivocally. Consider the fact that allegedly sex-specific differences are not observable in examinations of the structure of the brain itself, and that in small children "both hemispheres appear to be equally proficient."[24] At most, then, it would seem, the brain may come to control certain processes in sexually differentiated ways. Evidence suggests that the brain *develops* its powers through training and practice.[25] Brains of creatures presented with a wide variety of tasks and stimuli develop strikingly greater performance capacities than brains of creatures kept in impoverished environments. As Ruth Bleier points out, "the biology of the brain itself is shaped by the individual's environment and experiences."[26]

Bleier notes the difficulty of assessing the implications of lateralization research. She observes that there are just as many studies that find no sex differences as there are studies that do, and that variability within each sex is greater than variability between them.[27] Janet Sayers suggests that it is as plausible to argue that sex differences in the results of tests to measure spatial ability are the results of sex-specific strategies that subjects adopt to deal with the tests themselves as it is to attribute them to differences in brain organization. She points out that there is no conclusive demonstration that differences in brain organization actually "*cause* sex differences in spatial ability."[28] It is not easy to see, then, how these studies can plausibly support arguments about general differences in male and female cognitive abilities or about women's incapacity to enter such specific domains as engineering and architecture, where spatial abilities figure largely.

These are just some of the considerations that recommend caution in interpreting brain-lateralization studies. Differences in female and male brain functioning are just as plausibly attributable to sociocultural factors such as the sex-stereotyping of children's activities or to differing parental attitudes to children of different sexes, even from earliest infancy. It would be a mistake to rely on the research in developing a position about the epistemological significance of the sex of the knower, especially as its results are often elaborated and interpreted to serve political ends.[29]

Now Fuller, Gage, Ruddick, Firestone, Daly, and Covina evidently believe—albeit variously—in the effectiveness of *evaluative reversals* of alleged differences as a fundamental revolutionary move. Philosophers should acknowledge the superiority of feminine ideals in knowledge acquisition as much as in social life and institutions, and masculine ways of thought should give way, more generally, to feminine ways. These recommendations apply to theoretical content and to methodology, to rules for the conduct of inquiry, and to principles of justification and legitimation.

The general thesis that inspires these recommendations is that women have an edge in the development and exercise of just those attributes that merit celebration as feminine: in care, sensitivity, responsiveness and responsibility, intuition and trust. There is no doubt that these traits are commonly represented as constitutive of femininity. Nor is there much doubt that a society that valued them might be a better society than one that denigrates and discourages them. But these very traits are as problematic, both theoretically and practically, as they are attractive. It is not easy to separate their appeal from the fact that women—at least women of prosperous classes and privileged races—have been encouraged to cultivate them throughout so long a history of oppression and exploitation that they have become marks of acquiescence in powerlessness. Hence there is a persistent tension in feminist thought between a laudable wish to celebrate 'feminine' values as tools for the creation of a better social order and a fear of endorsing those same values as instruments of women's continued oppression.

My recurring critique, throughout this book, of theoretical appeals to an *essential* femininity is one I engage in from a position sensitive to the pull of both sides in this tension. By 'essentialism' I mean a belief in an essence, an inherent, natural, eternal female nature that manifests itself in such characteristics as gentleness, goodness, nurturance, and sensitivity. These are some of women's more positive attributes. Women are also represented, in essentialist thought, as naturally less intelligent, more dependent, less objective, more irrational, less competent, more scatterbrained than men: indeed, essential femaleness is commonly defined against a masculine standard of putatively *human* essence.

Essentialist attributions work both normatively and descriptively. Not only do they purport to describe how women essentially *are*, they are commonly enlisted in the perpetuation of women's (usually inferior) social status. Yet essentialist claims are highly contestable. Their diverse manifestations across class, race, and ethnicity attest to their having a sociocultural rather than a 'natural' source. Their deployment as instruments for keeping women in their place means that caution is always required in appealing to them—even though they often appear to designate women's *strengths*. Claims about masculine essence need also to be treated with caution, though it is worth noting that they are less commonly used to oppress men. Essential masculine aggressiveness, sexual needs, and ego-enhancing requirements are often added, rather, to reasons why women should remain subservient. Perhaps there are some essential female or male characteristics, but claims that there are always need to be evaluated and analyzed. The burden of proof falls on theorists who appeal to essences, rather than on those who resist them.

As I have noted, some of the thinkers I have cited advocate an evaluative reversal, in a tacit acceptance of stereotypical, essentialist conceptions of masculinity and femininity. To understand the import of the tension in feminist thought, these stereotypes need careful analysis. The issues of power and theoretical hegemony that are inextricably implicated in their maintenance need likewise to be analyzed. As an initial step toward embarking on this task I offer, in the remainder of this section, a critical analysis of three landmark articles that engage with mainstream epistemology with the intention of revealing grounds for feminist opposition to its traditional structures.

(i) In her early piece, "Methodocracy, Misogyny and Bad Faith: Sexism in the Philosophic Establishment," Sheila Ruth characterizes mainstream philosophy in its content, methodology, and practice as male, masculine, and masculinist. Noting, correctly, that most philosophers—even more in the late 1970s than in the 1990s—are men, Ruth maintains that the content of their philosophy reflects masculine interests and that their standard methodologies reflect imperialist masculine values, values whose normative status derives from their association with maleness. Ruth writes that "philosophical sexism, metasexism ... is epistemological, permeating philosophy to its roots—the structure of its methods and the logic of its criticism." She argues that "what should not be is the raising of ... male [intellectual] constructs to the status of universals—the identification of male constructs with allowable constructs so that women cannot 'legitimately' think, perceive, select, argue, etc. from their unique stance."[30] For Ruth, the sex of the knower *is* epistemologically significant at a fundamental level, with all-pervasive implications.

This essay attests to the surprise and anger occasioned by early 'second wave' feminist realizations that theories that had posed, for centuries, as universal, neutral, and impartial were, in fact, deeply invested in furthering the self-interest of a small segment of the human population. Such realizations brought with them a profound shock, which often resulted in an insistence on affirming contrary, feminine interests and values. These early contributions often appear flawed from the present stage of feminist theoretical development, and I shall draw attention to some of those flaws as reasons why I would not, today, wholeheartedly endorse Ruth's claims.[31] They are worthy of rearticulation, though, for this article is one of the classics of feminist philosophy which created space for the development of subsequent critiques.

There is much that is right about Ruth's contentions, but two interconnected problems make it impossible to agree completely with her: the assumptions that "male constructs" exercise a unified, univocal hegemony and that women occupy a single "unique stance." I have argued in the first section of this chapter that epistemological relativism is a strong position because it creates the possibility of raising questions

about the *identity* of knowers. It opens the way for analyses of the historical, racial, social, and cultural specificity of knowers and of knowledge. Now its value would be minimal were it possible to demonstrate that cognitive activity and knowledge have been conceived in exactly the same way by all knowers since the dawn of philosophy. Precisely because it allows the interplay of common threads *and* of specific variations, relativism has a significant explanatory capacity. This capacity is tacitly denied in an account such as Ruth's, based, as it apparently is, on implicit claims about essential, eternal conceptions of femininity and masculinity, mirrored in constant interpretations of knowing and knowledge. In the face of historical, ethnographic, political and class-based evidence to the contrary, the onus would fall on Ruth, should she still wish to defend these claims, to demonstrate the constancy of the concepts.

Their assumed rigidity presents a still more serious problem. The content Ruth gives to masculinity and femininity plays directly into their essentialist, stereotypical construal in late-twentieth-century western societies. Yet there is no better reason to believe that feminine and masculine characteristics are constant across a complex society at any one time than there is to believe in their historical or cross-cultural constancy. Norms of masculinity and femininity vary across race, class, age, and ethnicity (to name only a few of the axes) within any society at any time. An acceptance of the stereotypes results in a rigidity of thinking that limits possibilities of developing nuanced analyses. In this article it creates for Ruth the troubling necessity of defining her project both *against* and *with reference to* a taken-for-granted masculine norm. No single such norm is discernible in western thought, yet when Ruth's positive recommendations in favor of different philosophical styles are sketched out by contrast with that assumed norm, their explanatory power is diminished. Ruth is right to assert that women have had "no part in defining the content of philosophical speculation, but they have had even less influence over the categories of concern and the modes of articulation."[32] The predominance of feminine and masculine stereotypes in her argument points to an unhappy implication of such early arguments for evaluative reversal: namely, that had women had such influence, their contribution would have been as monolithic as the 'masculine' one.

The broadest of Ruth's claims remains her strongest: philosophy has oppressed women in ways that feminists are still learning to understand. My point is that analyses of this oppression need to be wary lest they replicate the very structures they deplore. Much depends, in the development of feminist projects, on how women's oppression is analyzed. It is important to prevent the reactive aspects of critical response from overwhelming its creative possibilities. Ruth's analysis leans rather too heavily toward the reactive mode.

(ii) In another early, landmark article, "The Social Function of the Empiricist Conception of Mind," Sandra Harding confronts stereotypes of femininity from a different direction. Her thesis is that "the empiricist model of mind supports social hierarchy by implicitly sanctioning 'underclass' stereotypes." Emphasizing the passivity of knowers in Humean* empiricism, Harding contends, first, that classical empiricism can allow no place for creativity, for historical self-consciousness, or for the adoption of a critical stance. Second, she discerns a striking similarity between 'the Humean mind' and stereotypical conceptions of women's minds: "formless, passive, and peculiarly receptive to direction from outside."[33] Her intention is to show that an espousal of empiricist theory, combined with an uncritical acceptance of feminine stereotypes, legitimates manipulative and controlling treatment of women in the social world. There are striking echoes, as Harding herself notes, with the Aristotelian view of woman's lack of rational authority: a lack that, for Aristotle, likewise justifies women's inferior social position.

Present-day empiricists would no doubt contend that Harding's equation of empiricism with a 'passive' epistemology and theory of mind has little validity, given the varieties of contemporary empiricism in its transformations under the influence of philosophers such as Quine.[34] Yet even if Harding has drawn only a caricature of 'the Humean mind', her account has a heuristic value in highlighting certain tendencies of orthodox, classical empiricism. Empiricism, and its latter-day positivist offspring, could indeed serve, either as a philosophy of mind or as a theory of knowledge, to legitimate under the guise of objectivity and impartial neutrality just the kinds of social practice feminists are concerned to eradicate. The impartiality of empiricist analysis, the interchangeability of its subjects of study, work to provide rationalizations for treating people as 'cases' or 'types', rather than as active, creative cognitive agents.[35] Such rationalizations are common in positivistic social science.

More intriguing is a 'double standard' Harding discerns in classical empiricist thought. The *explicit* picture of the Humean inquirer, she maintains, is of a person who is primarily passive, receptive, and hence manipulable. Yet the very existence of Hume's own philosophy counts as evidence that he himself escapes that characterization. His intellectual activity is marked by "a critical attitude, firm purposes and a willingness to struggle to achieve them, elaborate principles of inquiry and hypotheses to be investigated, clarity of vision, precision, and facility at rational argument."[36] This description of the *implicit* Humean inquirer, Harding notes, feeds into standard gender stereotypes, in which men come across as "effective historical agents" while women are incapable of historical agency.

Harding accuses the promulgators of the classical empiricist conception of mind of false consciousness. Their own theoretical activity exempts *their* minds from the very model for which they claim universal validity: the contention that no one is a self-directed agent, everyone is a blank tablet, cannot apply to the authors themselves. Hence the empiricists presuppose a we/they structure in which 'they' indeed are as the theory describes them, but 'we', by virtue of our theoretical creativity, escape the description. In consequence, "the empiricist model of mind ... functions as a self-fulfilling *prescription* beneficial to those already in power: treat people as if they are passive and need direction from others, and they will become or remain able to be manipulated and controlled."[37] Harding maintains that the implicit distinction between active empiricist theorist and passive ordinary inquirer maps onto the stereotypical active male/passive female distinction and acts to legitimate the social and political consequences of that stereotype in androcentered[†] power structures.

---

* Relating to David Hume: see the introduction to Hume elsewhere in this volume.
† Male-centered.

Now it is not easy to show that Harding is right either to find an implicit 'double standard' in Humean thought or to suggest that demarcations of the two 'kinds' of knower are appropriately drawn along sexual lines. Hume himself may have meant merely to distinguish a philosopher at his most sophisticated from an ordinary 'vulgar' thinker. His elitism may have been intellect- or class-related, rather than sex-related. If Harding is right, however, the Humean 'double standard' would suggest that the sex of the knower is epistemologically significant, in that it designates men alone as capable of active, creative, critical knowing—and of constructing epistemological theories. By contrast, women are capable only of receiving and shuffling information. Even if she is mistaken in her Humean attributions, then, the parallels Harding draws between the intellectual elitism that empiricism can create and sexual elitism find ample confirmation in the social world. The common relegation of women to low-status forms of employment, which differ from high-status employment partly in the kinds of knowledge, expertise, and cognitive authority they require, is just one confirming practice.[38]

What ensures Harding's paper a place in the history of feminist critiques of philosophy is less the detail of its Hume interpretation than its articulation of the political implications of metaphysical theses. In the face of challenges such as these, which have been more subtly posed both in Harding's later work and elsewhere as feminist thought has increased in sophistication, the neutrality of such theses can never be taken for granted. Should it be declared, the onus is on its declarers to demonstrate the validity of their claims. So despite the flaws in Harding's analysis, her article supports my contention that the sex of the knower is epistemologically significant. If metaphysical theories are marked by the maleness of their creators, then theories of knowledge informed by them cannot escape the marking. Whether the case can be made that both theoretical levels are thus marked, without playing into sexual stereotypes, is a difficult question, but the evidence points compellingly toward the conclusion that the sex of a philosopher informs his theory-building.

(iii) The influence of stereotypically sex-specific traits on conceptions of the proper way to do philosophy is instructively detailed in Janice Moulton's analysis of "The Adversary Method," as she perceptively names it. Moulton shows that a subtle conceptual "conflation of aggression and competence"[39] has produced a paradigm for philosophical inquiry that is modeled on adversarial confrontation between opponents. This conflation depends, above all, on an association of aggression with such positive qualities as energy, power, and ambition: qualities that count as prerequisites for success in the white, middle-class, male professional world. Moulton questions the validity of this association in its conferral of normative status on styles of behavior stereotypically described as male. Yet what is most seriously wrong with the paradigm, she argues, is not so much its maleness as its constitutive role in the production of truncated philosophical problems, inquiries, and solutions.

The adversarial method is most effective, Moulton claims, in structuring isolated disagreements about specific theses and arguments. Hence it depends for its success on the artificial isolation of such claims and arguments from the contexts that occasion their articulation. Adversarial argument aims to show that an opponent is wrong, often by attacking conclusions implicit in, or potentially consequent on, his basic or alleged premises.[40] Under the adversarial paradigm, the point is to confront the most extreme opposing position, with the object of showing that one's own position is defensible even against such stark opposition. Exploration, explanation, and understanding are lesser goals. The irony, Moulton claims, is that the adversarial paradigm produces bad reasoning, because it leads philosophers to adopt the mode of reasoning best suited to defeat an opponent—she uses "counterexample reasoning" to illustrate her point[41]—as the paradigmatic model for reasoning as such. Diverse modes of reasoning which might be more appropriate to different circumstances, tend to be occluded, as does the possibility that a single problem might be amenable to more than one approach.

Moulton's analysis lends support to the contention that the sex of the knower is significant at the 'metaepistemological' level where the legitimacy of epistemological problems is established. The connection between aggressive cognitive styles and stereotypes of masculine behavior is now a commonplace of feminist thought. Moulton's demonstration that such behavior constitutes the dominant mode—the paradigm—in philosophy, which has so long claimed to stand outside 'the commonplace', is compelling. She shows that mainstream philosophy bears the marks of its androcentric derivation out of a stereotypically constructed masculinity, whatever the limitations of that construction are.

Like all paradigms, the adversarial method has a specific location in intellectual history. While it demarcates the kinds of puzzle a philosopher can legitimately consider, a recognition of its historical specificity shows that this is not how philosophy has always been done nor how it must, of necessity, be done. In according the method (interim) paradigm status, Moulton points to the historical contingency of its current hegemony. The fact that many feminist philosophers report a sense of dissonance between the supposed gender neutrality of the method and their own feminine gender[42] puts the paradigm under serious strains. Such strains create the space and the possibilities for developing alternative methodological approaches. Whether the sex of the knower will be methodologically and/or epistemologically significant in such approaches must, for now, remain an open question.

Knowledge, Methodology, and Power

The adversarial method is but one manifestation of a complex interweaving of power and knowledge which sustains the hegemony of mainstream epistemology. Like the empiricist theory of the mind, it presents a public demeanor of neutral inquiry, engaged in the disinterested pursuit of truth. Despite its evident interest in triumphing over opponents, it would be unreasonable to condemn this disinterest as merely a pose. There is no reason to believe that practitioners whose work is informed by these methodological assumptions have ruthlessly or tyrannically adopted a theoretical stance for the express purpose of engaging in projects that thwart the intellectual pursuits of women or of other marginalized philosophers. Could such a purpose be discerned, the task of revealing the epistemological significance of the sex of the knower would be easy. Critics could simply offer such practitioners a clear demonstration of the errors of their ways and hope that, with a presumption of goodwill on their part, they would abandon the path of error for that of truth and fairness.

Taking these practitioners at their word, acknowledging the sincerity of their convictions about their neutral, objective, impartial engagement in the pursuit of truth, reveals the intricacy of this task. Certain sets of problems, by virtue of their complexity or their intrinsic appeal, often become so engrossing for researchers that they override and occlude other contenders for attention. Reasons for this suppression are often subtle and not always specifically articulable. Nor is it clear that the exclusionary process is wholly conscious. A network of sociopolitical relationships and intellectual assumptions creates an invisible system of acceptance and rejection, discourse and silence, ascendency and subjugation within and around disciplines. Implicit cultural presuppositions work with the personal idiosyncrasies of intellectual authorities to keep certain issues from placing high on research agendas. Critics have to learn how to notice their absence.

In "The Discourse on Language," Michel Foucault makes the astute observation that "within its own limits, every discipline recognizes true and false propositions, but it repulses a whole teratology[43] of learning."[44] The observation captures some of the subtleties involved in attempting to understand the often imperceptible workings of hegemonic, usually masculine power in mainstream philosophy. A discipline defines itself both by what it excludes (repulses) and by what it includes. But the self-definition process removes what is excluded (repulsed) from view so that it is not straightforwardly available for assessment, criticism, and analysis. Even in accepting mainstream avowals of neutral objectivity, critics have to learn to see what is repulsed by the disciplinarily imposed limits on methodology and areas of inquiry. The task is not easy. It is much easier to seek the flaws in existing structures and practices and to work at eradicating them than it is to learn to perceive what is not there to be perceived.

Feminist philosophy simply did not exist until philosophers learned to perceive the near-total absence of women in philosophical writings from the very beginning of western philosophy, to stop assuming that 'man' could be read as a generic term. Explicit denigrations of women, which became the focus of philosophical writing in the early years of the contemporary women's movement, were more readily perceptible. The authors of derogatory views about women in classical texts clearly needed power to be able to utter their pronouncements with impunity: a power they claimed from a 'received' discourse that represented women's nature in such a way that women undoubtedly merited the negative judgments that Aristotle or Nietzsche made about them. Women are now in a position to recognize and refuse these overt manifestations of contempt.

The covert manifestations are more intransigent. Philosophers, when they have addressed the issue at all, have tended to group philosophy with science as the most gender-neutral of disciplines. But feminist critiques reveal that this alleged neutrality masks a bias in favor of institutionalizing stereotypical masculine values into the fabric of the discipline—its methods, norms, and contents. In so doing, it suppresses values, styles, problems, and concerns stereotypically associated with femininity. Thus, whether by chance or by design, it creates a hegemonic philosophical practice in which the sex of the knower is, indeed, epistemologically significant. ∎

Suggestions for Critical Reflection

1. Code contrasts the traditional idea that knowledge claims should be assessed "on their own merits" with the claim that "the circumstances of knowledge acquisition" are relevant to their evaluation. Which of these two stances do you think is the most plausible—or epistemically responsible—on the face of it? After reading Code's article carefully, does she change your views?

2. Exactly *how* do "the circumstances of knowledge acquisition," and especially who the knower is, affect the evaluation of knowledge claims, on Code's view? For example, can some factual claim be true or justified if it is asserted by one knower but not if it is asserted by another? (Does Code in fact think that the circumstances of the knower are relevant to the *justification* of knowledge claims at all?) Are all types of knowledge claims equally relative to their knower, or are there differences between kinds of knowledge (e.g., between ethical knowledge and geographical knowledge)?

3. What is the significance of Code's claim that most pieces of knowledge are not 'all or nothing' but are a matter of *degree*?

4. Do you agree with Code—if this is indeed her view—that "there is no universal, unchanging framework or scheme for rational adjudication among competing knowledge claims"? How radical do you think this claim is? Is the kind of relativism that Code adopts, as she claims, an 'enabling' rather than a problematic position?

5. Code suggests that the nature and circumstances of the knower have not been ignored or treated neutrally in traditional epistemology. Rather, traditional epistemology—such as that of Descartes—has been shaped by tacit, often concealed, and sexist assumptions about the nature of the knower. What do you make of this claim? What is its significance for Code's project?

6. Why does Code reject essentialism about female nature? Is she pragmatically or theoretically right to do so? What is the significance of this stance for her version of feminist epistemology?

7. Code raises various doubts about the authors she considers—including concerns about whether their division of attributes into masculine and feminine are essentialist and stereotyping. If all such divisions are questionable, what would this mean for Code's claim that the sex of someone who makes knowledge-claims is relevant to the evaluation of those claims? Or that the dominant epistemological patterns have been masculine?

Notes

1 This question is the title of my paper published in *Metaphilosophy* 12 (July–October 1981): pp. 267–276. In this early essay I endorse an essentialism with respect to masculinity and femininity, and convey the impression that 'positive thinking' can bring an end to gender imbalances. I would no longer make these claims.

2 I consider some of these objections to relativism at greater length in "The Importance of Historicism for a Theory of Knowledge," *International Philosophical Quarterly* 22 (June 1982): pp. 157–174.

3 I discuss some of these accountability requirements, and the normative realism from which they derive, in my *Epistemic Responsibility* (Hanover, NH: University Press of New England, 1987).

4 René Descartes, *Meditations*, in *The Philosophical Works of Descartes*, trans. Elizabeth S. Haldane and G.R.T. Ross (Cambridge: Cambridge University Press, 1969), 1:149.

5 René Descartes, *Discourse on the Method of Rightly Conducting the Reason and Seeking for Truth in the Sciences*, in ibid., pp. 124, 120.

6 In this chapter I discuss the sex of the knower in a way that may seem to conflate biological sex differences with their cultural elaborations and manifestations as gender differences. I retain the older term—albeit inconsistently—for two reasons. The first, personally historical, reason connects this text with my first thoughts on these matters, published in my *Metaphilosophy* paper (see note [2], above). The second, philosophically historical, reason reflects the relatively recent appearance of 'gender' as a theoretical term of art. In the history of 'the epistemological project', which I discuss in these early chapters, 'sex' would have been the term used, had these questions been raised.

7 To cite just one example: in *The Theory of Epistemic Rationality* (Cambridge: Harvard University Press, 1987), Richard Foley appeals repeatedly to the epistemic judgments of people who are "like the rest of us" (p. 108). He contrasts their beliefs with beliefs that seem "crazy or bizarre or outlandish ... beliefs to most of the rest of us" (p. 114), and argues that an account of rational belief is plausible only if it can be presented from "some nonweird perspective" (p. 140). Foley contends that "an individual has to be at least minimally like us in order for charges of irrationality even to make sense" (p. 240). Nowhere does he address the question of who 'we' are. (I take this point up again in Chapter 7 [of *What Can She Know?*].)

8 Aristotle, *Politics*, trans. Benjamin Jowett, in *The Basic Works of Aristotle*, ed. Richard McKeon (New York: Random House, 1941), 1260b.

9 I discuss the implications of this lack of authority more fully in Chapters 9 and 6 [of *What Can She Know?*]. See Elizabeth V. Spelman, *Inessential Woman: Problems of Exclusion in Feminist Thought* (Boston: Beacon, 1988), for an interesting discussion of some more complex exclusions effected by Aristotle's analysis.

10 It would be inaccurate, however, to argue that this line is unbroken. Londa Schiebinger demonstrates that in the history of science—and, by implication, the history of the achievement of epistemic authority—there were many periods when women's intellectual achievements were not only recognized but respected. The "long line" I refer to is the dominant, historically most visible one. Schiebinger, *The Mind Has No Sex? Women in the Origins of Modern Science* (Cambridge: Harvard University Press, 1989).

11 *Humanist without Portfolio: An Anthology of the Writings of Wilhelm von Humboldt*, trans. with intro. by Marianne Cowan (Detroit: Wayne State University Press, 1963), p. 349.

12 I analyze this precise construal of objectivity in Chapter 2 of [of *What Can She Know?*].

13 See chap. 7, "Epistemic Community," of my *Epistemic Responsibility*.

14 I discuss the implications of these points for analyses of subjectivity in Chapter 1 [of *What Can She Know?*].

15 I owe this point—and the list—to Polly Young-Eisendrath, "The Female Person and How We Talk about Her," in Mary M. Gergen, ed., *Feminist Thought and the Structure of Knowledge* (New York: New York University Press, 1988).

16 Marilyn Frye points out: "Sex-identification intrudes into every moment of our lives and discourse, no matter what the supposedly primary focus or topic of the moment is. Elaborate, systematic, ubiquitous and redundant marking of a distinction between two sexes of humans and most animals is customary and obligatory. One *never* can ignore it." Frye, *The Politics of Reality: Essays in Feminist Theory* (Trumansburg, NY: Crossing Press, 1983), p. 19.

17 See Mary O'Brien, *The Politics of Reproduction* (London: Routledge & Kegan Paul, 1980).

18 Sara Ruddick, "Maternal Thinking," *Feminist Studies* 6 (1980): p. 348. I develop a critical analysis of Ruddick's position in Chapter 3 [of *What Can She Know?*]. It should be noted that in Ruddick's 1989 book, *Maternal Thinking: Toward a Politics of Peace* (Boston: Beacon, 1989), she addresses some of the issues I raise about the essentialism of this earlier article.

19 Margaret Fuller, *Woman in the Nineteenth Century* (1845; New York: Norton, 1971), p. 103.

20 Matilda Jocelyn Gage, *Women, Church, and State* (1893; Watertown, Mass.: Persephone, 1980), p. 238.

21 Shulamith Firestone, *The Dialectic of Sex: The Case for Feminine Revolution* (New York: Bantam, 1971), p. 175.

22 Mary Daly, *Gyn/Ecology: The Metaethics of Radical Feminism* (Boston: Beacon, 1978), pp. xiii, 53, 57, 320.

23 Gina Covina, "Rosy Rightbrain's Exorcism/ Invocation," in G. Covina and Laurel Galana, eds., *The Lesbian Reader* (Oakland, Calif.: Amazon, 1975), p. 96.

24 See Gordon Rattray Taylor, *The Natural History of the Mind* (London: Granada, 1979), p. 127. In an earlier article Taylor points out that "if the eyelids of an animal are sewn up at birth, and freed at maturity, it cannot see and will never learn to do so. The brain has failed to develop the necessary connections at the period when it was able to do so." Taylor, "A New View of the Brain," *Encounter* 36, 2 (1971): 30.

25 In this connection Oliver Sacks recounts an illuminating story of a fifty-nine-year-old, congenitally blind woman with cerebral palsy, whose manual sensory capacities, he determined, were intact and quite normal. But when he met her, she had no use of her hands, referring to them as "useless lumps of dough." It became apparent that her hands were functionless because she had never used them: "being 'protected', 'looked after', 'babied' since birth [had] prevented her from the normal exploratory use of the hands which all infants learn in the first months of life." This woman first learned to use her hands in her sixtieth year. Oliver Sacks, "Hands," in *The Man Who Mistook His Wife for a Hat and Other Clinical Tales* (New York: Summit, 1985), p. 57.

26 Ruth Bleier, "Lab Coat: Robe of Innocence or Klansman's Sheet?" in Teresa de Lauretis, ed., *Feminist Studies / Critical Studies* (Bloomington: Indiana University Press, 1986), p. 65.

27 Ibid., pp. 58–59.

28 Janet Sayers, *Biological Politics* (London: Tavistock, 1982), p. 103.

29 Sayers notes: "So germane do ... findings about sex differences in brain organization appear to the current political debate about the justice of continuing sexual inequalities in professional life that they are now regularly singled out for coverage in newspaper reports of scientific meetings." Ibid., p. 101. See Lynda Birke's elaboration of this point in her *Women, Feminism, and Biology* (Brighton: Harvester, 1986), p. 29.

30 Sheila Ruth, "Methodocracy, Misogyny, and Bad Faith: Sexism in the Philosophic Establishment," *Metaphilosophy* 10, 1 (1979): pp. 50, 56.

31 My *Metaphilosophy* article is another pertinent example. Allan Soble criticizes the essentialism of my argument in "Feminist Epistemology and Women Scientists," *Metaphilosophy* 10 (1983): pp. 291–307.

32 Ruth, "Methodocracy, Misogyny, and Bad Faith," p. 54. In my thinking about Ruth's article I am indebted to Jean Grimshaw's discussion in her *Philosophy and Feminist Thinking* (Minneapolis: University of Minnesota Press, 1986), pp. 53–55, 81–82.

33 Sandra Harding, "The Social Function of the Empiricist Conception of Mind," *Metaphilosophy* 10 (January 1979): pp. 39, 42.

34 See especially Lynn Hankinson Nelson, *Who Knows: From Quine to a Feminist Empiricism* (Philadelphia: Temple University Press, 1990). Because Nelson's book was published after my manuscript was completed, I have not discussed it in this book.

35 I discuss this consequence of empiricist thinking more fully in Chapter 2 [of *What Can She Know?*].

36 Harding, "Social Function of the Empiricist Conception of Mind," pp. 43, 44.

37 Ibid., p. 46.

38 An example of the hierarchy of cognitive relations created by such assumptions is the theme [of Chapter 6 of *What Can She Know?*].

39 Janice Moulton, "A Paradigm of Philosophy: The Adversary Method," in Sandra Harding and Merrill B. Hintikka, eds., *Discovering Reality* (Dordrecht: Reidel, 1983), p. 151.

40 I am agreeing with Moulton's association of the paradigm with maleness in using the masculine pronoun to refer to its practitioners—even though many women have learned to play the game well.

41 Moulton, "Paradigm of Philosophy," p. 159.

42 See, for example, Genevieve Lloyd's observation that "the exercise of writing feminist philosophy came out of [her] experience of dissonance between the supposed gender neutrality of philosophy and [her] gender." Lloyd, "Feminist Philosophy and the Idea of the Feminine" (manuscript, 1986), p. 22.

43 A 'teratology' is a collection of tales about marvellous and improbable creatures (such as sea monsters, or people with heads in their chests); Foucault's idea is that disciplines restrict themselves to what is familiar, and rule out or ignore the possibility of things that would be—from the perspective of the discipline—considered strange or unlikely.

44 Michel Foucault, "The Discourse on Language," in *The Archaeology of Knowledge*, trans. Alan Sheridan (New York: Pantheon, 1972), p. 223.

JENNIFER SAUL

Scepticism and Implicit Bias

Who Is Jennifer Saul?

Jennifer Saul is an American-born philosopher who worked for many years at the University of Sheffield in the UK and has recently moved to become Waterloo Chair in Social and Political Philosophy of Language at the University of Waterloo in Ontario, Canada. She is known for her work in both philosophy of language and feminist philosophy. Saul was born in Ohio to a progressive family of academics. She recalls attending her first feminist consciousness-raising meeting at four years old, accompanied by her grandmother, a mathematician who was active in the 1970s feminist movement.* She earned her MA and PhD at Princeton, specializing in analytic philosophy of language. As Saul notes, she hadn't yet entertained the possibility of feminist philosophy during her student years, believing that feminism was "too obviously correct to be something one could do philosophy about."† Ultimately, Saul came to recognize that social justice is connected in important ways to the very aspects of language that were already the focus of her work.

Saul's publications include *Feminism: Issues & Arguments* (2003), *Substitution, Simple Sentences and Intuitions* (2007), and *Lying, Misleading and What Is Said: An Exploration in Philosophy of Language and in Ethics* (2012). Saul co-founded two influential blogs: "Feminist Philosophers" and "What Is It Like to Be a Woman in Philosophy?"‡ She has been a vocal advocate for remedying the race and gender imbalance in academic philosophy, and in 2011 was awarded the Distinguished Woman Philosopher Award by the Society for Women in Philosophy.

What Is the Structure of This Reading?

Saul begins this paper by reviewing the scientific literature surrounding the phenomenon of implicit bias, illustrating a number of ways in which implicit biases appear to disadvantage some people in hiring processes, academic work, and other social interactions. She then argues that the doubt generated by the discovery of implicit bias entails a special sort of skepticism. While traditional philosophical skepticism is often seen as a form of "armchair philosophy," with little practical significance in our lives, the skepticism arising from bias-related doubt is far more troublesome, as it demands both attention and action. According to Saul, we ought to be more "unsettled" by implicit bias than by more traditional skeptical concerns such as the possibility that we are brains in vats. While we may have difficulty proving definitively that we are not brains in vats, in the case of bias-related doubt we actually have strong positive evidence from scientific studies indicating that we are frequently making errors. Moreover, if we are making bias-related errors we really should take action to change this given the harmful social consequences, whereas if we are brains in vats it's not clear that this would actually require us to change our actions.

In the final sections of this paper, Saul asks what we should do about these new concerns. We might attempt to use "counter-intuitive mechanical techniques" to reduce the effects of implicit bias, but Saul notes that the effectiveness of such techniques may be limited, as they typically target very specific associations and behaviors. The only complete solution, according to Saul, is to eradicate all types of prejudice and stereotype, which would result in nothing less than a "sweeping and radical transformation of our social world."

---

* Interview with Jennifer Saul, February 17, 2007, on the "What Is It Like to Be a Philosopher?" blog.
† Ibid.
‡ The title of the latter is an allusion to Thomas Nagel's "What Is It Like to Be a Bat?" (included in the Philosophy of Mind chapter of this volume).

Scepticism and Implicit Bias*

The goal of this paper is to explore the idea that what we know about implicit bias gives rise to something *akin to* a new form of scepticism. I am not wedded to the idea that the phenomenon I am pointing to should be called 'scepticism', but I am convinced that it is illuminating to examine the ways in which it does and does not resemble philosophical scepticism. I will call what I am discussing 'bias-related doubt'.

In some ways, bias-related doubt is stronger than traditional forms of scepticism, while in others it is weaker. In brief: I will be arguing that what we know about implicit biases shows us that we have very good reason to believe that we cannot properly trust our knowledge-seeking faculties. This does not mean that we might be mistaken *about everything*, or even everything in the external world (so it is weaker than traditional scepticism). But it does mean that we have *good reason* to believe that we are mistaken about a great deal (so it is stronger than traditional forms of scepticism). A further way in which bias-related doubt is stronger than traditional scepticism: this is doubt that demands action. With traditional scepticism, we feel perfectly fine about setting aside the doubts we have felt when we leave the philosophy seminar room. But with bias-related doubt, we don't feel fine about this at all. We feel a need to *do something* to improve our epistemic situation. Fortunately, though, it turns out that there is much we can do. However, much of what needs to be done cannot be done on a purely individual basis. So although scepticism has sometimes been treated by feminists as a paradigmatic case of the excesses of individualist philosophy,[1] this form of scepticism cannot be fully responded to individualistically.

1 Implicit Biases

There is a vast and still-growing literature on implicit bias, which I'll only be dipping into here. Very broadly speaking, these are largely unconscious tendencies to automatically associate concepts with one another.[2] Put like this, they don't sound very interesting or worrying. But the ones on which attention by philosophers has focused are both very interesting and very worrying. These are unconscious, automatic tendencies to associate certain traits with members of particular social groups, in ways that lead to some very disturbing errors: we tend to judge members of stigmatized groups more negatively, in a whole host of ways. Rather than attempt a general overview, I will give examples of the sorts of errors that will be our concern here.

CURRICULUM VITAE

CV studies take a common, and beautifully simple form. The experimenters ask subjects to rate what is in fact the same CV, varying whatever trait they want to study by (usually) varying the name at the top of it. When they do this, they find that the same CV is considered much better when it has a typically white rather than typically black name, a typically Swedish rather than typically Arab name, a typically male rather than typically female name, and so on. The right name makes the reader rate one as more likely to be interviewed, more likely to be hired, likely to be offered more money, and a better prospect for mentoring. These judgments are very clearly being affected by something that *should* be irrelevant—the social category of the person whose CV is being read. Moreover, the person making these mistaken judgments is surely unaware of the role that social category is playing in the formation of their views of the candidates. Significantly, the most recent of these studies (Moss-Racusin 2012), on the evaluation of women's CVs, showed that women were just as likely to make these problematic judgments as men. It also showed that these problems are not confined to an older generation: the tendencies were equally strong in all age groups.[3]

PRESTIGE BIAS

In a now-classic study, psychologists Peters and Ceci (1982) sent previously published papers to the top

---

* Jennifer Saul, "Scepticism and Implicit Bias," *Disputatio* 5, 37 (2013): 243–63.

psychology journals that had published them, but with false names and non-prestigious affiliations. Only 8% detected that the papers had already been submitted, and 89% were rejected, citing serious methodological errors (and not the one they should have cited—plagiarism). This makes it clear that institutional affiliation has a dramatic effect on the judgments made by reviewers (either positively, negatively, or both). These are experts in their field, making judgments about their area of expertise—psychological methodology—and yet they are making dramatically different judgments depending on the social group to which authors belong (member of prestigious vs non-prestigious psychology department).

PERCEPTION

Studies of so-called 'shooter bias' show us that implicit bias can even influence perception. In these studies, it has been shown that the very same ambiguous object is far more likely to be perceived as a gun when held by a young black man and something innocent (like a phone) when held like by a young white man.[4] (The same effect has been shown with men who appear Muslim versus men who appear non-Muslim (Unkelbach et al. 2008). In some of these experiments, the subjects' task is to shoot in a video game if and only if they see an image of a person carrying a gun. Subjects' 'shooting' is just as you'd expect given their perceptions. These show that implicit bias is getting to us even before we get to the point of reflecting upon the world—it affects our very perceptions of that world, again in worrying ways.[5]

MORAL AND POLITICAL CONSEQUENCES

Now let's explore some consequences of this. First, there are some obvious morally and politically significant consequences. We are very likely to make inaccurate judgments about who is the best candidate for a job, if some of the top candidates are known to be from stigmatised groups. We are very likely to mark inaccurately, if social group membership is known to us and the group we are marking is not socially homogeneous. We are very likely to make inaccurate judgments about which papers deserve to be published, if social group membership is known to us. We may

both over-rate members of some groups and under-rate others. Worse yet, we are misperceiving harmless objects as dangerous, and potentially acting on this in truly appalling ways. All of this *should* be tremendously disturbing to us. It means that we are being dramatically *unfair* in our judgments, even though we are doing so unintentionally. We are treating members of stigmatised groups badly, even if we desperately desire to treat them well. Moreover, what we are doing will help to ensure that this unfair treatment is continued: the results of these decisions will help to maintain the stereotypes that currently exist, which cause members of stigmatised groups to be treated unfairly. 'Vicious circle' seems a particularly apt phrase to describe the situation.

EPISTEMOLOGICAL CONSEQUENCES

But I want to focus now on some epistemological aspects of this situation. First, some relatively obvious ones, starting from those within philosophy. The unfairness described above means that there are almost certain to be some excellent students receiving lower marks and less encouragement than they should; some excellent philosophers not getting the jobs they should get; and where anonymous refereeing and editing is not practised, there is some excellent work not being published. Philosophy as a field is the worse for this: it is not as good as it could, or should, be. (For more on this, see Beebee and Saul 2011, Saul forthcoming.) Obviously, much the same will go on in other areas of academia, especially those that are as male-dominated as philosophy. Outside philosophy, there are similar effects, as the testimony of members of stigmatised groups is taken less seriously than it ought to be (Fricker 2007). Their views are less respected, and they are given less of an opportunity to participate fully in discussions and decision-making. As Chris Hookway (2010) has noted, a particular problem may lie in their *questions* not being taken seriously.

Now, some less obvious epistemological aspects of the situation, again focussing on philosophy. When we misjudge a paper's quality, we're making a mistake about the quality of an argument.[6] Moreover, our evaluation of that argument is being influenced by factors totally irrelevant to its quality: it's being influenced by our knowledge of the social group of its author. Worse yet, this influence operates below the level of consciousness—it's unavailable to inspection and rational evaluation. This means we may be accepting arguments we should not accept and rejecting arguments we should not reject. Many of our philosophical beliefs—those beliefs we take to have been arrived at through the most careful exercise of reason—are likely to be wrong.[7]

...

It is important to see that this is not *just* a matter of what Miranda Fricker (2007) has called testimonial injustice. Fricker argues that the social group to which a person belongs will often have a dramatic effect on our willingness to treat them as a credible source of knowledge. We will be less likely to accept the testimony of those from stigmatised groups. One thing implicit bias adds to this picture is just a matter of scale: research shows these problems to be far more widespread than would otherwise be apparent. But another, even more important addition, is that implicit bias doesn't just affect our judgments of people's *credibility* when deciding whether to accept their testimony or not. Mistaken as our credibility judgments are, at least we know that these are judgments about who to take seriously. We recognise that we are making judgments about people, and this is what we mean to be doing. The research on implicit bias shows us that we are actually being affected by biases about social groups *when we think we are evaluating evidence or methodology*. When considering testimony, it makes sense that we need to make judgments about how credible an individual is. But when psychologists assess the methodology of a study—or when philosophers assess the quality of an argument—they shouldn't be looking at the credibility of an individual at all. They should be looking just at the study, or the argument. And yet when implicit bias is at work, we are likely to be affected by the social group of the person presenting evidence or an argument even when we are trying to evaluate that evidence or argument itself. Implicit bias is not just affecting who we trust—it's affecting us when we think we're making judgments that have nothing to do with trust. It's leading us into errors based on social category membership when we think we're making judgments of scientific or argumentative merit.

But why should that unsettle us? We know already that most of what is currently accepted as science is likely to be proven false within centuries, and possibly decades. But notice: my claim is not that we're likely to be accepting some falsehoods, or even a lot of falsehoods. That's not unsettling. My claim is that we're likely to be *making errors*. Moreover, we're likely to be making errors of a very specific sort. It's *not* that we're likely to get some really difficult technical bits wrong, or that we're likely to get things wrong if we're really exhausted, or drunk. It's that we're likely to let the social identity of the person making an argument affect our evaluation of that argument. It is part of our self-understanding as rational enquirers that we will make certain sorts of mistakes. But not this sort of mistake. These mistakes are ones in which something that we actively think *should not* affect us does.

Worse yet, our errors are not confined to the professional arena, or to what we take to be carefully thought-out judgments about the quality of arguments that we encounter. The studies of shooter bias show us that as humans in the world, we are making errors in *perception* due to implicit bias. The very data from which we begin in thinking about the world—our perceptions—cannot be relied upon to be free of bias. Once more, this is clearly well beyond the worries raised by testimonial injustice.

The best way to see why these mistakes are—and should be—so unsettling to us as enquirers is to compare the situation of one who learns about implicit biases to the situations of people considering various sorts of sceptical scenarios.

2 Comparison to Sceptical Scenarios

2.1 COMPARISON TO TRADITIONAL SCEPTICISM

In a traditional sceptical scenario, we are confronted with a possibility that we can't rule out—that we're brains in vats,* or that tomorrow gravity might not

---

* This is an updated version of René Descartes's evil demon thought experiment; see Gilbert Harman, *Thought* (Princeton University Press, 1973), 5.

work any more.* Considering this scenario is meant to make us worry that we don't know (many of) the things that we take ourselves to know, or that we are unjustified in having (many of) the beliefs that we do. And a standard response is that these worries should not grip us, because we have no reason at all to suppose that these possibilities obtain. Doubt induced by implicit bias is unlike this: we have *very good reason* to suppose that we are systematically making errors caused by our unconscious biases related to social categories. In this way, then, the doubt provoked by implicit bias is stronger than that caused by considering sceptical arguments.

But, one might think, it's not really all that troubling. The doubt caused by implicit bias, surely, is a localized one. It seems, at first, to be like the sort of doubt we experience when we discover how poor we are at probabilistic reasoning. We have extremely good reason to think we're making errors when we make judgments of likelihood. But this sort of doubt doesn't trouble us all that much because we know exactly when we should worry and what we should do about it: if we find ourselves estimating likelihood, we should mistrust our instincts and either follow mechanical procedures we've learned or consult an expert (if not in person, then on the internet). This kind of worry is one that everyone can accept without feeling drawn into anything like scepticism. And it may seem at first that bias-related doubt is like this.

The problem starts to become vivid when we ask ourselves *when* we should be worried about implicit bias influencing our judgments. The answer is that we should be worried about it whenever we consider a claim, an argument, a suggestion, a question, etc. from a person whose apparent social group we're in a position to recognize. Whenever that's the case, there will be room for our unconscious biases to perniciously affect us. Most discussed in the literature so far (see Fricker 2007), we might make a mistaken judgment of credibility when assessing testimony. But we also might fail to listen properly to a contribution; fail to carefully consider a question; judge an argument to be less compelling or original than it is; think the evidence

presented is worse than it is. And, importantly, we can be adversely affected in a positive direction as well. When assessing a contribution from someone who our biases favour, we may grant more credibility than their testimony deserves; we may think their arguments are better than they are, perhaps failing to notice flaws that we would have noticed if the arguments were presented by someone else; we may take their evidence to be better than it is, and so on.

And *this* is going to happen a great deal. It happens whenever we are dealing with the social world in a non-anonymised† manner. Since the world is only rarely anonymised for us, this will happen nearly all the time. Much of our knowledge comes from testimony, or from arguments or evidence that we are presented with. Those testifying, or presenting the arguments or evidence, are usually people. And people are generally (though not always) perceived by us as members of social groups. Moreover, much of the knowledge we already have has come to us in this way. Our acceptance or rejection of testimony, arguments, evidence and the like has shaped the worldviews we have now. And this acceptance or rejection was, we can be fairly certain, distorted by the perceived social groups[8] of those presenting the testimony, arguments or evidence. Worse yet, we cannot even go back and attempt to consider or correct errors that we might have made—we are very unlikely to remember the sources of these beliefs of ours.

...

[Chris] Hookway writes that there are three key features to 'an interesting sceptical challenge'. (1990: 164)

1. It must make reference to 'part of our practice of obtaining information about our surroundings which we find natural, which it does not ordinarily occur to us to challenge.'
2. '[I]t must have a certain generality: challenges to the reliability of particular thermometers may lead us to lose confidence in that particular instrument; they do not lead us to lose confidence in ourselves as inquirers.'

---

*   This is an allusion to Hume's problem of induction (see the Hume selection in the Philosophy of Science section of this volume).

†   Anonymized material has all information about who it came from removed.

3. '[I]t must intimate that the feature of our practice which it draws attention to *could not* be defended.'

It seems to me that bias-related doubt easily meets each of these criteria. The practices called into question are ones that we normally don't think to question: our 'instinctive' sense that someone is credible, that a reason is convincing, or that an argument is compelling. There is definitely generality—this isn't like challenges just to probabilistic reasoning, which Hookway rightly flags as not that worrying because those challenges are very contained. Instead, it's challenges to the ordinary ways that we assess reasons, arguments evidence and testimony. Finally, the feature it calls attention to—our judgments are illicitly influenced by irrelevant matters in a way that frequently leads to injustice—is deeply indefensible.

What the literature on implicit bias shows us is that we *really should not* trust ourselves as inquirers. As Hookway argues (2003: 200), 'we can persevere with our inquiries only if we are confident that ... our reflection will take appropriate routes'. But we have now discovered that our reflection takes wholly inappropriate routes: we are not only failing to assess claims or arguments by methods that we endorse but we are instead assessing them by methods that we actively oppose. As he notes, only a part of the process of deliberation is conscious, and we need to be able to trust the habits of thought that underpin the unconscious bits (Hookway 1990: 11). We need to trust not just that they will guide us to truth but that they are based in values that we consider our own. Hookway raises the values concern when discussing an obsessive who is unable to stop repeatedly rehearsing doubts that he does not fully endorse, but the concern arises even more strongly in the case of biases against members of stigmatized groups. The literature on implicit bias shows us not just that our habits can't be relied on to lead us to truth, but also that—insofar as they can be described as based in values at all—they are likely to be based in values that we (most of us, anyway)

find repugnant. It is difficult to see how we could ever properly trust these again once we have reflected on implicit bias. And, Hookway (2000: Chapter 10) argues, self-trust is a necessary condition of responsible inquiry.

2.2 COMPARISON TO LIVE SCEPTICAL SCENARIOS

Bryan Frances's work on 'live sceptical scenarios' (Frances 2005), provides another instructive comparison. Frances characterizes traditional sceptical arguments as relying on the fact that certain hypotheses cannot be ruled out. He notes that responses to these often involve pointing out that, while these hypotheses cannot be ruled out, they are nonetheless not really *live*—they are so implausible that we can't really take them seriously. His book is devoted to arguing that there are sceptical hypotheses that are not like this. In his live sceptical scenarios, 'there are compelling scientific and philosophical reasons to think that the hypotheses are actually true'. Therefore, the traditional replies do not apply.

Now this looks quite a lot like what I have called Bias-Related Doubt. The hypotheses are ones for which there is compelling reason for thinking that they are true. But on closer inspection, it turns out that these reasons are far less compelling. The hypotheses in question are things like eliminativism* about belief and error theory about colour.† And the reasons for thinking that they are still live is that some sensible people who know a great deal endorse (or might endorse) these theories on the grounds of compelling scientific or philosophical reasons. But this falls a good deal short of what I have argued about bias-related doubt. Here the hypothesis is that we are frequently making errors that have their root in implicit bias. My claim is not just that the hypothesis is live—that sensible and knowledgeable people might endorse it on the basis of good reasons. Instead, it's that *we all have very good reason to believe that it is true*. And this is

---

*   Eliminativism about beliefs is the view that beliefs (and, usually, other mental states such as desires, thoughts, etc.) do not in fact exist; when we talk about a person "having a belief," we are simply mistaken; beliefs, etc., are not constituted by brain states or independent mental states either. Like witchcraft, they simply do not exist.

†   Error theory (about color) is the view that colors do not exist in reality, and that when we make statements about certain objects having certain colors (e.g., "The sky is blue") we are mistaken.

much stronger than the claim that a hypothesis is live. We will see that there are also differences with regard to how we should respond.

3 What Should We Do?

The scepticism created by learning about implicit bias differs dramatically from most other forms of scepticism in that it leads to the conclusion that we should change our behaviour. A striking feature of the sorts of scepticism that have tended to dominate discussion in recent times is that *even if* we became convinced by them, we would not feel the need to change anything about our behaviour: accepting that I don't know whether I'm a brain in a vat or not simply doesn't affect how I will go about living my life. Becoming a sceptic of the traditional sort doesn't lead me to decide differently about anything in the course of my every day life, or to alter my behaviour in any way.

But not all forms of scepticism are like these in their lack of impact on behaviour: Pyrrhonian scepticism* was meant to have a large and salutary impact on one's life. The convinced Pyrrhonian sceptic would learn to simply accept appearances rather than striving for belief.

> 'If he avoids "belief", the Pyrrhonist "acquiesces in appearances": he is guided by sensory appearances and by bodily needs and natural desires; he conforms to the prevailing customs and standards of his society.'[9]

Accepting appearances and conforming to prevailing customs and standards, of course, is very much *not* what a would-be responsible enquirer should feel moved to do after learning about implicit bias. For the literature on implicit bias shows that the way things appear to us is perniciously affected by biases that we are unaware of and would repudiate if we became aware of them. To put it bluntly, accepting appearances would mean acquiescing in one's reaction of fear at the sight of a black man; and acquiescing in one's greater sense of approval when looking at a CV with a man's name at the top of it. That these would not rise to the level of belief may mean that we're not committed to falsehoods. But the behaviours we would be led to would be just as troubling. As Hookway notes (1990: 18), the Pyrrhonist's 'is a very conservative outlook: the appearances he relies on are salient for him because of their conventional role.' Relying on the conventions of one's society is deeply cast into doubt by the literature on implicit bias.

The scepticism produced by implicit bias demands action. There are several reasons for this. The first reason is that the sceptical scenario is one that is troubling in a very different way from more traditional sceptical scenarios. If you actually are a brain in a vat, you're probably doing about as well with your life as you can. It's not clear that you would make different choices if you knew the scenario to hold. (And this is just as true for the live sceptical scenarios Frances considers, like those based in eliminativism or colour error theory.) But if you actually are basing lots of decisions on the social categories that people you encounter belong to, then you're clearly not doing as well as you can. You're making the wrong decisions epistemically speaking: taking an argument to be better than it is, perhaps; or wrongly discounting the view of someone you should listen to. You're also making the wrong decisions practically speaking: assigning the wrong mark to an essay, or rejecting a paper that you should accept. Finally, you're making the wrong decisions morally speaking: you are treating people unfairly; and you are basing your decisions on stereotypes that you find morally repugnant. So when the possibility is raised that you're doing this, it should not be possible to shrug it off in the way that it's perfectly reasonable to shrug off the brain in a vat possibility. Worse yet, it's not just the *possibility* that's raised: the research on implicit bias suggests that it's very likely that you're doing these things, with respect to at least some social categories.

But usually, you can't do anything at all to rule out the sceptical scenarios. And the same is true when it comes to any particular instance of the implicit bias sceptical scenario. Did I judge that woman's work to be less good than it was due to her gender? I will never

---

* Pyrrho (c. 360–c. 270 BCE) was a Greek philosopher who founded the school of Pyrrhonism, or Pyrrhonian skepticism, which was influential in the ancient Greek and Roman world. Its main tenet is that we should suspend belief concerning any proposition that is not completely evident.

know, because I won't get the opportunity to assess it without knowledge of her gender. And the same is true for certain more general versions: have I based much of what I think I know on epistemically irrelevant factors like social categories? I'm not going to be able to find out. So is there *anything* one can do? Not for past cases like these. However, I can act so as to reduce the likelihood of this happening in future instances.

Importantly, though, some of the most obvious things to do just don't work. Getting a woman to judge another woman's work is a poor check against bias, since both men and women are likely to hold biases causing them to negatively judge women's work (recall Moss-Racusin's 2012 CV study). Trying hard to be unprejudiced can backfire, if one doesn't go about it in just the right way (Legault et al. 2011). Reflecting on past instances in which one managed to do the right thing makes one *more* likely, not less likely to be biased (Moskowitz and Li). So what should one do?

Fortunately, there are some things we can do. Obviously anonymising can prevent us from even being aware of the social group that might trigger our implicit biases.[10] But anonymising is not a solution that's always available or appropriate, so it's fortunate that psychologists are discovering a lot of surprising interventions that seem to reduce the influence of implicit biases. We can spend time thinking about counter-stereotypical exemplars (members of stereotyped groups who don't fit the group stereotypes).[11] We can carefully form implementation intentions—not 'I will not be influenced by race' but 'when I see a black face I will think 'safe'' (Stewart and Payne 2008). We can spend a few hours engaging in Kawakami's negation training, in which we practice strongly negating stereotypes (Kawakami et al. 2000). But this might not work, unless we use Johnson's (2009) variant in which we think 'NO, THAT'S WRONG!' while pressing a space bar whenever presented with a stereotypical pairing. We can reflect on past instances in which we *failed* in efforts to be unbiased, thereby activating our motivation to control prejudice (Moskowitz and Li). And these are just a few examples.

Interestingly, some very effective interventions—like Kawakami's negation training—are widely viewed as far too demanding for widespread adoption. Alex Madva (manuscript), however, has argued extremely compellingly that these have been dismissed far too

quickly. And he has a point—what's a few hours of slightly tedious exercises if it can actually make me less prejudiced? The arguments I have presented here suggest that we may well also have very strong *epistemic* reasons as well for adopting these techniques. If we don't try to overcome the pernicious influences of these biases, we are not being responsible enquirers.[12]

Importantly, though, we are unlikely to completely eliminate the threat of error. Implicit bias could be affecting one's reasoning at almost any point—it is very hard to judge when social group membership is having a pernicious influence. So it is much trickier to correct for than other factors that are known to make one unreliable (e.g. 'don't make important decisions when drunk'). If we knew that we were about to enter a situation in which implicit biases might impair our thinking, and we knew exactly which biases would be relevant, we could formulate appropriate implementation intentions, like 'If I see black person, I will think "safe". But we don't in general know which stigmatized social groups we will encounter at which points, or what stereotype will be relevant. (Thinking 'safe' when we see a black person will not help us to more accurately assess the quality of their written work.) Moreover, we don't know what sorts of cognitive task might be relevant. So far, I have focused mostly on assessments of quality of argument, or of believability. But implicit biases surely affect other epistemically relevant matters as well: they might lead me to ask the wrong questions, or to neglect the right ones. Implementation intentions are a powerful device for controlling the expression of biases, but by their nature they target very specific behaviours. They cannot provide the general sort of reshaping of the cognitive faculties that would be needed to fully combat the influence of implicit biases. At the end of the paper, I'll discuss what this limitation to our individual corrective measures means for us.

4 Our Rational Capacities

Miranda Fricker is one of the few epistemologists who has thought long and hard about the negative epistemic effects of stereotypes. Her focus, however, is on the way that these affect evaluations of testimony from those that the stereotypes target, and she does not discuss the literature on implicit bias. This literature (as we have seen) shows the pernicious epistemic influence of stereotypes to extend far beyond evaluation of testimony. Still, Fricker's discussion is highly relevant: she argues that those who underrate the testimonies of others due to wrongful stereotyping of their social group are committing an injustice, and that they suffer from an epistemic vice.* This terminology seems wholly appropriate to apply to those in the grip of pernicious implicit biases. It seems worth examining, then, what she says about correcting for prejudices.

Fricker suggests that there are two ways to be a virtuous agent in terms of accepting testimony. The first is to be 'naively' virtuous—to simply have credibility judgments that are not influenced by prejudice. She admits that this will be difficult to manage with respect to the prejudices of the culture/sub-culture one grows up in. The next is to reflectively correct one's judgments—to, for instance, think 'I'm white, and I may fail to give sufficient credibility judgment to black people as a result.' Or, alternatively, to notice that despite consciously believing women to be the equals of men, one tends to always take a man's word over a woman's. Noticing these things, she suggests, allows one to consciously raise the credibility one assigns to members of stigmatized groups. And this possibility, she suggests, is essential to our status as rational enquirers:

> 'The claim that testimonial sensibility is a capacity of reason crucially depends on its capacity to adapt in this way, for otherwise it would be little more than a dead-weight social conditioning that looked more like a threat to the justification of a hearer's responses than a source of that justification.' (84)

Extending this idea in a natural way, we would expect the capacity to consciously, critically, reflectively correct for one's biases quite generally to be crucial to one's epistemic capacities being capacities of reason.

Before we learn about implicit bias and what to do about it, it is genuinely unclear to me whether we have this ability to critically and reflectively correct for our bias. We could perhaps claim that we had the *ability* to do that (once we learned about the evidence, etc.) but this claim would be so weak as not to amount to actually be very reassuring. Now, however, many of us do have the ability to critically and reflectively correct for our biases—at least once we have learned about their existence and studied the literature on what to do about them. Once we do that (and implement these techniques), we can responsibly claim that these capacities are not just dead-weight social conditioning. Importantly, though, this requires more than what Fricker imagined in her discussion: we are unlikely to notice through individualistic reflection the ways that our judgments are affected by social categories; and even when we do notice this we are unlikely to hit upon the right strategies for fighting it. The only way that we can engage in the necessary sort of correction is not individualistically or introspectively, but by informing ourselves about what scientists have discovered about humans like ourselves. The correction is dependent not just on our rational faculties but on the deliverances of science.

In order to inquire responsibly, we must instead recognize that our epistemic capacities are prone to errors that we cannot learn about through first-person reflection; and that we must correct them using counter-intuitive mechanical techniques that draw not upon our rational agency but upon automatic and unconscious responses. We can consciously enlist these unconscious responses, and use them to improve our epistemic responses, but we cannot do this through rational and critical reflection alone.

Moreover, as I noted in the previous section, individual efforts are inevitably limited.

To fully combat the influence of implicit biases, what we really need to do is to re-shape our social world. The stereotypes underlying implicit biases can only fully be broken down by creating more integrated neighborhoods and workplaces; by having women, people of colour and disabled people in positions of power; by having men in nurturing roles; and so on. The only way to be fully freed from the grip of bias-related doubt is to create a social world where the

---

* Saul describes Fricker's position in terms of virtue and vice, terminology that is often used in contemporary epistemology. An epistemic vice is a character trait that leads to bad knowledge practices; gullibility, dogmatism, and closed-mindedness are common examples, whereas conscientiousness and open-mindedness are epistemic virtues.

stereotypes that now warp our judgments no longer hold sway over us. And the way to do this is to end the social regularities that feed and support these stereotypes. Can this be done? Who knows. It is a massive task—one whose importance and magnitude Elizabeth Anderson makes clear (for the case of race) in her *The Imperative of Integration*. But if it is not, we would seem to be stuck with bias-related doubt, and with the consequent lack of trust in our cognitive faculties. And this is in itself quite a fascinating result. Scepticism is generally thought of as a highly individualistic epistemic issue. It's about the would-be knower doubting the guidance of her own mind. But bias-related doubt shows us a social dimension to this. We have seen that the social world gives rise to a powerful form of doubt, and one that can only be fully answered by a sweeping and radical transformation of our social world.[13] ∎

Suggestions for Critical Reflection

1. The main conclusion of this paper is that bias-related skepticism is far more worrisome than traditional philosophical skepticism. In what ways is bias-related skepticism said to be worse than traditional skepticism? Do you agree? What are the main components of Saul's argument for this conclusion?

2. Saul stresses that bias-related doubt is "not *just* a matter of what Miranda Fricker has called testimonial injustice." What does she mean by this? In what way does bias-related doubt go above and beyond testimonial injustice?

3. "The only way that we can engage in the necessary sort of correction is not individualistically or introspectively, but by informing ourselves about what scientists have discovered about humans like ourselves." Why does Saul say this, and how important is it? Is she right?

4. To what extent are people morally responsible for their own biases? Is society on the whole responsible? What are the implications of off-loading responsibility for biases from individuals onto society as a whole?

5. Have you observed implicit bias affecting your own judgment? If you have, how might you attempt to eliminate those biases? If you have not, how might you go about determining whether you are affected by implicit biases?

Notes

1 See, for example, Scheman 2002.

2 For a great deal more precision about the many different ways of characterizing implicit bias, and the many sorts of implicit biases there are, see Holroyd and Sweetman (forthcoming).

3 See, for example, Bertrand and Mullainathan 2004; Rooth 2007; Moss-Racusin et al. 2012; Steinpreis et al. 1999.

4 See, for example Correll et. al. 2002, 2007; Greenwald, Oakes, & Hoffman 2003; Payne 2001; Plant & Peruche 2005.

5 For much more on how perception is affected, see Siegel 2013.

6 Here I am assuming that philosophers will be prone to the same sorts of errors as others. They have not actually been studied.

7 I am *not* saying that we are affected only by biases. Of course, a part of what we are doing is applying our skill in evaluating philosophy, and sometimes we will get things right. My claim is just that these judgments will often be distorted, to a variable extent, by biases.

8 I phrase it this way because what affects us as audiences is what social group we *take* the speaker to be a member of, not what social group they are actually a member of.

9 Hookway (1990: 6).

10 This worked beautifully with orchestras, which began holding auditions behind screens, dramatically increasing their percentages of female members. And it is now standard practice in the UK to mark students' work anonymously, which is supported by the Union of Students for just this reason: <http://www.nusconnect.org.uk/campaigns/highereducation/archived/

learning-and-teaching-hub/anonymous-marking/>. For research on anonymous marking see Bradley 1984, 1993.

11 Blair 2002; Kang and Banaji 2006.

12 Madva also responds to criticisms that these techniques are not effective enough, and that they are too individualistic, focusing as they do on individual thinkers rather than societal reform.

13 I had very useful discussions of this paper with several different audiences: The ENFA5 Conference in Braga, Portugal; the Eastern APA audience in Washington DC; and the departmental seminars at Nottingham and Southampton. I have also benefitted enormously from discussions with Louise Antony, Ray Drainville, Miranda Fricker, Teresa Marques and especially Chris Hookway—to whom this paper owes an obvious and enormous debt. (Though the errors are all mine.)

References

Anderson, E. 2010. *The Imperative of Integration*. Princeton: Princeton University Press.

Beebee, H. and Saul, J. 2011. *Women in Philosophy in the UK: A Report*, published by the British Philosophical Association and the Society for Women in Philosophy. (<9-08/Women%20in%20Philosophy%20in%20the%20UK%20(BPA-SWIPUK%20Report).pdf>)

Bertrand, M. and Mullainathan, S. 2004. Are Emily and Greg more employable than Lakisha and Jamal? *American Economic Review*, 94, 991–1013.

Blair, I. 2002. The Malleability of Automatic Stereotypes and Prejudice. *Personality and Social Psychology Review*, 3, 242–261.

Bradley, C. 1984. Sex bias in the evaluation of students. *British Journal of Social Psychology*, 23: 2, 147–153.

Bradley, C. 1993. Sex bias in student assessment overlooked? *Assessment and Evaluation in Higher Education* 18:1, 3–8.

Correll, J., Park, B., Judd, C., & Wittenbrink, B. 2002. The police officer's dilemma: Using ethnicity to disambiguate potentially threatening individuals. *Journal of Personality and Social Psychology*, 83, 1314–1329.

Correll, J., Park, B., Judd, C., Wittenbrink, B., Sadler, M.S., & Keesee, T. 2007. Across the thin blue line: Police officers and racial bias in the decision to shoot. *Journal of Personality and Social Psychology*, 92, 1006–1023.

Frances, B. 2005. *Scepticism Comes Alive*. Oxford: Oxford University Press.

Fricker, M. 2007. *Epistemic Injustice: Power and the Ethics of Knowing*. Oxford: Oxford University Press.

Goldin, C. and Rouse, C. 2000. Orchestrating Impartiality: The Impact of 'Blind' Auditions on Female Musicians. *The American Economic Review*, 90:4, 715–741.

Greenwald, A.G., Oakes, M.A. and Hoffman, H. 2003b. Targets of discrimination: Effects of race on responses to weapons holders. *Journal of Experimental Social Psychology*, 39 399–405.

Holroyd, J. and Sweetman, J. Forthcoming.* The Heterogeneity of Implicit Bias. In *Implicit Bias and Philosophy*, ed. by M. Brownstein and J. Saul. Oxford: Oxford University Press.

Hookway, C. 1990. *Scepticism*. London: Routledge.

Hookway, C. 2000. *Truth, Rationality, and Pragmatism: Themes From Peirce*. Oxford: Oxford University Press.

Hookway, C. 2003. How to Be a Virtue Epistemologist. In *Intellectual Virtue: Perspectives from Ethics and Epistemology*, ed. by M. DePaul and L. Zagzebski. Oxford University Press.

Hookway, C. 2010. Some Varieties of Epistemic Injustice: Response to Fricker. *Episteme* 7:2, 151–163.

Johnson, I.R. 2009. *Just say 'No' (and mean it): Meaningful negation as a tool to modify automatic racial prejudice*. Doctoral dissertation, Ohio State University.

Kang, J. and Banaji, M. 2006. Fair Measures: A Behavioral Realist Revision of 'Affirmative Action'. *California Law Review* 94, 1063–1118.

Kawakami, K., Dovidio, J.F., Moll, J., Hermsen, S., and Russin, A. 2000. Just say no (to stereotyping): effects of training in the negation of stereotypic associations on stereotype activation. *Journal of Personality and Social Psychology*, 78, 871–888.

Legault, L., Gutsell, J., and Inzlicht, M. 2011. Ironic Effects of Antiprejudice Messages: How Motivational Interventions Can Reduce (But also Increase) Prejudice. *Psychological Science* 22(12), 1472–1477.

Madva, A. 2013. The Biases Against Debiasing. Paper presented at *Implicit Bias, Philosophy and Psychology Conference*, Sheffield, April 2013.

Moskowitz, G. and Li, P. 2011. Egalitarian Goals Trigger Stereotype Inhibition: A Proactive Form of Stereotype

---

* Now published: 2016.

Control, *Journal of Experimental Social Psychology* 47, 103–16.

Moss-Racusin, C., Dovidio, J., Brescoll, V., Graham, M., Handelsman, J. 2012. Science Faculty's Subtle Gender Biases Favor Male Students. *PNAS* 109(41), 16395–16396.

Payne, B.K. 2001. Prejudice and perception: The role of automatic and controlling processes in misperceiving a weapon. *Journal of Personality and Social Psychology*, 81, 181–192.

Peters, Douglas P. and Stephen J. Ceci. 1982. Peer-review practices of psychological journals: The fate of published articles, submitted again. *Behavioral and Brain Sciences* 5, 187–255.

Plant, E.A. and Peruche, B.M. 2005. The consequences of race for police officers' responses to criminal suspects. *Psychological Science*, 16, 180–183. *Price-Waterhouse v. Hopkins*, 109 S. Ct. 1775. (1989).

Rooth, D. 2007. Implicit discrimination in hiring: Real world evidence (IZA Discussion Paper No. 2764). Bonn, Germany: Forschungsinstitut zur Zukunft der Arbeit (Institute for the Study of Labor).

Saul, J. Forthcoming. Implicit Bias, Stereotype Threat and Women in Philosophy. In *Women in Philosophy: What Needs to Change?*, ed. by F. Jenkins and K. Hutchison.

Oxford: Oxford University Press. (Formerly titled 'Unconscious Influences and Women in Philosophy'.)*

Scheman, N. 2002. Though This Be Method, Yet there Is Madness in It: Paranoia and Liberal Epistemology. In *A Mind of One's Own: Feminist Essays on Reason and Objectivity*, ed. by L. Antony and C. Witt. Cambridge, MA: Westview.

Steinpreis, R., Anders, K., and Ritzke, D. 1999. The Impact of Gender on the Review of the Curricula Vitae of Job Applicants and Tenure Candidates: A National Empirical Study. *Sex Roles*, 41:7/8, 509–528.

Siegel, S. 2013. Can Selection Effects on Experience Influence Its Rational Role? *Oxford Studies in Epistemology* Vol. 4: 240–270.

Stewart, B.D. and Payne, B.K. 2008. Bringing Automatic Stereotyping under Control: Implementation Intentions as Efficient Means of Thought Control. *Personality and Social Psychology Bulletin*, 34, 1332–1345.

Unkelbach, C., Forgas, J., and Denson, T. 2008. The Turban Effect: The Influence of Muslim Headgear and Induced Affect on Aggressive Responses in the Shooter Bias Paradigm. *Journal of Experimental Social Psychology* 44:5, 1409–1413.

---

*   Now published: 2013.

LEE HESTER AND JIM CHENEY

Truth and Native American Epistemology

Who Are Lee Hester and Jim Cheney?

Lee Hester is Professor of American Indian Studies at the University of Science and Arts of Oklahoma, where he is also the Director of the department. Hester holds an MA and PhD in Philosophy from the University of Oklahoma. His scholarly interests extend beyond philosophy to American Indian Studies more broadly, and he has taught a wide range of courses in the area. His book *Political Principles and Indian Sovereignty* (2001) argues in favor of Native American sovereignty, contending that the denial of sovereignty to Native Americans contradicts the underlying principles of American democracy. A member of the Choctaw Nation of Oklahoma, Hester is a former President and Chairman of the Board of the Oklahoma Choctaw Tribal Alliance, a member of the Wordcraft Circle of Native Writers and Storytellers, a founding Board Member of the Choctaw Code Talkers Association, and Executive Director of the Meredith Indigenous Humanities Center, which helps to develop and implement humanities courses suited to individual Indigenous communities. He was awarded the Presidential Award of Excellence for Environmental Protection Services in 1973.

Jim Cheney was a Professor of Philosophy at the University of Wisconsin-Waukesha, where he taught for four decades. Cheney's teaching and scholarship focused on epistemology, environmental ethics, and North American Indigenous philosophy. He published numerous articles in the journal *Environmental Ethics*, including "Eco-Feminism and Deep Ecology" (1989), "Postmodern Environmental Ethics: Ethics of Bioregional Narrative" (1989), and "Naturalizing the Problem of Evil" (1997). Cheney, who also published under the name Shagbark Hickory, was a Rockefeller Foundation Visiting Humanities Fellow with the Native Philosophy Project at Lakehead University and the first Visiting Scholar in Residence of Ecophilosophy and Earth Education at Murdoch University in Australia. He died in 2016.

What Is the Structure of This Reading?

This article is the work of two authors who have each contributed half of the text. Both authors share the same overall purpose: to present an understanding of knowledge that is common in Native American traditions, and to contrast this understanding with Western philosophy's focus on scientific knowledge and its abstract notions of belief and truth.

In the first portion of the article, Jim Cheney outlines the challenges Native American epistemology poses to common Western understandings of knowledge. In Native American ways of knowing, Cheney finds alternatives first to the commonplace Western notion of truth, and then even to the Western notion of belief itself. He also contrasts Western epistemology's focus on "refutation and critical objection" with an aboriginal approach that seeks what he calls "responsible truth." The pursuit of responsible truth requires an ethically informed methodology, not one that treats knowledge as a set of abstract propositions that are true or false independent of experience and community. According to Cheney, Native American ways of knowing favor ethical maturity rather than the methodical accumulation of intellectual knowledge.

In the second half of the article, Lee Hester combines a traditional Western philosophical approach—the direct articulation of principles and arguments—with a traditional Native American approach based in storytelling. Using these methods, he outlines the role of practice, lived experience, and narrative in Native American ways of knowing. In doing so he takes up the metaphor, introduced by Cheney, of "the map and the territory"; while in Western epistemology the "map" of one's worldview is thought to correspond directly to the "territory" of the real world, in Native American epistemology the "map is not meant to be a high fidelity picture of the territory, but is an action guiding set of ideas" that are often expressed in narrative. He emphasizes the guiding role played by stories themselves, rather than any propositions or "truths" one might derive from them: "the narrative is as close to the truth as you can get."

Truth and Native American Epistemology*

I.

Two stories about Native American epistemology: one (Jim's) by a white Euro-American, the other (Lee's) by a Choctaw† Native American. Lee's story, though written to some extent in a language and style of Euro-American philosophy and foregoing many traditional teaching techniques, comes from a Native American world and—although he rightly states in his story that 'I [Lee] do not and cannot claim any special authority on these issues, I am neither a medicine-man nor an elder' (a statement that does not represent false humility, as we shall see)—there is the authority of one who speaks from a Native American world—no footnotes!—as contrasted with the lack of that authority in my story, which merely peeks into Native American worlds, gleaning small understandings as best I can.[1] For this reason, Lee's story follows—and indirectly comments on—mine.

The question 'How important is truth to knowledge and epistemology?'... has been a central concern in my work in environmental ethics and Native American philosophy. My reflections on this and related questions came to a focus in my work on the linked notions of 'ceremonial worlds' and narrative, which I began to think about while listening to indigenous people in Whitehorse, Yukon Territory in 1995 and in Thunder Bay, Ontario while working with the Native Philosophy Project during 1996–1997 (see Cheney and Weston, 1999). Ceremonial worlds are the worlds (or stories) within which we live, the worlds (myths, if you like) that have the power to orient us in

life. They define for us the nature of the sacred (that in which meaning is located, the more-than-human dimensions of our worlds), the natural and the human, and the relationships between them.[2] A starting place for me in developing the notion of a ceremonial world was Louise Profeit-LeBlanc's explication of the Northern Tutchone‡ term *tłi an oh* in response to a question posed to her concerning whether the stories she used in her work with at risk children were 'true'. In response, she used the term *tłi an oh* (usually glossed as 'what they say, it's true') and defined it as meaning 'correctly true', 'responsibly true' (a 'responsible truth'), 'true to what you believe in', 'what is good for you and the community' and 'rings true for everybody's well-being'.[3] Aside from the question of whether there is a concept of truth *simpliciter*§ in Northern Tutchone or only the concept of a *responsible* truth (and, presumably, its correlate: the concept of an irresponsible truth), *tłi an oh* does at least suggest a way of stepping beyond the 'defeat and confusion' Nelson Goodman and Catherine Elgin argue is built into the notions of truth and knowledge in contemporary Western philosophy.[4]

Making use of J.L. Austin's notion of the performative function of language,¶ a ceremonial world (in the fullest sense of the term) is an actively constructed portrait of the world intended to be responsibly true, one which rings true for everybody's well-being. It is a world built on the basis of an ethical-epistemological orientation of attentiveness (or, as Native Americans tend to put it, *respect*) rather than an epistemology of control. Such ceremonial worlds, built, as they are,

---

* Lee Hester and Jim Cheney, "Truth and Native American Epistemology," *Social Epistemology* 15, 4 (2001): 319–34.

† The Choctaw originally occupied what is now the Southeastern United States (Alabama, Florida, Mississippi, and Louisiana). People have, of course, lived in this area for thousands of years and the Choctaw people coalesced as a distinct group of tribes in the seventeenth century. They never went to war against the United States but nevertheless were forcibly relocated in 1831–33, as part of the 'Indian Removal,' in order for European Americans to take over their land.

‡ An Athabascan First Nation whose territory encompasses the central region of the Yukon Territory in Canada.

§ Latin term meaning "in the most complete sense, without qualification."

¶ Austin (1911–60) was an influential English philosopher of language, the author of *How to Do Things with Words* (1955). Among the things he emphasised is that language can be used to perform actions—such as to make a promise or to apologize—as well as to make (true or false) statements.

around the notion of responsible truth, are not developed piecemeal, but are synthetic* creations, adjusted holistically to all the concerns that arise from a focus on responsible truth: they must tie down to the world of everyday practice and experience in a way that makes it possible to survive; they must orient the community and its individuals on roads of life that allow for the flourishing of all members of the community as far as that is possible. The metaphysics or ontology of such a world will not be understood as *true* in the modern sense of the term. The issue is always (if implicitly) whether it is responsibly, or correctly, true; is it action guiding in the full sense just delineated?

In this full sense of the term, ceremonial worlds exist, so far as my experience goes, only in indigenous cultures. All of us live within ceremonial worlds in some sense, however, though nonindigenous ceremonial worlds tend to be diminished worlds. The ceremonial worlds of the West, for example, are diminished in the sense that they are not intended to be responsibly true worlds, ones that ring true for everybody's well-being. Nor are they worlds built on the basis of an ethical-epistemological orientation of attentiveness (respect). Rather, these worlds pretend to be value-neutral 'true' accounts of how the world really is. The so-called value-neutral project of building a 'true' account of the way the world is is severed from the project of creating a world in which humans can and do flourish. Moreover, these worlds tend to be built in accordance with epistemologies of domination and control; and it is within these worlds that we propose ethical theories and projects to *counter* domination and control. This peculiar and unfortunate situation arises because we do not see that our world-building projects are themselves founded (though implicitly) on epistemological foundations that all but guarantee that the explicitly ethical projects we set ourselves within these worlds will fail.

In a series of articles,[5] Vine Deloria, Jr has given us a portrait of epistemological relationships within the world of the 'old Indians, people who had known the life of freedom before they were confined to the reservations and subjected to Western religious and educational systems' that resonates remarkably with the notion of ceremonial worlds and takes it a significant step further.

'The real interest of the old Indians', Deloria says, 'was not to find the abstract structure of physical reality but rather to find the proper road along which, for the duration of a person's life, individuals were supposed to walk' (Deloria *et al.*, 1999, p. 46). This is key to understanding Native American epistemology: It is ethically informed;[6] any 'truths' that emerge in Native American worlds are 'responsible truths', in Louise Profeit-LeBlanc's sense of the term. 'Lacking a spiritual, social, or political dimension [in their scientific practice]', Deloria says, 'it is difficult to understand why Western peoples believe they are so clever. Any damn fool can treat a living thing as if it were a machine and establish conditions under which it is required to perform certain functions—all that is required is a sufficient application of brute force. The result of brute force is slavery' (Deloria *et al.*, 1999, p. 13). 'Science *forces* secrets from nature by experimentation, and the results of the experiments are thought to be knowledge. The traditional peoples *accepted* secrets from the rest of creation' (Deloria *et al.*, 1999, p. 135). Lacking an ethical dimension, the epistemology of Western scientific method produces something that can be called 'knowledge' only in an attenuated sense: 'We may elicit and force secrets from nature, but it is only answering the specific questions we ask it. It is not giving us the whole story as it would if it were specifically involved in the communication of knowledge' (Deloria *et al.*, 1999, p. 136).

Another, related, key to understanding Native American epistemology is its attitude with respect to anomalies—data or experiences that do not seem to fit into the patterns that have so far emerged in one's observations of nature.

> Within the life history of maturity one can be said to travel from information to knowledge to wisdom. Organisms gather information, and as the cumulative amount begins to achieve a critical mass, patterns of interpretation and explanation begin to appear—even thoughts seem to form themselves into societies at a certain level of complexity. Here it is that Western science prematurely derives its scientific 'laws' and assumes that the products of its own mind are inherent in the structure of the

---

* I.e., involving the combination of parts into a whole interrelated system.

universe. But American Indians allow the process to continue, recognizing that premature analysis will produce anomalies and give incomplete understanding. (Deloria *et al.*, 1999, p. 14)

At the point where 'patterns of interpretation and explanation' begin to emerge, the epistemological methods of Western science and Native American epistemological methods part ways. As Lee's story puts it, in Western science (and philosophy) *belief* enters the picture ('Western science prematurely derives its scientific "laws" and assumes that the products of its own mind are inherent in the structure of the universe') and the map is taken as a *true* account of the territory; the map is mistaken for the territory. For the Native American, both the map and the territory are real, but the map is not (is not understood as a true picture of) the territory. The Western understanding of 'true belief' is absent in Native American epistemology. As Deloria puts it in another context, 'it is important to note that [Indians] are dealing with recognitions, not beliefs that have an intellectual content; and recognitions, like perceptions, involve the totality of personality' (Deloria *et al.*, 1999, p. 362). Native Americans do not get stuck as Western thought does: 'An old chief of the Crow tribe from Montana was asked to describe the difference between his tribe and the whites who lived nearby. Pausing slightly and drawing his conclusions, he remarked that the white man has ideas [beliefs], the Indian has visions' (Deloria *et al.*, 1999, p. 15). Beliefs concern the map and mistake it for the territory; *visions* are integrating experiences at the core of ceremonial worlds that orient Native Americans culturally, spiritually, psychologically, politically, and in matters of subsistence and use of technology. 'Because Western science concentrates so heavily on information and theory, its product is youth, not maturity' (Deloria *et al.*, 1999, p. 15). There is a continuity in the maturation of Native American understanding from information to knowledge to maturity.

Traditional people preserve the whole vision, whereas scientists generally reduce the experience to its alleged constituent parts and inherent principles ... Science leaves anomalies, whereas the unexplained in traditional technology is held as a mystery, accepted, revered, but not discarded as useless. Science operates in fits and starts because the anomalies of one generation often become the orthodoxy of the next generation. (Deloria *et al.*, 1999, p. 135).

The Indian understands dreams, visions, and interspecies communications, when they are available, as a natural part of human experience ... [T]he task is to make sense of the experience or withhold judgment on its meaning until a sufficient number of similar experiences reveal the pattern of meaning that is occurring ... Wisdom ... increases with age. As a person gets older he or she is able to remember and understand a wide variety of events or activities that are species-, location-, and time-specific. Instead of matching generalizations with new phenomena, Indians match a more specific body of information with the immediate event or experience. Exceptions to the rule become a new set of specific behaviors that open new classifications for future information. (Deloria *et al.*, 1999, p. 67–68)

It is time to join the two keys to Native American epistemology so far discussed: the methodological points just made and the earlier point that this methodology is *ethically* informed. 'The old Indians', Deloria says,

were interested in finding the proper moral and ethical road upon which human beings should walk. All knowledge, if it is to be useful, was directed toward that goal. Absent in this approach was the idea that knowledge existed apart from human beings and their communities, and could stand alone for "its own sake." In the Indian conception, it was impossible that there could be abstract propositions that could be used to explore the structure of the physical world. Knowledge was derived from individual and communal experiences in daily life, in keen observation of the environment and in interpretive messages that they received from spirits in ceremonies, visions, and dreams. In formulating their understanding of the world, Indians did not discard any experience. Everything had to be included in the spectrum of knowledge and related to what was already known. (Deloria *et al.*, 1999, p. 43–44)

To use a phrase of Deloria's, we might call the idea that 'In formulating their understanding of the world,

Indians did not discard any experience. Everything had to be included in the spectrum of knowledge and related to what was already known' a 'principle of epistemological method'. Another principle of epistemological method appears, Deloria says, at the end of Black Elk's telling of how the Sioux* received the sacred pipe from White Buffalo Calf Woman and how she taught the people to communicate with the higher powers through the use of the pipe in ceremonies: 'This they tell', Black Elk said, 'and whether it happened so or not, I do not know; but if you think about it, you can see that it is true'. Deloria explicitly calls this statement 'a principle of epistemological method' (Deloria *et al.*, 1999, p. 44). The idea here is more complex than the first principle. As I read it, this second principle points to two ideas: that the account of Buffalo Calf Woman is not necessarily to be understood in literalist, historical terms; the account is to be understood as a depiction of one element of the ceremonial world within which the Oglala Lakota live[7] and that we must always consider (over the course of our entire lives) the ways (often multiple) that a particular story or experience might instruct us; stories and experience are to be understood as having often inexhaustible depth. A third principle of epistemological principle (not explicitly stated as such) is that 'Everything that humans experience has value and instructs us in some aspect of life' (Deloria *et al.*, 1999, p. 45).[8]

These three, closely-related principles might be contrasted with a more critical epistemological method that focuses on refutation and critical objection as the way to truth. In this epistemological style, for example, one might object that the second principle would certainly lead one astray and that the third principle is simply false (or, at least, has not been shown to be true). It should be noted, however, that to shift the burden of proof in this way does not so much *advance* the cause of 'truth' as it shuts down modes of reflecting on experience and stories that may very well lead to insight and knowledge and to 'responsible truth'. The point is similar to one Anthony Weston makes concerning Tom Birch's principle of universal

consideration in environmental ethics. Birch says that his principle demands that all things 'be taken as valuable, even though we may not yet know how or why, until they are proved otherwise' (Birch, 1993, p. 328). Weston comments: 'Actually, even more deeply, universal consideration requires us not merely to extend this kind of benefit of the doubt but actively to take up the case, so to speak, for beings so far excluded or devalued'. Weston then adds, precisely in line with the Native American view that at the heart of one's epistemological relation to the world there must be moral purpose, that 'ethics [a basic etiquette] is primary: ethics opens the way to knowledge, epistemology is value-driven, not vice versa' (Cheney and Weston, 1999, p. 120). Or, as Deloria himself puts it:

> In an epistemological sense, there is no question that the tribal method of gathering information is more sophisticated and certainly more comprehensive than Western science. In most tribal traditions, no data are discarded as unimportant or irrelevant. Indians consider their own individual experiences, the accumulated wisdom of the community that has been gathered by previous generations, their dreams, visions, and prophecies, and any information received from birds, animals, and plants as data that must be arranged, evaluated, and understood as a unified body of knowledge. This mixture of data from sources that the Western scientific world regards as highly unreliable and suspect produces a consistent perspective on the natural world. It is seen by tribal peoples as having wide application. Knowledge about plants and birds can form the basis of ethics, government, and economics as well as provide a means of mapping a large area of land. (Deloria *et al.*, 1999, p. 66–67)

This epistemological style of openness contrasts with the focus on extracting very specific pieces of information, understood within an equally specific set of concepts, that characterizes the controlled experiment of modern science. Deloria in fact contrasts Native

---

* The Sioux, also known as Očhéthi Šakówiŋ, are a large group of Native American and First Nation tribes with ancestral lands in the American Midwest and the Canadian Prairies. The Oglala Lakota are one of those tribes, living in what is now South Dakota.

American epistemology with Thomas Kuhn's understanding of science* as proceeding within paradigms and as being therefore highly selective both in its attention to data and the problems on which it chooses to focus.

Native American epistemological style, as depicted by Deloria, is even more radical than I have so far indicated. The principles of epistemological method so far mentioned are at least straightforwardly epistemological. But Deloria goes further. Many statements coming from Native American worlds that non-Native Americans would understand to be statements of *belief* (truth claims) concerning Native American world views are best understood as principles of epistemological method of a rather different sort than those so far mentioned. Consider, for example, Deloria's portrait of the universe as a moral universe:

> The real interest of the old Indians was not to discover the abstract structure of physical reality but rather to find the proper road along which, for the duration of a person's life, individuals were supposed to walk. This colorful image of the road suggests that the universe is a moral universe. That is to say, there is a proper way to live in the universe: There is a content to every action, behavior, and belief. The sum total of our life experiences has a reality. There is a direction to the universe, empirically exemplified in the physical growth cycles of childhood, youth, and old age, with the corresponding responsibility of every entity to enjoy life, fulfill itself, and increase in wisdom and the spiritual development of personality. Nothing has incidental meaning and there are no coincidences ... In the moral universe all activities, events, and entities are related, and consequently it does not matter what kind of existence an entity enjoys, for the responsibility is always there for it to participate in the continuing creation of reality. (Deloria *et al.*, 1999, p. 46)

These attributes of the moral universe have the same status as the three epistemological principles discussed above. That is, in relationship to the goal of finding the proper road upon which to walk, Native Americans paint a portrait of a moral universe that invites its own fulfillment (see Cheney and Weston, 1999, p. 125–129), they create a ceremonial world that gives direction to the quest for moral understanding and support for living in accordance with that moral understanding. The characteristics of the moral life are not deduced from, or suggested by, a prior, value-neutral account of the structure of the universe or 'metaphysics of morals'; rather, once again, 'ethics opens the way to knowledge, epistemology is value-driven, not vice versa'. This portrait of a moral universe is not properly understood as a set of false (or at least unproven) beliefs or assumptions. Such a view, in the words of Leroy Meyer and Tony Ramirez (Lakota), puts 'too much stock in the word "philosophy"'. As Deloria's account shows, to continue Meyer's and Ramirez's thought, 'there are alternative ways of intelligently engaging the world. To construe one's thinking in terms of belief is characteristic of a particular kind of world view' and indigenous peoples do not seem to 'conceive of experience in such an overtly intellectualized manner' (Meyer and Ramirez, 1996, p. 104).[9] Ceremonial worlds place communication and reciprocity with natural environments—rather than the desire to dominate those environments or to establish 'truth claims' about them—at the very heart of the production of knowledge and wisdom. Ethical maturity rather than true belief is the goal....

2.

Halito. Chim achukma? Sa-hoschifo-ut Lee Hester. *Chatah sia hoke*! Which is to say 'Hello. How are you? My name is Lee Hester. I am a citizen of the Choctaw Nation'. I begin my talks in this way to help emphasize the differences between Native American people and others living in North America. This greeting directly exemplifies differences in language and allegiance. To those that know the law, it points toward differences in legal status and the fact that there are laws that pertain only to American Indians. To everyone, it should point toward the deeper differences in culture and with some study, it perhaps hints at basic differences in world view, or what might from a native perspective be termed 'presence-in-the-world'. I do not and cannot

---

* See the selection from Thomas Kuhn in this volume.

claim any special authority on these issues, I am neither a medicine-man nor an elder. However, I am an enrolled member by blood, I prefer the term 'citizen', of an Indian Nation; I grew up in Oklahoma—which in the Choctaw language means 'Red People'—among Indian people, including my own relatives; my main associations are with Native American people. That, combined with a small amount of western philosophical training, may enable me to provide some observations—hopefully presented in a way which makes them meaningful.

The topic 'Truth and Native American Epistemology' is a grand one. One which I undoubtedly do not have all the 'answers' to, and maybe don't have any answers to. As I said, I will mainly present some observations, though my Euro-American philosophical training will drive me to some deductions based on the observations. Throughout this paper, I will use terms like 'Native American' or 'Indian' as if my conclusions are readily applicable to the peoples of all the sovereign Indian Nations. This is not necessarily true, though I do think there are many similarities from nation to nation. As Viola Cordova has said, any Native American has more in common with any other Native American than with any non-Indian. A short story will serve as a jumping off point for the rest of the talk. I have used this story elsewhere, so I hope I do not bore those of you that have heard it before.

A few years ago I was the professor of a course called 'Native American Identity'. I won't say I was 'teaching it' for many reasons. One of them is that I tried, as much as possible, to use members of the Native American community—particularly elders—as the real teachers. I like to think it is because I recognize that they are the ones who can truly teach it, not just that I am lazy.

One of our speakers was John Proctor, the oldest living Creek* medicine man. He is the uncle of Wanda Davis, a good friend of mine—so I was able to persuade him to spend a three-hour session with the class one evening. Mr. Proctor is a key practitioner of the traditional Creek religion. He is the medicine man for a stomp ground. 'Stomp ground' is the name given to the ceremonial grounds where the Creek practise their religion.

Mostly the students asked the kinds of questions you might expect. Since they thought of Mr. Proctor as a representative of a traditional religion, they asked him cosmogonic[†] or cosmological questions. I was surprised when one of the students asked the ultimate question ... Remember—this was a class on 'Indian Identity'. The student asked, 'What makes you Creek?'

Those of you familiar with the Native American traditions, or those that have attended one of my talks before, would expect the answer to be a rambling narrative that might *seem* not to be an answer at all. This is just what I expected. I settled back in my chair in preparation for Mr. Proctor's answer. Without hesitation he said, 'If you come to the stomp ground for four years, take the medicines and dance the dances, then you are Creek'. The answer was completely unexpected and thus even more forcefully illuminating. Mr Proctor had listed a set of *practices* which made someone Creek, or more properly in context, a member of the traditional Creek religion.

If you asked a member of just about any *Christian* religion what made them Christians, you would get a completely different answer. My Missionary Baptist relatives would tell you that to be Christian you have to 'Accept Jesus Christ as your personal Lord and Saviour'. Acceptance, faith—belief is at the core of Christian religion and not surprisingly at the core of Euro-American philosophy. Just think about how you would characterize different philosophical schools, or different figures in the Euro-American philosophical tradition. This school believed this... the central tenets of that school were... this famed philosopher thought that.... Beliefs, beliefs, beliefs.

Indeed, in the Euro-American philosophical tradition, it is unclear how one would go about doing epistemology at all without belief. The nature of justification, defeasibility,[‡] facticity, truth and a multitude of

---

* The Creek, often known as the Muscogee, are Indigenous peoples originally living in the Southeastern Woodlands of the US (crossing the boundaries of what are now Tennessee, Alabama, Georgia, and Florida), who were forcibly relocated to Oklahoma on the Trail of Tears in the 1830s.

† Having to do with cosmogony, accounts of the origin of the universe.

‡ A claim is defeasible if it can be defeated—if it is probably true, but possibly might not be.

other issues are up for grabs in epistemology, but there is one thing that is usually not questioned. Whatever knowledge may be, it would seem that it at least has to be a belief.

In the Euro-American philosophical tradition, the centrality of belief is clear. Though we may analyse what we are doing at great length, think up different ways of characterizing it, we go about asserting different views of 'the way things are'. These are generally expressed as propositions. To the extent that we buy into them, we 'believe' them. Sometimes, at least according to some epistemologists, we not only believe them but actually 'know' them.

John Proctor's answer points to a different way and the more I review my experiences in the Native American community the more I think that his answer is illuminating. It has helped me understand an interesting experience that I had while 'teaching' in Canada. Here I put the word 'teaching' in scare quotes, because I was more nearly learning than teaching. While in Canada I taught several classes, including an intro philosophy class attended by Daniel BigGeorge, an Anishnabe* who was a member of the Northern Wind drum group and a practitioner of some of the traditional religion. Daniel and I had several interesting encounters, but there was one that is particularly important to this talk.

Daniel came to me one day after class with a very serious demeanor. Generally he laughed and joked as is common among Native American people, but it was clear this time he had something important to say. He talked about the shaking tent ceremony and other ceremonies that a Euro-American might consider 'superstitious'. He ended by asking me if I believed in these ceremonies. I considered the question very carefully. Just what was my view? I have been trained in the Euro-American philosophical tradition, I have taught symbolic logic and other technical classes that are at the core of Western philosophy. Did I really 'believe' in the shaking tent?

I told Daniel that I could not say that I either believed or disbelieved in them. I have seen and experienced things that I do not comprehend in various traditional ceremonies. They are just part of my experience. I know my experiences, but I can't say what I experienced. He explained that he too did not 'believe' in them, though it was clear from what he said that he also did not 'disbelieve' in them. This was one of a couple of turning points in my relation to Daniel. Shortly after this exchange he invited me to come to a traditional ceremony welcoming the bears back after their winter hibernation. As a member of the Bear Clan, this was an important ceremony for Daniel. I was honoured to be invited. It was a great experience, one which I shall always cherish.

Now, I think that our discussion, among other things, may have been a test. As a mixed-blood I am often tested. In fact, at least one Western philosopher has suggested on the basis of how I look that I'm not a 'real' Indian. In the Indian community, the tests are a lot more subtle. If I had answered that I believed, then was I gullible, patronizing or trying to play 'real' Indian? The answer was bit more clear and just as negative if I answered that I disbelieved.

The way in which most ceremonies are approached also points to a form of what we might call non-belief. There is always an interesting mixture of reverence and irreverence in Indian ceremonies. Just about the time that things seem most serious, someone will usually crack a joke. Often it will be the very medicine-man or elder that is conducting the ceremony.

A group of four elders, presided over by Freda MacDonald, conducted a ceremony to consecrate a set of two eagle feathers. One was for Lorraine Brundige, the other for me. As a part of the ceremony, we passed around water for everyone to drink in turn. I was the first person to Freda's left, so I was the first to drink. When the water again reached Freda there was still some left. She passed it to me. I looked uncertain. She said, 'finish it'. I tossed it off at one gulp. Freda started laughing good-naturedly. 'Two feathers, two times around the circle', she explained. We all started joking about how I must be real thirsty, how people might think I was greedy for water and so on. It went on for some time. We finally finished the ceremony without a second circling of the water.

At the end of the ceremony, one of the elders I did not know from a nearby reserve began to talk to

---

*   The Anishnabe peoples historically live in the Northeast Woodlands and Subarctic of North America: Quebec, Ontario, Manitoba, and some of the US Midwest. This includes the Ojibway people.

me in Anishnabe. I had no clue what she was talking about. My Anishnabe is limited to *Meegwetch*, which is 'thank you', and *Ne'weeznin*, which is the closest I can come to 'Let's eat'. However, the elder was clearly imparting something of great importance, so I sat and listened to her intently. After a few minutes Freda began laughing again. 'Wrong kind of Indian', she said, 'he's a Choctaw not an Ojibway'.

Though it's clear that such joking is partly to alleviate tension, gloss over slip-ups and maintain harmony and good-will it also makes sense that this practice is much easier if you do not 'believe' in a western sense. Certainly we have all seen humour used for these purposes in Euro-American ceremonies, but I think those that have experienced both would say the jokes flow much more freely and with less provocation, if any, at a Native American ceremony.

At this point it is important to repeat that this does not mean Native Americans disbelieve in their traditions. Far from it. The traditions are approached with great reverence. Indeed, I think the difference in Native American and Euro-American approaches is so basic and subtle that the English language strains to express it. Unfortunately, since most philosophical dialogue in this country is in English, it is likely that when pressed to the limit it would be better to say that Native American people firmly believe in their tradition than to imply any less reverence.

This is because English has equated belief with truth. Now, I'm doing some Euro-American looking philosophy. I hope you don't mind. Euro-Philosophers express beliefs as propositions and assign them truth values. When we assert a belief we are asserting the truth of a certain picture of the world. There is, on one hand, our worldview ... whether we are Native American or Euro-American ... and on the other hand the world. What has been called metaphorically, 'the map and the territory'. I think most of us agree that we all live in the same territory. I think it is also clear that the maps held by the Native Americans and Euro-Americans are quite different. However, the main point of this talk is belief. Belief is our attitude

toward the relationship between the map and the territory. Western belief generally implies some kind of correspondence between the map and territory. The most extreme version of this is that we can have a completely clear and correct map, a one-to-one correspondence between the map and the territory. Or to put it in the vernacular, we can have the 'Truth'. This was clearly the project of the Enlightenment.* Even though modern thought has cast doubt on this, the West still clings to it.

I would characterize the attitude of Native Americans as one of agnosticism† concerning the relationship between their map and the territory. Though this may seem strange from a Western stance, it is actually very practical. Indeed, I would argue that it can even make a great deal of sense given modern Western understandings of the limits of knowledge....

The Native American map is not meant to be a high fidelity picture of the territory, but is an action guiding set of ideas. Indeed, the action guiding element is central. Remember the John Proctor story. Particular actions are what makes one Creek. One of the main puzzlements Indian people have expressed historically is how Europeans could assert the truth of their ideas, but act in ways that did not correspond to the truths they asserted. Popular sovereignty, religious freedom, the sanctity of property, peace, brotherhood and all the rest seem to be ignored nearly as often as they are upheld. Of course one answer is that there are bad people and bad governments who do not maintain their own lofty ideas. Though this is true, I think it is worsened by Western belief. If you are convinced that your map truly embodies the territory, despite the fact that it is necessarily incomplete or incorrect (and probably both) then you are going to make many false turns. Your actions will be contradictory. When you have mistaken the map for the territory, you will continue to claim that you have reached the right destination even when you are hopelessly lost....

The Western rejoinder might be, 'How can agnosticism concerning the connection between the map and territory be action guiding?' The answer is that

---

* The Enlightenment was a philosophical and cultural movement of the seventeenth and eighteenth centuries that emphasized individualism and the use of reason to question previously accepted doctrines.

† Agnosticism is the position that one does not—maybe even cannot—know the truth or falsity of statements in a given area.

it cannot, but it is an attitude which can be very helpful. Though Native Americans may not know what the connection is between their map and the territory, there are some things that they do know. Key among these is their experience. This includes their own actions and the observed consequences of those actions....

Knowledge is narrative of a life lived in the world. The individual stories are what you know. They may or may not provide a map of the world, but they do tell you about the consequences of your actions. You can learn much even if you believe little. You can even be taught. Here another short story might be useful.

After a long day's work I was supposed to help unload a bunch of tables and chairs at the new Choctaw center in Oklahoma City. Mr Amos Dorsey, an older full-blood Creek and I were going to work together. There was quite a bit of work to do and I wanted to get home, so I threw myself into the work—busily hustling back and forth. Mr Dorsey began to work too, but a bit slower and only after watching me for a second or two. Indeed, as he worked and watched me, I could almost swear he was actually going even slower. Eventually, it was as if he was going in slow-motion. Of course, part of that was due to my haste. As we worked and I fumed a bit at his slowness, I finally realized that somehow he was actually getting more done than I was. Mr Dorsey respected the task, understood the context and set about working efficiently. However, I think it was also an instance of teaching. I can not help but think he slowed down as he saw my thoughtless, disrespectful haste and then speeded up as he saw that I had learned my lesson and was working efficiently.

Now, we could assert some 'Truths' here. We might say that 'Haste makes waste'. Yet of course, the 'Early bird got the worm'. Just about any 'Truth' we might assert—particularly action guiding truths—are going to have contradictory 'Truths' that can be abstracted out of other stories. Thus we have the contradictory actions. This search for 'Truth' is the European tradition. The Native tradition does not abstract truths out

of the stories, the stories are often abstract enough in themselves without further removing them from reality. The narrative is as close to the truth as you can get. In the end, I think that the two epistemic systems may converge. As the Euro-American tradition refines its truths, resolving the contradictions by adding more and more exceptions and greater and greater complexity, these truths may eventually more nearly resemble stories. In the meantime, Indian people will be waiting at the fire already telling some good ones.

Acknowledgements

Lee Hester. I would like to thank the following people for their assistance with the Choctaw language: Dr. Marcia Haag, a linguist at the University of Oklahoma who has done extensive work on the Choctaw language, is always one of the first people that I call. Members of the Choctaw community of central Oklahoma including Mr. John Shoemaker, Mr. Buster Jefferson, and of course Mr. Henry Willis are the people that I look to as the ultimate sources. Mr. Ed Anderson and Ms. Mattie Coonce provided several years of enjoyable company and invaluable learning on the Choctaw language. Mrs. Lola Hester, my grandma, started it all trying to teach me some Choctaw while sitting under an *iti takkon* (peach tree) at her house.

Jim Cheney. I would like to thank my many First Nations teachers during my stay with the Native Philosophy Project in Thunder Bay, Ontario, particularly Lorraine Brundige, Viola Cordova, Lee Hester and Dennis McPherson, both for their generosity of spirit and for their insistence that my education would be better served by long lunches stretching into dinner with them than in any library, which indeed it was. I would also like to thank the faculty and staff of the Institute for Sustainability and Technology Policy, Murdoch University, Western Australia, for providing ideal conditions and intellectual context for writing this paper. ∎

Suggestions for Critical Reflection

1. Hester and Cheney suggest a replacement for the notion of truth "in the modern sense of the term." What is truth "in the modern sense of the term," and what do Hester and Cheney propose instead? What (if anything) would we lose by replacing the modern approach to truth with the approach they propose? What (if anything) would we gain?

2. What, according to Hester and Cheney, is the relationship between knowledge and action in indigenous epistemology? How (if at all) does this differ from a typical Western view of the relationship between knowledge and action?

3. Cheney writes that "Lee's story follows—and indirectly comments on—mine." How does Hester's portion of the text "comment on" Cheney's? To what extent (if at all) do Cheney's claims differ from Hester's?

4. In an article critiquing the concept of "indigenous knowledge," Kai Horsthemke argues that the concept of action guiding knowledge without belief is incoherent: "it is difficult to see how views about how one lives or ought to live, what one practices or ought to practice, etc., can be held in the absence of belief (i.e., beliefs about the utility, appropriateness and sustainability of one's practices, life, etc.) and of the corresponding desire for one's beliefs to be not only justified, but also true."* What do you think of this objection?

5. Can we ask whether the characterizations of Native American approaches given in this article are correct? Would doing so be inconsistent with those very approaches?

6. Compared to a typical (Western) philosophy paper, Hester's portion of this article is unconventional in its structure and approach. Does his portion of the paper enact the Native American approach to knowledge that he describes? If so, how?

7. Hester writes, "The Native tradition does not abstract truths out of the stories.... The narrative is as close to the truth as you can get." He also makes use of several anecdotes in his portion of the paper. What do these anecdotes communicate? To what extent (if at all) could the same meaning be captured in a set of abstract propositional statements as opposed to a narrative? Is the narrative version indeed "close[r] to the truth"?

8. Hester concludes that, "In the end, I think that the two epistemic systems may converge." Do you agree?

Notes

1 Yet there are some points of resonance between these worlds—the resonating reports from the Euro-American side usually being maverick minority reports (see Cheney, 1998). One such point of resonance with Native American worlds is Walker (1989). As Walker is to Native American ethical epistemology, so Nobel prize-winning cytologist Barbara McClintock is to Native American natural science epistemology (see Keller, 1985).

2 The reader must be forewarned at the outset about an easy confusion. Ceremonial worlds are not ceremonies. The 'real' world (of subsistence, say) is not separate from some 'ceremonial' world—as I use the term. I am not contrasting profane and sacred worlds. Nor does the term 'ceremonial world' mark off certain activities (ceremonies) from others (e.g. hunting). The real world in which hunting takes place is a ceremonial world (see Cheney and Hester, 2000, especially section IV, and Hyde, 1998).

3 In conversation at the Colloquium on Environment, Ethics, and Education, Yukon College, Whitehorse, Yukon Territory, 14–16 July 1995, and in a follow-up telephone conversation (see Cheney, 1996).

4 The 'defeat and confusion' of which Goodman and Elgin speak are the result of failings that contemporary epistemology has been quick to expose....

5 The six articles from which I draw are collected in Deloria *et al.*, 1999. Internal references (citing page numbers only) are to this collection. These articles are listed individually in the bibliography.

---

* Kai Horsthemke, "'Way-Centered' *versus* 'Truth-Centered' Epistemologies," *Education Sciences* 6, 1 (2016): 8.

6   A word of caution is necessary concerning the use of such phrases as 'ethically informed' in a Native American context. As Carol Geddes (Tlingit) explained in response to a question concerning the meaning of the Tlingit notion of respect (perhaps the central—certainly the most widely used—'ethical' concept among Native American peoples): 'It does not have a very precise definition in translation—the way it is used in English. It is more like awareness. It is more like knowledge and that is a very important distinction, because it is not like a moral law, it is more like something that is just a part of your whole awareness'

(Jickling, 1996, p. 279). For an extended discussion, see Hester *et al.* (2000).

7   Which does not mean that the account is not historically accurate, merely mythical, or the like. It means that the central role of the White Buffalo Calf Woman story and the ceremonies it conveys is to orient the people with respect to 'the proper moral and ethical road upon which human beings should walk'.

8   Emphasis added to the statements of the three principles of epistemological method.

9   With reference to the Canadian Inuit philosopher Gordon Christie.

References

Birch, T.H., 1993, Moral considerability and universal consideration. *Environmental Ethics*, 15, pp. 313–332.

Cheney, J., 2001, Truth, knowledge, and the wild world. In C. Preston (ed.) *Environment and Belief: The Placing of Knowledge* (Albany: State University of New York Press), forthcoming.*

Cheney, J., 1998, Rivers of thought: the confluence of aboriginal and western philosophy. In S. O'Meara and D.A. West (eds) *Indigenous Learning: Proceedings from the Second Biennial Aboriginal Peoples' Conference, 18–20 October, 1996* (Thunder Bay, ON: Aboriginal Resource and Research Centre).

Cheney, J., 1996, Sacred land. In B. Jickling (ed.) *A Colloquium on Environment, Ethics, and Education* (Whitehorse: Yukon College), pp. 61–68.

Cheney, J. and Hester, L., 2000, Ceremonial worlds and environmental sanity. *Strategies: Journal of Theory, Culture & Politics*, 13, 77–87.

Cheney, J. and Weston, A., 1999, Environmental ethics as environmental etiquette: toward an ethics-based epistemology. *Environmental Ethics*, 21, 115–134.

Deloria, B., Foehner, K., and Scinta, S. (eds) 1999, *Spirit & Reason: The Vine Deloria, Jr. Reader* (Golden, CO: Fulcrum Publishing).

Goodman, N. and Elgin, C.Z., 1988, A reconception of philosophy. In N. Goodman and C.Z. Elgin (eds) *Reconceptions in Philosophy and Other Arts and Sciences* (Indianapolis: Hackett Publishing), pp. 155–161.

Hester, L., McPherson, D., Booth, A., and Cheney, J., 2000, Indigenous worlds and Callicott's land ethic. *Environmental Ethics*, 22, 273–290.

Hyde, L., 1998, *Trickster Makes This World: Mischief, Myth, and Art* (New York: Farrar, Straus, and Giroux).

Jickling, B. (ed.), 1996, *A Colloquium on Environment, Ethics, and Education* (Whitehorse: Yukon College).

Meyer, L.N. and Ramirez, T., 1996, 'Wakinyan hotan' ('the thunderbeings call out'): the inscrutability of Lakota/Dakota metaphysics. In S. O'Meara and D.A. West (eds) *From Our Eyes: Learning from Indigenous People* (Toronto: Garamond Press).

---

*   Published as J. Cheney, "Truth, Knowledge and the Wild World," *Ethics and the Environment* 10, 2 (2005): 101–35.

Philosophy of Science

WHEN, IF EVER, ARE SCIENTIFIC INFERENCES JUSTIFIED?

The philosophy of science can be thought of as comprising two broad, intersecting streams: the epistemology of science and the metaphysics of science. The epistemology of science concerns itself with the justification, rationality, and objectivity of scientific knowledge and what is known as the "scientific method," while the metaphysics of science examines philosophical puzzles about the reality uncovered by the various sciences. Furthermore, each of these two types of investigation can be directed at science in general or at one of the particular sciences: there are thus sub-disciplines within the philosophy of science such as philosophy of physics, philosophy of mathematics, philosophy of biology, and philosophy of the social sciences.

Many of the threads of the epistemological strand of philosophy of science can be unraveled from the following question: *What, if anything, is the scientific method, and how rational is it?* Once one attempts to answer this question, a flurry of subsidiary questions arises: What is the methodological difference (if any) between science and other, non-scientific, areas of human endeavor (such as philosophy, history or astrology)? Do all the 'real' sciences share a common methodology? If not, can we discover a single, underlying unified science which is in principle capable of encompassing all the special sciences? How *rational* are the methods of science: how much reason do they give us to accept their conclusions? How *objective* are the methods of science: how much is science influenced by its social context and the personalities of individual scientists? Are the theories produced by science ever, in fact, true descriptions of reality, and is that what science should aspire to anyway? What exactly *is* a theory, anyway (for example, is it a set of mathematical equations, or a kind of model, or a more informal bundle of assumptions and claims)? How adequately does science explain the natural phenomena we want explained, and what counts as a scientific explanation? And so on. These and similar questions are investigated by philosophers of science.

Metaphysical questions about science can be thought of as centered on the following issue: *Are the principles and entities postulated by science actually real?* For example, many scientific theories postulate unobservable entities in order to explain the observed data. Most subatomic particles such as quarks, for instance, have never in any sense been *seen* by a scientist: rather, they are assumed to exist because their existence is the best explanation for a certain set of experimental data. In such situations, are we entitled to infer that such unobservable entities actually do exist, or should we instead treat them as instrumental fictions which are useful in generating observable predictions but which aren't real? (After all, plenty of unobserved entities which we now realize do not actually exist have been postulated by science in the past, such as the mythical substance phlogiston, which was invoked to explain many chemical properties, or the massless ether, which was thought to fill the gaps between objects and serve as the medium for the transmission of light. Why should our current theories be any luckier in the hypothetical entities they invent?)

One fundamental 'unobservable' principle of science, which has historically been of great interest to philosophers of science, is the principle of *causality*. The sense in which causality is unobservable was pointed out by the philosopher David Hume in the eighteenth century: although we certainly can and do observe that events of type *A* are always followed by events of type *B* (for example, that all objects propelled with force *x* will always accelerate at rate *y*), this necessarily falls short of being able to observe *causation* itself. All we actually see is what Hume called the "constant conjunction" of *A* things with *B* things, but we do not see the cause which lies behind and is the reason for this conjunction: that is, we do not *see* causal force, but we *infer* it from regularities which we detect in nature. So it is legitimate to ask questions like the following: *Are* there really causal laws lying behind the constant conjunctions we observe— are laws of nature real? If causal laws do exist, how can we reliably tell when we've identified one—how can we tell the difference between a genuine law and a merely accidental constant conjunction? And, if causal laws exist, what is their nature—for example, are they always deterministic, or can they be probabilistic (as quantum mechanics might be taken to suggest)?

The readings in this chapter focus primarily on the epistemological aspects of the philosophy of science: what is the method of science, and how rationally justifiable is it? It is natural to begin with something like the following account of science: scientists first accumulate facts about the world by conducting careful experiments, and then use these observations to support—or "verify"—one scientific theory rather than another. For example, one might think, by the careful observation of various chemical reactions, scientists are able to formulate and prove true general laws about the underlying chemistry. Furthermore, it is common to suppose that it is this experimental method which is unique to science and the source of its special epistemological power. The first selection collected here introduces a fundamental problem for this view of the scientific method, *the problem of induction*. Induction is, roughly, the process by which we infer general truths from particular observations (for example, inferring that all copper turns green by noticing that many old copper roofs are now green). The scientific method just described rests heavily on inductive inferences to move from a finite set of experimental observations to claims about laws of nature. But the question is: is induction rational? Are inductive inferences from the particular to the general justified? David Hume argues compellingly that inductive inferences are *not* rationally justified; and if he is right, then it follows that the scientific method—at least as we have so far understood it—is not rational.

The next two readings—the authors of which are reacting to the problem of induction—introduce two different accounts of the scientific method, in an effort to improve on the simplistic 'experimental' model described above. Carl Hempel presents a mature version of the influential logical positivist or verificationist account of science, while Karl Popper rejects verificationism and argues instead for a falsificationist view of science.

The fourth selection in this chapter, from Thomas Kuhn, introduces an important turn in late-twentieth-century philosophy away from the attempt to understand science as a rational enterprise and in favor of seeing it as a sociological phenomenon embedded in a particular historical context. Kuhn has thus been seen as launching an attack on the rationality of science.

Lastly, the article by Helen Longino asks "Can there be a feminist science?" and if so, how different would it look from historical, supposedly "value-free," science?

The philosophy of science has been a very active area of philosophy for a large part of the twentieth and the current century, and there are many good books which will take you beyond the readings included in this chapter. Among them are: Barker and Kitcher, *Philosophy of Science: A New Introduction* (Oxford University Press, 2013); Alan Chalmers, *What Is This Thing Called Science?* (Hackett, 2013); Curd, Cover and Pincock, eds., *Philosophy of Science: The Central Issues* (W.W. Norton, 2012); James Franklin, *What Science Knows: And How It Knows It* (Encounter Books, 2009); Peter Godfrey-Smith, *Theory and Reality: An Introduction to the Philosophy of Science* (University of Chicago Press, 2003); Ian Hacking, *Representing and Intervening* (Cambridge University Press, 1983); Philip Kitcher, *The Advancement of Science* (Oxford University Press, 1993); James Ladyman, *Understanding Philosophy of Science* (Routledge, 2001); W.H. Newton-Smith, *The Rationality of Science* (Routledge, 1991); Alexander Rosenberg, *The Philosophy of Science* (Routledge, 2011); and Bas van Fraassen, *The Scientific Image* (Oxford University Press, 1982). Useful references are *A Companion to the Philosophy of Science*, edited by W.H. Newton-Smith (Blackwell, 2001), Paul Humphreys, ed., *The Oxford Handbook of Philosophy of Science* (Oxford University Press, 2016), and Curd and Psillos, eds., *The Routledge Companion to Philosophy of Science* (Routledge, 2013).

DAVID HUME

FROM *An Enquiry Concerning Human Understanding*

There is a peculiarly painful chamber inhabited solely by philosophers who have refuted Hume. These philosophers, though in Hell, have not learned wisdom. They continue to be governed by their animal propensity towards induction. But every time that they make an induction, the next instance falsifies it. This, however, happens only during the first hundred years of their damnation. After that, they learn to expect that an induction will be falsified, and therefore it is not falsified until another century of logical torment has altered their expectation. Throughout all eternity surprise continues, but each time at a higher logical level. (Bertrand Russell)*

For some information on Hume's life and his overall philosophical project, please see the introduction to Hume in the Philosophy of Religion section of this volume.

What Is the Structure of This Reading?

An Enquiry Concerning Human Understanding first appeared (in 1748) under the title *Philosophical Essays Concerning Human Understanding*, and it does indeed consist of 12 somewhat loosely related philosophical essays. The underlying theme which ties the essays together is the primacy of experience and causal inference in establishing our ideas, especially such philosophically important ideas as necessity and probability, free will, and God.

Hume's argument in this reading has two parts. In the first part he argues there can be no rational justification for our expectations about those parts of the physical world we have not yet observed; in the second he presents his "skeptical solution of these doubts." First, in Section IV, Part I, he introduces a distinction between relations of ideas and matters of fact. He then argues that all empirical claims which go beyond "the present testimony of our senses, or the records of our memory" are based on reasonings "founded on the relation of cause and effect." How do we come to discover relations of cause and effect? Not, Hume argues, from "reasonings *a priori*" but from experience. In Part II, Hume addresses the question: "What is the foundation of all conclusions from experience?" and, for the remainder of this part, "contents himself" with a negative answer. He argues that conclusions from experience are not "founded on reasoning, or on any process of the understanding." Part of his argument here has the following structure: Hume tries to show that all experimental arguments rely upon the assumption that nature is generally uniform—the assumption that observed regularities in nature (like the whiteness of swans or day following night) will persist from the present into the future. He then argues—very ingeniously and persuasively—that this assumption is impossible to rationally justify. His conclusion is that inductive inferences are never rationally justifiable.

Hume's constructive project, presented in Section V, has the following pattern. He begins by describing the benefits of a generally skeptical frame of mind. Then he goes on to discuss the principle that *does* cause us to leap to inductive conclusions, since we have no rational reason to do so—this psychological principle, he suggests, is "custom or habit." In Part II, Hume gives us more detail about what he thinks is really going on when we come to have beliefs about the future: he argues that *belief* is a kind of involuntary feeling, "added" to our imagination of some event. That is, we can freely *imagine* almost any future event we like, but we usually cannot make ourselves *believe* that it will happen. This "extra" feeling of belief in a future event, Hume argues, can only be generated automatically in our minds by a certain sequence of past experiences.

---

* Bertrand Russell, "The Metaphysician's Nightmare" in *Nightmares of Eminent Persons* (Simon & Schuster, 1955). Note that Russell is not endorsing this view, which seems to misrepresent Hume's position on induction. Rather, he ascribes this quote to a fictional professor, Andrei Bumblowski.

Some Useful Background Information

1. Hume, like John Locke (see the Epistemology chapter of this volume), began his philosophy with a 'theory of ideas': it is useful to be aware of a few of the basics of this theory when reading this selection. For Hume, the smallest elements of thought are what he called *basic perceptions*. These can usefully be thought of as analogous to atoms, since these basic perceptions are, in Hume's view, bound together in various ways into larger units—*complex perceptions*—according to certain fundamental psychological laws; Hume called these laws "the principle of the association of ideas." Hume thought of this system as being the counterpart of Newtonian physics: on this view, physics is the science of matter, and Humean philosophy is the science of human nature or mind. Hume himself considered this general picture, and the use he made of it, to be his greatest contribution to human thought. It is especially notable that *rationality* plays relatively little part in Hume's naturalistic picture of human nature: instead, our ideas are connected together by deterministic laws based, for example, on their similarity or their history of "constant conjunction" (that is, a history of having always appeared together in the past). Finally, for Hume, these "laws of association" may defy further explanation: we might need to treat them as basic laws—brute regularities—just as the law of gravity was for Newton.

2. Unlike Locke, Hume divides his "perceptions" into two distinct sorts: *impressions* and *ideas*. Impressions are "all our sensations, passions and emotions, as they make their first appearance in the soul," and come in two flavors: *impressions of sensation* and *impressions of reflection*. Impressions of sensation, according to Hume, appear in the mind "from unknown causes," and the reasons for their occurrence are best studied by "anatomists and natural philosophers," rather than by those, like Hume himself, interested in studying human nature. Examples of such sensations might be a visual image of a cat on the mat, or the taste of a grape-flavored Popsicle. Impressions of reflection (such as disgust, pride, or desire) arise, usually, from our perception of and reaction to our own ideas. Finally, our *ideas* are, according to Hume, "the faint images" of impressions: that is, they are copies of earlier impressions (and so, causally dependent on them: you cannot possibly have an idea of something which you haven't previously experienced). Ideas, for Hume, have been described as "the mental tokens by which we reason," and would include, for example, our concepts of colors and shapes, of types of objects, of mathematical relationships, of historical individuals, of moral values, and so on.

3. Hume's arguments in this passage rely on two important distinctions, which it is helpful to have clear in your mind as you read. The first is the distinction, which is often called "Hume's fork," between *relations of ideas* and *matters of fact*. Relations of ideas are propositions whose truth or falsity can be discovered merely by thinking about the concepts involved, and which if true are necessarily true. For example, "a triangle has three sides" must be true since *by definition* triangles have three sides—it's just part of the concept *triangle* that it be three-sided. In modern jargon, relations of ideas are analytic *a priori* propositions.* The simplest kind of relation of ideas Hume calls "intuitively certain": these propositions are just self-evidently true to anyone who understands them, such as "1 is smaller than 2."† Other propositions, which are also relations of ideas, may be more complex and need to be shown by some kind of "demonstrative argument" (the proposition that 2^{16} is 65,536, for example, might not be immediately obvious, but it can be proven by a sequence of small and obvious steps).

---

* See the Introduction to the reading by Kant in the Epistemology chapter for an account of 'a priori,' 'a posteriori,' 'analytic' and 'synthetic.'

† If you have already read Descartes and Locke, you might notice that Hume's notion of 'intuition' is significantly different from that used by his philosophical predecessors. For example, Descartes's "I think therefore I am" would not count as 'intuitively certain' for Hume.

Matters of fact, by contrast, are synthetic *a posteriori* propositions—that is, only observation and experience can tell us whether they are true or false (and thus they cannot be *necessarily* true, but are only contingently true). An example might be, "sticking your finger inside a hot toaster really hurts." One of Hume's key claims is that propositions about relations of ideas never assert the existence of any non-abstract entities (such as physical objects), while claims about matters of fact often do.

4. The second important distinction used in this reading is one between *demonstrative arguments* and *experimental arguments*. Demonstrative arguments, for Hume, are deductively valid arguments where all the premises are relations of ideas. We can know that the conclusion of a demonstrative argument is true (indeed, necessarily true) without knowing anything about the actual world—this is why Hume often calls them "reasonings *a priori*." Experimental arguments are arguments of any other kind: that is, they are either arguments which have matters of fact among their premises, or arguments which are not deductive, or (most commonly) both.

5. Finally, a word about "induction." Although Hume does not actually use the word in this reading, Section IV, Part II of the *Enquiry* is usually thought of as presenting, for the first time, "the problem of induction." Induction is the modern term for the process of arriving at justified beliefs about the future on the basis of experience of the past; to put the same idea in another way, induction is the method for finding out what as-yet unobserved things are like on the basis of a sample of things we have observed. For example, we might notice that every swan we have ever seen has been white, and conclude that, very probably, the next swan we see will also be white. Furthermore, we might think, we've seen enough swans to justify concluding that probably *every* swan is white. Thus we use our experience of observing swans to draw inductive conclusions about unseen swans—generalizations about other swans in the world (such as Australian swans) and predictions about future

swans as yet unhatched. This method of reasoning is extremely common. It is what (apparently) supports much of our everyday behavior, such as getting up at a certain time in the morning to go to work or school, using a kettle to make tea, relying on the morning weather forecast to help us decide what to wear, expecting the bus to come at a certain time and place, and so on. All of these activities and beliefs are based on assuming that past experience is reliable evidence for expectations about the future. Science, too, is largely based on induction—physicists have only (indirectly) observed a tiny, infinitesimal fraction of all the electrons in the universe, for example, yet they assume that all electrons everywhere have the same charge.

We speak of "the problem of induction," because Hume has apparently shown us that we have no rational justification for induction. This would be an extremely radical conclusion if in fact it is so!

Some Common Misconceptions

1. Hume's philosophical concerns were not primarily negative or destructive: although he frequently attacks the role of reason in science and human affairs, and points out the limitations of our own experiential knowledge, he does not do so in order to leave us in a skeptical dead end. Instead, these attacks are part of his attempt to place the science of human nature upon a more reliable footing, by actually examining how we come to have the beliefs that we do.

2. Although there are differences of interpretation on this matter, it seems likely that Hume was not merely pointing out that inductive conclusions cannot be known *with certainty* to be true—that induction cannot be 100 per cent rationally justified. For that would simply be to say that induction is not deduction, which is trivial. (It is today part of the *definition* of an inductive, as opposed to deductive, argument that its conclusion may possibly be false even if all its premises are true, and this seems to correspond reasonably well with Hume's own distinction

between experimental and demonstrative methods of reasoning.) Instead, Hume is making the much more radical claim that the conclusions of inductive arguments *have no rational support at all*: they are not "founded on reasoning, or on any process of the understanding." Inductive arguments, if Hume is right, completely fail to justify their conclusions—their premises, if true, do not make their conclusions *any* more likely to be true. (Analogously, the argument "roses are red, violets are blue, therefore Tom Hanks will become President of America" is not rationally compelling since the truth of the premises—the respective colors of roses and violets—does nothing to make it more likely to be true that this particular actor will have successful political ambitions. See the introduction to this book for more information on inductive and deductive arguments.)

3. On the other hand, Hume is not arguing that induction does not actually *work*—he's not arguing that human beings are systematically *wrong* in their predictions about the future. On the contrary, he thinks that human beings are usually very successful in coming to have true beliefs about the future (that the sun will rise tomorrow, or that the next chunk of copper we mine from the earth will conduct electricity). And although it's admittedly a bit tricky to hold both that this is the case and that induction is not at all justified, it's not flat out inconsistent: it's perfectly coherent to say that lots of our beliefs are true but unjustified.

How Important and Influential Is This Passage?

An influential British philosopher named C.D. Broad once called inductive reasoning "the glory of Science ... [and] ... the scandal of Philosophy."* The scandal Broad had in mind was the failure of philosophers over the previous two hundred years to find a convincing answer to Hume's skeptical arguments—and this despite the wholesale (and apparently successful) reliance of the natural sciences on inductive arguments. If induction is not rationally justified, recall, then, that neither are most of the claims of physics, biology, chemistry, economics, and so on. Thus Hume, in effect, discovered and incisively formulated a serious new philosophical problem—the problem of induction. (H.H. Price once called Hume's discovery of this problem "one of the most important advances in the whole history of thought."†) This problem has very far-reaching consequences indeed, but it is so difficult a puzzle to solve that many philosophers feel Hume has not yet been satisfactorily answered. Hume's problem of induction is still a live problem today; various answers have been proposed but no single solution has yet found widespread acceptance. (If you have already read the selection from Kant in the previous chapter, you will be able to see how Kant produced what he thought would be a solution to this problem.)

Hume's own "skeptical solution" has been much less influential than his skeptical problem: even if Hume's account in Part V is successful (which many contemporary philosophers and psychologists doubt), it will still only be a *psychological* explanation for why we believe the things we do about the future, whereas what we seem to need to defend science—and most of our everyday beliefs—is a *rational justification* for induction.

---

* "The philosophy of Francis Bacon: An address delivered at Cambridge on the occasion of the Bacon tercentenary," 5 October 1926.
† "The Permanent Significance of Hume's Philosophy," *Philosophy* 15 (1940): 7–37.

FROM *An Enquiry Concerning Human Understanding**
SECTION IV: SCEPTICAL DOUBTS
CONCERNING THE OPERATIONS OF THE UNDERSTANDING

Part I

All the objects of human reason or enquiry may naturally be divided into two kinds, to wit,† *relations of ideas*, and *matters of fact*. Of the first kind are the sciences of geometry, algebra, and arithmetic; and in short, every affirmation which is either intuitively or demonstratively certain. *That the square of the hypotenuse‡ is equal to the square of the two sides*, is a proposition which expresses a relation between these figures. *That three times five is equal to the half of thirty*, expresses a relation between these numbers. Propositions of this kind are discoverable by the mere operation of thought, without dependence on what is anywhere existent in the universe. Though there never were a circle or triangle in nature, the truths demonstrated by Euclid§ would for ever retain their certainty and evidence.

Matters of fact, which are the second objects of human reason, are not ascertained in the same manner; nor is our evidence of their truth, however great, of a like nature with the foregoing. The contrary of every matter of fact is still possible; because it can never imply a contradiction, and is conceived by the mind with the same facility and distinctness, as if ever so conformable to reality. *That the sun will not rise to-morrow* is no less intelligible a proposition, and implies no more contradiction than the affirmation, *that it will rise*. We should in vain, therefore, attempt to demonstrate its falsehood. Were it demonstratively false, it would imply a contradiction, and could never be distinctly conceived by the mind.

It may, therefore, be a subject worthy of curiosity, to enquire what is the nature of that evidence which assures us of any real existence and matter of fact, beyond the present testimony of our senses, or the records of our memory. This part of philosophy, it is observable, has been little cultivated, either by the ancients or moderns; and therefore our doubts and errors, in the prosecution of so important an enquiry, may be the more excusable; while we march through such difficult paths without any guide or direction. They may even prove useful, by exciting curiosity, and destroying that implicit faith and security, which is the bane of all reasoning and free enquiry. The discovery of defects in the common philosophy, if any such there be, will not, I presume, be a discouragement, but rather an incitement, as is usual, to attempt something more full and satisfactory than has yet been proposed to the public.

All reasonings concerning matter of fact seem to be founded on the relation of *cause and effect*. By means of that relation alone we can go beyond the evidence of our memory and senses. If you were to ask a man, why he believes any matter of fact, which is absent; for instance, that his friend is in the country, or in France; he would give you a reason; and this reason would be some other fact; as a letter received from him, or the knowledge of his former resolutions and promises. A man finding a watch or any other machine in a desert island, would conclude that there had once been men in that island. All our reasonings concerning fact are of the same nature. And here it is constantly supposed that there is a connection between the present fact and that which is inferred from it. Were there nothing to bind them together, the inference would be entirely precarious. The hearing of an articulate voice and

---

*   Hume's *An Enquiry Concerning Human Understanding* was first published in 1748. This selection is taken from the 1777 "new edition," generally considered the final version authorized by Hume. Most of the spelling, capitalization, and punctuation have been modernized.

†   "To wit" is a phrase meaning "that is to say" or "namely."

‡   The hypotenuse is the side opposite the right angle of a right-angled triangle.

§   The foundational Greek mathematician, active around 300 BCE, whose *Elements* deduced the theorems of geometry from a small set of axioms.

rational discourse in the dark assures us of the presence of some person: Why? Because these are the effects of the human make and fabric, and closely connected with it. If we anatomize* all the other reasonings of this nature, we shall find that they are founded on the relation of cause and effect, and that this relation is either near or remote, direct or collateral. Heat and light are collateral effects of fire, and the one effect may justly be inferred from the other.

If we would satisfy ourselves, therefore, concerning the nature of that evidence, which assures us of matters of fact, we must enquire how we arrive at the knowledge of cause and effect.

I shall venture to affirm, as a general proposition, which admits of no exception, that the knowledge of this relation is not, in any instance, attained by reasonings *a priori*;† but arises entirely from experience, when we find that any particular objects are constantly conjoined with each other. Let an object be presented to a man of ever so strong natural reason and abilities; if that object be entirely new to him, he will not be able, by the most accurate examination of its sensible‡ qualities, to discover any of its causes or effects. Adam,§ though his rational faculties be supposed, at the very first, entirely perfect, could not have inferred from the fluidity and transparency of water that it would suffocate him, or from the light and warmth of fire that it would consume him. No object ever discovers,¶ by the qualities which appear to the senses, either the causes which produced it, or the effects which will arise from it; nor can our reason, unassisted by experience, ever draw any inference concerning real existence and matter of fact.

This proposition, *that causes and effects are discoverable, not by reason but by experience*, will readily be admitted with regard to such objects as we remember to have once been altogether unknown to us; since we must be conscious of the utter inability, which we then lay under, of foretelling what would arise from them. Present two smooth pieces of marble to a man who has no tincture of natural philosophy;** he will never discover that they will adhere together in such a manner as to require great force to separate them in a direct line, while they make so small a resistance to a lateral pressure. Such events, as bear little analogy to the common course of nature, are also readily confessed to be known only by experience; nor does any man imagine that the explosion of gunpowder, or the attraction of a loadstone,†† could ever be discovered by arguments *a priori*. In like manner, when an effect is supposed to depend upon an intricate machinery or secret structure of parts, we make no difficulty in attributing all our knowledge of it to experience. Who will assert that he can give the ultimate reason, why milk or bread is proper nourishment for a man, not for a lion or a tiger?

But the same truth may not appear, at first sight, to have the same evidence with regard to events, which have become familiar to us from our first appearance in the world, which bear a close analogy to the whole course of nature, and which are supposed to depend on the simple qualities of objects, without any secret structure of parts. We are apt to imagine that we could discover these effects by the mere operation of our reason, without experience. We fancy, that were we brought on a sudden into this world, we could at first have inferred that one billiard-ball would communicate motion to another upon impulse;‡‡ and that we needed not to have waited for the event, in order to pronounce with certainty concerning it. Such is the influence of custom,§§ that, where it is strongest, it not only covers our natural ignorance, but even conceals itself, and seems not to take place, merely because it is found in the highest degree.

But to convince us that all the laws of nature, and all the operations of bodies without exception, are

---

* Closely examine.

† Prior to—not based on—experience.

‡ "Sensible" means (here and elsewhere) able to be perceived or sensed.

§ According to the Old Testament, the first human being.

¶ Here (and sometimes elsewhere) "discovers" means reveals or discloses (rather than finds out).

** That is: no trace of knowledge of physical science.

†† A magnet (made from naturally occurring magnetic iron oxide).

‡‡ Impact, collision.

§§ Habit, repeated similar experience.

known only by experience, the following reflections may, perhaps, suffice. Were any object presented to us, and were we required to pronounce concerning the effect, which will result from it, without consulting past observation; after what manner, I beseech you, must the mind proceed in this operation? It must invent or imagine some event, which it ascribes to the object as its effect; and it is plain that this invention must be entirely arbitrary. The mind can never possibly find the effect in the supposed cause, by the most accurate scrutiny and examination. For the effect is totally different from the cause, and consequently can never be discovered in it. Motion in the second billiard-ball is a quite distinct event from motion in the first; nor is there any thing in the one to suggest the smallest hint of the other. A stone or piece of metal raised into the air, and left without any support, immediately falls: but to consider the matter *a priori*, is there any thing we discover in this situation which can beget the idea of a downward, rather than an upward, or any other motion, in the stone or metal?

And as the first imagination or invention of a particular effect, in all natural operations, is arbitrary, where we consult not experience; so must we also esteem the supposed tie or connection between the cause and effect, which binds them together, and renders it impossible that any other effect could result from the operation of that cause. When I see, for instance, a billiard-ball moving in a straight line towards another; even suppose motion in the second ball should by accident be suggested to me, as the result of their contact or impulse; may I not conceive, that a hundred different events might as well follow from that cause? May not both these balls remain at absolute rest? May not the first ball return in a straight line, or leap off from the second in any line or direction? All these suppositions are consistent and conceivable. Why then should we give the preference to one, which is no more consistent or conceivable than the rest? All our reasonings *a priori* will never be able to show us any foundation for this preference.

In a word, then, every effect is a distinct event from its cause. It could not, therefore, be discovered in the cause, and the first invention or conception of

it, *a priori*, must be entirely arbitrary. And even after it is suggested, the conjunction of it with the cause must appear equally arbitrary; since there are always many other effects, which, to reason, must seem fully as consistent and natural. In vain, therefore, should we pretend to determine any single event, or infer any cause or effect, without the assistance of observation and experience.

Hence we may discover the reason why no philosopher,* who is rational and modest, has ever pretended to assign the ultimate cause of any natural operation, or to show distinctly the action of that power, which produces any single effect in the universe. It is confessed, that the utmost effort of human reason is to reduce the principles, productive of natural phenomena, to a greater simplicity, and to resolve the many particular effects into a few general causes, by means of reasonings from analogy, experience, and observation. But as to the causes of these general causes, we should in vain attempt their discovery; nor shall we ever be able to satisfy ourselves, by any particular explication of them. These ultimate springs and principles are totally shut up from human curiosity and enquiry. Elasticity, gravity, cohesion of parts, communication of motion by impulse; these are probably the ultimate causes and principles which we shall ever discover in nature; and we may esteem ourselves sufficiently happy, if, by accurate enquiry and reasoning, we can trace up the particular phenomena to, or near to, these general principles. The most perfect philosophy of the natural kind only staves off our ignorance a little longer: as perhaps the most perfect philosophy of the moral or metaphysical kind serves only to discover larger portions of it. Thus the observation of human blindness and weakness is the result of all philosophy, and meets us at every turn, in spite of our endeavours to elude or avoid it.

Nor is geometry, when taken into the assistance of natural philosophy, ever able to remedy this defect, or lead us into the knowledge of ultimate causes, by all that accuracy of reasoning for which it is so justly celebrated. Every part of mixed mathematics† proceeds upon the supposition that certain laws are established by nature in her operations; and abstract reasonings

---

* The word "philosopher" at this time included natural scientists.
† Mathematical physics (mathematics applied to the physical world).

are employed, either to assist experience in the discovery of these laws, or to determine their influence in particular instances, where it depends upon any precise degree of distance and quantity. Thus, it is a law of motion, discovered by experience, that the moment* or force of any body in motion is in the compound ratio or proportion of its solid contents† and its velocity; and consequently, that a small force may remove the greatest obstacle or raise the greatest weight, if, by any contrivance or machinery, we can increase the velocity of that force, so as to make it an overmatch for its antagonist.‡ Geometry assists us in the application of this law, by giving us the just dimensions of all the parts and figures which can enter into any species of machine; but still the discovery of the law itself is owing merely to experience, and all the abstract reasonings in the world could never lead us one step towards the knowledge of it. When we reason *a priori*, and consider merely any object or cause, as it appears to the mind, independent of all observation, it never could suggest to us the notion of any distinct object, such as its effect; much less, show us the inseparable and inviolable connection between them. A man must be very sagacious§ who could discover by reasoning that crystal is the effect of heat, and ice of cold, without being previously acquainted with the operation of these qualities.

Part II

But we have not yet attained any tolerable satisfaction with regard to the question first proposed. Each solution still gives rise to a new question as difficult as the foregoing, and leads us on to farther enquiries. When it is asked, *What is the nature of all our reasonings concerning matter of fact?* the proper answer seems to be, that they are founded on the relation of cause and effect. When again it is asked, *What is the foundation of all our reasonings and conclusions concerning that relation?* it may be replied in one word, Experience. But if we still carry on our sifting humour,¶ and ask, *What is the foundation of all conclusions from experience?* this implies a new question, which may be of more difficult solution and explication. Philosophers, that give themselves airs of superior wisdom and sufficiency,** have a hard task when they encounter persons of inquisitive dispositions, who push them from every corner to which they retreat, and who are sure at last to bring them to some dangerous dilemma. The best expedient to prevent this confusion, is to be modest in our pretensions; and even to discover the difficulty ourselves before it is objected to us. By this means, we may make a kind of merit of our very ignorance.

I shall content myself, in this section, with an easy task, and shall pretend†† only to give a negative answer to the question here proposed. I say then, that, even after we have experience of the operations of cause and effect, our conclusions from that experience are *not* founded on reasoning, or any process of the understanding. This answer we must endeavour both to explain and to defend.

It must certainly be allowed, that nature has kept us at a great distance from all her secrets, and has afforded us only the knowledge of a few superficial qualities of objects; while she conceals from us those powers and principles on which the influence of those objects entirely depends. Our senses inform us of the colour, weight, and consistence‡‡ of bread; but neither sense nor reason can ever inform us of those qualities which fit it for the nourishment and support of a human body.

---

* Momentum.
† Mass.
‡ Here is what Hume means by this example (which comes from Newtonian physics). Imagine two bodies A and B: suppose that A has a mass of 2 and a velocity of 4 and that B has a mass of 6 and a velocity of 1. Thus the ratios of their respective masses will be 2:6 and their respective velocities 4:1. Then, A will have a higher momentum or force than B (despite only having one third the mass), since the "compound ratio" of its momentum to that of B will be 2×4 to 6×1, which is 8:6.
§ Mentally penetrating, insightful (Hume is being ironic).
¶ Searching frame of mind.
** Here "sufficiency" means ability.
†† Claim.
‡‡ Consistency, texture.

Sight or feeling conveys an idea of the actual motion of bodies; but as to that wonderful force or power, which would carry on a moving body for ever in a continued change of place, and which bodies never lose but by communicating it to others; of this we cannot form the most distant conception. But notwithstanding this ignorance of natural powers[1] and principles, we always presume, when we see like* sensible qualities, that they have like secret powers, and expect that effects, similar to those which we have experienced, will follow from them. If a body of like colour and consistence with that bread, which we have formerly eat,† be presented to us, we make no scruple of repeating the experiment,‡ and foresee, with certainty, like nourishment and support. Now this is a process of the mind or thought, of which I would willingly know the foundation. It is allowed on all hands that there is no known connection between the sensible qualities and the secret powers; and consequently, that the mind is not led to form such a conclusion concerning their constant and regular conjunction, by any thing which it knows of their nature. As to past *experience*, it can be allowed to give *direct* and *certain* information of those precise objects only, and that precise period of time, which fell under its cognizance: But why this experience should be extended to future times, and to other objects, which for aught we know, may be only in appearance similar; this is the main question on which I would insist. The bread, which I formerly eat, nourished me; that is, a body of such sensible qualities was, at that time, endued with§ such secret powers: but does it follow, that other bread must also nourish me at another time, and that like sensible qualities must always be attended with like secret powers? The consequence seems nowise necessary. At least, it must be acknowledged that there is here a consequence drawn by the mind; that there is a certain step taken; a process of thought, and an inference, which wants to be explained.¶ These two propositions are far from being

the same, *I have found that such an object has always been attended with such an effect*, and *I foresee, that other objects, which are, in appearance, similar, will be attended with similar effects*. I shall allow, if you please, that the one proposition may justly be inferred from the other: I know, in fact, that it always is inferred. But if you insist that the inference is made by a chain of reasoning, I desire you to produce that reasoning. The connection between these propositions is not intuitive. There is required a medium,** which may enable the mind to draw such an inference, if indeed it be drawn by reasoning and argument. What that medium is, I must confess, passes my comprehension; and it is incumbent on those to produce it, who assert that it really exists, and is the origin of all our conclusions concerning matter of fact.

This negative argument must certainly, in process of time, become altogether convincing, if many penetrating and able philosophers shall turn their enquiries this way and no one be ever able to discover any connecting proposition or intermediate step, which supports the understanding in this conclusion. But as the question is yet new, every reader may not trust so far to his own penetration, as to conclude, because an argument escapes his enquiry, that therefore it does not really exist. For this reason it may be requisite to venture upon a more difficult task; and enumerating all the branches of human knowledge, endeavour to show that none of them can afford such an argument.

All reasonings may be divided into two kinds, namely, demonstrative reasoning, or that concerning relations of ideas, and moral†† reasoning, or that concerning matter of fact and existence. That there are no demonstrative arguments in the case seems evident; since it implies no contradiction that the course of nature may change, and that an object, seemingly like those which we have experienced, may be attended with different or contrary effects. May I not clearly

---

*   Similar.

†   Eaten.

‡   Experience.

§   Endowed with, possessed of.

¶   Lacks explanation.

**   A ground of inference; a further premise.

††   Here "moral" means inductive or having at best only a probable conclusion. (Often, however, Hume uses the phrase "moral philosophy" in a somewhat different way, to mean the study of the nature of human beings, contrasted with "natural philosophy," the study of nature.)

and distinctly conceive that a body, falling from the clouds, and which, in all other respects, resembles snow, has yet the taste of salt or feeling of fire? Is there any more intelligible proposition than to affirm, that all the trees will flourish in December and January, and decay in May and June? Now whatever is intelligible, and can be distinctly conceived, implies no contradiction, and can never be proved false by any demonstrative argument or abstract reasoning *a priori*.

If we be, therefore, engaged* by arguments to put trust in past experience, and make it the standard of our future judgement, these arguments must be probable only, or such as regard matter of fact and real existence according to the division above mentioned. But that there is no argument of this kind, must appear, if our explication of that species of reasoning be admitted as solid and satisfactory. We have said that all arguments concerning existence are founded on the relation of cause and effect; that our knowledge of that relation is derived entirely from experience; and that all our experimental conclusions proceed upon the supposition that the future will be conformable to the past. To endeavour, therefore, the proof of this last supposition by probable arguments, or arguments regarding existence, must be evidently going in a circle, and taking that for granted, which is the very point in question.

In reality, all arguments from experience are founded on the similarity which we discover among natural objects, and by which we are induced to expect effects similar to those which we have found to follow from such objects. And though none but a fool or madman will ever pretend to dispute the authority of experience, or to reject that great guide of human life, it may surely be allowed a philosopher to have so much curiosity at least as to examine the principle of human nature, which gives this mighty authority to experience, and makes us draw advantage from that similarity which nature has placed among different objects. From causes which appear *similar*, we expect similar effects. This is the sum of all our experimental conclusions. Now it seems evident that, if this conclusion were formed by reason, it would be as perfect at first, and upon one instance, as after ever so long a course of experience.

But the case is far otherwise. Nothing so like as eggs; yet no one, on account of this appearing similarity, expects the same taste and relish† in all of them. It is only after a long course of uniform experiments in any kind, that we attain a firm reliance and security with regard to a particular event. Now where is that process of reasoning which, from one instance, draws a conclusion, so different from that which it infers from a hundred instances that are nowise different from that single one? This question I propose as much for the sake of information, as with an intention of raising difficulties. I cannot find, I cannot imagine any such reasoning. But I keep my mind still open to instruction, if any one will vouchsafe to bestow it on me.

Should it be said that, from a number of uniform experiments, we *infer* a connection between the sensible qualities and the secret powers; this, I must confess, seems the same difficulty, couched in different terms. The question still recurs, on what process of argument this *inference* is founded? Where is the medium, the interposing ideas, which join propositions so very wide of each other? It is confessed that the colour, consistence, and other sensible qualities of bread appear not, of themselves, to have any connection with the secret powers of nourishment and support. For otherwise we could infer these secret powers from the first appearance of these sensible qualities, without the aid of experience; contrary to the sentiment‡ of all philosophers, and contrary to plain matter of fact. Here, then, is our natural state of ignorance with regard to the powers and influence of all objects. How is this remedied by experience? It only shows us a number of uniform effects, resulting from certain objects, and teaches us that those particular objects, at that particular time, were endowed with such powers and forces. When a new object, endowed with similar sensible qualities, is produced, we expect similar powers and forces, and look for a like effect. From a body of like colour and consistence with bread we expect like nourishment and support. But this surely is a step or progress of the mind, which wants to be explained. When a man says, *I have found, in all past instances, such sensible qualities conjoined with such secret powers*: and when he says,

---

* Induced, persuaded.
† Pleasing flavor.
‡ Opinion.

similar sensible qualities will always be conjoined with similar secret powers, he is not guilty of a tautology,* nor are these propositions in any respect the same. You say that the one proposition is an inference from the other. But you must confess that the inference is not intuitive; neither is it demonstrative: Of what nature is it, then? To say it is experimental, is begging the question. For all inferences from experience suppose, as their foundation, that the future will resemble the past, and that similar powers will be conjoined with similar sensible qualities. If there be any suspicion that the course of nature may change, and that the past may be no rule for the future, all experience becomes useless, and can give rise to no inference or conclusion. It is impossible, therefore, that any arguments from experience can prove this resemblance of the past to the future; since all these arguments are founded on the supposition of that resemblance. Let the course of things be allowed hitherto ever so regular; that alone, without some new argument or inference, proves not that, for the future, it will continue so. In vain do you pretend to have learned the nature of bodies from your past experience. Their secret nature, and consequently all their effects and influence, may change, without any change in their sensible qualities. This happens sometimes, and with regard to some objects: why may it not happen always, and with regard to all objects? What logic, what process or argument secures you against this supposition? My practice, you say, refutes my doubts. But you mistake the purport of my question. As an agent, I am quite satisfied in the point; but as a philosopher, who has some share of curiosity, I will not say scepticism, I want to learn the foundation of this inference. No reading, no enquiry has yet been able to remove my difficulty, or give me satisfaction in a matter of such importance. Can I do better than propose the difficulty to the public, even though, perhaps, I have small hopes of obtaining a solution? We shall at least, by this means, be sensible of our ignorance, if we do not augment our knowledge.

I must confess that a man is guilty of unpardonable arrogance who concludes, because an argument has escaped his own investigation, that therefore it does not really exist. I must also confess that, though all the learned, for several ages, should have employed themselves in fruitless search upon any subject, it may still, perhaps, be rash to conclude positively that the subject must, therefore, pass all human comprehension. Even though we examine all the sources of our knowledge, and conclude them unfit for such a subject, there may still remain a suspicion, that the enumeration is not complete, or the examination not accurate. But with regard to the present subject, there are some considerations which seem to remove all this accusation of arrogance or suspicion of mistake.

It is certain that the most ignorant and stupid peasants—nay infants, nay even brute beasts—improve by experience, and learn the qualities of natural objects, by observing the effects which result from them. When a child has felt the sensation of pain from touching the flame of a candle, he will be careful not to put his hand near any candle; but will expect a similar effect from a cause which is similar in its sensible qualities and appearance. If you assert, therefore, that the understanding of the child is led into this conclusion by any process of argument or ratiocination,[†] I may justly require you to produce that argument; nor have you any pretence to refuse so equitable a demand.[‡] You cannot say that the argument is abstruse,[§] and may possibly escape your enquiry; since you confess that it is obvious to the capacity of a mere infant. If you hesitate, therefore, a moment, or if, after reflection, you produce any intricate or profound argument, you, in a manner, give up the question, and confess that it is not reasoning which engages us to suppose the past resembling the future, and to expect similar effects from causes which are, to appearance, similar. This is the proposition which I intended to enforce in the present section. If I be right, I pretend not to have made any mighty discovery. And if I be wrong, I must acknowledge myself to be indeed a very backward scholar; since I cannot now discover an argument which, it seems, was perfectly familiar to me long before I was out of my cradle.

---

*   Saying the same thing twice, in different words.
†   Reasoning.
‡   Neither do you have any reason to refuse such a fair demand.
§   Hidden.

SECTION V: SCEPTICAL SOLUTION OF THESE DOUBTS

Part I

The passion for philosophy, like that for religion, seems liable to this inconvenience,* that, though it aims at the correction of our manners, and extirpation† of our vices, it may only serve, by imprudent management, to foster a predominant inclination, and push the mind, with more determined resolution, towards that side which already *draws* too much,‡ by the bias and propensity of the natural temper. It is certain that, while we aspire to the magnanimous firmness of the philosophic sage, and endeavour to confine our pleasures altogether within our own minds, we may, at last, render our philosophy like that of Epictetus, and other *Stoics*,§ only a more refined system of selfishness, and reason ourselves out of all virtue as well as social enjoyment. While we study with attention the vanity of human life, and turn all our thoughts towards the empty and transitory nature of riches and honours, we are, perhaps, all the while flattering our natural indolence, which, hating the bustle of the world, and drudgery of business, seeks a pretence of reason to give itself a full and uncontrolled indulgence. There is, however, one species of philosophy which seems little liable to this inconvenience, and that because it strikes in with no disorderly passion of the human mind, nor can mingle itself with any natural affection or propensity; and that is the Academic or Sceptical philosophy.¶ The academics always talk of doubt and suspense of judgement, of danger in hasty determinations, of confining to very narrow bounds the enquiries of the understanding, and of renouncing all speculations which lie not within the limits of common life and practice. Nothing, therefore,

can be more contrary than such a philosophy to the supine indolence** of the mind, its rash arrogance, its lofty pretensions, and its superstitious credulity. Every passion is mortified by it, except the love of truth; and that passion never is, nor can be, carried to too high a degree. It is surprising, therefore, that this philosophy, which, in almost every instance, must be harmless and innocent, should be the subject of so much groundless reproach and obloquy.†† But, perhaps, the very circumstance which renders it so innocent is what chiefly exposes it to the public hatred and resentment. By flattering no irregular passion, it gains few partisans: by opposing so many vices and follies, it raises to itself abundance of enemies, who stigmatize it as libertine, profane, and irreligious.

Nor need we fear that this philosophy, while it endeavours to limit our enquiries to common life, should ever undermine the reasonings of common life, and carry its doubts so far as to destroy all action, as well as speculation. Nature will always maintain her rights, and prevail in the end over any abstract reasoning whatsoever. Though we should conclude, for instance, as in the foregoing section, that, in all reasonings from experience, there is a step taken by the mind which is not supported by any argument or process of the understanding; there is no danger that these reasonings, on which almost all knowledge depends, will ever be affected by such a discovery. If the mind be not engaged by argument to make this step, it must be induced by some other principle of equal weight and authority; and that principle will preserve its influence as long as human nature remains the same. What that principle is may well be worth the pains of enquiry.

---

* Unfitness
† Removal
‡ Pulls too much—i.e., toward the side we already favor.
§ Epictetus (c. 55–135 CE) was a leading Stoic of the Roman era. Stoicism was a philosophical movement that flourished between roughly 300 BCE and 200 CE, and its main doctrine was that the guiding principle of nature is Reason (*logos*) and the highest virtue is to live in harmony with this rational order.
¶ Hume means a kind of moderate skepticism, associated with Plato and the school he founded in Athens around 380 BCE, the Academy. This is to be contrasted with the extreme skepticism sometimes called Pyrrhonism, which seeks to suspend judgment on any question having conflicting evidence—which is to say, on nearly all questions.
** "Supine indolence": laziness.
†† Verbal abuse.

Suppose a person, though endowed with the strongest faculties of reason and reflection, to be brought on a sudden into this world; he would, indeed, immediately observe a continual succession of objects, and one event following another; but he would not be able to discover anything farther. He would not, at first, by any reasoning, be able to reach the idea of cause and effect; since the particular powers, by which all natural operations are performed, never appear to the senses; nor is it reasonable to conclude, merely because one event, in one instance, precedes another, that therefore the one is the cause, the other the effect. Their conjunction may be arbitrary and casual.* There may be no reason to infer the existence of one from the appearance of the other. And in a word, such a person, without more experience, could never employ his conjecture or reasoning concerning any matter of fact, or be assured of any thing beyond what was immediately present to his memory and senses.

Suppose, again, that he has acquired more experience, and has lived so long in the world as to have observed familiar objects or events to be constantly conjoined together; what is the consequence of this experience? He immediately infers the existence of one object from the appearance of the other. Yet he has not, by all his experience, acquired any idea or knowledge of the secret power by which the one object produces the other; nor is it by any process of reasoning, he is engaged to draw this inference. But still he finds himself determined to draw it: And though he should be convinced that his understanding has no part in the operation, he would nevertheless continue in the same course of thinking. There is some other principle which determines him to form such a conclusion.

This principle is custom or habit. For wherever the repetition of any particular act or operation produces a propensity to renew the same act or operation, without being impelled by any reasoning or process of the understanding, we always say, that this propensity is the effect of *custom*. By employing that word, we pretend not to have given the ultimate reason of such a propensity. We only point out a principle of human nature, which is universally acknowledged, and which

is well known by its effects. Perhaps we can push our enquiries no farther, or pretend to give the cause of this cause; but must rest contented with it as the ultimate principle, which we can assign, of all our conclusions from experience. It is sufficient satisfaction, that we can go so far, without repining† at the narrowness of our faculties because they will carry us no farther. And it is certain we here advance a very intelligible proposition at least, if not a true one, when we assert that, after the constant conjunction of two objects—heat and flame, for instance, weight and solidity—we are determined‡ by custom alone to expect the one from the appearance of the other. This hypothesis seems even the only one which explains the difficulty, why we draw, from a thousand instances, an inference which we are not able to draw from one instance, that is, in no respect, different from them. Reason is incapable of any such variation. The conclusions which it draws from considering one circle are the same which it would form upon surveying all the circles in the universe. But no man, having seen only one body move after being impelled by another, could infer that every other body will move after a like impulse. All inferences from experience, therefore, are effects of custom, not of reasoning.[2]

Custom, then, is the great guide of human life. It is that principle alone which renders our experience useful to us, and makes us expect, for the future, a similar train of events with those which have appeared in the past. Without the influence of custom, we should be entirely ignorant of every matter of fact beyond what is immediately present to the memory and senses. We should never know how to adjust means to ends, or to employ our natural powers in the production of any effect. There would be an end at once of all action, as well as of the chief part of speculation.

But here it may be proper to remark, that though our conclusions from experience carry us beyond our memory and senses, and assure us of matters of fact which happened in the most distant places and most remote ages, yet some fact must always be present to the senses or memory, from which we may first proceed in drawing these conclusions. A man, who

---

* A matter of chance.
† Complaining.
‡ Caused.

should find in a desert country the remains of pompous* buildings, would conclude that the country had, in ancient times, been cultivated by civilized inhabitants; but did nothing of this nature occur to him, he could never form such an inference. We learn the events of former ages from history; but then we must peruse the volumes in which this instruction is contained, and thence carry up our inferences from one testimony to another, till we arrive at the eyewitnesses and spectators of these distant events. In a word, if we proceed not upon some fact, present to the memory or senses, our reasonings would be merely hypothetical; and however the particular links might be connected with each other, the whole chain of inferences would have nothing to support it, nor could we ever, by its means, arrive at the knowledge of any real existence. If I ask why you believe any particular matter of fact, which you relate, you must tell me some reason; and this reason will be some other fact, connected with it. But as you cannot proceed after this manner, *in infinitum*,[†] you must at last terminate in some fact, which is present to your memory or senses; or must allow that your belief is entirely without foundation.

What, then, is the conclusion of the whole matter? A simple one; though, it must be confessed, pretty remote from the common theories of philosophy. All belief of matter of fact or real existence is derived merely from some object, present to the memory or senses, and a customary conjunction between that and some other object. Or in other words; having found, in many instances, that any two kinds of objects—flame and heat, snow and cold—have always been conjoined together; if flame or snow be presented anew to the senses, the mind is carried by custom to expect heat or cold, and to *believe* that such a quality does exist, and will discover itself upon a nearer approach. This belief is the necessary result of placing the mind in such circumstances. It is an operation of the soul,[‡] when we are so situated, as unavoidable as to feel the passion of love, when we receive benefits; or hatred, when we meet with injuries. All these operations are a species

of natural instincts, which no reasoning or process of the thought and understanding is able either to produce or to prevent.

At this point, it would be very allowable for us to stop our philosophical researches. In most questions we can never make a single step farther; and in all questions we must terminate here at last, after our most restless and curious enquiries. But still our curiosity will be pardonable, perhaps commendable, if it carry us on to still farther researches, and make us examine more accurately the nature of this *belief*, and of the *customary conjunction*, whence it is derived. By this means we may meet with some explications and analogies that will give satisfaction; at least to such as love the abstract sciences, and can be entertained with speculations, which, however accurate, may still retain a degree of doubt and uncertainty. As to readers of a different taste; the remaining part of this section is not calculated for them, and the following enquiries may well be understood, though it be neglected.

Part II

Nothing is more free than the imagination of man; and though it cannot exceed that original stock of ideas furnished by the internal and external senses, it has unlimited power of mixing, compounding, separating, and dividing these ideas, in all the varieties of fiction and vision. It can feign[§] a train of events, with all the appearance of reality, ascribe to them a particular time and place, conceive them as existent, and paint them out to itself with every circumstance, that belongs to any historical fact, which it believes with the greatest certainty. Wherein, therefore, consists the difference between such a *fiction* and *belief*? It lies not merely in any peculiar idea, which is annexed to such a conception as commands our assent, and which is wanting[¶] to every known fiction. For as the mind has authority over all its ideas, it could voluntarily annex this particular idea to any fiction, and consequently be able to believe whatever it pleases; contrary to what we

---

*   Splendid, full of pomp.
†   For ever, to infinity.
‡   Mind.
§   Simulate, imagine.
¶   Lacking.

find by daily experience. We can, in our conception, join the head of a man to the body of a horse; but it is not in our power to believe that such an animal has ever really existed.

It follows, therefore, that the difference between *fiction* and *belief* lies in some sentiment or feeling, which is annexed to the latter, not to the former, and which depends not on the will, nor can be commanded at pleasure. It must be excited by nature, like all other sentiments; and must arise from the particular situation, in which the mind is placed at any particular juncture. Whenever any object is presented to the memory or senses, it immediately, by the force of custom, carries the imagination to conceive that object, which is usually conjoined to it; and this conception is attended with a feeling or sentiment, different from the loose reveries of the fancy. In this consists the whole nature of belief. For as there is no matter of fact which we believe so firmly that we cannot conceive the contrary, there would be no difference between the conception assented to and that which is rejected, were it not for some sentiment which distinguishes the one from the other. If I see a billiard-ball moving toward another, on a smooth table, I can easily conceive it to stop upon contact. This conception implies no contradiction; but still it feels very differently from that conception by which I represent to myself the impulse and the communication of motion from one ball to another.

Were we to attempt a *definition* of this sentiment, we should, perhaps, find it a very difficult, if not an impossible task; in the same manner as if we should endeavour to define the feeling of cold or passion of anger, to a creature who never had any experience of these sentiments. Belief is the true and proper name of this feeling; and no one is ever at a loss to know the meaning of that term; because every man is every moment conscious of the sentiment represented by it. It may not, however, be improper to attempt a *description* of this sentiment; in hopes we may, by that means, arrive at some analogies, which may afford a more perfect explication of it. I say, then, that belief is nothing but a more vivid, lively, forcible, firm, steady conception of an object, than what the imagination alone is ever able to attain. This variety of terms, which may seem so unphilosophical, is intended only to express

that act of the mind, which renders realities, or what is taken for such, more present to us than fictions, causes them to weigh more in the thought, and gives them a superior influence on the passions and imagination. Provided we agree about the thing, it is needless to dispute about the terms. The imagination has the command over all its ideas, and can join and mix and vary them, in all the ways possible. It may conceive fictitious objects with all the circumstances of place and time. It may set them, in a manner, before our eyes, in their true colours, just as they might have existed. But as it is impossible that this faculty of imagination can ever, of itself, reach belief, it is evident that belief consists not in the peculiar nature or order of ideas, but in the *manner* of their conception, and in their *feeling* to the mind. I confess, that it is impossible perfectly to explain this feeling or manner of conception. We may make use of words which express something near it. But its true and proper name, as we observed before, is *belief*; which is a term that every one sufficiently understands in common life. And in philosophy, we can go no farther than assert, that *belief* is something felt by the mind, which distinguishes the ideas of the judgement from the fictions of the imagination. It gives them more weight and influence; makes them appear of greater importance; enforces them in the mind; and renders them the governing principle of our actions. I hear at present, for instance, a person's voice, with whom I am acquainted; and the sound comes as from the next room. This impression of my senses immediately conveys my thought to the person, together with all the surrounding objects. I paint them out to myself as existing at present, with the same qualities and relations, of which I formerly knew them possessed. These ideas take faster hold of my mind than ideas of an enchanted castle. They are very different to the feeling, and have a much greater influence of every kind, either to give pleasure or pain, joy or sorrow.

Let us, then, take in the whole compass* of this doctrine, and allow, that the sentiment of belief is nothing but a conception more intense and steady than what attends the mere fictions of the imagination, and that this *manner* of conception arises from a customary conjunction of the object with something present

---

* "Compass" here means "extent," and so to "take in the whole compass" is to summarize.

to the memory or senses: I believe that it will not be difficult, upon these suppositions, to find other operations of the mind analogous to it, and to trace up these phenomena to principles still more general.

We have already observed that nature has established connections among particular ideas, and that no sooner one idea occurs to our thoughts than it introduces its correlative,* and carries our attention towards it, by a gentle and insensible movement. These principles of connection or association we have reduced to three, namely, *resemblance, contiguity*† and *causation*; which are the only bonds that unite our thoughts together, and beget that regular train of reflection or discourse, which, in a greater or less degree, takes place among all mankind. Now here arises a question, on which the solution of the present difficulty will depend. Does it happen, in all these relations, that, when one of the objects is presented to the senses or memory, the mind is not only carried to the conception of the correlative, but reaches a steadier and stronger conception of it than what otherwise it would have been able to attain? This seems to be the case with that belief which arises from the relation of cause and effect. And if the case be the same with the other relations or principles of associations, this may be established as a general law, which takes place in all the operations of the mind.

We may, therefore, observe, as the first experiment to our present purpose, that, upon the appearance of the picture of an absent friend, our idea of him is evidently enlivened by the *resemblance*, and that every passion, which that idea occasions, whether of joy or sorrow, acquires new force and vigour. In producing this effect, there concur both a relation and a present impression. Where the picture bears him no resemblance, at least was not intended for‡ him, it never so much as conveys our thought to him: and where it is absent, as well as the person, though the mind may pass from the thought of the one to that of the other, it feels its idea to be rather weakened than enlivened by that transition. We take a pleasure in

viewing the picture of a friend, when it is set before us; but when it is removed, rather choose to consider him directly than by reflection in an image, which is equally distant and obscure.

The ceremonies of the Roman Catholic religion may be considered as instances of the same nature. The devotees of that superstition usually plead in excuse for the mummeries,§ with which they are upbraided, that they feel the good effect of those external motions, and postures, and actions, in enlivening their devotion and quickening their fervour, which otherwise would decay, if directed entirely to distant and immaterial objects. We shadow out the objects of our faith, say they, in sensible types and images, and render them more present to us by the immediate presence of these types, than it is possible for us to do merely by an intellectual view and contemplation. Sensible objects have always a greater influence on the fancy than any other; and this influence they readily convey to those ideas to which they are related, and which they resemble. I shall only infer from these practices, and this reasoning, that the effect of resemblance in enlivening the ideas is very common; and as in every case a resemblance and a present impression must concur, we are abundantly supplied with experiments to prove the reality of the foregoing principle.

We may add force to these experiments by others of a different kind, in considering the effects of *contiguity* as well as of *resemblance*. It is certain that distance diminishes the force of every idea, and that, upon our approach to any object; though it does not discover itself to our senses; it operates upon the mind with an influence, which imitates an immediate impression. The thinking on any object readily transports the mind to what is contiguous; but it is only the actual presence of an object, that transports it with a superior vivacity. When I am a few miles from home, whatever relates to it touches me more nearly than when I am two hundred leagues¶ distant; though even at that distance the reflecting on any

---

* The thing normally related or connected to it.
† Proximity in place or time
‡ Supposed to be.
§ Silly rituals.
¶ A league is roughly three miles (4.8 km).

thing in the neighbourhood of my friends or family naturally produces an idea of them. But as in this latter case, both the objects of the mind are ideas; notwithstanding there is an easy transition between them; that transition alone is not able to give a superior vivacity to any of the ideas, for want of some immediate impression.[3]

No one can doubt but causation has the same influence as the other two relations of resemblance and contiguity. Superstitious people are fond of the reliques of saints and holy men, for the same reason, that they seek after types or images, in order to enliven their devotion, and give them a more intimate and strong conception of those exemplary lives, which they desire to imitate. Now it is evident, that one of the best reliques, which a devotee could procure, would be the handywork of a saint; and if his clothes and furniture are ever to be considered in this light, it is because they were once at his disposal, and were moved and affected by him; in which respect they are to be considered as imperfect effects, and as connected with him by a shorter chain of consequences than any of those, by which we learn the reality of his existence.

Suppose, that the son of a friend, who had been long dead or absent, were presented to us; it is evident, that this object would instantly revive its correlative idea, and recall to our thoughts all past intimacies and familiarities, in more lively colours than they would otherwise have appeared to us. This is another phenomenon, which seems to prove the principle above mentioned.

We may observe, that, in these phenomena, the belief of the correlative object is always presupposed; without which the relation could have no effect. The influence of the picture supposes, that we *believe* our friend to have once existed. Contiguity to home can never excite our ideas of home, unless we *believe* that it really exists. Now I assert, that this belief, where it reaches beyond the memory or senses, is of a similar nature, and arises from similar causes, with the transition of thought and vivacity of conception here explained. When I throw a piece of dry wood into a fire, my mind is immediately carried to conceive, that it augments, not extinguishes the flame. This transition

of thought from the cause to the effect proceeds not from reason. It derives its origin altogether from custom and experience. And as it first begins from an object, present to the senses, it renders the idea or conception of flame more strong and lively than any loose, floating reverie of the imagination. That idea arises immediately. The thought moves instantly towards it, and conveys to it all that force of conception, which is derived from the impression present to the senses. When a sword is levelled at my breast, does not the idea of wound and pain strike me more strongly, than when a glass of wine is presented to me, even though by accident this idea should occur after the appearance of the latter object? But what is there in this whole matter to cause such a strong conception, except only a present object and a customary transition of the idea of another object, which we have been accustomed to conjoin with the former? This is the whole operation of the mind, in all our conclusions concerning matter of fact and existence; and it is a satisfaction to find some analogies, by which it may be explained. The transition from a present object does in all cases give strength and solidity to the related idea.

Here, then, is a kind of pre-established harmony between the course of nature and the succession of our ideas; and though the powers and forces, by which the former is governed, be wholly unknown to us; yet our thoughts and conceptions have still, we find, gone on in the same train with the other works of nature. Custom is that principle, by which this correspondence has been effected; so necessary to the subsistence of our species, and the regulation of our conduct, in every circumstance and occurrence of human life. Had not the presence of an object, instantly excited the idea of those objects, commonly conjoined with it, all our knowledge must have been limited to the narrow sphere of our memory and senses; and we should never have been able to adjust means to ends, or employ our natural powers, either to the producing of good, or avoiding of evil. Those, who delight in the discovery and contemplation of *final causes*,* have here ample subject to employ their wonder and admiration.

I shall add, for a further confirmation of the foregoing theory, that, as this operation of the mind,

---

* In this context, the purpose for the nature and arrangement of things in the universe.

by which we infer like effects from like causes, and *vice versa*, is so essential to the subsistence of all human creatures, it is not probable, that it could be trusted to the fallacious deductions of our reason, which is slow in its operations; appears not, in any degree, during the first years of infancy; and at best is, in every age and period of human life, extremely liable to error and mistake. It is more conformable to the ordinary wisdom of nature to secure so necessary an act of the mind, by some instinct or mechanical tendency, which may be infallible in its operations, may discover itself at the first appearance of life and thought, and may be independent of all the laboured deductions of the understanding. As nature has taught us the use of our limbs, without giving us the knowledge of the muscles and nerves, by which they are actuated; so has she implanted in us an instinct, which carries forward the thought in a correspondent course to that which she has established among external objects; though we are ignorant of those powers and forces, on which this regular course and succession of objects totally depends. ■

Suggestions for Critical Reflection

1. *Are* "all the objects of human reason or enquiry" divisible into exactly two piles: relations of ideas and matters of fact? What about, for example, the claim that a wall can't be simultaneously red all over and green all over: which of the two categories does this fall into? How about the statement that water is identical with H_2O?

2. Does Hume think we are being unreasonable or irrational if we continue to act as if inductive inferences are justified? Given what Hume has argued, what do you think?

3. What exactly would it mean to claim that the future resembles the past or that nature is "uniform"? Is nature uniform in *every* respect? (For example, is the sky always blue?) So what *kind* of uniformity do you think we need to look for?

4. Does the past reliability *of induction* provide evidence that future instances of induction will also be reliable? For example, on several hundred occasions in the past I inferred on the basis of previous experience that the Big Mac I was about to eat would not be poisonous, and each time I was right; do these several hundred instances of correct induction provide any evidence that induction is *generally* reliable? Why, or why not?

5. What's the difference (if any) between the psychological claim that people believe certain things about the future only out of habit, rather than because they have gone through some process of reasoning, and the claim that there is no rational justification available for our beliefs about the future? Which claim is Hume making?

6. Is it possible to formulate a skeptical problem about *deduction* that is similar to Hume's problem about induction?

7. What is the difference between believing something and merely imagining that it is true? Does Hume think that when we believe some future event will occur, as opposed to merely imagining it will occur, there is some *extra* idea present in our mind—a sort of idea of belief itself, added to the idea of the future event? Are Hume's views on the nature of belief plausible?

Notes

1 The word, Power, is here used in a loose and popular sense. The more accurate explication of it would give additional evidence to this argument. See Sect. 7 [not reprinted here].

2 Nothing is more usual than for writers, even, on *moral*, *political*, or *physical* subjects to distinguish between *reason* and *experience*, and to suppose, that these species of argumentation are entirely different from each other. The former are taken for the mere result of our intellectual faculties, which, by considering *a priori* the nature of things, and examining the effects, that must follow from their operation, establish particular principles of science and philosophy. The latter are supposed to be derived entirely from sense and observation, by which we learn what has actually resulted from the operation of particular objects, and are thence able to infer, what will, for the future, result from them. Thus, for instance, the limitations and restraints of civil government, and a legal constitution, may be defended, either from *reason*, which reflecting on the great frailty and corruption of human nature, teaches, that no man can safely be trusted with unlimited authority; or from *experience* and history, which inform us of the enormous abuses, that ambition, in every age and country, has been found to make so imprudent a confidence.

The same distinction between reason and experience is maintained in all our deliberations concerning the conduct of life; while the experienced statesman, general, physician, or merchant is trusted and followed; and the unpractised novice, with whatever natural talents endowed, neglected and despised. Though it be allowed, that reason may form very plausible conjectures with regard to the consequences of such a particular conduct in such particular circumstances; it is still supposed imperfect, without the assistance of experience, which is alone able to give stability and certainty to the maxims, derived from study and reflection.

But notwithstanding that this distinction be thus universally received, both in the active and speculative scenes of life, I shall not scruple to pronounce, that it is, at bottom, erroneous, at least, superficial.

If we examine those arguments, which, in any of the sciences above mentioned, are supposed to be mere effects of reasoning and reflection, they will be found to terminate, at last, in some general principle or, conclusion, for which we can assign no reason but observation and experience. The only difference between them and those maxims, which are vulgarly esteemed the result of pure experience, is, that the former cannot be established without some process of thought, and some reflection on what we have observed, in order to distinguish its circumstances, and trace its consequences: Whereas in the latter, the experienced event is exactly and fully familiar to that which we infer as the result of any particular situation. The history of a Tiberius or a Nero makes us dread a like tyranny, were our monarchs freed from the restraints of laws and senates: but the observation of any fraud or cruelty in private life is sufficient, with the aid of a little thought, to give us the same apprehension; while it serves as an instance of the general corruption of human nature, and shows us the danger which we must incur by reposing an entire confidence in mankind. In both cases, it is experience which is ultimately the foundation of our inference and conclusion.

There is no man so young and inexperienced, as not to have formed, from observation, many general and just maxims concerning human affairs and the conduct of life; but it must be confessed, that, when a man comes to put these in practice, he will be extremely liable to error, till time and farther experience both enlarge these maxims, and teach him their proper use and application. In every situation or incident, there are many particular and seemingly minute circumstances, which the man of greatest talent is, at first, apt to overlook, though on them the justness of his conclusions, and consequently the prudence of his conduct, entirely depend. Not to mention, that, to a young beginner, the general observations and maxims occur not always on the proper occasions, nor can be immediately applied with due calmness and distinction. The truth is, an unexperienced reasoner could be no reasoner at all, were he absolutely unexperienced; and when we assign that character to any one, we mean it only in a comparative sense, and suppose him possessed of experience, in a smaller and more imperfect degree.

3 'Naturane nobis, inquit, datum dicam, an errore quodam, ut, cum ea loca videamus, in quibus memoria dignos viros acceperimus multim esse versatos, magis moveamur, quam siquando eorum ipsorum aut facta audiamus aut scriptum aliquod legamus? Velut ego nunc moveor. Venit enim mihi Plato in mentem, quem accepimus primum hic disputare solitum; cuius etiam illi hortuli propinqui non memoriam solum mihi afferunt, sed ipsum videntur in conspectu meo hic ponere. Hic Speusippus, hic Xenocrates, hic eius auditor Polemo; cuius ipsa illa sessio fuit, quam videmus. Equidem etiam curiam nostram, Hostiliam dico, non hanc novam, quae mihi minor esse videtur postquam est maior, solebam intueri, Scipionem, Catonem, Laelium, nostrum vero in primis avum cogitare. Tanta vis admonitionis est*

in locis; ut non sine causa ex his memopriae deducta sit disciplina.'—Cicero de Finibus. Lib. v. ["Should I say," he asked, "that it is natural or just an error that makes us more greatly moved when we see places where, as we have been told, famous men spent a lot of time, than we are if, at some time or another, we hear about the things which they have done, or read something written by them? I, for example, feel moved at present. For Plato comes to my mind who, we know, was the first to hold regular discussions here: that garden nearby not only brings him to memory but seems to make me see

him. Here is Speusippus, here is Xenocrates, and here also is his pupil Polemo: it is the place where he used to sit that we see before us. Similarly, when I looked at our senate house (I mean the one Hostilius built and not the new building which seems to me lesser since it has been enlarged) I used to think of Scipio, Cato, and Lælius, and above all of my grandfather. Places can remind us of so much; it is not without good reason that the formal training of memory is based on them." Cicero, *On the Chief Good and Evil*, from Book V]

CARL HEMPEL

Scientific Inquiry: Invention and Test

Who Was Carl Hempel?

Carl Gustav ("Peter") Hempel—probably, with Popper and Kuhn, one of the three most influential philosophers of science of the twentieth century—was born in 1905 in Orianenberg, near Berlin, Germany. After attending high school in Berlin, at 18 he went to study mathematics and logic at the University of Göttingen with the famous mathematician David Hilbert. Although Hempel quickly fell in love with mathematical logic, he left Göttingen within the year to study at the University of Heidelberg, and then in 1924 moved back to Berlin where he studied physics with Hans Reichenbach and Max Planck, and logic with John von Neumann (all destined to become towering figures in their fields). Reichenbach introduced him to the members of a group of intellectuals called the Berlin Circle, and in 1929 Hempel took part in the historic first congress on scientific philosophy in Prague, organized by the founders of an important twentieth-century philosophical movement called "logical positivism." At that conference Hempel met the philosopher of science Rudolf Carnap, and was so impressed by him that he moved to Carnap's home town of Vienna, Austria; there, he attended classes by the logical positivists Carnap, Moritz Schlick, and Friedrich Waismann and took part in meetings of the group called the "Vienna Circle."

The Vienna and Berlin Circles of the 1920s and early 1930s were fairly informal, diverse, collaborative groups of "scientifically interested philosophers and philosophically interested scientists," as Hempel once put it. The members of these groups, especially the Vienna Circle, thought of themselves as decisively breaking with the past and founding a new, more effective kind of philosophical enterprise—a "modern scientific philosophy" built on the new techniques of logical analysis and modeled on the successful empirical methods of the exact sciences. The past history of philosophy, the new logical

empiricists (also known as logical positivists) declared, was one of fruitless strife; by contrast, in Hempel's words, "the Vienna Circle held that the purported problems of metaphysics constitute no genuine problems at all and that in an inquiry making use of an appropriately precise conceptual and linguistic apparatus, metaphysical questions could not even be formulated. They were pseudo-problems, devoid of any clear meaning."[*]

In 1934—just a week before Adolf Hitler anointed himself *Führer* of the German Third Reich—Hempel completed his PhD from the University of Berlin, with a dissertation on probability theory. In the previous year, shortly after Hitler was elected Chancellor of Germany, Hempel's supervisor Hans Reichenbach had been summarily dismissed from his Berlin chair because his father had been Jewish; Hempel himself was of pure "Aryan" stock, but his wife Eva Ahrends had partly "Jewish blood" and Hempel was frequently accused of the offense of "philosemitism," sympathy with the Jews. As a consequence, in 1934, Hempel fled Germany to Belgium, where he and Eva were supported by his friend and colleague Paul Oppenheim.

In 1937, because of Carnap's influence, Hempel was invited to become a Rockefeller research associate in philosophy at the University of Chicago, and Hempel officially emigrated to the United States in 1939. Between 1939 and 1948 Hempel taught at City College and Queens College in New York; during these years, Hempel's wife Eva died shortly after giving birth to a son, and Hempel married Diane Perlow. In 1948 he moved to Yale University, and in 1955 he was made Stuart Professor of Philosophy at Princeton, a post he held until his mandatory retirement at age 68 in 1973. Even after his retirement, Hempel continued to lecture at Princeton and then, as a visiting professor, at Jerusalem, Berkeley, Carleton College, and Pittsburgh; in 1977 (at the age of 72) he was made University Professor of Philosophy at the Univer-

---

[*]   "Empiricism in the Vienna Circle and in the Berlin Society for Scientific Philosophy: Recollections and Reflections" in F. Stadler, ed., *Scientific Philosophy: Origins and Developments* (Springer, 1993), 1.

sity of Pittsburgh, a post he held until 1985. Hempel died at Princeton, New Jersey, in 1997.

In a posthumous tribute, the well-known Princeton logician Richard Jeffrey wrote of Hempel:

> There was no arrogance in him; he got no thrill of pleasure from proving people wrong. His criticisms were always courteous, never triumphant. This quality was deeply rooted in his character. He was made so as to welcome opportunities for kindness, generosity, courtesy; and he gave his whole mind to such projects spontaneously, for pleasure, so that effort disappeared into zest. [His wife] Diane was another such player. (Once, in a restaurant, someone remarked on their politeness to each other, and she said, "Ah, but you should see us when we are alone together. [Pause] Then we are *really* polite.") And play it was, too. He was notably playful and incapable of stuffiness.*

Hempel is commonly credited with playing a leading role in developing the account of scientific explanation and prediction which came to be labeled the "Received View" by its critics in the last few decades of the twentieth century. (A more technical name for a central plank of this view is the *deductive-nomological* [D-N] or *covering law* model of scientific explanation.) According to this theory, the scientific explanation of a fact consists in the logical *deduction* of a statement that describes the fact (often called the "explanandum") from premises (the "explanans"), which include true scientific laws and statements of initial conditions. For example, a simple scientific explanation for why this piece of copper conducts electricity is that my bit of copper is "covered" by a general law which says that *all* copper conducts electricity under certain circumstances. In this case, the sentence (1) "This copper conducts electricity" is a *logical consequence* of the statements (2) "All copper conducts electricity under conditions C (e.g., the copper is pure, the metal is within a certain temperature range, etc.)" and (3) "Conditions C presently hold for this bit of copper"; according to Hempel, this logical relationship is why (2) and (3) count as *explaining* (1).

Furthermore, according to Hempel, scientific *prediction* turns out to be just the flip-side of explanation. One can start from an observation, and show that a certain theory *explains* that observation because the observation is deducible from the theory; or one can start with a theory, and show that the theory *predicts* some set of observations because they are logical consequences of the theory being true. Either way, in Hempel's view, the essential logical relationship between statements of laws and statements of observations is the same.

When it comes to the issue of *confirming* which scientific laws are true and which are not (i.e., which can feature in good explanations), one of the things Hempel is best known for is formulating, in 1945, "Hempel's paradox" (also known as the paradox of the ravens, or the paradox of confirmation). This puzzle calls into question the intuitive assumption that a general law is confirmed only by instances of that law—for example, the idea that the claim that "All ravens are black" is supported by observations of black ravens but not at all by the sighting of a white running shoe. Here is the paradox. A white running shoe is neither black nor a raven. Therefore, it appears that my shoe sighting is some evidence for the claim that all non-black things are non-ravens. But "all non-black things are non-ravens" is logically equivalent to "all ravens are black." Thus it turns out that—if our intuitive understanding of induction is correct—observations of white shoes (and blue jays, etc.) do in fact partially confirm the hypothesis that all ravens are black. But this seems absurd—it seems ridiculous to think that we could find out about birds by examining footwear; hence the paradox.

Various attempts have been made to deal with this puzzle. Hempel himself proposed that we resolve the paradox by accepting its apparently absurd conclusion: he held that *all* observations are relevant to any hypothesis, though some of them (such as sightings of white shoes) confirm it only much more weakly than others (sightings of black ravens).

What Is the Structure of This Reading?

In this reading Hempel argues that the traditional, or "narrow inductivist," view is incorrect, and that it should be replaced in our understanding of science by what he calls the "method of hypothesis."

---

*   Richard Jeffrey, "Preface," to Hempel's *Selected Philosophical Essays* (Cambridge University Press, 2000), ix.

Scientific Inquiry: Invention and Test[*]

The Role of Induction in Scientific Inquiry

We have considered some scientific investigations in which a problem was tackled by proposing tentative answers in the form of hypotheses that were then tested by deriving from them suitable test implications and checking these by observation or experiment.

But how are suitable hypotheses arrived at in the first place? It is sometimes held that they are inferred from antecedently collected data by means of a procedure called *inductive inference*, as contradistinguished from deductive inference, from which it differs in important respects.

In a deductively valid argument, the conclusion is related to the premisses in such a way that if the premisses are true then the conclusion cannot fail to be true as well. This requirement is satisfied, for example, by any argument of the following general form:

If *p*, then *q*.
It is not the case that *q*.

It is not the case that *p*.

Brief reflection shows that no matter what particular statements may stand at the places marked by the letters '*p*' and '*q*', the conclusion will certainly be true if the premisses are. In fact, our schema represents the argument form called *modus tollens*....

Another type of deductively valid inference is illustrated by this example:

Any sodium salt, when put into the flame of a Bunsen burner,[†] turns the flame yellow.
This piece of rock salt is a sodium salt.

This piece of rock salt, when put into the flame of a Bunsen burner, will turn the flame yellow.

Arguments of the latter kind are often said to lead from the general (here, the premiss about all sodium salts) to the particular (a conclusion about the particular piece of rock salt). Inductive inferences, by contrast, are sometimes described as leading from premises about particular cases to a conclusion that has the character of a general law or principle. For example, from premisses to the effect that each of the particular samples of various sodium salts that have so far been subjected to the Bunsen flame test did turn the flame yellow, inductive inference supposedly leads to the general conclusion that all sodium salts, when put into the flame of a Bunsen burner, turn the flame yellow. But in this case, the truth of the premisses obviously does *not* guarantee the truth of the conclusion; for even if it is the case that all samples of sodium salts examined so far did turn the Bunsen flame yellow, it remains quite possible that new kinds of sodium salt might yet be found that do not conform to this generalization. Indeed, even some kinds of sodium salt that have already been tested with positive result might conceivably fail to satisfy the generalization under special physical conditions (such as very strong magnetic fields or the like) in which they have not yet been examined. For this reason, the premisses of an inductive inference are often said to imply the conclusion only with more or less high probability, whereas the premisses of a deductive inference imply the conclusion with certainty.

The idea that in scientific inquiry, inductive inference from antecedently collected data leads to appropriate general principles is clearly embodied in the following account of how a scientist would ideally proceed:

> If we try to imagine how a mind of superhuman power and reach, but normal so far as the logical processes of its thought are concerned, ... would use the scientific method, the process would be as follows: First, all facts would be observed and recorded, *without selection* or *a priori* guess as to their relative importance. Secondly, the observed

---

[*]   From *Philosophy of Natural Science* (1st ed., 1967), 10–15.
[†]   A common piece of laboratory equipment that produces an adjustable gas flame.

and recorded facts would be analyzed, compared, and classified, *without hypothesis or postulates* other than those necessarily involved in the logic of thought. Third, from this analysis of the facts generalizations would be inductively drawn as to the relations, classificatory or causal, between them. Fourth, further research would be deductive as well as inductive, employing inferences from previously established generalizations.[1]

This passage distinguishes four stages in an ideal scientific inquiry: (1) observation and recording of all facts, (2) analysis and classification of these facts, (3) inductive derivation of generalizations from them, and (4) further testing of the generalizations. The first two of these stages are specifically assumed not to make use of any guesses or hypotheses as to how the observed facts might be interconnected; this restriction seems to have been imposed in the belief that such preconceived ideas would introduce a bias and would jeopardize the scientific objectivity of the investigation.

But the view expressed in the quoted passage—I will call it *the narrow inductivist conception of scientific inquiry*—is untenable, for several reasons....

First, our scientific investigation as here envisaged could never get off the ground. Even its first phase could never be carried out, for a collection of *all* the facts would have to await the end of the world, so to speak; and even all the facts *up to now* cannot be collected, since there are an infinite number and variety of them. Are we to examine, for example, all the grains of sand in all the deserts and on all the beaches, and are we to record their shapes, their weights, their chemical composition, their distances from each other, their constantly changing temperature, and their equally changing distance from the center of the moon? Are we to record the floating thoughts that cross our minds in the tedious process? The shapes of the clouds overhead, the changing color of the sky? The construction and the trade name of our

writing equipment? Our own life histories and those of our fellow investigators? All these, and untold other things, are, after all, among "all the facts up to now".

Perhaps, then, all that should be required in the first phase is that all the *relevant* facts be collected. But relevant to what? Though the author does not mention this, let us suppose that the inquiry is concerned with a specified *problem*. Should we not then begin by collecting all the facts—or better, all available data—relevant to that problem? This notion still makes no clear sense. Semmelweis sought to solve one specific problem, yet he collected quite different kinds of data at different stages of his inquiry.* And rightly so; for what particular sorts of data it is reasonable to collect is not determined by the problem under study, but by a tentative answer to it that the investigator entertains in the form of a conjecture or hypothesis. Given the conjecture that mortality from childbed fever was increased by the terrifying appearance of the priest and his attendant with the death bell, it was relevant to collect data on the consequences of having the priest change his routine; but it would have been totally irrelevant to check what would happen if doctors and students disinfected their hands before examining their patients. With respect to Semmelweis' eventual contamination hypothesis, data of the latter kind were clearly relevant, and those of the former kind totally irrelevant.

Empirical "facts" or findings, therefore, can be qualified as logically relevant or irrelevant only in reference to a given hypothesis, but not in reference to a given problem.

Suppose now that a hypothesis H has been advanced as a tentative answer to a research problem: what kinds of data would be relevant to H? Our earlier examples suggest an answer: A finding is relevant to H if either its occurrence or its nonoccurrence can be inferred from H. Take Torricelli's hypothesis, for example.† As we saw, Pascal‡ inferred from it that the mercury column in a barometer should grow shorter if the barometer were carried up a mountain. Therefore,

---

* Hempel is referring here to a case study he described earlier: that of the Viennese doctor Ignaz Semmelweis, who in the mid-nineteenth century discovered that incidences of childbed fever—a major cause of death in young mothers at that time—could be drastically reduced by disinfecting the hands of the attending doctors.

† This is also a reference to an earlier case study. Evangelista Torricelli (1608–47) hypothesized that the earth is surrounded by a sea of air which exerts pressure on the surface below because of its weight; thus, the higher one is off the ground, the less downward pressure the atmosphere would exert (since there is less air above one pushing down).

‡ Blaise Pascal (1623–62) was a French mathematician and physicist.

any finding to the effect that this did indeed happen in a particular case is relevant to the hypotheses; but so would be the finding that the length of the mercury column had remained unchanged or that it had decreased and then increased during the ascent, for such findings would refute Pascal's test implication and would thus disconfirm Torricelli's hypothesis. Data of the former kind may be called positively, or favorably, relevant to the hypothesis; those of the latter kind negatively, or unfavorably, relevant.

In sum, the maxim that data should be gathered without guidance by antecedent hypotheses about the connections among the facts under study is self-defeating, and it is certainly not followed in scientific inquiry. On the contrary, tentative hypotheses are needed to give direction to a scientific investigation. Such hypotheses determine, among other things, what data should be collected at a given point in a scientific investigation.

...

The second stage envisaged in our quoted passage is open to similar criticism. A set of empirical "facts" can be analyzed and classified in many different ways, most of which will be unilluminating for the purposes of a given inquiry. Semmelweis could have classified the women in the maternity wards according to criteria such as age, place of residence, marital status, dietary habits, and so forth; but information on these would have provided no clue to a patient's prospects of becoming a victim of childbed fever. What Semmelweis sought were criteria that would be significantly connected with those prospects; and for this purpose, as he eventually found, it was illuminating to single out those women who were attended by medical personnel with contaminated hands; for it was with this characteristic, or with the corresponding class of patients, that high mortality from childbed fever was associated.

Thus, if a particular way of analyzing and classifying empirical findings is to lead to an explanation of the phenomena concerned, then it must be based on hypotheses about how those phenomena are connected; without such hypotheses, analysis and classification are blind.

Our critical reflections on the first two stages of inquiry as envisaged in the quoted passage also undercut the notion that hypotheses are introduced only in the third stage, by inductive inference from antecedently collected data. But some further remarks on the subject should be added here.

Induction is sometimes conceived as a method that leads, by means of mechanically applicable rules, from observed facts to corresponding general principles. In this case, the rules of inductive inference would provide effective canons of scientific discovery; induction would be a mechanical procedure analogous to the familiar routine for the multiplication of integers, which leads, in a finite number of predetermined and mechanically performable steps, to the corresponding product. Actually, however, no such general and mechanical induction procedure is available at present; otherwise, the much studied problem of the causation of cancer, for example, would hardly have remained unsolved to this day. Nor can the discovery of such a procedure ever be expected. For—to mention one reason—scientific hypotheses and theories are usually couched in terms that do not occur at all in the description of the empirical findings on which they rest, and which they serve to explain. For example, theories about the atomic and subatomic structure of matter contain terms such as 'atom', 'electron', 'proton', 'neutron', 'psi-function', etc.; yet they are based on laboratory findings about the spectra of various gases, tracks in cloud and bubble chambers, quantitative aspects of chemical reactions, and so forth—all of which can be described without the use of those "theoretical terms". Induction rules of the kind here envisaged would therefore have to provide a mechanical routine for constructing, on the basis of the given data, a hypothesis or theory stated in terms of some quite novel concepts, which are nowhere used in the description of the data themselves. Surely, no general mechanical rule of procedure can be expected to achieve this. Could there be a general rule, for example, which, when applied to the data available to Galileo concerning the limited effectiveness of suction pumps, would, by a mechanical routine, produce a hypothesis based on the concept of a sea of air?

To be sure, mechanical procedures for inductively "inferring" a hypothesis on the basis of given data may be specifiable for situations of special, and relatively simple, kinds. For example, if the length of a copper rod has been measured at several different temperatures, the resulting pairs of associated values for temperature and length may be represented by points in a plane coordinate system, and a curve may be drawn through them in accordance with some particular rule of curve fitting. The curve then graphically represents a general quantitative hypothesis that expresses the length of the rod as a specific function of its temperature. But note that this hypothesis contains no novel terms; it is expressible in terms of the concepts of temperature and length, which are used also in describing the data. Moreover, the choice of "associated" values of temperature and length as data already presupposes a guiding hypothesis; namely, that with each value of the temperature, exactly one value of the length of the copper rod is associated, so that its length is indeed a function of its temperature alone. The mechanical curve-fitting routine then serves only to select a particular function as the appropriate one. This point is important; for suppose that instead of a copper rod, we examine a body of nitrogen gas enclosed in a cylindrical container with a movable piston as a lid, and that we measure its volume at several different temperatures. If we were to use this procedure in an effort to obtain from our data a *general* hypothesis representing the volume of the gas as a function of its temperature, we would fail, because the volume of a gas is a function both of its temperature and of the pressure exerted upon it, so that at the same temperature, the given gas may assume different volumes.

Thus, even in these simple cases, the mechanical procedures for the construction of a hypothesis do only part of the job, for they presuppose an antecedent, less specific hypothesis (i.e., that a certain physical variable is a function of one single other variable), which is not obtainable by the same procedure.

There are, then, no generally applicable "rules of induction", by which hypotheses or theories can be mechanically derived or inferred from empirical data. The transition from data to theory requires creative imagination. Scientific hypotheses and theories are not *derived* from observed facts, but *invented* in order to account for them. They constitute guesses at the connections that might obtain between the phenomena under study, at uniformities and patterns that might underlie their occurrence. "Happy guesses"[2] of this kind require great ingenuity, especially if they involve a radical departure from current modes of scientific thinking, as did, for example, the theory of relativity and quantum theory. The inventive effort required in scientific research will benefit from a thorough familiarity with current knowledge in the field. A complete novice will hardly make an important scientific discovery, for the ideas that may occur to him are likely to duplicate what has been tried before or to run afoul of well-established facts or theories of which he is not aware. ■

Suggestions for Critical Reflection

1. "What particular sorts of data it is reasonable to collect is not determined by the problem under study, but by a tentative answer to it that the investigator entertains in the form of a conjecture or hypothesis." Do you agree? What implications does this have for the working practice of scientists?

2. According to Hempel, there can be no possible mechanical rules for generating inductive generalizations from sets of data; that is, as it is sometimes put, there is no "logic of discovery." What are Hempel's reasons for claiming this, and are they persuasive? Even if there are no mechanical methods for scientific discovery, might there nevertheless be some useful non-mechanical methods—and if so, what might these look like?

3. Hempel suggests that, although induction is not a useful method for generating hypotheses, it is important for assessing how well supported a theory is by the evidence. How vulnerable does this make Hempel to the kind of skepticism about induction argued for by David Hume (see the Hume reading in this chapter)?

Notes

1   A.B. Wolfe, "Functional Economics," in *The Trend of Economics*, ed. R.G. Tugwell (New York: Alfred A. Knopf, Inc., 1924), p. 450 (italics are quoted).

2   This characterization was given already by William Whewell in his work *The Philosophy of the Inductive Sciences*, 2nd ed. (London: John W. Parker, 1847); II, 41. Whewell also speaks of "invention" as "part of induction" (p. 46). In the same vein, K. Popper refers to scientific hypotheses and theories as "conjectures"; see, for example, the essay "Science: Conjectures and Refutations" in his book, *Conjectures and Refutations* (New York and London: Basic Books, 1962). Indeed, A.B. Wolfe, whose narrowly inductivist conception of ideal scientific procedure was quoted earlier, stresses that "the limited human mind" has to use "a greatly modified procedure," requiring scientific imagination and the selection of data on the basis of some "working hypothesis" (p. 450 of the essay cited [above]).

KARL POPPER

Science: Conjectures and Refutations

Who Was Karl Popper?

Though Popper's reputation has perhaps waned somewhat since its peak in the 1970s, he is still generally considered one among a small handful of the greatest philosophers of science of the twentieth century. In his day he found a fervent following among prominent scientists such as Peter Medawar (a Nobel Prize winner for medicine, who in 1972 called him "incomparably the greatest philosopher of science that has ever been"*), neuroscientist John Eccles (another Nobel laureate, who urged his fellow scientists "to read and meditate upon Popper's writings on the philosophy of science and to adopt them as the basis of one's scientific life"†), and mathematician and astronomer Hermann Bondi (who once stated, "There is no more to science than its method, and there is no more to its method than Popper has said"‡).

Karl Raimund Popper was born in 1902 in Vienna, Austria, to Jewish parents who had converted to Protestantism. His parents were intellectual (his father's library is said to have contained 15,000 volumes) and financially comfortable until rampant inflation in Austria after World War I reduced his family to near-poverty. In his early and middle teens Popper was a Marxist, and then—after witnessing the appalling bloodshed of a brief Communist coup in neighboring Hungary—he became an enthusiastic and active Social Democrat. Vienna after the First World War was a city bubbling over with revolutionary new movements and ideas, and, for Popper, it was a thrilling time and place to be young. In addition to studying science and philosophy, Popper was involved with left-wing politics, social work with children, and also the Society for Private Concerts founded by the revolutionary atonal composer Arnold Schönberg (throughout his life, Popper had a great love of music).

During and after his education (he received his PhD in 1928), Popper worked as a schoolteacher in mathematics and physics, and occasionally as a cabinet-maker, but continued to pursue his interest in philosophy. However, his ideas were then, as for most of his career, out of tune with contemporary philosophical fashions: Otto Neurath, a member of the "Vienna Circle" of philosophers active during the 1920s and 1930s, nicknamed him "the Official Opposition" for his arguments against the then dominant philosophy of logical positivism. In 1934 Popper published his first book, *Logik der Forschung*—a heavily edited version of a book originally twice as long—which attacked the main ideas of the logical positivists. This book was later translated into English and published as *The Logic of Scientific Discovery* (1959).

In the 1930s, the Communists and other left wing parties in Austria, Germany, and Italy failed to effectively oppose the rise to power of fascism (believing it to be the last gasp of capitalism before the inevitable Communist revolution, and so offering only a half-hearted resistance) and Popper—accurately foretelling the annexation of Austria by Nazi Germany and the onset of a second European war—fled with his wife to New Zealand. There, from 1937 until 1945, he taught philosophy at the University of Canterbury, at Christchurch. He spent this period teaching himself Greek so he could study the Greek philosophers, and writing *The Open Society and Its Enemies* (published in 1943) which, through a critique of the political theories of Plato and Marx, defends the idea of liberty and democracy against that of totalitarianism. Popper considered this to be his contribution to the war against fascism.

According to Popper, no political ideology (either on the political right or left) can justify large-scale social engineering—it is simply impossible to formulate a demonstrably true, predictive theory of society, and so

---

* Peter Medawar, BBC Radio 3, 28 July 1972.
† John Eccles, *Facing Reality* (Springer-Verlag, 1970).
‡ Quoted in Bryan Magee, *Popper* (Routledge, 1974), p. 9.

we should never act as if we alone have the key to the truth about human nature. The proper function of social institutions in an "open society"—one in which any regime can be ousted without violence—is not large-scale utopian planning but, according to Popper, piecemeal reform with the object of minimizing, as much as possible, avoidable suffering. This way, the effectiveness of each small piece of legislation can be publicly assessed, and the society can move forward collectively after learning from its mistakes.

In 1946 Popper moved to England, where he was to live until his death in 1994. Despite his growing reputation (he was knighted in 1965), Popper was never offered a position at either Oxford or Cambridge* and he spent the rest of his career as a professor at the London School of Economics, still out of sync with the philosophical tendencies of the day which, during those years in England, were predominantly towards "linguistic" philosophy. Popper was impatient with endless discussion about the meanings of words, and denied that exact precision of terminology was either possible or desirable in science. Popper argued that a language is an instrument and what matters is what you *do* with that instrument; philosophers who devote their lives exclusively to the analysis of language are, as Bryan Magee has put it, like carpenters who devote all their time to sharpening their tools, but never use them except on each other. Popper wrote in the preface to *The Logic of Scientific Discovery*:

> Language analysts believe that there are no genuine philosophical problems, or that the problems of philosophy, if any, are problems of linguistic usage, or of the meaning of words. I, however, believe that there is at least one problem in which all thinking men are interested. It is the problem of cosmology: *the problem of understanding the world—including ourselves, and our knowledge, as part of the world.* All science is cosmology, I believe, and for me the interest of philosophy, no less than of science, lies solely in the contributions which it has made to it.

One of Popper's main contributions to the philosophy of science is his proposal of a solution to the 'problem of induction,' which involves the rejection of the previously orthodox view of the scientific method and its replacement with another. The essay reprinted here, "Science: Conjectures and Refutations," is an excellent (and in itself quite influential) summary of these arguments.

What Is the Structure of This Reading?

This article is Popper's own summary of his most important work in the philosophy of science. He begins by laying out the problem which he first became interested in: the problem of the *demarcation* between science and pseudo-science (i.e., of finding a criterion for what makes something a properly scientific theory). By comparing Einstein's relativity theory (an example of science) with the psychoanalytic theories of Freud and Adler (examples of pseudo-science), Popper argues that the proper mark of a scientific theory is its *falsifiability*.

In Section IV, Popper begins his discussion of the problem of induction. After laying out Hume's description of the problem (see the Hume reading in this chapter), he critiques Hume's psychologistic solution to the problem and uses this critique to motivate his own alternative account: the method of trial and error, or *conjectures and refutations*. In Section V, Popper suggests that this method of "trial and error" is ultimately rooted in the evolution of the human mind.

In Section VIII, Popper turns his attention to the "logic of science," and argues that it is simply a mistake to think that the scientific method is inductive: in fact, Popper asserts, real science proceeds by the method of conjecture and refutation, and scientists have in the past just misdescribed or misunderstood their own practices when they spoke of induction. Popper lays out his final solution to the problem of induction in Section IX, and in the last section of the paper he responds to various reformulations of the problem. Particularly important here is his distinction between the claim that science is a *rea-*

---

* This may have been partly to do with his combative personality. Despite advocating risky conjectures and public refutations, by all accounts Popper was a touchy character, quick to express scorn for those who doubted his ideas. On one famous occasion, at the Moral Sciences Club in Cambridge, he almost came to blows with Ludwig Wittgenstein and—legend has it—had to be restrained by Bertrand Russell (upon which, Wittgenstein stormed out of the room). See David Edmonds and John Eidinow, *Wittgenstein's Poker: The Story of a Ten-Minute Argument Between Two Great Philosophers* (Faber & Faber, 2001).

sonable practice for human beings to engage in, and the claim that our belief that science will eventually succeed in getting to the truth is a *rational* one: Popper supports the first claim, but unconditionally denies the second one.

Some Useful Background Information

1. Popper sought to replace the traditional inductivist view of science with a quite different account that denies induction plays any role in science at all. In order to see what Popper is reacting against, it is helpful to briefly review the traditional understanding of the scientific method. On this view (sometimes called the "Baconian" view, after Francis Bacon [1561–1626], the first philosopher to systematically lay out rules for good science) the scientist begins by making observations—by carrying out carefully controlled experiments at some outpost on the frontier between our knowledge and our ignorance. The results of these experiments are systematically recorded and shared with other workers in the field. As the body of data grows, certain regularities appear. Individual scientists formulate hypotheses which, if true, would explain all the known facts and reveal an underlying structure explaining the regularities in the data. They then attempt to confirm their hypotheses by performing experiments which will produce supporting evidence. Eventually, after enough experiments are done, some hypothesis is verified and is added to the body of confirmed scientific theory. Science moves on to the next point on the frontier.

   This process, known as the method of induction, was standardly thought to be what marked off scientific investigation from other kinds of intellectual pursuit: science, it might be said, is based on experimental *facts* (rather than, say, on claims rooted in tradition, authority, prejudice, habit, emotion, or whatever). It is this picture of science that Popper attempts to overturn, and replace with his own account of what scientists are actually up to.

2. Popper does not think that good scientific theories are good because they are true. As he once put it, "We cannot identify science with truth, for we think that both Newton's and Einstein's theories belong to science, but they cannot both be true, and they may well both be false."* A formative experience for Popper as a young philosopher was the replacement of Newtonian physics—previously the crown jewel of modern science—by Einstein's theories in the early decades of the twentieth century. Newtonian physics was, in 1900, the most successful, well-confirmed, and important scientific theory ever developed, and for more than two hundred years its laws had been unfailingly corroborated by literally billions of scientific observations and, furthermore, by underpinning the most impressive advances in technology in human history. Yet, despite the huge quantity of inductive evidence apparently confirming the truth of Newtonian physics, it turned out to be false. If this quantity of evidence could not verify a theory, Popper thought, then nothing could. Nothing in science is secure; every scientific theory is open to rejection or revision; all scientific 'knowledge' is probably false, though it aspires eventually to the truth. One of Popper's favorite quotations was from the early Greek philosopher Xenophanes (who lived about 500 BCE):

   > The gods did not reveal, from the beginning,
   > All things to us, but in the course of time
   > Through seeking we may learn and know things
   >   better.
   > But as for certain truth, no man has known it,
   > Nor shall he know it, neither of the gods
   > Nor yet of all the things of which I speak.
   > For even if by chance he were to utter
   > The final truth, he would himself not know it:
   > For all is but a woven web of guesses.†

3. Popper's approach to knowledge is self-consciously biological in orientation. Human beings, according to Popper, are problem-solving animals, and there is

---

* In *Modern British Philosophy*, ed. Bryan Magee (Oxford University Press, 1986), 78.
† These are fragments 18 and 34, according to the numbering of pre-Socratic fragments employed in H. Diels and W. Kranz, eds., *Die Fragmente der Vorsokratiker* (Weidmannsche Verlagsbuchhandlung, 1956). Translated and quoted by Popper in a section of *Conjectures and Refutations: The Growth of Scientific Knowledge* not included below.

continuity between simple examples of learning by trial and error in the lower animals and the method of conjecture and refutation in human science. The human search for knowledge is ultimately rooted, for Popper, in facts about our evolutionary history.

Some Common Misconceptions

1. Though Popper claims to have "solved the problem of induction," he did not do so by showing that induction *works*. Instead, he 'solves' the problem by issuing a complete ban on induction. The conclusions of science are never positively justified: they are never established as certainly true, or even as probable. In other words, Popper's "corroboration" is not the same thing as confirmation.

Conjectures are not inferences and refutations are not inductive; the failure to refute a hypothesis is *not* evidence in its favor, according to Popper.

2. Unlike the logical positivists, Popper does not dismiss pseudo-science as valueless or meaningless. Falsifiability is not, for him, a demarcation between sense and nonsense, but only between science and non-science. (For the logical positivists, verifiability was a demarcation of both kinds.) Thus, for Popper, although the methods of science have a privileged place in the rational human pursuit of the truth, domains other than science (such as art and religion) can still have substantial value, and can even prove to be valuable starting points—though never finishing posts—in the quest for knowledge.

Science: Conjectures and Refutations*

Mr. Turnbull had predicted evil consequences, ... and was now doing the best in his power to bring about the verification of his own prophecies. (Anthony Trollope)†

I.

When I received the list of participants in this course and realized that I had been asked to speak to philosophical colleagues I thought, after some hesitation and consultation, that you would probably prefer me to speak about those problems which interest me most, and about those developments with which I am most intimately acquainted. I therefore decided to do what I have never done before: to give you a report on my own work in the philosophy of science, since the autumn of 1919 when I first began to grapple with the problem, *"When should a theory be ranked as scientific?"* or *"Is there a criterion for the scientific character or status of a theory?"*

The problem which troubled me at the time was neither, "When is a theory true?" nor, "When is a theory acceptable?" My problem was different. I *wished to distinguish between science and pseudo-science*; knowing very well that science often errs, and that pseudo-science may happen to stumble on the truth.

I knew, of course, the most widely accepted answer to my problem: that science is distinguished from pseudo-science—or from 'metaphysics'—by its *empirical method*, which is essentially *inductive*, proceeding from observation or experiment. But this did not satisfy me. On the contrary, I often formulated my problem as one of distinguishing between a genuinely empirical method and a non-empirical or even a pseudo-empirical method—that is to say, a method which, although it appeals to observation and experiment, nevertheless does not come up to scientific standards. The latter method may be exemplified by astrology, with its stupendous mass of empirical

---

* This was originally a lecture given at Peterhouse College, Cambridge, in 1953. It was first published under the title "Philosophy of Science: A Personal Report" in 1957 in *British Philosophy in Mid-Century*, edited by C.A. Mace. The version reprinted here is from "Science: Conjectures and Refutations," in *Conjectures and Refutations: The Growth of Scientific Knowledge*, Copyright Karl L. Popper, 1963.

† *Phineas Finn* (1868), Chapter XXV.

evidence based on observation—on horoscopes and on biographies.

But as it was not the example of astrology which led me to my problem I should perhaps briefly describe the atmosphere in which my problem arose and the examples by which it was stimulated. After the collapse of the Austrian Empire* there had been a revolution in Austria: the air was full of revolutionary slogans and ideas, and new and often wild theories. Among the theories which interested me Einstein's theory of relativity was no doubt by far the most important. Three others were Marx's theory of history, Freud's psycho-analysis, and Alfred Adler's so-called 'individual psychology'.

There was a lot of popular nonsense talked about these theories, and especially about relativity (as still happens even today), but I was fortunate in those who introduced me to the study of this theory. We all—the small circle of students to which I belonged—were thrilled with the result of Eddington's eclipse observations† which in 1919 brought the first important confirmation of Einstein's theory of gravitation. It was a great experience for us, and one which had a lasting influence on my intellectual development.

The three other theories I have mentioned were also widely discussed among students at that time. I myself happened to come into personal contact with Alfred Adler, and even to co-operate with him in his social work among the children and young people in the working-class districts of Vienna where he had established social guidance clinics.

It was during the summer of 1919 that I began to feel more and more dissatisfied with these three theories—the Marxist theory of history, psychoanalysis, and individual psychology; and I began to feel dubious about their claims to scientific status. My problem perhaps first took the simple form, 'What is wrong with Marxism, psycho-analysis, and individual psychology? Why are they so different from physical theories, from Newton's theory, and especially from the theory of relativity?'

To make this contrast clear I should explain that few of us at the time would have said that we believed in the *truth* of Einstein's theory of gravitation. This shows that it was not my doubting the *truth* of those other three theories which bothered me, but something else. Yet neither was it that I merely felt mathematical physics to be more *exact* than the sociological or psychological type of theory. Thus what worried me was neither the problem of truth, at that stage at least, nor the problem of exactness or measurability. It was rather that I felt that these other three theories, though posing as sciences, had in fact more in common with primitive myths than with science; that they resembled astrology rather than astronomy.

I found that those of my friends who were admirers of Marx, Freud, and Adler, were impressed by a number of points common to these theories, and especially by their apparent *explanatory power*. These theories appeared to be able to explain practically everything that happened within the fields to which they referred. The study of any of them seemed to have the effect of an intellectual conversion or revelation, opening your eyes to a new truth hidden from those not yet initiated. Once your eyes were thus opened you saw confirming instances everywhere: the world was full of *verifications* of the theory. Whatever happened always confirmed it. Thus its truth appeared manifest; and unbelievers were clearly people who did not want to see the manifest truth; who refused to see it, either because it was against their class interest, or because of their repressions which were still 'un-analysed' and crying out for treatment.

The most characteristic element in this situation seemed to me the incessant stream of confirmations, of observations which 'verified' the theories in question; and this point was constantly emphasized by their adherents. A Marxist could not open a newspaper without finding on every page confirming evidence for his interpretation of history; not only in the news, but also in its presentation—which revealed the class bias of the paper—and especially of course in what the paper

---

* In 1918, with Austria-Hungary's defeat in World War I.
† Sir Arthur Stanley Eddington (1882–1944), during an expedition to Africa, observed the positions of stars visible around the sun during an eclipse, compared them to the positions of those same stars seen at night (when, of course, the sun is not in the same region of the sky), and deduced from the shift in their positions that the light from those stars must be bent by its passage through the sun's gravitational field.

did *not* say. The Freudian analysts emphasized that their theories were constantly verified by their 'clinical observations'. As for Adler, I was much impressed by a personal experience. Once, in 1919, I reported to him a case which to me did not seem particularly Adlerian, but which he found no difficulty in analysing in terms of his theory of inferiority feelings, although he had not even seen the child. Slightly shocked, I asked him how he could be so sure. 'Because of my thousandfold experience', he replied; whereupon I could not help saying: 'And with this new case, I suppose, your experience has become thousand-and-one-fold.'

What I had in mind was that his previous observations may not have been much sounder than this new one; that each in its turn had been interpreted in the light of 'previous experience', and at the same time counted as additional confirmation. What, I asked myself, did it confirm? No more than that a case could be interpreted in the light of the theory. But this meant very little, I reflected, since every conceivable case could be interpreted in the light of Adler's theory, or equally of Freud's. I may illustrate this by two very different examples of human behaviour: that of a man who pushes a child into the water with the intention of drowning it; and that of a man who sacrifices his life in an attempt to save the child. Each of these two cases can be explained with equal ease in Freudian and in Adlerian terms. According to Freud the first man suffered from repression (say, of some component of his Oedipus complex*), while the second man had achieved sublimation. According to Adler the first man suffered from feelings of inferiority (producing perhaps the need to prove to himself that he dared to commit some crime), and so did the second man (whose need was to prove to himself that he dared to rescue the child). I could not think of any human behaviour which could not be interpreted in terms of either theory. It was precisely this fact—that they always fitted, that they were always confirmed—which in the eyes of their admirers constituted the strongest argument in favour of these theories. It began to dawn on me that this apparent strength was in fact their weakness.

With Einstein's theory the situation was strikingly different. Take one typical instance—Einstein's prediction, just then confirmed by the findings of Eddington's expedition. Einstein's gravitational theory had led to the result that light must be attracted by heavy bodies (such as the sun), precisely as material bodies were attracted. As a consequence it could be calculated that light from a distant fixed star whose apparent position was close to the sun would reach the earth from such a direction that the star would seem to be slightly shifted away from the sun; or, in other words, that stars close to the sun would look as if they had moved a little away from the sun, and from one another. This is a thing which cannot normally be observed since such stars are rendered invisible in daytime by the sun's overwhelming brightness; but during an eclipse it is possible to take photographs of them. If the same constellation is photographed at night one can measure the distances on the two photographs, and check the predicted effect.

Now the impressive thing about this case is the *risk* involved in a prediction of this kind. If observation shows that the predicted effect is definitely absent, then the theory is simply refuted. The theory is *incompatible with certain possible results of observation*—in fact with results which everybody before Einstein would have expected.[1] This is quite different from the situation I have previously described, when it turned out that the theories in question were compatible with the most divergent human behaviour, so that it was practically impossible to describe any human behaviour that might not be claimed to be a verification of these theories.

These considerations led me in the winter of 1919–20 to conclusions which I may now reformulate as follows.

(1) It is easy to obtain confirmations, or verifications, for nearly every theory—if we look for confirmations.

(2) Confirmations should count only if they are the result of *risky predictions*; that is to say, if, unenlightened by the theory in question, we should have expected an event which was incompatible with the theory—an event which would have refuted the theory.

(3) Every 'good' scientific theory is a prohibition: it forbids certain things to happen. The more a theory forbids, the better it is.

---

* According to Freud, the Oedipus complex consists in subconscious sexual desire in a child (especially a boy) for the parent of the opposite sex, usually combined with repressed hostility towards the parent of the same sex.

(4) A theory which is not refutable by any conceivable event is non-scientific. Irrefutability is not a virtue of a theory (as people often think) but a vice.

(5) Every genuine *test* of a theory is an attempt to falsify it, or to refute it. Testability is falsifiability; but there are degrees of testability: some theories are more testable, more exposed to refutation, than others; they take, as it were, greater risks.

(6) Confirming evidence should not count *except when it is the result of a genuine test of the theory*; and this means that it can be presented as a serious but unsuccessful attempt to falsify the theory. (I now speak in such cases of 'corroborating evidence'.)

(7) Some genuinely testable theories, when found to be false, are still upheld by their admirers—for example by introducing *ad hoc** some auxiliary assumption, or by re-interpreting the theory *ad hoc* in such a way that it escapes refutation. Such a procedure is always possible, but it rescues the theory from refutation only at the price of destroying, or at least lowering, its scientific status. (I later described such a rescuing operation as a '*conventionalist twist*' or a '*conventionalist stratagem*'.)

One can sum up all this by saying that *the criterion of the scientific status of a theory is its falsifiability, or refutability, or testability*.

...

IV.

I have discussed the problem of demarcation[†] in some detail because I believe that its solution is the key to most of the fundamental problems of the philosophy of science. I am going to give you later a list of some of these other problems, but only one of them—the *problem of induction*—can be discussed here at any length.

I had become interested in the problem of induction in 1923. Although this problem is very closely connected with the problem of demarcation, I did not fully appreciate the connection for about five years.

I approached the problem of induction through Hume. Hume, I felt, was perfectly right in pointing out that induction cannot be logically justified. He held that there can be no valid logical[2] arguments allowing us to

establish "*that those instances, of which we have had no experience, resemble those, of which we have had experience*". Consequently "*even after the observation of the frequent or constant conjunction of objects, we have no reason to draw any inference concerning any object beyond those of which we have had experience*". For "shou'd it be said that we have experience"[3]—experience teaching us that objects constantly conjoined with certain other objects continue to be so conjoined—then, Hume says, "I wou'd renew my question, *why from this experience we form any conclusion beyond those past instances, of which we have had experience*". This "renew'd question" indicates that an attempt to justify the practice of induction by an appeal to experience must lead to an *infinite regress*. As a result we can say that theories can never be inferred from observation statements, or rationally justified by them.

I found Hume's refutation of inductive inference clear and conclusive. But I felt completely dissatisfied with his psychological explanation of induction in terms of custom or habit.

It has often been noticed that this explanation of Hume's is philosophically not very satisfactory. Hume, however, without doubt intended it as a *psychological* rather than a philosophical theory; for it tries to give a causal explanation of a psychological fact—*the fact that we believe in laws*, in statements asserting regularities or constantly conjoined kinds of events. Hume explains this fact by asserting that it is due to (i.e., constantly conjoined with) custom or habit. But even this reformulation of Hume's theory is unacceptable; for what I have just called a 'psychological fact' may itself be described as a custom or habit—our custom or our habit of believing in laws or regularities. It is neither surprising nor enlightening to hear that such a custom or habit can be explained as due to custom or habit, or conjoined with a custom or habit (even though a different one). Only when we remember that the words 'custom' and 'habit' are used by Hume, as they are in ordinary language, not merely to *describe* regular behaviour, but rather to *theorize about its origin* (ascribed to frequent repetition), can we reformulate his psychological theory in a more satisfactory way. Hume's theory becomes then the thesis that, like other habits, *our habit of believing in laws is the product of frequent repetition*—of the repeated

---

*   *Ad hoc* means "for the particular situation or case at hand and for no other" (Latin "to this").

†   That is, of demarcating between science and non-science.

observation that things of a certain kind are constantly conjoined with things of another kind.

This genetic-psychological theory is, as indicated, incorporated in ordinary language, and it is therefore hardly as revolutionary as Hume thought. It is no doubt an extremely popular psychological theory—part of 'common sense', one might say. But in spite of my love of both common sense and Hume, I felt convinced that this psychological theory was mistaken; and that it was in fact refutable on purely logical grounds.

Hume's psychology, which is the popular psychology, was mistaken, I felt, about at least three different things: (a) the typical result of repetition; (b) the genesis of habits; and especially (c) the character of those experiences or modes of behaviour which may be described as 'believing in a law' or 'expecting a law-like succession of events'.

(a) The typical result of repetition—say, of repeating a difficult passage on the piano—is that movements which at first needed attention are in the end executed without attention. We might say that the process becomes radically abbreviated, and ceases to be conscious: it becomes automatized, 'physiological'. Such a development, far from creating a conscious expectation of law-like succession, or a belief in a law, may on the contrary begin with a conscious belief and destroy it by making it superfluous. In learning to ride a bicycle we may start with the belief that we can avoid falling if we steer in the direction in which we threaten to fall, and this belief may be useful for guiding our movements. After sufficient practice we may forget the rule; in any case, we do not need it any longer. On the other hand, even if it is true that repetition may create unconscious expectations, these become conscious only if something goes wrong (we may not have heard the clock tick, but we may hear that it has stopped).

(b) Habits or customs do not, as a rule, *originate* in repetition. Even the habit of walking, or of speaking, or of feeding at certain hours, *begins* before repetition can play any part whatever. We may say, if we like, that they deserve to be called 'habits' or 'customs' only after repetition has played its typical part described under (a); but we must not say that the practices in question *originated* as the result of many repetitions.

(c) Belief in a law is not quite the same thing as behaviour which betrays an expectation of a law-like succession of events; but these two are sufficiently closely connected to be treated together. They may, perhaps, in exceptional cases, result from a mere repetition of sense impressions (as in the case of the stopping clock). I was prepared to concede this, but I contended that normally, and in most cases of any interest, they cannot be so explained. As Hume admits, even a single striking observation may be sufficient to create a belief or an expectation—a fact which he tries to explain as due to an inductive habit, formed as the result of a vast number of long repetitive sequences which had been experienced at an earlier period of life.[4] But this, I contended, was merely his attempt to explain away unfavourable facts which threatened his theory; an unsuccessful attempt, since these unfavourable facts could be observed in very young animals and babies—as early, indeed, as we like. "A lighted cigarette was held near the noses of the young puppies," reports F. Bäge. "They sniffed at it once, turned tail, and nothing would induce them to come back to the source of the smell and to sniff again. A few days later, they reacted to the mere sight of a cigarette or even of a rolled piece of white paper, by bounding away, and sneezing."[5] If we try to explain cases like this by postulating a vast number of long repetitive sequences at a still earlier age we are not only romancing, but forgetting that in the clever puppies' short lives there must be room not only for repetition but also for a great deal of novelty, and consequently of non-repetition.

But it is not only that certain empirical facts do not support Hume; there are decisive arguments of a *purely logical* nature against his psychological theory.

The central idea of Hume's psychological theory is that of *repetition, based upon similarity* (or 'resemblance'). This idea is used in a very uncritical way. We are led to think of the water-drop that hollows the stone: of sequences of unquestionably like events slowly forcing themselves upon us, as does the tick of the clock. But we ought to realize that in a psychological theory such as Hume's, only repetition-for-us, based upon similarity-for-us, can be allowed to have any effect upon us. We must respond to situations as if they were equivalent; *take* them as similar; *interpret* them as repetitions. In this way they become for us *functionally equal*. The clever puppies, we may assume, showed by their response, their way of acting or of reacting, that they recognized or interpreted the second situation as a repetition of the first: that they expected its main element, the objectionable smell, to be present. The situation was a repetition-for-them because they responded to it by *anticipating* its similarity to the previous one.

This apparently psychological criticism has a purely logical basis which may be summed up in the following simple argument. (It happens to be the one from which I originally started my criticism.) The kind of repetition envisaged by Hume can never be perfect; the cases he has in mind cannot be cases of perfect sameness; they can only be cases of similarity. Thus *they are repetitions only from a certain point of view*. (What has the effect upon me of a repetition may not have this effect upon a spider.) But this means that, for logical reasons, there must always be a point of view—such as a system of expectations, anticipations, assumptions, or interests— *before* there can be any repetition; which point of view, consequently, cannot be merely the result of repetition....

We must thus replace, for the purposes of a psychological theory of the origin of our beliefs, the naïve idea of events which *are* similar by the idea of events to which we react by *interpreting* them as being similar. But if this is so (and I can see no escape from it) then Hume's psychological theory of induction leads to an infinite regress, precisely analogous to that other infinite regress which was discovered by Hume himself, and used by him to explode the logical theory of induction. For what do we wish to explain? In the example of the puppies we wish to explain behaviour which may be described as *recognizing or interpreting* a situation as a repetition of another. Clearly, we cannot hope to explain this by an appeal to earlier repetitions, once we realize that the earlier repetitions must also have been repetitions-for-them, so that precisely the same problem arises again: that of *recognizing or interpreting* a situation as a repetition of another.

To put it more concisely, similarity-for-us is the product of a response involving interpretations (which may be inadequate) and anticipations or expectations (which may never be fulfilled). It is therefore impossible to explain anticipations, or expectations, as resulting from many repetitions, as suggested by Hume. For even the first repetition-for-us must be based upon similarity-for-us, and therefore upon expectations— precisely the kind of thing we wished to explain. (Expectations must come first, *before* repetitions.)

We see that there is an infinite regress involved in Hume's psychological theory.

Hume, I felt, had never accepted the full force of his own logical analysis. Having refuted the logical idea of induction he was faced with the following problem: how do we actually obtain our knowledge, as a matter of psychological fact, if induction is a procedure which is logically invalid and rationally unjustifiable? There are two possible answers: (1) We obtain our knowledge by a non-inductive procedure. This answer would have allowed Hume to retain a form of rationalism. (2) We obtain our knowledge by repetition and induction, and therefore by a logically invalid and rationally unjustifiable procedure, so that all apparent knowledge is merely a kind of belief—belief based on habit. This answer would imply that even scientific knowledge is irrational, so that rationalism is absurd, and must be given up. (I shall not discuss here the age-old attempts, now again fashionable, to get out of the difficulty by asserting that though induction is of course logically invalid if we mean by 'logic' the same as 'deductive logic', it is not irrational by its own standards, and as inductive logic admits; as may be seen from the fact that every reasonable man applies it *as a matter of fact*. As against this, it was Hume's great achievement to break this uncritical identification of the question of fact—*quid facti?*[*]—and the question of justification or validity—*quid juris?*[†] ...

It seems that Hume never seriously considered the first alternative. Having cast out the logical theory of induction by repetition he struck a bargain with common sense, meekly allowing the re-entry of induction by repetition, in the guise of a psychological fact. I proposed to turn the tables upon this theory of Hume's. Instead of explaining our propensity to expect regularities as the result of repetition, I proposed to explain repetition-for-us as the result of our propensity to expect regularities and to search for them.

Thus I was led by purely logical considerations to replace the psychological theory of induction by the following view. Without waiting, passively, for repetitions to impress or impose regularities upon us, we actively try to impose regularities upon the world. We try to

---

[*] What are the facts?

[†] What is the law? Kant opens the section of his *Critique of Pure Reason* called "The Transcendental Deduction of the Categories" with this legal distinction, as an analogy for the distinction he wants to make between two sorts of questions: How do we in fact think about things? and What entitles us to do so?

discover similarities in it, and to interpret it in terms of laws invented by us. Without waiting for premises we jump to conclusions. These may have to be discarded later, should observation show that they are wrong.

This was a theory of trial and error—of *conjectures and refutations*. It made it possible to understand why our attempts to force interpretations upon the world were logically prior to the observation of similarities. Since there were logical reasons behind this procedure, I thought that it would apply in the field of science also; that scientific theories were not the digest of observations, but that they were inventions—conjectures boldly put forward for trial, to be eliminated if they clashed with observations; with observations which were rarely accidental but as a rule undertaken with the definite intention of testing a theory by obtaining, if possible, a decisive refutation.

V.

The belief that science proceeds from observation to theory is still so widely and so firmly held that my denial of it is often met with incredulity. I have even been suspected of being insincere—of denying what nobody in his senses can doubt.

But in fact the belief that we can start with pure observations alone, without anything in the nature of a theory, is absurd; as may be illustrated by the story of the man who dedicated his life to natural science, wrote down everything he could observe, and bequeathed his priceless collection of observations to the Royal Society to be used as inductive evidence. This story should show us that though beetles may profitably be collected, observations may not.

Twenty-five years ago I tried to bring home the same point to a group of physics students in Vienna by beginning a lecture with the following instructions: "Take pencil and paper; carefully observe, and write down what you have observed!" They asked, of course, *what* I wanted them to observe. Clearly the instruction, "Observe!" is absurd.[6] (It is not even idiomatic, unless the object of the transitive verb can be taken as understood.) Observation is always selective. It needs a chosen object, a definite task, an interest, a point of view, a problem. And its description presupposes a descriptive language, with property words; it presupposes similarity and classification, which in their turn presuppose interests, points of view, and problems. "A hungry animal," writes Katz,[7] "divides the environment into edible and inedible things. An animal in flight sees roads to escape and hiding places.... Generally speaking, objects change ... according to the needs of the animal." We may add that objects can be classified, and can become similar or dissimilar, *only* in this way—by being related to needs and interests. This rule applies not only to animals but also to scientists: For the animal a point of view is provided by its needs, the task of the moment, and its expectations; for the scientist by his theoretical interests, the special problem under investigation, his conjectures and anticipations, and the theories which he accepts as a kind of background: his frame of reference, his 'horizon of expectations'.

The problem 'Which comes first, the hypothesis (*H*) or the observation (*O*)?' is soluble; as is the problem, 'Which comes first, the hen (*H*) or the egg (*O*)?'. The reply to the latter is, 'An earlier kind of egg'; to the former, 'An earlier kind of hypothesis'. It is quite true that any particular hypothesis we choose will have been preceded by observations—the observations, for example, which it is designed to explain. But these observations, in their turn, presupposed the adoption of a frame of reference: a frame of expectations: a frame of theories. If they were significant, if they created a need for explanation and thus gave rise to the invention of a hypothesis, it was because they could not be explained within the old theoretical framework, the old horizon of expectations. There is no danger here of an infinite regress. Going back to more and more primitive theories and myths we shall in the end find unconscious, *inborn* expectations.

The theory of inborn *ideas* is absurd, I think; but every organism has inborn *reactions* or *responses*; and among them, responses adapted to impending events. These responses we may describe as 'expectations' without implying that these 'expectations' are conscious. The new-born baby 'expects', in this sense, to be fed (and, one could even argue, to be protected and loved). In view of the close relation between expectation and knowledge we may even speak in quite a reasonable sense of 'inborn knowledge'. This 'knowledge', however, is not *valid a priori*;* an inborn expectation,

---

* It is not something that can be known with certainty, even independently of any experience of the world, to be true.

no matter how strong and specific, may be mistaken. (The newborn child may be abandoned, and starve.)

Thus we are born with expectations; with 'knowledge' which, although not *valid a priori*, is *psychologically or genetically a priori*, i.e., prior to all observational experience. One of the most important of these expectations is the expectation of finding a regularity. It is connected with an inborn propensity to look out for regularities, or with a *need to find* regularities, as we may see from the pleasure of the child who satisfies this need.

...

VIII.

Let us now turn from our logical criticism of the *psychology of experience* to our real problem—the problem of the *logic of science*....

From what I have said it is obvious that there was a close link between the two problems which interested me at that time: demarcation, and induction or scientific method. It was easy to see that the method of science is criticism, i.e., attempted falsifications. Yet it took me a few years to notice that the two problems—of demarcation and of induction—were in a sense one.

Why, I asked, do so many scientists believe in induction? I found they did so because they believed natural science to be characterized by the inductive method—by a method starting from, and relying upon, long sequences of observations and experiments. They believed that the difference between genuine science and metaphysical or pseudo-scientific speculation depended solely upon whether or not the inductive method was employed. They believed (to put it in my own terminology) that only the inductive method could provide a satisfactory *criterion of demarcation*.

I recently came across an interesting formulation of this belief in a remarkable philosophical book by a great physicist—Max Born's *Natural Philosophy of Cause and Chance*.[8] He writes: "Induction allows us to generalize a number of observations into a general rule: that night follows day and day follows night ... But while everyday life has no definite criterion for the validity of an induction, ... science has worked out a code, or rule of craft, for its application." Born nowhere reveals the contents of this inductive code

(which, as his wording shows, contains a "definite criterion for the validity of an induction"); but he stresses that "there is no logical argument" for its acceptance: "it is a question of faith"; and he is therefore "willing to call induction a metaphysical principle". But why does he believe that such a code of valid inductive rules must exist? This becomes clear when he speaks of the "vast communities of people ignorant of, or rejecting, the rule of science, among them the members of anti-vaccination societies and believers in astrology. It is useless to argue with them; I cannot compel them to accept the same criteria of valid induction in which I believe: the code of scientific rules." This makes it quite clear that *"valid induction" was here meant to serve as a criterion of demarcation between science and pseudo-science.*

But it is obvious that this rule or craft of "valid induction" is not even metaphysical: it simply does not exist. No rule can ever guarantee that a generalization inferred from true observations, however often repeated, is true. (Born himself does not believe in the truth of Newtonian physics, in spite of its success, although he believes that it is based on induction.) And the success of science is not based upon rules of induction, but depends upon luck, ingenuity, and the purely deductive rules of critical argument.

I may summarize some of my conclusions as follows:

(1) Induction, i.e., inference based on many observations, is a myth. It is neither a psychological fact, nor a fact of ordinary life, nor one of scientific procedure.

(2) The actual procedure of science is to operate with conjectures: to jump to conclusions—often after one single observation (as noticed for example by Hume and Born).

(3) Repeated observations and experiments function in science as *tests* of our conjectures or hypotheses, i.e., as attempted refutations.

(4) The mistaken belief in induction is fortified by the need for a criterion of demarcation which, it is traditionally but wrongly believed, only the inductive method can provide.

(5) The conception of such an inductive method, like the criterion of verifiability, implies a faulty demarcation.

(6) None of this is altered in the least if we say that induction makes theories only probable rather than certain....

IX.

If, as I have suggested, the problem of induction is only an instance or facet of the problem of demarcation, then the solution to the problem of demarcation must provide us with a solution to the problem of induction. This is indeed the case, I believe, although it is perhaps not immediately obvious.

For a brief formulation of the problem of induction we can turn again to Born, who writes: "...no observation or experiment, however extended, can give more than a finite number of repetitions"; therefore, "the statement of a law—B depends on A—always transcends experience. Yet this kind of statement is made everywhere and all the time, and sometimes from scanty material."[9]

In other words, the logical problem of induction arises from (*a*) Hume's discovery (so well expressed by Born) that it is impossible to justify a law by observation or experiment, since it "transcends experience"; (*b*) the fact that science proposes and uses laws "everywhere and all the time". (Like Hume, Born is struck by the "scanty material", i.e., the few observed instances upon which the law may be based.) To this we have to add (*c*) *the principle of empiricism* which asserts that in science, only observation and experiment may decide upon the *acceptance or rejection* of scientific statements, including laws and theories.

These three principles, (*a*), (*b*), and (*c*), appear at first sight to clash; and this apparent clash constitutes the *logical problem of induction*.

Faced with this clash, Born gives up (*c*), the principle of empiricism (as Kant and many others, including Bertrand Russell, have done before him), in favour of what he calls a "metaphysical principle"; a metaphysical principle which he does not even attempt to formulate; which he vaguely describes as a "code or rule of craft"; and of which I have never seen any formulation which even looked promising and was not clearly untenable.

But in fact the principles (*a*) to (*c*) do not clash. We can see this the moment we realize that the acceptance by science of a law or of a theory is *tentative only*; which is to say that all laws and theories are conjectures, or tentative *hypotheses* (a position which I have sometimes called "hypotheticism"); and that we may reject a law or theory on the basis of new evidence, without

necessarily discarding the old evidence which originally led us to accept it.[10]

The principle of empiricism (*c*) can be fully preserved, since the fate of a theory, its acceptance or rejection, is decided by observation and experiment—by the result of tests. So long as a theory stands up to the severest tests we can design, it is accepted; if it does not, it is rejected. But it is never inferred, in any sense, from the empirical evidence. There is neither a psychological nor a logical induction. *Only the falsity of the theory can be inferred from empirical evidence, and this inference is a purely deductive one.*

Hume showed that it is not possible to infer a theory from observation statements; but this does not affect the possibility of refuting a theory by observation statements. The full appreciation of this possibility makes the relation between theories and observations perfectly clear.

This solves the problem of the alleged clash between the principles (*a*), (*b*), and (*c*), and with it Hume's problem of induction.

X.

Thus the problem of induction is solved. But nothing seems less wanted than a simple solution to an age-old philosophical problem. Wittgenstein and his school hold that genuine philosophical problems do not exist;[11] from which it clearly follows that they cannot be solved. Others among my contemporaries do believe that there are philosophical problems, and respect them; but they seem to respect them too much; they seem to believe that they are insoluble, if not taboo; and they are shocked and horrified by the claim that there is a simple, neat, and lucid, solution to any of them. If there is a solution it must be deep, they feel, or at least complicated.

However this may be, I am still waiting for a simple, neat and lucid criticism of the solution which I published first in 1933 in my letter to the Editor of *Erkenntnis*,[12] and later in *The Logic of Scientific Discovery*.

Of course, one can invent new problems of induction, different from the one I have formulated and solved. (Its formulation was half its solution.) But I have yet to see any reformulation of the problem whose solution cannot be easily obtained from my old solution. I am now going to discuss some of these re-formulations.

One question which may be asked is this: how do we really jump from an observation statement to a theory?

Although this question appears to be psychological rather than philosophical, one can say something positive about it without invoking psychology. One can say first that the jump is not from an observation statement, but from a problem-situation, and that the theory must allow us *to explain* the observations which created the problem (that is, *to deduce* them from the theory strengthened by other accepted theories and by other observation statements, the so-called initial conditions). This leaves, of course, an immense number of possible theories, good and bad; and it thus appears that our question has not been answered.

But this makes it fairly clear that when we asked our question we had more in mind than, "How do we jump from an observation statement to a theory?" The question we had in mind was, it now appears, "How do we jump from an observation statement to a *good* theory?" But to this the answer is: by jumping first to *any* theory and then testing it, to find whether it is good or not; i.e., by repeatedly applying the critical method, eliminating many bad theories, and inventing many new ones. Not everybody is able to do this; but there is no other way.

Other questions have sometimes been asked. The original problem of induction, it was said, is the problem of *justifying* induction, i.e., of justifying inductive inference. If you answer this problem by saying that what is called an 'inductive inference' is always invalid and therefore clearly not justifiable, the following new problem must arise: how do you justify your method of trial and error? Reply: the method of trial and error is a *method of eliminating false theories* by observation statements; and the justification for this is the purely logical relationship of deducibility which allows us to assert the falsity of universal statements if we accept the truth of singular ones.

Another question sometimes asked is this: why is it reasonable to prefer non-falsified statements to falsified ones? To this question some involved answers have been produced, for example pragmatic answers. But from a pragmatic point of view the question does not arise, since false theories often serve well enough: most formulae used in engineering or navigation are known to be false, although they may be excellent approximations and easy to handle; and they are used with confidence by people who know them to be false.

The only correct answer is the straightforward one: because we search for truth (even though we can never be sure we have found it), and because the falsified theories are known or believed to be false, while the non-falsified theories may still be true. Besides, we do not prefer *every* non-falsified theory—only one which, in the light of criticism, appears to be better than its competitors: which solves our problems, which is well tested, and of which we think, or rather conjecture or hope (considering other provisionally accepted theories), that it will stand up to further tests.

It has also been said that the problem of induction is, "Why is it *reasonable* to believe that the future will be like the past?," and that a satisfactory answer to this question should make it plain that such a belief is, in fact, reasonable. My reply is that it is reasonable to believe that the future will be very different from the past in many vitally important respects. Admittedly it is perfectly reasonable to act on the assumption that it will, in many respects, be like the past, and that well-tested laws will continue to hold (since we can have no better assumption to act upon); but it is also reasonable to believe that such a course of action will lead us at times into severe trouble, since some of the laws upon which we now heavily rely may easily prove unreliable. (Remember the midnight sun!*) One might even say that to judge from past experience, and from our general scientific knowledge, the future will *not* be like the past, in perhaps most of the ways which those have in mind who say that it will. Water will sometimes not quench thirst, and air will choke those who breathe it. An apparent way out is to say that the future will be like the past *in the sense that the laws of nature will not change*, but this is begging the question. We speak of a 'law of nature' only

---

* Popper is here referring to the well-corroborated generalization that the sun will rise once and set once during every 24-hour period. This was refuted by the observation of the midnight sun—the sun north of the Arctic Circle or south of the Antarctic Circle—which, during the summer at the poles, rises and sets once every six months.

if we think that we have before us a regularity which does not change; and if we find that it changes then we shall not continue to call it a 'law of nature'. Of course our search for natural laws indicates that we hope to find them, and that we believe that there are natural laws; but our belief in any particular natural law cannot have a safer basis than our unsuccessful critical attempts to refute it.

I think that those who put the problem of induction in terms of the *reasonableness* of our beliefs are perfectly right if they are dissatisfied with a Humean, or post-Humean, sceptical despair of reason. We must indeed reject the view that a belief in science is as irrational as a belief in primitive magical practices—that both are a matter of accepting a 'total ideology', a convention or a tradition based on faith. But we must be cautious if we formulate our problem, with Hume, as one of the reasonableness of our *beliefs*. We should split this problem into three—our old problem of demarcation, or of how to *distinguish* between science and primitive magic; the problem of the rationality of the scientific or critical *procedure*, and of the role of observation within it; and lastly the problem of the rationality of our *acceptance* of theories for scientific and for practical purposes. To all these three problems solutions have been offered here.

One should also be careful not to confuse the problem of the reasonableness of the scientific procedure and the (tentative) acceptance of the results of this procedure—i.e., the scientific theories—with the problem of the rationality or otherwise *of the belief that this procedure will succeed*. In practice, in practical scientific research, this belief is no doubt unavoidable and reasonable, there being no better alternative. But the belief is certainly unjustifiable in a theoretical sense, as I have argued (in section V). Moreover, if we could show, on general logical grounds, that the scientific quest is likely to succeed, one could not understand why anything like success has been so rare in the long history of human endeavours to know more about our world.

Yet another way of putting the problem of induction is in terms of probability. Let *t* be the theory and *e* the evidence: we can ask for $P(t,e)$, that is to say, the probability of *t*, given *e*. The problem of induction, it is often believed, can then be put thus: construct a calculus of probability which allows us to work out for any theory *t* what its probability is, relative to any given empirical evidence *e*; and show that $P(t,e)$ increases with the accumulation of supporting evidence, and reaches high values—at any rate values greater than ½.

In *The Logic of Scientific Discovery* I explained why I think that this approach to the problem is fundamentally mistaken.[13] To make this clear, I introduced there the distinction between *probability* and *degree of corroboration or confirmation*. ... I explained in my book why we are interested in theories with a *high degree of corroboration*. And I explained why it is a mistake to conclude from this that we are interested in *highly probable* theories. I pointed out that the probability of a statement (or set of statements) is always the greater the less the statement says: it is inverse to the content or the deductive power of the statement, and thus to its explanatory power. Accordingly every interesting and powerful statement must have a low probability; and *vice versa*: a statement with a high probability will be scientifically uninteresting, because it says little and has no explanatory power. Although we seek theories with a high degree of corroboration, *as scientists we do not seek highly probable theories but explanations; that is to say, powerful and improbable theories*. The opposite view—that science aims at high probability—is a characteristic development of verificationism: if you find that you cannot verify a theory, or make it certain by induction, you may turn to probability as a kind of '*Ersatz*'* for certainty, in the hope that induction may yield at least that much.... ■

---

* Inferior substitute (from German "replacement").

Suggestions for Critical Reflection

1. Popper claimed to have solved the problem of induction. Did he? If not, did he at least solve the problem of showing how the methods of science could be rational despite Hume's arguments against the rationality of induction?

2. Popper stresses the importance of ruling out *ad hoc* modifications to theories. How helpful is this advice? How easy is it to tell when an adjustment to a theory is *ad hoc*, as opposed to when it is a legitimate improvement to a theory under the impact of new data? If it is not so easy, what implications (if any) does this have for Popper's account of science?

3. How plausible is Popper's suggestion that working scientists in fact adopt the method of conjecture and refutation (even though they may not realize they are doing so)? For example, do scientists deliberately pursue highly improbable claims (rather than less contentful, but more probable, hypotheses)? Do they then set out to falsify, rather than to verify, these theories? Do they abandon their theories when faced with single pieces of counter-evidence, rather than modify their theories to accommodate this new data? If scientists do *not* in fact use the methods Popper prescribes, how much of a problem is this for Popper's philosophy of science?

4. The attempted refutation of our conjectures, according to Popper, can never positively justify those conjectures, or justify us in thinking that they are probably true. On the other hand, according to Popper, the refutation of a conjecture is a step that takes us closer to the truth. Are these two claims compatible?

5. Popper says we ought to act on—provisionally, to believe—those theories that have survived extensive testing. How is this to be distinguished from induction?

6. Popper issues a ban on induction as an irrational method of doing science; but is his own method any more rational? That is, does it give us rational reasons for preferring one theory over another? Does it give us any reason to think scientific theories are getting better and better (i.e., closer to the truth)? Can Popper consistently assert that there is growth in scientific knowledge and that science is a rational activity?

Notes

1 This is a slight oversimplification, for about half of the Einstein effect may be derived from the classical theory, provided we assume a ballistic theory of light [that is, a Newtonian theory, thinking of light as tiny particles which would be influenced in standard fashion by a gravitational field.—ed.].

2 Hume does not say 'logical' but 'demonstrative', a terminology which, I think, is a little misleading. The following two quotations are from the *Treatise of Human Nature*, Book I, Part III, sections vi and xii. (The italics are all Hume's.)

3 This and the next quotation are from *loc. cit.*, section vi. See also Hume's *Enquiry Concerning Human Understanding*, section IV, Part II, and his *Abstract*, edited 1938 by J.M. Keynes and P. Sraffa, p. 15....

4 *Treatise*, section xiii; section xv, rule 4.

5 F. Bäge, 'Zur Entwicklung, etc.', *Zeitschrift f. Hundeforschung*, 1933; cp. D. Katz, *Animals and Men*, ch. VI, footnote.

6 See section 30 of *L.Sc.D.*

7 Katz, *loc. cit.*

8 Max Born, *Natural Philosophy of Cause and Chance*, Oxford, 1949, p. 7.

9 *Natural Philosophy of Cause and Chance*, p. 6.

10 I do not doubt that Born and many others would agree that theories are accepted only tentatively. But the widespread belief in induction shows that the far-reaching implications of this view are rarely seen.

11 Wittgenstein still held this belief in 1946....

12 [My *Logic of Scientific Discovery* (1959, 1960, 1961), here usually referred to as *L.Sc.D.*, is the translation of *Logik der Forschung* (1934), with a number of additional notes and appendices, including (on pp. 312–14) the letter to the Editor of *Erkenntnis* mentioned here in the text which was first published in *Erkenntnis*, 3, 1933, pp. 426 f.]

13 *L.Sc.D.*, ch. X, especially sections 80 to 83, also section 34 ff. See also my note 'A Set of Independent Axioms for Probability', *Mind*, N.S. 47, 1938, p. 275. ...

THOMAS KUHN

Objectivity, Value Judgment, and Theory Choice

Who Was Thomas Kuhn?

Thomas Kuhn's *The Structure of Scientific Revolutions* (first published in 1962) is the single most influential book in modern philosophy of science—and indeed, in the opinion of some, is perhaps the most influential book published in the second half of the twentieth century.* In it, Kuhn presented a view of science which seemed radically at variance with what most philosophers of science and scientists had previously supposed. Kuhn argued that most science—what he dubbed "normal science"—takes place against a background of unquestioned theoretical assumptions, which he called a *paradigm*. Typical scientists are not, contrary to popular opinion, objective, skeptical, and independent thinkers: rather, according to Kuhn, they are community-minded conservatives who accept what they have been taught by their elders and devote their energies to solving puzzles dictated to them by their theories. Indeed, according to Kuhn, scientists habitually attempt to *ignore* research findings that threaten the existing paradigm. Occasionally, however, the pressures from anomalies—especially inexplicable experimental results—generated within that paradigm become such that a crisis occurs within the scientific community and it is necessary for a *paradigm shift* (a phrase first coined by Kuhn) to take place. These episodes in the history of science are what Kuhn called "revolutions." For example, to caricature Kuhn (who did not hold that paradigm shifts are caused entirely by the actions of single individuals), Galileo's (imagined) experiments—dropping wood and lead balls from the Leaning Tower of Pisa—caused the extinction of the Aristotelian theory that bodies fall at a speed proportional to their weight; Lavoisier's discovery of oxygen signaled the death knell for the older "phlogiston" paradigm of chemistry; Darwin's theory of natural selection overthrew ideas of a world governed by design; and Einstein's theory of relativity completely replaced Newtonian physics. Science, in other words, is "a series of peaceful interludes punctuated by intellectually violent revolutions."† The old guard who worked within the previous paradigm then either undergo conversion to the new one, or simply die out and are replaced by younger scientists working in the new paradigm.

The most controversial and stimulating aspect of Kuhn's work has proved to be his claim that there can be no strictly rational reason to choose one new paradigm over another: that is, the adoption of scientific theories, according to Kuhn, is never and can never be a purely rational decision. According to the more extreme of Kuhn's adherents (though not—at least later in his career—Kuhn himself), this means that the logic and philosophy of science is to be replaced by the history and sociology of science: that is, science is best understood not as a rational or logical enterprise, but as a sociological phenomenon. Furthermore, Kuhn has apparently held that successive scientific paradigms are *incommensurable*: scientists before and after a theoretical revolution essentially speak a different language and think in completely different ways, and so—since no one can think within two different paradigms at once—it is not possible for anyone to *compare* the two paradigms and see which is better. If this is the case, it seems to follow that we have no good reason to believe that the history of science is a story of progress or of the cumulative acquisition of scientific knowledge; the scientific revolutions which supplant one paradigm with another do not take us any closer to the truth about the way the world is: they simply replace one set of theoretical puzzles with a new incompatible set. The essay reprinted here, "Objectivity, Value Judgment, and Theory Choice," summarizes some of Kuhn's mature views on these topics.

---

*   A report on the "most cited works of the twentieth century" issued by the Arts and Humanities Citation Index lists Lenin as the most cited author but *Structure*, by a fair margin, the most frequently mentioned book. *The Structure of Scientific Revolutions* has sold over a million copies and been translated into some 20 languages.

†   Nicholas Wade, "Thomas S. Kuhn: Revolutionary Theorist of Science," *Science* 197 (1977): 144.

Thomas Samuel Kuhn was born in Cincinnati, Ohio, in 1922, the son of an industrial engineer. He was educated in New York at a series of progressive, left-leaning schools—where, though bright, Kuhn by his own account felt anxious, isolated, and neurotic (feelings which apparently remained with him to some degree for the rest of his life)—and then in 1940 went to Harvard to take a degree in physics. His undergraduate degree completed in 1943, he joined the US army radar program as a physicist. Kuhn was assigned to work on radar profiles, first in the States and England, but was then sent to Europe in the wake of the Allied invasion—dressed in uniform so he would not be shot as a spy if captured behind enemy lines—to inspect captured German radar installations. He was present (by accident) when the victorious French general Charles de Gaulle entered Paris, and saw the German city of Hamburg after it had been flattened by Allied bombs.

After the war, Kuhn drifted into graduate work and received a PhD in physics from Harvard University in 1949. He remained at Harvard, teaching in the General Education in Science program, which was aimed at giving students in the humanities and social sciences a background in natural science. However, in 1955 Kuhn was denied tenure at Harvard—on the grounds that he was insufficiently specialized in any particular academic discipline, either physics or history or philosophy—and he moved to the University of California at Berkeley, where in 1961 he became a full professor of the history of science. In 1964 Kuhn transferred to Princeton and then in 1979, after a divorce, moved again and settled at the Massachusetts Institute of Technology, where he remarried and taught until his retirement in 1991. He died in 1996.

What Is the Structure of This Reading?

Kuhn begins this paper by summarizing passages in *The Structure of Scientific Revolutions* about rational theory choice and progress in science, and claiming that his position on these matters has been seriously misunderstood by many of the book's critics. He then lays out what are sometimes known as his "five ways": five criteria, which are shared by scientists, for rational theory choice. However,

he argues that these five criteria are insufficient to determine the choice of one theory over another—scientists can only adopt or refuse to adopt a theory on the basis of partly *subjective* criteria. Kuhn then argues that this claim—that there is no single, shared algorithm available for theory choice in science—is a philosophically substantial finding, partly because, on Kuhn's view, there is no distinction to be made between the "contexts of discovery and justification." Furthermore, Kuhn insists, science could not properly function if there were some shared set of criteria that determined what any rational scientist must believe; instead, we should think of the five ways as *values* which influence theory choice rather than *rules* which determine it. These five shared values are more or less permanent in the history of science, Kuhn goes on to claim, but they have no rational justification from outside of the practice of science, and furthermore they evolve and change with those practices. Lastly, Kuhn addresses the sense in which the idiosyncratic factors that supplement the five ways in theory choice are 'subjective,' and reaffirms and clarifies his claim that paradigms are "incommensurable": that is, roughly, that two scientists who adopt different theories face communication barriers at least as extreme as those faced by two people who speak different languages.

Some Useful Background Information

1. A notion central to Kuhn's critique of the rationality of science is that of *incommensurability*. Two things are 'incommensurable' if they cannot be compared—if one cannot be said to be better, or truer, or more preferable than the other. For example, the number seven and the taste of apples are incommensurable: there is no scale of values on which they can both be compared. In the philosophy of science, two theories (or other linguistic systems) are said to be incommensurable if the claims of one cannot be stated in the language of the other. From this it follows also that there can be no neutral third language in which the claims of both theories can be stated and compared*—that is, there can be no neutral standpoint from which we can assess the theories and say that one is better than the

---

*   Suppose there were some theoretical language—call it theory *C*—which is capable of stating both the claims of theory *A* and those of theory *B*; then it would follow that *A* and *B* are not incommensurable, since the statements of *A* could be

other. And from *this*, it seems to be an inescapable conclusion that we cannot give any content to the notion that science is progressing—that scientific theories are becoming closer approximations of the truth, for example—since we can no longer say that a later theory is better than an earlier one.

There are various reasons why one might think that scientific theories are incommensurable. One of the most influential arguments derives from a certain theory about how theoretical terms get their *meaning*. On this view (roughly), scientific terms like "electron" or "mass" do not, as ordinary words like "cow" and "yellow" may, get their meaning from being attached as labels to observable things in the world. (After all, we cannot *see* electrons, so how can we point to them in order to label them?) Instead, terms applied to theoretical entities get their meaning entirely from their *role in the theory*: for example, the meaning of the word "mass" is, roughly, *whatever it is* that performs the function that mass does in the mathematical equations which make up the theory. If all of this is right, then it seems to follow that *if you change the theory you also change the meanings of all the theoretical terms of that theory*. For example, mass plays a different role in Newton's theory than it does in relativity theory (e.g., mass is independent of velocity in classical mechanics but for Einstein mass increases as velocity does), and hence the word "mass" must mean something different in the two theories—that is, when Einstein talks about "mass" he is using a different language than when Newton talks about it, even though the words they use happen to look and sound the same.

2. Another notion of which Kuhn made influential use and which is often appealed to in arguments for incommensurability is the idea that all observation is "theory-laden." That is, it can be argued—and in fact is generally believed by philosophers of science—that it is impossible for a scientist to make any experimental observations of the world without relying upon certain theoretical assumptions, and furthermore that these observations are changed by those assumptions. For example, a scientist who uses equipment—such as a microscope, radio telescope, or fMRI machine—to make observations must rely upon many theoretical claims about the operation of that equipment, and what she believes she is seeing will depend upon how she believes the equipment operates. More fundamentally, it is thought that even unaided observations depend for their content upon the way a scientist categorizes or conceptualizes experience. For example, seventeenth-century chemists reported having seen phlogiston (a mythical substance) being emitted by burning objects as flames; a modern day chemist observes the same phenomenon and sees a violent oxidation reaction. A medieval scientist observing the dawn would have seen a moving sun and a static Earth; today's observer is aware that she is seeing the rotation of the Earth carrying the sun into view. Finally, for many scientists and engineers trained in the Aristotelian science of the Middle Ages, projectiles were apparently observed to behave just as they were theoretically expected to—they rose into the air in a straight line until the force of their flight was overcome by the force of their weight, and then fell straight down to the ground; nowadays, after Newton has changed our theoretical framework, we observe that projectiles really have a parabolic trajectory.

One of the implications of this—or at least of the most radical versions of this thesis, sometimes called "the collapse of the observation-theory distinction"—is, once again, a kind of incommensurability. If all observation is infected by theory, the argument goes, then there can be no neutral body of data that can be used to evaluate competing theories. The observations recorded by scientists trained in theory *A* will support that theory because they see what they expect to see; meanwhile the experiments conducted by the partisans of theory *B* will support *their* theory; since all observations are theory-laden, there are no neutral experimental results available with respect to the two theories, and so no data that can legitimately be used to falsify one or confirm the other.

---

translated into *C* and those *C*-statements in turn could be translated into the language of *B*, and hence the claims of *A* could be stated in the terms of *B* (and vice versa).

Objectivity, Value Judgment, and Theory Choice*

In the penultimate chapter of a controversial book fifteen years ago, I considered the ways scientists are brought to abandon one time-honored theory or paradigm in favor of another. Such decision problems, I wrote, "cannot be resolved by proof." To discuss their mechanism is, therefore, to talk "about techniques of persuasion, or about argument and counterargument in a situation in which there can be no proof." Under these circumstances, I continued, "lifelong resistance [to a new theory] ... is not a violation of scientific standards.... Though the historian can always find men— Priestley, for instance†—who were unreasonable to resist for as long as they did, he will not find a point at which resistance becomes illogical or unscientific." Statements of that sort[1] obviously raise the question of why, in the absence of binding criteria for scientific choice, both the number of solved scientific problems and the precision of individual problem solutions should increase so markedly with the passage of time. Confronting that issue, I sketched in my closing chapter a number of characteristics that scientists share by virtue of the training which licenses their membership in one or another community of specialists. In the absence of criteria able to dictate the choice of each individual, I argued, we do well to trust the collective judgment of scientists trained in this way. "What better criterion could there be," I asked rhetorically, "than the decision of the scientific group?"[2]

A number of philosophers have greeted remarks like these in a way that continues to surprise me. My views, it is said, make of theory choice "a matter for mob psychology."[3] Kuhn believes, I am told, that "the decision of a scientific group to adopt a new paradigm cannot be based on good reasons of any kind, factual or otherwise."[4] The debates surrounding such choices must, my critics claim, be for me "mere persuasive displays without deliberative substance."[5] Reports of this sort manifest total misunderstanding, and I have

occasionally said as much in papers directed primarily to other ends. But those passing protestations have had negligible effect, and the misunderstandings continue to be important. I conclude that it is past time for me to describe, at greater length and with greater precision, what has been on my mind when I have uttered statements like the ones with which I just began. If I have been reluctant to do so in the past, that is largely because I have preferred to devote attention to areas in which my views diverge more sharply from those currently received than they do with respect to theory choice.

What, I ask to begin with, are the characteristics of a good scientific theory? Among a number of quite usual answers I select five, not because they are exhaustive, but because they are individually important and collectively sufficiently varied to indicate what is at stake. First, a theory should be accurate: within its domain, that is, consequences deducible from a theory should be in demonstrated agreement with the results of existing experiments and observations. Second, a theory should be consistent, not only internally or with itself, but also with other currently accepted theories applicable to related aspects of nature. Third, it should have broad scope: in particular, a theory's consequences should extend far beyond the particular observations, laws, or subtheories it was initially designed to explain. Fourth, and closely related; it should be simple, bringing order to phenomena that in its absence would be individually isolated and, as a set, confused. Fifth—a somewhat less standard item, but one of special importance to actual scientific decisions—a theory should be fruitful of new research findings: it should, that is, disclose new phenomena or unnoted relationships among those already known.[6] These five characteristics—accuracy, consistency, scope, simplicity, and fruitfulness—are all standard criteria for evaluating the adequacy of a theory. If they had not been, I would

---

* This paper was originally given as the Machette Lecture delivered at Furman University in South Carolina in 1973. It was first published in *The Essential Tension: Selected Studies in Scientific Tradition and Change*, by Thomas Kuhn (University of Chicago Press, 1977), 320–39.

† Joseph Priestley (1733–1804) was an English scientist and theologian who discovered oxygen in 1774, though—in accordance with the terms of the then-current theory—he thought of it as "dephlogisticated air."

have devoted far more space to them in my book, for I agree entirely with the traditional view that they play a vital role when scientists must choose between an established theory and an upstart competitor. Together with others of much the same sort, they provide *the* shared basis for theory choice.

Nevertheless, two sorts of difficulties are regularly encountered by the men who must use these criteria in choosing, say, between Ptolemy's astronomical theory and Copernicus's,* between the oxygen and phlogiston theories of combustion,† or between Newtonian mechanics and the quantum theory.‡ Individually the criteria are imprecise: individuals may legitimately differ about their application to concrete cases. In addition, when deployed together, they repeatedly prove to conflict with one another; accuracy may, for example, dictate the choice of one theory, scope the choice of its competitor. Since these difficulties, especially the first, are also relatively familiar, I shall devote little time to their elaboration. Though my argument does demand that I illustrate them briefly, my views will begin to depart from those long current only after I have done so.

Begin with accuracy, which for present purposes I take to include not only quantitative agreement but qualitative as well. Ultimately it proves the most nearly decisive of all the criteria, partly because it is less equivocal than the others but especially because predictive and explanatory powers, which depend on it, are characteristics that scientists are particularly unwilling to give up. Unfortunately, however, theories cannot always be discriminated in terms of accuracy. Copernicus's system, for example, was not more accurate than Ptolemy's until drastically revised

by Kepler§ more than sixty years after Copernicus's death. If Kepler or someone else had not found other reasons to choose heliocentric astronomy, those improvements in accuracy would never have been made, and Copernicus's work might have been forgotten. More typically, of course, accuracy does permit discriminations, but not the sort that lead regularly to unequivocal choice. The oxygen theory, for example, was universally acknowledged to account for observed weight relations in chemical reactions, something the phlogiston theory had previously scarcely attempted to do. But the phlogiston theory, unlike its rival, could account for the metals' being much more alike than the ores from which they were formed. One theory thus matched experience better in one area, the other in another. To choose between them on the basis of accuracy, a scientist would need to decide the area in which accuracy was more significant. About that matter chemists could and did differ without violating any of the criteria outlined above, or any others yet to be suggested.

However important it may be, therefore, accuracy by itself is seldom or never a sufficient criterion for theory choice. Other criteria must function as well, but they do not eliminate problems. To illustrate I select just two—consistency and simplicity—asking how they functioned in the choice between the heliocentric and geocentric¶ systems. As astronomical theories both Ptolemy's and Copernicus's were internally consistent, but their relation to related theories in other fields was very different. The stationary central earth was an essential ingredient of received physical theory, a tight-knit body of doctrine which explained, among other things, how stones fall, how water pumps

---

* Ptolemy was a second-century CE astronomer from Alexandria, in Egypt, who based his astronomical theory on the belief that all heavenly bodies revolve around a stationary Earth. Nicholas Copernicus (1473–1543) was a Polish astronomer who advanced the competing theory that the Earth and other planets revolve around the sun.

† The former theory explains combustion as the violent chemical reaction of a substance with oxygen in the air around it; by contrast, the latter theory (which was current until the eighteenth century) postulated a volatile substance called phlogiston which is contained in all flammable materials and which is released as flame during combustion.

‡ According to Newtonian theory, light (and other forms of what we now think of as electromagnetic energy) consisted in the mechanical motions of particles in an all-enveloping, massless substance called "ether." Quantum theory is the modern scientific account of matter and energy; it is probabilistic rather than mechanical, and abandons the notion of a "medium" through which energy waves propagate.

§ Johannes Kepler (1571–1630), a German astronomer, is often considered the "father of modern astronomy" for his formulation of three fundamental laws of planetary motion.

¶ "Heliocentric" means centered on the sun; "geocentric" means centered on the Earth.

function, and why the clouds move slowly across the skies. Heliocentric astronomy, which required the earth's motion, was inconsistent with the existing scientific explanation of these and other terrestrial phenomena. The consistency criterion by itself, therefore, spoke unequivocally for geocentric tradition.

Simplicity, however, favored Copernicus, but only when evaluated in a quite special way. If, on the one hand, the two systems were compared in terms of the actual computational labor required to predict the position of a planet at a particular time, then they proved substantially equivalent. Such computations were what astronomers did, and Copernicus's system offered them no labor-saving techniques; in that sense it was not simpler than Ptolemy's. If, on the other hand, one asked about the amount of mathematical apparatus required to explain, not the detailed quantitative motions of the planets, but merely their gross qualitative features—limited elongation, retrograde motion, and the like—then, as every schoolchild knows, Copernicus required only one circle per planet, Ptolemy two.* In that sense the Copernican theory was the simpler, a fact vitally important to the choices made by both Kepler and Galileo and thus essential to the ultimate triumph of Copernicanism. But that sense of simplicity was not the only one available, nor even the one most natural to professional astronomers, men whose task was the actual computation of planetary position.

Because time is short and I have multiplied examples elsewhere, I shall here simply assert that these difficulties in applying standard criteria of choice are typical and that they arise no less forcefully in twentieth-century situations than in the earlier and better-known examples I have just sketched. When scientists must choose between competing theories, two men fully committed to the same list of criteria for choice may nevertheless reach different conclusions. Perhaps they interpret simplicity differently or have different convictions about the range of fields within which the consistency criterion must be met. Or perhaps they agree about these matters but differ about the relative weights to be accorded to these or to other criteria when several are deployed together. With divergences of this sort, no set of choice criteria yet proposed is of any use. One can explain, as the historian characteristically does, why particular men made particular choices at particular times. But for that purpose one must go beyond the list of shared criteria to characteristics of the individuals who make the choice. One must, that is, deal with characteristics which vary from one scientist to another without thereby in the least jeopardizing their adherence to the canons that make science scientific. Though such canons do exist and should be discoverable (doubtless the criteria of choice with which I began are among them), they are not by themselves sufficient to determine the decisions of individual scientists. For that purpose the shared canons must be fleshed out in ways that differ from one individual to another.

Some of the differences I have in mind result from the individual's previous experience as a scientist. In what part of the field was he at work when confronted by the need to choose? How long had he worked there; how successful had he been; and how much of his work depended on concepts and techniques challenged by the new theory? Other factors relevant to choice lie outside the sciences. Kepler's early election of Copernicanism was due in part to his immersion in the Neoplatonic and Hermetic† movements of his day; German Romanticism‡ predisposed those it affected toward both recognition

---

* In the Ptolemaic system, celestial orbits are described by "epicycles": that is, the orbits of the sun and planets form small circles, the centers of which move around the circumference of a larger circle centered on the Earth. For the Copernican system, of course, each planet's orbit is described by a single (elliptical) circle with the sun at its center.

† Neoplatonism is a school of thought—originating in the third century CE, and influential in medieval and Renaissance philosophy—which fused Plato's philosophy with religious doctrines, and which sees the universe as an emanation from an omnipresent, transcendent, unchanging One. Hermeticism, which was also popular during the Renaissance, involves allegiance to the doctrines found in a collection of occult writings on magical and religious topics which were (wrongly) thought to be the texts of an ancient Egyptian priesthood.

‡ Romanticism was a late eighteenth-century movement which reacted against the rationalism of the Enlightenment by embracing spontaneity, imagination, emotion, and inspiration. Among its themes was the belief that reality is ultimately spiritual, and that knowledge of nature cannot be achieved by rational and analytic means but only through

and acceptance of energy conservation; nineteenth-century British social thought had a similar influence on the availability and acceptability of Darwin's concept of the struggle for existence. Still other significant differences are functions of personality. Some scientists place more premium than others on originality and are correspondingly more willing to take risks; some scientists prefer comprehensive, unified theories to precise and detailed problem solutions of apparently narrower scope. Differentiating factors like these are described by my critics as subjective and are contrasted with the shared or objective criteria from which I began. Though I shall later question that use of terms, let me for the moment accept it. My point is, then, that every individual choice between competing theories depends on a mixture of objective and subjective factors, or of shared and individual criteria. Since the latter have not ordinarily figured in the philosophy of science, my emphasis upon them has made my belief in the former hard for my critics to see.

What I have said so far is primarily simply descriptive of what goes on in the sciences at times of theory choice. As description, furthermore, it has not been challenged by my critics, who reject instead my claim that these facts of scientific life have philosophic import. Taking up that issue, I shall begin to isolate some, though I think not vast, differences of opinion. Let me begin by asking how philosophers of science can for so long have neglected the subjective elements which, they freely grant, enter regularly into the actual theory choices made by individual scientists? Why have these elements seemed to them an index only of human weakness, not at all of the nature of scientific knowledge?

One answer to that question is, of course, that few philosophers, if any, have claimed to possess either a complete or an entirely well-articulated list of criteria. For some time, therefore, they could reasonably expect that further research would eliminate residual imperfections and produce an algorithm able to dictate rational, unanimous choice. Pending that achievement, scientists would have no alternative but to supply subjectively what the best current list of objective criteria still lacked. That some of them might still do

so even with a perfected list at hand would then be an index only of the inevitable imperfection of human nature.

That sort of answer may still prove to be correct, but I think no philosopher still expects that it will. The search for algorithmic decision procedures has continued for some time and produced both powerful and illuminating results. But those results all presuppose that individual criteria of choice can be unambiguously stated and also that, if more than one proves relevant, an appropriate weight function is at hand for their joint application. Unfortunately, where the choice at issue is between scientific theories, little progress has been made toward the first of these desiderata* and none toward the second. Most philosophers of science would therefore, I think, now regard the sort of algorithm which has traditionally been sought as a not quite attainable ideal. I entirely agree and shall henceforth take that much for granted.

Even an ideal, however, if it is to remain credible, requires some demonstrated relevance to the situations in which it is supposed to apply. Claiming that such demonstration requires no recourse to subjective factors, my critics seem to appeal, implicitly or explicitly, to the well-known distinction between the contexts of discovery and of justification.[7] They concede, that is, that the subjective factors I invoke play a significant role in the discovery or invention of new theories, but they also insist that that inevitably intuitive process lies outside of the bounds of philosophy of science and is irrelevant to the question of scientific objectivity. Objectivity enters science, they continue, through the processes by which theories are tested, justified, or judged. Those processes do not, or at least need not, involve subjective factors at all. They can be governed by a set of (objective) criteria shared by the entire group competent to judge.

I have already argued that that position does not fit observations of scientific life and shall now assume that that much has been conceded. What is now at issue is a different point: whether or not this invocation of the distinction between contexts of discovery and of justification provides even a plausible and useful idealization. I think it does not and can best

---

a kind of intuitive absorption into the spiritual process of nature.

* Things lacking but needed or desired.

make my point by suggesting first a likely source of its apparent cogency. I suspect that my critics have been misled by science pedagogy or what I have elsewhere called textbook science. In science teaching, theories are presented together with exemplary applications, and those applications may be viewed as evidence. But that is not their primary pedagogic function (science students are distressingly willing to receive the word from professors and texts). Doubtless *some* of them were *part* of the evidence at the time actual decisions were being made, but they represent only a fraction of the considerations relevant to the decision process. The context of pedagogy differs almost as much from the context of justification as it does from that of discovery.

Full documentation of that point would require longer argument than is appropriate here, but two aspects of the way in which philosophers ordinarily demonstrate the relevance of choice criteria are worth noting. Like the science textbooks on which they are often modelled, books and articles on the philosophy of science refer again and again to the famous crucial experiments: Foucault's pendulum,* which demonstrates the motion of the earth; Cavendish's demonstration of gravitational attraction;† or Fizeau's measurement of the relative speed of sound in water and air.‡ These experiments are paradigms of good reason for scientific choice; they illustrate the most effective of all the sorts of argument which could be available to a scientist uncertain which of two theories to follow;

they are vehicles for the transmission of criteria of choice. But they also have another characteristic in common. By the time they were performed no scientist still needed to be convinced of the validity of the theory their outcome is now used to demonstrate. Those decisions had long since been made on the basis of significantly more equivocal evidence. The exemplary crucial experiments to which philosophers again and again refer would have been historically relevant to theory choice only if they had yielded unexpected results. Their use as illustrations provides needed economy to science pedagogy, but they scarcely illuminate the character of the choices that scientists are called upon to make.

Standard philosophical illustrations of scientific choice have another troublesome characteristic. The only arguments discussed are, as I have previously indicated, the ones favorable to the theory that, in fact, ultimately triumphed. Oxygen, we read, could explain weight relations, phlogiston could not; but nothing is said about the phlogiston theory's power or about the oxygen theory's limitations. Comparisons of Ptolemy's theory with Copernicus's proceed in the same way. Perhaps these examples should not be given since they contrast a developed theory with one still in its infancy. But philosophers regularly use them nonetheless. If the only result of their doing so were to simplify the decision situation, one could not object. Even historians do not claim to deal with the full factual complexity of the situations they describe. But these

---

* This experiment was first performed in 1851 by the French physicist Jean Bernard Léon Foucault (1819–68) in order to show that the Earth spins around its axis. The oscillations of a weight swinging from a very long wire can be observed to slowly rotate (clockwise in the Northern hemisphere and anticlockwise in the Southern); however the pendulum itself must be moving in a straight line, since there is no outside force interrupting its movement; therefore, since the path of the pendulum seems to rotate with respect to the ground and yet we know that the pendulum is not rotating, it must be the *ground* which is spinning.

† Henry Cavendish (1731–1810) used a sensitive torsion balance to measure the value of the gravitational constant G and this allowed him to estimate the mass of the Earth for the first time. Cavendish's experimental apparatus involved a light, rigid six-foot long rod, suspended from a wire, with two small metal spheres attached to the ends of the rod. When the rod is twisted, the torsion of the wire exerts a force which is proportional to the angle of rotation of the rod, and Cavendish carefully calibrated his instrument to determine the relationship between the angle of rotation and the amount of torsional force. He then brought two large lead spheres near the smaller spheres attached to the rod: since all masses attract, the large spheres exerted a gravitational force upon the smaller spheres and twisted the rod a measurable amount. Once the torsional force balanced the gravitational force, the rod and spheres came to rest and Cavendish was able to determine the gravitational force of attraction between the masses.

‡ Armand-Hippolyte Fizeau (1819–96) is best known for experimentally determining the speed of light, and showing that different media (such as still water, moving water, and air) can affect the speed of propagation of light and sound.

simplifications emasculate by making choice totally unproblematic. They eliminate, that is, one essential element of the decision situation that scientists must resolve if their field is to move ahead. In those situations there are always at least some good reasons for each possible choice. Considerations relevant to the context of discovery are then relevant to justification as well; scientists who share the concerns and sensibilities of the individual who discovers a new theory are ipso facto* likely to appear disproportionately frequently among that theory's first supporters. That is why it has been difficult to construct algorithms for theory choice, and also why such difficulties have seemed so thoroughly worth resolving. Choices that present problems are the ones philosophers of science need to understand. Philosophically interesting decision procedures must function where, in their absence, the decision might still be in doubt.

That much I have said before, if only briefly. Recently, however, I have recognized another, subtler source for the apparent plausibility of my critics' position. To present it, I shall briefly describe a hypothetical dialogue with one of them. Both of us agree that each scientist chooses between competing theories by deploying some Bayesian algorithm† which permits him to compute a value for $p(T,E)$, i.e., for the probability of a theory T on the evidence E available both to him and to the other members of his group at a particular period of time. "Evidence," furthermore, we both interpret broadly to include such considerations as simplicity and fruitfulness. My critic asserts, however, that there is only one such value of p, that corresponding to objective choice, and he believes that all rational members of the group must arrive at it. I assert, on the other hand, for reasons previously given, that the factors he calls objective are insufficient to determine in full any algorithm at all. For the sake of the discussion I have conceded that each individual has an algorithm and that all their algorithms have much in common. Nevertheless, I continue to hold that the algorithms of individuals are all ultimately different by virtue of the subjective considerations with which each must complete the objective criteria before any computations can be done. If my hypothetical critic is liberal, he may now grant that these subjective differences do play a role in determining the hypothetical algorithm on which each individual relies during the early stages of the competition between rival theories. But he is also likely to claim that, as evidence increases with the passage of time, the algorithms of different individuals converge to the algorithm of objective choice with which his presentation began. For him the increasing unanimity of individual choices is evidence for their increasing objectivity and thus for the elimination of subjective elements from the decision process.

So much for the dialogue, which I have, of course, contrived to disclose the non sequitur‡ underlying an apparently plausible position. What converges as the evidence changes over time need only be the values of p that individuals compute from their individual algorithms. Conceivably those algorithms themselves also become more alike with time, but the ultimate unanimity of theory choice provides no evidence whatsoever that they do so. If subjective factors are required to account for the decisions that initially divide the profession, they may still be present later when the profession agrees. Though I shall not here argue the point, consideration of the occasions on which a scientific community divides suggests that they actually do so.

My argument has so far been directed to two points. It first provided evidence that the choices scientists make between competing theories depend not only on shared criteria—those my critics call objective—but also on idiosyncratic factors dependent on individual biography and personality. The latter are, in my critics' vocabulary, subjective, and the second part of my argument has attempted to bar some likely ways of denying their philosophic import. Let me now shift to a more positive approach, returning briefly to the

---

* Latin: "by that very fact."

† Thomas Bayes (1702–61) was an English clergyman who developed an influential theorem for calculating the probability of a hypothesis given a certain body of evidence. According to this theorem, in its simplest form, the probability of the hypothesis is the product of a) its prior probability (i.e., its probability before the evidence) and b) the probability of the evidence being as it is given the hypothesis, divided by the prior probability of that evidence. That is, $p(T,E) = (p(T) \times (p(E,T)) / p(E))$.

‡ A *non sequitur* is something that does not follow, e.g., a conclusion that does not logically follow from the premises.

list of shared criteria—accuracy, simplicity, and the like—with which I began. The considerable effectiveness of such criteria does not, I now wish to suggest, depend on their being sufficiently articulated to dictate the choice of each individual who subscribes to them. Indeed, if they were articulated to that extent, a behavior mechanism fundamental to scientific advance would cease to function. What the tradition sees as eliminable imperfections in its rules of choice I take to be in part responses to the essential nature of science.

As so often, I begin with the obvious. Criteria that influence decisions without specifying what those decisions must be are familiar in many aspects of human life. Ordinarily, however, they are called not criteria or rules, but maxims, norms, or values. Consider maxims first. The individual who invokes them when choice is urgent usually finds them frustratingly vague and often also in conflict one with another. Contrast "He who hesitates is lost" with "Look before you leap," or compare "Many hands make light work" with "Too many cooks spoil the broth." Individually maxims dictate different choices, collectively none at all. Yet no one suggests that supplying children with contradictory tags like these is irrelevant to their education. Opposing maxims alter the nature of the decision to be made, highlight the essential issues it presents, and point to those remaining aspects of the decision for which each individual must take responsibility himself. Once invoked, maxims like these alter the nature of the decision process and can thus change its outcome.

Values and norms provide even clearer examples of effective guidance in the presence of conflict and equivocation. Improving the quality of life is a value, and a car in every garage once followed from it as a norm. But quality of life has other aspects, and the old norm has become problematic. Or again, freedom of speech is a value, but so is preservation of life and property. In application, the two often conflict, so that judicial soul-searching, which still continues, has been required to prohibit such behavior as inciting to riot or shouting fire in a crowded theater. Difficulties like these are an appropriate source for frustration, but they rarely result in charges that values have no function or in calls for their abandonment. That response is barred to most of us by an acute consciousness that there are societies with other values and that these value differences result in other ways of life, other decisions about what may and what may not be done.

I am suggesting, of course, that the criteria of choice with which I began function not as rules, which determine choice, but as values, which influence it. Two men deeply committed to the same values may nevertheless, in particular situations, make different choices as, in fact, they do. But that difference in outcome ought not to suggest that the values scientists share are less than critically important either to their decisions or to the development of the enterprise in which they participate. Values like accuracy, consistency, and scope may prove ambiguous in application, both individually and collectively; they may, that is, be an insufficient basis for a *shared* algorithm of choice. But they do specify a great deal: what each scientist must consider in reaching a decision, what he may and may not consider relevant, and what he can legitimately be required to report as the basis for the choice he has made. Change the list, for example by adding social utility as a criterion, and some particular choices will be different, more like those one expects from an engineer. Subtract accuracy of fit to nature from the list, and the enterprise that results may not resemble science at all, but perhaps philosophy instead. Different creative disciplines are characterized, among other things, by different sets of shared values. If philosophy and engineering lie too close to the sciences, think of literature or the plastic arts. Milton's failure to set *Paradise Lost* in a Copernican universe does not indicate that he agreed with Ptolemy but that he had things other than science to do.

Recognizing that criteria of choice can function as values when incomplete as rules has, I think, a number of striking advantages. First, as I have already argued at length, it accounts in detail for aspects of scientific behavior which the tradition has seen as anomalous or even irrational. More important, it allows the standard criteria to function fully in the earliest stages of theory choice, the period when they are most needed but when, on the traditional view, they function badly or not at all. Copernicus was responding to them during the years required to convert heliocentric astronomy from a global conceptual scheme to mathematical machinery for predicting planetary position. Such predictions were what astronomers valued; in their absence, Copernicus would scarcely have been heard, something which had happened to the idea of a moving earth before. That his own version convinced very few is less important than his acknowledgment of the basis on which judgments would have to be reached if heliocentricism were to survive. Though idiosyncrasy must be invoked to explain why Kepler and Galileo were early converts to Copernicus's system, the gaps filled by their efforts to perfect it were specified by shared values alone.

That point has a corollary which may be more important still. Most newly suggested theories do not survive. Usually the difficulties that evoked them are accounted for by more traditional means. Even when this does not occur, much work, both theoretical and experimental, is ordinarily required before the new theory can display sufficient accuracy and scope to generate widespread conviction. In short, before the group accepts it, a new theory has been tested over time by the research of a number of men, some working within it, others within its traditional rival. Such a mode of development, however, *requires* a decision process which permits rational men to disagree, and such disagreement would be barred by the shared algorithm which philosophers have generally sought. If it were at hand, all conforming scientists would make the same decision at the same time. With standards for acceptance set too low, they would move from one attractive global viewpoint to another, never giving traditional theory an opportunity to supply equivalent attractions. With standards set higher, no one satisfying the criterion of rationality would be inclined to try out the new theory, to articulate it in ways which showed its fruitfulness or displayed its accuracy and scope. I doubt that science would survive the change. What from one viewpoint may seem the looseness and imperfection of choice criteria conceived as rules may, when the same criteria are seen as values, appear an indispensable means of spreading the risk which the introduction or support of novelty always entails.

Even those who have followed me this far will want to know how a value-based enterprise of the sort I have described can develop as a science does, repeatedly producing powerful new techniques for prediction and control. To that question, unfortunately, I have no answer at all, but that is only another way of saying that I make no claim to have solved the problem of induction. If science did progress by virtue of some shared and binding algorithm of choice, I would be equally at a loss to explain its success. The lacuna* is one I feel acutely, but its presence does not differentiate my position from the tradition.

It is, after all, no accident that my list of the values guiding scientific choice is, as nearly as makes any difference, identical with the tradition's list of rules dictating choice. Given any concrete situation to which the philosopher's rules could be applied, my values would function like his rules, producing the same choice. Any justification of induction, any explanation of why the rules worked, would apply equally to my values. Now consider a situation in which choice by shared rules proves impossible, not because the rules are wrong but because they are, as rules, intrinsically incomplete. Individuals must then still choose and be guided by the rules (now values) when they do so. For that purpose, however, each must first flesh out the rules, and each will do so in a somewhat different way even though the decision dictated by the variously completed rules may prove unanimous. If I now assume, in addition, that the group is large enough so that individual differences distribute on some normal curve, then any argument that justifies the philosopher's choice by rule should be immediately adaptable to my choice by value. A group too small, or a distribution excessively skewed by external historical pressures, would, of course, prevent the argument's transfer.[8] But those are just the circumstances under which scientific progress is itself problematic. The transfer is not then to be expected.

I shall be glad if these references to a normal distribution of individual differences and to the problem of induction make my position appear very close to more traditional views. With respect to theory choice, I have never thought my departures large and have been correspondingly startled by such charges as "mob psychology," quoted at the start. It is worth noting, however, that the positions are not quite identical, and for that purpose an analogy may be helpful. Many

---

* Hole or gap.

properties of liquids and gases can be accounted for on the kinetic theory* by supposing that all molecules travel at the same speed. Among such properties are the regularities known as Boyle's and Charles's law.† Other characteristics, most obviously evaporation, cannot be explained in so simple a way. To deal with them one must assume that molecular speeds differ, that they are distributed at random, governed by the laws of chance. What I have been suggesting here is that theory choice, too, can be explained only in part by a theory which attributes the same properties to all the scientists who must do the choosing. Essential aspects of the process generally known as verification will be understood only by recourse to the features with respect to which men may differ while still remaining scientists. The tradition takes it for granted that such features are vital to the process of discovery, which it at once and for that reason rules out of philosophical bounds. That they may have significant functions also in the philosophically central problem of justifying theory choice is what philosophers of science have to date categorically denied.

What remains to be said can be grouped in a somewhat miscellaneous epilogue. For the sake of clarity and to avoid writing a book, I have throughout this paper utilized some traditional concepts and locutions about the viability of which I have elsewhere expressed serious doubts. For those who know the work in which I have done so, I close by indicating three aspects of what I have said which would better represent my views if cast in other terms, simultaneously indicating the main directions in which such recasting should proceed. The areas I have in mind are: value invariance, subjectivity, and partial communication. If my views of scientific development are novel—a matter about which there is legitimate room for doubt—it is in areas such as these, rather than theory choice, that my main departures from tradition should be sought.

Throughout this paper I have implicitly assumed that, whatever their initial source, the criteria or values deployed in theory choice are fixed once and for all, unaffected by their participation in transitions from one theory to another. Roughly speaking, but only very roughly, I take that to be the case. If the list of relevant values is kept short (I have mentioned five, not all independent) and if their specification is left vague, then such values as accuracy, scope, and fruitfulness are permanent attributes of science. But little knowledge of history is required to suggest that both the application of these values and, more obviously, the relative weights attached to them have varied markedly with time and also with the field of application. Furthermore, many of these variations in value have been associated with particular changes in scientific theory. Though the experience of scientists provides no philosophical justification for the values they deploy (such justification would solve the problem of induction), those values are in part learned from that experience, and they evolve with it.

The whole subject needs more study (historians have usually taken scientific values, though not scientific methods, for granted), but a few remarks will illustrate the sort of variations I have in mind. Accuracy, as a value, has with time increasingly denoted quantitative or numerical agreement, sometimes at the expense of qualitative. Before early modern times, however, accuracy in that sense was a criterion only for astronomy, the science of the celestial region. Elsewhere it was neither expected nor sought. During the seventeenth century, however, the criterion of numerical agreement was extended to mechanics, during the late eighteenth and early nineteenth centuries to chemistry and such other subjects as electricity and heat, and in this century to many parts of biology. Or think of utility, an item of value not on my initial list. It too has figured significantly in scientific development, but far more strongly and steadily for chemists than for, say, mathematicians and physicists. Or consider scope. It is still an important scientific value, but important scientific advances have repeatedly been achieved at

---

* The kinetic theory is a theory of the thermodynamic behavior of matter, especially the relationships among pressure, volume, and temperature in gases. Among its central notions are that temperature depends on the kinetic energy of the rapidly moving particles of a substance, that energy and momentum are conserved in all collisions between particles, and that the average behavior of the particles in a substance can be deduced by statistical analysis.

† Boyle's law, formulated by Robert Boyle in 1662, is the principle that, at a constant temperature, the volume of a confined ideal gas varies inversely with its pressure. Charles's law, discovered by French scientist J.A.C. Charles in 1787, states that the volume of a fixed mass of gas held at a constant pressure varies directly with the absolute temperature.

its expense, and the weight attributed to it at times of choice has diminished correspondingly.

What may seem particularly troublesome about changes like these is, of course, that they ordinarily occur in the aftermath of a theory change. One of the objections to Lavoisier's new chemistry* was the roadblocks with which it confronted the achievement of what had previously been one of chemistry's traditional goals: the explanation of qualities, such as color and texture, as well as of their changes. With the acceptance of Lavoisier's theory such explanations ceased for some time to be a value for chemists; the ability to explain qualitative variation was no longer a criterion relevant to the evaluation of chemical theory. Clearly, if such value changes had occurred as rapidly or been as complete as the theory changes to which they related, then theory choice would be value choice, and neither could provide justification for the other. But, historically, value change is ordinarily a belated and largely unconscious concomitant of theory choice, and the former's magnitude is regularly smaller than the latter's. For the functions I have here ascribed to values, such relative stability provides a sufficient basis. The existence of a feedback loop through which theory change affects the values which led to that change does not make the decision process circular in any damaging sense.

About a second respect in which my resort to tradition may be misleading, I must be far more tentative. It demands the skills of an ordinary language philosopher, which I do not possess. Still no very acute ear for language is required to generate discomfort with the ways in which the terms "objectivity" and, more especially, "subjectivity" have functioned in this paper. Let me briefly suggest the respects in which I believe language has gone astray. "Subjective" is a term with several established uses: in one of these it is opposed to "objective," in another to "judgmental." When my critics describe the idiosyncratic features to which I appeal as subjective, they resort, erroneously I think,

to the second of these senses. When they complain that I deprive science of objectivity, they conflate that second sense of subjective with the first.

A standard application of the term "subjective" is to matters of taste, and my critics appear to suppose that that is what I have made of theory choice. But they are missing a distinction standard since Kant when they do so. Like sensation reports, which are also subjective in the sense now at issue, matters of taste are undiscussable. Suppose that, leaving a movie theater with a friend after seeing a western, I exclaim: "How I liked that terrible potboiler!" My friend, if he disliked the film, may tell me I have low tastes, a matter about which, in these circumstances, I would readily agree. But, short of saying that I lied, he cannot disagree with my report that I liked the film or try to persuade me that what I said about my reaction was wrong. What is discussable in my remark is not my characterization of my internal state, my exemplification of taste, but rather my *judgment* that the film was a potboiler. Should my friend disagree on that point, we may argue most of the night, each comparing the film with good or great ones we have seen, each revealing, implicitly or explicitly, something about how he *judges* cinematic merit, about his aesthetic. Though one of us may, before retiring, have persuaded the other, he need not have done so to demonstrate that our difference is one of judgment, not taste.

Evaluations or choices of theory have, I think, exactly this character. Not that scientists never say merely, I like such and such a theory, or I do not. After 1926 Einstein said little more than that about his opposition to the quantum theory. But scientists may always be asked to explain their choices, to exhibit the bases for their judgments. Such judgments are eminently discussable, and the man who refuses to discuss his own cannot expect to be taken seriously. Though there are, very occasionally, leaders of scientific taste, their existence tends to prove the rule. Einstein was one of the few, and his increasing isolation from the

---

* Antoine Laurent Lavoisier (1743–94) isolated the major components of air and water, disproved the phlogiston theory by determining the role of oxygen in combustion, and organized the classification of chemical compounds upon which the modern system is based. He formulated the concept of an element as being a simple substance that cannot be broken down by any known method of chemical analysis, and he showed that although matter changes state during a chemical reaction, its mass remains the same, thus leading him to propose the law of conservation of matter. Lavoisier was executed during the Reign of Terror after the French Revolution.

scientific community in later life shows how very limited a role taste alone can play in theory choice. Bohr,* unlike Einstein, did discuss the bases for his judgment, and he carried the day. If my critics introduce the term "subjective" in a sense that opposes it to judgmental—thus suggesting that I make theory choice undiscussable, a matter of taste—they have seriously mistaken my position.

Turn now to the sense in which "subjectivity" is opposed to "objectivity," and note first that it raises issues quite separate from those just discussed. Whether my taste is low or refined, my report that I liked the film is objective unless I have lied. To my judgment that the film was a potboiler, however, the objective-subjective distinction does not apply at all, at least not obviously and directly. When my critics say I deprive theory choice of objectivity, they must, therefore, have recourse to some very different sense of subjective, presumably the one in which bias and personal likes or dislikes function instead of, or in the face of, the actual facts. But that sense of subjective does not fit the process I have been describing any better than the first. Where factors dependent on individual biography or personality must be introduced to make values applicable, no standards of factuality or actuality are being set aside. Conceivably my discussion of theory choice indicates some limitations of objectivity, but not by isolating elements properly called subjective. Nor am I even quite content with the notion that what I have been displaying are limitations. Objectivity ought to be analyzable in terms of criteria like accuracy and consistency. If these criteria do not supply all the guidance that we have customarily expected of them, then it may be the meaning rather than the limits of objectivity that my argument shows.

Turn, in conclusion, to a third respect, or set of respects, in which this paper needs to be recast. I have assumed throughout that the discussions surrounding theory choice are unproblematic, that the facts appealed to in such discussions are independent of theory, and that the discussions' outcome is appropriately

called a choice. Elsewhere I have challenged all three of these assumptions, arguing that communication between proponents of different theories is inevitably partial, that what each takes to be facts depends in part on the theory he espouses, and that an individual's transfer of allegiance from theory to theory is often better described as conversion than as choice. Though all these theses are problematic as well as controversial, my commitment to them is undiminished. I shall not now defend them, but must at least attempt to indicate how what I have said here can be adjusted to conform with these more central aspects of my view of scientific development.

For that purpose I resort to an analogy I have developed in other places. Proponents of different theories are, I have claimed, like native speakers of different languages. Communication between them goes on by translation, and it raises all translation's familiar difficulties. That analogy is, of course, incomplete, for the vocabulary of the two theories may be identical, and most words function in the same ways in both. But some words in the basic as well as in the theoretical vocabularies of the two theories—words like "star" and "planet," "mixture" and "compound," or "force" and "matter"—do function differently. Those differences are unexpected and will be discovered and localized, if at all, only by repeated experience of communication breakdown. Without pursuing the matter further, I simply assert the existence of significant limits to what the proponents of different theories can communicate to one another. The same limits make it difficult or, more likely, impossible for an individual to hold both theories in mind together and compare them point by point with each other and with nature. That sort of comparison is, however, the process on which the appropriateness of any word like "choice" depends.

Nevertheless, despite the incompleteness of their communication, proponents of different theories can exhibit to each other, not always easily, the concrete technical results achievable by those who practice within each theory. Little or no translation is required

---

* Niels Bohr, a Danish physicist, made basic contributions to the theory of atomic structure between 1913 and 1915 and received a Nobel Prize in 1922. His model of the atom made essential use of quantum theory: he suggested that electrons in an atom move in orbits, and that when an electron moves to another orbit it gives off or absorbs a quantum of radiation.

to apply at least some value criteria to those results. (Accuracy and fruitfulness are most immediately applicable, perhaps followed by scope. Consistency and simplicity are far more problematic.) However incomprehensible the new theory may be to the proponents of tradition, the exhibit of impressive concrete results will persuade at least a few of them that they must discover how such results are achieved. For that purpose they must learn to translate, perhaps by treating already published papers as a Rosetta stone* or, often more effective, by visiting the innovator, talking with him, watching him and his students at work. Those exposures may not result in the adoption of the theory; some advocates of the tradition may return home and attempt to adjust the old theory to produce equivalent results. But others, if the new theory is to survive, will find that at some point in the language-learning process they have ceased to translate and begun instead to speak the language like a native. No process quite like choice has occurred, but they are practicing the new theory nonetheless. Furthermore, the factors that have led them to risk the conversion they have undergone are just the ones this paper has underscored in discussing a somewhat different process, one which, following philosophical tradition, it has labelled theory choice. ■

Suggestions for Critical Reflection

1. Kuhn quotes himself, from the *Structure of Scientific Revolutions*, as saying: "What better criterion [for which theory it is rational to adopt] could there be than the decision of the scientific group?" Do you agree with this claim? What better criterion *could* there be? If Kuhn is right about this, could the philosophy of science be replaced by the sociology of science (i.e., by the study of how groups of scientists come to consensus)?

2. What do you think is the philosophical value of studying the history of science? How much does the *actual* behavior of scientists show us about the ideal "scientific method"? In particular, do you think Kuhn establishes that the history of science reveals that there just *is* no completely rational method available to scientists?

3. Kuhn argues that not only do scientists possess no shared set of criteria for theory choice, but that science could not *survive* if there were a rational "scientific method" for confirming or discarding theories. Do you think he is right about this?

4. What do you think Kuhn made of the theories of science represented in this chapter by readings from Hempel and Popper? In what ways do you think his own account differs from theirs?

5. Both Hempel and, especially, Popper make a firm distinction between what Kuhn calls the context of discovery and the context of justification. How successful is Kuhn in arguing that there is no such distinction? What would be the implications if this distinction were collapsed?

6. Many critics have asserted that Kuhn's account of theory choice and paradigm shifts leaves no room for the notion that science *progresses* towards a closer and closer approximation to the *truth* about reality. On the basis of Kuhn's claims in this article, do you think that this is a fair criticism?

7. According to Kuhn, incommensurability follows from the theory-based meaning; but many philosophers of science nowadays disagree, arguing that even if meaning is theory-based, commensurability is based on sameness of reference, not of meaning. For example, even if Einstein and Newton mean different things when they use the word "mass," they are both referring to observable external phenomena, and so we can still do empirical tests to find out which theory is correct. For example,

---

* The Rosetta stone is a black basalt tablet discovered in 1799 by French troops near Rosetta, a northern Egyptian town in the Nile River delta. It can be seen in the British Museum in London and bears an inscription written in three different scripts—Greek, Egyptian hieroglyphic, and Egyptian demotic. This inscription provided the key to the code of (the hitherto baffling) Egyptian hieroglyphics.

Newton's theory predicts that the speed of light on Earth differs with direction; Einstein's predicts it does not. A crucial measuring experiment showed that Einstein was right. What do you think about this argument? How do you think Kuhn would reply to this argument?

8. One unfriendly critic of Kuhn, James Franklin, has said the following: "The basic content of Kuhn's book [*The Structure of Scientific Revolutions*] can be inferred simply by asking: what would the humanities crowd *want* said about science? Once the question is asked, the answer is obvious. Kuhn's thesis is that scientific theories are no better than ones in the humanities.... [S]cience is all theoretical talk and negotiation, which never really establishes anything" (from *The New Criterion*, June 2000). Given what Kuhn says in this article, to what degree do you think that Franklin gets Kuhn right?

Notes

1 *The Structure of Scientific Revolutions*, 2d ed. (Chicago, 1970), pp. 148, 151–52, 159. All the passages from which these fragments are taken appeared in the same form in the first edition, published in 1962.

2 Ibid., p. 170.

3 Imre Lakatos, "Falsification and the Methodology of Scientific Research Programmes," in I. Lakatos and A. Musgrave, eds., *Criticism and the Growth of Knowledge* (Cambridge, 1970), pp. 91–195. The quoted phrase, which appears on p. 178, is italicized in the original.

4 Dudley Shapere, "Meaning and Scientific Change," in R.G. Colodny, ed., *Mind and Cosmos: Essays in Contemporary Science and Philosophy*, University of Pittsburgh Series in the Philosophy of Science, vol. 3 (Pittsburgh 1966), pp. 41–85. The quotation will be found on p. 67.

5 Israel Scheffler, *Science and Subjectivity* (Indianapolis, 1967), p. 81.

6 The last criterion, fruitfulness, deserves more emphasis than it has yet received. A scientist choosing between two theories ordinarily knows that his decision will have a bearing on his subsequent research career. Of course he is especially attracted by a theory that promises the concrete successes for which scientists are ordinarily rewarded.

7 The least equivocal example of this position is probably the one developed in Scheffler, *Science and Subjectivity*, chap. 4.

8 If the group is small, it is more likely that random fluctuations will result in its members' sharing an atypical set of values and therefore making choices different from those that would be made by a larger and more representative group. External environment—intellectual, ideological, or economic—must systematically affect the value system of much larger groups, and the consequences can include difficulties in introducing the scientific enterprise to societies with inimical values or perhaps even the end of that enterprise within societies where it had once flourished. In this area, however, great caution is required. Changes in the environment where science is practiced can also have fruitful effects on research. Historians often resort, for example, to differences between national environments to explain why particular innovations were initiated and at first disproportionately pursued in particular countries, e.g., Darwinism in Britain, energy conservation in Germany. At present we know substantially nothing about the minimum requisites of the social milieux within which a sciencelike enterprise might flourish.

HELEN LONGINO

Can There Be a Feminist Science?

Who Is Helen Longino?

Helen E. Longino (born 1944) has been perhaps the most influential philosopher to apply contemporary feminist approaches to epistemology and philosophy of science. As an undergraduate, she majored in literary studies, moving to logic and philosophy of science for her graduate work at Johns Hopkins University. During the 1960s and 1970s, she was active in anti-war and feminist political action movements. As a faculty member at Mills College, Rice University, and University of Minnesota, she was strongly influential in establishing women's studies courses and programs. Her books include *Studying Human Behavior: How Scientists Investigate Aggression and Sexuality* (2013), *The Fate of Knowledge* (2001), and *Science as Social Knowledge* (1990). Longino is currently the Clarence Irving Lewis Professor of Philosophy at Stanford University. She has served as President of the Philosophy of Science Association and was elected to the American Academy of Arts and Sciences in 2016.

Some Useful Background Information

Longino's target for criticism is the long-held and (for a long time) universal view that the most important feature of good science is its *objectivity*—which was taken to mean that scientific practice, when working right, should be utterly uninfluenced by any values of the scientist, or of her culture or society—any values, that is, other than the internal scientific values of care in observation, honesty, thoroughness, and so on. The idea here was that nature itself—the external facts—should determine what's taken to be true by scientists.

Nobody thinks that real science always works this way: there are numerous high-profile examples brought to light of outright fraud, or unconscious bias, the result of what the scientist himself or the source of his funding, or the dominant culture, hopes to find. But the traditional view counts these as bad science. A very moderate feminist critique of science has, for decades, pointed out how male bias is among the factors that can make for bad science in this sense. Feminists point to deeply flawed scientific studies of the following sort: a study of the causes of heart-attack which studied only males as subjects, blithely considering their conclusions to be applicable to all humans; a study of societal dynamics which looked only at traditional male activities and roles; a study of cognitive abilities that rated subjects on the basis of typically male abilities, leading to the conclusion that women are intellectually less able.

But this is not Longino's critique. She does not merely point out that male-oriented assumptions lead to bad science, nor does she defend a distinctively female way of doing science. Instead, echoing Kuhn (see the previous reading), she notes that observations and data inevitably fall short of providing objective justification for scientific knowledge—science is never value free, because we always bring some values or other to bear on the connection between our evidence and our hypotheses. The objectivity of science does not consist in eliminating value judgments. Rather, science is properly objective only when it incorporates *diverse* values—when it avoids privileging one set of social values while ignoring others, and instead allows its claims to be scrutinized by a wide range of participants in an open and democratic way. "Her key idea is that the production of knowledge is a social enterprise, secured through the critical and cooperative interactions of inquirers. The products of this social enterprise are more objective, the more responsive they are to criticism from all points of view."[*]

---

[*] Elizabeth Anderson, "Feminist Epistemology and Philosophy of Science," *The Stanford Encyclopedia of Philosophy*, ed. Edward N. Zalta (Spring 2017).

What Is the Structure of This Reading?

Longino begins by mentioning various sorts of feminist approaches to science that her article will not take. Her subject will instead be a feminist critique of the idea that science should be impersonal, objective, and value-free; feminists, she argues, offer an alternative that makes for better science.

After a number of preliminaries, she reveals her central argument: that confirmation in science often essentially involves background assumptions, and that these assumptions are sometimes not merely established by simple observation or common sense, but are rather tied in with "contextual values"—not mere internal rules of science, but personal, social, or cultural values.

Some Common Misconceptions

1. Longino does not argue that there are typically feminine characteristics that should be represented more in scientific investigations. She does not reject this view wholesale; she merely argues that this is not what she will talk about.

2. Neither does Longino argue here for a position that some readers, seeing that this is a feminist treatment of scientific practice, might expect: that the current male science gets things all wrong, and that a replacement female science would do better. She mentions that her aim is not to replace one "absolutism" by another.

Can There Be a Feminist Science?*

This paper explores a number of recent proposals regarding "feminist science" and rejects a content-based approach in favor of a process-based approach to characterizing feminist science. Philosophy of science can yield models of scientific reasoning that illuminate the interaction between cultural values and ideology and scientific inquiry. While we can use these models to expose masculine and other forms of bias, we can also use them to defend the introduction of assumptions grounded in feminist political values.

I

The question of this title conceals multiple ambiguities. Not only do the sciences consist of many distinct fields, but the term "science" can be used to refer to a method of inquiry, a historically changing collection of practices, a body of knowledge, a set of claims, a profession, a set of social groups, etc. And as the sciences are many, so are the scholarly disciplines that seek to understand them: philosophy, history, sociology, anthropology, psychology. Any answer from the perspective of some one of these disciplines will, then, of necessity, be partial. In this essay, I shall be asking about the possibility of theoretical natural science that is feminist and I shall ask from the perspective of a philosopher. Before beginning to develop my answer, however, I want to review some of the questions that could be meant, in order to arrive at the formulation I wish to address.

The question could be interpreted as factual, one to be answered by pointing to what feminists in the sciences are doing and saying: "Yes, and this is what it is." Such a response can be perceived as question-begging, however. Even such a friend of feminism as Stephen Gould dismisses the idea of a distinctively feminist or even female contribution to the sciences. In a generally positive review of Ruth Bleier's book, *Science and Gender*, Gould (1984) brushes aside her connection between women's attitudes and values and the interactionist science she calls for. Scientists (male, of course) are already proceeding with wholist[†] and

---

* *Hypatia* 2, 3 (1987): 51–64.

† Wholism (usually spelled "holism") denotes a variety of positions which resist understanding larger unities as merely the sum of their parts, and asserts that we cannot explain or understand the parts without treating them as belonging to such larger wholes. This contrasts with positivism, which relies upon the assumption that observation is independent from theory and that confirming or disconfirming observations can be specified independently of the theory they are supposed to confirm or disconfirm.

interactionist* research programs. Why, he implied, should women or feminists have any particular, distinctive, contributions to make? There is not masculinist and feminist science, just good and bad science. The question of a feminist science cannot be settled by pointing, but involves a deeper, subtler investigation.

The deeper question can itself have several meanings. One set of meanings is sociological, the other conceptual. The sociological meaning proceeds as follows. We know what sorts of social conditions make misogynist science possible. The work of Margaret Rossiter (1982) on the history of women scientists in the United States and the work of Kathryn Addelson (1983) on the social structure of professional science detail the relations between a particular social structure for science and the kinds of science produced. What sorts of social conditions would make feminist science possible? This is an important question, one I am not equipped directly to investigate, although what I can investigate is, I believe, relevant to it. This is the second, conceptual, interpretation of the question: what sort of sense does it make to talk about a feminist science? Why is the question itself not an oxymoron,† linking, as it does, values and ideological commitment with the idea of impersonal, objective, value-free, inquiry? This is the problem I wish to address in this essay.

The hope for a feminist theoretical natural science has concealed an ambiguity between content and practice. In the content sense the idea of a feminist science involves a number of assumptions and calls a number of visions to mind. Some theorists have written as though a feminist science is one of the theories which encode a particular world view, characterized by complexity, interaction and wholism. Such a science is said to be feminist because it is the expression and valorization‡ of a female sensibility or cognitive temperament. Alternatively, it is claimed that women have certain traits (dispositions to attend to particulars, interactive rather than individualist and controlling social attitudes and behaviors) that enable them to understand the true character of natural processes (which are complex and interactive).[1] While proponents of this interactionist view see it as an improvement over most contemporary science, it has also been branded as soft—misdescribed as non-mathematical. Women in the sciences who feel they are being asked to do not better science, but inferior science, have responded angrily to this characterization of feminist science, thinking that it is simply new clothing for the old idea that women can't do science. I think that the interactionist view can be defended against this response, although that requires rescuing it from some of its proponents as well. However, I also think that the characterization of feminist science as the expression of a distinctive female cognitive temperament has other drawbacks. It first conflates feminine with feminist. While it is important to reject the traditional derogation of the virtues assigned to women, it is also important to remember that women are *constructed* to occupy positions of social subordinates. We should not uncritically embrace the feminine.

This characterization of feminist science is also a version of recently propounded notions of a 'women's standpoint' or a 'feminist standpoint' and suffers from the same suspect universalization that these ideas suffer from. If there is one such standpoint, there are many: as Maria Lugones and Elizabeth Spelman spell out in their tellingly entitled article, "Have We Got a Theory for You: Feminist Theory, Cultural Imperialism, and the Demand for 'The Woman's Voice,'" women are too diverse in our experiences to generate a single cognitive framework (Lugones and Spelman 1983). In addition, the sciences are themselves too diverse for me to think that they might be equally transformed by such a framework. To reject this concept of a feminist science, however, is not to disengage science from feminism. I want to suggest that we focus on science as practice rather than content, as process rather than product; hence, not on feminist science, but on doing science as a feminist.

The doing of science involves many practices: how one structures a laboratory (hierarchically or collectively), how one relates to other scientists (competitively

---

* This is the view, taken from a theoretical position in sociology, that derives social processes—in this case, the practice of science—from human interaction.

† Oxymoron: a contradictory or incongruous combination of terms.

‡ To valorize something is to enhance its value, usually artificially, or to assign a value to it.

or cooperatively), how and whether one engages in political struggles over affirmative action. It extends also to intellectual practices, to the activities of scientific inquiry, such as observation and reasoning. Can there be a feminist scientific inquiry? This possibility is seen to be problematic against the background of certain standard presuppositions about science. The claim that there could be a feminist science in the sense of an intellectual practice is either nonsense because oxymoronic as suggested above or the claim is interpreted to mean that established science (science as done and dominated by men) is wrong about the world. Feminist science in this latter interpretation is presented as correcting the errors of masculine, standard science and as revealing the truth that is hidden by masculine 'bad' science, as taking the sex out of science.

Both of these interpretations involve the rejection of one approach as incorrect and the embracing of the other as the way to a truer understanding of the natural world. Both trade one absolutism for another. Each is a side of the same coin, and that coin, I think, is the idea of a value-free science. This is the idea that scientific methodology guarantees the independence of scientific inquiry from values or value-related considerations. A science or a scientific research program informed by values is *ipso facto** "bad science." "Good science" is inquiry protected by methodology from values and ideology. This same idea underlies Gould's response to Bleier, so it bears closer scrutiny. In the pages that follow, I shall examine the idea of value-free science and then apply the results of that examination to the idea of feminist scientific inquiry.

II

I distinguish two kinds of values relevant to the sciences. Constitutive values, internal to the sciences, are the source of the rules determining what constitutes acceptable scientific practice or scientific method. The personal, social and cultural values, those group or individual preferences about what ought to be, I call contextual values, to indicate that they belong to the social and cultural context in which science is done (Longino 1983c). The traditional interpretation of the value-freedom of modern natural science amounts to a claim that its constitutive and contextual features are clearly distinct from and independent of one another, that contextual values play no role in the inner workings of scientific inquiry, in reasoning and observation. I shall argue that this construal of the distinction cannot be maintained.

There are several ways to develop such an argument. One scholar is fond of inviting her audience to visit any science library and peruse the titles on the shelves. Observe how subservient to social and cultural interests are the inquiries represented by the book titles alone! Her listeners would soon abandon their ideas about the value-neutrality of the sciences, she suggests. This exercise may indeed show the influence of external, contextual considerations on what research gets done/supported (i.e., on problem selection). It does not show that such considerations affect reasoning or hypothesis acceptance. The latter would require detailed investigation of particular cases or a general conceptual argument. The conceptual arguments involve developing some version of what is known in philosophy of science as the underdetermination thesis, i.e., the thesis that a theory is always underdetermined by the evidence adduced in its support, with the consequence that different or incompatible theories are supported by or at least compatible with the same body of evidence. I shall sketch a version of the argument that appeals to features of scientific inference.

One of the rocks on which the logical positivist program foundered was the distinction between theoretical and observational language. Theoretical statements contain, as fundamental descriptive terms, terms that do not occur in the description of data. Thus, hypotheses in particle physics contain terms like "electron," "pion," "muon," "electron spin," etc. The evidence for a hypothesis such as "A pion decays sequentially into a muon, then a positron" is obviously not direct observations of pions, muons and positrons, but consists largely in photographs taken in large and complex experimental apparati: accelerators, cloud chambers, bubble chambers. The photographs show all sorts of squiggly lines and spirals. Evidence for the hypotheses of particle physics is presented as statements that describe these photographs. Eventually, of

---

* Latin: by that very fact.

course, particle physicists point to a spot on a photograph and say things like "Here a neutrino hits a neutron." Such an assertion, however, is an interpretive achievement which involves collapsing theoretical and observational moments. A skeptic would have to be supplied a complicated argument linking the elements of the photograph to traces left by particles and these to particles themselves. What counts as theory and what as data in a pragmatic sense change over time, as some ideas and experimental procedures come to be securely embedded in a particular framework and others take their place on the horizons. As the history of physics shows, however, secure embeddedness is no guarantee against overthrow.

Logical positivists and their successors hoped to model scientific inference formally. Evidence for hypotheses, data, were to be represented as logical consequences of hypotheses. When we try to map this logical structure onto the sciences, however, we find that hypotheses are, for the most part, not just generalizations of data statements. The links between data and theory, therefore, cannot be adequately represented as formal or syntactic, but are established by means of assumptions that make or imply substantive claims about the field over which one theorizes. Theories are confirmed via the confirmation of their constituent hypotheses, so the confirmation of hypotheses and theories is relative to the assumptions relied upon in asserting the evidential connection. Confirmation of such assumptions, which are often unarticulated, is itself subject to similar relativization. And it is these assumptions that can be the vehicle for the involvement of considerations motivated primarily by contextual values (Longino 1979, 1983a).

The point of this extremely telescoped argument is that one can't give an a priori specification of confirmation that effectively eliminates the role of value-laden assumptions in legitimate scientific inquiry without eliminating auxiliary hypotheses (assumptions) altogether. This is not to say that all scientific reasoning involves value-related assumptions. Sometimes auxiliary assumptions will be supported by mundane inductive reasoning. But sometimes they will not be. In any given case, they may be metaphysical in character; they may be untestable with present investigative techniques; they may be rooted in contextual, value-related considerations. If, however, there is no a priori way to eliminate such assumptions

from evidential reasoning generally, and, hence, no way to rule out value-laden assumptions, then there is no formal basis for arguing that an inference mediated by contextual values is thereby bad science.

A comparable point is made by some historians investigating the origins of modern science. James Jacob (1977) and Margaret Jacob (1976) have, in a series of articles and books, argued that the adoption of conceptions of matter by 17th century scientists like Robert Boyle was inextricably intertwined with political considerations. Conceptions of matter provided the foundation on which physical theories were developed and Boyle's science, regardless of his reasons for it, has been fruitful in ways that far exceed his imaginings. If the presence of contextual influences were grounds for disallowing a line of inquiry, then early modern science would not have gotten off the ground.

The conclusion of this line of argument is that constitutive values conceived as epistemological (i.e., truth-seeking) are not adequate to screen out the influence of contextual values in the very structuring of scientific knowledge. Now the ways in which contextual values do, if they do, influence this structuring and interact, if they do, with constitutive values has to be determined separately for different theories and fields of science. But this argument, if it's sound, tells us that this sort of inquiry is perfectly respectable and involves no shady assumptions or unargued intuitively based rejections of positivism. It also opens the possibility that one can make explicit value commitments and still do "good" science. The conceptual argument doesn't show that all science is value-laden (as opposed to metaphysics-laden)—that must be established on a case-by-case basis, using the tools not just of logic and philosophy but of history and sociology as well. It does show that not all science is value-free and, more importantly, that it is not necessarily in the nature of science to be value-free. If we reject that idea we're in a better position to talk about the possibilities of feminist science.

III

In earlier articles (Longino 1981, 1983b; Longino and Doell 1983), I've used similar considerations to argue that scientific objectivity has to be reconceived as a function of the communal structure of scientific inquiry rather than as a property of individual scientists. I've then used these notions about scientific methodology to show that science displaying masculine bias is not *ipso facto* improper or 'bad' science; that the fabric of science can neither rule out the expression of bias nor legitimate it. So I've argued that both the expression of masculine bias in the sciences and feminist criticism of research exhibiting that bias are—shall we say—business as usual; that scientific inquiry should be expected to display the deep metaphysical and normative* commitments of the culture in which it flourishes; and finally that criticism of the deep assumptions that guide scientific reasoning about data is a proper part of science.

The argument I've just offered about the idea of a value-free science is similar in spirit to those earlier arguments. I think it makes it possible to see these questions from a slightly different angle.

There is a tradition of viewing scientific inquiry as somehow inexorable. This involves supposing that the phenomena of the natural world are fixed in determinate relations with each other, that these relations can be known and formulated in a consistent and unified way. This is not the old "unified science" idea of the logical positivists, with its privileging of physics. In its "unexplicated" or "pre-analytic" state, it is simply the idea that there is one consistent, integrated or coherent, true theoretical treatment of all natural phenomena. (The indeterminacy principle of quantum physics is restricted to our understanding of the behavior of certain particles which themselves underlie the fixities of the natural world. Stochastic† theories reveal fixities, but fixities among ensembles rather than fixed relations among individual objects or events.) The scientific inquirer's job is to discover those fixed relations. Just as the task of Plato's philosophers was to discover the fixed relations among forms and the task of Galileo's scientists was to discover the laws written in the language of the grand book of nature, geometry, so the scientist's task in this tradition remains the discovery of fixed relations however conceived. These ideas are part of the realist tradition in the philosophy of science.

It's no longer possible, in a century that has seen the splintering of the scientific disciplines, to give such a unified description of the objects of inquiry. But the belief that the job is to discover fixed relations of some sort, and that the application of observation, experiment and reason leads ineluctably to unifiable, if not unified, knowledge of an independent reality, is still with us. It is evidenced most clearly in two features of scientific rhetoric: the use of the passive voice as in "it is concluded that ..." or "it has been discovered that ..." and the attribution of agency to the data, as in "the data suggest...." Such language has been criticized for the abdication of responsibility it indicates. Even more, the scientific inquirer, and we with her, become passive observers, victims of the truth. The idea of a value-free science is integral to this view of scientific inquiry. And if we reject that idea we can also reject our roles as passive onlookers, helpless to affect the course of knowledge.

Let me develop this point somewhat more concretely and autobiographically. Biologist Ruth Doell and I have been examining studies in three areas of research on the influence of sex hormones on human behavior and cognitive performance: research on the influence of pre-natal, *in utero*, exposure to higher or lower than normal levels of androgens and estrogens on so-called 'gender-role' behavior in children, influence of androgens (pre- and post-natal) on homosexuality in women, and influence of lower than normal (for men) levels of androgen at puberty on spatial abilities (Doell and Longino, forthcoming).

The studies we looked at are vulnerable to criticism of their data and their observation methodologies. They also show clear evidence of androcentric bias‡—in the assumption that there are just two sexes and two genders (us and them), in the designation of appropriate and inappropriate behaviors for male and female children, in the caricature of lesbianism, in the assumption of male mathematical superiority. We did not find, however, that these assumptions mediated the inferences from data to theory that we found objectionable. These sexist assumptions did affect the way the data were described. What mediated the inferences from the alleged data (i.e., what functioned as auxiliary hypotheses or what provided auxiliary

---

* Normative means having to do with a value—a prescribed norm.
† Probabilistic.
‡ I.e., a bias in favor of the male point of view.

hypotheses) was what we called the linear model—the assumption that there is a direct one-way causal relationship between pre- or post-natal hormone levels and later behavior or cognitive performance. To put it crudely, fetal gonadal hormones organize the brain at critical periods of development. The organism is thereby disposed to respond in a range of ways to a range of environmental stimuli. The assumption of unidirectional programming is supposedly supported by the finding of such a relationship in other mammals; in particular, by experiments demonstrating the dependence of sexual behaviors—mounting and lordosis*—on peri-natal hormone exposure and the finding of effects of sex hormones on the development of rodent brains. To bring it to bear on humans is to ignore, among other things, some important differences between human brains and those of other species. It also implies a willingness to regard humans in a particular way—to see us as produced by factors over which we have no control. Not only are we, as scientists, victims of the truth, but we are the prisoners of our physiology.[2] In the name of extending an explanatory model, human capacities for self-knowledge, self-reflection, self-determination are eliminated from any role in human action (at least in the behaviors studied).

Doell and I have therefore argued for the replacement of that linear model of the role of the brain in behavior by one of much greater complexity that includes physiological, environmental, historical and psychological elements. Such a model allows not only for the interaction of physiological and environmental factors but also for the interaction of these with a continuously self-modifying, self-representational (and self-organizing) central processing system. In contemporary neurobiology, the closest model is that being developed in the group selectionist approach to higher brain function of Gerald Edelman and other researchers (Edelman and Mountcastle 1978). We argue that a model of at least that degree of complexity is necessary to account for the human behaviors studies in the sex hormones and behavior research and that if gonadal hormones function at all at these levels, they will probably be found at most to facilitate or inhibit neural processing in general. The strategy we take in our argument is to show that the degree of intentionality involved in the behaviors in question is greater than is presupposed by the hormonal influence researchers and to argue that this degree of intentionality implicates the higher brain processes.

To this point Ruth Doell and I agree. I want to go further and describe what we've done from the perspective of the above philosophical discussion of scientific methodology.

Abandoning my polemical mood for a more reflective one, I want to say that, in the end, commitment to one or another model is strongly influenced by values or other contextual features. The models themselves determine the relevance and interpretation of data. The linear or complex models are not in turn independently or conclusively supported by data. I doubt for instance that value-free inquiry will reveal the efficacy or inefficacy of intentional states or of physiological factors like hormone exposure in human action. I think instead that a research program in neuro-science that assumes the linear model and sex-gender dualism will show the influence of hormone exposure on gender-role behavior. And I think that a research program in neuroscience and psychology proceeding on the assumption that humans do possess the capacities for self-consciousness, self-reflection, and self-determination, and which then asks how the structure of the human brain and nervous system enables the expression of these capacities, will reveal the efficacy of intentional states (understood as very complex sorts of brain states).

While this latter assumption does not itself contain normative terms, I think that the decision to adopt it is motivated by value-laden considerations—by the desire to understand ourselves and others as self-determining (at least some of the time), that is, as capable of acting on the basis of concepts or representations of ourselves and the world in which we act. (Such representations are not necessarily correct, they are surely mediated by our cultures; all we wish to claim is that they are efficacious.) I think further that this desire on Ruth Doell's and my part is, in several ways, an aspect of our feminism. Our preference for a neurobiological model that allows for agency, for the efficacy of intentionality, is partly a validation of our (and everyone's) subjective experience of thought, deliberation, and choice. One of the tenets of feminist

---

*   Arching the spine backwards or downwards, which is a sexual response in some mammals (such as cats and mice).

research is the valorization of subjective experience, and so our preference in this regard conforms to feminist research patterns. There is, however, a more direct way in which our feminism is expressed in this preference. Feminism is many things to many people, but it is at its core in part about the expansion of human potentiality. When feminists talk of breaking out and do break out of socially prescribed sex-roles, when feminists criticize the institutions of domination, we are thereby insisting on the capacity of humans—male and female—to act on perceptions of self and society and to act to bring about changes in self and society on the basis of those perceptions. (Not overnight and not by a mere act of will. The point is that we act.) And so our criticism of theories of the hormonal influence or determination of so-called gender-role behavior is not just a rejection of the sexist bias in the description of the phenomena—the behavior of the children studied, the sexual lives of lesbians, etc.—but of the limitations on human capacity imposed by the analytic model underlying such research.[3]

While the argument strategy we adopt against the linear model rests on a certain understanding of intention, the values motivating our adoption of that understanding remain hidden in that polemical context. Our political commitments, however, presuppose a certain understanding of human action, so that when faced with a conflict between these commitments and a particular model of brain-behavior relationships we allow the political commitments to guide the choice.

The relevance of my argument about value-free science should be becoming clear. Feminists—in and out of science—often condemn masculine bias in the sciences from the vantage point of commitment to a value-free science. Androcentric bias, once identified, can then be seen as a violation of the rules, as "bad" science. Feminist science, by contrast, can eliminate that bias and produce better, good, more true or gender free science. From that perspective the process I've just described is anathema.* But if scientific methods generated by constitutive values cannot guarantee independence from contextual values, then that approach to sexist science won't work. We cannot restrict ourselves simply to the elimination of bias, but must expand our scope to include the detection of limiting and interpretive frameworks and the finding or construction of more appropriate frameworks. We need not, indeed should not, wait for such a framework to emerge from the data. In waiting, if my argument is correct, we run the danger of working unconsciously with assumptions still laden with values from the context we seek to change. Instead of remaining passive with respect to the data and what the data suggest, we can acknowledge our ability to affect the course of knowledge and fashion or favor research programs that are consistent with the values and commitments we express in the rest of our lives. From this perspective, the idea of a value-free science is not just empty, but pernicious.

Accepting the relevance to our practice as scientists of our political commitments does not imply simple and crude impositions of those ideas onto the corner of the natural world under study. If we recognize, however, that knowledge is shaped by the assumptions, values and interests of a culture and that, within limits, one can choose one's culture, then it's clear that as scientists/theorists we have a choice. We can continue to do establishment science, comfortably wrapped in the myths of scientific rhetoric, or we can alter our intellectual allegiances. While remaining committed to an abstract goal of understanding, we can choose to whom, socially and politically, we are accountable in our pursuit of that goal. In particular we can choose between being accountable to the traditional establishment or to our political comrades.

Such accountability does not demand a radical break with the science one has learned and practiced. The development of a "new" science involves a more dialectical evolution and more continuity with established science than the familiar language of scientific revolutions implies.

In focusing on accountability and choice, this conception of feminist science differs from those that proceed from the assumption of a congruence between certain models of natural processes and women's inherent modes of understanding.[4] I am arguing instead for the deliberate and active choice of an interpretive model and for the legitimacy of basing that choice on political considerations in this case. Obviously model choice is also constrained by (what we know of) reality, that is,

---

* Something one vehemently dislikes.

by the data. But reality (what we know of it) is, I have already argued, inadequate to uniquely determine model choice. The feminist theorists mentioned above have focused on the relation between the content of a theory and female values or experiences, in particular on the perceived congruence between interactionist, wholist visions of nature and a form of understanding and set of values widely attributed to women. In contrast, I am suggesting that a feminist scientific practice admits political considerations as relevant constraints on reasoning, which, through their influence on reasoning and interpretation, shape content. In this specific case, those considerations in combination with the phenomena support an explanatory model that is highly interactionist, highly complex. This argument is so far, however, neutral on the issue of whether an interactionist and complex account of natural processes will always be the preferred one. If it is preferred, however, this will be because of explicitly political considerations and not because interactionism is the expression of "women's nature."

The integration of a political commitment with scientific work will be expressed differently in different fields. In some, such as the complex of research programs having a bearing on the understanding of human behavior, certain moves, such as the one described above, seem quite obvious. In others it may not be clear how to express an alternate set of values in inquiry, or what values would be appropriate. The first step, however, is to abandon the idea that scrutiny of the data yields a seamless web of knowledge. The second is to think through a particular field and try to understand just what its unstated and fundamental assumptions are and how they influence the course of inquiry. Knowing something of the history of a field is necessary to this process, as is continued conversation with other feminists.

The feminist interventions I imagine will be local (i.e., specific to a particular area of research); they may not be exclusive (i.e., different feminist perspectives may be represented in theorizing); and they will be in some way continuous with existing scientific work. The accretion of such interventions, of science done by feminists as feminists, and by members of other disenfranchised groups, has the potential, nevertheless, ultimately to transform the character of scientific discourse.

Doing science differently requires more than just the will to do so and it would be disingenuous to pretend that our philosophies of science are the only barrier. Scientific inquiry takes place in a social, political and economic context which imposes a variety of institutional obstacles to innovation, let alone to the intellectual working out of oppositional and political commitments. The nature of university career ladders means that one's work must be recognized as meeting certain standards of quality in order that one be able to continue it. If those standards are intimately bound up with values and assumptions one rejects, incomprehension rather than conversion is likely. Success requires that we present our work in a way that satisfies those standards and it is easier to do work that looks just like work known to satisfy them than to strike out in a new direction. Another push to conformity comes from the structure of support for science. Many of the scientific ideas argued to be consistent with a feminist politics have a distinctively non-production orientation.[5] In the example discussed above, thinking of the brain as hormonally programmed makes intervention and control more likely than does thinking of it as a self-organizing complexly interactive system. The doing of science, however, requires financial support and those who provide that support are increasingly industry and the military. As might be expected they support research projects likely to meet their needs, projects which promise even greater possibilities for intervention in and manipulation of natural processes. Our sciences are being harnessed to the making of money and the waging of war. The possibility of alternate understandings of the natural world is irrelevant to a culture driven by those interests. To do feminist science we must change the social and political context in which science is done.

So: can there be a feminist science? If this means: is it in principle possible to do science as a feminist?, the answer must be: yes. If this means: can we in practice do science as feminists?, the answer must be: not until we change present conditions. ∎

Suggestions for Critical Reflection

1. Longino writes that she "rejects a content-based approach in favor of a process-based approach to characterizing feminist science." What do you think she means by this? Why is it important?

2. Longino describes a distinction between "contextual" and "constitutive" values in science? What is supposed to be the difference between them? What is Longino's own attitude towards this distinction in the end?

3. "If ... there is no a priori way to eliminate such [auxiliary] assumptions from evidential reasoning generally, and, hence, no way to rule out value-laden assumptions, then there is no formal basis for arguing that an inference mediated by contextual values is thereby bad science." What exactly is Longino saying here? Is she right?

4. How does Longino use her example of the study of the influence of sex hormones? What is the "background assumption" she thinks was at work in this study? What would a better version of this study look like?

5. "The idea of a value-free science is not just empty, but pernicious." Is it? Why?

6. A simple definition of feminism sees it as a movement to counter discrimination and injustice toward women. What else might be involved in feminism as an intellectual commitment? Is Longino's view of science properly conceived of as feminist—why or why not?

7. Longino does not advocate replacement of scientifically harmful "androcentric" values by supposedly scientifically superior feminist ones. What, exactly, does she advocate?

Notes

I am grateful to the Wellesley Center for Research on Women for the Mellon Scholarship during which I worked on the ideas in this essay. I am also grateful to audiences at UC Berkeley, Northeastern University, Brandeis University and Rice University for their comments and to the anonymous reviewers for *Hypatia* for their suggestions. An earlier version appeared as Wellesley Center for Research on Women Working Paper #63.

1 This seems to be suggested in Bleier (1984), Rose (1983) and in Sandra Harding's (1980) early work.

2 For a striking expression of this point of view see Witelson (1985).

3 Ideological commitments other than feminist ones may lead to the same assumptions and the variety of feminisms means that feminist commitments can lead to different and incompatible assumptions.

4 Cf. note [1], above.

5 This is not to say that interactionist ideas may not be applied in productive contexts, but that, unlike linear causal models, they are several steps away from the manipulation of natural processes immediately suggested by the latter. See Keller (1985), especially Chapter 10.

References

Addelson, Kathryn Pine. 1983. The man of professional wisdom. In *Discovering reality*, ed. Sandra Harding and Merrill Hintikka. Dordrecht: Reidel.

Bleier, Ruth. 1984. *Science and gender*. Elmsford, NY: Pergamon.

Doell, Ruth, and Helen E. Longino. N.d. *Journal of Homosexuality*. Forthcoming.*

Edelman, Gerald, and Vernon Mountcastle. 1978. *The mindful brain*. Cambridge, MA: MIT Press.

---

* Now in print: Ruth Doell and Helen Longino, "Sex Hormones and Human Behavior: A Critique of the Linear Model." *Journal of Homosexuality* 15, 3/4 (1988): 55–79.

Gould, Stephen J. 1984. Review of Ruth Bleier, *Science and gender. New York Times Book Review*, VVI, 7 (August 12): 1.

Harding, Sandra. 1980. The norms of inquiry and masculine experience. In *PSA 1980*, Vol. 2, ed. Peter Asquith and Ronald Giere. East Lansing, MI: Philosophy of Science Association.

Jacob, James R. 1977. *Robert Boyle and the English Revolution. A study in social and intellectual change*. New York: Franklin.

Jacob, Margaret C. 1976. *The Newtonians and the English Revolution, 1689–1720*. Ithaca, NY: Cornell University Press.

Keller, Evelyn Fox. 1985. *Reflections on gender and science*. New Haven, CT: Yale University Press.

Longino, Helen. 1979. Evidence and hypothesis. *Philosophy of Science* 46 (1): 35–56.

———. 1981. Scientific objectivity and feminist theorizing. *Liberal Education* 67 (3): 33–41.

———. 1983a. The idea of a value free science. Paper presented to the Pacific Division of the American Philosophical Association, March 25, Berkeley, CA.

———. 1983b. Scientific objectivity and logics of science. *Inquiry* 26 (1): 85–106.

———. 1983c. Beyond "bad science." *Science, Technology and Human Values* 8 (1): 7–17.

Longino, Helen, and Ruth Doell. 1983. Body, bias and behavior. *Signs* 9 (2): 206–227.

Lugones, Maria, and Elizabeth Spelman. 1983. Have we got a theory for you! Feminist theory, cultural imperialism and the demand for "the woman's voice." *Hypatia 1*, published as a special issue of *Women's Studies International Forum* 6 (6): 573–581.

Rose, Hilary. 1983. Hand, brain, and heart: A feminist epistemology for the natural sciences. *Signs* 9 (1): 73–90.

Rossiter, Margaret. 1982. *Women scientists in America: Struggles and strategies to 1940*. Baltimore, MD: Johns Hopkins University Press.

Witelson, Sandra. 1985. An exchange on gender. *New York Review of Books* (October 24).

Philosophy of Mind

WHAT IS THE PLACE OF MIND IN THE PHYSICAL WORLD?

The philosophy of mind has three main parts: the philosophy of psychology, philosophical psychology, and the metaphysics of mental phenomena. The philosophy of psychology (which can also be thought of as a branch of the philosophy of science) consists in the critical evaluation of the claims and methodologies of cognitive science. For example, in the first half of the twentieth century philosophers were involved with assessing the claims made by psychoanalytic theory (such as that of Sigmund Freud) and of psychological behaviorism, which controversially held that the only legitimate subject of psychological study is external human behavior. More recently, philosophers have played a role in creating and critiquing psychological models which are based on analogies between the human mind and computer programs.

For example, philosophers of mind examine the question of whether computers can "think"—manifest or model genuine intelligence—and whether the kind of information processing which is performed by the brain more resembles a familiar 'computational' type or a variety of more diffuse 'neural net' processing.

Philosophical psychology, by contrast, does not examine the science of psychology but instead engages in analysis of our ordinary, commonsensical concepts of the mental. It deals with such conceptual questions as the difference between deliberate action and mere behavior, the nature of memory and of perception, the no-

tion of rationality, the concept of personal identity, and so on.

Lastly, the metaphysics of the mind has to do with coming to understand the inherent nature of mental phenomena. The questions asked in this area are really at the heart of the philosophy of mind, and the four most important of them are the following:

1) What is the relationship between mind and brain? Of course, everyone knows that our minds and brains are closely connected: when certain things happen in our brains (perhaps caused by the ingestion of hallucinogenic chemicals), certain corresponding things happen in our minds. But what is the nature of this connection? Is the mind *nothing but* the physical brain (so that the brain processes *just are* the hallucinations), or is it something distinct from the brain, either because it is made of some different metaphysical 'stuff' (such as soul-stuff) or because it belongs to a different level or category of being (as a software program belongs to a different metaphysical category than the hard drive on which it is stored)?

2) What explains the fact that some of our mental states are directed at the world: how do some of our mental states come to be *meaningful*? The words on this page are meaningful because we use them as signs—when we learn to read, what we are learning is how to connect certain squiggles on the page with meaningful ideas. It is a much harder problem, however, to understand how bits

of our mind or brain can become signs, all by themselves, even though there is no one inside the head to 'read' them and give them meaning.

3) What explains the fact that some of our mental states have a certain qualitative *feel*? Put another way, where does *consciousness* come from? For example, the sensation of being tickled, or the smell of cooking onions, both have a distinctive feel to them: there is 'something it is like' for you to be tickled. However, if you think about it, this is a very unusual and quite puzzling fact; after all, for the vast majority of physical objects in the world, if you tickle them they don't feel a thing. So what makes *minds* special and unique in this respect? How do minds come to have a 'light on inside'—to be centers of consciousness and feeling in an unconscious, unfeeling universe? This is manifestly puzzling if you think of the mind as being nothing more than the three-and-a-bit-pound physico-chemical blob inside our skulls, but it turns out to be an extremely difficult problem for any theory of the mind. (In fact, arguably, it is the most difficult and pressing problem in all of philosophy.)

4) How do our mental states interact causally with the physical world? In particular, if our thoughts obey the laws of rationality instead of brute causality, then how can the workings of our mind be part of, or related to, the natural world? When I believe that this pesto sauce contains pine nuts, and I know that I am allergic to pine nuts and that if I eat any I will swell up like a balloon, and I don't want to swell up like a balloon, then it is (apparently) for this *reason* that I refuse to eat the pesto: my behavior is to be explained by the logical, rational connections between my beliefs and desires. The laws of physics, by contrast, are not rational laws. If a bullet ricochets off a lamppost and hits an innocent bystander during a bank robbery, it does not do so because it *ought* to bounce that way (nor does it do a bad thing because it has bounced *irrationally* or illogically)—its path is merely a physical consequence of the way it glanced off the metal of the lamppost. So, the laws of thought are rational and the laws of nature are non-rational: the problem is, then, how can thought be part of nature (be *both* rational and arational)? And if it is *not* part of nature, then how can it make things happen in the physical world (and vice versa)?

It is worth noting that, today, all of these questions are asked against the background of a default position called *physicalism*. Generally, in the sciences, we assume that the real world is nothing more than the physical world:

that all the things which exist are physical (roughly, made of either matter or energy) and obey exclusively physical laws (e.g., those described by fundamental physics). In most domains—such as chemistry, biology, or geology—this methodological assumption has proved fruitful; however, in psychology the question is much more vexed. In fact, the mind seems to be the last holdout of the nonphysical in the natural world. How can the feeling of pain or the taste of honey be made of either matter or energy? How can falling in love or choosing to become a politician be subject to the laws of physics? If the study of the human mind is ever to be integrated within the rest of (scientific) human knowledge, these phenomena will need to be accounted for in a physicalist framework: the big question is, can this be done, and how?

The issue in the philosophy of mind which is focused on in this chapter is the mind-body problem—what is the relationship between the mind and the brain?—and in particular the relationship between consciousness and the brain. Historically, there have been five main mind-body theories, and all five are introduced in the readings in this chapter. The traditional mind-body theory—the dominant story until about the middle of the twentieth century—is called *substance dualism*: on this view, mind and body are two completely different entities made up of two quite different substances: spirit and matter. The classic source for this view is Descartes's *Meditations*, which appears in the Epistemology chapter of this volume; Gilbert Ryle introduces the theory in this chapter, and then subjects it to a fairly devastating critique, calling it the "dogma of the Ghost in the Machine."

The next main mind-body theory to appear, dualism's successor, was called *behaviorism*: this theory holds that the mind is neither brain nor spirit, but instead consists in dispositions to behave in certain ways. Ryle is usually thought of as the primary philosophical practitioner and originator of this approach.

A natural approach to mental phenomena from a 'scientific' point of view is to attempt to reduce them to brain events. This tactic is called *mind-brain identity theory* in the philosophy of mind. The reading from Ned Block included here briefly describes both behaviorism and identity theory (which Block calls 'physicalism') and then introduces a fourth theory called *functionalism* which, by the time Block was writing in the late 1970s, was generally thought to have superseded all three prior theories. The essential idea behind functionalism is that the mind is best thought of as a sort of abstract information-processing device (rather like a computer program), and a mental state is really a kind of complex input-output relation between sensory stimuli and (internal and external) behavior. Block goes on, however, to raise a powerful critique of functionalism, suggesting that it may be in no better position than either the behaviorism or identity theory it replaced.

The following two articles raise worries for any theory that sets out to reduce the mind—and especially consciousness—to something wholly physical (which each of behaviorism, identity theory, and functionalism do). Thomas Nagel argues that some facts about consciousness are subjective in a particular way that poses problems for physicalism. As he puts it: "Without consciousness the mind-body problem would be much less interesting. With consciousness it seems hopeless." Frank Jackson formulates an influential argument against physicalism called the Knowledge Argument, and he uses this to defend the fifth theory of consciousness in this sequence, *property dualism*. The piece by David Chalmers re-emphasizes the difficulty of explaining consciousness in physical terms and proposes "that conscious experience be considered a fundamental feature [of the universe], irreducible to anything more basic" and describes what sort of theory that might look like. Lastly, the article by Amy Kind addresses head-on the following question: If consciousness is such a problem for physicalism or naturalism, why do we need to believe in (that kind of) consciousness at all?

The philosophy of mind has been a particularly active field for the past 50 years or so, and there are any number of good books available which will take you further into these fascinating questions. Some of the best are these: David Armstrong, *The Mind-Body Problem* (Westview, 1999); Keith Campbell, *Body and Mind* (University of Notre Dame Press, 1984); David Chalmers, *The Conscious Mind* (Oxford University Press, 1996); Paul Churchland, *Matter and Consciousness* (MIT Press, 2013); Tim Crane, *The Mechanical Mind* (Routledge, 2015); Daniel Dennett, *Consciousness Explained* (Little, Brown, 1991); Fred Dretske, *Naturalizing the Mind* (MIT Press, 1995); Edward Feser, *Philosophy of Mind: A Beginner's Guide* (OneWorld, 2006); Owen Flanagan, *The Science of the Mind* (MIT Press, 1991); Jerry Fodor, *Psychosemantics* (MIT Press, 1989); Stewart Goetz and Charles Taliaferro, *A Brief History of the Soul* (Wiley-Blackwell, 2011); John Heil, *Philosophy of Mind: A Contemporary Introduction* (Routledge, 2012); Ted Honderich, *Mind and Brain* (Oxford University Press, 1990); Jaegwon Kim, *Philosophy of Mind* (Routledge, 2010); Pete Mandik, *This Is Philosophy of Mind: An Introduction* (Wiley-Blackwell 2013); Colin McGinn, *The Character of Mind* (Oxford University Press, 1997); John Searle, *Mind: A Brief Introduction* (Oxford University Press, 2005); and Peter Smith and O.R. Jones, *The Philosophy of Mind* (Cambridge University Press, 1986). A good reference work on the philosophy of mind is *The Oxford Handbook of Philosophy of Mind*, edited by Brian P. McLaughlin and Ansgar Beckermann (Oxford University Press, 2011).

GILBERT RYLE

FROM *The Concept of Mind*

Who Was Gilbert Ryle?

Gilbert Ryle, who died in 1976, was one of the most influential figures in British philosophy in the 1950s and 1960s—he is often credited with a large part in reviving philosophy in Britain after World War II and with making Oxford University, for a period, the world center of philosophical activity. He was Waynflete Professor of Metaphysical Philosophy at Oxford from 1945 to 1968, and editor of *Mind*, the pre-eminent British journal of philosophy at the time, between 1948 and 1971.

Ryle was born in 1900 in the seaside town of Brighton, in the south of England. His father was a doctor who had a strong interest in philosophy and astronomy; he was in fact one of the founders of the Aristotelian Society, perhaps Britain's most important philosophical society for most of the twentieth century. In 1919 Ryle went to Queen's College, Oxford, to study Classics, but the subject that made the most impression on him was logic, which, he later wrote, unlike Classics, "felt to me like a grown-up subject, in which there were still unsolved problems."[*] He also spent a great deal of time rowing, and captained the Queen's College Boat Club. In 1923 he gained a first-class honors degree in "Greats" (Classical Studies and Philosophy) and in 1924 got *another* first-class undergraduate degree in "Modern Greats" (Philosophy, Politics, and Economics). In the same year he became a lecturer at Christ Church College.

Early in his career, in the 1930s, Ryle became preoccupied with the question of what philosophy itself is: what, if anything, is its special method and subject matter? It is not, he felt, merely the scholarly study of old texts, it's not just science without the experiments,[†] nor is it *simply* the examination of the meanings of words. His view, in the end, was that philosophy consists in the analysis of

certain kinds of meaningless expressions—with showing how certain combinations of ordinary words make no sense, and so resolving the problems created by these special kinds of nonsense. For example, "Florence hates the thought of going to hospital" is a grammatically misleading sentence, Ryle would say, since it appears to have the same form as "Florence hates Henry," which erroneously suggests that "the thought of going to hospital," like "Henry," is an expression which refers to an individual thing. This creates the apparent philosophical puzzle of trying to explain what kind of thing a thought is, and how a thought can be 'of' one thing rather than another, whereas Ryle would have us *dissolve* the problem by refusing to be trapped by surface grammar and insisting that talk of thoughts as "things" in this way is just *nonsense* created by our loose ways of speaking. Two early articles by Ryle which explore his view of the philosophical method are "Systematically Misleading Expressions" (1932) and "Categories" (1938); both can be found in the second volume of his *Collected Papers*.

Ryle's philosophical method should not be seen as entirely negative. It can be thought of as the attempt to map out the "logical geography" of the problems he considers. That is, he tries to expose the mistaken conceptual maps of other philosophers, and replace them with a new chart giving the correct locations of our ordinary concepts. *The Concept of Mind*, Ryle's first and best-known book and a modern classic of philosophy, applies this method to Cartesian dualism. As he once put it, Ryle was looking around for "some notorious and large-size Gordian Knot" upon which to "exhibit a sustained piece of analytical hatchet-work,"[‡] and he happened to settle upon our set of traditional—and in his view mistaken—assumptions about the nature of mind. His hatchet-work was immensely successful: partly because of the influence of *The Concept*

---

[*] "Autobiographical," in *Ryle: A Collection of Critical Essays*, ed. O.P. Wood and G. Pitcher (Doubleday, 1970), 2.

[†] Ryle was quite candid about his general ignorance of science and psychology, but he did not feel this harmed his philosophy.

[‡] "Autobiographical," 15.

of Mind, it is today almost (but not entirely) impossible to find a professional philosopher of mind who will admit to believing in the traditional dualism of Descartes (which makes mind and body separate substances).

With the coming of World War II in 1939, Ryle volunteered for military service and was commissioned in the Welsh Guards, where he was involved in intelligence work.* Immediately after the war Ryle was elected to the Waynflete chair of philosophy at Oxford, and when *The Concept of Mind* came out four years later Ryle was immediately established as a leading British philosopher. Representative book reviews by his peers noted that "this is probably one of the two or three most important and original works of general philosophy which have been published in English in the last twenty years"† and "it stands head and shoulders above its contemporaries."‡

During the next 30 years in which Ryle taught at Oxford and edited *Mind*, then perhaps the world's leading philosophical journal, he had a substantial impact on the growth and flourishing of the subject of philosophy in the second half of the twentieth century. Many of his students (such as A.J. Ayer, J.J.C. Smart, and Daniel Dennett) went on to become well-known philosophers; he was a constant presence at philosophical conferences all over the world (but especially the main British annual conference, the Joint Session of the Mind and Aristotelian Societies); and his editorship of *Mind* favored a new style of short, focused, analytical papers, and was deliberately encouraging to younger philosophers and philosophers from outside of Britain. Ryle retired from his Oxford chair in 1968, but remained philosophically active until his death in 1976.

What Is the Structure of This Reading?

"Descartes's Myth" is the first chapter of *The Concept of Mind*, which contains 10 chapters in all. The functions of this first chapter are (a) to lay out Ryle's target, Cartesian dualism, in preparation for Ryle's attack; (b) to describe generally the kind of logical error that dualism makes (a "category mistake"); and (c) to speculate about the historical origins of this mistake. The rest of the book consists, more or less, of a sequence of chapters each of which considers different aspects of mental life—such as intelligence, the will, emotion, sensation, imagination, and self-knowledge—and tries to expose the absurdities of the traditional Cartesian "logical geography" of these notions. In place of these faulty conceptual maps, Ryle argues for an account of the mind that generally treats mental states simply as dispositions or tendencies to behave in certain ways rather than others. Intelligence, for example, according to Ryle, should not be seen as something *additional* to behavior (a kind of ghostly mechanism which plans our behavior by judging possible actions according to a set of internally stored rules) but as itself a *kind* of behavior—a disposition to regularly perform task *X* well, in a variety of different contexts.

Some Useful Background Information

Ryle is often described as rejecting traditional dualism and replacing it with a new philosophical theory of the mind called *behaviorism*. Behaviorism, which was founded by the American psychologist John B. Watson in 1913 (and explained at length in his 1925 book *Behaviorism*), was originally intended to be an experimental method for psychology. Watson's view was that psychology ought to be a strictly empirical and "respectable" science; it therefore should not rely on the solitary introspective examination of one's own private mental states, but instead should restrict its data to objective, repeatable facts about "what an organism does and says." The business of psychology, then, should be the construction of psychological laws describing correlations between stimuli and reactions; psychology is best seen, not as the study of consciousness, but as the explanation and prediction of behavior. This form of behaviorism is usually called *methodological* (or *scientific*) *behaviorism*, and it is important to notice that it need not actually *deny* the existence of internal mental states but

---

* Unlike today perhaps, in those days 'military intelligence' was not considered a self-contradiction, and many of the brightest British minds were engaged in service that made good use of them.

† "Critical Review of *The Concept of Mind*," Stuart Hampshire, *Mind* 59 (1950): 237–55.

‡ "Intelligent Behaviour: A Critical Review of *The Concept of Mind*," J.L. Austin, *Times Literary Supplement*, 7 April 1950.

just says that the science of behavior can avoid talking about them.*

In the hands of the philosophers, behaviorism became not just a psychological method but a *theory* of the nature of mental states. In its purest form, this is the view that statements about mental phenomena can be completely analyzed in terms of (or reduced to, or translated into) statements about behavior and dispositions to behave. To have a mind *just is* to behave in a certain way. For example, to say that Othello is feeling jealous is, according to behaviorism, to say no more and no less than that he is behaving in a way characteristic of jealousy, or that he would behave in that way given suitable provocation. According to this theory, there are no internal "mental states" *in addition to* the patterns of human behavior. It is this kind of behaviorism—often called *logical* (or *analytic*) *behaviorism*—which is usually attributed to Gilbert Ryle (even though he himself, somewhat unconvincingly, denied that he was a behaviorist): indeed, *The Concept of Mind* is frequently cited as the central text of logical behaviorism.

Today, few if any philosophers are logical behaviorists. It is generally accepted that no analysis of the behavior corresponding to any particular belief or desire is possible, since what someone is disposed to do depends not only on a single belief but, in a potentially infinite variety of ways, on a whole system of connected beliefs. For example, the belief that a glass is half full of water will be associated with different behaviors depending on what else one believes about water (e.g., believing that it is a lethal acid), what one desires (e.g., whether or not you are thirsty), what one believes about the current perceptual conditions (e.g., thinking you are dreaming), and so on. There just is no single behavioral analysis of what it is to believe the glass is half full, and so that belief can't just *be* a set of behaviors.

Another major sticking point for behaviorism has been the worry that the behaviorist cannot treat mental states as being the *causes* of behavior since, for them, mentality just *is* a particular pattern of behavior. For example, a behaviorist cannot correctly say that someone winces because they feel pain, or is a crackerjack Scrabble player because they have a large vocabulary, since wincing and playing Scrabble well are *part* of what it is to feel pain or have a large vocabulary, rather than *effects* of those things.

Other forms of philosophical behaviorism live on today, however, in, for example, the following three modern theories:

1. *Analytical functionalism* is the view that the meanings of mental terms can be analyzed in terms of their role in our commonsense theory of behavior, "folk psychology." This view was held by, for example, David Lewis.
2. *Eliminative behaviorism* is a theory, associated with W.V. Quine, which denies any reality to internal mental states and talks only of overt behavior.
3. A theory developed by Donald Davidson, sometimes called *interpretivism*, holds that an "ideal interpreter" can have as complete and infallible access as is possible to the mental life of another person (because, for Davidson, to have a certain belief *just is* to be the kind of organism an ideal interpreter would attribute that belief to).

A Common Misconception

It is important to realize that the Ryle selection presented here, though itself a seminal piece of philosophy, is only a small part of a larger work. In this chapter, Ryle does not attempt to present all of his arguments against the doctrine of the ghost in the machine, nor does he explicitly describe his alternative behaviorist theory. Much of the power of Ryle's diagnosis comes from its initial plausibility, rather than from a battery of overt arguments. On the other hand, Ryle does make a couple of arguments, and it is also possible to see the seeds of other lines of argument being planted in this reading.

---

* Although, many behaviorists, such as Watson and B.F. Skinner, do in fact seem to have flirted with the notion that the mind can be eliminated—that it is just a kind of fiction designed to explain the complex movements of human bodies.

FROM *The Concept of Mind*
DESCARTES'S MYTH[*]

(1) *The Official Doctrine*

There is a doctrine about the nature and place of minds which is so prevalent among theorists and even among laymen that it deserves to be described as the official theory. Most philosophers, psychologists and religious teachers subscribe, with minor reservations, to its main articles and, although they admit certain theoretical difficulties in it, they tend to assume that these can be overcome without serious modifications being made to the architecture of the theory. It will be argued here that the central principles of the doctrine are unsound and conflict with the whole body of what we know about minds when we are not speculating about them.

The official doctrine, which hails chiefly from Descartes,[†] is something like this. With the doubtful exceptions of idiots[‡] and infants in arms every human being has both a body and a mind. Some would prefer to say that every human being is both a body and a mind. His body and his mind are ordinarily harnessed together, but after the death of the body his mind may continue to exist and function.

Human bodies are in space and are subject to the mechanical laws which govern all other bodies in space. Bodily processes and states can be inspected by external observers. So a man's bodily life is as much a public affair as are the lives of animals and reptiles and even as the careers of trees, crystals and planets.

But minds are not in space, nor are their operations subject to mechanical laws. The workings of one mind are not witnessable by other observers; its career is private. Only I can take direct cognisance of the states and processes of my own mind. A person

therefore lives through two collateral histories, one consisting of what happens in and to his body, the other consisting of what happens in and to his mind. The first is public, the second private. The events in the first history are events in the physical world, those in the second are events in the mental world.

It has been disputed whether a person does or can directly monitor all or only some of the episodes of his own private history; but, according to the official doctrine, of at least some of these episodes he has direct and unchallengeable cognisance. In consciousness, self-consciousness and introspection he is directly and authentically apprised of the present states and operations of his mind. He may have great or small uncertainties about concurrent and adjacent episodes in the physical world, but he can have none about at least part of what is momentarily occupying his mind.

It is customary to express this bifurcation of his two lives and of his two worlds by saying that the things and events which belong to the physical world, including his own body, are external, while the workings of his own mind are internal. This antithesis of outer and inner is of course meant to be construed as a metaphor, since minds, not being in space, could not be described as being spatially inside anything else, or as having things going on spatially inside themselves. But relapses from this good intention are common and theorists are found speculating how stimuli, the physical sources of which are yards or miles outside a person's skin, can generate mental responses inside his skull, or how decisions framed inside his cranium can set going movements of his extremities.

Even when 'inner' and 'outer' are construed as metaphors, the problem how a person's mind and body

---

[*] This is the first chapter of Ryle's book *The Concept of Mind*, published in 1949 (London: Routledge and Chicago: The University of Chicago Press) and copyright © 1984. Reproduced by permission of Taylor & Francis Books UK.

[†] See Descartes's *Meditations on First Philosophy* in the Epistemology chapter of this volume, especially the Second and Sixth Meditations.

[‡] The term "idiot" here comes from out-of-date clinical terminology where it means someone so mentally deficient as to be permanently incapable of rational conduct; it was often defined as a person having a "mental age" below three years.

influence one another is notoriously charged with theoretical difficulties. What the mind wills, the legs, arms and the tongue execute; what affects the ear and the eye has something to do with what the mind perceives; grimaces and smiles betray the mind's moods and bodily castigations* lead, it is hoped, to moral improvement. But the actual transactions between the episodes of the private history and those of the public history remain mysterious, since by definition they can belong to neither series. They could not be reported among the happenings described in a person's autobiography of his inner life, but nor could they be reported among those described in someone else's biography of that person's overt career. They can be inspected neither by introspection nor by laboratory experiment. They are theoretical shuttlecocks which are forever being bandied from the physiologist back to the psychologist and from the psychologist back to the physiologist.

Underlying this partly metaphorical representation of the bifurcation of a person's two lives there is a seemingly more profound and philosophical assumption. It is assumed that there are two different kinds of existence or status. What exists or happens may have the status of physical existence, or it may have the status of mental existence. Somewhat as the faces of coins are either heads or tails, or somewhat as living creatures are either male or female, so, it is supposed, some existing is physical existing, other existing is mental existing. It is a necessary feature of what has physical existence that it is in space and time; it is a necessary feature of what has mental existence that is in time but not in space. What has physical existence is composed of matter, or else is a function of matter; what has mental existence consists of consciousness, or else is a function of consciousness.

There is thus a polar opposition between mind and matter, an opposition which is often brought out as follows. Material objects are situated in a common field, known as "space", and what happens to one body in one part of space is mechanically connected with what happens to other bodies in other parts of space. But mental happenings occur in insulated fields, known as "minds", and there is, apart maybe from telepathy, no direct causal connexion between what happens in one mind and what happens in another. Only through the medium of the public physical world can the mind of one person make a difference to the mind of another. The mind is its own place and in his inner life each of us lives the life of a ghostly Robinson Crusoe.† People can see, hear and jolt one another's bodies, but they are irremediably blind and deaf to the workings of one another's minds and inoperative upon them.

What sort of knowledge can be secured of the workings of a mind? On the one side, according to the official theory, a person has direct knowledge of the best imaginable kind of the workings of his own mind. Mental states and processes are (or are normally) conscious states and processes, and the consciousness which irradiates them can engender no illusions and leaves the door open for no doubts. A person's present thinkings, feelings and willings, his perceivings, rememberings and imaginings are intrinsically 'phosphorescent'; their existence and their nature are inevitably betrayed to their owner. The inner life is a stream of consciousness of such a sort that it would be absurd to suggest that the mind whose life is that stream might be unaware of what is passing down it.

True, the evidence adduced recently by Freud‡ seems to show that there exist channels tributary to this stream, which run hidden from their owner. People are actuated§ by impulses the existence of which they vigorously disavow; some of their thoughts differ from the thoughts which they acknowledge; and some of the actions which they think they will to perform they do not really will. They are thoroughly gulled¶ by

---

* "Castigation" means "severe punishment."
† Protagonist of a 1719 novel by Daniel Defoe who spends many years alone on a desert island after being shipwrecked.
‡ Sigmund Freud (1856–1939) was an Austrian psychologist and the main founder of psychoanalysis. One of his central ideas was that the motives for human action are far more numerous and complex than is commonly thought, and that our most basic and constant motives—which result from various significant experiences throughout our life, and particularly in early childhood—are unconscious in the sense that it is difficult for us to acknowledge them and so we "repress" them.
§ Caused to act.
¶ Tricked or fooled.

some of their own hypocrisies and they successfully ignore facts about their mental lives which on the official theory ought to be patent to them. Holders of the official theory tend, however, to maintain that anyhow in normal circumstances a person must be directly and authentically seized of the present state and workings of his own mind.

Besides being currently supplied with these alleged immediate data of consciousness, a person is also generally supposed to be able to exercise from time to time a special kind of perception, namely inner perception, or introspection. He can take a (non-optical) 'look' at what is passing in his mind. Not only can he view and scrutinize a flower through his sense of sight and listen to and discriminate the notes of a bell through his sense of hearing; he can also reflectively or introspectively watch, without any bodily organ of sense, the current episodes of his inner life. This self-observation is also commonly supposed to be immune from illusion, confusion or doubt. A mind's reports of its own affairs have a certainty superior to the best that is possessed by its reports of matters in the physical world. Sense-perceptions can, but consciousness and introspection cannot, be mistaken or confused.

On the other side, one person has no direct access of any sort to the events of the inner life of another. He cannot do better than make problematic inferences from the observed behaviour of the other person's body to the states of mind which, by analogy from his own conduct, he supposes to be signalized by that behaviour. Direct access to the workings of a mind is the privilege of that mind itself; in default of such privileged access, the workings of one mind are inevitably occult* to everyone else. For the supposed arguments from bodily movements similar to their own to mental workings similar to their own would lack any possibility of observational corroboration. Not unnaturally, therefore, an adherent of the official theory finds it difficult to resist this consequence of his premisses, that he has no good reason to believe that there do exist minds other than his own. Even if he prefers to believe that to other human bodies there are harnessed minds not unlike his own, he cannot claim to be able to discover their individual characteristics, or the particular things that they undergo and do. Absolute solitude is on this showing the ineluctable destiny of the soul. Only our bodies can meet.

As a necessary corollary of this general scheme there is implicitly prescribed a special way of construing our ordinary concepts of mental powers and operations. The verbs, nouns and adjectives, with which in ordinary life we describe the wits, characters and higher-grade performances of the people with whom we have to do, are required to be construed as signifying special episodes in their secret histories, or else as signifying tendencies for such episodes to occur. When someone is described as knowing, believing or guessing something, as hoping dreading, intending or shirking something, as designing thus or being amused at that, these verbs are supposed to denote the occurrence of specific modifications in his (to us) occult stream of consciousness. Only his own privileged access to this stream in direct awareness and introspection could provide authentic testimony that these mental-conduct verbs were correctly or incorrectly applied. The onlooker, be he teacher, critic, biographer or friend, can never assure himself that his comments have any vestige of truth. Yet it was just because we do in fact all know how to make such comments, make them with general correctness and correct them when they turn out to be confused or mistaken, that philosophers found it necessary to construct their theories of the nature and place of minds. Finding mental-conduct concepts being regularly and effectively used, they properly sought to fix their logical geography. But the logical geography officially recommended would entail that there could be no regular or effective use of these mental-conduct concepts in our descriptions of, and prescriptions for, other people's minds.

(2) *The Absurdity of the Official Doctrine*

Such in outline is the official theory. I shall often speak of it, with deliberate abusiveness, as "the dogma of the Ghost in the Machine". I hope to prove that it is entirely false, and false not in detail but in principle. It is not merely an assemblage of particular mistakes. It is one big mistake and a mistake of a special kind. It

---

* Ryle does not literally mean "supernatural," but hidden from human view or beyond the normal range of human knowledge. (The word comes from the Latin for "secret" or "covered over.")

is, namely, a category-mistake. It represents the facts of mental life as if they belonged to one logical type or category (or range of types or categories), when they actually belong to another. The dogma is therefore a philosopher's myth. In attempting to explode the myth I shall probably be taken to be denying well-known facts about the mental life of human beings, and my plea that I aim at doing nothing more than rectify the logic of mental-conduct concepts will probably be disallowed as mere subterfuge.

I must first indicate what is meant by the phrase "Category-mistake". This I do in a series of illustrations.

A foreigner visiting Oxford or Cambridge* for the first time is shown a number of colleges, libraries, playing fields, museums, scientific departments and administrative offices. He then asks "But where is the University? I have seen where the members of the Colleges live, where the Registrar works, where the scientists experiment and the rest. But I have not yet seen the University in which reside and work the members of your University." It has then to be explained to him that the University is not another collateral institution, some ulterior counterpart to the colleges, laboratories and offices which he has seen. The University is just the way in which all that he has already seen is organized. When they are seen and when their coordination is understood, the University has been seen. His mistake lay in his innocent assumption that it was correct to speak of Christ Church, the Bodleian Library, the Ashmolean Museum† and the University, to speak, that is, as if "the University" stood for an extra member of the class of which these other units are members. He was mistakenly allocating the University to the same category as that to which the other institutions belong.

The same mistake would be made by a child witnessing the march-past of a division, who, having had pointed out to him such and such battalions, batteries, squadrons, etc., asked when the division was going to appear. He would be supposing that a division was a counterpart to the units already seen, partly similar to

them and partly unlike them. He would be shown his mistake by being told that in watching the battalions, batteries and squadrons marching past he had been watching the division matching past. The march past was not a parade of battalions, batteries, squadrons *and* a division; it was a parade of the battalions, batteries and squadrons *of* a division.

One more illustration. A foreigner watching his first game of cricket learns what are the functions of the bowlers, the batsmen, the fielders, the umpires and the scorers. He then says "But there is no one left on the field to contribute the famous element of team-spirit. I see who does the bowling, the batting and the wicket-keeping, but I do not see whose role it is to exercise *esprit de corps*." Once more, it would have to be explained that he was looking for the wrong type of thing. Team-spirit is not another cricketing-operation supplementary to all of the other special tasks. It is, roughly, the keenness with which each of the special tasks is performed, and performing a task keenly is not performing two tasks. Certainly exhibiting team spirit is not the same thing as bowling or catching, but nor is it a third thing such that we can say that the bowler first bowls *and* then exhibits team-spirit or that a fielder is at a given moment *either* catching *or* displaying *esprit de corps*.

These illustrations of category-mistakes have a common feature which must be noticed. The mistakes were made by people who did not know how to wield the concepts *University*, *division* and *team-spirit*. Their puzzles arose from inability to use certain items in the English vocabulary.

The theoretically interesting category-mistakes are those made by people who are perfectly competent to apply concepts, at least in the situations with which they are familiar, but are still liable in their abstract thinking to allocate those concepts to logical types to which they do not belong. An instance of a mistake of this sort would be the following story. A student of politics has learned the main differences between the British, the French, and the American

---

* Oxford and Cambridge, unlike most modern universities, are not single, unified institutions but consist of collections of 30 or 40 independent colleges and their facilities, plus a few general university buildings used by all the colleges, such as the Examination Schools at Oxford. One consequence of this is that neither Oxford nor Cambridge have a campus or even a central "University" building, but are spread out in various buildings across their respective towns.

† Christ Church College, the Bodleian, and the Ashmolean are all institutions at Oxford.

Constitutions, and has learned also the differences and connexions between the Cabinet, Parliament, the various Ministries, the Judicature and the Church of England. But he still became embarrassed when asked questions about the connexions between the Church of England, the Home Office and the British Constitution. For while the Church and the Home Office are institutions, the British Constitution is not another institution in the same sense of that noun. So inter-institutional relations which can be asserted or denied to hold between the Church and the Home Office cannot be asserted or denied to hold between either of them and the British Constitution. "The British Constitution" is not a term of the same logical type as "the Home Office" and "the Church of England". In a partially similar way, John Doe may be a relative, a friend, an enemy or a stranger to Richard Roe; but he cannot be any of these things to the Average Taxpayer. He knows how to talk sense in certain sorts of discussions about the Average Taxpayer, but he is baffled to say why he could not come across him in the street as he can come across Richard Roe.

It is pertinent to our main subject to notice that, so long as the student of politics continues to think of the British Constitution as a counterpart to the other institutions, he will tend to describe it as a mysteriously occult institution, and so long as John Doe continues to think of the Average Taxpayer as a fellow-citizen, he will tend to think of him as an elusive insubstantial man, a ghost who is everywhere yet nowhere.

My destructive purpose is to show that a family of radical category-mistakes is the source of the double-life theory. The representation of a person as a ghost mysteriously ensconced in a machine derives from this argument. Because, as is true, a person's thinking, feeling and purposive doing cannot be described solely in the idioms of physics, chemistry and physiology, therefore they must be described in counterpart idioms. As the human body is a complex organized unit, so the human mind must be another complex organized unit, though one made of a different sort of stuff and with a different sort of structure. Or, again, as the human body, like any other parcel of matter, is a field

of causes and effects, so the mind must be another field of causes and effects, though not (Heaven be praised) mechanical causes and effects.

(3) *The Origin of the Category-Mistake*

One of the chief intellectual origins of what I have yet to prove to be the Cartesian category-mistake seems to be this. When Galileo showed that his methods of scientific discovery were competent to provide a mechanical theory which should cover every occupant of space, Descartes found in himself two conflicting motives. As a man of scientific genius he could not but endorse the claims of mechanics, yet as a religious and moral man he could not accept, as Hobbes* accepted, the discouraging rider to those claims, namely that human nature differs only in degree of complexity from clockwork. The mental could not be just a variety of the mechanical.

He and subsequent philosophers naturally but erroneously availed themselves of the following escape-route. Since mental-conduct words are not to be construed as signifying the occurrence of mechanical processes, they must be construed as signifying the occurrence of non-mechanical processes; since mechanical laws explain movements in space as the effects of other movements in space, other laws must explain some of the non-spatial workings of minds as the effects of other non-spatial workings of minds. The difference between the human behaviours which we describe as intelligent and those which we describe as unintelligent must be a difference in their causation; so, while some movements of human tongues and limbs are the effects of mechanical causes, others must be the effects of non-mechanical causes, i.e., some issue from movements of particles of matter, others from workings of the mind.

The differences between the physical and the mental were thus represented as differences inside the common framework of the categories of "thing", "stuff", "attribute", "state", "process", "change", "cause" and "effect". Minds are things, but different sorts of things from bodies; mental processes are causes and

---

* Thomas Hobbes (1588–1679), English philosopher. He is best known for his political treatise *Leviathan*, but his work ranged widely in other areas. A thoroughgoing physicalist about mind, he alienated his sometime acquaintance Descartes by writing critical comments on his work.

effects, but different sorts of causes and effects from bodily movements. And so on. Somewhat as the foreigner expected the University to be an extra edifice, rather like a college but also considerably different, so the repudiators of mechanism represented minds as extra centres of causal processes, rather like machines but also considerably different from them. Their theory was a para-mechanical hypothesis.

That this assumption was at the heart of the doctrine is shown by the fact that there was from the beginning felt to be a major theoretical difficulty in explaining how minds can influence and be influenced by bodies. How can a mental process, such as willing, cause spatial movements like the movements of the tongue? How can a physical change in the optic nerve have among its effects a mind's perception of a flash of light? This notorious crux* by itself shows the logical mould into which Descartes pressed his theory of the mind. It was the self-same mould into which he and Galileo set their mechanics. Still unwittingly adhering to the grammar of mechanics, he tried to avert disaster by describing minds in what was merely an obverse† vocabulary. The workings of minds had to be described by the mere negatives of the specific descriptions given to bodies; they are not in space, they are not motions, they are not modifications of matter, they are not accessible to public observation. Minds are not bits of clockwork, they are just bits of not-clockwork.

As thus represented, minds are not merely ghosts harnessed to machines, they are themselves just spectral machines. Though the human body is an engine, it is not quite an ordinary engine, since some of its workings are governed by another engine inside it— this interior governor-engine being one of a very special sort. It is invisible, inaudible and it has no size or weight. It cannot be taken to bits and the laws it obeys are not those known to ordinary engineers. Nothing is known of how it governs the bodily engine.

A second major crux points the same moral. Since, according to the doctrine, minds belong to the same category as bodies and since bodies are rigidly governed by mechanical laws, it seemed to many theorists to follow that minds must be similarly governed by rigid non-mechanical laws. The physical world is a deterministic system, so the mental world must be a deterministic system. Bodies cannot help the modifications that they undergo, so minds cannot help pursuing the careers fixed for them. *Responsibility, choice, merit* and *demerit* are therefore inapplicable concepts— unless the compromise solution is adopted of saying that the laws governing mental processes, unlike those governing physical processes, have the congenial attribute of being only rather rigid. The problem of the Freedom of the Will was the problem how to reconcile the hypothesis that minds are to be described in terms drawn from the categories of mechanics with the knowledge that higher-grade human conduct is not of a piece with the behaviour of machines.

It is an historical curiosity that it was not noticed that the entire argument was broken-backed. Theorists correctly assumed that any sane man could already recognize the differences between, say, rational and non-rational utterances or between purposive and automatic behaviour. Else there would have been nothing requiring to be salved from mechanism. Yet the explanation given presupposed that one person could in principle never recognize the difference between the rational and the irrational utterances issuing from other human bodies, since he could never get access to the postulated immaterial causes of some of their utterances. Save for the doubtful exception of himself, he could never tell the difference between a man and a Robot. It would have to be conceded, for example, that, for all that we can tell, the inner lives of persons who are classed as idiots or lunatics are as rational as those of anyone else. Perhaps only their overt behaviour is disappointing; that is to say, perhaps "idiots" are not really idiotic, or "lunatics" lunatic. Perhaps, too, some of those who are classed as sane are really idiots. According to the theory, external observers could never know how the overt behaviour of others is correlated with their mental powers and processes and so they could never know or even plausibly conjecture whether their applications of mental-conduct concepts to these other people were correct or incorrect. It would then be hazardous or impossible

---

* The crux of a question is its most basic, critical, or deeply puzzling feature. (This term probably comes from the Medieval Latin phrase *crux interpretum*, or "torment of interpreters.")

† A thing's obverse is its complement or counterpart: e.g., the obverse of black is white, and the obverse of front is back.

for a man to claim sanity or logical consistency even for himself, since he would be debarred from comparing his own performances with those of others. In short, our characterizations of persons and their performances as intelligent, prudent and virtuous or as stupid, hypocritical and cowardly could never have been made, so the problem of providing a special causal hypothesis to serve as the basis of such diagnoses would never have arisen. The question, "How do persons differ from machines?" arose just because everyone already knew how to apply mental-conduct concepts before the new causal hypothesis was introduced. This causal hypothesis could not therefore be the source of the criteria used in those applications. Nor, of course, has the causal hypothesis in any degree improved our handling of those criteria. We still distinguish good from bad arithmetic, politic* from impolitic conduct and fertile from infertile imaginations in the ways in which Descartes himself distinguished them before and after he speculated how the applicability of these criteria was compatible with the principle of mechanical causation.

He had mistaken the logic of his problem. Instead of asking by what criteria intelligent behaviour is actually distinguished from non-intelligent behaviour, he asked "Given that the principle of mechanical causation does not tell us the difference, what other causal principle will tell it us?" He realized that the problem was not one of mechanics and assumed that it must therefore be one of some counterpart to mechanics. Not unnaturally psychology is often cast for just this role.

When two terms belong to the same category, it is proper to construct conjunctive† propositions embodying them. Thus a purchaser may say that he bought a left-hand glove and a right-hand glove, but not that he bought a left-hand glove, a right-hand glove and a pair of gloves. "She came home in a flood of tears and a sedan-chair"‡ is a well known joke based on the absurdity of conjoining terms of different types. It would have been equally ridiculous to construct the

disjunction. "She came home either in a flood of tears or else in a sedan-chair." Now the dogma of the Ghost in the Machine does just this. It maintains that there exist both bodies and minds; that there occur physical processes and mental processes; that there are mechanical causes of corporeal movements and mental causes of corporeal movements. I shall argue that these and other analogous conjunctions are absurd; but, it must be noticed, the argument will not show that either of the illegitimately conjoined propositions is absurd in itself. I am not, for example, denying that there occur mental processes. Doing long division is a mental process and so is making a joke. But I am saying that the phrase "there occur mental processes" does not mean the same sort of thing as "there occur physical processes", and, therefore, that it makes no sense to conjoin or disjoin the two.

If my argument is successful, there will follow some interesting consequences. First, the hallowed contrast between Mind and Matter will be dissipated, but dissipated not by either of the equally hallowed absorptions of Mind by Matter or of Matter by Mind, but in quite a different way. For the seeming contrast of the two will be shown to be as illegitimate as would be the contrast of "she came home in a flood of tears" and "she came home in a sedan-chair". The belief that there is a polar opposition between Mind and Matter is the belief that they are terms of the same logical type.

It will also follow that both Idealism and Materialism are answers to an improper question. The "reduction" of the material world to mental states and processes, as well as the "reduction" of mental states and processes to physical states and processes, presupposes the legitimacy of the disjunction "Either there exist minds or there exist bodies (but not both)". It would be like saying, "Either she bought a left-hand and right-hand glove or she bought a pair of gloves (but not both)".

It is perfectly proper to say, in one logical tone of voice, that there exist minds, and to say, in another

---

* Judicious, careful.

† A conjunction is an 'and' statement (e.g., "It's 2 AM and you're past curfew"); a disjunction is an 'or' sentence (e.g., "Either he's drunk or very nervous").

‡ Charles Dickens, *The Pickwick Papers*. A sedan chair is an enclosed chair carried on horizontal poles by two or four porters. This form of transport was common in Europe in the seventeenth and eighteenth centuries.

logical tone of voice, that there exist bodies. But these expressions do not indicate two different species of existence, for "existence" is not a generic word like "coloured" or "sexed". They indicate two different senses of "exist", somewhat as "rising" has different senses in "the tide is rising", "hopes are rising", and "the average age of death is rising". A man would be thought to be making a poor joke who said that three things are now rising, namely the tide, hopes and the average age of death. It would be just as good or bad a joke to say that there exist prime numbers and Wednesdays and public opinions and navies; or that there exist both minds and bodies. In the succeeding chapters I try to prove that the official theory does rest on a batch of category-mistakes by showing that logically absurd corollaries follow from it. The exhibition of these absurdities will have the constructive effect of bringing out part of the correct logic of mental-conduct concepts.

(4) Historical Note

It would not be true to say that the official theory derives solely from Descartes' theories, or even from a more widespread anxiety about the implications of seventeenth-century mechanics. Scholastic and Reformation theology* had schooled the intellects of the scientists as well as of the laymen, philosophers and clerics of that age. Stoic-Augustinian† theories of the will were embedded in the Calvinist‡ doctrines of sin and grace; Platonic and Aristotelian theories of the intellect shaped the orthodox doctrines of the immortality of the soul. Descartes was reformulating already prevalent theological doctrines of the soul in the new syntax of Galileo. The theologian's privacy of conscience became the philosopher's privacy of consciousness, and what had been the bogy of Predestination reappeared as the bogy of Determinism.§

It would also not be true to say that the two-worlds myth did no theoretical good. Myths often do a lot of theoretical good, while they are still new. One benefit bestowed by the para-mechanical myth was that it partly superannuated¶ the then prevalent para-political myth. Minds and their Faculties had previously been described by analogies with political superiors and political subordinates. The idioms used were those of ruling, obeying, collaborating and rebelling. They survived and still survive in many ethical and some epistemological discussions. As, in physics, the new myth of occult Forces was a scientific improvement on the old myth of Final Causes, so, in anthropological and psychological theory, the new myth of hidden operations, impulses and agencies was an improvement on the old myth of dictations, deferences and disobediences. ■

---

* Scholasticism was the educational tradition of the medieval universities and a system of thought which brought together Catholic doctrine with elements of classical Greek philosophy. The Reformation was a sixteenth-century movement to reform the Roman Catholic church which resulted in the establishment of the Protestant churches.

† Stoicism is an ancient philosophical system (founded by Zeno of Citium in about 300 BCE) which held, among other things, that the virtuous will should be brought into harmony with *logos*—the rational nature of things, or God. It had a great influence on early Christian thinkers, including Saint Augustine (354–430 CE), who defended the view that humans have free control of their will and so are responsible for their own sin.

‡ Calvinism is the theology of John Calvin (1509–64) and his followers. One of its central doctrines is that human actions are predetermined by God and that we are all sinners, but that God has bestowed his grace on some believers, allowing them to be redeemed by faith.

§ Predestination is the view that God has already decided, at the beginning of time, for every soul whether it will be saved or damned. (The theological problem then is: what use are faith or good works if our fate is already sealed?) Determinism is the thesis that all events or situations are determined or fixed by prior events or states of affairs: for example, the current situation of a physical particle might be said to be wholly determined by all its previous positions and interactions with other particles. (See the Free Will chapter of this volume.)

¶ Set aside; withdrew from active use.

Suggestions for Critical Reflection

1. Ryle's central conceptual tool in his critique of the doctrine of the ghost in the machine is the notion of a *category mistake*. How clear is this notion? Is it precise enough to do the job Ryle wants it to do?

2. Do you think that what Ryle describes as the "official doctrine" is now defunct? Should it be? Does Ryle persuade you that it is absurd?

3. A big part of Ryle's assault on the ghost in the machine is his attack on the "causal hypothesis." How radical would it be if we abandoned this view of the mind as "para-mechanical"? What consequences would this have for our understanding of the mind and human action?

4. On the basis of the evidence available in this reading, how behavioristic do you think Ryle is? How much does what he has to say about what the mind is *not* tell us about what he thinks the mind *is*? (This is, by the way, just an excerpt from his book. He does go on to try to say what the mind is.)

5. Ryle once said, "science talks about the world, while philosophy talks about talk about the world."* How much, if at all, does his admitted ignorance of psychology and neuroscience harm Ryle's arguments about the nature of the mind? What does your answer to this question suggest about the nature of philosophy?

---

* "Logic and Professor Anderson," *Australasian Journal of Philosophy* 28 (1950): 151.

NED BLOCK

FROM *Troubles with Functionalism*

Who Is Ned Block?

Ned Block is the Silver Professor of Philosophy, Psychology and Neural Science at New York University. Born in Chicago in 1942, he studied under Hilary Putnam, the famous philosopher of mind and one of the key originators of functionalism, at Harvard, where he received his PhD in 1971. He then taught at MIT until his move to NYU in 1996. Block is the author of scores of papers—several very influential—and the recipient of many prizes and honors. Across his career, his work stands out for its synthesis of philosophical and scientific approaches to the mind. Some of the key themes and arguments for which Block's work is most known appear in this reading, including the view that the phenomenal character of experiences—what they feel like—outstrips any functional or cognitive facts. This paper is also a good illustration of Block's role as the inventor of "some of the most memorable and powerful thought experiments in philosophy."*

What Is the Structure of This Reading?

Block is interested in three theories of what the mind is: (1) behaviorism—which says that having a mind is really nothing more nor less than tending to behave in particular ways under certain conditions; (2) physicalism—which is the position that mental properties are really complex neural properties; and (3) functionalism—which denies that mental states are either behavioral dispositions or neural states and holds instead that they are something more like input-output functions, perhaps rather like the input-output functions one might find in a computer program. By the time Block was writing, in the mid-1970s, it seemed that functionalism had decisively superseded both behaviorism and physicalism. One of the influential contributions of this paper is the way that Block lays out some key variants of functionalism—machine

functionalism, a priori functionalism, and psychofunctionalism—in a way that is helpful in getting a sense of what the theory actually is.

However, Block argues in this reading that functionalism is unlikely to be a true theory, as it suffers from problems that are analogous to those that functionalists identified in behaviorism and physicalism. Functionalists accuse behaviorists of what Block calls "liberalism": that is, being committed by their theory to ascribing mental states to entities that we are pretty sure do not have them (i.e., to things that merely *behave as if* they have a mind). Since behaviorism gives us false results, the argument goes, it cannot be a true theory. Conversely, functionalists accuse physicalists of what Block calls "chauvinism": that is, being committed by their theory to *denying* mental states to entities that we are sure *do* have them (i.e., thinking things that do not have typical human brains). The promise of functionalism, once the theory is properly formulated, is to hit the sweet spot between liberalism and chauvinism: that is, to be a theory that fits the facts. But Block's main conclusion in this reading is that no version of functionalism will be able to thread that needle.

This reading has the following structure:

i. Block defines functionalism, compares it to behaviorism and physicalism, and describes two important choice-points for the functionalist: machine vs. nonmachine functionalism, and analytic vs. empirical functionalism.

ii. In section 1.2 he mounts an argument to show that functionalism is too liberal: that it classifies systems—homunculi-headed robots—that lack mentality as having mentality. Two things are worth highlighting about this section. First, although Block uses the example of machine functionalism as the target of his criticism, he thinks his argument will apply against any form of functionalism.

---

* Philip Goff, "Consciousness, Function, and Representation: Collected Papers, by Ned Block," *Mind* 121 (2012): 780–84.

And second, Block identifies a specific reason why homunculi-headed robots do not have minds, even though functionalism says they should, and that is because they lack qualia (that is, subjective phenomenal experiences such as the taste of a banana or the smell of coffee): he calls this the Absent Qualia objection.

iii. Our selection then jumps to section 1.6 of Block's paper, where he tries to go beyond appealing to the intuitions we have about his thought-experiments, and attacks capital-F Functionalism more directly. In the portion included here, Block suggests that there is only one actual argument for the truth of Functionalism: that commonsense claims (platitudes) about mental states can be analyzed into claims about the relationship between sensory inputs, internal states, and behavioral outputs. But Block argues that we could break the relationship between the inputs-plus-inner-states and the behavioral outputs and yet still be committed to the occurrence of the relevant mental state (e.g., pain), and so no such analysis could be correct.

iv. We then skip to section 2.2, where Block directly attacks Psychofunctionalism by arguing that this version of functionalism, while it may fare better than Functionalism as a theory of nonqualitative mental states (such as beliefs or memories), is unable to explain qualitative mental states (qualia).

v. In section 3.1, Block continues his critique of Psychofunctionalism by arguing that, although it does a better job than Functionalism in avoiding liberalism, it is too closely tied to actual scientific theories of human psychology to avoid the danger of chauvinism, unless some principled theory of 'universal psychology' can be developed.

vi. Finally, in the last section of the paper, Block raises "the problem of the inputs and the outputs": this ultimate argument applies generally to all possible forms of functionalism (according to Block), and Block concludes that "I, for one, do not see how functionalism can describe inputs and outputs without falling afoul of either liberalism or chauvinism, or abandoning the original project of characterizing mentality in nonmental terms."

Some Useful Background Information

1. Block uses the term 'physicalism' in this reading in a particular way. In general, physicalism is the view that everything that exists is physical—that there are no non-physical things such a ghosts or souls. Block, however, has a more specific notion of physicalism in mind—that he calls *type physicalism*—which is the view that every type of thing, every property or kind, is a physical property or kind. In particular, on this view, if mental properties such as *being in pain* or *believing that dogs are mammals* are real properties at all, then they must turn out to be exactly the same properties as some complex physical property, such as undergoing neuronal activity with electrochemical profile X. This is important because functionalism is inconsistent with type physicalism, but not *token* physicalism—the view that each individual event is a physical event. So a functionalist would deny that kinds of mental events—e.g., beliefs that dogs are mammals—are not kinds of physical events, while still believing that each particular belief is a physical event (of some kind or other). In fact, most functionalists are token physicalists.

2. Block's description of functionalism makes use of the notion of a "Turing Machine." A Turing Machine is an abstract computing device named after Alan Turing, the British logician and mathematician who came up with the idea in 1936. It operates on an indefinitely long tape divided into squares which it 'rolls' along, scanning the square that is directly below it. Each square may contain a symbol from a finite alphabet, and when the machine reads a symbol (or detects the absence of a symbol) it is triggered to perform an action: the symbol on the tape can therefore be thought of as the input to the machine. In addition to reading these inputs, a Turing Machine is also capable of occupying any of a finite number of internal states. What action the machine will perform on any particular occasion is determined by these two things: the input, and the machine's current internal state. A Turing Machine can be programmed to perform two types of actions. It can change its internal state. Or it can produce some 'output': it can move one square to the left or right, or it can erase what

is on the input square, or it can write a symbol on the square.

Here is an example of a program for a Turing Machine (which starts in state S_1) telling it to count to three.

	q_0	q_1
S_1	$q_1 S_1$	L S_2
S_2	$q_1 S_2$	L S_3
S_3	$q_1 S_3$	H

All the possible internal states for our very simple machine are listed on the left and the possible inputs (symbols on the tape) are in the top row. The other cells describe what actions the machine will take for every combination of input and internal state. Suppose the machine starts in internal state S_1. Then, if it looks at the square below it and sees a blank—input q_0—it will produce output q_1 (i.e., write the symbol "1" on the tape) and stay in internal state S_1. On the other hand, if it had seen a 1 already written on the square, it would produce output L (i.e., move one square to the left) and go into internal state S_2. In state S_2, seeing a blank square it would write 1 and stay in S_2; while detecting a 1 already written would

cause it to move to the left without writing anything and to change its internal state to S_3; and so on. Following this program, as long as it is started in state S_1, the Turing Machine will produce a line of exactly three 1s and then halt its operation (output H).

A table of the type written above, which lays out the program for a Turing Machine, is called a Machine Table (or, sometimes, a State Table).

3. The difference between Functionalism and Psychofunctionalism can be thought of in terms of operationalizing the terms of either a common-sense psychological theory—the theory tacitly presupposed by everyday terms such as 'belief,' 'memory,' 'pain,' 'jealousy,' and so on—or of our best scientific theory of psychology, which might in principle use quite different categories. Capital-F Functionalism begins from the assumption that beliefs exist, for example, in more or less the way we currently think and speak about them, and then sets out to provide a functional analysis of 'belief' in terms of what beliefs do, i.e., what role they play, what causes them and what they in turn cause. By contrast, Psychofunctionalism begins from our best scientific theory of brains and behavior, and will identify mental states with whatever causal structures that theory tells us exist.

FROM *Troubles with Functionalism*[*]

The functionalist approach to the philosophy of mind is increasingly popular; indeed, it may now be dominant…. However, "functionalist" theories are the products of a number of rather different projects: attempts to reformulate logical behaviorism to avoid objections, attempts to exploit mind-machine analogies, attempts to apply empirical psychology to philosophy of mind, and attempts to argue for—or against—mental-neurological identity theses. Thus, though theories called 'functionalist' have a certain obvious family resemblance, it should not be surprising if there is no single doctrine about the nature of mind that all so-called functionalists share….

One characterization of functionalism that is probably vague enough to be accepted by most functionalists is: each type of mental state is a state consisting of a disposition to act in certain ways *and to have certain mental states*, given certain sensory inputs and certain mental states. So put, functionalism can be seen as a new incarnation of behaviorism. Behaviorism identifies mental states with dispositions to act in certain ways in certain input situations. But as critics have pointed out (Chisholm, 1957; Putnam, 1963), desire for goal G cannot be identified with, say, the disposition to do A in input circumstances in which A leads to G, since, after

---

[*] Ned Block, "Troubles with Functionalism," *Minnesota Studies in the Philosophy of Science* 9 (1978): 261–325.

all, the agent might not *know* A leads to G and thus might not be disposed to do A. Functionalism replaces behaviorism's "sensory inputs" with "sensory inputs and mental states"; and functionalism replaces behaviorism's "disposition to act" with "disposition to act and have certain mental states." Functionalists want to individuate mental states causally, and since mental states have mental causes and effects as well as sensory causes and behavioral effects, functionalists individuate mental states partly in terms of causal relations to other mental states. One consequence of this difference between functionalism and behaviorism is that there are organisms that according to behaviorism, have mental states but, according to functionalism, do not have mental states.

So, necessary conditions for mentality that are postulated by functionalism are in one respect stronger than those postulated by behaviorism. According to behaviorism, it is necessary and sufficient for desiring that G that a system be characterized by a certain set (perhaps infinite) of input-output relations; that is, according to behaviorism, a system desires that G just in case a certain set of conditionals of the form 'It will emit O given I' are true of it. According to functionalism, however, a system might have these input-output relations, yet not desire that G; for according to functionalism, whether a system desires that G depends on whether it has internal states which have certain causal relations to other internal states (and to inputs and outputs). Since behaviorism makes no such "internal state" requirement, there are possible systems of which behaviorism affirms and functionalism denies that they have mental states. One way of stating this is that, according to functionalism, behaviorism is guilty of *liberalism*—ascribing mental properties to things that do not in fact have them....

Furthermore, functionalism in both its machine and nonmachine versions* has typically insisted that characterizations of mental states should contain descriptions of inputs and outputs in *physical* language. Armstrong (1968), for example, says,

We may distinguish between 'physical behaviour', which refers to any merely physical action or passion of the body, and 'behaviour proper' which implies relationship to the mind.... Now, if in our formula ["state of the person apt for bringing about a certain sort of behaviour"] 'behaviour' were to mean 'behaviour proper', then we would be giving an account of mental concepts in terms of a concept that already presupposes mentality, which would be circular. So it is clear that in our formula, 'behaviour' must mean 'physical behaviour'. (p. 84)

Therefore, functionalism can be said to "tack down" mental states only at the periphery—i.e., through physical, or at least non-mental, specification of inputs and outputs. One major thesis of this chapter is that, because of this feature, functionalism fails to avoid the sort of problem for which it rightly condemns behaviorism. Functionalism, too, is guilty of liberalism, for much the same reasons as behaviorism. Unlike behaviorism, however, functionalism can naturally be altered to avoid liberalism—but only at the cost of falling into an equally ignominious failing.

The failing I speak of is the one that functionalism shows *physicalism* to be guilty of. By 'physicalism', I mean the doctrine that pain, for example, is identical to a physical (or physiological) state.[1†] As many philosophers have argued (notably Fodor, 1965, and Putnam, 1966; see also Block & Fodor, 1972), if functionalism is true, physicalism is false. The point is at its clearest with regard to Turing-machine[‡] versions of functionalism. Any given abstract Turing machine can be realized by a wide variety of physical devices; indeed, it is plausible that, given any putative correspondence between a Turing-machine state and a configurational physical (or physiological) state, there will be a possible realization of the Turing machine that will provide a counterexample to that correspondence. ... Therefore, if pain is a functional state, it cannot, for example, be a brain state, because creatures without brains can realize the same Turing machine as creatures with brains.

---

* See below, section 1.1.

† In the important endnote at this point, Block explains that what he's calling 'physicalism' is type physicalism, not token physicalism.

‡ See "Some Useful Background Information" above.

I must emphasize that the functionalist argument against physicalism does not appeal merely to the fact that one abstract Turing machine can be realized by systems of different *material composition* (wood, metal, glass, etc.). To argue this way would be like arguing that temperature cannot be a microphysical magnitude because the same temperature can be had by objects with *different* microphysical structures (Kim, 1972). Objects with different microphysical structures, e.g., objects made of wood, metal, glass, etc., can have many interesting microphysical properties in common, such as molecular kinetic energy of the same average value. Rather, the functionalist argument against physicalism is that it is difficult to see how there *could be* a nontrivial first-order* physical property in common to all and only the possible physical realizations of a given Turing-machine state. Try to think of a remotely plausible candidate! At the very least, the onus is on those who think such physical properties are conceivable to show us how to conceive of one.

One way of expressing this point is that, according to functionalism, physicalism is a *chauvinist* theory: it withholds mental properties from systems that in fact have them. In saying mental states are brain states, for example, physicalists unfairly exclude those poor brainless creatures who nonetheless have minds.[†]

A second major point of this paper is that the very argument which functionalism uses to condemn physicalism can be applied equally well against functionalism; indeed, any version of functionalism that avoids liberalism falls, like physicalism, into chauvinism....

1.1 More about What Functionalism Is

One way of providing some order to the bewildering variety of functionalist theories is to distinguish between those that are couched in terms of a Turing machine and those that are not.

A Turing-machine table lists a finite set of machine-table states, $S_1 ... S_n$; inputs, $I_1 ... I_m$; and outputs, $O_1 ... O_p$. The table specifies a set of conditionals of the form: if the machine is in state S_i and receives input I_j, it emits output O_k and goes into state S_l. That is, given any state and input, the table specifies an output and a next state. Any system with a set of inputs, outputs, and states related in the way specified by the table is described by the table and is a realization of the abstract automaton specified by the table....

One very simple version of machine functionalism (Block & Fodor, 1972) states that each system having mental states is described by at least one Turing-machine table of a specifiable sort and that each type of mental state of the system is identical to one of the machine-table states. Consider, for example, the Turing machine described in the accompanying table (cf. Nelson, 1975):

	S_1	S_2
nickel input	Emit no output Go to S_2	Emit a Coke Go to S_1
dime input	Emit a Coke Stay in S_1	Emit a Coke & a nickel Go to S_1

One can get a crude picture of the simple version of machine functionalism by considering the claim that S_1 = dime-desire, and S_2 = nickel-desire. Of course, no functionalist should claim that a Coke machine desires anything. Rather, the simple version of machine functionalism described in the table makes an analogous claim with respect to a much more complex machine table. Notice that machine functionalism specifies inputs and outputs explicitly, internal states implicitly.... To be described by this machine table, a device must accept nickels and dimes as inputs and dispense nickels and Cokes as outputs. But the states S_1 and S_2 can have virtually any natures, so long as those natures connect the states to each other and to the inputs and outputs specified in the machine

---

* A first-order property is one which is a property of an individual but not of other properties, such as tasting sweet or being an aunt. A second-order property is a property of (first-order) properties—e.g., being a color or being a family relationship—a third-order property is defined in terms of second-order properties, and so on.

† Block is not implying that there are humans with minds but no brains. He's saying that a type-physicalist, who identifies particular kinds of mental states with corresponding types of human brain-states, would deny those states to any creature without physical brain setups like humans have—to dogs, for example, or to (imaginary) Martians, who don't have brains at all, but still have beliefs, pains, etc.

table. All we are told about S_1 and S_2 are these relations; thus, in this sense, machine functionalism can be said to reduce mentality to input-output structures. This example should suggest the force of the functionalist argument against physicalism. Try to think of a first-order physical property that can be shared by all (and only) realizations for this machine table!

One can also categorize functionalists in terms of whether they regard functional identities as part of a priori psychology or empirical psychology. (Since this distinction crosscuts the machine/nonmachine distinction, I shall be able to illustrate nonmachine versions of functionalism in what follows.) The a priori functionalists (e.g., Smart, Armstrong, Lewis, Shoemaker) are the heirs of the logical behaviorists. They tend to regard functional analyses as analyses of the meanings of mental terms, whereas the empirical functionalists (e.g., Fodor, Putnam, Harman) regard functional analyses as substantive scientific hypotheses. In what follows, I shall refer to the former view as 'Functionalism' and the latter as 'Psychofunctionalism'. (I shall use 'functionalism' with a lowercase 'f' as neutral between Functionalism and Psychofunctionalism. When distinguishing between Functionalism and Psychofunctionalism, I shall always use capitals.) ...

This difference between Functionalism and Psychofunctionalism gives rise to a difference in specifying inputs and outputs. Functionalists are restricted to specification of inputs and outputs that are plausibly part of common-sense knowledge; Psychofunctionalists are under no such restriction. Although both groups insist on physical—or at least nonmental—specification of inputs and outputs, Functionalists require externally observable classifications (e.g., inputs characterized in terms of objects present in the vicinity of the organism, outputs in terms of movements of body parts). Psychofunctionalists, on the other hand, have the option to specify inputs and outputs in terms of internal parameters, e.g., signals in input and output neurons....

In discussing the various versions of functionalism, I have ... been rather vague about what psychology is supposed to be psychology *of*. Presumably, some animals,

e.g., dogs, are capable of many of the same mental states as humans, e.g., hunger, thirst, other desires, and some beliefs. Thus, if functionalism is true, we must suppose that there is a psychological theory that applies to people and some animals that says what it is in virtue of which both the animals and the people have beliefs, desires, etc. On the other hand, there are mental states people can have that dogs presumably cannot. Further, there may be mental states that some persons can have but others cannot. Some of us can suffer *weltschmerz*,* whereas others, perhaps, cannot. It is possible that there are no basic psychological differences between dogs, persons who can have *weltschmerz*, persons who cannot, etc. Perhaps the gross behavioral differences are due to different values of the same parameters in a single psychological theory that covers all the aforementioned creatures. An analogy: the same theory of nuclear physics covers both reactors and bombs, even though there is a gross difference in their behavior. This is due to different values of a single set of parameters that determine whether or not the reaction is controlled. Perhaps parameters such as information-processing capacity or memory space play the same role in psychology. But this is unlikely for scientific psychology, and it surely is not true for the common-sense psychological theories Functionalism appeals to. Thus, it seems likely that both Functionalism and Psychofunctionalism require psychological theories of different degrees of generality or level of abstraction—one for humans who can have *weltschmerz*, one for all humans, one for dogs and humans, etc. If so, different mental states may be identical to functional states at different abstractness levels. The same point applies to functional-equivalence relations. Two creatures may be functionally equivalent relative to one level of abstractness of psychological theory, but not with respect to another....

1.2 Homunculi-Headed Robots†

In this section I shall describe a class of devices that embarrass all versions of functionalism in that they indicate functionalism is guilty of liberalism—classifying systems that lack mentality as having mentality.

---

* German: world-weariness; depression caused by feeling how much the world falls short of the (romanticized) ideal.

† A homunculus is a tiny human or human-like creature. (The notion originated in sixteenth-century alchemy.) In honor of the author, these kinds of counter-examples to functionalism are sometimes fondly known as 'Blockheads.'

Consider the simple version of machine functionalism already described. It says that each system having mental states is described by at least one Turing-machine table of a certain kind, and each mental state of the system is identical to one of the machine-table states specified by the machine table. I shall consider inputs and outputs to be specified by descriptions of neural impulses in sense organs and motor-output neurons. This assumption should not be regarded as restricting what will be said to Psychofunctionalism rather than Functionalism. As already mentioned, every version of functionalism assumes *some* specification of inputs and outputs. A Functionalist specification would do as well for the purposes of what follows.

Imagine a body externally like a human body, say yours, but internally quite different. The neurons from sensory organs are connected to a bank of lights in a hollow cavity in the head. A set of buttons connects to the motor-output neurons. Inside the cavity resides a group of little men. Each has a very simple task: to implement a "square" of a reasonably adequate machine table that describes you. On one wall is a bulletin board on which is posted a state card, i.e., a card that bears a symbol designating one of the states specified in the machine table. Here is what the little men do: Suppose the posted card has a 'G' on it. This alerts the little men who implement G squares—'G-men' they call themselves.* Suppose the light representing input I_{17} goes on. One of the G-men has the following as his sole task: when the card reads 'G' and the I_{17} light goes on, he presses output button O_{191} and changes the state card to 'M'. This G-man is called upon to exercise his task only rarely. In spite of the low level of intelligence required of each little man, the system as a whole manages to simulate you because the functional organization they have been trained to realize is yours. A Turing machine can be represented as a finite set of quadruples (or quintuples, if the output is divided into two parts)—current state, current input; next state, next output. Each little man has the task corresponding to a single quadruple. Through the

efforts of the little men, the system realizes the same (reasonably adequate) machine table as you do and is thus functionally equivalent to you.

I shall describe a version of the homunculi-headed simulation, which is more clearly nomologically possible.† How many homunculi are required? Perhaps a billion are enough; after all, there are only about a billion neurons in the brain.

Suppose we convert the government of China to functionalism, and we convince its officials that it would enormously enhance their international prestige to realize a human mind for an hour. We provide each of the billion people in China (I chose China because it has a billion inhabitants) with a specially designed two-way radio that connects them in the appropriate way to other persons and to the artificial body mentioned in the previous example. We replace the little men with a radio transmitter and receiver connected to the input and output neurons. Instead of a bulletin board, we arrange to have letters displayed on a series of satellites placed so that they can be seen from anywhere in China. Surely such a system is not physically impossible. It could be functionally equivalent to you for a short time, say an hour. ...

What makes the homunculi-headed system (count the two systems as variants of a single system) just described a prima facie‡ counterexample to (machine) functionalism is that there is prima facie doubt whether it has any mental states at all—especially whether it has what philosophers have variously called "qualitative states," "raw feels," or "immediate phenomenological qualities." (You ask: What is it that philosophers have called qualitative states? I answer, only half in jest: As Louis Armstrong said when asked what jazz is, "If you got to ask, you ain't never gonna get to know."§) In Nagel's terms (1974), there is a prima facie doubt whether there is anything which it is like to be the homunculi-headed system.

The force of the prima facie counterexample can be made clearer as follows: Machine functionalism says that each mental state is identical to a machine-table

---

*   This is a small joke on Block's part: 'G-Man' is a mid-twentieth-century American slang term for Government-men, enforcement agents of the US government, such as FBI agents.
†   "Nomologically possible": consistent with the laws of nature.
‡   Latin: at first sight, before further investigation.
§   Though widely attributed to Louis Armstrong, it was "Fats" Waller who said, when asked to explain jazz, "Lady, if you got to ask, you ain't got it." Quoted in *Washington Post*, 17 July 1947.

state. For example, a particular qualitative state, Q, is identical to a machine-table state, S_q. But if there is nothing it is like to be the homunculi-headed system, it cannot be in Q even when it is in S_q. Thus, if there is prima facie doubt about the homunculi-headed system's mentality, there is prima facie doubt that Q = S_q, i.e., doubt that the kind of functionalism under consideration is true. Call this argument the Absent Qualia* Argument.

So there is prima facie doubt that machine functionalism is true. So what? After all, prima facie doubt is only prima facie. Indeed, appeals to intuition of this sort are notoriously fallible. I shall not rest on this appeal to intuition. Rather, I shall argue that the intuition that the homunculi-headed simulation described above lacks mentality (or at least qualia) has at least in part a rational basis, and that this rational basis provides a good reason for doubting that Functionalism (and to a lesser degree Psychofunctionalism) is true.

...

1.6 Is the Prima Facie Doubt Merely Prima Facie?

The Absent Qualia Argument rested on an appeal to the intuition that the homunculi-headed simulations lacked mentality, or at least qualia. I said that this intuition gave rise to prima facie doubt that functionalism is true. But intuitions unsupported by principled argument are hardly to be considered bedrock. Indeed, intuitions incompatible with well-supported theory (e.g., the pre-Copernican intuition that the earth does not move) thankfully soon disappear. Even fields like linguistics whose data consist mainly in intuitions often reject such intuitions as that the following sentences are ungrammatical (on theoretical grounds):

The horse raced past the barn fell.
The boy the girl the cat bit scratched died.

These sentences are in fact grammatical, though hard to process.[2]

Appeal to intuitions when judging possession of mentality, however, is *especially* suspicious. *No* physical mechanism seems very intuitively plausible as a seat of qualia, least of all a *brain*. Is a hunk of quivering gray stuff more intuitively appropriate as a seat of qualia than a covey of little men? If so, perhaps there is a prima facie doubt about the qualia of brain-headed systems too.

However, there is a very important difference between brain-headed and homunculi-headed systems. Since we know that *we are brain-headed systems*, and that *we* have qualia, we know that brain-headed systems can have qualia. So even though we have no theory of qualia which explains how this is *possible*, we have overwhelming reason to disregard whatever prima facie doubt there is about the qualia of brain-headed systems. Of course, this makes the Absent Qualia Argument partly *empirical*—it depends on knowledge of what makes us tick. But since this is knowledge we in fact possess, dependence on this knowledge should not be regarded as a defect.

There is another difference between us meat-heads and the homunculi-heads: they are systems designed to mimic us, but we are not designed to mimic anything (here I rely on another empirical fact). This fact forestalls any attempt to argue on the basis of an inference to the best explanation for the qualia of homunculi-heads. The best explanation of the homunculi-heads' screams and winces is not their pains, but that they were designed to mimic our screams and winces....

In spite of the widespread belief in forms of Functionalism, I know of only one kind of argument for it in the literature. It is claimed that Functional identities can be shown to be true on the basis of analyses of the meanings of mental terminology. According to this argument, Functional identities are to be justified in the way one might try to justify the claim that the state of being a bachelor is identical to the state of being an unmarried man. A similar argument appeals to commonsense platitudes about mental states instead of truths of meaning. Lewis says that Functional characterizations of mental states are in the province of "common sense psychology—folk

---

* Qualia (which is the plural form of the singular 'quale,' pronounced kwa-lay) are instances of subjective phenomenal consciousness: examples might be the taste of a banana, the smell of coffee, or the softness of a cat's fur—all of these understood as the conscious experience of those things (rather than the actual properties of these items, if there is a difference).

science, rather than professional science" (Lewis, 1972, p. 250....). And he goes on to insist that Functional characterizations should "include only platitudes which are common knowledge among us—everyone knows them, everyone knows that everyone else knows them, and so on" (Lewis, 1972, p. 256). I shall talk mainly about the "platitude" version of the argument. The analyticity version is vulnerable to essentially the same considerations....

Because of the required platitudinous nature of Functional definitions, Functionalism runs into serious difficulties with cases such as paralytics and disembodied brains hooked up to life-support systems. Suppose, for example, that C is a cluster of inputs and mental states which, according to Functionalism, issues in some characteristic behavior, B. We might take C to consist in part in: pain, the desire to be rid of the pain, the belief that an object in front of one is causing the pain, and the belief that the pain can easily be avoided by reverse locomotion. Let B be reverse locomotion. But a paralytic could typically have C without B. It might be objected, "If C typically issues in B, then one of the elements of C would have to be the belief that *B is possible*, but a paralytic would not have this belief." Reply: Imagine a paralytic who does not know he/she is paralyzed and who has the kind of hippocampal lesion that keeps him/her from learning,* or imagine a paralytic whose paralysis is *intermittent*. Surely someone in intense pain who believes the only way to avoid intense pain is by reverse locomotion and who believes he or she *might* be capable of reverse locomotion will (other things equal) attempt to locomote in reverse. This is as platitudinous as any of the platitudes in the Functionalist collection. But in the case of an intermittent paralytic, attempts to locomote in reverse might *typically fail*, and, thus, he/she might typically fail to emit B when in C. Indeed, one can imagine that a disease strikes worldwide, resulting in intermittent paralysis of this sort in all of us, so that *none* of us typically emits B in C.

It would seem that such a turn of events would require Functionalists to suppose that some of the mental states which make up C no longer occur. But this seems very implausible.

This objection is further strengthened by attention to brain-in-bottle examples. Perhaps the day will come when our brains will be periodically removed for cleaning. Imagine that this is done initially by treating neurons attaching the brain to the body with a chemical that allows them to stretch like rubber bands, so that no connections are disrupted. As technology advances, in order to avoid the inconvenience of one's body being immobilized while one's brain is serviced, brains are removed, the connections between brain and body being maintained by radio, while one goes about one's business. After a few days, the customer returns and has the brain reinserted. Sometimes, however, people's bodies are destroyed by accidents while their brains are being cleaned. If hooked up to input sense organs (but not output organs) these brains would exhibit *none* of the usual platitudinous connections between behavior and clusters of inputs and mental states. If, as seems plausible, these brains could have almost all the same ... mental states as we have, Functionalism is wrong....

2.2 Are Qualia Psychofunctional States?

I began this chapter by describing a homunculi-headed device and claiming there is prima facie doubt about whether it has any mental states at all, especially whether it has qualitative mental states like pains, itches, and sensations of red. The special doubt about qualia can perhaps be explicated by thinking about *inverted* qualia rather than *absent* qualia. It makes sense, or seems to make sense, to suppose that objects we both call green look to me the way objects we both call red look to you. It seems that we could be functionally equivalent even though the sensation fire hydrants evoke in you is qualitatively the same as the sensation grass evokes in me. Imagine an inverting lens which when placed in the eye of a subject results in exclamations like "Red things now look the way green things used to look, and vice versa." Imagine further, a pair of identical twins one of whom has the lenses inserted at birth. The twins grow up normally, and at age 21 are functionally equivalent. This situation offers at

---

*   I.e., damage to the hippocampus, which is the part of the brain associated with the formation of new memories about experienced events.

least some evidence that each's spectrum* is inverted relative to the other's. (See Shoemaker, 1975, footnote 17, for a convincing description of intrapersonal spectrum inversion.) However, it is very hard to see how to make sense of the analogue of spectrum inversion with respect to nonqualitative states. Imagine a pair of persons one of whom believes that p is true and that q (≠ p) is false, while the other believes that q is true and that p is false. Could these persons be functionally equivalent? It is hard to see how they could. Indeed, it is hard to see how two persons could have only this difference in beliefs and yet there be no possible circumstance in which this belief difference would reveal itself in different behavior....

In part because of this feature of qualia, I called the argument against functionalism the 'Absent Qualia Argument.' But there is another reason for firmly distinguishing between qualitative and nonqualitative mental states in talking about functionalist theories: Psychofunctionalism avoids Functionalism's problems with nonqualitative states, e.g., propositional attitudes like beliefs and desires. But Psychofunctionalism may be no more able to handle qualitative states than is Functionalism. The reason is that qualia may well not be in the domain of psychology.

To see this, let us try to imagine what a homunculi-headed realization of human psychology would be like. Current psychological theorizing seems directed toward the description of information-flow relations among psychological mechanisms. The aim seems to be to decompose such mechanisms into psychologically primitive mechanisms, "black boxes" whose internal structure is in the domain of psychology rather than in the domain of physiology. (See Fodor, 1968b, Dennett, 1975, and Cummins, 1975; interesting objections are raised in Nagel, 1969.) For example, a near-primitive mechanism might be one that matches two items in a representational system and determines if they are tokens of the same type. Or the primitive mechanisms might be like those in a digital computer, e.g., they might be (a) *add 1 to a given register*, and (b) *subtract 1 from a given register, or if the register contains 0, go to the nth (indicated) instruction*. (These operations can be combined to accomplish any digital computer operation; see Minsky, 1967, p. 206.) Consider a computer whose machine language code contains only two instructions corresponding to (a) and (b). If you ask how it multiplies or solves differential equations or makes up payrolls, you can be answered by being shown a program couched in terms of the two machine-language instructions. But if you ask how it adds 1 to a given register, the appropriate answer is given by a wiring diagram, not a program. The machine is hard-wired to add 1. When the instruction corresponding to (a) appears in a certain register, the contents of another register "automatically" change in a certain way. The computational structure of a computer is determined by a set of primitive operations and the ways nonprimitive operations are built up from them. Thus it does not matter to the computational structure of the computer whether the primitive mechanisms are realized by tube circuits, transistor circuits, or relays. Likewise, it does not matter to the psychology of a mental system whether its primitive mechanisms are realized by one or another neurological mechanism. Call a system a "realization of human psychology" if every psychological theory true of us is true of it. Consider a realization of human psychology whose primitive psychological operations are accomplished by little men, in the manner of the homunculi-headed simulations discussed. So, perhaps one little man produces items from a list, one by one, another compares these items with other representations to determine whether they match, etc.

Now there is good reason for supposing this system has some mental states. Propositional attitudes are an example. Perhaps psychological theory will identify remembering that P with having "stored" a sentencelike object which expresses the proposition that P (Fodor, 1975). Then if one of the little men has put a certain sentencelike object in "storage," we may have reason for regarding the system as remembering that P. But unless having qualia is just a matter of having certain information processing (at best a controversial proposal—see later discussion), there is no such theoretical reason for regarding the system as having qualia. In short, there is perhaps as much doubt about the qualia of this homunculi-headed system as

---

* The color spectrum. Imagine the color wheel spun 180° so that all the relations between the colors stay the same but now yellow is where blue was, cyan swapped with magenta, and so on.

there was about the qualia of the homunculi-headed Functional simulation discussed early in the chapter.

But the system we are discussing is ex hypothesi* something of which any true psychological theory is true. *So any doubt that it has qualia is a doubt that qualia are in the domain of psychology.*

It may be objected: "The kind of psychology you have in mind is *cognitive* psychology, i.e., psychology of thought processes; and it is no wonder that qualia are not in the domain of *cognitive* psychology!" But I *do not* have cognitive psychology in mind, and if it sounds that way, this is easily explained: nothing we know about the psychological processes underlying our conscious mental life has anything to do with qualia. What passes for the "psychology" of sensation or pain, for example, is (a) physiology, (b) psychophysics (i.e., study of the mathematical functions relating stimulus variables and sensation variables, e.g., the intensity of sound as a function of the amplitude of the sound waves), or (c) a grabbag of descriptive studies (see Melzack, 1972, Ch. 2). Of these, only psychophysics could be construed as being about qualia per se. And it is obvious that psychophysics touches only the *functional* aspect of sensation, not its qualitative character. Psychophysical experiments done on you would have the same results if done on any system Psychofunctionally equivalent to you, even if it had inverted or absent qualia. If experimental results would be unchanged whether or not the experimental subjects have inverted or absent qualia, they can hardly be expected to cast light on the nature of qualia.

Indeed, on the basis of the kind of conceptual apparatus now available in psychology, I do not see how psychology in anything like its present incarnation *could* explain qualia. We cannot now conceive how psychology could explain qualia, though we *can* conceive how psychology could explain believing, desiring, hoping, etc. (see Fodor, 1975). That something is currently inconceivable is not a good reason to think it is impossible. Concepts could be developed tomorrow that would make what is now inconceivable conceivable. But all we have to go on is what we know, and on the basis of what we have to go on, it looks like qualia are not in the domain of psychology....

3.1 Chauvinism vs. Liberalism

It is natural to understand the psychological theories Psychofunctionalism adverts to as theories of *human* psychology. On Psychofunctionalism, so understood, it is logically impossible for a system to have beliefs, desires, etc., except insofar as psychological theories true of us are true of it. Psychofunctionalism (so understood) stipulates that Psychofunctional equivalence to us is necessary for mentality.

... But even if Psychofunctional equivalence to us is a condition on our *recognition of mentality*, what reason is there to think it is a condition on mentality itself? Could there not be a wide variety of possible psychological processes that can underlie mentality, of which we instantiate only one type? Suppose we meet Martians and find that they are roughly Functionally (but not Psychofunctionally) equivalent to us. When we get to know Martians, we find them about as different from us as humans we know. We develop extensive cultural and commercial intercourse with them. We study each other's science and philosophy journals, go to each other's movies, read each other's novels, etc. Then Martian and Earthian psychologists compare notes, only to find that in underlying psychology, Martians and Earthians are very different. They soon agree that the difference can be described as follows. Think of humans and Martians as if they were products of conscious design. In any such design project, there will be various options. Some capacities can be built in (innate), others learned. The brain can be designed to accomplish tasks using as much memory capacity as necessary in order to minimize use of computation capacity; or, on the other hand, the designer could choose to conserve memory space and rely mainly on computation capacity. Inferences can be accomplished by systems which use a few axioms and many rules of inference, or, on the other hand, few rules and many axioms. Now imagine that what Martian and Earthian psychologists find when they compare notes is that Martians and Earthians differ as if they were the end products of maximally different design choices (compatible with rough Functional equivalence in adults). Should we reject our assumption that Martians can enjoy our films, believe their

---

* Latin: by assumption, as defined by the set-up of the hypothesis.

own apparent scientific results, etc.? Should they "reject" their "assumption" that we "enjoy" their novels, "learn" from their textbooks, etc.? Perhaps I have not provided enough information to answer this question. After all, there may be many ways of filling in the description of the Martian–human differences in which it would be reasonable to suppose there simply is no fact of the matter, or even to suppose that the Martians do not deserve mental ascriptions. But surely there are many ways of filling in the description of the Martian–Earthian difference I sketched on which it would be perfectly clear that even if Martians behave differently from us on subtle psychological experiments, they nonetheless think, desire, enjoy, etc. To suppose otherwise would be crude human chauvinism. (Remember theories are chauvinist insofar as they falsely *deny* that systems have mental properties and liberal insofar as they falsely *attribute* mental properties.)

So it seems as if in preferring Psychofunctionalism to Functionalism, we erred in the direction of human chauvinism. For if mental states are Psychofunctional states, and if Martians do not have these Psychofunctional states, then they do not have mental states either. In arguing that the original homunculi-headed simulations (taken as Functional simulations) had no mentality, I appealed, in effect, to the following principle: if the sole reason to think system x has mentality is that x was built to be Functionally equivalent to us, then differences between x and us in underlying information processing and/or neurophysiology are prima facie reasons to doubt whether x has mental states. But this principle does not dictate that a system can have mentality only insofar as it is Psychofunctionally equivalent to us. Psychofunctional equivalence to us is a sufficient condition for at least some aspects of mentality (those in the domain of psychology), but it is not obvious that it is a necessary condition of any aspects of mentality.

An obvious suggestion of a way out of this difficulty is to identify mental states with Psychofunctional states, taking the domain of psychology to include *all creatures with mentality*, including Martians. The suggestion is that we define "Psychofunctionalism" in terms of "universal" or "cross-system" psychology, rather than the human psychology I assumed earlier. Universal psychology, however, is a suspect discipline. For how are we to decide what systems should be

included in the *domain* of universal psychology? What systems are the generalizations of universal psychology based on? One possible way of deciding what systems have mentality, and are thus in the domain of universal psychology, would be to use some *other* developed theory of mentality, e.g., behaviorism or Functionalism. But such a procedure would be at least as ill-justified as the other theory used. Further, if Psychofunctionalism must presuppose some other theory of mind, we might just as well accept the other theory of mind instead.

Perhaps universal psychology will avoid this "domain" problem in the same way other branches of science avoid it or seek to avoid it. Other branches of science start with tentative domains based on intuitive and prescientific versions of the concepts the sciences are supposed to explicate. They then attempt to develop natural kinds in a way which allows the formulations of lawlike generalizations which apply to all or most of the entities in the prescientific domains. In the case of many branches of science—including biological and social sciences such as genetics and linguistics—the prescientific domain turned out to be suitable for the articulation of lawlike generalizations.

Now it may be that we shall be able to develop universal psychology in much the same way we develop Earthian psychology. We decide on an intuitive and prescientific basis what creatures to include in its domain, and work to develop natural kinds of psychological theory which apply to all or at least most of them. Perhaps the study of a wide range of organisms found on different worlds will one day lead to theories that determine truth conditions for the attribution of mental states like belief, desire, etc., applicable to systems which are pretheoretically quite different from us. Indeed, such cross-world psychology will no doubt require a whole new range of mentalistic concepts. Perhaps there will be families of concepts corresponding to belief, desire, etc., that is, a family of belieflike concepts, desirelike concepts, etc. If so, the cross-world psychology we develop shall, no doubt, be somewhat dependent on which new organisms we discover first. Even if cross-world psychology is in fact possible, however, there will certainly be many possible organisms whose mental status is indeterminate.

On the other hand, it may be that universal psychology is *not* possible. Perhaps life in the universe is such that we shall simply have no basis for reasonable decisions about what systems are in the domain of psychology and what systems are not.[3]

If cross-world psychology *is* possible, the problem I have been raising vanishes. Cross-world Psychofunctionalism avoids the liberalism of Functionalism and the chauvinism of human-Psychofunctionalism. But the question of whether cross-world psychology is possible is surely one which we have no way of answering now....

To summarize my conclusions so far: First, given the reasonable assumption that mental states are in the domain of psychology and/or physiology, the homunculi-head example shows that Functionalism is false. Second, none of the arguments in the literature for either Functionalism or Psychofunctionalism are persuasive. Third: the claim that beliefs and desires are Psychofunctional states is impervious to arguments based on homunculi-heads; but since there is a doubt that qualia are in the domain of psychology, there is a doubt that qualitative states are Psychofunctional states. Finally, I considered chauvinism/liberalism problems for Psychofunctionalism and concluded that some version of Psychofunctionalism may yet steer between the Scylla of liberalism and the Charybdis of chauvinism.* So, even if there is no good reason for thinking Psychofunctionalism true, still I have provided only weak reason for thinking it false. In the next section, I bring up a difficulty for Psychofunctionalism (and Functionalism) which may not be easily evaded.

3.2 The Problem of the Inputs and the Outputs

I have been supposing all along (as Psychofunctionalists often do—see Putnam, 1967) that inputs and outputs can be specified by neural impulse descriptions. But this is a chauvinist claim, since it precludes organisms without neurons (e.g., machines) from having functional descriptions. How can one avoid chauvinism with respect to specification of inputs and outputs? One way would be to characterize the inputs and outputs *only as* inputs and outputs. So the functional description of a person might list outputs by number: output₁, output₂, ... Then a system could be functionally equivalent to you if it had a set of states, inputs, and outputs causally related to one another in the way yours are, no matter what the states, inputs, and outputs were like. Indeed, though this approach violates the demand of some functionalists that inputs and outputs be physically specified, other functionalists—those who insist only that input and output descriptions be *nonmental*—may have had something like this in mind. This version of functionalism does not "tack down" functional descriptions at the periphery with relatively specific descriptions of inputs and outputs; rather, this version of functionalism treats inputs and outputs just as all versions of functionalism treat internal states. That is, this version specifies states, inputs, and outputs only by requiring that they *be* states, inputs, and outputs.

The trouble with this version of functionalism is that it is wildly liberal. Economic systems have inputs and outputs, e.g., influx and outflux of credits and debits. And economic systems also have a rich variety of internal states, e.g., having a rate of increase of GNP† equal to double the Prime Rate.‡ It does not seem impossible that a wealthy sheik could gain control of the economy of a small country, e.g., Bolivia, and manipulate its financial system to make it functionally equivalent to a person, e.g., himself. If this seems implausible, remember that the economic states, inputs, and outputs designated by the sheik to correspond to his mental states, inputs, and outputs need not be "natural" economic magnitudes. Our hypothetical sheik could pick *any* economic magnitudes at all—e.g., the fifth time derivative of the balance of payments. His only constraint is that the magnitudes he picks be economic, that their having such and such values be inputs, outputs, and states, and that he be able to set up a financial structure which realizes the intended causal structure. The mapping from psychological magnitudes to economic magnitudes could be as bizarre as the sheik requires.

This version of functionalism is far too liberal and must therefore be rejected. If there are any fixed

---

* Being between Scylla and Charybdis is an idiom similar to "between a rock and a hard place"; it means that you must make a hard choice between two bad options. In Homeric myth, Scylla and Charybdis are two monstrous naval hazards on opposite sides of the strait between Sicily and the Italian mainland, close enough together that ships can only avoid one by facing the other: Scylla is a six-headed sea monster and Charybdis a giant whirlpool.

† Gross National Product, a broad measure of a nation's total economic activity.

‡ The interest rate that banks charge their most creditworthy customers to borrow money.

points when discussing the mind-body problem, one of them is that the economy of Bolivia could not have mental states, no matter how it is distorted by powerful hobbyists. Obviously, we must be more specific in our descriptions of inputs and outputs. The question is: is there a description of inputs and outputs specific enough to avoid liberalism, yet general enough to avoid chauvinism? I doubt that there is.

Every proposal for a description of inputs and outputs I have seen or thought of is guilty of either liberalism or chauvinism. Though this paper has focused on liberalism, chauvinism is the more pervasive problem. Consider standard Functional and Psychofunctional descriptions. Functionalists tend to specify inputs and outputs in the manner of behaviorists: outputs in terms of movements of arms and legs, sound emitted and the like; inputs in terms of light and sound falling on the eyes and ears. As I argued earlier, this conception is chauvinist, since it denies mentality to brains in vats and to paralytics. But the chauvinism inherent in Functional descriptions runs deeper. Such descriptions are blatantly *species-specific*. Humans have arms and legs, but snakes do not—and whether or not snakes have mentality, one can easily imagine snakelike creatures that do. Indeed, one can imagine creatures with all manner of input-output devices, e.g., creatures that communicate and manipulate by emitting strong magnetic fields. Of course, one could formulate Functional descriptions for each such species, and somewhere in disjunctive heaven there is a disjunctive description* which will handle all species that ever actually exist in the universe (the description may be infinitely long). But even an appeal to such suspicious entities as infinite disjunctions will not bail out Functionalism, since even the amended view will not tell us what there is in common to pain-feeling organisms in virtue of which they all have pain. And it will not allow the ascription of pain to some hypothetical (but non-existent) pain-feeling creatures. Further, these are just the grounds on which functionalists typically acerbically reject the disjunctive theories sometimes advanced by desperate physicalists. If functionalists suddenly smile on wildly disjunctive states to save themselves from chauvinism, they will have no way of defending themselves from physicalism.

Standard Psychofunctional descriptions of inputs and outputs are also species-specific (e.g., in terms of neural activity) and hence chauvinist as well.

The chauvinism of standard input-output descriptions is not hard to explain. The variety of possible intelligent life is enormous. Given any fairly specific descriptions of inputs and outputs, any high-school-age science-fiction buff will be able to describe a sapient sentient being whose inputs and outputs fail to satisfy that description.

I shall argue that *any physical description* of inputs and outputs (recall that many functionalists have insisted on physical descriptions) yields a version of functionalism that is hopelessly chauvinist. Imagine yourself so badly burned in a fire that your optimal way of communicating with the outside world is via modulations of your EEG pattern† in Morse Code. You find that thinking an exciting thought produces a pattern that your audience agrees to interpret as a dot, and a dull thought produces a "dash." ... The "reverse" process is also presumably possible: others communicating with you in Morse Code by producing bursts of electrical activity that affect your brain (e.g., causing a long or short afterimage). Alternatively, if the cerebroscopes‡ that philosophers often fancy become a reality, your thoughts will be readable directly from your brain. Again, the reverse process also seems possible. In these cases, *the brain itself becomes one's input and output device*. But this possibility has embarrassing consequences for functionalism. You will recall, that as functionalists have emphasized in criticizing physicalism, a single mental state can be realized by an indefinite variety of physical states, that have no necessary and sufficient physical characterization. But if this functionalist point against physicalism is right, since the device which physically realizes mental states can serve as a mental system's input and output devices, *the same point applies to mental systems' input and output devices*. That is, on any sense of

---

* A description of something as being either A or B or C or ... (e.g., birds are either insect-eating or fruit-eating or seed-eating or meat-eating or omnivorous). A disjunction is simply an 'or' sentence.
† Waves showing electrical activity in the brain (picked up through electroencephalography [EEG]).
‡ Imagined scientific instruments capable of measuring neural activity and mental states.

'physical' in which the functionalist criticism of physicalism is correct, *there will be no physical characterizations that apply to all mental systems' inputs and outputs. Hence, any attempt to formulate a functional description with physical characterizations of inputs and outputs will exclude some systems with mentality, and thus will be chauvinist.*

If the functionalist argument against physicalism is right, any functional description that specifies inputs and outputs physically will be chauvinist. Moreover, mental or "action" terminology (e.g., 'punching the offending person') may not be used either, since to use such specifications of inputs or outputs would be to give up the functionalist program of characterizing mentality in nonmental terms. On the other hand, you recall, characterizing inputs and outputs simply *as* inputs and outputs is inevitably liberal. I, for one, do not see how functionalism can describe inputs and outputs without falling afoul of either liberalism or chauvinism, or abandoning the original project of characterizing mentality in nonmental terms. I do not claim that this is a conclusive argument against functionalism. Rather, like the functionalist argument against physicalism, it is perhaps best construed as a burden of proof argument. The functionalist says to the physicalist: "It is hard to see how there could be a single physical characterization of the internal state of every possible organism functionally equivalent to a human." I say to the functionalist: "It is very hard to see how there could be a single characterization of inputs and outputs that applies to all and only mental systems." In both cases, it seems enough has been said to make it the responsibility of those who think there could be such characterizations to sketch how they could be possible. ■

Suggestions for Critical Reflection

1. In this paper Block considers three main theories of mind—behaviorism, physicalism, and functionalism—and appears to raise serious problems for all of them. Where, then, does this leave us?

2. Block identifies a couple of different forms of vagueness that he suggests are inherent in functionalism understood broadly, but are difficult to resolve without grasping uncomfortable theoretical nettles. Functionalism gives a functional account of what mental states (or properties or other entities) are—it explains mental states by redescribing them in language that uses only input-output or causal role terms. But which mental states need to be explained, and what counts as explaining them correctly? According to Block, this can only be settled by relativizing functionalism to some psychological theory or other, since it is this theory that specifies what needs to be explained. Capital-F Functionalism, for example, assumes that what needs to be explained is the way we talk about the mind in English and other natural languages: beliefs, resentments, sensations, goals and so on. But trying to be precise about the psychological theory that functionalism cashes out is—Block suggests—harder and less comfortable than it seems. Is it a scientific theory? These change all the time—which scientific theory? Some unknown future theory? And how general can this theory be: does it apply to all thinkers (including any alien capable of thought), all mammals (including dogs and dolphins), all humans, all neurotypical humans, or just to humans of a particular cultural background? How worrying do you find this objection to be? Does it seem to you to suggest that functionalism is only vague right now, until we firm up the theory, or does it suggest that functionalism is inherently vague and can never be made clear in a satisfactory way?

3. Does Block assume a sharp distinction between qualitative and nonqualitative mental states (i.e., between qualia and cognition)? Is the distinction all that sharp—e.g., are emotional memories clearly either qualitative or cognitive? If the distinction is blurry, how does this affect Block's conclusions?

4. "If there are any fixed points when discussing the mind-body problem, one of them is that the economy of Bolivia could not have mental states, no matter how it is distorted by powerful hobbyists." Do you agree? There is a spectrum of imaginative thought-experiments used by Block to motivate his arguments: are there some cases on the spectrum that the functionalist might actually be able to accept, rather than to treat as counter-examples?

5. Many of the scenarios Block describes in this paper are made up: they are thought-experiments designed to elicit a particular intuition about the cases at hand. It is too quick to simply say that because these situations are non-actual they cannot be relevant. Any theory that says anything interesting goes beyond simply describing what is the case and makes commitments about what *would* be the case if the circumstances were different, so assessing the plausibility of what the theory tells us about non-actual cases is perfectly legitimate. It is also a useful way of drawing out the limits of a theory's content in order to understand better what it is committing us to. But the fact remains that, unlike a real experiment, the results of thought experiments do not present us with an empirical result but require interpretation. In other places in his writings, Block has suggested that the key to a reliable thought experiment is not that the hypothetical scenario itself is simple—they can be quite complex—but that the intuition which is being elicited is simple and unambiguous. What do you think about Block's use of thought experiments? Are they helpful or persuasive?

Notes

1   State type, not state token. Throughout the chapter, I shall mean by 'physicalism' the doctrine that says each distinct type of mental state is identical to a distinct type of physical state; for example, pain (the universal) is a physical state. Token physicalism, on the other hand, is the (weaker) doctrine that each particular datable pain is a state of some physical type or other. Functionalism shows that type physicalism is false, but it does not show that token physicalism is false....

2   Compare the first sentence with 'The fish eaten in Boston stank.' The reason it is hard to process is that 'raced' is naturally read as active rather than passive....

3   To take a very artificial example, suppose we have no way of knowing whether inhabitants of civilizations we discover are the builders of the civilizations or simulations the builders made before departing en masse.

References

Armstrong, D. *A materialist theory of mind*. London: Routledge & Kegan Paul, 1968.

Block, N. & Fodor, J. What psychological states are not. *Philosophical Review*, 1972, 81, 159–81.

Chisholm, Roderick. *Perceiving*. Ithaca: Cornell University Press, 1957.

Cummins, R. Functional analysis. *Journal of Philosophy*, 1975, 72, 741–64.

Dennett, D. Why the law of effect won't go away. *Journal for the Theory of Social Behavior*, 1975, 5, 169–87.

Fodor, J. Explanations in psychology. In M. Black (Ed.), *Philosophy in America*, London: Routledge & Kegan Paul, 1965.

Fodor, J. The appeal to tacit knowledge in psychological explanation. *Journal of Philosophy*, 1968b, 65, 627–40.

Fodor, J. *The language of thought*. New York: Crowell, 1975.

Kim, J. Phenomenal properties, psychophysical laws, and the identity theory. *The Monist*, 1972, 56(2), 177–92.

Lewis, D. Psychophysical and theoretical identifications. *Australasian Journal of Philosophy*, 1972, 50(3), 249–58.

Melzack, R. *The puzzle of pain*. New York: Basic Books, 1973.

Minsky, M. *Computation*. Englewood Cliffs: Prentice-Hall, 1967.

Nagel, T. The boundaries of inner space. *Journal of Philosophy*, 1969, 66, 452–58.

Nagel, T. What is it like to be a bat? *Philosophical Review*, 1974, 83, 435–50.

Nelson, R.J. Behaviorism, finite automata & stimulus response theory. *Theory and Decision*, 1975, 6, 249–67.

Putnam, H. Brains and behavior. 1963. Reprinted as are all Putnam's articles referred to here (except "On properties") in *Mind, language and reality; philosophical papers*, Vol. 2). London: Cambridge University Press, 1975.

Putnam, H. The mental life of some machines. 1966.

Putnam, H. The nature of mental states. (This was originally published under the title *Psychological Predicates*.) 1967.

Shoemaker, S. Functionalism and qualia. *Philosophical Studies*, 1975, 27, 271–315.

THOMAS NAGEL

What Is It Like to Be a Bat?

Who Is Thomas Nagel?

Thomas Nagel, an important American philosopher, was Professor of Law and Philosophy at New York University until his retirement in 2016. He was born in 1937 in Belgrade, Serbia, to German Jewish refugees, and the family moved to the US in 1939. Nagel was educated at Cornell (BA), Corpus Christi College, Oxford (BPhil), and Harvard (PhD, awarded in 1963). After working at Berkeley and Princeton, he moved to New York University in 1980. He is the author of a dozen books, including *The View from Nowhere* (1986) and *Mind and Cosmos: Why the Materialist Neo-Darwinian Conception of Nature Is Almost Certainly False* (2012), and many articles.

What Is Nagel's Overall Philosophical Project?

Throughout his career a main theme of Nagel's philosophical writing has been the difficulty of reconciling two fundamentally different points of view: our first-person, subjective, personal point of view, and the impartial, third-person, objective perspective.* The first-person perspective is typically thought of as being more partial than the third-person—partial both in the sense of being constrained by local horizons, and of being infected with personal concerns and biases. (For example, from *my* point of view it is right and natural to eat with a knife and fork, but this seems natural to me only because of the place and manner of my upbringing: speaking objectively, forks are no more nor less 'natural' than chopsticks or fingers.) As a result, subjective impressions are often thought of as being less reliable or 'true' than objective claims, and the first-person perspective tends to be treated as something to be avoided in serious knowledge-gathering enterprises such as science or good journalism. Nagel's guiding philosophical question is this: *could* we completely understand the universe from the third-person point of view—that is, is the subjective completely reducible to (or eliminable in favor of) the objective? As he puts it in one of his books, he wants to know "how to combine the perspective of a particular person inside the world with an objective view of that same world, the person and his viewpoint included."†

The short version of Nagel's response to this problem is the following:

1. The subjective perspective is ineliminable in various highly important ways, and a refusal to notice this can lead to philosophical errors. "Appearance and perspective are essential parts of what there is." Our objectivity is limited by the fact that we cannot leave our own viewpoints entirely behind.
2. However, objectivity is also to be valued and fostered as a crucial method of coming to understand aspects of the world as it is in itself. It is important that we struggle to transcend our local horizons and try to get a better view of our place in the universe.

Many of Nagel's books trace these themes, in one way or another. *The View from Nowhere*, published in 1986, is explicitly about the relation between the subjective and the objective. His first book, *The Possibility of Altruism* (1970), dealt with the conflict between personal and impersonal reasons for individual action, and one of his later books, *Equality and Partiality* (1991), examines the issue of reconciling individual claims with those of a group.

"What Is It Like to Be a Bat?" is Nagel's most famous and influential article. In it he applies his theme to the

---

* "First-person" and "third-person" are terms taken from grammatical categories: "I am hungry" is a first-person sentence, as it's about the speaker; "She/he/it is hungry" is a third-person sentence, as it's about a third party. ("You are hungry" would be an example of a second-person sentence.)

† Thomas Nagel, *The View from Nowhere* (Oxford University Press, 1986), 3.

philosophy of mind, and contends that all current third-person theories of the mind (such as identity-theory, behaviorism, or functionalism) are radically incomplete since they fail to capture "what it is like to be" conscious, and this subjective character of experience, Nagel suggests, is a central aspect of mentality. Nagel's most recent book, *Mind and Cosmos* (2012), argues controversially against a reductionist view of the emergence of consciousness.

In the preface to his book *Mortal Questions*, Nagel describes his view of philosophy, and it is worth repeating here:

> I believe one should trust problems over solutions, intuition over arguments, and pluralistic discord over systematic harmony. Simplicity and elegance are never reasons to think that a philosophical theory is true: on the contrary, they are usually grounds for thinking it false. Given a knockdown argument for an intuitively unacceptable conclusion, one should assume there is probably something wrong with the argument that one cannot detect—though it is always possible that the source of the intuition has been misidentified.... Often the problem has to be reformulated because an adequate answer to the original formulation fails to make the *sense* of the problem disappear.... Superficiality is as hard to avoid in philosophy as it is anywhere else. It is too easy to reach solutions that fail to do justice to the difficulty of the problems. All one can do is try to maintain a desire for answers, a tolerance for long periods without any, an unwillingness to brush aside unexplained intuitions, and an adherence to reasonable standards of clear expression and cogent argument.*

What Is the Structure of This Reading?

Nagel begins by saying that the problem of reducing the mental to the physical—of completely describing and explaining our mental life in physical, non-psychological terms—is uniquely difficult because of the nature of conscious experience, and he goes on to explain this by discussing the relation between subjective and objective facts, using bats as an example.

After an aside, where he discusses the relation between facts and conceptual schemes for representing those facts, Nagel proceeds to argue that subjective facts about consciousness make the mind-body problem intractable. One of his central claims is that the reduction of experience to neurophysiology (i.e., the physiology of the brain and nervous system) is importantly different from standard cases of reduction (e.g., the reduction of heat to mean molecular motion). Nagel then discusses what philosophical moral should be drawn from all this—what implications it has, for example, for the claim that mental states are identical with brain states. He closes by suggesting that we pursue a solution to the problem he has raised by trying to develop an "objective phenomenology" of the mental.

Some Useful Background Information

Nagel is reacting against attempts in the 1960s and early 1970s to *reduce* the mental to the physical—that is, to show that, properly understood, mental phenomena are nothing more than physical phenomena. There are two central varieties of reduction, sometimes called "ontological reduction" and "theory reduction." Ontological reduction consists in showing that objects (or properties or events) of the first type are identical with—or "realized by"—objects (properties, events) of the second: for example, it might be that genes are identical with DNA molecules, or that lightning is nothing but a kind of electrical discharge, or that the color purple is just reflected light of a particular wavelength. Theory reduction consists in showing that all the statements of one higher-level theory can be translated into (or otherwise deduced from) statements of another more fundamental theory: for example (roughly speaking), the Mendelian laws of genetics are entailed by molecular biology, and our commonsense 'theory' of temperature can be translated into the kinetic theory of matter.

Nagel's anti-reductive claim is, therefore, that any optimism we might feel, that mental entities such as beliefs and emotions can be shown to be identical with neurological or functional states, or that psychological theories can someday be translated into some non-psychological language, is seriously misguided.

---

* Thomas Nagel, *Mortal Questions* (Cambridge University Press, 1979), x–xi.

Some Common Misconceptions

1. It is sometimes thought Nagel argues that physicalism is false: that is, that the mental involves something *extra* over and above the physical. (This would make Nagel some kind of dualist.) However, Nagel does not claim this: instead, he argues that *existing* physicalist theories of the mental (behaviorism, identity theory, functionalism) must be wrong, and he suggests that, although physicalism may be true—or even demonstrably true—it will be very hard for us to understand *how* it can be true. That is, he worries about the difficulty of giving any kind of objective theory of the mind.

2. There are various kinds of 'subjectivity,' and it has sometimes puzzled people exactly which kind Nagel is worrying about (perhaps because Nagel himself does not distinguish between some of them). One variety of non-objectivity that Nagel is clear he is *not* endorsing, however, is a particular kind of privacy of the mental. Some philosophers (such as Descartes) have held that consciousness is radically private in the sense that we have a special kind of access to our own mental states which, in principle, we cannot have to physical states. If this were true, then I could look as hard as I liked at your brain (which is a physical object) and *never* see any of your mental states; it would mean that

the only access to consciousness must necessarily be from the first person, and thus that science would be forever excluded from studying and describing it. It is easy to see how this view might be confused with the one Nagel develops in this article, but nevertheless it is importantly different. For example, Nagel actually *denies* that we could never come to know anything at all about other people's consciousness, and even asserts that we can be corrected by other people when we make mistakes about what we ourselves are feeling (i.e., we are not 'incorrigible'). For Nagel, the problem is not some metaphysical difference of access to the mental and physical, but a problem about reconciling subjective and objective categories. Other versions of 'subjectivity' which may (or may not) be in play in this article include:

- having a particular point of view or perspective;
- being phenomenal or experiential (i.e., feeling a certain way);
- having a sense of oneself as being a subject—as being a creature that, for example, undergoes sensations, forms intentions to do things, and controls its own actions;
- being infallibly known or present to one's awareness (like the kind of raging toothache which is impossible to ignore and which one couldn't possibly be mistaken about).

What Is It Like to Be a Bat?*

Consciousness is what makes the mind-body problem really intractable. Perhaps that is why current discussions of the problem give it little attention or get it obviously wrong. The recent wave of reductionist euphoria has produced several analyses of mental phenomena and mental concepts designed to explain the possibility of some variety of materialism, psychophysical identification, or reduction.[1] But the problems dealt with are those common to this type of reduction and other types, and what makes the mind-body problem unique, and unlike the water–H_2O problem or the Turing machine–IBM machine problem[†] or the

---

* This article was first published in *The Philosophical Review* 83, 4 (1974): 435–50, published by Duke University Press.
† By "IBM machine" Nagel simply means a computer. See the introduction to Block's article, above, for a description of a Turing machine. Turing argued that any effective mathematical method or "algorithm"—and thus any computer program whatever—can in principle be run on a Turing machine; thus the "reduction" of any computation to the very few operations of that machine.

lightning–electrical discharge problem or the gene-DNA problem or the oak tree–hydrocarbon problem, is ignored.

Every reductionist has his favorite analogy from modern science. It is most unlikely that any of these unrelated examples of successful reduction will shed light on the relation of mind to brain. But philosophers share the general human weakness for explanations of what is incomprehensible in terms suited for what is familiar and well understood, though entirely different. This has led to the acceptance of implausible accounts of the mental largely because they would permit familiar kinds of reduction. I shall try to explain why the usual examples do not help us to understand the relation between mind and body—why, indeed, we have at present no conception of what an explanation of the physical nature of a mental phenomenon would be. Without consciousness the mind-body problem would be much less interesting. With consciousness it seems hopeless. The most important and characteristic feature of conscious mental phenomena is very poorly understood. Most reductionist theories do not even try to explain it. And careful examination will show that no currently available concept of reduction is applicable to it. Perhaps a new theoretical form can be devised for the purpose, but such a solution, if it exists, lies in the distant intellectual future.

Conscious experience is a widespread phenomenon. It occurs at many levels of animal life, though we cannot be sure of its presence in the simpler organisms, and it is very difficult to say in general what provides evidence of it. (Some extremists have been prepared to deny it even of mammals other than man.) No doubt it occurs in countless forms totally unimaginable to us, on other planets in other solar systems throughout the universe. But no matter how the form may vary, the fact that an organism has conscious experience *at all* means, basically, that there is something it is like to

be that organism. There may be further implications about the form of the experience; there may even (though I doubt it) be implications about the behavior of the organism. But fundamentally an organism has conscious mental states if and only if there is something that it is like to *be* that organism—something it is like *for* the organism.

We may call this the subjective character of experience. It is not captured by any of the familiar, recently devised reductive analyses of the mental, for all of them are logically compatible with its absence. It is not analyzable in terms of any explanatory system of functional states, or intentional states,* since these could be ascribed to robots or automata that behaved like people though they experienced nothing.[2] It is not analyzable in terms of the causal role of experiences in relation to typical human behavior—for similar reasons.[3] I do not deny that conscious mental states and events cause behavior, nor that they may be given functional characterizations. I deny only that this kind of thing exhausts their analysis. Any reductionist program has to be based on an analysis of what is to be reduced. If the analysis leaves something out, the problem will be falsely posed. It is useless to base the defense of materialism on any analysis of mental phenomena that fails to deal explicitly with their subjective character. For there is no reason to suppose that a reduction which seems plausible when no attempt is made to account for consciousness can be extended to include consciousness. Without some idea, therefore, of what the subjective character of experience is, we cannot know what is required of a physicalist theory.

While an account of the physical basis of mind must explain many things, this appears to be the most difficult. It is impossible to exclude the phenomenological† features of experience from a reduction in the same way that one excludes the phenomenal features of an ordinary substance from a physical or chemical

---

* See the introduction to the Block article, above, for an account of 'functional state.' An intentional state is one which has what philosophers call "intentionality," a technical term for 'aboutness' or, roughly, meaningfulness. Thus an intentional state is one which is about something else (such as the state of a register in a computer's CPU, as compared with, say, the position of a randomly chosen pebble on a beach).

† "Phenomenological" means having to do with phenomenology, and phenomenology is the description of the features of our lived conscious experience (as opposed to the features of what it is experience *of*). So, for example, the phenomenology of our perception of trees does not concern itself with actual trees and their relations to perceivers, but instead examines what it *feels* like to see a tree—what kind of (moving, temporal, emotionally resonant) picture we have in our head, if you like.

reduction of it—namely, by explaining them as effects on the minds of human observers.[4] If physicalism is to be defended, the phenomenological features must themselves be given a physical account. But when we examine their subjective character it seems that such a result is impossible. The reason is that every subjective phenomenon is essentially connected with a single point of view, and it seems inevitable that an objective, physical theory will abandon that point of view.

Let me first try to state the issue somewhat more fully than by referring to the relation between the subjective and the objective, or between the *pour-soi* and the *en-soi*.* This is far from easy. Facts about what it is like to be an *X* are very peculiar, so peculiar that some may be inclined to doubt their reality, or the significance of claims about them. To illustrate the connection between subjectivity and a point of view, and to make evident the importance of subjective features, it will help to explore the matter in relation to an example that brings out clearly the divergence between the two types of conception, subjective and objective.

I assume we all believe that bats have experience. After all, they are mammals, and there is no more doubt that they have experience than that mice or pigeons or whales have experience. I have chosen bats instead of wasps or flounders because if one travels too far down the phylogenetic tree,† people gradually shed their faith that there is experience there at all. Bats, although more closely related to us than those other species, nevertheless present a range of activity and a sensory apparatus so different from ours that the problem I want to pose is exceptionally vivid (though it certainly could be raised with other species). Even without the benefit of philosophical reflection, anyone who has spent some time in an enclosed space with an excited bat knows what it is to encounter a fundamentally *alien* form of life.

I have said that the essence of the belief that bats have experience is that there is something that it is like to be a bat. Now we know that most bats (the microchiroptera, to be precise) perceive the external world primarily by sonar, or echolocation, detecting the reflections, from objects within range, of their own rapid, subtly modulated, high-frequency shrieks. Their brains are designed to correlate the outgoing impulses with the subsequent echoes, and the information thus acquired enables bats to make precise discriminations of distance, size, shape, motion, and texture comparable to those we make by vision. But bat sonar, though clearly a form of perception, is not similar in its operation to any sense that we possess, and there is no reason to suppose that it is subjectively like anything we can experience or imagine. This appears to create difficulties for the notion of what it is like to be a bat. We must consider whether any method will permit us to extrapolate to the inner life of the bat from our own case,[5] and if not, what alternative methods there may be for understanding the notion.

Our own experience provides the basic material for our imagination, whose range is therefore limited. It will not help to try to imagine that one has webbing on one's arms, which enables one to fly around at dusk and dawn catching insects in one's mouth; that one has very poor vision, and perceives the surrounding world by a system of reflected high-frequency sound signals; and that one spends the day hanging upside down by one's feet in an attic. In so far as I can imagine this (which is not very far), it tells me only what it would be like for *me* to behave as a bat behaves. But that is not the question. I want to know what it is like for a *bat* to be a bat. Yet if I try to imagine this, I am restricted to the resources of my own mind, and those resources are inadequate to the task. I cannot perform it either by imagining additions to my present experience, or by imagining segments gradually subtracted from it, or by imagining some combination of additions, subtractions, and modifications.

To the extent that I could look and behave like a wasp or a bat without changing my fundamental structure, my experiences would not be anything like the experiences of those animals. On the other hand, it is doubtful that any meaning can be attached to the supposition that I should possess the internal neurophysiological constitution of a bat. Even if I could by gradual degrees be transformed into a bat, nothing in my present constitution enables me to imagine what

---

* *Pour-soi* (French) means "for itself" and *en-soi* means "in itself." In this context, the phrase refers to the contrast between consciousness and mere thing-hood.

† (Roughly) the scale of evolutionary development.

the experiences of such a future stage of myself thus metamorphosed would be like. The best evidence would come from the experiences of bats, if we only knew what they were like.

So if extrapolation from our own case is involved in the idea of what it is like to be a bat, the extrapolation must be incompletable. We cannot form more than a schematic conception of what it is like. For example, we may ascribe general *types* of experience on the basis of the animal's structure and behavior. Thus we describe bat sonar as a form of three-dimensional forward perception; we believe that bats feel some versions of pain, fear, hunger, and lust, and that they have other, more familiar types of perception besides sonar. But we believe that these experiences also have in each case a specific subjective character, which it is beyond our ability to conceive. And if there is conscious life elsewhere in the universe, it is likely that some of it will not be describable even in the most general experiential terms available to us.[6] (The problem is not confined to exotic cases, however, for it exists between one person and another. The subjective character of the experience of a person deaf and blind from birth is not accessible to me, for example, nor presumably is mine to him. This does not prevent us each from believing that the other's experience has such a subjective character.)

If anyone is inclined to deny that we can believe in the existence of facts like this whose exact nature we cannot possibly conceive, he should reflect that in contemplating the bats we are in much the same position that intelligent bats or Martians[7] would occupy if they tried to form a conception of what it was like to be us. The structure of their own minds might make it impossible for them to succeed, but we know they would be wrong to conclude that there is not anything precise that it is like to be us: that only certain general types of mental state could be ascribed to us (perhaps perception and appetite would be concepts common to us both; perhaps not). We know they would be wrong to draw such a skeptical conclusion because we know what it is like to be us. And we know that while it includes an enormous amount of variation and

complexity, and while we do not possess the vocabulary to describe it adequately, its subjective character is highly specific, and in some respects describable in terms that can be understood only by creatures like us. The fact that we cannot expect ever to accommodate in our language a detailed description of Martian or bat phenomenology should not lead us to dismiss as meaningless the claim that bats and Martians have experiences fully comparable in richness of detail to our own. It would be fine if someone were to develop concepts and a theory that enabled us to think about those things; but such an understanding may be permanently denied to us by the limits of our nature. And to deny the reality or logical significance of what we can never describe or understand is the crudest form of cognitive dissonance.

This brings us to the edge of a topic that requires much more discussion than I can give it here: namely, the relation between facts on the one hand and conceptual schemes or systems of representation on the other. My realism about the subjective domain in all its forms implies a belief in the existence of facts beyond the reach of human concepts. Certainly it is possible for a human being to believe that there are facts which humans never *will* possess the requisite concepts to represent or comprehend. Indeed, it would be foolish to doubt this, given the finiteness of humanity's expectations. After all, there would have been transfinite numbers even if everyone had been wiped out by the Black Death before Cantor* discovered them. But one might also believe that there are facts which *could* not ever be represented or comprehended by human beings, even if the species lasted forever—simply because our structure does not permit us to operate with concepts of the requisite type. This impossibility might even be observed by other beings, but it is not clear that the existence of such beings, or the possibility of their existence, is a precondition of the significance of the hypothesis that there are humanly inaccessible facts. (After all, the nature of beings with access to humanly inaccessible facts is presumably itself a humanly inaccessible fact.) Reflection on what it is like to be a bat seems to lead us,

---

* Georg Cantor (1845–1918) was a German mathematician. His theory of transfinite numbers is a mathematical theory of infinity which introduces a sequence of infinite cardinal numbers (called 'aleph-numbers' and written $\aleph_0, \aleph_1, \aleph_2, ...$) of increasing size. That is, intuitively, Cantor formalized the fact that some infinities are bigger than others.

therefore, to the conclusion that there are facts that do not consist in the truth of propositions expressible in a human language. We can be compelled to recognize the existence of such facts without being able to state or comprehend them.

I shall not pursue this subject, however. Its bearing on the topic before us (namely, the mind-body problem) is that it enables us to make a general observation about the subjective character of experience. Whatever may be the status of facts about what it is like to be a human being, or a bat, or a Martian, these appear to be facts that embody a particular point of view.

I am not adverting here to the alleged privacy of experience to its possessor. The point of view in question is not one accessible only to a single individual. Rather it is a *type*. It is often possible to take up a point of view other than one's own, so the comprehension of such facts is not limited to one's own case. There is a sense in which phenomenological facts are perfectly objective: one person can know or say of another what the quality of the other's experience is. They are subjective, however, in the sense that even this objective ascription of experience is possible only for someone sufficiently similar to the object of ascription to be able to adopt his point of view—to understand the ascription in the first person as well as in the third, so to speak. The more different from oneself the other experiencer is, the less success one can expect with this enterprise. In our own case we occupy the relevant point of view, but we will have as much difficulty understanding our own experience properly if we approach it from another point of view as we would if we tried to understand the experience of another species without taking up *its* point of view.[8]

This bears directly on the mind-body problem. For if the facts of experience—facts about what it is like *for* the experiencing organism—are accessible only from one point of view, then it is a mystery how the true character of experiences could be revealed in the physical operation of that organism. The latter is a domain of objective facts *par excellence**—the kind that can be observed and understood from many points of view and by individuals with differing perceptual systems. There are no comparable imaginative obstacles to the acquisition of knowledge about

bat neurophysiology by human scientists, and intelligent bats or Martians might learn more about the human brain than we ever will.

This is not by itself an argument against reduction. A Martian scientist with no understanding of visual perception could understand the rainbow, or lightning, or clouds as physical phenomena, though he would never be able to understand the human concepts of rainbow, lightning, or cloud, or the place these things occupy in our phenomenal world. The objective nature of the things picked out by these concepts could be apprehended by him because, although the concepts themselves are connected with a particular point of view and a particular visual phenomenology, the things apprehended from that point of view are not: they are observable from the point of view but external to it; hence they can be comprehended from other points of view also, either by the same organisms or by others. Lightning has an objective character that is not exhausted by its visual appearance, and this can be investigated by a Martian without vision. To be precise, it has a *more* objective character than is revealed in its visual appearance. In speaking of the move from subjective to objective characterization, I wish to remain noncommittal about the existence of an end point, the completely objective intrinsic nature of the thing, which one might or might not be able to reach. It may be more accurate to think of objectivity as a direction in which the understanding can travel. And in understanding a phenomenon like lightning, it is legitimate to go as far away as one can from a strictly human viewpoint.[9]

In the case of experience, on the other hand, the connection with a particular point of view seems much closer. It is difficult to understand what could be meant by the *objective* character of an experience, apart from the particular point of view from which its subject apprehends it. After all, what would be left of what it was like to be a bat if one removed the viewpoint of the bat? But if experience does not have, in addition to its subjective character, an objective nature that can be apprehended from many different points of view, then how can it be supposed that a Martian investigating my brain might be observing physical processes which were my mental processes (as he

---

* French: "the best example of its kind."

might observe physical processes which were bolts of lightning), only from a different point of view? How, for that matter, could a human physiologist observe them from another point of view?[10]

We appear to be faced with a general difficulty about psychophysical reduction. In other areas the process of reduction is a move in the direction of greater objectivity, toward a more accurate view of the real nature of things. This is accomplished by reducing our dependence on individual or species-specific points of view toward the object of investigation. We describe it not in terms of the impressions it makes on our senses, but in terms of its more general effects and of properties detectable by means other than the human senses. The less it depends on a specifically human viewpoint, the more objective is our description. It is possible to follow this path because although the concepts and ideas we employ in thinking about the external world are initially applied from a point of view that involves our perceptual apparatus, they are used by us to refer to things beyond themselves— toward which we *have* the phenomenal point of view. Therefore we can abandon it in favor of another, and still be thinking about the same things.

Experience itself, however, does not seem to fit the pattern. The idea of moving from appearance to reality seems to make no sense here. What is the analogue in this case to pursuing a more objective understanding of the same phenomena by abandoning the initial subjective viewpoint toward them in favor of another that is more objective but concerns the same thing? Certainly it *appears* unlikely that we will get closer to the real nature of human experience by leaving behind the particularity of our human point of view and striving for a description in terms accessible to beings that could not imagine what it was like to be us. If the subjective character of experience is fully comprehensible only from one point of view, then any shift to greater objectivity—that is, less attachment to a specific viewpoint—does not take us nearer to the real nature of the phenomenon: it takes us farther away from it.

In a sense, the seeds of this objection to the reducibility of experience are already detectable in successful cases of reduction; for in discovering sound to be, in reality, a wave phenomenon in air or other media, we leave behind one viewpoint to take up another, and the auditory, human or animal viewpoint that we leave behind remains unreduced. Members of radically different species may both understand the same physical events in objective terms, and this does not require that they understand the phenomenal forms in which those events appear to the senses of members of the other species. Thus it is a condition of their referring to a common reality that their more particular viewpoints are not part of the common reality that they both apprehend. The reduction can succeed only if the species-specific viewpoint is omitted from what is to be reduced.

But while we are right to leave this point of view aside in seeking a fuller understanding of the external world, we cannot ignore it permanently, since it is the essence of the internal world, and not merely a point of view on it. Most of the neobehaviorism of recent philosophical psychology results from the effort to substitute an objective concept of mind for the real thing, in order to have nothing left over which cannot be reduced. If we acknowledge that a physical theory of mind must account for the subjective character of experience, we must admit that no presently available conception gives us a clue how this could be done. The problem is unique. If mental processes are indeed physical processes, then there is something it is like, intrinsically,[11] to undergo certain physical processes. What it is for such a thing to be the case remains a mystery.

What moral should be drawn from these reflections, and what should be done next? It would be a mistake to conclude that physicalism must be false. Nothing is proved by the inadequacy of physicalist hypotheses that assume a faulty objective analysis of mind. It would be truer to say that physicalism is a position we cannot understand because we do not at present have any conception of how it might be true. Perhaps it will be thought unreasonable to require such a conception as a condition of understanding. After all, it might be said, the meaning of physicalism is clear enough: mental states are states of the body; mental events are physical events. We do not know *which* physical states and events they are, but that should not prevent us from understanding the hypothesis. What could be clearer than the words "is" and "are"?

But I believe it is precisely this apparent clarity of the word "is" that is deceptive. Usually, when we are told that *X* is *Y* we know *how* it is supposed to be true, but that depends on a conceptual or theoretical background and is not conveyed by the "is" alone. We know how both "*X*" and "*Y*" refer, and the kinds of things to which they refer, and we have a rough idea how the two referential paths* might converge on a single thing, be it an object, a person, a process, an event, or whatever. But when the two terms of the identification are very disparate it may not be so clear how it could be true. We may not have even a rough idea of how the two referential paths could converge, or what kind of things they might converge on, and a theoretical framework may have to be supplied to enable us to understand this. Without the framework, an air of mysticism surrounds the identification.

This explains the magical flavor of popular presentations of fundamental scientific discoveries, given out as propositions to which one must subscribe without really understanding them. For example, people are now told at an early age that all matter is really energy. But despite the fact that they know what "is" means, most of them never form a conception of what makes this claim true, because they lack the theoretical background.

At the present time the status of physicalism is similar to that which the hypothesis that matter is energy would have had if uttered by a pre-Socratic philosopher.† We do not have the beginnings of a conception of how it might be true. In order to understand the hypothesis that a mental event is a physical event, we require more than an understanding of the word "is." The idea of how a mental and a physical term might refer to the same thing is lacking, and the usual analogies with theoretical identification in other fields fail to supply it. They fail because if we construe the reference of mental terms to physical events on the usual model, we either get a reappearance of separate subjective events as the effects through which mental reference to physical events is secured, or else we get a false account of how mental terms refer (for example, a causal behaviorist‡ one).

Strangely enough, we may have evidence for the truth of something we cannot really understand.

Suppose a caterpillar is locked in a sterile safe by someone unfamiliar with insect metamorphosis, and weeks later the safe is reopened, revealing a butterfly. If the person knows that the safe has been shut the whole time, he has reason to believe that the butterfly is or was once the caterpillar, without having any idea in what sense this might be so. (One possibility is that the caterpillar contained a tiny winged parasite that devoured it and grew into the butterfly.)

It is conceivable that we are in such a position with regard to physicalism. Donald Davidson has argued that if mental events have physical causes and effects, they must have physical descriptions. He holds that we have reason to believe this even though we do not—and in fact *could* not—have a general psychophysical theory.[12] His argument applies to intentional mental events, but I think we also have some reason to believe that sensations are physical processes, without being in a position to understand how. Davidson's position is that certain physical events have irreducibly mental properties, and perhaps some view describable in this way is correct. But nothing of which we can now form a conception corresponds to it; nor have we any idea what a theory would be like that enabled us to conceive of it.[13]

Very little work has been done on the basic question (from which mention of the brain can be entirely omitted) whether any sense can be made of experiences' having an objective character at all. Does it make sense, in other words, to ask what my experiences are *really* like, as opposed to how they appear to me? We cannot genuinely understand the hypothesis that their nature is captured in a physical description unless we understand the more fundamental idea that they *have* an objective nature (or that objective processes can have a subjective nature).[14]

I should like to close with a speculative proposal. It may be possible to approach the gap between subjective and objective from another direction. Setting aside temporarily the relation between the mind and

---

* By "referential paths" Nagel means something like the various ways in which we fix the reference of our words to a certain thing (e.g., by personal acquaintance or by a description in a textbook). For example, I have at least two "referential paths" to the stuff picked out by the word *water*: it is the liquid which comes out of the tap in my kitchen, and it is the substance which has the molecular composition H_2O.

† A philosopher who lived before or around the time of Socrates (d. 399 BCE).

‡ Nagel presumably means the idea that our mental states are defined as whatever physically causes certain characteristic patterns of behavior (e.g., the word "pain" refers to the cause of pain behavior).

the brain, we can pursue a more objective understanding of the mental in its own right. At present we are completely unequipped to think about the subjective character of experience without relying on the imagination—without taking up the point of view of the experiential subject. This should be regarded as a challenge to form new concepts and devise a new method—an objective phenomenology not dependent on empathy or the imagination. Though presumably it would not capture everything, its goal would be to describe, at least in part, the subjective character of experiences in a form comprehensible to beings incapable of having those experiences.

We would have to develop such a phenomenology to describe the sonar experiences of bats; but it would also be possible to begin with humans. One might try, for example, to develop concepts that could be used to explain to a person blind from birth what it was like to see. One would reach a blank wall eventually, but it should be possible to devise a method of expressing in objective terms much more than we can at present, and with much greater precision. The loose intermodal* analogies—for example, "Red is like the sound of a trumpet"—which crop up in discussions of this subject are of little use. That should be clear to anyone who has both heard a trumpet and seen red. But structural features of perception might be more accessible to objective description, even though something would be left out. And concepts alternative to those we learn in the first person may enable us to arrive at a kind of understanding even of our own experience which is denied us by the very ease of description and lack of distance that subjective concepts afford.

Apart from its own interest, a phenomenology that is in this sense objective may permit questions about the physical[15] basis of experience to assume a more intelligible form. Aspects of subjective experience that admitted this kind of objective description might be better candidates for objective explanations of a more familiar sort. But whether or not this guess is correct, it seems unlikely that any physical theory of mind can be contemplated until more thought has been given to the general problem of subjective and objective. Otherwise we cannot even pose the mind-body problem without sidestepping it.[16] ∎

Suggestions for Critical Reflection

1. Many commentators suggest that Nagel collapses together two or three different kinds of subjectivity that would be better kept separate. Do you agree with this criticism? If so, how much of a problem (if any) does this cause for Nagel's arguments?

2. Do you think Nagel makes a good case for the claim that the reduction of, say, pain to some objectively-describable physical state is a very different ball game than the reduction of, for example, heat or liquidity to microphysical properties? If he's right about this, what philosophical implications are there (if any)?

3. Do you agree that there must be some facts—some things which are true—which could never be known by any human being, no matter how intelligent or well-informed?

4. Given Nagel's arguments, do you think that physicalism could possibly be true? That is, does Nagel leave open the possibility that everything that exists is, at bottom, physical (e.g., composed out of matter and energy)?

5. What do you think of Nagel's proposal for an "objective phenomenology"? What might such a theory look like? Is it even possible? Does Nagel *really* hold open the possibility of an objective description of the subjective character of experience?

---

*   Crossing between modes of sensation, such as sight and touch.

Notes

1 Examples are J.J.C. Smart, *Philosophy and Scientific Realism* (London, 1963); David K. Lewis, "An Argument for the Identity Theory," *Journal of Philosophy*, LXIII (1966), reprinted with addenda in David M. Rosenthal, *Materialism & the Mind-Body Problem* (Englewood Cliffs, N.J., 1971); Hilary Putnam, "Psychological Predicates" in Capitan and Merrill, *Art, Mind, & Religion* (Pittsburgh, 1967), reprinted in Rosenthal, *op. cit.*, as "The Nature of Mental States"; D.M. Armstrong, *A Materialist Theory of the Mind* (London, 1968); D.C. Dennett, *Content and Consciousness* (London, 1969). I have expressed earlier doubts in "Armstrong on the Mind," *Philosophical Review*, LXXIX (1970), 394–403; "Brain Bisection and the Unity of Consciousness," *Synthèse*, 22 (1971); and a review of Dennett, *Journal of Philosophy*, LXIX (1972). See also Saul Kripke, "Naming and Necessity" in Davidson and Harman, *Semantics of Natural Language* (Dordrecht, 1972), esp. pp. 334–342; and M.T. Thornton, "Ostensive Terms and Materialism," *The Monist*, 56 (1972).

2 Perhaps there could not actually be such robots. Perhaps anything complex enough to behave like a person would have experiences. But that, if true, is a fact which cannot be discovered merely by analyzing the concept of experience.

3 It is not equivalent to that about which we are incorrigible, both because we are not incorrigible about experience and because experience is present in animals lacking language and thought, who have no beliefs at all about their experiences.

4 Cf. Richard Rorty, "Mind-Body Identity, Privacy, and Categories," *The Review of Metaphysics*, XIX (1965), esp. 37–38.

5 By "our own case" I do not mean just "my own case," but rather the mentalistic ideas that we apply unproblematically to ourselves and other human beings.

6 Therefore the analogical form of the English expression "what it is *like*" is misleading. It does not mean "what (in our experience) it *resembles*," but rather "how it is for the subject himself."

7 Any intelligent extraterrestrial beings totally different from us.

8 It may be easier than I suppose to transcend inter-species barriers with the aid of the imagination. For example, blind people are able to detect objects near them by a form of sonar, using vocal clicks or taps of a cane. Perhaps if one knew what that was like, one could by extension imagine roughly what it was like to possess the much more refined sonar of a bat. The distance between oneself and other persons and other species can fall anywhere on a continuum. Even for other persons the understanding of what it is like to be them is only partial, and when one moves to species very different from oneself, a lesser degree of partial understanding may still be available. The imagination is remarkably flexible. My point, however, is not that we cannot *know* what it is like to be a bat. I am not raising that epistemological problem. My point is rather that even to form a *conception* of what it is like to be a bat (and a fortiori to know what it is like to be a bat) one must take up the bat's point of view. If one can take it up roughly, or partially, then one's conception will also be rough or partial. Or so it seems in our present state of understanding.

9 The problem I am going to raise can therefore be posed even if the distinction between more subjective and more objective descriptions or viewpoints can itself be made only within a larger human point of view. I do not accept this kind of conceptual relativism, but it need not be refuted to make the point that psycho-physical reduction cannot be accommodated by the subjective-to-objective model familiar from other cases.

10 The problem is not just that when I look at the "Mona Lisa," my visual experience has a certain quality, no trace of which is to be found by someone looking into my brain. For even if he did observe there a tiny image of the "Mona Lisa," he would have no reason to identify it with the experience.

11 The relation would therefore not be a contingent one, like that of a cause and its distinct effect. It would be necessarily true that a certain physical state felt a certain way. Saul Kripke (*op. cit.*) argues that causal behaviorist and related analyses of the mental fail because they construe, e.g., "pain" as a merely contingent name of pains. The subjective character of an experience ("its immediate phenomenological quality" Kripke calls it [p. 340]) is the essential property left out by such analyses, and the one in virtue of which it is, necessarily, the experience it is. My view is closely related to his. Like Kripke, I find the hypothesis that a certain brain state should *necessarily* have a certain subjective character incomprehensible without further explanation. No such explanation emerges from theories which view the mind-brain relation as contingent, but perhaps there are other alternatives, not yet discovered.

A theory that explained how the mind-brain relation was necessary would still leave us with Kripke's problem of explaining why it nevertheless appears contingent. That difficulty seems to me surmountable, in the following way. We may imagine something by representing it to ourselves either perceptually, sympathetically, or symbolically. I shall not try to say how symbolic imagination works, but part of what happens in the other two cases is this. To imagine something perceptually, we put ourselves in a conscious state resembling the state we would be in if we perceived it. To imagine something sympathetically, we put ourselves in a conscious state resembling the thing itself. (This method can be used only to imagine mental events and states—our own or another's.) When we try to imagine a mental state occurring without its associated brain state, we first sympathetically imagine the occurrence of the mental state: that is, we put ourselves into a state that resembles it mentally. At the same time, we attempt to perceptually imagine the non-occurrence of the associated physical state, by putting ourselves into another state unconnected with the first: one resembling that which we would be in if we perceived the nonoccurrence of the physical state. Where the imagination of physical features is perceptual and the imagination of mental features is sympathetic, it appears to us that we can imagine any experience occurring without its associated brain state, and vice versa. The relation between them will appear contingent even if it is necessary, because of the independence of the disparate types of imagination.

(Solipsism, incidentally, results if one misinterprets sympathetic imagination as if it worked like perceptual imagination: it then seems impossible to imagine any experience that is not one's own.)

12 See "Mental Events" in Foster and Swanson, *Experience and Theory* (Amherst, 1970); though I don't understand the argument against psychophysical laws.

13 Similar remarks apply to my paper "Physicalism," *Philosophical Review* LXXIV (1965), 339–356, reprinted with postscript in John O'Connor, *Modern Materialism* (New York, 1969).

14 This question also lies at the heart of the problem of other minds, whose close connection with the mind-body problem is often overlooked. If one understood how subjective experience could have an objective nature, one would understand the existence of subjects other than oneself.

15 I have not defined the term "physical." Obviously it does not apply just to what can be described by the concepts of contemporary physics, since we expect further developments. Some may think there is nothing to prevent mental phenomena from eventually being recognized as physical in their own right. But whatever else may be said of the physical, it has to be objective. So if our idea of the physical ever expands to include mental phenomena, it will have to assign them an objective character—whether or not this is done by analyzing them in terms of other phenomena already regarded as physical. It seems to me more likely, however, that mental-physical relations will eventually be expressed in a theory whose fundamental terms cannot be placed clearly in either category.

16 I have read versions of this paper to a number of audiences, and am indebted to many people for their comments.

FRANK JACKSON

FROM *Epiphenomenal Qualia* AND *What Mary Didn't Know*

Who Is Frank Jackson?

Frank Cameron Jackson was born in Australia in 1943. He studied mathematics and philosophy at the University of Melbourne and received his PhD in philosophy from La Trobe University. His main appointments have been in Australia: at the University of Adelaide, Monash University, and the Australian National University (ANU) in Canberra. At ANU, he served as Director of the Institute of Advanced Studies (1998–2001), Deputy Vice-Chancellor (Research) (2001), and Director of the Research School of Social Sciences (2004–07). He was Distinguished Professor at ANU from 2003 until his retirement in 2014, and between 2007 and 2013 he split his time with a half-time appointment at Princeton University. In 2006, Jackson was awarded the Order of Australia for his contributions to philosophy. He is the author of many books and articles on the philosophy of mind, philosophical logic, cognitive science, epistemology, metaphysics, and meta-ethics.

His thought-experiment involving Mary the 'color-blind' brain scientist, introduced in his article "Epiphenomenal Qualia," has been extremely influential and widely discussed; his later article "What Mary Didn't Know" deals with Mary's case in more detail.[*] Both articles are excerpted below. In these articles Jackson defends dualism about mind and body on the basis of the impossibility of providing a physical explanation of experience. It should be noted, however, that in articles published in 1995 and later Jackson recanted his dualism, commenting that "[m]ost contemporary philosophers given a choice between going with science and going with intuitions, go with science. Although I once dissented from the majority, I have capitulated and now see the interesting issue as being where the arguments from the intuitions against physicalism—the arguments that seem so compelling—go wrong."[†]

Jackson is also known, along with philosopher David Lewis, for his unfashionable defence of the relevance—indeed, the centrality—of conceptual analysis to philosophy, an approach sometimes nicknamed the Canberra Plan.[‡]

What Are the Structures of These Articles?

Jackson begins by defining physicalism as the position that "all (correct) information is physical information" and then declares that he considers physicalism false—that is, he thinks that some true facts are not physical facts. His goal in this paper is to go beyond appeals to intuition and to develop a compelling argument, based on obvious premises, that this is true. He calls this argument the "Knowledge Argument." Jackson lays out two thought experiments to develop this argument: Fred who can see two reds, and Mary the 'color-blind' brain scientist. Although in the original article he spends less time describing the Mary case, it is this which has come to be considered the core version of the Knowledge Argument.

Jackson, like most contemporary dualists, thinks it is likely that every physical event has a complete physical cause—he assumes there are no mysterious gaps in the physical explanations for the events in our brains,

---

[*]   It is the subject of an edited volume, *There's Something about Mary* (2004, edited by Ludlow, Nagasawa and Stoljar). Mary's plight was dramatized in the three-part UK documentary *Brainspotting* (1996), and also features (along with Jackson himself) in David Lodge's novel *Thinks ...* (2001).

[†]   "Mind and Illusion," in *Minds and Persons: Royal Institute of Philosophy Supplement* 53, ed. A. O'Hear (Cambridge University Press, 2003), 251.

[‡]   See his *From Metaphysics to Ethics: A Defense of Conceptual Analysis* (Oxford University Press, 1998).

or the ways our bodies behave. That is, although he is arguing that the physical sciences are incomplete, in the sense that they completely miss some key information about the universe (information about qualia), they are nevertheless complete* *within the domain of the physical*: we can fully explain physical phenomena using only physics. But what this means, on the face of it, is that non-physical qualia cannot be relevant to these explanations: we can completely understand neurology and human behavior without mentioning conscious states at all. This bizarre result is known as "epiphenomenalism," and the next section of Jackson's paper is devoted to coming to grips with it. His key point is that epiphenomenalism could be true—it's not just obvious that it's false—and that therefore the Knowledge Argument is not refuted by it.

The short selection from "What Mary Didn't Know" gives three responses to objections to Jackson's Mary argument in the earlier paper.

Some Useful Background Information

Epiphenomenalism about mind has a long philosophical history. It emerged with the growth of modern science, beginning in the Renaissance, as the tension between two strong intuitions grew: it gradually seemed more and more likely that physical events of every sort had physical causes only, while it struck most thinkers as obvious that the mental was a very different domain than the physical (and especially the physical as it was understood by modern science). Descartes, the most influential historical substance dualist, ran into a good deal of criticism because he held that mental events could cause physical ones. By the mid-twentieth century, the most common response to this difficulty was to deny dualism: to hold that mental events actually were physical ones, so could be causes (and effects) of other physical events. As we see in the Jackson article, a return to some sort of dualism seemed to require endorsing epiphenomenalism about the mental.

Epiphenomenal Qualia†

It is undeniable that the physical, chemical and biological sciences have provided a great deal of information about the world we live in and about ourselves. I will use the label 'physical information' for this kind of information, and also for information that automatically comes along with it. For example, if a medical scientist tells me enough about the processes that go on in my nervous system, and about how they relate to happenings in the world around me, to what has happened in the past and is likely to happen in the future, to what happens to other similar and dissimilar organisms, and the like, he or she tells me—if I am clever enough to fit it together appropriately—about what is often called the functional role of those states in me (and in organisms in general in similar cases). This information, and its kin, I also label 'physical'.

I do not mean these sketchy remarks to constitute a definition of 'physical information', and of the correlative notions of physical property, process, and so on, but to indicate what I have in mind here. It is well known that there are problems with giving a precise definition of these notions, and so of the thesis of Physicalism that all (correct) information is physical information. But—unlike some—I take the question of definition to cut across the central problems I want to discuss in this paper.

I am what is sometimes known as a "qualia freak".‡ I think that there are certain features of the bodily sensations especially, but also of certain perceptual experiences, which no amount of purely physical information includes. Tell me everything physical there is to tell about what is going on in a living brain, the kind of states, their functional role, their relation

---

*   Or will some day be complete.

†   From *The Philosophical Quarterly* 32, 127 (1982): 127–30, 133–36.

‡   Qualia (pronounced KWAH-lee-a; singular *quale* [KWAH-lay]) are subjective qualities of conscious experience; for example, pains, tastes, the visual experience of colors.

to what goes on at other times and in other brains, and so on and so forth, and be I as clever as can be in fitting it all together, you won't have told me about the hurtfulness of pains, the itchiness of itches, the pangs of jealousy, or about the characteristic experience of tasting a lemon, smelling a rose, hearing a loud noise or seeing the sky.

There are many qualia freaks, and some of them say that their rejection of Physicalism is an unargued intuition. I think that they are being unfair to themselves. They have the following argument. Nothing you could tell of a physical sort captures the smell of a rose, for instance. Therefore, Physicalism is false. By our lights this is a perfectly good argument. It is obviously not to the point to question its validity, and the premise is intuitively obviously true both to them and to me.

I must, however, admit that it is weak from a polemical point of view. There are, unfortunately for us, many who do not find the premise intuitively obvious. The task then is to present an argument whose premises are obvious to all, or at least to as many as possible. This I try to do in §I with what I will call "the Knowledge argument". In §II I contrast the Knowledge argument with the Modal argument and in §III with the "What is it like to be" argument. In §IV I tackle the question of the causal role of qualia. The major factor in stopping people from admitting qualia is the belief that they would have to be given a causal role with respect to the physical world and especially the brain; and it is hard to do this without sounding like someone who believes in fairies. I seek in §IV to turn this objection by arguing that the view that qualia are epiphenomenal* is a perfectly possible one.

I. The Knowledge Argument for Qualia

People vary considerably in their ability to discriminate colours. Suppose that in an experiment to catalogue this variation Fred is discovered. Fred has better colour vision than anyone else on record; he makes every discrimination that anyone has ever made, and moreover he makes one that we cannot even begin to make. Show him a batch of ripe tomatoes and he sorts them into two roughly equal groups and does so with complete consistency. That is, if you blindfold him, shuffle the tomatoes up, and then remove the blindfold and ask him to sort them out again, he sorts them into exactly the same two groups.

We ask Fred how he does it. He explains that all ripe tomatoes do not look the same colour to him, and in fact that this is true of a great many objects that we classify together as red. He sees two colours where we see one, and he has in consequence developed for his own use two words 'red$_1$' and 'red$_2$' to mark the difference. Perhaps he tells us that he has often tried to teach the difference between red$_1$ and red$_2$ to his friends but has got nowhere and has concluded that the rest of the world is red$_1$-red$_2$ colourblind—or perhaps he has had partial success with his children, it doesn't matter. In any case he explains to us that it would be quite wrong to think that because 'red' appears in both 'red$_1$' and 'red$_2$' that the two colours are shades of the one colour. He only uses the common term 'red' to fit more easily into our restricted usage. To him red$_1$ and red$_2$ are as different from each other and all the other colours as yellow is from blue. And his discriminatory behaviour bears this out: he sorts red$_1$ from red$_2$ tomatoes with the greatest of ease in a wide variety of viewing circumstances. Moreover, an investigation of the physiological basis of Fred's exceptional ability reveals that Fred's optical system is able to separate out two groups of wave-lengths in the red spectrum as sharply as we are able to sort out yellow from blue.

I think that we should admit that Fred can see, really see, at least one more colour than we can; red$_1$ is a different colour from red$_2$. We are to Fred as a totally red-green colour-blind person is to us. H.G. Wells' story "The Country of the Blind" is about a sighted person in a totally blind community.[1] This person never manages to convince them that he can see, that he has an extra sense. They ridicule this sense as quite inconceivable, and treat his capacity to avoid falling into ditches, to win fights and so on as precisely that capacity and nothing more. We would be making

---

* An epiphenomenon (plural *epiphenomena*) is something caused by some system of events, but having no effects in that system. An example is the sound made by a running car: it's caused by vibrations at various places in the car, but it has no effect on the car. An epiphenomenalist about mind holds that mental events are epiphenomena—physically caused, but having no mental or physical effect.

their mistake if we refused to allow that Fred can see one more colour than we can.

What kind of experience does Fred have when he sees red₁ and red₂? What is the new colour or colours like? We would dearly like to know but do not; and it seems that no amount of physical information about Fred's brain and optical system tells us. We find out perhaps that Fred's cones respond differentially to certain light waves in the red section of the spectrum that make no difference to ours (or perhaps he has an extra cone) and that this leads in Fred to a wider range of those brain states responsible for visual discriminatory behaviour. But none of this tells us what we really want to know about his colour experience. There is something about it we don't know. But we know, we may suppose, everything about Fred's body, his behaviour and dispositions to behaviour and about his internal physiology, and everything about his history and relation to others that can be given in physical accounts of persons. We have all the physical information. Therefore, knowing all this is *not* knowing everything about Fred. It follows that Physicalism leaves something out.

To reinforce this conclusion, imagine that as a result of our investigations into the internal workings of Fred we find out how to make everyone's physiology like Fred's in the relevant respects; or perhaps Fred donates his body to science and on his death we are able to transplant his optical system into someone else—again the fine detail doesn't matter. The important point is that such a happening would create enormous interest. People would say, "At last we will know what it is like to see the extra colour, at last we will know how Fred has differed from us in the way he has struggled to tell us about for so long". Then it cannot be that we knew all along all about Fred. But *ex hypothesi** we did know all along everything about Fred that features in the physicalist scheme; hence the physicalist scheme leaves something out.

Put it this way. *After* the operation, we will know *more* about Fred and especially about his colour experiences. But beforehand we had all the physical information we could desire about his body and brain, and indeed everything that has ever featured in physicalist accounts of mind and consciousness. Hence there is more to know than all that. Hence Physicalism is incomplete.

Fred and the new colour(s) are of course essentially rhetorical devices. The same point can be made with normal people and familiar colours. Mary is a brilliant scientist who is, for whatever reason, forced to investigate the world from a black and white room *via* a black and white television monitor. She specialises in the neurophysiology of vision and acquires, let us suppose, all the physical information there is to obtain about what goes on when we see ripe tomatoes, or the sky, and use terms like 'red', 'blue', and so on. She discovers, for example, just which wave-length combinations from the sky stimulate the retina, and exactly how this produces *via* the central nervous system the contraction of the vocal chords and expulsion of air from the lungs that results in the uttering of the sentence 'The sky is blue'. (It can hardly be denied that it is in principle possible to obtain all this physical information from black and white television, otherwise the Open University† would *of necessity* need to use colour television.)

What will happen when Mary is released from her black and white room or is given a colour television monitor? Will she *learn* anything or not? It seems just obvious that she will learn something about the world and our visual experience of it. But then it is inescapable that her previous knowledge was incomplete. But she had *all* the physical information. *Ergo* there is more to have than that, and Physicalism is false.

Clearly the same style of Knowledge argument could be deployed for taste, hearing, the bodily sensations and generally speaking for the various mental states which are said to have (as it is variously put) raw feels, phenomenal features or qualia. The conclusion in each case is that the qualia are left out of the physicalist story. And the polemical strength of the Knowledge argument is that it is so hard to deny the central claim that one can have all the physical information without having all the information there is to have.

...

---

*   Latin: by assumption, as defined by the set-up of the hypothesis.
†   A British university offering distance education, partly through broadcast lectures.

IV. The Bogey of Epiphenomenalism

Is there any really *good* reason for refusing to countenance the idea that qualia are causally impotent with respect to the physical world? I will argue for the answer no, but in doing this I will say nothing about two views associated with the classical epiphenomenalist position. The first is that mental *states* are inefficacious with respect to the physical world. All I will be concerned to defend is that it is possible to hold that certain *properties* of certain mental states, namely those I've called qualia, are such that their possession or absence makes no difference to the physical world. The second is that the mental is *totally* causally inefficacious. For all I will say it may be that you have to hold that the instantiation of *qualia* makes a difference to *other mental states* though not to anything physical. Indeed general considerations to do with how you could come to be aware of the instantiation of qualia suggest such a position.

Three reasons are standardly given for holding that a quale like the hurtfulness of a pain must be causally efficacious in the physical world, and so, for instance, that its instantiation must sometimes make a difference to what happens in the brain. None, I will argue, has any real force....

(i) It is supposed to be just obvious that the hurtfulness of pain is partly responsible for the subject seeking to avoid pain, saying 'It hurts' and so on. But, to reverse Hume, anything can fail to cause anything. No matter how often B follows A, and no matter how initially obvious the causality of the connection seems, the hypothesis that A causes B can be overturned by an over-arching theory which shows the two as distinct effects of a common underlying causal process.

To the untutored the image on the screen of Lee Marvin's fist moving from left to right immediately followed by the image of John Wayne's head moving in the same general direction looks as causal as anything. And of course throughout countless Westerns images similar to the first are followed by images similar to the second. All this counts for precisely nothing when we know the over-arching theory concerning how the relevant images are both effects of an underlying causal process involving the projector and the film. The epiphenomenalist can say exactly the same about the connection between, for example, hurtfulness and behaviour. It is simply a consequence of the fact that certain happenings in the brain cause both.

(ii) The second objection relates to Darwin's Theory of Evolution. According to natural selection the traits that evolve over time are those conducive to physical survival. We may assume that qualia evolved over time—we have them, the earliest forms of life do not—and so we should expect qualia to be conducive to survival. The objection is that they could hardly help us to survive if they do nothing to the physical world.

The appeal of this argument is undeniable, but there is a good reply to it. Polar bears have particularly thick, warm coats. The Theory of Evolution explains this (we suppose) by pointing out that having a thick, warm coat is conducive to survival in the Arctic. But having a thick coat goes along with having a heavy coat, and having a heavy coat is *not* conducive to survival. It slows the animal down.

Does this mean that we have refuted Darwin because we have found an evolved trait—having a heavy coat—which is not conducive to survival? Clearly not. Having a heavy coat is an unavoidable concomitant of having a warm coat (in the context, modern insulation was not available), and the advantages for survival of having a warm coat outweighed the disadvantages of having a heavy one. The point is that all we can extract from Darwin's theory is that we should expect any evolved characteristic to be either conducive to survival *or* a by-product of one that is so conducive. The epiphenomenalist holds that qualia fall into the latter category. They are a by-product of certain brain processes that are highly conducive to survival.

(iii) The third objection is based on a point about how we come to know about other minds. We know about other minds by knowing about other behaviour, at least in part. The nature of the inference is a matter of some controversy, but it is not a matter of controversy that it proceeds from behaviour. That is why we think that stones do not feel and dogs do feel. But, runs the objection, how can a person's behaviour provide any reason for believing he has qualia like mine, or indeed any qualia at all, unless this behaviour can be regarded as the *outcome* of the qualia. Man Friday's footprint was evidence of Man Friday* because footprints are

---

* Robinson Crusoe's first evidence that he is not alone on his island (in Daniel Defoe's 1719 novel of the same name).

causal outcomes of feet attached to people. And an epiphenomenalist cannot regard behaviour, or indeed anything physical, as an outcome of qualia.

But consider my reading in *The Times* that Spurs* won. This provides excellent evidence that *The Telegraph* has also reported that Spurs won, despite the fact that (I trust) *The Telegraph* does not get the results from *The Times*. They each send their own reporters to the game. *The Telegraph*'s report is in no sense an outcome of *The Times*', but the latter provides good evidence for the former nevertheless.

The reasoning involved can be reconstructed thus. I read in *The Times* that Spurs won. This gives me reason to think that Spurs won because I know that Spurs' winning is the most likely candidate to be what caused the report in *The Times*. But I also know that Spurs' winning would have had many effects, including almost certainly a report in *The Telegraph*.

I am arguing from one effect back to its cause and out again to another effect. The fact that neither effect causes the other is irrelevant. Now the epiphenomenalist allows that qualia are effects of what goes on in the brain. Qualia cause nothing physical but are caused by something physical. Hence the epiphenomenalist can argue from the behaviour of others to the qualia of others by arguing from the behaviour of others back to its causes in the brains of others and out again to their qualia.

You may well feel for one reason or another that this is a more dubious chain of reasoning than its model in the case of newspaper reports. You are right. The problem of other minds is a major philosophical problem, the problem of other newspaper reports is not. But there is no special problem of Epiphenomenalism as opposed to, say, Interactionism here.

There is a very understandable response to the three replies I have just made. "All right, there is no knockdown refutation of the existence of epiphenomenal qualia. But the fact remains that they are an excrescence.† They *do* nothing, they *explain* nothing, they serve merely to soothe the intuitions of dualists, and it is left a total mystery how they fit into the world view of science. In short we do not and cannot understand the how and why of them."

This is perfectly true; but is no objection to qualia, for it rests on an overly optimistic view of the human animal, and its powers. We are the products of Evolution. We understand and sense what we need to understand and sense in order to survive. Epiphenomenal qualia are totally irrelevant to survival. At no stage of our evolution did natural selection favour those who could make sense of how they are caused and the laws governing them, or in fact why they exist at all. And that is why we can't.

It is not sufficiently appreciated that Physicalism is an extremely optimistic view of our powers. If it is true, we have, in very broad outline admittedly, a grasp of our place in the scheme of things. Certain matters of sheer complexity defeat us—there are an awful lot of neurons—but in principle we have it all. But consider the antecedent probability that everything in the Universe be of a kind that is relevant in some way or other to the survival of *homo sapiens*. It is very low surely. But then one must admit that it is very likely that there is a part of the whole scheme of things, maybe a big part, which no amount of evolution will ever bring us near to knowledge about or understanding. For the simple reason that such knowledge and understanding is irrelevant to survival.

Physicalists typically emphasise that we are a part of nature on their view, which is fair enough. But if we are a part of nature, we are as nature has left us after however many years of evolution it is, and each step in that evolutionary progression has been a matter of chance constrained just by the need to preserve or increase survival value. The wonder is that we understand as much as we do, and there is no wonder that there should be matters which fall quite outside our comprehension. Perhaps exactly how epiphenomenal qualia fit into the scheme of things is one such.

This may seem an unduly pessimistic view of our capacity to articulate a truly comprehensive picture of our world and our place in it. But suppose we discovered living on the bottom of the deepest oceans a sort of sea slug which manifested intelligence. Perhaps survival in the conditions required rational powers. Despite their intelligence, these sea slugs have only a very restricted conception of the world by comparison

---

* The London soccer team Tottenham Hotspur.

† An abnormal disfiguring outgrowth.

with ours, the explanation for this being the nature of their immediate environment. Nevertheless they have developed sciences which work surprisingly well in these restricted terms. They also have philosophers, called slugists. Some call themselves tough-minded slugists, others confess to being soft-minded slugists.

The tough-minded slugists hold that the restricted terms (or ones pretty like them which may be introduced as their sciences progress) suffice in principle to describe everything without remainder. These tough-minded slugists admit in moments of weakness to a feeling that their theory leaves something out. They resist this feeling and their opponents, the soft-minded slugists, by pointing out—absolutely correctly—that no slugist has ever succeeded in spelling out how this mysterious residue fits into the highly successful view that their sciences have and are developing of how their world works.

Our sea slugs don't exist, but they might. And there might also exist super beings which stand to us as we stand to the sea slugs. We cannot adopt the perspective of these super beings, because we are not them, but the possibility of such a perspective is, I think, an antidote to excessive optimism.

What Mary Didn't Know[*]

...

I. Three Clarifications

The knowledge argument does not rest on the dubious claim that logically you cannot imagine what sensing red is like unless you have sensed red. Powers of imagination are not to the point. The contention about Mary is not that, despite her fantastic grasp of neurophysiology and everything else physical, she *could not imagine* what it is like to sense red; it is that, as a matter of fact, she *would not know*. But if physicalism is true, she would know; and no great powers of imagination would be called for. Imagination is a faculty that those who *lack* knowledge need to fall back on.

Secondly, the intensionality of knowledge[†] is not to the point. The argument does not rest on assuming falsely that, if S knows that *a* is *F* and if *a* = *b*, then S knows that *b* is *F*. It is concerned with the nature of Mary's total body of knowledge before she is released: is it complete, or do some facts escape it? What is to the point is that S may know that *a* is *F* and *know* that *a* = *b*, yet arguably not know that *b* is *F*, by virtue of not being sufficiently logically alert to follow the consequences through. If Mary's lack of knowledge were at all like this, there would be no threat to physicalism in it. But it is very hard to believe that her lack of knowledge could be remedied merely by her explicitly following through enough logical consequences of her vast physical knowledge. Endowing her with great logical acumen and persistence is not in itself enough to fill in the gaps in her knowledge. On being let out, she will not say "I could have worked all this out before by making some more purely logical inferences."

Thirdly, the knowledge Mary lacked which is of particular point for the knowledge argument against physicalism is *knowledge about the experiences of others*, not about her own. When she is let out, she has new experiences, color experiences she has never had before. It is not, therefore, an objection to physicalism that she learns *something* on being let out. Before she was let out, she could not have known facts about her experience of red, for there were no such facts to know. That physicalist and nonphysicalist alike can agree on. After she is let out, things change; and physicalism can happily admit that she learns this; after all, some physical things will change, for instance, her brain states and their functional roles. The trouble for physicalism is that, after Mary sees her first ripe tomato, she will realize how impoverished her conception of the mental life of *others* has been *all along*. She will

---

[*] From *The Journal of Philosophy* 83 (1986): 291–95.

[†] To say that knowledge is intensional is to say that one might know something when it is expressed in one way but not know *the same thing* when it is expressed another way. For example, I might know that Snoop Dogg is a rap musician but deny any knowledge of Calvin Cordozar Broadus, Jr. Yet they're the same person.

realize that there was, all the time she was carrying out her laborious investigations into the neurophysiologies of others and into the functional roles of their internal states, something about these people she was quite unaware of. All along their experiences (or many of them, those got from tomatoes, the sky, ...) had a feature conspicuous to them but until now hidden from her (in fact, not in logic). But she knew all the physical facts about them all along; hence, what she did not know until her release is not a physical fact about their experiences. But it is a fact about them. That is the trouble for physicalism.... ■

Suggestions for Critical Reflection

1. Anti-epiphenomenalists think that it's just obvious that our thoughts and feelings have causal influence on our other thoughts and feelings, and on our actions. Does Jackson give an adequate rebuttal to this idea? If he does not, what does this mean for the Knowledge Argument?

2. *Consider this objection; is it right?*
If Mary knows everything physical there is to know about colors and color-perception, then she *would* know what it's like to experience red things, even though while locked in her cell she'd never done that. To argue that there's something she doesn't know is simply to beg the question.

3. *Consider this objection; is it right?*
What Mary gets when she emerges from her room is not new knowledge of some sort of fact. Instead, it's merely a different way of knowing about some fact *that she already knew* in a different way. For example, perhaps now she is directly "acquainted" with something that before she knew "propositionally," that is via a description. Therefore the Knowledge Argument fails to show that there are any non-physical facts.

4. *Consider this objection; is it right?*
What Mary gets when she emerges from her room is not new knowledge of some sort of fact. Instead, it's a kind of knowledge that isn't about facts at all—it's knowing *how* to do something rather than knowing *that* something is true. For example, I know something new when I learn to swim but this isn't a matter of knowing new facts; it's a matter of having a new ability. Similarly, liberated-Mary has new abilities with respect to qualia: she can recognise them, remember them, re-identify them without using scientific instruments, etc. Therefore the Knowledge Argument fails to show that there are any non-physical facts.

5. "It may be that you have to hold that the instantiation of *qualia* makes a difference to *other mental states* though not to anything physical. Indeed general considerations to do with how you could come to be aware of the instantiation of qualia suggest such a position." This off-hand comment by Jackson opens a can of worms for the epiphenomenalist, a set of problems sometimes called the Paradox of Phenomenal Judgement. For example, if qualia have no causal effect on behaviour, then they have no causal effect on our *reports* of our own qualia (such as saying "Ouch, that really hurts!"). But in that case, in what sense can our reports of qualia (or our knowledge of our own qualia, our interest in the problem of consciousness, etc.) actually *be* about qualia, since they are not caused by them? Even worse, if we can't report on or know about qualia, why do we think they exist in the first place?

6. As mentioned above, Jackson now has changed his mind about the knowledge argument. Here's his account of what went wrong with his knowledge argument:

Intensionalism means that no amount of tub-thumping assertion by dualists (including by me in the past) that the *redness* of seeing red cannot be accommodated in the austere physicalist picture carries any weight. That striking feature is a feature of how things are being represented to be, and if, as claimed by the tub thumpers, it is transparently a feature that has no place in the physicalist picture, what follows is that physicalists should deny that anything has that striking feature. And this is no argument against physicalism. Physicalists can allow that people are sometimes in states that represent that things have a non-physical property. Examples are people who believe that there are fairies. What physicalists must deny is that such properties are instantiated.*

See if you can explain what he means here in your own terms: what might it be to deny that there is any such thing as "the *redness* of seeing red"? By contrast, how does Jackson try to deal with the intensionality of knowledge in "What Mary Didn't Know"? Who do you think is right, the earlier or the later Jackson?

Note

1 H.G. Wells, *The Country of the Blind and Other Stories* (London, n.d. [1911]).

---

* "Mind and Illusion," *op cit.*

DAVID CHALMERS

The Puzzle of Conscious Experience

Who Is David Chalmers?

David Chalmers was born in Sydney, Australia, in 1966. As a child he excelled in the sciences, especially mathematics, and he earned a bronze medal representing Australia at the notoriously challenging International Mathematical Olympiad in 1982. As a boy he also had synaesthesia, which is a condition where the stimulation of one sensory or cognitive pathway leads to experiences in a second, normally unconnected, sensory or cognitive pathway. In Chalmers, music produced strong color sensations in his mind. "Somewhat disappointingly most songs were murky shades of brown or olive green, but every now and then there was something distinctive. I remember that 'Here, There, and Everywhere' by the Beatles was bright red."*

His undergraduate degree, at the University of Adelaide, concentrated in mathematics and computer science, and he went to the University of Oxford as a Rhodes Scholar to do graduate work in mathematics. However, he had a growing interest in philosophy, and especially the problem of explaining consciousness. Influenced by Douglas Hofstadter's 1979 book *Gödel, Escher, Bach*, about the emergence of cognition from hidden neurological mechanisms, he made the radical decision to switch fields and moved to Indiana University to work in Hofstadter's Center for Research on Concepts and Cognition there. After completing his PhD in 1993 and a two-year post-doctoral fellowship at Washington University in St. Louis, Chalmers taught at UC Santa Cruz and the University of Arizona. In 1994 he gave an influential talk introducing what he called the "hard problem of consciousness" at the inaugural Toward a Science of Consciousness conference, and in 1996 he published the highly influential book *The Conscious Mind*.

Chalmers moved to the Australian National University in Canberra in 2004, and then to New York University, where he is University Professor of Philosophy and Neural Science and—along with Ned Block—co-director of the Center for Mind, Brain and Consciousness. He is also lead singer of the Zombie Blues band, and co-founder of the supremely useful PhilPapers,[†] a comprehensive online index, archive, and bibliography of philosophical writing.

What Is Chalmers's Overall Philosophical Project?

Chalmers is best known for arguing that the problem of integrating phenomenal consciousness—the subjective smells, sights, tastes and so on that make up our flow of conscious experience—into the physical world (and the natural sciences) is a uniquely difficult problem: indeed, what he calls "the hard problem." He does not argue specifically for dualism, but he does think we have compelling reasons to think that no physicalist account of consciousness could ever be successful. This is the subject of the article reprinted here.

In support of this, one of his central arguments is the so-called Zombie Argument (which lies in the background to, but is not explicitly described in, this paper). Zombies—of the philosophical rather than the Haitian or Hollywood variety—are theoretically constructed creatures stipulated to be identical in certain respects with ordinary human beings, but lacking in other respects. In Chalmers's argument, the zombies in question are identical to regular human beings in every physical way—they have brains just like ours, behave just like us, talk in the same way we do, etc.—but are different from human beings in that they lack conscious experience. From the outside your zombie twin is completely indiscernible from you, no matter what behavioral or scientific tests are performed; but 'from the inside' your zombie twin is

---

* From an interview on the website "What Is It Like to Be a Philosopher?" (28 September 2016).

† PhilPapers can be found at https://philpapers.org.

dark within. Its actions and utterances are not accompanied by any conscious sensations, such as pain, the taste of coffee, the sensation of seeing the vivid yellow of a maple tree in the fall....

The Zombie Argument itself can get somewhat complicated, and extensive discussion of the argument over the past twenty years has given rise to a substantial supporting philosophical apparatus. But the basic idea is fairly straightforward:

1. The zombies I have just described are *conceivable*. No one thinks they actually exist, but it is hard to deny that we can imagine them. We could, for example, write a perfectly coherent science fiction story in which a zombie is the protagonist.
2. Conceivability is a guide to logical possibility. We cannot imagine a square triangle or a male vixen, and these things are logically impossible. We can imagine a universe in which the laws of physics allow a pig-like creature to have wings and fly, or that we are subject to a complex deception and cats are actually robotic spies placed on Earth by an alien race, and—although these things are not true, or likely, or (at least in the first case) physically possible—they are nevertheless *logically* possible.
3. So zombies are logically possible.
4. But the logical possibility of zombies is incompatible with the truth of physicalism.
5. So physicalism is false.

A lot of the action here happens in premise 4, of course. Why should we believe it? The central idea is that if consciousness *just is* something physical, then it should not make sense to hold the physical constant while *changing* consciousness. That would be like trying to leave your house exactly as it is in every detail, while simultaneously performing home improvements; this doesn't even make sense, unless your house somehow is not the same thing as your home. Consider the case of 'zombie water': water that is physically exactly like regular water, but that has some difference such as that it is solid at room temperature. If you think hard about this case, you should see that it is actually logically impossible—it

is incoherent—because of the stipulation that zombie water is physically exactly like regular water. Nothing could have all the same microphysical properties and also be subject to all the same laws of physics and yet *not* be liquid at room temperature. Physics explains natural phenomena by showing that, if the physical theory is true, the thing to be explained *had* to be that way. So the apparent conceivability of zombies, while it might seem trivial at first sight, turns out to be hugely significant.*

The center of gravity of Chalmers's work is the problem of consciousness and its consequences, but he has also done influential work on language and meaning (including developing "two-dimensional semantics"), the metaphysics and epistemology of possibility, and artificial minds (including the threat of a "singularity"—a point beyond which artificial intelligence will enter a phase of runaway development beyond human control).

What Is the Structure of This Reading?

Chalmers begins with a distinction he thinks is fundamental to the philosophy of mind: between the functions carried out by the mental faculties, of gathering information from sensation, directing muscular activity, and so on, on the one hand, and the experiences of conscious life—of our impressions of shapes and colors, our feelings of pain and pleasure, our emotions and thoughts: in sum, our mental life—on the other. He's willing to grant that neuroscience could give a physicalist explanation of all of the former phenomena; his argument is that science can never begin to explain our mental life, to answer questions like: Why do we have *that* experience when we eat strawberries? Why are there any experiences at all? The first job of explanation he calls the "easy problem"—not meaning that it's easy to do, but rather just that science knows how to approach it, and it's scientifically doable; the second he calls the "hard problem"—not meaning that it's simply more difficult, but rather that it's really impossible for physical science.

After raising several examples that seem to show that neuroscience is inadequate to explain consciousness, Chalmers briefly considers and rejects the pros-

---

* Chalmers's landmark 1995 article laying out this argument and more than 20 responses by other philosophers are collected in *Explaining Consciousness: The Hard Problem*, ed. Jonathan Shear (MIT Press, 1999).

pect of solving the problem with "new tools of physical explanation." He proposes that the way forward instead is to postulate a new "fundamental component" for our theories that would allow them to connect together the physical and the phenomenal. He explores this idea— which, he suggests, is the only possible fruitful way of moving forward on the problem of consciousness— tentatively suggesting a version of this theory whereby "[p]erhaps information, or at least some information, has two basic aspects: a physical one and an experiential one." If this were so, he notes, then it might be that in some sense consciousness would be ubiquitous, making this a version of a theory called "panpsychism."

Some Useful Background Information

As science made enormous progress during the nineteenth and early twentieth centuries, a growing number of philosophers came to believe that the physical, scientific categories that had been deployed so successfully in explaining events elsewhere would someday have equal success in dealing with the mental; equally, more and more philosophers came to think that a unified view of reality was the correct one: a view that everything was made of one sort of physical stuff.

These two ideas, however, were separable. While (probably) most philosophers remained physicalist—believing that everything was ultimately constructed out of the same sort of matter, basically obeying the same sorts of laws—doubts grew during the second half of the twentieth century that physical explanation for mental events would be possible; that is, that there was, for example, a kind of brain event that happened every time anyone thought about dinner, that *constituted* thinking about dinner.

The most common theory denying the explicability of the mental by the physical came from the functionalists, who typically held that mental events were classified functionally—that is, by their typical causes and effects—and instances of a single mental type (e.g., wishing you had a hamburger now) might be realized by any of a possibly infinite number of different physical types of event. We can imagine, for example, that a Martian, whose brain was built on entirely different principles from ours, might also yearn for a hamburger, but this yearning might be identical in his case to a totally different physical brain event than in you. If there could not be a physical type corresponding, in an exceptionless way, to any mental type, then there could not be mental-physical bridge laws, and thus no physical explanation of the mental. (Most functionalists are, however, physicalists in the important sense that they believe that each particular mental event is also a physical event.)

Other arguments to the same conclusion relied on the basically normative character of mental ascriptions; the idea here is that whenever we assign beliefs and desires to others, we assume their rationality (otherwise their behavior might be correlated with any beliefs and desires whatever). Rationality is essentially an evaluative notion, thus having no place in physical sciences, like neurophysiology. Thus mental categories must cut up phenomena differently from physical ones; and again exceptionless "bridge" laws linking the two would be impossible. (Again, philosophers who accept this argument are generally physicalists.)

Chalmers, by contrast, accepts the idea that there are relations between the mental and the physical that can be described in terms of scientific laws. He denies, however, that these can be completely physical laws: they would have to describe correlations between the physical and the irreducibly mental.

The Puzzle of Conscious Experience*

Conscious experience is at once the most familiar thing in the world and the most mysterious. There is nothing we know about more directly than consciousness, but it is extraordinarily hard to reconcile it with everything else we know. Why does it exist? What does it do? How could it possibly arise from neural processes in the brain? These questions are among the most intriguing in all of science.

From an objective viewpoint, the brain is relatively comprehensible. When you look at this page, there is a whir of processing: photons strike your retina, electrical signals are passed up your optic nerve and between different areas of your brain, and eventually you might respond with a smile, a perplexed frown or a remark. But there is also a subjective aspect. When you look at the page, you are conscious of it, directly experiencing the images and words as part of your private, mental life. You have vivid impressions of the colors and shapes of the images. At the same time, you may be feeling some emotions and forming some thoughts. Together such experiences make up consciousness: the subjective, inner life of the mind.

For many years, consciousness was shunned by researchers studying the brain and the mind. The prevailing view was that science, which depends on objectivity, could not accommodate something as subjective as consciousness. The behaviorist movement in psychology, dominant earlier in this century, concentrated on external behavior and disallowed any talk of internal mental processes. Later, the rise of cognitive science focused attention on processes inside the head. Still, consciousness remained off-limits, fit only for late-night discussion over drinks.

Over the past several years, however, an increasing number of neuroscientists, psychologists and philosophers have been rejecting the idea that consciousness cannot be studied and are attempting to delve into its secrets. As might be expected of a field so new, there is a tangle of diverse and conflicting theories, often using basic concepts in incompatible ways. To help unsnarl the tangle, philosophical reasoning is vital.

The myriad views within the field range from reductionist theories, according to which consciousness can be explained by the standard methods of neuroscience and psychology, to the position of the so-called mysterians, who say we will never understand consciousness at all. I believe that on close analysis both of these views can be seen to be mistaken and that the truth lies somewhere in the middle.

Against reductionism I will argue that the tools of neuroscience cannot provide a full account of conscious experience, although they have much to offer. Against mysterianism I will hold that consciousness might be explained by a new kind of theory. The full details of such a theory are still out of reach, but careful reasoning and some educated inferences can reveal something of its general nature. For example, it will probably involve new fundamental laws, and the concept of information may play a central role. These faint glimmerings suggest that a theory of consciousness may have startling consequences for our view of the universe and of ourselves.

The Hard Problem

Researchers use the word "consciousness" in many different ways. To clarify the issues, we first have to separate the problems that are often clustered together under the name. For this purpose, I find it useful to distinguish between the "easy problems" and the "hard problem" of consciousness. The easy problems are by no means trivial—they are actually as challenging as most in psychology and biology—but it is with the hard problem that the central mystery lies.

The easy problems of consciousness include the following: How can a human subject discriminate sensory stimuli and react to them appropriately? How does the brain integrate information from many different sources and use this information to control behavior? How is it that subjects can verbalize their internal states? Although all these questions are associated with consciousness, they all concern the objective mechanisms

---

*   This article was published in *Scientific American* in December 1995. It was reprinted, slightly updated, in the Scientific American Special Edition *The Hidden Mind* 12, 1 (2002): 90–100.

of the cognitive system. Consequently, we have every reason to expect that continued work in cognitive psychology and neuroscience will answer them.

The hard problem, in contrast, is the question of how physical processes in the brain give rise to subjective experience. This puzzle involves the inner aspect of thought and perception: the way things feel for the subject. When we see, for example, we experience visual sensations, such as that of vivid blue. Or think of the ineffable sound of a distant oboe, the agony of an intense pain, the sparkle of happiness or the meditative quality of a moment lost in thought. All are part of what I call consciousness. It is these phenomena that pose the real mystery of the mind.

To illustrate the distinction, consider a thought experiment devised by the Australian philosopher Frank Jackson. Suppose that Mary, a neuroscientist in the 23rd century, is the world's leading expert on the brain processes responsible for color vision. But Mary has lived her whole life in a black-and-white room and has never seen any other colors. She knows everything there is to know about physical processes in the brain— its biology, structure and function. This understanding enables her to grasp all there is to know about the easy problems: how the brain discriminates stimuli, integrates information and produces verbal reports. From her knowledge of color vision, she knows how color names correspond with wave-lengths on the light spectrum. But there is still something crucial about color vision that Mary does not know: what it is like to experience a color such as red. It follows that there are facts about conscious experience that cannot be deduced from physical facts about the functioning of the brain.

Indeed, nobody knows why these physical processes are accompanied by conscious experience at all. Why is it that when our brains process light of a certain wavelength, we have an experience of deep purple? Why do we have any experience at all? Could not an unconscious automaton have performed the same tasks just as well? These are questions that we would like a theory of consciousness to answer.

Is Neuroscience Enough?

I am not denying that consciousness arises from the brain. We know, for example, that the subjective experience of vision is closely linked to processes in the visual cortex. It is the link itself that perplexes, however. Remarkably, subjective experience seems to emerge from a physical process. But we have no idea how or why this is.

Given the flurry of recent work on consciousness in neuroscience and psychology, one might think this mystery is starting to be cleared up. On closer examination, however, it turns out that almost all the current work addresses only the easy problems of consciousness. The confidence of the reductionist view comes from the progress on the easy problems, but none of this makes any difference where the hard problem is concerned.

Consider the hypothesis put forward by neurobiologists Francis Crick of the Salk Institute for Biological Studies in San Diego and Christof Koch of the California Institute of Technology. They suggest that consciousness may arise from certain oscillations in the cerebral cortex, which become synchronized as neurons fire 40 times per second. Crick and Koch believe the phenomenon might explain how different attributes of a single perceived object (its color and shape, for example), which are processed in different parts of the brain, are merged into a coherent whole. In this theory, two pieces of information become bound together precisely when they are represented by synchronized neural firings.

The hypothesis could conceivably elucidate one of the easy problems about how information is integrated in the brain. But why should synchronized oscillations give rise to a visual experience, no matter how much integration is taking place? This question involves the hard problem, about which the theory has nothing to offer. Indeed, Crick and Koch are agnostic about whether the hard problem can be solved by science at all.

The same kind of critique could be applied to almost all the recent work on consciousness. In his 1991 book *Consciousness Explained*, philosopher Daniel C. Dennett laid out a sophisticated theory of how numerous independent processes in the brain combine to produce a coherent response to a perceived event. The theory might do much to explain how we produce verbal reports on our internal states, but it tells us very little about why there should be a subjective experience behind these reports. Like other reductionist theories, Dennett's is a theory of the easy problems.

The critical common trait among these easy problems is that they all concern how a cognitive or behavioral function is performed. All are ultimately questions about how the brain carries out some task—how it discriminates stimuli, integrates information, produces reports and so on. Once neurobiology specifies appropriate neural mechanisms, showing how the functions are performed, the easy problems are solved.

The hard problem of consciousness, in contrast, goes beyond problems about how functions are performed. Even if every behavioral and cognitive function related to consciousness were explained, there would still remain a further mystery: Why is the performance of these functions accompanied by conscious experience? It is this additional conundrum that makes the hard problem hard.

The Explanatory Gap

Some have suggested that to solve the hard problem, we need to bring in new tools of physical explanation: non-linear dynamics, say, or new discoveries in neuroscience, or quantum mechanics. But these ideas suffer from exactly the same difficulty. Consider a proposal from Stuart R. Hameroff of the University of Arizona and Roger Penrose of the University of Oxford. They hold that consciousness arises from quantum-physical processes taking place in microtubules, which are protein structures inside neurons. It is possible (if not likely) that such a hypothesis will lead to an explanation of how the brain makes decisions or even how it proves mathematical theorems, as Hameroff and Penrose suggest. But even if it does, the theory is silent about how these processes might give rise to conscious experience. Indeed, the same problem arises with any theory of consciousness based only on physical processing.

The trouble is that physical theories are best suited to explaining why systems have a certain physical structure and how they perform various functions. Most problems in science have this form; to explain life, for example, we need to describe how a physical system can reproduce, adapt and metabolize. But consciousness is a different sort of problem entirely, as it goes beyond the scientific explanation of structure and function.

Of course, neuroscience is not irrelevant to the study of consciousness. For one, it may be able to reveal the nature of the neural correlate of consciousness—the brain processes most directly associated with conscious experience. It may even give a detailed correspondence between specific processes in the brain and related components of experience. But until we know why these processes give rise to conscious experience at

all, we will not have crossed what philosopher Joseph Levine has called the explanatory gap between physical processes and consciousness. Making that leap will demand a new kind of theory.

In searching for an alternative, a key observation is that not all entities in science are explained in terms of more basic entities. In physics, for example, space-time, mass and charge (among other things) are regarded as fundamental features of the world, as they are not reducible to anything simpler. Despite this irreducibility, detailed and useful theories relate these entities to one another in terms of fundamental laws. Together these features and laws explain a great variety of complex and subtle phenomena.

A True Theory of Everything

It is widely believed that physics provides a complete catalogue of the universe's fundamental features and laws. As physicist Steven Weinberg puts it in his 1992 book *Dreams of a Final Theory*, the goal of physics is a "theory of everything" from which all there is to know about the universe can be derived. But Weinberg concedes that there is a problem with consciousness. Despite the power of physical theory, the existence of consciousness does not seem to be derivable from physical laws. He defends physics by arguing that it might eventually explain what he calls the objective correlates of consciousness (that is, the neural correlates), but of course to do this is not to explain consciousness itself. If the existence of consciousness cannot be derived from physical laws, a theory of physics is not a true theory of everything. So a final theory must contain an additional fundamental component.

Toward this end, I propose that conscious experience be considered a fundamental feature, irreducible to anything more basic. The idea may seem strange at first, but consistency seems to demand it. In the 19th century it turned out that electromagnetic phenomena could not be explained in terms of previously known principles. As a consequence, scientists introduced electromagnetic charge as a new fundamental entity and studied the associated fundamental laws. Similar reasoning should be applied to consciousness. If existing fundamental theories cannot encompass it, then something new is required.

Where there is a fundamental property, there are fundamental laws. In this case, the laws must relate experience to elements of physical theory. These laws will almost certainly not interfere with those of the physical world; it seems that the latter form a closed system in their own right. Rather the laws will serve as a bridge, specifying how experience depends on underlying physical processes. It is this bridge that will cross the explanatory gap.

Thus, a complete theory will have two components: physical laws, telling us about the behavior of physical systems from the infinitesimal to the cosmological, and what we might call psychophysical laws, telling us how some of those systems are associated with conscious experience. These two components will constitute a true theory of everything.

Supposing for the moment that they exist, how might we uncover such psychophysical laws? The greatest hindrance in this pursuit will be a lack of data. As I have described it, consciousness is subjective, so there is no direct way to monitor it in others. But this difficulty is an obstacle, not a dead end. For a start, each one of us has access to our own experiences, a rich trove that can be used to formulate theories. We can also plausibly rely on indirect information, such as subjects' descriptions of their experiences. Philosophical arguments and thought experiments also have a role to play. Such methods have limitations, but they give us more than enough to get started.

These theories will not be conclusively testable, so they will inevitably be more speculative than those of more conventional scientific disciplines. Nevertheless, there is no reason they should not be strongly constrained to account accurately for our own first-person experiences, as well as the evidence from subjects' reports. If we find a theory that fits the data better than any other theory of equal simplicity, we will have good reason to accept it. Right now we do not have even a single theory that fits the data, so worries about testability are premature.

We might start by looking for high-level bridging laws, connecting physical processes to experience at an everyday level. The basic contour of such a law might be gleaned from the observation that when we are conscious of something, we are generally able to act on it and speak about it—which are objective, physical functions. Conversely, when some information is directly available for action and speech, it is generally conscious. Thus, consciousness correlates well with what we might call "awareness": the process by which information in the brain is made globally available to motor processes such as speech and bodily action.

Objective Awareness

The notion may seem trivial. But as defined here, awareness is objective and physical, whereas consciousness is not. Some refinements to the definition of awareness are needed, in order to extend the concept to animals and infants, which cannot speak. But at least in familiar cases, it is possible to see the rough outlines of a psychophysical law: where there is awareness, there is consciousness, and vice versa.

To take this line of reasoning a step further, consider the structure present in the conscious experience. The experience of a field of vision, for example, is a constantly changing mosaic of colors, shapes and patterns and as such has a detailed geometric structure. The fact that we can describe this structure, reach out in the direction of many of its components and perform other actions that depend on it suggests that the structure corresponds directly to that of the information made available in the brain through the neural processes of objective awareness.

Similarly, our experiences of color have an intrinsic three-dimensional structure that is mirrored in the structure of information processes in the brain's visual cortex. This structure is illustrated in the color wheels and charts used by artists. Colors are arranged in a systematic pattern—red to green on one axis, blue to yellow on another, and black to white on a third. Colors that are close to one another on a color wheel are experienced as similar. It is extremely likely that they also correspond to similar perceptual representations in the brain, as one part of a system of complex three-dimensional coding among neurons that is not yet fully understood. We can recast the underlying concept as a principle of structural coherence: the structure of conscious experience is mirrored by the structure of information in awareness, and vice versa.

Another candidate for a psychophysical law is a principle of organizational invariance. It holds that physical systems with the same abstract organization will give rise to the same kind of conscious experience, no matter what they are made of. For example, if the precise interactions between our neurons could be duplicated with silicon chips, the same conscious experience would arise. The idea is somewhat controversial, but I believe it is strongly supported by thought experiments describing the gradual replacement of neurons by silicon chips. The remarkable implication is that consciousness might someday be achieved in machines.

Theory of Consciousness

The ultimate goal of a theory of consciousness is a simple and elegant set of fundamental laws, analogous to the fundamental laws of physics. The principles described above are unlikely to be fundamental, however. Rather they seem to be high-level psychophysical laws, analogous to macroscopic principles in physics such as those of thermodynamics or kinematics. What might the underlying fundamental laws be? No one really knows, but I don't mind speculating.

I suggest that the primary psychophysical laws may centrally involve the concept of information. The abstract notion of information, as put forward in the 1940s by Claude E. Shannon of the Massachusetts Institute of Technology, is that of a set of separate states with a basic structure of similarities and differences between them. We can think of a 10-bit binary code as an information state, for example. Such information states can be embodied in the physical world. This happens whenever they correspond to physical states (voltages, say) and when differences between them can be transmitted along some pathway, such as a telephone line.

We can also find information embodied in conscious experience. The pattern of color patches in a visual field, for example, can be seen as analogous to that of the pixels covering a display screen. Intriguingly, it turns out that we find the same information states embedded in conscious experience and in underlying physical processes in the brain. The three-dimensional encoding of color spaces, for example, suggests that the information state in a color experience corresponds directly to an information state in the brain. Thus, we might even regard the two states as distinct aspects of a single information state, which is simultaneously embodied in both physical processing and conscious experience.

Aspects of Information

A natural hypothesis ensues. Perhaps information, or at least some information, has two basic aspects: a physical one and an experiential one. This hypothesis has the status of a fundamental principle that might underlie the relation between physical processes and experience. Wherever we find conscious experience, it exists as one aspect of an information state, the other aspect of which is embedded in a physical process in the brain. This proposal needs to be fleshed out to make a satisfying theory. But it fits nicely with the principles mentioned earlier—systems with the same organization will embody the same information, for example—and it could explain numerous features of our conscious experience.

The idea is at least compatible with several others, such as physicist John A. Wheeler's suggestion that information is fundamental to the physics of the universe. The laws of physics might ultimately be cast in informational terms, in which case we would have a satisfying congruence between the constructs in both physical and psychophysical laws. It may even be that a theory of physics and a theory of consciousness could eventually be consolidated into a single grander theory of information.

A potential problem is posed by the ubiquity of information. Even a thermostat embodies some information, for example, but is it conscious? There are at least two possible responses. First, we could constrain the fundamental laws so that only some information has an experiential aspect, perhaps depending on how it is physically processed. Second, we might bite the bullet and allow that all information has an experiential aspect—where there is complex information processing, there is complex experience, and where there is simple information processing, there is simple experience. If this is so, then even a thermostat might have experiences, although they would be much simpler than even a basic color experience, and there would certainly be no accompanying emotions or thoughts. This seems odd at first, but if experience is truly fundamental, we might expect it to be widespread. In any case, the choice between these alternatives should depend on which can be integrated into the most powerful theory.

Of course, such ideas may be all wrong. On the other hand, they might evolve into a more powerful proposal that predicts the precise structure of our conscious experience from physical processes in our brains. If this project succeeds, we will have good reason to accept the theory. If it fails, other avenues will be pursued, and alternative fundamental theories may be developed. In this way, we may one day resolve the greatest mystery of the mind. ∎

Suggestions for Critical Reflection

1. Chalmers says "I am not denying that consciousness arises from the brain." This is accurate, but perhaps a bit surprising. What does he think is the relationship between the brain and consciousness?

2. Valerie Gray Hardcastle suggests we

> Consider the following exchange. A water-mysterian wonders why water has this peculiar property [being wet]. She inquires and you give an explanation of the molecular composition of water and a brief story about the connection between micro-chemical properties and macro-phenomena. Ah, she says ... I am convinced that you have properly correlated water with its underlying molecular composition. I also have no reason to doubt ... your story about the macro-effects of chemical properties to be wrong. But I still am not satisfied, for you have left off in your explanation what I find most puzzling. Why *is* water H_2O? Why couldn't it be XYZ? Why couldn't it have some other radically different chemical story behind it? I can imagine a possible world in which water has all the macro-properties that it has now, but is not composed of H_2O ... What *can* one say? I think nothing. Water-mysterians are antecedently convinced of the mysteriousness of water and no amount of scientific data is going to change that perspective. Either you already believe that science is going to give you a correct identity statement, or you don't and you think that there is always going to be something left over, the wateriness of water.*

What analogy is Hardcastle drawing with Chalmers's position? The suggestion here is that consciousness-mysterianism is just as baseless as water-mysterianism, but that there are no arguments that could convince either mysterian that their positions are wrong. Do you agree?

3. Hardcastle points out that both materialists and dualists accept some facts as "brute facts"—unexplainable features of the universe, just the way it is; but she remarks that "it seems highly unlikely that some relatively chauvinistic *biological* fact should ever be brute." If this is to be a criticism of Chalmers, what's the "relatively chauvinistic biological fact" in his view? (What does "chauvinistic" mean in this context?) See if you can explain why Hardcastle thinks that this view is "highly unlikely."

4. What is Chalmers's "principle of organizational invariance"? What are its implications, if it's true? (Is it true?)

5. Chalmers imagines that some day psychophysical laws will be discovered. But if that's the case, would that allow "facts about conscious experience" to be "deduced from physical facts about the functioning of the brain"? If so, does this contradict what Chalmers claims about the "Mary" story?

6. At the end of the reading, Chalmers raises the prospect of panpsychism: the view that everything (or at least everything that "processes information," including certainly thermostats and All Wheel Drive traction systems, and possibly even natural processes such as convection) is conscious. How palatable is this notion? If we must reject it, what problems might this cause for Chalmers?

---

* "The Why of Consciousness: A Non-issue for Materialists," *Journal of Consciousness Studies* 3, 1 (1996): 7–13.

AMY KIND

How to Believe in Qualia

Who Is Amy Kind?

Amy Kind is an American philosopher who writes mainly about imagination, consciousness, and experience. She earned her MA and PhD at the University of California Los Angeles, and is now Russell K. Pitzer Professor of Philosophy at Claremont McKenna College in California. Kind co-edited two major texts on philosophy and the imagination—the *Routledge Handbook of Philosophy of Imagination* (2016) and *Knowledge Through Imagination* (2016)—and authored the textbook *Persons and Personal Identity* (2015) as well as numerous articles on cognition, qualia, and experience. Kind has described her research as an attempt to "put the image back in imagination."* She also runs a scholarly blog called "The Junkyard," which publishes posts about the philosophy of imagination by current academic philosophers. "Historically," she writes, "imagination has played a central role in the work of philosophers such as Aristotle, Descartes, Hume, Kant, Sartre, and many others...."†

What Is the Structure of This Reading?

In this paper, Kind addresses the issue of "qualia"—that is, the subjective, what-it's-like qualities of conscious experience. When we see a certain shade of color on an object, for example, our experience itself seems to be colorful in that way. When we hear a certain sound from an instrument, our experience may seem to have certain distinctive qualities that can be isolated and that are something other than representations of the instrument. These properties of experience are what philosophers call qualia (or, in the singular, a quale), and—largely because they appear to be in tension with

our best scientific theories of the world—some philosophers deny that they exist.

Kind's goal is to convince us that we should believe in qualia. The main motivation for "qualia realism," according to Kind, is simply the fact that we seem to experience qualia all the time. Some philosophers, however, deny this claim. According to these "opponents of qualia," we don't actually experience qualia; rather, what we experience is simply *things*, out there in the world, like trees, faces, thunder claps, coffee cups, etc. This claim—that we experience things directly, without any mysterious mediating mental objects like qualia—is what Kind refers to as the "transparency thesis." Kind's aim in this paper is to disprove this thesis, and in doing so demonstrate that qualia realism should be our default philosophical position. She does so by considering a number of mundane experiences (such as seeing a tree) and exotic ones (such as the afterimage on the back of your closed eyelids), arguing that these experiences give us good reason to think that qualia exist.

Some Useful Background Information

Kind writes that "[g]enerally speaking, the main proponents of the transparency thesis are representationalists." Representationalism about consciousness is the view that what is sometimes called phenomenal content—what it is like to eat an egg or watch a sunset—is (nothing more than) a variety of representational content. That is, the "pink" experience of watching a sunset is nothing other than the fact that the experience represents—is about—a pink sunset. The advantage of this approach is that representational content is, arguably, fairly well understood and able to be accounted for naturalistically. That is, we have theories of how

---

* Kind, "Putting the Image Back in Imagination," *Philosophy and Phenomenological Research* 62, 1 (2001): 85–109.
† Kind, "Welcome to the Junkyard" (2017), at *The Junkyard*, https://junkyardofthemind.com/blog/2017/4/3/welcome-to-the-junkyard-1

our mental states come to be about the things they are about, and those theories are compatible with a generally physicalist, naturalistic view of the world. If we can use these sorts of theories to explain phenomenal consciousness, then consciousness also can be naturalised. A key commitment of representationalism about consciousness, then, is that everything that makes consciousness special can be accounted for in terms of the *contents* of conscious states—what conscious states are *about*. Tacitly, this is a denial that conscious states—the vehicles carrying that content—have any properties *themselves* that are special in any mysterious way. That is, representationalism denies that qualia, understood as properties *of* conscious states, exist.*

How to Believe in Qualia[†]

Why should we believe that qualia[‡] exist? It would not be surprising if, when confronted with this question, the qualia realist were puzzled. "Look around you," she might say, "and then pause for just a moment and reflect on your experiences. Isn't there a redness to your experience of that soda can on your desk? And isn't there a sweetness to your experience as you take a sip from it? Surely your experiences have qualitative aspects—surely there is something your experiences are like." And thus, to many a qualia realist, the answer to the question posed above is simple. Why believe in qualia? Because our every experience reveals their existence.

Unfortunately, the matter cannot be resolved this easily. (If it could, then there would be no need to produce a collection of papers making the case for qualia.) The existence of qualia has long been under attack. Opponents of qualia typically fall into two camps. In the first camp, we have philosophers who admit that, at least on the face of it, the phenomenological[§] data support the existence of qualia. By their lights, however, there are strong theoretical reasons that count against qualia (typically that they cannot be accommodated within a physicalist[¶] framework). These opponents thus have the task of explaining why we should disregard the phenomenology of our experience. They must convince us why we should *not* believe in qualia.

In the second camp, however, are philosophers who deny the phenomenological data. Qualia realists have it wrong, they say. In fact, our experience does not reveal the existence of any qualia, for our experience is *transparent*—when we attend to our experiences, our attention goes right through to their objects. Such philosophers typically take these considerations of transparency to support a representationalist view

---

* Confusingly, there is also a position in the philosophy of perception called "representationalism" which holds that the world we see in conscious experience is not 'directly' the real world itself, but a virtual-reality replica of that world in an internal representation and hence that our perceptual access to reality is only 'indirect.' This is a distinct position from representationalism about consciousness—and is actually one that these kinds of representationalists typically deny. (Because otherwise the colors, smells, and tastes we experience would have to be properties of the inner representations somewhere between us and the world, and that is just another version of the problem of consciousness. Much more attractive, from a representationalist about consciousness's point of view, is to take the colors etc. we experience to be physical properties of objects out there in the world.)

† Amy Kind, "How to Believe in Qualia," in *The Case for Qualia*, ed. Edmond Wright (MIT Press, 2008), 285–98.

‡ In philosophy, "qualia" refers to the qualities of our subjective, conscious experiences—or what it is *like* to have a given experience.

§ In this context, "phenomenological" can be read roughly as "experiential," and "phenomenology" as something like "immediate first-hand experience."

¶ Physicalism is the view that the only things that exist are physical things.

of consciousness according to which the qualitative content of experience supervenes on,* or even reduces to, the intentional content† of experience. But for our purposes, what's important is that these philosophers deny that we have any reasons to believe in qualia—or, at the very least, that if we do have any such reasons, they are not provided by our experience. These opponents of qualia thus shift the burden of argument to the qualia realist. It is the qualia realist's responsibility, they say, to convince us why we should believe in qualia.

This essay aims to do just that. As I will suggest, these philosophers in the second camp are mistaken—the phenomenological data do support the existence of qualia. I will not address those philosophers in the first camp, that is, I do not take up the question of how qualia can be accommodated in a physicalist, or even naturalist, account of the mind (though the argument may suggest that it needs to be). But by showing that experience does, after all, support the existence of qualia, I aim to show that qualia realism should be our default position.

1 The Transparency Thesis

The view that our experience is transparent is generally thought to trace back at least to G.E. Moore,‡ who wrote, "When we try to introspect the sensation of blue, all we can see is the blue: the other element is as if it were diaphanous" (Moore 1903: 450). Although Moore subsequently qualifies this characterization of experience,[1] this remark has inspired many contemporary philosophers who present similar phenomenological descriptions. For example, consider the following passages from Michael Tye:

Focus your attention on a square that has been painted blue. Intuitively, you are directly aware of blueness and squareness as out there in the world away from you, as features of an external surface. Now shift your gaze inward and try to become aware of your experience itself, inside you, apart from its objects. Try to focus your attention on some intrinsic feature of the experience that distinguishes it from other experiences, something other than what it is an experience *of.* The task seems impossible: one's awareness seems always to slip through the experience to blueness and squareness, as instantiated together in an external object. In turning one's mind inward to attend to the experience, one seems to end up concentrating on what is outside again, on external features or properties. (Tye 1995: 30)[2]

If you are attending to how things *look* to you, as opposed to how they are independent of how they look, you are bringing to bear your faculty of introspection. But in so doing, you are not aware of any inner object or thing. The only objects of which you are aware are the external ones making up the scene before your eyes. Nor, to repeat, are you directly aware of any qualities of your experience. (Tye 2000: 46–47)

Likewise, consider Gilbert Harman's characterization of experience:

When Eloise sees a tree before her, the colors she experiences are all experienced as features of the tree and its surroundings. None of them are experienced as intrinsic features of her experience. Nor does she experience any features of anything as intrinsic features of her experiences. And that is true of you too. There is nothing special about Eloise's visual experience. When you see a tree, you do not experience any features as intrinsic features

---

* Some set of facts or properties A supervenes on another set of properties B just in case A cannot vary unless B varies. For example, facts about chairs supervene on facts about the atoms that those chairs are made of: a chair cannot change position, for example, unless its atoms do too.

† By "intentional content," Kind means the things that our experiences are *about.* "Representationalism," then, is the view that our experiences are nothing more than the things our experiences are about, and a theory of consciousness will be complete if it can fully explain the contents of our conscious experiences without needing to also explain any 'left over' properties of those experiences themselves (such as qualia).

‡ G.E. Moore (1873–1958) was a British philosopher known especially for his work in ethics and analytic philosophy. See the Epistemology chapter of this volume.

of your experience. Look at a tree and try to turn your attention to intrinsic features of your visual experience. I predict you will find that the only features there to turn your attention to will be features of the presented tree.... (Harman 1990: 39)

These passages support what I'll call the *transparency thesis*, that is, the claim that experience is transparent. Some philosophers who endorse considerations of transparency intend only a very weak claim, namely, that is *difficult* to attend directly to our experience, or that *typically* we don't attend directly to our experience. But I take it that philosophers like Harman and Tye want to endorse a stronger version of the claim. On their view, it is not simply difficult but *impossible* to attend directly to our experience. The only way to attend to our experience is by attending to the objects represented by that experience.[3] In what follows, I reserve the label "transparency thesis" for this strong claim.

As stated, even in this strong form, the transparency thesis is not itself a denial of the existence of qualia—or at least not straightforwardly so. In claiming that we cannot attend to qualia in attending to our experience, the transparency thesis remains silent on the question of whether qualia exist. But the transparency thesis nonetheless poses quite a threat to the qualia realist. First of all, we might plausibly suppose that any qualia worthy of the name must be introspectible, that is, introspectibility is essential to the nature of qualia.[4] If this is right, then the fact that the transparency thesis denies that qualia are available to introspection ends up being tantamount to a denial of their existence. But even if we were to accept that there could exist non-introspectible qualia, the transparency thesis would still have anti-qualia ramifications. For even if the transparency thesis is strictly speaking compatible with the existence of qualia, if qualia cannot be introspectively attended to then it looks like we no longer have any reason to believe that they exist. Insofar as our belief in qualia is driven by phenomenological considerations, our being deprived of those considerations leaves the belief entirely unjustified.[5]

Generally speaking, the main proponents of the transparency thesis are representationalists. In fact, many representationalists use the transparency thesis as support for their theory, claiming that representationalism offers the best explanation of the phenomenon of transparency. Tye, for example, claims

that phenomenal content reduces to a special sort of intentional content.[6] According to Tye, this helps us see "why visual phenomenal character is not a quality of an experience to which we have direct access (representational content is not a quality of the thing that has representational content)" (Tye 2000: 48–49).

In what follows, I will not take up the question of whether the transparency thesis can help motivate representationalism. Rather, I would like to focus instead on the prior question of whether the transparency thesis is true. To some extent, this will require us to look at the relationship between transparency and representationalism, since the defense of the first thesis often goes hand in hand with the defense of the second. But my primary focus here will be on transparency, not representationalism. To my mind, the pro-qualia case against transparency has not yet been satisfactorily made in the literature. Granted, qualia realists have produced numerous cases of apparent counterexamples to the transparency thesis—and I find many of these cases quite compelling. But, as you might expect, such examples are by no means uncontroversial. More important, however, is that most of the cases that have generated discussion are unusual in various respects—involving illusions, blurriness, or other non-ideal circumstances. Thus, the transparency theorist can often blunt the force of such examples. Even if he concedes that transparency fails in these "exotic" cases, he can still maintain that transparency holds for the vast majority of our experiences.[7] And it is not very satisfying for the qualia realist to rest her belief in qualia on a few unusual cases.

This essay thus aims to advance the debate past a discussion of these exotic examples. Once we understand how the exotic cases get their purchase as counterexamples to the transparency thesis, we can use this understanding to think about the more mundane cases for which the transparency thesis is supposed to be obvious. Having seen that we attend to qualia in certain exotic cases, we are reminded how we attend to qualia in the mundane cases as well. In short, by seeing why the transparency thesis is false, we are reminded how, and why, to believe in qualia.

2 The Exotic

The first exotic case to consider comes from blurry vision.[8] Suppose that someone who needs reading glasses peruses the morning newspaper while wearing his glasses. He sees the front page headlines clearly and sharply. When he takes off his glasses, however, his perception changes—he now has a blurry experience of those same headlines. Of course, this phenomenon is not limited to those who need reading glasses. Someone with perfect vision may achieve the same effect by unfocusing her eyes while reading the paper. When someone takes off his reading glasses, or unfocuses her eyes, there is a difference experientially—a phenomenal difference. How should this difference be best described? Does it seem that the words themselves are blurry, that is, that the blurriness is on the newspaper page itself? Or does it seem that the experience itself is blurry? Many people have the strong intuition that attending to the blurriness is different from attending to the words on the page. So insofar as the blurriness feels like an aspect of one's experience rather than an aspect of the headlines themselves, the case of blurry vision presents a problem for the transparency thesis.

A related case comes from phosphene experiences, that is, the color sensations created by pressure on the eyeball when one's eyelids are closed (Wright 1981; Block 1996). In offering this example, Block suggests that the phosphene experiences do not seem to be representing anything; we don't take the experience to suggest that there are colored moving expanses *out there* somewhere. Likewise in attending to the phosphene experiences, we don't seem to be attending to the object of the experience (some colored expanse *out there*) but rather to the experiences themselves.

A third kind of case comes from considering afterimages (see, e.g., Boghossian and Velleman 1989). In general, afterimages occur subsequent to the removal of some original (usually intense) stimulus. When a camera flash goes off, you might experience an afterimage in front of the photographer's face.[9] If you stare intently at a bright light for a little while and then close your eyes, there will be a lingering glow in the darkness. And if you stare at a green dot for half a minute and then shift your attention to a bright white piece of paper, you will visually experience a red dot similar in size and location to the green dot you had been staring at. But in none of these cases does it seem as if the afterimage represents something that is really there. When you close your eyes after looking at the bright light, for example, you don't take the lingering glow to be on the inner surface of your eyelids. When

you see the red afterimage against the white page, you don't take the redness to suggest the existence of a red dot on the page. As Block has suggested, afterimages "don't look as if they are really objects or as if they are really red. They look ... illusory" (Block 1996: 32, ellipsis in original; see also Wright 1983: 57–58).

If the above descriptions of these cases are correct, they seem to pose a significant threat both to representationalism and to the transparency thesis. Each of these cases suggests that there can be phenomenal content that does not reduce to representational content—either because there is no representational content (as in the afterimage and the phosphene cases), or because there is a difference in phenomenal content that does not correspond to representational content (as in the case of blurry vision). The cases thus pose a problem for the representationalists. And each of these cases also suggests that we can attend directly to our experiences without attending to the objects of our experiences—either because there is no object of our experience (again, as in the afterimage and the phosphene cases), or because the experience comes apart from the object that it represents (as in the case of blurry vision). They thus pose a problem for the transparency thesis.

Much of the ink spilled in response to these cases has focused specifically on defusing the threat to representationalism. Tye, for example, claims that in cases of blurry vision there is indeed a representational difference that can account for the phenomenal difference. Less information is presented when one takes off one's glasses: "In seeing blurrily, one undergoes sensory representations that fail to specify just where the boundaries and contours lie" (Tye 2000: 80). In the phosphene and afterimage cases, Tye thinks that by distinguishing what the experience represents *conceptually* from what it represents *nonconceptually*, we can dissipate the threat to representationalism (ibid.: 81–82).

These responses, however, do not do anything to dissipate the threat to the transparency thesis.[10] As a general strategy, the representationalist responses suggest that the proponents of the exotic cases understate the representational richness of the experiences. There is more representational content there than we might have initially believed. But admitting this does nothing to change our original sense of the phenomenology of the experience. It still seems to us, when we are having a blurry experience, that we can focus on the blurriness itself, rather than on just what the blurriness is blurriness *of*. Our attention to an afterimage does not seem to be attention to some worldly content—we do not see "right through" the experience in this case. Even if we can be convinced that the blurry image, the phosphene experience, and the afterimage have representational content, that in itself does not convince us that they are transparent.

3 Between the Exotic and the Mundane

We see something similar by considering a set of cases that fall on the spectrum somewhere between the exotic cases considered in section 2 and the mundane cases for which the transparency thesis has the most force. Recall that the transparency thesis derives its primary support from mundane visual experiences of, say, seeing a tree. But having begun with visual experience, proponents of transparency typically move on to perceptual experience generally, and then even to nonperceptual experiences as well. Tye, for example, explicitly claims that transparency holds across sensory modalities: "[T]he qualities of which we are directly aware via introspection ... are not qualities of the experiences of hearing, smelling, and tasting. Rather, they are qualities of public surfaces, sounds, odors, tastes, and so forth" (Tye 2000: 50). He also claims that transparency applies to bodily sensations, such as pains or itches. For the moment, let's grant the move from mundane visual cases to mundane cases in other perceptual modalities. Insofar as transparency is plausible for the mundane visual cases, it will be plausible for the mundane auditory cases, and similarly for the other perceptual modalities. Nonetheless, as we will see in this section, the plausibility of the transparency thesis becomes considerably more strained once we leave the perceptual realm.

One example frequently invoked in this context is the orgasm. As Block has forcefully argued (in, e.g., Block 1996: 33–34), it is difficult to specify what the representational content of an orgasm could be. All attempts seem to fall far short of capturing this phenomenally "impressive" experience. Similarly, if we think about introspecting an orgasm experience, it is difficult to see what it would mean to say that our experience is transparent. In attending to our experience, our attention goes right through to ... to where? In the mundane visual case, when I introspect my experience of a tree, my attention is supposed to go right through to the tree. But what would be the analogue of the tree in this case? The only possible suggestion would be some bodily location, but this doesn't seem faithful to the phenomenology of orgasms. And even if in attending to the orgasm we must attend to a particular bodily location, that doesn't seem to be all that we're doing.

A similar point can be made by thinking about pains. Does introspecting an experience of pain amount solely to attending to a particular bodily location? Here the transparency theorist must answer affirmatively. But this is a very hard position to defend. Moreover, it is not adequately defended simply by claiming, as Tye does, that whenever you become introspectively aware of a painful sensation, "your attention goes to *wherever you feel the pain*" (Tye 2000: 50). This claim is much weaker than the claim that your attention to the pain *consists* in your attention to the bodily location. Opponents of transparency can grant that when, for example, I have a pain in my toe, in order to focus on the pain I will have to focus at least in part on my toe. But there is a difference between saying that introspecting an experience of pain *involves* or even *requires* attending to a particular bodily location and saying that *all that there is* to introspecting an experience of pain is attending to a particular bodily location. Even if the former, weaker claim is plausible, it's the latter, stronger claim that the transparency thesis requires.

It's worth noting, however, that the weaker claim too can be called into question. In at least some cases, it seems that we can introspect pain without attending to a particular bodily location where the pain is felt. With some kinds of throbbing headaches, for example, I can introspectively attend to the throbbing pain without my attention going through to a particular part of my head—or so it seems to me. Some headaches are confined to one side or another, other headaches do not even seem to be especially localized. Given that I lack any sense of "where" the headache is, it seems odd to claim that my attention is directed in any but the most general sense at a bodily location.[11]

The same point applies to certain kinds of toothaches. I was once in need of a root canal in a tooth in the lower right side of my mouth, but I didn't know which particular tooth was the problem. I was in pain—in intense pain, in fact—and yet I could not myself pinpoint the precise location of the pain—even when I probed each tooth with my tongue or my finger. Eventually, the dentist pinpointed the problem spot for me by whacking the decaying tooth with a dental instrument. (I don't recommend having your dentist do this.) But his doing so changed my introspective experience. Only after he whacked the relevant tooth could I "find" the pain, and thus, only after he whacked the relevant tooth could I attend to the pain by attending to the tooth.[12]

The plausibility of the transparency thesis erodes further when considering emotions and moods. Emotional transparency is supposed to be relatively unproblematic, especially in comparison with the transparency of moods, since emotions at least tend to be associated with bodily occurrences. As Tye notes, "the qualities of which one is directly aware in introspecting felt emotions are frequently localized in particular parts of the body and experienced as such" (Tye 2000: 51). Anger might involve an increased pulse rate, fear might involve a tingling sensation along one's neck or a queasiness in one's stomach, and so on. This point enables Tye to treat emotional transparency analogously to the transparency of pain and other sensations. When we introspect pain, our attention is supposed to go to wherever we feel the pain. Likewise, when we introspect emotion, our attention is supposed to go wherever we feel the emotion: introspecting anger involves attention to one's increased pulse rate, introspecting fear involves attention to one's queasy stomach, and so on.

Is this all it involves? For the transparency theorist, the answer must be "yes." When we introspect an emotional experience, our attention must go right through to some bodily quality or other.[13] But this seems even less plausible for the case of emotions than it did for the case of pains. The typically tight connection between pains and bodily locations lends plausibility to the claim that we attend to bodily locations when we introspectively attend to pains. As I suggested above, however, the transparency theorist

needs to defend a stronger claim—that attention to pain *wholly consists* in attending to bodily locations—to show that experience is transparent. Since there is a much looser connection between emotions and bodily locations, it is harder to establish even the weak claim that we always attend to bodily locations when we introspectively attend to emotions. Matters are even worse for the transparency theorist when it comes to moods, where there is virtually no connection to bodily location. But even if Tye is right that the weak claim is true for emotions or moods, that would not be enough to show that our experience of emotions or moods is transparent.

4 The Mundane

At this point, it will be useful to distinguish explicitly four claims about experience that have been playing a role in our discussion. These claims split into two pairs. We can set out the claims as follows, letting "E" stand for an experience:

1. E has representational content.
2. The qualitative character of E consists wholly in its representational content (i.e., representationalism is true).
3. Attending to E involves attending to its representational content.
4. Attending to E consists wholly in attending to its representational content (i.e., the transparency thesis is true).[14]

Just as we should not confuse (1) with (2), we should not confuse (3) with (4). Moreover, just as (1) does not imply (2), (3) does not imply (4). Claim (1) is a necessary but not sufficient* condition for (2), just as (3) is a necessary but not sufficient condition for (4). Finally, whatever the relationship between (2) and (4)—a question I am here setting aside—it is clear that the truth of (1) implies neither (3) nor a fortiori[†] (4). On the other hand, however, the falsity of

---

* P is a necessary condition for Q if P must be true in order for Q to be true; P is a sufficient condition for Q if Q must be true in order for P to be true. So if P is a necessary but not sufficient condition for Q, P could be true while Q is false (but not vice versa).

† Latin: "from the stronger." An *a fortiori* inference is one that draws a weaker conclusion on the basis of a stronger conclusion that has already been reached.

(1) implies the falsity of both (3) and (4). If an experience lacks representational content, then our introspective attention to it cannot consist even in part of attention to representational content. So (1) is a necessary but not sufficient condition for all three of the subsequent claims.

Now let's think about how the transparency theorist attempts to accommodate apparent counterexamples to his thesis such as the exotic cases of section 2 and the nonperceptual cases of section 3. The exotic experiences like blurry vision and afterimages that we considered in section 2 threaten (4) primarily because they do not typically seem to have any representational content; for these experiences, that is, (1) seems false. But to defuse the threat of these cases, it is not enough for the transparency theorist to defend (1), that is, to find some representational content that they might have. Since (1) is not a sufficient condition for (4), defending (1) is only the first step. Even if these experiences do have some representational content, we need to be convinced that in attending to these experiences what we are doing—and *all* that we are doing—is attending to that representational content. And here the transparency theorist does not seem to have much to say.

For at least some of the nonperceptual experiences considered in section 3, the transparency theorist is on the same shaky ground that he is on with respect to the exotic cases. When it comes to orgasms and moods, it is hard to identify any representational content of the experience, that is, (1) seems false. But even for the nonperceptual experiences that plausibly do have representational content—experiences like pains and emotions—the transparency theorist is not on solid ground. The considerations he advances to help us see that we are attending to the representational content when we are attending to those experiences do not go far enough. They do not show us that *all* we are attending to when we are attending to the experiences is the representational content of the experience. In other words, even if (3) is true of these experiences, we need to be convinced of something more. And here again the transparency theorist does not seem to have much to say.

With these lessons learned from consideration of the apparent counterexamples to the transparency thesis, we are ready now to turn back to the mundane cases with which the transparency theorist begins—the very cases that are supposed to motivate the transparency thesis. What I want to suggest is that

our discussion of the apparent counterexamples to the transparency thesis opens up some new logical space for the opponents of the thesis to make a case against it. Once we see why transparency fails in the exotic cases, we can raise parallel questions about the mundane cases. Upon reflection, even the supposedly paradigmatic examples of transparency no longer seem as obviously transparent as they initially may have.

Look at a tree, we are instructed, and we are asked to try to turn our attention to intrinsic features of our visual experience. Proponents of transparency predict that we will fail. The only features there for us to turn our attention to are features of the presented tree (Harman 1990: 39). Our attention will always slip through to the greenness, and so on, as instantiated in the tree (see Tye 1995: 30). Keeping in mind our discussion above of the various counterexamples to transparency, however, I think this prediction is now called into question.

First, recall our discussion of the introspection of pain. Pain experience was alleged to be transparent because we cannot introspect it without attention to the bodily location where the pain is felt. However, as I discussed above, this fact alone does not establish the transparency of pain experience. The fact we attend to bodily location in introspectively attending to pain, even essentially so, does not mean that this is all we do. Likewise, the fact that we attend to worldly objects in introspectively attending to our perceptual experiences of worldly objects, even essentially so, does not mean that this is all we do. Compare a visual experience of a tree with a pain in your toe. The fact that you cannot help but attend to the tree when introspecting your visual experience of it no more establishes the transparency of visual experience than the fact that you cannot help but attend to your toe when introspecting the pain in your toe.

This conceptual point helps to create logical space for the failure of transparency, even with respect to perceptual experience. But of course, mere logical space is not enough. When we introspect our visual experiences, if we do not, or cannot, find anything else to attend to, then it looks like the transparency thesis will be correct for these experiences.

Here is where the moral gleaned from the exotic cases comes into play. Those cases showed us that transparency fails for at least some visual experiences. Insofar as those cases showed us how our introspective attention comes apart from the representational content of the experience, we can apply the lessons to the mundane cases. Consider again your visual experience of a tree. How can you attend to that experience without attending to the tree itself? To try to focus your attention away from the tree itself, think about afterimages, and about what you attend to when you are introspectively attending to your experience of afterimages. Now, once again, try to focus on that same aspect of your experience in your experience of the tree. You might try the following. Look at a tree, focus on your experience, and then close your eyes and image the tree. Focus in on the greenness on your imaged experience. Now reopen your eyes, so that you're looking at the tree. I predict that you *will* find features there, other than features of the presented tree, on which to train your attention. In particular, you can continue to attend to the greenness that you were attending to while your eyes were closed.

If I am right about this, the problems for the transparency thesis extend beyond the exotic cases. Even mundane visual experience—the very kind of experience that was supposed to be a paradigm case of transparency—is not transparent. Interestingly, we are helped to understand what's going on in the introspection of mundane cases by better understanding what's going on in the introspection of the exotic cases. Our reflection on why the counterexamples are problematic for the transparency thesis—on what we attend to when we are attending to our exotic experiences—enables us also to see what we are attending to in mundane experience.

5 Conclusion

When we introspect our ordinary perceptual experiences, the world gets in the way. The presence of external objects—the representational content of our experience—threatens to crowd out the qualia. But that doesn't mean the qualia are not there. As I have suggested in this essay, we are reminded that the qualia are there in ordinary experience by thinking carefully about experiences that are more out of the ordinary. In these other cases, there is no external object crowding out the qualia, and we can thus more easily focus our attention directly on them. And having reminded ourselves what we do in these more exotic cases, we can gain a better understanding of what we do in the more mundane cases.

In particular, I contend that when we attend introspectively to our experience—whether exotic or mundane—we are attending at least in part to qualia. Our experience is not, in fact, transparent. And thus, based on the support of the phenomenological data, it seems that we have every reason—or at least, all the reason we initially thought we had—to believe in the existence of qualia. ∎

Suggestions for Critical Reflection

1. Explain Kind's overarching argument against the "transparency thesis." On which points does Kind disagree with advocates of the transparency thesis?

2. Try to think of your own "exotic" instance of perception (akin to blurred vision, afterimages, and phosphene experiences, etc.). What makes this example different from more mundane cases? Does your example provide further evidence against the transparency thesis? Why or why not?

3. According to Kind, the transparency theorist is committed to the view that the experience of pain amounts "solely to attending to a particular bodily location"? Do you think this is a fair representation of the transparency theorist's account of pain? Can you think of a more refined account of pain that is compatible with the transparency thesis?

4. Suppose that representationalists about consciousness are correct and that when we perceive things we see "right through" the experience to the object itself, so that the properties we encounter, such as yellowness, pain, blurriness, or sweetness, are properties of the object not of our experience. The expectation is that the natural sciences will have no difficulty explaining these properties, since they are no longer mysterious mental qualia but just colors on the surfaces of objects and so on. But is this right—do the properties we encounter in experience, such as colors or tastes, really become less mysterious on this account? What

about the properties we encounter when we hallucinate or make mistakes (e.g., if we think we see a ghost)—that is, what if there is no object in our environment to actually have these properties (or to put it the way a representationalist might, what if the object of our experience is "merely intentional")?

5. On the other hand, if colors, smells, and so on are not properties 'in the world' but are properties of our mental experiences, then isn't this *even more* peculiar and problematic? For example, what sort of property is *only* 'visible' introspectively and (apparently) completely invisible when we look at brains 'from the outside'? Given what we know about the rest of science, can we really take the idea of qualia seriously?

6. A painting of a unicorn is called 'representational,' even though there's nothing it represents. What does that mean? Something like: we see it "as if" it could be a picture of something (even though we know it isn't). Does this analogy help the representationalist deal with after-images and other "exotic" perceptions?

7. Consider the following passage and try Kind's suggested experiment (whether with a tree or any other convenient object). Is this an accurate account of your experience?

> You might try the following. Look at a tree, focus on your experience, and then close your eyes and image the tree. Focus in on the greenness on your imaged experience. Now reopen your eyes, so that you're looking at the tree. I predict that you will find features there, other than features of the presented tree, on which to train your attention. In particular, you can continue to attend to the greenness that you were attending to while your eyes were closed.

Notes

1 The very next sentence (which, oddly, is often ignored) reads: "Yet it can be distinguished if we look attentively enough, and if we know that there is something to look for." See Kind 2003 for further discussion.

2 The quotation continues, "And this remains so, even if there really is no blue square in front of one—if, for example, one is subject to an illusion." As we will see in section 2, however, intuitions about transparency are much weaker with respect to illusions.

3 See Kind 2003, 2007, for further discussion of weak versus strong transparency.

4 See Kind 2001.

5 There might, however, be other (nonphenomenological) reasons to believe in qualia. See, e.g., Shoemaker 1994.

6 In particular, Tye thinks that the intentional content must be poised, abstract, and nonconceptual. This is what he calls his PANIC theory. See Tye 1995, 2000.

7 However, in Kind 2007, I deny that this sort of concessionary strategy saves representationalism.

8 See Block 1996; Boghossian and Velleman 1989; Wright 1975: 278.

9 It seems to me that this phenomenon was more dramatic in the "olden days" of actual flashbulbs. The flashes produced by today's digital cameras don't have quite the same effect.

10 For the purposes of this essay, I have set aside the question of the relationship between representationalism and the transparency thesis, but it's worth noting the following. If representationalism entails the transparency thesis, then showing that representationalism can accommodate the exotic cases would at least indirectly show that these cases do not pose a threat to the transparency thesis. But this alone would not help us to see where we went wrong in believing that we could attend directly to our experiences in the exotic cases.

11 Further support for this point might be derived from Ramachandran and Blakeslee's work on pain remapping (Ramachandran and Blakeslee 1999). In some amputees, touching one part of the body (such as the face) produces pain in the phantom limb.

12 For a different kind of example supporting this point, see Wright 1990: 3–14.

13 Strictly speaking, our attention need only go right through to some representational content or other, so if there were a plausible candidate for the representational content of emotions other than bodily states, the transparency theorist would not need to claim that attending to emotions involves attending to some bodily quality or other. Given the absence of a plausible alternative, however, the transparency theorist tends

to interpret emotional experience along similar lines to pain experience, i.e., as representing states of the body.

14 Although (3) is weaker than (4), it does not correspond directly to what I have elsewhere called weak transparency (Kind 2003). Whereas strong transparency claims that it is impossible to attend directly to our experience, weak transparency claims only that it is difficult (but not impossible) to do so. Nonetheless, if strong transparency turns out to be false, the truth of (3) might help to explain why weak transparency is true.

References

Block, N. 1996. Mental paint and mental latex. In *Philosophical Issues*, vol. 7: *Perception*, ed. E. Villanueva, 18–49. Atascadero, Calif.: Ridgeview.

Boghossian, P., and D. Velleman. 1989. Color as a secondary quality. *Mind* 98: 81–103.

Harman, G. 1990. The intrinsic quality of experience. In *Philosophical Perspectives*, vol. 4: *Action Theory and the Philosophy of Mind*, ed. J. Tomberlin, 31–52. Atascadero, Calif.: Ridgeview.

Kind, A. 2001. Qualia realism. *Philosophical Studies* 104: 143–162.

Kind, A. 2003. What's so transparent about transparency? *Philosophical Studies* 115: 225–244.

Kind, A. 2007. Restrictions on representationalism. *Philosophical Studies* 134, 3: 405–427.

Moore, G.E. 1903. The refutation of idealism. *Mind*, new series, 12: 433–453.

Ramachandran, V.S., and S. Blakeslee. 1999. *Phantoms in the Brain: Human Nature and the Architecture of the Mind*. London: Fourth Estate.

Shoemaker, S. 1994. Self-knowledge and "inner sense." *Philosophy and Phenomenological Research* 54: 249–314.

Tye, M. 1995. *Ten Problems of Consciousness*. Cambridge, Mass.: MIT Press/A Bradford Book.

Tye, M. 2000. *Consciousness, Color, and Content*. Cambridge, Mass.: MIT Press/A Bradford Book.

Wright, E.L. 1975. Perception: A new theory. *American Philosophical Quarterly* 14: 273–286.

Wright, E.L. 1981. Yet more on non-epistemic seeing. *Mind* 90: 586–591.

Wright, E.L. 1983. Introspecting images. *Philosophy* 58: 57–72.

Wright, E.L. 1990. Two more proofs of present qualia. *Theoria* 56: 3–22.

Free Will

DO WE HAVE FREE WILL?

The metaphysical topic which is addressed in this chapter is the problem of free will. This problem is generated by the following argument:

i. All human behavior is determined: that is, the state of the world at a particular time (e.g., the moment of your birth) entirely fixes what the state of the world will be at every moment into the future (e.g., now), and that includes fixing what actions you will ever perform.

ii. If determinism is true, then human beings are (in at least one important sense) not free to choose their actions—we could not have done otherwise than we did, and so we do not possess genuine free will.

iii. Therefore human beings do not have free will (and, furthermore, may lack moral responsibility for their actions, lead lives that have no meaning, and so on).

This is a straightforwardly valid argument. The problem, of course, is that both premises (i) and (ii) are highly plausible (or at least, can be made to seem so with a certain amount of argumentation), and yet the conclusion is, we hope and believe, *false*: we feel like free agents, able to choose to do one thing rather than another; we

believe that people often have moral (and other kinds of) responsibility for their action; we think that people can guide their own destinies in a meaningful way. The philosophical problem, therefore, is to say what, if anything, is wrong with the argument, and since the argument is valid the only way to criticize it is to call into question the truth of the premises. This means there are exactly three broad philosophical positions on the problem of free will:

The first position, usually called *hard determinism* or just *determinism*, is the view that the argument is sound: that is, both of the premises are true and hence freedom (and moral responsibility and so on) is a mere illusion. This stance is represented here by the reading from Paul Rée.

The second position, usually called *libertarianism* (or *metaphysical libertarianism*), accepts premise (ii) but argues that premise (i) is false—that is, libertarians agree that determinism is incompatible with freedom, but argue that we have free will because *indeterminism* is true. This stance is not fully represented in the readings in this chapter, but a key component of the argument—the defense of premise (ii)—is explored by Ishtiyaque Haji in the second reading. It is important to note that libertarianism is not the (very implausible) position that *none* of our actions are determined—it is the more limited view that *some*, probably the most important, of our actions are free in the sense that they are not fixed by what came before. So even if most of what we do is habitual, for example, as long as we have the capacity to wrestle with the big moral questions and make a (by their lights) genuinely free, genuinely novel, choice, then libertarianism would be true.

The third, and most popular (at least among philosophers), approach to free will is known as *soft determinism* or *compatibilism*. Compatibilists typically accept premise (i), determinism, but deny premise (ii): that is, they deny that the truth of determinism implies that we lack at least one important variety of freedom. Instead, they argue in a variety of ways that determinism is compatible with all the types of freedom worth wanting: that we can be *both* free and determined. A classic compatibilist account is reprinted here, from A.J. Ayer, followed by an extremely influential argument by Harry Frankfurt against the principle of alternate possibilities (PAP), a principle which if true would hold that an agent is morally responsible for an action only if that person could have done otherwise.

The last two readings exemplify a modern move away from simply considering the merits of libertarian versus compatibilist free will, toward more nuanced discussion of the metaphysics of moral responsibility which might suggest that the historical focus on determinism was misplaced. Peter Strawson influentially approached the question through a consideration of the "reactive attitudes" of gratitude and resentment, while Susan Wolf uses the lens of sanity and the "deep self."

Two quick notes about the terminology in this area, which can be confusing: First, "libertarianism" is the label both for a position in political philosophy that prioritizes political freedom, and for a position on the metaphysical question of free will. Although both stress human freedom, they are not deeply related: the first emphasizes political freedom—e.g., the freedom to vote or to practice your religion—while the latter affirms that the actions of human beings are sometimes undetermined and therefore free. We could be politically free even though we are, say, entirely physically or socially determined. It is, of course, the metaphysical and not the political usage of the term that we have in mind in this chapter.

Second, there are labels for *theoretical positions* about free will—"hard determinism," "libertarianism," and "compatibilism"—and labels for *premises* for the arguments for these positions—"determinism" or "indeterminism," "incompatibilism" or "compatibilism,"

and "moral responsibility." The labels are sometimes similar, and it is important to keep them straight as you think and write about free will. For example, "determinism" (used in this way) is the view that every action is completely fixed by what has happened in the past, and so we could never have done otherwise than we did. But this in itself is *not* a theory of free will—if it's true then it's the input to a theory, or a constraint on theories ... but both the hard determinist and the compatibilist endorse determinism.

There are many decent collections of articles on the problem of free will, including Robert Kane, ed., *Free Will* (Blackwell, 2009) and *The Oxford Handbook of Free Will* (Oxford University Press, 2011); Derk Pereboom, ed., *Free Will* (Hackett, 2009); Timothy O'Connor, ed., *Agents, Causes, and Events* (Oxford University Press, 1995); and Gary Watson, ed., *Free Will* (Oxford University Press, 2003). Useful and accessible single-author discussions of the problem of free will include Daniel Dennett, *Elbow Room* (MIT Press, 1985); Sam Harris, *Free Will* (Free Press, 2012); Ted Honderich, *How Free Are You?* (Oxford University Press, 1993); Robert Kane, *A Contemporary Introduction to Free Will* (Oxford University Press, 2005); Graham McFee, *Free Will* (McGill-Queen's University Press, 2000); Fischer, Kane, Pereboom, and Vargas, *Four Views on Free Will* (Wiley-Blackwell, 2007); Michael McKenna and Derk Pereboom, *Free Will: A Contemporary Introduction* (Routledge, 2016); Timothy O'Connor, *Persons and Causes* (Oxford University Press, 2000); Matthew Talbert, *Moral Responsibility: An Introduction* (Polity, 2016); and Jennifer Trusted, *Free Will and Responsibility* (Oxford University Press, 1984).

Finally, here are a few influential books on free will: Richard Double, *The Non-Reality of Free Will* (Oxford University Press, 1991); John Martin Fischer, *The Metaphysics of Free Will* (Blackwell, 1996); Ted Honderich, *A Theory of Determinism* (2 vols., Oxford University Press, 1988); Alfred Mele, *Free: Why Science Hasn't Disproved Free Will* (Oxford University Press, 2014); Murphy and Brown, eds., *Did My Neurons Make Me Do It?: Philosophical and Neurobiological Perspectives on Moral Responsibility and Free Will* (Oxford University Press, 2009); Derk Pereboom, *Living without Free Will* (Cambridge University Press, 2001); Galen Strawson, *Freedom and Belief* (Oxford University Press, 1986); Peter van Inwagen, *An Essay on Free Will* (Oxford University Press, 1983); and Daniel Wegner, *The Illusion of Conscious Will* (MIT Press, 2005).

PAUL RÉE

FROM *The Illusion of Free Will*

Who Was Paul Rée?

Paul Rée, a German philosopher and psychologist, is most remembered for his association with the German philosopher Friedrich Nietzsche and for his uncompromising moral relativism and atheism. Born in 1849, Rée was the son of a wealthy Prussian landowner. In his early twenties he fought in the Franco-Prussian war of 1870–71, in which Prussian troops advanced into France and decisively defeated the French army at Sedan (a town near the Belgian border). The outcome was the fall of the French Second Empire and the establishment of a new, united German Empire—the first Reich—under its first chancellor, Prince Otto Leopold von Bismarck. On his return from the war, wounded, Rée went to Switzerland to recuperate and, abandoning the law studies he had begun before the war, devoted himself to the study of philosophy and psychology. In 1875 he received a doctorate in philosophy from the University of Halle (a city in central Germany), and also published a book of psychological aphorisms, *Psychologische Beobachtungen*.

In 1873 Rée had met Nietzsche in Basel, and after the publication of Rée's *Psychological Observations*, Nietzsche wrote him a letter complimenting the work. As a result, the two struck up a close friendship— which Nietzsche's biographer, Walter Kaufmann, has called "among the best things which ever happened to Nietzsche"[*]—that lasted about seven years. However, Rée was ethnically Jewish (though not a religious practitioner), and several of Nietzsche's anti-Semitic friends and his unpleasant sister resented Rée's influence on Nietzsche.[†] In 1882, after Nietzsche bitterly broke off his relationship with the tempestuous and bewitching Lou Salomé, to whom Rée had originally introduced him, Rée's friendship with the famous philosopher came to an end, and they never spoke again. Later, Rée was to

dismiss Nietzsche's ethical writings as "a mixture of insanity and nonsense."

In 1877 Rée published *Ursprung der moralischen Empfindungen* (*The Origin of the Moral Sentiments*). In this book, strongly influenced by Charles Darwin and David Hume, Rée argued that there are no universally true moral principles, and that what is regarded as morally right or wrong, in any given society, is a function of its needs and cultural conditions. *The Illusion of Free Will*, in which Rée advocates abandoning notions of moral responsibility in practical as well as philosophical life, was published in 1885, when Rée was 36. In the same year, he published *Die Entstehung des Gewissens* (*The Origin of Conscience*) and in the process of writing this book he became concerned about his own lack of knowledge of the natural sciences. The next year Rée enrolled at the University of Munich to study medicine. After obtaining his MD, Rée returned to his family estate in Stibbe, West Prussia. There he practiced medicine, charging no fees, and when his own medical knowledge fell short in particular cases, paid all the hospital expenses for the peasants and laborers who were his patients.

For the last 10 years of his life, Rée led an isolated, ascetic existence living at Stibbe with his brother, and spent much of his time working on a major book that would encapsulate all his philosophical reflections. Rée told a friend that when it was finished he would give up philosophy, but that since he could not live without doing philosophy, there would be nothing left for him but to die. This is more or less what happened: in 1900, when his book was almost completed, Rée, a passionate mountain climber, returned to live in Switzerland and the following year fell to his death from the icy ridge of a Swiss mountain. His book, *Philosophie*, was published posthumously in 1903 and, to this day, has been almost completely ignored. In this work, Rée roundly

---

[*]   Walter Kaufmann, *Nietzsche: Philosopher, Psychologist, Antichrist* (Princeton University Press, 1978), 48.
[†]   There's some controversy about whether Nietzsche himself was anti-Semitic.

condemned metaphysics as a system of "fairy tales" and "lies," and argued that religions "are true neither in the literal nor in an allegorical sense—they are untrue in every sense. Religion issues from a marriage of error and fear."

What Is the Structure of This Reading?

This selection contains most of Chapters 1 and 2 of Paul Rée's 1885 book *Die Illusion der Willensfreiheit* (*The Illusion of Free Will*). The final (third) chapter of the book, which is not reprinted here, contains a detailed critique of Immanuel Kant's views on free will. Rée begins by defining freedom of the will as the ability to act as "an absolute beginning"—i.e., a thought or action is free, according to Rée, only in the case where it is not the necessary result of prior causes. Rée then goes on to argue that *no* event is uncaused, and thus that there can be no such thing as free will. To show this, he first examines the example of an act of decision in a donkey and then extends similar considerations to human beings. He insists that even actions performed solely from a sense of duty are not genuinely free, and he argues that one must be careful to distinguish between correct and incorrect senses of the claim "I can do what I want." Finally, he diagnoses our mistaken belief in free will as being the result of ignorance of the causes of our own actions. Because we do not see how our actions are caused, we fallaciously assume that they are not caused.

In section 5, which marks the start of Chapter 2 of his book, Rée explores the implications for morality of the truth of determinism. He argues that if all our actions are necessary effects of prior causes, then we cannot be held morally responsible for them: we cannot legitimately be praised or blamed for our actions. True philosophers, Rée hints, will try to rid themselves of the bad habit of assigning moral responsibility. On the other hand, we certainly do *prefer* some actions (and some types of people) over others, and this is legitimate; but our preferences themselves are to be explained as causal effects of our genetic inheritance and social upbringing.

Some Useful Background Information

There is a useful and commonly made philosophical distinction which is helpful for understanding Rée's position on free will: the contrast between necessary and sufficient conditions. *A* is a *necessary* condition for *B* if *B* could not have occurred (or been true) without *A*—that is, if there would be no *B* unless *A*. For example, being connected to a power supply is a necessary condition for a bulb to light up (the bulb could not light unless connected to a source of electricity). On the other hand, *A* is a *sufficient* condition for *B* if the occurrence (or truth) of *A* is *sufficient* for the occurrence (or truth) of *B*—that is, if *B* happens every time *A* does. Being connected in the right way to a properly functioning circuit with an adequate source of power, under normal physical circumstances, with the power switch in the "on" position is, altogether, a sufficient circumstance for a bulb to light.

It follows from this that if *A* is a sufficient condition for *B*, then if *A* occurs *B* must *necessarily* occur as well.* (On the other hand, if *A* is merely a necessary condition for *B*, the occurrence of *A* only tells us that *B* *may* happen, but not that it actually will.)

---

* This claim is a bit more complicated than it seems, however, because of the various flavors which necessity can come in: for example, the fact that *B* always follows *A* in the actual world perhaps means that *B* is a '*physically* necessary' consequence of *A*, but it need not follow that *B* follows from *A* by *logical* necessity.

FROM *The Illusion of Free Will**

CHAPTERS 1 AND 2

1. Nothing Happens without a Cause

...To say that the will is not free means that it is subject to the law of causality. Every act of will is in fact preceded by a sufficient cause. Without such a cause the act of will cannot occur; and, if the sufficient cause is present, the act of will must occur.

To say that the will is free would mean that it is not subject to the law of causality. In that case every act of will would be an absolute beginning [a first cause] and not a link [in a chain of events]: it would not be the effect of preceding causes.

The reflections that follow may serve to clarify what is meant by saying that the will is not free.... Every object—a stone, an animal, a human being—can pass from its present state to another one. The stone that now lies in front of me may, in the next moment, fly through the air, or it may disintegrate into dust or roll along the ground. If, however, one of these *possible* states is to be *realized*, its sufficient cause must first be present. The stone will fly through the air if it is tossed. It will roll if a force acts upon it. It will disintegrate into dust, given that some object hits and crushes it.

It is helpful to use the terms "potential" and "actual" in this connection. At any moment there are innumerably many potential states. At a given time, however, only *one* can become actual, namely, the one that is triggered by its sufficient cause.

The situation is no different in the case of an animal. The donkey that now stands motionless between two piles of hay† may, in the next moment, turn to the left or to the right, or he may jump into the air or put his head between his legs. But here, too, the sufficient cause must first be present if of the *possible* modes of behavior one is to be *realized*.

Let us analyze one of these modes of behavior. We shall assume that the donkey has turned toward the bundle on his right. This turning presupposes that certain muscles were contracted. The cause of this muscular contraction is the excitation of the nerves that lead to them. The cause of this excitation of the nerves is a state of the brain. It was in a state of decision. But how did the brain come to be in that condition? Let us trace the states of the donkey back a little farther.

A few moments before he turned, his brain was not yet so constituted as to yield the sufficient cause for the excitation of the nerves in question and for the contraction of the muscles; for otherwise the movement would have occurred. The donkey had not yet "decided" to turn. If he then moved at some subsequent time, his brain must in the meantime have become so constituted as to bring about the excitation of the nerves and the movement of the muscles. Hence the brain underwent some change. To what causes is this change to be attributed? To the effectiveness of an impression that acts as an external stimulus, or to a sensation that arose internally; for example, the sensation of hunger and the idea of the bundle on the right, by jointly affecting the brain, change the way in which it is constituted so that it now yields the sufficient cause for the excitation of the nerves and the contraction of the muscles. The donkey now "wants" to turn to the right; he now turns to the right.

Hence, just as the position and constitution of the stone, on the one hand and the strength and direction of the force that acts upon it, on the other, necessarily determine the kind and length of its flight, so the

---

* Paul Rée's *Die Illusion der Willensfreiheit* was first published in Berlin in 1885. This selection was translated by Stefan Bauer-Mengelberg and edited by Paul Edwards and Arthur Pap (who also supplied the section headings) in 1973.

† This philosophical example is known as "Buridan's Ass," named for the fourteenth-century French philosopher Jean Buridan. The example is not found in Buridan's writing, but was used by critics to parody his account of free will in similar situations. Aristotle gives this example in *On the Heavens* 295b. In the usual use of the donkey example, it is halfway between two equally attractive bundles, so is unable to move and starves.

movement of the donkey—his turning to the bundle on the right—is no less necessarily the result of the way in which the donkey's brain and the stimulus are constituted at a given moment. That the donkey turned toward this particular bundle was determined by something trivial. If the bundle that the donkey did not choose had been positioned just a bit differently, or if it had smelled different, or if the subjective factor—the donkey's sense of smell or his visual organs—had developed in a somewhat different way, then, so we may assume, the donkey would have turned to the left. But the cause was not complete there, and that is why the effect could not occur, while with respect to the other side, where the cause was complete, the effect could not fail to appear.

For the donkey, consequently, just as for the stone, there are innumerably many *potential* states at any moment; he may walk or run or jump, or move to the left, to the right, or straight ahead. But only the one whose sufficient cause is present can ever become *actual*.

At the same time, there is a difference between the donkey and the stone in that the donkey moves because he wants to move, while the stone moves because it is moved. We do not deny this difference. There are, after all, a good many other differences between the donkey and the stone. We do not by any means intend to prove that this dissimilarity does not exist. We do not assert that the donkey is a stone, but only that the donkey's every movement and act of will has causes just as the motion of the stone does. The donkey moves because he wants to move. But that he wants to move at a given moment, and in this particular direction, is causally determined.

Could it be that there was no sufficient cause for the donkey's wanting to turn around—that he simply wanted to turn around? His act of will would then be an absolute beginning. An assumption of that kind is contradicted by experience and the universal validity of the law of causality. By experience, since observation teaches us that for every act of will some causes were the determining factors. By the universal validity of the law of causality, since, after all, nothing happens anywhere in the world without a sufficient cause. Why, then, of all things should a donkey's act of will come into being without a cause? Besides, the state of willing, the one that immediately precedes the excitation of the motor nerves, is no different in principle from other states—that of indifference, of lassitude, or of weariness. Would anyone believe that all of these states exist without a cause? And if one does not believe that, why should just the state of willing be thought to occur without a sufficient cause?

It is easy to explain why it seems to us that the motion of the stone is necessary while the donkey's act of will is not. The causes that move the stone are, after all, external and visible. But the causes of the donkey's act of will are internal and invisible; between us and the locus of their effectiveness lies the skull of the donkey. Let us consider this difference somewhat more closely. The stone lies before us as it is constituted. We can also see the force acting upon it, and from these two factors, the constitution of the stone and the force, there results, likewise visible, the rolling of the stone. The case of the donkey is different. The state of his brain is hidden from our view. And, while the bundle of hay is visible, its effectiveness is not. It is an internal process. The bundle does not come into visible contact with the brain but acts at a distance. Hence the subjective and the objective factor—the brain and the impact that the bundle has upon it—are invisible.

Let us suppose that we could depict the donkey's soul in high relief, taking account of and making visible all those states, attitudes, and feelings that characterize it before the donkey turns. Suppose further that we could see how an image detaches itself from the bundle of hay and, describing a visible path through the air, intrudes upon the donkey's brain and how it produces a change there in consequence of which certain nerves and muscles move. Suppose, finally, that we could repeat this experiment arbitrarily often, that, if we returned the donkey's soul into the state preceding his turning and let exactly the same impression act upon it, we should always observe the very same result. Then we would regard the donkey's turning to the right as necessary. We would come to realize that the brain, constituted as it was at that moment, had to react to such an impression in precisely that way.

In the absence of this experiment it seems as though the donkey's act of will were not causally determined. We just do not see its being causally determined and consequently believe that no such determination takes place. The act of will, it is said, is the cause of the turning, but it is not itself determined; it is said to be an absolute beginning.

The opinion that the donkey's act of will is not causally determined is held not only by the outsider;

the donkey himself, had he the gift of reflection, would share it. The causes of his act of will would elude him, too, since in part they do not become conscious at all and in part pass through consciousness fleetingly, with the speed of lightning. If, for example, what tipped the scales was that he was closer by a hair's breadth to the bundle on the right, or that it smelled a shade better, how should the donkey notice something so trivial, something that so totally fails to force itself upon his consciousness?

In *one* sense, of course, the donkey is right in thinking "I could have turned to the left." His state at the moment, his position relative to the bundle, or its constitution need merely have been somewhat different, and he really would have turned to the left. The statement "I could have acted otherwise" is, accordingly, true in this sense: turning to the left is one of the movements possible for me (in contrast, for example, to the movement of flying); it lies within the realm of my possibilities.

We arrive at the same result if we take the law of inertia as our point of departure. It reads: every object strives to remain in its present state. Expressed negatively this becomes: without a sufficient cause no object can pass from its present state to another one. The stone will lie forever just as it is lying now; it will not undergo the slightest change if no causes—such as the weather or a force—act upon it to bring about a change. The donkey's brain will remain in the same state unchanged for all eternity if no causes—the feeling of hunger or fatigue, say, or external impressions—bring about a change.

If we reflect upon the entire life of the donkey *sub specie necessitatis*,* we arrive at the following result. The donkey came into the world with certain properties of mind and body, his genetic inheritance. Since the day of his birth, impressions—of the companions with whom he frolicked or worked, his feed, the climate— have acted upon these properties. These two factors, his inborn constitution and the way in which it was formed through the impressions of later life, are the cause of all of his sensations, ideas, and moods, and of all of his movements, even the most trivial ones. If, for example, he cocks his left ear and not the right one, that is determined by causes whose historical development could be traced back ad infinitum;† and likewise when he stands, vacillating,‡ between the two bundles. And when action, the act of feeding, takes the place of vacillation, that, too, is determined: the idea of the one bundle now acts upon the donkey's mind, when it has become receptive to the idea of that particular sheaf, in such a way as to produce actions.

2. Human Beings and the Law of Causality

Let us now leave the realm of animals and proceed to consider man. Everything is the same here. Man's every feeling is a necessary result. Suppose, for example, that I am stirred by a feeling of pity at this moment. To what causes is it to be attributed? Let us go back as far as possible. An infinite amount of time has elapsed up to this moment. Time was never empty; objects have filled it from all eternity. These objects ... have continually undergone change. All of these changes were governed by the law of causality; not one of them took place without a sufficient cause.

We need not consider what else may have characterized these changes. Only their *formal* aspect, only this *one* point is of concern to us: no change occurred without a cause.

At some time in the course of this development, by virtue of some causes, organic matter was formed, and finally man. Perhaps the organic world developed as Darwin described it. Be that as it may, it was in any case due to causes that I was born on a particular day, with particular properties of body, of spirit, and of heart. Impressions then acted upon this constitution; I had particular governesses, teachers, and playmates. Teaching and example in part had an effect and in part were lost upon me; the former, when my inborn constitution made me receptive to them, when I had an affinity for them. And that is how it has come to be, through

---

* Latin: "under the aspect of necessity"—that is, seen from the standpoint of necessity. (This expression is modeled on philosopher Baruch Spinoza's coinage *sub specie aeternitatis*, "under the aspect of eternity," which Spinoza uses in his *Ethics* [1677] to characterize the highest form of knowledge as that in which the world is seen from the standpoint of timelessness or eternity.)

† Latin: "without limit, forever."

‡ Swaying indecisively between one course of action and another.

the operation of [a chain of] causes, that I am stirred by a feeling of pity at this moment. The course of the world would have had to be somewhat different if my feelings were to be different now.

It is of no consequence for the present investigation whether the inborn capacity for pity, for taking pleasure in another's pain, or for courage remains constant throughout life or whether teaching, example, and activity serve to change it. In any case the pity or pleasure in another's pain, the courage or cowardice, that a certain person feels or exhibits at a given moment is a necessary result, whether these traits are inborn—an inheritance from his ancestors—or were developed in the course of his own life.

Likewise every intention, indeed, every thought that ever passes through the brain, the silliest as well as the most brilliant, the true as well as the false, exists of necessity. In that sense there is no freedom of thought. It is necessary that I sit in this place at this moment, that I hold my pen in my hand in a particular way, and that I write that every thought is necessary; and if the reader should perchance be of the opinion that this is not the case, i.e., if he should believe that thoughts may not be viewed as effects, then he holds this false opinion of necessity also.

Just as sensations and thoughts are necessary, so, too, is action. It is, after all, nothing other than their externalization, their objective embodiment. Action is born of sensations and thoughts. So long as the sensations are not sufficiently strong, action cannot occur, and when the sensations and thoughts are constituted so as to yield the sufficient cause for it, then it must occur; then the appropriate nerves and muscles are set to work. Let us illustrate this by means of an action that is judged differently at different levels of civilization, namely, murder.* Munzinger,† for example, says that among the Bogos‡ the murderer, the terror of the neighborhood, who never tires of blood and murder, is a man of respect. Whoever has been raised with such views will not be deterred from murder either by external or by internal obstacles. Neither the police nor his

conscience forbids him to commit it. On the contrary, it is his habit to praise murder; his parents and his gods stimulate him to commit it, and his companions encourage him by their example. And so it comes to be that, if there is a favorable opportunity, he does the deed. But is this not terribly trivial? After all, everyone knows that an act of murder is due to *motives*! True, but almost no one (except perhaps a philosopher) knows that an act of murder, and indeed every action, has a *cause*. Motives are a part of the cause. But to admit that there are motives for an action is not yet to recognize that it is causally determined, or to see clearly that the action is determined by thoughts and sensations—which in turn are effects—just as the rolling of a ball is determined by a force. But it is this point, and only this one, to which we must pay heed.

Let us now consider the act of murder from the same point of view in the case of civilized peoples. Someone raised at a higher level of civilization has learned from childhood on to disapprove of murder and to regard it as deserving punishment. God, his parents, and his teachers—in short, all who constitute an authority for him—condemn acts of this kind. It is, moreover, inconsistent with his character, which has been formed in an era of peace. Lastly, too, fear of punishment will deter him. Can murder prosper on such soil? Not easily. Fear, pity, the habit of condemning murder—all these are just so many bulwarks that block the path to such an action. Nevertheless need, passion, or various seductive influences will perhaps remove one after another of these bulwarks. Let us consider the cause of an act of murder more closely. First it is necessary to distinguish between two components, the subjective and the objective, in the total cause. The *subjective* part of the cause consists of the state of the murderer at the moment of the deed. To this we must assign all ideas that he had at the time, the conscious as well as the unconscious ones, his sensations, the temperature of his blood, the state of his stomach, of his liver—of each and every one of his bodily organs. The *objective* component consists of the appearance of the victim, the locality in which the deed took place,

---

* The German word Rée used here was *Raubmord*, a compound noun denoting a combination of murder and robbery (with overtones of pillage and rape).

† Werner Munzinger (1832–75) was a Swiss linguist and explorer. He spent many years traveling in Eritrea, Abyssinia, and the Sudan, three countries in northeast Africa south of Egypt (Abyssinia is now called Ethiopia).

‡ The Bogos were a tribe living in the highlands of northern Abyssinia and southern Eritrea. Munzinger described the customs of the Bogos in his 1859 book *Über die Sitten und das Recht der Bogos*.

and the way it was illuminated. The act of murder was necessarily consummated at that moment because these impressions acted upon a human being constituted in that particular way at the time. "Necessarily" means just that the act of murder is an effect; the state of the murderer and the impressions acting upon it are its cause. If the cause had not been complete, the effect could not have occurred. If, for example, the murderer had felt even a trifle more pity at that moment, if his idea of God or of the consequences that his deed would have here on earth had been somewhat more distinct, or if the moon had been a little brighter, so that more light would have fallen upon the victim's face and his pleading eyes—then, perhaps, the cause of the act of murder would not have become complete, and in consequence the act would not have taken place.

Thus for man, as for animal and stone, there are at any moment innumerably many *potential* states. The murderer might, at the moment when he committed the murder, have climbed a tree instead or stood on his head. If, however, instead of the murder one of these actions were to have become *actual*, then its sufficient cause would have had to be present. He would have climbed a tree if he had had the intention of hiding, or of acting as a lookout, that is to say, if at that moment he had had other ideas and sensations. But this could have been the case only if the events that took place in the world had been somewhat different [stretching back in time] ad infinitum.

3. Determinism and Will-Power

But I can, after all, break through the network of thoughts, sensations, and impressions that surrounds me by resolutely saying "I will not commit murder!" No doubt. We must, however, not lose sight of the fact that a resolute "I will" or "I will not" is also, wherever it appears, a necessary result; it does not by any means exist without a cause. Let us return to our examples. Although the Bogo really has reasons only to commit murder, it is nevertheless possible for a resolute "I will not commit murder" to assert itself. But is it conceivable that this "I will not" should occur without a sufficient cause? Fear, pity, or some other feeling, which in turn is an effect, overcomes him and gives rise to this "I will

not" before the cause of the murder has yet become complete. Perhaps Christian missionaries have had an influence upon him; hence the idea of a deity that will visit retribution on him for murder comes before his soul, and that is how the "I will not" comes to be. It is easier to detect the causes of the resolute "I will not commit murder" in someone raised at a higher level of civilization; fear, principles, or the thought of God in most cases produce it in time.

A resolute will can be characteristic of a man. No matter how violently jealousy, greed, or some other passion rages within him, he does not want to succumb to it; he does not succumb to it. The analogue of this constitution is a ball that, no matter how violent a force acts upon it, does not budge from its place. A billiard cue will labor in vain to shake the earth. The earth victoriously resists the cue's thrusts with its mass. Likewise man resists the thrusts of greed and jealousy with the mass of his principles. A man of that kind, accordingly, is free—from being dominated by his drives. Does this contradict determinism? By no means. A man free from passion is still subject to the law of causality. He is necessarily free. It is just that the word "free" has different meanings. It may be correctly predicated of man in every sense except a single one: he is not free from the law of causality. Let us trace the causes of his freedom from the tyranny of the passions.

Let us suppose that his steadfastness of will was not inherited, or, if so, merely as a disposition. Teaching, example, and, above all, the force of circumstances developed it in him. From early childhood on he found himself in situations in which he had to control himself if he did not want to perish. Just as someone standing at the edge of an abyss can banish dizziness by thinking "If I become dizzy, then I will plunge," so thinking "If I yield to my excitation—indeed, if I so much as betray it*—I will perish" has led him to control of his drives.

It is often thought that those who deny that the will is free want to deny that man has the ability to free himself from being dominated by his drives. However, one can imagine man's power to resist passions to be as great as one wants, even infinitely great; that is to say, a man may possibly resist even the most violent passion: his love of God or his principles have still more power over him than the passion. The question whether even

---

* Reveal it, let it show.

the most resolute act of will is an effect is entirely independent of this.

But is being subject to the law of causality not the weak side of the strong? By no means. Is a lion weak if he can tear a tiger apart? Is a hurricane weak if it can uproot trees? And yet the power by means of which the lion dismembers and the storm uproots is an effect, and not an absolute beginning. By having causes, by being an effect, strength is not diminished.

Just as resolute willing is to be considered an effect, so is irresolute willing. A vacillating man is characterized by the fact that he alternately wants something and then doesn't want it. To say that someone contemplating murder is still vacillating means that at one time the desire for possessions, greed, and jealousy predominate—then he wants to commit murder, at another time fear of the consequences, the thought of God, or pity overcomes him, and then he does not want to commit murder. In the decisive moment, when his victim is before him, everything depends upon which feeling has the upper hand. If at that moment passion predominates, then he wants to commit murder; and then he commits murder.

We see that, from whatever point of view we look at willing, it always appears as a necessary result, as a link [in a chain of events], and never as an absolute beginning.

But can we not prove by means of an experiment that willing is an absolute beginning? I lift my arm because I *want* to lift it.... Here my *wanting* to lift my arm is the cause of the lifting, but this wanting, we are told, is not itself causally determined; rather, it is an absolute beginning. I simply want to lift my arm, and that is that. We are deceiving ourselves. This act of will, too, has causes; my intention to demonstrate by means of an experiment that my will is free gives rise to my wanting to lift my arm. But how did this intention come to be? Through a conversation, or through reflecting on the freedom of the will. Thus the thought "I want to demonstrate my freedom" has the effect that I want to lift my arm. There is a gap in this chain. Granted that my intention to demonstrate that my will is free stands in some relation to my wanting to lift my arm, why do I not demonstrate my freedom by means of some other movement? Why is it *just my arm* that I want to lift? This specific act of will on my part has not yet been causally explained. Does it perhaps not have causes? Is it an uncaused act of will? Let us note first that someone who

wishes to demonstrate that his will is free will usually really extend or lift his arm, and in particular his right arm. He neither tears his hair nor wiggles his belly. This can be explained as follows. Of all of the parts of the body that are subject to our voluntary control, there is none that we move more frequently than the right arm. If, now, we wish to demonstrate our freedom by means of some movement, we will automatically make that one to which we are most accustomed.... Thus we first have a conversation about or reflection on the freedom of the will; this leads to the intention of demonstrating our freedom; this intention arises in an organism with certain [physiological] habits [such as that of readily lifting the right arm], and as a result we want to lift (and then lift) the right arm.

I remember once discussing the freedom of the will with a left-handed man. He asserted "My will is free; I can do what I want." In order to demonstrate this he extended his *left* arm.

It is easy to see, now, what the situation is with regard to the assertion "I can do what I want." In one sense it is indeed correct; in another, however, it is wrong. The *correct* sense is to regard willing as a cause and action as an effect. For example, I can kill my rival if I want to kill him. I can walk to the left if I want to walk to the left. The causes are *wanting* to kill and *wanting* to walk; the effects are killing and walking. In some way every action must be preceded by the act of willing it, whether we are aware of it or not. According to this view, in fact, I can do *only* what I want to do, and only if I want to do it. The *wrong* sense is to regard willing *merely* as a cause, and not at the same time as the effect of something else. But, like everything else, it is cause *as well as effect*. An absolutely initial act of will does not exist. Willing stands in the middle: it brings about killing and walking to the left; it is the effect of thoughts and sensations (which in turn are effects).

4. Ignorance of the Causation of Our Actions

Hence our volition (with respect to some action) is always causally determined. But it seems to be free (of causes); it seems to be an absolute beginning. To what is this appearance due?

We do not perceive the causes by which our volition is determined, and that is why we believe that it is not causally determined at all.

How often do we do something while "lost in thought"! We pay no attention to what we are doing, let alone to the causes from which it springs. While we are thinking, we support our head with our hand. While we are conversing, we twist a piece of paper in our hand. If we then reflect on our behavior—stimulated perhaps by a conversation about the freedom of the will—and if we are quite incapable of finding a sufficient cause for it, then we believe that there was no sufficient cause for it at all, that, consequently, we could have proceeded differently at that moment, e.g., supporting our head with the left hand instead of the right....

To adduce yet another example: suppose that there are two eggs on the table. I take one of them. Why not the other one? Perhaps the one I took was a bit closer to me, or some other trivial matter, which would be very difficult to discover and is of the kind that almost never enters our consciousness, tipped the scales. If I now look back but do not see why I took *that* particular egg, then I come to think that I could just as well have taken the other.

Let us replace "I could have taken the other egg" by other statements containing the expression "I could have." For example, I could, when I took the egg, have chopped off my fingers instead, or I could have jumped at my neighbor's throat. Why do we never adduce such statements ... but always those contemplating an action close to the one that we really carried out? Because at the moment when I took the egg, chopping off my fingers and murder were far from my mind. From this point of view the two aspects of our subject matter—the fact that acts of will are necessary and that they appear not to be necessary—can be perceived especially clearly. *In fact* taking the other egg was at that moment just as impossible as chopping off a finger. For, whether a nuance of a sensation or a whole army of sensations and thoughts is lacking in the complete cause obviously does not matter; the effect cannot occur so long as the cause is incomplete. But it *seems* as though it would have been possible to take the other egg at that moment; if something almost happened, we think that it could have happened.

While in the case of unimportant matters we perhaps do not notice the causes of our act of will and therefore think that it has no causes, the situation is quite different—it will be objected—in the case of important matters. We did not, after all, marry one girl rather than another while "lost in thought." We did not close the sale of our house while "lost in thought." Rather, everyone sees that motives determined such decisions. In spite of this, however, we think "I could have acted differently." What is the source of this error?

In the case of unimportant matters we do not notice the cause of our action at all; in the case of important ones we perceive it, but not adequately. We do, to be sure, see the separate parts of the cause, but the special relation in which they stood to one another at the moment of the action eludes us.

Let us first consider another example from the realm of animals. A vixen* vacillated whether to sneak into the chicken coop, to hunt for mice, or to return to her young in her den. At last she sneaked into the chicken coop. Why? Because she wanted to. But why did she want to? Because this act of will on her part resulted from the relation in which her hunger, her fear of the watchdog, her maternal instinct, and her other thoughts, sensations, and impressions stood to one another at that time. But a vixen with the gift of reflection would, were she to look back upon her action, say "I could have willed differently." For, although she realizes that hunger influenced her act of will, the *degree* of hunger on the one hand, and of fear and maternal instinct on the other, present at the moment of the action elude her. Having become a different animal since the time of the action, perhaps because of it, she thinks—by way of a kind of optical illusion—that she was that other animal already then. It is the same in the case of man. Suppose, for example, that someone has slain his rival out of jealousy. What does he himself, and what do others, perceive with respect to this action? We see that on the one hand jealousy, the desire for possessions, hatred, and rage were present in him, and on the other fear of punishment, pity, and the thought of God. We do not, however, see the particular relation in which hatred and pity, and rage and fear of punishment, stood to one another at the moment of the deed. If we could see this, keep it fixed, and recreate it experimentally, then everyone would regard this action as an effect, as a necessary result.

---

* Female fox.

Let us now, with the aid of our imagination, suppose that the sensations and thoughts of the murderer at the moment of the deed were spread out before us, clearly visible as if on a map. From this reflection we shall learn that *in fact* we are lacking such an overview, and that this lack is the reason why we do not ascribe a cause (or "necessity") to the action.

The kaleidoscopically changing sensations, thoughts, and impressions would, in order for their relation to one another to become apparent, have to be returned to the state in which they were at the moment of the deed, and then made rigid, as if they were being nailed to their place. But beyond that, the thoughts and sensations would have to be spatially extended and endowed with a colored surface; a stronger sensation would have to be represented by a bigger lump. A clearer thought would have to wear, say, a bright red color, a less clear one a gray coloration. Jealousy and rage, as well as pity and the thought of God, would have to be plastically exhibited* for us in this way. We would, further, have to see how the sight of the victim acts upon these structures of thoughts and sensations, and how there arises from these two factors first the desire to commit murder and then the act of murder itself.

Moreover, we would have to be able to repeat the process, perhaps as follows: we return the murderer to the state of mind that he had some years before the act of murder; we equip his mind with precisely the same thoughts and sensations, and his body with the same constitution. Then we let the very same impressions act upon them; we bring him into contact with the same people, let him read the same books, nourish him with the same food, and, finally, we will place the murdered person, after having called him back to life, before the murderer with the very same facial expression, in the same illumination and at the same distance. Then, as soon as the parts of the cause have been completely assembled, we would always see that the very same effect occurs, namely, wanting to commit, and then committing, murder.

Finally, too, we would have to vary the experiment, in the manner of the chemists; we would have to be able now to weaken a sensation, now to strengthen it, and to observe the result that this produces.

If these conditions were fulfilled, if we could experimentally recreate the process and also vary it, if we were to see its components and, above all, their relation to one another with plastic clarity before us—on the one hand, the *degree* of jealousy and of rage present at the moment; on the other, the *degree* of fear of punishment and of pity—then we would acknowledge that wanting to commit murder and committing murder are necessary results. But as it is we merely see that, on the one hand, jealousy and related feelings, and, on the other, pity and the idea of God, were present in the murderer. But, since we do not see the particular relation in which the sensations and thoughts stood to one another at the moment of the deed, we simply think that the *one* side could have produced acts of will and actions as well as the *other*, that the murderer could, at the moment when he wanted to commit and did commit murder, just as well have willed and acted differently, say compassionately.

It is the same if we ourselves are the person who acts. We, too, think "I could have willed differently." Let us illustrate this by yet another example. Yesterday afternoon at 6:03 o'clock I sold my house. Why? Because I wished to do so. But why did I wish to do so? Because my intention to change my place of residence, and other circumstances, caused my act of will. But was I compelled to will? Could I not have postponed the sale or forgone it altogether? It seems so to me, because I do not see the particular relation in which my thoughts, sensations, and impressions stood to one another yesterday afternoon at 6:03 o'clock.

Thus: we do not see the sufficient cause (either not at all, in the case of unimportant matters; or inadequately, in the case of important ones); consequently it does not exist for us; consequently we think that our volition and our actions were not causally determined at all, that we could just as well have willed and acted differently. No one would say "I could have willed differently" if he could see his act of will and its causes displayed plastically before him, in an experiment permitting repetition.

But who are the mistaken "we" of whom we are speaking here? Patently the author does not consider himself to be one of them. Does he, then, set himself, along with a few fellow philosophers, apart from the

---

* Modeled in three dimensions.

rest of mankind, regarding them as ignorant of the truth? Well, it really is not the case that mankind has always concerned itself with the problem of the freedom of the will and only a small part arrived at the result that the will is not free; rather, in precivilized ages no one, and in civilized ages almost no one, concerned himself with this problem. But of the few who did address themselves to this question, as the history of philosophy teaches us, almost all recognized that there is no freedom of the will. The others became victims of the illusion described above, without ever coming to grips with the problem in its general form (is the will subject to the law of causality or not?)....

5. Determinism Is Inconsistent with Judgments of Moral Responsibility

We hold ourselves and others responsible without taking into account the problem of the freedom of the will.

Experience shows that, if someone has lied or murdered, he is told that he has acted reprehensibly and deserves punishment. Whether his action is uncaused or whether, like the other processes in nature, it is subject to the law of causality—how would people come to raise such questions in the ordinary course of their lives? Or has anyone ever heard of a case in which people talking about an act of murder, a lie, or an act of self-sacrifice discussed these actions in terms of the freedom of the will? It is the same if we ourselves are the person who acted. We say to ourselves "Oh, if only I had not done this! Oh, if only I had acted differently!" or "I have acted laudably, as one should act." At best a philosopher here or there chances upon the question whether our actions are causally determined or not, certainly not the rest of mankind.

Suppose, however, that someone's attention is directed to the fact that the will is not free. At first it will be very difficult to make this plausible to him. His volition is suspended from threads that are too nearly invisible, and that is why he comes to think that it is not causally determined at all. At last, however—so we shall assume—he does come to recognize that actions are effects, that their causes are thoughts and impressions, that these must likewise be viewed as effects, and

so on. How will he then judge these actions? Will he continue to maintain that murder is to be punished by *reprisal* and that benevolent actions are to be considered *meritorious*? By no means. Rather, the first conclusion that he will—validly—draw from his newly acquired insight is that we cannot hold anyone responsible. "*Tout comprendre c'est tout pardonner*";* no one can be made to answer for an *effect*.

In order to illustrate this important truth, that whoever considers intentions to be effects will cease to assign merit or blame for them, let us resume discussion of the examples above. From early childhood on the Bogo ... has learned to praise murder. The praiseworthiness of such an action already penetrated the consciousness of the child as a secondary meaning of the word "murder," and afterward it was confirmed by every impression: his gods and his fellow men praise murder. In consequence he involuntarily judges acts of murder to be praiseworthy, no matter whether it was he himself or someone else who committed them. Let us assume, now, that a philosopher had succeeded in persuading the Bogos that the act of murder and the intention to practice cruelty are causally determined. Then their judgment would undergo an essential modification.

To conceive of actions and intentions as causally determined, after all, means the following. We go back in the history of the individual, say to his birth, and investigate which of his characteristics are inborn and to what causes they are due.[1] Then, ever guided by the law of causality, we trace the development or transformation of these properties; we see how impressions, teachings, and examples come to him and, if his inborn constitution has an affinity for them, are taken up and transformed by it, otherwise passing by without leaving a trace. Finally we recognize that the keystone, the necessary result of this course of development, is the desire to commit murder and the act of murder.

A Bogo who looks upon murder and the intention to practice cruelty in this way—that is, as an effect—will say that it is impossible to regard them as meritorious.

But will he now look upon these actions with apathy, devoid of all feeling? By no means. He will still consider them to be pleasant or unpleasant, agreeable or disagreeable.

---

* French: "To understand all is to forgive all," a European proverb dating back to at least the eighteenth century, expressed most famously using these words by Tolstoy in *War and Peace* (1868).

When the action is directed against himself, he will perceive it as pleasant or as unpleasant; the prospect of being murdered is unpleasant for everyone, whether he considers the action to be causally determined or uncaused.

Similarly our liking or dislike for the character of a human being will persist even if we regard it as the result of causes. To say that I find someone agreeable means that I am drawn to him; I like him. Of a landscape, too, one says that it is agreeable, and, just as this liking cannot be diminished even if we consider the trees, meadows, and hills to be the result of causes, so our liking for the character of a human being is not diminished if we regard it *sub specie necessitatis*. Hence to the Bogo who has come to see that murder is causally determined it is still agreeable or disagreeable. Usually he will consider it to be agreeable. He will say that it warms the cockles of his heart to observe such an action; it accords with his wild temperament, as yet untouched by civilization. Therefore he will, in view of the necessity, suspend only the specifically moral practice of regarding it as meritorious. But his liking may become love, and even esteem and reverence. It will be objected, however, that "I revere a mode of behavior" entails "I consider it meritorious for a person to behave in that way," and similarly for esteem. To be sure, the words "reverence" and "esteem" *frequently* have this meaning, and *to the extent that they do* a determinist would cease using them. But all words that denote human feelings have not only one, but several meanings. They have, if I may express it in that way, a harem of meanings, and they couple now with this one, now with that one. So, if I "revere" someone, it means also that I esteem him, that he impresses me, and that I wish to be like him.... Reverence and esteem in *this* sense can coexist with determinism.

Hence the Bogo who conceives of the intention to practice cruelty and the act of murder as effects can nevertheless consider them to be agreeable or disagreeable, and in a certain sense he can also have esteem and reverence for them, but he will not regard them as meritorious.

Let us now consider the act of murder at high levels of civilization. Civilization, as it progressed, stigmatized murder and threatened penalties for it on earth and in heaven. This censure already penetrates the consciousness of the child as a secondary meaning of the word "murder" and afterward is confirmed through every impression. All the people whom one knows, all

the books that one reads, the state with its institutions, pulpit and stage always use "murder" in a censorious sense. That is how it comes to be that we involuntarily declare an act of murder to be blameworthy, be it that others or that we ourselves, driven by passion, committed it. Whether the action was determined by causes or uncaused—that question is raised neither by the person who acted nor by the uninvolved observers. But *if* it is raised, if someone considers the act of murder *sub specie necessitatis*, then he ceases to regard it as blameworthy. He will then no longer want to see punishment in the proper sense—suffering as retribution—meted out for it, but merely punishment as a safety measure.[2] The feelings of liking and dislike, however, will continue to exist even then. On the whole, someone raised at a high level of civilization will have a feeling of dislike for acts of murder; he will not feel drawn to whoever commits it; he will not like him. For such an act does not accord with his temperament, which was formed as he was engaged in non-violent occupations. In spite of the recognition that the action was necessary, this dislike can at times grow to revulsion, and even to contempt—given that the latter notion is stripped of the specifically moral elements that it contains (the attribution of blame). It will then mean something like this: I do not want to be like that person.

The situation is the same in the case of benevolent actions and those performed out of a sense of duty; we cease to regard them as meritorious if we consider them to be effects. Let us look more closely at actions performed out of a sense of duty. To say that someone acts out of a sense of duty means that he performs an action, perhaps contrary to his inclinations, because his conscience commands him to do it. But how does conscience come to issue such commandments? As follows: with some actions (and intentions) there is linked for us from early childhood on a categorical "thou shalt do (or have) them"; for example, "you *should* help everyone as much as possible." If someone then makes this habitual judgment into the guiding principle of his behavior, if he helps a person because his conscience commands "thou *shalt* help thy fellow man," then he is acting "out of a sense of duty".... If we want to consider such an action from the point of view of eternity and necessity, we shall have to proceed as follows: we investigate (1) the constitution of the child who receives the teaching "thou shalt help," (2) the constitution of those who give it to him. The child absorbing this doctrine has some inborn constitution of nerves, of blood, of imagination, and of reason. The commandment "thou shalt help" is impressed upon this substance with some degree of insistence; the deity, heaven, hell, approval of his fellow men and of his own conscience—these ideas are presented to him, depending upon his teachers, as being more or less majestic and inspiring. And the child transforms them with greater or lesser intensity, depending upon his receptivity. The ultimate constitution of a man, the preponderance within him of the sense of duty over his own desires, is in any case a necessary result, a product of his inborn constitution and the impressions received. To someone who contemplates this, such a temperament may, to be sure, still seem agreeable (perhaps because he himself is or would like to be similarly constituted), but no one can regard as *meritorious* behavior that he conceives to be an *effect*.

But what if we ourselves are the person who acted? Then the circumstances are analogous; then, too, liking and dislike remain, while the attribution of merit or blame (the "pangs of conscience") disappears.

Our own action, too, can remain agreeable or become disagreeable for us after it has occurred. It is agreeable if the disposition from which we acted persists after the action; it will become disagreeable if we change our frame of mind. Suppose, for example, that we have acted vengefully and are still in the same mood; then the act of revenge is still agreeable, whether we conceive it to be an effect or not. If, however, a feeling of pity takes the place of our desire for revenge, then we come to dislike our action; we cannot stand our earlier self—the less so, the more pronounced our feeling of pity is. The reflection that the action is an effect in no way affects this feeling of dislike, perhaps of disgust, or even of revulsion for ourselves. We say to ourselves that the desire for revenge was, to be sure, necessarily stronger than the ideas and impressions that stood in its way, hence the action took place necessarily, too; but now it happens that pity is necessarily present, and, along with it, regrets that we acted as we did....

6. Can We Abandon Judgments of Moral Responsibility?

But is it really possible to shake off feelings of guilt so easily? Do they disappear, like a spook, when the magic word *effect* is pronounced? Is the situation with respect to this feeling not quite like that with regard to dislike? It was, to be sure, necessary that I took revenge, but now

I necessarily feel dislike for my own action, along with guilt. I can no more prevent the onset of the one feeling than of the other. But if the feeling of guilt asserts itself in spite of the recognition that actions are effects, should we not suspect that our holding others responsible, too, will persist in spite of this insight? Did we commit an error somewhere? Is it that responsibility and necessity do not exclude each other? The situation is as follows. The reason why we assign moral praise to some actions and moral censure to others has already been mentioned repeatedly. Censure already penetrates the consciousness of the child as a secondary meaning of the words "murder," "theft," "vengefulness," and "pleasure in another's pain," and praise as a secondary meaning of the words "benevolence" and "mercy." That is why censure seems to him to be a constituent part of murder, and praise, of benevolence. At a later point in his life, perhaps in his twentieth year, the insight comes to him from somewhere that all actions are effects and therefore cannot earn merit or blame. What can this poor little insight accomplish against the accumulated habits of a lifetime of judging? The habit of mind of assigning blame for actions like murder makes it very difficult to think of them without this judgment. It is all very well for reason to tell us that we may not assign blame for such actions, since they are effects—our habit of judging, which has become a feeling, will see to it that it is done anyway. But—let habit confront habit! Suppose that, whenever someone involuntarily wants to assign blame or merit for an action, he ascends to the point of view of eternity and necessity. He then regards the action as the necessary result of [a chain of events stretching back into] the infinite past. Through that way of looking at things the *instinctive* association between the action and the judgment will be severed, if not the first time, then perhaps by the thousandth. Such a man will shed the habit of assigning blame or merit for any action whatsoever.

In fact, of course, human beings almost never behave like that; this way of looking at things is completely foreign to them. Furthermore, human beings determine their actions by considering whether they will make them happy or unhappy; but shedding the habit of making judgments [of moral responsibility] would hardly increase their happiness....

The situation with respect to a person's character is no different from that with respect to his individual actions. *Customarily* one assigns blame or merit, whether to himself or to others, for a single action: a single act of cheating or of giving offense. But *sometimes* we go back from the action to its source, to a person's character. In reality, of course, character, in its broadest as well as its smallest traits, is just as necessary as an individual action; it is the product of [a chain of events stretching back into] the infinite past, be it that it was inherited in its entirety or that it was formed in part during the individual's lifetime. But with regard to character, too, hardly anyone adopts this point of view. Just as in the case of particular actions, character is regarded neither as free nor as necessary; that is to say, people do not raise the question at all whether the law of causality is applicable also to actions and character. Hence one assigns blame and merit for character as for actions, though they are effects; for one does not see that they are effects. If one sees this, if one regards character *sub*

specie necessitatis, then he ceases to assign blame or merit for it. Liking and dislike, on the other hand, nevertheless persist even then: a character closely related to mine will garner my liking, my love, and perhaps even, in the sense mentioned above, my esteem and reverence—whether I conceive of it as an effect or not.

Hence we assign blame or merit for character and actions out of the habit of judging, without concerning ourselves with the question whether they are causally determined or not. We cease to assign blame or merit for character and actions as soon as we recognize that they are causally determined (if we ignore the remnants of our habits).

Let us recapitulate: the character, the intentions, and the actions of every human being are effects, and it is impossible to assign blame or merit for effects. ■

Suggestions for Critical Reflection

1. "To say that the will is not free means that it is subject to the law of causality." Is this right? Or could the will somehow be *both* free and subject to causal laws?
2. Rée admits that "man has the ability to free himself from being dominated by his drives." Does this undermine his claim that determinism is incompatible with moral responsibility?
3. Rée suggests that anyone who comes to properly grasp the truth of determinism will immediately abandon any belief in moral responsibility (though perhaps will be unable to shake off the habit of making moral judgments). Is this claim plausible? How strong are his reasons for making it?
4. Here are two claims:
   a. Some event *A* will occur *whenever* its sufficient cause is present.
   b. Some event *A* will occur *only* when its sufficient cause is present.
   Do these two claims say different things (i.e., could one be true when the other one is false)? Does Rée

clearly differentiate between the two of them? How might the difference between the two claims cause problems for Rée's argument?
5. "Observation teaches us that for every act of will, some causes were the determining factors." Is this true and, if so, is it sufficient to establish determinism?
6. One of the consequences of Rée's determinism, he suggests, is that people can *only* do what they want to do—that is, according to Rée, it is impossible to deliberately do something that you do not want to do. Does this seem right to you? Does it actually follow from the thesis of determinism?
7. Is it *fair* to prefer some people over others, to seek the company of the former, and to shun the latter, if they are not responsible for their character traits? For example, is it okay to dislike depressed people if it's not their fault they are depressed? Is the question of 'fairness' even appropriate, if human beings have no free will?

Notes

1 An investigation as detailed as that is, of course, never possible in practice.

2 Punishments are causes that prevent the repetition of the action punished.

ISHTIYAQUE HAJI

FROM *Incompatibilism's Allure*

Who Is Ishtiyaque Haji?

Ishtiyaque Haji is a Professor of Philosophy at the University of Calgary, Alberta. He is the author of seven books and many papers on free will, moral responsibility, and philosophical psychology. He studied at Simon Fraser University and received his PhD from the University of Massachusetts, Amherst.

What Is the Structure of This Reading?

This reading summarizes some of the main reasons why "a number of thoughtful people might be drawn to libertarianism. The libertarian affirms that determinism is incompatible with moral responsibility and free action but at least some of us, at times, perform free actions for which we are morally responsible. These people might reason that it seems much more plausible that we are, at least on occasion, morally responsible for what we do than that we are not responsible for any of our behavior."*

The chapter begins by describing two case studies that encourage the reader to reflect on our judgments about moral responsibility, and in particular to consider the intuition that blame-worthiness is *incompatible* with certain kinds of determination of our behavior. Haji then organizes this intuition into five possible arguments for incompatibilism, plus a further sixth argument to the effect that we are not responsible for any of our actions regardless of the truth of determinism. Finally, Haji briefly considers a different route to incompatibilism that starts from a principled defense of libertarianism against its alternatives, and then concludes from this that compatibilism must be false.

Haji is agnostic about the truth of determinism, and his concern here is to assess the *compatibility* of determinism, if it turned out to be true, with free will and moral responsibility. His own position, at the end of his book, is that, despite its attractions the main libertarian positions "have significant shortcomings" and we might have to be content with what he calls "semicompatibilism": the view that although determinism is incompatible with our freedom to do otherwise, it does not undermine moral responsibility. He has developed a more restricted form of responsibility that he calls "moral appraisability"—which is in some ways similar to the "reactive attitudes" described by P.F. Strawson in his reading in this chapter—and argues that using this notion allows us to make progress on the "age-old grand puzzle" of free will.

FROM *Incompatibilism's Allure*†

1.1 The Robert Harris Case

Robert Alton Harris' heartrending story is the sort of tragic drama that impels many of us to think deeply about free action, responsibility, and moral luck. The kind of impact, pertinent to our concerns, which Harris' case may well have on our moral thinking can be highlighted perspicuously by following Gary Watson's presentation of its details.[1] The picture of Harris that emerges from the *Los Angeles Times* article,

---

* *Incompatibilism's Allure*, 27.

† This is taken from the introductory chapter to Haji's *Incompatibilism's Allure: Principal Arguments for Incompatibilism* (Broadview Press, 2009).

"Icy Killer's Life Steeped in Violence," is one of a ruthless, brutal murderer.[2] This is a portrayal which, at least initially and customarily, foments attitudes of anger and resentment toward Harris. But as the history of the young man's life on Death Row unravels—as we learn, Watson explains, about how Harris came to be the mean and perverse youth that he was—typically, our negative attitudes are held in check. Some of the details of the case should bear this out.

On July 5, 1978, Robert, 25, and his brother, Daniel, 18, were trying to hotwire a car that they intended to use in a bank robbery. Unable to start the car, Harris decided to take another car in which two youths, John Mayeski and Michael Baker, on their way to a nearby lake for a day of fishing, were eating lunch. Approaching the car and pointing a Luger* at Mayeski's head, Harris crawled into the back seat and ordered the 16-year-olds to drive east. Daniel followed in the Harrises' car. On reaching a secluded canyon area, Harris informed the boys about the planned robbery, and assured them that they would not be hurt. He even offered to leave some of the stolen money in their car to pay for its use. It was agreed that the Harris brothers would leave to rob the bank and that Mayeski and Baker would walk back into town and report the car stolen. As the two boys started to walk away, Harris slowly raised the Luger and shot Mayeski in the back. Harris then chased Baker down a hill and shot him four times. Mayeski was still alive when Harris made his way back. Harris walked over to the boy, put the Luger to his head and fired. Recalling the aftermath of the shooting, Daniel remarked, "[Robert] was swinging the rifle and pistol in the air and laughing. God, that laugh made blood and bone freeze in me."[3]

After the shooting, the Harris brothers drove to a friend's house. Harris began to feast on what was left of the slain youths' lunch. He offered his brother an apple turnover; Daniel became nauseated and ran into the bathroom. "Harris was in an almost lighthearted mood. He smiled and told Daniel that it would be amusing if the two of them were to pose as police officers and inform the parents that their sons were killed."[4] Thinking that somebody might have heard the shots and that the police could be searching for the bodies, Harris told Daniel that they should scout the street near the bodies and perhaps kill some police in the area. Later, as they prepared to rob the bank, "Harris pulled out the Luger, noticed blood stains and remnants of flesh on the barrel as a result of the point-blank shot, and said, 'I really blew that guy's brains out.' And then, again, he started laughing."[5]

Does it matter to our first reaction—that Harris is an archetypal candidate for blame—how he came to be so? The article is sensitive to this issue as well. During an interview with one of Robert's sisters, Barbara, Barbara "put her palms over her eyes and said softly, 'I saw every grain of sweetness, pity and goodness in him destroyed.... It was a long and ugly journey before he reached that point.'"[6]

Harris was born on January 15, 1953, several hours after his mother, six and one-half months pregnant, was kicked in the stomach by her insanely jealous husband who claimed that the child was not his. Because of the premature birth, Robert was a tiny baby; he was kept alive in an incubator and spent months at the hospital. All of the children had horrendous childhoods, but Robert fell victim to abuse that was unusually brutal even in the Harris family. The pain and permanent injury Robert's mother suffered because of the birth, and the constant abuse to which her husband subjected her, turned her against her son. She began to blame all of her problems on Robert and grew to hate the child. Harris suffered from a learning disability and a speech problem. There was no money, though, for therapy. Barbara reported that when he was at school Harris felt stupid and his classmates teased him, and when he was at home he was abused.

"He wanted love so bad he would beg for any kind of physical contact.... He'd come up to my mother and just try to rub his little hands on her leg or her arm. He just never got touched at all. She'd just push him away or kick him".... All nine children are psychologically crippled ... [Barbara continued], but most have been able to lead useful lives. But Robert was too young, and the abuse lasted too long ... for him ever to have had a chance to recover.... [At age 14] Harris was sentenced to a federal youth detention center [for car theft]. He was one of the youngest inmates there, Barbara

---

* A World War II-era pistol.

Harris said, and he grew up "hard and fast." ... Harris was raped several times ... and he slashed his wrists twice in suicide attempts. He spent more than four years behind bars as a result of an escape, an attempted escape and a parole violation.... The centers were "gladiator schools," Barbara Harris said, and Harris learned to fight and to be mean. By the time he was released from federal prison at 19, all his problems were accentuated.... "The only way he could vent his feelings was to break or kill something," Barbara Harris said. "He took out all the frustrations of his life on animals. He had no feeling for life, no sense of remorse. He reached the point where there wasn't that much left of him."[7]

Reflecting on this section of the *Times'* report, it is natural to wonder to what extent Harris was responsible for becoming the sort of person that he was. Was the pathway of his life fully set in stone by parental and societal neglect, social or genetic conditioning, sheer bad luck, and the like, or did he have any hand in molding it? If the former, and this inclines us to mitigate or remove blame, then we may be well on the way toward *incompatibilism*, loosely, the view that blameworthiness—or, more generally, moral responsibility—is incompatible with being "determined" in certain ways. We might see Harris's actions as "determined" in the sense that their sources—the desires, beliefs, values, and so forth—the springs of action that collectively made up his psychological life—were "foreign" or "alien" to him; "foreign" in a robust sense in which, for example, we are comfortable in proclaiming that the desires that a child acquires as a result of *indoctrination* rather than as an outcome of *education* are not "really" the child's own. Is this ever the case? Real-life cases are engagingly (and sometimes, for purposes of analysis, distressingly) messy. For this reason, to unearth different routes to incompatibilism ... it may be more helpful to turn to thought experiments in which various parameters can be controlled.

1.2 The Ann/Beth Cases

Ponder, then, a more clinical imaginary case that Alfred Mele advances. The case resembles Harris' in one vital respect: the central figure's springs of action do not seem to be "truly the agent's own" in that she did not have a hand in their acquisition. Ann and Beth are both philosophy professors but Ann is far more dedicated to the discipline. Wanting more production out of Beth and not scrupulous about how he gets it, the dean of the University enlists the help of new-wave neurologists who "implant" Ann's hierarchy of values into easy-going Beth. Understand 'values' in this way: "S at least *thinly values X* at a time if and only if at that time S both has a positive motivational attitude toward X [for instance, S is favorably inclined toward X or S wants X] and believes X to be good."[8] The pro-attitudes* "implanted" in Beth are *practically unsheddable*. A pro-attitude is practically unsheddable for a person at a time if, given her psychological constitution at that time, ridding herself of that attitude is not a "psychologically genuine option" under any but extraordinary circumstances.[9] It is important to keep in mind that if, for example, a desire is unsheddable for a person at a time, that desire need not be irresistible at that time. A parent's desire to care for her child may be unsheddable at some time but it need not then be irresistible. This "induction" of values into Beth results in her becoming the psychological twin of Ann in some respects. But the induction leaves unscathed values, beliefs, desires, and so forth which pre-manipulated Beth possessed and which can co-exist more or less harmoniously with the newly engineered-in pro-attitudes. Such psychological tampering is, thus, consistent with failing to undermine personal identity: pre-manipulated Beth is identical to† her post-manipulated later self.

An agent's action expresses a belief, or it expresses a pro-attitude such as a desire, or, more generally, it expresses an actional spring, only if that actional spring plays a (nondeviant) causal role in the production of

---

* A pro-attitude is a favorable attitude towards, or preference for, something.

† Haji does not mean that Beth is exactly the same in every way after her dean's psychological meddling (which of course she is not); he means that she nevertheless is *the same person* as she was before, and she hasn't turned into a different individual—just as you are the same person as the 13-year-old you, although you may have quite different attributes now than you had then.

that action. Again, an actional spring just is a causal antecedent of an action such as a desire, belief, or value. Regarding the first few actions of Beth which express engineered-in actional springs, we would want to say that these implanted elements are not "truly Beth's own." Owing to their not being Beth's own, a number of us would be inclined to agree that these actions of Beth are not free and that Beth is not morally responsible for them. We may refer to this case as "**Ann/Beth-1**."

"**Ann/Beth-2**" is just like **Ann/Beth-1** save that in **Ann/Beth-2** the implanted desires are both unsheddable for Beth *and* irresistible. Again, many of us would be drawn to the view that victimized Beth's actions that express these desires (and other implanted antecedents of action) in this second variation of the case are not ones for which she is responsible. And at least some of us would want to add that Beth is not responsible for these actions because, among other things, they are the inevitable causal upshots of antecedents, such as irresistible engineered-in desires, with respect to the acquisition of which she had no control. But then it is a short step from this sort of reasoning to the much more troubling conclusion that all our actions are already determined—"in the cards" so to speak, because they are the *inevitable* causal consequences, not of manipulators, but of facts in the far distant past and the laws of nature. And if this is so, then none of us is responsible for any of our actions. As some theorists steeped in the free will literature will put it, it appears that causal determinism is incompatible with free action and moral responsibility, or more simply, it appears that incompatibilism may well be true.

...

1.4 Different Pathways to Incompatibilism

... [I]t is not so difficult to see why one might think that determinism rules out free action and, thus, moral responsibility on the credible assumption that if a person is morally responsible for an action, then that action is free. In the second version of the **Ann/Beth** case—**Ann/Beth-2**—Beth's first post-transformation action, *A*, causally issues from an irresistible desire. (Assume that *A* consists in Beth's

expending considerable time on refereeing a paper.) Some may find it tempting to argue in this way:

THE LACK OF FREEDOM ARGUMENT

(1) The causal antecedents of Beth's *A*-ing (her pertinent desires, for example) are irresistible.
(2) If the causal antecedents of Beth's *A*-ing are irresistible, then Beth cannot but do *A*.
(3) If Beth cannot but do *A*, then Beth does not do *A* freely.
(4) If Beth does not do *A* freely, then Beth is not morally responsible for *A*-ing.
(5) Therefore, Beth is not morally responsible for *A*-ing.

What underlies this argument is the intuitive and highly attractive picture that *free* agents have more than one path or option genuinely open to them on various occasions in their lives. On this picture, the paths into the future branch out from the present—"the future is a garden of forking paths," as John Martin Fischer following Borges* says—and it is "up to us" on which pathway we tread; it is "up to us" how we choose and act.[10] So although we may have chosen and acted in one way, we could, given the same past and the laws, have chosen and acted in another way. If determinism is true, though, then at every instant, the future is a branchless extension of the past. So if determinism is true, no one is free to choose among alternative pathways into the future.

It is worth probing deeper into how, precisely, **Ann/Beth-2** motivates *incompatibilism*—it's worth examining how exactly this case helps to energize the view that determinism is incompatible with free action and responsibility. Among others, Peter van Inwagen has argued that if determinism is true, then none of our actions is "up to us"; they are not up to us in the sense that *we could not have done otherwise*. He summarizes his intriguing **Consequence Argument** in this way:

> If determinism is true, then our acts are the consequences of the laws of nature and events in the remote past. But it is not up to us what went

---

* See Jorge Luis Borges's 1941 short story "The Garden of Forking Paths."

on before we were born, and neither is it up to us what the laws of nature are. Therefore, the consequences of these things (including our present acts) are not up to us.[11]

Conjoined with the premise that if our acts are not up to us—if we lack the freedom to do otherwise—we do not perform them freely and are not morally responsible for them, the **Consequence Argument** yields incompatibilism as its conclusion. In **Ann/Beth-2**, Beth's first post-transformation act, A, is inevitable because this action is performed, in part, on the basis of a desire that is irresistible. Suppose we accept van Inwagen's conclusion that if determinism is true, then we never have the freedom to do other than what we in fact do; all our actions are inevitable insofar as they are the causal upshots of the distant past and the laws. We can then avail ourselves of this sort of argument:

THE PROTO-CONSEQUENCE ARGUMENT

(1A) If determinism is true, then Beth cannot but do A.
(2A) If Beth cannot but do A, then Beth does not do A freely.
(3A) If Beth does not do A freely, then Beth is not morally responsible for A-ing.
(4A) Therefore, if determinism is true, then Beth is not morally responsible for A-ing.

The second version of the **Ann/Beth** case suggests another route to incompatibilism. One might reason that manipulated Beth is not responsible for acquiring the engineered-in springs of action, including the irresistible desire, on the basis of which she exerts considerable efforts in refereeing a paper. Nor is she responsible for the fact that if she acquires these springs, then she referees the paper. But then it seems to follow that she is not responsible for refereeing the paper either. In short, this line of reasoning relies on a principle of this sort: if you are not responsible for one thing, and you are not responsible for this thing's leading to a second—that is, you are not responsible for the "conditional fact" that if the first occurs or obtains, so does the second—you are not responsible for the second thing. Exploiting this principle, it may be proposed that,

pretty clearly, no one is even partly morally responsible for the state of the universe at a distant time in the past—a time at which there were no human beings, for instance—and no one is even partly morally responsible for the laws being what they are. Assuming that determinism is true, no one is even partly morally responsible for the fact that the combination of the distant past (the complete state of the universe at a time in the past) and the laws entail all events, including our actions. These two claims appear to sanction the result that no one is even partly responsible for one's actions. Unlike the **Proto-Consequence Argument**, in working toward incompatibilism this **Direct Argument** does not invoke the **Principle of Alternative Possibilities**—that persons are morally responsible for what they have done only if they could have done otherwise. It appears to sidestep this principle altogether. In brief, compare this direct argument for Beth's not being responsible—*direct* because it works around the **Principle of Alternative Possibilities** altogether—with the prior argument for the same conclusion:

THE DIRECT ARGUMENT

(1B) No one is even partly responsible for what the state of the universe at a time close to the Big Bang was and for the laws being what they are.
(2B) Assuming determinism, no one is even partly responsible for the fact that the combination of the distant past (the complete state of the universe at a time close to the Big Bang) and the laws entails that Beth performs A (at the time when she does perform A).
(3B) If (1B) and (2B), then Beth is not morally responsible for performing A.
(4B) Therefore, Beth is not morally responsible for performing A.

Inspection reveals that there is no premise in the **Direct Argument** that neatly corresponds to premise (2A) of the **Proto-Consequence Argument**. So, it seems, there is no premise in the **Direct Argument** that appeals to the **Principle of Alternative Possibilities**.

Reflecting on Harris' case, we might be tempted by the view that it is obvious that Harris did moral wrong in killing the youths; he ought not to have killed them. If we think of the morally deontic* notions of right, wrong, and obligation, it would not be unusual to be drawn to the principle that "ought" implies "can": if you morally ought to do something, then you can do it. If it is true, for example, that you cannot open the safe and defuse the bomb therein because you don't know the combination, then you can't have a moral *obligation* to open the safe. The moral "ought" expresses a kind of necessity or requirement. Morality cannot *require* you to do what you *cannot* do. But if "ought" implies "can," then surely "ought not" implies "can refrain from"; if you ought not to do something—if it is wrong for you to do it—then you can refrain from doing it. So it seems that there is a requirement of alternative possibilities for wrongness: you can't do wrong unless you could have refrained from doing what you do. Suppose, though, that determinism *does* undermine alternative possibilities; suppose, that is, that if determinism is true, then you cannot refrain from doing what you do. We now have another pathway that the **Deontic Argument** exposes to incompatibilism:

THE DEONTIC ARGUMENT

(1C) If determinism is true, then you can't refrain from doing what you do.

(2C) If you can't refrain from doing what you do, then whatever you do is not wrong (because you can't do wrong unless you could have avoided doing what you did).

(3C) If whatever you do is not wrong, then you can't be morally blameworthy for anything that you do.

(4C) Therefore, if determinism is true, you can't be morally blameworthy for anything that you do.

Harris' case and both **Ann/Beth** cases invite yet another argument for incompatibilism. Various varieties of manipulation, or social conditioning, or indoctrination undermine moral responsibility. Arguably, the kind of treatment to which Harris was subject during his early childhood is responsibility-subverting. The manipulation in the **Ann/Beth** cases also seems to be manipulation of a responsibility-subverting sort. Focusing on the **Ann/Beth** cases, one might plausibly propose that the type of manipulation involved in these cases undercuts responsibility because its victim (Beth), as a result of being manipulated, is not the "ultimate originator" of her engineered-in springs of action; so she is not the ultimate source of the actions that causally derive from these springs. To be responsible, though, for our choices, actions, and so forth, these things must originate "in us." It is a condition of responsibility that we be the ultimate originators or sources of our intentional behavior. As Beth fails to satisfy this condition, Beth is not morally responsible for them. *She* is not the ultimate source of her actions that express her implanted desires, beliefs, etc.; maybe the *manipulator* carries the burden of responsibility. But now assume, again, that determinism is true. Then there is a sense in which all our actions, including all our decisions, originate in the distant past and the laws of nature, sources over which we have no control. Given the thought that if we are not the ultimate sources of our actions we are not responsible for them, it follows that if determinism is true, we are not responsible for any of our actions. So we have this sort of argument for incompatibilism:

THE MANIPULATION ARGUMENT

(1D) Actions that result from manipulation of the sort displayed in the **Ann/Beth** cases are actions for which an agent is not morally responsible. (Or, as we may say, actions that derive from a causal history involving *menacing manipulation*—manipulation that undermines responsibility—aren't ones for which an agent is responsible.)

(2D) Actions that result from a deterministic causal history are relevantly similar to those that derive from a causal history involving menacing manipulation (in either case, the agent is not the ultimate source of her actions).

(3D) If (1D) and (2D), then determinism undermines moral responsibility.

(4D) Therefore, determinism undermines moral responsibility.

This version of the **Manipulation Argument** attempts to convince us that cases of responsibility-undercutting manipulation are relevantly similar to

---

* *Intrinsically* right or wrong, and so *intrinsically* obligatory or forbidden. 'Intrinsically' here is in contrast to: because of consequences, because of (in)compatibility with good character, etc.

actions that are causally determined: just as, in virtue of being manipulated in the manner in which she is, Beth is not the ultimate originator of her actions, and, thus, is not morally responsible for them, so in virtue of her actions being causally determined, Beth is not their ultimate originator and, hence, bears no responsibility for them.

Finally, all the cases with which we commenced might spur an argument—the **Impossibility Argument**—for the stronger conclusion that we are not responsible for any of our actions *regardless* of the truth of determinism. This conclusion is, of course, consistent with the incompatibilist's claim that determinism rules out moral responsibility. In roughly hewn strokes, the line of reasoning for this forceful conclusion unfolds in this way: If Beth is not responsible for the way she is at a particular time—if she is not, for example, responsible for having the desires, values, or beliefs with which she finds herself at a particular time—then she is not responsible for actions that express these causal antecedents. But if she is to be responsible for these causal antecedents—if she is to be responsible for these desires, for instance—she must be responsible for earlier actions or behavior as a result of which she acquired these desires. To be responsible, though, for these earlier actions, she would have had to have been responsible for the springs of these earlier actions. But to have been responsible for these earlier springs, she would have had to have been responsible for still earlier actions that led to the acquisition of these earlier springs, and so forth. Thus, responsibility for an action requires what is impossible: it requires having made an *infinite* number of choices. In premise and conclusion form, the **Impossibility Argument** can be restated in this way:

THE IMPOSSIBILITY ARGUMENT

(1E) The actions we perform depend on certain facts about what we are like in relevant mental respects, or *how we are.*

(2E) If (1E), then if we are responsible for any of our acts, then we are responsible for being in the relevant ways how we are.

(3E) If we are responsible for being in the relevant ways how we are, then we can or could be responsible for an *infinite* series of "character-forming" actions.

(4E) It is not the case that we can or could be responsible for an *infinite* series of "character-forming" actions.

(5E) Therefore, it is false that we are responsible for any of our acts.

The **Impossibility Argument** and the **Manipulation Argument** share a common kernel: both place a great deal of stock in the idea that if we are to be responsible for our actions, these actions must originate "in us"; we must be their "final source." The **Manipulation Argument** seeks to convince us that, just as in cases involving manipulation that is responsibility-undermining, we are not responsible for our actions because our actions ultimately originate in sources external to us (they originate in the manipulator), so with causally determined actions, we are not responsible for them because they have their ultimate sources in the distant past and the laws. The **Impossibility Argument**, in slight contrast, seeks to persuade us that responsibility does require that we be the ultimate originators of our actions, but that it is impossible for us to be such originators. If this skeptical argument is sound, then it indirectly supports incompatibilism in this way: if we are not responsible for our actions regardless of whether determinism is true, then we are not responsible for our actions even if determinism is true.

Some theorists may be drawn to incompatibilism via yet another route. These theorists may first affirm that we *are* morally responsible for at least some of our behavior. This leaves open two possibilities:

1. The incompatibilist account is true, so this moral responsibility is consistent only with a libertarian account of action.*
2. The *compatibilist account of free action and responsibility* is true: this attempts to show that free action and responsibility are compatible with determinism.

---

* A view combining the positions that we have free will and that (therefore) determinism is false.

Then they might reason that, among the leading competing compatibilist and libertarian accounts of free action and responsibility, the best account is a libertarian one. They may, for example, call upon the **Manipulation Argument** to cast doubt on compatibilist rivals. Or, for instance, they might reason that ultimate origination is a requirement of free action and responsibility but no compatibilist competitor is up to the task of providing a suitably rich account of such origination. Their overall strategy would be to examine critically both compatibilist and libertarian contenders and then see which wins the day. In the view of these theorists it is a form of libertarianism that prevails. But if some version of libertarianism is true, then incompatibilism is victorious.

On one libertarian snapshot of free action, if you perform an action at a certain time, that action is free only if, given *exactly* the same past and the laws up until the time (or just prior to the time) at which you perform the action, you could then have performed some alternative instead. If determinism is true, this is impossible; you do not have such "genuine alternatives." For, assuming determinism, if you perform an action at a certain time, the past and the laws entail that you perform that action at that time. So if the past and the laws are "held fixed" right up to or just prior to the time at which you perform an action, it appears that it is not possible that, at that time, you perform some alternative instead. What may underlie this libertarian vision of free action? Either the garden-of-forking-paths picture of free action—the thought that free action and responsibility require that you have genuine alternatives so that it is "up to you" on which pathway into the future you tread; or the idea that responsibility requires that you be an ultimate originator of your choices or actions, something that is not possible if determinism is true; or, perhaps, both of these things. ∎

Suggestions for Critical Reflection

1. What is your reaction to the Harris case? Do the details of Harris's life make you less inclined to blame him for his actions, and if so why do you think that is?

2. What is the stipulated difference between the Ann/Beth-1 and Ann/Beth-2 cases? Why does this change matter to the question of free will, do you think?

3. Which of the six arguments for incompatibilism raised by Haji do you think is the strongest? Are there any reasons to believe in incompatibilism that you think Haji might have missed?

4. The arguments for incompatibilism described in this reading tend to move from an intuition that Harris and/or Beth are not free or responsible, to a general claim that (if determinism is true) none of us are ever free. Examine how the arguments make this transition (if they do), and assess how plausibly they do so.

5. Haji says that "if 'ought' implies 'can,' then surely 'ought not' implies 'can refrain from.'" Does this follow? Even if it does not, how plausible do you find the latter claim?

Notes

1 Gary Watson, "Responsibility, and the Limits of Evil: Variations on a Strawsonian Theme," in Fisher and Ravizza, eds., *Perspectives on Moral Responsibility* (Ithaca, NY: Cornell UP, 1993).

2 Miles Corwin, *Los Angeles Times* (16 May 1982). Copyright, 1982, *Los Angeles Times*.

3 Watson 1993, p. 132.

4 Watson 1993, p. 132.

5 Watson 1993, p. 132.

6 Watson 1993, p. 134.

7 Watson 1993, pp. 135–36.

8 Alfred Mele, *Irrationality: An Essay on Akrasia, Self-Deception, and Self-Control* (NY: Oxford UP, 1995), 116.

9   Mele 1995, p. 172; Mele, *Free Will and Luck* (NY: Oxford UP, 2006), 164–65.

10 John M. Fischer, "Compatibilism," in Fischer, Kane, Pereboom and Vargas, *Four Views on Free Will* (Oxford: Blackwell, 2007), 46.

11 Peter van Inwagen, *An Essay on Free Will* (Oxford: Oxford UP, 1983), 16.

A.J. AYER

Freedom and Necessity

Who Was A.J. Ayer?

Sir Alfred Jules Ayer (1910–89), known to all his friends as Freddie, was born into a wealthy European-origin family in London. He attended the pre-eminent English private school Eton, then went on scholarship to Oxford. He served as an officer in a British espionage and sabotage unit during World War II, then taught at University College London and at Oxford.

When only 24, Ayer wrote *Language, Truth, and Logic*, the book that made his name. In it, he briefly, simply, and persuasively to many, argued for logical positivism, a form of radical empiricism that had been developed largely by the group of philosophers called the Vienna Circle, whose ideas Ayer had picked up while studying with them in Austria. Logical positivism dominated Anglophone philosophy for decades; while objections (especially to Ayer's rather simplified version) came thick and fast, everyone was at least aware of it as a philosophical force to be reckoned with.

While *Language, Truth, and Logic* was by far his bestseller, Ayer wrote a good deal of other important work, especially in epistemology. While his work is not now generally included in lists of all-time philosophical landmarks, he was considered, in terms of influence if not of originality, second only to Bertrand Russell among the English philosophers of his day. He was also known for his advocacy of humanism and was the first executive director of the British Humanist Association, a charitable organization working towards "a tolerant world where rational thinking and kindness prevail."*

Ayer was extraordinarily well-known by the British public. He wrote and spoke on all sorts of popular issues, all over the media. In those days, TV networks programmed witty intellectual chatter, and Ayer was a master at this. He loved his celebrity, and hobnobbed with the famous and influential. He was knighted in 1970.

What Is the Structure of This Reading?

The problem Ayer will talk about, clearly set out in the first few paragraphs of his article, is how free action—action for which one is morally responsible—is possible, given the assumption that all human action, like everything else in the world, is determined by causes, and, given the causes, could not have been otherwise. That is, he lays out the tension between determinism and the view that moral responsibility requires that we could have done otherwise than we did. He critically scrutinizes the plausibility of determinism, but then asks whether the denial of determinism—the view that some of our actions are not caused but random—will help the defender of moral responsibility in any case. If the kind of freedom required for morality is not the absence of causality, then what is it? According to Ayer, freedom in this sense is instead the absence of *constraint*, and he goes on to define what he means by this. "[I]t is not when my action has any cause at all, but only when it has a special sort of cause, that it is reckoned not to be free."

Ayer concludes by attempting to explain and defuse the tendency many philosophers have of counting causal determination as constraining. A constrained action, he argues, is one that you'll do whatever you decide, if anything. But free actions, on his understanding, are those in which your decision is operative: they would not have occurred had you not decided to do them. Your decision, for a determinist, is itself causally determined; but that's not relevant. The fact that the causal chain behind the action includes your decision is what makes it a "free" action, an action for which you're responsible.

---

* https://humanism.org.uk/about/

Freedom and Necessity*

When I am said to have done something of my own free will it is implied that I could have acted otherwise; and it is only when it is believed that I could have acted otherwise that I am held to be morally responsible for what I have done. For a man is not thought to be morally responsible for an action that it was not in his power to avoid. But if human behaviour is entirely governed by causal laws, it is not clear how any action that is done could ever have been avoided. It may be said of the agent that he would have acted otherwise if the causes of his action had been different, but they being what they were, it seems to follow that he was bound to act as he did. Now it is commonly assumed both that men are capable of acting freely, in the sense that is required to make them morally responsible, and that human behaviour is entirely governed by causal laws: and it is the apparent conflict between these two assumptions that gives rise to the philosophical problem of the freedom of the will.

Confronted with this problem, many people will be inclined to agree with Dr. Johnson: 'Sir, we *know* our will is free, and *there's* an end on't.'† But, while this does very well for those who accept Dr. Johnson's premiss, it would hardly convince anyone who denied the freedom of the will. Certainly, if we do know that our wills are free, it follows that they are so. But the logical reply to this might be that since our wills are not free, it follows that no one can know that they are: so that if anyone claims, like Dr. Johnson, to know that they are, he must be mistaken. What is evident, indeed, is that people often believe themselves to be acting freely; and it is to this 'feeling' of freedom that some philosophers appeal when they wish, in the supposed interests of morality, to prove that not all human action is causally determined. But if these philosophers are right in their assumption that a man cannot be acting freely if his action is causally determined, then the fact that someone feels free to do, or

not to do, a certain action does not prove that he really is so. It may prove that the agent does not himself know what it is that makes him act in one way rather than another: but from the fact that a man is unaware of the causes of his action, it does not follow that no such causes exist.

So much may be allowed to the determinist; but his belief that all human actions are subservient to causal laws still remains to be justified. If, indeed, it is necessary that every event should have a cause, then the rule must apply to human behaviour as much as to anything else. But why should it be supposed that every event must have a cause? The contrary is not unthinkable. Nor is the law of universal causation a necessary presupposition of scientific thought. The scientist may try to discover causal laws, and in many cases he succeeds; but sometimes he has to be content with statistical laws, and sometimes he comes upon events which, in the present state of his knowledge, he is not able to subsume under any law at all.‡ In the case of these events he assumes that if he knew more he would be able to discover some law, whether causal or statistical, which would enable him to account for them. And this assumption cannot be disproved. For however far he may have carried his investigation, it is always open to him to carry it further; and it is always conceivable that if he carried it further he would discover the connection which had hitherto escaped him. Nevertheless, it is also conceivable that the events with which he is concerned are not systematically connected with any others: so that the reason why he does not discover the sort of laws that he requires is simply that they do not obtain.

Now in the case of human conduct the search for explanations has not in fact been altogether fruitless. Certain scientific laws have been established; and with the help of these laws we do make a number of successful predictions about the ways in which different people

---

* This paper first appeared in *Polemic* No. 5 in 1946; it is reprinted here from Ayer's *Philosophical Essays* (Palgrave Macmillan, 1972).

† Samuel Johnson (1709–84) was a prominent English essayist and the compiler of the first great *Dictionary of the English Language*; he is quoted in James Boswell's *Life of Johnson* (1769: Aetat. 60).

‡ "Subsume under any law at all": to explain by showing that something is an instance of a general law of nature.

440 | FREE WILL

will behave. But these predictions do not always cover every detail. We may be able to predict that in certain circumstances a particular man will be angry, without being able to prescribe the precise form that the expression of his anger will take. We may be reasonably sure that he will shout, but not sure how loud his shout will be, or exactly what words he will use. And it is only a small proportion of human actions that we are able to forecast even so precisely as this. But that, it may be said, is because we have not carried our investigations very far. The science of psychology is still in its infancy and, as it is developed, not only will more human actions be explained, but the explanations will go into greater detail. The ideal of complete explanation may never in fact be attained: but it is theoretically attainable. Well, this may be so: and certainly it is impossible to show *a priori** that it is not so: but equally it cannot be shown that it is. This will not, however, discourage the scientist who, in the field of human behaviour, as elsewhere, will continue to formulate theories and test them by the facts. And in this he is justified. For since he has no reason *a priori* to admit that there is a limit to what he can discover, the fact that he also cannot be sure that there is no limit does not make it unreasonable for him to devise theories, nor, having devised them, to try constantly to improve them.

But now suppose it to be claimed that, so far as men's actions are concerned, there is a limit: and that this limit is set by the fact of human freedom. An obvious objection is that in many cases in which a person feels himself to be free to do, or not to do, a certain action, we are even now able to explain, in causal terms, why it is that he acts as he does. But it might be argued that even if men are sometimes mistaken in believing that they act freely, it does not follow that they are always so mistaken. For it is not always the case that when a man believes that he has acted freely we are in fact able to account for his action in causal terms. A determinist would say that we should be able to account for it if we had more knowledge of the circumstances, and had been able to discover the appropriate natural laws. But until those discoveries have been made, this remains only a pious hope. And may it not be true that, in some cases at least, the reason why we can give no causal explanation is that no

causal explanation is available; and that this is because the agent's choice was literally free, as he himself felt it to be?

The answer is that this may indeed be true, inasmuch as it is open to anyone to hold that no explanation is possible until some explanation is actually found. But even so it does not give the moralist what he wants. For he is anxious to show that men are capable of acting freely in order to infer that they can be morally responsible for what they do. But if it is a matter of pure chance that a man should act in one way rather than another, he may be free but he can hardly be responsible. And indeed when a man's actions seem to us quite unpredictable, when, as we say, there is no knowing what he will do, we do not look upon him as a moral agent. We look upon him rather as a lunatic.

To this it may be objected that we are not dealing fairly with the moralist. For when he makes it a condition of my being morally responsible that I should act freely, he does not wish to imply that it is purely a matter of chance that I act as I do. What he wishes to imply is that my actions are the result of my own free choice: and it is because they are the result of my own free choice that I am held to be morally responsible for them.

But now we must ask how it is that I come to make my choice. Either it is an accident that I choose to act as I do or it is not. If it is an accident, then it is merely a matter of chance that I did not choose otherwise; and if it is merely a matter of chance that I did not choose otherwise, it is surely irrational to hold me morally responsible for choosing as I did. But if it is not an accident that I choose to do one thing rather than another, then presumably there is some causal explanation of my choice: and in that case we are led back to determinism.

Again, the objection may be raised that we are not doing justice to the moralist's case. His view is not that it is a matter of chance that I choose to act as I do, but rather that my choice depends upon my character. Nevertheless he holds that I can still be free in the sense that he requires; for it is I who am responsible for my character. But in what way am I responsible for my character? Only, surely, in the sense that there is a causal connection between what I do now and what

---

*   Latin: before conducting the experiments (before experience).

I have done in the past. It is only this that justifies the statement that I have made myself what I am: and even so this is an over-simplification, since it takes no account of the external influences to which I have been subjected. But, ignoring the external influences, let us assume that it is in fact the case that I have made myself what I am. Then it is still legitimate to ask how it is that I have come to make myself one sort of person rather than another. And if it be answered that it is a matter of my strength of will, we can put the same question in another form by asking how it is that my will has the strength that it has and not some other degree of strength. Once more, either it is an accident or it is not. If it is an accident, then by the same argument as before, I am not morally responsible, and if it is not an accident we are led back to determinism.

Furthermore, to say that my actions proceed from my character or, more colloquially, that I act in character, is to say that my behaviour is consistent and to that extent predictable: and since it is, above all, for the actions that I perform in character that I am held to be morally responsible, it looks as if the admission of moral responsibility, so far from being incompatible with determinism, tends rather to presuppose it. But how can this be so if it is a necessary condition of moral responsibility that the person who is held responsible should have acted freely? It seems that if we are to retain this idea of moral responsibility, we must either show that men can be held responsible for actions which they do not do freely, or else find some way of reconciling determinism with the freedom of the will.

It is no doubt with the object of effecting this reconciliation that some philosophers* have defined freedom as the consciousness of necessity. And by so doing they are able to say not only that a man can be acting freely when his action is causally determined, but even that his action must be causally determined for it to be possible for him to be acting freely. Nevertheless this definition has the serious disadvantage that it gives to the word 'freedom' a meaning quite different from any that it ordinarily bears. It is indeed obvious that if we are allowed to give the word 'freedom' any meaning that we please, we can find a meaning that will reconcile it with determinism: but this is no more a solution of our present problem than the fact that the word 'horse' could be arbitrarily used to mean what is ordinarily meant by 'sparrow' is a proof that horses have wings. For suppose that I am compelled by another person to do something 'against my will'. In that case, as the word 'freedom' is ordinarily used, I should not be said to be acting freely: and the fact that I am fully aware of the constraint to which I am subjected makes no difference to the matter. I do not become free by becoming conscious that I am not. It may, indeed, be possible to show that my being aware that my action is causally determined is not incompatible with my acting freely: but it by no means follows that it is in this that my freedom consists. Moreover, I suspect that one of the reasons why people are inclined to define freedom as the consciousness of necessity is that they think that if one is conscious of necessity one may somehow be able to master it. But this is a fallacy. It is like someone's saying that he wishes he could see into the future, because if he did he would know what calamities lay in wait for him and so would be able to avoid them. But if he avoids the calamities then they don't lie in the future and it is not true that he foresees them. And similarly if I am able to master necessity, in the sense of escaping the operation of a necessary law, then the law in question is not necessary. And if the law is not necessary, then neither my freedom nor anything else can consist in my knowing that it is.

Let it be granted, then, that when we speak of reconciling freedom with determinism we are using the word 'freedom' in an ordinary sense. It still remains for us to make this usage clear: and perhaps the best way to make it clear is to show what it is that freedom, in this sense, is contrasted with. Now we began with the assumption that freedom is contrasted with causality: so that a man cannot be said to be acting freely if his action is causally determined. But this assumption has led us into difficulties and I now wish to suggest that it is mistaken. For it is not, I think, causality that freedom is to be contrasted with, but constraint. And while it is true that being constrained to do an action entails being caused to do it, I shall try to show that the converse does not hold. I shall try to show that

---

* Karl Marx is a prominent example of a philosopher who makes this claim, building on the tradition of Kant and Hegel.

from the fact that my action is causally determined it does not necessarily follow that I am constrained to do it: and this is equivalent to saying that it does not necessarily follow that I am not free.

If I am constrained, I do not act freely. But in what circumstances can I legitimately be said to be constrained? An obvious instance is the case in which I am compelled by another person to do what he wants. In a case of this sort the compulsion need not be such as to deprive one of the power of choice. It is not required that the other person should have hypnotized me, or that he should make it physically impossible for me to go against his will. It is enough that he should induce me to do what he wants by making it clear to me that, if I do not, he will bring about some situation that I regard as even more undesirable than the consequences of the action that he wishes me to do. Thus, if the man points a pistol at my head I may still choose to disobey him: but this does not prevent its being true that if I do fall in with his wishes he can legitimately be said to have compelled me. And if the circumstances are such that no reasonable person would be expected to choose the other alternative, then the action that I am made to do is not one for which I am held to be morally responsible.

A similar, but still somewhat different, case is that in which another person has obtained an habitual ascendancy over me.* Where this is so, there may be no question of my being induced to act as the other person wishes by being confronted with a still more disagreeable alternative: for if I am sufficiently under his influence this special stimulus will not be necessary. Nevertheless I do not act freely, for the reason that I have been deprived of the power of choice. And this means that I have acquired so strong a habit of obedience that I no longer go through any process of deciding whether or not to do what the other person wants. About other matters I may still deliberate; but as regards the fulfilment of this other person's wishes, my own deliberations have ceased to be a causal factor in my behaviour. And it is in this sense that I may be said to be constrained. It is not, however, necessary

that such constraint should take the form of subservience to another person. A kleptomaniac† is not a free agent, in respect of his stealing, because he does not go through any process of deciding whether or not to steal. Or rather, if he does go through such a process, it is irrelevant to his behaviour. Whatever he resolved to do, he would steal all the same. And it is this that distinguishes him from the ordinary thief.

But now it may be asked whether there is any essential difference between these cases and those in which the agent is commonly thought to be free. No doubt the ordinary thief does go through a process of deciding whether or not to steal, and no doubt it does affect his behaviour. If he resolved to refrain from stealing, he could carry his resolution out. But if it be allowed that his making or not making this resolution is causally determined, then how can he be any more free than the kleptomaniac? It may be true that unlike the kleptomaniac he could refrain from stealing if he chose: but if there is a cause, or set of causes, which necessitate his choosing as he does, how can he be said to have the power of choice? Again, it may be true that no one now compels me to get up and walk across the room: but if my doing so can be causally explained in terms of my history or my environment, or whatever it may be, then how am I any more free than if some other person had compelled me? I do not have the feeling of constraint that I have when a pistol is manifestly pointed at my head; but the chains of causation by which I am bound are no less effective for being invisible.

The answer to this is that the cases I have mentioned as examples of constraint do differ from the others: and they differ just in the ways that I have tried to bring out. If I suffered from a compulsion neurosis, so that I got up and walked across the room, whether I wanted to or not, or if I did so because somebody else compelled me, then I should not be acting freely. But if I do it now, I shall be acting freely, just because these conditions do not obtain; and the fact that my action may nevertheless have a cause is, from this point of view, irrelevant. For it is not when my action has any

---

* If someone has an "habitual ascendancy over me," this would mean that I obey that person unquestioningly, as a matter of habit.

† Kleptomania is a mental disorder characterized by an obsessive, recurring impulse to steal, regardless of economic need or profit.

cause at all, but only when it has a special sort of cause, that it is reckoned not to be free.

But here it may be objected that, even if this distinction corresponds to ordinary usage, it is still very irrational. For why should we distinguish, with regard to a person's freedom, between the operations of one sort of cause and those of another? Do not all causes equally necessitate? And is it not therefore arbitrary to say that a person is free when he is necessitated in one fashion but not when he is necessitated in another?

That all causes equally necessitate is indeed a tautology*, if the word 'necessitate' is taken merely as equivalent to 'cause': but if, as the objection requires, it is taken as equivalent to 'constrain' or 'compel', then I do not think that this proposition is true. For all that is needed for one event to be the cause of another is that, in the given circumstances, the event which is said to be the effect would not have occurred if it had not been for the occurrence of the event which is said to be the cause, or *vice versa*, according as causes are interpreted as necessary, or sufficient, conditions: and this fact is usually deducible from some causal law which states that whenever an event of the one kind occurs then, given suitable conditions, an event of the other kind will occur in a certain temporal or spatio-temporal relationship to it. In short, there is an invariable concomitance† between the two classes of events; but there is no compulsion, in any but a metaphorical sense. Suppose, for example, that a psycho-analyst is able to account for some aspect of my behaviour by referring it to some lesion‡ that I suffered in my childhood. In that case, it may be said that my childhood experience, together with certain other events, necessitates my behaving as I do. But all that this involves is that it is found to be true in general that when people have had certain experiences as children, they subsequently behave in certain specifiable ways; and my case is just another instance of this general law. It is in this way indeed that my behaviour is explained. But from the fact that my behaviour is capable of being explained, in the sense that it can be subsumed under some natural law, it does not follow that I am acting under constraint.

If this is correct, to say that I could have acted otherwise is to say, first, that I should have acted otherwise if I had so chosen; secondly, that my action was voluntary in the sense in which the actions, say, of the kleptomaniac are not; and thirdly, that nobody compelled me to choose as I did: and these three conditions may very well be fulfilled. When they are fulfilled, I may be said to have acted freely. But this is not to say that it was a matter of chance that I acted as I did, or, in other words, that my action could not be explained. And that my actions should be capable of being explained is all that is required by the postulate of determinism.

If more than this seems to be required it is, I think, because the use of the very word 'determinism' is in some degree misleading. For it tends to suggest that one event is somehow in the power of another, whereas the truth is merely that they are factually correlated. And the same applies to the use, in this context, of the word 'necessity' and even of the word 'cause' itself. Moreover, there are various reasons for this. One is the tendency to confuse causal with logical necessitation, and so to infer mistakenly that the effect is contained in the cause. Another is the uncritical use of a concept of force which is derived from primitive experiences of pushing and striking. A third is the survival of an animistic conception of causality, in which all causal relationships are modelled on the example of one person's exercising authority over another. As a result we tend to form an imaginative picture of an unhappy effect trying vainly to escape from the clutches of an overmastering cause. But, I repeat, the fact is simply that when an event of one type occurs, an event of another type occurs also, in a certain temporal or spatio-temporal relation to the first. The rest is only metaphor. And it is because of the metaphor, and not because of the fact, that we come to think that there is an antithesis between causality and freedom.

Nevertheless, it may be said, if the postulate of determinism is valid, then the future can be explained in terms of the past: and this means that if one knew

---

* An expression that says the same thing twice, in different words.
† Co-occurrence or co-existence.
‡ Abnormal or damaged brain tissue; an injury.

enough about the past one would be able to predict the future. But in that case what will happen in the future is already decided. And how then can I be said to be free? What is going to happen is going to happen and nothing that I do can prevent it. If the determinist is right, I am the helpless prisoner of fate.

But what is meant by saying that the future course of events is already decided? If the implication is that some person has arranged it, then the proposition is false. But if all that is meant is that it is possible, in principle, to deduce it from a set of particular facts about the past, together with the appropriate general laws, then, even if this is true, it does not in the least entail that I am the helpless prisoner of fate. It does not even entail that my actions make no difference to the future: for they are causes as well as effects; so that if they were different their consequences would be different also. What it does entail is that my behaviour can be predicted: but to say that my behaviour can be predicted is not to say that I am acting under constraint. It is indeed true that I cannot escape my destiny if this is taken to mean no more than that I shall do what I shall do. But this is a tautology, just as it is a tautology that what is going to happen is going to happen. And such tautologies as these prove nothing whatsoever about the freedom of the will.

Suggestions for Critical Reflection

1. Consider the following case. An ingenious physiologist has hooked up wires to your brain; by pushing buttons, he can cause you to have a variety of "volitions"; these are what Ayer would presumably count as decisions to act, so he would count your resulting actions as free. But it is plausible to claim that in this case you would be entirely unfree—merely the physiologist's puppet. Which position is right? Where does the other position go wrong?

2. You've been called to act as a witness for the prosecution in a criminal trial, and friends of the accused tell you that all of your family will be in great danger if you testify honestly. You decide that all you can do is to lie to the court, and say you can't remember anything. This is ordinarily an immoral act, but is it under the circumstances? Are you constrained to act as you did? (Compare Ayer's example of someone's holding a gun to your head.)

If this is genuine constraint, then does that mean you're not morally responsible for lying?

3. It is important to Ayer's case that he can make a clear and principled contrast between the kind of causation of behavior which is a constraint and the kind which is not. Is his distinction clear? Is his distinction principled—that is, does it seem to get at something deep that seems to make a difference to our moral judgments?

4. Fatalism is the position that something will happen in the future *no matter what*. In the last few paragraphs, Ayer attempts to distinguish determinism from fatalism, and to argue that it is the second, not the first, that is incompatible with responsibility and freedom. Try to explain his argument, in your own words. Some philosophers think that determinism and fatalism are the same thing. Why do you think they would say this? Who is right?

HARRY G. FRANKFURT

Alternate Possibilities and Moral Responsibility

Who Is Harry Frankfurt?

Harry Frankfurt (b. 1929) taught at Ohio State University, Yale University, Harpur College, and Rockefeller University, as well as Princeton, where he is now Professor Emeritus. He has published eight books and dozens of academic articles on topics in ethics, free will, philosophy of mind, and early modern philosophy. Frankfurt is perhaps best known for his work on autonomy and moral responsibility, and his writing has been widely praised for its clarity and concision. In addition to his academic scholarship, Frankfurt has also published non-fiction writing suitable to a general audience.

His 2005 book *On Bullshit* was a *New York Times* best-seller, receiving popular media coverage and leading to a television interview on *The Daily Show with Jon Stewart*. *On Bullshit* examines acts of deceptive communication in which the speaker attempts to persuade others by disregarding the truth of what is being said, as opposed to lies, in which the speaker attempts to deliberately hide the truth. In 2006 he published a follow-up book, *On Truth*.

What Is the Structure of This Reading?

Frankfurt frames this paper as an argument against what he calls "the principle of alternate possibilities." This widely-held principle, which has at times been used in arguments against the possibility of free will, holds that "a person is morally responsible for what he has done only if he could have done otherwise." The intuitive appeal of this principle can be seen most easily in cases of coercion: we don't typically say that someone is guilty of a crime or other moral transgression if that person was coerced into action by someone else—say, by being held at gunpoint. Similarly, if we found that someone had caused unwarranted harm to another but we then discovered that some sort of physical obstruction would have made it impossible for them to do otherwise, we might conclude that they are not morally responsible for what they've done. If, for example, a person knowingly drove their vehicle into someone else, we would likely find them innocent of what would otherwise be a horrific moral transgression if in fact the vehicle's steering and braking mechanisms had malfunctioned, preventing any other course of action.

Frankfurt argues that the principle of alternate possibilities is false. In order to do this, he needs only to show that there is at least one case in which a person is responsible for their actions and yet could not have done otherwise. Frankfurt offers a series of related examples involving a fictional person named Jones, distinguishing them from one another by the use of subscript numbers: $Jones_1$, $Jones_2$, $Jones_3$, and $Jones_4$. In each of these cases, Jones is said to have performed some immoral action, and in each case Jones is unable to do other than he has done due to some external condition: a coercive threat in the first three cases; a more direct form of control in the fourth. If the principle of alternate possibilities were true, then Jones would not be responsible for his actions in any of these scenarios. And yet, Frankfurt argues, he is clearly morally responsible in at least some of them (in particular, $Jones_4$), and so the principle of alternate possibilities cannot be true. Toward the end of this reading, Frankfurt proposes that a modified version of the principle may be true, and this revised version would accurately distinguish between the cases in which Jones is responsible and those in which he is not.

A Common Misconception

This paper concerns the moral responsibility of people, not their legal responsibility. In order to establish his arguments, Frankfurt stipulates the intentions and reasoning of the people in his examples. In reality, and in a courtroom, we cannot, of course, know a person's intentions with certainty. So, even if Frankfurt is right about the truth of the principle of alternate possibilities, this may not mean that we should abandon the principle in our legal and everyday practices.

Alternate Possibilities and Moral Responsibility*

A dominant role in nearly all recent inquiries into the free-will problem has been played by a principle which I shall call "the principle of alternate possibilities." This principle states that a person is morally responsible for what he has done only if he could have done otherwise. Its exact meaning is a subject of controversy, particularly concerning whether someone who accepts it is thereby committed to believing that moral responsibility and determinism are incompatible. Practically no one, however, seems inclined to deny or even to question that the principle of alternate possibilities (construed in some way or other) is true. It has generally seemed so overwhelmingly plausible that some philosophers have even characterized it as an *a priori* truth.† People whose accounts of free will or of moral responsibility are radically at odds evidently find in it a firm and convenient common ground upon which they can profitably take their opposing stands.

But the principle of alternate possibilities is false. A person may well be morally responsible for what he has done even though he could not have done otherwise. The principle's plausibility is an illusion, which can be made to vanish by bringing the relevant moral phenomena into sharper focus.

I

In seeking illustrations of the principle of alternate possibilities, it is most natural to think of situations in which the same circumstances both bring it about that a person does something and make it impossible for him to avoid doing it. These include, for example, situations in which a person is coerced into doing something, or in which he is impelled to act by a hypnotic suggestion, or in which some inner compulsion drives him to do what he does. In situations of these kinds there are circumstances that make it impossible for the person to do otherwise, and these very circumstances also serve to bring it about that he does whatever it is that he does.

However, there may be circumstances that constitute sufficient conditions‡ for a certain action to be performed by someone and that therefore make it impossible for the person to do otherwise, but that do not actually impel the person to act or in any way produce his action. A person may do something in circumstances that leave him no alternative to doing it, without these circumstances actually moving him or leading him to do it—without them playing any role, indeed, in bringing it about that he does what he does.

An examination of situations characterized by circumstances of this sort casts doubt, I believe, on the relevance to questions of moral responsibility of the fact that a person who has done something could not have done otherwise. I propose to develop some examples of this kind in the context of a discussion of coercion and to suggest that our moral intuitions concerning these examples tend to disconfirm the principle of alternate possibilities. Then I will discuss the principle in more general terms, explain what I think is wrong with it, and describe briefly and without argument how it might appropriately be revised.

II

It is generally agreed that a person who has been coerced to do something did not do it freely and is not morally responsible for having done it. Now the doctrine that coercion and moral responsibility are mutually exclusive may appear to be no more than a somewhat particularized version of the principle of alternate possibilities. It is natural enough to say of a person who has been coerced to do something that he could not have done otherwise. And it may easily seem that being coerced deprives a person of freedom and of moral responsibility simply because it is a special

---

* Harry Frankfurt, "Alternate Possibilities and Moral Responsibility," *The Journal of Philosophy* 66, 23 (1969): 829–39.
† A truth that can be derived from reason alone, independent of experience. In this context, the expression may be taken to mean that the principle is thought to be necessarily true, without the need of further evidence.
‡ A set of conditions is *sufficient* for X if those conditions will cause X regardless of whether or not any other conditions hold.

case of being unable to do otherwise. The principle of alternate possibilities may in this way derive some credibility from its association with the very plausible proposition that moral responsibility is excluded by coercion.

It is not right, however, that it should do so. The fact that a person was coerced to act as he did may entail both that he could not have done otherwise and that he bears no moral responsibility for his action. But his lack of moral responsibility is not entailed by his having been unable to do otherwise. The doctrine that coercion excludes moral responsibility is not correctly understood, in other words, as a particularized version of the principle of alternate possibilities.

Let us suppose that someone is threatened convincingly with a penalty he finds unacceptable and that he then does what is required of him by the issuer of the threat. We can imagine details that would make it reasonable for us to think that the person was coerced to perform the action in question, that he could not have done otherwise, and that he bears no moral responsibility for having done what he did. But just what is it about situations of this kind that warrants the judgment that the threatened person is not morally responsible for his act?

This question may be approached by considering situations of the following kind. Jones decides for reasons of his own to do something, then someone threatens him with a very harsh penalty (so harsh that any reasonable person would submit to the threat) unless he does precisely that, and Jones does it. Will we hold Jones morally responsible for what he has done? I think this will depend on the roles we think were played, in leading him to act, by his original decision and by the threat.

One possibility is that Jones$_1$ is not a reasonable man: he is, rather, a man who does what he has once decided to do no matter what happens next and no matter what the cost. In that case, the threat actually exerted no effective force upon him. He acted without any regard to it, very much as if he were not aware that it had been made. If this is indeed the way it was, the situation did not involve coercion at all. The threat did not lead Jones$_1$ to do what he did. Nor was it in fact sufficient to have prevented him from doing otherwise: if his earlier decision had been to do something else, the threat would not have deterred him in the slightest. It seems evident that in these circumstances

the fact that Jones$_1$ was threatened in no way reduces the moral responsibility he would otherwise bear for his act. This example, however, is not a counterexample either to the doctrine that coercion excuses or to the principle of alternate possibilities. For we have supposed that Jones$_1$ is a man upon whom the threat had no coercive effect and, hence, that it did not actually deprive him of alternatives to doing what he did.

Another possibility is that Jones$_2$ was stampeded by the threat. Given that threat, he would have performed that action regardless of what decision he had already made. The threat upset him so profoundly, moreover, that he completely forgot his own earlier decision and did what was demanded of him entirely because he was terrified of the penalty with which he was threatened. In this case, it is not relevant to his having performed the action that he had already decided on his own to perform it. When the chips were down he thought of nothing but the threat, and fear alone led him to act. The fact that at an earlier time Jones$_2$ had decided for his own reasons to act in just that way may be relevant to an evaluation of his character; he may bear full moral responsibility for having made *that* decision. But he can hardly be said to be morally responsible for his action. For he performed the action simply as a result of the coercion to which he was subjected. His earlier decision played no role in bringing it about that he did what he did, and it would therefore be gratuitous to assign it a role in the moral evaluation of his action.

Now consider a third possibility. Jones$_3$ was neither stampeded by the threat nor indifferent to it. The threat impressed him, as it would impress any reasonable man, and he would have submitted to it wholeheartedly if he had not already made a decision that coincided with the one demanded of him. In fact, however, he performed the action in question on the basis of the decision he had made before the threat was issued. When he acted, he was not actually motivated by the threat but solely by the considerations that had originally commended the action to him. It was not the threat that led him to act, though it would have done so if he had not already provided himself with a sufficient motive for performing the action in question.

No doubt it will be very difficult for anyone to know, in a case like this one, exactly what happened. Did Jones$_3$ perform the action because of the threat, or were his reasons for acting simply those which had already persuaded him to do so? Or did he act on the basis of two motives, each of which was sufficient for his action? It is not impossible, however, that the situation should be clearer than situations of this kind usually are. And suppose it is apparent to us that Jones₃ acted on the basis of his own decision and not because of the threat. Then I think we would be justified in regarding his moral responsibility for what he did as unaffected by the threat even though, since he would in any case have submitted to the threat, he could not have avoided doing what he did. It would be entirely reasonable for us to make the same judgment concerning his moral responsibility that we would have made if we had not known of the threat. For the threat did not in fact influence his performance of the action. He did what he did just as if the threat had not been made at all.

III

The case of Jones₃ may appear at first glance to combine coercion and moral responsibility, and thus to provide a counterexample to the doctrine that coercion excuses. It is not really so certain that it does so, however, because it is unclear whether the example constitutes a genuine instance of coercion. Can we say of Jones₃ that he was coerced to do something, when he had already decided on his own to do it and when he did it entirely on the basis of that decision? Or would it be more correct to say that Jones₃ was not coerced to do what he did, even though he himself recognized that there was an irresistible force at work in virtue of which he had to do it? My own linguistic intuitions lead me toward the second alternative, but they are somewhat equivocal.* Perhaps we can say either of these things, or perhaps we must add a qualifying explanation to whichever of them we say.

This murkiness, however, does not interfere with our drawing an important moral from an examination of the example. Suppose we decide to say that Jones₃ was *not* coerced. Our basis for saying this will clearly be that it is incorrect to regard a man as being coerced to do something unless he does it *because of* the coercive force exerted against him. The fact that an

irresistible threat is made will not, then, entail that the person who receives it is coerced to do what he does. It will also be necessary that the threat is what actually accounts for his doing it. On the other hand, suppose we decide to say that Jones₃ *was* coerced. Then we will be bound to admit that being coerced does not exclude being morally responsible. And we will also surely be led to the view that coercion affects the judgment of a person's moral responsibility only when the person acts as he does because he is coerced to do so—i.e., when the fact that he is coerced is what accounts for his action.

Whichever we decide to say, then, we will recognize that the doctrine that coercion excludes moral responsibility is not a particularized version of the principle of alternate possibilities. Situations in which a person who does something cannot do otherwise because he is subject to coercive power are either not instances of coercion at all, or they are situations in which the person may still be morally responsible for what he does if it is not because of the coercion that he does it. When we excuse a person who has been coerced, we do not excuse him because he was unable to do otherwise. Even though a person is subject to a coercive force that precludes his performing any action but one, he may nonetheless bear full moral responsibility for performing that action.

IV

To the extent that the principle of alternate possibilities derives its plausibility from association with the doctrine that coercion excludes moral responsibility, a clear understanding of the latter diminishes the appeal of the former. Indeed the case of Jones₃ may appear to do more than illuminate the relationship between the two doctrines. It may well seem to provide a decisive counterexample to the principle of alternate possibilities and thus to show that this principle is false. For the irresistibility of the threat to which Jones₃ is subjected might well be taken to mean that he cannot but perform the action he performs. And yet the threat, since Jones₃ performs the action without regard to it, does not reduce his moral responsibility for what he does.

---

* In describing this question in terms of "linguistic intuitions," Frankfurt emphasizes that the answer depends on how we define and use the term "coercion," and competent English-speakers may disagree about this.

The following objection will doubtless be raised against the suggestion that the case of Jones₃ is a counterexample to the principle of alternate possibilities. There is perhaps a sense in which Jones₃ cannot do otherwise than perform the action he performs, since he is a reasonable man and the threat he encounters is sufficient to move any reasonable man. But it is not this sense that is germane to the principle of alternate possibilities. His knowledge that he stands to suffer an intolerably harsh penalty does not mean that Jones₃, strictly speaking, *cannot* perform any action but the one he does perform. After all it is still open to him, and this is crucial, to defy the threat if he wishes to do so and to accept the penalty his action would bring down upon him. In the sense in which the principle of alternate possibilities employs the concept of "could have done otherwise," Jones₃'s inability to resist the threat does not mean that he cannot do otherwise than perform the action he performs. Hence the case of Jones₃ does not constitute an instance contrary to the principle.

I do not propose to consider in what sense the concept of "could have done otherwise" figures in the principle of alternate possibilities, nor will I attempt to measure the force of the objection I have just described.[1] For I believe that whatever force this objection may be thought to have can be deflected by altering the example in the following way.[2] Suppose someone—Black, let us say—wants Jones₄ to perform a certain action. Black is prepared to go to considerable lengths to get his way, but he prefers to avoid showing his hand unnecessarily. So he waits until Jones₄ is about to make up his mind what to do, and he does nothing unless it is clear to him (Black is an excellent judge of such things) that Jones₄ is going to decide to do something *other* than what he wants him to do. If it does become clear that Jones₄ is going to decide to do something else, Black takes effective steps to ensure that Jones₄ decides to do, and that he does do, what he wants him to do.[3] Whatever Jones₄'s initial preferences and inclinations, then, Black will have his way.

What steps will Black take, if he believes he must take steps, in order to ensure that Jones₄ decides and acts as he wishes? Anyone with a theory concerning what "could have done otherwise" means may answer this question for himself by describing whatever measures he would regard as sufficient to guarantee that, in the relevant sense, Jones₄ cannot do otherwise. Let

Black pronounce a terrible threat, and in this way both force Jones₄ to perform the desired action and prevent him from performing a forbidden one. Let Black give Jones₄ a potion, or put him under hypnosis, and in some such way as these generate in Jones₄ an irresistible inner compulsion to perform the act Black wants performed and to avoid others. Or let Black manipulate the minute processes of Jones₄'s brain and nervous system in some more direct way, so that causal forces running in and out of his synapses and along the poor man's nerves determine that he chooses to act and that he does act in the one way and not in any other. Given any conditions under which it will be maintained that Jones₄ cannot do otherwise, in other words, let Black bring it about that those conditions prevail. The structure of the example is flexible enough, I think, to find a way around any charge of irrelevance by accommodating the doctrine on which the charge is based.[4]

Now suppose that Black never has to show his hand because Jones₄, for reasons of his own, decides to perform and does perform the very action Black wants him to perform. In that case, it seems clear, Jones₄ will bear precisely the same moral responsibility for what he does as he would have borne if Black had not been ready to take steps to ensure that he do it. It would be quite unreasonable to excuse Jones₄ for his action, or to withhold the praise to which it would normally entitle him, on the basis of the fact that he could not have done otherwise. This fact played no role at all in leading him to act as he did. He would have acted the same even if it had not been a fact. Indeed, everything happened just as it would have happened without Black's presence in the situation and without his readiness to intrude into it.

In this example there are sufficient conditions for Jones₄'s performing the action in question. What action he performs is not up to him. Of course it is in a way up to him whether he acts on his own or as a result of Black's intervention. That depends upon what action he himself is inclined to perform. But whether he finally acts on his own or as a result of Black's intervention, he performs the same action. He has no alternative but to do what Black wants him to do. If he does it on his own, however, his moral responsibility for doing it is not affected by the fact that Black was lurking in the background with sinister intent, since this intent never comes into play.

V

The fact that a person could not have avoided doing something is a sufficient condition of his having done it. But, as some of my examples show, this fact may play no role whatever in the explanation of why he did it. It may not figure at all among the circumstances that actually brought it about that he did what he did, so that his action is to be accounted for on another basis entirely. Even though the person was unable to do otherwise, that is to say, it may not be the case that he acted as he did *because* he could not have done otherwise. Now if someone had no alternative to performing a certain action but did not perform it because he was unable to do otherwise, then he would have performed exactly the same action even if he *could* have done otherwise. The circumstances that made it impossible for him to do otherwise could have been subtracted from the situation without affecting what happened or why it happened in any way. Whatever it was that actually led the person to do what he did, or that made him do it, would have led him to do it or made him do it even if it had been possible for him to do something else instead.

Thus it would have made no difference, so far as concerns his action or how he came to perform it, if the circumstances that made it impossible for him to avoid performing it had not prevailed. The fact that he could not have done otherwise clearly provides no basis for supposing that he *might* have done otherwise if he had been able to do so. When a fact is in this way irrelevant to the problem of accounting for a person's action it seems quite gratuitous to assign it any weight in the assessment of his moral responsibility. Why should the fact be considered in reaching a moral judgment concerning the person when it does not help in any way to understand either what made him act as he did or what, in other circumstances, he might have done?

This, then, is why the principle of alternate possibilities is mistaken. It asserts that a person bears no moral responsibility—that is, he is to be excused—for having performed an action if there were circumstances that made it impossible for him to avoid performing it. But there may be circumstances that make it impossible for a person to avoid performing some action without those circumstances in any way bringing it about that he performs that action.

It would surely be no good for the person to refer to circumstances of this sort in an effort to absolve himself of moral responsibility for performing the action in question. For those circumstances, by hypothesis, actually had nothing to do with his having done what he did. He would have done precisely the same thing, and he would have been led or made in precisely the same way to do it, even if they had not prevailed.

We often do, to be sure, excuse people for what they have done when they tell us (and we believe them) that they could not have done otherwise. But this is because we assume that what they tell us serves to explain why they did what they did. We take it for granted that they are not being disingenuous, as a person would be who cited as an excuse the fact that he could not have avoided doing what he did but who knew full well that it was not at all because of this that he did it.

What I have said may suggest that the principle of alternate possibilities should be revised so as to assert that a person is not morally responsible for what he has done if he did it because he could not have done otherwise. It may be noted that this revision of the principle does not seriously affect the arguments of those who have relied on the original principle in their efforts to maintain that moral responsibility and determinism are incompatible. For if it was causally determined that a person perform a certain action, then it will be true that the person performed it because of those causal determinants. And if the fact that it was causally determined that a person perform a certain action means that the person could not have done otherwise, as philosophers who argue for the incompatibility thesis characteristically suppose, then the fact that it was causally determined that a person perform a certain action will mean that the person performed it because he could not have done otherwise. The revised principle of alternate possibilities will entail, on this assumption concerning the meaning of 'could have done otherwise', that a person is not morally responsible for what he has done if it was causally determined that he do it. I do not believe, however, that this revision of the principle is acceptable.

Suppose a person tells us that he did what he did because he was unable to do otherwise; or suppose he makes the similar statement that he did what he did because he had to do it. We do often accept statements like these (if we believe them) as valid excuses, and such statements may well seem at first glance to invoke the revised principle of alternate possibilities. But I think that when we accept such statements as valid excuses it is because we assume that we are being told more than the statements strictly and literally convey. We understand the person who offers the excuse to mean that he did what he did *only because* he was unable to do otherwise, or *only because* he had to do it. And we understand him to mean, more particularly, that when he did what he did it was not because that was what he really wanted to do. The principle of alternate possibilities should thus be replaced, in my opinion, by the following principle: a person is not morally responsible for what he has done if he did it only because he could not have done otherwise. This principle does not appear to conflict with the view that moral responsibility is compatible with determinism.

The following may all be true: there were circumstances that made it impossible for a person to avoid doing something; these circumstances actually played a role in bringing it about that he did it, so that it is correct to say that he did it because he could not have done otherwise; the person really wanted to do what he did; he did it because it was what he really wanted to do, so that it is not correct to say that he did what he did only because he could not have done otherwise. Under these conditions, the person may well be morally responsible for what he has done. On the other hand, he will not be morally responsible for what he has done if he did it only because he could not have done otherwise, even if what he did was something he really wanted to do. ■

Suggestions for Critical Reflection

1. The effectiveness of Frankfurt's argument depends on the success of his purported counter-examples. Do you agree with Frankfurt's intuitions about which versions of Jones are responsible? Why or why not?

2. In Frankfurt's counter-examples, Jones is alleged to be morally responsible because he has decided on a course of action independent of the restrictions on his alternate possibilities. But if coercion is not the cause of Jones's decisions, what is? Are these decisions themselves determined by prior conditions, and if so, does this have any bearing on the question of Jones's responsibility?

3. The broader philosophical debate on free will often assumes that either a great many of our actions are performed freely or none of them are, and so we're either very often responsible for our actions (if we have free will) or never responsible (if we do not). In this paper, Frankfurt's claims about moral responsibility seem to pertain to only a much smaller subset of actions involving uncommon scenarios of restriction on possible action. How does Frankfurt's argument bear on the broader debate about free will and responsibility?

4. Suppose you are tasked with assessing the moral guilt of an apparently-coerced person, and yet you are unable to determine the interplay between the apparent coercion and the person's actions. That is, because you can't directly observe the person's reasoning, you don't know whether their case is more similar to that of $Jones_1$, $Jones_2$, etc. How should you proceed? Is it best to adopt something like the principle of alternate possibilities as a practical rule in guiding our judgments about responsibility? Why or why not?

5. Consider this case: A child has fallen into a swimming pool, and $Jones_4$ hears her cries for help. He can swim, and could easily have saved the child, but he's too busy watching TV and doesn't want to get his clothes wet, so he does nothing. But he couldn't have saved the child even had he decided to, because the gate to the swimming pool had (unknown to anybody) been locked, and nobody could have gotten in on time. Is $Jones_4$ morally responsible for the child's death? Does Frankfurt's analysis apply here? Is it helpful?

Notes

1. The two main concepts employed in the principle of alternate possibilities are "morally responsible" and "could have done otherwise." To discuss the principle without analyzing either of these concepts may well seem like an attempt at piracy. The reader should take notice that my Jolly Roger is now unfurled.

2. After thinking up the example that I am about to develop I learned that Robert Nozick, in lectures given several years ago, had formulated an example of the same general type and had proposed it as a counterexample to the principle of alternate possibilities.

3. The assumption that Black can predict what $Jones_4$ will decide to do does not beg the question of determinism. We can imagine that $Jones_4$ has often confronted the alternatives—A and B—that he now confronts, and that his face has invariably twitched when he was about to decide to do A and never when he was about to decide to do B. Knowing this, and observing the twitch, Black would have a basis for prediction. This does, to be sure, suppose that there is some sort of causal relation between $Jones_4$'s state at the time of the twitch and his subsequent states. But any plausible view of decision or of action will allow that reaching a decision and performing an action both involve earlier and later phases, with causal relations between them, and such that the earlier phases are not themselves part of the decision or of the action. The example does not require that these earlier phases be deterministically related to still earlier events.

4. The example is also flexible enough to allow for the elimination of Black altogether. Anyone who thinks that the effectiveness of the example is undermined by its reliance on a human manipulator, who imposes his will on $Jones_4$, can substitute for Black a machine programmed to do what Black does. If this is still not good enough, forget both Black and the machine and suppose that their role is played by natural forces involving no will or design at all.

P.F. STRAWSON

Freedom and Resentment

Who Was P.F. Strawson?

Sir Peter Frederick Strawson was born in 1919 in the London suburb of Ealing. His family was fairly poor: his parents were both schoolteachers, but his mother gave up teaching when she married, and his father, who suffered from poor health after World War I, died in 1936. Strawson's early interests were languages and English literature, and in 1937 he won a scholarship to read English at St. John's College, Oxford. "I am, or was, a competent versifier," he later wrote, "and if I had been able to choose my talents, I would have chosen to be a poet. But of course I could not, and am not."* Nevertheless, on his arrival at Oxford, Strawson decided to change his degree course from English to the honors school of Politics, Philosophy and Economics (PPE). This was partly due to his already growing interest in philosophy, partly because he felt his enjoyment of literature would not be enhanced by a professional career in English, and partly because in 1937 he had "the perhaps rather priggish thought that since ... the political future and the civilization of Europe seemed threatened, I ought to be better equipped than I was with understanding of politics and economics."

By the end of his undergraduate degree Strawson knew he wanted to be a professional philosopher, but World War II intervened and in 1940 he was called up into the Royal Artillery. He was promoted through the ranks, briefly commanded a radar station near the south coast of England, and then became a Captain in the Royal Electrical and Mechanical Engineers. The wartime activity he later claimed he was most proud of was his role as a defending officer for soldiers facing courts martial, where he was frequently able to have the severity of their sentences reduced by pleading mitigating circumstances. In 1945 he married Grace Martin (whom he nicknamed, and since always called, "Ann") and was shipped off to join the occupying Allied army in Italy and Austria.

After Strawson's return from the war, he started his academic career, on the strength of his undergraduate degree and Oxford references, as an assistant lecturer in Philosophy at the University College of North Wales, Bangor. In 1947, he won the competitive examination for the John Locke Scholarship at Oxford (a prize of £80 at the time) and, on the basis of this, was made a philosophy tutor at University College, Oxford. The next year he was made a Fellow of the college (moving to Magdalen College and assuming the Waynflete Chair of Metaphysical Philosophy in 1968, retiring in 1987). Strawson was knighted in 1977.

From the mid-1950s until his death in 2006, Strawson lectured throughout the world, and he had a special fondness for India. He had four children, one of whom, Galen, has become a well-known philosopher in his own right.

What Was Strawson's Overall Philosophical Project?

Strawson's main research interest was the philosophy of logic and language, and especially the phenomena of predication and reference to individuals. One of his earlier articles remains perhaps his most famous. "On Referring," published in *Mind* in 1950, criticized Bertrand Russell's logical theory of descriptions for ignoring the ways in which we actually use and understand describing phrases. In the same year, he also wrote an influential paper on the topic of truth, and in 1959 published his best-known book, *Individuals*, in which he introduced a distinction between "descriptive" and "revisionary" metaphysics. Descriptive metaphysics, which Strawson defended, is the project of describing

---

* "Intellectual Autobiography," in *The Philosophy of P.F. Strawson* (The Library of Living Philosophers Volume XXVI), ed. Lewis Edwin Hahn (Open Court, 1998).

and analyzing "the actual structure of our thought about the world."* (For example, Strawson argued that *material bodies* and *persons* are the two fundamental and different categories of our worldview.) By contrast, revisionary metaphysics, which Strawson attacked, supposedly attempts to replace the actual structure of our beliefs about the world with a fictional one which is aesthetically, morally, or intellectually preferable. Strawson thought of Kant as the paradigm practitioner of descriptive metaphysics—and in 1966 published a well-received book on Kant's metaphysics called *The Bounds of Sense*—but accused Descartes, Leibniz, and Berkeley of being revisionary.

A major methodological theme of Strawson's philosophy was his focus on language, and he was known as a leading example of "Oxford linguistic philosophy." His concern was to analyze the structure of language as it is actually spoken, in all its complexity, rather than attempting to replace it with a simpler and more formalized logical language. His slogan was "ordinary language has no exact logic," and he defended this view in his *Introduction to Logical Theory*, published in 1952. He also defended a view he called "naturalism," which resists attempts, grounded in philosophical theorizing or skepticism, to modify the fundamental opinions that come to us naturally: for example, we naturally assume we know things about the external world, and Strawson rejected any attempt on the part of philosophy to show us otherwise.

What Is the Structure of This Reading?

Strawson begins by drawing a four-part distinction between philosophers who (1) don't know what determinism is, (2) are pessimists about the moral implications of determinism, (3) are optimists about the moral implications of determinism, or (4) are moral skeptics. Strawson confesses he belongs to the first group, but his argument addresses the second and third positions. Strawson states he wants to "reconcile" them and, in the second paragraph of section I of the paper, outlines how this is to be done. In section II, he further describes the problem to which his reconciliation will be a solution. However, instead of moving straight into a discussion of

moral praise and blame he instead discusses attitudes that are in some sense "closer to home": he talks about *gratitude* and *resentment* and their relation to determinism. His idea is that if he can say something useful in this relatively fresh area, then he might be able to transfer those insights to the more contested issue of morality and determinism.

In sections III and IV, Strawson first deals with what he calls the *participant reactive attitudes* we have toward other people with whom we have relations, and he focuses on two questions: What are the conditions under which these attitudes vary—that is, when are they more or less appropriate? Could we do without these reactive attitudes, or decide not to have them anymore? In the course of discussing the first question, he distinguishes between two sorts of cases: those where, for some reason, we do not resent a particular *action* by someone, even though we continue to think of that person as someone to whom gratitude or resentment might normally be appropriate; and cases where, for some reason, we no longer treat a particular *person* as an object of gratitude or resentment. (Furthermore, Strawson distinguishes between two sub-groups of the second class of cases, but he mainly discusses only the second of these.)

Having got all this straight, Strawson moves to his second question and asks, "What effect would, or should, the acceptance of the truth of a general thesis of determinism have upon these reactive attitudes?" His answer is rather subtle but, in short, amounts to "none." Even without knowing exactly what determinism is, Strawson claims, we can see that our reasons for feeling, or not feeling, gratitude and resentment are completely independent of theoretical claims about determinism.

Strawson is now ready to directly approach the more standard question: Is determinism incompatible with moral responsibility? He begins section V of the paper by describing moral attitudes toward the actions of others as the "vicarious analogues" of personal reactive attitudes (and so suggesting that considerations in previous sections of the paper are relevant to the current one). He also discusses what he calls the "self-reactive" attitudes, which include our own sense of our moral responsibility. Strawson's discussion of the moral attitudes now parallels that of the personal reactive attitudes: that is, he

---

* *Individuals: An Essay in Descriptive Metaphysics* (Methuen, 1959), 9.

asks first what conditions affect the appropriateness of our moral judgments, and second, whether we could or should entirely dispense with these judgments in the face of determinism.

In the final part of the paper, Strawson suggests that optimists and pessimists both make mistakes in their views, and that his discussion has shown how the two positions can be reconciled in light of "the facts" about freedom and resentment. His discussion of these issues is, as always, sophisticated, but the essence of what Strawson is saying is that the optimist needs to take more seriously the "moral phenomenology" of our attitudes, and the pessimist needs to abandon his "metaphysics."

A Common Misconception

Strawson is not attempting to *answer* the philosophical question of free will as it is traditionally posed, but instead to *side-step* or dissolve it. He does not directly defend compatibilism (as it is normally understood) because he does not argue that determinism is compatible with free will and moral responsibility; rather, he argues that the question of determinism is simply *irrelevant* to questions about our moral attitudes.

Some Useful Background Information

In section II of his paper, Strawson distinguishes between "negative" and "positive" conceptions of freedom. Negative freedom is, standardly, freedom *from* constraints or coercion; in this sense you are free to do something if nobody will interfere with your attempt to do it. Positive freedom, by contrast, is the ability *to* perform some particular action if you want to—it is a kind of autonomy or, as it is often put, "self-determination." Thus, for example, very poor people in a democratic society might have a great deal of negative freedom but relatively little positive freedom, since they lack resources or opportunities: for instance, becoming an actuarial accountant or traveling to see the Taj Mahal in India is not against the law or socially disapproved of, so in one sense people are free to do these things; but many lack the money, the time, or the knowledge to do them, and so lack *positive* freedom in those respects. A distinction, between negative and positive freedom, was drawn by Kant in the third chapter of his *Foundations of the Metaphysics of Morals* (1785), and it was influentially developed by Isaiah Berlin in "Two Concepts of Liberty," a paper delivered at Oxford University in 1958 and published in *Four Essays on Liberty* (Oxford University Press, 1969).

Freedom and Resentment*

I.

Some philosophers say they do not know what the thesis of determinism is. Others say, or imply, that they do know what it is. Of these, some—the pessimists perhaps—hold that if the thesis is true, then the concepts of moral obligation and responsibility really have no application, and the practices of punishing and blaming, of expressing moral condemnation and approval, are really unjustified. Others—the optimists perhaps—hold that these concepts and practices in no way lose their *raison d'être*[†] if the thesis of determinism is true. Some hold even that the justification of these concepts and practices requires the truth of the thesis. There is another opinion which is less frequently voiced: the opinion, it might be said, of the genuine moral sceptic. This is that the notions of moral guilt, of blame, of moral responsibility are inherently confused and that we can see this to be so if we consider the consequences either of the truth of determinism or

---

*   This paper was written to be presented to the British Academy in 1960. It is reproduced here from the *Proceedings of the British Academy*, Volume 48 (1963).
†   French: purpose, reason for being.

of its falsity. The holders of this opinion agree with the pessimists that these notions lack application if determinism is true, and add simply that they also lack it if determinism is false. If I am asked which of these parties I belong to, I must say it is the first of all, the party of those who do not know what the thesis of determinism is. But this does not stop me from having some sympathy with the others, and a wish to reconcile them. Should not ignorance, rationally, inhibit such sympathies? Well, of course, though darkling, one has some inkling—some notion of what sort of thing is being talked about. This lecture is intended as a move towards reconciliation; so is likely to seem wrongheaded to everyone.

But can there be any possibility of reconciliation between such clearly opposed positions as those of pessimists and optimists about determinism? Well, there might be a formal withdrawal on one side in return for a substantial concession on the other. Thus, suppose the optimist's position were put like this: (1) the facts as we know them do not show determinism to be false; (2) the facts as we know them supply an adequate basis for the concepts and practices which the pessimist feels to be imperilled by the possibility of determinism's truth. Now it might be that the optimist is right in this, but is apt to give an inadequate account of the facts as we know them, and of how they constitute an adequate basis for the problematic concepts and practices; that the reasons he gives for the adequacy of the basis are themselves inadequate and leave out something vital. It might be that the pessimist is rightly anxious to get this vital thing back and, in the grip of his anxiety, feels he has to go beyond the facts as we know them; feels that the vital thing can be secure only if, beyond the facts as we know them, there is the further fact that determinism is false. Might he not be brought to make a formal withdrawal in return for a vital concession?

II.

Let me enlarge very briefly on this, by way of preliminary only. Some optimists about determinism point to the efficacy of the practices of punishment, and of moral condemnation and approval, in regulating behaviour in socially desirable ways.[1] In the fact of their efficacy, they suggest, is an adequate basis for these practices; and this fact certainly does not show

determinism to be false. To this the pessimists reply, all in a rush, that *just* punishment and *moral* condemnation imply moral guilt and guilt implies moral responsibility and moral responsibility implies freedom and freedom implies the falsity of determinism. And to this the optimists are wont to reply in turn that it is true that these practices require freedom in a sense, and the existence of freedom in this sense is one of the facts as we know them. But what 'freedom' means here is nothing but the absence of certain conditions the presence of which would make moral condemnation or punishment inappropriate. They have in mind conditions like compulsion by another, or innate incapacity, or insanity, or other less extreme forms of psychological disorder, or the existence of circumstances in which the making of any other choice would be morally inadmissible or would be too much to expect of any man. To this list they are constrained to add other factors which, without exactly being limitations of freedom, may also make moral condemnation or punishment inappropriate or mitigate their force: as some forms of ignorance, mistake, or accident. And the general reason why moral condemnation or punishment are inappropriate when these factors or conditions are present is held to be that the practices in question will be generally efficacious means of regulating behaviour in desirable ways only in cases where these factors are *not* present. Now the pessimist admits that the facts as we know them include the existence of freedom, the occurrence of cases of free action, in the negative sense which the optimist concedes; and admits, or rather insists, that the existence of freedom in this sense is compatible with the truth of determinism. Then what does the pessimist find missing? When he tries to answer this question, his language is apt to alternate between the very familiar and the very unfamiliar.[2] Thus he may say, familiarly enough, that the man who is the subject of justified punishment, blame or moral condemnation must really *deserve* it; and then add, perhaps, that, in the case at least where he is blamed for a positive act rather than an omission, the condition of his really deserving blame is something that goes beyond the negative freedoms that the optimist concedes. It is, say, a genuinely free identification of the will with the act. And this is the condition that is incompatible with the truth of determinism.

The conventional, but conciliatory, optimist need not give up yet. He may say: Well, people often decide to do things, really intend to do what they do, know just what they're doing in doing it; the reasons they think they have for doing what they do, often really are their reasons and not their rationalizations. These facts, too, are included in the facts as we know them. If this is what you mean by freedom—by the identification of the will with the act—then freedom may again be conceded. But again the concession is compatible with the truth of the determinist thesis. For it would not follow from that thesis that nobody decides to do anything; that nobody ever does anything intentionally; that it is false that people sometimes know perfectly well what they are doing. I tried to define freedom negatively. You want to give it a more positive look. But it comes to the same thing. Nobody denies freedom in this sense, or these senses, and nobody claims that the existence of freedom in these senses shows determinism to be false.

But it is here that the lacuna* in the optimistic story can be made to show. For the pessimist may be supposed to ask: But *why* does freedom in this sense justify blame, etc.? You turn towards me first the negative, and then the positive, faces of a freedom which nobody challenges. But the only reason you have given for the practices of moral condemnation and punishment in cases where this freedom is present is the efficacy of these practices in regulating behaviour in socially desirable ways. But this is not a sufficient basis, it is not even the right *sort* of basis, for these practices as we understand them.

Now my optimist, being the sort of man he is, is not likely to invoke an intuition of fittingness at this point. So he really has no more to say. And my pessimist, being the sort of man he is, has only one more thing to say; and that is that the admissibility of these practices, as we understand them, demands another kind of freedom, the kind that in turn demands the falsity of the thesis of determinism. But might we not induce the pessimist to give up saying this by giving the optimist something more to say?

III.

I have mentioned punishing and moral condemnation and approval; and it is in connection with these practices or attitudes that the issue between optimists and pessimists—or, if one is a pessimist, the issue between determinists and libertarians—is felt to be particularly important. But it is not of these practices and attitudes that I propose, at first, to speak. These practices or attitudes permit, where they do not imply, a certain detachment from the actions or agents which are their objects. I want to speak, at least at first, of something else: of the non-detached attitudes and reactions of people directly involved in transactions with each other; of the attitudes and reactions of offended parties and beneficiaries; of such things as gratitude, resentment, forgiveness, love, and hurt feelings. Perhaps something like the issue between optimists and pessimists arises in this neighbouring field too; and since this field is less crowded with disputants, the issue might here be easier to settle; and if it is settled here, then it might become easier to settle it in the disputant-crowded field.

What I have to say consists largely of commonplaces. So my language, like that of commonplaces generally, will be quite unscientific and imprecise. The central commonplace that I want to insist on is the very great importance that we attach to the attitudes and intentions towards us of other human beings, and the great extent to which our personal feelings and reactions depend upon, or involve, our beliefs about these attitudes and intentions. I can give no simple description of the field of phenomena at the centre of which stands this commonplace truth; for the field is too complex. Much imaginative literature is devoted to exploring its complexities; and we have a large vocabulary for the purpose. There are simplifying styles of handling it in a general way. Thus we may, like La Rochefoucauld,† put self-love or self-esteem or vanity at the centre of the picture and point out how it may be caressed by the esteem, or wounded by the indifference or contempt, of others. We might

---

* Latin: the missing part, hole, or gap.

† François de Marsillac, duc de la Rochefoucauld (1613–80), was a French writer known for his moralistic aphorisms, published as *Réflections* in 1665. His reflections on human conduct led him to believe that self-interest was its driving force.

speak, in another jargon, of the need for love, and the loss of security which results from its withdrawal; or, in another, of human self-respect and its connection with the recognition of the individual's dignity. These simplifications are of use to me only if they help to emphasize how much we actually mind, how much it matters to us, whether the actions of other people—and particularly of *some* other people—reflect attitudes towards us of goodwill, affection, or esteem on the one hand or contempt, indifference, or malevolence on the other. If someone treads on my hand accidentally, while trying to help me, the pain may be no less acute than if he treads on it in contemptuous disregard of my existence or with a malevolent wish to injure me. But I shall generally feel in the second case a kind and degree of resentment that I shall not feel in the first. If someone's actions help me to some benefit I desire, then I am benefited in any case; but if he intended them so to benefit me because of his general goodwill towards me, I shall reasonably feel a gratitude which I should not feel at all if the benefit was an incidental consequence, unintended or even regretted by him, of some plan of action with a different aim.

...

We should think of the many different kinds of relationship which we can have with other people—as sharers of a common interest; as members of the same family; as colleagues; as friends; as lovers; as chance parties to an enormous range of transactions and encounters. Then we should think, in each of these connections in turn, and in others, of the kind of importance we attach to the attitudes and intentions towards us of those who stand in these relationships to us, and of the kinds of *reactive* attitudes and feelings to which we ourselves are prone. In general, we demand some degree of goodwill or regard on the part of those who stand in these relationships to us, though the forms we require it to take vary widely in different connections. The range and intensity of our *reactive* attitudes towards goodwill, its absence or its opposite vary no less widely. I have mentioned, specifically, resentment and gratitude; and they are a usefully opposed pair. But, of course, there is a whole continuum of reactive attitude and feeling stretching on both sides of these and—the most comfortable area—in between them.

The object of these commonplaces is to try to keep before our minds something it is easy to forget when we are engaged in philosophy, especially in our cool, contemporary style, viz. what it is actually like to be involved in ordinary interpersonal relationships, ranging from the most intimate to the most casual.

IV.

It is one thing to ask about the general causes of these reactive attitudes I have alluded to; it is another to ask about the variations to which they are subject, the particular conditions in which they do or do not seem natural or reasonable or appropriate; and it is a third thing to ask what it would be like, what it *is* like, not to suffer them. I am not much concerned with the first question; but I am with the second; and perhaps even more with the third.

Let us consider, then, occasions for resentment: situations in which one person is offended or injured by the action of another and in which—in the absence of special considerations—the offended person might naturally or normally be expected to feel resentment. Then let us consider what sorts of special considerations might be expected to modify or mollify this feeling or remove it altogether. It needs no saying now how multifarious these considerations are. But, for my purpose, I think they can be roughly divided into two kinds. To the first group belong all those which might give occasion for the employment of such expressions as 'He didn't mean to', 'He hadn't realized', 'He didn't know'; and also all those which might give occasion for the use of the phrase 'He couldn't help it', when this is supported by such phrases as 'He was pushed', 'He had to do it', 'It was the only way', 'They left him no alternative', etc. Obviously these various pleas, and the kinds of situations in which they would be appropriate, differ from each other in striking and important ways. But for my present purpose they have something still more important in common. None of them invites us to suspend towards the agent, either at the time of his action or in general, our ordinary reactive attitudes. They do not invite us to view the *agent* as one in respect of whom these attitudes are in any way inappropriate. They invite us to view the *injury* as one in respect of which a particular one of these attitudes is inappropriate. They do not invite us to see the *agent* as other than a fully responsible agent. They invite us to see the *injury* as one for which he was not fully, or at all, responsible. They do not suggest that the agent is in any way an inappropriate object of that kind of demand for goodwill or regard which is reflected in our ordinary reactive attitudes. They suggest instead that the fact of injury was not in this case incompatible with that demand's being fulfilled, that the fact of injury was quite consistent with the agent's attitude and intentions being just what we demand they should be.[3] The agent was just ignorant of the injury he was causing, or had lost his balance through being pushed or had reluctantly to cause the injury for reasons which acceptably override his reluctance. The offering of such pleas by the agent and their acceptance by the sufferer is something in no way opposed to, or outside the context of, ordinary inter-personal relationships and the manifestation of ordinary reactive attitudes. Since things go wrong and situations are complicated, it is an essential and integral element in the transactions which are the life of these relationships.

The second group of considerations is very different. I shall take them in two subgroups of which the first is far less important than the second. In connection with the first subgroup we may think of such statements as 'He wasn't himself', 'He has been under very great strain recently', 'He was acting under post-hypnotic suggestion'; in connection with the second, we may think of 'He's only a child', 'He's a hopeless schizophrenic', 'His mind has been systematically perverted', 'That's purely compulsive behaviour on his part'. Such pleas as these do, as pleas of my first general group do not, invite us to suspend our ordinary reactive attitudes towards the agent, either at the time of his action or all the time. They do not invite us to see the agent's action in a way consistent with the full retention of ordinary inter-personal attitudes and merely inconsistent with one particular attitude. They invite us to view the agent himself in a different light from the light in which we should normally view one who has acted as he has acted. I shall not linger over the first subgroup of cases....

The second and more important subgroup of cases allows that the circumstances were normal, but presents the agent as psychologically abnormal—or as morally undeveloped. The agent was himself; but he is warped or deranged, neurotic or just a child. When we

see someone in such a light as this, all our reactive attitudes tend to be profoundly modified. I must deal here in crude dichotomies and ignore the ever-interesting and ever-illuminating varieties of cases. What I want to contrast is the attitude (or range of attitudes) of involvement or participation in a human relationship, on the one hand, and what might be called the objective attitude (or range of attitudes) to another human being, on the other. Even in the same situation, I must add, they are not altogether *exclusive* of each other; but they are, profoundly, *opposed* to each other. To adopt the objective attitude to another human being is to see him, perhaps, as an object of social policy; as a subject for what, in a wide range of sense, might be called treatment; as something certainly to be taken account, perhaps precautionary account, of; to be managed or handled or cured or trained; perhaps simply to be avoided, though *this* gerundive* is not peculiar to cases of objectivity of attitude. The objective attitude may be emotionally toned in many ways, but not in all ways: it may include repulsion or fear, it may include pity or even love, though not all kinds of love. But it cannot include the range of reactive feelings and attitudes which belong to involvement or participation with others in inter-personal human relationships; it cannot include resentment, gratitude, forgiveness, anger, or the sort of love which two adults can sometimes be said to feel reciprocally, for each other. If your attitude towards someone is wholly objective, then though you may fight him, you cannot quarrel with him, and though you may talk to him, even negotiate with him, you cannot reason with him. You can at most pretend to quarrel, or to reason, with him.

Seeing someone, then, as warped or deranged or compulsive in behaviour or peculiarly unfortunate in his formative circumstances—seeing someone so tends, at least to some extent, to set him apart from normal participant reactive attitudes on the part of one who so sees him, tends to promote, at least in the civilized, objective attitudes. But there is something curious to add to this. The objective attitude is not only something we naturally tend to fall into in cases like these, where participant attitudes are partially or wholly inhibited by abnormalities or by immaturity. It

---

* A gerund is a grammatical term for any noun formed from a verb, such as "running" or "smoking." "Gerundive," on the other hand, is a noun formed from a Latin verb (*gerere*, "to do") and means something that must or should be done.

is also something which is available as a resource in other cases too. We look with an objective eye on the compulsive behaviour of the neurotic or the tiresome behaviour of a very young child, thinking in terms of treatment or training. But we *can* sometimes look with something like the same eye on the behaviour of the normal and the mature. We *have* this resource and can sometimes use it: as a refuge, say, from the strains of involvement; or as an aid to policy; or simply out of intellectual curiosity. Being human, we cannot, in the normal case, do this for long, or altogether. If the strains of involvement, say, continue to be too great, then we have to do something else—like severing a relationship. But what is above all interesting is the tension there is, in us, between the participant attitude and the objective attitude. One is tempted to say: between our humanity and our intelligence. But to say this would be to distort both notions.

What I have called the participant reactive attitudes are essentially natural human reactions to the good or ill will or indifference of others towards us, as displayed in *their* attitudes and actions. The question we have to ask is: What effect would, or should, the acceptance of the truth of a general thesis of determinism have upon these reactive attitudes? More specifically, would, or should, the acceptance of the truth of the thesis lead to the decay or the repudiation of all such attitudes? Would, or should, it mean the end of gratitude, resentment, and forgiveness; of all reciprocated adult loves; of all the essentially *personal* antagonisms?

But how can I answer, or even pose, this question without knowing *exactly* what the thesis of determinism is? Well, there is one thing we do know; that if there is a coherent thesis of determinism, then there must be a sense of 'determined' such that, if that thesis is true, then all behaviour whatever is determined in that sense. Remembering this, we can consider at least what possibilities lie formally open; and then perhaps we shall see that the question can be answered *without* knowing exactly what the thesis of determinism is. We can consider what possibilities lie open because we have already before us an account of the ways in which particular reactive attitudes, or reactive attitudes in general, may be, and, sometimes, we judge, should be, inhibited. Thus I considered earlier a group of considerations which tend to inhibit, and, we judge, should inhibit, resentment, in particular cases of an agent causing an injury, without inhibiting reactive attitudes in general towards that agent. Obviously this group of considerations cannot strictly bear upon our question; for that question concerns reactive attitudes in general. But resentment has a particular interest; so it is worth adding that it has never been claimed as a consequence of the truth of determinism that one or another of *these* considerations was operative in every case of an injury being caused by an agent; that it would follow from the truth of determinism that anyone who caused an injury *either* was quite simply ignorant of causing it *or* had acceptably overriding reasons for acquiescing reluctantly in causing it *or...*, etc. The prevalence of this happy state of affairs would not be a consequence of the reign of universal determinism, but of the reign of universal goodwill. We cannot, then, find here the possibility of an affirmative answer to our question, even for the particular case of resentment.

Next, I remarked that the participant attitude, and the personal reactive attitudes in general, tend to give place, and it is judged by the civilized should give place, to objective attitudes, just in so far as the agent is seen as excluded from ordinary adult human relationships by deep-rooted psychological abnormality—or simply by being a child. But it cannot be a consequence of any thesis which is not itself self-contradictory that abnormality is the universal condition.

Now this dismissal might seem altogether too facile; and so, in a sense, it is. But whatever is too quickly dismissed in this dismissal is allowed for in the only possible form of affirmative answer that remains. We can sometimes, and in part, I have remarked, look on the normal (those we rate as 'normal') in the objective way in which we have learned to look on certain classified cases of abnormality. And our question reduces to this: could, or should, the acceptance of the determinist thesis lead us always to look on everyone exclusively in this way? For this is the only condition worth considering under which the acceptance of determinism could lead to the decay or repudiation of participant reactive attitudes.

It does not seem to be self-contradictory to suppose that this might happen. So I suppose we must say that it is not absolutely inconceivable that it should happen. But I am strongly inclined to think that it is, for us as we are, practically inconceivable. The human commitment to participation in ordinary interpersonal relationships is, I think, too thorough-going and deeply rooted for us to take seriously the thought that a general theoretical conviction might so change our world that, in it, there were no longer any such things as inter-personal relationships as we normally understand them; and being involved in inter-personal relationships as we normally understand them precisely is being exposed to the range of reactive attitudes and feelings that is in question.

This, then, is a part of the reply to our question. A sustained objectivity of inter-personal attitude, and the human isolation which that would entail, does not seem to be something of which human beings would be capable, even if some general truth were a theoretical ground for it. But this is not all. There is a further point, implicit in the foregoing, which must be made explicit. Exceptionally, I have said, we can have direct dealings with human beings without any degree of personal involvement, treating them simply as creatures to be handled in our own interest, or our side's, or society's—or even theirs. In the extreme case of the mentally deranged, it is easy to see the connection between the possibility of a wholly objective attitude and the impossibility of what we understand by ordinary inter-personal relationships. Given this latter impossibility, no other civilized attitude is available than that of viewing the deranged person simply as something to be understood and controlled in the most desirable fashion. To view him as outside the reach of personal relationships is already, for the civilized, to view him in this way. For reasons of policy or self-protection we may have occasion, perhaps temporary, to adopt a fundamentally similar attitude to a 'normal' human being; to concentrate, that is, on understanding 'how he works', with a view to determining our policy accordingly, or to finding in that very understanding a relief from the strains of involvement. Now it is certainly true that in the case of the abnormal, though not in the case of the normal, our adoption of the objective attitude is a consequence of our viewing the agent as *incapacitated* in some or all respects for ordinary interpersonal relationships. He is thus incapacitated, perhaps, by the fact that his picture of reality is pure fantasy, that he does not, in a sense, live in the real world at all; or by the fact that his behaviour is, in part, an unrealistic acting out of unconscious purposes; or by the fact that he is an idiot, or a moral idiot.* But there is something else which, *because* this is true, is equally certainly *not* true. And that is that there is a sense of 'determined' such that (1) if determinism is true, all behaviour is determined in this sense, and (2) determinism might be true, i.e. it is not inconsistent with the facts as we know them to suppose that all behaviour might be determined in this sense, and (3) our adoption of the objective attitude towards the abnormal is the result of a prior embracing of the belief that the behaviour, or the relevant stretch of behaviour, of the human being in question *is* determined in this sense. Neither in the case of the normal, then, nor in the case of the abnormal is it true that, when we adopt an objective attitude, we do so *because* we hold such a belief. So my answer has two parts. The first is that we cannot, as we are, seriously envisage ourselves adopting a thoroughgoing objectivity of attitude to others as a result of theoretical conviction of the truth of determinism; and the second is that when we do in fact adopt such an attitude in a particular case, our doing so is not the consequence of a theoretical conviction which might be expressed as 'Determinism in this case', but is a consequence of our abandoning, for different reasons in different cases, the ordinary inter-personal attitudes.

...

V.

The point of this discussion of the reactive attitudes in their relation—or lack of it—to the thesis of determinism was to bring us, if possible, nearer to a position of compromise in a more usual area of debate. We are not now to discuss reactive attitudes which are essentially those of offended parties or beneficiaries. We are to discuss reactive attitudes which are essentially not those, or only incidentally are those, of offended parties or beneficiaries, but are nevertheless, I shall claim, kindred attitudes to those I have discussed. I

---

* By "idiot" Strawson does not merely mean someone who is stupid or foolish. He is using clinical terminology (now out of date—and considered offensive) to mean someone sufficiently mentally deficient to be permanently incapable of rational conduct, often defined as having a mental age below three years. A "moral idiot" would be someone incapable of moral understanding or action.

put resentment in the centre of the previous discussion. I shall put moral indignation—or, more weakly, moral disapprobation—in the centre of this one.

The reactive attitudes I have so far discussed are essentially reactions to the quality of others' wills towards us, as manifested in their behaviour: to their good or ill will or indifference or lack of concern. Thus resentment, or what I have called resentment, is a reaction to injury or indifference. The reactive attitudes I have now to discuss might be described as the sympathetic or vicarious* or impersonal or disinterested or generalized analogues of the reactive attitudes I have already discussed. They are reactions to the qualities of others' wills, not towards ourselves, but towards others. Because of this impersonal or vicarious character, we give them different names. Thus one who experiences the vicarious analogue of resentment is said to be indignant or disapproving, or morally indignant or disapproving. What we have here is, as it were, resentment on behalf of another, where one's own interest and dignity are not involved; and it is this impersonal or vicarious character of the attitude, added to its others, which entitle it to the qualification 'moral'....

The personal reactive attitudes rest on, and reflect, an expectation of, and demand for, the manifestation of a certain degree of goodwill or regard on the part of other human beings towards ourselves; or at least on the expectation of, and demand for, an absence of the manifestation of active ill will or indifferent disregard. (What will, in particular cases, *count* as manifestations of good or ill will or disregard will vary in accordance with the particular relationship in which we stand to another human being.) The generalized or vicarious analogues of the personal reactive attitudes rest on, and reflect, exactly the same expectation or demand in a generalized form; they rest on, or reflect, that is, the demand for the manifestation of a reasonable degree of goodwill or regard, on the part of others, not simply towards oneself, but towards all those on whose behalf moral indignation may be felt, i.e., as we now think, towards all men. The generalized and non-generalized

forms of demand, and the vicarious and personal reactive attitudes which rest upon, and reflect, them are connected not merely logically. They are connected humanly; and not merely with each other. They are connected also with yet another set of attitudes which I must mention now in order to complete the picture. I have considered from two points of view the demands we make on others and our reactions to their possibly injurious actions. These were the points of view of one whose interest was directly involved (who suffers, say, the injury) and of others whose interest was not directly involved (who do not themselves suffer the injury). Thus I have spoken of personal reactive attitudes in the first connection and of their vicarious analogues in the second. But the picture is not complete unless we consider also the correlates of these attitudes on the part of those on whom the demands are made, on the part of the agents. Just as there are personal and vicarious reactive attitudes associated with demands on others for oneself and demands on others for others, so there are self-reactive attitudes associated with demands on oneself for others. And here we have to mention such phenomena as feeling bound or obliged (the 'sense of obligation'); feeling compunction; feeling guilty or remorseful or at least responsible; and the more complicated phenomenon of shame.

All these three types of attitude are humanly connected. One who manifested the personal reactive attitudes in a high degree but showed no inclination at all to their vicarious analogues would appear as an abnormal case of moral egocentricity, as a kind of moral solipsist.† Let him be supposed fully to acknowledge the claims to regard that others had on him, to be susceptible of the whole range of self-reactive attitudes. He would then see himself as unique both as one (*the* one) who had a general claim on human regard and as one (*the* one) on whom human beings in general had such a claim. This would be a kind of moral solipsism. But it is barely more than a conceptual possibility; if it is that. In general, though within varying limits, we

---

*   Experienced as if one were taking part in the sensations or feelings of another. For example, reading a book about kayaking down the Mackenzie River to the Beaufort Sea might give one a vicarious feeling of excitement or adventure.

†   A solipsist is someone who does not recognize the existence of anyone but themselves. Strictly speaking, solipsism is the philosophical position that nothing exists (or can be known to exist) except one's own self and the contents of its consciousness; Strawson is using the term in the more general ordinary sense to mean extreme egoism or selfishness—the view that nothing is of value except one's own interests.

demand of others for others, as well as of ourselves for others, something of the regard which we demand of others for ourselves. Can we imagine, besides that of the moral solipsist, any other case of one or two of these three types of attitude being fully developed, but quite unaccompanied by any trace, however slight, of the remaining two or one? If we can, then we imagine something far below or far above the level of our common humanity—a moral idiot or a saint. For all these types of attitude alike have common roots in our human nature and our membership of human communities.

Now, as of the personal reactive attitudes, so of their vicarious analogues, we must ask in what ways, and by what considerations, they tend to be inhibited. Both types of attitude involve, or express, a certain sort of demand for inter-personal regard. The fact of injury constitutes a prima facie* appearance of this demand's being flouted or unfulfilled. We saw, in the case of resentment, how one class of considerations may show this appearance to be mere appearance, and hence inhibit resentment, *without* inhibiting, or displacing, the sort of demand of which resentment can be an expression, without in any way tending to make us suspend our ordinary interpersonal attitudes to the agent. Considerations of this class operate in just the same way, for just the same reasons, in connection with moral disapprobation or indignation; they inhibit indignation without in any way inhibiting the sort of demand on the agent of which indignation can be an expression, the range of attitudes towards him to which it belongs. But in this connection we may express the facts with a new emphasis. We may say, stressing the moral, the generalized aspect of the demand: considerations of this group have no tendency to make us see the agent as other than a morally responsible agent; they simply make us see the injury as one for which he was not morally responsible. The offering and acceptance of such exculpatory pleas as are here in question in no way detracts in our eyes from the agent's status as a term of moral relationships.† On the contrary, since things go wrong and situations are complicated, it is an essential part of the life of such relationships.

But suppose we see the agent in a different light: as one whose picture of the world is an insane delusion; or as one whose behaviour, or a part of whose behaviour, is unintelligible to us, perhaps even to him, in terms of conscious purposes, and intelligible only in terms of unconscious purposes; or even, perhaps, as one wholly impervious to the self-reactive attitudes I spoke of, wholly lacking, as we say, in moral sense. Seeing an agent in such a light as this tends, I said, to inhibit resentment in a wholly different way. It tends to inhibit resentment because it tends to inhibit ordinary interpersonal attitudes in general, and the kind of demand and expectation which those attitudes involve; and tends to promote instead the purely objective view of the agent as one posing problems simply of intellectual understanding, management, treatment, and control. Again the parallel holds for those generalized or moral attitudes towards the agent which we are now concerned with. The same abnormal light which shows the agent to us as one in respect of whom the personal attitudes, the personal demand, are to be suspended, shows him to us also as one in respect of whom the impersonal attitudes, the generalized demand, are to be suspended. Only, abstracting now from direct personal interest, we may express the facts with a new emphasis. We may say: to the extent to which the agent is seen in this light, he is not seen as one on whom demands and expectations lie in that particular way in which we think of them as lying when we speak of moral obligation; he is not, to that extent, seen as a morally responsible agent, as a term of moral relationships, as a member of the moral community.

…What concerns us now is to inquire, as previously in connection with the personal reactive attitudes, what relevance any general thesis of determinism might have to their vicarious analogues. The answers once more are parallel; though I shall take them in a slightly different order. First, we must note, as before, that when the suspension of such an attitude or such attitudes occurs in a particular case, it is *never* the consequence of the belief that the piece of behaviour in question was determined in a sense such that all behaviour *might be*, and, if determinism is true, all behaviour *is*, determined

---

* Latin: "at first sight" or "on the face of it."
† As one side ("term") of a moral relation.

in that sense. For it is not a consequence of any general thesis of determinism which might be true that nobody knows what he's doing or that everybody's behaviour is unintelligible in terms of conscious purposes or that everybody lives in a world of delusion or that nobody has a moral sense, i.e. is susceptible of self-reactive attitudes, etc. In fact no such sense of 'determined' as would be required for a general thesis of determinism is ever relevant to our actual suspensions of moral reactive attitudes. Second, suppose it granted, as I have already argued, that we cannot take seriously the thought that theoretical conviction of such a general thesis would lead to the total decay of the personal reactive attitudes. Can we then take seriously the thought that such a conviction—a conviction, after all, that many have held or said they held—would nevertheless lead to the total decay or repudiation of the vicarious analogues of these attitudes? I think that the change in our social world which would leave us exposed to the personal reactive attitudes but not at all to their vicarious analogues, the generalization of abnormal egocentricity which this would entail, is perhaps even harder for us to envisage as a real possibility than the decay of both kinds of attitude together. Though there are some necessary and some contingent differences between the ways and cases in which these two kinds of attitudes operate or are inhibited in their operation, yet, as general human capacities or pronenesses, they stand or lapse together.
....

VI.

And now we can try to fill in the lacuna which the pessimist finds in the optimist's account of the concept of moral responsibility, and of the bases of moral condemnation and punishment; and to fill it in from the facts as we know them. For, as I have already remarked, when the pessimist himself seeks to fill it in, he rushes beyond the facts as we know them and proclaims that it cannot be filled in at all unless determinism is false.

Yet a partial sense of the facts as we know them is certainly present to the pessimist's mind. When his opponent, the optimist, undertakes to show that the truth of determinism would not shake the foundations of the concept of moral responsibility and of the practices of moral condemnation and punishment, he typically refers, in a more or less elaborated way, to the efficacy of these practices in regulating behaviour in socially desirable ways. These practices are represented solely as instruments of policy, as methods of individual treatment and social control. The pessimist recoils from this picture; and in his recoil there is, typically, an element of emotional shock. He is apt to say, among much else, that the humanity of the offender himself is offended by *this* picture of his condemnation and punishment.

The reasons for this recoil—the explanation of the sense of an emotional, as well as a conceptual, shock—we have already before us. The picture painted by the optimists is painted in a style appropriate to a situation envisaged as wholly dominated by objectivity of attitude. The only operative notions invoked in this picture are such as those of policy, treatment, control. But a thoroughgoing objectivity of attitude, excluding as it does the moral reactive attitudes, excludes at the same time essential elements in the concepts of *moral* condemnation and *moral* responsibility. This is the reason for the conceptual shock. The deeper emotional shock is a reaction, not simply to an inadequate conceptual analysis, but to the suggestion of a change in our world. I have remarked that it is possible to cultivate an exclusive objectivity of attitude in some cases, and for some reasons, where the object of the attitude is not set aside from developed inter-personal and moral attitudes by immaturity or abnormality. And the suggestion which seems to be contained in the optimist's account is that such an attitude should be universally adopted to all offenders. This is shocking enough in the pessimist's eyes. But, sharpened by shock, his eyes see further. It would be hard to make *this* division in our natures. If to all offenders, then to all mankind. Moreover, to whom could this recommendation be, in any real sense, addressed? Only to the powerful, the authorities. So abysses seem to open.[4]

But we will confine our attention to the case of the offenders. The concepts we are concerned with are those of responsibility and guilt, qualified as 'moral', on the one hand—together with that of membership of a moral community; of demand, indignation, disapproval and condemnation, qualified as 'moral', on the other hand—together with that of punishment. Indignation, disapproval, like resentment, tend to inhibit or at least to limit our goodwill towards the object of these attitudes, tend to promote an at least partial and temporary withdrawal of goodwill; they do so in proportion as they are strong; and their strength is in general proportioned to what is felt to be the magnitude of the injury and to the degree to which the agent's will is identified with, or indifferent to, it. (These, of course, are not contingent connections.) But these attitudes of disapprobation and indignation are precisely the correlates of the moral demand in the case where the demand is felt to be disregarded. The making of the demand *is* the proneness to such attitudes. The holding of them does not, as the holding of objective attitudes does, involve as a part of itself viewing their object other than as a member of the moral community. The partial withdrawal of goodwill which *these* attitudes entail, the modification *they* entail of the general demand that another should, if possible, be spared suffering, is, rather, the consequence of *continuing* to view him as a member of the moral community; only as one who has offended against its demands. So the preparedness to acquiesce in that infliction of suffering on the offender which is an essential part of punishment is all of a piece with this whole range of attitudes of which I have been speaking. It is not only moral reactive attitudes towards the offender which are in question here. We must mention also the self-reactive attitudes of offenders themselves. Just as the other-reactive attitudes are associated with a readiness to acquiesce in the infliction of suffering on an offender, within the 'institution' of punishment, so the self-reactive attitudes are associated with a readiness on the part of the offender to acquiesce in such infliction *without* developing the reactions (e.g., of resentment) which he would normally develop to the infliction of injury upon him; i.e. with a readiness, as we say, to accept punishment[5] as 'his due' or as 'just'.

I am not in the least suggesting that these readinesses to acquiesce, either on the part of the offender himself or on the part of others, are always or commonly accompanied or preceded by indignant boilings or remorseful pangs; only that we have here a continuum of attitudes and feelings to which these readinesses to acquiesce themselves belong. Nor am I in the least suggesting that it belongs to this continuum of attitudes that we should be ready to acquiesce in the infliction of injury on offenders in a fashion which we

saw to be quite indiscriminate or in accordance with procedures which we knew to be wholly useless. On the contrary, savage or civilized, we have some belief in the utility of practices of condemnation and punishment. But the social utility of these practices, on which the optimist lays such exclusive stress, is not what is now in question. What is in question is the pessimist's justified sense that to speak in terms of social utility alone is to leave out something vital in our conception of these practices. The vital thing can be restored by attending to that complicated web of attitudes and feelings which form an essential part of the moral life as we know it, and which are quite opposed to objectivity of attitude. Only by attending to this range of attitudes can we recover from the facts as we know them a sense of what we mean, i.e. of *all* we mean, when, speaking the language of morals, we speak of desert, responsibility, guilt, condemnation, and justice. But we *do* recover it from the facts as we know them. We do not have to go beyond them. Because the optimist neglects or misconstrues these attitudes, the pessimist rightly claims to find a lacuna in his account. We can fill the lacuna for him. But in return we must demand of the pessimist a surrender of his metaphysics.

Optimist and pessimist misconstrue the facts in very different styles. But in a profound sense there is something in common to their misunderstandings. Both seek, in different ways, to over-intellectualize the facts. Inside the general structure or web of human attitudes and feelings of which I have been speaking, there is endless room for modification, redirection, criticism, and justification. But questions of justification are internal to the structure or relate to modifications internal to it. The existence of the general framework of attitudes itself is something we are given with the fact of human society. As a whole, it neither calls for, nor permits, an external 'rational' justification. Pessimist and optimist alike show themselves, in different ways, unable to accept this.[6] The optimist's style of over-intellectualizing the facts is that of a characteristically incomplete empiricism, a one-eyed utilitarianism.* He seeks to find an adequate basis for certain social practices in calculated consequences, and loses sight (perhaps wishes to lose sight) of the human attitudes of

---

* Utilitarianism is (roughly) the ethical theory that an action is morally good insofar as it produces a net quantity of pleasure or happiness over pain or unhappiness.

which these practices are, in part, the expression. The pessimist does not lose sight of these attitudes, but is unable to accept the fact that it is just these attitudes themselves which fill the gap in the optimist's account. Because of this, he thinks the gap can be filled only if some general metaphysical proposition is repeatedly verified, verified in all cases where it is appropriate to attribute moral responsibility. This proposition he finds it as difficult to state coherently and with intelligible relevance as its determinist contradictory. Even when a formula has been found ('contra-causal freedom' or something of the kind) there still seems to remain a gap between its applicability in particular cases and its supposed moral consequences. Sometimes he plugs this gap with an intuition of fittingness—a pitiful intellectualist trinket for a philosopher to wear as a charm against the recognition of his own humanity.

...

If we sufficiently, that is *radically*, modify the view of the optimist, his view is the right one. It is far from wrong to emphasize the efficacy of all those practices which express or manifest our moral attitudes, in regulating behaviour in ways considered desirable; or to add that when certain of our beliefs about the efficacy of some of these practices turn out to be false, then we may have good reason for dropping or modifying those practices. What *is* wrong is to forget that these practices, and their reception, the reactions to them, really *are* expressions of our moral attitudes and not merely devices we calculatingly employ for regulative purposes. Our practices do not merely exploit our natures, they express them. Indeed the very understanding of the kind of efficacy these expressions of our attitudes have turns on our remembering this. When we do remember this, and modify the optimist's position accordingly, we simultaneously correct its conceptual deficiencies and ward off the dangers it seems to entail, without recourse to the obscure and panicky metaphysics of libertarianism. ■

Suggestions for Critical Reflection

1. Some people find it a bit too easy to lose the forest for the trees when reading Strawson's article. To guard against this, try to formulate exactly what Strawson's final position *is* on the problem of free will and morality. For example, is he, in the end, more sympathetic to the optimist side or to the pessimists? If the optimist and pessimist positions require modification, how does Strawson think they should be modified? What concessions must each side make for the sake of reconciliation?

2. Along similar lines, what exactly is Strawson's *argument* that the truth or falsity of determinism is not relevant to our moral attitudes? Once it's clear, how persuasive is this argument?

3. Strawson admits some people might feel his analysis "leaves the real question unanswered," and (in a couple of places) defends himself against this claim. What do you think? For example, does Strawson simply *ignore* the standard worry that determinism means we "could not have done otherwise" and thus that we are not morally responsible for our actions? If so, does he do this legitimately? Alternatively, do you think Strawson

spends too much time discussing whether we *could* abandon our moral judgments if determinism is true, when really he should be discussing whether we *should* do so?

4. What do you think of Strawson's claim that "a sustained objectivity of inter-personal attitude ... does not seem to be something of which human beings would be capable"? Is this true? Would Strawson's argument survive if it is *not* true—that is, is this an essential premise for his argument? For Strawson, is this just an *empirical* claim, or might it somehow be conceptually or logically true (e.g., because of the "logic" of reactive and moral language)?

5. Some say Strawson's article works by making the (fairly radical) assumption that talk of freedom and responsibility is talk, not about truths or facts, but instead about human *attitudes*. Do you think this diagnosis is correct? If so, how does the nature of the debate change?

Notes

1 Cf. P.H. Nowell-Smith, 'Freewill and Moral Responsibility', *Mind*, vol. LVII, 1948.

2 As Nowell-Smith pointed out in a later article: 'Determinists and Libertarians', *Mind*, vol. LXIII, 1954.

3 Perhaps not in every case *just* what we demand they should be, but in any case *not* just what we demand they should not be. For my present purpose these differences do not matter.

4 Peered into by Mr. J.D. Mabbott, in his article 'Freewill and Punishment', published in *Contemporary British Philosophy*, 3rd ser., London, Allen & Unwin, 1956.

5 Of course not *any* punishment for *anything* deemed an offence.

6 Compare the question of the justification of induction. The human commitment to inductive belief-formation is original, natural, non-rational (not *irrational*), in no way something we choose or could give up. Yet rational criticism and reflection can refine standards and their application, supply 'rules for judging of cause and effect'. Ever since the facts were made clear by Hume, people have been resisting acceptance of them.

SUSAN WOLF

Sanity and the Metaphysics of Responsibility

Who Is Susan Wolf?

Susan Wolf (b. 1952) received her PhD from Princeton University and is currently the Edna J. Koury Professor of Philosophy at the University of North Carolina, Chapel Hill. She previously taught at Johns Hopkins University, the University of Maryland, and Harvard University. Wolf works primarily in ethics, often drawing connections with philosophy of mind, moral psychology, aesthetics, and other areas. She has written a number of influential and provocative papers, such as "Moral Saints," in which she argues that moral perfection "does not constitute a model of personal well-being toward which it would be particularly rational or good or desirable for a human being to strive." In more recent years, Wolf has published a number of books, including *The Variety of Values: Essays on Morality, Meaning, and Love* (2014) and *Meaning in Life and Why It Matters* (2012). In 2002 she was awarded a Distinguished Achievement Award from the Andrew W. Mellon Foundation, which cited her as "one of the most original and distinguished philosophers of her generation."

What Is the Structure of This Reading?

Wolf begins her paper by describing a fairly widespread compatibilist strategy designed to show that moral responsibility is consistent with determinism; she calls this tactic the "deep-self" view, and illustrates it using the work of Harry Frankfurt, Gary Watson, and Charles Taylor. Wolf presents a metaphysical objection to this compatibilist line, gives an initial response to the objection, but then reformulates the problem (using the example of JoJo) and concludes that it really does strike against the deep-self position. She suggests the solution lies, not in abandoning the deep-self view, but in supplementing it. However, she argues, it is best supplemented not with a new kind of power or control but with a condition of *sanity*. She calls this new theory the "sane deep-self view," and argues first that sanity is *necessary* for free will and then that having a sane self in control of one's own will is *sufficient* for freedom.

Wolf then compares the sane deep-self view with the plain deep-self view with which she began. The plain deep-self view gives us the ability to *revise* our selves, but that (Wolf has argued) is not enough for freedom of the will; it does not give us the ability to *create* our selves, but this (Wolf has also argued) is metaphysically impossible. Instead, the sane deep-self view finds a place somewhere between these two positions and defines freedom as the ability to *correct* our selves. Wolf closes by trying to answer two objections which might be raised against her account of free will.

Sanity and the Metaphysics of Responsibility*

Philosophers who study the problems of free will and responsibility have an easier time than most in meeting challenges about the relevance of their work to ordinary, practical concerns. Indeed, philosophers who study these problems are rarely faced with such challenges at all, since questions concerning the conditions of responsibility come up so obviously and so frequently in everyday life. Under scrutiny, however, one might question whether the connections between philosophical and nonphilosophical concerns in this area are real.

---

* This essay first appeared in *Responsibility, Character, and the Emotions: New Essays in Moral Psychology*, ed. Ferdinand David Schoeman (Cambridge University Press, 1987), 46–62.

In everyday contexts, when lawyers, judges, parents, and others are concerned with issues of responsibility, they know, or think they know, what in general the conditions of responsibility are. Their questions are questions of application: Does this or that particular person meet this or that particular condition? Is this person mature enough, or informed enough, or sane enough to be responsible? Was he or she acting under posthypnotic suggestion* or under the influence of a mind-impairing drug? It is assumed, in these contexts, that normal, fully developed adult human beings are responsible beings. The questions have to do with whether a given individual falls within the normal range.

By contrast, philosophers tend to be uncertain about the general conditions of responsibility, and they care less about dividing the responsible from the nonresponsible agents than about determining whether, and if so why, any of us are ever responsible for anything at all.

In the classroom, we might argue that the philosophical concerns grow out of the nonphilosophical ones, that they take off where the nonphilosophical questions stop. In this way, we might convince our students that even if they are not plagued by the philosophical worries, they ought to be. If they worry about whether a person is mature enough, informed enough, and sane enough to be responsible, then they should worry about whether that person is metaphysically free enough, too.

The argument I make here, however, goes in the opposite direction. My aim is not to convince people who are interested in the apparently nonphilosophical conditions of responsibility that they should go on to worry about the philosophical conditions as well, but rather to urge those who already worry about the philosophical problems not to leave the more mundane, prephilosophical problems behind. In particular, I suggest that the mundane recognition that *sanity* is a condition of responsibility has more to do with the murky and apparently metaphysical problems which surround the issue of responsibility than at first meets

the eye. Once the significance of the condition of sanity is fully appreciated, at least some of the apparently insuperable metaphysical aspects of the problem of responsibility will dissolve.

My strategy is to examine a recent trend in philosophical discussions of responsibility, a trend that tries, but I think ultimately fails, to give an acceptable analysis of the conditions of responsibility. It fails due to what at first appear to be deep and irresolvable metaphysical problems. It is here that I suggest that the condition of sanity comes to the rescue. What at first appears to be an impossible requirement for responsibility—the requirement that the responsible agent have created her- or himself—turns out to be the vastly more mundane and noncontroversial requirement that the responsible agent must, in a fairly standard sense, be sane.

Frankfurt, Watson, and Taylor

The trend I have in mind is exemplified by the writings of Harry Frankfurt, Gary Watson, and Charles Taylor. I will briefly discuss each of their separate proposals, and then offer a composite view that, while lacking the subtlety of any of the separate accounts, will highlight some important insights and some important blind spots they share.

In his seminal article "Freedom of the Will and the Concept of a Person,"[1] Harry Frankfurt notes a distinction between freedom of action and freedom of the will. A person has freedom of action, he points out, if she (or he) has the freedom to do whatever she wills to do—the freedom to walk or sit, to vote liberal or conservative, to publish a book or open a store, in accordance with her strongest desires. Even a person who has freedom of action may fail to be responsible for her actions, however, if the wants or desires she has the freedom to convert into action are themselves not subject to her control. Thus, the person who acts under posthypnotic suggestion, the victim of brain-washing, and the kleptomaniac† might all possess freedom of action. In the standard contexts in which these

---

*   A suggestion made when someone is under hypnosis, intended to make the subject act in a certain way when conscious.

†   Kleptomania is a mental disorder characterized by an obsessive, recurring impulse to steal, regardless of economic need or profit.

examples are raised, it is assumed that none of the individuals is locked up or bound. Rather, these individuals are understood to act on what, at one level at least, must be called *their own desires*. Their exemption from responsibility stems from the fact that their own desires (or at least the ones governing their actions) are not up to them. These cases may be described in Frankfurt's terms as cases of people who possess freedom of action, but who fail to be responsible agents because they lack freedom of the will.

Philosophical problems about the conditions of responsibility naturally focus on an analysis of this latter kind of freedom: What *is* freedom of the will, and under what conditions can we reasonably be thought to possess it? Frankfurt's proposal is to understand freedom of the will by analogy to freedom of action. As freedom of action is the freedom to do whatever one wills to do, freedom of the will is the freedom to will whatever one wants to will. To make this point clearer, Frankfurt introduces a distinction between first-order and second-order desires. First-order desires are desires to do or to have various things; second-order desires are desires about what desires to have or what desires to make effective in action. In order for an agent to have both freedom of action and freedom of the will, that agent must be capable of governing his or her actions by first-order desires and capable of governing his or her first-order desires by second-order desires.

Gary Watson's view of free agency[2]—free and responsible agency, that is—is similar to Frankfurt's in holding that an agent is responsible for an action only if the desires expressed by that action are of a particular kind. While Frankfurt identifies the right kind of desires as desires that are supported by second-order desires, however, Watson draws a distinction between "mere" desires, so to speak, and desires that are *values*. According to Watson, the difference between free action and unfree action cannot be analyzed by reference to the logical form of the desires from which these various actions arise, but rather must relate to a difference in the quality of their source. Whereas some of my desires are just appetites or conditioned responses I find myself "stuck with," others are expressions of judgments on my part that the objects I desire are good. Insofar as my actions can be governed by the latter type of desire—governed, that is, by my values or valuational system—they are actions that I perform freely and for which I am responsible.

Frankfurt's and Watson's accounts may be understood as alternate developments of the intuition that in order to be responsible for one's actions, one must be responsible for the self that performs these actions. Charles Taylor, in an article entitled "Responsibility for Self,"[3] is concerned with the same intuition. Although Taylor does not describe his view in terms of different levels or types of desire, his view is related, for he claims that our freedom and responsibility depends on our ability to reflect on, criticize, and revise our selves. Like Frankfurt and Watson, Taylor seems to believe that if the characters from which our actions flowed were simply and permanently *given* to us, implanted by heredity, environment, or God, then we would be mere vehicles through which the causal forces of the world traveled, no more responsible than dumb animals or young children or machines. But like the others, he points out that, for most of us, our characters and desires are not so brutely implanted— or, at any rate, if they are, they are subject to revision by our own reflecting, valuing, or second-order desiring selves. We human beings—and as far as we know, only we human beings—have the ability to step back from ourselves and decide whether we are the selves we want to be. Because of this, these philosophers think, we are responsible for ourselves and for the actions that we produce.

Although there are subtle and interesting differences among the accounts of Frankfurt, Watson, and Taylor, my concern is with features of their views that are common to them all. All share the idea that responsible agency involves something more than intentional agency. All agree that if we are responsible agents, it is not just because our actions are within the control of our wills, but because, in addition, our wills are not just psychological states *in* us, but expressions of characters that come *from* us, or that at any rate are acknowledged and affirmed *by* us. For Frankfurt, this means that our wills must be ruled by our second-order desires; for Watson, that our wills must be governable by our system of values; for Taylor, that our wills must issue from selves that are subject to self-assessment and redefinition in terms of a vocabulary of worth. In one way or another, all these philosophers seem to be saying that the key to responsibility lies in the fact that responsible agents are those for whom it is not just the case that their actions are within the control of their wills, but also the case that their wills are within the control of their *selves* in some deeper sense. Because, at one level, the differences among Frankfurt, Watson, and Taylor may be understood as differences in the analysis or interpretation of what it is for an action to be under the control of this deeper self, we may speak of their separate positions as variations of one basic view about responsibility: the *deep-self* view.

The Deep-Self View

Much more must be said about the notion of a deep self before a fully satisfactory account of this view can be given. Providing a careful, detailed analysis of that notion poses an interesting, important, and difficult task in its own right. The degree of understanding achieved by abstraction from the views of Frankfurt, Watson, and Taylor, however, should be sufficient to allow us to recognize some important virtues as well as some important drawbacks of the deep-self view.

One virtue is that this view explains a good portion of our pretheoretical intuitions about responsibility. It explains why kleptomaniacs, victims of brainwashing, and people acting under posthypnotic suggestion may not be responsible for their actions, although most of us typically are. In the cases of people in these special categories, the connection between the agents' deep selves and their wills is dramatically severed—their wills are governed not by their deep selves, but by forces external to and independent from them. A different intuition is that we adult human beings can be responsible for our actions in a way that dumb animals, infants, and machines cannot. Here the explanation is not in terms of a split between these beings' deep selves and their wills; rather, the point is that these beings *lack* deep selves altogether. Kleptomaniacs and victims of hypnosis exemplify individuals whose selves are *alienated* from their actions; lower animals and machines, on the other hand, do not have the sorts of selves from which actions *can* be alienated, and so they do not have the sort of selves from which, in the happier cases, actions can responsibly flow.

At a more theoretical level, the deep-self view has another virtue: It responds to at least one way in which the fear of determinism presents itself.

A naive reaction to the idea that everything we do is completely determined by a causal chain that extends backward beyond the times of our births involves thinking that in that case we would have no control over our behavior whatsoever. If everything is determined, it is thought, then what happens happens, whether we want it to or not. A common, and proper, response to this concern points out that determinism does not deny the causal efficacy an agent's desires might have on his or her behavior. On the contrary, determinism in its more plausible forms tends to affirm this connection, merely adding that as one's behavior is determined by one's desires, so one's desires are determined by something else.[4]

Those who were initially worried that determinism implied fatalism, however, are apt to find their fears merely transformed rather than erased. If our desires are governed by something else, they might say, they are not *really* ours after all—or, at any rate, they are ours in only a superficial sense.

The deep-self view offers an answer to this transformed fear of determinism, for it allows us to distinguish cases in which desires are determined by forces foreign to oneself from desires which are determined *by* one's self—by one's "real," or second-order desiring, or valuing, or deep self, that is. Admittedly, there are cases, like that of the kleptomaniac or the victim of hypnosis, in which the agent acts on desires that "belong to" him or her in only a superficial sense. But the proponent of the deep-self view will point out that even if determinism is true, ordinary adult human action can be distinguished from this. Determinism implies that the desires which govern our actions are in turn governed by something else, but that something else will, in the fortunate cases, be our own deeper selves.

This account of responsibility thus offers a response to our fear of determinism; but it is a response with which many will remain unsatisfied. Even if my actions are governed by my desires and my desires are governed by my own deeper self, there remains the question: Who, or what, is responsible for this deeper self? The response above seems only to have pushed the problem further back.

Admittedly, some versions of the deep-self view, including Frankfurt's and Taylor's, seem to anticipate this question by providing a place for the ideal that an agent's deep self may be governed by a still deeper self. Thus, for Frankfurt, second-order desires may themselves be governed by third-order desires, third-order desires by fourth-order desires, and so on. Also, Taylor points out that, as we can reflect on and evaluate our prereflective selves, so we can reflect on and evaluate the selves who are doing the first reflecting and evaluating, and so on. However, this capacity to recursively create endless levels of depth ultimately misses the criticism's point.

First of all, even if there is no *logical* limit to the number of levels of reflection or depth a person may have, there is certainly a psychological limit—it is virtually impossible imaginatively to conceive a fourth-, much less an eighth-order, desire. More important, no matter how many levels of self we posit, there will still, in any individual case, be a last level—a deepest self about whom the question "What governs it?" will arise, as problematic as ever. If determinism is true, it implies that even if my actions are governed by my desires, and my desires are governed by my deepest self, my deepest self will still be governed by something that must, logically, be external to myself altogether. Though I can step back from the values my parents and teachers have given me and ask whether these are the values I really want, the "I" that steps back will itself be a product of the parents and teachers I am questioning.

The problem seems even worse when one sees that one fares no better if determinism is false. For if my deepest self is not determined by something external to myself, it will still not be determined by *me*. Whether I am a product of carefully controlled forces or a result of random mutations, whether there is a complete explanation of my origin or no explanation at all, *I* am not, in any case, responsible for my existence; I am not in control of my deepest self.

Thus, though the claim that an agent is responsible for only those actions that are within the control of his or her deep self correctly identifies a necessary condition for responsibility—a condition that separates the hypnotized and the brainwashed, the immature and the lower animals from ourselves, for example—it fails to provide a sufficient condition of responsibility that puts all fears of determinism to rest. For one of the fears invoked by the thought of determinism seems to be connected to its implication that we are but intermediate links in a causal chain, rather than ultimate, self-initiating sources of movement

and change. From the point of view of one who has this fear, the deep-self view seems merely to add loops to the chain, complicating the picture but not really improving it. From the point of view of one who has this fear, responsibility seems to require being a prime mover unmoved,* whose deepest self is itself neither random *nor* externally determined, but is rather determined *by* itself—who is, in other words, self-created.

At this point, however, proponents of the deep-self view may wonder whether this fear is legitimate. For although people evidently can be brought to the point where they feel that responsible agency requires them to be ultimate sources of power, to the point where it seems that nothing short of self-creation will do, a return to the internal standpoint of the agent whose responsibility is in question makes it hard to see what good this metaphysical status is supposed to provide or what evil its absence is supposed to impose.

From the external standpoint, which discussions of determinism and indeterminism encourage us to take up, it may appear that a special metaphysical status is required to distinguish us significantly from other members of the natural world. But proponents of the deep-self view will suggest this is an illusion that a return to the internal standpoint should dispel. The possession of a deep self that is effective in governing one's actions is a sufficient distinction, they will say. For while other members of the natural world are not in control of the selves that they are, we, possessors of effective deep selves, are in control. We can reflect on what sorts of beings we are, and on what sorts of marks we make on the world. We can change what we don't like about ourselves, and keep what we do. Admittedly, we do not create ourselves from nothing. But as long as we can revise ourselves, they will suggest, it is hard to find reason to complain. Harry Frankfurt writes that a person who is free to do what he wants to do and also free to want what he wants to want has "all the freedom it is possible to desire or to conceive."[5] This suggests a rhetorical question: If you are free to control your actions by your desires, and free to control your desires by your deeper desires, and free to control those desires by still deeper desires, what further kind of freedom can you want?

---

* Something that initiates a chain of causation (events) but is not itself caused (an event). The classic example of a (putative) "prime mover" is God: see the selection from Aquinas in the Philosophy of Religion section.

The Condition of Sanity

Unfortunately, there is a further kind of freedom we can want, which it is reasonable to think necessary for responsible agency. The deep-self view fails to be convincing when it is offered as a complete account of the conditions of responsibility. To see why, it will be helpful to consider another example of an agent whose responsibility is in question.

JoJo is the favorite son of Jo the First, an evil and sadistic dictator of a small, undeveloped country. Because of his father's special feelings for the boy, JoJo is given a special education and is allowed to accompany his father and observe his daily routine. In light of this treatment, it is not surprising that little JoJo takes his father as a role model and develops values very much like Dad's. As an adult, he does many of the same sorts of things his father did, including sending people to prison or to death or to torture chambers on the basis of whim. He is not *coerced* to do these things, he acts according to his own desires. Moreover, these are desires he wholly *wants* to have. When he steps back and asks, "Do I really want to be this sort of person?" his answer is resoundingly "Yes," for this way of life expresses a crazy sort of power that forms part of his deepest ideal.

In light of JoJo's heritage and upbringing—both of which he was powerless to control—it is dubious at best that he should be regarded as responsible for what he does. It is unclear whether anyone with a childhood such as his could have developed into anything but the twisted and perverse sort of person that he has become. However, note that JoJo is someone whose actions are controlled by his desires and whose desires are the desires he wants to have: That is, his actions are governed by desires that are governed by and expressive of his deepest self.

The Frankfurt-Watson-Taylor strategy that allowed us to differentiate our normal selves from the victims of hypnosis and brainwashing will not allow us to differentiate ourselves from the son of Jo the First. In the case of these earlier victims, we were able to say that although the actions of these individuals were, at one level, in control of the individuals themselves, these individuals themselves, qua* agents, were not the selves they more deeply wanted to be. In this respect, these people were unlike our happily more integrated selves. However, we cannot say of JoJo that his self, qua agent, is not the self he wants it to be. It is the self he wants it to be. From the inside, he feels as integrated, free, and responsible as we do.

Our judgment that JoJo is not a responsible agent is one that we can make only from the outside—from reflecting on the fact, it seems, that his deepest self is not up to him. Looked at from the outside, however, our situation seems no different from his—for in the last analysis, it is not up to any of us to have the deepest selves we do. Once more, the problem seems metaphysical—and not just metaphysical, but insuperable. For, as I mentioned before, the problem is independent of the truth of determinism. Whether we are determined or undetermined, we cannot have created our deepest selves. Literal self-creation is not just empirically, but logically impossible.

If JoJo is not responsible because his deepest self is not up to him, then we are not responsible either. Indeed, in that case responsibility would be impossible for anyone to achieve. But I believe the appearance that literal self-creation is required for freedom and responsibility is itself mistaken.

The deep-self view was right in pointing out that freedom and responsibility requires us to have certain distinctive types of control over our behavior and our selves. Specifically, our actions need to be under the control of our selves, and our (superficial) selves need to be under the control of our deep selves. Having seen that these types of control are not enough to guarantee us the status of responsible agents, we are tempted to go on to suppose that we must have yet another kind of control to assure us that even our deepest selves are somehow up to us. But not all the things necessary for freedom and responsibility must be types of power and control. We may need simply to *be* a certain way, even though it is not within our power to determine whether we are that way or not.

Indeed, it becomes obvious that at least one condition of responsibility is of this form as soon as we remember what, in everyday contexts, we have known all along—namely, that in order to be responsible, an agent must be *sane*. It is not ordinarily in our

---

* Latin: "considered in the capacity of."

power to determine whether we are or are not sane. Most of us, it would seem, are lucky, but some of us are not. Moreover, being sane does not necessarily mean that one has any type of power or control an insane person lacks. Some insane people, like JoJo and some actual political leaders who resemble him, may have complete control of their actions, and even complete control of their acting selves. The desire to be sane is thus not a desire for another form of control; it is rather a desire that one's self be connected to the world in a certain way—we could even say it is a desire that one's self be *controlled by* the world in certain ways and not in others.

This becomes clear if we attend to the criteria for sanity that have historically been dominant in legal questions about responsibility. According to the M'Naughten Rule,* a person is sane if (1) he knows what he is doing and (2) he knows that what he is doing is, as the case may be, right or wrong. Insofar as one's desire to be sane involves a desire to know what one is doing—or more generally, a desire to live in the real world—it is a desire to be controlled (to have, in this case, one's *beliefs* controlled) by perceptions and sound reasoning that produce an accurate conception of the world, rather than by blind or distorted forms of response. The same goes for the second constituent of sanity—only, in this case, one's hope is that one's *values* be controlled by processes that afford an accurate conception of the world.[6] Putting these two conditions together, we may understand sanity, then, as the minimally sufficient ability cognitively and normatively† to recognize and appreciate the world for what it is.

There are problems with this definition of sanity, at least some of which will become obvious in what follows, that make it ultimately unacceptable either as a gloss on or an improvement of the meaning of the term in many of the contexts in which it is used. The definition offered does seem to bring out the interest sanity has for us in connection with issues of

responsibility, however, and some pedagogical as well as stylistic purposes will be served if we use sanity hereafter in this admittedly specialized sense.

The Sane Deep-Self View

So far I have argued that the conditions of responsible agency offered by the deep-self view are necessary but not sufficient. Moreover, the gap left open by the deep-self view seems to be one that can be filled only by a metaphysical, and, as it happens, metaphysically impossible addition. I now wish to argue, however, that the condition of sanity, as characterized above, is sufficient to fill the gap. In other words, the deep-self view, supplemented by the condition of sanity, provides a satisfying conception of responsibility. The conception of responsibility I am proposing, then, agrees with the deep-self view in requiring that a responsible agent be able to govern her (or his) actions by her desires and to govern her desires by her deep self. In addition, my conception insists that the agent's deep self be sane, and claims that this is *all* that is needed for responsible agency. By contrast to the plain deep-self view, let us call this new proposal the *sane deep-self view*.

It is worth noting, to begin with, that this new proposal deals with the case of JoJo and related cases of deprived childhood victims in ways that better match our pretheoretical intuitions. Unlike the plain deep-self view, the sane deep-self view offers a way of explaining why JoJo is not responsible for his actions without throwing our own responsibility into doubt. For, although like us, JoJo's actions flow from desires that flow from his deep self, unlike us, JoJo's deep self is itself insane. Sanity, remember, involves the ability to know the difference between right and wrong, and a person who, even on reflection, cannot see that having someone tortured because he failed to salute you is wrong plainly lacks the requisite ability.

---

* This (also known as the McNaughten rule, and by various other spellings as well) is a British legal principle governing decisions as to the criminal responsibility of insane persons. In 1843 Daniel M'Naughten, laboring under the insane belief that the British government was persecuting him, mistook the prime minister's secretary for the prime minister himself and murdered him. He was tried, but acquitted on grounds of insanity (and committed to Bethlehem Hospital, a London asylum). Because of the difficulty and prominence of the case, the House of Lords—at the time, England's supreme court—sent a number of questions about insanity and criminal responsibility to the judges of England, who returned answers in the form of rules: the M'Naughten rules.

† Cognition has to do with representing what is true, normativity with what is right (morally right).

Less obviously, but quite analogously, this new proposal explains why we give less than full responsibility to persons who, though acting badly, act in ways that are strongly encouraged by their societies—the slaveowners of the 1850s, the Nazis of the 1930s, and many male chauvinists of our fathers' generation, for example. These are people, we imagine, who falsely believe that the ways in which they are acting are morally acceptable, and so, we may assume, their behavior is expressive of or at least in accordance with these agents' deep selves. But their false beliefs in the moral permissibility of their actions and the false values from which these beliefs derived may have been inevitable, given the social circumstances in which they developed. If we think that the agents could not help but be mistaken about their values, we do not blame them for the actions those values inspired.[7]

It would unduly distort ordinary linguistic practice to call the slaveowner, the Nazi, or the male chauvinist even partially or locally insane. Nonetheless, the reason for withholding blame from them is at bottom the same as the reason for withholding it from JoJo. Like JoJo, they are, at the deepest level, unable cognitively and normatively to recognize and appreciate the world for what it is. In our sense of the term, their deepest selves are not fully *sane*.

The sane deep-self view thus offers an account of why victims of deprived childhoods as well as victims of misguided societies may not be responsible for their actions, without implying that we are not responsible for ours. The actions of these others are governed by mistaken conceptions of value that the agents in question cannot help but have. Since, as far as we know, our values are not, like theirs, unavoidably mistaken, the fact that these others are not responsible for their actions need not force us to conclude that we are not responsible for ours.

But it may not yet be clear why sanity, in this special sense, should make such a difference—why, in particular, the question of whether someone's values are unavoidably *mistaken* should have any bearing on their status as responsible agents. The fact that the sane deep-self view implies judgments that match our intuitions about the difference in status between characters like JoJo and ourselves provides little support for it if it cannot also defend these intuitions. So we must consider an objection that comes from the point of view we considered earlier which rejects the intuition that a relevant difference can be found.

Earlier, it seemed that the reason JoJo was not responsible for his actions was that although his actions were governed by his deep self, his deep self was not up to him. But this had nothing to do with his deep self's being mistaken or not mistaken, evil or good, insane or sane. If JoJo's values are unavoidably mistaken, our values, even if not mistaken, appear to be just as unavoidable. When it comes to freedom and responsibility, isn't it the unavoidability, rather than the mistakenness, that matters?

Before answering this question, it is useful to point out a way in which it is ambiguous: The concepts of avoidability and mistakenness are not unequivocally distinct. One may, to be sure, construe the notion of avoidability in a purely metaphysical way. Whether an event or state of affairs is unavoidable under this construal depends, as it were, on the tightness of the causal connections that bear on the event's or state of affairs' coming about. In this sense, our deep selves do seem as unavoidable for us as JoJo's and the others' are for them. For presumably we are just as influenced by our parents, our cultures, and our schooling as they are influenced by theirs. In another sense, however, our characters are not similarly unavoidable.

In particular, in the cases of JoJo and the others, there are certain features of their characters that they cannot avoid *even though these features are seriously mistaken, misguided, or bad*. This is so because, in our special sense of the term, these characters are less than fully sane. Since these characters lack the ability to know right from wrong, they are unable to revise their characters on the basis of right and wrong, and so their deep selves lack the resources and the reasons that might have served as a basis for self-correction. Since the deep selves we unavoidably have, however, are sane deep selves—deep selves, that is, that unavoidably *contain* the ability to know right from wrong—we unavoidably do have the resources and reasons on which to base self-correction. What this means is that though in one sense we are no more in control of our deepest selves than JoJo et al.,* it does not follow in our case, as it does in theirs, that we would be the way we are, even if it is a bad or wrong way to be. However, if this does not follow, it seems to me, our absence of control at the deepest level should not upset us.

Consider what the absence of control at the deepest level amounts to for us: Whereas JoJo is unable to control the fact that, at the deepest level, he is not fully sane, we are not responsible for the fact that, at the deepest level, we are. It is not up to us to *have* minimally sufficient abilities cognitively and normatively to recognize and appreciate the world for what it is. Also, presumably, it is not up to us to have lots of other properties, at least to begin with—a fondness for purple, perhaps, or an antipathy for beets. As the proponents of the plain deep-self view have been at pains to point out, however, we do, if we are lucky, have the ability to revise our selves in terms of the values that are held by or constitutive of our deep selves. If we are lucky enough both to have this ability and to have our deep selves be sane, it follows that although there is much in our characters that we did not choose to have, there is nothing irrational or objectionable in our characters that we are compelled to keep.

Being sane, we are able to understand and evaluate our characters in a reasonable way, to notice what there is reason to hold on to, what there is reason to eliminate, and what, from a rational and reasonable standpoint, we may retain or get rid of as we please. Being able as well to govern our superficial selves by our deep selves, then, we are able to change the things we find there is reason to change. This being so, it seems that although we may not be *metaphysically* responsible for ourselves—for, after all, we did not create ourselves from nothing—we are *morally* responsible for ourselves, for we are able to understand and appreciate right and wrong, and to change our characters and our actions accordingly.

Self-creation, Self-revision, and Self-correction

At the beginning of this chapter, I claimed that recalling that sanity was a condition of responsibility would dissolve at least some of the appearance that responsibility was metaphysically impossible. To see how this is so, and to get a fuller sense of the sane deep-self view, it may be helpful to put that view into perspective by comparing it to the other views we have discussed along the way.

As Frankfurt, Watson, and Taylor showed us, in order to be free and responsible we need not only to be able to control our actions in accordance with our desires, we need to be able to control our desires in accordance with our deepest selves. We need, in other words, to be able to *revise* ourselves—to get rid of some desires and traits, and perhaps replace them with others on the basis of our deeper desires or values or reflections. However, consideration of the fact that the selves who are doing the revising might themselves be either brute products of external forces or arbitrary outputs of random generation made us wonder whether the capacity for self-revision was enough to assure us of responsibility—and the example of JoJo added force to the suspicion that it was not. Still, if the ability to revise ourselves is not enough, the ability to create ourselves does not seem necessary either. Indeed, when you think of it, it is unclear why anyone should want self-creation. Why should anyone be disappointed at having to accept the idea that one has to get one's start somewhere? It is an idea that most of us have lived with quite contentedly all along. What we do have reason to want, then, is something more than the ability to revise ourselves, but less than the ability to create ourselves. Implicit in the sane deep-self view is the idea that what is needed is the ability to *correct* (or improve) ourselves.

Recognizing that in order to be responsible for our actions, we have to be responsible for our selves, the sane deep-self view analyzes what is necessary in order to be responsible for our selves as (1) the ability to evaluate ourselves sensibly and accurately, and (2) the ability to transform ourselves insofar as our evaluation tells us to do so. We may understand the exercise of these abilities as a process where by we *take* responsibility for the selves that we are but did not ultimately create. The condition of sanity is intrinsically connected to the first ability; the condition that we be able to control our superficial selves by our deep selves is intrinsically connected to the second.

---

* Latin: "and others."

The difference between the plain deep-self view and the sane deep-self view, then, is the difference between the requirement of the capacity for self-revision and the requirement of the capacity for self-correction. Anyone with the first capacity can *try* to take responsibility for himself or herself. However, only someone with a sane deep self—a deep self that can see and appreciate the world for what it is—can self-evaluate sensibly and accurately. Therefore, although insane selves can try to take responsibility for themselves, only sane selves will properly be accorded responsibility.

Two Objections Considered

At least two problems with the sane deep-self view are so glaring as to have certainly struck many readers. In closing, I shall briefly address them. First, some will be wondering how, in light of my specialized use of the term "sanity," I can be so sure that "we" are any saner than the nonresponsible individuals I have discussed. What justifies my confidence that, unlike the slaveowners, Nazis, and male chauvinists, not to mention JoJo himself, we are able to understand and appreciate the world for what it is? The answer to this is that nothing justifies this except widespread inter-subjective agreement* and the considerable success we have in getting around in the world and satisfying our needs. These are not sufficient grounds for the smug assumption that we are in a position to see the truth about *all* aspects of ethical and social life. Indeed, it seems more reasonable to expect that time will reveal blind spots in our cognitive and normative outlook, just as it has revealed errors in the outlooks of those who have lived before. But our judgments of responsibility can only be made from here, on the basis of the understandings and values that we can develop by exercising the abilities we do possess as well and as fully as possible.

If some have been worried that my view implicitly expresses an overconfidence in the assumption that we are sane and therefore right about the world, others will be worried that my view too closely connects sanity with being right about the world, and fear that my view implies that anyone who acts wrongly or has false beliefs about the world is therefore insane and so not responsible for his or her actions. This seems to me to be a more serious worry, which I am sure I cannot answer to everyone's satisfaction.

First, it must be admitted that the sane deep-self view embraces a conception of sanity that is explicitly normative. But this seems to me a strength of that view, rather than a defect. Sanity is a normative concept, in its ordinary as well as in its specialized sense, and severely deviant behavior, such as that of a serial murderer or a sadistic dictator, does constitute evidence of a psychological defect in the agent. The suggestion that the most horrendous, stomach-turning crimes could be committed only by an insane person—an inverse of Catch-22,† as it were—must be regarded as a serious possibility, despite the practical problems that would accompany general acceptance of that conclusion.

But, it will be objected, there is no justification, in the sane deep-self view, for regarding only horrendous and stomach-turning crimes as evidence of insanity in its specialized sense. If sanity is the ability cognitively and normatively to understand and appreciate the world for what it is, then *any* wrong action or false belief will count as evidence of the absence of that ability. This point may also be granted, but we must be careful about what conclusion to draw. To be sure, when someone acts in a way that is not in accordance with acceptable standards of rationality and reasonableness, it is always appropriate to look for an explanation of why he or she acted that way. The hypothesis that the person was unable to understand and appreciate that an action fell outside acceptable bounds will always be a possible explanation. Bad performance on a math test always suggests the possibility that the testee is stupid. Typically, however, other explanations will be possible, too—for example,

---

*   That is, widespread agreement in judgment by lots of different people.
†   In the original Catch-22, from Joseph Heller's 1961 book (of the same name) about US airmen during the Italian campaign of World War II, a US military regulation creates a deadlock comprising two mutually exclusive sets of conditions. As a military doctor explains in the novel, "[pilot] Orr was crazy and could be grounded. All he had to do was ask; and as soon as he did he would be no longer crazy and would have to fly more missions. Orr would be crazy to fly more missions and sane if he didn't, but if he was sane he had to fly them. If he flew them he was crazy and didn't have to; but if he didn't want to he was sane and had to."

that the agent was too lazy to consider whether his or her action was acceptable, or too greedy to care, or, in the case of the math testee, that he or she was too occupied with other interests to attend class or study. Other facts about the agent's history will help us decide among these hypotheses.

This brings out the need to emphasize that sanity, in the specialized sense, is defined as the *ability* cognitively and normatively to understand and appreciate the world for what it is. According to our common-sense understandings, having this ability is one thing and exercising it is another—at least some wrong-acting, responsible agents presumably fall within the gap. The notion of "ability" is notoriously problematic, however, and there is a long history of controversy

about whether the truth of determinism would show our ordinary ways of thinking to be simply confused on this matter. At this point, then, metaphysical concerns may voice themselves again—but at least they will have been pushed into a narrower, and perhaps a more manageable, corner.

The sane deep-self view does not, then, solve all the philosophical problems connected to the topics of free will and responsibility. If anything, it highlights some of the practical and empirical problems, rather than solves them. It may, however, resolve some of the philosophical, and particularly, some of the metaphysical problems, and reveal how intimate are the connections between the remaining philosophical problems and the practical ones. ■

Suggestions for Critical Reflection

1. How satisfying a view of moral responsibility do you find the "deep-self" view? Do you agree that freedom of the will consists, essentially, in having the right kind of *control* over one's *will*? What else might it be (i.e., what else, if anything, might the libertarian be looking for)?

2. How plausible is Wolf's suggestion that the metaphysical problem of free will seems much less serious from "the internal standpoint"? Does this mean that it really *is* less serious? What exactly do you think Wolf means by the distinction between "internal" and "external" standpoints?

3. Do you agree that JoJo is not responsible for his actions? If not, how much of a problem is this for Wolf's arguments?

4. Compare JoJo with KayKay, who is deep-self rational and moral, but who is enticed by the advantages of some horrible action; KayKay struggles with this enticement, but at last gives in, with great shame afterward. JoJo (according to Wolf) is insane, so not responsible; KayKay is sane, so is responsible. So it would seem that JoJo should not be blamed or punished but KayKay should be. Is that correct?

5. Why does Wolf say that "literal self-creation is not just empirically, but logically impossible"? Is she right?

6. Wolf claims sanity has both a cognitive and a normative component: that is, to be sane one must both have reasonable *beliefs* and have reasonable *values*. Does this definition seem plausible? In particular, do we normally think morally unreasonable people should be considered *insane*?

7. Even if Wolf's definition of "sanity" is not a standard one, is the notion she describes useful for her purpose? That is, is it true that "the deep-self view, supplemented by the condition of sanity [in Wolf's sense], provides a satisfying conception of responsibility"?

8. If, as Wolf admits, we are not responsible for our own sanity, can we really be held responsible for the results of that sanity (including its effects on our own characters)? And if so, why are insane people (according to Wolf) *not* responsible for the results of their *in*sanity?

9. Can we be sure that, on Wolf's definition, *any* of us are really sane? If none of us are *fully* sane, then what does this mean about the freedom of our wills? For example, are only *some* of our actions free, and if so, which ones?

Notes

1   Harry Frankfurt, "Freedom of the Will and the Concept of a Person," *Journal of Philosophy* LXVIII (1971), 5–20.

2   Gary Watson, "Free Agency," *Journal of Philosophy* LXXII (1975), 205–20.

3   Charles Taylor, "Responsibility for Self," in A.E. Rorty, ed., *The Identities of Persons* (Berkeley: University of California Press, 1976), pp. 281–99.

4   See, e.g., David Hume, *A Treatise of Human Nature* (Oxford: Oxford University Press, 1967), pp. 399–406, and R.E. Hobart, "Free Will as Involving Determination and Inconceivable Without It," *Mind* 43 (1934).

5   Frankfurt, p. 16.

6   Strictly speaking, perception and sound reasoning may not be enough to ensure the ability to achieve an accurate conception of what one is doing and especially to achieve a reasonable normative assessment of one's situation. Sensitivity and exposure to certain realms of experience may also be necessary for these goals. For the purpose of this essay, I understand "sanity" to include whatever it takes to enable one to develop an adequate conception of one's world. In other contexts, however, this would be an implausibly broad construction of the term.

7   Admittedly, it is open to question whether these individuals were in fact unable to help having mistaken values, and indeed, whether recognizing the errors of their society would even have required exceptional independence or strength of mind. This is presumably an empirical question, the answer to which is extraordinarily hard to determine. My point here is simply that *if* we believe they are unable to recognize that their values are mistaken, we do not hold them responsible for the actions that flow from these values, and *if* we believe their ability to recognize their normative errors is impaired, we hold them less than fully responsible for the relevant actions.

Personal Identity

Who are you? What makes you *you*? One way to think about this is to think about the things about yourself that could be changed while still leaving you the same person. We'll approach this issue by imagining changes over time: you start out being just the way you are now, and have been, and then a radical change happens. The question is: will you still exist in a quite different form? Or would this mean that you cease to exist? How different could your body be? You could lose a limb or change sex and still be you, most people assume, but what if 'you' changed into a different species, or lost your biological body (if you became a robot or a ghost, for example)? How much could your psychology change while still being the psychology of the same person? How much personality change would result in you becoming a different person? What if you had severe amnesia and could no longer remember anything that happened to you before last week, or if all your memories of that time were replaced by false memories—are you still the same person 'you' were then?

This chapter deals with these issues. The approach we take to them is broadly metaphysical. Informally, one might think of their 'personal identity' as involving the values and beliefs about oneself that one feels especially committed to: perhaps you define yourself as being a musician, being from New Zealand, being a lesbian, being a good hockey player, or having red hair. This kind of self-identity might be something that is largely up to you—you can decide what it is about yourself that you think is particularly important—and it might change over time. It might even involve beliefs about yourself that aren't true (if you falsely believe that you are the lost heir to the Russian throne, for example). In this chapter, however, when we talk about personal identity what we have in mind is some fact of the matter that is not up to you—that is what it is independently of what you believe about it. Just as, we might think, there is something that makes gold gold, or a giraffe a giraffe, or the White House the White House, in the same way there is something that makes you you—our task is to work out what it is.* And, many philosophers think, the question of *personal* identity—what makes individual persons the persons they are—is especially interesting and significant. It turns out (arguably) to be a lot more philosophically puzzling than the question of what makes gold gold. Furthermore, the stakes are higher: we are especially interested in what it takes for a person—ourselves, for example—to continue to exist, rather than to cease to exist; and we are also interested in what makes something a person rather than a non-person, since this might well have important moral and legal implications.

The question of personal identity is one that has a long and complex philosophical history, but to simplify the terrain somewhat we can say that there are four basic positions on the self:

1. Biological views. Roughly, we are our bodies, or parts of our bodies. If your body changes enough you will cease to exist (and possibly another different person will come into existence). On some versions of this view, what makes a human person the particular person that they are is a biological fact about them, not all that different from what makes any animal the animal it is.

2. Psychological views. There is something about our psychological states that makes us the persons we are. For us to persist through time as the same person only requires that there be some appropriate kind of continuity in our psychology—for example, for our past and present mental states to be connected through memories, or by an unbroken stream of consciousness, or for our psychology to be unified by our status as agents who can make plans and carry them out.

3. Substance dualist views. Our selves are a special kind of non-physical object—something like a soul or an ego. These selves typically are intimately attached to a physical body, but that connection is only contingent and we would continue to be the

same person even with a different body or no body at all so long as our soul persists.

4. Non-self views. Personal identity is a comforting myth. There is no such thing as the persistence of a person through time, and none of the biological and psychological facts about us require appeal to the notion of a self. (Consider the Buddhist doctrine of *anattā* or non-self, for example.)

The readings in this chapter focus on the strategy of understanding personal identity in terms of psychological continuity—that is, option 2. above. The modern form of this view originates with John Locke, in the first selection in this chapter. There, Locke argues that what makes us the person we are is our consciousness, rather than our bodies, and furthermore that an individual consciousness is tied together over time by being connected through memories. In the next reading, Bernard Williams call this view into question: he first presents a thought-experiment that seems to clearly support Locke's theory, but then shows that what is essentially the same set of circumstances can be presented in such a way that we develop *opposite* intuitions and become convinced to reject the psychological-continuity theory. This leaves us unsure of where we stand on personal identity, and the following article by Daniel Dennett hammers home, in a very entertaining way, the complexities and perplexities of the issue. The next reading is a very influential article by Derek Parfit in which he argues that psychological continuity fails as an account of personal identity, and suggests that psychological *connectedness*—which can be a matter of degree, and can connect us to more than one possible past or future self—is a more important element in personal survival than continuity. Finally, the paper by Marya Schechtman contrasts two important versions of the psychological-continuity theory: the Lockean view that we are a unified consciousness, or subject of experience, vs. a more modern view, influenced by Kant, that holds that persons are agents with a unified set of life plans and short-term goals.

If you want to explore the philosophy of the self further—and perhaps investigate the other three approaches that are not foregrounded here—there are

---

* The identity relation in question, then, is what is sometimes known as 'numerical identity': it is a relation every thing bears to itself, and to nothing else.

many resources available. Some good collections of articles include: John Perry, ed., *Personal Identity* (University of California Press, 2008); Martin and Barresi, eds., *Personal Identity* (Blackwell, 2003); Bermúdez, Marcel, and Eilan, eds., *The Body and the Self* (MIT Press, 1995); S. Gallagher, ed., *The Oxford Handbook of the Self*, (Oxford University Press, 2011); Gallagher and Shear, eds., *Models of the Self* (Imprint Academic, 1999); and Amelie O. Rorty, ed., *The Identities of Persons* (University of California Press, 1976).

Some relatively recent influential books are: L.R. Baker, *Persons and Bodies: A Constitution View* (Cambridge University Press, 2000); R. Chisholm, *Person and Object* (Open Court, 1976); B. Garrett, *Personal Identity and Self-Consciousness* (Routledge, 1998); A. Kind, *Persons and Personal Identity* (Polity Press, 2015); G. Kopf, *Beyond Personal Identity: Dōgen, Nishida, and a Phenomenology of No-Self* (Routledge, 2001); E.J. Lowe, *Subjects of Experience* (Cambridge University Press, 1996);

H. Noonan, *Personal Identity* (Routledge, 2003); E. Olson, *The Human Animal: Personal Identity without Psychology* (Oxford University Press, 1997); D. Parfit, *Reasons and Persons* (Oxford University Press, 1984); J. Perry, *Identity, Personal Identity, and the Self* (Hackett, 2002); Shoemaker and Swinburne, *Personal Identity* (Wiley-Blackwell, 1991); P. Snowdon, *Persons, Animals, Ourselves* (Oxford University Press, 2014); P. Unger, *Identity, Consciousness, and Value* (Oxford University Press, 1990); and K.V. Wilkes, *Real People: Personal Identity without Thought Experiments* (Oxford University Press, 1988).

A few representative articles include: W.R. Carter, "How to Change Your Mind," *Canadian Journal of Philosophy* 19 (1989): 1–14; M. Johnston, "Human Beings," *Journal of Philosophy* 84 (1987): 59–83; T. Nagel, "Brain Bisection and the Unity of Consciousness," *Synthèse* 22 (1971): 396–413; and D. Parfit, "We Are Not Human Beings," *Philosophy* 87 (2012): 5–28.

JOHN LOCKE

FROM *An Essay Concerning Human Understanding*

For information on Locke's life and overall philosophical project, please see the introduction to Locke earlier in the Epistemology chapter of this volume.

What Is the Structure of This Reading?

In this selection from the *Essay Concerning Human Understanding* (1690), Locke evaluates the concept of identity to determine how we decide that one thing is the same at different intervals in time. In the case of living beings, Locke argues, identity is based upon participation in the same life. It is possible for a living thing to change particles and still be the same: a tree may shed its leaves, and still have the same identity.

For people, Locke notes, the situation is more complex. It is difficult to determine what we mean when we say that a young person in the past and an old person in the present share an identity (that is, are the same individual). Locke proposes that we distinguish between one's identity as a "human" (or "man," in Locke's dated phrasing) and as a "person." In his view, a human persists over time much as a tree does, in that one can be called the same human so long as the same living body has persisted from one moment to the next. A person, on the other hand, is "a thinking intelligent being, that has reason and reflection, and can consider itself as itself, the same thinking thing, in different times and places; which it does only by that consciousness which is inseparable from thinking, and, as it seems to me, essential to it." Because it is consciousness that makes one a person, it is the persistence of consciousness that makes one the same person from one moment to the next, according to Locke.

A person's body may change—it may, for example, develop wrinkles—but the person will remain the same as long as they have the same consciousness. And what counts as the same consciousness, from an earlier time to a later, is that the later one can remember the experiences of the earlier one. Memory conjoins the past and present, allowing a person to persist over time. Locke offers the example of a prince's consciousness and memories suddenly transferring into the body of a cobbler. Locke claims that in

such a scenario, we would hold that the prince now *is* the person inhabiting the cobbler's body; his ability to recollect the prince's memories establishes that he is the same person that previously inhabited the princely body. This shows that personal identity is a matter of shared consciousness and memory, and not a matter of bodily continuity.

Some Useful Background Information

1. Locke's contention that consciousness is the seat of personal identity builds upon the ideas of his philosophical predecessor René Descartes (see the Descartes selection from the Epistemology chapter of this volume). Descartes famously held that the thinking subject or "cogito" is the foundation of the self. Locke's contribution to Descartes's theory of identity is the notion that personhood is found in connected consciousness: a person's identity stretches only as far back as they can recall.

2. On the other hand Locke, unlike Descartes, asserts that selves are not substances—continuity of substance is a quite different issue than continuity of self, writes Locke, and it is quite coherent to suppose one self surviving through a change of substance, or two substances combining to compose one connected consciousness and hence one self, or even one substance composing two different selves at different times. This is in line with Locke's general skepticism about the possibility of having a clear idea what substance actually is. (See the Locke reading in the Epistemology chapter for more on this.)

3. When Locke brings up the possibility of a cat or parrot exercising reason, he is responding to Aristotle's famous definition of "man" as a "rational animal." Locke rejects Aristotle's account of human existence, because it is possible to imagine an animal gaining intellectual and discursive capabilities on par with those of a human. If a parrot is able to reason as well as a human, this does not mean that a parrot is therefore human, as Aristotle's theory would seem to require.

FROM *An Essay Concerning Human Understanding**

BOOK II, CHAPTER XXVII: OF IDENTITY AND DIVERSITY

§8. An animal is a living organized body; and consequently the same animal, as we have observed, is the same continued life communicated to different particles of matter, as they happen successively to be united to that organized living body. And whatever is talked of other definitions, ingenious observation puts it past doubt, that the idea in our minds, of which the sound man in our mouths is the sign,† is nothing else but of an animal of such a certain form: since I think I may be confident, that, whoever should see a creature of his own shape or make, though it had no more reason all its life than a cat or a parrot, would call him still a man; or whoever should hear a cat or a parrot discourse, reason, and philosophize, would call or think it nothing but a cat or a parrot; and say, the one was a dull irrational man, and the other a very intelligent rational parrot.... For I presume it is not the idea of a thinking or rational being alone that makes the idea of a man in most people's sense: but of a body, so and so shaped, joined to it: and if that be the idea of a man, the same successive body not shifted all at once, must, as well as the same immaterial spirit, go to the making of the same man.

§9. This being premised, to find wherein personal identity consists, we must consider what *person* stands for; which, I think, is a thinking intelligent being, that has reason and reflection, and can consider itself as itself, the same thinking thing, in different times and places; which it does only by that consciousness which is inseparable from thinking, and, as it seems to me, essential to it: it being impossible for anyone to perceive without perceiving that he does perceive. When we see, hear, smell, taste, feel, meditate, or will anything, we know that we do so. Thus it is always as to our present sensations and perceptions: and by this everyone is to himself that which he calls self; it not

being considered in this case whether the same self be continued in the same or diverse substances. For, since consciousness always accompanies thinking, and it is that which makes everyone to be what he calls self, and thereby distinguishes himself from all other thinking things, in this alone consists personal identity, i.e. the sameness of a rational being: and as far as this consciousness can be extended backwards to any past action or thought, so far reaches the identity of that person; it is the same self now it was then; and it is by the same self with this present one that now reflects on it, that that action was done.

§10. But it is farther inquired, whether it be the same identical substance. This few would think they had reason to doubt of, if these perceptions, with their consciousness, always remained present in the mind, whereby the same thinking thing would be always consciously present, and, as would be thought, evidently the same to itself. But that which seems to make the difficulty is this, that this consciousness being interrupted always by forgetfulness, there being no moment of our lives wherein we have the whole train of all our past actions before our eyes in one view, but even the best memories losing the sight of one part whilst they are viewing another; and we sometimes, and that the greatest part of our lives, not reflecting on our past selves, being intent on our present thoughts, and in sound sleep having no thoughts at all, or at least none with that consciousness which remarks our waking thoughts: I say, in all these cases, our consciousness being interrupted, and we losing the sight of our past selves, doubts are raised whether we are the same thinking thing, i.e. the same substance or no. Which, however reasonable or unreasonable, concerns not personal identity at all: the question being what makes the same person; and not whether it be

---

* Locke's *An Essay Concerning Human Understanding* was first published in 1690. The excerpts given here are from the sixth edition of 1710, reprinted from Locke's 10-volume *Collected Works* (first published in 1714 and reprinted with corrections in 1823).

† "Of which the sound man in our mouths is the sign": of which the symbol (for the idea) is the word "man."

the same identical substance, which always thinks in the same person; which in this case matters not at all: different substances, by the same consciousness (where they do partake in it) being united into one person, as well as different bodies by the same life are united into one animal, whose identity is preserved, in that change of substances, by the unity of one continued life. For, it being the same consciousness that makes a man be himself to himself, personal identity depends on that only, whether it be annexed solely to one individual substance, or can be continued in a succession of several substances. For as far as any intelligent being can repeat the idea of any past action with the same consciousness it had of it at first, and with the same consciousness it has of any present action; so far it is the same personal self. For it is by the consciousness it has of its present thoughts and actions, that it is self to itself now, and so will be the same self, as far as the same consciousness can extend to actions past or to come; and would be by distance of time, or change of substance, no more two persons, than a man be two men by wearing other clothes today than he did yesterday, with a long or a short sleep between: the same consciousness uniting those distant actions into the same person, whatever substances contributed to their production.

§11. That this is so, we have some kind of evidence in our very bodies, all whose particles, whilst vitally united to this same thinking conscious self, so that we feel when they are touched, and are affected by, and conscious of good or harm that happens to them, are a part of ourselves; i.e. of our thinking conscious self. Thus, the limbs of his body are to everyone a part of himself; he sympathizes and is concerned for them. Cut off a hand, and thereby separate it from that consciousness he had of its heat, cold, and other affections, and it is then no longer a part of that which is himself, any more than the remotest part of matter. Thus, we see the substance whereof personal self consisted at one time may be varied at another, without the change of personal identity; there being no question about the same person, though the limbs which but now were a part of it, be cut off.

§12. But the question is, "whether if the same substance which thinks be changed, it can be the same person; or, remaining the same, it can be different persons?"

And to this I answer, first, This can be no question at all to those who place thought in a purely material animal constitution, void of an immaterial substance. For whether their supposition be true or no, it is plain they conceive personal identity preserved in something else than identity of substance; as animal identity is preserved in identity of life, and not of substance. And therefore those who place thinking in an immaterial substance only, before they can come to deal with these men, must show why personal identity cannot be preserved in the change of immaterial substances, or variety of particular immaterial substances, as well as animal identity is preserved in the change of material substances, or variety of particular bodies: unless they will say, it is one immaterial spirit that makes the same life in brutes,* as it is one immaterial spirit that makes the same person in men; which the Cartesians† at least will not admit, for fear of making brutes thinking things too.

§13. But next, as to the first part of the question, "whether, if the same thinking substance (supposing immaterial substances only to think) be changed, it can be the same person?" I answer, that cannot be resolved, but‡ by those who know what kind of substances they are that do think; and whether the consciousness of past actions can be transferred from one thinking substance to another. I grant, were the same consciousness the same individual action, it could not: but it being a present representation of a past action, why it may not be possible, that that may be represented to the mind to have been, which really never was, will remain to be shown. And therefore how far the consciousness of past actions is annexed to any individual agent, so that another cannot possibly have it, will be hard for us to determine, till we know what kind of action it is that cannot be done without a reflex act of perception accompanying it, and how performed by thinking substances, who cannot think without being conscious of it. But that which we call the same

---

*   Animals.

†   Followers of French philosopher René Descartes.

‡   In this context, "but" means "except."

consciousness, not being the same individual act, why one intellectual substance may not have represented to it, as done by itself, what it never did, and was perhaps done by some other agent; why, I say, such a representation may not possibly be without reality of matter of fact, as well as several representations in dreams are, which yet whilst dreaming we take for true, will be difficult to conclude from the nature of things. And that it never is so, will by us, till we have clearer views of the nature of thinking substances, be best resolved into the goodness of God, who, as far as the happiness or misery of any of his sensible creatures is concerned in it, will not, by a fatal error of theirs, transfer from one to another that consciousness which draws reward or punishment with it. How far this may be an argument against those who would place thinking in a system of fleeting animal spirits, I leave to be considered. But yet to return to the question before us, it must be allowed, that, if the same consciousness (which, as has been shown, is quite a different thing from the same numerical figure or motion in body) can be transferred from one thinking substance to another, it will be possible that two thinking substances may make but one person. For the same consciousness being preserved, whether in the same or different substances, the personal identity is preserved.

§14. As to the second part of the question, "whether the same immaterial substance remaining, there may be two distinct persons?" which question seems to me to be built on this, whether the same immaterial being, being conscious of the action of its past duration, may be wholly stripped of all the consciousness of its past existence, and lose it beyond the power of ever retrieving it again; and so as it were beginning a new account from a new period, have a consciousness that cannot reach beyond this new state. All those who hold pre-existence* are evidently of this mind; since they allow the soul to have no remaining consciousness of what it did

in that pre-existent state, either wholly separate from body, or informing any other body; and if they should not, it is plain, experience would be against them. So that personal identity, reaching no further than consciousness reaches, a pre-existent spirit not having continued so many ages in a state of silence, must needs make different persons. Suppose a Christian, Platonist,† or a Pythagorean‡ should, upon God's having ended all his works of creation the seventh day, think his soul hath existed ever since; and should imagine it has revolved in several human bodies, as I once met with one, who was persuaded his had been the soul of Socrates; (how reasonably I will not dispute; this I know, that in the post he filled, which was no inconsiderable one, he passed for a very rational man, and the press§ has shown that he wanted¶ not parts or learning) would anyone say, that he, being not conscious of any of Socrates's actions or thoughts, could be the same person with Socrates? Let anyone reflect upon himself, and conclude that he has in himself an immaterial spirit, which is that which thinks in him, and, in the constant change of his body keeps him the same; and is that which he calls himself: Let his also suppose it to be the same soul that was in Nestor** or Thersites,†† at the siege of Troy (for souls being, as far as we know anything of them in their nature, indifferent to any parcel of matter, the supposition has no apparent absurdity in it), which it may have been, as well as it is now the soul of any other man: but he now having no consciousness of any of the actions either of Nestor or Thersites, does or can he conceive himself the same person with either of them? can he be concerned in either of their actions? attribute them to himself, or think them his own more than the actions of any other men that ever existed? So that this consciousness not reaching to any of the actions of either of those men, he is no more one self with either of them, than if the soul of immaterial spirit that now informs‡‡ him, had been created, and began to exist, when it began to inform his present body; though it were ever so true,

---

* The existence of the soul before birth in a body.
† A follower of the philosophy of Plato, who maintained that the soul is the seat of a person's identity.
‡ A follower of the Greek philosopher Pythagoras, who believed in reincarnation and the immortality of the soul.
§ Media publicity.
¶ Lacked.
** In Homer's *Odyssey*, Nestor is an Argonaut and king of Pylos.
†† In Homer's *Iliad*, Thersites was a Greek soldier.
‡‡ Directs, guides.

that the same spirit that informed Nestor's or Thersites's body were numerically the same that now informs his. For this would no more make him the same person with Nestor, than if some of the particles of matter that were once a part of Nestor were now a part of this man; the same immaterial substance, without the same consciousness, no more making the same person, by being united to any body, than the same particle of matter, without consciousness united to any body, makes the same person. But let him once find himself conscious of any of the actions of Nestor, he then finds himself the same person with Nestor.

§15. And thus may we be able, without any difficulty, to conceive the same person at the resurrection, though in a body not exactly in make or parts the same which he had here, the same consciousness going along with the soul that inhabits it. But yet the soul alone, in the change of bodies, would scarce to anyone, but to him that makes the soul the man, be enough to make the same man. For should the soul of a prince, carrying with it the consciousness of the prince's past life, enter and inform the body of a cobbler, as soon as deserted by his own soul, everyone sees he would be the same person with the prince, accountable only for the prince's actions: but who would say it was the same man? The body too goes to the making the man, and would, I guess, to every body determine the man in this case; wherein the soul, with all its princely thoughts about it, would not make another man: but he would be the same cobbler to everyone besides himself. I know that, in the ordinary way of speaking, the same person, and the same man, stand for one and the same thing. And indeed everyone will always have a liberty to speak as he pleases, and to apply what articulate sounds to what ideas he thinks fit, and change them as often as he pleases. But yet when we will inquire what makes the same spirit, man, or person, we must fix the ideas of spirit, man, or person in our minds; and having resolved with ourselves what we mean by them, it will not be hard to determine, in either of them, or the like, when it is the same, and when not.

§16. But though the same immaterial substance or soul does not alone, wherever it be, and in whatsoever state, make the same man; yet it is plain, consciousness, as far as ever it can be extended, should it be to ages past, unites existences and actions, very remote in time,

into the same person, as well as it does the existences and actions of the immediately preceding moment: so that whatever has the consciousness of present and past actions, is the same person to whom they both belong. Had I the same consciousness that I saw the ark and Noah's flood, as that I saw an overflowing of the Thames last winter, or as that I write now; I could no more doubt that I who write this now, that saw the Thames overflowed last winter, and that viewed the flood at the general deluge, was the same self, place that self in what substance you please, than that I who write this am the same myself now whilst I write (whether I consist of all the same substance material or immaterial, or no) that I was yesterday. For as to this point of being the same self, it matters not whether this present self be made up of the same or other substances; I being as much concerned, and as justly accountable for any action that was done a thousand years since, appropriated to me now by this self-consciousness, as I am for what I did the last moment.

§17. Self is that conscious thinking thing, whatever substance made up of (whether spiritual or material, simple or compounded, it matters not), which is sensible, or conscious of pleasure and pain, capable of happiness or misery, and so is concerned for itself, as far as that consciousness extends. Thus everyone finds that, whilst comprehended under that consciousness, the little finger is as much a part of himself as what is most so. Upon separation of this little finger, should this consciousness go along with the little finger, and leave the rest of the body, it is evident the little finger would be the person, the same person; and self then would have nothing to do with the rest of the body. As in this case it is the consciousness that goes along with the substance, when one part is separate from another, which makes the same person, and constitutes this inseparable self; so it is in reference to substances remote in time. That with which the consciousness of this present thinking thing can join itself, makes the same person, and is one self with it, and with nothing else; and so attributes to itself, and owns all the actions of that thing, as its own, as far as that consciousness reaches, and no further; as everyone who reflects will perceive.

§18. In this personal identity, is founded all the right and justice of reward and punishment; happiness and misery being that for which everyone is concerned for himself, and not mattering what becomes of any substance not joined to, or affected with that consciousness. For as it is evident in the instance I gave but now, if the consciousness went along with the little finger when it was cut off, that would be the same self which was concerned for the whole body yesterday, as making part of itself, whose actions then it cannot but admit as its own now. Though if the same body should still live, and immediately from the separation of the little finger have its own peculiar consciousness, whereof the little finger knew nothing; it would not at all be concerned for it, as a part of itself, or could own any of its actions, or have any of them imputed to him.

§19. This may show us wherein personal identity consists; not in the identity of substance, but, as I have said, in the identity of consciousness; wherein if Socrates and the present mayor of Queenborough* agree, they are the same person: if the same Socrates waking and sleeping do not partake of the same consciousness, Socrates waking and sleeping is not the same person. And to punish Socrates waking for what sleeping Socrates thought, and waking Socrates was never conscious of, would be no more of right, than to punish one twin for what his brother-twin did, whereof he knew nothing, because their outsides were so like, that they could not be distinguished; for such twins have been seen.

§20. But yet possibly it will still be objected, suppose I wholly lose the memory of some parts of my life, beyond a possibility of retrieving them, so that perhaps I shall never be conscious of them again; yet am I not the same person that did those actions, had those thoughts that I once was conscious of, though I have now forgot them? To which I answer, that we must here take notice what the word I is applied to: which, in this case, is the man only. And the same man being presumed to be the same person, I is easily here supposed to stand also for the same person. But if it be possible for the same man to have distinct incommunicable consciousness at different times, it is past doubt the same man would at different times make different persons; which, we see, is the sense of

mankind in the solemnest declaration of their opinions; human laws not punishing the mad man for the sober man's actions, nor the sober man for what the mad man did, thereby making them two persons: which is somewhat explained by our way of speaking in English when we say such an one is not himself, or is beside himself; in which phrases it is insinuated, as if those who now, or at least first used them, thought that self was changed; the self-same person was no longer in that man.

§21. But yet it is hard to conceive that Socrates, the same individual man, should be two persons. To help us a little in this, we must consider what is meant by Socrates, or the same individual man.

First, it must be either the same individual, immaterial, thinking substance; in short, the same numerical soul, and nothing else.

Secondly, or the same animal, without any regard to an immaterial soul.

Thirdly, or the same immaterial spirit united to the same animal.

Now, take which of these suppositions you please, it is impossible to make personal identity to consist in anything but consciousness, or reach any further than that does.

For, by the first of them, it must be allowed possible that a man born of different women, and in distant times, may be the same man. A way of speaking, which whoever admits, must allow it possible for the same man to be two distinct persons, as any two that have lived in different ages, without the knowledge of one another's thoughts.

By the second and third, Socrates in this life, and after it, cannot be the same man any way, but by the same consciousness; and so making human identity to consist in the same thing wherein we place personal identity, there will be difficulty to allow the same man to be the same person. But then they who place human identity in consciousness only, and not in something else, must consider how they will make the infant Socrates the same man with Socrates after the resurrection. But whatsoever to some men makes a man, and consequently the same individual man, wherein perhaps few are agreed, personal identity can

---

* A small town in Kent, in southeast England.

by us be placed in nothing but consciousness (which is that alone which makes what we call self) without involving us in great absurdities.

§22. But is not a man drunk and sober the same person? Why else is he punished for the fact he commits when drunk, though he be never afterwards conscious of it? Just as much the same person as a man that walks, and does other things in his sleep, is the same person, and is answerable for any mischief he shall do in it. Human laws punish both, with a justice suitable to their way of knowledge; because, in these cases, they cannot distinguish certainly what is real, what counterfeit: and so the ignorance in drunkenness or sleep is not admitted as a plea. For though punishment be annexed to personality, and personality to consciousness, and the drunkard perhaps be not conscious of what he did; yet human judicatures* justly punish him, because the fact is proved against him, but want of consciousness cannot be proved for him. But in the great day,† wherein the secrets of all hearts shall be laid open, it may be reasonable to think, no one shall be made to answer for what he knows nothing of; but shall receive his doom,‡ his conscience accusing or excusing him. ...

Suggestions for Critical Reflection

1. Locke argues as follows: "since consciousness always accompanies thinking, and it is that which makes everyone to be what he calls self, and thereby distinguishes himself from all other thinking things, in this alone consists personal identity." Is this a good argument?

2. Locke seems to emphasize a first-person, subjective perspective on personal identity—"being the same consciousness that makes a man be himself to himself"—rather than a third-person or objective perspective. Is this the right approach to personal identity? Are we experts on what makes us us?

3. Locke recognizes that it is possible for humans to "lose themselves," and cease to be the person they once were. Do you agree with this idea? Why or why not? Are there circumstances in which someone can become a different person?

4. How would Locke respond to the phenomenon of "false memories," that is, memories that are influenced by external pressures? Would he suggest that a person who misremembers their past experiences is identical with their past self? Why or why not?

5. Locke's theory entails that a person who cannot remember committing a crime while drunk should not be held responsible, because "they" did not really perform the criminal acts. Locke suggests that the law punishes people for acts committed while drunk simply because it is difficult to determine when people are lying about their memories. Do you agree with Locke's position in this issue? Why or why not?

6. You most probably remember nothing from age one. Does that mean that the one-year-old was not you? Suppose you remember nothing that happened to you ten days ago. But nine days ago, you remembered what had happened to you ten days ago; and eight days ago you remembered experiences from nine days ago, and so on up to today. Would that make you the same person you were ten days ago, according to Locke?

7. Thomas Reid argued that Locke mistakes the evidence we have for the existence of a stable personal identity—memory—with personal identity itself.§ Memory, Reid claims, is the testimony of the self, but not the cause of the self. Analyze this claim. To what extent might Reid's revision of

---

* Law courts
† The Last Judgment, or Judgment Day, at the Second Coming of Christ.
‡ Judgment, reward or punishment.
§ Thomas Reid, "Of Mr. Locke's Account of Our Personal Identity," in *Essays on the Intellectual Powers of Man* (1785).

Locke's theory eradicate the "strange" suppositions that Locke's ideas necessitate? How would Locke respond to Reid's objection?

8. David Hume suggests that we never actually experience a "self." Instead, we only ever encounter a flow of changing sensations. The self, he argues, is nothing more than a cluster of perceptions. How might Locke answer Hume? Which view do you find more persuasive? Why?

BERNARD WILLIAMS

The Self and the Future

Who Was Bernard Williams?

His obituary in the London *Times* (14 June 2003) called Sir Bernard Williams "the most brilliant and most important British moral philosopher of his time," remarking that his work "effortlessly spanned the entire discipline of philosophy." Born in 1929 in Essex, England, Williams turned to philosophy as a part of his education in Classics at Oxford. After serving as an RAF pilot in the early-1950s, he taught at Oxford, then at University College London, Bedford College, and, from 1967 until 1988, Cambridge. While at Cambridge, Williams participated in several governmental commissions, including the 1979 Committee on Obscenity and Censorship, in which he recommended against prohibiting supposed "obscene" texts that caused no discernible harm. Unhappy with Thatcherite educational policy, he moved in 1987 to UC Berkeley, but returned in 1990 to Oxford following Margaret Thatcher's resignation. The author of numerous influential books of philosophy, including *Morality: An Introduction to Ethics* (1972), *Shame and Necessity* (1993), and *Truth and Truthfulness* (2002), Williams was knighted in 1999 and died in 2003.

What Is the Structure of This Reading?

Williams begins by laying out a simple thought experiment. Suppose that, through some sort of undescribed process, person A and person B are changed such that after the process their personalities and memories seem to have been swapped. That is, the body that originally belonged to person A now has the memories and behavior that originally belonged to person B, and vice versa.

On first analysis, Williams claims, we might be inclined to say that the two people have changed bodies. That is, we might say that the person now occupying body A is in fact now "person B" and that the person occupying body B is in fact now "person A." Under this interpretation, the thought experiment provides evidence for the claim that personal identity is a mental trait associated with memory and other psychological attributes; wherever your memory goes, so do you. Indeed, John Locke made this argument using a similar thought experiment over two centuries earlier, discussing an imagined case in which a prince's memories are transferred into the body of a cobbler (see the Locke reading earlier in this chapter). Williams then offers a further twist on the experiment. Suppose the same procedure will take place, but afterward one person will be treated pleasantly and the other will be tortured. If asked their preference prior to the experiment, person A would probably desire for body B to receive the pleasant treatment, which again supports the conclusion that personal identity is ensconced within one's memories, not one's body.

However, Williams then makes further adjustments to the thought experiment, running through a number of other variations that may pull us toward the contrary position. Suppose there is no person B at all, but that you are in person A's shoes and you are told that your body will soon be tortured. However, you are also told that your memory will be erased beforehand. In this scenario, Williams argues, you *would* have good reason to fear the torture, and if anything the knowledge that your memory will be erased beforehand only compounds that fear. And yet, if personal identity is just the continuity of memory, then you shouldn't have any reason to fear the torture, as the tortured individual would no longer share your memory and so cannot *be* you. If Williams is correct in saying that you have reason to fear the future torture in this new scenario, this would seem to show that in an important sense "you" are the person inhabiting your body, regardless of whether your memory persists.

This new scenario seems to pull us toward the conclusion that the "self" is the body in an important sense, which is quite opposite our earlier interpretation of the original A-and-B scenario. Williams then offers a series of intermediate scenarios that further test our intuitions. He suggests that these complexities should caution us against uncritically accepting overly "neat" solutions to problems of personal identity.

The Self and the Future*

Suppose that there were some process to which two persons, *A* and *B*, could be subjected as a result of which they might be said—question-beggingly†— to have *exchanged bodies*. That is to say—less question-beggingly—there is a certain human body which is such that when previously we were confronted with it, we were confronted with person *A*, certain utterances coming from it were expressive of memories of the past experiences of *A*, certain movements of it partly constituted the actions of *A* and were taken as expressive of the character of *A*, and so forth; but now, after the process is completed, utterances coming from this body are expressive of what seem to be just those memories which previously we identified as memories of the past experiences of *B*, its movements partly constitute actions expressive of the character of *B*, and so forth; and conversely with the other body.

There are certain important philosophical limitations on how such imaginary cases are to be constructed, and how they are to be taken when constructed in various ways. I shall mention two principal limitations, not in order to pursue them further here, but precisely in order to get them out of the way.

There are certain limitations, particularly with regard to character and mannerisms, to our ability to imagine such cases even in the most restricted sense of our being disposed to take the later performances of that body which was previously *A*'s as expressive of *B*'s character; if the previous *A* and *B* were extremely unlike one another both physically and psychologically, and if, say, in addition, they were of different sex, there might be grave difficulties in reading *B*'s dispositions in any possible performances of *A*'s body. Let us forget this, and for the present purpose just take *A* and *B* as being sufficiently alike (however alike that has to be) for the difficulty not to arise; after the experiment, persons familiar with *A* and *B* are just *overwhelmingly struck* by the *B*-ish character of the doings associated

with what was previously *A*'s body, and conversely. Thus the feat of imagining an exchange of bodies is supposed possible in the most restricted sense. But now there is a further limitation which has to be overcome if the feat is to be not merely possible in the most restricted sense but also is to have an outcome which, on serious reflection, we are prepared to describe as *A* and *B* having changed bodies—that is, an outcome where, confronted with what was previously *A*'s body, we are prepared seriously to say that we are now confronted with *B*.

It would seem a necessary condition of so doing that the utterances coming from that body be taken as genuinely expressive of memories of *B*'s past. But memory is a causal notion; and as we actually use it, it seems a necessary condition on *x*'s present knowledge of *x*'s earlier experiences constituting memory of those experiences that the causal chain linking the experiences and the knowledge should not run outside *x*'s body. Hence if utterances coming from a given body are to be taken as expressive of memories of the experiences of *B*, there should be some suitable causal link between the appropriate state of that body and the original happening of those experiences to *B*. One radical way of securing that condition in the imagined exchange case is to suppose, with Shoemaker,‡ that the brains of *A* and of *B* are transposed. We may not need so radical a condition. Thus suppose it were possible to extract information from a man's brain and store it in a device while his brain was repaired, or even renewed, the information then being replaced: it would seem exaggerated to insist that the resultant man could not possibly have the memories he had before the operation. With regard to our knowledge of our own past, we draw distinctions between merely recalling, being reminded, and learning again, and those distinctions correspond (roughly) to distinctions between no new input, partial new input, and total new input with

---

* Bernard Williams, "The Self and the Future," *The Philosophical Review* 79, 2 (1970): 161–80.

† "Begging the question" is a logical fallacy or error in reasoning, in which the conclusion of an argument is included as an assumption within one of the argument's premises.

‡ Sydney Shoemaker proposed a series of thought experiments about personal identity that involved cases of brain transplantation. See, for example, Sydney Shoemaker, "Personal Identity: A Materialist's Account," *Personal Identity*, ed. Sydney Shoemaker and Richard Swinburne (Blackwell, 1984).

regard to the information in question; and it seems clear that the information-parking case just imagined would not count as new input in the sense necessary and sufficient for "learning again." Hence we can imagine the case we are concerned with in terms of information extracted into such devices from A's and B's brains and replaced in the other brain; this is the sort of model which, I think not unfairly for the present argument, I shall have in mind.

We imagine the following. The process considered above exists; two persons can enter some machine, let us say, and emerge changed in the appropriate ways. If A and B are the persons who enter, let us call the persons who emerge the *A-body-person* and the *B-body-person*: the A-body-person is that person (whoever it is) with whom I am confronted when, after the experiment, I am confronted with that body which previously was A's body—that is to say, that person who would naturally be taken for A by someone who just saw this person, was familiar with A's appearance before the experiment, and did not know about the happening of the experiment. A non-question-begging description of the experiment will leave it open which (if either) of the persons A and B the A-body-person is; the description of the experiment as persons "changing bodies" of course implies that the A-body-person is actually B.

We take two persons A and B who are going to have the process carried out on them. (We can suppose, rather hazily, that they are willing for this to happen; to investigate at all closely at this stage why they might be willing or unwilling, what they would fear, and so forth, would anticipate some later issues.) We further announce that one of the two resultant persons, the A-body-person and the B-body-person, is going after the experiment to be given $100,000, while the other is going to be tortured. We then ask each A and B to choose which treatment should be dealt out to which of the persons who will emerge from the experiment, the choice to be made (if it can be) on selfish grounds.

Suppose that A chooses that the B-body-person should get the pleasant treatment and the A-body-person the unpleasant treatment; and B chooses conversely (this might indicate that they thought that "changing bodies" was indeed a good description of the outcome). The experimenter cannot act in accordance with both these sets of preferences, those expressed by A and those expressed by B. Hence there is one clear sense in which A and B cannot both get what

they want: namely, that if the experimenter, before the experiment, announces to A and B that he intends to carry out the alternative (for example), of treating the B-body-person unpleasantly and the A-body-person pleasantly—then A can say rightly, "That's not the outcome I chose to happen," and B can say rightly, "That's just the outcome I chose to happen." So, evidently, A and B before the experiment can each come to know either that the outcome he chose will be that which will happen, or that the one he chose will not happen, and in that sense they can get or fail to get what they wanted. But is it also true that when the experimenter proceeds *after* the experiment to act in accordance with one of the preferences and not the other, then one of A and B will have got what he wanted, and the other not?

There seems very good ground for saying so. For suppose the experimenter, having elicited A's and B's preference, says nothing to A and B about what he will do; conducts the experiment; and then, for example, gives the unpleasant treatment to the B-body-person and the pleasant treatment to the A-body-person. Then the B-body-person will not only complain of the unpleasant treatment as such, but will complain (since he has A's memories) that that was not the outcome he chose, since he chose that the B-body-person should be well treated; and since A made his choice in selfish spirit, he may add that he precisely chose in that way because he did not want the unpleasant things to happen to *him*. The A-body-person meanwhile will express satisfaction both at the receipt of the $100,000, and also at the fact that the experimenter has chosen to act in the way that he, B, so wisely chose. These facts make a strong case for saying that the experimenter has brought it about that B did in the outcome get what he wanted and A did not. It is therefore a strong case for saying that the B-body-person really is A, and the A-body-person really is B; and therefore for saying that the process of the experiment really is that of changing bodies. For the same reasons it would seem that A and B in our example really did choose wisely, and that it was A's bad luck that the choice he correctly made was not carried out, B's good luck that the choice he correctly made was carried out. This seems to show that to care about what happens to me in the future is not necessarily to care about what happens to *this* body (the one I now have); and this in turn might be taken to show that in some sense of

Descartes's obscure phrase, I and my body are "really distinct"* (though, of course, nothing in these considerations could support the idea that I could exist without a body at all).

These suggestions seem to be reinforced if we consider the cases where *A* and *B* make other choices with regard to the experiment. Suppose that *A* chooses that the *A*-body-person should get the money, and the *B*-body-person get the pain, and *B* chooses conversely. Here again there can be no outcome which matches the expressed preferences of both of them: they cannot both get what they want. The experimenter announces, before the experiment, that the *A*-body-person will in fact get the money, and the *B*-body-person will get the pain. So *A* at this stage gets what he wants (the announced outcome matches his expressed preference). After the experiment, the distribution is carried out as announced. Both the *A*-body-person and the *B*-body-person will have to agree that what is happening is in accordance with the preference that *A* originally expressed. The *B*-body-person will naturally express this acknowledgement (since he has *A*'s memories) by saying that this is the distribution he chose; he will recall, among other things, the experimenter announcing this outcome, his approving it as what he chose, and so forth. However, he (the *B*-body-person) certainly does not like what is now happening to him, and would much prefer to be receiving what the *A*-body-person is receiving—namely, $100,000. The *A*-body-person will on the other hand recall choosing an outcome other than this one, but will reckon it good luck that the experimenter did not do what he recalls choosing. It looks, then, as though the *A*-body-person has gotten what he wanted, but not what he chose, while the *B*-body-person has gotten what he chose, but not what he wanted. So once more it looks as though they are, respectively, *B* and *A*; and that in this case the original choices of both *A* and *B* were unwise.

Suppose, lastly, that in the original choice *A* takes the line of the first case and *B* of the second: that is, *A* chooses that the *B*-body-person should get the money and the *A*-body-person the pain, and *B* chooses

exactly the same thing. In this case, the experimenter would seem to be in the happy situation of giving both persons what they want—or at least, like God, what they have chosen. In this case, the *B*-body-person likes what he is receiving, recalls choosing it, and congratulates himself on the wisdom of (as he puts it) his choice; while the *A*-body-person does not like what he is receiving, recalls choosing it, and is forced to acknowledge that (as he puts it) his choice was unwise. So once more we seem to get results to support the suggestions drawn from the first case.

Let us now consider the question, not of *A* and *B* choosing certain outcomes to take place after the experiment, but of their willingness to engage in the experiment at all. If they were initially inclined to accept the description of the experiment as "changing bodies" then one thing that would interest them would be the character of the other person's body. In this respect also what would happen after the experiment would seem to suggest that "changing bodies" was a good description of the experiment. If *A* and *B* agreed to the experiment, being each not displeased with the appearance, physique, and so forth of the other person's body; after the experiment the *B*-body-person might well be found saying such things as: "When I agreed to this experiment, I thought that *B*'s face was quite attractive, but now I look at it in the mirror, I am not so sure"; or the *A*-body-person might say "When I agreed to this experiment I did not know that *A* had a wooden leg; but now, after it is over, I find that I have this wooden leg, and I want the experiment reversed." It is possible that he might say further that he finds the leg very uncomfortable, and that the *B*-body-person should say, for instance, that he recalls that he found it very uncomfortable at first, but one gets used to it: but perhaps one would need to know more than at least I do about the physiology of habituation to artificial limbs to know whether the *A*-body-person would find the leg uncomfortable: that body, after all, has had the leg on it for some time. But apart from this sort of detail, the general line of the outcome regarded from this point of view seems to confirm our previous conclusions about the experiment.

---

* In his *Meditations on First Philosophy*, René Descartes grounds several conclusions, including the distinction between mind and body, on claims that they are "clearly and distinctly" different or that their separateness is "really distinct." See the reading from Descartes in the Epistemology chapter for more information.

Now let us suppose that when the experiment is proposed (in non-question-begging terms) *A* and *B* think rather of their psychological advantages and disadvantages. *A*'s thoughts turn primarily to certain sorts of anxiety to which he is very prone, while *B* is concerned with the frightful memories he has of past experiences which still distress him. They each hope that the experiment will in some way result in their being able to get away from these things. They may even have been impressed by philosophical arguments to the effect that bodily continuity is at least a necessary condition of personal identity: *A*, for example, reasons that, granted the experiment comes off, then the person who is bodily continuous with him will not have this anxiety, while the other person will no doubt have some anxiety—perhaps in some sense his anxiety—and at least that person will not be he. The experiment is performed and the experimenter (to whom *A* and *B* previously revealed privately their several difficulties and hopes) asks the *A*-body-person whether he has gotten rid of his anxiety. This person presumably replies that he does not know what the man is talking about; he never had such anxiety, but he did have some very disagreeable memories, and recalls engaging in the experiment to get rid of them, and is disappointed to discover that he still has them. The *B*-body-person will react in a similar way to questions about his painful memories, pointing out that he still has his anxiety. These results seem to confirm still further the description of the experiment as "changing bodies." And all the results suggest that the only rational thing to do, confronted with such an experiment, would be to identity oneself with one's memories, and so forth, and not with one's body. The philosophical arguments designed to show that bodily continuity was at least a necessary condition of personal identity would seem to be just mistaken.

Let us now consider something apparently different. Someone in whose power I am tells me that I am going to be tortured tomorrow. I am frightened, and look forward to tomorrow in great apprehension. He adds that when the time comes, I shall not remember being told that this was going to happen to me, since shortly before the torture something else will be done to me which will make me forget the announcement. This certainly will not cheer me up, since I know perfectly well that I can forget things, and that there is such a thing as indeed being tortured unexpectedly because I had forgotten or been made to forget a prediction of the torture: that will still be a torture which, so long as I do know about the prediction, I look forward to in fear. He then adds that my forgetting the announcement will be only part of a larger process: when the moment of torture comes, I shall not remember any of the things I am now in a position to remember. This does not cheer me up, either, since I can readily conceive of being involved in an accident, for instance, as a result of which I wake up in a completely amnesiac state and also in great pain; that could certainly happen to me, I should not like it to happen to me, nor to know that it was going to happen to me. He now further adds that at the moment of torture I shall not only not remember the things I am now in a position to remember, but will have a different set of impressions of my past, quite different from the memories I now have. I do not think that this would cheer me up, either. For I can at least conceive the possibility, if not the concrete reality, of going completely mad, and thinking perhaps that I am George IV* or somebody; and being told that something like that was going to happen to me would have no tendency to reduce the terror of being told authoritatively that I was going to be tortured, but would merely compound the horror. Nor do I see why I should be put into any better frame of mind by the person in charge adding lastly that the impressions of my past with which I shall be equipped on the eve of torture will exactly fit the past of another person now living, and that indeed I shall acquire these impressions by (for instance) information now in his brain being copied into mine. Fear, surely, would still be the proper reaction: and not because one did not know what was going to happen, but because in one vital respect at least one did know what was going to happen—torture, which one can indeed expect to happen to oneself, and to be preceded by certain mental derangements as well.

If this is right, the whole question seems now to be totally mysterious. For what we have just been

---

* George IV (1762–1830) was the king of Britain, Ireland, and Hanover from 1820 until 1830. He was known for his opulent lifestyle, gluttony, and preoccupation with fashion and the arts.

through is of course merely one side, differently represented, of the transaction which we considered before; and it represents it as a perfectly hateful prospect, while the previous considerations represented it as something one should rationally, perhaps even cheerfully, choose out of the options there presented. It is differently presented, of course, and in two notable respects; but when we look at these two differences of presentation, can we really convince ourselves that the second presentation is wrong or misleading, thus leaving the road open to the first version which at the time seemed so convincing? Surely not.

The first difference is that in the second version the torture is throughout represented as going to happen to *me*: "you," the man in charge persistently says. Thus he is not very neutral. But should he have been neutral? Or, to put it another way, does his use of the second person have a merely emotional and rhetorical effect on me, making me afraid when further reflection would have shown that I had no reason to be? It is certainly not obviously so. The problem just is that through every step of his predictions I seem to be able to follow him successfully. And if I reflect on whether what he has said gives me grounds for fearing that I shall be tortured, I could consider that behind my fears lies some principle such as this: that my undergoing physical pain in the future is not excluded by any psychological state I may be in at the time, with the platitudinous* exception of those psychological states which in themselves exclude experiencing pain, notably (if it is a psychological state) unconsciousness. In particular, what impressions I have about the past will not have any effect on whether I undergo the pain or not. This principle seems sound enough.

It is an important fact that not everything I would, as things are, regard as an evil would be something that I should rationally fear as an evil if it were predicted that it would happen to me in the future and also predicted that I should undergo significant psychological changes in the meantime. For the fact that I regard that happening, things being as they are, as an evil can be dependent on factors of belief or character which might themselves be modified by the psychological changes in question. Thus if I am appallingly subject to acrophobia,† and am told that I shall find myself on top of a steep mountain in the near future, I shall to that extent be afraid; but if I am told that I shall be psychologically changed in the meantime in such a way as to rid me of my acrophobia (and as with the other prediction, I believe it), then I have no reason to be afraid of the predicted happening, or at least not the same reason. Again, I might look forward to meeting a certain person again with either alarm or excitement because of my memories of our past relations. In some part, these memories operate in connection with my emotion, not only on the present time, but projectively forward: for it is to a meeting itself affected by the presence of those memories that I look forward. If I am convinced that when the time comes I shall not have those memories, then I shall not have just the same reasons as before for looking forward to that meeting with the one emotion or the other. (Spiritualism, incidentally, appears to involve the belief that I have just the same reasons for a given attitude toward encountering people again after I am dead, as I did before: with the one modification that I can be sure it will all be very nice.)

Physical pain, however, the example which for simplicity (and not for any obsessional reason) I have taken, is absolutely minimally dependent on character or belief. No amount of change in my character or my beliefs would seem to affect substantially the nastiness of tortures applied to me; correspondingly, no degree of predicted change in my character and beliefs can unseat the fear of torture which, together with those changes, is predicted for me.

I am not at all suggesting that the *only* basis, or indeed the only rational basis, for fear in the face of these various predictions is how things will be relative to my psychological state in the eventual outcome. I am merely pointing out that this is one component; it is not the only one. For certainly one will fear and otherwise reject the changes themselves, or in very many cases one would. Thus one of the old paradoxes of hedonistic utilitarianism;‡ if one had assurances that undergoing certain operations and being attached

---

* Banal, uninteresting.
† Fear of heights.
‡ A moral theory that advocates acting in such a way as to maximize pleasure and minimize pain.

to a machine would provide one for the rest of one's existence with an unending sequence of delicious and varied experiences, one might very well reject the option, and react with fear if someone proposed to apply it compulsorily; and that fear and horror would seem appropriate reactions in the second case may help to discredit the interpretation (if anyone has the nerve to propose it) that one's reason for rejecting the option voluntarily would be a consciousness of duties to others which one in one's hedonic state would leave undone. The prospect of contented madness or vegetableness is found by many (not perhaps by all) appalling in ways which are obviously not a function of how things would then be for them, for things would then be for them not appalling. In the case we are at present discussing, these sorts of considerations seem merely to make it clearer that the predictions of the man in charge provide a double ground of horror: at the prospect of torture, and at the prospect of the change in character and in impressions of the past that will precede it. And certainly, to repeat what has already been said, the prospect of the second certainly seems to provide no ground for rejecting or not fearing the prospect of the first.

I said that there were two notable differences between the second presentation of our situation and the first. The first difference, which we have just said something about, was that the man predicted the torture for *me*, a psychologically very changed "me." We have yet to find a reason for saying that he should not have done this, or that I really should be unable to follow him if he does; I seem to be able to follow him only too well. The second difference is that in this presentation he does not mention the other man, except in the somewhat incidental role of being the provenance of the impressions of the past I end up with. He does not mention him at all as someone who will end up with impressions of the past derived from me (and, incidentally, with $100,000 as well—a consideration which, in the frame of mind appropriate to this version, will merely make me jealous).

But why *should* he mention this man and what is going to happen to him? My selfish concern is to be told what is going to happen to me, and now I know: torture, preceded by changes of character, brain operations, changes in impressions of the past. The knowledge that one other person, or none, or many will be similarly mistreated may affect me in other ways, of sympathy, greater horror at the power of this tyrant, and so forth; but surely it cannot affect my expectations of torture? But—someone will say—this is to leave out exactly the feature which, as the first presentation of the case showed, makes all the difference: for it is to leave out the person who, as the first presentation showed, will be you. It is to leave out not merely a feature which should fundamentally affect your fears, it is to leave out the very person for whom you are fearful. So of course, the objector will say, this makes all the difference.

But can it? Consider the following series of cases. In each case we are to suppose that after what is described, A is, as before, to be tortured; we are also to suppose the person A is informed beforehand that just these things followed by the torture will happen to him:

i. A is subjected to an operation which produces total amnesia;
ii. amnesia is produced in A, and other interference leads to certain changes in his character;
iii. changes in his character are produced, and at the same time certain illusory "memory" beliefs are induced in him; these are of a quite fictitious kind and do not fit the life of any actual person;
iv. the same as (*iii*), except that both the character traits and the "memory" impressions are designed to be appropriate to another actual person, B;
v. the same as (*iv*), except that the result is produced by putting the information into A from the brain of B, by a method which leaves B the same as he was before;
vi. the same happens to A as in (*v*), but B is not left the same, since a similar operation is conducted in the reverse direction.

I take it that no one is going to dispute that A has reasons, and fairly straightforward reasons, for fear of pain when the prospect is that of situation (*i*); there seems no conceivable reason why this should not extend to situation (*ii*), and the situation (*iii*) can surely introduce no difference of principle—it just seems a situation which for more than one reason we should have grounds for fearing, as suggested above. Situation (*iv*) at least introduces the person B, who was the focus of the objection we are now discussing. But it does not seem to introduce him in any way which makes a material difference; if I can expect pain through a transformation which involves new "memory"-impressions, it would seem a purely external fact, relative to that, that the "memory"-impressions had a model. Nor, in (*iv*), do we satisfy a causal condition which I mentioned at the beginning for the "memories" actually being memories; though notice that if the job were done thoroughly, I might well be able to elicit from the *A*-body-person the kinds of remarks about his previous expectations of the experiment—remarks appropriate to the original *B*—which so impressed us in the first version of the story. I shall have a similar assurance of this being so in situation (*v*), where, moreover, a plausible application of the causal condition is available.

But two things are to be noticed about this situation. First, if we concentrate on *A* and the *A*-body-person, we do not seem to have added anything which from the point of view of his fears makes any material difference; just as, in the move from (*iii*) to (*iv*), it made no relevant difference that the new "memory"-impressions which precede the pain had, as it happened, a model, so in the move from (*iv*) to (*v*) all we have added is that they have a model which is also their cause: and it is still difficult to see why that, to him looking forward, could possibly make the difference between expecting pain and not expecting pain. To illustrate that point from the case of character: if *A* is capable of expecting pain, he is capable of expecting pain preceded by a change in his dispositions—and to that expectation it can make no difference, whether that change in his dispositions is modeled on, or indeed indirectly caused by, the dispositions of some other person. If his fears can, as it were, reach through the change, it seems a mere trimming how the change is in fact induced. The second point about situation (*v*) is that if the crucial question for *A*'s fears with regard to what befalls the *A*-body-person is whether the *A*-body-person is or is not the person *B*,[1] then that condition has not yet been satisfied in situation (*v*): for there we have an undisputed *B* in addition to the *A*-body-person, and certainly those two are not the same person.

But in situation (*vi*), we seemed to think, that is finally what he is. But if *A*'s original fears could reach through the expected changes in (*v*), as they did in (*iv*) and (*iii*), then certainly they can reach through in (*vi*). Indeed, from the point of view of *A*'s expectations and

fears, there is less difference between (*vi*) and (*v*) than there is between (*v*) and (*iv*) or between (*iv*) and (*iii*). In those transitions, there were at least differences—though we could not see that they were really relevant differences—in the content and cause of what happened to him; in the present case there is absolutely no difference at all in what happens to him, the only difference being in what happens to someone else. If he can fear pain when (*v*) is predicted, why should he cease to when (*vi*) is?

I can see only one way of relevantly laying great weight on the transition from (*v*) to (*vi*); and this involves a considerable difficulty. This is to deny that, as I put it, the transition from (*v*) to (*vi*) involves merely the addition of something happening to *somebody else*; what rather it does, it will be said, is to involve the reintroduction of *A* himself, as the *B*-body-person; since he has reappeared in this form, it is for this person, and not for the unfortunate *A*-body-person, that *A* will have his expectations. This is to reassert, in effect, the viewpoint emphasized in our first presentation of the experiment. But this surely has the consequence that *A* should not have fears for the *A*-body-person who appeared in situation (*v*). For by the present argument, the *A*-body-person in (*vi*) is not *A*; the *B*-body-person is. But the *A*-body-person in (*v*) is, in character, history, everything, exactly the same as the *A*-body-person in (*vi*); so if the latter is not *A*, then neither is the former. (It is this point, no doubt, that encourages one to speak of the difference that goes with (*vi*) as being, on the present view, the reintroduction of *A*.) But no one else in (*v*) has any better claim to be *A*. So in (*v*), it seems, *A* just does not exist. This would certainly explain why *A* should have no fears for the state of things in (*v*)—though he might well have fears for the path to it. But it rather looked earlier as though he could well have fears for the state of things in (*v*). Let us grant, however, that that was an illusion, and that *A* really does not exist in (*v*); then does he exist in (*iv*), (*iii*), (*ii*), or (*i*)? It seems very difficult to deny it for (*i*) and (*ii*); are we perhaps to draw the line between (*iii*) and (*iv*)?

Here someone will say: you must not insist on drawing a line—borderline cases are borderline cases, and you must not push our concepts beyond their limits. But this well-known piece of advice, sensible as it is in many cases, seems in the present case to involve an extraordinary difficulty. It may intellectually comfort observers of *A*'s situation; but what is *A* supposed to make of it? To be told that a future situation is a borderline one for its being myself that is hurt, that it is conceptually undecidable whether it will be me or not, is something which, it seems, I can do nothing with; because, in particular, it seems to have no comprehensible representation in my expectations and the emotions that go with them.

If I expect that a certain situation, *S*, will come about in the future, there is of course a wide range of emotions and concerns, directed on *S*, which I may experience now in relation to my expectation. Unless I am exceptionally egoistic, it is not a condition on my being concerned in relation to this expectation, that I myself will be involved in *S*—where my being "involved" in *S* means that I figure in *S* as someone doing something at that time or having something done to me, or, again, that will have consequences affecting me at that or some subsequent time. There are some emotions, however, which I will feel only if I will be involved in *S*, and fear is an obvious example.

Now the description of *S* under which it figures in my expectations will necessarily be, in various ways, indeterminate; and one way in which it may be indeterminate is that it leave open whether I shall be involved in *S* or not. Thus I may have good reason to expect that one out of us five is going to get hurt, but no reason to expect it to be me rather than one of the others. My present emotions will be correspondingly affected by this indeterminacy. Thus, sticking to the egoistic concern involved in fear, I shall presumably be somewhat more cheerful than if I knew it was going to be me, somewhat less cheerful than if I had been left out altogether. Fear will be mixed with, and qualified by, apprehension; and so forth. These emotions revolve around the thought of the eventual determination of the indeterminacy; moments of straight fear focus on its really turning out to be me, of hope on its turning out not to be me. All the emotions are related to the coming about of what I expect: and what I expect in such a case just cannot come about save by coming about in one of the ways or another.

There are other ways in which indeterminate expectations can be related to fear. Thus I may expect

(perhaps neurotically*) that something nasty is going to happen to me, indeed expect that when it happens it will take some determinate form, but have no range, or no closed range, of candidates for the determinate form to rehearse in my present thought. Different from this would be the fear of something radically indeterminate—the fear (one might say) of a nameless horror. If somebody had such a fear, one could even say that he had, in a sense, a perfectly determinate expectation: if what he expects indeed comes about, there will be nothing more determinate to be said about it after the event than was said in the expectation. Both these cases of course are cases of *fear* because one thing that is fixed amid the indeterminacy is the belief that it is to me to which the things will happen.

Central to the expectation of *S* is the thought of what it will be like when it happens—thought which may be indeterminate, range over alternatives, and so forth. When *S* involves me, there can be the possibility of a special form of such thought: the thought of how it will be for me, the imaginative projection of myself as participant in *S*.[2]

I do not have to think about *S* in this way, when it involves me; but I may be able to. (It might be suggested that this possibility was even mirrored in the language, in the distinction between "expecting to be hurt" and "expecting that I shall be hurt"; but I am very doubtful about this point, which is in any case of no importance.)

Suppose now that there is an *S* with regard to which it is for conceptual reasons undecidable whether it involves me or not, as is proposed for the experimental situation by the line we are discussing. It is important that the expectation of *S* is not *indeterminate* in any of the ways we have just been considering. It is not like the nameless horror, since the fixed point of that case was that it was going to happen to the subject, and that made his state unequivocally fear. Nor is it like the expectation of the man who expects one of the five to be hurt; his fear was indeed equivocal, but its focus, and that of the expectation, was that when *S* came about, it would certainly come about in one way or the other. In the present case, fear (of the torture, that is to say, not of the initial experiment) seems

---

* Neuroticism is a personality trait that involves responding negatively to perceived stressors, and treating minor problems as major catastrophes.

neither appropriate, nor inappropriate, nor appropriately equivocal. Relatedly, the subject has an incurable difficulty about how he may think about *S*. If he engages in projective imaginative thinking (about how it will be for him), he implicitly answers the necessarily unanswerable question; if he thinks that he cannot engage in such thinking, it looks very much as if he also answers it, though in the opposite direction. Perhaps he must just refrain from such thinking; but is he just refraining from it, if it is incurably undecidable whether he can or cannot engage in it?

It may be said that all that these considerations can show is that fear, at any rate, does not get its proper footing in this case; but that there could be some other, more ambivalent, form of concern which would indeed be appropriate to this particular expectation, the expectation of the conceptually undecidable situation. There are, perhaps, analogous feelings that actually occur in actual situations. Thus material objects do occasionally undergo puzzling transformations which leave a conceptual shadow over their identity. Suppose I were sentimentally attached to an object to which this sort of thing then happened; then it might be that I could neither feel about it quite as I did originally, nor be totally indifferent to it, but would have some other and rather ambivalent feeling toward it. Similarly, it may be said, toward the prospective sufferer of pain, my identity relations with whom are conceptually shadowed, I can feel neither as I would if he were certainly me, nor as I would if he were certainly not, but rather some such ambivalent concern.

But this analogy does little to remove the most baffling aspect of the present case—an aspect which has already turned up in what was said about the subject's difficulty in thinking either projectively or non-projectively about the situation. For to regard the prospective pain-sufferer *just* like the transmogrified* object of sentiment, and to conceive of my ambivalent distress about his future pain as just like ambivalent distress about some future damage to such an object, is of course to leave him and me clearly distinct

from one another, and thus to displace the conceptual shadow from its proper place. I have to get nearer to him than that. But is there any nearer that I can get to him without expecting his pain? If there is, the analogy has not shown us it. We can certainly not get nearer by expecting, as it were, *ambivalent* pain; there is no place at all for that. There seems to be an obstinate bafflement to mirroring in my expectations a situation in which it is conceptually undecidable whether I occur.

The bafflement seems, moreover, to turn to plain absurdity if we move from conceptual undecidability to its close friend and neighbor, conventionalist decision.[†] This comes out if we consider another description, overtly conventionalist, of the series of cases which occasioned the present discussion. This description would reject a point I relied on in an earlier argument—namely, that if we deny that the *A*-body-person in (*vi*) is *A* (because the *B*-body-person is), then we must deny that the *A*-body-person in (*v*) is *A*, since they are exactly the same. "No," it may be said, "this is just to assume that we say the same in different sorts of situation. No doubt when we have the very good candidate for being *A*—namely, the *B*-body-person—we call him *A*; but this does not mean that we should not call the *A*-body-person *A* in that other situation when we have no better candidate around. Different situations call for different descriptions." This line of talk is the sort of thing indeed appropriate to lawyers deciding the ownership of some property which has undergone some bewildering set of transformations; they just have to decide, and in each situation, let us suppose, it has got to go to somebody, on as reasonable grounds as the facts and the law admit. But as a line to deal with a person's fears or expectations about his own future, it seems to have no sense at all. If *A*'s fears can extend to what will happen to the *A*-body-person in (*v*), I do not see how they can be rationally diverted from the fate of the exactly similar person in (*vi*) by his being told that someone would have a reason in the latter situation which he would not have in the former for deciding to call another person *A*.

---

* Changed into a different, fantastical shape.

† Conventionalism is the idea that philosophical claims and distinctions are decisions that we make, rather than determinations of objective truth. In this context, the idea is that, for the conventionalist, there is no independent truth on these questions of identity; rather, we can choose to describe these situations as we wish on practical grounds.

Thus, to sum up, it looks as though there are two presentations of the imagined experiment and the choice associated with it, each of which carries conviction, and which lead to contrary conclusions. The idea, moreover, that the situation after the experiment is conceptually undecidable in the relevant respect seems not to assist, but rather to increase, the puzzlement; while the idea (so often appealed to in these matters) that it is conventionally decidable is even worse. Following from all that, I am not in the least clear which option it would be wise to take if one were presented with them before the experiment. I find that rather disturbing.

Whatever the puzzlement, there is one feature of the arguments which have led to it which is worth picking out, since it runs counter to something which is, I think, often rather vaguely supposed. It is often recognized that there are "first-personal" and "third-personal" aspects of questions about persons, and that there are difficulties about the relations between them. It is also recognized that "mentalistic" considerations (as we may vaguely call them) and considerations of bodily continuity are involved in questions of personal identity (which is not to say that there are mentalistic and bodily criteria of personal identity). It is tempting to think that the two distinctions run in parallel: roughly, that a first-personal approach concentrates attention on mentalistic considerations, while a third-personal approach emphasizes considerations of bodily continuity. The present discussion is an illustration of exactly the opposite. The first argument, which led to the "mentalistic" conclusion that A and B would change bodies and that each person should identify himself with the destination of his memories and character, was an argument entirely conducted in third-personal terms. The second argument, which suggested the bodily continuity identification, concerned itself with the first-personal issue of what A could expect. That this is so seems to me (though I will not discuss it further here) of some significance.

I will end by suggesting one rather shaky way in which one might approach a resolution of the problem, using only the limited materials already available.

The apparently decisive arguments of the first presentation, which suggested that A should identify himself with the B-body-person, turned on the extreme neatness of the situation in satisfying, if any could, the description of "changing bodies." But this neatness is basically artificial; it is the product of the will of the experimenter to produce a situation which would naturally elicit, with minimum hesitation, that description. By the sorts of methods he employed, he could easily have left off earlier or gone on further. He could have stopped at situation (*v*), leaving B as he was; or he could have gone on and produced two persons each with A-like character and memories, as well as one or two with B-like characteristics. If he had done either of those, we should have been in yet greater difficulty about what to say; he just chose to make it as easy as possible for us to find something to say. Now if we had some model of ghostly persons in bodies, which were in some sense actually moved around by certain procedures, we could regard the neat experiment just as the *effective* experiment: the one method that really did result in the ghostly persons changing places without being destroyed, dispersed, or whatever. But we cannot seriously use such a model. The experimenter has not in the sense of that model *induced* a change of bodies; he has rather produced the one situation out of a range of equally possible situations which we should be most disposed to call a change of bodies. As against this, the principle that one's fears can extend to future pain whatever psychological changes precede it seems positively straightforward. Perhaps, indeed, it is not; but we need to be shown what is wrong with it. Until we are shown what is wrong with it, we should perhaps decide that if we were the person A then, if we were to decide selfishly, we should pass the pain to the B-body-person. It would be risky: that there is room for the notion of a *risk* here is itself a major feature of the problem. ∎

Suggestions for Critical Reflection

1. Consider the role of fear in Williams's inquiry. To what degree does he presume that fears about future experiences attest to the status of personal identity? Is this an effective way to assess these thought experiments?

2. Williams claims that "no one is going to dispute" that a person has reasons to fear future pain in a scenario where their memory will be completely erased prior to that pain. Is he right about this? Would it be irrational to argue otherwise?

3. Williams remarks that, "To be told that a future situation is a borderline one for its being myself that is hurt ... is something which, it seems, I can do nothing with." Is he correct to say that we would not be satisfied with an inconclusive solution to these issues of personal identity when we run the risk of future pain? Why or why not?

4. In the final paragraph of his article, Williams observes that his initial description of the body-swapping thought experiment, which suggested that personhood could skip between bodies by following one's memory, seemed at first glance to be "neat" and satisfying. But on further analysis, it is at best an oversimplification, and perhaps incorrect. Consider the appeal of "neat" answers to complex philosophical problems. Are you more likely to agree with a philosophical theory if it seems simple and satisfying? Why or why not?

Notes

1 This of course does not have to be the crucial question, but it seems one fair way of taking up the present objection.

2 For a more detailed treatment of issues related to this, see *Imagination and the Self*, British Academy (London, 1966); reprinted in P.F. Strawson (ed.), *Studies in Thought and Action* (Oxford, 1968).

DANIEL C. DENNETT

Where Am I?

Who Is Daniel Dennett?

Born in Boston in 1942, Daniel Clement Dennett spent his early childhood in Beirut, Lebanon, where his father was stationed as a secret agent in the OSS.* After his father died on a mission in 1947, Dennett returned to the United States. He began his post-secondary studies at Wesleyan University, then transferred to Harvard, where he attended courses taught by the celebrated philosopher W.V.O. Quine. At Quine's recommendation, Dennett pursued his graduate studies at Oxford, where he was supervised by Gilbert Ryle, a towering figure in Anglophone philosophy at the time. At the age of 23, Dennett received an Assistant Professorship at the University of California at Irvine, where he taught until 1971. Dennett then moved to Tufts University in Massachusetts, where he is now University Professor and Austin B. Fletcher Professor of Philosophy, and Director of the Center for Cognitive Studies.

Although his formal education was almost exclusively devoted to philosophy, Dennett has a strong bent for practical issues and problems and for finding out "how things work." He has described himself as "playing catch-up" since graduate school on the scientific areas most closely connected to his research, especially psychology, biology, and computer science.

What Is Dennett's Overall Philosophical Project?

One of the first thinkers to seriously consider the philosophical significance of artificial intelligence and cognitive science, Dennett believes that it is deeply incorrect to identify our self with a *res cogitans*, or "mental substance." It is possible, he claims, to perceive mind-like qualities in objects that cannot possibly contain mental "stuff." Through what he calls "the intentional stance," we can interpret non-thinking objects—such as computers—as though they were rational agents with motivations and beliefs.

The central plank of Dennett's theory of mental content is that, as he puts it, "brains are syntactic engines that can mimic the competence of semantic engines." By this he means that brains are complex, mechanical systems which follow the laws of physics and not the principles of rationality. However, Dennett suggests, evolution has 'designed' the human brain so that its mechanical (or "syntactic") processes closely resemble those of a system intelligently manipulating meaningful symbols (semantics). Meaning is something that brains—and thus human beings—seem to have only *from the outside*. Moreover, since this is, in Dennett's view, all there is to having mental content, any system which is complex enough to act as if it has beliefs or desires—such as a thermostat, a simple robot, or an ant—really does have those mental states in just the same way as a human being, though in a more rudimentary form.

Dennett's theory of consciousness is equally radical and is called the Multiple Drafts Model. He develops it as a foil to a more traditional model of consciousness, which he labels (after René Descartes) the "Cartesian Theater." According to this traditional picture, consciousness consists in a sort of metaphorical theater where all the data of consciousness 'come together' into a single experience at a particular time, which is 'observed' by the self. Dennett rejects nearly all the elements of the Cartesian theater: the idea of a self, a mind's eye, or a central place where all the pieces of a single conscious image come together.

Instead, he thinks of consciousness as the multiple, simultaneous processing of various different bits of data, distributed across the brain and even across time. For example, the processing of the visual information about my room as it was at 11:29 a.m. might be occurring a few moments later than the processing of the aural information about the room at that time, and will certainly take place

---

* The Office of Strategic Services, a wartime intelligence agency of the United States during World War II and predecessor of the CIA.

at a different location in my brain. Furthermore, there is no particular point at which this processing 'stops' and spills its results into consciousness—my perceptions of the state of my office at 11:29 are subject to constant adjustment and revision as they go on, and there is no particular threshold they cross to become conscious. Thus, according to Dennett, there just *is* no "mental image" in our minds when we are conscious and so, roughly, the traditional "problem of consciousness" is dissolved.

What Is the Structure of This Reading?

Dennett begins by providing a lengthy fictional introduction about being tasked by the government to carry out a secret mission, which sets the stage for a thought experiment about a human body operated remotely by a brain in a vat. Dennett describes a situation in which his brain is preserved in Texas, and responsible for electronically controlling his body in Oklahoma. Dennett's opening is noteworthy, not only for its creativity and comedy, but also for its personalization of a philosophical issue. The thought experiment in the text concerns not an abstract individual or token figure, but the author, Daniel C. Dennett himself.

Following his description of the fictional circumstances that led to the disconnection of his body and brain, Dennett raises his essay's central question: in a situation where a person's body is separated from—but still controlled by—their brain, "where" in space is that person? Dennett suggests that there are three possible answers to this question. The first is that "he" is located in his body. The second is that "he" is located in his brain. The third is that "he" is wherever his point of view is located—that is, "wherever he thinks he is." It may be possible, Dennett suggests, for a person to change where they are in space through acts of imagination.

Dennett imagines changes that might occur in his experience of the world as a result of the separation of brain and body. Via a discussion of his body being lost, and his brain being linked to a new body, Dennett then considers a series of possible complications that the ability to separate a person's brain and body would cause. For example, Dennett wonders whether it is possible for a person to be in two places at once, to exist as a disembodied self, to switch bodies while remaining the same person, to make a computer reproduction of a human brain, or for two persons to share the same identity.

Where Am I?[*]

Now that I've won my suit under the Freedom of Information Act,[†] I am at liberty to reveal for the first time a curious episode in my life that may be of interest not only to those engaged in research in the philosophy of mind, artificial intelligence, and neuroscience but also to the general public.

Several years ago I was approached by Pentagon[‡] officials who asked me to volunteer for a highly dangerous and secret mission. In collaboration with NASA and Howard Hughes,[§] the Department of

Defense was spending billions to develop a Supersonic Tunneling Underground Device, or STUD. It was supposed to tunnel through the earth's core at great speed and deliver a specially designed atomic warhead "right up the Red's[¶] missile silos," as one of the Pentagon brass put it.

The problem was that in an early test they had succeeded in lodging a warhead about a mile deep under Tulsa, Oklahoma, and they wanted me to retrieve it for them. "Why me?" I asked. Well, the mission

[*] Daniel C. Dennett, "Where Am I?" in *Brainstorms: Philosophical Essays on Mind and Psychology* (MIT Press, 1978). This talk was presented first at the Chapel Hill Colloquium, October 1976, and subsequently at MIT, in December 1976, and at the University of Alabama, in April 1978.

[†] An American law that allows ordinary citizens to access information from the government.

[‡] The headquarters of the United States Department of Defense.

[§] Hughes was a wealthy American businessperson and pilot well known for his eccentric behavior.

[¶] "Red" is a pejorative term for communist. In this context, it refers to the Soviet Union.

involved some pioneering applications of current brain research, and they had heard of my interest in brains and of course my Faustian* curiosity and great courage and so forth…. Well, how could I refuse? The difficulty that brought the Pentagon to my door was that the device I'd been asked to recover was fiercely radioactive, in a new way. According to monitoring instruments, something about the nature of the device and its complex interactions with pockets of material deep in the earth had produced radiation that could cause severe abnormalities in certain tissues of the brain. No way had been found to shield the brain from these deadly rays, which were apparently harmless to other tissues and organs of the body. So it had been decided that the person sent to recover the device should *leave his brain behind*. It would be kept in a safe place where it could execute its normal control functions by elaborate radio links. Would I submit to a surgical procedure that would completely remove my brain, which would then be placed in a life-support system at the Manned Spacecraft Center in Houston? Each input and output pathway, as it was severed, would be restored by a pair of microminiaturized radio transceivers, one attached precisely to the brain, the other to the nerve stumps in the empty cranium. No information would be lost, all the connectivity would be preserved. At first I was a bit reluctant. Would it really work? The Houston brain surgeons encouraged me. "Think of it," they said, "as a mere *stretching* of the nerves. If your brain were just moved over an *inch* in your skull, that would not alter or impair your mind. We're simply going to make the nerves indefinitely elastic by splicing radio links into them."

I was shown around the life-support lab in Houston and saw the sparkling new vat in which my brain would be placed, were I to agree. I met the large and brilliant support team of neurologists, hematologists, biophysicists, and electrical engineers, and after several days of discussions and demonstrations I agreed to give it a try. I was subjected to an enormous array of blood tests, brain scans, experiments, interviews, and the like. They took down my autobiography at great length, recorded tedious lists of my beliefs, hopes, fears, and tastes. They even listed my favorite stereo recordings and gave me a crash session of psychoanalysis.

The day for surgery arrived at last and of course I was anesthetized and remember nothing of the operation itself. When I came out of anesthesia, I opened my eyes, looked around, and asked the inevitable, the traditional, the lamentably hackneyed postoperative question: "Where am I?" The nurse smiled down at me. "You're in Houston," she said, and I reflected that this still had a good chance of being the truth one way or another. She handed me a mirror. Sure enough, there were the tiny antennae poling up through their titanium ports cemented into my skull.

"I gather the operation was a success," I said. "I want to go see my brain." They led me (I was a bit dizzy and unsteady) down a long corridor and into the life-support lab. A cheer went up from the assembled support team, and I responded with what I hoped was a jaunty salute. Still feeling lightheaded, I was helped over to the life-support vat. I peered through the glass. There, floating in what looked like ginger ale, was undeniably a human brain, though it was almost covered with printed circuit chips, plastic tubules, electrodes, and other paraphernalia. "Is that mine?" I asked. "Hit the output transmitter switch there on the side of the vat and see for yourself," the project director replied. I moved the switch to OFF, and immediately slumped, groggy and nauseated, into the arms of the technicians, one of whom kindly restored the switch to its ON position. While I recovered my equilibrium and composure, I thought to myself: "Well, here I am sitting on a folding chair, staring through a piece of plate glass at my own brain … But wait," I said to myself, "shouldn't I have thought, 'Here I am, suspended in a bubbling fluid, being stared at by my own eyes'?" I tried to think this latter thought. I tried to project it into the tank, offering it hopefully to my brain, but I failed to carry off the exercise with any conviction. I tried again. "Here am *I*, Daniel Dennett, suspended in a bubbling fluid, being stared at by my own eyes." No, it just didn't work. Most puzzling and confusing. Being a philosopher of firm physicalist conviction, I believed unswervingly that the tokening[†] of my thoughts

---

* Faust is a character from literature and folklore who made a deal with the devil to exchange his soul for knowledge.
† Some type of thing is *tokened* when a particular instance of that type is brought into existence.

was occurring somewhere in my brain: yet, when I thought "Here I am," where the thought occurred to me was *here*, outside the vat, where I, Dennett, was standing staring at my brain.

I tried and tried to think myself into the vat, but to no avail. I tried to build up to the task by doing mental exercises. I thought to myself, "The sun is shining *over there*," five times in rapid succession, each time mentally ostending* a different place: in order, the sunlit corner of the lab, the visible front lawn of the hospital, Houston, Mars, and Jupiter. I found I had little difficulty in getting my "there"s to hop all over the celestial map with their proper references. I could loft a "there" in an instant through the farthest reaches of space, and then aim the next "there" with pinpoint accuracy at the upper left quadrant of a freckle on my arm. Why was I having such trouble with "here"? "Here in Houston" worked well enough, and so did "here in the lab," and even "here in this part of the lab," but "here in the vat" always seemed merely an unmeant mental mouthing. I tried closing my eyes while thinking it. This seemed to help, but still I couldn't manage to pull it off, except perhaps for a fleeting instant. I couldn't be sure. The discovery that I couldn't be sure was also unsettling. How did I know *where* I meant by "here" when I thought "here"? Could I *think* I meant one place when in fact I meant another? I didn't see how that could be admitted without untying the few bonds of intimacy between a person and his own mental life that had survived the onslaught of the brain scientists and philosophers, the physicalists and behaviorists. Perhaps I was incorrigible† about where I *meant* when I said "here." But in my present circumstances it seemed that either I was doomed by sheer force of mental habit to thinking systematically false indexical‡ thoughts, or where a person is (and hence where his thoughts are tokened for purposes of semantic analysis) is not necessarily where his brain, the physical seat of his soul, resides. Nagged by confusion, I attempted to orient myself by

falling back on a favorite philosopher's ploy. I began naming things.

"Yorick,"§ I said aloud to my brain, "you are my brain. The rest of my body, seated in this chair, I dub 'Hamlet.'" So here we all are: Yorick's my brain, Hamlet's my body, and I am Dennett. *Now*, where am I? And when I think "where am I?", where's that thought tokened? Is it tokened in my brain, lounging about in the vat, or right here between my ears where it *seems* to be tokened? Or nowhere? Its *temporal* coordinates give me no trouble; must it not have spatial coordinates as well? I began making a list of the alternatives.

1. *Where Hamlet goes there goes Dennett*. This principle was easily refuted by appeal to the familiar brain-transplant thought experiments so enjoyed by philosophers. If Tom and Dick switch brains, Tom is the fellow with Dick's former body—just ask him; he'll claim to be Tom and tell you the most intimate details of Tom's autobiography. It was clear enough, then, that my current body and I could part company, but not likely that I could be separated from my brain. The rule of thumb that emerged so plainly from the thought experiments was that in a brain-transplant operation, one wanted to be the *donor* not the recipient. Better to call such an operation a *body* transplant, in fact. So perhaps the truth was,

2. *Where Yorick goes there goes Dennett*. This was not at all appealing, however. How could I be in the vat and not about to go anywhere, when I was so obviously outside the vat looking in and beginning to make guilty plans to return to my room for a substantial lunch? This begged the question¶ I realized, but it still seemed to be getting at something important. Casting about for some support for my intuition, I hit upon a legalistic sort of argument that might have appealed to Locke.

Suppose, I argued to myself, I were now to fly to California, rob a bank, and be apprehended. In which state would I be tried: in California, where the

---

* Pointing out, indicating, referring to.
† Incapable of being corrected—in this context because no one else can have better evidence than you can and so no one could be in a position to correct you.
‡ An indexical is an expression whose reference can shift from context to context, such as "here," "now," and "I."
§ A character in Shakespeare's *Hamlet*, whose skull is held by the protagonist during the famous "Alas, poor Yorick! I knew him, Horatio ..." speech.
¶ Presupposed what was supposed to be proved.

robbery took place, or in Texas, where the brains of the outfit were located? Would I be a California felon with an out-of-state brain, or a Texas felon remotely controlling an accomplice of sorts in California? It seemed possible that I might beat such a rap just on the undecidability of that jurisdictional question, though perhaps it would be deemed an interstate, and hence Federal, offense. In any event, suppose I were convicted. Was it likely that California would be satisfied to throw Hamlet into the brig, knowing that Yorick was living the good life and luxuriously taking the waters in Texas? Would Texas incarcerate Yorick, leaving Hamlet free to take the next boat to Rio? This alternative appealed to me. Barring capital punishment or other cruel and unusual punishment, the state would be obliged to maintain the life-support system for Yorick though they might move him from Houston to Leavenworth,* and aside from the unpleasantness of the opprobrium, I, for one, would not mind at all and would consider myself a free man under those circumstances. If the state has an interest in forcibly relocating persons in institutions, it would fail to relocate *me* in any institution by locating Yorick there. If this were true, it suggested a third alternative.

3. *Dennett is wherever he thinks he is.* Generalized, the claim was as follows: At any given time a person has a *point of view* and the location of the point of view (which is determined internally by the content of the point of view) is also the location of the person.

Such a proposition is not without its perplexities, but to me it seemed a step in the right direction. The only trouble was that it seemed to place one in a heads-I-win/tails-you-lose situation of unlikely infallibility as regards location. Hadn't I myself often been wrong about where I was, and at least as often uncertain? Couldn't one get lost? Of course, but getting lost *geographically* is not the only way one might get lost. If one were lost in the woods one could attempt to reassure oneself with the consolation that at least one knew where one was: one was right *here* in the familiar surroundings of one's own body. Perhaps in

this case one would not have drawn one's attention to much to be thankful for. Still, there were worse plights imaginable, and I wasn't sure I wasn't in such a plight right now.

Point of view clearly had something to do with personal location, but it was itself an unclear notion. It was obvious that the content of one's point of view was not the same as or determined by the content of one's beliefs or thoughts. For example, what should we say about the point of view of the Cinerama† viewer who shrieks and twists in his seat as the roller-coaster footage overcomes his psychic distancing? Has he forgotten that he is safely seated in the theater? Here I was inclined to say that the person is experiencing an illusory shift in point of view. In other cases, my inclination to call such shifts illusory was less strong. The workers in laboratories and plants who handle dangerous materials by operating feedback-controlled mechanical arms and hands undergo a shift in point of view that is crisper and more pronounced than anything Cinerama can provoke. They can feel the heft and slipperiness of the containers they manipulate with their metal fingers. They know perfectly well where they are and are not fooled into false beliefs by the experience, yet it is as if they were inside the isolation chamber they are peering into. With mental effort, they can manage to shift their point of view back and forth, rather like making a transparent Necker cube‡ or an Escher§ drawing change orientation before one's eyes. It does seem extravagant to suppose that in performing this bit of mental gymnastics, they are transporting *themselves* back and forth.

Still their example gave me hope. If I was in fact in the vat in spite of my intuitions, I might be able to train myself to adopt that point of view even as a matter of habit. I should dwell on images of myself comfortably floating in my vat, beaming volitions to that familiar body *out there*. I reflected that the ease or difficulty of this task was presumably independent of the truth about the location of one's brain. Had I been practicing before the operation, I might now

---

* A US federal prison located in Kansas.
† A wide-screen movie projection process producing a strong illusion of surrounding reality.
‡ ▱ An optical illusion—a cube that seems to shift front surfaces from lower-left to upper-right.
§ An artist whose woodcuts, lithographs, and mezzotints are noted for their inclusion of mathematical themes and impossible objects.

be finding it second nature. You might now yourself try such a *trompe l'oeil*.* Imagine you have written an inflammatory letter which has been published in the *Times*, the result of which is that the government has chosen to impound your brain for a probationary period of three years in its Dangerous Brain Clinic in Bethesda, Maryland. Your body of course is allowed freedom to earn a salary and thus to continue its function of laying up income to be taxed. At this moment, however, your body is seated in an auditorium listening to a peculiar account by Daniel Dennett of his own similar experience. Try it. Think yourself to Bethesda, and then hark back longingly to your body, far away, and yet *seeming* so near. It is only with long-distance restraint (yours? the government's?) that you can control your impulse to get those hands clapping in polite applause before navigating the old body to the rest room and a well-deserved glass of evening sherry in the lounge. The task of imagination is certainly difficult, but if you achieve your goal the results might be consoling.

Anyway, there I was in Houston, lost in thought as one might say, but not for long. My speculations were soon interrupted by the Houston doctors, who wished to test out my new prosthetic nervous system before sending me off on my hazardous mission. As I mentioned before, I was a bit dizzy at first, and not surprisingly, although I soon habituated myself to my new circumstances (which were, after all, well nigh indistinguishable from my old circumstances). My accommodation was not perfect, however, and to this day I continue to be plagued by minor coordination difficulties. The speed of light is fast, but finite, and as my brain and body move farther and farther apart, the delicate interaction of my feedback systems is thrown into disarray by the time lags. Just as one is rendered close to speechless by a delayed or echoic hearing of one's speaking voice so, for instance, I am virtually unable to track a moving object with my eyes whenever my brain and my body are more than a few miles apart. In most matters my impairment is scarcely detectable, though I can no longer hit a slow curve ball with the authority of yore. There are

some compensations of course. Though liquor tastes as good as ever, and warms my gullet while corroding my liver, I can drink it in any quantity I please, without becoming the slightest bit inebriated, a curiosity some of my close friends may have noticed (though I occasionally have *feigned* inebriation, so as not to draw attention to my unusual circumstances). For similar reasons, I take aspirin orally for a sprained wrist, but if the pain persists I ask Houston to administer codeine to me *in vitro*.† In times of illness the phone bill can be staggering.

But to return to my adventure. At length, both the doctors and I were satisfied that I was ready to undertake my subterranean mission. And so I left my brain in Houston and headed by helicopter for Tulsa. Well, in any case, that's the way it seemed to me. That's how I would put it, just off the top of my head as it were. On the trip I reflected further about my earlier anxieties and decided that my first postoperative speculations had been tinged with panic. The matter was not nearly as strange or metaphysical as I had been supposing. Where was I? In two places, clearly: both inside the vat and outside it. Just as one can stand with one foot in Connecticut and the other in Rhode Island, I was in two places at once. I had become one of those scattered individuals we used to hear so much about. The more I considered this answer, the more obviously true it appeared. But, strange to say, the more true it appeared, the less important the question to which it could be the true answer seemed. A sad, but not unprecedented, fate for a philosophical question to suffer. This answer did not completely satisfy me, of course. There lingered some question to which I should have liked an answer, which was neither "Where are all my various and sundry parts?" nor "What is my current point of view?" Or at least there seemed to be such a question. For it did seem undeniable that in some sense *I* and not merely *most of me* was descending into the earth under Tulsa in search of an atomic warhead.

When I found the warhead, I was certainly glad I had left my brain behind, for the pointer on the specially built Geiger counter I had brought with me was

---

* French: "deceive the eye"; an artistic technique that allows three-dimensional objects to be rendered in two dimensions so realistically that they seem to be real objects, not paintings.
† Latin: "in the glass"; normally used with reference to experiments and procedures done in test tubes, petri dishes, etc.

off the dial. I called Houston on my ordinary radio and told the operation control center of my position and my progress. In return, they gave me instructions for dismantling the vehicle, based upon my on-site observations. I had set to work with my cutting torch when all of a sudden a terrible thing happened. I went stone deaf. At first I thought it was only my radio earphones that had broken, but when I tapped on my helmet, I heard nothing. Apparently the auditory transceivers had gone on the fritz. I could no longer hear Houston or my own voice, but I could speak, so I started telling them what had happened. In mid-sentence, I knew something else had gone wrong. My vocal apparatus had become paralyzed. Then my right hand went limp—another transceiver had gone. I was truly in deep trouble. But worse was to follow. After a few more minutes, I went blind. I cursed my luck, and then I cursed the scientists who had led me into this grave peril. There I was, deaf, dumb, and blind, in a radioactive hole more than a mile under Tulsa. Then the last of my cerebral radio links broke, and suddenly I was faced with a new and even more shocking problem: whereas an instant before I had been buried alive in Oklahoma, now I was disembodied in Houston. My recognition of my new status was not immediate. It took me several very anxious minutes before it dawned on me that my poor body lay several hundred miles away, with heart pulsing and lungs respirating, but otherwise as dead as the body of any heart-transplant donor, its skull packed with useless, broken electronic gear. The shift in perspective I had earlier found well nigh impossible now seemed quite natural. Though I could think myself back into my body in the tunnel under Tulsa, it took some effort to sustain the illusion. For surely it was an illusion to suppose I was still in Oklahoma: I had lost all contact with that body.

It occurred to me then, with one of those rushes of revelation of which we should be suspicious, that I had stumbled upon an impressive demonstration of the immateriality of the soul based upon physicalist principles and premises. For as the last radio signal between Tulsa and Houston died away, had I not changed location from Tulsa to Houston at the speed of light? And had I not accomplished this without any increase in mass? What moved from A to B at such speed was surely myself, or at any rate my soul or mind—the massless center of my being and home of my consciousness. My *point of view* had lagged some-what behind, but I had already noted the indirect bearing of point of view on personal location. I could not see how a physicalist philosopher could quarrel with this except by taking the dire and counterintu-itive route of banishing all talk of persons. Yet the notion of personhood was so well entrenched in every-one's world view, or so it seemed to me, that any denial would be as curiously unconvincing, as systematically disingenuous, as the Cartesian negation, "non sum."[1]*

The joy of philosophic discovery thus tided me over some very bad minutes or perhaps hours as the helplessness and hopelessness or my situation became more apparent to me. Waves of panic and even nau-sea swept over me, made all the more horrible by the absence of their normal body-dependent phenom-enology.† No adrenaline rush of tingles in the arms, no pounding heart, no premonitory salivation. I did feel a dread sinking feeling in my bowels at one point, and this tricked me momentarily into the false hope that I was undergoing a reversal of the process that landed me in this fix—a gradual undisembodiment. But the isolation and uniqueness of that twinge soon convinced me that it was simply the first of a plague of phantom body hallucinations that I, like any other amputee, would be all too likely to suffer.

My mood then was chaotic. On the one hand, I was fired up with elation of my philosophic discovery and was wracking my brain (one of the few familiar things I could still do), trying to figure out how to communicate my discovery to the journals; while on the other, I was bitter, lonely, and filled with dread and uncertainty. Fortunately, this did not last long, for my technical support team sedated me into a dreamless sleep from which I awoke, hearing with magnificent fidelity the familiar opening strains of my favorite Brahms piano trio. So that was why they had wanted a list of my favorite recordings! It did not take me long to realize that I was hearing the music without ears. The

---

*   René Descartes suggested that the thinking subject is the site of the self, famously declaring *cogito ergo sum*, "I think therefore I am." Here, Dennett is negating the Cartesian self, as *non sum* literally means "I am not."

†   "Phenomenology" can be read, roughly, as "experiences" in this context.

output from the stereo stylus was being fed through some fancy rectification circuitry directly into my auditory nerve. I was mainlining Brahms, an unforgettable experience for any stereo buff. At the end of the record it did not surprise me to hear the reassuring voice of the project director speaking into a microphone that was now my prosthetic ear. He confirmed my analysis of what had gone wrong and assured me that steps were being taken to re-embody me. He did not elaborate, and after a few more recordings, I found myself drifting off to sleep. My sleep lasted, I later learned, for the better part of a year, and when I awoke, it was to find myself fully restored to my senses. When I looked into the mirror, though, I was a bit startled to see an unfamiliar face. Bearded and a bit heavier, bearing no doubt a family resemblance to my former face, and with the same look of spritely intelligence and resolute character, but definitely a new face. Further self-explorations of an intimate nature left me no doubt that this was a new body, and the project director confirmed my conclusions. He did not volunteer any information on the past history of my new body and I decided (wisely, I think in retrospect) not to pry. As many philosophers unfamiliar with my ordeal have more recently speculated, the acquisition of a new body leaves one's *person* intact. And after a period of adjustment to a new voice, new muscular strengths and weaknesses, and so forth, one's *personality* is by and large also preserved. More dramatic changes in personality have been routinely observed in people who have undergone extensive plastic surgery, to say nothing of sex-change operations, and I think no one contests the survival of the person in such cases. In any event I soon accommodated to my new body, to the point of being unable to recover any of its novelties to my consciousness or even memory. The view in the mirror soon became utterly familiar. That view, by the way, still revealed antennae, and so I was not surprised to learn that my brain had not been moved from its haven in the life-support lab.

I decided that good old Yorick deserved a visit. I and my new body, whom we might as well call Fortinbras,* strode into the familiar lab to another round of applause from the technicians, who were of course congratulating themselves, not me. Once more I stood before the vat and contemplated poor Yorick, and on a whim I once again cavalierly flicked off the output transmitter switch. Imagine my surprise when nothing unusual happened. No fainting spell, no nausea, no noticeable change. A technician hurried to restore the switch to ON, but still I felt nothing. I demanded an explanation, which the project director hastened to provide. It seems that before they had even operated on the first occasion, they had constructed a computer duplicate of my brain, reproducing both the complete information-processing structure and the computational speed of my brain in a giant computer program. After the operation, but before they had dared to send me off on my mission to Oklahoma, they had run this computer system and Yorick side by side. The incoming signals from Hamlet were sent simultaneously to Yorick's transceivers and to the computer's array of inputs. And the outputs from Yorick were not only beamed back to Hamlet, my body; they were recorded and checked against the simultaneous output of the computer program, which was called "Hubert"† for reasons obscure to me. Over days and even weeks, the outputs were identical and synchronous, which of course did not *prove* that they had succeeded in copying the brain's functional structure, but the empirical support was greatly encouraging.

Hubert's input, and hence activity, had been kept parallel with Yorick's during my disembodied days. And now, to demonstrate this, they had actually thrown the master switch that put Hubert for the first time in on-line control of my body—not Hamlet, of course, but Fortinbras. (Hamlet, I learned, had never been recovered from its underground tomb and could be assumed by this time to have largely returned to the dust. At the head of my grave still lay the magnificent bulk of the abandoned device, with the word STUD emblazoned on its side in large letters—a circumstance which may provide archeologists of the next century with a curious insight into the burial rites of their ancestors.)

---

* A character in *Hamlet* who arrives at the end of the play, after most of the main characters are dead, and is crowned king of Denmark.
† A Germanic name that literally means "bright mind." It is also the first name of Dennett's contemporary, Hubert Dreyfus, a well-known critic of the idea that the mind can be replicated by computer software.

The laboratory technicians now showed me the master switch, which had two positions, labeled *B*, for Brain (they didn't know my brain's name was Yorick), and *H*, for Hubert. The switch did indeed point to *H*, and they explained to me that if I wished, I could switch it back to *B*. With my heart in my mouth (and my brain in its vat), I did this. Nothing happened. A click, that was all. To test their claim, and with the master switch now set at *B*, I hit Yorick's output transmitter switch on the vat and sure enough, I began to faint. Once the output switch was turned back on and I had recovered my wits, so to speak, I continued to play with the master switch, flipping it back and forth. I found that with the exception of the transitional click, I could detect no trace of a difference. I could switch in mid-utterance, and the sentence I had begun speaking under the control of Yorick was finished without a pause or hitch of any kind under the control of Hubert. I had a spare brain, a prosthetic device which might some day stand me in very good stead, were some mishap to befall Yorick. Or alternatively, I could keep Yorick as a spare and use Hubert. It didn't seem to make any difference which I chose, for the wear and tear and fatigue on my body did not have any debilitating effect on either brain, whether or not it was actually causing the motions of my body, or merely spilling its output into thin air.

The one truly unsettling aspect of this new development was the prospect, which was not long in dawning on me, of someone detaching the spare—Hubert or Yorick, as the case might be—from Fortinbras and hitching it to yet another body—some Johnny-come-lately Rosencrantz or Guildenstern.* Then (if not before) there would be *two* people, that much was clear. One would be me, and the other would be a sort of super-twin brother. If there were two bodies, one under the control of Hubert and the other being controlled by Yorick, then which would the world recognize as the true Dennett? And whatever the rest of the world decided, which one would be *me*? Would I be the Yorick-brained one, in virtue of Yorick's causal priority and former intimate relationship with the original Dennett body, Hamlet? That seemed a bit legalistic, a bit too redolent of the arbitrariness of consanguinity† and legal possession, to be convincing at the metaphysical level. For suppose that before the arrival of the second body on the scene, I had been keeping Yorick as the spare for years, and letting Hubert's output drive my body—that is, Fortinbras—all that time. The Hubert-Fortinbras couple would seem then by squatter's rights (to combat one legal intuition with another) to be the true Dennett and the lawful inheritor of everything that was Dennett's. This was an interesting question, certainly, but not nearly so pressing as another question that bothered me. My strongest intuition was that in such an eventuality *I* would survive so long as *either* brain-body couple remained intact, but I had mixed emotions about whether I should want both to survive.

I discussed my worries with the technicians and the project director. The prospect of two Dennetts was abhorrent to me, I explained, largely for social reasons. I didn't want to be my own rival for the affections of my wife, nor did I like the prospect of the two Dennetts sharing my modest professor's salary. Still more vertiginous and distasteful, though, was the idea of knowing *that much* about another person, while he had the very same goods on me. How could we ever face each other? My colleagues in the lab argued that I was ignoring the bright side of the matter. Weren't there many things I wanted to do but, being only one person, had been unable to do? Now one Dennett could stay at home and be the professor and family man while the other could strike out on a life of travel and adventure—missing the family of course, but happy in the knowledge that the other Dennett was keeping the home fires burning. I could be faithful and adulterous at the same time. I could even cuckold myself—to say nothing of other more lurid possibilities my colleagues were all too ready to force upon my overtaxed imagination. But my ordeal in Oklahoma (or was it Houston?) had made me less adventurous, and I shrank from this opportunity that was being offered (though of course I was never quite sure it was being offered to *me* in the first place).

---

* In *Hamlet*, they are friends of prince Hamlet who are used as pawns by King Claudius to influence young Hamlet's behavior.

† The property of being a blood relation to another person; it is carefully defined in many legal codes to specify when marriages are permitted and how the inheritance of property occurs.

There was another prospect even more disagreeable: that the spare, Hubert or Yorick as the case might be, would be detached from any input from Fortinbras and just left detached. Then, as in the other case, there would be two Dennetts, or at least two claimants to my name and possessions, one embodied in Fortinbras, and the other sadly, miserably disembodied. Both selfishness and altruism bade me take steps to prevent this from happening. So I asked that measures be taken to ensure that no one could ever tamper with the transceiver connections or the master switch without my (our? no, *my*) knowledge and consent. Since I had no desire to spend my life guarding the equipment in Houston, it was mutually decided that all the electronic connections in the lab would be carefully locked. Both those that controlled the life-support system for Yorick and those that controlled the power supply for Hubert would be guarded with fail-safe devices, and I would take the only master switch, outfitted for radio remote control, with me wherever I went. I carry it strapped around my waist and—wait a moment—here it is. Every few months I reconnoiter the situation by switching channels. I do this only in the presence of friends, of course, for if the other channel were, heaven forbid, either dead or otherwise occupied, there would have to be somebody who had my interests at heart to switch it back, to bring me back from the void. For while I could feel, see, hear, and otherwise sense whatever befell my body, subsequent to such a switch, I'd be unable to control it. By the way, the two positions on the switch are intentionally unmarked, so I never have the faintest idea whether I am switching from Hubert to Yorick or vice versa. (Some of you may think that in this case I really don't know *who* I am, let alone where I am. But such reflections no longer make much of a dent on my essential Dennettness, on my own sense of who I am. If it is true that in one sense I don't know who I am then that's another one of your philosophical truths of underwhelming significance.)

In any case, every time I've flipped the switch so far, nothing has happened. *So let's give it a try ...*

"THANK GOD! I THOUGHT YOU'D NEVER FLIP THAT SWITCH! You can't imagine how horrible it's been these last two weeks—but now you know, it's your turn in purgatory. How I've longed for this moment! You see, about two weeks ago—excuse me, ladies and gentlemen, but I've got to explain this to my ... um, brother, I guess you could say, but he's just told you the facts, so you'll understand—about two weeks ago our two brains drifted just a bit out of synch. I don't know whether *my* brain is now Hubert or Yorick, any more than you do, but in any case, the two brains drifted apart, and of course once the process started, it snowballed, for I was in a slightly different receptive state for the input we both received, a difference that was soon magnified. In no time at all the illusion that I was in control of my body—our body—was completely dissipated. There was nothing I could do—no way to call you. YOU DIDN'T EVEN KNOW I EXISTED! It's been like being carried around in a cage, or better, like being possessed—hearing my own voice say things I didn't mean to say, watching in frustration as my own hands performed deeds I hadn't intended. You'd scratch our itches, but not the way I would have, and you kept me awake, with your tossing and turning. I've been totally exhausted, on the verge of a nervous breakdown, carried around helplessly by your frantic round of activities, sustained only by the knowledge that some day you'd throw the switch.

"Now it's your turn, but at least you'll have the comfort of knowing *I* know you're in there. Like an expectant mother, I'm eating—or at any rate tasting, smelling, seeing—for *two* now, and I'll try to make it easy for you. Don't worry. Just as soon as this colloquium is over, you and I will fly to Houston, and we'll see what can be done to get one of us another body. You can have a female body—your body could be any color you like. But let's think it over. I tell you what—to be fair, if we both want this body, I promise I'll let the project director flip a coin to settle which of us gets to keep it and which then gets to choose a new body. That should guarantee justice, shouldn't it? In any case, I'll take care of you, I promise. These people are my witnesses.

"Ladies and gentlemen, this talk we have just heard is not exactly the talk *I* would have given, but I assure you that everything he said was perfectly true. And now if you'll excuse me, I think I'd—we'd—better sit down."[2] ∎

Suggestions for Critical Reflection

1. What is the relationship between brain and body? In Dennett's story, would it be more accurate to say that Dennett "is" the disembodied brain, or that he is the brain-less body? Does either explanation seem correct?

2. At one point in his story, Dennett considers what would occur if he committed a crime while his body and brain were separated. He wonders if the trial would occur in the state where his body was located, or the state where his brain was preserved. What does this rumination indicate about the broader implications of Dennett's inquiry? Are there practical reasons why it is important to figure out where the self really is? Imagine that you are standing on the Connecticut–Rhode Island border, and you shoot somebody also standing on the border. Which state would you be tried in? The one in which the gun was? Or the one with the bullet-hole? Or the one with your brain? Or the one with most of your brain (in case the border bisects your head)?

3. Dennett imagines the existence of an electronically reproduced brain. If the technology to replicate brains electronically existed, what would the implications be for artificial intelligence? Would this entail that robots could be given brains, and therefore selves? Does Dennett leave open the possibility of ascribing personhood to machines?

4. René Descartes argued that, because it is possible to imagine living on without a body, the foundation of the self must be found within the mind, within the mental substance he believed to underwrite thinking (see the reading from Descartes in the Epistemology chapter, especially meditations 2, 3, and 6). What might Descartes say about the situations described in Dennett's story?

5. Dennett couches his speculations about personal identity within a short piece of narrative fiction, rather than a more conventional philosophical essay. Why do you think he chose to do this? What effect does the form of Dennett's text have upon its content? In other words, what are the consequences, benefits, and drawbacks of these arguments appearing within a short story?

Notes

1 Cf. Jaakko Hintikka, "Cogito ergo sum: Inference or Performance?" *The Philosophical Review*, LXXI, 1962, pp. 3–22.

2 Anyone familiar with the literature on this topic will recognize that my remarks owe a great deal to the explorations of Sydney Shoemaker, John Perry, David Lewis and Derek Parfit, and in particular to their papers in Amelie Rorty, ed., *The Identities of Persons*, 1976.

DEREK PARFIT

Personal Identity

Who Was Derek Parfit?

Derek Antony Parfit was born in 1942 in Chengdu, China, the son of two doctors who provided training to a Chinese Christian mission.* After studying at Eton College, England, he earned a degree in history in 1964 from the University of Oxford, and then pursued a fellowship at Harvard and Columbia. In 1984, Parfit published *Reasons and Persons*, a text that earned him a reputation as one of the world's leading philosophers. He served as a research fellow at All Soul's College, Oxford, and was also a visiting professor at Harvard, Rutgers, and New York University. In two volumes in 2011, and a third in 2017, he published his second and final book *On What Matters*, which synthesized the three leading ethical theories: virtue ethics, deontology, and consequentialism. Parfit thought and wrote about philosophy almost continuously, all day every day, but he was also an extreme perfectionist, constantly revising and distilling his writing down to shorter and clearer passages, and so he published relatively sparsely. Outside of his academic career, Parfit was an amateur photographer, especially of architecture, and a philanthropist known to be generous both intellectually and financially. Parfit died in 2017 at the age of 74. Fortified by his philosophical beliefs, Parfit was reportedly unfrightened by death (though he regretted not being able to do all the philosophy he still wished to do): "My death will break the more direct relations between my present experiences and future experiences, but it will not break various other relations. This is all there is to the fact that there will be no one living who will be me. Now that I have seen this, my death seems to me less bad."[†]

What Is Parfit's Overall Philosophical Project?

Parfit's central purpose is to take on metaphysical questions that make a difference in how humans lead their lives. To this end, he primarily engages philosophical questions that relate to ethical conduct, such as those involved with free will, time, and personal identity. Parfit attacks the idea that individuals exist in isolation, and that self-interest should be the primary criterion for rational action. In his view, personal identity—the notion that an enduring self connects me to "my" past and future experiences—is misguided. What matters, Parfit claims, are our psychological relations to people, who may be "future selves" separated from us by time, or people across the world separated from us by space. Because personal identity is unimportant, Parfit argues, we have just as much of an obligation to help the world's poor in the present as we do to accumulate wealth for ourselves in the future.

What Is the Structure of This Reading?

Parfit begins by observing that there are situations where the criteria we typically use to determine personal identity fail. He suggests that these situations reveal that some questions about personal identity have no definite answer. But, he wants to show, this isn't a problem because the important philosophical questions that seem to be connected to the issue of personal identity can be separated from it and answered independently.

In section I he closely examines a situation where one self becomes divided into two, and argues that the best

---

* His parents gradually grew disillusioned with evangelizing Christianity in a culture already rich with sophisticated value systems and religious beliefs; meanwhile, the seven-year-old Derek became devout, declaring that he wanted to become a monk. By the age of eight, however, he too had lost his Christian faith, deciding that a good God would not send people to Hell ("How to Be Good," profile of Parfit in *The New Yorker* by Larissa MacFarquhar, 5 September 2011).

† Reported in Derek Parfit's obituary in the London *Times*, 4 January 2017.

response to this kind of case is to accept that one person can survive as two different people. From this it follows that survival cannot be a matter of continuing personal identity, since two different things cannot both be identical to—the same thing as—one thing. In section II, Parfit endorses psychological continuity as a criterion of identity: it works well, he suggests, in cases where there are no splits—non-branching cases—and if there *are* splits or branches, then identity does not apply in any case so the search for a criterion is inapplicable.

In section III Parfit explains how we can make sense of psychological continuity—for example, remembering your past—without presupposing personal identity. Then in section IV he uses the idea of the fusion of two selves to argue that survival can be a matter of degree, rather than something which is all-or-nothing. In doing so, he distinguishes the relations of psychological continuity and psychological *connectedness*, and argues that connectedness is a more important element in survival than continuity. In section V he draws upon his analysis of psychological connectedness to develop a way of talking about important philosophical issues, such as the survival of the self, without depending on the (binary, one-to-one) idea of personal identity.

He concludes by suggesting that there are two significant ethical consequences that arise when we replace the concept of identity with relations of degree. The first is that there is no pressing reason to care more for your future self than for people in the world not identical to you, because many other people may be just as related to you as your own future self. The second is that selfish fears about death can be diminished, because the relationship between one's present and one's future self is not as strong as we ordinarily think.

Personal Identity[*1]

We can, I think, describe cases in which, though we know the answer to every other question, we have no idea how to answer a question about personal identity. These cases are not covered by the criteria of personal identity that we actually use.

Do they present a problem?

It might be thought that they do not, because they could never occur. I suspect that some of them could. (Some, for instance, might become scientifically possible.) But I shall claim that even if they did they would present no problem.

My targets are two beliefs: one about the nature of personal identity, the other about its importance.

The first is that in these cases the question about identity must have an answer.

No one thinks this about, say, nations or machines. Our criteria for the identity of these do not cover certain cases. No one thinks that in these cases the questions "Is it the same nation?" or "Is it the same machine?" must have answers.

Some people believe that in this respect they are different. They agree that our criteria of personal identity do not cover certain cases, but they believe that the nature of their own identity through time is, somehow, such as to guarantee that in these cases questions about their identity must have answers. This belief might be expressed as follows: "Whatever happens between now and any future time, either I shall still exist, or I shall not. Any future experience will either be *my* experience, or it will not."

This first belief—in the special nature of personal identity—has, I think, certain effects. It makes people assume that the principle of self-interest is more rationally compelling than any moral principle. And it makes them more depressed by the thought of aging and of death.

I cannot see how to disprove this first belief. I shall describe a problem case. But this can only make it seem implausible.

Another approach might be this. We might suggest that one cause of the belief is the projection of our emotions. When we imagine ourselves in a problem case, we do feel that the question "Would it be me?" must have an answer. But what we take to be a

* Derek Parfit, "Personal Identity," *The Philosophical Review* 80, 1 (1971): 3–27. This was Parfit's first published philosophy paper.

bafflement about a further fact may be only the bafflement of our concern.

I shall not pursue this suggestion here. But one cause of our concern is the belief which is my second target. This is that unless the question about identity has an answer, we cannot answer certain important questions (questions about such matters as survival, memory, and responsibility).

Against this second belief my claim will be this. Certain important questions do presuppose a question about personal identity. But they can be freed of this presupposition. And when they are, the question about identity has no importance.

I

We can start by considering the much-discussed case of the man who, like an amoeba, divides.[2]

Wiggins has recently dramatized this case.[3] He first referred to the operation imagined by Shoemaker.[4] We suppose that my brain is transplanted into someone else's (brainless) body, and that the resulting person has my character and apparent memories of my life. Most of us would agree, after thought, that the resulting person is me. I shall here assume such agreement.[5]

Wiggins then imagined his own operation. My brain is divided, and each half is housed in a new body. Both resulting people have my character and apparent memories of my life.

What happens to me? There seem only three possibilities: (1) I do not survive; (2) I survive as one of the two people; (3) I survive as both.

The trouble with (1) is this. We agreed that I could survive if my brain were successfully transplanted. And people have in fact survived with half their brains destroyed. It seems to follow that I could survive if half my brain were successfully transplanted and the other half were destroyed. But if this is so, how could I *not* survive if the other half were also successfully transplanted? How could a double success be a failure?

We can move to the second description. Perhaps one success is the maximum score. Perhaps I shall be one of the resulting people.

The trouble here is that in Wiggins' case each half of my brain is exactly similar, and so, to start with, is each resulting person. So how can I survive as only one of the two people? What can make me one of them rather than the other?

It seems clear that both of these descriptions— that I do not survive, and that I survive as one of the people—are highly implausible. Those who have accepted them must have assumed that they were the only possible descriptions.

What about our third description: that I survive as both people?

It might be said, "If 'survive' implies identity, this description makes no sense—you cannot be two people. If it does not, the description is irrelevant to a problem about identity."

I shall later deny the second of these remarks. But there are ways of denying the first. We might say, "What we have called 'the two resulting people' are not two people. They are one person. I do survive Wiggins' operation. Its effect is to give me two bodies and a divided mind."

It would shorten my argument if this were absurd. But I do not think it is. It is worth showing why.

We can, I suggest, imagine a divided mind. We can imagine a man having two simultaneous experiences, in having each of which he is unaware of having the other.

We may not even need to imagine this. Certain actual cases, to which Wiggins referred, seem to be best described in these terms. These involve the cutting of the bridge between the hemispheres of the brain.* The aim was to cure epilepsy. But the result appears to be, in the surgeon's words, the creation of "two separate spheres of consciousness,"[6] each of which controls one half of the patient's body. What is experienced in each is, presumably, experienced by the patient.

There are certain complications in these actual cases. So let us imagine a simpler case.

Suppose that the bridge between my hemispheres is brought under my voluntary control. This would enable me to disconnect my hemispheres as easily as if I were blinking. By doing this I would divide my mind.

---

* The corpus callosum, a thick bundle of nerves connecting the two cerebral hemispheres of the brain (in placental mammals) enabling communication between them.

And we can suppose that when my mind is divided I can, in each half, bring about reunion.

This ability would have obvious uses. To give an example: I am near the end of a maths exam, and see two ways of tackling the last problem. I decide to divide my mind, to work, with each half, at one of two calculations, and then to reunite my mind and write a fair copy of the best result.

What shall I experience?

When I disconnect my hemispheres, my consciousness divides into two streams. But this division is not something that I experience. Each of my two streams of consciousness seems to have been straightforwardly continuous with my one stream of consciousness up to the moment of division. The only changes in each stream are the disappearance of half my visual field and the loss of sensation in, and control over, half my body.

Consider my experiences in what we can call my "right-handed" stream. I remember that I assigned my right hand to the longer calculation. This I now begin. In working at this calculation I can see, from the movements of my left hand, that I am also working at the other. But I am not aware of working at the other. So I might, in my right-handed stream, wonder how, in my left-handed stream, I am getting on.

My work is now over. I am about to reunite my mind. What should I, in each stream, expect? Simply that I shall suddenly seem to remember just having thought out two calculations, in thinking out each of which I was not aware of thinking out the other. This, I submit, we can imagine. And if my mind was divided, these memories are correct.

In describing this episode, I assumed that there were two series of thoughts, and that they were both mine. If my two hands visibly wrote out two calculations, and if I claimed to remember two corresponding series of thoughts, this is surely what we should want to say.

If it is, then a person's mental history need not be like a canal, with only one channel. It could be like a river, with islands, and with separate streams.

To apply this to Wiggins' operation: we mentioned the view that it gives me two bodies and a divided mind. We cannot now call this absurd. But it is, I think, unsatisfactory.

There were two features of the case of the exam that made us want to say that only one person was involved. The mind was soon reunited, and there was only one body. If a mind was permanently divided and its halves developed in different ways, the point of speaking of one person would start to disappear. Wiggins' case, where there are also two bodies, seems to be over the borderline. After I have had his operation, the two "products" each have all the attributes of a person. They could live at opposite ends of the earth. (If they later met, they might even fail to recognize each other.) It would become intolerable to deny that they were different people.

Suppose we admit that they are different people. Could we still claim that I survived as both, using "survive" to imply identity?

We could. For we might suggest that two people could compose a third. We might say, "I do survive Wiggins' operation as two people. They can be different people, and yet be me, in just the way in which the Pope's three crowns are one crown."*[7]

This is a possible way of giving sense to the claim that I survive as two different people, using "survive" to imply identity. But it keeps the language of identity only by changing the concept of a person. And there are obvious objections to this change.[8]

The alternative, for which I shall argue, is to give up the language of identity. We can suggest that I survive as two different people without implying that I am these people.

When I first mentioned this alternative, I mentioned this objection: "If your new way of talking does not imply identity, it cannot solve our problem. For that is about identity. The problem is that all the possible answers to the question about identity are highly implausible."

We can now answer this objection.

We can start by reminding ourselves that this is an objection only if we have one or both of the beliefs which I mentioned at the start of this paper.

The first was the belief that to any question about personal identity, in any describable case, there must

---

* The tiara worn by the Catholic pope includes three tiers or "crowns"; there are various interpretations as to the meaning of these crowns.

be a true answer. For those with this belief, Wiggins' case is doubly perplexing. If all the possible answers are implausible, it is hard to decide which of them is true, and hard even to keep the belief that one of them must be true. If we give up this belief, as I think we should, these problems disappear. We shall then regard the case as like many others in which, for quite unpuzzling reasons, there *is* no answer to a question about identity. (Consider "Was England the same nation after 1066?")*

Wiggins' case makes the first belief implausible. It also makes it trivial. For it undermines the second belief. This was the belief that important questions turn upon the question about identity. (It is worth pointing out that those who have only this second belief do not think that there must *be* an answer to this question, but rather that we must decide upon an answer.)

Against this second belief my claim is this. Certain questions do presuppose a question about personal identity. And because these questions *are* important, Wiggins' case does present a problem. But we cannot solve this problem by answering the question about identity. We can solve this problem only by taking these important questions and prizing them apart from the question about identity. After we have done this, the question about identity (though we might for the sake of neatness decide it) has no further interest.

Because there are several questions which presuppose identity, this claim will take some time to fill out.

We can first return to the question of survival. This is a special case, for survival does not so much presuppose the retaining of identity as seem equivalent to it. It is thus the general relation which we need to prize apart from identity. We can then consider particular relations, such as those involved in memory and intention.

"Will I survive?" seems, I said, equivalent to "Will there be some person alive who is the same person as me?"

If we treat these questions as equivalent, then the least unsatisfactory description of Wiggins' case is, I think, that I survive with two bodies and a divided mind.

Several writers have chosen to say that I am neither of the resulting people. Given our equivalence, this implies that I do not survive, and hence, presumably, that even if Wiggins' operation is not literally death, I ought, since I will not survive it, to regard it *as* death. But this seemed absurd.

It is worth repeating why. An emotion or attitude can be criticized for resting on a false belief, or for being inconsistent. A man who regarded Wiggins' operation as death must, I suggest, be open to one of these criticisms.

He might believe that his relation to each of the resulting people fails to contain some element which is contained in survival. But how can this be true? We agreed that he *would* survive if he stood in this very same relation to only *one* of the resulting people. So it cannot be the nature of this relation which makes it fail, in Wiggins' case, to be survival. It can only be its duplication.

Suppose that our man accepts this, but still regards division as death. His reaction would now seem wildly inconsistent. He would be like a man who, when told of a drug that could double his years of life, regarded the taking of this drug as death. The only difference in the case of division is that the extra years are to run concurrently. This is an interesting difference. But it cannot mean that there are *no* years to run.

I have argued this for those who think that there must, in Wiggins' case, be a true answer to the question about identity. For them, we might add, "Perhaps the original person does lose his identity. But there may be other ways to do this than to die. One other way might be to multiply. To regard these as the same is to confuse nought† with two."

For those who think that the question of identity is up for decision, it would be clearly absurd to regard Wiggins' operation as death. These people would have to think, "We could have chosen to say that I should be one of the resulting people. If we had, I should not have regarded it as death. But since we have chosen to

---

* The date of the successful invasion of England, and overthrow of its monarchy, by the Norman-French William the Conqueror.
† Zero.

say that I am neither person, I *do*." This is hard even to understand.[9]

My first conclusion, then, is this. The relation of the original person to each of the resulting people contains all that interests us—all that matters—in any ordinary case of survival. This is why we need a sense in which one person can survive as two.[10]

One of my aims in the rest of this paper will be to suggest such a sense. But we can first make some general remarks.

II

Identity is a one–one relation.* Wiggins' case serves to show that what matters in survival need not be one–one.

Wiggins' case is of course unlikely to occur. The relations which matter are, in fact, one–one. It is because they are that we can imply the holding of these relations by using the language of identity.

This use of language is convenient. But it can lead us astray. We may assume that what matters *is* identity and, hence, has the properties of identity.

In the case of the property of being one–one, this mistake is not serious. For what matters is in fact one–one. But in the case of another property, the mistake *is* serious. Identity is all-or-nothing. Most of the relations which matter in survival are, in fact, relations of degree. If we ignore this, we shall be led into quite ill-grounded attitudes and beliefs.

The claim that I have just made—that most of what matters are relations of degree—I have yet to support. Wiggins' case shows only that these relations need not be one–one. The merit of the case is not that it shows this in particular, but that it makes the first break between what matters and identity. The belief that identity *is* what matters is hard to overcome. This is shown in most discussions of the problem cases which actually occur: cases, say, of amnesia or of brain damage. Once Wiggins' case has made one breach in this belief, the rest should be easier to remove.[11]

To turn to a recent debate: most of the relations which matter can be provisionally referred to under the heading "psychological continuity" (which includes causal continuity). My claim is thus that we use the language of personal identity in order to imply such continuity. This is close to the view that psychological continuity provides a criterion of identity.

Williams has attacked this view with the following argument. Identity is a one–one relation. So any criterion of identity must appeal to a relation which is logically one–one. Psychological continuity is not logically one–one. So it cannot provide a criterion.[12]

Some writers have replied that it is enough if the relation appealed to is always in fact one–one.[13]

I suggest a slightly different reply. Psychological continuity is a ground for speaking of identity when it is one–one.

If psychological continuity took a one–many or branching form, we should need, I have argued, to abandon the language of identity. So this possibility would not count against this view.

We can make a stronger claim. This possibility would count in its favor.

The view might be defended as follows. Judgments of personal identity have great importance. What gives them their importance is the fact that they imply psychological continuity. This is why, whenever there is such continuity, we ought, if we can, to imply it by making a judgment of identity.

If psychological continuity took a branching form, no coherent set of judgments of identity could correspond to, and thus be used to imply, the branching form of this relation. But what we ought to do, in such a case, is take the importance which would attach to a judgment of identity and attach this importance directly to each limb of the branching relation. So this case helps to show that judgments of personal identity do derive their importance from the fact that they imply psychological continuity. It helps to show that when we can, usefully, speak of identity, this relation is our ground.

This argument appeals to a principle which Williams put forward.[14] The principle is that an important judgment should be asserted and denied only on importantly different grounds.

---

* A relation of one thing to one thing (as opposed to, say, a two–one relation—such as the typical relation of biological parents to their first child, or a three–one relation—such as the way the three branches of the federal government make up the US government).

Williams applied this principle to a case in which one man is psychologically continuous with the dead Guy Fawkes,* and a case in which two men are. His argument was this. If we treat psychological continuity as a sufficient ground for speaking of identity, we shall say that the one man is Guy Fawkes. But we could not say that the two men are, although we should have the same ground. This disobeys the principle. The remedy is to deny that the one man is Guy Fawkes, to insist that sameness of the body is necessary for identity.

Williams' principle can yield a different answer. Suppose we regard psychological continuity as more important than sameness of the body.[15] And suppose that the one man really is psychologically (and causally) continuous with Guy Fawkes. If he is, it would disobey the principle to deny that he is Guy Fawkes, for we have the same important ground as in a normal case of identity. In the case of the two men, we again have the same important ground. So we ought to take the importance from the judgment of identity and attach it directly to this ground. We ought to say, as in Wiggins' case, that each limb of the branching relation is as good as survival. This obeys the principle.

To sum up these remarks: even if psychological continuity is neither logically, nor always in fact, one–one, it can provide a criterion of identity. For this can appeal to the relation of *non-branching* psychological continuity, which is logically one–one.[16]

The criterion might be sketched as follows. "*X* and *Y* are the same person if they are psychologically continuous and there is no person who is contemporary with either and psychologically continuous with the other." We should need to explain what we mean by "psychologically continuous" and say how much continuity the criterion requires. We should then, I think, have described a sufficient condition for speaking of identity.[17]

We need to say something more. If we admit that psychological continuity might not be one–one, we need to say what we ought to do if it were not one–one. Otherwise our account would be open to the objections that it is incomplete and arbitrary.[18]

I have suggested that if psychological continuity took a branching form, we ought to speak in a new way, regarding what we describe as having the same significance as identity. This answers these objections.[19]

We can now return to our discussion. We have three remaining aims. One is to suggest a sense of "survive" which does not imply identity. Another is to show that most of what matters in survival are relations of degree. A third is to show that none of these relations needs to be described in a way that presupposes identity.

We can take these aims in the reverse order.

III

The most important particular relation is that involved in memory. This is because it is so easy to believe that its description must refer to identity.[20] This belief about memory is an important cause of the view that personal identity has a special nature. But it has been well discussed by Shoemaker[21] and by Wiggins.[22] So we can be brief.

It may be a logical truth that we can only remember our own experiences. But we can frame a new concept for which this is not a logical truth. Let us call this "*q*-memory."

To sketch a definition[23] I am *q*-remembering an experience if (1) I have a belief about a past experience which seems in itself like a memory belief, (2) someone did have such an experience, and (3) my belief is dependent upon this experience in the same way (whatever that is) in which a memory of an experience is dependent upon it.

According to (1) *q*-memories seem like memories. So I *q*-remember *having* experiences.

This may seem to make *q*-memory presuppose identity. One might say, "My apparent memory of *having* an experience is an apparent memory of *my* having an experience. So how could I *q*-remember my having other people's experiences?"

This objection rests on a mistake. When I seem to remember an experience, I do indeed seem to remember *having* it.[24] But it cannot be a part of what I seem to remember about this experience that I, the person who now seems to remember it, am the person who had this experience.[25] That I am is something that I

---

* Guy Fawkes (1570–1606) attempted to assassinate King James I of England and blow up the English Parliament as part of the so-called Gunpowder Plot in 1605.

automatically assume. (My apparent memories sometimes come to me simply as the belief that *I* had a certain experience.) But it is something that I am justified in assuming only because I do not in fact have q-memories of other people's experiences.

Suppose that I did start to have such q-memories. If I did, I should cease to assume that my apparent memories must be about my own experiences. I should come to assess an apparent memory by asking two questions: (1) Does it tell me about a past experience? (2) If so, whose?

Moreover (and this is a crucial point) my apparent memories would now come to me as q-memories. Consider those of my apparent memories which do come to me simply as beliefs about my past: for example, "I did that." If I knew that I could q-remember other people's experiences, these beliefs would come to me in a more guarded form: for example, "Someone—probably I—did that." I might have to work out who it was.

I have suggested that the concept of q-memory is coherent. Wiggins' case provides an illustration. The resulting people, in his case, both have apparent memories of living the life of the original person. If they agree that they are not this person, they will have to regard these as only q-memories. And when they are asked a question like "Have you heard this music before?" they might have to answer "I am sure that I q-remember hearing it. But I am not sure whether I remember hearing it. I am not sure whether it was I who heard it, or the original person."

We can next point out that on our definition every memory is also a q-memory. Memories are, simply, q-memories of one's own experiences. Since this is so, we could afford now to drop the concept of memory and use in its place the wider concept q-memory. If we did, we should describe the relation between an experience and what we now call a "memory" of this experience in a way which does not presuppose that they are had by the same person.[26]

This way of describing this relation has certain merits. It vindicates the "memory criterion" of personal identity against the charge of circularity.[27] And it might, I think, help with the problem of other minds.

But we must move on. We can next take the relation between an intention and a later action. It may be a logical truth that we can intend to perform only our own actions. But intentions can be redescribed as q-intentions. And one person could q-intend to perform another person's actions.

Wiggins' case again provides the illustration. We are supposing that neither of the resulting people is the original person. If so, we shall have to agree that the original person can, before the operation, q-intend to perform their actions. He might, for example, q-intend, as one of them, to continue his present career, and, as the other, to try something new.[28] (I say "q-intend *as* one of them" because the phrase "q-intend *that* one of them" would not convey the directness of the relation which is involved. If I intend that someone else should do something, I cannot get him to do it simply by forming this intention. But if I am the original person, and he is one of the resulting people, I can.)

The phrase "q-intend *as* one of them" reminds us that we need a sense in which one person can survive as two. But we can first point out that the concepts of q-memory and q-intention give us our model for the others that we need: thus, a man who can q-remember could q-recognize, and be a q-witness of, what he has never seen; and a man who can q-intend could have q-ambitions, make q-promises, and be q-responsible for.

To put this claim in general terms: many different relations are included within, or are a consequence of, psychological continuity. We describe these relations in ways which presuppose the continued existence of one person. But we could describe them in new ways which do not.

This suggests a bolder claim. It might be possible to think of experiences in a wholly "impersonal" way. I shall not develop this claim here. What I shall try to describe is a way of thinking of our own identity through time which is more flexible, and less misleading, than the way in which we now think.

This way of thinking will allow for a sense in which one person can survive as two. A more important feature is that it treats survival as a matter of degree.

IV

We must first show the need for this second feature. I shall use two imaginary examples.

The first is the converse of Wiggins' case: fusion. Just as division serves to show that what matters in survival need not be one–one, so fusion serves to show that it can be a question of degree.

Physically, fusion is easy to describe. Two people come together. While they are unconscious, their two bodies grow into one. One person then wakes up.

The psychology of fusion is more complex. One detail we have already dealt with in the case of the exam. When my mind was reunited, I remembered just having thought out two calculations. The one person who results from a fusion can, similarly, *q*-remember living the lives of the two original people. None of their *q*-memories need be lost.

But some things must be lost. For any two people who fuse together will have different characteristics, different desires, and different intentions. How can these be combined?

We might suggest the following. Some of these will be compatible. These can coexist in the one resulting person. Some will be incompatible. These, if of equal strength, can cancel out, and if of different strengths, the stronger can be made weaker. And all these effects might be predictable.

To give examples—first, of compatibility: I like Palladio* and intend to visit Venice. I am about to fuse with a person who likes Giotto† and intends to visit Padua. I can know that the one person we shall become will have both tastes and both intentions. Second, of incompatibility: I hate red hair, and always vote Labour. The other person loves red hair, and always votes Conservative.‡ I can know that the one person we shall become will be indifferent to red hair, and a floating voter.§

If we were about to undergo a fusion of this kind, would we regard it as death?

Some of us might. This is less absurd than regarding division as death. For after my division the two resulting people will be in every way like me, while after my fusion the one resulting person will not be wholly similar. This makes it easier to say, when faced with fusion, "I shall not survive," thus continuing to regard survival as a matter of all-or-nothing.

This reaction is less absurd. But here are two analogies which tell against it.

First, fusion would involve the changing of some of our characteristics and some of our desires. But only the very self-satisfied would think of this as death. Many people welcome treatments with these effects.

Second, someone who is about to fuse can have, beforehand, just as much "intentional control" over the actions of the resulting individual as someone who is about to marry can have, beforehand, over the actions of the resulting couple. And the choice of a partner for fusion can be just as well considered as the choice of a marriage partner. The two original people can make sure (perhaps by "trial fusion") that they do have compatible characters, desires, and intentions.

I have suggested that fusion, while not clearly survival, is not clearly failure to survive, and hence that what matters in survival can have degrees.

To reinforce this claim we can now turn to a second example. This is provided by certain imaginary beings. These beings are just like ourselves except that they reproduce by a process of natural division.

We can illustrate the histories of these imagined beings with the aid of a diagram. (See below.) The lines on the diagram represent the spatiotemporal paths which would be traced out by the bodies of these beings. We can call each single line (like the double line) a "branch"; and we can call the whole structure a "tree." And let us suppose that each "branch" corresponds to what is thought of as the life of one individual. These individuals are referred to as "A," "B + 1," and so forth.

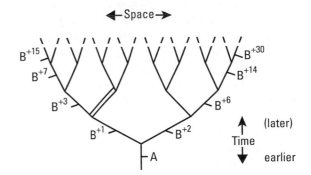

* Andrea Palladio was a sixteenth-century Italian architect best known for the buildings he designed in Venice.
† Giotto di Bondone was an Italian painter and architect whose most famous work is the decoration of the Scrovegni Chapel in Padua, c. 1305.
‡ Labour refers to the most prominent left-wing political party in Britain, and Conservative to the most prominent right-wing party.
§ Someone with no allegiance to any one political party.

Now, each single division is an instance of Wiggins' case. So *A*'s relation to both *B* + 1 and *B* + 2 is just as good as survival. But what of *A*'s relation to *B* + 30?

I said earlier that what matters in survival could be provisionally referred to as "psychological continuity." I must now distinguish this relation from another, which I shall call "psychological connectedness."

Let us say that the relation between a *q*-memory and the experience *q*-remembered is a "direct" relation. Another "direct" relation is that which holds between a *q*-intention and the *q*-intended action. A third is that which holds between different expressions of some lasting *q*-characteristic.

"Psychological connectedness," as I define it, requires the holding of these direct psychological relations. "Connectedness" is not transitive, since these relations are not transitive.* Thus, if *X q*-remembers most of *Y*'s life, and *Y q*-remembers most of *Z*'s life, it does not follow that *X q*-remembers most of *Z*'s life. And if *X* carries out the *q*-intentions of *Y*, and *Y* carries out the *q*-intentions of *Z*, it does not follow that *X* carries out the *q*-intentions of *Z*.

"Psychological continuity," in contrast, only requires overlapping chains of direct psychological relations. So "continuity" *is* transitive.

To return to our diagram. *A is* psychologically continuous with *B* + 30. There are between the two continuous chains of overlapping relations. Thus, *A* has *q*-intentional control over *B* + 2, *B* + 2 has *q*-intentional control over *B* + 6, and so on up to *B* + 30. Or *B*+ 30 can *q*-remember the life of *B* + 14, *B* + 14 can *q*-remember the life of *B* + 6, and so on back to *A*.[29]

A, however, need *not* be psychologically connected to *B* + 30. Connectedness requires direct relations. And if these beings are like us, *A* cannot stand in such relations to every individual in his indefinitely long "tree." *Q*-memories will weaken with the passage of time, and then fade away. *Q*-ambitions, once fulfilled, will be replaced by others. *Q*-characteristics will gradually change. In general, *A* stands in fewer and fewer direct psychological relations to an individual in his "tree" the more remote that individual is. And if the individual is (like *B* + 30) sufficiently remote, there may be between the two *no* direct psychological relations.

Now that we have distinguished the general relations of psychological continuity and psychological connectedness, I suggest that connectedness is a more important element in survival. As a claim about our own survival, this would need more arguments than I have space to give. But it seems clearly true for my imagined beings. *A* is as close psychologically to *B* + 1 as I today am to myself tomorrow. *A* is as distant from *B* + 30 as I am from my great-great-grandson.

Even if connectedness is not more important than continuity, the fact that one of these is a relation of degree is enough to show that what matters in survival can have degrees. And in any case the two relations are quite different. So our imagined beings would need a way of thinking in which this difference is recognized.

V

What I propose is this.

First, *A* can think of any individual, anywhere in his "tree," as "a descendant self." This phrase implies psychological continuity. Similarly, any later individual can think of any earlier individual on the single path[30] which connects him to *A* as "an ancestral self."

Since psychological continuity is transitive, "being an ancestral self of" and "being a descendant self of" are also transitive.

To imply psychological connectedness I suggest the phrases "one of my future selves" and "one of my past selves."

These are the phrases with which we can describe Wiggins' case. For having past and future selves is, what we needed, a way of continuing to exist which does not imply identity through time. The original person does, in this sense, survive Wiggins' operation: the two resulting people are his later selves. And they can each refer to him as "my past self." (They can share a past self without being the same self as each other.)

Since psychological connectedness is not transitive, and is a matter of degree, the relations "being a past self of" and "being a future self of" should themselves be treated as relations of degree. We allow for

---

* A relation R is transitive when, if *a* is related by R to *b*, and *b* is related by R to *c*, then *a* must be related by R to *c*. "Is larger than" is an example of a transitive relation, while "gave birth to" is not.

this series of descriptions: "my most recent self," "one of my earlier selves," "one of my distant selves," "hardly one of *my* past selves (I can only *q*-remember a few of his experiences)," and, finally, "not in any way one of *my* past selves—just an ancestral self."

This way of thinking would clearly suit our first imagined beings. But let us now turn to a second kind of being. These reproduce by fusion as well as by division.[31] And let us suppose that they fuse every autumn and divide every spring. This yields the following diagram:

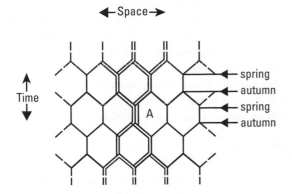

←Space→

If *A* is the individual whose life is represented by the three-lined "branch," the two-lined "tree" represents those lives which are psychologically continuous with *A*'s life. (It can be seen that each individual has his own "tree," which overlaps with many others.)

For the imagined beings in this second world, the phrases "an ancestral self" and "a descendant self" would cover too much to be of much use. (There may well be pairs of dates such that every individual who ever lived before the first date was an ancestral self of every individual who ever will live after the second date.) Conversely, since the lives of each individual last for only half a year, the word "I" would cover too little to do all of the work which it does for us. So part of this work would have to be done, for these second beings, by talk about past and future selves.

We can now point out a theoretical flaw in our proposed way of thinking. The phrase "a past self of" implies psychological connectedness. Being a past self of is treated as a relation of degree, so that this phrase can be used to imply the varying degrees of psychological connectedness. But this phrase can imply only the degrees of connectedness between different lives. It cannot be used within a single life. And our way

of delimiting successive lives does not refer to the degrees of psychological connectedness. Hence there is no guarantee that this phrase, "a past self of," could be used whenever it was needed. There is no guarantee that psychological connectedness will not vary in degree within a single life.

This flaw would not concern our imagined beings. For they divide and unite so frequently, and their lives are in consequence so short, that within a single life psychological connectedness would always stand at a maximum.

But let us look, finally, at a third kind of being.

In this world there is neither division nor union. There are a number of everlasting bodies, which gradually change in appearance. And direct psychological relations, as before, hold only over limited periods of time. This can be illustrated with a third diagram (given below). In this diagram the two shadings represent the degrees of psychological connectedness to their two central points.

←Space→

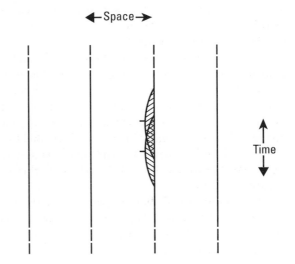

These beings could not use the way of thinking that we have proposed. Since there is no branching of psychological continuity, they would have to regard themselves as immortal. It might be said that this is what they are. But there is, I suggest, a better description.

Our beings would have one reason for thinking of themselves as immortal. The parts of each "line" are all psychologically continuous. But the parts of each "line" are not all psychologically connected. Direct psychological relations hold only between those parts which are close to each other in time. This gives our beings a reason for *not* thinking of each "line" as corresponding to one single life. For if they did, they would have no way of implying these direct relations. When a speaker says, for example, "I spent a period doing such and such," his hearers would not be entitled to assume that the speaker has any memories of this period, that his character then and now are in any way similar, that he is now carrying out any of the plans or intentions which he then had, and so forth. Because the word "I" would carry none of these implications, it would not have for these "immortal" beings the usefulness which it has for us.[32]

To gain a better way of thinking, we must revise the way of thinking that we proposed above. The revision is this. The distinction between successive selves can be made by reference, not to the branching of psychological continuity, but to the degrees of psychological connectedness. Since this connectedness is a matter of degree, the drawing of these distinctions can be left to the choice of the speaker and be allowed to vary from context to context.

On this way of thinking, the word "I" can be used to imply the greatest degree of psychological connectedness. When the connections are reduced, when there has been any marked change of character or style of life, or any marked loss of memory, our imagined beings would say, "It was not I who did that, but an earlier self." They could then describe in what ways, and to what degree, they are related to this earlier self.

This revised way of thinking would suit not only our "immortal" beings. It is also the way in which we ourselves could think about our lives. And it is, I suggest, surprisingly natural.

One of its features, the distinction between successive selves, has already been used by several writers. To give an example, from Proust:* "we are incapable, while we are in love, of acting as fit predecessors of the next persons who, when we are in love no longer, we shall presently have become...."[33]

Although Proust distinguished between successive selves, he still thought of one person as being these different selves. This we would not do on the way of thinking that I propose. If I say, "It will not be me, but one of my future selves," I do not imply that I will be that future self. He is one of my later selves, and I am one of his earlier selves. There is no underlying person who we both are.

To point out another feature of this way of thinking. When I say, "There is no person who we both are," I am only giving my decision. Another person could say, "It will be you," thus deciding differently. There is no question of either of these decisions being a mistake. Whether to say "I," or "one of my future selves," or "a descendant self" is entirely a matter of choice. The matter of fact, which must be agreed, is only whether the disjunction applies. (The question "Are *X* and *Y* the same person?" thus becomes "Is *X* at least* an ancestral [or descendant] self of *Y*?")

VI

I have tried to show that what matters in the continued existence of a person are, for the most part, relations of degree. And I have proposed a way of thinking in which this would be recognized.

I shall end by suggesting two consequences and asking one question.

It is sometimes thought to be especially rational to act in our own best interests. But I suggest that the principle of self-interest has no force. There are only two genuine competitors in this particular field. One is the principle of biased rationality: do what will best achieve what you actually want. The other is the principle of impartiality: do what is in the best interests of everyone concerned.

The apparent force of the principle of self-interest derives, I think, from these two other principles.

The principle of self-interest is normally supported by the principle of biased rationality. This is because most people care about their own future interests.

Suppose that this prop is lacking. Suppose that a man does not care what happens to him in, say, the

---

* Marcel Proust was a French author, best known for his novel, *À la recherche du temps perdu* ("In Search of Lost Time"), published in seven parts between 1913 and 1927. Proust's writing is characterized by detailed reminiscences on the past, which are often sparked by chance encounters with objects in the present.

more distant future. To such a man, the principle of self-interest can only be propped up by an appeal to the principle of impartiality. We must say, "Even if you don't care, you ought to take what happens to you then equally into account." But for this, as a special claim, there seem to me no good arguments. It can only be supported as part of the general claim, "You ought to take what happens to everyone equally into account."[34]

The special claim tells a man to grant an *equal* weight to all the parts of his future. The argument for this can only be that all the parts of his future are *equally* parts of *his* future. This is true. But it is a truth too superficial to bear the weight of the argument. (To give an analogy: The unity of a nation is, in its nature, a matter of degree. It is therefore only a superficial truth that all of a man's compatriots are *equally* his compatriots. This truth cannot support a good argument for nationalism.)[35]

I have suggested that the principle of self-interest has no strength of its own. If this is so, there is no special problem in the fact that what we ought to do can be against our interests. There is only the general problem that it may not be what we want to do.

The second consequence which I shall mention is implied in the first. Egoism, the fear not of near but of distant death, the regret that so much of one's *only* life should have gone by—these are not, I think, wholly natural or instinctive. They are all strengthened by the beliefs about personal identity which I have been attacking. If we give up these beliefs, they should be weakened.

My final question is this. These emotions are bad, and if we weaken them we gain. But can we achieve this gain without, say, also weakening loyalty to, or love of, other particular selves? As Hume* warned, the "refined reflections which philosophy suggests ... cannot diminish ... our vicious passions ... without diminishing ... such as are virtuous. They are ... applicable to all our affections. In vain do we hope to direct their influence only to one side."[36]

That hope *is* vain. But Hume had another: that more of what is bad depends upon false belief. This is also my hope. ■

Suggestions for Critical Reflection

1. Parfit's theory of personal identity is often compared to the Buddhist doctrine of no-self—to the point that Tibetan monks have been reported to chant excerpts from his books. To what extent does Parfit advocate the erasure of the self? How does Parfit's theory of degrees of relation relate to the Buddhist idea that all things in the universe are related to one another?

2. Parfit develops a concept he calls *q*-memory. Why does he do this—what part of his overall argument is this? How clear is his explanation of *q*-memory? Are all our memories really *q*-memories?

3. "Now that we have distinguished the general relations of psychological continuity and psychological connectedness, I suggest that connectedness is a more important element in survival." Is Parfit able to show this? How radical is this conclusion, if it is true?

4. Parfit recognizes that a weakened conception of personal identity may inadvertently result in people losing loyalty towards or love for others. Is identity a precondition for love or loyalty? Why or why not?

5. Parfit suggests that his critique of personal identity may soften fears that people have around death. Do you agree with this claim? Why or why not?

6. Parfit claims that his view has practical ethical consequences, in that it may lead us to abandon the principle of self-interest. Does his view also suggest that we should change our understanding of personal responsibility? Does our criminal justice system rely on a certain conception of the self?

---

* David Hume (1711–76) was an important Scottish philosopher. For more on Hume, see the Philosophy of Religion and Philosophy of Science chapters of this volume.

7. The Mississippi river has, at several places in it, long islands dividing it into two streams which rejoin down-river. Suppose we drive to the bank of the east stream at one such place. (Call that stream 'Eastie'.) "That's the Mississippi!" I say. But later we drive on the other side to the west stream ('Westie'). "That's the Mississippi again!" I say. If what I said was true, then Eastie = the Mississippi (where the equals sign means *identity*), and Westie = the Mississippi, but Eastie ≠ Westie. Does this approach to identity conflict with Parfit's? If so, who is correct?

8. Suppose that you can expect to live for another 60 years, and that you're pretty sure that 60 years from now you'll have no psychological connectedness whatever with your present self. On those grounds, would Parfit say that you really should have no motivation to think long-term: don't bother brushing your teeth, or putting money into a retirement fund?

Notes

1 I have been helped in writing this by D. Wiggins, D.F. Pears, P.F. Strawson, A.J. Ayer, M. Woods, N. Newman, and (through his publications) S. Shoemaker.

2 Implicit in John Locke, *Essay Concerning Human Understanding*, ed. by John W. Yolton (London, 1961), Vol. II, Ch. XXVII, sec. 18, and discussed by (among others) A.N. Prior in "Opposite Number," *Review of Metaphysics*, II (1957–1958), and "Time, Existence and Identity," *Proceedings of the Aristotelian Society*, LVII (1965–1966); J. Bennett in "The Simplicity of the Soul," *Journal of Philosophy*, LXIV (1967); and R. Chisholm and S. Shoemaker in "The Loose and Popular and the Strict and the Philosophical Senses of Identity," in *Perception and Personal Identity: Proceedings of the 1967 Oberlin Colloquium in Philosophy*, ed. by Norman Care and Robert H. Grimm (Cleveland, 1967).

3 In *Identity and Spatio-Temporal Continuity* (Oxford, 1967), p. 50.

4 In *Self-Knowledge and Self-Identity* (Ithaca, N.Y., 1963), p. 22.

5 Those who would disagree are not making a mistake. For them my argument would need a different case. There must be some multiple transplant, faced with which these people would both find it hard to believe that there must be an answer to the question about personal identity, and be able to be shown that nothing of importance turns upon this question.

6 R.W. Sperry, in *Brain and Conscious Experience*, ed. by J.C. Eccles (New York, 1966), p. 299.

7 Cf. David Wiggins, *op. cit*, p. 40.

8 Suppose the resulting people fight a duel. Are there three people fighting, one on each side, and one on both? And suppose one of the bullets kills. Are there two acts, one murder and one suicide? How many people are left alive? One? Two? (We could hardly say, "One and a half.") We could talk in this way. But instead of saying that the resulting people *are* the original person—so that the pair is a trio—it would be far simpler to treat them as a pair, and describe their relation to the original person in some new way. (I owe this suggested way of talking, and the objections to it, to Michael Woods.)

9 Cf. Sydney Shoemaker, in *Perception and Personal Identity: Proceedings of the 1967 Oberlin Colloquium in Philosophy, loc. cit.*

10 Cf. David Wiggins, *op. cit.*, p. 54.

11 Bernard Williams' "The Self and the Future," *Philosophical Review*, LXXIX (1970), 161–180, is relevant here. He asks the question "Shall I survive?" in a range of problem cases, and he shows how natural it is to believe (1) that this question must have an answer, (2) that the answer must be all-or-nothing, and (3) that there is a "risk" of our reaching the *wrong* answer. Because these beliefs are so natural, we should need in undermining them to discuss their causes. These, I think, can be found in the ways in which we misinterpret what it is to remember (cf. Sec. III below) and to anticipate (cf. Williams' "Imagination and the Self," *Proceedings of the British Academy*, LII [1966], 105–124); and also in the way in which certain features of our egoistic concern—e.g., that it is simple, and applies to all imaginable cases—are "projected" onto its object. (For another relevant discussion, see Terence Penelhum's *Survival and Disembodied Existence* [London, 1970], final chapters.)

12 "Personal Identity and Individuation," *Proceedings of the Aristotelian Society*, LVII (1956–1957), 229–253; also *Analysis*, 21 (1960–1961), 43–48.

13 J.M. Shorter, "More about Bodily Continuity and Personal Identity," *Analysis*, 22 (1961–1962), 79–85; and Mrs. J.M.R. Jack (unpublished), who requires that this truth be embedded in a causal theory.

14 *Analysis*, 21 (1960–1961), 44.

15 For the reasons given by A.M. Quinton in "The Soul," *Journal of Philosophy*, LIX (1962), 393–409.

16 Cf. S. Shoemaker, "Persons and Their Pasts," to appear in the *American Philosophical Quarterly*, and "Wiggins on Identity," *Philosophical Review*, LXXIX (1970), 542.

17 But not a necessary condition, for in the absence of psychological continuity bodily identity might be sufficient.

18 Cf. Bernard Williams, "Personal Identity and Individuation," *Proceedings of the Aristotelian Society*, LVII (1956–1957), 240–241, and *Analysis*, 21 (1960–1961), 44; and also Wiggins, *op. cit.*, p. 38: "if coincidence under [the concept] *f* is to be *genuinely* sufficient we must not withhold identity ... simply because transitivity is threatened."

19 Williams produced another objection to the "psychological criterion," that it makes it hard to explain the difference between the concepts of identity and exact similarity (*Analysis*, 21 [1960–1961], 48). But if we include the requirement of causal continuity we avoid this objection (and one of those produced by Wiggins in his note 47).

20 Those philosophers who have held this belief, from Butler onward, are too numerous to cite.

21 *Op. cit.*

22 In a paper on Butler's objection to Locke (not yet published).

23 I here follow Shoemaker's "quasi-memory." Cf. also Penelhum's "retrocognition," in his article on "Personal Identity," in the *Encyclopedia of Philosophy*, ed. by Paul Edwards.

24 As Shoemaker put it, I seem to remember the experience "from the inside" (*op. cit.*).

25 This is what so many writers have overlooked. Cf. Thomas Reid: "My memory testifies not only that this was done, but that it was done by me who now remember it" ("Of Identity," in *Essays on the Intellectual Powers of Man*, ed. by A.D. Woozley [London, 1941], p. 203). This mistake is discussed by A.B. Palma in "Memory and Personal Identity," *Australasian Journal of Philosophy*, 42 (1964), 57.

26 It is not logically necessary that we only *q*-remember our own experiences. But it might be necessary on other grounds. This possibility is intriguingly explored by Shoemaker in his "Persons and Their Pasts" (*op. cit.*). He shows that *q*-memories can provide a knowledge of the world only if the observations which are *q*-remembered trace out fairly continuous spatiotemporal paths. If the observations which are *q*-remembered traced out a network of frequently interlocking paths, they could not, I think, be usefully ascribed to persisting observers, but would have to be referred to in some more complex way. But in fact the observations which are *q*-remembered trace out single and separate paths; so we can ascribe them to ourselves. In other words, it is epistemologically necessary that the observations which are *q*-remembered should satisfy a certain general condition, one particular form of which allows them to be usefully self-ascribed.

27 Cf. Wiggins' paper on Butler's objection to Locke.

28 There are complications here. He could form *divergent* *q*-intentions only if he could distinguish, in advance, between the resulting people (e.g., as "the left-hander" and "the right-hander"). And he could be confident that such divergent *q*-intentions would be carried out only if he had reason to believe that neither of the resulting people would change their (inherited) mind. Suppose he was torn between duty and desire. He could not solve this dilemma by *q*-intending, as one of the resulting people, to do his duty, and, as the other, to do what he desires. For the one he *q*-intended to do his duty would face the same dilemma.

29 The chain of continuity must run in one direction of time. *B* + 2 is not, in the sense I intend, psychologically continuous with *B* + 1.

30 Cf. David Wiggins, *op. cit.*

31 Cf. Sydney Shoemaker in "Persons and Their Pasts," *op. cit.*

32 Cf. Austin Duncan Jones, "Man's Mortality," *Analysis*, 28 (1967–1968), 65–70.

33 *Within a Budding Grove* (London, 1949), I, 226 (my own translation).

34 Cf. Thomas Nagel's *The Possibility of Altruism* (Oxford, 1970), in which the special claim is in effect defended as part of the general claim.

35 The unity of a nation we seldom take for more than what it is. This is partly because we often think of nations, not as units, but in a more complex way. If we thought of ourselves in the way that I proposed, we might be less likely to take our own identity for more than what it is. We are, for example, sometimes told, "It is irrational to act against your own interests. After all, it will be *you* who will regret it." To this we could reply, "No, not me. Not even one of my future selves. Just a descendant self."

36 "The Sceptic," in "Essays Moral, Political and Literary," *Hume's Moral and Political Philosophy* (New York, 1959), p. 349.

MARYA SCHECHTMAN

Experience, Agency, and Personal Identity

Who Is Marya Schechtman?

Marya Schechtman (b. 1960) obtained her PhD in 1988 from Harvard University, writing a dissertation on issues of personal identity and bioethics—two topics that continue to be the focus of her research. She also has interests in practical reasoning and Existentialism. Schechtman's first book, *The Constitution of Selves* (1996), identified conceptual slippage and equivocation in the work of contemporary theorists of identity. Her most recent book, *Staying Alive* (2014), broadens this inquiry and addresses the connections between metaphysical and practical questions of personal identity. Since 1988, she has held a position at the University of Illinois at Chicago, where she is Professor of Philosophy and the Associate Dean of the College of Liberal Arts and Sciences.

What Is the Structure of This Reading?

In this article Schechtman describes how internal tensions in the metaphysical debate about persons as continuing psychological subjects have led to a focus instead on practical philosophy and the notion of persons as unified agents. However, she goes on to argue, an account of personal identity wholly in terms of agency "is likely to remain unsatisfying" and she advocates for an integrated approach that draws upon both the unity of the subject and the unity of agency.

After introducing her topic in section I, in section II of the paper Schechtman draws upon the work of philosopher Peter Unger to motivate the view that "a *person* is most fundamentally an experiencing subject, and survival must involve the unity of an experiencing subject over time." But then in section III she outlines how Derek Parfit has argued forcefully that this apparently attractive idea cannot be understood coherently.

One response to Parfit's critique would be to give up on the idea that there is any psychological criterion for personal identity, but instead (in section IV) Schechtman describes how some philosophers have reacted by developing a different psychological criterion. Instead of the view that we are "subjects" of experience whose survival over time is a matter of having a unified consciousness, some philosophers such as John Perry, Carol Rovane, and Christine Korsgaard have proposed the view that "agency" is essential to personhood—that is, the view that we do (and perhaps must) conceive ourselves in terms of our decisions and intentions, including life plans and short-term goals that give us reasons to act.

In section V, though, Schechtman subjects the agency view of selfhood to a critique, drawing upon the writings of existential philosopher Albert Camus, who claimed that our lives have no intrinsic meaning and that we must "find our value instead in the raw fact of our consciousness." The agency-based account seems unable to explain why we *care* about continuing to exist into the future. Schechtman concludes that we should return to a view of personal identity as being the continuing subject of conscious experience, but that this view can be changed and strengthened by incorporating insights from the agency view—"we must think of subjectivity and agency as inherently intertwined, and thus of unity of agency and unity of consciousness as separate but interdependent unities."

Experience, Agency, and Personal Identity[*1]

I. Introduction

Questions of personal identity are raised in many different philosophical contexts. In metaphysics the question at issue is that of personal identity over time, or of what relation a person at one time must bear to a person at another time in order for them to be, literally, the same person. There are two standard responses to this question in the current literature. One considers a person as essentially a biological entity and defines the identity of the person over time in terms of the continued existence of a single organism. The other follows John Locke in accepting a distinction between persons and human beings and defines the identity of a person in terms of the continued flow of psychological life.[2] This second response—the "psychological continuity theory"—has a great deal of appeal and enjoys a great many supporters. Both positions are still very much alive in the current discussion, suggesting that at the very least each response expresses some important aspect of our thought about what we are and how we continue. In what follows I will leave aside the dispute *between* these two accounts of identity and will focus only on the psychological side. Understanding what fuels the idea that personal identity should be defined in psychological terms, and what a viable psychological account of identity would look like, is an important goal in its own right and will put us in a better position to understand the relation between psychological and biological accounts of identity.

A central element in the motivation and defense of the psychological continuity theory of personal identity comes from the intimate connection between the concepts of identity and survival. One obvious way of understanding what it means for a person to survive is for there to be someone in the future who is she. Since surviving is, to put it mildly, a matter of the utmost practical importance, it seems that whatever relation defines personal identity over time should also bear the importance we attach to survival. Psychological continuity theorists argue that when we ask ourselves which kind of continuation—physical or psychological—seems to bear this importance, the latter emerges as the better candidate. This view trades on the intuition that a situation where a person's body continues to function but his psychological life comes to an end (as in, e.g., a case of irreversible coma or total possession) seems like a failure to survive, while a situation in which psychological life continues despite the death of a person's body (as in, e.g., some of the traditional religious depictions of an afterlife) seems like a case of personal continuation.

It remains, however, for psychological continuity theorists to describe in more detail the kind of psychological continuation that constitutes survival. The initial and most natural idea is that persons should be construed as experiencing subjects, and that personal identity should be defined in terms of a deep unity of consciousness throughout an entire life, but this unity turns out to be difficult to define coherently. For this and other reasons, some identity theorists who support a psychologically based view have shifted from a picture of the person as a subject to a picture of the person as an agent,[†] and from a definition of personal identity in terms of a deep phenomenological unity[‡] to a definition in terms of the unity of agency. This shift leaves us with the question of whether unity of agency is a strong enough relation to provide an account of what it is for a person, literally, to survive.

Some resources for answering this question can be found in other areas of philosophy—in particular,

---

* Published in *Social Philosophy and Policy* 22, 2 (2005): 1–24.

† In philosophy, "agency" usually refers to the ability to act and make decisions; an "agent" is a being that is able to make choices and do things. A "subject," by contrast, is usually thought of as being endowed with consciousness, which is able to experience things and possess beliefs and desires.

‡ Phenomenology is a philosophical approach that examines the nature of experience and the "phenomena" that appear within consciousness. In this context, "phenomenological unity" refers to the idea that identity is based on a continuous chain of conscious experiences.

in discussions of free will, practical reason, and the theory of action, which I will refer to collectively with the term "practical philosophy." A prominent strand of thought there suggests that having deeply held projects and commitments is essential to being a person, and describes how a person can literally disintegrate from a lack of such projects and commitments. While this discussion does make a strong case that unity of agency must be part of any acceptable psychological account of the persistence of the person, the original intuition that some sort of deep unity of consciousness is required for personal survival runs deep, and a view couched entirely in terms of unity of agency is unlikely to be fully satisfying. Fortunately, the insights gleaned by following out the shift toward a view of the person as agent can help point to a way that something like phenomenological unity of consciousness might be introduced without so much difficult metaphysical baggage.

My main goal here is to follow out the way in which a picture of persons as essentially agents has found its way into the metaphysical discussion of personal identity, and to assess where this leaves us in our attempts to understand the conditions of personal persistence. I begin by showing how the internal pressures of the metaphysical discussion lead to the introduction of an understanding of persons as agents, and how work in practical philosophy can help support the plausibility of this understanding as a response to the metaphysical question of personal persistence. After this I discuss why a response to this question wholly in terms of agency is likely to remain unsatisfying, and I point very briefly to a possible strategy for reintroducing an understanding of the person as subject as part of a more integrated account.

II. What Matters in Survival and Peter Unger's Distinction

As I have already mentioned, the central considerations supporting the psychological continuity theory are based on the idea that it is psychological rather than physical continuation that captures what

matters to us in survival. As discussion of this view has unfolded, many psychological continuity theorists have found reason to put aside the question of personal identity per se and ask directly about the conditions of survival and what we find important in it. The main impetus for this switch is a difficulty with using psychological continuity as a criterion of personal identity. Psychological continuity—at least as usually defined by these theories—does not have the logical form of an identity relation. The continuity relation, unlike identity itself, can be one–many, intransitive,* and a matter of degree. Derek Parfit famously argues that this does not undermine the psychological continuity theory but rather reveals that what really underlies our interest in the question of personal identity over time is the issue of survival.[3] In ordinary circumstances, survival will involve identity; the person as whom one survives will be oneself. However, in certain imaginable science fiction scenarios, Parfit argues, it may be possible to survive as someone else. This might happen, for instance, if a person could split amoeba-like into two qualitatively identical people. Such a division hardly seems like death, he argues, yet the two resulting people, since they are clearly not identical with one another, cannot both be identical to the original person on pain of intransitivity. This "fission" scenario is thus a case in which a person enjoys what we take to be significant in survival despite the fact that there is no one in the future to whom she is identical.[4]

Parfit holds that our interest in questions of identity is an artifact of the fact that in ordinary circumstances survival requires identity with some future person. Once we see that we can have what matters in survival without identity, we can see that our main interest is with survival rather than identity itself. The question of whether or not we are going to survive undoubtedly bears a special significance for us. As John Perry puts it: "You learn that someone will be run over by a truck tomorrow; you are saddened, feel pity, and think reflectively about the frailty of life; one bit of information is added, that someone is you, and a whole different set of emotions rise in

---

* A relation R is intransitive if *a* can be in relation R to *b*, and *b* can be in relation R to *c*, but *a* might not be in relation R to *c*. For example, 'being a predator of' is an intransitive relation. Identity is a transitive relation.

your breast."[5] What we are after with questions of diachronic* personal identity (that is, questions about the conditions for the persistence of a single person over time), says Parfit, is the question of what relation to the future carries this importance—"what matters" in survival. Many theorists of personal identity who would define it in psychological terms have thus shifted their emphasis from identity to what matters in survival.

It might seem as if the shift of focus to "what matters" automatically turns the discussion to a more metaphorical or psychological notion than that with which we started, since we are now asking what makes our continuation a good rather than what makes us, literally, still alive. Most psychological continuity theorists would deny this, however. The survival they are trying to define is, they insist, quite literal, and the sense of "what matters" at issue should be read that way. This point is made most explicitly by Peter Unger, who says that there are different things we could mean by "what matters in survival," and that it is important for us to keep clear on which of them is under consideration. He distinguishes between three different uses of this term. One, to which I will return later, concerns the question of which features of survival *constitute* it as survival. For present purposes, the most important distinction is between the other two senses, which he calls the "desirability" and the "prudential" senses of "what matters." According to the desirability sense,

> 'what matters in survival' will mean much the same as this: what it is that one gets out of survival that makes continued survival a desirable thing for one, a better thing, at least, than is utter cessation. On this desirability use, if one has what matters in survival, then, from a self-interested perspective, one has reason to continue rather than opt for sudden painless termination.[6]

This is contrasted with the prudential use, which determines,

from the perspective of a person's concern for herself, or from a slight rational extension of that perspective, what future being there is or, possibly, which future beings there are, for whom the person rationally should be "intrinsically" concerned. Saying that this rational concern is "intrinsic" means, roughly, that, even apart from questions of whether or not he might advance the present person's projects, there is this rational concern for the welfare of the future being.[7]

Unger suggests that there is a question of whether a future will be mine to experience—whether I will undergo what happens in it—which at least seems quite independent of my values, goals, ideals, or character traits.

If we are looking to answer literal, metaphysical questions about our survival, Unger argues, we should be looking for the relation that underlies the more fundamental, prudential connection between different moments of a person's life. The desirability sense of what matters may be an important thing to define in its own right, but it is not, he says, "highly relevant to questions of our survival."[8] To test for the prudential sense of what matters, Unger suggests that we use the "avoidance of future pain test." We are to imagine ourselves connected to a future person in some way, and then imagine that person being subjected to horrible torture or excruciating pain. The question we are to ask is whether our horror of the future pain is sympathetic in nature or rather the sort of concern we would feel if we were anticipating our own future pain. The latter response suggests that we have what matters in survival in the fundamental sense at issue in metaphysical discussions of personal survival.

Unger himself believes that attention to this question will lead us to a more biologically based account of personal survival, albeit one that requires the continuity of minimal psychological capacities (what he calls "core" psychology). Traditional psychological continuity theorists have rejected Unger's solution, but they seem to accept his basic insight. They suggest that the avoidance of future pain test

---

* Happening over time (as opposed to 'synchronic,' which means at a moment in time). You as a one-year-old are diachronically identical with you at present; you at present are synchronically identical with the person reading this footnote.

reveals that what matters fundamentally in survival is the legitimate *anticipation* of future experiences. To survive we must bear a connection to the future that makes it rational for us to expect to have experiences then. These theorists do not accept Unger's solution because they deny, for reasons given by Locke, that the continuity of the body can itself be what legitimates anticipation of future experiences. (Locke famously argues through the use of hypothetical cases that continuity of body—or soul—with no continuity of consciousness cannot provide what we seek in survival.) For such anticipation we need a deep phenomenological connection to the future—a unity of consciousness over time. Continuity of the body might turn out to be one source of such a phenomenological connection; it might even turn out to be the only source. This would, however, be a contingent fact, and even if it were true it would not be the continuity of the body per se, but rather the unity of consciousness it produced, that would make our intrinsic concern for some future person rational. On this view, then, a *person* is most fundamentally an experiencing subject, and survival must involve the unity of an experiencing subject over time. This is, in many ways, a very natural and appealing picture of what is involved in our survival as persons, but it is difficult to develop a coherent theory based on this picture, as the next section will explain.

III. Derek Parfit's Argument against the Person as Experiencing Subject

A compelling initial picture of what constitutes literal survival for those who take a psychological approach to this question is, as we have seen, a unity of consciousness over time.[9] Derek Parfit has argued quite forcefully, however, that this natural first idea of what defines survival cannot be defended—or even defined—in the end. He provides several arguments explicitly directed at the idea that personal identity cannot be defensibly defined in terms of the unity of a subject of experiences, but most of the fundamental insights behind these arguments can be found in the Teletransportation and Branch-Line cases with which he opens his discussion of personal identity in *Reasons and Persons*.[10] This pair of cases uncovers both the hold this conception of personal continuation has on us, and its problematic nature. In Teletransportation,

a subject enters a booth where his body is scanned and dematerialized. A molecule-for-molecule duplicate of the original body is built on the destination planet, a duplicate who by hypothesis replicates the intrinsic character of the original person's psychological states exactly. The question is whether this is an efficient means of travel to distant planets, or death and replacement by an imposter. Parfit acknowledges that we are quite likely to think of it as the latter. Despite the exact similarity of the newly formed individual to the original person, we may well fear that the replica will lack a deep attachment to that person present in ordinary survival. We fear that while in ordinary survival one will *feel* one's future experiences, in Teletransportation one will feel nothing in the future—one's point of view, which would continue in the ordinary case, is snuffed out.

The presupposition underlying this fear is that there is a deep unity of consciousness within a given life that may be absent in our connection to a replica. It is not immediately obvious exactly what this deep unity of consciousness is, but the basic idea can be understood on the model of co-consciousness at a time. At a given time there is a brute difference between a set of experiences being present in a single consciousness and their being parts of distinct consciousnesses. This is why, for example, a decision about whether to tolerate a small pain in my shoulder now to avoid an excruciating pain in my foot now is different in kind from a decision about whether to tolerate a small pain in my shoulder now to avoid *your* experiencing an excruciating pain in *your* foot now. The fear of Teletransportation reveals the supposition that we have a relation to our future experiences which is relevantly like the relation we have to our own present ones. This is why the decision about whether to suffer a small pain now to avoid an excruciating pain *later* is also different from the decision about whether to suffer a small pain now to keep someone else from suffering an excruciating pain later.[11] This difference is, of course, what the avoidance of future pain test proposed by Unger is testing for. When we fear that we will not survive Teletransportation, we are expressing the possibility that this connection to the future may not hold in cases of replication. In more concrete terms, we suspect that my attitude toward the replica's potential pains should be more like my attitude toward the potential pains of others than toward my own.

Since a teletransported replica is, by stipulation, completely identical to the original person in terms of the *contents* of her consciousness, whatever difference there is between ordinary survival and having a replica cannot be defined in terms of these contents. The previous discussion makes it clear, however, that it is supposed to be a difference in the *quality of experience*. To make the case that there could be such a difference, we thus need to be able to understand a phenomenological distinction between really continuing and being replaced by a replica which is not defined in terms of the contents of consciousness. Parfit's claim is that there is no defensible way to define such a distinction. The difference we are seeking cannot be explained by the fact that in one case we retain our original body, since the psychological account is based on the intuition that we could in theory have what counts as survival without continuation of the body. If the sameness of body plays a crucial role, it will have to be because continuing in a single body is experientially different from being replaced by a replica, and we still need to say something about the nature of this phenomenological difference.[12] Parfit thinks that we might have been able to make sense of this mysterious unity of consciousness over time if we accepted the view that we are simple, immaterial souls (although the Lockean arguments make this questionable in any event), but argues that there is no reason to believe such a thing, and many reasons not to.[13]

Of course, the inability to define the deep unity of consciousness that we assume in our own lives—and fear might be absent in replication—may not be enough to convince us that it does not exist. It seems as if we actively experience this continuity and connection in our own lives. Moreover, it seems all too possible to imagine the flow of our own psychological life terminated or diverted despite the existence of a replica with qualitatively identical contents of consciousness. Kathleen Wilkes makes this point quite effectively in a footnote in *Real People: Personal Identity without Thought Experiments*. Discussing the transporter depicted on the science fiction series *Star Trek*, she says:

Captain Kirk, so the story goes, disintegrates at place p and reassembles at place p*. But perhaps, instead, he dies at p and a doppelganger emerges at p*. What is the difference? One way of illustrating the difference is to suppose there is an afterlife: a heaven, or hell, increasingly supplemented by yet more Captain Kirks all cursing the day they ever stepped into the molecular disintegrator.[14]

Once the viewpoint of the original Captain Kirk is reintroduced, it seems natural to assume there is a unified flow of consciousness between the original Kirk and the disembodied Kirk—a flow of consciousness that does not exist between the original Kirk and his doppelganger. If we now simply take out the assumption of an afterlife, we can see that the connection between the original and doppelganger remains phenomenologically deficient.

Parfit himself is very sensitive to the pull of this idea, and this is why he introduces the variation on his Teletransportation case that he calls the "Branch-Line case." In the Branch-Line case, the traveler is scanned and a blueprint made, but the original body is not dematerialized. Instead, it is damaged in such a way that it can live only a few more days. At the same time, a healthy replica is built on the distant planet (here Mars) as in simple Teletransportation. There are now two people who are psychologically continuous (in Parfit's sense) with the original person: the replica on Mars and the person with the original body on Earth. It seems clear, Parfit acknowledges, that the connection between the person on Earth (now traveling on a branch line of psychological continuation) and the replica does not contain what matters most fundamentally in survival. Parfit imagines himself on the branch line talking to his replica on Mars:

Since my Replica knows that I am about to die, he tries to console me with the same thoughts with which I recently tried to console a dying friend. It is sad to learn, on the receiving end, how unconsoling these thoughts are. My Replica then assures me that he will take up my life where I leave off. He loves my wife, and together they will care for my children. And he will finish the book that I am writing.... All these facts console me a little. Dying when I know that I shall have a Replica is not quite as bad as, simply, dying. Even so, I shall soon lose consciousness, forever.[15]

The replica is as like the branch-line person in terms of contents of consciousness as a person is like herself in the near future, but there is all the difference in the world for this person between her psychological life continuing several more decades and its being terminated while the replica continues for those decades—or so it seems. This is why, Parfit acknowledges, "it is natural to assume that my prospect, on the Branch Line, is almost as bad as ordinary death." Nonetheless, he goes on to say, "[a]s I shall argue later, I ought to regard having a Replica as being about as good as ordinary survival."[16]

He offers a variety of considerations in favor of this claim. These include a collection of arguments for a reductionist view of persons, arguments against the possibility of directly experiencing a deep unity of consciousness over time in our own lives, and thought experiments aimed at making it more plausible that the person on the branch line could survive as the replica. The case most directly addressing this issue is, importantly, not a science fiction case, but one that is part of a real life. Parfit describes a sleeping pill he has taken that takes a short time to work. After taking the pill, the person remains fully conscious for a while, but when he awakens he has no memory of the time between taking the pill and falling asleep. Parfit reports that having once taken such a pill, he apparently solved a practical problem before falling asleep, for he found a note the next morning under his razor advising him of the solution, despite having no memory of solving the problem or writing the note. He argues that the person who has taken such a pill can know, like the person on the branch line, that his stream of consciousness will end before morning, but he is unlikely to face this prospect as if he is facing death. Yet, Parfit argues, in terms of intrinsic relations of consciousness or phenomenology the relation of the person who takes this sleeping pill to the person in the morning is no different from the relation of the branch-line person to his replica on Mars. There are, indeed, a host of differences between the two cases, but they do not seem to be *intrinsic* differences, and so if we want to say that these make

the difference between surviving and not surviving we will have given up on the idea that the importance of survival is linked to a deep diachronic unity of consciousness.

While there is much to understand—and to take exception to—in Parfit's arguments, the underlying theme is, I think, fairly simple and quite persuasive. What his arguments do at their most effective is direct us to commonplace examples of survival and undermine our conviction that there is any deep unity of consciousness there. The sleeping-pill case, for instance, tells us less about a heart-damaged person with a replica on Mars than about what happens to us all the time. We do not need to take sleeping pills to have gaps in our consciousness, or to know sometimes that what we are thinking and experiencing in the present will be entirely lost to future consciousness—this is why people make lists and keep journals. This challenge is reinforced by the sort of empirical work used by Daniel Dennett and Andy Clark, among others, to reveal that our unity of consciousness—even at a time—is not all that casual introspection might lead us to believe.[17]

Whatever the upshot of detailed engagement with Parfit's many arguments, he raises a powerful and serious challenge to one deep-seated understanding of what is involved in our survival, and its importance. A tempting and natural way to think about our continuation is in terms of a flow of consciousness that connects current experience to future experience in something like the way our current experiences are connected to one another. It is this flow of consciousness that seems to allow us to really have experiences in the future—to *be* there in the sense that is most important. Parfit's repeated challenge to this picture, emblemized in the Teletransportation and Branch-Line cases, is essentially David Hume's*—that if we take the time to really look, we can find no such unity in our own lives. This is why Parfit finally says of Teletransportation: "I want the person on Mars to be me in a specially intimate way in which no future person will ever be me. My continued existence never involves this deep further fact. What I fear will be missing is *always*

---

* The Scottish philosopher David Hume (1711–76) argues that the self is nothing more than a fleeting cluster of perceptions. He suggests that the commonplace idea that there is an enduring identity underlying our experiences is unjustified. See the readings from Hume elsewhere in this volume.

missing."[18] He thus draws the following conclusion: it is not, as he claimed earlier, that Teletransportation is about as good as ordinary survival, but rather that "ordinary survival is *about as bad as*, or little better than, Teletransportation. *Ordinary survival is about as bad as being destroyed and having a Replica*."[19]

If Parfit succeeds in his challenge—which many think he does—the only psychological connection between one's present and one's future is a relation of similarity or association between the contents of consciousness at different times. Since our sense of the importance of survival seems to be based—at least largely—on the assumption of a deep, phenomenological connection to the future, that importance needs to be reassessed in light of Parfit's challenge. The most extreme possibility is that the psychological relations we really do bear to the future have no intrinsic importance, and hence that survival itself is not actually very important. As counterintuitive as this conclusion is, Parfit suggests that it is defensible, and in some ways liberating.[20]

This conclusion is not forced on us, however. To avoid it, one need only show that some relation that we really do bear to the future justifies, at least partially, the importance we attribute to survival. This might be done by revisiting the original arguments that favor a psychological account of identity and turning instead toward a biologically based view—a view that places the significance of survival in biological connections.[21] But the importance of survival might also be salvaged within the framework of a psychologically based view if it could be shown that the psychological relation that we do have to our futures can still bear the importance we attribute to survival despite the fact that it is not the deep phenomenological connection we thought we had. This strategy has been fairly popular, and it is here that we see a turn to a view of persons as agents in the metaphysical literature on personal identity.

IV. The Turn toward Agency

A. JOHN PERRY'S DISTINCTION BETWEEN THE IMPORTANCE AND CONSTITUTION OF IDENTITY

One good example of the switch to an agency-based approach to survival can be found in John Perry's work.

Like Unger, Perry distinguishes between different senses of "what matters in survival." His distinction, however, is not quite the same as Unger's. He says that the phrase "what matters in survival" can mean either "*what is of importance*" in survival or "what makes a case of survival a case of survival."[22] Unger's prudential and desirability senses would thus both fall under Perry's category of importance. Although Perry is a psychological continuity theorist, he holds a version of this view in which identity-constituting psychological continuity is intimately interlinked with continuity of body. He therefore claims that not only is a person's replica not *identical* to her, but, strictly speaking, she does not *survive* as her replica either (he thus uses "survival" in a different sense than I have been using it). The puzzles which Parfit and others find concerning identity and survival, Perry argues, frequently involve a conflation of the two senses of "what matters" as he has defined them. The confusion stems from the expectation that the relation that defines survival will be intrinsically important, and when it is found not to be, this is taken as a challenge to the psychological continuity theory. What we need to understand, says Perry, is that the importance of survival—in both Unger's prudential sense and his desirability sense—is derivative rather than immediate.

To make this point, and to show from what the importance of survival derives, Perry uses a variant on Unger's avoidance of future pain test. He imagines a scenario in which a person, by pushing a button, can prevent someone from experiencing terrible pain the next day, and asks whether a person has different sorts of reasons to press the button if the pain she prevents will be her own—reasons that go beyond the simple fact that anyone's pain is bad and should, all things equal, be prevented. Perry argues that a person does, at least usually, have special reasons to push the button to prevent her own pain, but also that they are not the sorts of reasons we typically take her to have. On Perry's view, the legitimacy of our concerns about our future pains is not based on a deep phenomenological connection to the future, but instead derives from our concern for our projects. Each of us has many projects, and we have reasons to see those projects carried out. If we are in excruciating pain, we are less likely to be able to see our projects through, and so we have reasons to avoid excruciating pain. Given that we are the people most likely to carry out our own projects, we thus have special reasons to avoid our own pains. Perry is aware, of course, that in some instances there may be others who can carry out our projects better than we can. He adds, however, that it is extremely improbable that there is anyone else who could and would carry out *all* of our projects better than we would, and therefore our concern for our projects gives us reason to be specially concerned for ourselves.

Perry also acknowledges that the asymmetry between the likelihood that a person will carry out her projects and the likelihood that someone else will is a contingent rather than a logically necessary one. In the types of thought experiments used in the personal identity literature, this truism may not hold. Teletransportation, for instance, replicates a person's entire psychological life. In Perry's terminology, the people in these cases will not "survive" as their replicas, but the replicas will, by definition, be just as likely to carry out their projects as they would, and in just the same way. What is important in survival in the most fundamental sense will thus be captured in these cases, even though the original person does not, in Perry's sense, survive.[23] Perry agrees with Parfit that the importance of identity and survival is derivative and does not depend upon a deep, phenomenological connection between the different temporal parts of a person's life. It depends instead, he says, on our interest in carrying out our projects—that is, our interests as agents.

B. CAROL ROVANE AND THE RECONNECTION OF CONSTITUTION AND IMPORTANCE

The shift to a view of the person as agent is also made by Carol Rovane in *The Bounds of Agency: An Essay in Revisionary Metaphysics*. Rovane does not enter the debate in direct response to the challenge of explaining the importance of survival or capturing phenomenological unity, and so she does not explicitly address these issues. She does, however, undertake to offer a psychological account of personal identity that will capture its practical importance (and, although she does not herself use the distinction between identity and survival, the practical importance of survival as

well). More specifically, Rovane sets herself the goal of providing an account of identity that explains the normative injunction* that rational unity should be achieved within the point of view of a single person, but not beyond.[24] To achieve her goal Rovane offers a normative analysis of personal identity. "According to the normative analysis, the condition of personal identity is the condition that gives rise to a certain normative commitment, namely, the commitment to achieve overall rational unity."[25] Although her view is quite complex, the features relevant for our purposes are well-articulated in an analysis she offers of where her view stands relative to Locke's. She agrees with Locke, she says, that personal identity should be defined in terms of the unity of a first-person point of view, but adds that her "analysis will reject Locke's specific account of what a first person point of view is. He construed it as the phenomenological point of view of a unified consciousness. In contrast, the normative analysis takes it to be the rational point of view of an agent."[26] Central to Rovane's view is the claim that a rational and phenomenological point of view need not—indeed, likely will not—coincide.

Rovane thus argues that the view that personal survival should be defined in terms of a phenomenological unity does not explain the normative injunction to take into account all of one's own states, but not anyone else's, in deliberations about what to do. Instead she offers a view in which identity is defined in terms of unity of agency. This unity requires as a background condition many of the types of psychological connections that are present in the psychological continuity theory, but "in addition, the set must include certain substantive practical commitments that serve as *unifying projects*."[27] There is, of course, a great deal more to her view than I have described here, but it is the fundamental insight that is important for our purposes. Translated into the terminology we have been using, Rovane says that the bounds of self-interested concern will be set not by phenomenological unity, but by agential unity, and thus that both what constitutes survival and what matters in it will be our continuation as rational agents, not as experiencing subjects.

---

* A normative injunction is an instruction telling you what you ought to do.

C. RESOURCES IN PRACTICAL PHILOSOPHY—CHRISTINE KORSGAARD AND HARRY FRANKFURT

The idea that persons should be viewed primarily as agents, and the unity of persons as the unity of agency, is not, of course, limited to discussions in the metaphysics of personal identity. It is a standard position in practical philosophy* as well. For the most part, the discussions of identity in metaphysics and practical philosophy have proceeded independently. This is unfortunate, as insights found in practical philosophy provide useful resources for those interested in developing an agent-based view of personal identity. However, one important point of contact between these two discussions can be found in Christine Korsgaard's essay "Personal Identity and the Unity of Agency: A Kantian Response to Parfit."[28] Here Korsgaard explicitly takes on Parfit's arguments against a deep unity in the life of a person. She urges the Kantian† position that "subject" and "agent" represent two perspectives we can take on persons, but says that if we wish to find what unifies a person, we must understand persons under the latter description rather than the former. The unity of a person's life, she says, is a unity of agency, not of experience.

Korsgaard accepts Parfit's argument that there is no unity of consciousness of the sort we tend to assume. She very elegantly describes the naive view of phenomenological unity as follows:

> The sphere of consciousness presents itself as something like a room, a place, a lit-up area, within which we do our thinking, imagining, remembering and planning, and from which we observe the world, the passing scene. It is envisioned as a tunnel or a stream, because we think that one moment of consciousness is somehow directly continuous with others, even when interrupted by deep sleep or anesthesia. We are inclined to think that memory is a deeper thing than it is, that it is *direct* access to an earlier stage

of a continuing self, and not merely one way of knowing what happened. And so we may think of amnesia, not merely as the loss of knowledge, but as a door that blocks an existing place.[29]

Like Parfit, Korsgaard denies the accuracy of this picture of consciousness and acknowledges that if we are looking for a significant unity within the life of a person we will not find it by looking for a unified subject of experiences. If we think about persons as agents, however, a meaningful, nonarbitrary unity is easy to find. Korsgaard writes: "[S]uppose Parfit has established that there is no deep sense in which I am identical to the subject of experiences who will occupy my body in the future. ... I will argue that I nevertheless have reasons for regarding myself as the same rational agent as the one who will occupy my body in the future." She goes on to clarify that "these reasons are not metaphysical, but practical."[30]

When we start out thinking of persons as agents, we will immediately come upon the obvious fact that as agents, we must act, and that means we must decide what to do—or not do, as the case may be. Once we concentrate on this aspect of human existence, Korsgaard says, it will be easy to see that in order to act we must conceive of ourselves as unified agents. To show this, she begins by asking us to consider what underlies our sense that we are unified *at* a time, and says that there are two elements of this unity. First, the need for unity is forced upon us by the fact that, at least in our world, we control one and only one body. If we are divided about what to do, we need to overcome our division to be able to act coherently and effectively. "You are a unified person at any given time because you must act, and you have only one body with which to act."[31] The second element is the "unity implicit in the *standpoint* from which you deliberate and choose." She says that "it may be that what actually happens when you make a choice is that the strongest of your conflicting desires wins, but that is not the way you think of it when you deliberate. When you deliberate, it is as if

---

* A branch (or style) of philosophy that considers the value and implementation of philosophical concepts and approaches in everyday existence. While traditional metaphysics asks lofty questions about the nature of reality, practical philosophy considers pragmatic concerns about how we ought to live in the world.

† Influenced by the philosophy of Immanuel Kant (1724–1804).

there were something over and above all your desires, something that is *you* and *chooses* which one to act on."[32] According to Korsgaard, this sense of ourselves as choosing necessitates that we have *reasons* for choosing one course of action over the others, and "it is these reasons, rather than the desires themselves, which are expressive of your will."[33] You must have a sense of yourself as a unified chooser with reasons in order to act.

Korsgaard goes on to argue that *this* unity, unlike unity of consciousness, can easily be seen as stretching over time as well as holding at a time. A person needs to coordinate action and motives over time as well as at a time, since almost anything we want to do will take at least a bit of time to unfold. Imagine, she says, that my body really is occupied by a series of subjects, changing from moment to moment. It is clear that they had better learn to cooperate "if together we are going to have any kind of a *life*."[34] But more than this, the need to think of oneself as a unified agent acting from reasons means that we must identify ourselves with those reasons, and those reasons may, and probably will, "automatically carry us into the future."[35] If you understand yourself as an agent "implementing something like a particular plan of life, you need to identify with your future in order to be *what you are even now*."[36] The basis for our unity over time is thus the necessity of acting once we are thrust on the scene, and not some metaphysical fact. As Korsgaard sums it up: "You normally think you lead one continuing life because you are one person, but according to this argument the truth is the reverse. You are one continuing person because you have one life to lead."[37]

Korsgaard realizes that to many it will seem that she has ignored the central issue. There may be some good practical reasons to act *as if* we will persist into the future, and to view ourselves as unified, but this does not really unify us. She rejects this description of the situation, however, for two reasons. First, she agrees with Parfit that our naive conception of the unity of a person rests on the assumption of a deep unity of consciousness over time, and that there is no such unity to be found in our actual lives, let alone in bizarre science fiction cases. Second, and most important, while our sense of our unity as agents may rest on practical rather than metaphysical facts, these facts are by no means trivial or arbitrary. It is not just an accident or convention that we take the body as the most relevant unit of agency; things would go badly for us if we didn't—indeed, after a while there might well not be any "us" for whom things would go badly. She allows, as does Rovane, that there can be units of agency bigger (and presumably also smaller) than the body—families, tribes, bowling leagues, or our teenaged selves might qualify. There is no denying, however, the necessity of viewing ourselves as unified agents (whatever the size of the unit), nor of taking a human life as a particularly basic such unit. Such unification is necessary, even if the necessity is not metaphysical.

The basic picture behind this view is developed further in recent work in practical reasoning that starts from the picture of the person as an agent and stresses the fundamental importance of our unity as agents, suggesting that our very survival depends upon it. Much of this work is Korsgaard's own. This picture is laid out in great detail in her book *The Sources of Normativity* and in her *Locke Lectures*. In the latter she tells us:

> Because human beings are self-conscious, we are conscious of threats to our psychic unity or integrity. Sometimes these threats spring from our own desires and impulses. The element of truth in the image of the miserable sinner who must repress his unruly desires in order to be good rests in the fact that we deliberate in the face of threats to our integrity, and act against them. What is false about the picture is the idea that we must repress these threats *in order to be good*. Rather, we must repress them in order to be one, to be unified, to be whole. We must repress them in order to maintain our personal or practical identity.[38]

If we do not unify ourselves as agents, we are in danger of real disintegration.

This general picture is shared by Harry Frankfurt. Although his view of personal identity differs from Korsgaard's in many important respects, he shares with her the idea that we must maintain unity of will to have any sort of life at all. Frankfurt tells us: "[T]here is, I believe, a quite primitive human need to establish and to maintain volitional unity.* Any threat to that unity—that is, any threat to the cohesion of the self—tends to alarm a person, and to mobilize him for an attempt at 'self-preservation.'"[39] Although the term appears in scare quotes, elsewhere Frankfurt links these issues to "self-preservation" "only in an unfamiliarly literal sense—in the sense of sustaining not the *life* of the organism but the *persistence of the self*."[40] By giving us a way to think about unity of agency as central to our real persistence as persons, the work of Korsgaard and Frankfurt in practical philosophy adds a great deal to the plausibility of the approach suggested by Perry and Rovane. It provides a deep, nonarbitrary unity over the course of our lives that is not a unity of consciousness.

V. Unity of Consciousness Again

The switch to an agency-based view of persons and personal identity, especially supplemented by work in practical philosophy, represents an important development in our thought about these issues. There is a compelling case for the view that unity of agency is a real and important feature of personal identity. The question that remains, however, is whether this sort of unity is really strong enough to bear the kind of importance we attribute to survival. It may be that there is no unity of consciousness of the sort we typically assume there to be throughout the life of a person, and also that unity of agency is a more important unity than we generally take it to be, but that does not mean that it has the kind of visceral significance our naive-but-problematic notion of unity of consciousness did. To use Parfit's idiom, it is not clear whether an agency-based approach to personal identity is an alternative above and beyond those he conceived, or whether it is a version of the "moderate claim," giving survival some importance, but not as much as we originally believed.

When we look at a view like Perry's or Rovane's, it certainly seems the latter. Of course we care about our projects, but if *all* there is to survival is the continuity of projects, the difference between surviving and

being survived by like-minded folk does seem trivial. Korsgaard and Frankfurt offer resources for seeing an agency-based view as more of a real alternative to the Parfitian approach. The brute importance of unity of agency, not as a nicety or refinement of our lives, but as a condition of them, suggests that this sort of unity may well be considered the condition of survival as we ordinarily conceive it. On this view, unity of agency is not a consolation for not having unity of consciousness, but the unity that carries the significance we usually attribute to survival. This perspective, however, works better when we look at the short term, and it becomes more problematic when we look on the time scale of a human life. Korsgaard makes an excellent case for the need for unity of agency in the short term as a precondition for taking any action, and thus as a precondition for anything we might recognize as a person. The need for unity of agency over the long term, however, is a more tenuous thing. I do need a unified will at a time to eat, drink, or get out of bed, but I don't necessarily need a unified will over time to do those things.

Korsgaard, of course, argues that in a real sense I do need a unified will over time to take even minimal actions now. The move here depends rather heavily on the need to have *reasons* for action. To unify my will now, on her view, I need to see myself as having reasons for my choices, and it is these reasons that carry me into the future by taking the form of general laws. This is why the necessity of unification of agency over time is based on the view of oneself as "implementing a life plan" or having "any kind of a life." So here the necessity of unification looks less like it comes from the desire to have *a* life and more like it comes from the desire to have a *meaningful* life. Frankfurt's position is similar in this respect. Although he does not think we need reasons to act, he does think we need to have fairly stable commitments to what we care about. His rationale for this claim is the same as Korsgaard's; such stability is necessary to have a meaningful life. In their later work, both philosophers thus stress the connection between unity of agency and a life that is "worth living." Korsgaard does this, for instance, in her discussion of our identification with a variety of "practical identities"—identities as mother, friend, patriot,

---

* To have a volition is just to make a choice or to will something; in this context, "volitional unity" means the same thing as "unity of will."

union member, etc.—which provide us with reasons for action. She defines these practical identities as "a description under which you value yourself, a description under which you find your life to be worth living and your actions to be worth undertaking."[41] And Frankfurt describes a life of ambivalence as follows: "For someone who is unlikely to have any stable preferences or goals," he says,

> the benefits of freedom are, at the very least, severely diminished. The opportunity to act in accordance with his own inclinations is a doubtful asset for an individual whose will is so divided that he is moved both to decide for a certain alternative and to decide against it. Neither of the alternatives can satisfy him, since each entails the frustration of the other. The fact that he is free to choose between them is likely only to make his anguish more poignant and more intense.[42]

This provides us with a powerful motivation for seeking volitional unity over time, to be sure, but it does not make an overwhelming case for the fact that such unity is what defines our persistence. The distinction between a life integrated enough to be *a* life and one integrated enough to be a *meaningful* life thus becomes blurred.

This is problematic for agency-based accounts of personal identity because it seems all too possible for a person to live a life that has no meaning or direction, or to lose meaning only to find it again, and then perhaps lose it again. These are all crises *within* the life of a person and not crises that signify the end of a life. This idea is well-expressed in the opening question of Camus's* *Myth of Sisyphus*—"why not suicide?" Camus denies the existence of a transcendent meaning that could unify a life, and asks whether and why we should go to the trouble of living if life has no meaning. While I do not mean to imply that Camus has a completely convincing conception of the nature of human existence, I do think he represents well one strain of thought that persists in our thinking about ourselves and our lives. The relation of this strain of thought to a position like Korsgaard's is complex, and worth investigating.

To begin, it might seem as if the very coherence of Camus's question challenges Korsgaard's position as

I have interpreted it. If we are worried about having to live in the future despite the fact that life has no over-arching significance, it would seem that no such significance is required to continue living a life. But this is too quick. Even if we accept (as I do) that Camus is talking about suicide not only as the act of killing an organism, but as the act of killing a psychological self, his question in many ways supports Korsgaard's position far more than it challenges it. Camus is saying that without meaning we wonder whether it is worth the effort of living. This means we do feel as if we have to decide what to do about the future—whether to perpetuate ourselves into it in a way that guarantees that we will have to keep acting and so take on the responsibility of deciding what to do, or whether to spare ourselves that effort. Considering such a drastic step, and for this reason, certainly suggests that we are identifying ourselves as the very agents who will be called upon to act in the future. This is why we need to make decisions now about what to do then. Suicide is a decision about what to do in one's future; it is the decision to do nothing.

The challenge to Korsgaard raised by Camus, such as it is, comes rather in the way that he argues that suicide is not an appropriate or rational reaction to the recognition that life has no meaning. Life can be lived all the better, he says, because it has no meaning. We can find a reason to live in the perpetual, self-expressive struggle against the arationality of the world. It is important to note that in some respects Camus and Korsgaard offer the same solution to the problem of meaninglessness. Neither relies on a transcendent purpose, outside of our natures, that provides our reason to live. Reasons for living and value must be provided by us, and are provided by us via our expression of ourselves as value-conferring or reason-giving beings. In fact, toward the end of *The Sources of Normativity*, Korsgaard gives an analysis of what is wrong with suicide that is in many ways very like Camus's.[43] There is, however, an important difference. Korsgaard's picture involves our taking the reasons we give ourselves seriously, which means recognizing that they give meaning to our lives insofar as we are true to them, and threaten to make our lives disintegrate into meaninglessness if we are not. Camus, on the other hand,

---

* Albert Camus (1913–60) was a French existentialist philosopher and author.

suggests that we can only have a life worth living if we refuse to take these human meanings seriously, if we reject stability and find our value instead in the raw fact of our consciousness. Now, sometimes by "consciousness" he means consciousness *of* our condition—the continued awareness that we assert ourselves by struggling hopelessly against the absurd. But he also often means just the capacity to have experience—any experience. He tells us that "what counts is not the best living but the most living,"[44] that "no depth, no emotion, no passion, and no sacrifice could render equal in the eyes of the absurd man (even if he wished it so) a conscious life of forty years and a lucidity spread over sixty years,"[45] and that "the present and the succession of presents before a constantly conscious soul is the ideal of the absurd man."[46]

I do not mean to urge Camus's view as more accurate than Korsgaard's, but in its extremity it points to an important element that is not given sufficient emphasis in her account—the value that we put on the sheer fact of being conscious, independent of any practical implications. Of course, Korsgaard does not deny that we care about consciousness, but I think Camus's picture shows more than just that; it shows how much we care about being perpetuated into the future as the same experiencing subject. The subject who is conscious now wants to act, and wants meaning, but she also just plain wants to *be there* in the future, with or without purpose. Two more months, even if there are no loose ends to tie up or projects to complete, are two more months. This does not mean that pain and depression cannot make the negative value of continuation so great that it is no longer deemed worthwhile—this is when we see suicide as an understandable response. But the significance of being there, just to be there, just to keep having experiences, just to have *a* life and not necessarily a *meaningful* life is, I think, an important part of "what matters in survival."

So, we seem to be back to the idea that the agency-based account of personal identity is some form of Parfit's moderate claim. The kind of survival that seems so important to us—the survival that psychological accounts of identity are trying to capture—requires a deep unity of consciousness over time, something that we now have reason to believe we do not, and cannot, have. This would mean that Parfit was right in claiming we are merely under an *illusion* that this unity exists, and therefore take identity and survival to have

an importance that they do not actually have. But this is too quick. Our discussion of agency-based accounts of identity has hinted that they may be able to give us something more like our naive conception of psychological continuation than we might have thought. These hints are the suggestions that our conception of ourselves as unified agents can have a profound impact on the quality of our conscious experience, and on our experience of ourselves as persisting *subjects* as well as agents. Korsgaard talks about the way in which our reasons for action "carry us into the future" as agents, but they may also do so as subjects. In conceiving of ourselves as continuing as agents, we project ourselves into the future as subjects as well—imagining what will bring us satisfaction, when we will be filled with regret, what is likely to tempt us away from our purpose, and so on. To experience ourselves as unified agents, we may well also have to experience ourselves as unified subjects, and vice versa.

Another aspect of this connection is mentioned by Frankfurt in his discussion of why we need final ends. He has told us already that we need to have stable commitments that constrain our will (with our approval) because otherwise life will be meaningless, but he puts a particularly interesting gloss on this claim when he tells us that if we fail to find something we care about in this way we will get bored, and, he says,

> the avoidance of boredom is a profound human need. Our aversion to being bored is not a matter simply of distaste for a rather unpleasant state of consciousness. The aversion expresses our sensitivity to a much more basic threat. It is of the essence of boredom that we don't care about what is going on. We therefore experience an attenuation of psychic vitality or liveliness. In its most familiar manifestations, being bored involves a reduction in the sharpness and focus of attention. The general level of mental energy diminishes. Our responsiveness to conscious stimuli flattens out and shrinks. Distinctions are not noticed and not made, so that our conscious field becomes increasingly homogeneous. As boredom progresses, it entails an increasing diminution of significant differentiation within consciousness.[47]

He goes on to explain:

At the limit, when consciousness is totally undifferentiated, this homogenization is tantamount to the cessation of conscious experience altogether. When we are bored, in other words, we tend to fall asleep. Any substantial increase in the extent to which we are bored undermines, then, the very continuation of conscious mental life. That is, it threatens the extinction of the active self. What is expressed by our interest in avoiding boredom is therefore not simply a resistance to discomfort, but a quite primitive urge for psychic survival.[48]

It is not just activity that is threatened if we do not have long-term commitments; it is our very consciousness. The danger, of course, is not just literally falling asleep, but rather failing to project one's consciousness into the future in the ways we usually do.

Interestingly enough, Camus makes just the opposite claim. He says that we need to reject long-term commitments and the meaning derived from them if we are to retain our consciousness. Commitment breeds complacency, and a rote, mechanistic implementation of a life-plan dulls our consciousness. If we are to be really alive, and remain really conscious, he says, we must think of ourselves as faced with the world afresh at each moment. Undoubtedly there is some truth to both of these perspectives. A failure to have passions may well dull consciousness, and so may falling into a routine. Moreover, there is probably less of a distinction between Frankfurt and Korsgaard on the one hand and Camus on the other than it at first appears. While Frankfurt and Korsgaard do require stability, they also emphasize that as agents we are forced to keep our commitments in place, essentially by perpetually rechoosing them. These issues are too complex to sort out here. For the present, I am interested only in making the more general point that the quality of our consciousness is going to be affected in a variety of ways by our recognition that we are agents and by our conception of ourselves as unified agents. The agency view thus need not be seen simply as a *substitution* of a picture of persons as agents for a picture of persons as subjects, but rather as a new way of thinking about persons as subjects, and the way in which subjects might be unified over time.

This discussion suggests that while we do, indeed, feel that a continuation of consciousness is a crucial part of the survival of the person, it is not the bare continuation of sentience isolated by Unger's prudential sense of what matters, nor the formal connections of similarity and association between the contents of consciousness offered by psychological continuity theorists. It is, rather, a continuing sense of ourselves as subjects moving through the world and experiencing it. This experience of ourselves as unified subjects may well require at some point the structure and organization that comes from conceiving of ourselves as unified agents, and may arise only under the practical exigencies* of living in the world. This does not mean that this experience is not of independent value, nor that it cannot outlast the sorts of identifications and reasons that unify an agent over the long term. There may thus be a meaningful and significant question of whether I can anticipate having experience in the future that cannot simply be answered by looking at how I unify myself as an agent, even if the answer is not totally independent of that fact. The relations to which I am pointing are, admittedly, very vague at this point. If, however, there is reason to believe that they really exist, there is reason to think that we can come up with a more satisfying account of personal identity by uncovering and understanding them.

VI. Conclusion

The psychological approach to problems of personal identity seems to capture one very important aspect of our conception of what we are and the conditions of our persistence. It is not easy, however, to articulate the insight it provides. Originally it seems that the insight is that we are fundamentally subjects of experience, and that our survival requires a persistence of experiencing subjects. The naive understanding of this persistence is in terms of a deep, metaphysical unity of consciousness over time. Parfit and others have argued effectively that it is hard even to make this naive understanding coherent, let alone give reasons for believing that we have it in ordinary survival. This argument seems to imply that ordinary survival

---

* Practical exigencies are practical demands or requirements.

cannot have the importance we usually attribute to it, perhaps having no importance at all.

An alternative approach has developed suggesting that persons should be conceived as most fundamentally agents rather than subjects of experience, and thus that the unity of a person over time should be defined in terms of unity of agency rather than unity of subject. This approach is seen in both metaphysics and practical philosophy. Perry and Rovane offer their alternatives within the context of the metaphysical debate, while Korsgaard and Frankfurt develop theirs mostly within the context of discussions of practical reason. I have suggested that as revealing as these views are, they still seem to leave out the importance our conception of ourselves as experiencing subjects has for us, an importance that is described in Camus's *Myth of Sisyphus*. Using hints found in the development of agency-based views of personal identity, however, I have pointed to a possible reintroduction of the picture of the person as subject into the agency-based views we have considered.

Coming from a Kantian perspective, Korsgaard says that persons are both subjects and agents, and we can take one perspective or the other depending on our purposes. I have suggested that for these purposes we must think of subjectivity and agency as inherently intertwined, and thus of unity of agency and unity of consciousness as separate but interdependent unities. In this way we can hope to regain a meaningful unity of consciousness as part of personal survival. Like the unity of agency described by Korsgaard, it will not have a metaphysical basis, but it will be nonarbitrary and deeply important nonetheless. ■

Suggestions for Critical Reflection

1. Schechtman rejects Parfit's conclusion that "the psychological relations we really do bear to the future have no intrinsic importance, and hence that survival itself is not actually very important." Why does she do so? Is she right?

2. Schechtman suggests that metaphysical considerations of the issue of personal identity would benefit from an encounter with the insights of practical philosophy. Consider this claim. What can we learn from integrating insights about familiar human experiences with contemplations about the nature of reality?

3. Schechtman follows French philosopher Albert Camus in proposing that there is something appealing about the simple fact of remaining alive. She suggests that the desirability of persisting as a conscious being reveals that there is a problem with agency-based theories of identity, which hold that what we really want from "survival" is someone to carry out our projects. Do you agree with this position? Does staying alive matter more to you than guaranteeing that someone will complete your life's work? Why or why not?

4. In the first part of her paper Schechtman outlines problems with a view of personal identity as consisting in the unity of consciousness, and she positions the unity of agency as an improvement over this idea. At the end of her paper, however, she reintroduces the unity of consciousness as a required component of our conception of personal identity and suggests that combining it with the unity of agency makes an attractive overall picture of personal identity. What do you think this theory would look like? How does it address the weaknesses she has identified in the two positions taken separately? Is it even possible to integrate these two competing theories of personal identity?

Notes

1 I am indebted to many friends and colleagues for their input in the course of writing this essay. I would like especially to thank David DeGrazia, Anthony Laden, Ray Martin, Marc Slors, and the editors of *Social Philosophy and Policy*.

2 There are, of course, other positions that are and have been defended. Historically it has been popular to define personal identity in terms of the persistence of an immaterial soul, and this view still has its defenders. Others see identity as irreducible and unanalyzable. Continuity of organism and continuity of psychological life are, however, generally acknowledged as the basic candidates for an account of personal identity in the current discussion, and the vast majority of authors in the area defend one or the other of them.

3 In fact, Parfit shifts his use of the term "survival" over the course of his work. In Derek Parfit, "Personal Identity," *Philosophical Review* 80 (1971): 3–27, he suggests that survival can come apart from identity, and suggests that we are interested in questions of survival. In his book *Reasons and Persons* (Oxford: Clarendon Press, 1984), Parfit seems to imply that, strictly speaking, survival requires identity, and that we are interested in "what matters in survival." I will be using the terminology in the former sense. For a full discussion of the evolution in Parfit's use of this term, see Marvin Belzer, "Self-Conception and Personal Identity" [*Social Philosophy and Policy* 22 (2005): 126–164].

4 Parfit, *Reasons and Persons*, chap. 12.

5 John Perry, "The Importance of Being Identical," in Amélie Oksenberg Rorty, ed., *The Identities of Persons* (Berkeley: University of California Press, 1976), 67.

6 Peter Unger, *Identity, Consciousness, and Value* (New York: Oxford University Press, 1990), 93.

7 Ibid., 94.

8 Ibid., 93.

9 As mentioned in note 2, for terminological simplicity in what follows I will refer to having what matters in this fundamental sense simply as "survival," meaning that in my use survival does not automatically imply identity.

10 Parfit, *Reasons and Persons*, 199–201.

11 Of course, in either case we may decide that suffering the small pain is the better thing to do. We can care as much or more about the pains of others as we do about our own. The point is just that the considerations that go into the decision making are different in each case.

12 Of course, at this point we might revert to a biological criterion, saying that our special concern about our own futures is not based on a deep unity of consciousness, but only on the fact that the organism currently having experience will be present, sentient, and in pain in the future. There are many considerations in favor of this position, and Parfit also offers many arguments against it. For the present, I am only interested in following out the intuitions behind psychological accounts of identity. I will, therefore, only consider what would be required to make this approach work, and see where this leads us.

13 Parfit, *Reasons and Persons*, 227–28.

14 Kathleen Wilkes, *Real People: Personal Identity without Thought Experiments* (Oxford: Clarendon Press, 1994), 46n.

15 Parfit, *Reasons and Persons*, 201.

16 Ibid.

17 See, for instance, Andy Clark, *Being There* (Cambridge, MA: MIT Press, 1998); and Daniel Dennett, *Consciousness Explained* (Boston: Little, Brown, and Co., 1991).

18 Parfit, *Reasons and Persons*, 208.

19 Ibid.

20 Ibid., 281–82.

21 This approach has become increasingly popular lately. A prominent example is Eric Olson's book *The Human Animal: Personal Identity without Psychology* (New York: Oxford University Press, 1997).

22 Perry, "The Importance of Being Identical," 85–86.

23 That is, the person does not survive as Perry uses the term—as I am using the term "survival," however, the person does survive.

24 This normative injunction says that "when I deliberate I ought to resolve all of the contradictions and conflicts within my own point of view, but I need not resolve all of my disagreements with you. Likewise, I ought to rank all of my preferences, but this ranking need not reflect your preferences. And more generally, when I arrive at all-things-considered judgments I should take into account all of my beliefs, desires, and so forth, but not yours." Carol Rovane, *The Bounds of Agency* (Princeton, NJ: Princeton University Press, 1998), 24.

25 Ibid., 23.

26 Ibid., 19.

27 Ibid., 31.

28 Christine Korsgaard, "Personal Identity and the Unity of Agency: A Kantian Response to Parfit," *Philosophy and Public Affairs* 18 (Spring 1989).

29 Ibid., 116.

30 Ibid., 109.

31 Ibid., 111.

32 Ibid.

33 Ibid., 113.

34 Korsgaard therefore holds that personal identity will, in our world, be tied to the identity of the human being. She stresses that this is a contingent fact, however, in the sense that in a world where people had their bodies replaced with replicas on a regular basis, and these replicas continued their lives in something like the ordinary way, the unity of the agent could involve more than one body. See ibid., 113.

35 Ibid.

36 Ibid., 113–14.

37 Ibid., 113.

38 Christine Korsgaard, *Locke Lectures*, Lecture I, 18.

39 Harry Frankfurt, "Autonomy, Necessity, and Love," in Frankfurt, *Necessity, Volition, and Love* (Cambridge: Cambridge University Press, 1999), 139.

40 Harry Frankfurt, "On the Usefulness of Final Ends," in Frankfurt, *Necessity, Volition, and Love*, 89.

41 Christine Korsgaard, *The Sources of Normativity* (Cambridge: Cambridge University Press, 1996), 101.

42 Harry Frankfurt, "The Faintest Passion," in Frankfurt, *Necessity, Volition, and Love*, 102.

43 Korsgaard, *The Sources of Normativity*, 160–64.

44 Albert Camus, *The Myth of Sisyphus and Other Essays*, trans. Justin O'Brien (New York: Vintage International, 1991), 63.

45 Ibid.

46 Ibid., 63–64.

47 Frankfurt, "On the Usefulness of Final Ends," 89.

48 Ibid.

PERMISSIONS ACKNOWLEDGMENTS

Adams, Marilyn McCord. Excerpt from "Horrendous Evils and the Goodness of God," *Proceedings of the Aristotelian Society*, Supplementary Volume 63 (1989): 297–310. Reprinted by permission of the Aristotelian Society.

Anselm of Canterbury, Saint. Excerpts from *Anselm of Canterbury: The Major Works*, translated by M.J. Charlesworth and edited by Brian Davies and G.R. Evans. Oxford World's Classics, 1998. Reprinted with the permission of Oxford University Press.

Ayer, A.J. "Freedom and Necessity," Chapter 12 of *Philosophical Essays*. Copyright © 1972, Palgrave Macmillan. Reprinted with the permission of SNCSC.

Block, Ned. Excerpt from "Troubles with Functionalism," *Minnesota Studies in Philosophy of Science* 9 (1978): 261–331. Copyright © 1978 by the University of Minnesota. All rights reserved. Reprinted with the permission of Ned Block and the University of Minnesota Press.

Chalmers, David. "The Puzzle of Conscious Experience," from *Scientific American*, December 1995. Reprinted with the permission of David Chalmers.

Code, Lorraine. "Is the Sex of the Knower Epistemologically Significant?" Chapter 1 of *What Can She Know? Feminist Theory and the Construction of Knowledge*. Copyright © 1991 by Cornell University. Used by permission of the publisher, Cornell University Press.

Dennett, Daniel C. "Where Am I?" pages 310–23 of *Brainstorms: Philosophical Essays on Mind and Psychology*. Copyright © 1981 Massachusetts Institute of Technology. Reprinted with the permission of The MIT Press.

Frankfurt, Harry. "Alternate Possibilities and Moral Responsibilities," Chapter 1 of *The Importance of What We Care About: Philosophical Essays*. Cambridge University Press, 1998. Originally published in *Journal of Philosophy* LXVI (66.23), December 1969. Reprinted with the permission of Joan Gilbert and The Journal of Philosophy.

Gettier, Edmund. "Is Justified True Belief Knowledge?" *Analysis* 23.6 (June 1963): 121–23. Reprinted by permission of Oxford University Press.

Hempel, Carl. "Scientific Inquiry: Invention and Test," from *Philosophy of Natural Science*, 1st ed., copyright © 1967. Reprinted by permission of Pearson Education Inc., New York.

Hester, Lee, and Jim Cheney. Excerpt from "Truth and Native American Epistemology," *Social Epistemology* 15.4 (2001): 319–34. Reprinted by permission of the publisher, Taylor & Francis Ltd. http://www.tandfonline.com

Jackson, Frank. Excerpt from "Epiphenomenal Qualia," *Philosophical Quarterly* 32.127 (1982): 127–36. Reprinted by permission of Oxford University Press. Excerpt from "What Mary Didn't Know," *Journal of Philosophy* 83 (May 1986): 291–95. Reprinted with the permission of Frank Jackson and The Journal of Philosophy.

Kant, Immanuel. "Introduction," from *The Critique of Pure Reason*, 2nd ed., edited by Norman Kemp Smith. Copyright © 2007 Palgrave Macmillan. Reprinted with the permission of SNCSC.

Kind, Amy. "How to Believe in Qualia," pages 285–98 of *The Case for Qualia*, edited by Edmond Wright. Copyright © 2008 Massachusetts Institute of Technology. Reprinted with the permission of The MIT Press.

Kuhn, Thomas. "Objectivity, Value Judgment and Theory Choice," from *The Essential Tension: Selected Studies in Scientific Tradition and Change*. Chicago: The University of Chicago Press. Copyright © 1977 by The University of Chicago.

Longino, Helen. "Can There Be a Feminist Science?" *Hypatia* 2.3 (1987): 51–64. Copyright © 1987 by Hypatia, Inc. Reprinted with the permission of the publisher, John Wiley & Sons, Inc.

Mackie, J.L. "Evil and Omnipotence," *Mind* (New Series) 64.254 (April 1955): 200–12. Reprinted by permission of Oxford University Press.

Moore, G.E. "Proof of an External World," *Proceedings of the British Academy* 25 (1939): 273–300. Reprinted with the permission of Dr. Thomas Baldwin.

Nagel, Thomas. "What Is It Like to Be a Bat?" *The Philosophical Review* 83.4 (October 1974): 435–50.

Parfit, Derek. "Personal Identity," *The Philosophical Review* 80.1 (Jan. 1971): 3–27.

Pascal, Blaise. "The Wager," from *Pensées*, translated by W.F. Trotter. E.P. Dutton & Co., 1958.

Plato. "The Allegory of the Cave," from *The Republic*, translated by Benjamin Jowett, 1892.

Popper, Karl. Excerpts from "Science: Conjectures and Refutations," in *Conjectures and Refutations: The Growth of Scientific Knowledge*, copyright © Karl L. Popper 1963; copyright © The Estate of Sir Karl Popper 2002. Reprinted with the permission of the University of Klagenfurt/Karl Popper Library.

Rée, Paul. "The Illusion of Free Will" ("Die Illusion der Willensfreiheit"), Chapters 1 and 2, from *Die Illusion der Willensfreiheit* (1885) translated by Stefan Bauer-Mengelberg, in *A Modern Introduction to Philosophy*, 3rd ed., edited by Paul Edwards and Arthur Pap. The Free Press, 1973.

Ryle, Gilbert. "Descartes' Myth," Chapter 1 of *The Concept of Mind*, copyright © 1984. London: Routledge; Chicago: The University of Chicago Press. Reproduced by permission of Taylor & Francis Books UK.

Saul, Jennifer. "Scepticism and Implicit Bias," *Disputatio* 5.37 (2013): 243–63. Reprinted with the permission of Jennifer Saul.

Schechtman, Marya. "Experience, Agency, and Personal Identity," *Social Philosophy and Policy* 22.2 (July 2005): 1–24. Copyright © 2005 Social Philosophy and Policy Foundation. Reproduced with permission.

Strawson, P.F. Excerpt from "Freedom and Resentment," *Proceedings of the British Academy*, Volume 48. London: Oxford University Press. Copyright © British Academy 1963, pp. 187–211.

Williams, Bernard. "The Self and the Future," *The Philosophical Review* 79.2 (April 1970): 161–80.

Wolf, Susan. "Sanity and the Metaphysics of Responsibility," from *Responsibility, Character and the Emotions: New Essays in Moral Psychology*, edited by Ferdinand David Schoeman. Copyright © Cambridge University Press, 1987. Reprinted with permission.

Images

Introduction
"Top Hat," by Eli W. Buel, ca. 1870. https://commons.wikimedia.org/wiki/File:Accession_Number-_1969-0183-0156_(2720792408).jpg

Philosophy of Religion
"Sunlight Seeping through Heavy Tungnath Clouds," by Sriramskumar, 2016. Licensed under the Creative Commons Attribution-Share Alike 4.0 International license, https://creativecommons.org/licenses/by-sa/4.0/deed.en

Epistemology
"Self Portrait with Leica," by Ilse Bing, collection of Michael Mattis and Judith Hochberg. Copyright © Estate of Ilse Bing.

Philosophy of Science
"Self Portrait," by Nadar (Gaspard-Félix Tournachon), n.d. National Library of France, Prints and Photographs Department, FOL-EO-15 (3), https://gallica.bnf.fr/ark:/12148/btv1b105358981

Philosophy of Mind
"Faradisation du muscle frontal," by Guillaume-Benjamin-Amand Duchennede Boulogne, ca. 1854–1856. The Horace W. Goldsmith Foundation Fund, through Joyce and Robert Menschel, 2013. Metropolitan Museum of Art (US), 2013.229

Free Will
"Silvan Omerzu's Interpretation of Pinocchio Ostržek," by Miha Fras, 2015. Licensed under the Creative Commons Attribution-No Derivatives 4.0 International license, https://creativecommons.org/licenses/by-nd/4.0/

Personal Identity
[No title], Anonymous, n.d. Licensed under the CC0 1.0 Universal Public Domain Dedication license, https://creativecommons.org/publicdomain/zero/1.0/

From the Publisher

A name never says it all, but the word "Broadview" expresses a good deal of the philosophy behind our company. We are open to a broad range of academic approaches and political viewpoints. We pay attention to the broad impact book publishing and book printing has in the wider world; for some years now we have used 100% recycled paper for most titles. Our publishing program is internationally oriented and broad-ranging. Our individual titles often appeal to a broad readership too; many are of interest as much to general readers as to academics and students.

Founded in 1985, Broadview remains a fully independent company owned by its shareholders—not an imprint or subsidiary of a larger multinational.

For the most accurate information on our books (including information on pricing, editions, and formats) please visit our website at www.broadviewpress.com. Our print books and ebooks are also available for sale on our site.

broadview press
www.broadviewpress.com